Frommer's®

Canada

16th Edition

by Leslie Brokaw, Pamela Cuthbert, James Hale, Andrew Hempstead, Paul Karr, Chris McBeath, Bill McRae, Kirsten Murphy, Donald Olson, Barbara Ramsay Orr & Christie Pashby

John Wiley & Sons Canada, Ltd.

Published by:
JOHN WILEY & SONS CANADA, LTD.
6045 Freemont Blvd.
Mississauga, ON L5R 4J3

ISBNs 978-0-470-93653-5 (print); 978-0-470-94554-4 (ePdf); 978-1-118-00748-8 (eMobi); 978-1-118-00749-5 (ePub)

Editor: Gene Shannon
Production Editor: Pamela Vokey
Editorial Assistant: Katie Wolsley
Cartographer: Lohnes + Wright
Photo Editor: Richard Fox
Production by Wiley Indianapolis Composition Services

Front cover photo: Canoe on Lake by Mountain, Lower Waterfowl Lake, Mount Cephren, Alberta, Canada
Back cover photo: Toronto Casa Loma, exterior

SPECIAL SALES

For reseller information, including discounts and premium sales, please call our sales department: Tel. 416/646-7992. For press review copies, author interviews, or other publicity information, please contact our marketing department: Tel. 416/646-4584; Fax: 416/236-4448.

Manufactured in the United States of America

1 2 3 4 5 RRD 15 14 13 12 11

CONTENTS

12 NORTH TO ONTARIO'S LAKELANDS & BEYOND 450

13 MANITOBA & SASKATCHEWAN 480

14 ALBERTA & THE ROCKIES 528

15 VANCOUVER 616

16 VICTORIA & BRITISH COLUMBIA 674

17 THE YUKON, NORTHWEST TERRITORIES & NUNAVUT 761

APPENDIX: CANADA IN DEPTH 824

LIST OF MAPS

ABOUT THE AUTHORS

Leslie Brokaw has been writing for Frommer's since 2006, authoring or contributing to recent editions of *Frommer's Montreal Day by Day, Frommer's Canada,* and *Frommer's New England*, as well as *Frommer's Montreal & Quebec City*.

Toronto native **Pamela Cuthbert** is an award-winning food writer and editor published in *Macleans, Saveur, The Walrus, The Toronto Star, The Economist, Common Dreams,* and elsewhere. A past editor with *Time Out Toronto*, she has also contributed to other books, including *The Edible City* and the *Slow Food Almanac*. She lives in her hometown with her husband and young son.

An Ottawa native, **James Hale** is a writer, editor and broadcaster with a keen interest in urban life around the world. He divides his time between providing communications counsel to government and corporate clients and writing about jazz for publications that include *DownBeat* and *Signal To Noise*. He also maintains a music blog, jazzchronicles.blogspot.com.

Andrew Hempstead is a travel writer and photographer who has traveled widely throughout Canada from his home in Banff, Alberta. In addition to this book, he has authored guidebooks to Alberta, Atlantic Canada, British Columbia, the Canadian Rockies, Newfoundland & Labrador, Nova Scotia, and Vancouver, and has co-authored guidebooks to Australia and New Zealand.

Paul Karr has written, co-authored, or edited more than 25 guidebooks, including *Vancouver & Victoria For Dummies; Frommer's Nova Scotia, New Brunswick & Prince Edward Island; Frommer's New England; Frommer's Vermont, New Hampshire & Maine;* and *Frommer's Maine Coast.* He also has contributed to *Frommer's Irreverent Guides* to Rome and Vancouver. In addition, he has written articles for *Sierra* and *Sports Illustrated,* among other publications. He divides his time among New England, both coasts of Canada, Europe, and Japan.

A full-time writer who globe-trots and scribes for a living, author **Chris McBeath** makes her home in the islands of the Pacific Northwest. Chris tweets, blogs, and maintains a travel website (www.greatestgetaways.com) on her various travels and contributes to publications worldwide.

Bill McRae was born and raised in rural eastern Montana, though he spent the better years of his youth attending university in Great Britain, France, and Canada. He has previously written about Montana, Utah, and Oregon for Moon Publications and about the Pacific Northwest and Seattle for Lonely Planet. Other publications he has written for include *National Geographic*, Microsoft Expedia, and *1,000 Places to See in the U.S.A. and Canada Before You Die* for Workman Press. Bill also is co-author of *Frommer's British Columbia & the Canadian Rockies.*

Kirsten Murphy is a self-taught photojournalist who grew up in Vancouver, lived in Zimbabwe and now calls Yellowknife home. Her photos appear in the *Globe and Mail*, *National Post* and *Up Here* magazine. She is a regular contributor to Canadian Press Images and was the official blogger for Tropicana's Arctic Sun commercial in January 2010. For the last two years, Kirsten hosted an award winning, syndicated radio show about Arctic climate change on CKLB Radio in Yellowknife.

Donald Olson is a novelist, playwright, and travel writer. Donald Olson's travel stories have appeared in *The New York Times*, *Travel & Leisure*, *Sunset*, *National Geographic* books, and many other publications. He is the author of *England For Dummies* (winner of the 2002 Lowell Thomas Travel Writing Award for Best Guidebook), *London For Dummies*, *Germany For Dummies*, *Frommer's London from $95 a Day*, *Frommer's Portable London from $95 a Day*, and *Frommer's Irreverent Guide to London.*

Barbara Ramsay Orr has been writing about world travel, food, wine, and culture for over 20 years and is still gobsmacked by the beauty of her home turf. Her work has appeared in most of the major publications in Canada, in international publications, and online. She maintains a trio of blogs that document her encounters with food, with the world, and with the local scene in Niagara, and has won awards for both her writing and her travel photography.

Christie Pashby has been writting for Frommer's for a decade, contributing to titles like *Frommer's Argentina*, *Frommer's Chile*, and *Best Hikes in British Columbia* and authoring *Frommer's Banff and the Canadian Rockies Day by Day* and *Frommer's Alberta*. She divides her time between the Canadian Rockies and Bariloche, Argentina. A freelance journalist and translator, her website is www.patagonialiving.com.

HOW TO CONTACT US

In researching this book, we discovered many wonderful places—hotels, restaurants, shops, and more. We're sure you'll find others. Please tell us about them, so we can share the information with your fellow travelers in upcoming editions. If you were disappointed with a recommendation, we'd love to know that, too. Please write to:

Frommer's Canada, 16th Edition
John Wiley & Sons Canada, Ltd. • 6045 Freemont Blvd. • Mississauga, ON L5R 4J3

AN ADDITIONAL NOTE

Please be advised that travel information is subject to change at any time—and this is especially true of prices. We therefore suggest that you write or call ahead for confirmation when making your travel plans. The authors, editors, and publisher cannot be held responsible for the experiences of readers while traveling. Your safety is important to us, however, so we encourage you to stay alert and be aware of your surroundings. Keep a close eye on cameras, purses, and wallets, which are all favorite targets of thieves and pickpockets.

FROMMER'S STAR RATINGS, ICONS & ABBREVIATIONS

Every hotel, restaurant, and attraction listing in this guide has been ranked for quality, value, service, amenities, and special features using a **star-rating system.** In country, state, and regional guides, we also rate towns and regions to help you narrow down your choices and budget your time accordingly. Hotels and restaurants are rated on a scale of zero (recommended) to three stars (exceptional). Attractions, shopping, nightlife, towns, and regions are rated according to the following scale: zero stars (recommended), one star (highly recommended), two stars (very highly recommended), and three stars (must-see).

In addition to the star-rating system, we also use seven **feature icons** that point you to the great deals, in-the-know advice, and unique experiences that separate travelers from tourists. Throughout the book, look for:

special finds—those places only insiders know about

fun facts—details that make travelers more informed and their trips more fun

kids—best bets for kids and advice for the whole family

special moments—those experiences that memories are made of

overrated—places or experiences not worth your time or money

insider tips—great ways to save time and money

great values—where to get the best deals

The following **abbreviations** are used for credit cards:

AE American Express | **DISC** Discover | **V** Visa
DC Diners Club | **MC** MasterCard

TRAVEL RESOURCES AT FROMMERS.COM

Frommer's travel resources don't end with this guide. Frommer's website, **www.frommers.com**, has travel information on more than 4,000 destinations. We update features regularly, giving you access to the most current trip-planning information and the best airfare, lodging, and car-rental bargains. You can also listen to podcasts, connect with other Frommers.com members through our active-reader forums, share your travel photos, read blogs from guidebook editors and fellow travelers, and much more.

1

THE BEST OF CANADA

Planning a trip to such a vast and diverse country can present you with a bewildering array of choices. We've scoured all of Canada in search of the best places an experiences, and in this chapter, we share our very perso and opinionated choices. We hope they'll give you some ideas and g started.

THE best TRAVEL EXPERIENCES

nic driving

- **Exploring the Cabot Trail** (Nova Scotia): This a surplus of loop around Cape Breton Highlands National Pa area. You can dramatic coastal scenery. Take a few days to e at, and dabble hike blustery headlands, scope for whales o around a cove or two in a sea kayak. See ch
- **Hiking Gros Morne National Park** (Newf When the Earth's land masses broke apart and shifted 50 rs ago, a piece of the mantle, the very shell of the planet ward to form awe-some tableland mountains of rock ek or more trekking coastal trails, venturing to scenic d strolling alongside landlocked fjords. See "Gros Mo ek," in chapter 6.
- **Watching the World Go by at Cafe** (Québec): Tables are set out at Place d'Armes n the Quartier du Petit-Champlain in Lower Town and-Allée. It's a quality-of-life invention the Québ ed. See chapter 8.
- **Checking Out Toronto nd Music** (Ontario): Sure, Toronto likes its block h are usually housed at the Royal Alexandra or t theaters. However, the offer-ings from the Ca Opera Atelier, Tafelmusik, and the Lorraine Kim People are innovative and con-sistently excelle e Canadian Opera Company or the National B ge at their new home—the Four Seasons Centr rts—is breathtaking. See "Toronto After Dark," i

- **Seeing the Polar Bears in Churchill** (Manitoba): In October or November, travel by train or plane to Churchill and the shores of Hudson Bay to view hundreds of magnificent polar bears, which migrate to the bay's icy shores and even lope into Churchill itself. In the evening, you can glimpse the famous aurora borealis (northern lights). Either take **VIA Rail**'s *Hudson Bay* train (✆ **888/VIA-RAIL** in Canada or 800/561-3949 in the U.S.), a 2-night/1-day trip from Winnipeg, or fly in on **Calm Air** (✆ **800/839-2256**). See "Churchill, the World's Polar Bear Capital," in chapter 13.
- **Horseback Riding in the Rockies** (Alberta): Rent a cabin on a rural guest ranch and get back in the saddle again. Spend a day fishing, then return to the lodge for a count[illegible] dance or barbecue. Ride a horse to a backcountry chalet in the rugged mountai[illegible] wilderness. Forget the crowded park highways and commercialized resort tow[illegible], and just relax. **Brewster's Kananaskis Guest Ranch** (✆ **800/691-5085** or [illegible]/673-3737) in Kananaskis Village, near Banff, offers a variety of guided ho[illegible]ck trips, including food, lodging, and the horse you ride in on. See p. 562.
- **Sailing the [illegible]t Bear Rainforest** (British Columbia): About halfway up BC's west coast is [illegible]lated region of mountains, fjords, bays, rivers, and inlets. It's one of the last pla[illegible]ere grizzly bears are still found in large numbers, plus salmon, killer whales, [illegible]nd porpoises. **Maple Leaf Adventures** (✆ **888/599-5323** or 250/386-72[illegible]) [illegible] a number of trips on a 28m (92-ft.) schooner to this magic part of the worl[illegible] [illegible] 681.

THE be[illegible] FAMILY VACATIONS

- **Fundy National Pa[illegible]** [illegible]**ity** (New Brunswick): You'll find swimming, hiking, and kayaking at thi[illegible]ary national park—and plenty of attractions and programs for kids, to[illegible] [illegible]ook biking in the hills east of the park, or rappelling and rock climbi[illegible] [illegible]Enrage, either. See "Fundy National Park," in chapter 4.
- **Prince Edward Island** [illegible]he red-sand beaches here might turn white swim trunks a bit pinkis[illegible] [illegible] to beat a day or two splashing around these tepid waters while admi[illegible] [illegible]nd landscapes. The island possesses several children's amusemen[illegible] [illegible]ll. See chapter 5.
- **Mont-Tremblant Ski Reso[illegible]** [illegible]ébec): The pearl of the Laurentians is Mont-Tremblant, just an h[illegible] [illegible]om Montréal and the highest peak in eastern Canada at 968m (3,[illegible] [illegible] in the winter for skiers and snowboarders from all over and [illegible] [illegible]d the top resort in eastern North America by Ski magazine. D[illegible] [illegible]n particularly heavy in the resort town; the area gains back som[illegible] [illegible] summer with thinned-out traffic. See "North into the Lauren[illegible] chapter 7.
- **Ottawa** (Ontario): In this famil[illegible] [illegible] your kids can watch soldiers strut their stuff and red-coated N[illegible] [illegible]questrian and musical skills. Canoeing or skating on the cana[illegible] [illegible]awa boasts a host of lively museums to explore—such as [illegible] Museum, the Canadian Museum of Civilization, and the [illegible]chnology Museum. See chapter 9.
- **The Muskoka Lakes** (Ontario): Th[illegible] [illegible]esorts that welcome families. Kids can swim, canoe, bike [illegible] [illegible] most resorts offer

children's programs, parents can enjoy a rest, as well. And once you tell the small fries that Santa's Village is open year-round in the town of Bracebridge, you won't be able to keep them away. See "The Muskoka Lakes," in chapter 12.

- **Whistler/Blackcomb Ski Resorts** (British Columbia): Whistler and Blackcomb's twin ski resorts offer lots of family-oriented activities. You'll find everything from downhill and cross-country skiing, snowboarding, snowshoeing, and snowmobiling lessons in winter to horseback riding, mountain biking, in-line skating, swimming, kayaking, and rafting summer trips designed for families with school-age children. See "Whistler," in chapter 16.
- **Travel the Klondike Gold Rush Route** (The Yukon): Follow the Klondike Gold Rush, traveling from Skagway, Alaska, up and over White Pass, to the Yukon's capital, Whitehorse. Canoe through the once-daunting Miles Canyon on the mighty Yukon River. Drive to Dawson City and visit the gold fields, walk the boardwalks of the old town center, and listen to recitations of Robert Service poetry. Pan for gold and attend an old-fashioned musical revue at the opera house. Inexpensive public campgrounds abound in the Yukon, making this one of the more affordable family vacations in western Canada. See chapter 17.

THE best NATURE & WILDLIFE VIEWING

- **Whales at Digby Neck** (Nova Scotia): For a cha[illegible]ee fin, minke, or humpback whales, choose from a plethora of whale-[illegible] outfitters located along this narrow peninsula of remote fishing villa[illegible]t, sperm, blue, and pilot whales, along with the infrequent orcas, have [illegible] seen over the years. Getting to the tip of the peninsula is half the f[illegible]uires two ferries. See "From Digby to Yarmouth," in chapter 3.
- **Birds and Caribou on the Avalon Peni**[illegible]wfoundland): In one busy day, you can see a herd of caribou, the larg[illegible]olony in North America, and an extraordinary gannet colony visible fr[illegible] cliffs. See "The Southern Avalon Peninsula," in chapter 6.
- **Whales at Baie Ste-Catherine** (Q[illegible]ut a 2-hour drive north of Québec City in the upper Charlevoix regi[illegible] of resident minke and beluga whales are joined by blue, fin, and hu[illegible]s in the summers. Mid-June to early October is the best time to s[illegible] can be spotted from land, but whale-watching cruises offer clos[illegible]ebsite www.whales-online.net provides up-to-date info on activity[illegible]e "Upper Charlevoix: Baie Ste-Catherine & Tadoussac," in chapte[illegible]
- **Pelicans in Prince Alb**[illegible]**k** (Saskatchewan): On Lavallee Lake roosts the second-largest p[illegible] North America. Bison, moose, elk, caribou, black bear, and re[illegible]ee in this 400,000-hectare (1 million-acre) wilderness. See "[illegible]onal Park," in chapter 13.
- **Orcas off Vanc**[illegible]sh Columbia): The waters surrounding Vancouver Island teem[illegible] whales), as well as harbor seals, sea lions, bald eagles, and ha[illegible] porpoises. In Victoria, **Seafun Safaris Whale Watching** is c[illegible]ies offering whale-watching tours in Zodiacs and covered boats [illegible]6.

THE best VIEWS

- **Cape Enrage** (New Brunswick): Just east of Fundy National Park, you'll find a surprisingly harsh coastal terrain of high rocky cliffs pounded by the sea. Route 915 offers a wonderful detour off the beaten path. See "Fundy National Park," in chapter 4.
- **Signal Hill** (Newfoundland): Signal Hill marks the entrance to St. John's harbor. Besides the history that was made here, it's uncommonly scenic, with views of a coast that hasn't changed in 500 years. The North Head Trail is one of Newfoundland's most dramatic—and it's entirely within city limits. See p. 193.
- **Bonavista Peninsula** (Newfoundland): The peninsula's northernmost tip offers a superb v tage point for spotting icebergs, even into midsummer. You'll also see puffins, w les, and one of the most scenic lighthouses in eastern Canada. See "The Bona ta Peninsula," in chapter 6.
- **Terrasse D erin in Québec City** (Québec): Every narrow street, leafy plaza, sidewalk ca horse-drawn calèche, and church spire in Québec City breathes recollections he provincial cities of the mother country of France. Atop the bluff overlook he St. Lawrence River, this handsome boardwalk promenade, with its green- hite–topped gazebos, looks much as it did 100 years ago, when ladies with para nd gentlemen with top hats strolled it on sunny afternoons, with the turrets Château Frontenac as a backdrop. At night, the river below is the color of liq ercury, and music from the *boîtes* in Lower Town echoes faintly. See chapte
- **Niagara Falls** (On his is still a wonder of nature, despite its commercial exploitation. You ca nce the falls from the cockpit of a helicopter or from the decks of the *Mai ist,* which takes you into the roaring maelstrom. The least intimidating vie n the Skylon Tower. See "Niagara-on-the-Lake & Niagara Falls," in chap
- **Agawa Canyon** (Ontar the northern Ontario wilderness that inspired the Group of Seven, tak va Canyon Train Tour on a 184km (114-mile) trip from the Soo to Hear he Agawa Canyon, where you can spend a few hours exploring scenic w vistas. The train snakes through a vista of deep ravines and lakes, hug sides and crossing gorges on skeletal trestle bridges. See "Some Northe ighlights: Driving along Highways 11 & 17," in chapter 12.
- **Moraine Lake in Banff Natio rta): Ten snow-clad peaks towering up to 3,000m (9,843 ft.) rear up hind this gem-blue tiny lake. Rent a canoe and paddle to the mount "Banff National Park," in chapter 14.
- **Vancouver** (British Columbia): t beautiful setting of any city in Canada or indeed the world, th us places to take in the view of mountains, city, and ocean: on t peaks of **Grouse Mountain**, accessible via a quick tram ride; or of your harbor-side hotel room in the **Pan Pacific Hotel Vanco** t way remains the cheapest: Round about sunset, wander to Engl the corner of Denman and Davie streets, grab an ice cream or a all, and watch as the sun shimmers red, and then descends be land, lighting the Coast Mountains, Vancouver, and English Ba w. See chapter 15.

THE most DRAMATIC DRIVES

- **Cape Breton's Cabot Trail** (Nova Scotia): This 300km (186-mile) loop through the uplands of Cape Breton Highlands National Park is a world-class excursion. You'll see Acadian fishing ports, pristine valleys, and some of the most picturesque coastline anywhere. See chapter 3.
- **Viking Trail** (Newfoundland): Travelers looking to leave the crowds behind needn't look any farther. This beautiful drive to Newfoundland's northern tip is wild and solitary, with views of curious geology and a wind-raked coast. And you'll end up at one of the world's great historic sites—L'Anse aux Meadows. See "The Great Northern Peninsula," in chapter 6.
- **Icefields Parkway** (Hwy. 93 through Banff and Jasper national parks, Alberta): This is one of the world's grandest mountain drives. Cruising along it is like a trip back to the ice ages. The parkway climbs past glacier-notched peaks to the Columbia Icefields, a sprawling cap of snow, ice, and glacier at the very crest of the Rockies. See "Banff National Park," in chapter 14.
- **Highway 99** (British Columbia): The Sea to Sky Highway from Vancouver to Lillooet takes you from a dramatic seacoast past glaciers, pine forests, and a waterfall that cascades from a mountaintop and through Whistler's majestic glacial mountains. The next leg of the 4-hour drive winds up a series of switchbacks to the thickly forested Cayoosh Creek valley and on to the craggy mountains surrounding the Fraser River Gold Rush town of Lillooet. See chapter 16.
- **Dempster Highway** (from Dawson City to Inuvik, Northwest Territories): Canada's most northerly highway, the Dempster is a year-round gravel road across the top of the world. From Dawson City, the road winds over the Continental Divide three times, crosses the Arctic Circle, and fords the Peel and Mackenzie rivers by ferry before reaching Inuvik, a First Nations community on the mighty Mackenzie River delta. See chapter 17.

THE best WALKS & RAMBLES

- **Halifax's Waterfront** (Nova Scotia): Take your time strolling along Halifax's working waterfront. You can visit museums, board an historic ship or two, enjoy a snack, and take an inexpensive ferry ride across the harbor and back. Come evening, there's fiddle and guitar playing at the pubs. See "Halifax," in chapter 3.
- **Cape Breton Highlands National Park** (Nova Scotia): You'll find bog and woodland walks aplenty at Cape Breton, but the best trails follow rugged cliffs along the open ocean. The Skyline Trail is among the most dramatic pathways in the province. See "Cape Breton Highlands National Park," in chapter 3.
- **Green Gardens Trail** (Gros Morne, Newfoundland): This demanding hike at Gros Morne National Park takes you on a 16km (9.9-mile) loop, much of which follows coastal meadows atop fractured cliffs. It's demanding but worth every step. See "Gros Morne National Park," in chapter 6.
- **Vieux-Montréal** (Montréal, Québec): The architectural heritage of the historic Vieux-Montréal, or "Old Montréal," district and the Vieux-Port (Old Port) waterfront promenade adjacent has been substantially preserved. Several small but intriguing museums are housed in historic buildings, and restored 18th- and 19th-century structures have been adapted for use as shops, galleries, boutique hotels,

cafes, studios, bars, and apartments. In the evening, many of the finer buildings are illuminated. Today, especially in summer, activity centers around Place Jacques-Cartier, where street performers, strolling locals, and tourists congregate. See chapter 7.

- **Toronto's Art & Design District** (Ontario): The stretch of Queen Street that runs west of Bathurst Avenue has been reinvented as the Art & Design District. This isn't just a marketing ploy—the title is well deserved. The area is home to the Museum of Contemporary Canadian Art and to private art collections such as the Stephen Bulger Gallery; it's also the neighborhood to see some of the best local design talent, with block after block of unique boutiques, small but edgy galleries, and plenty of cafes. See chapter 10.
- **Lake Superior Provincial Park** (Ontario): Follow any trail in this park to a rewarding vista. The 16km (9.9-mile) Peat Mountain Trail leads to a panoramic view close to 150m (about 492 ft.) above the surrounding lakes and forests. The moderate Orphan Lake Trail offers views over the Orphan Lake and Lake Superior, plus a pebble beach and Baldhead River falls. The 26km (16-mile) Toawab Trail takes you through the Agawa Valley to the 25m (82-ft.) Agawa Falls. See "Some Northern Ontario Highlights: Driving along Highways 11 & 17," in chapter 12.
- **Johnston Canyon** (Banff National Park, Alberta): Just 24km (15 miles) west of Banff, Johnston Creek cuts a deep, very narrow canyon through limestone cliffs. The trail winds through tunnels, passes waterfalls, edges by shaded rock faces, and crosses the chasm on footbridges before reaching a series of iridescent pools, formed by springs that bubble up through highly colored rock. See "Banff National Park," in chapter 14.
- **Plain of Six Glaciers Trail** (Lake Louise, Alberta): From Chateau Lake Louise, a lakeside trail rambles along the edge of emerald-green Lake Louise, and then climbs to the base of Victoria Glacier. At a rustic teahouse, you can order a cup of tea and a scone—each made over a wood-burning stove—and gaze up at the rumpled face of the glacier. See "Banff National Park," in chapter 14.
- **Stanley Park** (Vancouver, British Columbia) is something of a miracle—a huge, lush park (one of the largest city parks in the world) right on the edge of a densely populated urban neighborhood. Stroll the famous seawall that skirts the entire park, visit a striking collection of First Nation totem poles, or simply wander among the giant trees and magnificent plantings. See p. 651.
- **Long Beach** (Vancouver Island, British Columbia): Part of Pacific Rim National Park, Long Beach is more than 16km (10 miles) long and hundreds of meters wide, and is flanked by awe-inspiring rainforests of cedar, fir, and Sitka spruce. Beyond the roaring surf, you'll see soaring eagles, basking sea lions, and occasionally even migrating gray whales. See chapter 16.

THE best BIKING ROUTES

- **Nova Scotia's South Shore:** Not in a hurry to get anywhere? Peddling peninsulas and coasting along placid inlets is a great tonic for the weary soul. You'll pass through graceful villages such as Shelburne, Lunenburg, and Chester, and rediscover a quiet way of life en route. See "The South Shore," in chapter 3.
- **Prince Edward Island:** This island province sometimes seems like it was created specifically *for* bike touring. The villages here are reasonably spaced apart, hills are virtually nonexistent, the coastal roads are picturesque in the extreme, and a new

island-wide bike path offers detours through marshes and quiet woodlands. See chapter 5.

- **Montréal's Lachine Canal** (Montréal, Québec): Montréal boasts an expanding network of more than 350km (217 miles) of cycling paths and year-round bike lanes on city streets. The Lachine Canal was inaugurated in 1824 so ships could bypass the Lachine Rapids on the way to the Great Lakes, and the canal now has a nearly flat 11km (6.8-mile) bicycle path on either side of it that travels peacefully alongside locks and over small bridges. You can rent bikes in the Old Port. See "Outdoor Activities & Spectator Sports," in chapter 7.
- **Québec's Route verte (Green Route):** In 2007, the province officially inaugurated the *Route verte,* a 4,000km (2,485-mile) bike-path network that stretches from one end of Québec to the other and links up all regions and cities. The idea is modeled on the Rails-to-Trails program in the U.S. and cycling routes in Denmark and Great Britain. Inns along the route are especially focused on serving bikers, with covered and locked storage for overnight stays and carb-heavy meals. See p. 249.
- **Niagara Region** (Ontario): The flatlands here make for terrific biking terrain. A bike path runs along the Niagara Parkway, which follows the Niagara River. You'll bike past fruit farms, vineyards, and gardens with picnicking spots. See "Niagara-on-the-Lake & Niagara Falls," in chapter 11.
- **Highways 1 and 93 through Banff and Jasper National Parks** (Alberta): Also called the Icefields Parkway, this well-maintained wide highway winds through some of the world's most dramatic mountain scenery. Take the Bow Valley Parkway, between Banff and Lake Louise, and Parkway 93A between Athabasca Falls and Jasper for slightly quieter peddling. Best of all, there are seven hostels (either rustic or fancy) at some of the most beautiful sights along the route, so you don't have to weigh yourself down with camping gear. See chapter 14.
- **Stanley Park Seawall** (Vancouver, British Columbia): Vancouver's Seawall surrounds the Stanley Park shoreline on the Burrard Inlet and English Bay. Built just above the high-tide mark, it offers nonstop breathtaking views, no hills, and no cars. See chapter 15.

THE best CULINARY EXPERIENCES

- **Fresh Lobster** (Nova Scotia and New Brunswick): Wherever you see wooden lobster traps piled on a wharf, you'll know a fresh lobster meal isn't far away. The most productive lobster fisheries are around Shediac, New Brunswick, and all along Nova Scotia's Atlantic coast. Sunny days are ideal for cracking open a crustacean while sitting at a wharf-side picnic table, preferably with a locally brewed beer close at hand. See chapters 3 and 4.
- **Newfoundland Berries:** The unforgiving rocky and boggy soil of this blustery island resists most crops, but it also produces some of the most delicious berries in Canada. Look for roadside stands or pick your own blueberries, strawberries, partridgeberries, or bakeapples. Many restaurants add these berries to desserts (cheesecake, custard) when they're in season, too. See chapter 6.
- **Pigging Out in Montréal** (Montréal, Québec): See what its cultish fans have been raving about. **Au Pied de Cochon** (✆ **514/281-1114**) looks like just another storefront restaurant, but it's packed to the walls 6 nights a week because of its slabs

of meat, especially pork. "The Big Happy Pig's Chop," weighing in at more than a pound, is emblematic. Foie gras comes in nearly a dozen combinations, including stuffed into a ham hock, with *poutine,* and in a goofy creation called Duck in a Can—which does, indeed, come sealed in a can with a can opener. See p. 236.

- **Indulging in a Tasting Menu Dinner in Québec City** (Québec): Higher-end establishments in both Montréal and Québec City are increasingly offering menus that let you sample the chef's wildest concoctions, and "surprise menus" are equally popular—you don't know what you're getting until it's right in front of you. The imaginative menu at **Laurie Raphaël** (**© 418/692-4555**) has included silky-smooth foie gras on a teeny ice-cream paddle with a drizzle of port reduction, Alaskan snow crab with a bright-pink pomegranate terrine, and an egg yolk "illusion" of thickened orange juice encapsulated in a skin of pectin served in a puddle of maple syrup. Dazzling! See p. 287.
- **Indulging in Toronto's Gastronomic Scene** (Ontario): Toronto is blessed with a host of stellar chefs, such as Mark McEwan (**Bymark; © 416/777-1144**), Lynn Crawford (**RubyWatchCo; © 416/465-0100**), Chris McDonald (**Cava; © 416/979-9918**), Anthony Walsh (**Canoe Restaurant and Bar; © 416/364-0054**), and Jamie Kennedy (**Gilead Bistro & Cafe; © 416/288-0680**). This is your chance to find out why they're household names. See "Where to Dine," in chapter 10.
- **Tasting the World in Toronto** (Ontario): The United Nations has called Toronto the world's most multicultural city, so it's no surprise that the restaurant scene reflects that diversity. Whether you try the excellent sushi at **Hiro Sushi** (**© 416/304-0550**), tasty Ethiopian cooking at **Lalibela** (**© 416/535-6615**), classic French cuisine at **Loire** (**© 416/850-8330**), or imaginatively updated Greek at **Pan on the Danforth** (**© 416/466-8158**), your taste buds will thank you. See "Where to Dine," in chapter 10.
- **Dining along the Wine Route** (Ontario): The Niagara Region enjoys its own unique microclimate, a fact that explains why this is one of the lushest, most bountiful parts of Canada. Sampling the local wines is a great way to spend an afternoon, particularly if you add lunch and dinner to your itinerary at a vineyard restaurant such as **On the Twenty** (**© 905/562-7313**) or **Vineland Estates** (**© 888/846-3526** or 905/562-7088). See "Niagara-on-the-Lake & Niagara Falls," in chapter 11.
- **Cutting Edge in Winnipeg** (Manitoba): Winnipeg's restaurant of the moment, the two-story **Mise** (**© 204/284-7916**), takes local ingredients as a base for an inventive mix of traditional and contemporary dishes. In summer, the patio is a much-sought-after location to savor dishes like candied-salmon watermelon salad and slow roasted pork back ribs. See p. 499.
- **Going Organic in Calgary** (Alberta): You'll walk through a quiet tree-filled park on an island in the Bow River to reach the bustling **River Café** (**© 403/261-7670**). An immense wood-fired oven and grill produces soft, chewy flat breads and smoky grilled meats and vegetables, all organically grown and freshly harvested. On warm summer evenings, picnickers loll in the grassy shade, nibbling this and that from the cafe's picnic-like menu. See p. 545.
- **Dining at a Hotel in Lake Louise** (Alberta): At its cozy dining room in an old log lodge, the **Post Hotel** (**© 800/661-1586** or 403/522-3989) serves up the kind of sophisticated yet robust cuisine that perfectly fits the backdrop of glaciered peaks, deep forest, and glassy streams. Both the wine list and the cooking are

French and hearty, with the chef focusing on the best of local ingredients—lamb, salmon, and Alberta beef. After spending time out on the trail, a meal here will top off a quintessential day in the Rockies. See p. 586.

- **Serving Up Exquisite Canadian Cuisine in Edmonton** (Alberta): The **Hardware Grill** (✆ **780/423-0969**) is a stylish restaurant in an historic storefront with one of western Canada's finest dining rooms. The chef captures the best of local produce and meats without being slave to the indigenous foods movement, instead taking a Pan-Canadian view of fine dining. Fresh BC oysters and salmon, Alberta steaks, Québec foie gras, and Maritime lobsters are artfully prepared, and it's especially exciting to make a meal of the menu's ample selection of small plates—savoring these exquisite culinary explosions is the gastronomic equivalent of foreplay. See p. 612.
- **Enjoying Dim Sum in Vancouver's Chinatown** (British Columbia): With its burgeoning Chinese population, Vancouver's Chinatown has more than half a dozen dim-sum parlors where you can try steamed or baked barbecued-pork buns, dumplings filled with fresh prawns and vegetables, or steamed rice-flour crepes filled with spicy beef. One favorite is **Sun Sui Wah** (✆ **604/872-8822**). See p. 649.
- **Eating Local in Lotus Land** (British Columbia): Self-sufficiency is the new watchword on the west coast, with top chefs sourcing all their ingredients locally. On Vancouver Island, the **Sooke Harbour House** (✆ **800/889-9688** or 250/642-3421) offers lamb from nearby Salt Spring Island, seasoned with herbs from the chef's own garden. See p. 703. In Vancouver, the **Raincity Grill** (✆ **604/685-7337**) makes a specialty of fresh-caught seafood and local game, while the vast selection of BC wines by the glass makes dinner an extended road trip through the west coast wine country, with no need for a designated driver. See p. 645.

THE best FESTIVALS & SPECIAL EVENTS

- **International Busker Festival** (Halifax, Nova Scotia): In early August, the 10-day International Busker Festival brings together talented street performers from around the world, performing in their natural habitat. Best of all, it's free. See p. 76.
- **Newfoundland and Labrador Folk Festival** (St. John's, Newfoundland): How did such a remote island develop such a deep talent pool? That's one of the questions you'll ponder while tapping your feet at this 3-day festival, which is laden with local talent. It's cheap, folksy, and fun. See p. 22.
- **Montréal Jazz Festival** (Montréal, Québec): The city has a long tradition in jazz, and this enormously successful July festival has been celebrating America's art form since 1979. Spread out over 11 days, close to 150 indoor shows are scheduled. Wynton Marsalis, Harry Connick, Jr., and even Bob Dylan have been featured in recent years, with smaller shows that highlight everything from Dixieland to the most experimental. See p. 261.
- **Carnaval de Québec** (Québec): Never mind that temperatures in Québec can plummet in February to –40°F (–40°C). Canadians happily pack the family up to come out and play for the 17 days of the city's winter festival. There's a monumental ice palace, dog-sled racing, ice sculptures competitions, outdoor hot-tubbing, zip-line rides over crowds, and dancing at night at outdoor concerts. See p. 296.

- **Toronto International Film Festival** (Ontario): Second only to Cannes, this film festival draws Hollywood's leading luminaries to town for 10 days in early September; more than 250 films are on show. See p. 22.
- **Stratford Festival** (Ontario): This world-famous festival of superb repertory theater, launched by Tyrone Guthrie in 1953, has featured major players such as the late Sir Alec Guinness, Christopher Plummer, Dame Maggie Smith, and the late Sir Peter Ustinov. Productions, which run from May to October or early November on four stages, range from classic to contemporary. You can also participate in informal discussions with company members. See "Stratford & the Stratford Festival," in chapter 11.
- **Festival du Voyageur** (Winnipeg, Manitoba): There's no better antidote to February cabin fever than a midwinter festival, and this is western Canada's largest. The festival celebrates the French-Canadian trappers and explorers called *voyageurs* who traveled the waterways of Canada in canoes. Held in St. Boniface (Winnipeg's French Quarter), the festival brings together traditional French-Canadian food, music, and high spirits. See p. 488.
- **Calgary Stampede** (Alberta): In all North America, there's nothing quite like the Calgary Stampede. Of course, it's the world's largest rodeo, but it's also a series of concerts, an art show, an open-air casino, a carnival, a street dance—you name it, it's undoubtedly going on somewhere. In early July, all of Calgary is converted into a party, and everyone's invited. See "Calgary," in chapter 14.
- **Celebration of Light** (Vancouver, British Columbia): This 4-night fireworks extravaganza in late July and early August (www.vancouverfireworks.ca) takes place over English Bay. Three of the world's leading manufacturers are invited to represent their countries in competition against one another, setting their best displays to music. On the fourth night, all three companies launch their finales. Up to 500,000 people show up each night. The best seats are at the "Bard on the Beach" Shakespeare festival across False Creek. See chapter 15.

THE best LUXURY HOTELS & RESORTS

- **Keltic Lodge** (Cape Breton Island, Nova Scotia; © **800/565-0444** or 902/285-2880): It's got grand natural drama in the sea-pounded cliffs that surround it, plus a generous measure of high culture. (Jackets on men at dinner, please!) The adjacent golf course is stupendous, and some of the national park's best hikes are close at hand. See p. 97.
- **Kingsbrae Arms Relais & Châteaux** (St. Andrews, New Brunswick; © **506/529-1897**): This deluxe inn manages the trick of being opulent and comfortable at the same time. The shingled manse is lavishly appointed, beautifully landscaped, and well situated for exploring charming St. Andrews. See p. 115.
- **Dalvay by the Sea** (Grand Tracadie, Prince Edward Island; © **902/672-2048**): This intimate resort (it has fewer than 35 rooms and cottages total) is on a quiet stretch of beach. The Tudor mansion was built by a business partner of John D. Rockefeller, and the woodwork alone is enough to keep you entertained during your stay. Bring your bike. See p. 154.
- **Hôtel Le St-James** (Montréal, Québec; © **866/841-3111** or 514/841-3111): Old Montréal's surge of designer hotels spans the spectrum from super-minimalist

to gentlemen's club. The opulent Le St-James sits squarely at the gentlemen's-club end of the range. A richly paneled entry leads to a grand hall with carved urns, bronze chandeliers, and balconies with gilded metal balustrades, and the 60 units are furnished with entrancing antiques and impeccable reproductions. A stone-walled, candle-lit spa offers massage and full-body water therapy. See p. 222.

- **Fairmont Le Château Frontenac** (Québec City; © **800/441-1414** or 418/692-3861): The turreted hotel opened in 1893 and has hosted Queen Elizabeth and Prince Philip; during World War II, Winston Churchill and Franklin D. Roosevelt had the entire place to themselves for a conference. Luxurious rooms are outfitted with regal decor and elegant château furnishings. Bathrooms have marble touches, and every mattress was replaced in 2006 or 2007. Fairmont Gold floors, with a separate concierge and a lounge with an honor bar, offer expansive views of the St. Lawrence River and the old city below. See p. 279.
- **Park Hyatt Toronto** (Ontario; © **800/233-1234** or 416/925-1234): Talk about having it all—the Park Hyatt boasts a beautifully renovated Art Deco building, a creative dining room (Annona), a serene spa, top-notch service, and one of the best views in the city from the rooftop terrace lounge (where they mix a mighty martini, too). This is a place to relax and let yourself be pampered. See p. 384.
- **Langdon Hall** (Cambridge, Ontario; © **800/268-1898** or 519/740-2100): This quintessential English country house, built in 1902 for the granddaughter of John Jacob Astor, is now a small hotel where you can enjoy 81 hectares (200 acres) of lawns, gardens, and woodlands. The guest rooms feature the finest amenities, fabrics, and furnishings. Facilities include a full spa, a pool, a tennis court, a croquet lawn, and an exercise room. The airy dining room overlooking the lily pond offers fine continental cuisine. See p. 446.
- **Delta Bessborough** (Saskatoon, Saskatchewan; © **800/268-1133** or 306/244-5521): Canada is famous for its historic, turn-of-the-20th-century luxury hotels built by the railways, but none is more unexpected than this massive French château in the midst of the Saskatchewan prairies. Beautifully restored, the Bessborough is more than a relic—it's a celebration of the past. Expect exemplary service, comfortable rooms, and the giddy feeling that you're on the Loire, not the South Saskatchewan River. See p. 522.
- **The Fairmont Chateau Lake Louise** (Banff National Park, Alberta; © **800/441-1414** or 403/522-3511): First of all, there's the view: Across a tiny gem-green lake rise massive cliffs shrouded in glacial ice. And then there's the hotel: Part hunting lodge, part European palace, the Chateau is its own community, with sumptuous boutiques, sports-rental facilities, seven dining areas, two bars, magnificent lobby areas, and beautifully furnished guest rooms. See p. 586.
- **Fairmont Hotel Macdonald** (Edmonton, Alberta; © **800/441-1414** or 780/424-5181): When the Canadian Pacific bought and refurbished this landmark hotel in the 1980s, all the charming period details were preserved, while all the inner workings were modernized and brought up to snuff. The result is a regally elegant but friendly small hotel, a real class act. See p. 608.
- **Westin Bayshore Resort & Marina** (Vancouver, British Columbia; © **800/937-8461** or 604/682-3377): Vancouver's only resort hotel with its own marina, the Westin Bayshore looks out across the Burrard Inlet to the mountains and west to the vast expanse of Stanley Park. The finishes throughout are top quality, the beds divine, the pool is one of the largest in North America, and the size of the hotel

(which includes a spa and conference center) makes it like a small, luxurious city. See p. 636.

- **The Wickaninnish Inn** (Tofino, British Columbia; © **800/333-4604** in North America or 250/725-3100): No matter which room you book in this beautiful new lodge, you'll wake to a magnificent view of the untamed Pacific. The inn is on a rocky promontory, surrounded by an old-growth spruce and cedar rainforest, and the sprawling sands of Long Beach. In summer, try golfing, fishing, or whale-watching. In winter, shelter by the fire in the Pointe restaurant and watch the wild Pacific storms roll in. See p. 733.
- **Brentwood Bay Lodge & Spa** (Victoria, British Columbia; © **888/544-2079** or 250/544-2079): Every detail has been carefully considered and beautifully rendered in this contemporary timber-and-glass lodge located on a pristine inlet about 20 minutes north of downtown Victoria. With its contemporary rooms, fabulous spa, fine-dining room, and host of amenities, guests experience the luxurious best of the Pacific Northwest. See p. 702.
- **Four Seasons Resort Whistler** (Whistler, British Columbia; © **888/935-2460** or 604/935-3400): This grand—even monumental—hotel is the classiest place to stay in Whistler, which is saying something. This is a hotel with many moods, from the Wagnerian scale of the stone-lined lobby, to the precise gentility of the guest rooms, to the faint and welcome silliness of the tiled and back-lit stone fixtures of the restaurant. This is a great hotel that's not afraid to make big statements. See p. 749.

THE best BED & BREAKFASTS

- **Shipwright Inn** (Charlottetown, Prince Edward Island; © **888/306-9966** or 902/368-1905): This in-town, nine-room B&B is within easy walking distance of all of the city's attractions yet has a settled and pastoral feel. It's informed by a Victorian sensibility without being over the top about it. See p. 158.
- **Banberry House** (St. John's, Newfoundland; © **877/579-8226** or 709/579-8006): This centrally located B&B boasts stained glass from 1892 by the same craftsman who worked on a nearby basilica. It is full of carefully preserved historical authenticity, and the breakfast features local delicacies made on-site, with the menu changing daily. See p. 195.
- **Beild House** (Collingwood, Ontario; © **888/322-3453** or 705/444-1522): On Fridays, you can sit down to a splendid five-course dinner before retiring to the bed that belonged to the duke and duchess of Windsor. A sumptuous breakfast will follow the next morning. This handsome 1909 house contains 11 rooms, 7 with private bathrooms. See p. 455.
- **Banff Boutique Inn** (Banff, Alberta; © **403/762-4636**): A local couple with a passion for inn-keeping have turned an old-fashioned building (originally built as a European-style *pension* in 1943) into a lovely inn, with modern decor and mountain hospitality. The excellent breakfast spread includes a wide variety of home-baked goodies and is served in a cozy room with contemporary works by local artists. See p. 576.
- **The Albion Manor** (Victoria, British Columbia; © **877/389-0012**): Recent renovations have worked miracles, transforming this 1892 heritage house into an art-inspired home. The artist-owners have a background in staging international expos,

so decor incorporates whimsical sculptures (sometimes edgy and always theatrical), Victorian-era antiques, and well-traveled pieces from Morocco to Papua New Guinea for an eclectic, one-of-a-kind ambiance. Nearly every item has a story. Guest rooms, beds, and lounges are exceptionally comfortable, with intriguing items. See p. 700.

THE best CAMPING & WILDERNESS LODGES

- **Green Park Provincial Park** (Tyne Valley, Prince Edward Island; © **902/831-7912**): Can't afford your own well-maintained estate? This provincial campground makes a decent substitute. Set on a quiet inlet, the 88-hectare (217-acre) park is built around an extravagant gingerbread mansion that's still open to the public. See "Prince County," in chapter 5.
- **Gros Morne National Park** (Newfoundland): Backpackers will find wild, spectacular campsites in coastal meadows along the remarkable Green Gardens Trail; car campers should head for Trout River Pond, at the foot of one of Gros Morne's dramatic landlocked fjords. See "Gros Morne National Park," in chapter 6.
- **Arowhon Pines** (Algonquin Park, Ontario; © **866/633-5661,** 705/633-5661 in summer, or 416/483-4393 in winter): Located 8km (5 miles) off the highway down a dirt road, this is one of the most entrancing places anywhere. You can enjoy peace, seclusion, and natural beauty, plus comfortable accommodations and good fresh food. There are no TVs or phones—just the call of the loons, the gentle lapping of the water, the croaking of the frogs, and the splash of canoe paddles cutting the surface of the lake. See p. 467.
- **Tunnel Mountain** (Banff, Alberta; © **403/762-1500**): If you find Banff too expensive and too crowded, these campgrounds—three within 5km (3 miles) of town—are a great antidote. Most sites have full hookups, with showers and real toilets. And you'll pay just one-tenth of what hotel dwellers are paying for equally good access to the Rockies. See "Banff National Park," in chapter 14.
- **Clayoquot Sound** (British Columbia): The best place to camp in BC is on a wild beach on the shores of this vast forested fjord, with only the eagles for company by day and an endless supply of burnable driftwood at night. Much of the coastline is Crown or public land, so there are limitless places to camp (and it's free). The only trick is you need a kayak to take you there. Along the way, you'll see 1,000-year-old trees, glaciers, whales, and bald eagles. See chapter 16.

2 PLANNING YOUR TRIP TO CANADA

Canada is a vast country—in fact, it is the world's second-largest nation. This chapter can save you money, time, and headaches as you plan your visit.

The Regions in Brief

Bounded by the Atlantic, Pacific, and Arctic oceans, Canada is a land of extraordinary natural beauty, with dramatic land and seascapes, and vibrant cosmopolitan cities. The country is divided into 10 provinces and 3 territories.

NOVA SCOTIA

The heart of Canada's maritime provinces, Nova Scotia has brooding landscapes, wild seacoasts, and historic fishing villages. Its name means New Scotland, after all. Centered on a beautiful natural harbor, Halifax is one of Canada's most charming small cities, with an abundance of 19th-century stone architecture. See chapter 3.

NEW BRUNSWICK

Wedged between the Gulf of St. Lawrence and the Bay of Fundy, New Brunswick is truly maritime. At Fundy National Park, you can view some of the world's most powerful tides along a wilderness coastline. Grand Manan and Campobello Islands are famed for wildlife and birding opportunities. The cities of Fredericton and Saint John ooze historic charm. See chapter 4.

PRINCE EDWARD ISLAND

Canada's smallest province is a green and bucolic island in the Gulf of St. Lawrence that's seemingly far from the stress and hurry of one's regular life. The capital city of Charlottetown is a lovely brick-built city clustered around a quiet bay, but the real attraction here is the surrounding countryside covered with farms (a setting that served as the inspiration for *Anne of Green Gables*) and the beaches along the island's north coast. See chapter 5.

NEWFOUNDLAND & LABRADOR

So remote that part of the province occupies its own time zone, Newfoundland and Labrador form Canada's wild east. Rocky and windswept, its long history includes the Vikings and other seafaring adventurers. Today, craggy fishing villages, and the austere tablelands and fjords of Gros Morne National Park, attract travelers who value isolation and dramatic landscapes. See chapter 6.

QUEBEC

Canada's French-speaking homeland, Québec boasts two fascinating cities. Montréal, in many ways the cultural center of Canada, has a rich history, excellent food, a vibrant arts scene, and an indomitable sense of style. Québec City is at once a modern capital and one of the most historic cities in North America. Dating from the 17th century, it is the only walled city north of Mexico. See chapters 7 and 8.

ONTARIO

A vast province dominated by the Great Lakes, Ontario is home to Ottawa, the governmental capital of Canada, and Toronto, the country's bustling business capital. To the west is farmland and Stratford, home to the world-class Stratford Festival, famed for its theatrical performances. See chapters 9 through 12.

MANITOBA

Dominated by its capital, hardworking but artsy Winnipeg, Manitoba is the land bridge between eastern and western Canada. Half farmland, half lake, the province is Canada's heartland. Winnipeg has long been a center for trade, transport, and industry; more recently, it's become a scrappy Mecca for the arts, with great galleries, classical music and dance institutions, and a rousing rock-band subculture. See chapter 13.

SASKATCHEWAN

Located where the Great Plains meet the northern arboreal forests, Saskatchewan is too easily neglected as the flyover province. In fact, its immigrant pioneer history is fascinating, and its two largest cities, Regina and Saskatoon, boast excellent hotels and restaurants. To the north, Prince Albert National Park preserves a vast expanse of linked lakes where the prairies meet the northern forests. See chapter 13.

ALBERTA

Famed for the stunning scenery of the Canadian Rockies, Alberta boasts Banff and Jasper national parks, which contain some of the most dramatic mountain landscapes on Earth. Calgary is a gleaming metropolis, with impressive hotels and restaurants, and a Texas-like Western swagger. Out on the eastern prairies, paleontologists—and eager travelers—unearth fossils at digs near the dinosaur capital of Drumheller. See chapter 14.

BRITISH COLUMBIA

BC is Canada's California. In this most westerly province, Vancouver is one of the most cosmopolitan of North American cities, facing as much to Asia as to traditional cultural centers along the Atlantic seaboard. Victoria is a city of genteel English ways, while the rugged Pacific coast is a haven for outdoor adventurers. See chapters 15 and 16.

THE YUKON

Born of a gold rush, the Yukon preserves its historic prospecting past at former mining camps such as Whitehorse and Dawson City. The rip-snorting days of gambling halls, dog sledding, and claim jumping isn't history yet here, and the Yukon makes an excellent destination for travelers of all interests. To the north, seasonal roads lead past the Arctic Circle to the tundra of the far north. See chapter 17.

THE NORTHWEST TERRITORIES

Vast and largely untracked, the Northwest Territories encompass the outback fishing nirvanas of Great Slave Lake and Great Bear Lake. Yellowknife is its bustling capital, still proud of its rich mining heritage. Near the mouth of the mighty Mackenzie River, Inuvik and other Inuvialuit settlements are centers of traditional northern life. See chapter 17.

NUNAVUT

Canada's newest territory, Nunavut is the Inuit homeland, encompassing Arctic Ocean islands and coastline. The population and cultural center is Baffin Island, where alluring Native art and Ice Age landscapes draw adventurous travelers. See chapter 17.

VISITOR INFORMATION & MAPS

In addition to the provincial tourism websites listed below, take a look at the official tourism and travel site for Canada at **www.canada.travel.** Each of the provinces and territories can provide excellent road maps for free or a small fee:

Canada

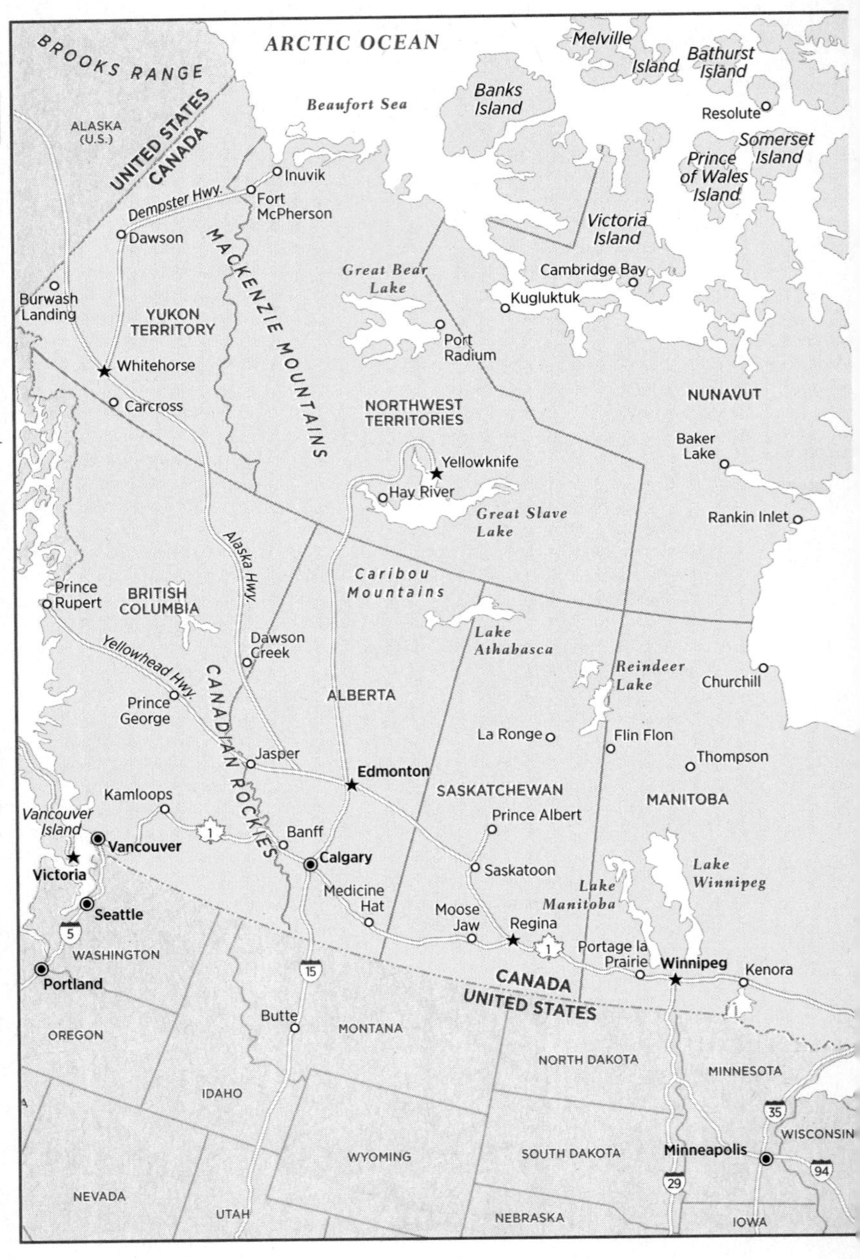
ARCTIC OCEAN
BROOKS RANGE
Beaufort Sea
Melville Island
Bathurst Island
Banks Island
Resolute
Somerset Island
Prince of Wales Island
ALASKA (U.S.)
UNITED STATES
CANADA
Inuvik
Dempster Hwy.
Fort McPherson
Victoria Island
Dawson
MACKENZIE MOUNTAINS
Great Bear Lake
Cambridge Bay
Burwash Landing
Kugluktuk
YUKON TERRITORY
Port Radium
Whitehorse
Carcross
NORTHWEST TERRITORIES
NUNAVUT
Baker Lake
Yellowknife
Hay River
Great Slave Lake
Rankin Inlet
Alaska Hwy.
Caribou Mountains
Prince Rupert
BRITISH COLUMBIA
Dawson Creek
Lake Athabasca
Yellowhead Hwy.
Reindeer Lake
Churchill
CANADIAN ROCKIES
Prince George
ALBERTA
La Ronge
Flin Flon
Thompson
Jasper
Edmonton
SASKATCHEWAN
MANITOBA
Kamloops
Vancouver Island
1
Prince Albert
Banff
Vancouver
Victoria
Calgary
Saskatoon
Lake Winnipeg
Lake Manitoba
Medicine Hat
Seattle
Moose Jaw
Regina
5
1
Portage la Prairie
Winnipeg
WASHINGTON
Kenora
15
Portland
CANADA
UNITED STATES
Butte
OREGON
MONTANA
NORTH DAKOTA
MINNESOTA
IDAHO
35
WISCONSIN
WYOMING
SOUTH DAKOTA
Minneapolis
94
29
NEVADA
UTAH
NEBRASKA
IOWA

2

PLANNING YOUR TRIP TO CANADA | Visitor Information & Maps

- **Nova Scotia Dept. of Tourism, Culture, and Heritage:** P.O. Box 456, Halifax, NS B3J 2R5; ✆ **800/565-0000** or 902/425-5781; www.novascotia.com.
- **Tourism New Brunswick:** P.O. Box 12345, Campbellton, NB E3N 3T6; ✆ **800/561-0123;** www.tourismnewbrunswick.ca.
- **Tourism Prince Edward Island:** P.O. Box 2000, Charlottetown, PEI C1A 7N8; ✆ **800/463-4734** or 902/368-4444; www.tourismpei.com.
- **Newfoundland and Labrador Tourism:** P.O. Box 8700, St. John's, NL A1B 4J6; ✆ **800/563-6353** or 709/729-2830; www.newfoundlandandlabradortourism.com.
- **Tourisme Québec:** P.O. Box 979, Montréal, QC H3C 2W3; ✆ **877/266-5687** or 514/873-2015; www.bonjourquebec.com.
- **Ontario Tourism:** 10 Dundas St. E., Ste. 900, Toronto, ON M7A 2A1; ✆ **800/668-2746;** www.ontariotravel.net.
- **Travel Manitoba:** 7th Floor, 155 Carlton St., Winnipeg, MB R3C 3H8; ✆ **800/665-0040** or 204/927-7800; www.travelmanitoba.com.
- **Tourism Saskatchewan:** 189–1621 Albert St., Regina, SK S4P 2S5; ✆ **877/237-2273** or 306/787-9600; www.sasktourism.com.
- **Travel Alberta:** P.O. Box 2500, Edmonton, AB T5J 2Z4; ✆ **800/252-3782** or 780/427-4321; www.travelalberta.com.
- **Tourism British Columbia:** 200 Burrard St., Plaza Level, Vancouver, BC V6C 3L6; ✆ **800/435-5622** or 604/683-2000; www.hellobc.com.
- **Tourism Yukon:** P.O. Box 2703, Whitehorse, YT Y1A 2C6; ✆ 800-661-0494**;** www.travelyukon.com.
- **NWT Tourism:** P.O. Box 610, Yellowknife, NWT X1A 2N5; ✆ **800/661-0788** or 867/873-7200; www.spectacularnwt.com.
- **Nunavut Tourism:** P.O. Box 1450, Iqaluit, NU X0A 0H0; ✆ **866/686-2888** or 867/979-6551; www.nunavuttourism.com.

For general information about Canada's national parks, contact **Parks Canada National Office** (25 N Eddy St., Hull, QC K1A 0M5; ✆ **888/773-8888;** www.pc.gc.ca).

CITY SITES Internet city guides are a good way to navigate without getting lost in the virtual countryside. Here are some to check out for Canada's top cities:

- **Montréal:** www.tourisme-montreal.org (Tourism Montréal)
- **Québec:** www.quebecregion.com (Québec City Tourism)
- **Ottawa:** www.ottawatourism.ca (Ottawa Tourism)
- **Toronto:** www.toronto.com (Toronto.com), www.seetorontonow.com (Tourism Toronto), www.toronto.ca (City of Toronto)
- **Winnipeg:** www.tourismwinnipeg.com (Tourism Winnipeg)
- **Saskatoon:** www.tourismsaskatoon.com (Tourism Saskatoon)
- **Calgary:** www.visitcalgary.com (Tourism Calgary)
- **Banff National Park:** www.banfflakelouise.com (Banff Lake Louise Tourism)
- **Edmonton:** www.edmonton.com (Edmonton Economic Development Corporation)
- **Vancouver:** www.tourism-vancouver.com (Tourism Vancouver)
- **Victoria:** www.tourismvictoria.com (Tourism Victoria), www.victoria.ca (City of Victoria)

ENTRY REQUIREMENTS

Passports

For information on how to get a passport, go to "Passports" in the "Fast Facts" section of this chapter—the websites listed provide downloadable passport applications, as well as the current fees for processing passport applications. For information on passport requirements for entering Canada, visit the Citizenship and Immigration Canada website at www.cic.gc.ca.

It is no longer possible to enter Canada and return to the U.S. by showing a government-issued photo ID (such as a driver's license) and proof of U.S. citizenship (such as a birth or naturalization certificate). The **Western Hemisphere Travel Initiative (WHTI),** which took full effect in 2009, requires all U.S. citizens returning to the U.S. from Canada to have a U.S. passport (this includes children under age 18).

In other words, if you are a U.S. citizen traveling to Canada by air, sea, or land, you must have a valid U.S. passport or a new passport card in order to get back into the U.S.

In addition to carrying a passport from their home country, permanent U.S. residents who aren't U.S. citizens must also be prepared to present their Alien Registration Cards (green cards). Also, if you plan to drive into Canada, be sure to bring your car's registration papers and proof of insurance.

An important point: In addition to a passport, any person under 18 traveling alone needs a letter from a parent or guardian granting him or her permission to travel to Canada. The letter must give the traveler's name and the trip's duration.

Although it is rare, immigration officials may prevent the entry of visitors who appear to pose a health risk, those they doubt will be able to support themselves and their dependents in Canada, or those whose willingness and means to return to their home country is in doubt.

Immigration officials can prevent the entry of foreign nationals who have a criminal record. This includes any convictions for driving while intoxicated; anyone with a felony conviction will find it very challenging to enter Canada.

BRINGING CHILDREN INTO CANADA

If you are traveling to Canada with children, you should carry identification for each child. Divorced parents who share custody of their children should carry copies of the legal custody documents. Adults who are not parents or guardians should have written permission from the parents or guardians to supervise the children. When traveling with a group of vehicles, parents or guardians should travel in the same vehicle as the children when arriving at the border. Customs officers are looking for missing children and may ask questions about children traveling with you.

Visas

Citizens of the U.S., most European countries, most former British colonies, and certain other countries (Israel, Korea, and Japan, for instance) do not need visas but must carry passports to enter Canada. Entry visas are required for citizens of more than 130 countries. Visas must be applied for and received from a Canadian embassy before arriving in Canada. For more information on entry requirements to Canada, see the Citizenship and Immigration Canada website at **www.cic.gc.ca.**

Customs

For information on what you can bring into and take out of Canada, go to "Customs" in the "Fast Facts" section of this chapter.

WHEN TO GO

When to go to Canada depends a lot on what you plan to do when you get there. Although much of Canada lies above the 49th parallel, and therefore has long and often intense winter weather, this isn't particularly a negative if you are going to Canada to ski or snowboard. Although some tourist facilities in small centers are closed in winter, most remain open (after all, Canadians live in Canada year-round and require a full network of services).

Summer, from late June to August, brings the finest weather and not surprisingly, the largest influx of travelers. Prices are highest, accommodations are frequently booked up, and crowds fill the national parks. In many ways, the fall months, particularly September and October, are the best time to travel, as the weather is frequently very pleasant, the crowds have dispersed, and accommodation prices are lower than summer. If you are looking for value, spring is another good time to visit Canada.

The Weather

In Canada's southern reaches, where most of the population lives, the weather is similar as that in the northern United States. As you head north, the climate becomes harsher, meaning long and extremely cold winters, and brief but surprisingly warm summers (with lots of insects).

As a general rule, **spring** runs mid-March to mid-June, **summer** mid-June to mid-September, **fall** mid-September to mid-November, and **winter** mid-November to mid-March. Pick the season best suited to your tastes and temperament, and remember that your vehicle should be winterized November through March and that snow can fall in the mountains at any time of year. September and October bring autumn foliage and great opportunities for photographers.

Evenings tend to be cool everywhere, particularly on or near water. In summer, you'll need a supply of insect repellent if you're planning on outdoor activities such as hiking or camping.

With the huge size of some provinces and territories, you naturally get considerable climate variations inside their borders. Québec, for instance, sprawls all the way from the temperate south to the Arctic, and the weather varies accordingly. For up-to-date weather conditions and forecasts across Canada, check out Environment Canada's weather center online at **www.weatheroffice.gc.ca**.

Daily Mean Temperature & Total Precipitation for Vancouver, BC

	JAN	FEB	MAR	APR	MAY	JUNE	JULY	AUG	SEPT	OCT	NOV	DEC
TEMP (°F)	38	41	45	40	46	62	66	67	61	42	48	39
TEMP (°C)	3	5	7	4	8	17	19	19	16	6	9	4
PRECIPITATION (IN.)	5.9	4.9	4.3	3.0	2.4	1.8	1.4	1.5	2.5	4.5	6.7	7.0

Daily Mean Temperature & Total Precipitation for Calgary, AB

	JAN	FEB	MAR	APR	MAY	JUNE	JULY	AUG	SEPT	OCT	NOV	DEC
TEMP (°F)	26	31	38	51	62	69	74	73	63	55	37	28
TEMP (°C)	−4	0	3	11	16	21	23	23	17	13	3	-2
PRECIPITATION (IN.)	.5	.4	.6	1	2.1	3	2.8	1.9	1.9	.6	.5	.5

Daily Mean Temperature & Total Precipitation for Winnipeg, MB

	JAN	FEB	MAR	APR	MAY	JUNE	JULY	AUG	SEPT	OCT	NOV	DEC
TEMP (°F)	8	15	29	50	66	74	79	77	66	52	31	14
TEMP (°C)	-13	-10	-2	10	19	23	26	25	19	11	-1	-10
PRECIPITATION (IN.)	.8	.6	.9	1.4	2.4	3.3	2.8	3	2	1.2	.8	.7

Daily Mean Temperature & Total Precipitation for Toronto, ON

	JAN	FEB	MAR	APR	MAY	JUNE	JULY	AUG	SEPT	OCT	NOV	DEC
TEMP (°F)	28	29	39	53	65	75	80	78	70	57	45	33
TEMP (°C)	-3	-2	4	12	18	24	27	26	21	14	7	1
PRECIPITATION (IN.)	1.8	1.8	2.2	2.5	2.6	2.7	3	3.3	2.9	2.5	2.8	2.6

Daily Mean Temperature & Total Precipitation for Montreal, QC

	JAN	FEB	MAR	APR	MAY	JUNE	JULY	AUG	SEPT	OCT	NOV	DEC
TEMP (°F)	22	24	36	51	65	74	79	76	68	55	41	27
TEMP (°C)	-6	-4	2	11	19	23	26	25	20	13	5	-3
PRECIPITATION (IN.)	2.5	2.2	2.7	2.9	2.7	3.2	3.4	3.9	3.4	3	3.7	3.4

Daily Mean Temperature & Total Precipitation for Halifax, NS

	JAN	FEB	MAR	APR	MAY	JUNE	JULY	AUG	SEPT	OCT	NOV	DEC
TEMP (°F)	29	29	37	46	59	68	74	73	66	55	45	34
TEMP (°C)	-2	-2	3	8	15	20	23	23	19	13	7	1
PRECIPITATION (IN.)	5.8	4.7	4.8	4.9	4.4	3.9	3.8	4.3	3.7	5.1	6.1	6.6

Canada Calendar of Events

Canadians love a festival, and not even the chill of winter will keep them from celebrating. The Canadian festival calendar is jammed with events celebrating ethnic cultures, food and wine, historical events and characters, the arts, rodeos, music and theater—even salmon, lobsters, and whales. Following is a seasonal list of festival highlights from across Canada; see individual chapters for more festival options.

For an exhaustive list of events beyond those listed here, check http://events.frommers.com, where you'll find a searchable, up-to-the-minute roster of what's happening in cities all over the world.

WINTER

Winter Carnival (✆ **418/626-3716;** www.carnaval.qc.ca) is a celebration of all things winter in Québec City. February.

Festival du Voyageur (✆ **204/237-7692;** www.festivalvoyageur.mb.ca) is Winnipeg's celebration of the 18th-century French voyagers who explored Canada by canoe, with music, wine, and winter fun. February.

Yukon Quest (✆ **867/668-4711;** www.yukonquest.com) brings hundreds of sled dogs and mushers to Whitehorse, Yukon, for one of the world's top dog-sledding events. February.

SPRING

Pacific Rim Whale Festival (✆ **250/726-4641;** www.pacificrimwhalefestival.org) celebrates the yearly return of up to 20,000 gray whales to the waters off Tofino and Ucluelet, Vancouver Island. March.

Canadian Tulip Festival (✆ **888/465-1867;** http:/tulipfestival.ca) features thousands of tulips in bloom, plus art fairs and concerts, in Ottawa, Canada's capital. May.

SUMMER

Stratford Shakespeare Festival (✆ **800/567-1600;** www.stratfordfestival.ca) presents over a dozen theatrical productions, a mix of Shakespeare and contemporary works, in a delightful Ontario country town. May through October.

Montreal International Fireworks Competition (✆ **514/397-2000;** www.internationaldesfeuxloto-quebec.com) is North America's largest fireworks competition, with fireworks makers from around the world competing for Jupiter trophies, the pinnacle of pyrotechnics. June through August.

Calgary Stampede (✆ **800/661-1767;** www.calgarystampede.com) is the world's largest and richest rodeo and Calgary's opportunity to celebrate its cowboy past. July.

Vancouver Folk Music Festival (✆ **604/602-9798;** www.thefestival.bc.ca) is one of North America's top folk music events, bringing Summer of Love musical stylings to a gorgeous bayside park. July.

RCMP Training Academy Sunset Retreat Ceremony (✆ **306/780-5838;** www.rcmp-grc.gc.ca/depot) is a stirring drill practice and flag ceremony with dress-uniformed Mounties plus pipe-and-bugle bands at Regina's century-old RCMP training facility. July through mid-August.

Banff Summer Arts Festival (✆ **800/413-8368;** www.banffcentre.ca) is a celebration of classical and jazz music in the heart of the Canadian Rockies. July through August.

International Busker Festival (www.buskers.ca) brings street musicians and performers from around the world to Halifax's bustling waterfront. August.

Newfoundland and Labrador Folk Festival (✆ **709/576-8508;** www.nlfolk.com) is a major folk music festival held at the center of St. Johns, Newfoundland. August.

FALL

Toronto International Film Festival (✆ **416/968-3456;** www.tiff.net) is a glittering celebration of stars and cinema, and the world's second-largest film festival. September.

Celtic Colours (✆ **888/355-7744;** www.celtic-colours.com) is the largest Celtic music and arts festival outside of Britain, held on Cape Breton Island, Nova Scotia. October.

Okanagan Wine Festival (✆ **250/861-6654;** www.thewinefestivals.com) celebrates BC's Okanagan Valley's fall harvest with wine tastings, winery open houses, and dining events. October.

GETTING THERE

By Plane

Vancouver (YVR), Calgary (YYC), Toronto (YYZ), and Montréal (YUL) serve as the dominant hubs for international flights and are served by most international carriers, including British Airways, Air France, Qantas, Singapore Airlines, Lufthansa, SAS, and most U.S. airlines. Smaller airports, such as Halifax and Winnipeg, also have international flights, particularly in summer.

Air Canada (✆ **888/247-2262;** www.aircanada.com) is the country's largest air carrier, with flights to Canada from all major U.S. cities, as well as South America, Europe, and Asia. Canada's second-largest airline is **WestJet** (✆ **888/937-8538;** www.westjet.com), which flies into the country from major U.S. cities such as Los Angeles, Phoenix, New York, and Orlando.

By Car

Because Canada has the longest open border on Earth, it makes sense that many U.S.-based travelers will consider taking their own car to Canada as a road-trip destination. There are scores of border crossings between Canada and the U.S. (the U.S. freeway system enters at 13 different locations). However, not all border crossings keep the same hours, and many are closed at night. Before you set off to cross the border at a remote location, ascertain if it will be open when you arrive.

In addition to having the proper ID to cross into Canada, drivers may also be asked to provide proof of car insurance and show the car registration. If you're driving a rental car, you may be asked to show the rental agreement. It's always a good idea to clean your car of perishable foodstuff before crossing the border; fruits, vegetables, and meat products may be confiscated and may lead to a full search of the car. Remember that firearms are allowed across the border only in special circumstances; handguns are almost completely outlawed.

RENTAL CARS Canada has scores of rental-car companies, including **Hertz** (✆ **800/654-3001** in the U.S. or 800/263-0600 in Canada; www.hertz.com), **Avis** (✆ **800/331-1212;** www.avis.com), **Dollar** (✆ **800/800-3665;** www.dollar.com), **Thrifty** (✆ **800/847-4389;** www.thrifty.com), **Budget** (✆ **800/527-0700** in the U.S. or 800/268-8900 in Canada; www.budget.com), **Enterprise** (✆ **800/261-7331;** www.enterprise.com), and **National** (✆ 800/**877/222-9058;** www.nationalcar.com). Nevertheless, rental companies regularly sell out during the tourist season, from around mid-June through August. Therefore, it's a good idea to make reservations as far in advance as possible.

Check out **Breezenet.com,** which offers car-rental discounts with some of the most competitive rates around. Also worth visiting are Orbitz, Hotwire, Travelocity, and Priceline, all of which offer competitive online car-rental rates.

International visitors should note that insurance and taxes are almost never included in quoted rental car rates. Be sure to ask your rental agency about additional fees for these. They can add a significant cost to your car rental.

Several rental-car agencies offer roadside assistance programs in Canada. In case of an accident, a breakdown, a dead battery, a flat tire, a dry gas tank, getting stuck, or locking yourself out of your car, call your agency's 24-hour number. For **Hertz,** call ✆ 800/654-5060; for **Avis,** call ✆ 800/354-2847; for **Dollar,** call ✆ 800/235-9393; for **Budget,** call ✆ 800/354-2847; for **National,** call ✆ 800/268-9711; and for **Enterprise,** call ✆ 800/307-6666.

None of the above rental agencies enforce a mandatory upper-age cutoff for renting cars to seniors, but individual franchisers can impose their own age limits. The minimum age for renting cars in Canada is usually 21, though rates are high. Standard rates for drivers kick in at 25 years of age.

Members of the **American Automobile Association (AAA)** should remember to take their membership cards since the **Canadian Automobile Association** (**CAA;** ✆ **800/222-4357;** www.caa.ca) extends privileges to them in Canada.

By Train

Amtrak (✆ **800/872-7245;** www.amtrak.com) can get you to the Canadian border, where you can connect up with Canada's **VIA Rail** (✆ **888/842-7245;** www.viarail.ca) system. On the East Coast, Amtrak's *Adirondack* starts at New York City's Penn Station and travels daily via Albany and upstate New York to Montréal. The *Maple Leaf* links New York City and Toronto via Albany, Rochester, Buffalo, and Niagara Falls, departing daily from Penn Station. On the West Coast, the *Cascades* runs from Eugene, Oregon, to Vancouver, British Columbia, with stops in Portland and Seattle. Amtrak-operated buses may also connect segments of these routes.

Amtrak and VIA Rail both offer their own rail passes, which give you 15, 30, or 45 days of unlimited economy-class travel. Remember that the passes don't include meals; you can buy meals on the train or carry your own food.

By Bus

Greyhound (in Canada © **800/661-8747,** www.greyhound.ca; in the U.S. © 800/231-2222, www.greyhound.com) operates the major intercity bus system in Canada, with frequent cross-border links to cities in the U.S. northern tier (many more than what's offered by Amtrak). In general, Greyhound offers cross-border service along routes where the U.S. freeway system enters Canada.

By Ferry

Ferries operate from Maine to Nova Scotia, and from Seattle, Anacortes, and Port Angeles, Washington, to Victoria, British Columbia. For details, see the relevant chapters.

MONEY & COSTS

Prices for goods and services are comparable between Canada and the U.S.—particularly now that the Canadian dollar has been close to par with its U.S. counterpart for a number of years. On a day-to-day basis, traveling in Canada will cost about the same as traveling in the U.S., as long as restraint is used when making hotel and dining selections. European travelers will find that Canadian prices for comparable goods and services are generally lower than those in their home countries.

Currency

Canadian currency is counted in dollars and cents, just like the currency system in the U.S. However, in addition to pennies, nickels, dimes, and quarters, there are one- and two-dollar coins (there are no one- or two-dollar bills). Dollar coins are bronze-plated coins and bear the picture of a loon—hence their nickname, "loonies." There's also a two-toned $2 coin, which is sometimes referred to as a "toonie." Paper currency begins with $5 bills.

Exchanging currency is pretty straightforward, particularly if you are changing U.S. dollars into Canadian. Most banks on both sides of the border will exchange U.S. and Canadian currency, even if they don't normally advertise as foreign exchange services. However, the easiest way to procure Canadian currency is simply to withdraw money from an ATM (see below).

Often, Canadian businesses will accept U.S. dollars in payment, making the currency value exchange, if any, at the till.

It's always advisable to bring money in a variety of forms on a vacation: a mix of cash, credit cards, and traveler's checks. You should also exchange enough petty cash to cover airport incidentals, tipping, and transportation to your hotel before you leave home, or withdraw money upon arrival at an airport ATM.

ATMs

The easiest and best way to get cash away from home is from an ATM (automated teller machine), sometimes referred to as a "cash machine" or a "cashpoint." ATMs also offer the best exchange rates. Avoid exchanging money at commercial exchange bureaus and hotels, which often have the highest transaction fees.

The **Cirrus** (© **800/424-7787;** www.mastercard.com) and **PLUS** (© **800/843-7587;** www.visa.com) networks span the globe. Go to your bank card's website to find ATM locations at your destination. Be sure you know your daily withdrawal limit before you depart. ***Note:*** Many banks impose a fee every time you use a card at another bank's ATM, and that fee can be higher for international transactions (up to $5 or more) than for domestic ones (where they're rarely more than $2). In addition, the bank from which you withdraw cash may charge its own fee. For international withdrawal fees, ask your bank.

Credit Cards

Credit cards are a safe way to carry money. They also provide a convenient record of all your expenses, and they generally offer relatively good exchange rates. You can withdraw cash advances from your credit cards at banks or ATMs but high fees make credit card cash advances a pricey way to get cash. Keep in mind that you'll pay interest from the moment of your withdrawal, even if you pay your monthly bills on time. Also, note that many banks now assess a 1% to 3% "transaction fee" on **all** charges you incur abroad (whether you're using the local currency or your native currency).

Canadian businesses honor the same credit cards as in the U.S. and the U.K. Visa and MasterCard are the most common, though American Express is also normally accepted in hotels and restaurants catering to tourists. Discover and Diners Club cards are somewhat less frequently accepted.

For tips and telephone numbers to call if your wallet is stolen or lost, go to "Lost & Found" in the "Fast Facts" section of this chapter.

Traveler's Checks

You can buy traveler's checks at most banks. They are offered in denominations of $20, $50, $100, $500, and sometimes $1,000. Generally, you'll pay a service charge ranging from 1% to 4%.

The most popular traveler's checks are offered by **American Express** (© **800/221-7282**); **Visa** (© **800/732-1322**)—AAA members can obtain Visa checks for a $9.95 fee (for checks up to $1,500) at most AAA offices or by calling © **866/339-3378;** and **MasterCard** (© **800/223-9920**).

Be sure to keep a record of the traveler's checks serial numbers separate from your checks in the event that they are stolen or lost. You'll get a refund faster if you know the numbers.

All the above companies also offer traveler's checks denominated in Canadian dollars. If you are planning to use traveler's checks frequently while in Canada, there are advantages to buying them in Canadian dollars, as there is usually no fee to reimburse them, and they can be used like cash in most retail situations.

TRAVEL INSURANCE

The cost of travel insurance varies widely, depending on the destination, the cost and length of your trip, your age and health, and the type of trip you're taking, but expect to pay between 5% and 8% of the vacation itself. You can get estimates from various providers through **InsureMyTrip.com.** Enter your trip cost and dates, your age, and other information, for prices from more than a dozen companies.

U.K. citizens and their families who make more than one trip abroad per year may find an annual travel insurance policy works out cheaper. Check **www.moneysupermarket.com,** which compares prices across a wide range of providers for single- and multi-trip policies.

Most big travel agents offer their own insurance and will probably try to sell you their package when you book a holiday. Think before you sign. **Britain's Consumers'**

Association recommends that you insist on seeing the policy and reading the fine print before buying travel insurance. **The Association of British Insurers** (© **020/7600-3333;** www.abi.org.uk) gives advice by phone and publishes *Holiday Insurance,* a free guide to policy provisions and prices. You might also shop around for better deals: Try **Columbus Direct** (© **0870/033- 9988;** www.columbusdirect.com).

Trip-Cancellation Insurance

Trip-cancellation insurance will help retrieve your money if you have to back out of a trip or depart early, or if your travel supplier goes bankrupt. Trip cancellation traditionally covers such events as sickness, natural disasters, and State Department advisories. The latest news in trip-cancellation insurance is the availability of **expanded hurricane coverage** and the **"any-reason"** cancellation coverage—which costs more but covers cancellations made for any reason. You won't get back 100% of your prepaid trip cost, but you'll be refunded a substantial portion. **TravelSafe** (© **888/885-7233;** www.travelsafe.com) offers both types of coverage. Expedia also offers any-reason cancellation coverage for its air-hotel packages.

For details, contact one of the following recommended insurers: **Access America** (© **800/284-8300;** www.accessamerica.com), **Travel Insured International** (© **800/243-3174;** www.travelinsured.com), and **Travelex Insurance Services** (© **800/228-9792;** www.travelex-insurance.com).

Medical Insurance

For international travel, most U.S. health plans (including Medicare and Medicaid) do not provide coverage, and the ones that do often require you to pay for services upfront and reimburse you only after you return home.

As a safety net, you may want to buy travel medical insurance, particularly if you're traveling to a remote or high-risk area where emergency evacuation might be necessary. If you require additional medical insurance, try **MEDEX Assistance** (© **800/732-5309;** www.medexassist.com) or **Travel Assistance International** (© **800/821-2828;** www.travelassistance.com).

Lost-Luggage Insurance

On international flights (including U.S. portions of international trips), baggage coverage is limited to approximately US$9 per pound, up to approximately US$635 per checked bag. If you plan to check items more valuable than what's covered by the standard liability, see if your homeowner's policy covers your valuables, get baggage insurance as part of your travel-insurance package, or buy Travel Guard's "BagTrak" product.

If your luggage is lost, immediately file a lost-luggage claim at the airport, detailing the luggage contents. Most airlines require that you report delayed, damaged, or lost baggage within 4 hours of arrival. The airlines are required to deliver luggage, once found, directly to your house or destination free of charge.

HEALTH

In general, Canada poses no particular health threats to travelers. Nonetheless, you may want to check your government's travel advisory site for any last-minute alerts.

If you suffer from a chronic illness, consult your doctor before your departure. For conditions such as epilepsy, diabetes, or heart problems, wear a **MedicAlert**

identification tag (✆ **888/633-4298;** www.medicalert.org), which will immediately alert doctors to your condition and give them access to your records through MedicAlert's 24-hour hotline.

Pack **prescription medications** in your carry-on luggage and carry prescription medications in their original containers, with pharmacy labels—otherwise they won't make it through airport security. Also, bring along copies of your prescriptions in case you lose your pills or run out. Don't forget an extra pair of contact lenses or prescription glasses. Carry the generic name of prescription medicines, in case a local pharmacist is unfamiliar with the brand name.

General Availability of Health Care

Canada's health-care system is similar to that in other Western countries, except that its health insurance for Canadian citizens is managed nationally by the federal government. Hospitals, clinics, and pharmacies are as common as in the U.S. and western Europe. Contact the **International Association for Medical Assistance to Travelers** (IAMAT; ✆ **716/754-4883,** or 416/652-0137 in Canada; www.iamat.org) for tips on travel and health concerns in Canada. **Travel Health Online** (www.tripprep.com), sponsored by a consortium of travel medicine practitioners, may also offer helpful advice on traveling abroad. You can find listings of reliable medical clinics overseas at the **International Society of Travel Medicine** (www.istm.org).

What To Do If You Get Sick Away From Home

Most Canadian hospitals have emergency rooms open 24 hours for emergency care. In addition, most cities also have walk-in clinics where nonemergency treatment is available. Look in the local Yellow Pages under "Clinics, Medical" for walk-in clinics; these clinics usually take charge cards, though they may be able to bill your private insurance directly. You can also inquire at your hotel, as some hotels have relationships with private practitioners to treat the emergency needs of guests.

Pharmacies are common, and most large cities have at least one 24-hour operation. You'll have no trouble having prescriptions filled; in fact, prescription drugs are substantially cheaper in Canada than in the U.S. Also, certain drugs are available over the counter in Canada that are available only by prescription in the U.S.

In most cases, your existing health plan will provide the coverage you need, though you may need to pay upfront and request reimbursement later. But double-check; you may want to buy **travel medical insurance** instead. Bring your insurance ID card with you when you travel.

For American travelers, Medicare and Medicaid do not provide coverage for medical costs outside the U.S. Before leaving home, find out what medical services your health insurance covers. To protect yourself, consider buying medical travel insurance (see "Medical Insurance," under "Travel Insurance," above).

Very few health insurance plans pay for medical evacuation back to your home country (which can cost US$10,000 and up). A number of companies offer medical evacuation services anywhere in the world. If you're ever hospitalized more than 150 miles from home, **Medjet Assist** (✆ **800/527-7478;** www.medjetassistance.com) will pick you up and fly you to the hospital of your choice virtually anywhere in the world in a medically equipped and staffed aircraft 24 hours a day, 7 days a week. Annual memberships are US$250 individual, US$385 family; you can also purchase short-term memberships.

SAFETY

Staying Safe

Canada is one of the least violent countries on Earth—at least outside of the hockey arena. Using common sense, most travelers should experience few if any threatening situations during a trip to Canada. In fact, most Canadians are unfailingly polite and helpful.

The weather and wildlife are probably a greater threat to the average traveler than violence from other human beings. If driving in winter, be sure to have winter tires or carry traction devices such as chains, plus plenty of warm clothes and a sleeping bag.

Wildlife is really only dangerous if you put yourself into their habitat: Being in the wrong place at the wrong time can be dangerous. Elk can often seem tame, particularly those that live near human civilization. However, during calving season, mother elk can mistake your doting attention as an imminent attack on her newborn.

Moose are also dangerous, as they are truly massive and, when surprised, are apt to charge first and ask questions later. Give a moose plenty of room, and resist the temptation to feed them snacks. Chances are they will come looking for more. Also be careful when driving in areas where moose are common, particularly at sunset—if you collide with a moose, you will come out on the losing end.

Bears are the most dangerous wilderness denizens to humans. Canada is home to grizzly bears, one of the largest carnivores in North America, and to black bears, a smaller, less fearsome cousin (unless you're visiting Churchill in late fall or traveling along the polar ice floes, you're extremely unlikely to see a polar bear). Grizzly bears tend to keep their distance from humans, preferring the remote backcountry to inhabited areas. However, black bears can coexist much more readily with humans and, in some ways, pose a more persistent threat. Never come between a bear and her cubs, or stand in the way of a bear's food source. Never hike alone in the backcountry and, if camping, keep food items away from tents.

Dealing with Discrimination

Canada has one of the most open and cosmopolitan cultures in the world and an extremely ethnically diverse population. Gay and lesbian rights are enshrined in federal law. It's unlikely that travelers will encounter discrimination while visiting Canada. It's possible to get into heated conversations regarding U.S. foreign policy, but little discrimination will result from this kind of dispute over political issues.

SPECIALIZED TRAVEL RESOURCES

Travelers with Disabilities

Most disabilities shouldn't stop anyone from traveling. There are more options and resources for disabled travelers than ever before.

A clearinghouse of official Canadian federal government information on disability issues, including those related to travel and transportation, is available from **Persons with Disabilities Online** at www.pwd-online.gc.ca. The **Canadian Paraplegic Association** (**© 613/723-1913;** www.canparaplegic.org) can offer advice for mobility-challenged travelers, as well as address issues for those with spinal-cord injuries or with other physical disabilities. From the national website, you can click to find provincial organizations.

Organizations that offer a vast range of resources and assistance to disabled travelers include **MossRehab** (✆ **800/225-5667;** www.mossresourcenet.org); the **American Foundation for the Blind** (AFB; ✆ **800/232-5463;** www.afb.org); and **SATH** (**Society for Accessible Travel & Hospitality;** ✆ **212/447-7284;** www.sath.org).

Access-Able Travel Source (www.access-able.com) offers a comprehensive database on travel agents from around the world with experience in accessible travel; destination-specific access information; and links to such resources as service animals, equipment rentals, and access guides.

Many travel agencies offer customized tours and itineraries for travelers with disabilities. Among them are **Flying Wheels Travel** (✆ **507/451-5005;** www.flyingwheelstravel.com) and **Accessible Journeys** (✆ **800/846-4537** or 610/521-0339; www.disabilitytravel.com).

Flying with Disability (www.flying-with-disability.org) is a comprehensive information source on airplane travel. **Avis** (✆ **888/879-4273;** www.avis.com) has an "Avis Access" program that offers services for customers with special travel needs. These include specially outfitted vehicles with swivel seats, spinner knobs, and hand controls; mobility scooter rentals; and accessible bus service. Be sure to reserve well in advance.

Also check out the quarterly online magazine ***Emerging Horizons*** (www.emerginghorizons.com), available by subscription (US$17 per year; US$22 international).

The "Accessible Travel" link at **Mobility-Advisor.com** (www.mobility-advisor.com) offers a variety of travel resources to disabled persons.

British travelers should visit the website www.tourismforall.org.uk to access a wide range of travel information and resources for disabled and elderly people.

Gay & Lesbian Travelers

Canada is one of the most gay-tolerant travel destinations in the world. Witness the fact that gay marriage is legal in Canada and that the entire nation has nondiscrimination protection for gays and lesbians. While not every rural town is ready for the circuit-party set, most gay travelers will encounter little adversity.

A good clearinghouse for information on gay Canada is the website **www.gaycanada.com,** which features news and links to gay-owned or -friendly accommodations and business across Canada. Another guide for gay-based travel information for destinations worldwide is www.gay.com.

The **International Gay and Lesbian Travel Association** (IGLTA; ✆ **954/630-1637;** www.iglta.org) is the trade association for the gay and lesbian travel industry, and offers an online directory of gay- and lesbian-friendly travel businesses and tour operators.

Many agencies offer tours and travel itineraries specifically for gay and lesbian travelers. San Francisco–based **Now, Voyager** (✆ **800/255-6951;** www.nowvoyager.com) offers worldwide trips and cruises, and **Olivia** (✆ **800/631-6277;** www.olivia.com) offers lesbian cruises and resort vacations.

Gay.com Travel (✆ **800/929-2268** or 415/644-8044; www.gay.com/travel), is an excellent online successor to the popular ***Out & About*** print magazine. It provides regularly updated information about gay-owned, gay-oriented, and gay-friendly lodging, dining, sightseeing, nightlife, and shopping establishments in every important destination worldwide. The Canadian website **GayTraveler** (www.gaytraveler.ca) offers ideas and advice for gay travel all over the world.

The following travel guides are available at many bookstores, or you can order them from any online bookseller: ***Spartacus International Gay Guide,*** 35th edition (Bruno Gmünder Verlag; www.spartacusworld.com) and the ***Damron*** guides (www.damron.com), with separate, annual books for gay men and lesbians.

Senior Travel

Mention the fact that you're a senior while traveling in Canada, and frequently you can receive discounted admission prices to cultural and tourist attractions. In most Canadian cities, people over the age of 65 qualify for reduced admission to theaters, museums, festivals, and other attractions, as well as discounted fares on public transportation. It is less common to receive discounts on lodging, though it does happen, so it is worth asking when you make your lodging reservations.

Members of **AARP** (601 E St. NW, Washington, DC 20049; ✆ **888/687-2277;** www.aarp.org) get discounts on hotels, airfares, and car rentals, although these benefits are not as widespread in Canada as the U.S; visit the website for CARP (www.carp.ca), the equivalent Canadian association, for information on reciprocal benefits. AARP offers members a wide range of benefits, including *AARP: The Magazine* and a monthly newsletter. Anyone over 50 can join.

Many reliable agencies and organizations target the 50-plus market. Formerly known as Elderhostel, **Road Scholar** (✆ **800/454-5768;** www.roadscholar.org) arranges worldwide study programs for those aged 55 and over. **ElderTreks** (✆ **800/741-7956** or 416/588-5000; www.eldertreks.com) offers small-group tours to off-the-beaten-path or adventure-travel locations, restricted to travelers 50 and older.

A recommended publication offering travel resources and discounts for seniors is the quarterly magazine ***Travel 50 & Beyond*** (www.travel50andbeyond.com). Alison Gardner's website **www.travelwithachallenge.com** is a Canadian-based online magazine aimed at senior travelers.

Family Travel

Canada makes an especially great family-vacation destination because of its fantastic national park system and abundance of recreational activities. Destinations such as the Canadian Rockies are especially attractive, as outfitters make it easy to arrange guided hiking, biking, white-water rafting, and horseback riding excursions simply by talking to your hotel's concierge. Destinations on both the Atlantic and Pacific coast provide opportunities to learn to sea kayak or to journey out onto the seas to view marine wildlife, while the prairie provinces feature guest ranches and Old West activities.

To locate accommodations, restaurants, and attractions that are particularly kid-friendly, refer to the "Kids" icon throughout this guide.

Recommended family travel websites include **Family Travel Forum** (www.familytravelforum.com), a comprehensive site that offers customized trip planning; **Family Travel Network** (www.familytravelnetwork.com), an online magazine providing travel tips; and **TravelWithYourKids.com** (www.travelwithyourkids.com), a comprehensive site written by parents for parents offering sound advice for long-distance and international travel with children.

Student Travel

The **International Student Travel Confederation** (**ISTC;** www.istc.org) was formed in 1949 to make travel around the world more affordable for students. Check out its website for comprehensive travel services information and details on how to get an **International Student Identity Card (ISIC),** which qualifies students for substantial savings on rail passes, plane tickets, entrance fees, and more. It also provides students with basic health and life insurance and a 24-hour help line. The card is valid for a maximum of 18 months. You can apply for the card online or in person at **STA Travel** (✆ **800/781-4040** in North America; www.statravel.com), the biggest student travel agency in the world; check out the website to locate STA Travel offices worldwide. If you're no longer a student but are still under 26, you can get an **International Youth Travel Card (IYTC),** which entitles you to some discounts. **Travel CUTS** (✆ **866/246-9762;** www.travelcuts.com) offers similar services for both Canadians and U.S. residents. Irish students may prefer to turn to **USIT** (✆ **01/602-1904;** www.usit.ie), an Ireland-based specialist in student, youth, and independent travel.

Single Travelers

On package vacations, single travelers are often hit with a "single supplement" to the base price. To avoid it, you can agree to room with other single travelers or find a compatible roommate before you go, from one of the many roommate-locator agencies.

Travel Buddies Singles Travel Club (✆ **800/998-9099;** www.travelbuddies worldwide.com), based in Canada, runs small, intimate, single-friendly group trips and will match you with a roommate free of charge. **TravelChums** (www.travel chums.com) is an Internet-only travel-companion matching service with elements of an online personals-type site, hosted by the respected New York–based Shaw Guides travel service.

Many reputable tour companies offer singles-only trips. **Singles Travel International** (✆ **877/765-6874;** www.singlestravelintl.com) offers singles-only escorted tours to places like London, Alaska, Fiji, and the Greek Islands.

Single travelers should also check out Eleanor Berman's classic ***Traveling Solo: Advice and Ideas for More Than 250 Great Vacations,*** 6th edition (Globe Pequot), updated in 2008; and ***No Strings Attached: The Savvy Guide to Solo Travel*** (Capital Books) by Leslie Atkins.

Traveling with Pets

Dogs, cats, and most pets can enter Canada with their owners, though you must have proof of rabies vaccinations within the last 36 months for pets over 3 months old.

Finding hotels that allow pets is easy with www.petswelcome.com, www.pettravel.com, and www.travelpets.com. Several hotel chains make a point of welcoming pets, including Motel 6, Fairmont, and Westin.

SUSTAINABLE TOURISM/ ECO-TOURISM

Each time you take a flight or drive a car, carbon dioxide (CO_2) is released into the atmosphere. You can help neutralize this danger to our planet through "carbon offsetting"—paying someone to reduce your CO_2 emissions by the same amount you've added. Carbon offsets can be purchased in the U.S. from companies such as **Carbonfund** (www.carbonfund.org) and **TerraPass** (www.terrapass.org), and from **Climate Care** (www.jpmorganclimatecare.com) in the U.K.

Although one could argue that any vacation that includes an airplane flight can't be truly "green," you can go on holiday and still contribute positively to the environment. You can offset carbon emissions from your flight in other ways. Choose forward-looking companies that embrace responsible development practices, helping preserve destinations for the future by working alongside local people. An increasing number of sustainable tourism initiatives can help you plan a family trip and leave as small a "footprint" as possible on the places you visit.

Responsible Travel (www.responsibletravel.com) contains a great source of sustainable travel ideas run by a spokesperson for responsible tourism in the travel industry. **Sustainable Travel International** (www.sustainabletravelinternational.org) promotes responsible tourism practices, issues an annual "Green Gear & Gift Guide," and has a sustainable travel blog.

You can find eco-friendly travel tips, statistics, and touring companies and associations—listed by destination under "Your Travel Choice"—at the International Ecotourism Society website, www.ecotourism.org. **Ecotourismlogue.com** is part online magazine and part eco-directory that lets you search for touring companies in several categories (water-based, land-based, spiritually oriented, and so on).

In the U.K., **Tourism Concern** (www.tourismconcern.org.uk) works to reduce social and environmental problems connected to tourism and find ways of improving tourism so that local benefits are increased.

The **Association of British Travel Agents** (**ABTA;** www.abta.com) acts as a focal point for the U.K. travel industry and is one of the leading groups spearheading responsible tourism.

The **Association of Independent Tour Operators** (**AITO;** www.aito.co.uk) is a group of specialist operators leading the field in making holidays sustainable.

FROMMERS.COM: THE complete TRAVEL RESOURCE

It should go without saying, but we highly recommend **Frommers.com.** We think you'll find our expert advice and tips; independent reviews of hotels, restaurants, attractions, and preferred shopping and nightlife venues; vacation giveaways; and an online booking tool indispensable before, during, and after your travels. We publish the complete contents of over 300 travel guides in our **Destinations** section, covering thousands of places worldwide to help you plan your trip. Each weekday, we publish original articles reporting on **Deals & News** via our free **Frommers.com Newsletter** to help you save time and money and travel smarter. We're betting you'll find our **Events** listings (http://events.frommers.com) an invaluable resource; it's an up-to-the-minute roster of what's happening in cities everywhere—including concerts, festivals, lectures, and more. We've also added **podcasts, blogs, Twitter feeds, Facebook updates, interactive maps,** and hundreds of new images across the site. Check out our **Community** area, featuring **Forums** where you can join in conversations with thousands of fellow Frommer's travelers, post trip reports, and upload travel photos.

STAYING CONNECTED

Telephones

The Canadian phone system is similar to the system in the United States. Canadian phone numbers have 10 digits: The first three numbers are the area code, which corresponds to a province or division thereof, plus a seven-digit local number. Ten-digit dialing (dialing the area code for local calls) is in effect in many parts of Ontario and Québec and all of Alberta and British Columbia. To call a number within the same locality elsewhere in Canada, all you have to dial is the seven-digit local number. If you're making a long-distance call (out of the area or province), you need to precede the local number with 1, plus the area code and seven-digit local number.

Pay phones are easy to find, particularly in hotels and at public transportation hubs. You can use coins to operate the phone (dial the number, then insert coins as directed by the automated voice), or credit cards. It's far cheaper to use prepaid phone cards, which are widely available in pharmacies, gas stations, and post offices. Phone cards are available in various denominations and can be used to make either domestic or international calls. Or you can order virtual phone cards over the Internet on websites such as **www.pingo.com** and **www.zaptel.com;** these phone card services are activated immediately and can be "recharged" through the company website.

TO MAKE INTERNATIONAL CALLS Dial the international access code 011, followed by the country code (1 for the U.S., 44 for the U.K., 353 for Ireland, 61 for Australia, and 64 for New Zealand), then dial the city code (without the initial 0 for U.K. and Ireland numbers) and then the number.

FOR DIRECTORY ASSISTANCE Dial ✆ **411** if you're looking for a number inside Canada or the U.S. Fees for these directory assistance calls range from C$1.25 to C$3.50. For international directory assistance, dial 00 and ask for the international directory-assistance operator. These calls cost C$7.95 each. It is free to use Web-based phone directories, such as www.whitepages.com or www.anywho.com, to research phone numbers.

FOR OPERATOR ASSISTANCE If you need operator assistance in making a call, dial 0.

TOLL-FREE NUMBERS Numbers beginning with 800, 888, 877, and 866 within Canada are toll-free.

Cellphones

Most U.S. travelers with cellphones will find that their phones will probably work just fine in Canada. Call your service provider to make certain, but nearly all U.S. providers have reciprocal relationships with national Canadian networks. Calls on a U.S. phone using a Canadian network can be expensive, however, usually more than the standard roaming charges incurred within the U.S.

For cellphone users from Asia, Australia, and Europe, the situation is a bit more complicated. The three letters that define much of the world's wireless capabilities are **GSM** (Global System for Mobile Communications), a big, seamless network that makes for easy cross-border cellphone use throughout Europe and dozens of other countries worldwide. In Canada and the U.S., GSM networks are less common. In the U.S., T-Mobile, AT&T Wireless, and Cingular offer some GSM services; in Canada, Rogers is the dominant GSM network user.

ONLINE traveler's TOOLBOX

Veteran travelers visit these sites to make their trips easier. Following is a selection of handy online tools to bookmark and use.

- **Airplane Food** (www.airlinemeals.net)
- **Airplane Seating** (www.seatguru.com)
- **Foreign Languages for Travelers** (www.travlang.com)
- **Maps** (www.mapquest.com or http://maps.google.com)
- **MasterCard ATM Locator** (www.mastercard.com)
- **Time and Date** (www.timeanddate.com)
- **Travel Warnings** (http://travel.state.gov, www.fco.gov.uk/travel, www.voyage.gc.ca, or www.smartraveller.gov.au)
- **Universal Currency Converter** (www.xe.com/ucc)
- **Visa ATM Locator** (www.visa.com)
- **Weather** (www.intellicast.com or www.theweathernetwork.com)

GSM phones function with a removable plastic SIM card, encoded with your phone number and account information. If your cellphone is on a GSM system and you have a world-capable multiband phone such as many Sony Ericsson, Motorola, or Samsung models, you can make and receive calls across civilized areas around much of the globe. Just call your wireless operator and ask for "international roaming" to be activated on your account. Unfortunately, per-minute charges can be high.

For some, **renting** a phone when visiting Canada may be a good idea. A quick search of the Web reveals many cellphone rental companies that provide service in Canada, including **Rogers** (© **888/764-3771;** www.rogers.com), **Cellular Abroad** (© **800/287-5072;** www.cellularabroad.com), and **Planet Omni** (© **800/707-0031;** www.planetomni.com). Cellphone rental charges range from C$30 to C$35 a week, but fees can quickly mount, as you'll also need to buy a SIM card and pay dearly (up to C80¢ a minute) for both incoming and outgoing calls. To rent a phone, you'll need to contact the rental company in advance of your departure and await the arrival of your phone.

Buying a phone once you arrive in Canada can be more economically attractive. Two of Canada's largest carriers, **Rogers** (www.rogers.com) and **Telus Mobility** (www.telusmobility.com) offer pay-as-you-go plans, which don't require users to sign up for lengthy contract plans. Once you arrive at your destination, stop by a local cellphone shop (both Rogers and Telus Mobility have stores everywhere in urban centers; the websites give locations) and ask for the cheapest pay-as-you-go package. You'll need to purchase a phone, but if you resist splurging on a high-end model, these can cost as little as C$50. Pay-as-you-go plans start at C$1 per day, or C25¢ per minute, depending on the plan. Incoming calls are free. The downside is that you'll end up with a non-GSM phone, but you'll be prepared for your next trip to Canada or the States.

Voice over Internet Protocol (VoIP)

If you have Web access while traveling, you might consider a broadband-based telephone service (in technical terms, **Voice over Internet Protocol,** or **VoIP**), such as Skype (www.skype.com) or Vonage (www.vonage.com), which allows you to make free international calls if you use its services from your smartphone or laptop, or in a cybercafe. The people you're calling must also use the service for it to work; check the sites for details.

Internet/E-Mail

WITHOUT YOUR OWN COMPUTER

To find cybercafes in your destination check **www.cybercaptive.com** and **www.cybercafe.com.**

All major airports have **Internet kiosks** that provide basic Web access for a per-minute fee that's usually higher than cybercafe prices. Check out copy shops like **FedEx Office** or **UPS Stores**, which offer computer stations with fully loaded software (as well as Wi-Fi). Most libraries also offer desktop computers with free Internet access.

WITH YOUR OWN COMPUTER

More and more hotels, resorts, airports, cafes, and retailers are going **Wi-Fi** (wireless fidelity), becoming "hot spots" that offer free high-speed Wi-Fi access or charge a small fee for usage. To find public Wi-Fi hot spots at your destination, go to **www.jiwire.com;** its Wi-Fi Finder holds the world's largest directory of public wireless hot spots.

Wherever you go, bring a **connection kit** of the right power and phone adapters, and a spare Ethernet network cable—or find out whether your hotel supplies them to guests. (Both phone and electrical cables in Canada are exactly the same as the U.S.)

PACKAGES FOR THE INDEPENDENT TRAVELER

Packages are simply a way to buy the airfare, accommodations, and other elements of your trip (such as car rentals, airport transfers, and sometimes even activities) at the same time and often at discounted prices.

One good source of package deals is the airlines themselves, including **Air Canada,** which offers an array of package deals specially tailored to trim the costs of your vacation. Collectively, these packages come under the title "Air Canada Vacations." This term covers a whole series of travel bargains, ranging from city packages to fly/drive tours, escorted tours, motor-home travel, and ski holidays. For details, pick up the brochure from an Air Canada office or follow the links at www.aircanadavacations.com.

Other airlines offer Canadian package holidays, including **American Airlines Vacations** (✆ **800/321-2121;** www.aavacations.com), **Delta Vacations** (✆ **800/800-1504;** www.deltavacations.com), **Continental Airlines Vacations** (✆ **800/829-7777;** www.covacations.com), and **United Vacations** (✆ **888/854-3899;** www.unitedvacations.com).

Several big online travel agencies—Expedia, Travelocity, Orbitz, and Lastminute—also do a brisk business in packages. Travel packages are also listed in the travel section of your local Sunday newspaper. Or check ads in national travel magazines such as *Budget Travel, Travel + Leisure, National Geographic Traveler,* and *Condé Nast Traveler.*

ASK before YOU GO

Before you invest in a package deal or an escorted tour:

- Always ask about the **cancellation policy.** Can you get your money back? Is there a deposit required?
- Ask about the **accommodations choices and prices** for each. Then look up the hotels' reviews in a Frommer's guide and check their rates online for your specific dates of travel. Also, find out what types of rooms are offered.
- Request a complete **schedule** (escorted tours only).
- Ask about the **size** and demographics of the group (escorted tours only).
- Discuss what is included in the **price** (transportation, meals, tips, airport transfers, etc.; escorted tours only).
- Finally, look for **hidden expenses.** Ask whether airport departure fees and taxes, for example, are included in the total cost—they rarely are.

ESCORTED GENERAL-INTEREST TOURS

Escorted tours are structured group tours, with a group leader. The price usually includes everything from airfare to hotels, meals, tours, admission costs, and local transportation.

Collette Vacations (62 Middle St., Pawtucket, RI 02860; ✆ **800/468-5955;** www.collettevacations.com) offers a wide variety of escorted trips by bus and train, including several in the Atlantic provinces, the Pacific Northwest, and the Rockies. A 10-day Fall Foliage tour of Nova Scotia focuses on the stunning colors of Cape Breton Island. Shorter trips explore the Toronto/Niagara area, and some combine scheduled VIA Rail service with bus travel.

Brewster Transportation and Tours (✆ **877/791-5500;** www.brewster.ca) offers a wide variety of tours throughout Canada, both escorted and independent. Their offerings include motorcoach and train excursions, ski and other winter vacations, city and resort combination packages, chartered day tours by bus, and independent driving tours. Highlights include a visit to the Columbia Icefields in Jasper National Park, Alberta, and one to Yellowknife, Northwest Territories, to view the aurora borealis.

Travel by train lets you see the Rockies as you never would in a bus or behind the wheel of a car. **Rocky Mountaineer Vacations** (✆ **877/460-3200;** www.rockymountaineer.com) bills its *Rocky Mountaineer* as "The Most Spectacular Train Trip in the World." During daylight hours between mid-April and mid-October, this sleek blue-and-white train winds past foaming waterfalls, ancient glaciers, towering snow-capped peaks, and roaring mountain streams. The *Rocky Mountaineer* gives you the options of traveling east from Vancouver; traveling west from Jasper, Calgary, or Banff; or taking round-trips. The company's *Sea to Sky Climb* train links Vancouver with Whistler while travel to/from Whistler and Jasper via Prince George is a fourth route. There are also packages that include links to the Inside Passage from Prince Rupert to Victoria. Tours range from 2 to 12 days, with stays in both the mountains and cities.

John Steel Railtours (✆ **800/988-5778** or 604/886-3427; www.johnsteel.com) offers both escorted and independent tour packages, many through the Rockies and the west and a few in other regions, which combine train and other forms of travel. VIA Rail operates the train portions of John Steel tours. Packages run from 5 to 12 days, at all times of year, depending on the route, and combine stays in major cities and national parks.

Despite the fact that escorted tours require big deposits and predetermine hotels, restaurants, and itineraries, many people derive security and peace of mind from the structure they offer. Escorted tours—whether they're navigated by bus, motorcoach, train, or boat—let travelers sit back and enjoy the trip without having to drive or worry about details. They take you to the maximum number of sights in the minimum amount of time with the least amount of hassle. They're particularly convenient for people with limited mobility, and they can be a great way to make new friends.

On the downside, you'll have little opportunity for serendipitous interactions with locals. The tours can be jam-packed with activities, leaving little room for individual sightseeing, whim, or adventure—plus, they often focus on the heavily touristed sites, so you miss out on many a lesser-known gem.

THE OUTDOOR ADVENTURE PLANNER

Outfitters & Adventure-Travel Operators

Most outfitters offer trips in specific geographic areas only, though some larger outfitters package trips across the country. In the chapters that follow, we'll recommend lots of local operators and tell you about the outings they run. We've found a few, though, that operate in more than one region of Canada.

The Great Canadian Adventure Company (✆ **888/285-1676** or 780/414-1676; www.adventures.ca) offers over 40 different types of guided activities and expeditions—including all of the standards, plus such options as First Nations and Inuit cultural tours, helicopter- or snowcat-transported backcountry skiing and snowboarding, and a submersible excursion—in every province and just about every nook of the country.

Canadian River Expeditions (✆ **800/297-6927** or 867/668-3180; www.nahanni.com) offers white-water and naturalist float trips in rivers across western and northern Canada, with the South Nahanni River a specialty.

Canusa Cycle Tours (✆ **800/938-7986;** www.canusa-cat.com) offers guided cycle tours along some of western Canada's most scenic highways, including the Icefields Parkway between Lake Louise and Jasper.

Ecosummer Expeditions (✆ **800/465-8884** or 250/674-0102; www.ecosummer.com) offers a wide variety of wildlife viewing, sea kayaking, white-water rafting, dog sledding, photography, and other expeditions in British Columbia, the Yukon, the Northwest Territories, and Nunavut. Ecosummer also offers trips to Greenland and Central America.

Black Feather (✆ **888/849-7668** or 705/746-1372; www.blackfeather.com) leads kayaking, canoeing, and hiking trips in British Columbia, the Northwest Territories, Nunavut, Ontario, and Labrador. Some tours are family-oriented, while others are women-only.

An Outfitter vs. Planning Your Own Trip

A basic consideration for most people who embark on an adventure vacation is time versus money. If you have time on your hands and have basic skills in dealing with sports and the outdoors, then planning your own trip can be fun. On the other hand, making one phone call and writing one check makes a lot more sense if you don't have a lot of time and lack the background to safely get you where you want to go.

TRANSPORTATION & EQUIPMENT In general, the more remote the destination, the more you should consider an outfitter. In many parts of Canada, simply getting to the area where your trip begins requires a great deal of planning. Frequently, outfitters will have their own airplanes or boats, or work in conjunction with someone who does. These transportation costs are usually included in the price of an excursion and are usually cheaper than the same flight or boat trip on a chartered basis.

The same rule applies to equipment rental. Getting your kayak or canoe to an out-of-the-way lake can be an adventure in itself. But hire an outfitter, and they'll take care of the hassle.

Another option is to use an outfitter to "package" your trip. Some outfitters offer their services to organize air charters and provide equipment for a fee but leave you to mastermind the trip.

SAFETY Much of Canada is remote and given to weather extremes. What might be considered a casual camping trip or boating excursion in more populated or temperate areas can become life-threatening in the Canadian backcountry—which often starts right at the edge of town. Almost all outfitters are certified as first-aid providers, and most carry two-way radios or satellite phones in case there's a need to call for help. Local outfitters also know the particular hazards of the areas where they lead trips. In some areas, such as the Arctic, where hazards range from freakish weather to ice-floe movements and polar bears, outfitters are nearly mandatory.

OTHER PEOPLE Most outfitters will lead groups on excursions only after signing up a minimum number of participants. This is usually a financial consideration for the outfitter, but for participants this can be both good and bad news. Traveling with the right people can add to the trip's enjoyment, but the wrong companions can lead to exasperation and disappointment. If you're sensitive to other peoples' idiosyncrasies, ask the potential outfitter specific questions regarding who else is going on the trip.

Selecting an Outfitter

An outfitter will be responsible for your safety and your enjoyment of the trip, so make certain you choose one wisely. All outfitters should be licensed or accredited by the province and should be happy to provide you with proof. This means they're bonded, carry the necessary insurance, and have the money and organizational wherewithal to register with the province. This rules out fly-by-night operations and college students who've decided to set up business for the summer. If you're just starting to plan an excursion, ask the provincial tourist authority for its complete list of licensed outfitters.

Often, a number of outfitters offer similar trips. When you've narrowed down your choice, call and talk to those outfitters. Ask questions and try to get a sense of who these people are; you'll be spending a lot of time with them, so make sure you feel comfortable. If you have special interests, such as bird- or wildlife-watching, be sure to mention them. A good outfitter will also take your interests into account when planning a trip.

If there's a wide disparity in prices between outfitters for the same trip, find out what makes the difference. Some companies economize on food. If you don't mind having cold cuts for each meal of your weeklong canoe expedition, then perhaps the least expensive outfitter is okay. However, if you prefer a cooked meal, alcoholic beverages, or a choice of entrees, then be prepared to pay more. On a long trip, it may be worth it to you.

Ask how many years an outfitter has been in business and how long your particular escort has guided this trip. While a start-up outfitting service can be perfectly fine, you should know what level of experience you're buying. If you have questions, especially for longer or more dangerous trips, ask for referrals.

What to Pack

Be sure that it's clearly established between you and your outfitter what you're responsible for bringing along. If you need to bring a sleeping bag, find out what weight of bag is suggested for the conditions you'll encounter. If you have any special dietary requirements, find out whether you can be accommodated or need to pack and prepare accordingly.

While it's fun and relatively easy to amass the equipment for a backcountry expedition, none of it will do you any good if you don't know how to use it. Even though compasses aren't particularly accurate in the North, bring one along and know how to use it (or consider using a GPS device). Detailed maps are always a good idea. If you're trekking without guidance, make sure you have the skills appropriate to your type of expedition, plan your packing well (with contingencies for changes in weather), and bring along a good first-aid kit.

For all summer trips in Canada, make sure to bring along insect repellent, as mosquitoes can be particularly numerous and hungry. If you know you're heading into bad mosquito country, consider buying specialized hats with mosquito netting attached, or full mosquito jackets. Sunglasses are a must, even above the Arctic Circle. The farther north you go in summer, the longer the sun stays up; the low angle of the sun can be particularly annoying. In winter, the glare off snow can cause sun blindness. For the same reasons, sunscreen is a necessity.

Summer weather is changeable in Canada. If you're planning outdoor activities, be sure to bring along wet-weather gear, even in high summer. The more exposure you'll have to the elements, the more you should consider bringing high-end Gore-Tex and artificial-fleece outerwear. The proper gear can make the difference between a miserable time and a great adventure.

If you're traveling in Canada in winter, you'll want to have the best winter coat, gloves, and boots you can afford. A coat with a hood is especially important, as winter winds can blow for days at a time.

GETTING AROUND CANADA

By Car

Once in Canada, drivers will find that roads are generally in good condition. There are two major highway routes that cross Canada east to west. Highway 1—the Trans-Canada Highway—which is largely four-lane, travels from Victoria on the Pacific to St. John's in Newfoundland a total of 8,000km (4,971 miles)—with some ferries along the way. The Yellowhead Highway (Hwy. 16) links Winnipeg to Prince Rupert in BC along a more northerly route.

GASOLINE As in the United States, the trend in Canada is toward self-service stations, and in some areas, you may have difficulty finding the full-service kind. Though Canada (specifically, Alberta) is a major oil producer, gasoline isn't particularly cheap. Gas sells by the liter and pumps for anywhere from about C95¢ to C$1.50 per liter, or about C$4 to C$6 per U.S. gallon. (Note that the term "gallon" in Canada usually refers to the imperial gallon, which amounts to about 1.2 U.S. gal.) Gasoline prices vary from region to region, with prices highest in northern regions.

DRIVING RULES Canadian driving rules are similar to regulations in the United States. Wearing seat belts is compulsory (and enforced) in all provinces for all passengers. Children under 5 must be in child restraints. Motorcyclists must wear helmets. Throughout the country, pedestrians have the right of way, and crosswalks are sacrosanct. The speed limit on the auto routes (limited-access highways) is usually 110kmph (68 mph). In all provinces but Québec, right turns on red are permitted after a full stop, unless another rule is posted. The use of handheld cellphones while driving is prohibited in most jurisdictions. Drivers must carry proof of insurance in Canada at all times.

SAMPLE DRIVING DISTANCES BETWEEN MAJOR CITIES Here are some sample driving distances between major Canadian cities. The distances are calculated based on a particular route, possibly the fastest, but not necessarily the shortest: Montréal to Vancouver, 4,910km (3,051 miles); Vancouver to Halifax, 6,295km (3,912 miles); Toronto to Victoria, 4,700km (2,920 miles); Winnipeg to St. John's, 5,100km (3,169 miles); Calgary to Montréal, 3,710km (2,305 miles); St. John's to Vancouver, 7,625km (4,738 miles); Ottawa to Victoria, 4,810km (2,989 miles). To get driving directions online, check MapQuest (www.mapquest.com), Google Maps (http://maps.google.com), or Yahoo! Maps (http://maps.yahoo.com) and select Driving Directions.

By Plane

Getting around Canada by air is easy, with two major airlines serving the country from coast to coast and dozens of smaller airlines linking out-of-the-way places to larger population centers. For information, contact **Air Canada** (✆ **888/937-8538;** www.aircanada.com) or **WestJet** (✆ **888/937-8538;** www.westjet.com).

In the last decade, Canada has undergone a renaissance in domestic air-travel pricing. It's usually cheaper to fly between Canadian cities than take the bus or train.

By Train

Most of Canada's passenger rail traffic is carried by the government-owned **VIA Rail** (✆ **888/842-7245** or 514/989-2626; www.viarail.ca). You can traverse the continent very comfortably in sleeping cars, parlor coaches, bedrooms, and roomettes. Virtually all of Canada's major cities (save St. John's, Regina, Calgary, and Victoria) are connected by rail, though service is less frequent than it used to be. Some luxury trains, such as the *Canadian,* boast dome cars with panoramic picture windows, hot showers, and dining cars. Reduced regular fares are available for students, seniors, and children traveling with adults.

The problem with traveling on VIA Rail, particularly in western Canada, is that the train runs only 3 days a week. If you want to link your visit between destinations in

Alberta and British Columbia with a train journey, you may be out of luck unless your schedule is very flexible. Also, if sightseeing and not just transport is part of your vacation agenda, then you may also find that your train journey takes place overnight. Because of the way the train is scheduled in many parts of rural Canada, there's just one schedule per train, so the leg between Winnipeg and Edmonton, for instance, will always be overnight, no matter which train you take.

You can buy a **Canrailpass,** C$941 in high season and C$588 in low season, giving you seven one-way trips in economy-class in one 21-day period throughout the VIA Rail national network. Seniors 60 and over, students, and children 17 and under receive a 10% discount on all fares. Class upgrades are available for a fee each time you ride. A similar but less expensive package is available for seven one-way trips on the Québec-Windsor corridor (Toronto, Niagara Falls, Ottawa, Montréal, and Québec City) within a 10-day period.

By Bus

While many visitors may not relish the option of traveling by bus while in Canada, in fact, **Greyhound Canada** (© **800/661-8747;** www.greyhound.ca) offers far superior service and coverage than does Greyhound in the U.S. Not only are the buses newer and cleaner, and the bus stations better kept up than in the U.S., Greyhound is often the only option for public transport in many parts of Canada due to the relatively minimal coverage by VIA Rail.

TIPS ON ACCOMMODATIONS

Travelers to Canada are lucky: The quality of hotels and lodging in Canada is very high. In fact, along with the Swiss, Canadians seem to have a natural gift for the hospitality industry.

A national accommodations rating system is in place in Canada. Called **Canada Select,** it rates lodgings between one and five stars based on the evaluation of independent adjudicators. The system is more prominent in some provinces than in others; it is also completely voluntary, so the absence of stars doesn't necessarily mean that the property is substandard. In fact, the Canada Select program is most popular and meaningful for smaller inns and B&Bs, where an independent evaluation is often reassuring.

Generally speaking, most travelers would be comfortable staying in accommodations with at least three stars. These accommodations may not be fancy, but they will be clean and pleasant. Four-star accommodations are usually top-notch. It's worthwhile noting that the gradations between four and five stars have to do with features that may not directly affect the comfort or pleasure of your stay—types of curtains, types of door locks, and so on. In other words, you may not even recognize the supposed superiority of a five-star property over one with four stars.

Every Canadian city has a selection of upscale luxury or business hotels. The preeminent Canadian chain of luxury hotels is **Fairmont Hotels and Resorts** (© **800/257-7544;** www.fairmont.com), which is the company that now controls many of the historic and utterly fabulous hotels built by the Canadian railroads around the turn of the 20th century. These include a number of hotels that are practically symbols of Canada, such as the Empress in Victoria, the Château Lake Louise, the Banff Springs, and the Château Frontenac in Québec City. These Fairmont hotels have been lovingly restored, but you'll have to decide if their rates are worth it to you—certainly, a stay at one of these vintage beauties will be a highlight of any stay in Canada (some Fairmont hotels are modern, though of equally high quality).

Many hotel chains familiar from the U.S. and Europe are also found in Canada, including Hilton, Radisson, Hyatt, Ramada, and Westin. An excellent Canadian-based chain of upscale business hotels is **Delta Hotels and Resorts** (✆ **888/890-3222;** www.deltahotels.com). Delta hotels (not related to the airline) are very high quality and are frequently among the top hotels in major Canadian cities and resort towns. A smaller chain of hotels in western Canada is **Coast Hotels & Resorts** (✆ **800/716-6199;** www.coasthotels.com), which also keeps very high standards. As in other parts of North America, the **Best Western** chain (✆ **800/780-7234;** www.bestwestern.com) is well represented in Canada and offers a guarantee of good, midlevel quality.

Canada is also known for its small inns and bed-and-breakfasts. There are many more high-quality B&B inns available than this guide could possibly cover. However, the text usually offers the phone number and website information to contact local B&B organizations. A good Canada-wide clearinghouse for B&Bs is the website **www.bbcanada.com.**

Another Canadian specialty is its backcountry lodges and country inns. These are sometimes located in remote regions, at the end of a long and bumpy road, or accessible only on foot. However, the lodges found in this guide are rustic in spirit only and offer high-quality lodging and dining in beautiful and remote areas.

TIPS ON DINING

Dining habits in Canada are quite similar to those in the U.S. Evening meals are generally eaten between 6 and 8pm. A tip of 15% to 20% is usually expected for good service. The quality of food in Canada is generally quite high; you'll have no problem finding excellent dining options across the country.

Canada is a country of recent immigrants. You can ask locals for recommendations to the best neighborhood Chinese, Lebanese, Pakistani, Jamaican, or other ethnic restaurant. As these restaurants tend to come and go pretty quickly, they may not appear in this guide. However, almost every Canadian city and town has an offering of ethnic restaurants that will provide inexpensive and delicious dining.

Traditional Canadian cooking is often excellent. In Atlantic Canada, this will include wondrous all-you-can-eat lobster buffets in out-of-the-way diners and church basements, while in Québec, it will include rotisserie chicken, smoked beef, and the heart-stopping but delicious fast food called *poutine* (fried potatoes with cheese and gravy). Out west, Alberta beef is on most menus, and along the Pacific coast, wild salmon and halibut are almost always available in restaurants, right off the boat and absolutely fresh.

However, Canada is also home to a more modern cooking ethic that focuses on organic, locally grown meats and produce, and fresh fish and seafood; unusual meats such as bison and game meats such as venison, elk, moose, and caribou are also common on upscale menus. New Canadian cuisine is frequently excellent. It is intensely dedicated to local products, but it also draws on the combined strength of pioneer cooking, including the traditional cooking of French and British settlers, as well as the subtle cuisines of more recent immigrant communities, particularly from Asia.

If you haven't heard of—much less tried—Canadian wines, you're in for a treat. The Niagara area of Ontario is famed for its dessert ice wines, while the Okanagan

Valley in British Columbia is home to a burgeoning wine industry featuring excellent vintages made from traditional French varietals. Most Canadian towns and cities also have a number of brewpubs that feature locally brewed beer and ales, as well as flavorful casual dining.

[Fast FACTS] CANADA

AAA Members of the **American Automobile Association (AAA)** are covered by the **Canadian Automobile Association (CAA)** while traveling in Canada. Bring your membership card and proof of insurance. The 24-hour hotline for emergency service is ✆ **800/222-4357.** Most mobile phones can call ✆ ***CAA** (*222) to reach emergency road service. See www.caa.ca for more. The AAA card also provides discounts at many hotels and restaurants.

American Express See the city chapters that follow for the locations of individual American Express offices. To report lost or stolen traveler's checks, call ✆ **800/668-2639.**

ATM Networks See "Money & Costs," p. 24.

Business Hours Standard business hours in Canada are similar to those in the U.S., usually 10am to 6pm. It is common for stores to be closed on Sundays, particularly outside of the larger cities and major tourist areas.

Customs **What You Can Bring Into Canada** Customs regulations are generous in most respects but get pretty complicated when it comes to firearms, plants, meats, and pets. You can bring in free of duty up to 50 cigars, 200 cigarettes, and 200g (7 oz.) of tobacco, providing you're over 18. Those of age (18 or 19, depending on the province) are also allowed about 1.1L liters (37 oz.) of liquor, 1.5 liters (51 oz.) of wine, or 24 355mL (12-oz.) containers of beer. Dogs, cats, and most pets can enter Canada with their owners, though you must have proof of rabies vaccinations within the last 36 months for pets over 3 months old.

Canada has complex requirements, restrictions, and limits that apply to importing meat, eggs, dairy products, fresh fruits and vegetables, and other food from around the world. You can avoid problems by not bringing such goods into Canada.

As for firearms, visitors can bring rifles for the purposes of hunting into Canada during hunting season. Handguns and automatic rifles are generally not allowed. Fishing tackle poses no problems, but the bearer must possess a nonresident license for the province or territory where he or she plans to use it. For more details concerning Customs regulations, contact the **Canada Border Service Agency** (✆ **800/461-9999** within Canada or 204/983-3500; www.cbsa.gc.ca).

What You Can Take Home from Canada

U.S. Citizens: Returning U.S. citizens who have been away for at least 48 hours are allowed to bring back, once every 30 days, US$800 worth of merchandise duty-free. You'll be charged a flat rate of 3% duty on the next US$1,000 worth of purchases. Be sure to have your receipts handy. With some exceptions, you cannot bring fresh fruits and vegetables into the United States. For travelers 18 and older, the $800 duty-free exemption includes the following maximums: 2L (68 oz.) of alcohol, 100 cigars, or 200 cigarettes. For specifics on what you can bring back and the corresponding fees, download the invaluable free pamphlet *Know Before You Go* online at **www.cbp.gov.** (Click on "Travel," and then click on "Know Before You Go"). Or contact the **U.S. Customs and Border Protection (CBP;** ✆ **877/227-5511** or 703/526-4200) and request the pamphlet.

U.K. citizens: Returning U.K. citizens have a duty-free customs allowance of £390. This amount includes the following maximums: 200 cigarettes or 50 cigars, or 250g (9 oz.) of tobacco;

4L (135 oz.) of table wine; 1L (34 oz.) of spirits or strong liqueurs (over 22% volume); or 2L (68 oz.) of fortified wine. People under 17 cannot have the tobacco or alcohol allowance. For more information, contact **HM Revenue & Customs** at ✆ **0845/010-9000** (from outside the U.K., 020/8929-0152), or consult their website at www.hmrc.gov.uk.

Australian Citizens: The duty-free allowance in Australia is A$900 or, for those under 18, A$450. Citizens can bring in 250 cigarettes or 250g (8¾ oz.) of loose tobacco, and 2.3L (78 oz.) of alcohol (for travelers 18 and older). If you're returning with valuables you already own, such as foreign-made cameras, you should file form B263, which can be downloaded from www.customs.gov.au. A helpful brochure available from Australian consulates or Customs offices is "Know Before You Go." For more information, call the **Australian Customs Service** at ✆ **1300/363-263,** or log on to www.customs.gov.au.

New Zealand Citizens: The duty-free allowance for New Zealand is NZ$700. Citizens over 17 can bring in 200 cigarettes, 50 cigars, or 250g (8¾ oz.) of tobacco (or a mixture of all three if their combined weight doesn't exceed 250g/8¾ oz.), plus 4.5L (152 oz.) of wine and beer, or three 1.1L (37 oz.) bottles of liquor. New Zealand currency does not carry import or export restrictions. Fill out a certificate of export, listing the valuables you are taking out of the country; that way, you can bring them back without paying duty. For more information, contact **New Zealand Customs** (✆ **0800/428-786** or 09/300-5399; www.customs.govt.nz).

Drugstores Drugstores and pharmacies are found throughout Canada. As in the U.S., there are a number of national chain pharmacies, including Shoppers Drug Mart and Rexall. In addition, many larger grocery stores in Canada also have in-store pharmacies. Many prescription-only drugs in the United States are available over the counter in Canada, and pharmacists are more likely to offer casual medical advice than their counterparts in the States. If you're not feeling well, a trip to see a pharmacist may save you a trip to the doctor.

Electricity Canada uses the same electrical plug configuration and current as the United States: 110 to 115 volts, 60 cycles.

Embassies & Consulates

All embassies are in Ottawa, the national capital; the **U.S. embassy** is at 490 Sussex Dr., Ottawa, ON K1N 1G8 (✆ **613/688-5335;** http://ottawa.usembassy.gov). The mailing address for the embassy's consular services is P.O. Box 866, Station B, Ottawa, ON K1P 5T1. For the other embassies in Ottawa, see "Fast Facts: Ottawa," in chapter 9.

U.S. consulates are in the following locations: **Nova Scotia, Newfoundland, New Brunswick,** and **Prince Edward Island**—Suite 904, Purdy's Wharf Tower II, 1969 Upper Water St., Halifax (✆ **902/429-2480**); **Québec**—2 rue de la Terrasse-Dufferin (behind Château Frontenac), Québec City (✆ **418/692-2095**), and 1155 St. Alexander St., Montréal (✆ **514/398-9695**); **Ontario**—360 University Ave., Toronto (✆ **416/595-1700,** or 416/201-4100 for emergency after-hours calls); **Alberta, Saskatchewan, Manitoba,** and the **Northwest Territories**—615 Macleod Trail SE, 10th Floor, Calgary (✆ **403/266-8962**); **British Columbia** and the **Yukon**—Mezzanine, 1095 W. Pender St., Vancouver (✆ **604/685-4311**).

The **British High Commission** is at 80 Elgin St., Toronto (✆ **613/237-1530;** http://ukincanada.fco.gov.uk), and an **Australian consulate general** is at Suite 1100, South Tower, 175 Bloor St. E., Toronto (✆ **416/323-3909;** www.canada.embassy.gov.au).

Emergencies Dial ✆ **911** in an emergency.

Holidays National holidays are celebrated throughout the country; all government facilities and banks are closed, but some department stores and a scattering of smaller shops stay open. If the holiday falls on a weekend, the following Monday is observed.

Language Canada has two official languages, English and French. French is the dominant language in Québec; however, most Québecers can also speak passable English, particularly if they work in the tourism industry. However, it's a good idea to dust off your high-school French if you're traveling to Québec destinations outside of Montréal or Québec City. Not only is it a courtesy to address people in their native tongue, you'll be treated with greater respect if you don't start barking English orders to waiters and hotel staff.

Liquor Laws Laws regarding beer, wine, and liquor vary from province to province. In some provinces, all beer, wine, and spirits are sold only in government liquor stores, which keep very restricted hours and are usually closed on Sundays. Alberta and Québec have liquor laws that resemble those in the United States. In those provinces and Manitoba, the minimum drinking age is 18; in all others, it's 19.

Lost & Found Be sure to tell all of your credit card companies the minute you discover your wallet has been lost or stolen and file a report at the nearest police precinct. Your credit card company or insurer may require a police report number or record of the loss. Most credit card companies have an emergency toll-free number to call if your card is lost or stolen; they may be able to wire you a cash advance immediately or deliver an emergency credit card in a day or two. Visa's North American emergency number is ✆ **800/847-2911** or 410/581-9994. American Express cardholders and traveler's check holders should call ✆ **800/221-7282.** MasterCard holders should call ✆ **800/627-8372** or 636/722-7111. For other credit cards, call the toll-free number directory at ✆ **800/555-1212.**

If you need emergency cash over the weekend when all banks and American Express offices are closed, you can have money wired to you via **Western Union** (✆ **800/325-6000** in the U.S. or 800/325-0000 in Canada; www.westernunion.com).

Mail Standard mail in Canada is carried by **Canada Post** (✆ **800/607-6301** or 416/979-8822; www.canadapost.ca). At press time, it costs C57¢ to send a letter or postcard within Canada and C$1 to send a letter or postcard from Canada to the United States. Airmail service to other countries is C$1.70 for the first 30g (1 oz.). Rates go up frequently. If you put a return address on your letter, make sure it's Canadian; otherwise, leave it without. Expect a letter from Canada to take at least a week to reach its U.S. destination.

Measurements Canada uses the metric system, though many Canadians still use miles to measure distance and are familiar with other U.S. forms of measurement. See the chart on the inside front cover of this book for details on converting metric measurements to nonmetric equivalents.

Newspapers & Magazines In addition to local newspapers, the *Globe and Mail* and the *National Post,* both based out of Toronto, are distributed nationally. *Maclean's* is a Canadian weekly newsmagazine.

Passports Allow plenty of time before your trip to apply for a passport; processing normally takes 3 weeks but can take much longer during busy periods (especially spring). And keep in mind that if you need a passport in a hurry, you'll pay a higher processing fee.

For Residents of Australia: You can pick up an application from your local post office or any branch of Passports Australia, but you must schedule an interview at the passport office to present your application materials. Call the **Australian Passport Information Service** at ✆ **131-232** or visit the government website at www.passports.gov.au.

For Residents of Ireland: You can apply for a 10-year passport at the **Passport Office,** Setanta Centre, Molesworth Street, Dublin 2 (✆ **01/671-1633;** www.irlgov.ie/iveagh). Those under age 18 and over 65 must apply for a 3-year passport. You can also apply at 1A South Mall, Cork (✆ **021/272-525**), or at most main post offices.

For Residents of New Zealand: You can pick up a passport application at any New Zealand Passports Office or download it from their website. Contact the **Passports Office** at ✆ **0800/225-050** in New Zealand or 04/474-8100, or log on to www.passports.govt.nz.

For Residents of the United Kingdom: To pick up an application for a standard 10-year passport (5-year passport for children under 16), visit your nearest passport office, major post office, or travel agency, or contact the **United Kingdom Passport Service** at ✆ **0870/521-0410** or search its website at www.ukpa.gov.uk.

For Residents of the United States: Whether you're applying in person or by mail, you can download passport applications from the U.S. State Department at **http://travel.state.gov.** To find your regional passport office, either check the U.S. State Department website or call the **National Passport Information Center** toll-free number (✆ **877/487-2778**) for automated information.

Police In emergencies, dial ✆ **911.**

Safety See the section "Safety," earlier in this chapter.

Smoking Smoking indoors is much more restricted in Canada than in much of the U.S. or Europe. All of the country's 13 provinces and territories have now passed smoking bans prohibiting cigarettes in the workplace and public buildings, bars, and restaurants. In some jurisdictions, there are even regulations on how closely one can smoke to public entrances to buildings.

Taxes Throughout Canada, you will be charged a federal **goods and services tax (GST),** a 5% tax on virtually all goods and services. In all provinces except Alberta, there is an additional **provincial sales tax (PST)** of between 5% and 10% added to purchases and financial transactions, and all provinces and some municipalities levy a hotel room tax of up to 5%. Some provinces (Ontario, British Columbia, Nova Scotia, and New Brunswick) instead levy a 12% to 15% **harmonized sales tax (HST),** which combines their provincial sales taxes with the GST. Some hotels and shops include the GST or HST in their prices; others add it on separately.

As of April 2007, the Canadian government no longer offers GST or HST rebates of hotel bills or the cost of goods you've purchased in Canada.

Time Zone Six time zones are observed in Canada. In winter, when it's 6:30pm Newfoundland standard time, it's 6pm Atlantic Standard Time (Labrador, Prince Edward Island, New Brunswick, and Nova Scotia); 5pm Eastern Standard Time (Québec and most of Ontario); 4pm Central Standard Time (northwestern Ontario, Manitoba, and most of Saskatchewan); 3pm Mountain Standard Time (northwestern Saskatchewan, Alberta, eastern British Columbia, and the Northwest Territories); and 2pm Pacific Standard Time (the Yukon and most of British Columbia).

Each year, on the second Sunday in March, Daylight Saving Time comes into effect in most of Canada, and clocks are advanced by 1 hour. On the first Sunday in November, Canada reverts to standard time. The only province that doesn't observe Daylight Saving Time is Saskatchewan.

Tipping For good service in a restaurant, tip 15% to 20%. Tip hairdressers or taxi drivers 10%. Bellhops get C$1 per bag for luggage taken to your room; for valets who fetch your car, a C$2 tip should suffice.

Water The water in Canada is renowned for its purity. You can drink water directly from the tap anywhere in the country. Bottled water is also widely available.

NOVA SCOTIA

by Paul Karr

3

Nova Scotia is more than just a pretty picture. Apparently humdrum on the surface, it resists characterization at every turn—and turns out to be friendly as all get-out. Sure, upon entry it feels much more cultured and British than wild, a better place to buy a wool sweater and shoot a round of golf than to actually get your feet wet. But then you stumble upon the blustery, boggy uplands and crags of Cape Breton Highlands National Park, and hear the wild strains of some local Celtic band's fiddling emanating from a tiny pub, and you start to realize that people here are both tougher than you thought and full of spunk—closer to Newfies, maybe, then Brits.

Yes, this is a place of rolling hills and cultivated farms, especially near the Northumberland Straits on the northern shore—but it's also got a vibrant, edgy arts and entertainment scene in Halifax, a city possessing more intriguing street life than plenty of cities three times its size. The place has been called a "San Francisco in miniature" (though it's really more like a small Boston).

This is a province that has truly earned its name—"Nova Scotia" is just grammar-school Latin for "New Scotland"—with Highland Games, kilts, and more than a touch of brogue. Yet it also possesses rich little enclaves of Acadian culture, both on the far shore of Cape Breton and along the southwestern coast between Digby and Yarmouth. (Want to see a really huge wooden church in the unlikeliest of places? It's here.)

But this province is also a good vacation for the sort of traveler who's not yet ready to tackle Nepal. You can do low-key Sunday drives here 7 days a week without a traffic jam. The scene changes almost kaleidoscopically as you wind along Nova Scotia's roads: from dense forests to bucolic farmlands, from ragged coastline cliffs to melancholy bogs, from historic villages with tall ships lazing about at port to dynamic little downtowns serving up everything from fish and chips and a pint to the occasional gourmet eatery. Pretty much the only terrain Nova Scotia doesn't offer is, well, desert.

In fact, the province is twice blessed. Many of the best parts are compact enough that you needn't spend all your time in a car—thanks, Halifax and the South Shore. Yet it has less than a million residents (one in three live in Halifax), making most of it empty enough to provide lots of space when you're seeking a clear head and a nearly private beach. Even in the most thickly populated sections, it's still possible to feel a sense of remoteness here, of being surrounded by a big ocean and long history.

More than once while traveling through the back roads of Nova Scotia, I've had the sense I was traveling through the New England of 60 or 70 years ago—the one that captivated writers and painters long before anyone referred to tourism as an "industry." I still get that sense here, sometimes—a sense of peace, quiet, and mannered culture. It's not gone, not yet, and with a little exploring you can find it, too.

EXPLORING THE PROVINCE

Visitors to Nova Scotia should spend a little time poring over a map (and this travel guide) before leaving home. It's a good idea to narrow down your options, because numerous loops, circuits, and side-trips are possible here—and the permutations only multiply once you factor in various ferry links to the United States, New Brunswick, Prince Edward Island, and Newfoundland. You don't want to spread yourself *too* thin. So figuring out where to go—and how to get there—is the hardest work you'll need to do in a place that is quite easy to travel around once you've arrived there.

Essentials

VISITOR INFORMATION Every traveler to Nova Scotia should get a copy of the massive (400-plus-page) official tourism guide. It's comprehensive, colorful, well-organized, and free, listing most hotels, campgrounds, and attractions within the province, plus brief descriptions and current prices. (Restaurants are given only limited coverage, however; investigate those using this book and your own nose for eats.)

The tome, called the *Nova Scotia Doers' & Dreamers' Guide,* becomes available each year around March. Contact the province by phone (© **800/565-0000** or 902/424-5000), mail (Nova Scotia Department of Tourism, Culture, and Heritage, P.O. Box 456, Halifax, NS B3J 2R5), or Internet (www.novascotia.com). You can wait until you arrive in the province to obtain the visitor's guide, of course. But then you won't be able to do much advance planning.

TOURIST OFFICES The provincial government administers about a dozen official **Visitor Information Centres** (known as "VICs") throughout the province. These mostly seasonal centers (see box) are amply stocked with brochures and tended by knowledgeable staffers. In addition, virtually every town of any note has a local tourist information center filled with racks of brochures covering the entire province and staffed with local people who know the area. You won't ever be short of information. Also be sure to request the province's excellent free road map, which will begin to give you a sense of how few roads there actually are here. (What the map *doesn't* convey is how big the province is. Driving takes time here.)

For general questions about travel in the province, call **Nova Scotia's information hot line** at © **800/565-0000** (North America) or 902/424-5000 (outside North America).

Getting There

BY CAR & FERRY Most travelers reach Nova Scotia overland by car from New Brunswick. Plan on at least a 4-hour drive from the U.S. border at Calais, Maine, to Amherst (at the New Brunswick–Nova Scotia border).

To shorten the long drive around the Bay of Fundy, a 3-hour ferry (also operated by Bay Ferries) known as the *Princess of Acadia* links **Saint John, New Brunswick,** with **Digby, Nova Scotia.** Remarkably, this ferry sails daily year-round, with two sailings per day during peak travel periods. In 2010, the peak season one-way fare

Nova Scotia & Prince Edward Island

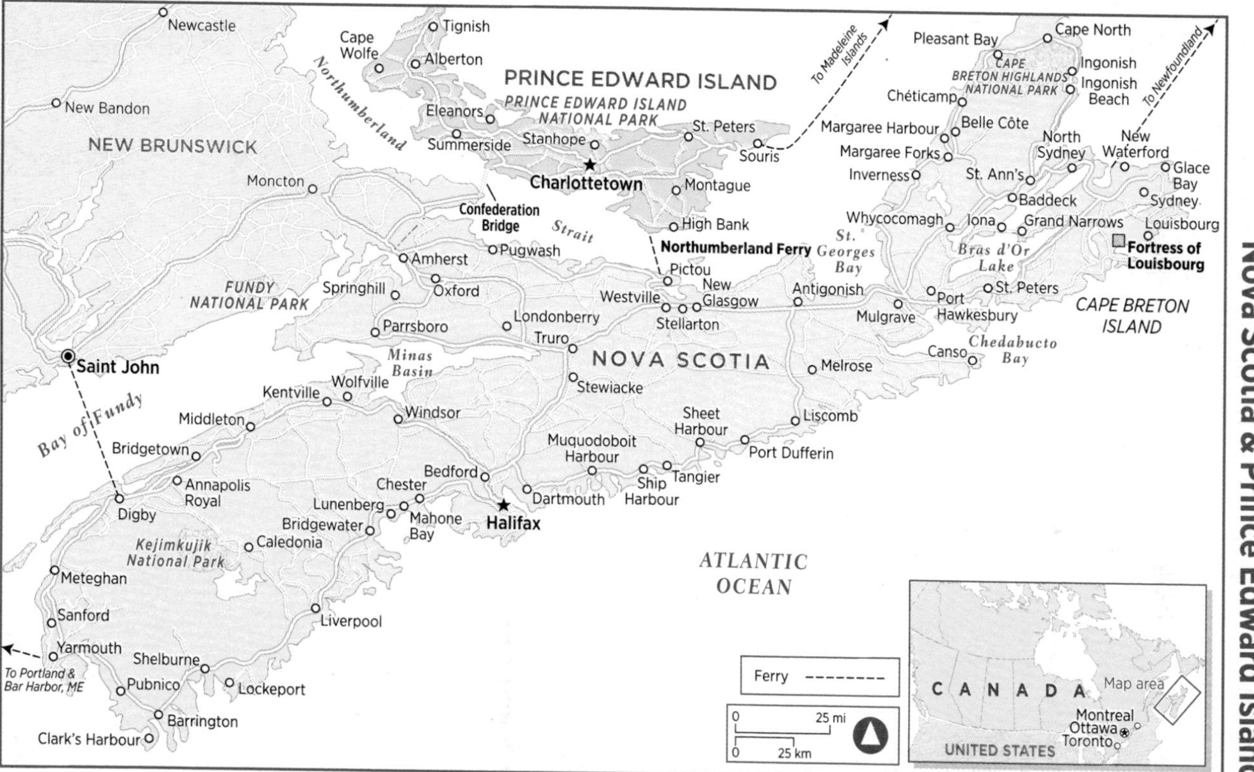

(charged June through October) was C$40 for adults, C$25 for children age 6 to 13, C$5 per child under age 6, and C$30 for students and seniors. Your car itself costs an additional C$80 (more for trucks, vans, and buses), plus a C$20 fuel surcharge. Fares are a bit cheaper outside the peak travel months, and if you walk on and return within 30 days, there are also discounts available on the round-trip. Note that AAA and CAA members receive C$10 discounts on the automobile portion of the fare. Complete up-to-the-minute schedules and fares for the *Princess of Acadia* can be found at www.nfl-bay.com or by calling © **888/249-SAIL** [7245].

For those traveling farther afield, ferries also connect Prince Edward Island to Caribou, Nova Scotia, and Newfoundland to North Sydney, Nova Scotia.

You can view the latest **updated highway conditions** around the province of Nova Scotia by logging onto the province's transportation website at **http://511.gov.ns.ca/map.** This map shows both road construction projects and unusual weather conditions affecting traffic flow.

BY PLANE Halifax is the air hub of the Atlantic Provinces. **Air Canada** (© **888/247-2262;** www.aircanada.com) provides daily direct service from New York and Boston using its commuter partner **Jazz** (www.flyjazz.ca), which also flies directly to Sydney, Charlottetown, Saint John, and St. John's, as well as several more remote destinations in eastern Canada. But other contenders are jumping into the fray, as well: **Continental** (© **800/231-0856;** www.continental.com) flies direct from Newark to Halifax several times daily in summer, for one. American Airlines' **American Eagle** (© **800/433-7300;** www.aa.com) commuter service flies small planes from New York's LaGuardia Airport back and forth to Halifax. If you're coming from anywhere other than New York, however, you will probably need to connect in Montréal or Toronto, which can turn into a half-day excursion or more.

BY TRAIN **VIA Rail** (© **888/842-7245;** www.viarail.ca) offers train service 6 days a week on the *Ocean* run between Halifax and Montréal; the entire trip takes between 18 and 21 hours depending on direction, with a basic summertime fare of about C$250 each way, not counting sleeping accommodations (which can add considerably to the cost). Discounts for those buying at least 1 week in advance are sometimes possible.

As I said, sleeping berths and private cabins are available at extra cost—the cheapest bed, in a double-bunked cabin, is about twice the cost of the no-bed fare—and VIA has created an even higher class of service (summer-only) known as the Sleeper Touring class aboard the *Ocean*. This class offers all-inclusive meals, sleeping accommodations, exclusive access to lounges and a panoramic car, and continuing presentations from an onboard educator about Maritime Province culture and history.

The *Ocean* runs daily (except Tuesdays) each direction year-round, with standard overnight sleeper-cabin service; the Easterly option is available from mid-June through mid-October. Check the VIA Rail website for routes, schedules, and booking.

The Great Outdoors

Nova Scotia's terrific official travel guide (the aforementioned *Doers' & Dreamers' Guide*) contains a very helpful "Outdoors" section in the back that's full of detailed listings of camping outfitters, bike shops, whale-watching tour operators, and the like. More specific information on the province's adventure outfitters can also be obtained from the trade association for providers, the **Nova Scotia Adventure Tourism Association,** 1099 Marginal Rd., Suite 201, Halifax, NS B3H 4P7 (© **800/948-4267** or 902/423-4480).

BIKING The low hills of Nova Scotia and the gentle, mostly empty roads make for wonderful cycling. Cape Breton is the most challenging of the province's destinations; the south coast and Bay of Fundy regions yield wonderful ocean views while making fewer cardiovascular demands on the cyclist. A number of bike outfitters can aid in your trip planning. **Freewheeling Adventures** (✆ **800/672-0775** or 902/857-3600; www.freewheeling.ca) is highly recommended for its guided bike tours throughout Nova Scotia (as well as Prince Edward Island and Newfoundland). Want to go it alone? Walter Sienko's guide, *Nova Scotia & the Maritimes by Bike: 21 Tours Geared for Discovery* (1995) is very helpful in planning a local bike excursion.

Also, for a good introduction to cycling in Nova Scotia and beyond point your Web browser to the website of **Atlantic Canada Cycling** (www.atl-canadacycling.com) and click on "Tour Planning" for brief introductions to the regions of Nova Scotia and their respective characteristics (including strength of local winds). The site also offers group bicycle tours and events, and sells books and maps.

BIRD-WATCHING More than 400 species of birds have been spotted in Nova Scotia, ranging from odd and exotic birds blown off course in storms to majestic **bald eagles,** of which perhaps 250 nesting pairs reside in Nova Scotia, mostly on Cape Breton Island. Many whale-watching tours also offer specialized seabird-spotting tours, including trips to **puffin colonies.**

CAMPING With backcountry options rather limited, Nova Scotia's forte is drive-in camping. The 20 or so provincial parks offer some 1,500 campsites among them, and campgrounds are uniformly clean, friendly, well managed, and reasonably priced. For a brochure and map listing all provincial campsites, contact the **Nova Scotia Department of Natural Resources/Parks and Recreation Division** (✆ **902/662-3030**). The division's website is located at **www.parksnovascotia.ca** and is well organized. As usual, the province's *Doers' & Dreamers' Guide* contains the fullest campground listings available in print.

Also check with the Campground Owners Association of Nova Scotia: Its website at **www.campingnovascotia.com** lists a number of privately held campgrounds. The free and helpful *Campers Guide,* available at visitor information centers, lists this information as well.

CANOEING Nova Scotia offers an abundance of accessible canoeing on inland lakes and ponds. The premier destination is **Kejimkujik National Park** in the southern interior, which has plenty of backcountry sites accessible by canoe. A number of other fine canoe trips allow paddlers and portagers to venture off for hours or days. General information on paddling routes, classes, events, and local clubs is available from the organization **Canoe Kayak Nova Scotia,** 5516 Spring Garden Rd., 4th floor, Halifax, NS B3J 1G6 (✆ **902/425-5454,** ext. 316). The group's website can be found at **www.ckns.ca**.

FISHING Saltwater fishing tours are easily arranged on charter boats berthed at many of the province's harbors. Inquire locally at visitor information centers or consult the "Boat Tours & Charters" section of the *Doers' & Dreamers' Guide.* No fishing license is required for *most* saltwater species for those on charters. For questions, current fishing regulations, or lists of licensed fishing guides, check out the Nova Scotia **Department of Fisheries and Aquaculture** website at **www.gov.ns.ca/fish.**

Committed freshwater anglers come to Nova Scotia in pursuit of the tragically dwindling Atlantic salmon, which requires a license separate from that for other freshwater fish. **Salmon licenses** must be obtained from a provincial office, campground, or licensed outfitter. Other freshwater species popular with anglers are brown trout, shad, smallmouth bass, rainbow trout, and speckled trout. Again, for up-to-date information contact the Department of Fisheries and Aquaculture (see above).

GOLF Nova Scotia lays claim to more than 50 golf courses. Among the most memorable are the government-owned **Highland Links** (✆ **800/441-1118** or 902/285-2600; www.highlandlinksgolf.com) course in Ingonish, which features a dramatic oceanside setting, and **Bell Bay Golf Club** (✆ **800/565-3077** or 902/295-1333; www.bellbaygolfclub.com) near Baddeck—which is also wonderfully scenic and has appeared in *Golf Digest.* Highland Links costs C$91 plus tax for 18 holes in peak season; Bell Bay, C$79 for 18 holes in peak season. Both cost less during spring and fall, and Sunday or twilight rates are sometimes also available.

Golf Nova Scotia (✆ **800/565-0000,** ext. 007; www.golfnovascotia.com), run by the tourism office, represents about 30 well-regarded properties around the province and can arrange customized golfing packages at its member courses. A handy directory of Nova Scotia's golf courses (with phone numbers) is published as a separate brochure and in the "Outdoors" section of the *Doers' & Dreamers' Guide* as well.

HIKING & WALKING Serious hikers make tracks for **Cape Breton Highlands National Park,** which is home to the most dramatic terrain in the province. But other options abound—trails are found throughout Nova Scotia, although in many cases they're a matter of local knowledge. (Ask at the visitor information centers.) Published hiking guides are widely available at local bookstores. Especially helpful are the back-pocket-size guides published by **Nimbus Publishing;** call for a catalog (✆ **800/646-2879** or 902/454-7404; www.nimbus.ns.ca).

WHALE-WATCHING When on the Nova Scotia coast, you're never far from a whale-watching operation. Around two dozen such tour outfits offer trips in search of finback, humpback, pilot, and minke whales, among others. The richest waters for whale-watching are on the Fundy Coast, where the endangered right whale is often seen feeding in summer; thus, Digby Neck (the thin strand of land extending southwest from the town of Digby) has the highest concentration of whale-watching excursions in the province, but you'll find them in many other coves and harbors, as well. Ask staff at local visitor information centers to direct you to the whales, or check the provincial tourism guide, which contains a very good listing of whale-watchers.

WOLFVILLE ★

90km (56 miles) NW of Halifax, 234km (145 miles) NE of Yarmouth

The trim Victorian village of Wolfville (pop. 3,800) has a distinctively New England feel to it, both in its handsome architecture and its compact layout—a small commercial downtown just 6 blocks long is surrounded by shady neighborhoods of elegant homes. And it's not hard to trace that sensibility back to its source: The area was largely populated in the wake of the American Revolution by transplanted New Englanders, who forced off the original Acadian settlers.

The town's mainstay these days is handsome **Acadia University,** which has nearly as many full-time students as there are residents of Wolfville. The university's presence gives the small village an edgier, more youthful air. Don't miss the university's **Art Gallery** ★ (✆ **902/585-1373**; http://gallery.acadiau.ca), which showcases both contemporary and historic Nova Scotian art; it's located at 10 Highland Ave. (at the corner of Main St.) and is open Tuesday through Sunday from noon to 4pm, year-round. Admission is free.

Exploring Wolfville

Strolling through the village is a good way to spend a half-day; the towering elms and maples that shade the extravagant Victorian architecture make for an ideal walk. Begin at the **Wolfville Tourist Bureau** (✆ **877/999-7117** or 902/542-7000) at 11 Willow Ave. (in Willow Park) on the northern edge of the downtown area; it's open daily from mid-April through October. For a good printable map of Wolfville's downtown area, go to **www.downtownwolfville.com** and click on "Maps & Guides."

At **Blomidon Provincial Park** (✆ **902/584-2332**), 24km (15 miles) north of Route 101 (exit 11), some 14km (8.7 miles) of trail take walkers through forest and along the coast. Among the most dramatic trails is the 6km (3.7-mile) **Jodrey Trail ★**, which follows towering cliffs that offer broad views over the Minas Basin. It's open from mid-May through early October.

Grand-Pré National Historic Site ★ Long before relocated New Englanders arrived in this part of Canada, hardworking Acadians had already vastly altered the local landscape. They did it in large part by constructing a series of dikes outfitted with ingenious log valves, which allowed farmers to convert the saltwater marshes to productive farmland. At Grand-Pré, a short drive east of Wolfville just off Route 1, you can learn about these dikes, along with the history of the Acadians who populated the Minas Basin from 1680 until their expulsion in 1755. More a memorial park than a history exhibit, Grand-Pré ("great meadow") features superbly tended grounds excellent for picnics or contemplative strolls. Among the handful of buildings on the grounds is a graceful stone church, built in 1922 on the presumed site of the original Acadian church. Evangeline Bellefontaine, the revered (albeit fictional) heroine of Longfellow's epic poem, was said to have been born here; look for the tragic heroine's iconic statue in the garden, created in 1920 by Canadian sculptor Philippe Hérbert.

2241 Grand-Pré Rd. (P.O. Box 150), Grand-Pré B0P 1M0. ✆ **902/542-4040.** www.grand-pre.com. Admission C$7.80 adults, C$6.55 seniors, C$3.90 children age 6–16, C$20 families. Daily mid-May to mid-Oct 9am–6pm. Closed mid-Oct to mid-May.

Where to Stay

Gingerbread House Inn ★ The ornate, brightly painted Gingerbread House Inn was originally the carriage house for the building now housing Victoria's Historic Inn (see below). A former owner went woodshop-wild, adding all manner of swirly accoutrements and giving the place a convincingly authentic air. Most guest rooms here are now an updated and modern interpretation of the gingerbread style and are quite comfortable, though the two units in the back are darker and smaller than the rest. Each room has its own private exterior entrance, adding to the privacy, and each has its own feel: The airy Gaspereau suite has a modern-city loft feel, with luxe touches such as a sleek propane fireplace, big-screen television, and big eight-person hot tub beneath a mural of a lake. But the Country and Sunrise suites are much more, well, gingerbread with their exposed unvarnished wood, throw rugs, rocking chairs, and the like. Even some of the simpler rooms sport hot tubs. Breakfasts here are elaborate.

8 Robie Tufts Dr. (P.O. Box 819), Wolfville, NS B4P 1X1. ✆ **888/542-1458** or 902/542-1458. Fax 902/542-4718. www.gingerbreadhouse.ca. 9 units. May–Oct C$115–C$129 double, C$165–C$199 suite; Nov–Apr C$85–C$119 double, C$135–C$199 suite. Rates include full breakfast. Ask about golf packages.

AE, MC, V. No children permitted in suites. **Amenities:** Dining room. *In room:* A/C, TV, DVD, fireplace, Jacuzzi (some), no phone.

Tattingstone Inn ★★ This handsome Italianate-Georgian mansion, named after one of Harwood's forebears' ancestral town in England, dates from 1874 and overlooks the village's main drag. It has changed hands but not its feeling. The inn is still furnished with a mix of reproductions and antiques, of traditional and modern art. The place isn't as over-the-top Victorian as one might guess when first laying eyes on the manse; instead, the inn is decorated with a deft touch that mixes informal country antiques with regal Empire pieces. Rooms in the carriage house are a little smaller than those in the main house, but still pleasant—and they showcase fine examples of modern Canadian art. Ask about the blue-and-cream "Toad Hall" room in the carriage house if you value privacy: There's a living room downstairs with an electric fireplace and an exposed-beam ceiling, while the upstairs sports a queen bed and two-person Jacuzzi. The Tattingstone's spacious, semi-formal dining room is refined; diners eat off white tablecloths beneath stern Doric columns. The heated outdoor pool is a bonus, as is the enclosed sun porch, which nicely captures the lambent early evening light.

620 Main St. (P.O. Box 98), Wolfville, NS B4P 1E8. ✆ **800/565-7696** or 902/542-7696. www.tattingstone.ns.ca. 10 units. July–Oct C$118–C$178 double; Nov–June C$98–C$165 double. Rates include full breakfast. AE, MC, V. **Amenities:** Restaurant; outdoor pool; steam room; tennis court. *In room:* A/C, TV/VCR, hair dryer, Jacuzzi (some), fireplace (some), no phone.

Victoria's Historic Inn ★★ Victoria's Historic Inn was constructed by apple mogul William Chase in 1893, and remains architecturally elaborate today. The sturdy Queen Anne–style building features bold pediments and pavilions adorned with balusters and ornate Stick-style trim. Inside, it feels like you've wandered into a Victorian parlor. Whereas the nearby Tattingstone Inn (see above) resists theme decor, Victoria's Historic Inn embraces it wholeheartedly: there's a Cranberry Room, a Sunflower Room, a Nautical Room, and so on. There's also dense mahogany and cherry woodwork throughout, along with some exceptionally intricate ceilings. Several of the inn's suites have fireplaces and Jacuzzis. The deluxe two-room Chase Suite (the most expensive unit), for instance, features a large sitting room with a gas fireplace, double Jacuzzi, queen bed, and an oak mantle. Less expensive third-floor rooms are smaller and somewhat less historic in flavor.

600 Main St., Wolfville, NS B4P 1E8. ✆ **800/556-5744** or 902/542-5744. Fax 902/542-7794. www.victoriashistoricinn.com. 15 units. Apr–Oct C$118–C$245 double and suite; Nov–Mar C$108–C$175 double and suite. Rates include full breakfast. AE, MC, V. *In room:* A/C, TV/VCR, Jacuzzi (some).

Where to Dine

Most of the inns in Wolfville also open their dining rooms at night and serve fancy food to the public, with prices to match.

Al's Homestyle Café DELI This lowbrow, family-operated diner/deli is located in the nearby hamlet of Canning, about 10 miles northwest of Wolfville along Route 358. It has been a local favorite for years. Al Waddell no longer owns the place, but his popular recipes for sausages live on—choose from flavors like Polish, German, hot Italian, and honey garlic. They also pack the sausages to go. A sausage on a bun plus a cup of soup will run you less than C$5.

9819 Main St., Canning. ✆ **902/582-7270.** Most selections less than C$5. V. Mon–Sat 8am–6pm; Sun 11am–5pm.

ANNAPOLIS ROYAL ★★

197km (122 miles) W of Halifax, 128km (80 miles) NE of Yarmouth

For anyone curious about Canada's early history, Annapolis Royal is one of Nova Scotia's absolute don't-miss destinations. This is arguably Nova Scotia's most historic town—it bills itself, with some justification, as "Canada's birthplace"—and remains a treat to visit. Because the region was overlooked by later economic growth (the bulk of the trade and fishing moved to the Atlantic side of the peninsula), it requires very little in the way of imagination to see Annapolis Royal as it once was. The original settlement was rebuilt on the presumed site of explorer Samuel de Champlain's famous 1604 visit; the old Fort Anne still overlooks the upper reaches of the basin, much as it did when abandoned in 1854; and the village maintains much of its original historic charm, with narrow streets and historic buildings facing a placid waterfront.

Essentials

GETTING THERE Annapolis is located at exit 22 off Route 101. It is 200km (124 miles) from Halifax, and 129km (80 miles) from Yarmouth.

VISITOR INFORMATION The **Annapolis Royal and Area Visitor Information Centre** (© **902/532-5454**) is 1km (⅔ mile) north of the town center at 236 Prince Albert Rd. (follow Prince Albert Rd. and look for the Annapolis Royal Tidal Generating Station). It's usually open daily in summer 8am to 8pm, and 10am to 6pm in spring and fall. Also check the town's official tourism site at **www.annapolisroyal.com** for more local details.

Exploring the Town

It's pretty amazing to stop and think, as you stroll down lower **St. George Street**, that you're walking down the oldest street in Canada. You'll pass numerous historic structures, marked on the town's walking-tour map, which you can obtain at the tourist office (see previous section.)

In the evening, there's often entertainment in downtown Annapolis Royal at **King's Theatre,** 209 St. George St. (© **902/532-5466;** www.kingstheatre.ca). Shows range from movies to musical performances to variety shows to touring plays—and there are plenty of offerings for kids, too. Stop by or call to find out what's happening.

Fort Anne National Historic Site ★ What you'll likely remember about a visit here are the impressive grassy earthworks that cover some 14 hectares (35 acres) of high ground overlooking the confluence of the Annapolis River and Allains Creek. The French built the first fort here around 1643. Since then, dozens of buildings and fortifications have occupied this site. You can visit the 1708 gunpowder magazine (the oldest building among all the Canadian National Historic Sites), then look through a museum located in the 1797 British field officers' quarters. The model of this site as it appeared in 1710 is especially intriguing. If you find all the history a bit tedious, ask a guide for a croquet set and practice your technique on the green lawns. A good strategy for visiting is to come during the day to tour the museum and get a feel for the lay of the land. Then return later for the evening sunset, long after the bus tours have departed, to walk the **Perimeter Trail ★**, an easy 530m (⅓-mile-long) path that traces along the top of the star-shaped fort and features good river and valley vistas.

Entrance on St. George St. © **902/532-2397.** Admission C$3.90 adults, C$3.40 seniors, C$1.90 children, C$9.80 families. May 15–Oct 15 9am–6pm; off season by appointment (grounds open year-round).

Port-Royal National Historic Site ★ Canada's first permanent settlement, Port Royal was located on an attractive point with sweeping views of the Annapolis Basin. After spending the dreadful winter of 1604 on an island in the St. Croix River (along the current Maine–New Brunswick border), the survivors moved to this better-protected location. Settlers lived here for 8 years in a high style that approached decadency given such bleak surroundings. Many of the handsome, compact, French-style farmhouse buildings originally here were designed by Samuel de Champlain to re-create the comfort they might have enjoyed at home. Although the original settlement was abandoned and eventually destroyed, this 1939 reproduction is convincing in all the details. You'll find costumed interpreters engaged in traditional handicrafts like woodworking. Allow 1 or 2 hours to wander and explore it.

10km (6¼ miles) south of Rte. 1, Granville Ferry (turn left shortly after passing the tidal generating station). ✆ **902/532-2898.** Admission C$3.90 adults, C$3.40 seniors, C$1.90 children, C$9.80 families. May 15–Oct 15 daily 9am–6pm. Closed Oct 16–May 14.

Where to Stay

Garrison House Inn ★ The historic Garrison House sits across the road from Fort Anne in the town center; it has been taking in guests since 1854, when it first opened to accommodate officers at the fort. Rooms are nicely appointed with antiques. Room no. 2 is attractive with its wide pine floors, braided rug, and wing-back chairs, although it faces the street; room no. 7 is tucked in back, well away from the hubbub, and has two skylights and a big window to let in light. The inn's very good restaurant (see below) includes a screened-in veranda with food and drink service.

350 St. George St., Annapolis Royal, NS B0S 1A0. ✆ **866/532-5750** or 902/532-5750. Fax 902/532-5501. www.garrisonhouse.ca. 7 units. C$69–C$149 double. AE, MC, V. Street parking. Open May–Nov; call in advance for weekends rest of year. **Amenities:** Restaurant; bar. *In room:* AC, TV/DVD, Jacuzzi (1 unit), no phone.

King George Inn ★ ☺ This place is the opposite of a modern, sleek hotel. The handsome King George was built as a sea captain's mansion in 1868, and also served a stint as a rectory before becoming an inn. It's still fittingly busy and cluttered for its era; guest rooms are furnished entirely in antiques, mostly country Victorian pieces. Think commodes, bowls, pitchers, rocking chairs, Oriental rugs, and Tara-worthy lamps. Most of the rooms have queen-size beds—ask if you want a king or two doubles—and the two family suites have separate bedrooms with a shared bathroom. The best room in the house might be no. 7, the Duchess of Kent suite, with its Jacuzzi and small private deck off the back of the house overlooking the garden. A second Jacuzzi room was added later, in the Queen Victoria suite, which also has a king bed, bay window, and gigantic headboard (if you're into that). The inn features a pump organ and a 19th-century grand piano, and helpfully provides bikes for guests.

548 Upper St. George St., Annapolis Royal, NS B0S 1A0. ✆ **888/799-5464.** www.kinggeorgeinn.20m.com. 8 units. C$75–C$150 double. MC, V. Closed Jan–Apr. **Amenities:** Bikes. *In room:* A/C, hair dryer, no phone.

Queen Anne Inn ★★ You can't miss this Second Empire mansion, built in 1865, on your way into town. Like the Hillsdale House across the street, the Queen Anne (built for the sister of the Hillsdale's owner) has benefited from a preservation-minded owner, who restored the Victorian detailing to its former luster. There's a zebra-striped dining-room floor (alternating planks of oak and maple) and a grand central staircase. The guest rooms are quite elegant and furnished appropriately for the Victorian era, although some have been updated to include Jacuzzis. Featherbeds and handmade soaps are other nice touches, and a dining room is open to the public for dinner 5 nights a week. There's also a two-story carriage house here split into two bi-level suite units, good for families. As if that weren't enough, the parklike grounds with their towering elms are shady and inviting. And breakfast is a three-course affair.

494 St. George St., Annapolis Royal, NS B0S 1A0. ✆ **877/536-0403** or 902/532-7850. Fax 902/532-2078. www.queenanneinn.ns.ca. 12 units. June–Oct C$109–C$209 double and suite; May C$99–C$139 double and suite. Rates include full breakfast. MC, V. Closed Nov–Apr. **Amenities:** Dining room. *In room:* TV, Jacuzzi (some), no phone.

Where to Dine

The Garrison House ★★ ECLETIC The Garrison House Inn's restaurant is arguably the most intimate, attractive, and innovative of Annapolis Royal's eating choices. Three cozy dining rooms in the inn each have a different feel: some with colonial colors, some with contemporary styling, most with black Windsor chairs and piscine art. (Check out the room with the green floors and the humpback whale.) Chef-owner Patrick Redgrave's menu ranges all over the world without ever losing its Canadian footing. Start with Thai shrimp soup, a seafood chowder, mushroom risotto, or mussels steamed in wine and finished with habanero cream. Main dishes might include Digby scallops, a Vietnamese coconut milk curry, grilled chicken, strip loin of beef, salmon poached in bourbon and glazed with maple, "mumbo-jumbo" jambalaya—or just the catch of the day.

350 St. George St. (inside the Garrison House Inn). ✆ **866/532-5750** or 902/532-5750. Reservations recommended in summer. Main courses C$14–C$27. AE, MC, V. May–Oct daily 5:30–8:30pm; Nov–Apr open by arrangement.

Ye Olde Town Pub PUB FARE For a more relaxed bite than other places around town, head by this genial local pub located centrally in town and housed in an 1884 brick building that was once a bank (hence the bars on the windows). It's said to be the smallest pub in Nova Scotia—in the entire history of the province. But they've got a big heart. There's beer, of course, but also a kitchen that serves vittles all day, a kids' menu, and even Wi-Fi internet access for those who just can't hoist a pint without updating their Twitter accounts about it at the same time.

9 Church St. ✆ **902/532-2244.** Daily 11am–11pm.

FROM DIGBY TO YARMOUTH

The South Shore—that stretch of coast between Yarmouth and Halifax—serves to confirm popular conceptions of Nova Scotia about small fishing villages and shingled homes. But the 113km (70-mile) shoreline from Digby to Yarmouth seems determined to confound those same conceptions. Here, rather than picture-postcard views, you'll find Acadian enclaves, fishing villages with more corrugated steel than weathered shingle, miles of uncrowded sandy beaches, and spruce-topped basalt cliffs that seem like they could be transplanted from Labrador.

Digby & Digby Neck

The port town of **Digby** is home to the world's largest inshore scallop fleet. These boats drag the ocean bottom nearby and bring back the succulent Digby scallops famous throughout Canada. The town itself is an active and historic community, too, where life centers around the fishing boats, convivial neighborhoods of wood-frame houses, and no-frills seafood eating places. (It also serves as Nova Scotia's gateway for those arriving from Saint John, New Brunswick, via ferry. The ferry terminal is on Route 303, just west of Digby.)

Just south, **Digby Neck** is a long, bony finger of ridges, bogs, dense forests, beaches, and expansive ocean views. Although neither the neck nor the islands have much in the way of services for tourists, they're worth the drive if you're a connoisseur of end-of-the-world remoteness. The town of **Sandy Cove** is picture-perfect, with its prominent church steeples rising from the forest; **Tiverton** on Long Island and **Westport** on Brier Island are unadorned fishing villages. You get the distinct feeling that life hasn't changed much here in the past few decades. And, in fact, it really hasn't.

ESSENTIALS

GETTING THERE Digby is Nova Scotia's gateway for those arriving from **Saint John,** New Brunswick, via ferry. The ferry terminal is on Route 303, west of Digby. If you're indeed arriving by ferry and want to visit the town before pushing on, look sharp for signs directing you downtown from the bypass, lest you end up on Route 101 and headed out of town by mistake. Coming from the rest of Nova Scotia, take exit 26 off Route 101 to reach Digby.

From Digby, Route 217 runs about 45 miles south to **Brier Island.** Two **ferries** bridge the islands, and they run 24 hours a day, year-round. The first boat leaves **East Ferry** (about a 45-min. drive from Digby) on the mainland for **Tiverton,** Long Island every half-hour; the second ferry departs Long Island for **Brier Island** on the hour. The ferries are timed so that you can drive directly from one ferry to the next, if you don't dally too much on the road between. The fare is C$5 for each ferry (C$10 total), and you pay each full fare on the outbound leg, no fare returning north.

VISITOR INFORMATION The province maintains a **visitor information center** (✆ **902/245-2201**) in Digby on Route 303 (on your right shortly after you disembark from the Saint John ferry), at 237 Shore Rd. It's open from early May through October. There's also a **municipal tourist information center** on the harbor at 110 Montague Row (✆ **902/245-5714**), open daily from May until mid-October.

On Long Island, you can pick up local information inside **the Islands Museum** (✆ **902/839-2034**) in Tiverton. The museum opens from June through late September and is free to enter.

EXPLORING THE AREA

Brier Island is a great destination for mountain bikers. Just 6 by 2km wide (4 by 1½ miles), it's the right scale for spending a slow afternoon poking around the dirt roads that lead to two of the island's red-and-white lighthouses. Brier Island maps are available free at island stores and lodges. If you park your car on the Long Island side and take your bike over on the ferry, you'll save money; there's no charge for bikes or pedestrians. You can rent a bike cheaply at the local youth hostel, the **Digby Backpackers Inn** (✆ **902/245-4573**) at 168 Queen St. (see "Where to Stay & Dine," below).

HIKING On **Long Island,** two short but rewarding woodland hikes bring you to open vistas of St. Mary's Bay and the Bay of Fundy. The trailhead for the first, the 800m (half-mile) hike to **Balancing Rock ★★**, is about 4km (2½ miles) south of the **Tiverton** ferry on Route 217; look for a well-marked parking area on the left. The trail crosses through swamp, bog, and forest and is straight and flat—until the last

91m (300 ft.), when it plummets nearly straight down a sheer bluff to the ocean's edge via some 169 steps. At the base, a series of boardwalks leads you over the surging ocean to get a dead-on view of the basalt column balancing improbably atop another column.

For the second short hike, return to the parking lot and drive 5km (3 miles) south to the **picnic area** on the right. From the parking lot atop the hill, a hike of about 1km (a half-mile) descends gradually through a forest of moss, ferns, and roots to the Fundy shore. Note that the coastline here looks almost lunar, its dark rock marbled with thin streaks of quartz. You're likely to have this coast all to yourself, since few travelers ever venture here.

Farther along, **Brier Island** is also laced with **hiking trails** offering fantastic opportunities for seaside exploration. Pick up one of the maps offered free around the island. One good place to take a walk is at the **Grand Passage Lighthouse** (turn right after disembarking the ferry and continue until you can't go any farther). Park near the light and walk through the stunted pines to the open meadows on the western shore, where you can pick up a **coastal trail**.

WHERE TO STAY & DINE

In addition to the choices listed below, there are two hostels in the area. The **Digby Backpackers Inn** ★ (✆ **902/245-4573;** www.digbyhostel.com), at 168 Queen St., is newish and good. Run by an international couple, it offers dorm beds for C$25 a night and double rooms for C$60; all bathrooms are shared, but breakfast is included. The **Brier Island Hostel** (✆ **902/839-2273;** www.brierislandhostel.com), on Brier Island, offers beds for C$18 adults, C$9 children 6 and under.

Brier Island Lodge ★ 🎁 Built to jump-start local ecotourism, the Brier Island Lodge is a basic but great find thanks to eye-popping views. You'll find a rustic-modern motif, with log-cabin construction and soaring glass windows overlooking the Grand Passage 40m (131 ft.) below; most rooms overlook the ocean and a lighthouse. Inside, they feature all the usual motel amenities, plus a few unexpected touches (double Jacuzzis in the pricier rooms). A well-regarded dining room serves up traditional favorites, and local fishermen congregate in an airy lounge in the evening to play cards and watch a satellite TV. Hiking trails connect directly from the lodge to the Fundy shore. Breakfasts feature fresh eggs from hens at the adjacent farm. But don't plan on sleeping in; as the lodge notes, "When the sun comes up, our roosters will be happy to let you know."

Brier Island (P.O. Box 39), Westport, NS B0V 1H0. ✆ **800/662-8355** or 902/839-2300. Fax 902/839-2006. www.brierisland.com. 40 units. C$79–C$149 double. MC, V. **Amenities:** Dining room; lounge; bike rental. *In room:* A/C, TV, Jacuzzi (4 rooms).

Digby Pines Golf Resort and Spa ★★ ☺ Red-roofed Digby Pines is situated on 121 hectares (300 acres), with marvelous views of the Annapolis Basin. The imposing stucco-and-stone resort is surrounded by the aforementioned pines, and it's a throwback to an era when moneyed families headed to fashionable resorts for the entire summer. Built in 1929 in Norman château style, the inn is owned by the province of Nova Scotia—which does a good job emphasizing comfort over mere historic re-creation. The gracious lobby features old-world touches like Corinthian capitals, floral couches, and parquet floors; guest rooms vary in size and views (ask for a water-view room; there's no extra charge), and are basically furnished and equipped with ceiling fans. Thirty or so cottages have one to three bedrooms each (guests share the living rooms), most featuring fireplaces, air-conditioning, and mini-refrigerators. A spa offers a full menu of treatments and services, an 18-hole Stanley Thompson–designed golf course threads its way through the pines, and the kids' program is exemplary.

Shore Rd. (P.O. Box 70), Digby, NS B0V 1A0. ✆ **800/667-4637** or 902/245-2511. Fax 902/245-6133. www.digbypines.ca. 147 units. C$159–C$442 double. Packages available. AE, DC, DISC, MC, V. Closed mid-Oct to mid-May. **Amenities:** Restaurant; bar; babysitting; bike rentals; children's center; concierge; golf course; health club; heated outdoor pool; sauna; spa; 2 tennis courts. *In room:* A/C (cottages only), TV, fridge (cottages only), hair dryer.

Yarmouth

Yarmouth is a pleasant burg that offers some noteworthy historic architecture dating from the golden ages of seafaring. But this town's not terribly unique, and thus not high on the list of places to spend a few days. It's a little too big (pop. 7,200) to be charming, a little too small to generate any urban buzz or vitality. It does have the flavor of a handy pit stop rather than a true destination, even if recent redevelopment efforts have spruced up the waterfront and added some evening entertainment options during the summer. Take time to follow the self-guided walking tour, enjoy a meal, or wander around the waterfront, which is slowly reawakening from its torpor.

ESSENTIALS

GETTING THERE Yarmouth is at the convergence of two of the province's principal highways, routes 101 and 103. It's approximately 300km (186 miles) from Halifax.

VISITOR INFORMATION The **Yarmouth Visitor Centre** (✆ **902/742-5033**) is at 228 Main St., just up the hill from the ferry in a modern, shingled building you simply can't miss. Both provincial and municipal tourist offices are located here, open June through mid-October daily from about 8am to 7pm.

EXPLORING THE AREA

The tourist bureau and the local historical society publish a very informative walking-tour brochure covering downtown Yarmouth. It's well worth requesting at the Yarmouth Visitor Centre (see above). The guide offers general tips on what to look for in local architectural styles (how do you tell the difference between Georgian and Classic Revival?), as well as brief histories of significant buildings. The entire tour is 4km (2½ miles) long.

The most scenic side trip—an ideal excursion by bike or car—is to **Cape Forchu** and the **Yarmouth Light** ★. Head west on Main Street (Rte. 1) for 2km (1¼ miles) from the visitor center, then turn left at the horse statue. The road winds out to the cape, past seawalls and working lobster wharves, meadows, and old homes. When the road finally ends, you'll have arrived at the red-and-white-striped concrete lighthouse that marks this harbor's entrance. Ramble around the dramatic rock-and-grass bluffs—part of Leif Ericson Picnic Park—that surround the lighthouse, and don't miss the short trail out to the point below the light.

Art Gallery of Nova Scotia (Western Branch) ★★ ☺ A satellite of the famous art gallery in Halifax, this AGNS is housed in the former Royal Bank building at the heart of Yarmouth's downtown. Its changing exhibits draw from the mothership's permanent collections, and might include a rumination on the history of flight; a curated showing of folk art from the Maritimes; or a collection of tall-ship paintings. The museum fills a much-needed gap in Yarmouth's cultural scene, and staff here even offer various summer art classes and workshops. Plus this: If you visit this museum first, you can deduct the admission from the price of your admission later at the Halifax museum. If you went to the Halifax museum first, this one's free. For that reason alone, you should definitely duck in here whenever you're in town and at a loss for things to do (or waiting for the ferry).

340 Main St. ✆ **902/749-2248.** Admission C$5 adults, C$4 seniors, C$3.50 students, C$2 children age 6 to 17, C$12 families; admission free with proof of visit to AGNS Halifax. Daily 10am–5pm, Thurs to 8pm in summer.

Firefighters' Museum of Nova Scotia ☺ This two-story museum will appeal mostly to confirmed fire buffs, historians, and impressionable young children. The museum is home to a varied collection of early firefighting equipment, with hand-drawn pumpers the centerpiece of the collection. Kids love the 1933 vintage Chev Bickle Pumper because they can don helmets and take the wheel for some pretend-I'm-a-fireman time. Also showcased here are uniforms, badges, and pennants. Also look for the collection of photos of notable Nova Scotia fires. If you're into that.

451 Main St. ✆ **902/742-5525.** Admission C$3 adults, C$2.50 seniors, C$1.50 children, C$6 families. July–Aug Mon–Sat 9am–9pm, Sun 10am–5pm; June and Sept Mon–Sat 9am–5pm; Oct–May Mon–Fri 9am–4pm, Sat 1–4pm.

WHERE TO STAY

Yarmouth is also home to a number of chain motels, mostly on Main St.

Guest-Lovitt House ★★ A helpful reader tipped me off to this grandiose-looking mansion just blocks from Yarmouth's ferry terminal, now a small B&B owned by two locals that might be the town's best lodgings. Four rooms await the traveler, each with a four-poster king or queen bed draped in white covers, lacy drapes, television with DVD player, and lightly floral wallpapers or pastel schemes to accent. Antique furnishings in each room include touches such as fireplaces, writing desks, wingback chairs, loveseats, and even—in the case of the Dr. Webster Room—a little private balcony. An outdoor hot tub provides faux-California experiences, a good breakfast is included, and there's a gazebo for sitting. Two of the rooms can be combined into a suite (at a discount) when need be.

12 Parade St., Yarmouth, NS B5A 3A4. ✆ **866/742-0372** or 902/742-0372. 4 units. C$119-C$159 double. Rates include full breakfast. AE, MC, V. **Amenities:** Jacuzzi. *In room:* TV, hair dryer.

Harbour's Edge B&B ★ 🎁 Now this is truth in advertising: This attractive early Victorian home (built 1864) sits on a quiet hectare (2½ acres) and 76m (250 ft.) of harbor frontage, where the scenery changes twice per day with the tides. This was the very first parcel of land in Yarmouth to be owned by a European, but before that local native peoples had camped and fished here for ages. Today you can lounge on the lawn watching herons, hawks, and kingfishers, and it's hard to believe you're just a few minutes from a big international ferry terminal. The inn opened in 1997 after 3 years of restoration, and rooms are lightly furnished to highlight the architectural integrity of the design. All four rooms sport high ceilings and handsome spruce floors. The attractive Audrey Kenney Room is biggest, but the Clara Caie has better views of the harbor (though the private bathroom and its claw-foot tub are down the hall). The Georgie Allen has a private hallway and clear harbor view, as well. You'll feel safe here, too, because one of the two innkeepers is a Mountie: a Canadian cop.

12 Vancouver St., Yarmouth, NS B5A 2N8. ✆ **902/742-2387.** www.harboursedge.ns.ca. 4 units. C$135–C$150 double. Rates include full breakfast. MC, V. Head toward Cape Forchu (see above); watch for the inn shortly after turning at the horse statue. *In room:* Hair dryer, no phone.

WHERE TO DINE

Quick-N-Tasty ☺ SEAFOOD The name about says it all. This country-cooking joint a mile or two from the incoming ferries from Maine has long been a hit with locals. The restaurant is adorned with the sort of paneling that was au courant in the 1970s, and meals are likewise old-fashioned and generous. The emphasis here is on seafood; you can order fish either fried or broiled, but go for the hot open-faced lobster club sandwich—it's gaining international foodie acclaim. The seafood casserole and the blueberry desserts are also notable.

Rte. 1, Dayton (from downtown Yarmouth, follow Rte. 3 west to Rte. 1). ✆ **902/742-6606.** Sandwiches C$3–C$12; main courses C$7–C$18. AE, DC, MC, V. Daily 11am–8pm. Closed mid-Dec to Feb. Just east of Yarmouth on the north side of Rte. 1.

Rudder's Seafood Restaurant & Brewpub ★ BREWPUB Yarmouth's first (and Nova Scotia's fourth) brewpub opened in 1997 on the waterfront. It occupies an old warehouse dating from the mid-1800s, where you can see the wear and tear of the decades on the battered floor and in the stout beams and rafters. The place has been nicely spruced up, though, and the menu features creative pub fare plus Acadian and Cajun specialties (like rappie pie and jambalaya), as well as lobster suppers and planked salmon. The steaks are quite good, as is the beer. In summer, there's outdoor seating on a deck with a view of the harbor across the parking lot.

96 Water St. ✆ **902/742-7311.** Sandwiches C$4–C$11; entrees C$10–C$24. AE, DC, MC, V. Mid-Apr to mid-Oct daily 11am–11pm (shorter hours in spring and fall). Closed mid-Oct to mid-Apr.

THE SOUTH SHORE ★★

The Atlantic coast between Yarmouth and Halifax is that quaint, maritime Nova Scotia you see on laminated place mats and calendars. Lighthouses and weathered, shingled buildings perch at the rocky edge of the sea, as if tenuously trespassing on the ocean's good graces. But as rustic and beautiful as this area is, you might find it a bit monotonous to visit *every* quaint village along this coastline—which involves some 300-plus kilometers (200-plus miles) of slow, twisting road along water's edge. If your heart is set on fully exploring this fabled landscape, then, be sure to leave enough time for the many nooks and crannies along this stretch of the coast. Towns such as Lunenburg, Mahone Bay, and Peggy's Cove are well worth the time.

Shelburne

Shelburne is a historic town with unimpeachable pedigree. Settled in 1783 by United Empire Loyalists fleeing New England after the Revolution and the Treaty of Paris, the town swelled with newcomers until by 1784 it is believed to have had a population of 10,000—larger than the Montréal, Halifax, or Québec of the time. With the recent declines in both boat building and fishing, however, the town had edged back into that dim economic twilight familiar to other seaside villages, and the waterfront began to deteriorate in spite of valiant preservation efforts.

Then Hollywood came calling. In 1992, the film *Mary Silliman's War* was filmed here. The producers found the waterfront to be a reasonable facsimile of 1776 Fairfield, Connecticut. The film crew spruced up the town a bit, and buried local power lines along the waterfront. Two years later, director Roland Joffe arrived to film *The Scarlet Letter*. Those film crews buried more power lines, built 15 "historic" structures near the waterfront (most demolished after filming), dumped tons of rubble to create dirt lanes, and generally made the place look like 17th-century Boston. It still does today.

ESSENTIALS

GETTING THERE Shelburne is about 209km (130 miles) southwest of Halifax on Route 3. It's a short hop from Route 103 via either exit 25 (southbound) or exit 26 (northbound).

VISITOR INFORMATION The local **visitor information center** (© **902/875-4547**) is in a tidy waterfront building at the corner of King and Dock streets. It's open daily mid-May to October.

EXPLORING SHELBURNE

The central historic district runs along the waterfront, where you can see legitimately old buildings, Hollywood fascimiles (see above), and spectacular views of the harbor from small, grassy parks. There's a lot more in the district, too, including a helpful little tourist office at the bend in the road (see above), gift shops, a B&B (the Cooper's Inn, reviewed below), a husband-and-wife team of coopers making barrels in an open shop (technically, it's not open to the public, but ask nicely for a look), a kayaking and outdoor adventure center, and the **Sea Dog Saloon** (© **902/875-2862**) at the very end of the road at 1 Dock St. A block inland from the water is Shelburne's commercial stretch, where you can find services that include banks, shops, and snacks.

Shelburne Historic Complex ★ ☺ The historic complex is an association of four local museums located within steps of each other. The most engaging is the **Dory Shop Museum,** right on the waterfront. On the first floor you can admire examples of the simple, elegant boatbuilding craft (said to be invented in Shelburne) and view videos about the late Sidney Mahaney, a master builder who worked in this shop from the time he was 17 until he was 96. Then head upstairs, where all the banging is going on. While you're there, ask about the difference between a Shelburne dory and a Lunenburg dory.

The **Shelburne County Museum** features a potpourri of locally significant artifacts from the town's Loyalist past. Most intriguing is the 1740 fire pumper; it was made in London and imported here in 1783. Behind the museum is the austerely handsome **Ross-Thomson House,** built in 1784 through 1785. The first floor contains a general store as it might have looked in 1784, with bolts of cloth and cast-iron teakettles. Upstairs is a militia room with displays of antique and reproduction weaponry. The fourth museum, the **Muir-Cox Shipyard** and its Interpretive Centre, was added most recently and features maritime displays of barks, sailboats, yachts, and more. If you're interested in these sorts of things, you could easily spend a half-day here, particularly if you're bringing children who are captivated by the craftspeople.

Dock St. (P.O. Box 39), Shelburne, NS B0T 1W0. © **902/875-3219.** Admission to all 4 museums C$8 adults, free for children under 16; individual museums C$3 adults, free for children under 16; all museums free on Sunday mornings. June to mid-Oct daily 9:30am–5:30pm (Dory Shop, June to Sept). Closed mid-Oct to May.

WHERE TO STAY

Just across the harbor from Shelburne, **The Islands Provincial Park** ★ (© **902/875-4304**) offers 62 quiet campsites on 500 waterside acres from May through September. Some sites are right on the harbor, with a front-row seat and great views of the historic village; ask about those sites' availability first. There are no hookups for RVs here, another reason to consider it as a quiet overnight getaway. Campsites here cost C$23 apiece.

The Cooper's Inn ★★ 🎁 Facing the harbor in the Dock Street historic area, the impeccably historic Cooper's Inn was originally built by Loyalist merchant George Gracie in 1785. Subsequent additions and updates have been historically sympathetic. The downstairs sitting rooms set the mood nicely, with worn wood floors, muted wall colors (mustard and khaki green), and classical music in the background. A courtyard with a pond and bell fountain is a tranquil recent addition. Rooms in the main building feature painted wood floors (they're carpeted in the cooper-shop annex) and are decorated in a comfortably historic-country style. A third-floor suite features wonderful detailing, two sleeping alcoves, and harbor views—worth the extra cost. The George Gracie Room has a four-poster bed and water view, the small Roderick Morrison Room a wonderful claw-foot tub perfect for a late-evening soak, and the Harbour Suite a harbor-view tub and massage chair.

36 Dock St., Shelburne, NS B0T 1W0. ✆ **800/688-2011** or 902/875-4656. www.thecoopersinn.com. 8 units. C$100–C$185 double and suite. Rates include full breakfast. MC, V. **Amenities:** 2 dining rooms. *In room:* TV/VCR, hair dryer, kitchenette (1 unit).

WHERE TO DINE

In addition to the two choices listed below (one fancy, one very downscale), **Lothar's Café** (✆ **902/875-3697**), at 149 Water St., is also a good option when in town. Chef Lothar (yes, really) serves a sort of Swiss-Austrian-Germanic cuisine, plus fondue for dessert—and, of course, fried fish, this being Nova Scotia. It's closed Tuesdays and Wednesdays.

Charlotte Lane Café ★★ CAFE The 2008 closing of the venerable Shelburne Cafe and bakery on Dock Street left a huge gap in this town's local food scene. But have no fear: The Charlotte Lane Café rushed into that gap and has since successfully bridged it. Situated on a tiny lane between the village's waterfront and its main commercial street, it's a bit hard to find, but worth it once you do. The kitchen's eclectic lunch and dinner items range from straightforward pasta dishes to Thai-spiced tofu and noodles, racks of lamb with a port wine-orange sauce, seared scallops, and a filet mignon-lobster combination. You can go heavy or light, since the salads and starters like eggplant picatta are good as well. There's a wine list, too, plus the likes of brown sugar-and-buttermilk apple pie, sticky toffee pudding, sorbets, and baked cheesecakes for dessert.

13 Charlotte Lane (btw. Water and Dock sts.). ✆ **902/875-3314.** Lunch items C$10, dinner items and larger entrees C$16–C$21. MC, V. Tues–Sat 9am–11pm.

Mr. Fish ★ 💲 SEAFOOD You can't miss this little fried-fish stand on the side of busy Route 3, near a shopping center; what the place lacks in location, it more than makes up for in character and good simple seafood. Matronly line cooks fry messes of haddock, scallops, and shrimp, perfectly jacketed in light crusts, and the local clientele streams in for takeout. As if that weren't good enough, they then dole out great fries and crunchy coleslaw on the side—and a smile. You eat outside on the picnic tables (but watch for bees); if it's raining, you'll have to eat in your car.

104 King St. (Rte. 3, north of town center). ✆ **902/875-3474.** Meals C$3–C$13. V. Mon–Sat 11am–7pm (Fri and holidays until 9pm); Sun noon–7pm.

Lunenburg ★★★

Lunenburg is just plain lovable, compressing everything you came to see in Nova Scotia into one tidy package: ocean tides, fishing boats, terrain, architecture, museums, and fish. It's one of Nova Scotia's most historic *and* most appealing villages, a fact recognized in 1995 when UNESCO declared the old downtown a World Heritage Site.

The town was first settled in 1753, primarily by German, Swiss, and French colonists. It was laid out on the "model town" plan then in vogue. (Savannah, Georgia, and Philadelphia, Pennsylvania, are also laid out using similar plans.) The plan consists of seven north–south streets, intersected by nine east–west streets. Lunenburg is located on a harbor and flanked by steep hills—yet the town's planners decided not to bend the rules for geography. As a result, some of the town's streets go straight uphill, and can be exhausting to walk.

Still, it's worth trying. About three-quarters of the buildings in the compact downtown date from the 18th and 19th centuries, many of them are possessed of a distinctive style and are painted in bright pastel colors. Looming over it all is the red-and-white **Lunenburg Academy,** with its exaggerated mansard roof, pointy towers, and extravagant use of ornamental brackets. (The first two floors are still used as a public school, though, so the interior is open to the public only on special occasions.)

ESSENTIALS

GETTING THERE Lunenburg is 100km (62 miles) southwest of Halifax on Route 3.

VISITOR INFORMATION The **Lunenburg Visitor Information Centre** (© **888/615-8305** or 902/634-8100) is located at the top of Blockhouse Hill Road. It's open daily from May through October, usually from 9am to 8pm. It's not in an obvious location, but the brown "?" signs posted around town—and helpful locals—can point you there. Staff here are especially good at helping you find a place to spend the night if you've arrived without reservations. You can also call up local information on the Web at **www.lunenburgns.com**.

EXPLORING LUNENBURG

Leave plenty of time to explore Lunenburg by foot. An excellent walking-tour brochure is available at the tourist office on Blockhouse Hill Road, though supplies are limited. If that's gone, contact the **Lunenburg Board of Trade** (© **902/634-3170**) for an excellent local and regional map.

St. John's Anglican Church ★★★ at the corner of Duke and Cumberland streets has got to be one of the most impressive architectural sights in all of eastern Canada—even though it's a reconstruction. The original structure, built in 1754 of oak timbers shipped from Boston, was built in simple New England meetinghouse style. Then, between 1840 and 1880, the church went through a number of additions and was overlaid with ornamentation and shingles to create an amazing example of the "carpenter Gothic" style—one in which many local residents were baptized and attended services throughout their adult lives. All this changed on Halloween night of 2001, however: A fire nearly razed the place, gutting its precious interior and much of the ornate exterior as well. In June of 2005, however, the church reopened after a painstaking 3-year restoration project using new materials but the old design. It's a must-see, and it's free to enter.

While exploring the steep streets of the town, note the architectural influence of its European settlers—especially the Germans. Some local folks made their fortunes from the sea, but serious money was also made by local carpenters who specialized in the ornamental brackets that elaborately adorn dozens of homes here. Many of these homes feature a distinctive architectural element known as the "Lunenburg bump"—a five-sided dormer-and-bay-window combo installed directly over an extended front door. (Other homes feature the simpler, more common Scottish dormer.) Also look for double or triple roofs on some projecting dormers, giving them the appearance of wedding cakes.

Several boat tours operate from the waterfront, most tied up near the Fisheries Museum. **Lunenburg Whale Watching Tours** (✆ **902/527-7175;** www.novascotiawhalewatching.com) sails in pursuit of several species of whales, along with seals and seabirds, on 3-hour excursions. There are four departures daily from May through October, with reservations recommended (and all bookings must be confirmed 24 hours in advance with a phone call). Cost is C$48 per adult, C$30 for children age 5 to 14, and C$18 for children under 5 (though infants are free). Alternately, if you have less time, **Star Charters** (✆ **877/386-3535** or 902/634-3535; www.novascotiasailing.com) takes visitors on shorter, mellow 90-minute tours of Lunenburg's inner harbor five times daily from June through October on the *Eastern Star,* a 46-ft. wooden ketch. These tours cost C$24 for adults, C$15 for students, C$11 for children, and C$52 for a full family. (Rates are C$3 higher for sunset cruises, which depart around 7pm.)

Fisheries Museum of the Atlantic ★ ☺ The sprawling Fisheries Museum is professionally designed and curated, and deserves credit for taking a topic some consider dull—fishing—and actually making it relatively fun for kids to learn about. The museum has also been upgraded and expanded to keep pace with the times. You'll find aquarium exhibits on the first floor, including a touch-tank for kids and answers to questions like "Do fish sleep?" Look for the massive 7kg (15-lb.) lobster here, estimated to be more than 30 years old. Detailed dioramas depict the whys and hows of fishing from dories, colonial schooners, and other historic vessels. There's a newer exhibit called "Sea Monsters," too (look for me there), and a third-floor section on "Rum Runners." While here you'll learn a whole bunch about the *Bluenose,* a replica of which ties up in Lunenburg when it's not touring elsewhere (see "The *Bluenose*" box, below). Outside, you can tour several other vessels—a trawler and a salt-bank schooner among them—and visit a working boat shop and a scallop-shucking house. Allow at least 2 hours to probe all the corners of this engaging museum, which is appropriately right on the waterfront.

On the waterfront. ✆ **866/579-4909** or 902/634-4794. http://museum.gov.ns.ca/fma. Mid-May to mid-Oct admission C$10 adults, C$7 seniors, C$3 children age 6–17, C$22 families; rest of the year C$4 per person (children free). May–Oct daily 9:30am–5:30pm (July–Aug to 7pm); Nov–Apr Mon–Fri, 9:30am–4pm.

WHERE TO STAY

Alicion Bed & Breakfast ★★ 🎁 Newish owners Lorne and Janet Johanson run this small B&B, formerly the Senator Bed & Breakfast, out of a large, shipshape house in a serene residential neighborhood within walking distance of Lunenburg's Old Town. It gets raves from Frommer's readers. Surprisingly for the house's size, there are only three guest rooms available here; of the three, two have Jacuzzi-like jetted "hydrotherapy" tubs, and the third—furnished with two twin beds, rather than a double—has a Victorian claw-foot tub. The owners have gone "green" with the property, adding organic fabrics and foods to an already excellent lodging.

66 McDonald St. (P.O. Box 1215), Lunenburg, NS B0J 2C0. ✆ **877/634-9358** or 902/634-9358. www.alicionbb.com. 3 units. C$135–C$155 double. Rates include full breakfast. MC, V. **Amenities:** Bikes. *In room:* Jacuzzi (2 units), no phone.

THE bluenose

Take an old Canadian dime—one minted before 2001—out of your pocket and have a close look. That graceful schooner on one side? That's the *Bluenose*, Canada's most recognized and most storied ship.

The *Bluenose* was built in Lunenburg in 1921 as a fishing schooner. But it wasn't just any schooner. It was an exceptionally fast schooner.

U.S. and Canadian fishing fleets had raced informally for years. Starting in 1920, the *Halifax Herald* sponsored the International Fisherman's Trophy, which was captured that first year by Americans sailing out of Massachusetts. Peeved, the Nova Scotians set about taking it back. And did they ever. The *Bluenose* retained the trophy for 18 years running, despite the best efforts of Americans to recapture it. The race was shelved as World War II loomed; in the years after the war, fishing schooners were displaced by long-haul, steel-hulled fishing ships, and the schooners sailed into the footnotes of history. The *Bluenose* was sold in 1942 to labor as a freighter in the West Indies. Four years later it foundered and sank off Haiti.

The replica *Bluenose II* was built in 1963 from the same plans as the original, in the same shipyard, and even by some of the same workers. It has been owned by the province since 1971, and sails throughout Canada and beyond as Nova Scotia's seafaring ambassador. The *Bluenose*'s location varies from year to year, and it schedules visits to ports in Canada and the United States. In midsummer, it typically alternates between Lunenburg and Halifax, during which time visitors can sign up for 2-hour harbor sailings (C$40 adults, C$25 children age 3 to 12). To hear about the ship's schedule, call the ***Bluenose II* Preservation Trust** (✆ **866/579-4909** ext. 234 or 902/634-4794 ext 234). Find each summer's sailing schedule online at **http://museum.gov.ns.ca/bluenose**.

Kaulbach House ★★ Under new ownership by a pair of Brits since 2007, this is one of very few local inns to have upscaled with the times. I mean, the place actually has flatscreen TVs and Wi-Fi. But it also has history: The house is decorated elaborately, as befits its architecture. Rooms are furnished in simple Victorian style, rendered somewhat less oppressive by welcoming, un-Victorian color schemes (one room is even ruby red). The biggest and best room (the Bluenose Suite) is on the top floor; it features two sitting areas and a great view; the former servants' quarters, on street level, are smaller. The owners have also spruced up the rooms a good bit with great shower heads, fresh flowers, fluffy robes, CD player clock-radios, and DVD players. The included three-course breakfast is also worth coming for, and the parlor/living room feels as Victorian as they come. And it's a good choice in one more regard: It's one of the few small Lunenburg inns in which all guest rooms have their own private bathrooms.

75 Pelham St. (P.O. Box 1348), Lunenburg, NS B0J 2C0. ✆ **800/568-8818** or 902/634-8818. www.kaulbachhouse.com. 6 units. C$99–C$169 double. Off-season discounts available. Rates include full breakfast. MC, V. Closed Nov–May. *In room:* A/C, TV/DVD, hair dryer, no phone.

Lennox Inn Bed & Breakfast ★ In 1991, this handsome but simple house in a quiet residential area of Lunenburg was condemned and slated for demolition. Robert Cram didn't want to see it go, so he bought it and spent several years restoring it to its original 1791 appearance, filling it with antiques and period reproduction furniture. It's also painted deep red. Things are more rustic than opulent here (the wood-floored rooms are pretty spare), but the Lennox should be first on your list in Lunenburg if you're into a period feel and historic homes. In fact, the inn claims, quite plausibly, to be the oldest unchanged inn in all of Canada (it was once a tavern back in the day). Three of the four spacious second-floor rooms here still have their original plaster, and all four have their original fireplaces (though they don't any longer work) and period prints. The rooms also have skinny four-poster beds and French wingback chairs (you half expect Betsy Ross to appear around a corner); my favorite of the four is probably the Fox Room, on the southwest corner—it has its own bathroom, one of two units that do. Amazingly, the owner has gone ahead and added Wi-Fi access recently. A country breakfast is served in the former drinking room; be sure to note the ingenious old bar.

69 Fox St. (P.O. Box 254), Lunenburg, NS B0J 2C0. ✆ **888/379-7605** or 902/521-0214. www.lennoxinn.com. 4 units, 2 with shared bathroom. C$95–C$120 double. Rates include full breakfast. MC, V. Open year-round; by reservation only mid-Oct to Apr. *In room:* No phone.

Lunenburg Arms Hotel & Spa ★★ In a town where nearly all the lodgings consist of former seamen's homes, this hotel converted from a gutted former tavern-boardinghouse stands out as a modern and welcome alternative. It's what passes for a boutique hotel in these parts, offering an updated look, rooms that are wheelchair-accessible, an elevator, and wiring for high-speed Internet access—amenities you don't often find in small-town Nova Scotia. Rooms are furnished in pleasant carpeting, and the queen and king beds wouldn't look out of place in a New York hotel. Yet there are also thoughtfully homey touches such as wood-laminate floors and a stuffed teddy bear (or two) placed in each room. (Pets are welcomed with open paws, as well.) The smallish bathrooms feature pedestal sinks and all-new fixtures. No two rooms are laid out exactly alike, so examine a couple if possible to get the configuration you want—some rooms have Jacuzzis, some feature knockout harbor views, and there are two bi-level loft suites with the beds up small sets of stairs. The Arms also has a spa featuring Aveda products; its facilities include a soaker tub, a hot tub, and aromatherapy-delivering steam showers. The hotel restaurant, **Tin Fish** (see below), is very good.

94 Pelham St., Lunenburg, NS B0J 2C0. ✆ **800/679-4950** or 902/640-4040. Fax 902/640-4041. www.lunenburgarms.com. 26 units. Peak season C$129–C$199 double, C$199–C$269 suite; off-peak C$89–C$169 double and suite. AE, MC, V. **Amenities:** Dining room; conference room; spa. *In room:* A/C, TV, hair dryer.

WHERE TO DINE

Historic Grounds Coffee House ★ CAFE Jeff and Teri Green's youthful coffeehouse in the heart of formerly unhip Lunenburg serves up more than just great coffee. They also do hearty breakfasts, chowders, sandwiches, salads, and fish cakes throughout most of the day, and always with a smile. Wash your meal down with real Italian espresso or—especially in summer—an addictive coffee drink they call a frappé (not an American-style frappe, but instead more like a frozen espresso). Ice cream and interesting dessert items are also available, as are sodas and smoothies. Get a table on the small balcony if you can snag one—they've got one of the best dining views in town, at a fraction of the cost you'd pay for a meal anywhere else.

100 Montague St. ✆ **902/634-9995.** Lunch items C$3.95–C$8.95. AE, DISC, MC, V. June to mid-Sept Mon–Fri 7:30am–10pm, Sat–Sun 8am–10pm; mid-Sept to May daily 7:30am–6pm.

Old Fish Factory Restaurant ★ SEAFOOD I'm tempted to call this the "Ole Factory," since the fish on the docks don't always smell sweet. But in fact this place's aroma won't offend you. The large and popular restaurant is housed—as you'd guess—in a huge old fish-processing plant (which it shares with a good fisheries museum; see "Exploring Lunenburg," earlier). The place sometimes seems to swallow whole bus tours at once, Jonah-like, so come early and angle for a window seat or a spot on the patio. The specialty here is seafood (no shocker there), which tends to involve platters of fish prepared variously. At lunch you can order fish cakes, a fish sandwich, or a Cape Sable salmon filet, but at dinnertime the options widen: Lobster is served at least four different ways, and chefs whip up bouillabaisse, snow crab, local haddock, scallops in a honey butter—even offbeat choices like curried mango seafood pasta or baked halibut sided with strawberry salsa. (There's also steak, lamb, pork chops, and chicken for more terrestrial tasters.) Or just grab a cold one at the Ice House bar. Touristy? Yes. Good food? Actually, yes.

68 Bluenose Dr. (at the Fisheries Museum). ✆ **800/533-9336** or 902/634-3333. www.oldfishfactory.com. Reservations recommended. Lunch C$9–C$18; dinner C$17–C$29. AE, DC, DISC, MC, V. Daily 11am–9pm. Closed late Oct to early May.

Tin Fish ★ CANADIAN A new addition to Lunenburg's restaurant menu, Tin Fish is the house restaurant of the Lunenburg Arms (see "Where to Stay," above). It mostly features straight-ahead Canadian food, but done classier than the fried grub that predominates elsewhere around town. Start with scallops on the half-shell in Bechamel sauce, crab cakes, mussels, or a tomato tart, then move on to entrees like local haddock peppered and fried in a panko crust, rack of lamb, planked salmon, barbecued striploin, breast of duck, or a maple-curry pasta. Even the vegetarian entrée, a grilled phyllo wrap filled with goat cheese, slivered almonds, and grilled veggies, is good. Eat inside by the fireplace, at the bar, or out on the stylish terrace opening onto a quiet street.

94 Pelham St. ✆ **800/679-4950** or 902/640-4040. Reservations accepted. Lunch C$10–C$15; dinner C$18–C$28. AE, MC, V. Daily 7am–10pm.

Mahone Bay ★★

The village of Mahone Bay, settled in 1754 by European Protestants, is picture-perfect Nova Scotia at its best. It's tidy and trim, with an eclectic Main Street that snakes along the lovely eponymous bay and is lined with inviting shops, markets, and eateries. Locals are friendly and knowledgeable. The winds attract plenty of sailboats to the bay. And the town's **three churches,** grouped closely together, are among the most famous in the province—expect churcharazzi politely clicking away. This is a town that's remarkably well cared for by its 900 of so full-time residents, a growing number of whom live here and commute to Halifax (about an hour away). Architecture buffs will find a range of styles to keep them ogling, too.

ESSENTIALS

GETTING THERE Mahone Bay lies 10km (6 miles) east of Lunenburg on Route 3.

VISITOR INFORMATION One of the best **visitor information centers** (✆ **888/624-6151** or 902/624-6151; www.mahonebay.com) in Nova Scotia is located at 165 Edgewater St., near the three church steeples. It's open daily in summer from around 9am until 7:30pm, only until 5:30pm in the shoulder seasons.

EXPLORING THE TOWN

The free **Mahone Bay Settlers Museum,** 578 Main St. (✆ **902/624-6263**), provides a historic context for your explorations. From June through early September, it's open Monday to Saturday 10am to 5pm and Sundays 1 to 5pm. After Labour Day, they sometimes open on request; call if you want to have a look. A good selection of historic decorative arts is on display here. Before leaving, be sure to request a copy of "Three Walking Tours of Mahone Bay," a handy brochure that outlines easy historic walks around the compact downtown.

Thanks to the looping waterside routes nearby, this is a popular destination for bikers. And the deep, protected harbor offers superb sea kayaking. If you'd like to give kayaking a go, contact **East Coast Outfitters** (✆ **877/852-2567** or 902/852-2567), based in the Peggy's Cove area near Halifax. They offer half-day introductory classes and a 5-day coastal tour of the area. Among the more popular adventures is the day-long introductory tour, in which paddlers explore the complex shoreline and learn about kayaking in the process. The price is about C$115 per person, C$35 extra for an optional lobster lunch. Rentals are also available, starting at about C$50 per half-day for a single kayak. (You can also rent for just an hour or two, but what fun is that?)

WHERE TO STAY

You'll find a clutch of bed-and-breakfast choices along Mahone Bay's Main Street, and also on the roads leading to surrounding coves; consult the **Chamber of Commerce** website (www.mahonebay.com) for a fairly complete listing.

Right in the center of town, the lovely **Mahone Bay Bed & Breakfast** at 558 Main St. (✆ **866/239-6252** or 902/624-6388) is a Victorian option with four rooms at rates from C$95 to C$135 per night. This restored, bright yellow house was built in the 1860s by one of the town's many former shipbuilders; expect plenty of wicker, a widow's walk, and some rather arresting curvature on the front detail of the home.

Amber Rose Inn ★★ There are only three units in this family-owned Main Street inn carved out of a blue heritage home built in 1875. But all three are good-sized suites with whirlpools, all are air-conditioned, and all have Wi-Fi access. The affordable rates make this place a steal. Rooms are sparely furnished (in a good way), rose-themed, and floral-printed; they're also accented by plentiful flowers and gardens outside. The side entrance has a lovely little porch with bird feeders, great for reading a magazine and taking in the coastal light. Morning breakfasts are included and run to strudels, pancakes, quiche, waffles, and eggs Benedict.

319 W. Main St. (Box 450), Mahone Bay, NS B0J 2E0. ✆ **902/624-1060.** Fax 902/624-0363. www.amberroseinn.com. 3 units. C$95–C$135 suite. Rates include full breakfast. AE, MC, V. Closed Jan–Apr. *In room:* A/C, TV, hair dryer.

WHERE TO DINE

Mahone Bay's little main street has more than its share of places in which you can nosh, though most of them are priced in "tourodollars": which is to say, higher than they probably should be.

Maybe that's why the seasonally open **Gazebo Cafe ★** at 567 Main St. (✆ **902/624-6484**) still remains my favorite casual eating spot in the town. Affable and affordable, the place dishes up filling, healthy sandwiches and thick bowls of seafood chowder. They also do juices, smoothies, and top-notch coffee. Fresh desserts are delivered several times weekly. This place is becoming the de facto arts headquarters of the town, so check the bulletin board for news about local art shows and musical performances, some of which even occasionally take place right at the cafe. If you're coming in fall, call ahead; every year's schedule is different. They might be closing up shop, or they might be serving lunch straight through until Christmas.

Innlet Café ★★ SEAFOOD/GRILL The Kralicks, the Bavarian owners of the Innlet, are carrying on the place's long tradition as Mahone Bay residents' upscale night out on the town. Everything here is good, though there's perhaps less of an emphasis on seafood now than there used to be, and more steaks, stir-fries, pastas, and the like. (Being German, the Kralicks couldn't resist sticking apple strudel on the dessert menu, either; try it.) The best seats in the house are on the stone patio, with its fine view of the harbor and the famous three steeples. If you end up sitting inside, though, that's okay: The airiness of the interior make it just as inviting. The atmosphere here is informal and relaxed, never stuffy. There's a wine list and cocktails. 249 Edgewater St. ✆ **902/624-6363.** www.innletcafe.com. Reservations recommended for dinner. Most main course items C$12–C$21. MC, V. Daily 11:30am–9pm.

Chester ★★

Chester is a short drive off Route 103 and has the feel of a moneyed summer colony somewhere on the New England coast back in the roaring '20s. In any case, the town was first settled in 1759 by immigrants from New England and Great Britain, and today it has a population of about 1,600. The village is noted for its regal homes and quiet streets, along with the numerous islands offshore. The atmosphere here is uncrowded, untrammeled, lazy, and slow—the way life used to be in summer resorts throughout the world. Change may be on the horizon: Canadian actors and authors have apparently discovered the place and are snapping up waterfront homes in town and on the islands as private retreats, giving a bit of cultural edge to the lazy feel of the spot. There's not really a public beach here, but the views and boat rides are more than enough to compensate.

ESSENTIALS

GETTING THERE Chester is located on Route 3 and is a short drive off Route 103, 21km (13 miles) east of Mahone Bay.

VISITOR INFORMATION The **Chester Visitor Information Centre** (✆ **902/275-4616;** www.chesterns.com) is inside the old train station on Route 3, on the south side of town. It's open daily from 9am to 7pm.

EXPLORING THE TOWN

Like so many other towns in Nova Scotia, Chester is best seen from your car. But unlike other towns, where the center of gravity seems to be in the commercial district, here the focus is on the graceful, shady residential areas that radiate out from the tiny main street.

In your rambles, plan to head down **Queen Street** to the waterfront, then veer around on South Street, admiring the views out toward the mouth of the harbor. Continue on South Street past the yacht club, past the statue of the veteran (in a kilt), past the sundial in the small square. Then you'll come to a beautiful view of Back Harbour. At the foot of the small park is a curious municipal saltwater pool, filled at high tide. On warmer days, you'll find what appears to be half the town out splashing and shrieking in the bracing water.

In the evening, the intimate **Chester Playhouse** ★★, 22 Pleasant St. (✆ **800/363-7529** or 902/275-3933; www.chesterplayhouse.ca), hosts plays, concerts, a summer theater festival, and other high-quality events from March through

December; it's a town institution, and absolutely a must-visit if you're a theater or folk music buff. Theater festival tickets are usually around C$25 per person for adults, cheaper for children; musical performance ticket prices vary. Call or check the Playhouse's website for a schedule or to purchase tickets.

WHERE TO STAY

Graves Island Provincial Park ★★ ☺ This 50-hectare (124-acre) estatelike park is one of the province's more elegant-looking campgrounds, as befits moneyed Chester. The park has expanded to 80-odd sites, many of them dotting a high grassy bluff with outstanding views out to the spruce-clad islands of Mahone Bay; camping is available from mid-May through to the end of the first week of September. There's also a boat launch, swimming area, and playground for the kids.

Route 3 (3km/1¾ miles north of the village on East River). ✆ **902/275-4425.** 84 sites. C$23 per site.

Mecklenburgh Inn ★★ This appealing, brightly painted inn, built around 1900, is located on a low hill in one of Chester's residential neighborhoods. Rather than being prepossessing, the building has a fun, lived-in feel (motto: "The door is always open"), dominated by two broad porches on the first and second floors which invariably are populated with guests rocking on Adirondack chairs and watching the town wander by below. (They wander here because they have to: The town post office is just next door.) This place has been ticking along with a casual bonhomie since the late 1980s, though Wi-Fi access has been added and all rooms finally have private bathrooms (three of the four with claw-foot tubs, one with a shower only). Rooms are modern Victorian and generally quite bright, with pine flooring whose beauty has been newly restored. Other touches include recently upgraded amenities such as French truffles, Frette linens, bathrobes, and pillow-topped mattresses. Yet it's still a relative bargain for the price, considering how nice the touches are.

78 Queen St., Chester, NS B0J 1J0. ✆ **866/838-4638** or 902/275-4638. www.mecklenburghinn.ca. 4 units. C$95–C$155 double. Rates include full breakfast. AE, V. Closed Jan–Apr. *In room:* Hair dryer, no phone.

WHERE TO DINE

If it's baked goods you crave, **Julien's Pastry Shop** (✆ **902/275-2324**) at 43 Queen St. does them extremely well, as does the Kiwi Café (see below).

Kiwi Café ★★ CAFE A little enclave of New Zealand culture on the nautical coast of Nova Scotia? Yes, indeed. The former Luigi's bookshop-cafe right in the heart of downtown Chester was sold in 2004 and reinvented as the Kiwi, a thank-goodness-it's-still-fun place in what can be an occasionally starchy town. Proprietress Lynda Flynn—yes, she's really from New Zealand, and received training in the culinary arts in Auckland—serves up eggs and bagels (try the lobster scramble) for breakfast, plus an assortment of sandwiches, wraps, panini, fresh soups, Nova Scotian fish cakes with mango salsa, and gourmet salads for lunch. Wash it down with wine, Nova Scotia beer, or a good blended Halifax-roasted-coffee drink. On the go? No problem: Grab a "Dinner in a Box" (Flynn also runs a catering business) or some New Zealand honey from the little provisions shop on the premises. And don't forget a piece of hummingbird cake. A great little find, full of good cheer.

19 Pleasant St. ✆ **902/275-1492.** www.kiwicafechester.com. Main courses C$4.50–C$8.50. V. Daily 8:30am–4pm.

La Vista ★★ CONTINENTAL/SEAFOOD This dining room, located inside the Oak Island Resort spa and convention center just north of Chester down a side peninsula, offers an upscale alternative to traveling diners in the Chester area. And the views out those windows—well, just be there at sunset on a clear day. That's all I can say. Start off with a bowl of seafood chowder flavored heavily with dill, some French onion soup with Gruyère, a smoked-salmon Napoleon, Thai crab cakes, or a plate of local mussels steamed in white wine; then move on to a piece of sesame-crusted salmon over basmati rice, cedar-planked salmon with maple butter, pan-roasted halibut with pepper and lemongrass, roasted tenderloin with a Stilton crust, shrimp-and-lobster pasta, or whatever else has been invented for the season. The signature, decadent "Cordon Oak Island" stuffs a chicken with apple-wood smoked cheddar and Black Forest ham, but then tops it with (what else?) maple cream.

36 Treasure Dr. (inside the Oak Island Resort), Western Shore. ✆ **800/565-5075** or 902/627-2600. Main courses C$18–C$23. MC, V. Daily 7am–2pm and 5–9pm. Take Hwy. 103 to exit 9, continue 2km (1¼ miles) to Rte 3, turn onto Rte 3, continue 5km (3 miles) to resort.

HALIFAX ★★

322km (200 miles) NE of Yarmouth

Halifax is the biggest city in the Maritime Provinces by far, yet it doesn't *feel* big at all—in just the way that Boston and San Francisco don't feel like huge cities. It actually feels like a collection of loosely connected neighborhoods, which is in fact what it is; you often forget this is one of the central economic engines of eastern Canada.

Established in 1749, the city was named for George Montagu Dunk, second earl of Halifax. (Residents agree it was a huge stroke of luck that the city avoided being named Dunk, Nova Scotia.) The city plodded along as a colonial backwater for the better part of a century, superceded by nearby towns building more boats (Shelburne and Lunenberg, to name two); one historian even wrote of Halifax as "a rather degenerate little seaport town."

But the city's natural advantages—that well-protected harbor, its location near major fishing grounds and shipping lanes—eventually caused Halifax to overtake its rivals and emerge as an industrial port and military base for the ages. Relatively speaking, of course. And then, at long last, so came the tourists and scholars and urban escapees from Toronto: In recent decades, this city has grown aggressively (it annexed several adjacent suburbs in 1969) and carved out a niche for itself as the commercial and financial hub of the Maritimes.

Today it's also the cultural cutting edge of eastern Canada. Pop singer Sarah MacLachlan grew up here, and it's also the hometown of professional hockey's "next Gretzky," young Sidney Crosby of the Pittsburgh Penguins—a big deal in hockey-crazed Canada. (Crosby's 2009 victory parade with the Stanley Cup snarled downtown's streets, but nobody complained.) So long as you're not allergic to beer, good food, ocean breezes, and good music, I think it's fair to say you'll never be at a loss for something to do during your time here.

Essentials

GETTING THERE

BY PLANE Many travelers arrive in Halifax by air. Halifax's **Stanfield International Airport** (airport code YHZ) is 34km (21 miles) north of the city center in Elmsdale; to get there, take Route 102 to exit 6. Airlines serving Halifax currently include Air Canada (and its commuter airline Jazz), WestJet, American Eagle, CanJet, Provincial, Continental Express, Delta, and Icelandair. Take a cab (a flat fare of

C$53 by law); rent a car (plenty of big-name chain options in the terminal); or take the **Airporter** (✆ **902/873-2091**) shuttle bus, which makes frequent runs to major downtown hotels daily from 6:30am to 11:15pm. The rate is C$21 per person one-way.

BY CAR Coming from New Brunswick and the west, the most direct route to Halifax by car is via Route 102 from Truro; allow 2 or 2½ hours to drive here once you cross the invisible provincial border at Amherst. From the ferry docks at Yarmouth, it's a 3½-hour drive up the coast if you don't stop and linger anywhere—but you will. Figure on a full day.

BY RAIL **VIA Rail** (✆ **888/842-7245**) offers train service 6 days a week between Halifax and Montréal. The entire trip takes between 18 and 21 hours, depending on direction. Stops include Moncton and Campbellton (with bus connections to Québec). Halifax's train station, at Barrington and Cornwallis streets, is within walking distance of downtown attractions.

VISITOR INFORMATION

There's a ton of tourist info here. The city's **tourist information booth** (✆ **902/490-5963**) in **Scotia Square** (two blocks below The Citadel) and the government-run **visitor information center** (VIC) (✆ **902/424-4248**) on the waterfront at 1655 Lower Water St. (Sackville Landing) are both open daily, year-round until 9pm in summer, until 4:30pm and 6pm, respectively, in winter. Each is staffed with friendly folks who will point you in the right direction or help you make room reservations.

There's **another provincial VIC** at Halifax's **airport** (see "By Plane," above), also open year-round, while a helpfully central *fourth* **seasonal VIC** opens downtown at 1598 Argyle St. (corner of Sackville) from mid-May through mid-October only. As if that weren't enough, tourism office staff cruise the waterfront and boardwalk on Segway scooters during the summer months. For online information about the city, visit **www.halifaxinfo.com**.

GETTING AROUND

Parking in Halifax can be problematic. Long-term metered spaces are in high demand downtown, and many of the parking lots and garages fill up fast. If you're headed downtown for a brief visit, you can usually find a 2-hour meter. But if you're looking to spend the day in town, I'd suggest venturing out early and snagging a spot in an affordable parking lot or garage. There's plentiful parking near Sackville Landing, or try along Lower Water Street (south of the Maritime Museum of the Atlantic), where you can sometimes park all day for around C$6.

Metro Transit operates buses throughout the city. Route and timetable information is available at the information centers or by phone (✆ **902/490-4000**). Bus fare is C$2.25 for adults, C$1.50 for seniors and children.

Daily throughout the summer (early July through late October), a bright green bus named **FRED** cruises a loop through the downtown, passing each stop about every 30 minutes from 10:30am until 5pm. It's free. Stops include the Maritime Museum, Water Street, the Grand Parade, the Citadel, and Barrington Place. Request a schedule and map at the visitor center. FRED, by the way, stands for Free Rides Everywhere Downtown. But it's still a cool name.

SPECIAL EVENTS & FESTIVALS

The annual **Royal Nova Scotia International Tattoo** (✆ **902/420-1114;** www.nstattoo.ca) features military and marching bands totaling some 2,000-plus military

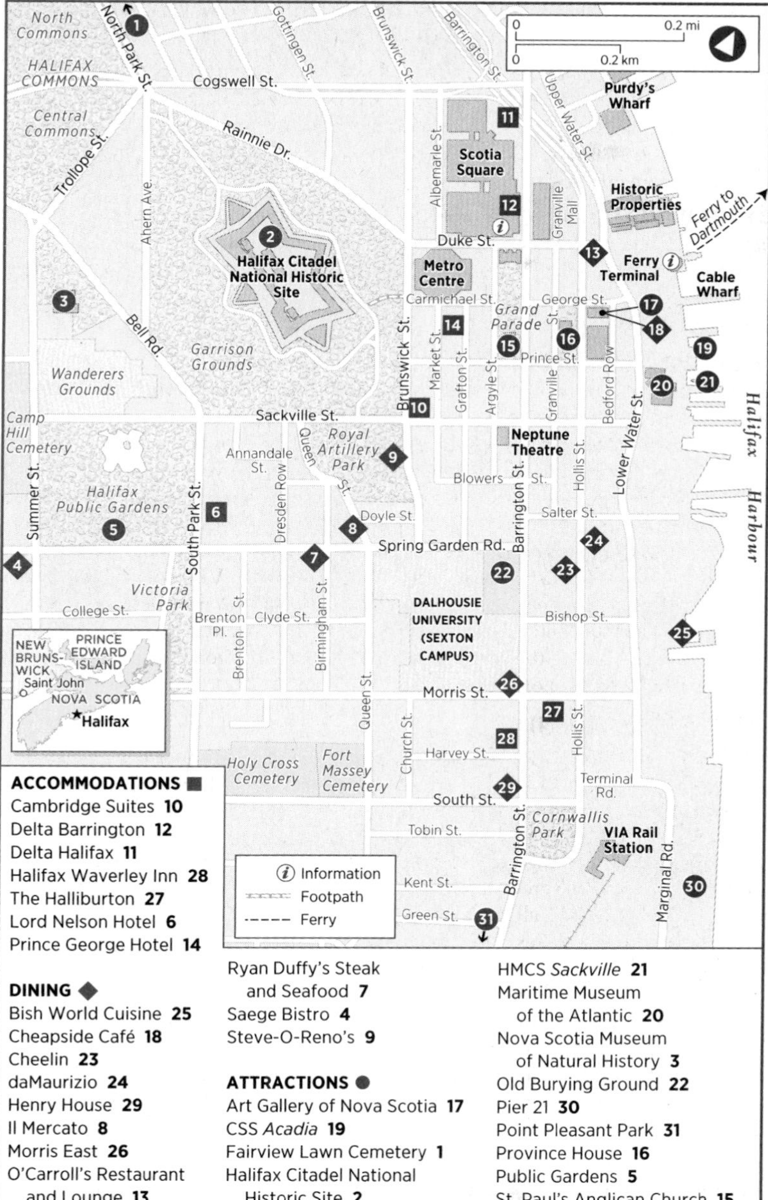
North Commons
North Park St.
HALIFAX COMMONS
Cogswell St.
Gottingen St.
Brunswick St.
Barrington St.
Upper Water St.
Purdy's Wharf
Central Commons
Trollope St.
Rainnie Dr.
Albemarle St.
Scotia Square
Historic Properties
Ferry to Dartmouth
Granville Mall
Ahern Ave.
Halifax Citadel National Historic Site
Duke St.
Metro Centre
Ferry Terminal
Cable Wharf
Carmichael St.
George St.
Grand Parade
Bell Rd.
Garrison Grounds
Market St.
Prince St.
Wanderers Grounds
Grafton St.
Argyle St.
Granville St.
Bedford Row
Lower Water St.
Halifax Harbour
Camp Hill Cemetery
Sackville St.
Royal Artillery Park
Annandale St.
Queen St.
Neptune Theatre
Hollis St.
Blowers St.
Halifax Public Gardens
Summer St.
Dresden Row
Doyle St.
Salter St.
South Park St.
Spring Garden Rd.
Victoria Park
College St.
Brenton Pl.
Clyde St.
Birmingham St.
Brenton St.
DALHOUSIE UNIVERSITY (SEXTON CAMPUS)
Bishop St.
NEW BRUNSWICK
PRINCE EDWARD ISLAND
Saint John
NOVA SCOTIA
Halifax
Morris St.
Church St.
Harvey St.
Holy Cross Cemetery
Fort Massey Cemetery
South St.
Terminal Rd.
Tobin St.
Cornwallis Park
VIA Rail Station
Kent St.
Green St.
Marginal Rd.
0 0.2 mi
0 0.2 km
Information
Footpath
Ferry
ACCOMMODATIONS ■
Cambridge Suites 10
Delta Barrington 12
Delta Halifax 11
Halifax Waverley Inn 28
The Halliburton 27
Lord Nelson Hotel 6
Prince George Hotel 14
DINING ◆
Bish World Cuisine 25
Cheapside Café 18
Cheelin 23
daMaurizio 24
Henry House 29
Il Mercato 8
Morris East 26
O'Carroll's Restaurant and Lounge 13
Ryan Duffy's Steak and Seafood 7
Saege Bistro 4
Steve-O-Reno's 9
ATTRACTIONS ●
Art Gallery of Nova Scotia 17
CSS Acadia 19
Fairview Lawn Cemetery 1
Halifax Citadel National Historic Site 2
HMCS Sackville 21
Maritime Museum of the Atlantic 20
Nova Scotia Museum of Natural History 3
Old Burying Ground 22
Pier 21 30
Point Pleasant Park 31
Province House 16
Public Gardens 5
St. Paul's Anglican Church 15

and civilian performers. The rousing event takes place over the course of a week in early July and is held indoors at the Halifax Metro Center. Tickets are C$31 to C$62 per adult, depending on the position of your seating, less for seniors and children.

The annual **Atlantic Jazz Festival** (✆ **902/492-2225**; www.jazzeast.com) has performances ranging from global and avant-garde to local and traditional music each July. Venues include area nightclubs and outdoor stages, and prices vary considerably; consult the website for the latest details and specifics of performance and price.

In early August, expect to see a profusion of street performers ranging from folk singers and fire-eaters to clowns and jugglers. They descend on Halifax each summer for the 10-day **Halifax International Busker Festival** (www.buskers.ca). Performances take place along the waterfront walkway all day long and are often quite remarkable. The festival is free, though donations are requested—you can donate *and* get complete info by buying a comprehensive festival guide for just C$2 on the waterfront before and during the festival. Any hotel reception desk in town worth its salt should also be able to give you updated info on what's happening where.

The **Atlantic Film Festival ★★★** (✆ **902/422-6965** or 422-3456; www.atlanticfilm.com) offers screenings of more than 150 films at theaters around Halifax over a 10-day period in mid-September. The focus is largely on Canadian filmmaking, with an emphasis on independent productions and shorts, and the quality level is high. (The 2009 offerings included *We Are Wizards,* Josh Koury's documentary on the Harry Potter phenomenon, and *Real Time,* with Randy Quaid as a humane hit man.) Panel discussions with industry players are also part of the festival, meaning you get a chance to see mid-level directors and stars up close and personal. Some films are free, while others cost C$5 to C$15 each to view.

Exploring Halifax

Halifax is fairly compact, thus easily reconnoitered on foot or by using the excellent public transportation in town. The major landmark is the **Citadel**—that stone fortress looming over downtown from a grassy height. (From the ramparts, you can look into the windows of the 10th floor of downtown skyscrapers.) The Citadel is only 9 blocks uphill from the **waterfront**—9 *steep* blocks—and the entire downtown's so small that you can easily see both the downtown sights and the waterfront in a single day, if that's all you have.

Another lively neighborhood worth seeking out runs along **Spring Garden Road** between the Public Gardens and the library (at Grafton St.). Here you'll find intriguing boutiques, bars, and restaurants along these 6 blocks, set amid a Bohemian street scene. If you have strong legs, start on the waterfront and walk uphill and over the Citadel, descend to the lovely **Public Gardens** (see later), then return via Spring Garden Road to your downtown hotel, enjoying a drink and a bite along the way.

THE WATERFRONT ★

Halifax's rehabilitated waterfront is most inviting between Sackville Landing (at the foot of Sackville St.) and the Casino Nova Scotia (near Purdy Wharf). Don't venture much farther north than that—the waterside path becomes a gauntlet of tall drab office towers and their big unpleasant vents. On sunny summer afternoons, this good stretch of waterfront bustles with tourists enjoying the harbor, business folks sneaking ice-cream cones, and skateboarders trying to make (or stay out of) trouble. Plan on about 2 to 3 hours to tour and gawk this section from end to end.

Sackville Landing is a good place to start a waterfront walking tour. In addition to the attractions listed below, the waterfront walkway is also studded with other small diversions, intriguing shops, takeout food emporia, and minor monuments. Think of it as an alfresco scavenger hunt.

The waterfront's shopping core is located in and around the 3-block **Historic Properties,** near the Marriott. These buildings of wood and stone are Canada's oldest surviving warehouses, and were once the heart of the city's shipping industry. Today, their historic architecture provides ballast for the somewhat precious boutiques and restaurants they now house instead. Especially appealing is the granite-and-ironstone **Privateers' Warehouse,** which dates from 1813.

If you're feeling like a pub crawl might be in order, the Historic Properties area is also a good place to wander around during the early evening. There's a contagious energy that spills out of the handful of public houses here as workers get off work and tipple pints: You'll find a bustling camaraderie and live music.

Maritime Museum of the Atlantic ★★★ ☺ All visitors to Nova Scotia with even a passing interest in local history owe themselves a stop at this standout museum, situated on a prime piece of waterfront. The exhibits are involving and well executed, and you'll be surprised how fast 2 hours can fly. Visitors are greeted by a cool 3m (10-ft.) lighthouse lens from 1906, then proceed through a series of shipbuilding and seagoing displays. Visit the deckhouse of a coastal steamer (ca. 1940) and learn the colorful history of Samuel Cunard, the Nova Scotia native (born in 1787) who founded the Cunard Steam Ship Co. to carry royal mail—but established a travel dynasty instead. Another highlight is the shocking exhibit on the tragic Halifax explosion of 1917, when two warships collided in the harbor not far from this museum, detonating tons of TNT; more than 1,700 people died, and windows were shattered *60 miles* away.

But perhaps the most poignant exhibit here is just a single deck chair from the *Titanic*—a reminder that 150 victims of that disaster are buried here in Halifax, where the rescue efforts were centered. Also memorable are an "Age of Steam" exhibit; Queen Victoria's barge; an interesting "Shipwreck Treasures of Nova Scotia" section with its stories and artifacts from more than a dozen local shipwrecks; and recreations of a ship's chandlery, sail loft, and carpenter's shop. This is a fascinating place for adult and teens to visit, especially on a rainy day.

1675 Lower Water St. ✆ **902/424-7490.** www.maritime.museum.gov.ns.ca. May–Oct admission C$8.75 adults, C$7.75 seniors, C$4.75 children 6–17, C$23 family; Nov–Apr, admission discounted about 50%. May–Oct daily 9:30am–5:30pm (to 8pm Tues); Nov–Apr closed Mon and only 1–5pm Sun.

CSS *Acadia* This unusually handsome 1913 steam-powered vessel is part of the Maritime Museum (their "largest artifact"). The *Acadia* was used by the Canadian government to chart the ocean bottom for 56 years until its retirement in 1969. Much of the ship is now open for self-guided tours, including the captain's quarters, upper decks, wheelhouse, and oak-paneled chart room. If you want to see more of the ship, ask about guided half-hour tours (they take place four times daily), which offer access to the engine room and more. Allow a half-hour to an hour to take it in.

1675 Lower Water St. (on the water, in front of Maritime Museum). ✆ **902/424-7490.** Admission C$2 per person or free with Maritime Museum ticket, which costs C$8.75 adults, C$7.75 seniors, C$4.75 children 6–17, C$23 family. Mon–Sat 9:30am–5:30pm; Sun 1–5:30pm.

HMCS *Sackville* This blue-and-white corvette (a speedy warship smaller than a destroyer) is tied up along a wood-planked wharf behind a small visitor center. There's a short multimedia presentation to provide some background. The ship is outfitted just as it was in 1944, maintained as a memorial to the Canadians who served in World War II. Plan to spend about a half-hour if you're inclined to visit.

Sackville Landing (summer), HMC dockyard (winter). ✆ **902/429-2132.** Admission C$4 adults, C$2 seniors and students, C$9 family. June–Oct daily 10am–5pm; off-season hours vary.

Pier 21 ★ ☺ Between 1928 and 1971 more than one million immigrants arrived in Canada at Pier 21, Canada's version of America's Ellis Island. In 1999, the pier was restored and reopened, filled with engaging interpretive exhibits that vividly evoke the confusion and anxiety of the immigration experience. The pier is divided roughly into three sections: the boarding of the ship amid the cacophony of many languages, the crossing of the Atlantic (a half-hour multimedia show recaptures the voyage in a shiplike theater), and the dispersal of recent arrivals throughout Canada via passenger train. For those seeking more in-depth information (they say one in five Canadians today can trace a link back to Pier 21), there's also a reference library and computer resources. Plan to spend an hour here, but only if you're into immigration history.

1055 Marginal Rd. (on the waterfront behind the Westin Hotel). ✆ **902/425-7770.** www.pier21.ca. C$8.50 adults, C$7.50 seniors, C$5 children 6–16, C$21 family. May–Nov daily 9:30am–5:30pm; Dec–March Tues–Sat 10am–5pm; Apr Mon–Sat 10am–5pm.

THE CITADEL & DOWNTOWN

Downtown Halifax cascades 9 blocks down a hill between the imposing stone Citadel and the city's waterfront. There's no fast-and-ready tour route; don't hesitate to follow your own whims, ducking down quiet sidestreets and into bars or striding along the main roads as you wish. A good spot to regain your bearings periodically is the **Grand Parade,** where military recruits once practiced their drills. It's a lovely piece of urban landscape—a broad terrace carved into a hill, presided over on either end by **St. Paul's** (see below) and Halifax's **City Hall**, a sandstone structure built between 1887 and 1890 and exuberantly adorned with all the usual Victorian architectural trifles: prominent clock tower, dormers, pediments, arched windows, pilasters, Corinthian columns. (Alas, there's not much to see inside.)

If the weather is nice, the Grand Parade is also a prime spot to bring an alfresco lunch and enjoy some people-watching.

Art Gallery of Nova Scotia Located in a pair of sandstone (yes, again) buildings between the waterfront and the Grand Parade, Halifax's Art Gallery is arguably the premier gallery in the Maritimes, with a nice focus on local and regional art. Yet you'll also find a selection of other works by Canadian, British, and European artists, too, and well-chosen exhibits of folk and Inuit art. In 1998, the gallery expanded to include the Provincial Building next door, where the entire tiny house of Nova Scotian folk artist Maud Lewis was reassembled and put on display. More good news: The admission price has come down a bit in recent years, and this museum can be comfortably perused in 60 to 90 minutes. Overwhelmed? Sign up for the once-a-day tours. Also consider a lunch break in the attractive Cheapside Café (see "Where to Dine," later).

1723 Hollis St. (at Cheapside). ✆ **902/424-5280.** Admission C$10 adults, C$8 seniors, C$5 students, C$3 children age 6–17, C$20 families. Daily 10am–5pm (Thurs to 9pm). Tours daily at 2:30pm (second tour 7pm Thurs only).

Halifax Citadel National Historic Site ★★ The Citadel is the perfect introduction of Halifax: It provides a good geographic first look at the city, and anchors it in history, as well. Even if a big stone fort weren't here, it would still be worth the uphill trek to this site just for the astounding views—the panoramic sweep across downtown, the city's harbor, and the Atlantic Ocean make for some great sightseeing. And the ascent to your goal quickly makes it obvious why this spot was chosen for Halifax's most formidable defense: there's simply no sneaking up on the place. Four forts have occupied this same hilltop since Col. Edward Cornwallis was posted to the colony in 1749, but today the Citadel has been restored to look much as it did in 1856, when the fourth and final fort was built out of concern over American expansionist ideas. Yet the fort has never been attacked, perhaps a testament to its effectiveness as a deterrent. In a sprawling gravel and cobblestone courtyard, you'll find convincingly costumed interpreters in kilts and bearskin hats marching in unison, playing bagpipes, and firing a cannon at noon. (The former barracks and other chambers are home to exhibits about life at the fort.)

Citadel Hill. ✆ **902/426-5080.** Admission June to mid-Sept C$12 adults, C$10 seniors, C$5.80 children 6–16, C$29 families; May and mid-Sept to Oct C$7.80 adults, C$6.55 seniors, C$3.90 children 6–16, C$20 families; free rest of the year. July–Aug daily 9am–6pm; May–June and Sept–Oct daily 9am–5pm. Nov–Apr, visitor center closed but grounds open. No guides or tours in fall or winter.

Nova Scotia Museum of Natural History ★ ☺ Situated on the far side of the Citadel from downtown, this modern, midsize museum offers a good introduction to the flora and fauna of Nova Scotia. Galleries include geology, botany, mammals, and birds, plus exhibits of archaeology and Mi'kmaq culture. There's a cool butterfly house, filled with the winged wonders from July to September. Also noteworthy are an extensive collection of lifelike ceramic fungus and a colony of honeybees that freely come and go from their indoor acrylic hive through a tube connected to the outdoors. Allow an hour, or more if your kids are really excited by this sort of science.

1747 Summer St. ✆ **902/424-7353.** Admission C$5.75 adults, C$5.25 seniors, C$3.75 children 6–17, C$12–C$17 families; admission free on Wed nights 5–8pm. June to mid-Oct Mon–Sat 9:30am–5:30pm (Wed until 8pm), Sun noon–5:30pm; mid-Oct to May, closed Mon.

Province House ★ Canada's oldest seat of government, the three-story stone Province House has been home to the tiny Nova Scotian legislature since 1819. This exceptional Georgian building is a superb example of the rigorously symmetrical Palladian style. And like a jewel box, its dour stone exterior hides gems of ornamental detailing and artwork inside, especially the fine plasterwork, which is rare in a Canadian building from this era. A free well-written booklet is available when you enter; it provides helpful background about the building's history and architecture. If the legislature is in session (it's not always), you can obtain a visitor's pass and sit up in the gallery, watching the business of the province unfold. They also offer tours, which you book by calling the information number below. History buffs should allow an hour for this visit.

1726 Hollis St. (near Prince St.). ✆ **902/424-4661.** www.gov.ns.ca/legislature. Free admission. July–Aug Mon–Fri 9am–5pm, Sat–Sun and holidays 10am–4pm; Sept–June Mon–Fri 9am–4pm.

St. Paul's Anglican Church ★★ Forming one end of the Grand Parade, this classically handsome white Georgian building was the first Anglican cathedral established outside of England, and as such is Canada's oldest Protestant place of worship. It was once the figurehead for all church doings in eastern Canada—all the way to Ontario. That makes it pretty significant. (Part of the 1749 church was fabricated in Boston and erected in Halifax with the help of a royal endowment from King George II.) Later, history continued happening here: A piece of flying debris from the great explosion of 1917 (see "Maritime Museum of the Atlantic," p. 77) is lodged in the wall over the doors to the nave. Just a quick visit is enough to get a sense of the place, especially the fine stained-glass windows; take one of the summertime guided tours if you want to see more. But you're also allowed to be amazed by the exterior.

1749 Argyle St. (on the Grand Parade near Barrington St.). ✆ **902/429-2240.** www.stpaulshalifax.org. Mon–Fri 9am–4:30pm; Sun services 8, 9:15, and 11am. Free guided tours June–Aug Mon–Sat; call for scheduling.

GARDENS & OPEN SPACE

Fairview Lawn Cemetery ★ When the *Titanic* went down on April 15, 1912, nearly 2,000 people died. Ship captains from Halifax were recruited to help retrieve the corpses. (You can learn about this grim mission at the Maritime Museum, described on p. 77.) Some 121 victims, mostly ship crewmembers, were buried at this quiet cemetery located a short drive north of downtown Halifax. Some of the simple graves have names, but many others only bear numbers. Plaques and signs highlight some poignant stories from the tragedy. It's definitely worth an hour or more for *Titanic* fans; others might just spend a few minutes here. (Without a car, though, skip it entirely—too far.) A brochure with driving directions to this and two other *Titanic* cemeteries in the city can be obtained either at the Maritime Museum or the city's visitor information centers.

Chisholm Ave., off Connaught Ave. (about 2½ miles northwest of the Citadel). ✆ **902/490-4883.** Daylight hours year-round.

Old Burying Ground Fully restored in 1991, this was the first burial ground in Halifax, and between 1749 and 1844 some 12,000 people were interred here. (Only 1 in 10 graves is marked with a headstone, however.) You'll find examples of 18th- and 19th-century gravestone art—especially winged heads and winged skulls. (No rubbings are allowed, however.) Also exceptional is the Welsford-Parker Monument from 1855, which honors Nova Scotians who fought in the Crimean War. An ornate statue near the grounds' entrance features a lion with a Medusa-like mane. Go at dusk, when the grounds are imbued with a quiet grace, a few hours before sunset. The light slants through the trees and city traffic seems far, far away. Cemetery buffs could spend an hour or more; others can easily drop by for 10 minutes en route to downtown attractions or eateries.

Corner of Spring Garden and Barrington. ✆ **902/429-2240.** Free admission. June–Sept 9am–5pm; guides until late Aug. Closed rest of year.

Point Pleasant Park ★★ Point Pleasant is one of Canada's finer urban parks, and there's no better place for a walk along the water on a balmy day. This 73-hectare (180-acre) park occupies a wooded peninsula today, but for years it actually served as one of the linchpins in the city's military defense. Look carefully and you'll find the ruins of early forts, plus a nicely preserved Martello tower. (Halifax still has a 999-year lease from Great Britain for this park, for which it pays 1 shilling—about US10¢—per year.) You'll also find a lovely gravel carriage road around the point, a small swimming beach, miles of walking trails, and groves of graceful fir trees. The park is located about 2km (1¼ miles) south of the Public Gardens. Take note, though, that no bikes are allowed on weekends or holidays; you'll need to use pedi-power.

Point Pleasant Dr. (south end of Halifax; head south on S. Park St. near Public Gardens and continue on Young). Free admission. Daylight hours.

Public Gardens ★★ ☺ The Public Gardens took seed in 1753, when they were founded as a private venture. The tract was acquired by the Nova Scotia Horticultural

A ROAD TRIP TO peggy's cove ★★

About 42km (26 miles) southwest of Halifax is the fishing village of **Peggy's Cove ★★** (pop. 120), which offers postcard-perfect tableaus: an octagonal lighthouse (surely one of the most photographed in the world), tiny fishing shacks, and graceful fishing boats bobbing in the postage stamp-size harbor. The bonsai-like perfection hasn't gone unnoticed by the big tour operators, however, so it's a rare summer day when you're not sharing the experience with a few hundred of your close, personal bus-tour friends. The village is home to a handful of B&Bs and a gallery, but scenic values draw the day-trippers with cameras. While there, make sure to check out the touching **Swissair Flight 111 Memorial ★** among the rocks just before the turnoff to the cove; this site memorializes the passengers of that flight, which crashed into the Atlantic just off the coast.

Society in 1836, and these gardens assumed their present look around 1875 during the peak of the Victorian era. As such, the garden is one of Canada's Victorian masterpieces, rarer and more evocative than any mansard-roofed mansion. You'll find here wonderful examples of 19th-century trends in outdoor landscaping, from the "naturally" winding walks and ornate fountains to the duck ponds and Victorian band shell. (Stop by the shell at 2pm any summer Sunday to catch a free concert.) There are plenty of leafy trees, lush lawns, cranky ducks who have lost their fear of humans, and little ponds. You'll also usually find everyone from octogenarians to kids feeding pigeons there, and smartly uniformed guards slowly walk the grounds. The overseers have also been commendably stingy with memorial statues, plaques, and other falderol.

Spring Garden Rd. and S. Park St. Free admission. Spring to late fall 8am–dusk.

Where to Stay

EXPENSIVE

Cambridge Suites Hotel Halifax ★ ☺ The attractive, modern Cambridge Suites is nicely located near the foot of the Citadel, well positioned for exploring the city. It's perfect for families—about 40 of the units are two-room suites, bigger spaces featuring kitchenettes with microwaves and extra phones. Expect above-average service and a comfortable, inoffensive decor. They also offer the usual business-hotel amenities such as a fitness center, free Wi-Fi throughout the property, and a business center. **Dofsky's Grill** on the first floor is open for all three meals, palatable if not thrilling. Look for pasta, blackened haddock, burgers, jerk chicken, and the like.

1583 Brunswick St., Halifax, NS B3J 3P5. ✆ **888/417-8483** or 902/420-0555. Fax 902/420-9379. www.cambridgesuiteshalifax.com. 200 units. C$119–C$299 suite. Children under 18 stay free in parent's room. AE, DC, MC, V. Valet or self-parking C$15. **Amenities:** Restaurant; babysitting; concierge; health club; Jacuzzi; room service; sauna. *In room:* A/C, TV/VCR, fridge (some units), hair dryer, kitchenette (some units), minibar.

Delta Barrington ★ Convenience and location are the reasons to consider booking into the Delta Barrington, located just 1 block from both the waterfront and the Grand Parade—and connected to the Metro Centre and much of the rest of downtown by a covered walkway. It's a large modern hotel, yes, but was designed and furnished with an eye more to comfort than flash. Guest rooms are decorated in a contemporary country decor, with pine headboards and country-style reproduction furniture. The king rooms are spacious, furnished with sofas and easy chairs. Some rooms face the pedestrian plaza and have been soundproofed to block out the noise from below, though the downside is that these windows don't open. (Most other rooms in the hotel have windows that do open.) Thus the quietest rooms face the courtyard, but lack a view. The hotel restaurant, the **Stone Street Café,** serves an attractive upscale menu that's mostly constructed of fish and lobster prepared various upscale ways, but you can also order rack of lamb, pappardelle, beef tenderloin, and the like. Also ask about the hotel's affordable "Seafood Festival" dinner specials.

1875 Barrington St., Halifax, NS B3J 3L6. ✆ **877/814-7706** or 902/429-7410. Fax 902/420-6524. www.deltabarrington.com. 200 units. C$134–C$294 double. AE, DC, DISC, MC, V. Valet parking C$20. Small pets allowed. **Amenities:** Restaurant; babysitting; children's programs; concierge; Jacuzzi; indoor pool; room service; sauna. *In room:* A/C, TV, hair dryer, minibar.

Delta Halifax ★ The Delta Halifax (formerly the Hotel Halifax, which was formerly the Chateau Halifax) is a slick and modern downtown hotel that offers premium services. It's located just a block off the waterfront, to which it's connected via a skyway, although navigating the skyway involves an annoying labyrinth of parking garages and charmless concrete structures. The lobby is street-side, and guests—largely business travelers during the week—take elevators above a six-floor parking garage to reach their rooms. Ask for a room in the "resort wing" near the pool, which feels farther away from the chatter of downtown and the press of business. A number of rooms have balconies and many have harbor views; ask when you book. Rooms are in two classes—either 300 or 500 square feet—and all are furnished simply and unexceptionably with standard-issue hotel furniture. The **Crown Bistrot** restaurant (run by the same chef as the Delta Barrington's cafe) offers good Continental, Asian, and Maritime-inflected cuisine, while **Sam Slick's Lounge** next door features Friday-night piano and a surprisingly varied bar menu.

1990 Barrington St., Halifax, NS B3J 1P2. ✆ **877/814-7706** or 902/425-6700. Fax 902/425-6214. www.deltahalifax.com. 296 units. C$134–C$284 double. AE, MC, V. Valet parking C$23, self-parking C$20. **Amenities:** Restaurant; bar; babysitting; concierge; health club; Jacuzzi; indoor pool; limited room service; sauna. *In room:* A/C, TV, hair dryer, minibar.

The Halliburton ★★ The Halliburton is a well-appointed, well-run, elegant country inn located in the heart of downtown. Named after former resident Sir Brenton Halliburton (Nova Scotia's first chief justice), the inn is spread out among three town-house-style buildings connected via gardens and sun decks in the rear (though not internally). The main building was constructed in 1809, but only converted into an inn in 1995; it was somehow modernized without the loss of its considerable charm. All guest rooms here are subtly furnished with fine antiques, yet few are so rare that you'd fret about damaging them. (The rooms also feature iPod-playing clock-radios, flatscreen TVs, and Wi-Fi access.) Things are rich and masculine in tone here, and light on frilly stuff. Among the best units: room no. 113, small but with a lovely working fireplace and unique skylighted bathroom. Room nos. 102 and 109 are suites with wet bars and fireplaces; there's also a studio apartment. Halliburton is popular with business travelers, yet it's also a romantic spot for couples to hide out in. The intimate first-floor dining room **Stories ★** serves dinner nightly.

5184 Morris St., Halifax, NS B3J 1B3. ✆ **888/512-3344** or 902/420-0658. Fax 902/423-2324. www.halliburton.ns.ca. 29 units. C$145–C$350 double; off-season discounts available. Rates include continental breakfast and free parking (limited; first-come, first-serve). AE, MC, V. **Amenities:** Restaurant; babysitting; room service. *In room:* A/C, TV, hair dryer.

The Lord Nelson Hotel & Suites ★ The Lord Nelson was built in 1928, and was for years the city's preeminent lodging. It gradually sank in esteem, however, and somehow eventually ended up as a flophouse. In 1998, the hotel was purchased and got a long-overdue, top-to-bottom renovation. It certainly has location going for it: It's right across from the lovely Public Gardens and abuts lively Spring Garden Road. Rooms are furnished with Georgian reproductions. The business-class Flagship Rooms feature desks, ergonomic office chairs, robes, free local calls, and morning newspapers. The hotel charges a premium for rooms facing the street or gardens, but they're probably worth it; others face into a somewhat bleak courtyard. You can tipple a pint off the lobby at the Victory Arms, a cozy and convincing English-style pub serving British fare like bangers and mash and fish and chips (of course) but also rotating more inventive dishes like Singapore noodles, Kobe beef burgers, nan-based pizzas, and Cajun-spiced codfish sandwiches. This hotel is particularly pet-friendly.

1515 South Park St., Halifax, NS B3J 2L2. ✆ **800/565-2020** or 902/423-6331. Fax 902/491-7148. www.lordnelsonhotel.com. 260 units. C$139–C$259 double. AE, DC, DISC, MC, V. Valet parking C$25, self-parking C$20. Pets allowed with C$100 deposit. **Amenities:** Restaurant; bar; babysitting; concierge; health club; limited room service; sauna. *In room:* A/C, TV, hair dryer.

The Prince George Hotel ★ This contemporary and large downtown hotel features understated styling, polished wainscoting, carpeting, and the discreet use of marble, though it still feels a bit sterile and stuffy. In any case, expect modern and comfortably appointed rooms, most with balconies and all with a selection of complimentary tea and coffee, coffeemakers, and hair dryers. This hotel is nicely situated near the Citadel and restaurants and is linked to much of the rest of downtown via underground passageways; parking is beneath the hotel. The hotel's **Gio restaurant ★** on the first floor features contemporary bistro styling, with a zippy menu to match: Dinner options have included Kobe burgers, crab club sandwiches, stuffed chicken, Thai noodles, elk (!) tenderloin, grilled tuna, steak frites, and haddock in an almond-butter sauce. If you're in town on a Sunday, an attractive and popular Sunday brunch is served at the hotel's **Terrace** restaurant for C$30 per person—reservations are required.

1725 Market St., Halifax, NS B3J 3N9. ✆ **800/565-1567** or 902/425-1986. Fax 902/429-6048. www.princegeorgehotel.com. 206 units. C$149–C$299 double. AE, DC, DISC, MC, V. Valet parking C$25, self-parking C$20. **Amenities:** Restaurant; babysitting; concierge; Jacuzzi; indoor pool; limited room service; sauna. *In room:* A/C, TV, minibar, hair dryer.

MODERATE

Waverley Inn ★ The Waverley is adorned in high Victorian style, as befits its 1866 provenance. Flamboyant playwright Oscar Wilde was a guest here in 1882, and perhaps he had a hand in the decorating scheme? There's walnut trim, red upholstered furniture, and portraits of sourpuss Victorians at every turn. Headboards in the guest rooms are especially elaborate—some look like props from Gothic horror movies. Among the rooms, no. 130 has a unique Chinese wedding bed and a Jacuzzi, and it's one of about ten rooms in the inn with private Jacuzzis. Some rooms have canopy beds. The inn now also offers free Wi-Fi access in every room and a free Internet terminal in the lobby.

1266 Barrington St., Halifax, NS B3J 1Y5. ✆ **800/565-9346** or 902/423-9346. Fax 902/425-0167. www.waverleyinn.com. 34 units. Mid-May to Oct C$129–C$229 double; Nov to mid-May C$109–C$179 double. Rates include full breakfast, snacks, afternoon tea, and parking. DC, MC, V. *In room:* A/C, TV, hair dryer (some units), Jacuzzi (some units), no phone (some units).

INEXPENSIVE

The 75-bed **Halifax Heritage House Hostel** (✆ **902/422-3863**) is located at 1253 Barrington St., within walking distance of many downtown attractions including the city farmer's market and a number of convivial bars. You'll usually share rooms with other travelers (several private and family rooms are available, though); there are lockers in each room, shared bathrooms for all, and a shared, fully equipped kitchen. Bring coins for the Internet terminals and the coin-op laundry. Rates are C$26 and up per person in dormitories, C$57 and up for a double bed in a private room.

A short distance from downtown, but convenient to bus lines, are the dorm rooms at **Dalhousie University** (✆ **888/271-9222** or 902/494-8840), which rents out a range of one-, two-, and three-bedroom units when school isn't in session from mid-May through mid-August.

Where to Dine

EXPENSIVE

Bish World Cuisine ★★★ 🎁 FUSION Maurizio strikes again! The culinary wizard behind the popular daMaurizio (see below) in The Brewery market daringly opened a second high-tone eatery—across the street from his first—and, against the odds in a tough economic moment, it's already supplanting his original fine-dining establishment as the "in" place. Tucked into a harborside location at the back of the upscale Bishop's Landing development, Bish combines Asian and Continental influences to fine effect, much like a hot young chef in Tokyo or L.A. would do. Exhibit A: appetizers of panko-encrusted scallops with ponzu glazes; tuna tartare; jumbo shrimp with green curry, bok choy, and Thai basil; mussels and frites; oyster fritters served with horseradish crème fraîche; Dungeness crab cakes with a lime-chili aioli; and Southern-style barbeque ribs paired with Johnnycakes. Exhibit B: main courses of charred Atlantic salmon with carbonara sauce; miso sea bass with udon; bouillabaisse with garlic baguettes; Nova Scotia lobster over angelhair pasta; sesame-seared tuna; a local version of surf-and-turf (filet mignon and roasted lobster); duck à l'orange; sugarcane- and rum-lacquered pork loin; and a huge Angus rib steak with herbed frites, black and white ketchup (whatever that is), and sauteed wild mushrooms.

1475 Lower Water St. (in Bishop's Landing, entrance at end of Bishop St.). ✆ **902/425-7993.** Reservations highly recommended. Main courses C$28–C$39. AE, DC, MC, V. Mon–Sat 5:30–10pm.

daMaurizio ★★★ ITALIAN Everything daMaurizio touches turns to gold, even though it's no longer owned by its founder. Located inside a cleverly adapted former brewery, its vast space has been divided into a complex of hives with columns and exposed brick that add to the atmosphere and heighten the anticipation of the meal. The decor shuns fancy trimmings for simplicity. Start with an appetizer such as a bowl of San Marzano tomato soup with garlic, a plate of calamari quick-fried with tomato and chiles, a salad with grapefruit and candied walnuts, or some mussels in white wine. The main courses here tax even the most decisive diner: on a given night, *secondi* (pasta dishes) might include gnocchi with garlic and onions, penne with veal, or ravioli stuffed with lobster or mascarpone in a truffle cream sauce. But you're only getting started. The main courses might run to seared fillet of salmon served with mango, cucumber, and lime mostarda; grilled prime rib of pork, finished nicely with apricots, sherry, ginger, honey, and chili; handmade ravioli stuffed with braised beef and flavored with truffle oil; veal scaloppine with lobster and cream sauce; veal chops with sage and port wine sauce; a grilled pepper-crusted Angus tenderloin, flambéed with brandy, veal stock, and cream; a grilled rack of lamb served with a cabernet reduction; seared jumbo scallops; or branzino with a citrusy compote.

1479 Lower Water St. (in The Brewery). ✆ **902/423-0859.** Reservations highly recommended. Main courses C$27–C$34; pasta dishes C$10–C$16. AE, DC, MC, V. Mon–Sat 5–10pm.

MODERATE

O'Carroll's ★★ SEAFOOD/CONTINENTAL Is O'Carroll's the city's "Most Improved" in the past 5 years? Maybe. A dusky, Gaelic-influenced sort of spot laid out in white tablecloths, potted plants, and stained-glass lamps, it's still a good place for a filling seafood meal. But the kitchen has really changed directions recently, in the process becoming a lot fancier (and better) than the average fish house. Chef Colin Stone now serves inventive entrees in the dining room like seared Kobe beef, braised lamb, and cedar-planked salmon with a whisky-maple glaze. (Yes, they still serve steaks and big seafood medleys.) Lunch is equally classy, with lamb burgers, spring rolls, lobster ravioli, Malaysian shrimp curries—but also ribeye steaks, finnan haddie, Digby scallops, and local steamed lobsters. Even the pub section has gone upscale, eschewing greasy pub grub for smoked-chicken-and-pear salads and lobster bisque.

1860 Upper Water St. ✆ **902/423-4405.** Reservations recommended. Main courses C$8–C$19 at lunch, C$15–C$22 at dinner, C$10–C$14 in the pub. AE, MC, V. Restaurant daily 11am–2:30pm and 5–11pm; pub daily 11am–11pm; weekend hours may vary.

Ryan Duffy's STEAKHOUSE Located on the upper level of a small shopping mall on Spring Garden, Ryan Duffy's may at first strike you as a knockoff of an American chain such as Friday's or Olive Garden. It's not. The house specialty here is steak, for which the place is justly famous. The beef comes from corn-fed Hereford, Black Angus, and Shorthorn, and is nicely tender. Steaks are grilled over natural wood charcoal to order (no broiling here; Hallelujah), and can be dressed up with garlic, cilantro butter, or other extras as you wish. The more expensive cuts, such as the strip loin, are trimmed right at the table and are so juicy you might not need a knife. They'll even cook it "blue rare" if you want it that way. If you don't feel like steak, though, there's a lot less to get excited about on the menu here—bear that in mind.

5640 Spring Garden Rd. ✆ **902/421-1116.** Reservations recommended. Main courses C$9–C$15 at lunch, C$19–C$38 at dinner. AE, DC, MC, V. Mon–Fri 11:30am–2pm and 5–10pm; Sat–Sun 5–10pm.

Saege Bistro ★★ FUSION Here's an up-and-coming star to watch on the Halifax scene: Geir Simensen's Saege Bistro, a member of the family-owned catering team that handles the Cheapside Café (see below). Think of it as "Scandinavia meets Canada" (with a sprinkling from the rest of the world). Lunches run to Norwegian fish cakes, corn-crusted crab cakes, schnitzel, Asian stir-fries, lobster ravioli with pesto cream, and mussels steamed in Calvados; dinners to bouillabaisse, seared Digby scallops, pork chops, cumin rack of lamb, and salmon with coconut and peach chutney—not to mention plenty of interesting pizzas and pastas. Dessert could be a lemon flan, a gianduja torte, a pistachio mousse with mango sorbet, or a chile-and-chocolate *pot de crème*—yum. Saege also does a nice and extremely affordable Sunday **brunch** ★ with items like real muesli, huevos rancheros, and brioche French toast filled with apple chutney. I hope this place has staying power.

5883 Spring Garden Rd. ✆ **902/429-1882.** www.saege.ca. Reservations recommended. Main courses C$9–C$21 at lunch, C$15–C$26 at dinner. AE, DC, MC, V. Tues–Fri 11:30am–10pm; Sat–Sat 9:30am–10pm; Sun 9:30am–9pm.

INEXPENSIVE

Morris East ★★ (✆ **902/444-7663;** www.morriseast.com), an excellent thin-crust pizza joint (though it's fancier than "joint" suggests), uses a wood-fired oven; sometimes you can smell the place before you can see it. It's at 5212 Morris St. on the west side, about a block from Henry House (see below).

Cheapside Café ★★ ☺ CAFE Yes, it's cheap, but that's not the point; the name actually comes from an open market that once occupied this street, named after a similar market in London. This cheerful and lively cafe is tucked inside the Provincial Building, one of two structures housing the Art Gallery of Nova Scotia, and it's a fantastic find. Run by the same proprietress as the late, lamented Sweet Basil Bistro, it's my place of choice in downtown Halifax for sandwiches and sweets. The interior is almost like a small museum, with fun artwork on the walls and table settings. The daily card of soups and sandwiches might feature choices like jerked pork tenderloin on rye with an apple-blackberry compote, open-faced shrimp sandwiches with dill mayonnaise, phyllo with chevre and mushrooms, or grilled red pepper and Portobello sandwiches. And desserts really are over the top.

1723 Hollis St. (inside the Art Gallery of Nova Scotia). ✆ **902/425-4494.** Sandwiches and entrees C$9–C$12. MC, V. Tues–Sat 10am–5pm (Thurs to 8pm); Sun 11am–2:30pm.

Cheelin ★ CHINESE Possibly Halifax's best Chinese restaurant, Cheelin manages to achieve a seemingly improbable balance between authentic Asian cuisine and a funkier, Haligonian vibe. The Szechuan- and Beijing-influenced kitchen serves normally hard-to-find dishes like *mapo* tofu (spicy tofu, cubed and stir-fried, often mixed with ground pork or beef) and *yu xiang* pork (pork with Szechuan sauce, usually made from some combination of ginger, garlic, sesame, vinegar, or fish flavoring). Yet the brightly painted, pastel interior and the hip young staff and crowd—plus a few hip dishes like scallops with mango sauce—tell you that you're in Halifax. They deliver to downtown hotels.

1496 Lower Water St. (inside The Brewery). ✆ **902/422-2252.** Most items C$10–C$15. AE, MC, V. Mon 11am–2:30pm; Tues–Sat 11am–2:30pm and 5:30–10pm; Sun 5:30–10pm.

Henry House ★ BREWPUB Eastern Canada's first brewpub is housed in an austere building on the far western reaches of Barrington Street, down near the youth hostel. The starkly handsome 1834 stone building in which it's housed has a medium-fancy dining room upstairs with red tablecloths and captains' chairs, plus a pub downstairs that's more informal (and louder). You can order off the same menu at either spot, and the food's mostly what you'd expect at a brewpub, though better-tasting. Entrees could include beer-battered fish, salmon, steak sandwiches, a smoked-salmon club sandwich, burgers, beef-and-beer stew, fish cakes with beans, or a chicken-and-leek pie. The half-dozen locally brewed beers here are fresh and good, as is the black-and-tan and amber-and-tan.

1222 Barrington St. ✆ **902/423-5660.** www.henryhouse.ca. Main courses C$8–C$15. AE, DC, MC, V. Mon–Sat 11:30am–12:30am; Sun noon–11pm.

Il Mercato ★★ ITALIAN Another leg in the daMaurizio Bish empire, this fun bistro features light-colored Tuscan sponged walls and big rustic terra-cotta tiles on the floor, which set an appropriate mood amid the clamor of Spring Garden. I like this place a lot. Come early or else expect to wait (no reservations are accepted). You'll find a great selection of meals at prices that approach bargain level. Start by selecting antipasti from the deli counter in the front (you point; the waitstaff will bring them to your table). The focaccias are superb and come with salad, while the ravioli filled with roast chicken and wild mushrooms is sublime. There are plenty of pastas and thin-crust pizzas on the menu, too, while non-Italian entrees include a grilled rack of lamb with Dijon, veal scallopine, a seafood medley cooked up with peppers, and a strip steak topped with gorgonzola. The desserts, Italian coffees, aperitifs, and cocktails are similarly tasty. Try a toffee crunch, a chocolate tart, a sambuca, a Campari, or an espresso if you like—but save room for the fantastic homemade gelati, too.

5650 Spring Garden Rd. ✆ **902/422-2866.** www.il-mercato.ca. Reservations not accepted. Main courses and pastas C$10–C$20. AE, DC, MC, V. Mon–Sat 11am–11pm.

Steve-O-Reno's ★ CAFE Tucked on a quaint side street off Spring Garden Road, this coffee shop is also a popular lunch stop for the locals. You'll have your choice of potent coffee and other beverages (such as chai tea latte), along with inventive fruit smoothies, a small selection of sandwiches and salads, and a pleasantly relaxed atmosphere. They do everything well and inexpensively, and the hip young staff is friendly and cheerful as can be. There's also a second, drive-through location of Steve-O's on Robie Street, open similar hours.

1536 Brunswick St. ✆ **902/429-3034.** Meals C$4–C$6. No credit cards. Mon–Sat 7:30am–6pm; Sun 8am–6pm.

Halifax by Night

THE PERFORMING ARTS **Shakespeare by the Sea** ★ (✆ **902/422-0295**) stages a whole line of bardic and non-bardic productions July through Labour Day at several alfresco venues around the city. Most are held at Point Pleasant Park, where the ruins of old forts and buildings are used as the stage settings for delightful performances, with the audience sprawled on the grass, many enjoying picnic dinners with their *Taming of the Shrew.* Shows are technically free, though the players suggest a donation of C$15. The occasional more elaborate productions at other locations (past shows have included *King Lear* at the Citadel and *Titus Andronicus* at the park's Martello tower) have limited seating, with ticket prices that might range up to C$30.

The Neptune Theatre, 1593 Argyle St. (✆ **902/429-7070;** www.neptunetheatre.com), benefited from a big, multimillion-dollar renovation and now also runs an intimate 200-seat studio theater. Top-notch dramatic productions are offered throughout the year. (The main season runs September through May, with a summer season filling in the gap with eclectic performances.) Main-stage tickets range generally from around C$15 to C$45.

THE CLUB & BAR SCENE

Halifax's young and thirsty congregate in pubs, nightclubs, and on street corners along two streets that converge at the public library: Grafton Street and Spring Garden Road. **Economy Shoe Shop** (✆ **902/423-7463**), at 1663 Argyle St., is a cafe-bar where many of Halifax's prettiest people wind up sooner or later. In the evening (and late afternoons on Sat), you'll find lively Maritime music and good beer at the **Lower Deck Pub** (✆ **902/425-1501**) in the Historic Properties complex on the waterfront. There's music nightly, and on Saturday afternoons (out on the patio in summer). Local rock bars include the **Marquee Club** at 2037 Gottingen St. (✆ **902/429-3020**). **The Maxwell's Plum** at 1600 Grafton St. (✆ **902/423-5090**) is an English pub where peanut shells litter the floor and patrons quaff from a list of dozens of 150 import and Canadian draft and bottled beers.

Also check out ***The Coast,*** a free newspaper widely available around town, for good listings of upcoming performances.

THE EASTERN SHORE

Heading from Halifax to Cape Breton Island (or vice versa), you need to choose between two routes. If you're burning to get to your destination, take **Route 102** to Route 104 (the Trans-Canada Highway, the one with the maple leaf). If you're in no particular hurry and are more content venturing down narrow lanes, destination unknown, though, allow a couple of days to wind along the Eastern Shore, mostly along **Route 7.** (Official tourism material refers to this stretch as the Marine Drive.) Along the way you'll be rewarded with glimpses of a rugged coastline that's wilder and more remote than the coast south of Halifax. Gas up: Communities here are farther apart, less genteel, and stocked with far fewer services—or tourists.

Essentials

GETTING THERE Routes 107 and 7 run along or near the coast from Dartmouth to Stillwater (near Sherbrooke). Other local routes—including numbers 211, 316, 16, and 344—continue onward along the coast to the causeway to Cape Breton. An excursion along the entire coastal route—from Dartmouth to Cape Breton Island with a detour to Canso—is about 400km (250 miles) in length. Driving time would vary wildly, depending on your capacity for making detours.

VISITOR INFORMATION Several tourist information centers are staffed along the route. You'll find the best stocked and most helpful centers in **Sheet Harbour** inside the **MacPhee House Museum** (next to the waterfall; ✆ **902/885-2595**); in **Sherbrooke Village,** in the little yellow building at the entrance to the historic complex that also serves as the museum's info center (✆ **902/522-2400**); and in **Canso** at 1297 Union St., on the waterfront (✆ **902/366-2170**). All are open daily in summer.

A Driving Tour of the Eastern Shore

This section assumes you'll drive northeastward from Halifax toward Cape Breton. If you're traveling the opposite direction, just hold this book upside down. (I'm kidding.)

Between Halifax and Sheet Harbour, the route plays hide-and-seek with the coast, touching coastal views periodically and then veering inland again. The most scenic areas are around wild, open-vista **Ship Harbour** and **Spry Harbour,** noted for its attractive older homes and the islands looming offshore.

At the **Fisherman's Life Museum** (✆ **902/889-2053**) in Jeddore Oyster Pond, you'll get a glimpse of life on the Eastern Shore a century ago. The humble white-shingle-and-green-trim cottage was built by James Myers in the 1850s; early in this century it became the property of his youngest son, Ervin, who raised a dozen daughters here—a popular stop for local boys, evidently—and the home and grounds have been restored to look as they might have around 1900 or 1920. It's replete with hooked rugs and a reproduction pump organ, among other period touches. A walk through the house and barn and down to the fishing dock won't take much more than 20 minutes or so. The museum is open June through mid-October, daily, from 9am until 5pm. Admission is C$3.50 adults, C$2.50 seniors and children age 6 to 17, C$7.75 families. It's located on Route 7 and is well marked.

At the town of Lake Charlotte you can opt for a side road that weaves along the coast (look for signs for Clam Harbour). The road alternately follows wooded coves and passes through inland forests; about midway you'll see signs for a turn to **Clam Harbour Beach Park ★**, one of the best beaches on this coast. A long, broad crescent beach attracts sunbathers and swimmers from Halifax and beyond; it also helps that there's a boardwalk, clean sand, and toilets and changing rooms here, plus lifeguards supervising the action on summer weekends.

Between Ship and Spry harbours is the town of Tangier, home to the great tour outfit **Coastal Adventures** (✆ **877/404-2774** or 902/772-2774), which specializes in kayak tours. It's run by Scott Cunningham, who literally wrote the book on Nova Scotia kayaking (he's the author of the definitive guide to paddling this coast). This well-run operation is situated on a beautiful island-dotted part of the coast, but it specializes in multiday trips throughout Atlantic Canada. You can write (P.O. Box 77, Tangier, NS B0J 3H0) or call for a brochure well in advance of your trip, or check the company's website at **www.coastaladventures.com.**

There's also a terrific little fish-smoking business just outside Tangier, **J. Willie Krauch & Sons ★** (✆ **800/758-4412** or 902/772-2188). The Krauch family (pronounced *craw,* not *crotch,* thank goodness) sells wood-smoked Atlantic salmon, mackerel, and eel in an unpretentious little store; they'll also give you a tour of the premises, if you like, where you can check out the old-style smoking process in action. Take some to go for a picnic. It's open until around 6pm daily.

Continuing northeast, **Sheet Harbour** is a pleasant little town of 800 or so souls, with a campground open May through September, a couple small grocery stores, two motels, and a **visitor information center** (✆ **902/885-2595**), behind which is a short nature trail and boardwalk that descends along low, rocky cascades. Inland from Sheet Harbour on Route 374 you can find the **Liscomb Game Sanctuary,** a popular destination for the sort of hearty explorers who come equipped with their own maps, compasses, canoes, and fishing rods. (There are few services to speak of here.)

Way out on the eastern tip of Nova Scotia's mainland is the end-of-the-world town of **Canso** (pop. 900), which is currently in the process of being assimilated by the bigger nearby village of Guysborough, but no matter. It's still a rough-edged fishing town and oil port, windswept and foggy. The main attraction here is the ruined fort at the **Grassy Island National Historic Site** (✆ **902/295-2069**). A park-run boat takes you out to the island, which once housed a bustling community of fishermen and traders from New England, where a small interpretive center on the waterfront (open daily 10am to 6pm June to mid-September) features artifacts recovered from the island and boat schedules. Admission to the island and park are by voluntary donation in a box; pay what you wish.

If you're coming to Canso in summer, also watch out for the annual music festival held the first week of July to honor late Canadian folk musician Stan Rogers, who perished in an airline fire in Cincinnati in 1983 at the age of just 33. The **Stan Rogers Folk Festival** (✆ **888/554-7826;** www.stanfest.com), also known in these parts as StanFest, focuses on the craft of songwriting. But big names do sometimes play here. Day passes start at C$33 per adult.

Route 16 between the intersection of Route 316 and Guysborough is an especially **scenic drive.** This road runs high and low along brawny hills, giving soaring views of Chedabucto Bay and grassy hills across the way. Also pleasant, although not quite as distinguished, is Route 344 from Guysborough to the Canso causeway. That road twists, turns, and drops through woodlands with some nice views of the strait. It might make you wish you were the owner of a large and powerful motorcycle.

Sherbrooke Village ★★ ☺ About half of the town of Sherbrooke comprises Sherbrooke Village, a historic section surrounded by low fences, water, and fields. You'll have to pay admission to wander around, but the price is well worth it: This is the largest restored village in all of Nova Scotia, and is unique in several respects. For one, almost all the buildings here are on their original sites (only two have been moved). That's very rare in museums like this. Second, many of the homes are still occupied by local residents—and other private homes are interspersed with the ones open to visitors. So it's not just a historic exhibit. About two dozen buildings have been restored and opened to the public, from a convincing general store to an operating blacksmith shop and post office. Look also for the former temperance hall, courthouse, printery, boatbuilding shop, drugstore, and schoolhouse. All are capably staffed by genial interpreters in costume, who can tell you what life was like around here from the 1860s forward. Be sure to ask about the source of the town's early prosperity; you might be surprised. You could easily spend up to a half-day here, depending on your (or your kids') interest level.

Rte. 7, Sherbrooke. ✆ **888/743-7845** or 902/522-2400. http://museum.gov.ns.ca/sv. Admission C$10 adults, C$8 seniors, C$4.25 children age 6 to 17, C$28 families. June to mid-Oct daily 9:30am–5pm.

Where to Stay & Dine

Liscombe Lodge Resort ★★ ☺ This modern complex, owned and operated by the province, consists of a central lodge plus a series of smaller cottages and outbuildings. It's situated on a remote part of the coast, adjacent to hiking trails and a popular boating area at the mouth of the Liscomb River. The lodge bills itself as a nature lover's resort, and indeed it offers access to both forest and sea. But it's not exactly wilderness here; the well-tended lawns, modern architecture, shuffleboard, marina, free Wi-Fi, and outdoor chessboard testify to the middle-to-upper income summer-campness of the place. What makes it great for vacationing families are the tons of kid-friendly offerings (table tennis, horseshoe pitches, and so forth). Outdoor types will enjoy the guided kayak trips, hikes, and bird watches. Rooms here are modern and motel-like; the cottages and chalets have multiple bedrooms: again, good for families. The dining room is open to the public and serves resort fare (steaks, fish).

Rte. 7, Liscomb Mills, NS B0J 2A0. ✆ **800/665-6343** or 902/779-2307. Fax 902/779-2700. www.signatureresorts.com. 54 units. C$140–C$350 double. Packages and meal plans available. AE, DC, DISC, MC, V. Closed mid-Oct to mid-May. Pets allowed in chalets. **Amenities:** Restaurant; free bikes; fitness center; indoor pool; whirlpool; sauna; shuffleboard; tennis court. *In room:* TV, VCR (some units), fridge (some units), hair dryer, no phone.

SeaWind Landing Country Inn ★★ What to do when your boatbuilding business tanks because the fish no longer bite? How about opening an inn? That's what a local couple did, and this lovely 8-hectare (20-acre) oceanfront compound was the happy result. (They sold the property in 2008, but the original feel remains intact.) Some of the guest rooms are located in the handsome, 130-year-old home, which has been tastefully modernized and updated. The rest are in a more recent outbuilding, whose rooms feature a whitewashed brightness, terrific peninsula and ocean views, and double Jacuzzis. (Pay less than C$100 for a room with a Jacuzzi? Here, yes.) The innkeepers are very knowledgeable about local art—much of the work on display in the inn was created locally—and they have compiled a literate, helpful guide to the region for guests. The property also has three private sand beaches, and coastal boat tours and picnic lunches can be arranged for an extra charge. The inn also serves dinner as part of some of its packages, featuring local products and wines.

1 Wharf Rd., Charlos Cove, NS B0H 1T0. ✆ **800/563-4667.** www.seawindlanding.com. 10 units. C$95–C$169 double. Packages available. AE, MC, V. Closed mid-Oct to mid-May. **Amenities:** Dining room. *In room:* Hair dryer, Jacuzzi (most units), no phone.

CAPE BRETON ISLAND ★★★

Isolated and craggy Cape Breton Island—Nova Scotia's northernmost land mass—should be tops on a list of don't-miss destinations for travelers to Nova Scotia, especially those who like outdoor adventures or great views. The island's chief draw is **Cape Breton Highlands National Park,** a knockout park up at the top of the island's western lobe. There's also the historic fort at **Louisbourg** and scenic **Bras d'Or Lake,** an inland saltwater lake that nearly cleaves the island in two. Above all, there are the drives: It's hard to find a road on this island that's *not* a scenic route. Some of the vistas are wild and dramatic, some green and pastoral, but all of them will have you clicking your camera furiously.

For convenience, I've divided this section into two parts: one on the bulk of Cape Breton Island, and then one on Cape Breton Highlands National Park itself. (For specific information on the park, jump ahead to the next section on p. 101.)

Essentials

GETTING THERE Cape Breton Island lies across the Canso Causeway, 262km (163 miles) from the New Brunswick border at Amherst and 272km (169 miles) from Halifax—a little less than 3 hours' drive from either point if you take the fastest route. After the causeway, it then takes 2 to 3 hours to reach the national park; Baddeck, Mabou, the Margaree Valley, and Louisbourg can be reached in 1 to 2 hours' driving.

VISITOR INFORMATION A number of tiny local tourist information centers dot Cape Breton Island, but you're best off grabbing a pile of info at the bustling **Port Hastings Info Centre** (✆ **902/625-4201**), which is on your right just after you cross the causeway onto the island. It's open daily from around 8am until about 8:30pm most of the year, closed only from January through April.

SPECIAL EVENTS **Celtic Colours ★★★** (✆ **877/285-2321** or 902/562-6700; www.celtic-colours.com) is a big, island-wide annual music shindig timed to approximate the peak of the lovely highland foliage in early October. Few tourists know about it, and the concentration of local Celtic musicians getting together for good times and music beneath lovely foliage is simply breathtaking if you're into this sort of thing. It usually begins in the second week of October and lasts more than 10 days: a foot-stompin', pennywhistlin', fiddle-playin' 10 days. *Ceilidh* nights (see below) cost about C$20, and popular local performers sell out months in advance; check the website or call well ahead if you've got your heart set on a particular act. Otherwise, just buy a ticket to anything. You can't go wrong. Stages and venues are scattered all over Cape Breton Island, but the heaviest concentration of events takes place near the festival headquarters in Sydney.

Mabou & Vicinity ★★

The little village of Mabou sits on a deep, protected inlet along the island's western shore. This former coal-mining town has made itself over as a lobster-fishing town, though you don't come here for crustaceans; the seafood is shipped out to Halifax. Instead, come for lovely scenery and culture. The town itself consists of a short main street, a clump of homes, a gas station, a few eateries and services, plus (if you can find it) a scenic little beach.

Local residents are strongly oriented toward **music**; this tiny town has produced not only several international hit Celtic music acts and a former premier of Nova Scotia (Rodney MacDonald), a step dancer and fiddler who was elected in 2006. Evening entertainment here revolves around fiddle playing, square dancing, and the traditional gathering of musicians and storytellers known as a ***ceilidh*** ★★★ (*kay-lee*). These planned and impromptu musical events take place in pubs, civic buildings, outdoors, people's homes . . . anywhere. To find out what's going on, stop by the village **grocery store, The Mull** pub right across the street, or the **Red Shoe** pub (see "Where to Dine," below) and scope out their bulletin boards and calendars. You might also check with the **Strathspey Place Theatre** (✆ **902/945-5300;** www.strathspeyplace.com) on Route 19. It offers occasional Celtic music events too, usually for C$15 to C$20.

In a handsome valley between Mabou and Inverness is the distinctive post-and-beam **Glenora Distillery** ★ (✆ **800/839-0491** or 902/258-2662). This modern distillery—North America's only single-malt whisky ("scotch") producer—began producing spirits from the pure local stream in 1990, and selling it in 2000. Production runs take place each fall, but tours of the facility are offered throughout the year. Tours cost C$7 and last about a half-hour (offered daily 9am–5pm), culminating in welcome free samples; they also conveniently end near the gift shop, where you can buy local music CDs, gift glasses, even bottles of the whisky itself (for at least C$80 a pop).

WHERE TO STAY

Glenora Inn & Distillery ★★ When was the last time you spent the night sleeping next to a huge illicit stash of moonshine? Okay, I exaggerate. A little. This distiller of single-malt whisky (see above) offers nine modern hotel rooms over a courtyard next to a pub, beside the distillery. They're contemporary yet rustic, with easy access to said pub and a restaurant (which often feature live performers from the area). There are also a half-dozen attractive log chalets, of one to three bedrooms each, with woody interiors on the hills overlooking the distillery. These are perfect for either lovebirds or families. Each chalet has a Jacuzzi, satellite TV, and wonderful view of the mist-covered valley below. It all has the feel of being tucked in a remote vale in the Scottish Highlands. Note that the inn's pub doesn't open until mid-June, the restaurant until early July.

Rte. 19, Glenville, NS B0E 1X0. ✆ **800/839-0491.** www.glenoradistillery.com. 15 units. C$125–C$175 double; C$175–C$295 chalet. AE, MC, V. Closed mid-Oct to mid-May. **Amenities:** Restaurant; bar. *In room:* TV, Jacuzzi (some units).

Mabou River Inn ★★ 🎁 Located not far from the river and adjacent to the Mother of Sorrows Pioneer Shrine (dedicated to the settlers of the Mabou area), this former boarding school was converted twice, first into a winning youth hostel and then into this homey little inn just off the main road. Hosts Donna and David Cameron keep things running smoothly and dispense great advice; nature lovers will appreciate the opportunity to hike, kayak, fish, and mountain-bike on the scenic Ceilidh Trail using the inn's rental equipment, while night owls can stroll a few minutes across the bridge and into town to check out the local traditional music offerings

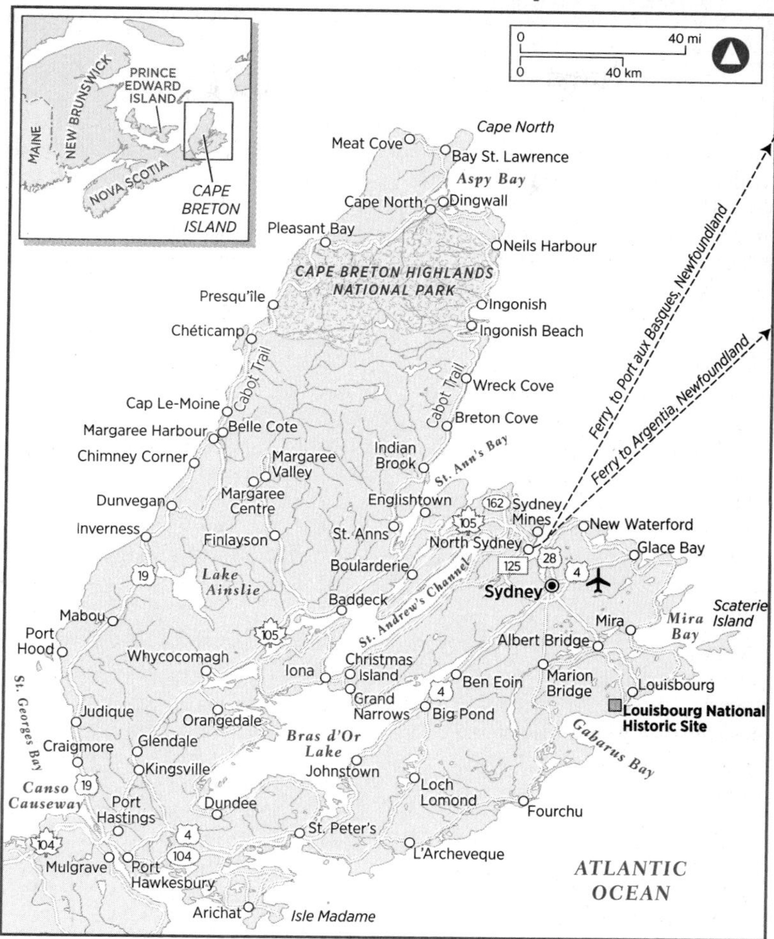

that fill Mabou in summer. Note that while all nine of the main inn rooms come with their own private bathrooms, you need to put on your slippers and walk to get to seven of them. There are also three two-bedroom apartment suites good for families, since they come with TVs, VCRs, kitchens, and phones. The kitchen and dining room for guests are useful: at night the staff cooks up good pizzas and serves beer and wine with them.

19 Southwest Ridge Rd. (P.O. Box 255), Mabou, NS B0E 1X0. ✆ **888/627-9744** or 902/945-2356. Fax 902/945-2605. www.mabouriverinn.com. 12 units. C$89–C$99 double; C$135–C$145 suite. AE, MC, V. **Amenities:** Restaurant; bike and sea kayak rentals. *In room:* TV/VCR (some units), kitchenette (some units), no phone (some units).

WHERE TO DINE

The Red Shoe Pub ★★ CANADIAN You can't find a more local pub than "the Shoe" (as it's known here), owned by the famous Rankin family of musicians and open from June through mid-October. I remember when this was a gloriously hazy dive of fiddle music, cigarette smoke, sassy waitresses, and heavy pub fare. Not now: The province is smoke-free, and the menu has been completely revamped—you can get a goat-cheese panini, a pulled-pork sandwich, some beautifully caloric Nova Scotia poutine, a bowl of seafood chowder with cheddar biscuits, steak frites, or char-broiled salmon. There are requisite ales on tap and in bottles, of course. The real highlight, though, is the daily scheduled musical performances in the pub—the next Celtic music star might be playing for a small donation or cover charge on the night you swing by.

Main St. (Hwy. 19), Mabou. ✆ **902/945-2996.** Entrees C$9–C$19. MC, V. June–mid Oct Mon–Wed daily 11:30am–11pm; Thurs–Sat 11:30am–2am; Sun noon–11pm.

Margaree Valley ★

West of Baddeck and south of Chéticamp, the **Margaree Valley** consists of the area from the village called Margaree Valley (near the headwaters of the Margaree River) to Margaree Harbor, downriver on Cape Breton's west coast. Some seven small Margaree-themed communities are clustered along this valley floor, a world apart from the rugged drama of the surf-battered coast—it's more reminiscent of Vermont than Maine. In autumn, the foliage here is often among eastern Canada's best.

The **Margaree River** is a bona fide celebrity in fishing circles—widely regarded as one of the most productive Atlantic salmon rivers in North America, and the salmon have continued to return to spawn here in recent years, which is unfortunately *not* the case on many other waterways of Atlantic Canada. The river has been closed to all types of fishing except fly-fishing since the 1880s, and in 1991 it was designated a Canadian Heritage River.

Learn about the river's heritage at the **Margaree Salmon Museum ★** (✆ **902/248-2848**) in North East Margaree. The handsome museum building features a brief video about the life cycle of the salmon, and its exhibits include fishermen photos, antique rods (including an impressive 16-footer), examples of seized poaching equipment—plus hundreds of skillfully hand-tied salmon flies. (You've got to be a buff to appreciate those, maybe.) If you want to fish, museum docents can help you find a guide to bring you out on the river; late spring and early fall are usually the times of year when the fish are biting. The museum is open daily mid-June through mid-October, 9am to 5pm. Admission is C$2 per adult, C$1 per child.

Also make a point of dropping by **Cape Breton Clay ★★** (✆ **902/235-2467;** www.capebretonclay.com), northeast of the salmon museum. Margaree Valley native Bell Fraser's work is truly unique. Fish, crab, lobster, starfish, ear of corn, and other motifs are worked into her platters and bowls in ways that surprise and delight. The shop is open from June through mid-October, 10am to 5pm, and it's definitely worth a stop; individual pieces might run from C$60 to C$300.

WHERE TO STAY

The Normaway Inn ★ Down a drive lined with Scotch pines, the Normaway is a throwback—though it's catching up with the times now. Built in 1928 and run by the same family since the 1940s, it was once the sort of place anglers dressed in tweed. It's no longer a luxury getaway; families and honeymooners come to the

500-acre compound for fresh air, quiet, and local music. Ten rooms are situated in the main lodge, which is rugged in a loveable stonework-and-exposed beam way; first-floor rooms, which are bigger and have corner windows, are probably the best of the lot. There are also 17 cottages spread around the property—configurations and views vary considerably; none have kitchens or air-conditioning, but newer cottages have touches like whirlpool tubs, and all but two have woodstoves. The newest additions are three expensive suites in the MacPherson House, about a quarter-mile from the lodge. Expect barn dances, simplicity, weak Wi-Fi, and the odd mosquito in your cabin.

P.O. Box 121, Margaree Valley, NS B0E 2C0. ✆ **800/565-9463** or 902/248-2987. Fax 902/248-2600. www.normaway.com. 30 units. C$99–C$149 double; C$179–C$269 suite; C$139–C$189 cottage. 2-night minimum stay (some dates) July–Aug. MAP meal plans available. DC, MC, V. Closed late Oct to May. Pets allowed in cottages only. **Amenities:** Dining room; free bikes; tennis court. *In room:* No phone.

Chéticamp

The Acadian town of **Chéticamp** is the western gateway to Cape Breton Highlands National Park, and the center of French-speaking culture on Cape Breton. The change is rather obvious as you drive northward from Margaree Harbour—the family names suddenly go from MacDonald to Doucet, and the cuisine turns on its head all at once. The town is an assortment of restaurants, boutiques, and tourist establishments spread along a Main Street closely hugging the harbor. A winding **boardwalk ★** follows harbor's edge through much of town, and this is a great spot to stretch your legs from the drive and have a look at the local geography. Chéticamp Island sits just across the water; the mighty coastal hills of the national park are visible just up the coast.

Chéticamp is famous worldwide for its hooked rugs, a craft perfected here by the early Acadian settlers. Those curious about the craft should allow time for a stop at Les Trois Pignons, which houses the **Elizabeth LeFort Gallery** and **the Hooked Rug Museum ★** (✆ **902/224-2642;** www.lestroispignons.com). It is located on Main Street in the north end of town and displays some 300 fine tapestries, many created by Elizabeth LeFort, who was Canada's premier rug-hooking artist for many decades until she passed away in 2005—check out her tableau of U.S. presidents from 1959, which required 1.7 *million* loops to be hooked. You can also view tools used for the craft. The museum and gallery are usually open from mid-May to early October, daily 9am to 5pm (until 7pm in July and August). Admission is C$5 per adult, C$4 for seniors, C$3.50 students, C$12 for families, and free for children 5 and under.

In the 1930s, artisans formed the **Co-operative Artisanale de Chéticamp,** located at 5067 Main St. (✆ **902/224-2170**). A selection of hooked rugs—from tiny ones on up—are sold here, along with other trinkets and souvenirs. There's often a weaver or other craftsperson at work in the shop. A small local museum downstairs (admission is free) chronicles the life and times of the early Acadian settlers and their descendants. It's closed from mid-October to May.

WHERE TO STAY

A handful of motels service the thousands of travelers who pass through each summer. **Laurie's Motor Inn,** on Main Street (✆ **800/959-4253** or 902/224-2400), has more than 50 motel rooms and newer suites in a string of buildings situated right in town; rates run from C$99 to C$299 per night (mostly toward the lower end of that range). The inn also manages some nice rental homes and apartments around town for longer stays; inquire if you're interested in something bigger or need cooking facilities.

Pilot Whale Chalets ★ These spare, modern cottages each have at least two bedrooms and full housekeeping facilities, including microwaves, TVs, VCRs, gas barbecues for firing up steaks, coffeemakers, decks, and woodstoves; some even have Jacuzzis and fireplaces, as well. They're plain but attractive, and their best feature is the great view northward toward the coastal mountains. The lodge has also added some basement apartment suites to several of the cottages, which does impinge upon the privacy of both cottage dwellers and suite dwellers. All rooms now have phones, DVD players, and tubs; for more space and comfort, ask about the three-bedroom cottage with king beds, two bathrooms with whirlpools, Wi-Fi, and a private laundry—it sleeps up to six people. A small beach sits adjacent to the hotel property.

Rte. 19, Chéticamp, NS B0E 1H0. ✆ **902/224-1040.** Fax 902/224-1540. www.pilotwhalechalets.com. 13 units. C$95–C$115 double; C$159–C$249 cabin. AE, MC, V. *In room:* TV/VCR/DVD, kitchenette (some units), Jacuzzi (some units).

WHERE TO DINE

La Boulangerie Aucoin (✆ **902/224-3220**) has been a staple of Chéticamp daily life since the 1950s. Located just off the Cabot Trail between the town and the national park (look for signs), the place is full of fresh-baked goods; ask what's just out of the oven when you get to the counter. Among the potential options: croissants, scones, fresh bread, and (yum) berry pies. This is a great place to fuel up on snacks before setting off into the park.

Restaurant Acadien ACADIAN This local restaurant is attached to a crafts shop on the south side of town (the Co-operative Artisanale; see above) and has the feel of a cafeteria. Servers wear costumes inspired by traditional Acadian dress, and the menu draws heavily on tried-and-true Acadian cuisine, just as you'd expect it to. Look for *fricot* (a sort of chicken-and-potato soup), stewed potatoes, and the meat pies for which this region is renowned. They also do lobster, fried fish, turkey dinners, and other more traditionally Anglo fare. Also on the menu: baked beans, bottled beer, blood pudding (for the brave of heart) and butterscotch and blueberry pies (among others).

15067 Main St. ✆ **902/224-3207.** Reservations recommended. Breakfast items C$3.50–C$5; lunch and dinner entrees C$4–C$17. AE, MC, V. Daily 7am–9pm. Closed Nov to mid-May.

Ingonish ★

The Ingonish area includes a gaggle of similarly named towns—Ingonish Centre, Ingonish Ferry, South Ingonish Harbour—which collectively add up to a population of perhaps 1,300 or so (on a good day). Like Chéticamp on the peninsula's east side, Ingonish serves as a gateway to the national park and is home to a park visitor information center and a handful of motels and restaurants. There's really no critical mass of services in any one of the villages, though—instead, they're spread along a lengthy stretch of the Trail. So you never quite feel you've arrived in town. You pass a liquor store, some shops, a bank, a post office, a handful of cottages. And that's it—suddenly you're there, in the wild park.

For golfers, the windswept **Highlands Links course ★★★** (✆ **800/441-1118** or 902/285-2600; www.highlandslinksgolf.com)—adjacent to the Keltic Lodge (see "Where to Stay," below) but under completely separate management—is considered one of the best in Nova Scotia, if not all of Atlantic Canada. It's a 6,600-yard, links-style course with stupendous views and some stupendously difficult holes. Peak-season rounds cost about C$90 per adult (C$27 to C$45 for children); spring and fall rates are about C$20 lower, and twilight rates are also available. Ask about packages whenever booking a hotel room in the area, and be sure to reserve your tee time in advance.

South of Ingonish, the **Cabot Trail** ★★★ climbs and descends the 1,000-ft. promontory of Cape Smokey, which explodes into panoramic views from the top. At the highest point, there's a free **provincial park**—really little more than a picnic area and a trailhead—where you can cool your engines and admire the views. A 10km (6-mile) hiking trail studded with unforgettable viewpoints leads to the tip of the cape along the high bluffs.

WHERE TO STAY

A number of serviceable cottage courts and motels are located in the area. (If you're booking by phone, be sure to find out *which* Ingonish you're staying in; the town names in this area all sound the same, which could create confusion.)

In addition to the choice below, **Glenghorm Beach Resort** in Ingonish (✆ **800/565-5660** or 902/285-2049) has about 75 units on a spacious 8-hectare (20-acre) property that fronts a sandy beach. Calling it a resort is a little bit of a stretch. Some rooms feature painted cinderblock walls and decor that's plain and a bit dated, though others feel a bit fresher and nicer. The expensive two-bedroom deluxe suite on the second floor is quite nice, though, featuring Jacuzzi tubs, kitchen units, and fireplaces. (Other suites are in a building out back, and aren't as nice.) Options include motel rooms and efficiencies, along with cottages and some elaborate suites. Prices are C$95 to C$129 for the motel rooms, C$115 to C$189 for the cottages, and C$195 to C$399 for one- and two-bedroom suites.

Keltic Lodge Resort & Spa ★★ ☺ Owned and operated by the province, the Keltic Lodge is reached after a dramatic drive through a grove of white birch trees and across an isthmus topping big cliffs. The vaguely Tudor-looking resort is also impressive at first glance, and the views are just extraordinary. Yet most rooms here remain furnished plainly, with run-of-the-mill motel-type furniture; you might expect more for the price. Some units are located in the more modern Inn at Keltic building a few hundred yards away. It has better views though a more sterile character. The cute log-cabinesque cottages are better, set among the birches—half with two bedrooms, half with four—but you'll need to share space with other travelers. If you rent one bedroom of a cottage, for instance, you'll share your living room with one to three other sets of guests; that may or may not be the sort of "resort" experience you wanted. Escape to the Highland Links golf course (see above), a spa (with full treatments, yoga classes, and a hair salon), or the nice heated outdoor swimming pool (with one of the best pool views in the province). The resort is nice to young kids, too—free meals, bedtime snacks, and various programs and recreational offerings.

Middle Head Peninsula, Ingonish Beach, NS B0C 1L0. ✆ **800/565-0444** or 902/285-2880. Fax 902/285-2859. www.kelticlodge.ca. 105 units. C$175–C$442 double and cottage. Rates include breakfast and dinner. Packages available. AE, DC, DISC, MC, V. Closed late Oct to late May. **Amenities:** 2 restaurants; lounge; children's programs; golf course; outdoor pool; spa. *In room:* A/C (2 units), TV, fridge (some units), fireplace (some units), hair dryer, no phone.

Baddeck

Although **Baddeck** (pronounced *Bah*-deck) is some distance from the national park, it's often considered the de facto "capital" of the Cabot Trail. That's not because the town is especially vibrant or fascinating; rather, it's partly because Baddeck is centrally positioned on the island, and partly because the main drag happens to offer more hotels, B&Bs, and restaurants than any other town on the loop. (That's how thinly populated it is up here.) There are also a clutch of practical services here you can't easily find on the Trail: grocery stores, Laundromats, gas stations, and the like.

Baddeck does have one claim to fame: For years, it was the summertime home of telephone inventor Alexander Graham Bell, now memorialized at a national historic site (see below). It's also a compact, easy town to explore by foot and is scenically located on the shores of big Bras d'Or (say bra-*door*) Lake. If you're on a tight schedule and plan to drive the Cabot Trail in just a day (figure on 6–8 hours), this might be the best place to bed down afterward, if only because it's on the way to Sydney and/or Louisbourg.

If, however, your intention is to spend a few days exploring the hiking trails, bold headlands, and remote coves of the Trail and the national park (which I certainly recommend), find an inn farther north; this town's single street can get claustrophobically packed with tourists and tour buses, and outside of Bell's home there's really little else to recommend doing here.

The friendly **Baddeck Welcome Center** (✆ **902/295-1911**) is located just south of the village at the intersection of routes 105 and 205. It's open daily from June through mid-October.

EXPLORING THE TOWN

Baddeck is much like a modern New England village, skinny and centered around a single main street (called Chebucto St. rather than Main St.) just off the lake. You can ask for a free walking-tour brochure at the welcome center, although a complete tour of all the highlights probably won't take you much more than 15 or 20 minutes.

Government Wharf (head down Jones St. from the Yellow Cello restaurant) is where you go for summer boat tours, the best way to experience Bras d'Or Lake up close. **Loch Bhreagh Boat Tours** (✆ **902/295-2016**), for one, offers thrice-daily sightseeing tours on a 13m (42-ft.) cruiser motorboat. They pass Alexander Graham Bell's palatial former estate and other attractions at this end of the lake. (Moonlight tours are available by arrangement, if you've got a big enough group together.)

About 180m (200 yards) offshore is **Kidston Island ★**, owned by the town of Baddeck. It has a wonderful sand beach with lifeguards and an old lighthouse to explore. The local Lion's Club offers frequent pontoon boat shuttles across St. Patrick's Channel, warm and clear weather permitting; the crossing is free, but donations are encouraged.

Alexander Graham Bell National Historic Site ★★ ☺ Each summer for much of his life, Alexander Graham Bell—of Scottish descent, but his family emigrated to Canada when he was young—fled the heat and humidity of Washington, D.C., for this hillside retreat perched above Bras d'Or Lake. The mansion, still owned and occupied by the Bell family, is visible across the harbor from various points around town. Today it's part homage, part science center. The modern exhibit center highlights Bell's amazing mind; you'll find exhibits on his invention of the telephone at age 29, of course, but also information about other projects: ingenious kites, hydrofoils, and airplanes, for instance. Bell also invented the metal detector—who knew? Science buffs will love the place, and most visitors are surprised to learn Bell actually died in this home. (He's buried on the mountaintop.) Then there's an extensive "discovery" section, where kids are encouraged to apply their intuition and creativity to science problems. All in all, it's a very well-thought-out attraction—and attractive, too.

Chebucto St., Baddeck. ✆ **902/295-2069.** Admission C$7.80 adults, C$6.55 seniors, C$3.90 youth age 6–16, C$20 families. June daily 9am–6pm; July to mid-Oct daily 8:30am–6pm; May and mid- to late Oct daily 9am–5pm. Late Oct to Apr by appointment only.

WHERE TO STAY & DINE

If the places below are booked, you could just as easily try **Auberge Gisele's Inn,** 387 Shore Rd. (✆ **800/304-0466** or 902/295-2849), a nicely modern 75-room hotel that's open May to late October and popular with bus tours; regular rooms cost C$115 to C$150, upgraded rooms and suites run from C$140 up as high as C$300 (with fireplace and Jacuzzi). There's also the cost-effective **Cabot Trail Motel** (✆ **902/295-2580**) on Route 105 about a mile west of Baddeck, with 38 motel units and four chalets overlooking the lake, a nice little heated outdoor pool, and private saltwater beach. Its rates run from C$95 to C$125 per night.

Green Highlander Lodge The Green Highlander is located atop the Yellow Cello, a popular eatery on Baddeck's main drag. The three rooms here are decorated in a sort of gentleman's fishing camp motif, quite simple but pleasing. Rooms are named after Atlantic salmon flies; Blue Charm has a private sitting room and blue-quilted twin beds, while all three have private decks with views looking out toward Kidston Island. Ask about moonlight paddle trips, kayak rentals, and the private beach located 2km (a mile) away. The inn also manages a cottage nearby, hewn in unvarnished wood paneling with a kitchenette and propane grill for al fresco cookery on the deck.

525 Chebucto St. (Box 128), Baddeck, NS B0E 1B0. ✆ **866/470-5333** or 902/295-2303. Fax 902/295-1592. www.greenhighlanderlodge.com. 3 units. C$90–C$120 double. Rates include full breakfast. AE, MC, V. Closed Nov to Apr. **Amenities:** Restaurant, kayak rentals. *In room:* TV, hair dryer.

Telegraph House ★ Rooms in this 1861 hotel on Baddeck's main street are divided between the original building, an annex of motel units on a hill behind it, and a set of cabins. This is actually where Alexander Graham Bell stayed when he first visited Baddeck. (Oddly enough, rooms here *don't* have phones; what would Bell think?) The bigger motel rooms in back are fairly charmless, but do have small decks with glimpses of the lake; some of the newest rooms in the main lodge now have lovely polished wood floors and whirlpool baths; you can even stay in Bell's room, a Victorian space of flowery wallpaper print. The cottages are quite small, yet they're as brightly furnished as a child's playroom, and come with air-conditioning and whirlpool tubs. The dining room serves breakfast plus straightforward lunches and dinners of meat, fish, fowl, and huge desserts. Fiddle and piano music sometimes fill the inn, and guests can linger on the front or side porches.

479 Chebucto St. (P.O. Box 8), Baddeck, NS B0E 1B0. ✆ **888/263-9840** or 902/295-1100. Fax 902/295-1136. www.baddeck.com/telegraph. 41 units. C$75–C$125 double; C$100–C$225 cottage. AE, MC, V. **Amenities:** Restaurant. *In room:* A/C (some units), TV (some units), Jacuzzi (some units), no phone.

Louisbourg ★★

Louisbourg, on Cape Breton's remote and windswept easternmost coast, was once one of Canada's most impressive French settlements. Despite its brief prosperity and durable construction, the colony basically disappeared after the British forced the French out (for the second and final time) in 1760. Through the miracle of archaeology and historic reconstruction, much of the imposing settlement has now been re-created, and today this is among Canada's most ambitious national historic parks.

However, a visit does require some effort. This attraction isn't on the way to anyplace else, and it's a very long and inconvenient detour from the National Park. Only go if you're craving an Acadian history fix.

EXPLORING THE VILLAGE

The hamlet of Louisbourg—which you pass through en route to the historic park—is low-key. A short **boardwalk** with interpretive signs runs along the town's tiny waterfront. (You'll get a glimpse of the historic site across the water.) Nearby is a cool faux-Elizabethan theater, the **Louisbourg Playhouse** ★ (✆ **902/733-2996;** www.louisbourgplayhouse.com), at 11 Aberdeen St. The playhouse was originally built near the old town by Disney for the movie *Squanto*. After production wrapped, Disney donated it to the village, which dismantled it and moved it to a side street near the harbor. Various performances and concerts are staged here throughout the summer.

As you come into town on Route 22, you'll pass the **Sydney and Louisbourg Railway Museum** (✆ **902/733-2720**), which shares the gabled railway depot with the local **visitor information center** (same phone). The museum commemorates the former railway, which shipped coal from the mines to Louisbourg harbor between 1895 and 1968. You can visit some of the old rolling stock (including an 1881 passenger car) and view the roundhouse. It's open daily from mid-May through mid-October; in July and August, from 8am to 8pm, and in spring and fall from 9am to 5pm. Admission is free. There's a gift shop here, as well.

Since you're already here, you might detour a few additional miles out of your way to **Lighthouse Point** ★, the site of Canada's very first lighthouse. (The lighthouse you see there today is a replacement version, however.) The rocky coastline at this spot is quite dramatic and undeveloped, and open—no trees. It's a great spot for a little hike, a picnic, and some photographs. Look sharp for Havenside Road, which diverges from the main paved road near the visitor information center/railway museum in the center of town. You might pass lobstermen at work on the way.

Fortress of Louisbourg National Historic Site ★★ ☺ Though it feels like the end of the world today, the village of Louisbourg has had three lives. The first was early in the 18th century, when the French colonized the area aggressively and built a stone fortress—imposing but not impregnable, because the British captured it in 1745. The fort was returned to the French following negotiations in Europe. War soon broke out again, however, and the British recaptured it in 1758 (and blew it up for good measure). That appeared to be the end, but the Canadian government decided to recreate about a quarter of the stone-walled town in the 1960s, based on a few documents about what had been there. The park is built to show life as it might have been in 1744, as an important French military capital and seaport that had not yet been captured; you arrive at the site after walking through an interpretive center and taking a short bus ride. (Keeping cars at a distance definitely enhances the historic feeling.) Past an impressive gatehouse—complete with a costumed guard on the lookout for English spies—wander narrow lanes and poke through faux-historic buildings, some of which contain informative exhibits, others of which are furnished with convincing reproductions. Chicken, geese, and other barnyard animals peck and cluck away, and vendors hawk freshly baked bread from wood-fired ovens. It really does feel like old Europe. Ask for the free tour, and allow at least 4 hours for the experience.

Louisbourg, NS. ✆ **902/733-2280** or 733-3546. June–Sept admission C$18 adult, C$15 seniors, C$8.80 children, C$44 families; May and Oct admission discounted 60%. July–Aug daily 9am–5:30pm; mid-May to June and Sept to mid-Oct daily 9:30am–5pm. Limited services last 2 weeks of May and last 2 weeks of Oct. Closed Nov to mid-May.

WHERE TO STAY & DINE

Louisbourg has a handful of informal, family-style restaurants such as **The Grubstake** at 7499 Main St. (✆ **902/733-2308**), open mid-June to early October from noon to about 9pm, and the **Lobster Kettle** at 41 Commercial St. (✆ **902/733-2723**).

Cranberry Cove Inn ★★ You can't miss this attractive in-town inn en route to the fortress: it's the three-story Victorian farmhouse painted cranberry red. Inside, it's decorated in a light Victorian motif. Upstairs rooms are carpeted and furnished on themes. Anne's Hideaway is the smallest, but has a nice old tub and butterfly collection; Isle Royale is done up in Cape Breton tartan patterns. The quirky Field and Stream room comes with a twig headboard, mounted deer head, and stuffed pheasant. Meals in the dining room match the inn's exterior—the included breakfast sprinkles cranberries into the mix. Dinner is served nightly (only to guests who have paid for package deals) in a handsome first-floor dining room of polished wood floors and cherry furniture. Entrees could range from charbroiled salmon to cranberry-marinated chicken. Note that, due to the three-story open staircase, this inn really isn't suitable for those with toddlers.

12 Wolfe St., Louisbourg, NS B1C 2J2. ✆ **800/929-0222** or 902/733-2171. www.louisbourg.com/cranberrycove. 7 units. C$105–C$160 double. Rates include full breakfast. Meal plans available. MC, V. Closed Nov–Apr. **Amenities:** Dining room. *In room:* TV, hair dryer, Jacuzzi (some units).

Louisbourg Harbour Inn Bed & Breakfast ★★ This yellow clapboard inn is just a block off Louisbourg's main street and overlooks the fishing wharves, harbor, and fortress. The lovely pine floors within are nicely restored, and guest rooms are tidy and attractive and well thought out. (Six of the eight units face the ocean, while five have Jacuzzis.) Some are fussier than others—expect busy floral bedspreads—but all of them are comfortable. The best rooms are probably on the third floor, up the stairs; room no. 6 is bright and cheerful, while room no. 7 is spacious and boasts a handsome wooden bed and a pair of rockers overlooking the fish pier.

9 Lower Warren St., Louisbourg, NS B1C 1G6. ✆ **888/888-8466** or 902/733-3222. 8 units. C$110–C$180 double. Rates include breakfast. MC, V. Closed mid-Oct to mid-June. *In room:* Fridge (some units), Jacuzzi (some units), no phone.

CAPE BRETON HIGHLANDS NATIONAL PARK ★★★

Cape Breton Highlands National Park is one of the two crown-jewel national parks in Atlantic Canada (Gros Morne in Newfoundland is the other). Covering nearly 1,000 sq. km (370 sq. miles) and stretching across a rugged peninsula from the Atlantic to the Gulf of St. Lawrence, this park is famous for its starkly beautiful terrain. It also features one of the most dramatic coastal drives in North America: think Big Sur, but greener. One of the great pleasures of this park is that it holds something for everyone, from tourists who prefer to sightsee from the comfort of their cars to those who prefer backcountry hiking in the company of bear and moose.

The **Cabot Trail ★★★**, a paved road built in 1939, winds dramatically along the flanks of these mountains, offering extraordinary vistas and camera shots at every turn. On the park's eastern flank—the Atlantic side—the terrain's a bit less spectacular, but those lush green hills still offer a backdrop that's exceptionally beautiful.

Essentials

GETTING THERE As mentioned, access to the park is via the **Cabot Trail,** which is very well marked by provincial signage. The entire loop is about 305km (190 miles), though the section that passes through the national park—from the entrance at Chéticamp to the one at Ingonish—is only about 105km (65 miles). You'll drive slowly to take in the vistas. Although the loop can be done in either direction, I would encourage you to drive it in a clockwise direction; the visitor center in Chéticamp offers a far more detailed introduction to the park.

VISITOR INFORMATION Two **visitor information centers** are located at either end of the park, in **Chéticamp** and **Ingonish.** Both are open daily from mid-May through mid-October, 8am to 8pm in summer (Jul–Aug) and 9am to 5pm during the shoulder seasons. The Chéticamp center has much more extensive information about the park, including a slide presentation, natural history exhibits, a cool large-scale relief map, and a very good bookstore specializing in the natural and cultural history. The park's main phone number is ✆ **902/224-2306.**

FEES Entrance permits are required from mid-May through mid-October and can be purchased either at information centers or at tollhouses at the two main park entrances. Permits are required for any activity along the route, even stopping to admire the view. Daily fees are C$7.80 adults, C$6.80 seniors, C$3.90 children age 6 to 16, and C$20 families. If you'll stay in the vicinity of this park for a week or more, buy an **annual pass,** which saves you money; the yearly pass is about C$98 for families, about C$39 per adult.

Camping

The park has five drive-in campgrounds. The biggest are at **Chéticamp** (on the west side) and **Broad Cove** (on the east), both of which have the commendable policy of never turning a camper away; even if all regular sites are full, they'll still find a place for you to pitch a tent or park your RV. All these campgrounds are well run and well maintained, though Chéticamp and Broad Cove have the most facilities, including three-way hookups for RVs.

Rates run from around C$18 to C$38 per night, depending on the level of services you require, time of year, and the campground you've selected. Remember that you're also required to buy park entry (or have a park pass in hand) when camping at Cape Breton, and that you can only make advance reservations at Chéticamp, where half the sites are set aside for advance bookings using the website **www.pccamping.ca.** At all the other campgrounds, it's first-come, first-served. Winter camping is allowed in some park campsites, as well, for a flat fee of C$15.

The park also has a stunning backcountry campsite at **Fishing Cove ★★**, set on a pristine, scenic cove. It's an 8km (5-mile) hike into the site from your car, and there's no potable drinking water once you arrive; pack enough in. (No campfires are allowed there, either.) Once there, however, you can watch for pilot whales at sunset from the cliffs to your heart's content. The site costs C$9.80 per night; make arrangements at one of the visitor information centers.

Hiking

The park offers no fewer than 25 distinct hiking tracks departing from the Cabot Trail. Many excursions are quite short and have the feel of a casual stroll rather than a vigorous tramp, but those determined to get a workout will find suitable trails, too. All the trails are listed, with brief descriptions, on the reverse side of the map you get when you pay your park entry fee at the gates.

The **Skyline Trail ★★★** offers oodles of altitude and views, without the climbing. You ascend a tableland from Chéticamp by car, then follow a 9km (6-mile) loop out along dramatic bluffs and through wind-stunted spruces and firs. A spur trail descends to a high, exposed point overlooking the surf; it's capped by blueberry bushes. Moose are often spotted along this trail, though it's a very popular trek for visitors and thus often crowded. (An exceedingly rare fatal coyote attack occurred on the trail in 2009; check with park staff about the trail's current status.)

Farther along the Cabot Trail, **Lone Shieling ★** is an easy 800m (½-mile) loop through lush hardwood forest in a valley that's home to 350-year-old sugar maples. The re-created hut of a Scottish crofter (shepherd) is another cool feature.

If you're looking to leave the crowds behind, the **Glasgow Lakes Lookoff ★** is a relatively gentle 9km (6-mile) round-trip hike that takes you through barrens and scrubby forest to a rocky bald overlook with distant views of the ocean and some highland lakes. This trail is alternately swampy and rocky, so wear rugged footwear.

On the eastern shore, try the 4km (2½-mile) **hike to Middle Head ★★**, which starts beyond the Keltic Lodge resort. This dramatic, rocky peninsula thrusts well out into the Atlantic. The trail is wide and relatively flat, and you'll cross open meadows with wonderful views both to the north and south. The tip of the peninsula is grassy and open, a good spot from which to watch for passing whales—or see waves crashing in after a storm. Allow about 2 hours for a relaxed walk out to the point and back.

NEW BRUNSWICK

by Paul Karr

4

For whatever reason, New Brunswick isn't usually considered a top priority when first-time travelers begin hatching plans to visit the eastern provinces. Even within Canada, the province is as well known for its pulp mills, industrial forests, cargo ports, and refineries (Irving Oil is based here) as for its cute villages, high tides, fresh air, or friendly locals.

And to foreigners? The place is mostly confused with the same-named city in New Jersey. Either that, or it's viewed as a place to be driven through as quickly as possible en route to Nova Scotia and Prince Edward Island.

Rest assured, though: New Brunswick *does* have pockets of wilderness and scenic beauty that equal those anywhere in eastern Canada, and plenty of great cultural offerings. (FDR was crazy about the place.) This province's appeals are just a bit less obvious than those of, say, Cape Breton.

So you'll need to do a little homework before heading there, but if you do, you can definitely cobble together a number of fun excursions taking in the province's variegated landscapes. You can lounge in surprisingly warm ocean waters lapping up on sandy beaches that hold their own to anything Prince Edward Island's got to offer. You can shutterbug it on rocky, surf-pounded headlands that look like the far shores of Newfoundland. You can gape at huge tides that will stun the kids with their drop and power. You can even browse through a chocolate museum (which must be the best idea for a museum by anyone, anywhere, ever).

You could also make time to explore a salty, pubby maritime city, Saint John, that makes a nice run at copying Halifax's mix of arts, culture, beer, and a busy working harbor.

Some weather-numbers watchers claim this province has the warmest summers and sunniest winters in the country, on average—and the provincial tourism commission has been all too eager to jump on these stats as proof that there's something magical here. But I think that's missing the point. I don't think they need to reach so far.

My advice is just this: Go explore New Brunswick beyond the highways, beyond the first glance. Do that, and you'll find it to be a place full of lovely landscapes, friendly locals, and fun things to do.

EXPLORING THE PROVINCE

Here's a bit of advice: It's important to come to New Brunswick with a strategy already in hand, one that takes into account geography and driving times. That's because the key tourist attractions here aren't close to each other at all, and there are no superspeedways to get you from one to the next quickly. You'd hate to spend most of your vacation looking out the window of a car.

If you're drawn to rugged beauty, plan to focus mostly on the **Fundy Coast** with its stupendous dropping tides, rocky cliffs, and boreal landscape. This part of the coastline actually feels a lot more remote and northerly than the more densely settled (and tamer-looking) northeastern coast.

Those who want to sip a pint to the strains of traditional music, shop at a great farmer's market, or visit a museum or gourmet restaurant? Swing through **Saint John** and its lovely associated fishing towns instead. Those interested in Franco history or sandy beaches, on the other hand, should keep moving and drive north to the **Gulf of St. Lawrence,** which brings Acadian heritage, seafood, whale-watches, and a laid-back feel to the table.

Those simply interested in hurrying *through* the province to get to Prince Edward Island or Nova Scotia? Well, you've paged to the wrong chapter of this book. Take at least a day to detour through Fundy National Park to see **Cape Enrage** and **Hopewell Rocks**—two of among eastern Canada's most dramatic attractions. If nothing else, you'll be able to tell your friends that New Brunswick should never again be written off on any tour of eastern Canada.

Essentials

VISITOR INFORMATION New Brunswick publishes several free annual directories and guides that are helpful in planning a trip to the province, including the comprehensive *Experience New Brunswick* vacation planner listing attractions, accommodations, campgrounds, and adventure packages, as well as the official New Brunswick travel map. Contact the **New Brunswick Department of Tourism and Parks,** P.O. Box 12345, Campbellton, NB E3N 3T6 (✆ **800/561-0123;** www.tourismnewbrunswick.ca).

TOURIST OFFICES The province staffs six official visitor information centers; more than 50 cities, towns, and villages also have their own municipal information centers. A complete listing of phone numbers for these centers can be found in the *Experience New Brunswick* guide, or look for "?" direction signs on the highway. Phone numbers and addresses for the appropriate visitor information centers are provided in each section of this chapter.

Getting There

BY PLANE The province's main airports are at Fredericton (the provincial capital), Saint John, and Moncton, all of which are chiefly served by **Air Canada** (✆ **888/247-2262;** www.aircanada.com) and the major car-rental companies. **Continental** (✆ **800/231-0856;** www.continental.com) also flies nonstop from Newark, New Jersey's, Liberty International Airport to Moncton, while **WestJet** (✆ **888/937-8538;** www.westjet.com) links Saint John and Moncton with Toronto.

BY TRAIN Canada's government-operated cross-country railroad, **VIA Rail** (✆ **888/842-7245;** www.viarail.ca), offers train service through the province to and from Montréal 6 days a week (no departures on Tues) year-round. The train follows a northerly route to and from Halifax, with stops in **Campbellton, Miramichi,** and **Moncton.** Check the VIA Rail website for more details on routes, schedules, stopping times in New Brunswick, and online booking.

BY CAR The Trans-Canada Highway bisects the province, entering from Québec at St. Jacques. It follows the Saint John River Valley before veering through Moncton and exiting into Nova Scotia at the hamlet of Aulac. The entire distance is about 530km (329 miles). The fastest route from New York City or New England to New Brunswick, however, is the **Maine Turnpike** (a toll road). Take the turnpike north to Bangor, Maine, then slice east on Route 9 to connect to Route 1. Continue to Calais, Maine which is just across the river from **St. Stephen,** New Brunswick.

A more scenic variation is to drive across a bridge onto **Campobello Island** from Lubec, Maine (see the "Passamaquoddy Bay" section, below), then take a ferry to Deer Island, drive the length of the island, and board a second ferry to the mainland.

Those headed to **Fredericton** or **Moncton** can speed their trips somewhat by following the Maine Turnpike to its conclusion, then continuing north on I-95 all the way to Houlton, Maine, and beyond; you'll connect with the Trans-Canada after crossing the border.

BY FERRY **Bay Ferries** (✆ **888/249-7245;** www.nfl-bay.com) operates the ferry known as the *Princess of Acadia* that links **Saint John** with Digby, Nova Scotia. The ferry sails year-round, with one to two crossings daily (travel time: 3 hours) each way. The peak-season (June through October) one-way fares in 2010 were C$40 for adults, C$30 for seniors, C$25 for children ages 6 to 13, C$5 per child under 6, and C$80 and up per vehicle, plus a C$20 fuel surcharge; fares are cheaper during the rest of the year. Also, adults and kids get a 25% discount on round-trips completed within 30 days (vehicle fare is discounted 15%), so be sure to buy a round-trip ticket if you'll return the same way you came. Reservations for the ferry in summer are advised.

The Great Outdoors

The province has put together a campaign to encourage visitors of all budgets to explore its outdoor attractions and activities. The provincial travel guide outlines dozens of multiday and day adventures ranging from a C$10 guided hike at Fundy National Park to fancy biking packages that include overnight inn accommodations and gourmet dinners. For more information on these programs, call the tourism department at ✆ **800/561-0123** or check the official website of the province's parks at **www.nbparks.ca.**

BACKPACKING Among the best destinations for a backcountry hike in this province are **Mount Carleton Provincial Park** (p. 109) and **Fundy National Park** (p. 131), both of which maintain backcountry campsites for visitors. The two landscapes are quite different to hike through, however—see the appropriate sections for more information on each park, then take your pick.

BICYCLING The islands and peninsulas of **Passamaquoddy Bay** lend themselves nicely to cruising in the slow lane—especially Campobello Island (p. 110),

New Brunswick & the Gaspé Peninsula

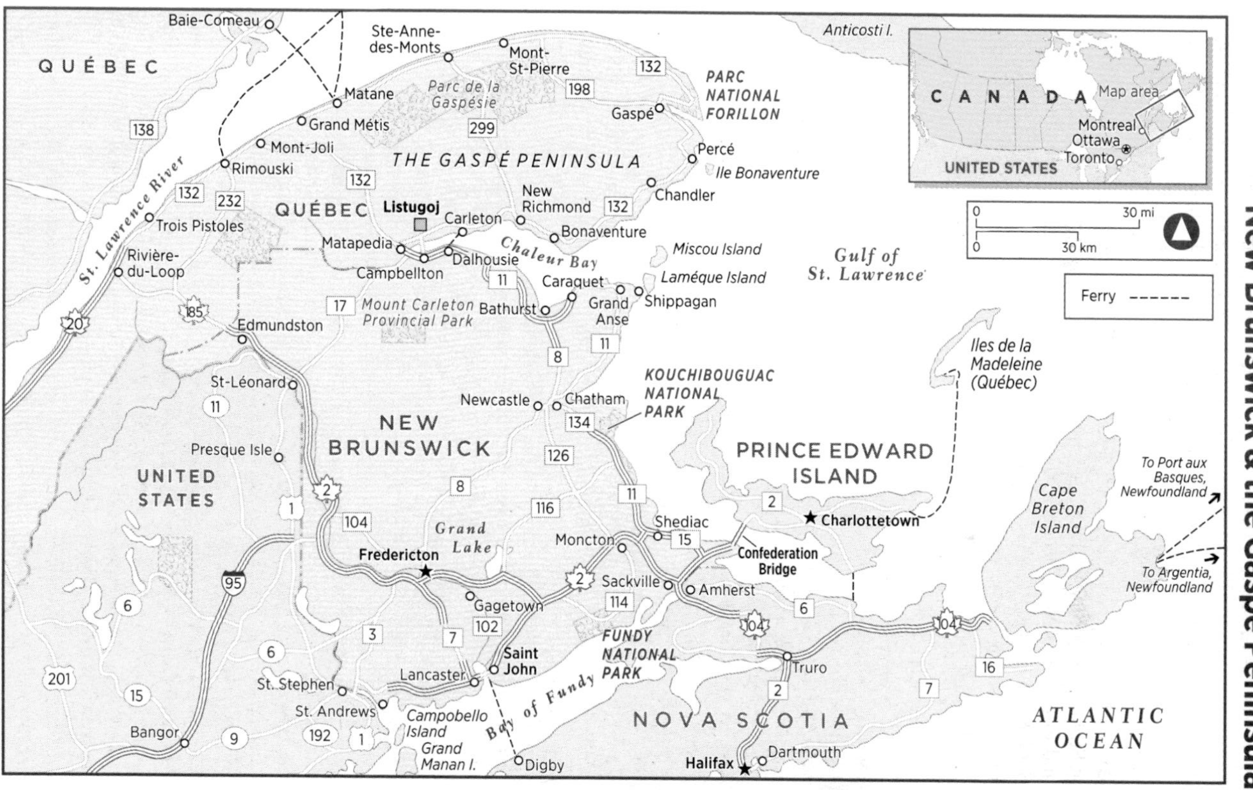

which also has good dirt roads for mountain biking. **Grand Manan** (p. 115) holds lots of appeal for cyclists, too, even if the main road (Rte. 776) has some rather narrow shoulders and some pretty quick local drivers. Some of the best coastal biking is around **Fundy National Park**—especially the back roads to Cape Enrage and the **Fundy Trail Parkway,** an 11km (7-mile) multi-use trail that hugs the coast west of the national park. Along the Acadian Coast, **Kouchibouguac National Park** has limited but unusually nice biking trails through mixed terrain (rentals are available in the park).

A handy guide is *Biking to Blissville,* by Kent Thompson. It covers 35 rides in the Maritimes and costs C$15, plus tax and shipping. Look in local bookshops, check online, or contact the publisher directly: **Goose Lane Editions,** 500 Beaverbrook Ct., Suite 500, Fredericton, NB E3B 5X4 (✆ **888/926-8377** or 506/450-4251; www.gooselane.com).

BIRD-WATCHING **Grand Manan** is the province's most notable destination for birders, right on the Atlantic flyway. (The great John James Audubon lodged here while studying and drawing bird life more than 150 years ago.) Over the course of a typical year, as many as 275 species could be observed on the island; September is often the best month for sightings. Boat tours from Grand Manan can also take you farther out to **Machias Seal Island,** with its colonies of puffins, Arctic terns, and razorbills. It's fun to swap information with other birders, too; during the ferry ride, look for excitable folks with binoculars and floppy hats dashing from one side of the boat to the other and back.

Campobello Island's mixed terrain attracts a good mixture of birds, including the sharp-shinned hawk, common eider, and black guillemot. Ask for a checklist and map at the visitor center. Shorebird enthusiasts also flock to **Shepody Bay National Wildlife Area,** which maintains preserves in the mudflats between **Alma** (near the entrance to Fundy National Park) and Hopewell Cape. There's good birding in the marshes around **Sackville,** near the Nova Scotia border, too.

CANOEING New Brunswick has some 3,500km (2,175 miles) of inland waterways, plus countless lakes and protected bays. Canoeists can find everything from glass-smooth waters to daunting rapids. In Kouchibouguac National Park, for example, there's a rental and tour concession based at **Ryans Recreational Equipment Rental Centre** (✆ **506/876-8918**), open from mid-May to mid-September (open weekends from mid-May to mid-June and the final week of the season). More experienced canoeists looking for a longer expedition should head for the **St. Croix River** along the U.S. border.

FISHING The **Miramichi River** has long attracted anglers lured by its wily Atlantic salmon. Some experts consider it to be among the best salmon rivers on the planet, even if diminished runs have plagued recent years (as they have all rivers in the Maritimes). There are strict laws regarding river fishing of the salmon: The fish must be caught using flies, not hooks, and nonresidents must hire a licensed guide when fishing for them. For other freshwater species, including bass, as well as open-ocean saltwater angling, the rules are less restrictive. Regulations are available from the **Fish and Wildlife Branch** of the Department of Natural Resources (✆ **506/453-2440;** www.gnb.ca/0254).

GOLF In St. Andrews, the **Algonquin hotel**'s redesigned golf course is a beauty—more than 100 years old, it was retouched by Donald Ross' plans in the 1920s, then rethought and expanded in the late 1990s—easily ranking among eastern Canada's top 10. That's right: It's behind the big-name stars on Cape Breton Island and Prince Edward Island. The course now features 9 newer inland holes (the front 9), in addition to the 9 original seaside holes that become increasingly spectacular as you approach the point of land separating New Brunswick from Maine. All 18 of them are challenging, so bring your "A" game. Service and upkeep are impeccable, and there's both a snack bar on premises and a roving club car with sandwiches and drinks. Greens fees are C$49 to C$99 for 18 holes (carts extra; discount at twilight time). Lessons are offered, and there's a short-game practice area with a huge putting green in addition to the usual driving range. Call ✆ **888/460-8999** or 506/529-8165 for tee times and other details. In Fredericton, lovely **Kingswood** (✆ **800/423-5969** or 506/443-3333; www. kingswoodpark.com/golf.php)—located inside a family entertainment park—was recognized by *Golf Digest* as the best new Canadian golf course in 2003. It features 27 holes, a par-3 course, and a double-ended driving range. A round of 18 holes costs C$54 to C$69.

HIKING The province's highest point is on top of **Mount Carleton Provincial Park** (✆ **506/235-0793**), in the center of a vast area of woodlands far from all major population centers. Several demanding hikes in the park yield glorious views. The park's open daily from mid-May through mid-October and costs C$7 to enter; you get there either by following Route 17 from **Campbellton** or taking various local roads (routes 105, 108, and then 385, to be specific) from the border crossing at Limestone, Maine. This should take less than 3 hours from either Campbellton or Caribou, Maine. There's also superb hiking at **Fundy National Park,** with a mix of coastal and woodland hikes on well-marked trails. The multi-use, 11km (7-mile) **Fundy Trail Parkway** ★★ has terrific views of the coast and is wheelchair-accessible.

A Hiking Guide to New Brunswick by Marianne Eiselt (Goose Lane Editions, ✆ **888/926-8377;** www.gooselane.com) is an excellent local guide to hiking trails.

SEA KAYAKING The huge tides that make kayaking so fascinating along the **Bay of Fundy** also make it exceptionally dangerous—even the strongest kayakers are no match for these fierce ebb tides if they're in the wrong place. Fortunately, a number of skilled sea-kayaking guides work the province.

Among the most extraordinary places to explore in New Brunswick is **Hopewell Rocks.** At high tide, there are plenty of sea caves and narrow channels to explore. **Baymount Outdoor Adventure** (✆ **877/601-2660** or 506/734-2660), run by the Faulkners in Hillsborough, offers 90-minute sea kayak tours of Hopewell Rocks from June through early September for C$55 adults, C$45 children, or C$180 per family.

Other good kayak outfitters along the coast include **FreshAir Adventure** (✆ **800/545-0020** or 506/887-2249) in Alma (near Fundy National Park) and Bruce Smith's **Seascape Kayak Tours** (✆ **866/747-1884** or 506/747-1884) in Deer Island.

WHALE-WATCHING The **Bay of Fundy** is rich with plankton, and therefore rich with whales. Some 15 types of whales can be spotted in the bay, including finback, minke, humpback, the infrequent orca, and the endangered right whale. Whale-watching expeditions sail throughout the summer from various docks, wharves, and ports including Campobello Island, Deer Island, Grand Manan, St. Andrews, and St. George. Any visitor information center can point you in the right direction; the province's travel guide also lists lots of tours, which typically cost around C$40 to C$50 for 2 to 4 hours of whale-watching.

AROUND PASSAMAQUODDY BAY

The **Passamaquoddy Bay** region is often the first point of entry for those arriving overland from the United States. The deeply indented bay is wracked by massive tides that produce currents powerful enough to stymie even the sturdiest fishing boats. It's a place of deep fogs, spruce-clad islands, bald eagles, and little development. Fortunately for you, it's also home to a grand old summer colony and a peninsula that boasts several five-star inns and a rambling turn-of-the-20th-century resort.

Campobello Island ★

Campobello is a compact island (about 16km/10 miles long and 5km/3 miles wide) at the mouth of Passamaquoddy Bay. It's connected by a graceful modern bridge to Lubec, Maine, and is much easier to get to from the United States than from Canada. (To get here from the Canadian mainland without driving through the United States requires two ferries, one of which operates only during the summer.) This is a great quick trip into Canada if you're already in Downeast Maine; from Bar Harbor, Maine, it's about a 2½-hour drive—into another world that feels a century or more older. Campobello has been home to both humble fishermen and wealthy families over the years, yet both have coexisted quite amicably. Today, the island is a mix of elegant summer mansions and simpler local homes.

ESSENTIALS

GETTING THERE Campobello Island is accessible year-round from the United States. From Route 1 in Whiting, Maine, take Route 189 to Lubec, then cross the free **FDR International Bridge** from the mainland onto Campobello.

In summer only, there's a second option. From **St. George** on the Canadian mainland, drive down Route 172 to the dock at **L'Etete.** Board the free **provincial ferry** that runs year-round (operates on the half-hour 7am to 5pm, hourly until 10pm) to **Deer Island**'s northern tip. Then drive the length of that island to Cummings Cove—it's only about 24km (15 miles or 20 minutes' drive)—and board the small ferry to Campobello. This second ferry is operated by **East Coast Ferries** (✆ **877/747-2159** or 506/747-2159; www.eastcoastferries.nb.ca) from late June through September, running once per hour from 8:30am to 6:30pm. The ride takes about a half-hour. The fare is C$16 for a car and driver, plus C$3 for each additional passenger and a small fuel surcharge (currently C$2). You can retrace your steps for another C$16, or drive on across the border into Maine. Remember: ferry times are in local Atlantic time, one hour *ahead* of Eastern Standard Time.

VISITOR INFORMATION The **Campobello Welcome Center,** 44 Rte. 774, Welshpool, NB E5E 1A3 (✆ **506/752-7043**), is on the right side just after you cross the bridge from Lubec. It's usually open from mid-May until early September, 9am to 7pm, then from around 10am until 6pm through mid-October.

EXPLORING THE ISLAND

Roosevelt Campobello International Park ★★ This free park in Welshpool, on Rte. 774 (✆ **506/752-2922;** www.fdr.net), is truly international, run by a commission with representatives from both the U.S. and Canada. It offers scenic coastlines, 14km (9 miles) of walking trails on 1,130 hectares (2,800 acres)—and tons of history, thanks to Franklin Delano Roosevelt's still-looming presence here. Like any number of affluent Americans, FDR's family made annual treks to this prosperous summer colony to experience cool air and presumed near-magical powers of restoration. ("The extensive forests of balsamic firs seem to affect the atmosphere of this region, causing a quiet of the nervous system and inviting sleep," reported one 1890 real-estate brochure.) The future U.S. president came to this island every summer between 1883 and 1921, when he was stricken with polio. Franklin and his siblings spent those summers exploring the coves and sailing around the bay, and he later always recalled his time here fondly. (His phrase "beloved island" still gets no rest in local advertising.) You'll learn a lot about Roosevelt and his early life both at the visitor center, where you can watch a short film, and during a self-guided tour of his family's elaborate mansion, which is still covered in cranberry-colored shingles. For a "cottage" this big, it's surprisingly comfortable and intimate.

The park's visitor center closes down in late October until mid-May, but the extensive grounds and parklands remain open year-round sunrise to sunset; maps and walk suggestions are available at the visitor center.

459 Rte. 774, Welshpool. ✆ **506/752-2922.** www.fdr.net. Free admission. Daily 10am–6pm; last tour at 5:45pm. Visitor center closed mid-Oct to mid-May; grounds open year-round.

WHERE TO STAY & DINE

There's camping at **Herring Cove Provincial Park** (✆ **506/752-7010**). Nightly fees at the 88 sites range from C$22 (for a simple site) to C$35 (for a rustic shelter to somewhat protect you from the elements) with discounts for seniors. For indoor options, see below.

Lupine Lodge ★ ☺ In 1915, cousins of the Roosevelts built this handsome compound of log buildings not far from the family cottage. A busy road runs between the lodge and the water, but the buildings are located on a small rise and have the feel of being removed from traffic. Guest rooms are in two long lodges adjacent to the main building and restaurant. The rooms with bay views cost a bit more but are worth it—they're slightly bigger and furnished in a more rustic style. All units have queen beds (some rooms add a double bed or fireplace) plus access to a deck overlooking the bay. You won't find phones, TVs, luxe bathrooms, or wireless Internet here, but you will find a pleasing vibe—they welcome even small children, and will pack a lunch for your explorations. The lodge's attractive **dining room** is a good place for a meal, exuding summer with its log walls, double stone fireplace, views of fishing fleets on the bay, and mounted moose and swordfish. Three meals are served daily (blueberry pancakes are great at breakfast), and dinners have been improved: Entrees now include choices like maple-glazed salmon, pasta, and a turkey dinner, in addition to the longtime favorites such as steak, seafood, lobster rolls, and lobster stew.

610 Rte. 774, Welshpool, Campobello Island, NB E5E 1A5. ✆ **888/912-8880** or 506/752-2555. www.lupinelodge.com. 11 units. C$100–C$180 double. MC, V. Closed mid Oct–late May. **Amenities:** Restaurant. *In room:* No phone.

Owen House, A Country Inn & Gallery This three-story clapboard captain's house dates from 1835 and sits on 4 tree-filled hectares (10 acres) at the edge of the bay. First-floor common rooms are decorated in a Victorian manner, with Persian and braided carpets and mahogany furniture; watch the water from a nautical-feeling sun room that has big windows. The guest rooms are a mixed bag, furnished with a mixture of antique and modern furniture. Some units are bright and filled with salty air (room no. 1 is biggest and most expensive, with waterfront views on two sides and attractive antiques such as a cane chair and an iron-frame bed). Others are simpler, dark, or tucked beneath stairs. The four third-floor rooms share two bathrooms—the innkeepers can assign one of the bathrooms privately to room nos. 7 or 8 for an extra charge—but they also have excellent views. Bedspreads are frumpy, while the wooden floors are handsome.

11 Welshpool St., Welshpool, Campobello Island, NB E5E 1G3. ✆ **506/752-2977.** www.owenhouse.ca. 9 units, 4 with shared bathroom. C$104–C$210 double. Rates include full breakfast. MC, V. Closed Nov–Apr. No children under 6 in Aug. *In room:* No phone.

St. Andrews ★★

The village of St. Andrews—or St. Andrews-by-the-Sea, as the chamber of commerce persists in calling it—traces its roots back to a bunch of Loyalists. After the American Revolution, New Englanders who supported the British in the struggle needed a new life. They landed first at seaside Castine, Maine, which they thought was safely on British soil. But it wasn't; the St. Croix River was later determined to be the true border between Canada and the United States. Forced to uproot once more, these Loyalists dismantled their homes, loaded the pieces aboard ships, and rebuilt them on the welcoming peninsula of St. Andrews. And you know what? Some of these remarkably resilient saltbox houses *still* stand in the town today.

St. Andrews is beautifully situated at the tip of a long, wedge-shaped peninsula. Thanks to its location off the beaten track, this village hasn't been spoiled much by modern development, and walking the wide, shady streets—especially around the Algonquin—reminds one of a simpler time, as do hundreds of century-old homes in the town. A number of appealing boutiques and shops are spread along Water Street on the town's shoreline, and it's easy to grab a boat tour on the docks, too. I definitely recommend this town if you're seeking a tame, easy touristic dip into New Brunswick. The Tudor-style Algonquin hotel is the area's social hub and defining landmark.

ESSENTIALS

GETTING THERE St. Andrews is located on Route 127, which dips southward from Route 1 between St. Stephen and St. George. It's an easy drive north from **St. Stephen** or south from **Saint John** (more scenic coming from Saint John); the turnoff is well marked from both directions. **Acadian Bus Lines** (✆ **800/567-5151;** www.acadianbus.com) runs one daily bus between St. Andrews and Saint John; the trip takes less than 90 minutes, and the adult one-way fare is C$25, C$43 round-trip. Even better, the bus line offers discounts to children, students, and seniors.

VISITOR INFORMATION St. Andrews' seasonal **Welcome Centre** (✆ **800/563-7397** or 506/529-3556) is located at 46 Reed Ave., on your left as you enter the village. Look for the handsome 1914 home overarched by broad-crowned trees (which is also home to the local **Chamber of Commerce**). The center opens daily from mid-May through mid-October; the rest of the year, contact the Chamber at the same address or by calling ✆ **506/529-3555.**

EXPLORING ST. ANDREWS

The local chamber of commerce produces two brochures, a town map and directory, and the St. Andrews-by-the-Sea historic guide, all of which are free. Also look for *A Guide to Historic St. Andrews,* produced by the St. Andrews Civic Trust. Many of the private dwellings in St. Andrews even feature plaques with information on their origins—look for them especially on the sides of the town's saltbox-style homes.

The village's compact and handsome downtown flanks **Water Street,** the long commercial street paralleling the bay. You'll find understated commercial architecture here, much of it from the turn of the 20th century, in a variety of styles. Allow an hour or so for browsing through the boutiques and art galleries. There's also a mix of restaurants and inns.

Two blocks inland on King Street, get a dose of local history at the **Ross Memorial Museum** ★, 188 Montague St. (✆ **506/529-5124**). This brick Georgian mansion was built in 1824; in 1945, it was left to the town by American reverend Henry Phipps Ross and his wife Sarah Juliette Ross, who only lived there 7 years before dying within days of each other. The house was full of their eclectic and intriguing collection of period furniture, carpets, and paintings—and it has remained that way. The museum is open June through mid-October, Monday through Saturday from 10am to 4:30pm. Admission is by donation—leave a few dollars. Just uphill from the museum, at the head of King Street, is the steadily growing **Kingsbrae Garden** (see below).

Toward the western end of Water Street, you'll come to Joe's Point Road at the foot of Harriet Street. The stout wooden **blockhouse** that sits just off the water behind low grass-covered earthworks was built by townspeople during the War of 1812, when the colonials anticipated a U.S. attack (which never came). It's administered to visitors as the **Blockhouse National Historic Site** (✆ **506/529-4270**), open June through August; entry is just C90¢ per person.

Kingsbrae Garden ☺ This 11-hectare (27-acre) public garden opened in 1998, is on the former grounds of a long-gone estate. Its designers incorporated the existing hedges and trees, but also planned attractive open spaces around the mature plants. The grounds include almost 2,000 varieties of trees (including old-growth forest), shrubs, and plants; among the notable features are a day lily collection, extensive rose garden, small maze, fully functional Dutch windmill that circulates water through two duck ponds, and a children's garden with an elaborate Victorian-mansion playhouse. The Garden Cafe has a patio and excellent views over the lawns to the bay below. There's also a gift shop and art gallery on the premises. Those with a horticultural bend should plan to spend a few hours here, strolling and enjoying it; as a quick picnic stop with the family, though, it's a bit expensive. (Walk to one of the town's local parks instead.)

220 King St. ✆ **866/566-8687** or 506/529-3335. Admission C$9.75 adults, C$8 students and seniors, C$24 families, free for children under 6. Gardens open mid-May to mid-Oct daily 9am–6pm; café, mid-May to mid-Oct daily 10am–5pm. Closed mid-Oct to mid-May.

Ministers Island Historic Site/Covenhoven ★★ This rugged, 202-hectare (500-acre) island is linked to the mainland by a sandbar at low tide, and 2-hour-long tours are strictly scheduled around the tides. (Call for times.) Though prices have increased considerably recently, this is still a very interesting trip. You meet your tour guide on the mainland, then drive your car out in a convoy across the ocean floor to the once-magical island estate built in 1890 by Sir William Van Horne. Van Horne, originally from Illinois, was president and chief visionary of the Canadian Pacific Railway; he also built the gray sandstone mansion known as Covenhoven as a vacation home with 50 rooms (including 17 bedrooms!), a circular bathhouse (where he painted landscapes), and one of Canada's largest, most impressive barns. The estate also featured heated greenhouses (partly powered by windmill) that once grew grapes, mushrooms, and enormous, 2-pound peaches. When Van Horne was stuck working in Montréal, he shipped dairy products from the creamery and vegetables from the greenhouse to himself daily—by rail, of course. (He extended the rail line here.) You'll learn all this, and much more, on the tours. Just don't expect the mansion to be in pristine condition; since nobody lives here anymore, it's frankly falling apart, and restoring it would take big bucks. Appreciate it for what it was—and remember to get back to dry land before high tide.

Rte. 127 (northeast of St. Andrews), Chamcook. ✆ **506/529-5081.** Tours C$14 adults, C$11 seniors and students, C$45 families, free for children 6 and under. Tours mid-May to mid-Oct; closed mid-Oct to mid-May.

WHERE TO STAY

Those traveling on a budget instead of seeking the luxury digs below might head for the low-slung **Picket Fence Motel,** 102 Reed Ave. (✆ **506/529-8985**). This trim and tidy property offers 17 cost-effective rooms, all with air-conditioning, close to the handsome Algonquin golf course (see "Golf," earlier) and within walking distance of St. Andrews' village center. The queen- and double-bedded rooms cost C$65 to C$80 double. There's also the **Europa Inn** (✆ **506/529-3818;** www.europainn.com) in the heart of town at 48 King St. The inn's owners rent out a series of rooms, suites, and an apartment. Nightly rates run from C$69 (for a simple room, off-season) to C$149 (for a suite in high season). Helpfully, the suites and apartment all have kitchenettes or full kitchens.

The Fairmont Algonquin ★★ The Algonquin's pedigree dates from 1889, when it opened its doors to wealthy vacationers seeking respite from the city heat. The original structure was destroyed by fire in 1914, but surviving annexes were rebuilt in Tudor style; in 1993 an architecturally similar addition was built across the road, linked by a gatehouse-inspired bridge. This red-tile-roofed resort commands your attention through its sheer size and bearing—and kilt-wearing, bagpipe-playing staff. Several long blocks from the water's edge, the inn is perched on a hill and affords panoramic bay views from a second-floor roof garden and many of the guest rooms. Rooms have been updated, and are comfortable and tasteful. In addition to its outstanding seaside golf course (see "Golf," earlier), there's now a spa at the hotel with a full card of treatments ranging from facials and nail services to body wraps and massage. The resort's dining room ★, open May through October, is one of the better spots in town to eat—it's often bustling with summer folks, and the kitchen produces surprisingly creative meals.

184 Adolphus St., St. Andrews, NB E5B 1T7. ✆ **800/441-1414** or 506/529-8823. Fax 506/529-7162. www.fairmont.com. 234 units. C$99–C$459 double; C$299–C$1,169 suite. Rates include continental breakfast. AE, DC, MC, V. Free valet parking. Small cats and dogs C$25 per night. **Amenities:** 2 restaurants; 2 bars; babysitting; bike rentals; children's programs; concierge; golf course; health club; Jacuzzi; outdoor heated pool; sauna; spa; 2 tennis courts; game room; salon. *In room:* TV, hair dryer, minibar.

Kingsbrae Arms Relais & Châteaux ★★★ Part of the Relais & Châteaux network, this Kingsbrae Arms is an expensive, luxe five-star inn with an upscale European feel. Located at the top of King Street, it occupies a manor house built by jade merchants in 1897. The inn employs a heated pool amid rose gardens at the foot of a lawn to good effect, and sits immediately next door to Kingsbrae Garden (see above); some guest rooms have wonderful views of the gardens, others a panoramic sweep of the bay. Guests are pampered by high-thread-count sheets, thick robes, and guest-services suite stocked with complimentary snacks and refreshments. Some rooms also have Jacuzzis and steam showers—while all of them sport gas fireplaces, CD players, Wi-Fi access, satellite televisions, and Bulgari bath products. Two suites in the carriage house are especially suited for those bringing pets or young children along on the trip.

219 King St., St. Andrews, NB E5B 1Y1. ✆ **506/529-1897.** www.kingsbrae.com. 8 units. C$395–C$995. Packages available. 2-night minimum; July–Aug 3-night minimum. 5% room service charge additional. AE, MC, V. Closed Nov–Apr. Pets allowed with advance permission. **Amenities:** Babysitting. *In room:* A/C, TV, hair dryer, Jacuzzi (some units).

WHERE TO DINE

Some locals also swear by **The Gables,** 143 Water St. (✆ **506/529-3440**), a waterside spot that features middling food and service. You mostly come to sit out on the patio (on plastic chairs), watch the water, and feel like—well, a tourist. The menu is seafood, lobster, and burgers, but don't get your hopes up too high.

Europa ★★ 🎁 CONTINENTAL In an intriguing yellow building that once housed a movie theater and dance hall, Bavarian husband-and-wife transplants Markus and Simone Ritter whip up French-, Swiss-, and Austrian-accented cuisine for a 35-seat room. Starters could run to French onion soup; a colorful bell pepper soup; lobster bisque; smoked salmon with *rösti* and capers; or scallops seared in Mornay sauce and baked with cheese (a house specialty). Main courses usually include several versions of schnitzel (grilled pork or veal steak) with different fillings, toppings, and sauces; steak Béarnaise; duck a l'Orange; rack of lamb; haddock in lemon butter or champagne sauce; and tiger shrimp with mango chutney. Finish with a chocolate mousse, almond parfait, or homemade ice cream or sorbet. The wine list is surprisingly strong. All in all, a lovely slice of Europe—just as the name promises.

48 King St. ✆ **506/529-3818.** Reservations recommended. Main courses C$18–C$27. MC, V. Mid-May to Sept daily 5pm–9pm; Oct Tues–Sat 5pm–9pm; Nov to mid-Feb Thurs–Sat 5pm–9pm. Closed mid-Feb to mid-May.

GRAND MANAN ISLAND ★

Geologically rugged, profoundly peaceful, and indisputably remote, Grand Manan—a handsome island of 2,700 year-round residents—is just a 90-minute ferry ride from the port of Blacks Harbour, which is just southeast of St. George. Despite being located incredibly close to Maine, this is a much-prized destination for adventurous travelers; sometimes, even a highlight of their vacation. Yet the island remains a mystifying puzzle to others who fail to be taken in by its rough-hewn charm. Either this is your kind of place, or it isn't; maybe there's no in-between. One way to find out is to visit.

Hiking the island's trails, don't be surprised if you come across knots of quiet people peering intently through binoculars—these are the birders (not the Cather fans), on a quest to see all 300 or so species of birds that either nest here or stop by during their long migrations. This is *the* place to pad your "life list" if you're accumulating one, with birds ranging from bald eagles to puffins (you'll need to pay for a boat tour to catch a glimpse of the latter). You're practically guaranteed to see something you've never seen before.

Essentials

GETTING THERE Grand Manan is reached from Blacks Harbour on the Canadian mainland via frequent ferry service in summer. **Coastal Transport car ferries** (**© 506/642-0520;** www.coastaltransport.ca), each capable of hauling 60 cars, depart from the mainland and the island every 2 hours between 7:30am and 5:30pm during July and August, three to four times daily the rest of the year. The round-trip fare is C$11 per adult, C$5.40 per child age 5 to 12, and C$33 per car. Boarding the ferry on the mainland is free; you buy tickets when you leave the island.

The island is exceptionally popular in summer. You might wait in line, or you might not get a spot on the ferry at all. Reserve your return trip at least a day ahead to avoid getting stranded on the island overnight (unless that's what you want), and get in line early to secure a spot, too. As for departing from Blacks Harbour for the island, one time-tested strategy is to bring a picnic lunch, arrive an hour or 2 early, put your car in the line, then head for the grassy waterfront park adjacent to the wharf and eat al fresco. It's a nicely attractive spot; there's even an island to explore during low tide while you wait.

VISITOR INFORMATION The island's **Visitor Information Centre** (**© 888/525-1655** or 506/662-3442), is located at the island's museum (see "Exploring the Island," below) in the village of Grand Harbour, one of three villages on the island's eastern shore; the center is open weekdays and Sunday afternoons through the summer, until it closes down in mid-September until the following June. If you come when it's closed, ask at island stores or inns for a free island map published by the **Grand Manan Tourism Association** (www.grandmanannb.com), which also has a listing of key island phone numbers.

Exploring the Island

Start exploring before you even land. As you come abreast of the island aboard the ferry, head for the starboard (right) side: You'll soon see the so-called **Seven Days' Work** in the rocky cliffs of Whale's Cove, a spot where seven layers of hardened lava and sill (intrusive igneous rock) have come together to create a sort of geological Dagwood sandwich.

Get an even better understanding of the local landscape at the **Grand Manan Museum** (**© 506/662-3424**) in Grand Harbour. The museum's geology exhibit, in the basement, teaches you what to look for as you roam around the island. Serious birders might enjoy the collections donated by island birder Allan Moses upstairs, which feature 200-plus stuffed and mounted birds behind glass; I'm guessing animal-rights types would want to skip it, though. The museum also houses an impressive lighthouse lens from the Gannet Rock Lighthouse, plus a collection of various items that have washed up here at one time or another from shipwrecks. The museum is open from June to September, Monday through Friday, 9am to 5:30pm; it's also open Saturdays (same hours) in July and August. Admission is C$4 for adults, C$2 for seniors and students, and free for children under 12.

The relatively flat and compact island is perfect for cycling; the only stretches to avoid are some fast, less scenic segments of Route 776. Any of the side roads offer superb biking, and the paved cross-island road to **Dark Harbour** is especially nice; when you get there, you'll find a scenic little harbor with a few cabins, dories, and salmon pens. Eat your Wheaties before coming: This route is wild and hilly for a stretch, but then offers a memorably scenic coast down to the ocean on the island's western side as your reward.

Bike rentals are available at **Adventure High** ★ (✆ **800/732-5492** or 506/662-3563; www.adventurehigh.com) on Route 776 in **North Head,** not far from the ferry. If you're fit enough, consider leaving your car at Blacks Harbour and taking only a bike onto the boat, then returning on the last ferry; you'll save money and burn calories. The outfitter also offers sea kayak tours around the island, for those who prefer to get a rarely-seen, whale's-eye view of the impressive cliffs. Bikes rent for C$22 per day, C$16 for a half-day. Kayak tours run from C$40 for a 2-hour sunset tour to C$99 for a full day's excursion. The same folks can even rent you a cabin—or add a lobster dinner on the beach to your kayak trip, for an extra charge.

While Grand Manan is about as quiet as it gets, you can find even more silence and solitude (and cross one more island off your "life list") by driving to **White Head Island,** population 190 on a good day. To get there, drive to Ingalls Head (follow Ingalls Head Rd. from Grand Harbour) and catch a free ferry to the island. You walk along the shore to a lighthouse guarding the passage between Battle Beach and Sandy Cove. The ferry holds 10 cars and sails year-round, up to 10 times per day during the summer.

Whale-Watching & Boat Tours

A fine way to experience island ecology is to mosey offshore. Several outfitters offer complete nature tours, providing a nice sampling of the world above and beneath the sea. On an excursion you might see minke, finback, or humpback whales, along with exotic birds including puffins and phalaropes. **Sea Watch Tours** (✆ **877/662-8562** or 506/662-8552; www.seawatchtours.com), run by Peter and Kenda Wilcox, operates a series of excursions from late June through September, with whale sightings guaranteed or your money back, aboard a 13m (43-ft.) vessel with canopy. Rates run C$63 to C$85 for adults and C$43 to C$45 per child 12 or younger.

Where to Stay

The Anchorage Provincial Park ★ (✆ **506/662-7022**) has about 100 campsites scattered about forest and field, available mid-May through mid-September. There's a small beach and a hiking trail on the property, and it's well situated for exploring the southern part of the island. It's very popular midsummer; call before you board the ferry to ask about campsite availability. Sites are C$24 to C$35, some with hookups for RVs, others better suited for a simple tent—including some involving crude shelters to help you fend off the weather.

Inn at Whale Cove Cottages ★★ The Inn at Whale Cove is a family-run compound set in a grassy meadow overlooking the aforementioned cove. The original building is a farmhouse dating to 1816, restored with a selection of simple country antiques; three guest rooms here are comfortable. Sally's Attic has a small deck with a big view, though Miss Henrietta's only sports a single bed. The living room features good reading material and a fireplace. Six cottages are scattered about the property, varying in size from one to four bedrooms; most rent only by the week, a few by the night. (One was built by author Willa Cather.) The John's Flat and Cove View units are the most modern, sporting extra bedrooms and dining rooms, decks, televisions, laundry service, and (in one case) a Jacuzzi. The 4 hectares (10 acres) of grounds, especially the pathway to the beach, are lovely. Innkeeper Laura Buckley received culinary training in Toronto and the **dining room ★** demonstrates a deft touch with Continental cuisine. Dinners are served nightly from June through mid-October, weekends only in May and early June.

26 Whale Cove Cottage Rd., North Head, Grand Manan, NB E0G 2M0. © **506/662-3181.** 9 units. C$125–C$160 double; C$800–C$950 per week cottage. Rates include full breakfast. MC, V. All but 1 unit closed Nov–Apr. Dogs allowed in all but 1 unit, C$5 per day. **Amenities:** Dining room. *In room:* TV (2 units), Jacuzzi (1 unit), kitchenette (3 units).

Where to Dine

Options for dining out aren't exactly extravagant on Grand Manan, but the Inn at Whale Cove Cottages (see "Where to Stay," above) serves great meals incorporating fresh local ingredients. **Shorecrest Lodge** (© **506/662-3216**) in North Head, another local inn, has a country-style dining room with fireplace and hardwood floors, and serves a menu of seafood, pizza, chicken, and beef daily during the summer months. You'll also encounter a few other family restaurants and grocers along the main road, as well.

The seasonal, summer-only **North Head Bakery ★** (© **506/662-8862**) on Route 776 is superb and has been baking with traditional methods and whole grains since 1990. Breads made here daily include a crusty, seven-grain loaf and a delightful egg-and-butter bread—nor should the chocolate-chip cookies be overlooked. The bakery is on the main road, on the left as you're heading south from the ferry.

If you're here on Saturday morning between late June and early September, check out the weekly **farmer's market** in North Head.

SAINT JOHN ★

152km (94 miles) SW of Moncton, 112km (70 miles) SE of Fredericton

Centered on a good-size commercial harbor, **Saint John** is New Brunswick's largest city, the center of much of this province's industry. Spread out over a low hill with good rocky views, the downtown boasts elaborate Victorian flourishes on its rows of commercial buildings. A few impressive mansions are tucked into the side streets, their interiors featuring intricate wood carving—appropriately so, since timber barons built most of those.

Saint John

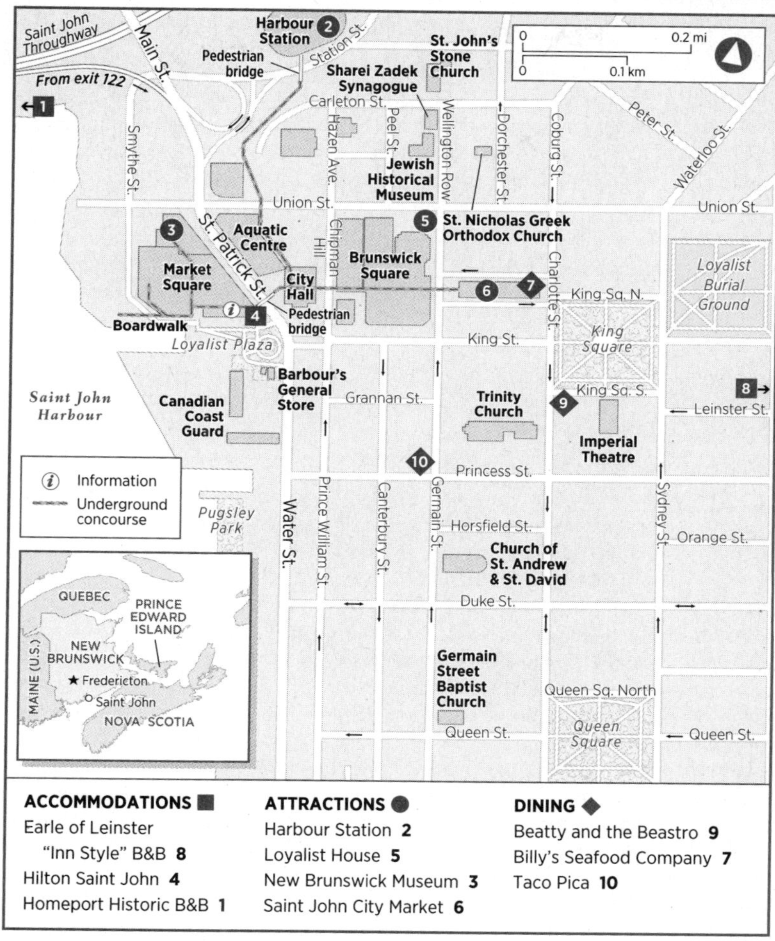

There's an industrial grittiness to the city, which can be either unappealing or charming. Just don't expect a tidy garden city with lots of neat homes; this isn't that sort of place. Instead, Saint John offers plenty of brick architecture in various states of repair. Throughout downtown you'll see its past and present front and center: big shipping terminals, oil storage tanks, and paper mills. But don't give up. The central downtown district—once you find it—is laid out in gridlike blocks and squares, good for walks waiting for the ferry to Digby, bites to eat, and a pint of beer. You might even stay a night or 2, just to get a break from the cute-village train that Atlantic Canada can sometimes be.

This is a place full of life, not a postcard: Streets often bustle with skateboarders, merchants, carousers, out-for-the-weekenders, and local old-timers casing the public market for discount produce.

Essentials

GETTING THERE

BY PLANE Saint John's **airport,** coded YSJ (✆ **506/638-5555;** www.saintjohnairport.com), has regular flights to and from Montréal, Toronto, and Halifax on **Air Canada** (✆ **888/237-2262;** www.aircanada.com). **WestJet** (✆ **800/538-5696;** www.westjet.com) also operates flights from Toronto. There are auto-rental kiosks in the terminal, and a taxi ride into the city costs about C$30.

BY FERRY Year-round **ferry service** connects Saint John with Digby, Nova Scotia. For more details, see "Exploring New Brunswick" at the beginning of this chapter.

BY CAR Saint John is located on Route 1. It's 106km (66 miles) from the U.S. border at St. Stephens and 427km (265 miles) around the bend from Halifax. If you're driving north from Maine on Route 1, note that there is a **C50¢ toll** to cross the Saint John Harbour Bridge (though you can actually avoid it by taking slower Route 100). Reach downtown by taking exit 122 or 123 off Route 1.

VISITOR INFORMATION Saint John (www.tourismsaintjohn.com) is fully stocked with three visitor information centers (VICs). Arriving from the west, look for the contemporary triangular building near the Route 1 off-ramp: This is the **Route 1 West visitor information center** (✆ **506/658-2940**), open from mid-May through early October until 8pm in mid-summer (until 6pm in the shoulder seasons). You'll find a trove of information and brochures here.

There's another seasonal VIC, the **Reversing Falls information center** (✆ **506/658-2937**), inside the observation building overlooking those falls on Route 100, which is also labeled on maps as Bridge Road. Get there from Route 1 by taking exit 119 or 119B; just like the Route 1 center, this VIC opens from mid-May through mid-October.

If you're already downtown, or you're visiting town outside the peak seasons, look for the **City Centre Tourist Information Centre** (✆ **886/463-8639** or 506/658-2855) inside Market Square, a central shopping mall just off the waterfront. You find the info center by entering the mall at street level, at the corner of St. Patrick and Water streets. It's open 6 days a week (closed Sun) year-round, mid-June to mid-Sept 9am to 7pm and the rest of the year 9am to 5:30 or 6pm.

Exploring Saint John

If the weather's good, begin by wandering around the **waterfront.** Tourism Saint John has published several walking-tour brochures that offer plenty of history and architectural trivia, including a rundown of the oddly fascinating gargoyles and sculpted heads that adorn downtown's 19th-century buildings. If you have time for only one walk, architecture buffs should go on **"Prince William's Walk,"** an hour-long, self-guided tour of the city's impressive commercial buildings. (Personally, though, I like to wing it and just wander.) You can obtain these tour brochures at the **Market Square information center** (see Visitor Information, above).

Wherever you ramble, be sure to drop by the **Saint John City Market** (detailed below) and to work the **Old Burial Ground ★** (across from King's Square) into your itinerary; it's a good place to rest for a spell. The ancient cemetery dates from 1784, but it was renovated quite recently—note the beaver fountain, which is supposed to be symbolic of the city's hardworking citizens. I think.

If you have a car, you'll also want to visit some of the city's **nature preserves.** And if the weather's disagreeable (it could be), head indoors. Saint John has helpfully linked up downtown's malls and shops through an elaborate network of underground passageways and overhead pedestrian walkways dubbed **"The Inside Connection" ★**. The various spurs of the network don't only touch shopping destinations, either: two major hotels, as well as the museum, city library, city market, sports arena, and gleaming aquatic center are linked in, too.

Loyalist House ★ A mandatory destination for antiques buffs or Anglophiles, this stately white Georgian mansion was built in 1817 for the Merritts, a family of wealthy Loyalists from New York. Inside you'll find an extraordinary collection of furniture; most pieces were original to the house and have never left. Especially notable are the extensive holdings of Duncan Phyfe Sheraton furniture and a rare piano-organ combination. The house also features its original brass knocker; doors steamed and bent to fit into the curved sweep of the stairway; and intricate carvings on the wooden chair rails. It even managed to avoid being burnt to the ground during a great fire that razed much of the city in 1877. Tours of the home last 30 to 45 minutes, but the house is open only for a few months out of the year. If you're here some other time, round up an interested group (or a family reunion), give these folks a call, and ask them nicely if they can open up the house. They just might.

120 Union St. ✆ **506/652-3590.** C$3 adults, C$1 children, C$7 families. July to mid-Sept daily 10am–5pm (last admission 4:45pm); mid-May to June Mon–Fri 10am–5pm; Sept–Apr by appointment only.

New Brunswick Museum ★★ ☺ The imposing-looking New Brunswick Museum is a must-stop for anyone seriously curious about this province's natural or cultural history. Collections are displayed on three open floors, an exhaustive mixture of traditional artifacts and quirky objects. Exhibits include the complete interior of Sullivan's Bar (where longshoremen used to slake their thirst a few blocks away); a massive section of ship's frame; wonderful geological exhibits; and even a sporty white Bricklin from a failed stab at auto-manufacturing in the province during the mid-'70s. (Most frightful-looking exhibit? Maybe the "permanent wave" machine from a 1930s beauty parlor.) The "Wind, Wood, and Sail" gallery describes 19th-century shipbuilding in the province, right down to obscure details about oakum, tar, and deadeyes. There's also a Hall of Great Whales, with skeletons and scale models of the giant mammals, including a 12m (40-ft.) right whale. Allow at least 2 hours to enjoy the eclectic, uncommonly well-displayed exhibits here.

1 Market Sq. ✆ **506/643-2300.** Admission C$6 adults, C$4.75 seniors, C$3.25 students and children 4–18, C$13 families. Mon–Fri 9am–5pm (Thurs until 9pm), Sat 10am–5pm, Sun noon–5pm. Closed Mon Nov to mid-May.

Saint John City Market ★★ Hungry travelers, venture here at your peril. This spacious, bustling marketplace is crammed with vendors hawking meat, fresh seafood, cheeses, flowers, baked goods, and bountiful fresh produce. (You can even sample *dulse,* a snack of dried seaweed from the Bay of Fundy—though some travelers have compared the experience to that of licking a wharf.) The market was built in 1876, and has been a constant draw for city residents ever since. Note the construction of the roof—local lore claims it resembles an inverted ship because it was made by boatbuilders who didn't know how to build anything else. Also look for small, enduring traces of tradition: The handsome iron gates at either end have been in place since 1880, and a loud bell is rung daily by the Deputy Market Clerk to signal the opening and closing of the market. A number of vendors offer meals to go, and there's bright seating in an enclosed terrace on the south side. It's definitely worth an hour or two, and perfectly positioned for an eating break for either the road- or walking-tour weary. Just don't make the mistake of coming on a Sunday or a Canadian holiday: it'll be closed.

47 Charlotte St. (facing King's Square). ✆ **506/658-2820.** Mon–Fri 7:30am–6pm; Sat 7:30am–5pm. Closed Sun and holidays.

Where to Stay

Budget travelers should head for Manawagonish Road, where most of the city's lower-priced motels congregate. A bonus: Unlike most motel strips, this one's actually reasonably attractive as it winds along a high ridge west of town, providing views out to the Bay of Fundy. It's about a 10-minute ride from town. Nightly rates at many of the mom-and-pop motels on the strip are unbelievably low, sometimes as low as the C$60 range even during summer. The chain property **Econo Lodge Inn & Suites,** 1441 Manawagonish Rd. (✆ **800/55-ECONO** [553-2666] or **506/635-8700**), is more expensive but a bit more comfortable, and rooms have those sweeping views.

In-town camping is available summers at **Rockwood Park** (✆ **506/652-4050**), though it's a lot more like car camping than in-the-wild camping. Eighty or so sites are spread across a rocky hill; unfortunately, many overlook downtown, the highway, and a railyard (expect nighttime noise). RVs requiring full hookups are directed to an area resembling a parking lot. Other sites vary widely in privacy and scenery. Rates start at around C$18 for a tent site and around C$24 for hookups. Follow signs to the park from either exit 122 or exit 125 off Route 1.

Earle of Leinster "Inn Style" Bed & Breakfast The Earle of Leinster, a handsome Victorian row house in a working-class neighborhood not far from King's Square, is a welcoming, casual place rather than a fancy one; it feels like a small European hotel. There's a kitchen and free self-serve washer and dryer for guests, plus a pool table and TV in the basement. The Fitzgerald and Lord Edward rooms in the main house are the most historic, with high ceilings and regal furniture; most of the rest are out in the carriage house and feel motel-like, though a second-floor loft is quite spacious and some units resemble mini-suites with their microwave ovens. All units have Wi-Fi access; bathrooms, while private, are on the small side.

96 Leinster St., Saint John, NB E2L 1J3. ✆ **506/652-3275.** www.earleofleinster.com. 7 units. C$93–C$115 double. Rates include full breakfast. AE, DC, MC, V. Pets allowed. **Amenities:** Laundry. *In room:* TV/VCR, fridge, hair dryer, kitchenette (some units), no phone.

Hilton Saint John ★★ This 12-story waterfront hotel was built in 1984, and has all the amenities you'd expect from an upscale chain hotel: you're trading personality and charm for dependability. Rooms on the top two floors have been updated and upgraded to include perks like electronic safes, cordless phones, bigger desks, free high-speed Internet, and terry-cloth robes. They also have the best views and big comfy beds. It helps that this hotel boasts probably the best location of any in Saint John, overlooking the harbor yet also just steps from the rest of downtown by street or indoor walkway. Windows in all guest rooms open, allowing in the sea breeze, and the business center is well stocked. This Hilton is connected to the city's convention center, so it attracts large groups of conventioneers and tons of associated events; ask whether anything's scheduled before you book if you don't want to be overwhelmed. The hotel's lounge offers light meals through midnight, while the main dining room serves more refined food in an understated harborside setting nightly.

1 Market Sq., Saint John, NB E2L 4Z6. ✆ **800/561-8282** in Canada, 800/445-8667 in the U.S., or 506/693-8484. Fax 509/657-6610. www.hiltonsaintjohn.com. 197 units. C$119–C$219 double. AE, DC, DISC, MC, V. Self-parking C$17 per night. Pets allowed. **Amenities:** 2 restaurants; bar; lounge; babysitting; concierge; fitness room; Jacuzzi; indoor pool; game room; salon; 24-hr. room service; sauna. *In room:* A/C, TV, hair dryer, minibar.

Homeport Historic Bed & Breakfast ★★ ☺ This architecturally impressive home was built by a prominent shipbuilding family (hence the name), and sits high atop a rocky ridge on the north side of Route 1 overlooking downtown and the harbor. Built around 1858—that's before Canada was even Canada yet—it's one of southern New Brunswick's best options for an overnight if you're a fan of old houses. Rooms here are furnished with materials gleaned from local auctions and shops; look for sleigh beds and (nonworking) marble fireplaces, for instance. The Veranda Room is particularly spacious, with fine harbor views and afternoon sunlight; the walls are decorated with steel engravings commemorating the laying of the first trans-Atlantic cable, floors are of hand-cut pine, and there's locally made antique furniture. The Harbour Master Suite has a four-poster bed and small sitting room good for those traveling with a child or two. As well, all units have individually controlled heat—a rarity in small inns. Breakfasts are served family-style around a long antique table in the dining room.

80 Douglas Ave. (take exit 121 or 123 to Main St.), Saint John, NB E2K 1E4. ✆ **888/678-7678** or 506/672-7255. www.homeport.nb.ca. 10 units. C$109–C$175 double and suite. Rates include full breakfast. AE, MC, V. Free parking. *In room:* A/C, TV, fridge (1 unit); kitchenette (1 unit).

Where to Dine

For lunch, also don't overlook Saint John's **city market** (see above)—grab a light meal and some fresh juice in the market to go, then eat it either in the alley atrium or right on King's Square.

Beatty and the Beastro ★★ 🎁 CONTINENTAL Ignore the silly name; this big-windowed establishment fronting King's Square is one of the best-looking eateries in Saint John, showing off a modern, European look. Service is cordial and efficient, and the food's very good. Lunch includes soups, salads, omelets, curry wraps, and elaborate gourmet sandwiches (but the simple grilled fish sandwich isn't bad, either). Critics have praised the lamb dinner entree, the preparation of which varies nightly according to the chef's desire; the house curries are good, as are chicken parmigiana, schnitzel served with spaetzle, the steaks, chicken Florentine, and a Hungarian-influenced chicken dish (lots of paprika) of the restaurant's own creation. When dessert time rolls around, try a piece of butterscotch pie, coconut cream pie, or lemon chess pie—each has a large local cheering section.

60 Charlotte St. (on King's Sq.). ✆ **506/652-3888.** Reservations recommended on weekends. Main courses C$7–C$10 at lunch, C$20–C$21 at dinner. AE, DC, MC, V. Mon–Fri 11:30am–3pm and 5:30–9pm; Sat 5:30–10pm. Closed Sun.

Billy's Seafood Company ★★ ☺ SEAFOOD It's not fancy but it's not a dive; it's just right. Billy Grant's seafood eatery off King's Square gets big points for its friendly staff, fresh-off-the-boat seafood (they sell it to City Market customers during the day), better pricing than the tourist-oriented seafood restaurants on the waterfront, and great attitude toward kids. They really know how to cook fish here without *over*cooking it. Specialties of the house include cedar-planked salmon, Billy's bouillabaisse, and delicious lighter entrees: lobster rolls, oysters-and-chips, and a chicken breast club sandwich. They also serve steak, pasta, and even a rack of lamb if you're somehow not in the mood for fish.

49-51 Charlotte St. (at City Market). ✆ **888/933-3474** or 506/672-3474. www.billysseafood.com. Reservations suggested. Entrees C$6–C$29. AE, DC, MC, V. Mon–Thurs 11am–10pm; Fri–Sat 11am–11pm; Sun 4–9pm. Closed Sun Jan–Mar.

Taco Pica ★ LATIN AMERICAN Here's something refreshingly different: a restaurant that's cooperatively owned by the chefs, servers, and managers, and some of their friends. (Its full name is "Taco Pica Worker Cooperative Restaurant.") It's bright, festive, and just a short stroll off King Street. The restaurant developed a devoted local following when it opened in the mid-'90s, thanks to a menu that's a notch above the usual staid local adaptations of Latin American and Mexican fare. Reliable dishes prepared here by the Guatemalan staff include *pepian* (a spicy beef stew with chayote); garlic shrimp; and shrimp tacos with potatoes, peppers, and cheese. Vegetarian items are also available, as are a good variety of fresh juices and libations—fruit margaritas definitely put out the fire in a hot dish. Insiders' tip: There's sometimes a live guitarist at night, and the place even occasionally turns into an impromptu Latin-flavored dance club on weekend nights (after the dinner service, of course).

96 Germain St. ✆ **506/633-8492.** Reservations recommended on weekends. Main courses C$8–C$17. AE, MC, V. Mon–Sat 10am–10pm. Closed Sun and holidays.

FREDERICTON

174km (108 miles) W of Moncton, 112km (70 miles) NW of Saint John

Few outsiders probably realize that the capital of New Brunswick is *not* Saint John: It's the city of Fredericton, a compact, historic place of brick and concrete that unfolds along the banks of the wide Saint John River. Its handsome buildings, broad streets, and wide sidewalks make the place feel more like a big village than a small city. Two icons announce you've arrived: the stately elm trees here that somehow resisted Dutch elm disease, and the Union Jack occasionally fluttering from buildings, attesting to long-standing ties with Mother England.

The city is divided into three zones: malls and motels atop the hills near the Trans-Canada Highway; the impressive, Georgian-style University of New Brunswick on a hillside just south of town; and downtown itself, a casual blend of modern and historic buildings.

Fredericton

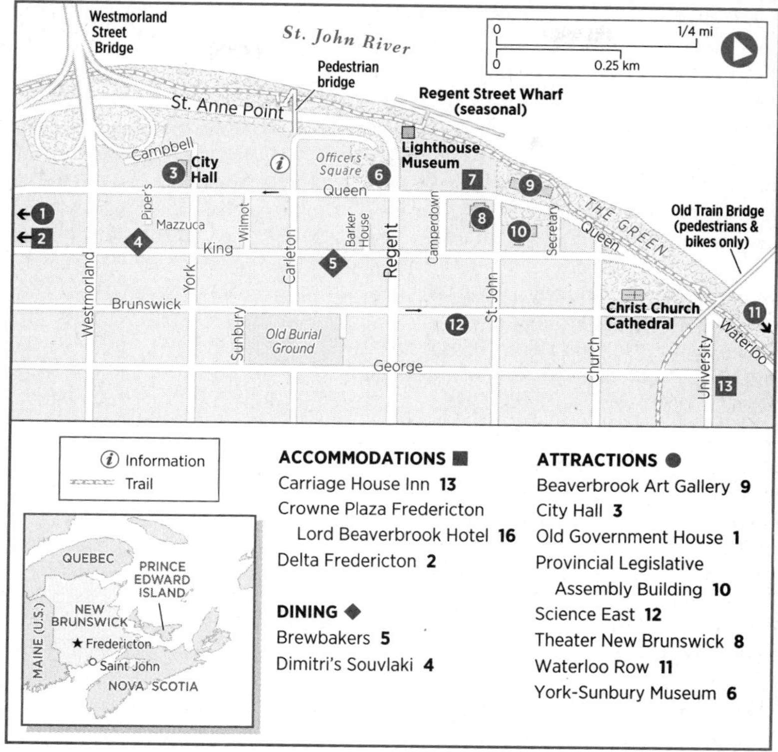

Most visitors focus on the **downtown.** The main artery—where you'll find the bulk of the attractions and restaurants—is **Queen Street,** which parallels the river. An ill-considered four-lane highway separates much of the center from the actual river banks, but you can reach water's edge either via **The Green,** a pathway that follows the river, or by crossing a pedestrian bridge at the foot of Carleton Street.

Once you've seen the river, it's time to get to know the buildings and people. With a population of just 50,000 (not including its 'burbs), Fredericton is low-key. There's really no single must-see attraction here, but strolling the streets gives you a sense of history and place. If New Brunswick's main allure for you lies in its shimmering sea, deep woods, high tides, and wide open spaces, you won't miss much by skipping Fredericton. But if your passions include history—especially the history of British settlements in North America—it's well worth the detour.

Essentials

GETTING THERE BY PLANE **Fredericton International Airport** (**© 506/ 460-0920;** www.frederictonairport.ca), coded YFC, is located 10 minutes southeast of downtown on Route 102 and is served by cab and rental-car companies. For flight information, contact **Air Canada** (© **888/247-2262;** www.aircanada.com), which is basically the only carrier here. The airline connects Fredericton daily with Montréal, Halifax, and Toronto.

GETTING THERE BY CAR Fredericton's not on the way to anything. Fortunately, though, it's only about 112km (70 miles)—a little more than an hour's drive—north from Saint John via Route 7. From the U.S.-Canadian border at Houlton, Maine, it's about the same distance: Take Route 95 to Woodstock, New Brunswick, then turn onto the Trans-Canada Highway and follow it east for an hour. Look for signs directing you downtown. (From the west, follow Woodstock Road, which tracks along the river. From Saint John, look for Route 7 to Regent Street, and then turn right down the hill.)

VISITOR INFORMATION Always careful to cater to visitors, Fredericton maintains several central visitor information centers. There's one in **City Hall** at 397 Queen St. (© **506/460-2129**), open May through October; one in an Irving Big Stop gas station, near the airport; and a third at **King's Landing** (© **506/460-2191**), at 20 Kings Landing Rd. just west of town in River Valley, open from mid-May through early October. No matter which one you find first, ask for a Visitor Parking Pass, which allows visitors from outside the province to park free at city lots and meters in town for several days without penalty. You can also request travel information in advance by visiting the city's website at **www.tourismfredericton.ca** or by calling © **888/888-4768** or 506/460-2129.

Exploring Fredericton

The free ***Fredericton Visitor Guide,*** available at the information centers and many hotels around town, includes a well-written and informative **walking tour** of the downtown area. It's worth tracking down before exploring the city.

City Hall, at 397 Queen St., is an elaborate Victorian building with a prominent brick tower and a 2.5m (8-ft.) clock dial. The second-floor City Council Chamber occupies what used to be Fredericton's opera house until the 1940s. Small, folksy tapestries adorn the **visitor's gallery** and tell the town's history. Learn about these tapestries—and the rest of the building—during free tours, offered twice daily from mid-May through mid-October (both in English and French). Contact the tourism office (© **506/460-2129**) to arrange a tour.

Officers' Square, on Queen Street between Carleton and Regent streets, is a handsome city park now, but in 1785 it was the center of the city's military activity; it was chiefly used for drills, first as part of the British garrison and then, until 1914, by the Canadian Army. Today, the only soldiers are local actors who put on a little show for the tourists. Concerts and dramatic events are also staged on the square during summer. That handsome colonnaded stone building facing the parade grounds is the former officers' quarters, now the **York-Sunbury Museum** (see below).

In the center of the square, there's a prominent statue of a robed Lord Beaverbrook. It's a name you hear a lot in Fredericton—a street, a museum, and a hotel also bear his name—though it wasn't actually his name; he was born Max Aitken in Newcastle, New Brunswick. Aitken amassed a fortune, primarily in publishing, during his life and was made a lord in Britain in 1917, using the name of a stream near Newcastle where he had fished as a boy. Aitken later donated an art collection and a modern building to house it in (the Beaverbrook Art Gallery, natch), along with a modern playhouse, now home to the **Theatre New Brunswick,** built the same year Beaverbrook died (1964).

Two blocks upriver from Officers' Square are the Soldiers' Barracks, housed in a similarly grand stone building. Check your watch against a sundial high on the end of the barracks, a replica of the original timepiece. A small exhibit explains the life of enlisted men during the 18th century.

Fredericton is well noted for its distinctive architecture, especially its neighborhoods of fine Victorian and Queen Anne residences. Particularly attractive is **Waterloo Row ★**, a group of privately owned historic homes—some grand, some less so—just south of the downtown area. Follow the river bank south (near the University of New Brunswick) to find these houses.

One entertaining and enlightening way to learn about the city's history is to sign up for a walking tour with the **Calithumpians Theatre Company ★**. Costumed guides offer free tours in July and August, pointing out highlights with anecdotes and dramatic tales. Recommended is the nighttime "Haunted Hike" tour, done by lantern light, which runs 6 nights each week (no Sunday tours). The tour takes about 2 hours and costs C$13 for adults, C$8 for children; meet at The Coach House at the corner of Church and Queen streets (behind Gallery 78). Call the theater company at **✆ 506/457-1975** for more information.

If you're in town on a Saturday, do not miss the **Boyce Farmers' Market ★** (**✆ 506/451-1815**) at 665 George St. (corner of Regent St.)—it's adjacent to **Science East** (see below). This award-winning market, which runs from about 6am until about 1pm, has existed here in one form or another since the late 18th century (although the current building was constructed in the 1950s, and later expanded). Something approaching 200 vendors—butchers, bakers, even some candlestick makers—still hawk everything from fresh produce to crafts, croissants, and artisanal smoked meats, just as they always have done. *Harrowsmith* magazine once selected this market as one of the top farmer's markets in Canada. It's well worth an hour of your Saturday morning.

Also don't miss any event hosted by the local artists' coop **Gallery Connexion** (**✆ 506/454-1433;** www.galleryconnexion.ca). Currently without a permanent home or studio space, the collective nonetheless soldiers on, presenting talks, video artworks, exhibitions, musical performances, and other events. Check the website or call the gallery office, located (for now) at the Fredericton Playhouse.

Beaverbrook Art Gallery ★ This surprisingly impressive museum overlooks the waterfront and is home to an extensive collection of British paintings, including works by Reynolds, Gainsborough, Constable, and Turner. Antiques buffs gravitate to the rooms with period furnishings and early decorative arts, while others find themselves drawn to Dalí's massive *Santiago El Grande* and studies for an ill-fated portrait of Winston Churchill. Exhibits of modern art are increasing. Other shows have touched on more conventional ground, such as 19th-century French realism and a show on the cities of Canada drawn from The Seagram Collection. This gallery is especially strong when showing the art of First Nations (native Canadian) artists. Stop by, or check the website, to find out what's currently on display.

703 Queen St. **✆ 506/458-2028.** www.beaverbrookartgallery.org. Admission C$8 adults, C$6 seniors, C$3 students, C$18 families; Thurs evenings after 5:30pm pay what you wish. Tues–Wed and Fri–Sat 9am–5:30pm, Thurs 9am–9pm, Sun noon to 5:30pm. Closed Mon Jan–May.

Old Government House ★ Government House, constructed in 1828, was built as the official residence of the lieutenant governor and governor of the province of locally quarried sandstone in a rigorously classical style. It features a Palladian symmetry and intricate plasterwork. During various periods of time it housed a school, a military hospital, and a detachment of Mounties; spared from the wrecking ball, the home was restored and reopened in 1999, and is now once again the official residence of the lieutenant governor, who has an apartment on the third floor and an office on the second floor. Bilingual tours begin in the basement interpretive center and last about 45 minutes. You hike sweeping staircases and view extraordinarily high-ceilinged reception rooms; there's an art gallery on the second floor, and the rooms are full of intriguing period pieces and fixtures. Ask the helpful guides anything.

51 Woodstock Rd. (next to the Sheraton hotel). ✆ **506/453-2505.** www.gnb.ca/lg/ogh. Free admission. Mid May–Aug tours Mon–Sat 10am–4pm and Sun noon–4pm; off season by appointment only.

Provincial Legislative Assembly Building ★★ New Brunswick's official Assembly Building, built in 1880, boasts an exterior in bulbous, extravagant Second Empire style, but the dressed-up interior is the star. Behind heavy doors that look like the gates of Oz, you find a creaky, wooden place that's surprisingly welcoming. In the small rotunda, look first for the prints from John James Audubon's elephant folio, which are kept on display in a special case. The assembly chamber itself nearly takes your breath away, especially when viewed from the visitor gallery on the upper floors. (To get there, you climb a graceful wood spiral stairway housed in its own rotunda.) The chamber is over-the-top ornate in that fussy Victorian way all out of proportion to the legislative humdrum. Note the regal trappings, including a portrait of a young Queen Elizabeth. Half-hour-long tours are available; plan to spend at least an hour here if you really love old buildings. ***Note:*** At press time, this building was closed to tours due to ongoing renovations. Call ahead to learn its current status.

706 Queen St. (across from the Beaverbrook Art Gallery). ✆ **506/453-2506.** www.gnb.ca/legis. Free admission. June to mid-Aug daily 9am–5pm.

Science East ★★ ☺ Children usually enjoy a visit to this science center for two reasons: First, it's located in an old jail, a sturdy stone structure built in the 1840s (and still used as a jail as late as 1996). And then there are the great exhibits: more than 150 interactive displays in all, both indoors and out. Kids can fool around with a huge kaleidoscope, use a periscope to people-watch, check out a solar-powered water fountain, make patterns with a laser beam, even create a miniature tornado—though, truth be told, the dungeon museum probably will impress them more than all that. It's an ideal place to visit with the kids on a chilly or rainy day, and there's lots to do outside here on nice days, too. This is one of Canada's preeminent science museums, and if you have kids with a spark of curiosity, this place is easily worth up to 2 hours of your time.

668 Brunswick St. ✆ **506/457-2340.** www.scienceeast.nb.ca. Admission C$8 adults, C$7 seniors, C$5 children under 16 or students, C$22 families. June–Aug Mon–Sat 10am–5pm, Sun noon–4pm; rest of the year, Mon–Fri noon–5pm, Sat 10am–5pm, closed Sun.

Outside of Town

Kings Landing Historical Settlement ★★ Kings Landing, on the bank of the Saint John River, is about 32km (20 miles)—and 150 years—away from Fredericton.

The huge (121-hectare/300-acre) authentic re-creation brings to life the New Brunswick from the years 1790 to 1910: It consists of about 20 historic homes and buildings. The aroma of baking bread mixes with the smells of horses and livestock (make what you will of that), and the blacksmith's hammer clashes with church bells while costumed "settlers" chat about their lives. The best buildings—nearly all built by Loyalists relocated from New England—include Hagerman House (furniture by cabinetmaker John Warren Moore), Ingraham House (regional furniture and a formal English garden), and Morehouse House (an interesting kitchen and a clock Benedict Arnold left behind). The C. B. Boss Sash and Door Factory is a simulated turn-of-the-20th-century manufacturing plant. There's also an ox barn, a farmhouse, several churches, and a scenic little cove to enjoy.

Afterward, hitch a ride on the sloven wagon—a low-slung work wagon distinctive to the Maritimes (it was invented in Saint John)—or lunch at the King's Head Inn, which served travelers along the Saint John River more than a century ago and offers grub and grog such as ale, chicken pie, and corn chowder.

20 Kings Landing Rd. (exit 253 off the Trans-Canada Hwy., on Rte. 2 west). ✆ **506/363-4999.** www.kingslanding.nb.ca. Admission C$16 adults, C$14 seniors, C$13 students over 16, C$11 children 6–16, C$37 families. June to mid-Oct daily 10am–5pm. Closed mid-Oct to May.

Where to Stay

In addition to the properties listed below, a clutch of motels and chain hotels are bunched up in a bustling mall zone on the hillside above town (along Regent and Prospect sts.), about 10 minutes' drive from downtown.

The Carriage House Inn ★ 🎁 Fredericton's premier B&B is a short stroll from the riverfront pathway, in a quiet residential neighborhood—and B&B travelers love it. A former mayor and local lumber baron built the imposing three-story Victorian home in 1875; inside, it's all dark wood trim, deep colors, floral-printed sofas, and a few steep stairs. Rooms—nine of which are queen-bedded, one of which is double-bedded—are furnished with plenty of period art and antiques; some public areas of the inn are so cluttered with these artifacts, in fact, that you feel you're actually inside a museum instead of a hotel. High-speed Wi-Fi is available in the house, and delicious big breakfasts are included with the rate; they're served in the sunny ballroom at the rear of the mansion by bilingual hosts, who get raves far and wide for their hospitality. This is not a luxury inn, but it's a very restful place if you're the sort who doesn't mind sleeping in historic old homes. And, helpfully, it's open year-round.

230 University Ave., Fredericton, NB E3B 4H7. ✆ **800/267-6068** or 506/452-9924. Fax 506/452-2770. www.carriagehouse-inn.net. 10 units. C$99–C$129 double. Rates include full breakfast. AE, MC, V. "Small, well-trained pets" allowed. **Amenities:** Restaurant. *In room:* A/C, TV, hair dryer.

Crowne Plaza Fredericton Lord Beaverbrook Hotel ★ ☺ This hulking waterfront hotel looks boxy and dour from the street. But inside, the mood lightens, thanks to interesting composite stone floors, Georgian pilasters, and happy chandeliers. The indoor pool and recreation area downstairs are positively whimsical, a sort of tiki-room grotto motif that kids love. Guest rooms are appointed with traditional reproduction furniture in dark wood—freshened up since Crowne Plaza acquired the property—though the standard, lowest-priced rooms can be somewhat dim and most windows don't open (ask for a room with windows that do open if that's important to you). However, the suites here are spacious, and many have excellent river views. Some Jacuzzi suites have now been added, but this is still an old-fashioned hotel at its heart; those looking for a more modern feel should check out the Delta (see below) before booking. There are several choices for dining: The **Terrace Room** is the main dining area, with an indoor gazebo, tapestries, and a deck overlooking the river. The more intimate **Governor's Room** has higher aspirations, with French-inflected dinner entrees. Finally, the **Maverick Room** (once known as the James Joyce Irish Pub) is the spot for a pint and a snack.

659 Queen St., Fredericton, NB E3B 5A6. ✆ **877/579-7666** or 506/455-3371. Fax 506/455-1441. www.cpfredericton.com. 168 units. $109–$199 double; suites up to $599. Packages available. AE, DC, MC, V. **Amenities:** 3 restaurants; pub; babysitting; Jacuzzi; indoor pool; sauna. *In room:* A/C, TV, hair dryer, Jacuzzi (some units).

Delta Fredericton ★★ This resort hotel, built only in 1992, occupies a prime location on the river about a 10-minute walk from downtown via the riverfront pathway. In summer, life revolves around an outdoor pool (with its own poolside bar) on a deck overlooking the river. Sundays the lobby is taken over by an over-the-top brunch buffet. Though obviously up to date, the Delta's interior is done with classical styling; some suites are positively huge, and some come with Jacuzzis and river balconies. The hotel's lounge is an active and popular nightspot, especially on weekends. Across the lobby is **Bruno's Seafood & Chophouse,** a good alternative to the restaurants downtown. The chef usually cooks with whatever's fresh at the farmer's market; look for seasonal and regional specialties (even fiddleheads in early summer), local vegetables and fruits in season, and good steaks.

225 Woodstock Rd., Fredericton, NB E3B 2H8. ✆ **888/462-8800** or 506/457-7000. Fax 506/457-7000. www.deltafredericton.com. 222 units. C$119–C$219 double; suites C$249–C$800. AE, DC, MC, V. Free parking. Pets accepted. **Amenities:** Restaurant; 2 bars; babysitting; fitness room; Jacuzzi; heated indoor pool and heated outdoor pool; room service; sauna. *In room:* A/C, TV, minibar, hair dryer, fridge (some units), Jacuzzi (some units).

Where to Dine

Brewbakers ★★ ITALIAN Brewbakers is a fun pub, cafe, and restaurant on three levels in a cleverly adapted downtown building. It's a bustling and informal spot—a meeting spot of sorts for the town—creatively cluttered with art and artifacts. Lunch hours and early evenings get very busy. The cafe section is quieter, as is a mezzanine dining room above the cafe, while the third floor bustles with the open kitchen. Lunch features sandwiches that get fancier every year: smoked salmon, pulled pork, triple-cream Brie, and oven-roasted peppers with garlicky mayo are just samples of what might be on the card. For dinner, pastas are the main attraction, served up with the usual array of sauces, and recent years have brought haute cuisine (a maple-curry-chicken-cream pasta is just one offering). Other good nighttime choices include pizzas, pan-roasted scallops, strip loin, and herb-crusted tenderloin. The cocktail menu has been expanded to take in some Asian- and martini-influenced libations, too—this place is almost hip now.

546 King St. ✆ **506/459-0067.** Reservations recommended. Main courses C$8–C$16 at lunch, C$18–C$28 at dinner. AE, DC, MC, V. Mon–Thurs 11:30am–10pm; Fri 11:30am–11pm; Sat 4–11pm; Sun 4–10pm.

Dimitri's Souvlaki GREEK Dimitri's is hard to find and easy to walk past. But the generic, chain-restaurant interior belies decent cooking for budget-conscious diners. You'll get a big plate of food here without spending a lot of money.

Greek specialties include moussaka (with and without meat), souvlaki, and *dolmades*. Deluxe dinner plates are served with excellent potatoes—hearty wedges cooked crispy on the outside, yet hot and soft within.

349 King St. (in Piper's Lane area). ✆ **506/452-8882.** Main courses C$8–C$18. AE, DC, MC, V. Mon–Sat 11am–10pm.

FUNDY NATIONAL PARK ★★

The **Fundy Coast** (between Saint John and Alma) is for the most part wild, remote, and unpopulated. It's criss-crossed by few roads other than the Fundy Drive, making it difficult to explore deeply—unless you happen to have brought a boat with you, which I'm guessing you didn't. The best access to this coast is at **Fundy National Park,** a gem of a destination that's hugely popular in summer with travelers of an outdoors bent. Families often settle in here for a week or so, filling their days with activities in and around the park such as hiking, sea kayaking, biking, and splashing around in a seaside pool.

Nearby there are also some lovely drives, plus an innovative adventure center at **Cape Enrage.** You can even vary your adventuring according to the weather: if a muffling fog moves in and smothers the coastline (and it might), head inland for a hike to a waterfall through lush forest. If it's a day of brilliant sunshine, on the other hand, venture along the rocky shores by foot, bike, or boat, and bring a camera.

Essentials

GETTING THERE Route 114 runs through the center of Fundy National Park. If you're coming from the west, follow the prominent national park signs just east of **Sussex**. If you're coming from Prince Edward Island or Nova Scotia, head southward on Route 114 from Moncton.

VISITOR INFORMATION The park's main **Visitor Centre** (✆ **506/887-6000**) is located just inside the **Alma** (eastern) entrance to the park. The stone building is open daily during peak season from 8am to 10pm, and until 4:30pm the rest of the year. You can watch a video presentation, peruse a handful of exhibits on wildlife and tides, and shop at the nicely stocked nature bookstore. The smaller **Wolfe Lake Information Centre** (✆ **506/432-6026**) is at the park's western entrance; it's open until 6pm daily, from late June through late August.

The small town of **Alma** also maintains a seasonal information center at 8584 Main St. (✆ **506/887-6127**), open from late spring through September.

FEES Park entry fees are charged from mid-May to mid-October. The fee is C$7.80 adults, C$6.80 seniors, C$3.90 children ages 6 to 16, and C$20 families. Seasonal and annual passes are also available.

Exploring the Park

Most national park activities are centered around the Alma (eastern) side of the park, where the park entrance has a cultivated and manicured air, as if part of a landed estate. Here you'll find stone walls, well-tended lawns, and attractive landscaping, along with a golf course, amphitheater, lawn bowling, and tennis.

Also in this area is a **heated saltwater pool,** set near the bay with a sweeping ocean view. There's a lifeguard on duty, and it's a popular destination for families. The pool is open from late June through early September. Entrance costs C$3.40 adults, C$2.90 seniors, C$1.65 children, and C$8.80 for families.

Sea kayaking tours are a great way to get an up-close look at the marine environment here—but you want expert help when kayaking the world's highest tides. **FreshAir Adventure** (✆ **800/545-0020** or 506/887-2249) in Alma offers tours that range from 2 hours to several days. The half-day tours explore marsh and coastline (C$48–C$60 per person, including snack); the full-day adventure includes a hot meal and 6 hours of exploring the wild shores (C$90–C$110 per person).

Birders are always pleased to learn that some 250-plus species have been sighted within park boundaries, and almost half of them breed here. Notably, the endangered peregrine falcon has been reintroduced to the bay's steep cliffs.

The park maintains miles and miles of scenic **trails** for hikers and walkers, with good signage and stairs where necessary. These range from a 20-minute loop to a 4-hour trek, and they pass through varied terrain. The trails are arranged such that several can be linked into a full 48km (30-mile) backpacker's loop, dubbed the **Fundy Circuit** (which typically requires 3 to 5 nights camping in the backcountry; preregistration is required, so check in at the visitor center if you're serious about doing it).

Among the most accessible hikes is the **Caribou Plain Trail ★**, a 3km (2-mile) loop that provides a wonderful introduction to the local terrain. You hike along a beaver pond, across a raised peat bog via boardwalk, then through lovely temperate forest. Read the interpretive signs to learn about deadly "flarks" which lurk in bogs and can swallow a moose whole. **Third Vault Falls Trail ★★** is an 8km (5-mile), in-and-back hike that takes you to the park's highest waterfall (it's about 14m/46 ft. high). The trail is largely a flat stroll through leafy woodlands—until you begin a steady descent into a mossy gorge. You round a corner and there you are, suddenly facing the cataract. How cool is that?

All the park's trails are covered in the pullout trail guide you'll find in *Salt & Fir,* the visitors' guide you receive when you pay your entry fee at the gatehouse.

CAMPING The national park maintains four drive-in campgrounds and about 15 backcountry sites. The two main campgrounds are near the Alma entrance. **Headquarters Campground ★** is within walking distance of Alma, the saltwater pool, and numerous other attractions. Since it overlooks the bay, this campground tends to be cool and subject to fogs. **Chignecto North Campground ★** is higher on the hillside, sunnier, and warmer. You can hike down to Alma on an attractive hiking trail in 1 to 2 hours. Both campgrounds have hookups for RVs, flush toilets, and showers, and both can be reserved in advance online (✆ **877/737-3783;** www.pccamping.ca); sites cost C$16 to C$35 per night, depending on services offered.

The **Point Wolfe** and **Wolfe Lake** campgrounds lack RV hookups and are slightly more primitive, but they are the preferred destinations for campers seeking a quieter camping experience. Rates at Point Wolfe, where showers and flush toilets are available, are about C$25 and it too can be reserved online via Canada's national parks campground website at **www.pccamping.ca**. Wolfe Lake lacks showers and has only pit toilets—thus a night there costs only about C$16. Call the park directly to reserve.

Backcountry sites are scattered throughout the park, with only one located directly on the coast (at the confluence of the coast and Goose River). Ask at the visitor centers for more information or to reserve a site (mandatory). Backcountry camping fees are about C$10 per person per night.

A Side Trip to Hopewell Rocks

There's no better place in Canada to witness the extraordinary power of ocean tides than at the **Hopewell Rocks ★★★** (✆ **877/734-3429;** www.thehopewellrocks.ca), located about 40km (25 miles) northeast of Fundy National Park on Route 114. Think of it as a natural sculpture garden. At low tide (the best time to visit), these eroded columns as high as 15m (50 feet) stand on the ocean floor like Brancusi or Easter Island statues, and you can walk right out among them and gawk. (They're sometimes called the "flowerpots," on account of the trees and plants that still flourish on their narrowing summits.) But don't linger: Most of those rocks will be under water in a few hours.

When you arrive, park at the visitor center and restaurant and wander down to the shore. (There's also a shuttle service that runs from the interpretive center to the rocks for a small fee.) Signboards fill you in on the natural history of the rocks. If you've come at low tide, you can descend the steel staircase to the sea floor and admire these wondrous free-standing rock sculptures, chiseled by waves and tides.

Even the **visitor center** is a pleasant place to spend some time. It not only has intriguing exhibits (look for the satellite photos of the area, and a time-lapse video of the tides) but the cafeteria-style restaurant has terrific views from its floor-to-ceiling windows and serves good, simple food.

The park charges an entry fee of C$8.50 adults, C$7.25 students and seniors, C$6.25 children ages 5 to 18, and C$23 families. It's open daily mid-May to mid-June, 9am to 5pm, then 8am to 8pm from mid-June until mid-August (mid-Aug to late Aug to 6pm only), and from 9am to 5pm from September until it closes in mid-October. Note that the site can get crowded at peak times, which is understandable given its uniqueness and beauty, but might not jive with your ideal of peace and quiet. If your schedule allows it, come early in the day, when most travelers are still in bed.

If you arrive at the top half of the tide, consider a sea kayak tour around the islands and caves. **Baymount Outdoor Adventures** (✆ **877/601-2660** or 506/734-2660) runs 90-minute kayak tours of Hopewell Rocks from June through early September for C$55 per adult, C$45 per child, or C$180 per family. Caving tours of nearby caverns are also offered by this family outfit; contact them for details.

Where to Stay

Broadleaf Guest Ranch ★ ☺ The two-bedroom cottages at this homey, family-operated ranch are a great choice for families or couples traveling together, particularly those with an interest in horses: The ranch offers rides of varying duration; cattle checks; even some basic spa packages. (Think of it as a dude ranch without the snakes.) Cottages here sport full kitchens, small sitting areas with gas stoves, and lovely sweeping views of the 607-hectare (1,500-acre) ranch property and bay. You won't mistake these lodgings for a luxury experience: Bedrooms are furnished with bunkbeds (a single over a double). While un-fancy, staying here is like sinking into a favorite chair: comforting. So is the home-cooking that Broadleaf dishes up in a large, cafeteria-style dining area. In addition to the cottages, there are three simple bed-and-breakfast rooms in the main house, a little 9-site campground (with hookups) in an apple orchard, and an annex known as "Broadleaf Too."

5526 Rte. 114, Hopewell Hill NB E4H 3N5. ✆ **800/226-5405** or 506/882-2349. Fax 506/882-2075. www.broadleafranch.com. 7 units. Main inn rooms C$60 double; chalets and apartments C$150–C$200. Packages available. MC, V. **Amenities:** Restaurant; bike rentals; room service; spa; watersports equipment. *In room:* TV/VCR (some units), kitchenette (some units), no phone.

Fundy Highlands Inn and Chalets ★ ☺ This property's 24 cottages—managed by provincial natives Doug and Donna Stewart—are furnished with color televisions, beach towels, and kitchenette units. Some of the cottages even have built-in bunk beds, a good choice for travelers with young children. It's also notable for its grounds, rose beds, and good views of the bay and coastline from many of the cottages' windows. If the chalets are all fully booked up, the same owners run the adjacent **Fundy Park Motel,** with 20 basic rooms for C$69 to C$89 each; all of the motel rooms have kitchenettes, too, and second-floor rooms have a veranda. Just be aware that all rooms in the motel are furnished with bunk beds only.

8714 Rte. 114, Fundy National Park, NB E4H 4V3. ✆ **877/883-8639** or 506/887-2930. www.fundyhighlandchalets.com. 24 units. Cottages C$79–$C105. Packages available. MC, V. *In room:* TV, kitchenette.

Where to Dine

Amid the scattering of seafood takeout and lobster shops in and around the park, one good picnic pick is **Butland's** (✆ **506/887-2190;** www.fundylobster.com) at 8607 Main St. in Alma beside the town wharf. They sell locally caught crustaceans, scallops, and smoked salmon. You can cook the lobster yourself in your cabin, or have these guys do it; there are no tables here. The shack is open daily from mid-May through Labor Day, then weekends until New Year's.

There's also a bakery in Alma, **Kelly's Bake Shop,** at 8587 Main St. (✆ **506/887-2460**), open year-round. They serve big, locally famous sticky buns.

MONCTON

152km (94 miles) NE of Saint John, 174km (108 miles) E of Fredericton

Moncton makes a claim that it's the crossroads of the Maritimes, and it hasn't been bashful about using this lucky geographic position (it *is* at the crossing of several major highways) to promote itself as a regional business hub. As a result, the majority of downtown's hotels and restaurants here cater to people in suits, rather than travelers, at least on the weekdays. But there is some life here; take a walk down Main Street at night or on a weekend, and you'll spot spiky hairdos, flannel, skateboards, and other youthful fashion accouterments.

For families, Moncton offers a decent way station if you're traveling with kids. A concentration of family-friendly attractions, including **Crystal Palace** (see "Exploring Moncton," below), offer entertaining—if somewhat pricey—ways to fill an idle afternoon.

Essentials

GETTING THERE BY PLANE Moncton's small **international airport** (www.gmia.ca) is about 11km (7 miles, or 10 minutes) from downtown via Route 132; you basically head straight out Main St. and cross the river. (From the airport, take Rue

Champlain straight into town.) **Air Canada** (✆ **888/AIR-CANA** [247-2262]; www.aircanada.com) has long served the city, and Canadian carrier **WestJet** (✆ **888/937-8538;** www.westjet.com) now also connects Moncton with Toronto and other points in Canada. From the U.S., **Continental** (✆ **800/231-0856;** www.continental.com) flies to and from Newark daily. At last count, there were four international-chain car rental agencies at the airport.

GETTING THERE BY TRAIN The **VIA Rail** (✆ **888/842-7245;** www.viarail.com) *Ocean* train from Montréal to Halifax stops in Moncton 6 days a week. Moncton's station is located on Main Street, next to Highfield Square.

GETTING THERE BY CAR Moncton is at the crossroads of several major routes through New Brunswick, including Route 2 (the Trans-Canada Hwy.) and Route 15.

VISITOR INFORMATION There's a downtown visitor information center located centrally in **Bore Park,** just off Main Street at 10 Bendview Court (✆ **506/853-3540**), open daily from mid-May through September. The city's tourism website is located at **www.gomoncton.com.**

Exploring Moncton

Moncton's downtown is easily reconnoitered on foot—if you can find parking. (Look for lots a block just north and south of Main St.) **Downtown Moncton, Inc.,** publishes a nicely designed "Historic Walking Tour" brochure that touches upon some of the most significant buildings; ask for it at the visitor center.

The most active stretch of Main Street is the section between City Hall and the train underpass: an accumulation of cafes, newsstands, hotels, and restaurants, plus a handful of shops. There's also quite a mix of architectural styles here, the earliest examples of which testify to Moncton's former prosperity and prominence as a regional center of commerce.

Crystal Palace ★ ☺ The indoor amusement park at Crystal Palace can make a rainy day with the kids go by quickly. The spacious, enclosed park includes a four-screen cinema, shooting arcades, numerous games (ranging from Skee-Ball to video games), a medium-size roller coaster, a carousel, swing ride, laser tag, bumper cars, miniature airplane and truck rides, miniature golf, batting cages, and even a virtual-reality ride. The park especially appeals to kids under the age of 12, though teens will likely find a few video games to occupy them, too. Families can stay virtually inside the park by booking a room at the adjoining Ramada Plaza Crystal Palace Hotel (see "Where to Stay," below).

At Champlain Place Shopping Centre (Trans-Canada Hwy., exit 504-A W.), 499 Paul St., Dieppe. ✆ **506/859-4386** or 877/856-4386 (eastern Canada only). www.crystalpalace.ca. Free admission. Rides are 1–4 tickets each (book of 25 C$23); unlimited ride bracelets C$23 adults, C$20 children shorter than 4 ft., C$73 families. Game tokens C$20 per 100. Late June to early Sept daily 10am–10pm; rest of year Mon–Thurs noon–8pm, Fri noon–9pm, Sat 10am–9pm, Sun 10am–8pm.

Where to Stay

In addition to the properties listed below, a welter of inexpensive and mid-priced chain hotels have set up shop near the complex of services around the attraction known as Magnetic Hill. Double rooms range from as little as C$65 up to as high as C$199, though they tend toward the lower end of that range. To reach these hotels from the Trans-Canada Hwy, take exit 450.

Delta Beauséjour ★ The downtown Delta Beauséjour, constructed in the 1970s, is boxy, bland, and concrete (what else would you expect from the '70s?), and the entrance courtyard is somewhat sterile and off-putting. But inside, the decor is more inviting. Rooms are appointed in usual business-hotel style; a third-floor indoor pool offers year-round swimming, while a pleasant outdoor deck overlooks the distant marshes of the Petitcodiac River. The hotel is a favorite among corporate travelers, but in summer and on weekends leisure travelers largely get it to themselves. In addition to the elegant **Windjammer** restaurant (dinner only; see "Where to Dine," below), the hotel also has **Triiio** (a restaurant/lounge serving three meals a day) and a cafeteria space serving breakfast, lunch, and snacks all day.

750 Main St., Moncton, NB E1C 1E6. ✆ **888/351-7666** or 506/854-4344. Fax 506/858-0957. www.deltahotels.com. 310 units. C$129–C$199 double. Rates include continental breakfast. AE, DC, MC, V. **Amenities:** 3 restaurants; bar; babysitting; fitness center; indoor heated pool; 24-hr. room service. *In room:* A/C, TV, fax (some units), minibar.

Ramada Plaza Moncton ★ This modern, three-story chain hotel adjoins the Crystal Palace amusement park (see above), a short walk from the region's largest mall. As such, it's surrounded by acres of asphalt and has little in the way of native charm. Most rooms are modern (a number are suites), unexceptional but well furnished with amenities like mini-fridges and minibars. But there's a surprise here: a handful of "fantasy suites" that go way over the top with themes like "Deserted Island" (you sleep in a thatched hut) and "Rock 'n' Roll" (you sleep in a bed that's a replica of a pink '59 Cadillac). This is corny kitschy hostelry the way it used to be. Some of this Ramada's rooms face the hotel's tropics-themed indoor pool, but others face that vast parking lot, so book carefully. For entertainment, there's the amusement park right outside the hotel, obviously. The hotel's restaurant, McGinnis Landing, serves basic pub grub and buffet brunches. It's a bit pricey, but the restaurant does cater well to kids' appetites. Some of the hotel's package offerings include tickets to the amusement park.

499 Paul St., Dieppe, NB E1A 6S5. ✆ **800/561-7108** or 506/858-8584. Fax 506/858-5486. www.crystalpalacehotel.com. 115 units. C$90–C$275 double. Packages available. AE, DC, DISC, MC, V. **Amenities:** Restaurant; bar; babysitting; Jacuzzi; indoor pool; room service; sauna *In room:* A/C, TV, fridge, hair dryer, minibar.

Where to Dine

If you're visiting this area in summer, also check out the seasonal (mid-May through mid-October) restaurants that spring up along **Pointe-du-Chêne wharf ★**, a marina complex on the waterfront in **Shediac** about 24km (15 miles) east of the city via routes 11 and 15. You'll find everything from fish and chips to barbecue to ice cream here—even some adult beverages.

City Grill ★ CANADIAN Once an Australian-themed steakhouse, this popular downtown eatery totally recast itself in 2008 with a quieter, more refined vibe. Gone are the oversized steak knives and boomerangs replaced with prints of city skylines and a black-and-white color scheme. The kitchen now integrates some of the old (steaks are still very much on the menu) with much healthier choices such as salads, pizzas, and food cooked over one of eastern Canada's only working charcoal grills—hence the name.

130 Westmoreland St. ✆ **506/857-8325.** Call-ahead seating in lieu of reservations. Lunches C$9–C$15; dinners C$17–C$28. AE, DC, DISC, MC, V. Mon–Thurs 11:30am–2pm and 5–10pm; Fri 11:30am–2pm and 5–11pm; Sat 5–11pm.

The Windjammer ★★ SEAFOOD/CONTINENTAL Tucked off the lobby of Moncton's top business hotel is The Windjammer. This is probably the city's best restaurant—and some Canadian observers consider it one of the country's top hotel eateries. With its heavy wood and nautical theme, it resembles the private officers' mess of an exclusive ship. But this is no fish-and-chips joint. Chef Stefan Müller's menu is ambitious, with appetizers like seafood chowder, smoked lobster tails, a cold seafood "martini," and mussels steamed in apple wine. Entrees from the sea might include a garlicky-gingery filet of salmon, some herb-rubbed Arctic char, a pan-roasted black cod, or lobster cooked whichever way you like it. The chef also serves land-based fare such as bison steak, veal chops, oven-roasted rack of lamb, maple-and-cherry-glazed duck, and a beef tenderloin flambé prepared right at tableside (flames and all) and then garnished with a peppercorn sauce. It's expensive for New Brunswick, but an excellent find in an unlikely place.

750 Main St. (inside the Delta Beauséjour). ✆ **506/877-7137.** Reservations recommended. Main courses C$20–C$42. AE, DC, MC, V. Mon–Sat 5:30–10pm.

KOUCHIBOUGUAC NATIONAL PARK ★

Much is made of the fact that big **Kouchibouguac National Park** (local slang: "the Kooch") has all sorts of ecosystems worth studying, from sandy barrier islands to ancient peat bogs. But that's like saying Disney has nice lakes: It misses the point. In fact, this artfully designed park is a wonderful destination for cycling, hiking, and beach-going, too—yes, it has beaches. If you're an outdoorsy type, plan to spend a few days here doing nothing but exercising. The varied natural wonders (which *are* spectacular) will just be an added bonus—a big one. The only group this park might disappoint is gung-ho hikers. There isn't any hard-core hiking or climbing, just gentle walking and strolling.

Essentials

GETTING THERE Kouchibouguac National Park is located about 112km (70 miles) north of Moncton; figure less than 90 minutes' driving time. The exit for the park, off Route 11, is well marked.

VISITOR INFORMATION The park is open daily from April through November, while a **Visitor Reception Centre** (✆ **506/876-2443**) opens daily from mid-May until mid-October. The visitor center is just off Route 134, a short drive past the park entrance. (It's open from 8am to 8pm from June through August, 9am to 5pm in the shoulder seasons.) There's a slide show here to introduce you to the park's attractions, plus some field guides.

FEES A daily pass costs C$7.80 adults, C$6.80 seniors, C$3.90 children 6 to 16, and C$20 families. (Rates are discounted 50 to 60% from April through June and from October through November.) Seasonal passes are also available, but are only worth the dough if you're planning to visit for more than 3 days. Though there are no formal checkpoints here, occasional roadblocks during the summer check for pass-holding compliance. Note that, for a small extra charge, you can also get a helpful map of the park at the information center.

Exploring the Park

The hiking and biking trails are as short and undemanding as they are appealing. The one hiking trail that requires slightly more fortitude is the **Kouchibouguac River Trail,** which runs for some 13km (8 miles) along the banks of the river.

The **Bog Trail ★** runs just 2km (a mile and a quarter) in each direction, but it opens the door to a wonderfully alien world: The 4,500-year-old bog here is a classic domed bog, made of peat created by decaying shrubs and other plants. At the bog's edge you'll find a wooden tower ascended by a spiral staircase that affords a panoramic view of the eerie habitat.

Callanders Beach and **Cedar Trail ★** are both located at the end of a short dirt road. There's an open field with picnic tables here, a small protected beach on the lagoon (with fine views of dunes across the way), and an 800m (about a half mile or so) hiking trail along a boardwalk that passes through a cedar forest, past a salt marsh, and through a mixed forest. This is a good alternative for those who prefer to avoid the crowds (again, relatively speaking) at Kellys Beach.

Beaches

The park features about 16km (10 miles) of sandy beaches, mostly along barrier islands of sandy dunes, delicate grasses and flowers, and nesting plovers and sandpipers. **Kellys ★** is the principal beach, one of the best-designed and best-executed recreation areas in eastern Canada. At a forest's edge, a short walk from the main parking area, you can find showers, changing rooms, a snack bar, and some interpretive exhibits. From here, you walk about 480m (⅓-mile) across a winding boardwalk that's plenty fascinating as it crosses a salt marsh, lagoons, and some of the best-preserved dunes in the province.

The long, sandy beach here features water that's comfortably warm, with waves that are usually mellow—they lap rather than roar, unless a storm's passing offshore. Lifeguards oversee a roped-off section about 91m (300 ft.) long; elsewhere, though, you're on your own. For kids, there's supervised swimming on a sandy stretch of the quiet lagoon.

Ryans ★★ (✆ **506/876-8918**)—a cluster of buildings between the campgrounds and Kellys Beach—is the recreational center where you can rent bikes, kayaks, paddleboats, and canoes seasonally. All rent relatively cheaply, even the double kayaks. Canoes can be rented for longer excursions. And since Ryans is located on a lagoon, you can explore around the dunes or upstream on the winding river.

Where to Stay & Dine

South Kouchibouguac ★, the main campground, is centrally located and very nicely laid out with 300-plus sites, most rather large and private. The 50 or so sites with electricity are nearer the river and somewhat more open, while the newest sites (nos. 1–35) lack grassy areas for pitching a tent—campers there must pitch their tents on gravel pads. Bring a thick sleeping pad or ask for another site. Sites here cost C$22 to C$29 per night, depending on time of year and the level of comfort you require. Reservations are accepted for about half of the sites; call © **506/876-2443** starting in late April. The remaining sites are doled out first-come, first-served.

Other camping options include remote, semiprimitive **Côte-à-Fabien,** across the river on Kouchibouguac Lagoon. It lacks showers and some sites require a short walk, but it's more appealing for tenters. The cost is C$16 per night. The park also maintains three backcountry sites: **Sipu** on the Kouchibouguac River (accessible by canoe or foot only), **Petit Large** (accessed by foot or bike), and **Pointe-à-Maxime** (by canoe or kayak only; no drinking water). These sites all cost C$9.90 per night.

THE ACADIAN PENINSULA

The **Acadian Peninsula** is the bulge on the northeast corner of New Brunswick, forming one of the arms of the **Baie des Chaleurs** (Québec's Gaspé Peninsula forms the other). It's a land of tidy, nondescript houses, miles of shoreline (much of it beaches), harbors filled with commercial fishing boats, and residents proud of their Acadian heritage. You'll see the Stella Maris flag—the French tricolor with a single gold star in the field of blue—everywhere up here.

One thing it's *not* is wild and remote. On a map it looks like this coastline should be that way, but it's not. Farmhouses dot the roads, and you'll occasionally come upon brilliant meadows of hawkweed or lupine, but this part of the province is more given over to prefab housing on little lots between the sea and boring two-lane highways. Other than the superb Acadian Village historical museum near Caraquet (see p. 140), there are few organized attractions in this region. It's more a place to unwind while walking on a beach or watching fishing boats than to do heavy-duty sightseeing.

Essentials

GETTING THERE Route 11 is the main highway serving the Acadian Peninsula. Caraquet is about 260km (160 miles, or 3½ hours' drive) north from Moncton, about 160km (100 miles, or 2-plus hours) north from the entrance to Kouchibouguac National Park.

VISITOR INFORMATION The **Caraquet Tourism Information,** 35 du Carrefour Ave. (© **506/726-2676**), is a seasonal (mid-May through August) office that offers convenient access to other activities in the harbor (see below) and has plenty of parking. The village of **Shippagan** dispenses its information from a wooden lighthouse near the Marine Centre at 200 Hotel de Ville Ave. (© **506/336-3993**); it's only open from June through August.

Caraquet ★

The historic beach town of Caraquet—widely regarded as the spiritual capital of Acadian New Brunswick—is the town that keeps going and going. (Geographically speaking, anyway.) It's spread thinly along a single commercial boulevard that parallels the beach; this town once claimed the honorific "longest village in the world" when it ran to some 20km (13 miles) long. As a result, Caraquet lacks a well-defined downtown, an urban center of gravity, an identity; there's one stoplight, where Boulevard St-Pierre Est changes to Boulevard St-Pierre Ouest. (Most of the establishments mentioned below are somewhere on this boulevard.)

A good place to start a tour is the **Carrefour de la Mer,** 51 Blvd. St-Pierre Est, a modern complex overlooking the man-made harbor. It has a spare, Scandinavian feel to it, and you'll find the tourist information office (see above), a seafood restaurant, a snack bar, a children's playground, and two short strolls that lead to picnic tables on jetties with fine harbor views.

Village Historique Acadien ★★ New Brunswick sometimes seems awash in Acadian museums and historic villages. But if you only have time to see one, this is the place to visit. Some 45 buildings—most transported from villages elsewhere on the peninsula—depict life as it was lived in Acadian settlements between 1770 and 1890. The buildings are set amongst hundreds of acres of woodlands, marshes, and fields. You'll learn all about the exodus and settlement of the Acadians from costumed guides, who also demonstrate skills ranging from letterpress printing to blacksmithing. Rotating exhibits of local art are also shown each season. And that's not all: The village opened a large addition in 2002 which focuses on more recent eras; this section's buildings (mostly replicas) continue the saga, showing Acadian life from 1890 to 1939 with a special focus on industry. Plan on spending 2 to 4 hours in total on the site. The attractive yellow Chateau Albert Hotel, which houses students enrolled in workshops in traditional Acadian arts and crafts, is also open to the public, and is inexpensive; its simple rooms lack phones and televisions (to fit the period), but there's a dining room, convivial bar area, and lost-in-time vibe.

Rte. 11 (6 miles west of Caraquet). ✆ **506/726-2600.** www.villagehistoriqueacadien.com. Summer admission C$16 adults, C$14 seniors, C$11-C$13 children 6 and over, C$37 families; late Sept rates discounted about 60%. Early June to mid-Sept daily 10am–6pm; mid-Sept to late Sept 10am–5pm. Closed late Sept to early June.

WHERE TO STAY & DINE

Hôtel Paulin ★★ A three-story red clapboard building with a green-shingled mansard roof, the Hotel Paulin was built in 1891 as the first hotel in Caraquet and is still best in town; it has been operated by a member of the Paulin family for the past three generations. Located just off the main boulevard and overlooking the bay, it's an attractively Victorian place that's gone just a bit more upscale with the times over the past decade—adding units and raising prices to match. The lobby's decor features royal blue wainscoting, canary-yellow walls, and stuffed furniture upholstered in white with blue piping. Rooms and suites are comfortably if sparely furnished in flowery duvets and still more antiques. (Four newish luxury suites on the top floor are more stylish and contemporary, adding luxe touches like granite and mahogany styling; the Albert Suite has a lovely, modern bath.) However, not all units here have a true ocean view; ask when booking. The hotel's first floor houses a handsome, well-regarded **restaurant ★★** featuring seafood and fusion and French influences (think grilled pizzas, tricked-up lobster, seafood grills, and pears with goat cheese). Spa services are also being added.

143 Blvd. St-Pierre Ouest, Caraquet, NB E1W 1B6. ✆ **866/727-9981** or 506/727-9981. Fax 506/727-4808. www.hotelpaulin.com. 16 units. Mid-June to mid-Sept C$195–C$315 double and suite; mid-Sept to mid-June C$179–C$235 double and suite. Minimum 2-night stay first 2 wks of Aug. MC, V. **Amenities:** Restaurant; massage; spa. *In room:* A/C, TV, hair dryer, no phone.

Grande-Anse

Grande-Anse is a wide-spot-in-the-road village of low, modern homes near bluffs overlooking the bay, lorded over by the stone Saint Jude church. The best view of the village—and a pretty good spot for a picnic—is along the bluffs just below the church. (Look for the sign indicating QUAI 45m/147 ft. west of the church.) Here you'll find a small man-made harbor with a fleet of fishing boats, a small sandy beach, and some grassy bluffs where you can park overlooking the bay.

If you'd prefer picnic tables, head a few miles westward to **Pokeshaw Park,** open from mid-June through August. Just offshore is a large kettle-shaped island ringed with cliffs that rise from the waves, long ago separated from the cliffs on which you're now standing. An active cormorant rookery thrives among the trees. There's a small picnic shelter for use in inclement weather; the park's open daily from 9am to 9pm, and a small admission fee is charged.

For an ocean swimming experience, head to **Plage Grande-Anse,** located 2km (a mile) east of the town. This handsome beach has a snack bar near the parking area and is open from 10am to 9pm daily. There's a small entrance fee for adults.

PRINCE EDWARD ISLAND

by Paul Karr

Prince Edward Island (PEI) may not be the world's most exciting vacation spot, but it's a place that has always inspired travelers I know to do exactly the one thing they came here to do: relax.

5

There's something about this richly hued landscape of blue seas, henna-colored cliffs capped with purple flowers, and green, green fields that triggers a pleasant disconnection with the hurry-scurry, Twitter-it-now pace of modern life. Indeed, even *change* is slow here: Over the past 120 years the island's population has grown by just 30,000.

PEI was first sighted and explored in 1534 by the tireless French explorer Jacques Cartier, who discovered Mi'kmaq native Canadians living here. Over the next 2 centuries, dominion over the island bounced between Great Britain and France (who called the place Isle-St-Jean). Great Britain was awarded the island in 1763 as part of the Treaty of Paris that was hashed out to settle the Revolutionary War; a little more than a century later, the first Canadian Confederation was held in Charlottetown and resulted in the official creation of Canada in 1867. (To be fair, though, PEI didn't actually join this new confederation until 1873; a careful lot, these folks.)

The island is British and civil through and through, which means people are friendly. It's also very small, yet there are numerous side roads—roads that are usually (but not always) well marked. In any case, it's difficult to become disoriented here. Still, you should try. Whether you're on a bike or in a car, it can be quite pleasurable getting lost on the back roads, secure in the knowledge that you'll eventually end up either at the junction of another road—or at the sea.

For all its stuttery steps toward modernity, this island is still largely steeped in the slower pace of an earlier era. Milkmen still make their rounds; you return soda bottles for refilling, not recycling; and gas-station attendants cheerfully pump your gas and wash your windows without your ever needing to ask. Take a cue from this slow cadence and schedule 1 or 2 extra days into your vacation, with absolutely no plans, in a cabin or cottage. Even if it rains, you probably won't regret it.

EXPLORING THE ISLAND

Essentials

VISITOR INFORMATION Tourism PEI publishes a comprehensive **free visitor's guide** to island attractions and lodgings that's well worth picking up. It is available at all information centers on the island, or in advance by calling ✆ **800/463-4734** or 902/368-4444. The official PEI website is located at **www.gentleisland.com**.

TOURIST OFFICES PEI's splashy main information center is in something called **Gateway Village** (✆ **902/437-8570**), just as you arrive on the island via the Confederation Bridge (see below). It's a good spot for gathering brochures and asking last-minute questions.

Getting There

BY PLANE The island's main airport, Charlottetown Airport (call sign YYG; www.flypei.com), is a few miles north of the city. In summer, you can get here easily from either the U.S. or Canada. **Air Canada** (✆ **888/247-2262;** www.aircanada.com) commuter flights from Halifax take just a half-hour, and the airline also flies daily to Toronto and Montréal. Calgary-based **WestJet** (✆ **888/937-8538;** www.westjet.com) also connects Charlottetown with Toronto. **Delta** (✆ **800/221-1212;** www.delta.com) runs direct weekend summertime service from Boston's Logan and New York's JFK airports.

A taxi ride into Charlottetown from the airport costs a flat fee of C$12 for the first passenger, plus C$3 each for additional passengers; two strangers can even share a single cab into town for a city-mandated fare of C$9 each. (Cabs also run to other parts of the island, for higher flat fares.) There are also limousine firms and several chain auto-rental outfits in the terminal.

BY CAR By car, you'll either arrive by ferry (see below) or drive onto the island via the big **Confederation Bridge** (✆ **888/437-6565** or 902/437-7300), which opened with great fanfare in 1997. You'll also sometimes hear this bridge referred to as the "fixed link". The dramatic 13km (8-mile) bridge is open 24 hours a day and takes 10 to 12 minutes to cross. Unless you're high up in a van, a truck, or an RV, however, your views are mostly obstructed by the concrete barriers that form the guardrails along both sides.

The round-trip bridge toll as of 2010 was C$42.50 round-trip for passenger cars (more for vehicles with more than two axles); the toll is collected when you leave the island, not when you enter it. (If you drive on in a rental car and fly off, you escape the toll altogether.) Credit cards are accepted at the bridge plaza.

BY FERRY For those arriving from Cape Breton Island or other points east, **Northumberland Ferries Limited** (✆ **888/249-7245;** www.nfl-bay.com) provides seasonal service between Caribou, Nova Scotia (just north of Pictou) and Woods Island, PEI. Ferries with a 250-car capacity run from May to mid-December. During peak season (June to mid-Oct), ferries depart each port approximately every 90 minutes throughout the day, with the last ferry departing as late as 8pm or 9:30pm in mid-summer depending on which direction you are traveling. The crossing takes about 75 minutes.

No reservations are accepted, except for buses; thus, it's best to arrive at least an hour before departure to boost your odds of securing a berth on the next boat. Early-morning ferries tend to be less crowded. Fares are C$63 for a regular-size car (more for campers and RVs), plus C$16 per person (C$14 for seniors, free for kids under age 12). There's a small fuel surcharge, as well, and major credit cards are honored.

The Great Outdoors

BICYCLING There's no finer destination in Atlantic Canada for relaxed cycling than Prince Edward Island. The modest size of this island, the gentleness of the hills, and the loveliness of the landscapes all make for memorable biking trips. Although you won't find much (or any) rugged mountain biking here, you can find plenty of idyllic excursions, especially in the northern and eastern portions of the island.

And there's a great bike trail here: the **Confederation Trail ★★★**, an impressive system of several hundred miles of pathway built along the ripped-up trackbed of an ill-fated provincial railway running from the island's far northwestern shore to its northeastern corner; branch trails stretch to downtown Charlottetown and towns like Souris, Montague, and Georgetown. On trail, stop by the **Trailside Inn & Café** at 109 Main St. in Mount Stewart (✆ **888/704-6595;** www.trailside.ca), where several spurs of the trail converge. You can rent from **MacQueen's Island Tours & Bike Shop,** 430 Queen St. in Charlottetown (✆ **800/969-2822** or 902/368-2453; www.macqueens.com), which also organizes tour packages, or **Smooth Cycle** at 330 University Ave. (✆ **800/310-6550** from eastern Canada or 902/566-5530).

FISHING If you're interested in deep-sea fishing, head to the north coast, where you'll find plenty of fishing captains and outfitters happy to take you out on the big waves. The greatest concentrations of services are at the harbors of North Rustico and Covehead Bay; rates are quite reasonable, generally about C$20 for 3 hours or so.

Trout fishing holes on the island attract inland anglers, although, as always, the very best spots are a matter of local knowledge. A good place to start your inquiries is at **Going Fishing** in the Sherwood Shopping Centre at 161 St. Peters Rd. in Charlottetown (✆ **902/367-3444**). The store specializes in fly-fishing equipment, but also stocks conventional rods and reels as well.

Information on fishing licenses can be obtained from any visitor information center, or by contacting the province's **Department of Fisheries, Aquaculture & Rural Development,** P.O. Box 2000, Charlottetown, PEI C1A 7N8 (✆ **902/368-6330**).

GOLF While it can never possess the scenic grandeur of Nova Scotia's top courses, PEI's reputation for golf has soared in recent years thanks largely to a slew of new, renovated, and expanded courses—and the LPGA success of Charlottetown native Lorie Kane. The island now possesses ten of Canada's top 100 courses, according to the national *Globe & Mail* newspaper.

One of the best-regarded courses is the **Links at Crowbush Cove ★** (✆ **800/235-8909** or 902/368-5761); greens fees run C$79 to C$99 per person. Another favorite is the **Brudenell River Golf Course** (✆ **800/235-8909** or 902/652-8965), near Montague along the eastern shore at the Rodd Brudenell River Resort. Greens fees here are C$59 to C$79 per person.

Golf PEI (✆ **866/465-3734**), a trade association, publishes a booklet and website outlining the essentials of 21 member island courses. Request a copy from island

Prince Edward Island

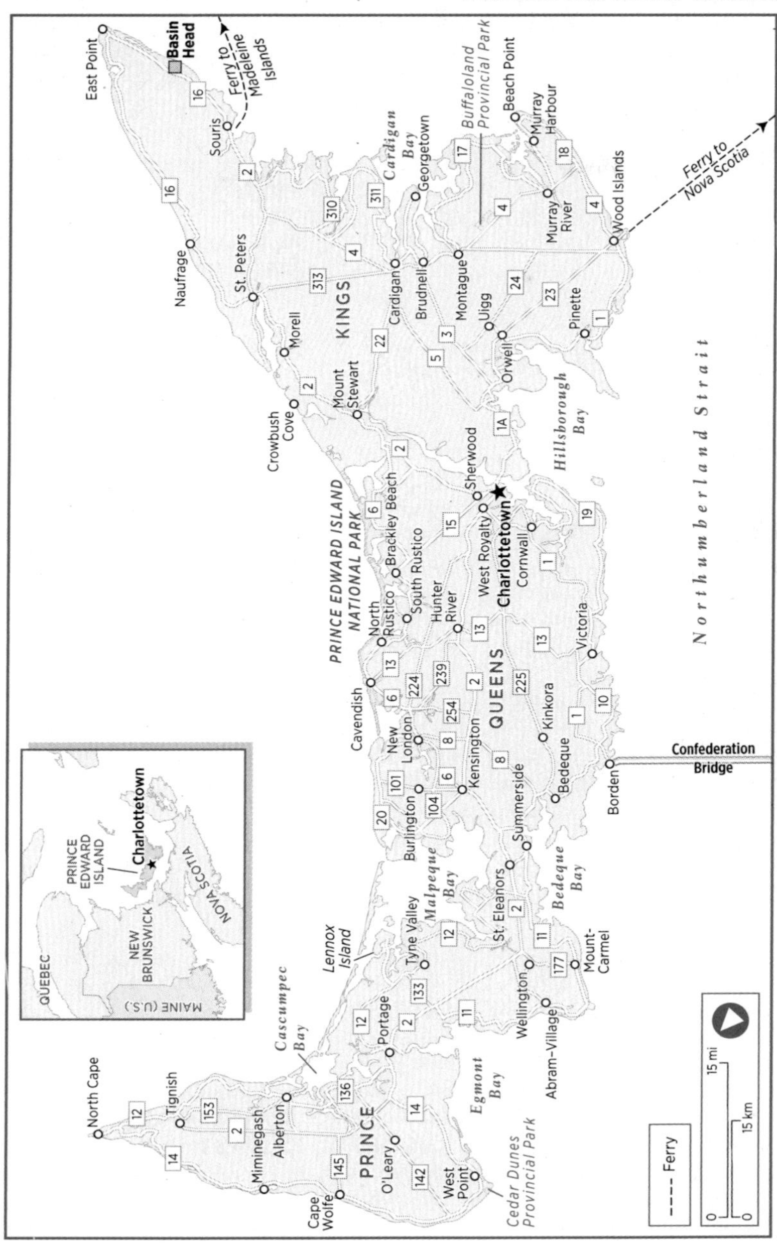

information centers or from the provincial tourist information office, or check the website at **www.golfpei.com;** the organization's mailing address is 565 N. River Rd., Charlottetown, PEI C1E 1J7.

SWIMMING PEI's chief attraction is its red sand beaches, which are generally excellent for swimming. You'll find them ringing the island, tucked in between dunes and crumbling cliffs. Thanks to the moderating influence of the Gulf of St. Lawrence, the water temperature is more humane here than elsewhere in Atlantic Canada. The most popular beaches (by far) are at **Prince Edward Island National Park** along the north coast, but you can easily find other local or provincial beaches with great swimming by asking anywhere locally.

Good choices include **Cedar Dunes Provincial Park** (on the island's southwestern coast), **Red Point Provincial Park** (on its northeastern shore), and **Panmure Island Provincial Park** on the southeastern coast.

QUEENS COUNTY

Queens County occupies the center of PEI. It's home to the island's largest city (**Charlottetown**), which is also the provincial capital, and hosts the greatest concentration of traveler services by far. The county is neatly cleaved by the Hillsborough River, which is spanned by a bridge at Charlottetown. **Cavendish** on the north shore is the most tourist-oriented place in the entire province; it has built a vigorous tourist industry around one fictional literary character (Anne of Green Gables) who fictionally lived here in a fictional time but is now bringing in very real touro-dollars. On the other hand, much of the rest of the county—besides Charlottetown, of course—is extremely pastoral and untrammeled.

Essentials

GETTING THERE Route 2 is the fastest way to travel east or west through the county, though it really lacks the charm of the quieter byways. Route 6 is the main route along the county's northern coast; unlike Route 2, following this highway is not a straight line but rather involves a number of turns at stop signs at intersections. Keep a sharp eye on the road signs or you'll lose the trail.

VISITOR INFORMATION The snazzy, well-stocked little **Cavendish Visitor Information Centre** (© **800/463-4734** or 902/963-7830) is open daily from mid-June through mid-October. It's located just north of the intersection of routes 13 and 6.

Cavendish: Anne's Hometown

Cavendish is the home of the fictional red-headed Anne of Green Gables, a somewhat heroic figure in Canadian children's literature (and, in fact, Anne is well known around the world, though most Americans probably have never heard of her). She's a simple but plucky girl who perseveres through the sheer force of her optimism. And her fictional hometown is—make that was—a nice enough area, featuring a bucolic mix of woodlands, fields, rolling hills, and sandy dunes, the ideal setting for the pastoral novels that made Anne so famous.

However, the enduring popularity of the novels has attracted droves of curious tourists over the years, and it didn't take savvy entrepreneurs long at all to figure

THE BIRTH OF anne shirley

Visitors to Prince Edward Island owe it to themselves to think about picking up a copy of *Anne of Green Gables* at some point. Not that you won't enjoy your stay here without doing so, but if you don't read it, you might feel a bit out of touch and unable to understand the inside references that seem to seep into many aspects of PEI culture.

Some background: in 1908 island native Lucy Maud Montgomery published *Anne of Green Gables*, her first book—and it was an instant smash. The book is a fictional account of one Anne Shirley, a precocious and bright 11-year-old who's mistakenly sent from Nova Scotia to the farm of the taciturn and dour Matthew and Marilla Cuthbert.

Anne's vivid imagination and outsized vocabulary get her into a series of ever-more-hilarious pickles, from which she generally emerges beloved by everyone who encounters her. It's a bright, bittersweet story, and it went on to huge popular success, spawning a number of sequels.

out that this place could support a mini-Disney's worth of children's attractions, hotels, and eateries. The bucolic character of Anne's town has thus been severely compromised. At least most attractions are set back from the road—and the beaches are excellent.

SEEING EVERYTHING ANNE

Green Gables Heritage Place ✋ The best place to start an Anne tour is at Green Gables itself, but this place somewhat disappoints, even if it is the closest thing we have to the "real" fictional Green Gables. (The author's birthplace or favorite home, covered above and below, are equally authentic destinations.) The farmhouse here dates from the mid-19th century and belonged to cousins of Montgomery's grandfather; it is considered the chief inspiration for the Cuthbert farm in the books, and has since been furnished according to descriptions in the books. The home is operated by Parks Canada as part of the larger Lucy Maud Montgomery's Cavendish National Historic Site; as such, the parks department operates a helpful visitor center on the site where you can watch a short film about Montgomery, view a handful of exhibits, and explore the farm and trails. Come very early or very late in the day to avoid the biggest crowds.

2 Palmer's Lane (just off Rte. 6), Cavendish (just west of intersection with Rte. 13). ✆ **902/963-7874** or 963-7871 (off-season). Admission mid-June to late Aug, C$7.80 adults, C$6.55 seniors, C$3.90 children, C$20 families; rates discounted 25% May to mid-June and late Aug to Oct; rates discounted 50% Nov to Apr. May–Oct daily 9am–5pm; Apr and Nov, Sun–Thurs 10am–4pm; Dec to March by appointment only.

Cavendish Cemetery ★ This historic cemetery, protected by a grove of trees, was founded in 1835 and is best known as the final resting spot for author Lucy Maud Montgomery. It's not hard to find her gravesite: Follow the pavement blocks from the arched entryway, which is across from the Anne Shirley Motel. She's buried beneath the same headstone as her husband, the Rev. Ewen MacDonald (thus the stone reads "MacDonald," not Montgomery).

Intersection of routes 13 and 6, Cavendish. Free admission. Open daily dawn–dusk.

Avonlea ★ ☺ This development of faux historic buildings opened in 1999, with the idea of creating the sort of a village center you might find in the Anne novels. And, of course, the true goal is to entice paying tourists. The facility is on a big lot among amusement parks and motels, but several Anne-related buildings and artifacts are located at the site, including the actual one-room schoolhouse in which Montgomery taught (moved here from Belmont, about 48km/30 miles away) and a Presbyterian church she occasionally attended (moved about 16km/10 miles from Long River). There's also a variety show, hayrides, staff in period dress, a restaurant, several stores, and tea, ice cream, and candy. But for what it delivers, it's a bit overpriced—except in September, when the cost of admission plunges.

8779 Rte. 6, Cavendish. ✆ **902/963-3050.** www.avonlea.ca. Day-pass admission C$19 adults, C$17 seniors, C$15 children 3–18, C$65 families; Sept admission C$10 per person flat fee. Musical variety show, small extra charge. Mid-June daily 10am–5pm; July–Aug 10am–6pm; Sept 10am–4pm. Closed Oct to mid-June.

Lucy Maud Montgomery Birthplace A few miles south of the Silver Bush Anne of Green Gables Museum is this simple white home, where the author was born in 1874. Today the house is once again decorated in the Victorian style of Montgomery's era, and it includes mementos like the author's wedding dress and scrapbook. Just like Silver Bush, this is historically authentic and worth an hour for die-hard Anne fans.

Intersection of routes 6 and 20, New London. ✆ **902/886-2099** or 902/836-5502. Admission C$3 adults, C50¢ children 6–12. Mid-May to mid-Oct daily 9am–5pm. Closed mid-Oct to mid-May.

Site of Lucy Maud Montgomery's Cavendish Home ★ Finally! The place where the girl behind the girl lived…sort of. Author Montgomery lived in a house on this site with her grandparents, Alexander and Lucy Macneill, from 1876 (when she was 21 months old) until 1911. She wrote *Anne of Green Gables* and her other books at the home, which unfortunately is no longer standing; visitors can roam the grounds and read interpretive signs and plaques about the property's literary history. There's also a small bookshop featuring books by and about the author. Again, as with so many others around the area, this site is mainly of interest to die-hard Anne buffs. Admission is by donation; drop in something like C$3 per adult.

Rte. 6. Cavendish (just east of Rte. 13 intersection). ✆ **902/963-2231.** Admission by donation. Mid-May to Oct daily 9am–5pm (July–Aug to 6pm). Closed Nov to mid-May.

Anne of Green Gables Museum at Silver Bush ★ About 19km (12 miles) west of Cavendish, near the intersection of routes 6 and 20, is Silver Bush, also known as the Anne of Green Gables Museum. While technically unrelated to Anne herself, this simple two-story home of white clapboard probably *did* sow some seeds of influence for the story: Lucy Maud Montgomery's aunt and uncle lived here, the authoress passed many days in childhood in this house visiting family, and she even married here in 1911. The surrounding countryside is lovely and untouched by time, and the building still holds some of Montgomery's furniture, linens, photos, and other personal effects. For the best view of the lake that may have inspired the "Lake of Shining Waters," take the horse-drawn carriage ride.

Rte. 20, Park Corner (about 6 miles north of intersection with Rte. 6). ✆ **800/665-2663** or 902/886-2884 (weekends only). Admission C$3 adults, C$1 children age 6–16. May and Oct daily 11am–4pm; June and Sept daily 10am–4pm; July–Aug daily 9am–5pm.

WHERE TO STAY

Cavendish Beach Cottages ★★ ☺ Location, location, location. This compound of about a dozen closely spaced cottages is located on a grassy rise within PEI's lovely national park (the area where the best beaches are), just past the gatehouse to the park. The pine-paneled units come in one-, two-, and three-bedroom configurations, and while they won't win any prizes for design each does have a queen bed (most add another double bed or two, as well). And all of them feature direct ocean views, cable television, air-conditioning (not that you'll need it), kitchenettes with microwaves and dishwashers, and outdoor propane barbecue grills. Some have tubs while others have showers only, but generally speaking these are a great choice for couples and families—all the more so, since every cottage is no more than a 2-minute walk from the beach. The swingsets, playhouse, and picnic tables are the capper. There's also easy access right onto Gulf Shore Drive, where you find some of PEI's best walking and biking trails. No pets are allowed in the cottages, and all units are non-smoking.

1445 Gulf Shore Dr., Cavendish C0A 1N0 (mailing address P.O. Box 3088, Charlottetown, PEI C1A 7N9). ✆ **902/963-2025.** Fax 902/963-2025. www.cavendishbeachcottages.com. 13 units. Mid-June to Aug C$145–C$215 double, May to mid-June and Sept–early Oct C$95–C$140 double. MC, V. Closed early Oct to mid-May. *In room:* A/C, TV, kitchenette, no phone.

Green Gables Bungalow Court ★★ Managed by the same folks as the good Cavendish Beach Cottages (see above) and located next to the "official" Green Gables house, this pleasant cluster of one- and two-bedroom cottages began as a government make-work project promoting tourism in the 1940s. As a result, the cottages are actually quite sturdily built, and they've been nicely arrayed beneath tall pines. Now that they've had some fresh coats of paints and repairs, they're also nice to look at, with painted shutters, flower boxes, little decks, and shady trees. Prices vary according to size; a large two-bedroom bungalow costs about 50% more than a tiny "efficiency" cottage. All units have kitchens with refrigerators, utensils, and coffeemakers, plus outdoor gas grills; some one-bedroom units have TVs, though they're in the minority. The beach is about a kilometer (⅔ of a mile) away, and there's a nice heated outdoor pool, kids' play area, high-speed Internet access, and coin-op laundry, too.

8663 Cavendish Rd. (Rte. 6), Cavendish, PEI C0A 1N0. ✆ **800/965-3334** or 902/963-2722. www.greengablesbungalowcourt.com. 40 cottages. C$70–C$149 double, C$699–C$999 weekly. AE, MC, V. Closed Oct–June. **Amenities:** Heated outdoor pool. *In room:* TV (some units), fridge, kitchenette, no phone.

WHERE TO DINE

Café on the Clyde ★★ ☺ CANADIAN This cafe is part of the popular Prince Edward Island Preserve Co., itself a worthwhile stop for the delicious homemade preserves sold here. But now foodies have a second reason to make the trip: Light meals are served in a bright, modern-looking dining room just off the showroom. The cafe serves three meals a day: Breakfasts run to French toast, granola, bread with the eponymous preserves, or a hearty country platter, while lunch choices include seafood chowder, sandwiches and wraps, fish cakes, lobster quiche, and those famous PEI mussels. Dinner could be cedar-planked salmon with blueberry sauce, a seafood baked, or rib-eye steak. Finish with maple ice cream crepes or one of the other delectable cakes, pies, or cheesecakes. There's also beer and wine, a kids' menu, and jazz guitar (on weekend nights). Just be prepared for the tour-bus crowd: Buses get their own parking lot here, close to the door. Still, this is a legitimate dining destination in an area where eats are few and far between.

Intersection of routes 224 and 258 (4 miles south of Rte. 6, on Rte. 13), New Glasgow. © **902/964-4301.** Reservations recommended for dinner. Main courses C$7–C$10 at breakfast and lunch, C$13–C$17 at dinner. AE, DC, MC, V. July–Aug daily 9am–9pm; June and Sept limited hours. Closed Oct–May.

Olde Glasgow Mill Restaurant ★ CANADIAN This casual restaurant, originally built as a late-19th-century feed mill in twee little New Glasgow, has been a restaurant since 1997 and is nicely shielded from the tourist throngs over in Cavendish. The place overlooks a small pond and features an eclectic assortment of regional meals. Appetizers include seafood chowder, along with salads and PEI mussels. Lunch entrees are uncomplicated (pizza, crepes, salads, turkey burgers, fajitas), while dinner is a more serious affair. Once you get beyond the expected items (Atlantic salmon; scallops), you'll find such choices as a rack of lamb encrusted in herbs, served with the traditional mint; lobster thermidor; peppered steaks; chicken glazed with maple and stuffed with vegetables and Brie; and a few inventive pastas, adulterated with such elements as basil, curry, seafood, and zucchini. A six-course "chef's tasting menu" kicks things up a notch higher still.

5592 Rte. 13, New Glasgow. © **902/964-3313.** Reservations recommended. Lunch C$9–C$12; dinner C$14–C$29. AE, MC, V. June–early Oct Mon–Sat noon–10pm, Sun 10am–10pm. Closed early Oct–May.

North & South Rustico to Brackley Beach

A few miles east of Cavendish are the Rusticos, of which there are five in all: North Rustico, South Rustico, Rusticoville, Rustico Harbour, and Anglo Rustico. (Don't feel bad if you can't keep them straight.) It's a fun, relaxing place to head if you're seeking beaches, small harbors, and friendly locals.

The region was first "settled" by Acadians in 1790, and many present-day residents are descendants of those original settlers. **North Rustico** ★ clusters around a scenic harbor with views out toward Rustico Bay. Leave time for parking, walking around, perusing deep-sea fishing opportunities (see below), and peeking into shops. The village curves around Rustico Bay to end at North Rustico Harbour, a sand spit with fishing wharves, summer cottages, and a couple of informal restaurants. A wood-decked promenade follows the water's edge from town to harbor, a worthy destination for a quiet afternoon ramble or a picnic. Also here is **Outside Expeditions** (© **800/207-3899** or 902/963-3366; www.getoutside.com), one of PEI's best outfitters; they offer sea kayaking excursions around the harbor and into surrounding areas (see "Sea Kayaking," earlier in this chapter).

To find **South Rustico** ★★, turn off Route 6 onto **Route 243** and ascend the low hill overlooking the bay. Here you'll find a handsome cluster of buildings that were once home to some of the most prosperous Acadian settlers. Among the structures is the sandstone **Farmers' Bank of Rustico Museum** ★ (© **902/963-3168**), beside the church. The bank was established with the help of a visionary local cleric, the Reverend Georges-Antoine Belcourt, in 1864 to help local farmers get their operations into the black; Father and parishioners actually built the bank themselves, timber by timber, stone by stone. It then operated for some 30 years and helped inspire the credit union movement in North America before it was, ironically, forced to shut down by legislative banking reforms. The bank is open for tours from June through September, Monday through Saturday, 9:30am to 5:30pm, and Sundays 1 to 5:30pm. (You can call during the off-season and try to schedule a walk-through, as well.) Admission costs C$4 per adult, C$3 per senior, C$2 per student, and C$8 per family.

Right next door to the bank, there are two more structures worth checking out. **Doucet House ★**, a sturdy log building of Acadian construction dating from 1772, was the home of Jean Doucet, who arrived in these parts on a type of boat called a "shallop." It's believed that this might be the oldest extant home on the entire island. The house was moved from its waterside location in 1999 and completely restored—which it badly needed—and period furnishings have since been added to bring back that ages-old flavor. Its opening hours and admissions fees are the same as those for the Farmers' Bank; in fact, one ticket gets you into both.

Finally, there's the handsome **St. Augustine's Parish Church** (dating from 1838, with a cemetery beyond), also next door. You can't miss it: it's enormous, at a bend in the road. If the church's door is open, have a look around the graceful structure.

Brackley Beach ★ is the gateway to the eastern section of PEI's national park, and it has the fewest services of any town in these parts. It's just a quiet area, with no village center to speak of; it can be best appreciated by those who prefer their beach vacations untouched by civilization or noise.

WHERE TO STAY

Barachois Inn ★★ Topped by a fine mansard roof, the proudly Victorian Barachois (pronounced bar-a-*schwa*) Inn was built in 1880 by a local merchant. It's located right amongst an impressive concentration of historic buildings (the Farmers' Bank, Doucet House, and a church among them) overlooking the bay in North Rustico; you can enjoy both the historic village and the inn's fine garden during the space of a single evening stroll. Innkeepers Judy and Gary MacDonald bought the place as derelict property in 1982 and swiftly restored it, adding modern art to counterpoint the severe architecture and period antiques in which it's furnished. Depending on which room you book, you might find a canopy bed or claw-foot tubs when you arrive and turn your key; note that rooms on the third floor are a bit cozier than the spacious second-floor suites, though any room beneath these slanted eaves feels far removed from urban bustle. The newer MacDonald House next door adds four executive-style rooms and modern luxuries like a sauna, exercise bike, and meeting room—yet its architecture nicely echoes that of the original home. Packages abound; you can even book one that includes an Anne of Green Gables–themed carriage ride, gourmet dinner at a local restaurant, and a packed picnic lunch.

2193 Church Rd. (Hunter River R.R. 3), Rustico, PEI C0A 1N0. ✆ **800/963-2194.** www.barachoisinn.com. 8 units, 1 with private bathroom in hallway. C$125–C$235 double. Rates include full breakfast. Packages available. AE, MC, V. Closed Nov–Mar. **Amenities:** Sauna. *In room:* A/C, TV/VCR, hair dryer, kitchenette, no phone.

Shaw's Hotel ★★ ☺ You can't miss Shaw's, a delightfully old-fashioned hotel inside a Victorian farmhouse with a (fire-engine red!) mansard roof, down a tree-lined dirt road beside an inlet. This place has been in the same family since 1860, and even with a few recent touchups—a sun deck, bar, and dining-room expansion were completed in 1999 and more than two-thirds of the beds are now in outlying cottages—it still has the feel of a farm-stay vacation . . . during the 19th century. More than a dozen guest rooms are located in the upstairs section of the main building; they're "boardinghouse style," a euphemism for "smallish." The 27 free-standing cottages on the property are the real stars, though they vary considerably in size and vintage; none are lavish, but they have the essentials (kitchenettes or cube refrigerators) and a few are downright comfy: double Jacuzzi, anyone? A few also have televisions, which the main inn lacks. While these newer cottages are fine, the older ones do have a certain rustic charm. (This is still the sort of place where you walk down a sandy lane to the beach.) The handsome dining room serves breakfast and dinner daily—guests can join a MAP plan for about $40 per person extra—with dinner choices that might include filet mignon, poached halibut, pasta with cream sauce, prime rib, rack of lamb, or lobster. (Yet it's not the stuffy place you'd expect from such a menu.) Abundant children's programs in summer, a kids' menu in the dining room, and a playground on premises all make Shaw's a good choice for families, too.

Rte. 15, Brackley Beach, PEI C1E 1Z3. ✆ **902/672-2022.** Fax 902/672-3000. www.shawshotel.ca. 38 units. C$75–C$145 double; C$120–C$240 suite; C$190–C$710 cottage. MAP plan about $80 per night additional (double occupancy). Packages available. AE, MC, V. Closed Nov to late May. "Well-mannered" dogs allowed in cottages only. **Amenities:** Restaurant; bar; babysitting; canoe, kayak, and bike rentals; children's program. *In room:* TV (some units), fridge (some units), kitchenette (some units), no phone.

WHERE TO DINE

This is perhaps PEI's best dining region. In addition to the selections listed below, you should consider sampling the fare from the resort dining rooms at **Shaw's Hotel** (see "Where to Stay," above) and at **Dalvay by the Sea ★★** (described in the "Prince Edward Island National Park" section of this chapter on p. 154). Both are excellent. There's also a great local restaurant in Margate, the **Shipwright's Café,** about 24km (15 miles) due west of North Rustico on Route 6 (see p. 167).

The Dunes Café ★★ CAFE Once simply the house cafe/coffeehouse of a local gallery, the Dunes has gradually and consistently improved its cooking and upped its menu's ante—to the point where it's no longer just an afterthought, but rather serves lunches and dinners equal to those almost anywhere in rural PEI. Foodies are taking notice. This is a great spot for a gourmet lunch or dinner of island fish chowder, crab cakes, grilled chorizo, Asian spice-cured salmon gravlax, seafood cioppino, shrimp (or vegan) Pad Thai, curries, lamb-feta burgers, or one of the salads; it's amazing how the chef balances fresh local ingredients with international spices and influences. They also serve good coffee here, of course, as well as tea and knockout house cocktails at night—drinks like the gingery "A Dunes Life," the islandy "Fruit Oasis," and a "Capetown Collins" made with roiboos tea. The restaurant's kids' menu is considerate of the little ones.

Rte. 15, Brackley Beach. ✆ **902/672-1883.** www.dunesgallery.com. Lunch main courses C$8–C$14, dinner entrees C$17–C$32. MC, V. June–Sept daily 11:30am–10pm. Closed Nov–May.

PRINCE EDWARD ISLAND NATIONAL PARK ★★

Located along PEI's sandy north-central coast, Prince Edward Island National Park is big and small all at once. In total, the park encompasses just 40 skinny kilometers

(25 miles) of red-sand beaches and wind-sculpted dunes topped by marram grass; salt marshes; and gentle inlets. Even what length it possesses is broached in several places by broad estuarine inlets that connect to harbors; as a result, you can't drive the entire park's length in one stretch, but rather must break away from the coastal road (and views) and backtrack inland.

But this is *the* reason many people come to PEI. These bright red beaches and dunes define the island. There's little point in trying to tour the whole length of the park, since these beaches are all similar-looking to each other. It's better to simply pick out *one* stretch of beach (say, near your hotel), stake a claim, and settle in for a few days.

Essentials

GETTING THERE From downtown Charlottetown, Route 15 (which passes the airport, then continues north) is the most direct route to central sections of the national park. To reach the lovely eastern sections and Dalvay by the Sea, you can also drive east on Route 2, then turn north on Route 6 at Bedford. Alternately, to reach the Cavendish (western) area and the attractive Rusticos most quickly, take Route 2 west to Hunter River, then turn north on Route 13. The entire drive from city to beach is probably 30 or 40km (20 or 25 miles) at most, yet it can still take up to 45 minutes or more, depending on traffic conditions. To follow the park, travel west on Route 6.

VISITOR INFORMATION The **Cavendish Visitor Information Centre** (✆ **800/463-4734** or 902/963-7830), north of the intersection of routes 6 and 13, furnishes information on the park's destinations and activities. It opens daily from mid-May through early September. Inside the park, the modern **Greenwich Interpretation Centre** (✆ **902/961-2514**) is open from 10am to 5pm, June through September. For other questions or during the off-season, the park administration (located in Charlottetown) can be reached at ✆ **902/672-6350.**

FEES The park is open year-round. Between June and early September, however, visitors must stop at one of the two tollhouses and pay entry fees. From July through September, the fees are C$7.80 adults, C$6.80 seniors, C$3.90 children ages 6 to 16, and C$20 per family; all these rates are discounted by 50% in June. Ask about multiday passes if you plan to visit for more than 3 days.

Exploring the Park

Hiking is limited in both quantity and drama in PEI National Park, especially when compared with the trails in Atlantic Canada's other national parks, but you can still find a number of pleasant strolls here. (Of course, there's also the beach, which is perfect for long leisurely walks.) The park maintains more than a dozen trails in all, adding up to a total of 45km (28 miles), so there's plenty of room to roam. Among the most appealing is the **Homestead Trail ★**, which departs from the Cavendish campground. The trail offers both a 6km (4-mile) loop and an 8km (5-mile) loop and skirts wheat fields, woodlands, and estuaries, with frequent views of the distinctively lumpy dunes at the west end of the national park.

Cycling the seaside roads in the park is sublime. Traffic is generally light, and it's easy to make frequent stops along the way to explore beaches, woodlands, or the marshy edges of inlets. The two **shoreline roads ★★** within the national park—between Dalvay and Rustico Island, and from Cavendish to North Rustico Harbour—are especially beautiful as sunset edges into twilight. As a bonus, there are snack bars located both at Brackley Beach and again at Covehead Bay.

You can rent bikes easily in Charlottetown (see above), or right on the beach from **Dalvay Beach Bike Rentals** (✆ **888/366-2955** or 902/672-2048). The facility is located at the venerable Dalvay by the Sea resort (see "Where to Stay & Dine," below). These folks even smartly offer a half-day package deal that includes a packed picnic lunch for two for about C$15 more.

Beaches

PEI National Park is home to two kinds of sandy beaches: popular, sometimes crowded strands with changing rooms, lifeguards, snack bars, and other amenities; and all the rest. Where you go depends on your temperament. If it's not a day at the beach without the aroma of other people's coconut tanning oil, head for **Brackley Beach** or **Cavendish Beach**. (The latter is within walking distance of the Green Gables house and many amusements, thus making it good for families with kids; see "Cavendish," earlier in this chapter, for full details on said attractions.)

If you'd just as soon be left alone with the waves, sun, and sand, though, you need to head a bit farther afield—or just keep walking very far down the beaches from parking lots until you have left the crowds behind. I won't reveal the very best spots, for fear they'll get crowded. Get thee a map of the national park, and study it closely. A hint: "Fewer facilities" almost always translates to "far fewer people."

Where to Stay & Dine

Prince Edward Island National Park maintains excellent campgrounds, which open for the short season in mid-June, with hundreds of sites in total. This is one of the best ways to enjoy the island, and it's not very expensive: Campground fees start at about C$25 per night, with serviced sites costing no more than C$35 per night.

The most popular (and first to fill) is **Cavendish,** located just off Route 6 west of Green Gables and in the park's western reaches. It has hundreds of sites, spread among piney forest and open, sandy bluffs; sites at the edge of the dunes overlooking the beach are the most popular, but most sites aren't especially private or scenic. This campground closes for the season at the end of September.

The **Stanhope ★** campground lies just across the park road from lovely Stanhope Beach, on the eastern side of the park (you enter through Brackley Beach). Most sites here are forested, and you're afforded more privacy here than at Cavendish; all things considered, it's a better choice. Two-way hookups, free showers, and kitchen shelters are offered. It's also open much later—until mid-November, amazingly, though I don't know anyone who has camped then. Reserve either one online (**www.pccamping.ca**) or by phone (✆ **877/737-3783** or 405/505-8302); the reservations system shuts down for the season early in September.

Also see listings for "Cavendish: Anne's Hometown," earlier in this chapter, and "North & South Rustico to Brackley Beach," above.

Dalvay by the Sea ★★ This imposing Tudor mansion was built in 1895 by Alexander MacDonald, a partner of John D. Rockefeller. It's unusually large for a private home, but feels intimate for a luxury inn. There are glimpses of the ocean across the road from the upper floors, though the home's design focuses on the freshwater pond out front. Inside, you'll be taken aback by extraordinary cedar woodwork in the main entryway and a grand stone fireplace. The 26 guest rooms are elegantly appointed, solid, and quiet, they have also been kept free of any phones or televisions to emphasize the natural setting. In the evening you hear the sounds of the sea (the inn overlooks one of the park's best beaches). Eight newer, three-bedroom pine cottages are in big demand thanks to their size, open design, and amenities like wet bars and propane stoves; book these well ahead. Dalvay added a new pavilion-style **dining room ★★** in 1999; it blends nicely with the architecture, and has good views of the gardens and pond. The hotel also serves afternoon tea each day from 2 to 4pm. Idea: Hike off all the calories at one of the walking trails nearby.

Rte. 6, Grand Tracadie (P.O. Box 8, Little York), PEI C0A 1P0. ✆ **888/368-2955** or 902/672-2048. Fax 902/672-2741 (summer only). www.dalvaybythesea.com. 34 units. June to late Sept C$284–C$404 MAP double, C$484–C$524 MAP cottage; extra charges for all children above age 3 and more than 2 adults. Rates include full breakfast and dinner. B&B rates and packages also available. National park entrance fees also charged. 2-night minimum in summer. AE, DC, MC, V. Closed late Sept to May. **Amenities:** 2 dining rooms; bike rentals; canoeing; croquet; horseshoes; lawn bowling; tennis court. *In room:* Fridge (cottages only), minibar (cottages only), no phone.

CHARLOTTETOWN ★

56km (35 miles) E of Borden-Carleton, 61km (38 miles) NW of Wood Islands

Charlottetown remains one of Atlantic Canada's most graceful and relaxed cities, and one of my favorite to visit. Named for Queen Charlotte (wife of the infamous King George III), metro Charlottetown and its suburbs are now home to about 60,000 people—nearly one of every two islanders. To Canadians, the city is everlastingly famous for hosting the 1864 conference that 3 years later led to the creation of the independent Dominion of Canada. For that reason, you're never far away from the word *confederation,* which graces buildings, malls, bridges, everything.

The downtown has a brisk feel to it, with its mixture of modern and Victorian commercial buildings, government and cultural centers, buttoned-down bureaucrats and punks/folkies/artists hanging out around town. In the historic district you'll find leafy streets, amazing churches on almost every street corner, and large, and elegant homes dating from various eras (the most dramatic were built in the late 19th century).

Essentials

GETTING THERE Coming by car from the mainland and across the Confederation Bridge, Route 1 (the Trans-Canada Hwy.) makes more or less a straight shot east into downtown Charlottetown. From the Woods Island ferry, you also take Route 1 (in fact, the route begins at the ferry dock), except you go west.

Charlottetown Airport (www.flypei.com) is just north of the city center. In summer, you can get here easily from either the U.S. or Canada via several carriers. **Air Canada** (✆ **888/247-2262;** www.aircanada.com) offers daily flights from Halifax, Toronto, and Montréal, and **WestJet** (✆ **888/937-8538;** www.westjet.com) also connects Charlottetown with Toronto.

If you're coming from Montréal by VIA Rail train, debark at Moncton and take an **Acadian** (✆ **800/567-5151;** www.acadianbus.com) bus to Charlottetown; the cost is C$35 per adult for the trip, which takes about 3 hours. If you're coming from

Charlottetown

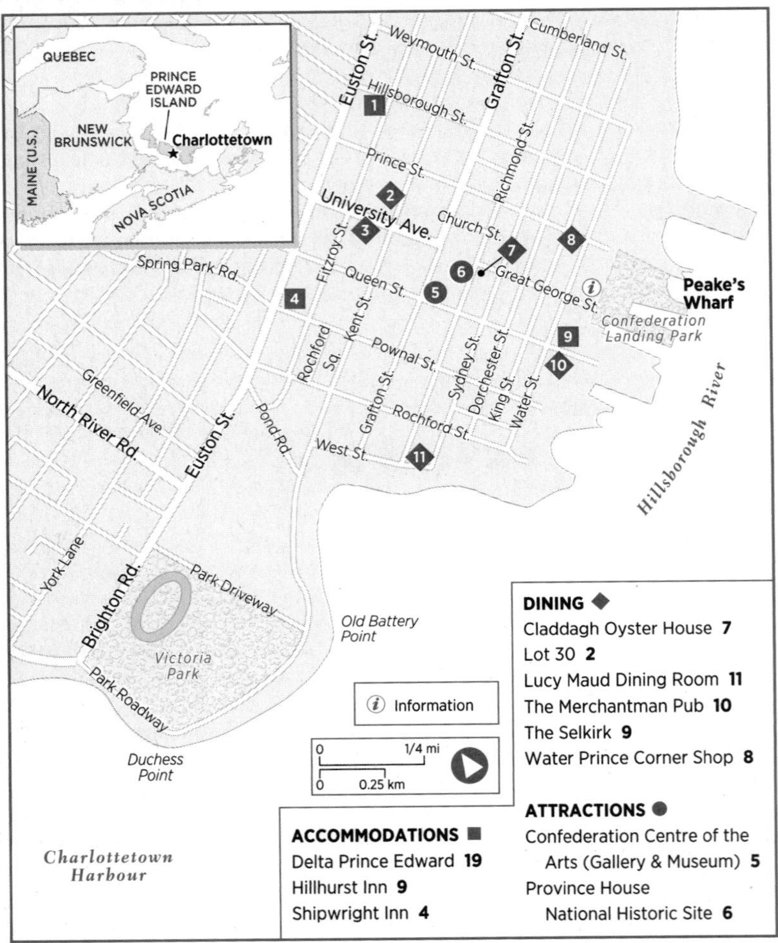

Halifax, **PEI Express Shuttle** (✆ **877/877-1771;** www.peishuttle.com) operates one daily van trip between Charlottetown and Halifax. The trip takes 4 to 5 hours and costs C$60 one-way for adults, C$55 for students and seniors, C$45 for children under age 12.

VISITOR INFORMATION The city's main **Visitor Information Centre** (✆ **902/368-7795**) is in a little historic building right beside the modern brick structure with a pavilion known as **Founders' Hall.** It's at the very end of Prince Street, at the entrance to Confederation Landing Park. (Brown question-mark signs also help direct you there.) This place is loaded with helpful staffers, an interactive computer kiosk, a cafe, free Internet, and an ample supply of brochures; there's also a vacancy board to let you know where rooms are currently available around town, and it's the jumping-off point for city-sponsored walking tours (for a charge). The center is open daily in July and August, weekdays only in the off season.

Exploring Charlottetown

Charlottetown is a compact city that's easy to walk around in. Focus on three areas: the waterfront, the downtown area near Province House and the Confederation Court Mall, and the parks and residential areas near Victoria Park.

You're best off first heading to the **information center** (see above), by the waterfront, for a little orientation and then starting your first tour right from there. That's because parking is generally scarce downtown, but relatively abundant near the visitor center, both on the street and in free and paid lots. At the visitor center, be sure to ask for a map and one of the free walking-tour brochures.

The **waterfront** is anchored by **Peake's Wharf,** a collection of touristy boutiques and eats that attracts hordes in summer. Next to the wharf is **Confederation Landing Park** ★, an open, modern park with a boardwalk along water's edge; lush lawns; and benches nicely situated for lazing about awhile with the kids. There's also a big marina, where you can scope out the pleasure craft.

From the wharf, stroll up **Great George Street** ★★★, one of the best-looking streets in eastern Canada with its leafy trees, perfectly scaled Georgian row houses, and stately churches. At the top of Great George Street, stop into the **Province House** and **Confederation Centre of the Arts** (see below), then explore downtown's shops and restaurants.

Confederation Centre Art Gallery ★ Part of the Confederation Centre of the Arts (which includes three theaters), this is the largest art gallery in Atlantic Canada. The center is housed in a bland, gray, boxy complex of sandstone and glass—a casualty of the "modern" architecture wave that swept the continent in the 1960s and 1970s. (Canadian writer Will Ferguson has referred to the building as "one of the greatest unprosecuted crimes of urban planning in Canadian history.") Inside, however, the gallery is spacious and well arranged on two levels, featuring displays from a 15,000-piece permanent collection as well as imaginatively curated changing exhibits. And admission is free. Shows might range from an exhibit on Canadian legal history to knit rugs from war-torn Afghanistan, from Uruguayan paintings to photographs of islands.

145 Richmond St. ✆ **902/628-6142.** www.confederationcentre.com. Mid-May to late Aug daily 9am–5pm; rest of the year Wed–Sat 11am–5pm, Sun 1pm–5pm.

Province House National Historic Site ★ PEI's official legislative building, this imposing landmark of sandstone was built in 1847 in an area set aside by town fathers for administration and churches. When it served as a colonial legislature, the massive building rose up from vacant lots of dust and mud; but today, as the provincial legislature, it's ringed by handsome trees and an inviting lawn. A bustling downtown area lies just beyond it. The building occupies a special spot in Canada's history: This is the place where the details of the Confederation were hammered out in 1864. (During the 1980s, the building was restored to appear as it would have looked in that year.) The Legislative Assembly, where the island's legislators have been meeting since 1847, is surprisingly tiny—but PEI's legislature has just 27 members, the smallest in Canada. Especially impressive is the second-floor Confederation Chamber.

2 Palmer's Lane. ✆ **902/566-7626.** Free admission (donations requested). June–Oct daily 8:30am–5pm; rest of the year Mon–Fri 8:30am–5pm.

Where to Stay

For those traveling on a tight budget, there are also a number of moderately priced motels situated along the main access roads running into town (coming from the Confederation Bridge) and beside the airport.

Delta Prince Edward ★★ ☺ A 10-story hotel overlooking the harbor, the Prince Edward is stocked with business-travel amenities like coffeemakers, hair dryers, very helpful customer service, and cordless phones (in about half the rooms). The very best "deluxe" rooms are furnished in reproduction Georgian-style furniture, and have two-person Jacuzzis; others have more standard oak and beige laminate furnishings. Higher rooms have better views, and there's a premium for water views, but the city views are actually nicer than those—and you can usually still glimpse the water anyway. The hotel added a new class of apartment-like "Home Suites" in 2009, good for extended stays. There's now a day spa here, as well. The venerable **Selkirk** restaurant (see below) is one of the city's top fine-dining venues.

18 Queen St., Charlottetown, PEI C1A 8B9. ✆ **888/890-3222** or 902/566-2222. Fax 902/566-2282. www.deltaprinceedward.com. 211 units. Peak season C$169–C$390 double, C$225–C$905 suite; call for off-season rates. Packages available. AE, DC, DISC, MC, V. Valet parking C$19, self parking C$15 per day. Pets allowed. **Amenities:** Restaurant; lounge; babysitting; concierge; fitness room; Jacuzzi; indoor pool; room service; sauna; spa; golf simulator. *In room:* A/C, TV, minibar, hair dryer, Jacuzzi (some units).

Hillhurst Inn ★ A fine mansion built in a fine neighborhood three blocks northeast of Province House around the turn of the 19th century, Hillhurst features a number of nice touches—including some extraordinarily detailed woodworking carved by early shipbuilders throughout the home. Rooms here vary in size and style, but all have been upgraded over time for a modern age; all now have phones, air-conditioning, televisions, and so forth. Two even have Jacuzzis. As is often the case, third-floor rooms require a bit of a hike, and are smaller and cozier than rooms on the second floor. Only drawback? Many of the bathrooms are on the smallish side (some had to be shoehorned into former closets), and the furnishings are perhaps a bit less historic and creative than those at the comparatively priced Shipwright down the street.

181 Fitzroy St., Charlottetown, PEI C1A 1S3. ✆ **877/994-8004** or 902/894-8004. Fax 902/892-7679. www.hillhurst.com. 9 units. Mid-June to late Sept C$135–C$235 double; spring and fall C$99–C$165 double. Closed Dec–Apr. Rates include full breakfast. AE, DISC, MC, V. Free parking. *In room:* A/C, TV, hair dryer, Jacuzzi (some units).

Shipwright Inn ★★★ The Shipwright has a settled, pastoral feel to it—a perfect combination, and very PEI. The sturdy Victorian home was built in the 1860s by a local shipbuilder, and later expertly renovated and refurbished. It's decorated in period furniture, without the over-the-top Victorian floral thing that dampens so many B&Bs. Rooms here are kitted out with surprisingly modern amenities such as phones, televisions, and VCR or DVD players. All rooms also show off gorgeous wooden floors (some made from ship-planking). Among the best units are those with something extra: The romantic Officer's Wardroom, a suite with an Asian feel, has a living room, private balcony, fireplace, headboard made from the inn's original doors, and a skylight-view Jacuzzi. The Crow's Nest unit features a king bed, claw-foot Jacuzzi (really), double-sided fireplaces, attractive unvarnished wood furniture, and a shared deck. The other seven units, including some relatively simple ones, are also each distinctive and handsome; staff here are unfailingly helpful.

51 Fitzroy St., Charlottetown, PEI C1A 1R4. ✆ **888/306-9966** or 902/368-1905. Fax 902/628-1905. www.shipwrightinn.com. 9 units. Mid-May to mid-Oct C$149–C$299 double; rest of the year C$99–C$199 double. Rates include full breakfast. AE, DC, MC, V. Free parking. **Amenities:** Dining room; massage. *In room:* A/C, TV, fridge (most units), hair dryer, Jacuzzi (some units), kitchenette (some units), minibar.

Where to Dine

Claddagh Oyster House ★ SEAFOOD The famous PEI oysters and mussels, are the focus of this eatery; seafood chowder is good as a starter, as are the lobster spaghetti, lobster strudel, and lobster-crab cakes with a lemony remoulade. Seafood entrees include boiled lobster, a seafood platter, seared scallops with ginger-pea puree, and PEI-farmed halibut; there are also grilled steaks, Moroccan-spiced rack of lamb, a beef tenderloin topped with crab and sided with whipped potato, and other landlubber entrees. There are no harbor views here, but the preparation and service here are a notch above that at most other fish joints. There's also a great, convivial vibe as locals pop in for the live Irish music and beer downstairs.

131 Sydney St. ✆ **902/892-9661.** Reservations recommended. Main courses C$22–C$30; oysters C$2 each. AE, DISC, MC, V. Mon–Fri 11:30am–2pm; Sun–Thurs 5–10pm; Fri–Sat 5–10:30pm.

Lot 30 ★★★ FUSION Celeb chef Gordon Bailey returns with this downtown fine-dining spot, featuring creative seafood appetizers such as white wine and white-cheddar steamed mussels, a cioppino incorporating seared salmon, house-cured pork, or voluptuous salads constructed of cashews, feta, lobster, and other goodies. Entrees are more spread out between land and sea, running to such choices as butter-poached lobster with fingerling potatoes, beef short ribs, ribeye steaks, pan-roasted salmon with Thai black rice, baked Arctic char, bacony sea scallops, grilled duck breast with Yukon gnocchi, and duets of lamb or pork prepared two distinct ways. The rotating desserts are as fancy and well prepared as you'd expect them to be: panna cotta, crème brûlées, a chocolate-peanut butter mousse with peanut sauce, and assorted other tarts and cakes. If you're a serious foodie, don't pass up a chance to dine here while on island.

151 Kent St. ✆ **902/629-3030.** www.lot30restaurant.ca. Reservations recommended. Main courses $20–$35. MC, V. Tues–Sun 5–9pm. Closed Jan.

Lucy Maud Dining Room ★★ REGIONAL The Lucy Maud is located on the respected Culinary Institute of Canada's Charlottetown campus. The building is a bit institutional and charmless, and the 80-seat dining room has much the feel of a hotel restaurant. But nice touches like custom china offset the lack of personality, and there's a lovely view of the bay and Victoria Park from the big windows. Best of all, diners taste some excellent island cuisine, prepared and served by Institute chefs in training. Lunch and dinner menus change every semester. Typical dinner entrees could be anything from duck or venison (the kitchen is known for its venison) to chicken, steaks, and seafood prepared with local twists such as blueberry puree. There's always salmon on the menu, and sometimes a curry-inflected seafood chowder.

4 Sydney St. ✆ **902/894-6868.** Reservations recommended. Main courses C$8–C$13 at lunch, C$15–C$28 at dinner. AE, MC, V. Tues–Fri 11:30am–1:30pm; Tues–Sat 6–8pm. Closed holiday weekends and Oct–May.

The Merchantman Pub ★★ 🎁 FUSION More upscale than a bar, less fancy than a sit-down dining room, the Merchantman broke new ground when it opened in the mid-'90s. It's as close a thing to a "gastropub" (pub serving gourmet food) as there is on this island; even the nachos are gourmet. The kitchen specializes in seafood, often cooked with Thai or Cajun spices, but they cook a little of everything. Start with lobster bruschetta (yes, please), bacon-dusted scallops, local mussels or oysters, crab cakes, or a bowl of chowder. You could then move on to hearty sandwiches, island fish cakes, or a burger from the pub menu and be plenty happy. Gourmet items include beef medallions in whiskey lemon butter sauce; seared rainbow trout; lobster linguine; rack of lamb in a rhubarb-wine sauce; or a piece of barbecue-roasted salmon. Sweetish desserts, including a maple tart, complete the menu.

23 Queen St. ✆ **902/892-9150.** Pub and gourmet items C$8–C$25. MC, V. Mon–Thurs 11:30am–10pm; Fri–Sat 11:30am–11pm; Sun 11am–10pm.

The Selkirk ★★★ CANADIAN/FUSION Charlottetown's most stylish restaurant is right in the lobby of the high-end Delta Prince Edward hotel (see "Where to Stay," above). Yet it has a more informal character than many hotel dining rooms, with an eclectic mix of chairs and a piano player providing a soundtrack. The menu is also more ambitious and creative than it has to be; lunch choices begin with fish and chips and burgers, but also include steak sandwiches, veggie Wellington, and pasta carbonara with scallops. Dinners might start with a grilled chicken brochette, a bowl of local seafood chowder, wine-steamed island mussels, or a salad of local greens and goat cheese; main courses could include a lobster dinner, a cut of beef tenderloin, a filet of haddock, or some pan-seared scallops. Standard hotel-dining selections, to be sure, but they're prepared right—and for a price that's not nearly as high as you'd expect.

18 Queen St. (in the Delta Prince Edward). ✆ **902/566-2222.** Reservations recommended. Lunch entrees C$12–C$21; dinner entrees C$18–C$25. AE, DC, DISC, MC, V. Mon–Fri 7am–1:30pm and 5:30–9pm; Sat 7–11am and 5:30–9pm; Sun 7am–2pm and 5:30–9pm.

Water Prince Corner Shop ★★ 🎁 SEAFOOD You don't often find a lobster pound in the heart of a historic district of a city, but that's what this place is: a hidden gem, tucked into an attractive building at Water and Prince streets. It looks at first glance like a newsstand or convenience store. Inside, though, you'll find one of the city's most convivial seafood joints, serving lobster dinners, seafood chowder, cooked mussels, and lobster rolls to an appreciative mixture of tourists and locals. There's a liquor license if you want to tip a few, and simpler items like burgers and chicken fingers for the kids or the shellfish-allergic.

141 Water St. ✆ **902/368-3212.** Reservations recommended. Lunch C$4.95–C$11, dinner C$6.95–C$25. AE, DISC, DC, MC, V. May–June and Sept–Oct daily 9am–8pm; July–Aug daily 9am–10pm.

KINGS COUNTY

After a visit to Charlottetown and the island's central towns, Kings County comes as a bit of a surprise. It's far more tranquil and uncluttered than Queens County, and the landscapes feature woodlots alternating with corn, grain, and potato fields.

Although locals play up this county's two largest commercial centers—**Souris** and **Montague**—it's good to keep in mind that each of these coastal hamlets has a population of less than 2,000. So don't arrive here expecting attractions to amuse and entertain you; you'll have to do that yourself. Fortunately, this is prime cycling territory, and walks on the empty beaches are another good tonic for life. Long drives in the country, with occasional stops for eats or to snap photos, are usually the order of the day.

Essentials

GETTING THERE Several of the island's main roads, including Highways 1, 2, 3, and 4, connect Kings County with Charlottetown and the western flank of the island. So it's easy to get here; get out a map, plot a cool route, and point your car north and west. If you're coming from Nova Scotia, the **Woods Island** ferry docks up on the southern coast, though fewer and fewer travelers seem to take that route anymore. See "Exploring Prince Edward Island," earlier in this chapter, for more about the ferry.

VISITOR INFORMATION There's a provincial **Visitor Information Centre** at 95 Main St. in **Souris** (which is also Route 2; ✆ **902/687-7030**), open daily from mid-June through mid-October. There's another VIC at the head of pretty **St. Peters Bay,** on Route 2 at the intersection of routes 313 and 16 (✆ **902/961-3540**); this info center, which borders the Confederation Trail, opens daily June through October.

Montague

Montague may be the Kings County region's main commercial hub, but it's a hub in pretty low gear: compact and attractive, with a handsome business district on a pair of flanking hills sloping down to a bridge across the Montague River. (In fact, a century and a half ago, the town was called Montague Bridge.) Shipbuilding was the economic mainstay in the 19th century; today, though, dairy and (surprise) tobacco farming are the main local endeavors.

EXPLORING THE OUTDOORS

Cruise Manada ★ (✆ **800/986-3444** or 902/838-3444; www.cruisemanada.com) offers good seal- and bird-watching tours daily during peak season aboard restored fishing boats that protect passengers from the weather; the cost is C$22 adults, C$20 seniors and students, C$12 children ages 5 to 13. Trips depart from the marina on the Montague River (it's just below the visitor center, in the old railway depot) once to three times daily in July and August, once daily from mid-May through the end of June and throughout September. Reservations are advised; allow at least 2 hours for the trip.

Southeast of Montague (en route to Murray River) is **Buffaloland Provincial Park ★** (✆ **902/652-8950**), home to a small herd of buffalo. These magnificent animals were a gift to PEI from the province of Alberta, and they now number about two dozen. Walk down the fenced-in corridor into the paddock and ascend the wooden platform for the best view of these gentle, shaggy beasts. The park is right off Route 4, about 6km (4 miles) outside town; watch for signs. Like so many PEI parks, it's free.

Brudenell River Provincial Park ★ is one of the province's best parks and is a great spot to work up an athletic glow on a sunny afternoon. You'll find two well-regarded golf courses, a golf academy, a full-blown resort (see "Where to Stay," below), tennis, lawn bowling, a wildflower garden, a playground, a campground, and nature trails. Kids' programs—which might include Frisbee golf, shoreline scavenger hunts, and crafts workshops—are scheduled daily in summer. You can also rent watercraft within the park. The park is open daily from mid-May through early October, and is free to enter. Head north of Montague on Route 4, then east on Route 3 to the park signs.

WHERE TO STAY

Rodd Brudenell River Resort ★★ ☺ The seasonal (open May through October), attractive Brudenell River Resort was built in 1991, and its open, vaguely Frank Lloyd Wright–influenced design reflects this recent vintage. This is an especially popular destination for golfers. Guests choose from among three types of lodgings. The hotel proper has about 100 well-appointed guest rooms and suites, most with a balcony or terrace looking out onto either the river or one of the resort's showpiece **golf courses ★★**. The expensive, modern "gold cottages" each have two bedrooms, a Jacuzzi, a wet bar, cathedral ceilings, kitchens with dishwashers, fireplaces, decks, barbecue sets, and big-screen TVs; they can be split in half, so you might share a cottage with another set of guests, but the halves are fully divided. "Country cabins" lower down by the river are budget-friendly but *much* less impressive. In addition to the excellent golf courses, the resort has indoor and outdoor pools and a spa.

Rte. 3 (P.O. Box 67), Cardigan, PEI C0A 1G0. ✆ **800/565-7633** or 902/652-2332. Fax 902/652-2886. www.rodd-hotels.ca. 181 units. C$139–C$260 double, C$90–C$183 cabin, C$167–C$568 suite and cottage. Packages available. AE, DC, MC, V. Closed mid-Oct to early May. Pets allowed (C$10 per pet per night). **Amenities:** 2 restaurants; bar; babysitting; canoe/kayak/bike rentals; children's center; 3 golf courses; golf school; fitness center; Jacuzzi; indoor and outdoor pools; sauna; spa; 2 tennis courts. *In room:* A/C, TV, fridge (some units), hair dryer, kitchenette (some units), minibar (some units).

WHERE TO DINE

Windows on the Water Café ★★ SEAFOOD If you haven't yet dined on those internationally famous PEI mussels yet, this enjoyable seasonal cafe is the place to do it. The blue mussels are steamed in a *mirepoix* (French vegetable soup stock) adulterated with flavors of sesame, ginger, and garlic—a tasty take. Dinnertime main courses here could include sole stuffed with crab; fish burgers; or peppered steak served with sautéed vegetables. Lunches are lighter, but still great—chicken salads, house-made maritime fish cakes, and the like. For dessert, the bread pudding is highly recommended. If the weather's good, ask for a seat on the (covered) deck and enjoy a great view of the Montague River; if not, that's okay, because the open dining room is lively enough on its own.

106 Sackville St. (corner of Main St.), Montague. ✆ **902/838-2080.** Reservations recommended. Main courses C$7–C$10 at lunch, C$15–C$21 at dinner. AE, DC, MC, V. June–Sept daily 11:30am–9:30pm. Closed Oct–May.

Souris & Northeast PEI

Some 42km (26 miles) northeast of Montague is the town of Souris, an active fishing town attractively set on a gentle hill overlooking the harbor. Souris (pronounced Soo-*ree*) is French for "mouse"—so named because early settlers here were beset by voracious field mice that destroyed their crops. The town is the launching base for an excursion to the Magdalen Islands, and it also makes a good base for exploring northeastern PEI.

EXPLORING THE AREA

Several good beaches can be found ringing this wedge-shaped peninsula that points toward Nova Scotia's Cape Breton Island. **Red Point Provincial Park** (✆ **902/357-3075**) lies about 13km (8 miles) northeast of Souris, on Route 16. Open from June through mid-September, it offers a handsome beach and supervised swimming, along with a **campground** that's popular with families.

Just a little farther along Route 16 there's another inviting (and often empty) beach at **Basin Head,** which features a **"singing sands" beach ★** that allegedly sings (actually, it more like squeaks) when you walk on it. The dunes here are especially nice. Look also for the nearby **Basin Head Fisheries Museum ★** (✆ **902/357-7233**), a provincially operated museum that offers insight into the life of the inshore fisherman. Admission is C$4 adults, C$3.50 students, and C$12 families (free for children under 12). It's open daily 9am to 5pm, then closed from mid-September through May.

At the island's far eastern tip is the aptly named **East Point Lighthouse ★** (✆ **902/357-2106**). You can simply enjoy the dramatic setting or take a tour of the building from mid-June through early September. Ask for your East Point ribbon while you're here; if you also made it to the North Cape Lighthouse on PEI's western shore, you'll receive a Traveler's Award documenting you've traveled the island tip-to-tip. Admission to the octagonal lighthouse tower is C$3 adults, C$2 seniors and students, C$1 children, and C$8 families. There's also a craft shop on-site purveying jewelry, soap, sand paintings, local books and music, and other island goods.

WHERE TO STAY & DINE

Inn at Bay Fortune ★★ This lovely brick-and-shingle compound on 18 hectares (45 acres) of bayside grounds in the hamlet of Bay Fortune was built by playwright Elmer Harris in 1910 as a summer home, and it quickly became the nucleus for a colony of artists, actors, and writers. Current innkeeper David Wilmer bought it from an actress in the 1980s, then renovated thoroughly—about half the units have fireplaces, and some have Jacuzzis—though it still retains solid furniture, old-home angles and quirks, and an absence of phones, TVs, or air-conditioning units. He also added a six-room wing of more luxurious rooms, including the wonderful bi-level North Tower room no. 4 with its high ceiling, propane fireplace, and balcony overlooking the lodge and bay; the view is simply awesome. There's also a Jacuzzi. The best view, though, might be from South Tower room no. 4, up a narrow staircase—it feels like another planet once you reach this perchlike unit. Towers all booked up? The Green Room has a cool little rooftop deck with bay views, patio furniture, and an umbrella. Newer rooms here are bigger than the older ones, yet all are cozy with mixes of antiques and custom-made furniture. Wilmer has done a good job.

758 Rte. 310 (turn south off Rte. 2 about 5 miles west of Souris), Bay Fortune, PEI C0A 2B0. ✆ **902/687-3745**. Fax 902/687-3540. www.innatbayfortune.com. 17 units. C$135–C$150 double, C$200–C$335 suite; suite off-season discounts available. Rates include full breakfast. Packages available. DC, MC, V. Closed mid-Oct to mid-May. **Amenities:** Restaurant. *In room:* Fireplace (some units), Jacuzzi (some units), no phone.

Inn at Spry Point ★★ This rambling house was built in the 1970s on a remote point of land as an experiemental community—think windmills, solar power, greenhouses, trout ponds, and hippy-dippy talk. But oil prices dropped, interest in conservation waned, and the experiment faded. Enter David Wilmer, owner of the Inn at Bay Fortune (see above). He bought the property and brought it up to date (no small task). All 15 units have king-sized beds and most are tastefully, airily appointed with comfortable sitting areas (11 of them are considered suites). They're rather minimalist in effect, with white wood walls and beams, white bed covers, simple flooring, wooden dressers, and French chairs. Most have private balconies, and several have a little garden terrace as well; suite no. 6 has a deep whirlpool soaker tub and shower from which you can see the grounds. Outside, walk trails traversing red-clay cliffs with views of the Northumberland Strait. Later, dine in the outstanding **dining room ★★**, whose chef features locally grown organic produce and island seafood.

Spry Pt. Rd. (turn off from Rte. 310 about 6 miles south of Rte. 2), Little Pond, PEI COA 2B0. ✆ **888/687-3745** or 902/583-2400. Fax 902/583-2176. www.innatsprypoint.com. 15 units. C$159–C$299 double. Rates include full breakfast. Packages available. DC, MC, V. Closed mid-Sept to late June. **Amenities:** Restaurant room service. *In room:* A/C.

PRINCE COUNTY

Prince County encompasses the western end of PEI, and offers a mixture of lush agricultural landscapes, rugged coastline, and unpopulated sandy beaches. Generally speaking, this region is more ragged around the edges (in a working-farm, working-waterfront kind of way) than prettier, more polished and postcard-friendly places on the island in Kings and Queens counties. In other words: Real people live and work here. Respect them. Within this unrefined landscape, however, you can find pockets of charm such as the village of **Victoria** on the south coast (at the county line) and in **Tyne Valley** near the north coast, which is vaguely reminiscent of a Cotswold hamlet.

Essentials

GETTING THERE Route 2 is the main highway connecting Prince County with the rest of the island; almost all of the smaller feeder routes in these parts eventually lead you to or from Route 2.

VISITOR INFORMATION The best source of travel information for the county is **Gateway Village** (✆ **902/437-8570**) at the end of the Confederation Bridge, described in the introduction to this chapter (see "Essentials," p. 143). It's open daily, year-round.

Victoria ★★

The town of **Victoria**—a short detour off Route 1 between the Confederation Bridge and Charlottetown—is a tiny, scenic village that has attracted a clutch of artists, boutique owners, and craftspeople. What there is of the village is perfect for strolling—parking is near the wharf and off the streets, keeping the narrow lanes free for foot traffic. Wander these short, shady streets while admiring the architecture, much of which is in an elemental, farmhouse style in clapboard or shingles and constructed with sharply creased gables. The village, which was first settled in 1767, has utterly escaped the creeping sprawl that has plagued so many otherwise attractive places on-island. The entire place consists of a total of four square blocks, surrounded by potato fields and the Northumberland Strait.

EXPLORING VICTORIA

The **Victoria Seaport Lighthouse Museum** (no phone) is located inside the shingled, square **lighthouse** ★ near the town parking lot. (You can't miss it.) You'll find a rustic local history museum with the usual assortment of artifacts from the past century or so. It's open daily in summer; admission is by donation.

In the middle of town is the cute, well-regarded **Victoria Playhouse** ★ (✆ **902/658-2025**). Built in 1913 as a community hall, the building has a unique raked stage (it drops 17cm/7 inches over 6m/21 ft. to create the illusion of space), four beautiful stained-glass lamps, and a proscenium arch—pretty unusual for a community hall. Plays staged here from July through mid-September attract folks out from Charlottetown for the night. It's hard to say which is more fun: the performances or the fact of a professional play being staged in a small town with absolutely nothing else going on. There's also a Monday-night concert series, with performers offering up everything from traditional folk to Latin jazz. Most tickets are C$26 adults, C$24 seniors, and C$20 students, though a few performances are priced higher; matinees cost about C$18.

WHERE TO STAY

Orient Hotel ★ The Orient has been a Victoria mainstay for years—a 1926 guide says the inn offered rooms for C$2.50 per night. (Of course, back then a trip to the bathroom required a walk to the carriage house.) The place has since been modernized, and all rooms now have private bathrooms, but the hotel still retains much of its original charm and quirkiness, too. The century-old building with bright yellow shingles and maroon trim is at the edge of the village, overlooking fields that turn purple in late summer. Rooms are painted in warm pastel tones and furnished in flea-market antiques; most have good water views, and all have phones, ceiling fans, and televisions. **Mrs. Proffit's Tea Room,** on the first floor, serves light lunches (sandwiches, lobster rolls, soup, salad) plus an afternoon tea featuring good scones.

34 Main St. (P.O. Box 55), Victoria, PEI C0A 2G0. ✆ **800/565-6743** or 902/658-2503. 8 units. C$80–C$150 double and suite. Rates include full breakfast. Packages available. MC, V. Closed mid-Oct to mid-May. Not suitable for children under 12. **Amenities:** Tea room. *In room:* TV.

WHERE TO DINE

Landmark Café ★ CAFE The Landmark occupies a small green building that was once this town's general store and post office. Today it does still peddle something—the pots and jars hung up on the walls—but the food is now squarely the main focus here, not the crockery. The menu, while limited, is inviting, served in a funky, slightly bohemian setting that keeps the same summer people and locals coming back, year after year. Daily offerings usually include sandwiches and lobster rolls for lunch, and such things as steamed mussels, salads, lasagna, meat pie, salmon, and good filet mignon for dinner. Yes, there's a wine list.

12 Main St. ✆ **902/658-2286.** Reservations recommended. Sandwiches around C$6; main courses C$11–C$16. MC, V. Daily 11:30am–9:30pm. Closed mid-Sept to late June.

Tyne Valley ★

The village of **Tyne Valley,** just off Malpeque Bay, is one of the most attractive and pastoral areas in all of western PEI. It's also exceptionally tiny, even for this island. You'll quickly discover that there's little to do here, yet much to admire: verdant barley and potato fields surrounding a village of gingerbread-like homes, plus azure inlets nosing in on the view from the long distance. A former shipbuilding center, Tyne Valley now attracts artisans and others in search of the slow lane; the gorgeous scenery is a bonus. A handful of good restaurants, inns, and shops cater to summer visitors.

EXPLORING TYNE VALLEY

Just north of the village on Route 12 is lovely **Green Park Provincial Park ★★** (✆ **902/831-7912**), open from mid-June through early September. Once the site of an active shipyard, this 80-hectare (200-acre) park is now a lush riverside destination with emerald lawns and leafy trees. It still has the feel of a turn-of-the-20th-century estate—which, in fact, it was. In the heart of the park is the extravagant 1865 gingerbread mansion built by James Yeo, a merchant, shipbuilder, and landowner who in his time was the island's wealthiest and most powerful man.

The historic Yeo House and the **Green Park Shipbuilding Museum ★** (✆ **902/831-7947**), open June through September, are now the park's centerpieces. Managed by the province's museum and heritage foundation, they together provide a good glimpse into the prosperous lives of shipbuilders during the golden ages of PEI shipbuilding. The museum and house are open daily from mid-June through mid-September, 9am to 5pm. Admission is C$5 adults, C$3.50 students, C$14 families, and free for children under 12.

When leaving the area and returning to Charlottetown, consider taking a brief, highly scenic detour along the bay on **Route 12 ★** from Tyne Valley to MacDougall—it's a little bit longer than going straight back to Route 2 immediately, but much more rewarding.

WHERE TO STAY

Green Park Provincial Park ★★ (✆ **902/831-7912**), on Route 12 just outside Tyne Valley, may be the most gracious and lovely park on the entire island, and it offers camping on 58 grassy and wooded sites overlooking an arm of Malpeque Bay for about C$23 to C$30 per night.

Caernarvon Cottages and Gardens ★ ☺ The sense of quiet and the views over Malpeque Bay across the road are the lures at this attractive, well-maintained cottage complex a few minutes' drive from Tyne Valley. Four cute red-roofed pine cottages, built around 1990, are furnished simply but pretty comfortably: Each has two bedrooms, cathedral ceilings, a sleeping loft, an outdoor gas barbecue, a porch with a bay view, board games, and a kitchen well-kitted out with a stove, toaster, dishwasher, and that great, island-made Paderno cookware. There's a playground out back, and croquet sets and kites available for loan. One caveat: The owner keeps large, energetic dogs (pets are welcome here).

4697 Rte. 12 (about 7 or 8 miles south of Tyne Valley), Bayside, PEI, C0B 1Y0. ✆ **800/514-9170** or 902/854-3418. www.cottagelink.com/caernarvon. 7 units. C$125 double and cottage; C$700–C$750 weekly cottage double occupancy. Inn rates include full breakfast. V. Cottages closed mid-Sept to mid-June (sometimes opened upon request). Pets welcome in cottages. *In room:* TV/DVD (some units), hair dryer, kitchenette (some units), no phone.

The Doctor's Inn B&B ★ A stay at this tiny, year-round inn is a bit like visiting relatives you didn't realize you had. Upstairs in the handsome, right-in-town farmhouse are three plain guest rooms (one with a single bed) sharing a bathroom. That might seem annoying, but you can rent two rooms here for less than the cost of one room at most other PEI inns. There's lots of wood trim, an upstairs sitting area, and extensive, certified-organic gardens out back to wander to—or even buy something from. The inn is also just 3 to 5km (2 or 3 miles) from nice Green Park Provincial Park (see "Exploring Tyne Valley," above). Best of all, the innkeepers serve up one of eastern Canada's most memorable meals in their **dining room ★★**. Diners gather for appetizers in a sitting room, then move to a large oval dining-room table for woodstove-baked bread and salads of produce from the gardens. Entrees are cooked on the same stove in the same old-fashioned kitchen; look for such things as scallops, Arctic char, salmon, or veal, and finish with a homemade dessert. Dinner is served as a four-course meal with wine for C$45 to C$55 per person.

Rte. 167 (at junction with Rte. 12), Tyne Valley, PEI C0B 2C0. ✆ **902/831-3057.** www.peisland.com/doctorsinn. 3 units. C$60 double. Rates include breakfast. MC, V. "Well-mannered" pets welcome. **Amenities:** Dining room. *In room:* No phone.

WHERE TO DINE

The best food in this area is the nightly dinner service at **The Doctor's Inn ★★** (see "Where to Stay," above). Non-inn guests are requested to reserve at least 24 hours in advance, so that the inn can be sure to have enough seats for its paying guests.

The Shipwright's Café ★★ REGIONAL This friendly and locally popular restaurant moved to the village of Margate in 2001. It's elegant yet informal, and you'd be comfortable here in neat jeans or sport clothes. Expect great service, a short but serviceable wine list, and salads with organic greens to begin your meal. Dishes here include lunchtime lamb wraps, chili tostadas, curried mussels, iced or broiled-with-cheese local oysters, and the "Margate Clipper" (a lobster sandwich on potato bread with greens). Dinners run more to fish cakes, herb-crusted Atlantic salmon with lime salsa, vegetable pot pie, seafood paella with bread and aioli, tournedos of beef, and a chowder rich with plenty of those famous plump PEI mussels. It's a great local find—*if* you can find it.

11869 Rte. 6 (at junction of Rte. 233), Margate, PEI C0B 1M0. ✆ **902/836-3403.** Reservations recommended. Lunch items C$9–C$20; dinner entrees C$15–C$20 (more for lobster). MC, V. June–Sept daily 11:30am–3:30pm and 5–8:30pm. Closed Oct–May.

6 NEWFOUNDLAND & LABRADOR

The rustic majesty that is Newfoundland and Labrador can be summed up in two words: "people" and "place." Both are unforgettable. The inhabitants of this isolated locale are as real as it gets. They are unpretentious, thoughtful, and witty. They'll charm you with their accents and their generous spirit. Though their lifestyle is neither opulent nor lavish, they will never hesitate to help a person in need. It comes from living in a harsh environment, where a helping hand can make the difference between survival and some other, ugly, alternative.

Newfoundland and Labrador's landscape and its animal inhabitants are equally remarkable. There are fjords and mountain vistas of stunning beauty. Places where sky meets horizon in blazing color, and where stands of spruce flow in an evergreen sea. Here, salmon launch themselves against the current and traffic slows for road-hopping rabbits. It is a place where howling winds have blown trains off their tracks and arctic air chills your backbone. As any local will tell you, this is the most blessedly cursed union of land, sea, air, and sky on creation. Come here once, and you'll have a perpetual longing to return.

Up until the last decade, Newfoundland was virtually undiscovered as a tourist destination. Even most Canadians hadn't been to "the Rock." But over the past 10 years, the province has put great effort into promoting itself throughout North America and on the global stage. Newfoundland and Labrador has revealed itself to the world as an exciting, unique, and even trendy destination.

EXPLORING NEWFOUNDLAND & LABRADOR

The first thing you need to realize is that Newfoundland and Labrador is big—very big—compared to the rest of Atlantic Canada. To see highlights of the entire province, you'll likely need at least 2 weeks. If you can't afford the time or resources for a lengthy visit, select a few regions and focus on those. The wonderfully slower pace of Newfoundland and Labrador is best enjoyed if you don't have to rush through it.

Cape Chidley
Ungava Bay
Hebron
QUÉBEC
Nain
Davis Inlet
Hopedale
Makkovik
Lobstick Lake
Michikamau Lake
502
Rigolet
LABRADOR
Esker
501
Twin Falls
Labrador City
Wabush
500
Churchill River
520
Lake Melville
Cartwright
Happy Valley-Goose Bay
Mud Lake
MEALY MOUNTAINS
Kenamu River
389
510
Pinware
Battle Harbour
L'Anse-au-Loup
Red Bay
L'Anse aux Meadows National Historic Site
L'Anse-Amour
Blanc-Sablon
St. Anthony
St. Barbe
430
Harrington Harbour
GROS MORNE NATIONAL PARK
Englee
Sept-Iles
Baie Verte
Anticosti Island
Twillingate
TERRA NOVA NATIONAL PARK
Lewisporte
330
Corner Brook
Deer Lake
Grand Falls
Gander
Bonavista
235
230
Stephenville
Gulf of St. Lawrence
NEWFOUNDLAND
80
St. John's
360
480
70
Port aux Basques
210
Argentia
NEW BRUNSWICK
PRINCE EDWARD ISLAND
Havre-Aubert
Grand Bank
100
St-Pierre & Miquelon (FRANCE)
St-Pierre
10
90
Summerside
Fredericton
Charlottetown
Moncton
North Sydney
Cape Breton Island
Saint John
NOVA SCOTIA
ATLANTIC OCEAN
Digby
Halifax
Yarmouth
Sable I.
Ferry
0 150 mi
0 150 km
U.S.
CANADA
Map area
Montreal
Ottawa
Toronto
UNITED STATES

Essentials

VISITOR INFORMATION Contact **Newfoundland & Labrador Tourism** to request a free *Travel Guide, Hunting and Fishing Guide,* or *Highway Map*. Reach them by mail at P.O. Box 8700, St. John's, NL A1B 4J6; call ✆ **800/563-6353** or 709/729-2830; or visit **www.newfoundlandandlabrador.com.** The **Newfoundland & Labrador Road Distance Database** (www.stats.gov.nl.ca/datatools/roaddb/distance) is a helpful online tool for computing driving distances and times between most cities and towns.

Getting There

BY PLANE

Air Canada is the biggest player in Canada, offering two flight options: Air Canada's regular air service and its regional carrier Jazz. Between the two, you'll find connections from destinations around the world to St. John's, Gander, Deer Lake, and Happy Valley–Goose Bay. Call **Air Canada** at ✆ **888/247-2262** or visit them on the Web at **www.aircanada.com.**

WestJet is a low-fare airline from Western Canada that flies into St. John's from Halifax, with connections from there across the country. To compare prices, see **www.westjet.com** or call ✆ **888/937-8538.**

BY CAR

The vast majority of visitors arriving in Newfoundland by road do so by catching a ferry from North Sydney, Nova Scotia (see "By Ferry," below), to either Port-aux-Basques, from where it's 905km (562 miles) to St. John's, or Argentia, a 90-minute drive to the capital.

The only road access to the province is from Baie Comeau, Quebec, from where it's 570km (354 miles) of partly paved road to the Quebec/Newfoundland and Labrador border. From the border, the Trans-Labrador Highway continues eastward to Goose Bay. This is a remote, lightly traveled region of Canada, with few services and much advance planning needed for safe travel.

BY FERRY

Marine Atlantic offers service between North Sydney, Nova Scotia, and two points in Newfoundland. The shorter of the two is the 6-hour journey to Port aux Basques. Ferry service on this route operates year-round, with one-way fares of C$29 adults, C$15 children, and C$8 and up for vehicles. Extras include dorm beds (C$17) and cabins (from C$105).

If your primary destination is St. John's, you can take the approximately 14-hour sailing to Argentia, which is a 1½-hour drive from the capital city. This is a seasonal service that operates from mid-June to mid-September. One-way fares include C$81 adults, C$41 children, and C$168 and up for vehicles. A dorm bed is C$29 and cabins are C$153.

Advance reservations are recommended for all sailings, and a C$25 deposit, payable through a major credit card, is required for reservations booked more than 48 hours prior to departure.

Contact **Marine Atlantic** at ✆ **800/341-7981** or 902/794-5200, or reserve online at **www.marine-atlantic.ca.**

Getting Around

BY PLANE

Traveling by air is the best option if your time is limited. One suggestion would be to fly into St. John's, spend a few days touring the Avalon Peninsula, and then fly across to Deer Lake and pick up another rental car for exploring Gros Morne National Park.

BY CAR

The **Trans-Canada Highway** (also known as Hwy. 1) starts in St. John's and heads west 905km (562 miles) across the province to Channel-Port-aux-Basques (about a 12-hr. drive), where you can hop the ferry to Nova Scotia. It is paved, but just two lanes wide most of the way.

You'll have the most fun—and meet the most interesting people—if you get off the Trans-Canada and take the smaller arteries into the coastal communities.

Other than the Trans-Canada Highway, which has speeds of 90 or 100kmph (around 56–62 mph), the smaller regional routes have a maximum speed of 80kmph (around 50 mph), with speed limits being reduced to 50kmph (31 mph) once you enter many communities.

Warning: The island of Newfoundland is home to more than 150,000 moose. Extreme caution and reduced speeds are recommended when traveling any time between sunset and sunrise, as that's when the massive animals are most likely to be about.

BY FERRY

Provincial Ferry Services operate along 16 different routes. Some are short hops—in the case of Portugal Cove to Bell Island, an enjoyable day trip from St. John's.

For more extensive travel, there are three sailings you should be aware of. Between May and early January, daily ferry service crosses the Strait of Belle Isle from St. Barbe (Western Newfoundland) to Blanc-Sablon (Quebec), from where Route 510 winds up the southern Labrador coast. The one-way fare is C$7.50 for adults, C$6 for seniors and children, and C$23 per vehicle and driver. In Labrador, through summer, a passenger and freight ferry departs Happy Valley–Goose Bay, calling at some 20 isolated villages as far north as Nain, Labrador. The trip takes 2 days each way. Reservations are recommended for both routes; call ✆ **866/535-2567.** You can check schedules at **www.tw.gov.nl.ca/ferryservices.**

The Great Outdoors

BIKING Bike touring in Newfoundland is not for the out-of-shape. It's not that the hills here are necessarily brutal (though many are). It's the *weather* that can be downright demoralizing. Expect more than a handful of blustery days, complete with horizontal rains that seem to swirl around from every direction and can bring forward pedaling progress to a standstill.

Freewheeling Adventures, P.O. Box 100, Norris Point, NL A0K 3V0 (✆ **800/672-0775** or 902/857-3612; www.freewheeling.ca), runs van-supported trips based in hotels and B&Bs.

Aspenwood Tours, P.O. Box 622, Springdale, NL A0J 1T0 (✆ **709/673-4255**), arranges mountain biking trips in and around the central sections of Newfoundland.

BIRD-WATCHING If you're from a temperate climate, bird-watching doesn't get much more interesting or exotic than in Newfoundland and Labrador: It's one of the most intensive areas on the continent (and the world) for certain birds. Seabirds typically attract the most attention, and eastern Newfoundland and the Avalon Peninsula are especially rich in bird life. Just south of St. John's—it's offshore from Route 10, near Deer Lake—is **Witless Bay Ecological Reserve** (**© 709/635 4520**), a cluster of several islands hosting the largest colony of breeding puffins and kittiwakes in the western Atlantic. On the southern Avalon Peninsula, **Cape St. Mary's** features a remarkable sea stack just yards from easily accessible cliffs that's home to a cacophonous colony of northern gannets.

CAMPING Campgrounds are scattered across the province. The season is short, with campgrounds usually opening sometime in June, and then closing for the season by the end of September. All campgrounds are detailed in the annual *Travel Guide*. For a free copy, contact **Newfoundland and Labrador Tourism** at **© 800/563-6353** or 709/729-2830, or order online at www.newfoundlandlabrador.com.

FISHING Newfoundland and Labrador are legendary among serious anglers, especially those stalking the cagey Atlantic salmon, which can weigh up to 18kg (40 lbs.). Other prized species include landlocked salmon, lake trout, brook trout, and northern pike. More than 100 fishing-guide services on the island and mainland can provide everything from simple advice to complete packages that include bush-plane transportation, lodging, and personal guides. One fishing license is needed for Atlantic salmon, one for other fish, so be sure to read the current *Newfoundland & Labrador Hunting and Fishing Guide* closely for current regulations. It's available at most visitor centers, or by calling **© 800/563-6353.** To request it by mail, write the provincial tourism office at P.O. Box 8700, St. John's, NL A1B 4J6.

GOLFING If you're a golfer, you'll be pleased to learn that Newfoundland and Labrador has a number of fine courses. You'll find some of them in St. John's. The best-groomed 18-hole course in the city is the Osprey (one of two courses at Clovelly), but if you want more of a challenge, look to the Admiral's Green, located in Pippy Park. For an online guide to the province's golf courses, visit **www.golf newfoundland.ca.**

HIKING & WALKING Newfoundland has hundreds of trails, many along the coast leading to abandoned communities. Some places are finally realizing the recreational potential for these trails, and are now publishing maps and brochures directing you to them. The Bonavista Peninsula and the Eastport Peninsula, both on Newfoundland's east coast, are two areas that are attracting attention for world-class trails that were all but overlooked until recently.

The best-maintained trails are at **Gros Morne National Park ★★★**, which has around 100km (60 miles) of trails. In addition to these, there's also off-track hiking on the dramatic Long Range for backpackers equipped to set out for a couple of days. Ask at the park visitor center for more information.

SEA KAYAKING With all its protected bays and inlets, Newfoundland is ideal for exploring by sea kayak. But there's a catch: the super-frigid water. You'll need to be well prepared in the event you end up in the drink. Experts traveling with their own gear can pick and choose their destinations; the area northeast of **Terra Nova National Park,** with its archipelago centering around St. Brendan's Island, is one great choice. Novices should stick to guided tours. The aforementioned **Aspenwood** (✆ **709/673-4255**) in Springdale does half- and full-day guided paddles and rentals, in addition to its mountain-biking options; **Eastern Edge Kayak Adventures** (✆ (**866/782-5925** or 709/773-2201) offers tours and clinics of 1 day and up, mostly on the Avalon Peninsula. **Coastal Safari** (✆ **877/888-3020** or 709/579-3977; www.coastalsafari.com), based in St. John's, is a similar outfitter offering extended paddling tours from May through the end of August.

WESTERN NEWFOUNDLAND

If you're traveling in an east-west direction across the island, Western Newfoundland is the grand finale to a wondrous adventure. If, however, this is your entry point to Newfoundland, it's an enticing prelude to an unforgettable vacation. Either way, it's a memory in the making. **Stephenville to Port-aux-Basques** is a scenic 2-hour drive, with sections of highway hugging the ocean. **Corner Brook,** the province's second largest city, spills over steep hills to a large harbor. A popular ski resort and fishing in the Humber River are the main draws.

Essentials

GETTING THERE Port aux Basques is at the southwestern end of the Trans-Canada Highway (Route 1), 218km (135 miles) south of Corner Brook. Most people who come here do so because of its ferry terminal. See "Exploring Newfoundland & Labrador," earlier, for details on the Nova-Scotia-to-Port-aux-Basques ferry. Corner Brook is 53km (33 miles) southwest of Deer Lake along the Trans-Canada Highway (Rte. 1) and 218km (135 miles) north of the Port aux Basques Ferry Terminal. It's 687km (427 miles) west of St. John's.

Western Newfoundland is served by two airports, **Deer Lake,** 50km (30 miles) east of Corner Brook, and **Stephenville,** 80km (50 miles) south of Corner Brook. Both offer service to St. John's, and Goose Bay, Labrador. There are car-rental agencies at both airports and there is a shuttle available from Deer Lake to Corner Brook.

VISITOR INFORMATION Port aux Basques' **Visitor Information Centre** (✆ **709/695-2262)** is on the Trans-Canada Highway, 4km (2½ miles) from the ferry terminal, at the turnoff to downtown. The center is open June to August daily from 9am until 10pm. Through summer and the rest of the year, it also opens for all ferry arrivals. **Corner Brook Tourist Chalet,** located at 11 Confederation Dr. (✆ **709/634-5831;** www.cornerbrook.com), provides information on all of Western Newfoundland. The center is open year-round, from June 15 to September 15 daily from 9am until 9pm, and the rest of the year Monday to Friday from 9am until 5pm.

Port aux Basques & Stephenville

Port aux Basques gets its name from its French heritage, as this region was originally settled by Basque fishermen in the 1500s. Today, Port aux Basques has around 4,500 residents and is home to a Marine Atlantic ferry terminal, which receives year-round ferry service from North Sydney, Nova Scotia. The community is also referred to as Channel–Port aux Basques. North of Port aux Basques is Stephenville (pop. 5,500), a good base for exploring the lovely Port au Port Peninsula or Barachois Pond Provincial Park, both just minutes away from town.

Originally built for U.S. servicemen based at the local Air Force base, **Harmon Seaside Links (✆ 709/643-4322;** www.harmonseasidelinks.com) is a golf course with all the elements of a Scottish links course, including wide fairways lined with fescue grass and ocean views. The 18-hole course is off Route 460 in Stephenville. It has club and power-cart rentals, as well as a driving range. Green fees are C$35. The course is closed November to April.

The Stephenville area has several festivals during the summer, including the **Stephenville Theatre Festival** (**✆ 709/643-4553;** www.stf.nf.ca) that runs during July and August. Outside the venue are impressive murals, while an interior gallery features changing art exhibits. Tickets for main-stage productions are C$24 adults, C$22 seniors, and C$10 children.

WHERE TO STAY & DINE

Cape Anguille Lighthouse Inn ★★ For a completely different experience, consider spending the night in this lighthouse keeper's home, which sits high atop cliffs on Cape Anguille. The adjacent lighthouse is still in operation—and your hosts are the keeper Leonard Patry, who was born at the lighthouse, and his family. The guest rooms are simple yet clean and practical. It's worth the extra C$10 for those with ocean views. In keeping with the get-away-from-it-all theme, the rooms do not have televisions or phones. Meals are available with advance notice. ***Tip:*** Birdwatchers will love the cape and adjacent Codroy Valley, with over 200 species recorded, and some (such as great blue herons) at the northern extent of their range.

Turn off Trans-Canada Hwy. at Doyles, 37km (23 miles) north of Port aux Basques to Cape Anguille. ✆ **877/254-6586** or 709/634-2285. www.linkumtours.com. 6 units. C$100 double. Rates include full breakfast. MC, V. Free parking. Closed Nov–Apr. *In room:* No phone.

Hartery's Family Restaurant ★ NEWFOUNDLAND If you're looking for a more traditional Newfoundland atmosphere and a good meal, I recommend Hartery's. They serve a large variety of dishes and are well known for their traditional "Jiggs Dinner" (boiled beef and cabbage), served all day Thursday and a steal at C$9. They also serve a very nice seafood platter for C$25.

109 Main St., Stephenville. ✆ **709/643-2242.** Reservations recommended for Thursday Jiggs Dinner. Main courses C$8–C$25. MC, V. Mon–Fri 9am–9pm; Sat–Sun 11am–9pm.

Corner Brook

Its proximity to the open waters of the Gulf of St. Lawrence makes Corner Brook a favorite stopover for cruise ships sailing Canada's east coast. That's just one of many appealing aspects to Corner Brook's spectacular location. The community is in a hilly lowland region surrounded by the Long Range Mountains—a continuation of the Appalachian belt stretching up from the New England states—so the natural beauty is stunning.

EXPLORING CORNER BROOK

Corner Brook has a couple of attractions, but it's also worth considering the coastal drive along the southern side of the Humber Arm. Route 450 begins right in town and passes a string of fishing villages en route to Lark Harbour, at the end of the road 50km (31 miles) from town. Aside from admiring the coastal panorama, allow time for a stop in delightfully named **Blow Me Down Provincial Park,** where the Bay of Islands spreads out to the north, and to the south, you can easily spot

the barren rust-colored peaks of the Blow Me Down Mountains. Allow 3 hours for the round-trip.

Marble Mountain Resort ★★★ Atlantic Canada's biggest and best winter resort destination. Rising steeply from the Humber River, Marble Mountain has a peak elevation of only 546m (1,791 ft.), but receives an amazing 5m (16 ft.) of snowfall per year. There are 37 runs, ranging from novice to expert, with 27 groomed trails, seven mogul runs, and three runs through glades of trees. Freestylers are catered to with a half-pipe, snocross park, and terrain park. Marble Mountain operates a high-speed detachable quad chair, two more quad chairs, and a platter lift. Not only will the steepness of the slopes catch your eye, so will the magnificent post-and-beam day lodge, where you find multiple eateries, a ski school, and a rental shop.

While winter is most definitely high season, it's also worth stopping by in summer. A short but steep trail leads to photogenic Steady Brook Falls (allow 30 min. for the round-trip), while the super-fit who slog their way to the summit of Marble Mountain will be rewarded with sweeping mountain and river views. This trail takes around 2 hours to complete.

Rte. 1, Steady Brook, 12km (7½ miles) north of Corner Brook. ✆ **888/462-7253** or 709/637-7601. www.skimarble.com. Lift pass C$49 adults, C$37 seniors and students, C$25 children 12 and under. Ski lifts operate late Dec to early Apr.

WHERE TO STAY & DINE

There are quite a few places to stay and eat in Corner Brook, but I always prefer spending the night at one of the appealing Steady Brook lodgings, 12km (7½ miles) north of town at the base of Marble Mountain.

Marble Inn Resort ★★ Marble Inn is on the banks of the Humber River 12km (7½ miles) north of Corner Brook—within walking distance of the alpine resort. The maroon-colored cedar-shake cottages range in size from one to four bedrooms. Amenities and services differ from unit to unit, with some having full kitchens and others having kitchenettes. Several have a fireplace and Jacuzzi. ***Hint:*** The cottages have a distinctive woodsy feel and are best suited for families, but for a slice of luxury, choose one of the two-bedroom riverside suites, which feature stainless steel kitchen appliances, comfortable living areas, and laundry facilities. Some units come with a Jacuzzi or fireplace.

Madison's Grill, the resort's restaurant, is an excellent choice for dinner, even if you have rented a kitchen-equipped unit. The healthy, wide-ranging menu offers something for everyone, including family-friendly choices such as a whole lasagna for four people. It's open daily for dinner and Sunday for lunch.

21 Dogwood Dr., Steady Brook, 12km (7½ miles) north of Corner Brook. ✆ **877/497-5673** or 709/634-2237. www.marbleinn.com. 12 cottages, 7 inn rooms, 9 suites. C$119–C$299 cottages; C$139 inn rooms; C$329 suites. Midweek and off-season discounts apply. Inquire about ski-pass discounts. MC, V. **Amenities:** Restaurant; exercise room; pool; sauna; playground; guided tours; ski packages. *In room:* TV/DVD player, kitchen/kitchenette.

Bay of Islands Bistro ★★ CONTEMPORARY/CANADIAN Bay of Islands Bistro is one of the best restaurants west of the capital—it has an innovative menu with a wide range of offerings. This is the high-caliber kind of restaurant you'd expect to find in a major city, and a wonderful find in a smaller city such as Corner Brook. On a rather uninspiring main street, the setting, in a renovated residence surrounded by bland buildings, is also a surprise. The emphasis is on local and seasonal produce and seafood, which is given a modern makeover and beautifully presented. Also notable is the professional service. The dinner prices are higher than you'll find in most other restaurants in town, but lunches, including gourmet sandwiches, are well priced.

13 West St., Corner Brook. ✆ **709/639-3463.** Reservations recommended. Main courses C$17–C$33. AE, DC, MC, V. Tues–Thurs noon–9:30pm; Fri–Sat noon–10:30pm; Sun noon–9:30pm.

GROS MORNE NATIONAL PARK

Gros Morne is larger than life, bordered by the Long Range Mountains and tapering to 90m (295-ft.) oceanic depths mere meters from shore. In between is an unbelievable biotic richness: old-growth forests, coastal lowlands, glacier-scarred landscapes, and a place where continents collided. The best way to really appreciate it is via a boat tour, hiking, rock climbing, skiing, or snowmobiling. In short, you have to get out there!

Unless you're the hardy type, the weather may hamper your enjoyment of the park. Between the prevailing southwest winds and the proximity of the Gulf of St. Lawrence, there is, on average, precipitation every 2 days during the summer months. From late September (for the higher elevations) on through the winter months, that dripping wetness translates into an impressive snowfall—up to 1,000 centimeters (394 in., or 33 ft.) in some areas, making Gros Morne ideal for backcountry skiing.

The weather in Gros Morne can be quite unpredictable, so be prepared with clothing for all types, and be sure to get a pre-trip orientation from a park warden before you head off into the backcountry. You'll find hiking trails for every experience level, with the most difficult being the 16km (10-mile) trail to the summit of Gros Morne Mountain, the highest peak in the park at 850m (2,789 ft.). ***Warning:*** Pay special attention to prudent food handling when picnicking, camping, or hiking the backcountry so that you're not surprised by a hungry black bear.

Essentials

GETTING THERE The park entrance is 30km (19 miles) northwest of Deer Lake along Route 430. From this point, it's an additional 40km (25 miles) to Rocky Harbour, the park's main service center. From farther afield, it's 340km (211 miles) to Rocky Harbour from the ferry terminal at Port aux Basques and 640km (398 miles) to the park from St. John's. Alternatively, you can fly into Deer Lake from Halifax, St. John's, Toronto, or Montréal, and rent a car. **Deer Lake Regional Airport** (**© 709/635-3601;** www.deerlakeairport.com) is serviced by Air Canada, Air Labrador, Provincial Airlines, and WestJet. Four car-rental agencies have outlets at the airport (Avis, Budget, Hertz, and National), and an information desk is located by the baggage carousel. Other airport services include Wi-Fi, a gift shop, a restaurant, and an ATM.

VISITOR INFORMATION The most comprehensive information on Gros Morne is available in the park's **Discovery Centre** (**© 709/458-2417**), on Route 431 near the community of Woody Point. It's open mid-May to June daily 9am to 5pm; July to August daily 9am to 6pm (until 9pm Sunday and Wednesday); and September to early October daily 9am to 5pm. The main **Park Visitor Centre** (**© 709/458-2066**), near Rocky Harbour, is open mid-May to late June daily 9am to 5pm; late June to early September daily 9am to 9pm; and early September to October daily 9am to 5pm. You can also get information at the **park entrance kiosk,** on Route 430 near the southeastern entrance to the park at Wiltondale. The kiosk does not have a telephone and is open mid-May to mid-October daily 10am until 6pm.

Parks Canada publishes a wonderful visitor's guide called the *Tuckamore,* which provides detailed information about services in and around the park. You'll be given a copy upon paying your entrance fee; you can also get the same information online at **www.pc.gc.ca/grosmorne.**

FEES All park visitors must pay an entry fee. A day pass is C$10 for adults, C$8 for seniors 65 and over, C$5 for children 6 to 16 years, and free for children 5 and under. Family passes are C$20. If you're continuing up the northern peninsula from Gros Morne, consider the **Viking Trail Pass,** which covers park entrance for 1 week, as well as admission to four national historic sites along the northern peninsula. The cost is C$44 for adults, C$36 for seniors 65 years and over, C$22 for children 6 to 16, free for children 5 and under, and C$89 for families. Your park entrance fee gives you access to park services, including the wonderful Discovery Centre.

Exploring Gros Morne

The orange-yellow moonscape of the **Tablelands ★★** is an easily accessible geological wonder along Route 431. The Tablelands are an excellent example of plate tectonics (so much so that the park has been declared a UNESCO World Heritage Site) in which 470-million-year-old ultrabasic rock was brought to the Earth's surface as a result of faulting. In plain English, it means that this is what the world would look like if you turned it inside out.

Regardless of how much time you have in Gros Morne, the one activity you simply must do is take a 2½-hour narrated cruise on **Western Brook Pond.** Western Brook Pond isn't what we traditionally think of as a pond. It's a 16km-long (10-mile), 165m-deep (541-ft.) inland fjord created during the Glacial Epoch. Access to the departure point is at the end of a 3km (1.9-mile) walking trail (allow at least 40 minutes, or an hour if you walk at a leisurely pace) beginning 27km (17 miles) north of Rocky Harbour. During June and September, there is only a 1pm sailing. In July and August, there are three daily sailings: 10am, and 1 and 4pm. The cost is C$48 adults, C$23 children 12 to 16, C$19 children 11 and under, and C$115 families. Tours are operated by **Bon Tours** (✆ **888/458-2016** or 709/458-2016; www.bontours.ca).

Whether it's an evening stroll along an interpretive trail or a trek to the summit of the park's namesake mountain, you should plan to hike at least one trail while visiting the park. The trail to the 806m (2,644-ft.) summit of **Gros Morne Mountain,** second-highest peak in Newfoundland, is the premier day hike in all of Newfoundland and Labrador. But this 8km (5-mile) trail that starts just above sea level is very strenuous and only for fit and prepared hikers. Covered in tussock grasses and alpine plants, views are nothing short of stupendous, stretching across Bonne Bay to the ocean. You should allow at least 7 hours for the round-trip and be prepared with stout hiking boots, plenty of drinking water, snacks, and rain gear. It is also important you check the weather forecast and trail conditions at the visitor center before heading out.

One of the most popular overnight treks is the 35km (22-mile) **Long Range Traverse,** which usually takes 4 or 5 days. The trail head is reached by joining the boat tour on Western Brook Pond, which drops you off at the far end of the lake. From this point, it's a steep climb to the summit of the Long Range Plateau, where the unmarked trail heads south through total wilderness, before eventually joining the Gros Mountain Trail. The trail is open July to mid-October. Permits are required for all hikers attempting the Long Range Traverse. The cost is C$84 per person, plus a reservation fee of C$25per booking. For details, call ✆ **709/458-2477.**

There are also some pretty amazing cross-country skiing opportunities in Gros Morne. If you're a beginner, the trails around Rocky Harbour and in the north of the park will be best suited to your abilities: The terrain is relatively gentle, with rolling hills and no steep inclines.

Whether you're looking to do some skiing, hiking, sea kayaking, backpacking, or snowshoeing, there are a number of guided tours available. **Gros Morne Adventures**

(✆ **800/685-4624** or 709/458-2722; www.grosmorneadventures.com) will customize a tour for you any time of the year. Try the *Gros Morne Explorer,* a 6 day hike through some of the park's most scenic trails that runs June through September. The cost, including transfers from Deer Lake, lodging, and meals, is C$1,695. Guided kayaking programs range from 2 hours to a full day. You can also rent single or double kayaks and go off on your own, if you're an experienced kayaker.

Where to Stay & Dine

You'll be pleased by the wealth of motel, inn, and B&B accommodation choices located in communities encircled by the park but outside park boundaries. If, however, you're hoping to stay in a luxury hotel, you're going to be disappointed—there aren't any, though there is always ample room at the best lodgings of all, where amenities include pine-needle carpets and starlight canopies.

During July and August, accommodations in Gros Morne—both campsites and motel rooms—can be difficult to come by. It's best to make your reservations as soon as you know you'll be coming.

There are several decent restaurants in the area, but not as many as you might think given the size of the park. It's the nature of the destination; most people aren't here for fine dining. They prefer to picnic or barbecue.

Entente Cordiale 🎁 Overlooking the ocean from beyond the park's northern boundary is Entente Cordiale, a delightfully welcoming bed-and-breakfast named for a 1904 agreement in which the French gave up their rights to Newfoundland's west coast. The trim, two-story wood-frame home is large by Newfoundland standards and is surrounded by an eye-catching driftwood fence. Inside are six comfortable guest rooms, two with unobstructed ocean views and the others with partial water views. A light breakfast is included in the rates, and dinner is available upon request.

The hosts will encourage you to spend time strolling along the sandy beach fronting Portland Creek or, for those looking for adventure, pepper you with suggestions that may include visiting Portland Creek Inner Pond and East Brook Gulch. They can also help with the logistics of hiking the 50km (31-mile) Four Ponds Traverse.

Main Rd., Portland Creek. ✆ **800/316-1899** or 709/898-2288. www.ententecordiale.com. 6 units. C$80–C$90 double. MC, V. Rates include breakfast. Closed Oct to mid-June. *In room:* No phone.

Java Jack's ★★ NEWFOUNDLAND Originally a cafe—as the name suggests—Java Jack's has grown into a great little restaurant within the confines of a restored heritage home brightened by a canary-yellow exterior. You could start with warm potato salad or fish cakes made with halibut, then move onto my favorite main, the Bubbly Bake, a richly flavored dish filled with local seafood. Still hungry? Try the Dark Tickle chocolates, made locally. Regardless of what you order, your meal will take full advantage of herbs and vegetables from the restaurant garden, which is also the source of flowers set on every table.

88 Main St., Rocky Harbour ✆ **709/458-3004.** Reservations not accepted. Main courses C$17–C$25. MC, V. Daily 9am–9pm.

Seaside Restaurant ★ SEAFOOD This casual restaurant is in a restored waterfront building along the boardwalk in Trout River, a picturesque fishing village at the end of Route 431. The decor is suitably nautical, with the most-sought-after tables on an upstairs balcony with sweeping ocean views. You can order light meals such as salads, but it is the simple presentations of local seafood, including chowders, crab, lobster, and cod, that get the most attention.

Rte. 431, Trout River. ✆ **709/451-3461.** Reservations not necessary. Main courses C$9–C$18. MC, V. Mid-May to mid-Oct daily noon–10pm.

Sugar Hill Inn ★★★ One of the more luxurious places to stay while in Gros Morne (and one of the only places that has air-conditioning) is Sugar Hill Inn. Most impressive is the King Suite. It features a king-size bed, private Jacuzzi for two, and gorgeous leather couch. This room is popular—especially with honeymooners—so be sure to book early. There is also a nice cottage with queen-size bed, Jacuzzi tub, and a private deck. Every room has a hardwood floor, and most have a private entrance.

The Sugar Hill Inn offers a set three-course menu nightly in a classy dining room. The specialty of the house is fresh local seafood, with choices dependent on availability—you may be invited to try halibut, cod, salmon, shrimp, or scallops. It's one of the very few restaurants in the province where *nothing* is deep-fried. One staple are the desserts made fresh daily (the baked custard with blueberry sauce is simply divine). Dining is by reservation only—primarily for guests of the inn—and is served from 6:30 to 8:30pm.

Norris Point Rd., Norris Point. ✆ **888/299-2147** or 709/458-2147. www.sugarhillinn.ca. 11 units. C$145–C$225 double. C$15 additional person. Off-season discounts. AE, MC, V. Free parking. Closed Oct–Jan. **Amenities:** Restaurant; lounge; sauna. *In room:* A/C, TV.

Camping in Gros Morne

A good number of visitors come to Gros Morne to camp and thus to fully appreciate the great outdoors. The campgrounds are justifiably popular, so reservations are wise. Contact the **Parks Canada Campground Reservation Service** (✆ **877/737-3783;** www.pccamping.ca). For general information on camping in Gros Morne, contact the **Park Visitor Centre** (✆ **709/458-2417;** www.pc.gc.ca/grosmorne).

Berry Hill Campground ★ With 146 wooded campsites, including four walk-in sites especially for tent campers, this is the park's largest campground. It also has the most facilities, as well as a hiking trail. It is close to Rocky Harbour, where grocery stores and restaurants can be found. If you want to combine culture with camping, you'll be pleased to know that the shuttle for the Gros Morne Theatre Festival makes a campground pickup.

Rte. 430, Rocky Harbour. 146 sites. C$26 per site; C$7 per firewood bundle. AE, MC, V. Closed mid-Sept to mid-June. **Amenities:** Shower and washroom facilities; water; kitchen shelter; dump station; picnic tables; fire pits; playground; hiking.

Trout River Pond Campground ★ Campsites at Trout River are larger and more sheltered than in some other parts of the park and provide awesome views of the Tablelands and Trout River Pond. The drinking water is good, but it's still not a bad idea to filter it. This is a popular spot because of the nearby beach, boat tour, and boat launch. Although the most isolated auto-accessible campground in the park, it's also the best base for exploring the Tablelands, the Green Gardens area, and the community of Trout River.

Rte. 431, Trout River. 44 sites. C$26 unserviced site; C$7 per firewood bundle. AE, MC, V. Open mid-June to mid-Sept. **Amenities:** Kitchen shelter; picnic tables; swimming; fishing; hiking; playground; washrooms w/showers; water; fire pits.

NORTHERN PENINSULA

The Bonne Bay entrance to the northern peninsula is a dazzling panorama of surreal extremes: You'll scale near-perpendicular mountain heights through some of the tallest trees in the province, following a twining blacktop on what seems a perpetual climb, until a sudden final crest reverses your direction into a similarly stunning descent. All the while, your vehicle is regularly overtaken by tractor-trailers, logging trucks, and speeding grannies, who are obviously immune to the natural wonder.

It calms down considerably after that. As is typical elsewhere in the province, the highway follows traditional coastal settlement patterns. Virtually all settlement in the province is along the coast, a reflection of the importance of the fishery and ocean access to early settlers. From Cow Head north, the topography is mostly flat, with stands of tuckamore (trees whose growth has been stunted by wind and sea) to the right and the Atlantic Ocean to the left. Here and there, you'll encounter stretches of barrens and bog, much like the scenery along the Burin Peninsula.

Essentials

GETTING THERE Port au Choix is 13km (8 miles) off of Route 430, and 230km (143 miles) north of Deer Lake. Both the main highway and the paved access road are in good condition, but you won't find a lot of services along the way—so be sure to tank up and have a few snacks with you before heading out. It's a 2½-hour drive from Port au Choix to St. Anthony.

Port au Choix

As the approximate halfway point between Deer Lake and St. Anthony, Port au Choix is a convenient stopover on the northern peninsula. With a population of 1,200, it's one of the larger communities en route and has a good number of services/facilities (for example, a bank, a post office, and restaurants). But the main reason to detour from the highway is to visit the site where archaeologists are uncovering evidence of ancient native cultures.

Port au Choix National Historic Site ★★ Archaeological findings confirm that over the last 4,500 years, five cultures inhabited the barren peninsula extending into the Gulf of St. Lawrence, beyond the modern-day town of Port au Choix. Although these earliest residents didn't leave a written record, from 30 years of archaeological digs, we have a good idea of the way these ancient people lived and adapted to the harsh environment. The best place to learn about the site is the **Parks Canada Visitor Centre,** which is signposted through town, on the peninsula itself. Here, you can see a wonderful assortment of displays about the Maritime Archaic Indians, Groswater Paleoeskimos, Dorset Paleoeskimos, and more recent native cultures. Artifacts of note include stone axes, hunting tools, and bone carvings. Don't miss the life-size replica of a Dorset-Paleoeskimo dwelling from about 1,500 years ago. Whale bones were used to frame the structure, and animal skins insulated it from the region's harsh weather. The well-curated displays, such as the assortment of ancient stone and bone tools from the region's four prehistoric cultures, make for an enjoyably edifying experience.

Once you've seen the indoor displays, plan on exploring the rest of the historic site on foot. Check at the visitor center for scheduled guided hikes, which generally depart daily through summer at 1:30pm.

Port au Choix National Historic Site. ✆ **709/861-3522.** www.pc.gc.ca/portauchoix. C$8 adults, C$7 seniors, C$4 children 6 to 16, free for children 5 and under; C$20 families. June–Sept daily 9am–6pm.

WHERE TO STAY & DINE

There is one motel in town, as well as a B&B, a small inn, and a couple of good restaurants—making it the best place to stay while in the area.

Anchor Café ★ SEAFOOD You won't have any problem recognizing the Anchor Café—the front of the building is shaped like the bow of a boat. It's a casual, fun (albeit kitschy) establishment decorated with lobster pots, fishing nets, and a sou'westered mannequin. With such an obvious fishing theme, it's no surprise this wheelchair-friendly restaurant specializes in local seafood. Of special note are any items that include coldwater shrimp (those tasty little shrimp you see on shrimp rings), which are caught in local waters and processed in the waterfront factory across the road. The cod and shrimp chowder can be a meal in itself, or head straight for mains such as blackened halibut. The Anchor Café is on the main road through town and directly opposite the waterfront.

Main St., Port au Choix. ✆ **709/861-3665.** Reservations not necessary. Main courses C$6–C$18. MC, V. May–June and Sept–Oct daily 10am–10pm; July–Aug daily 9am–11pm.

Sea Echo Motel There's a wise manager in charge here: The hanging plastic seafood and lighthouse replica, while charming in the adjacent restaurant, are thankfully absent in the unremarkable decor of this motel's very spacious rooms. You'll be surprised at just how much space there is: besides the bed(s), there are nightstands, a bureau, a love seat, a table with two chairs, and still ample room to move around. It's not advertised as wheelchair accessible, but I don't think maneuvering around this single-story structure will be a problem for travelers with disabilities.

Fisher St., Port au Choix. ✆ **709/861-3777.** www.seaechomotel.ca. 33 units. C$92–C$115 double. AE, DC, MC, V. Free parking. **Amenities:** Restaurant; lounge; gift shop. *In room:* TV, hair dryer, Wi-Fi.

L'Anse aux Meadows

At a barren outpost on a flat headland jutting bravely into the North Atlantic, you'll find several innocuous grassy mounds that are both a UNESCO World Heritage Site and a National Historic Site. These "mounds" are the footprints of the first European settlement in North America. Although the Viking Norsemen who first arrived on these shores more than 1,000 years ago didn't make a permanent home of what they called *Vinland*, they left evidence of their passage in the foundations of the original sod structures that once housed them.

The community of L'Anse aux Meadows is 40km (25 miles) north of St. Anthony (turn off Rte. 430 onto Rte. 436) and surrounding villages offer a limited number of services, including welcoming bed-and-breakfasts and one of Newfoundland's best restaurants. Visitor information is available at **L'Anse aux Meadows National Historic Site** (✆ **709/623-2608;** www.pc.gc.ca/eng/lhn-nhs/nl/meadows/index.aspx). The center is open June to early October daily 9am to 6pm.

L'Anse aux Meadows National Historic Site ★★★ Embark on your Viking journey at the visitor center, just off Route 436 and within site of the first European settlement in North America. The details of your adventure will be revealed in a 30-minute video (offered in the theater) that details the discovery of the site by Dr.

Helge Ingstad and his wife, Dr. Anne Stine. As Norwegians, Ingstad and Stine had a strong interest in determining the exact location of *Vinland,* the legendary location referenced in the Norse sagas.

After watching the video, examine the many artifacts that confirm the Vikings' presence here as far back as A.D. 1000. You'll even see a model of how the settlement would have looked when it was inhabited. From there, it's on to the real thing. A short walk along a gravel path takes you to the excavated foundations of the Viking settlement, where the use of each structure is detailed. Beyond this point are reconstructions of the sod and timber buildings that the Vikings called home all those years ago. Costumed interpreters will educate and entertain you with demonstrations of their various crafts. "Gunnar" shares the secret of navigation and ship construction, "Harald" illustrates the power of forge and anvil, while "Thora" proves that Viking women are a force to be reckoned with (she plans to divorce her impractical dreamer of a husband—Bjorn, the "brains" behind the expedition—when they return to civilization).

Rte. 436, L'Anse aux Meadows. ✆ **709/623-2608.** www.pc.gc.ca/eng/lhn-nhs/nl/meadows/index.aspx. C$12 adults, C$10 seniors over 64, C$6 children 6–16, free for children 5 and under; C$28 families. Mid-June to early Oct daily 9am–6pm.

WHERE TO STAY & DINE

Norseman Restaurant ★★★ SEAFOOD Without a doubt, the Norseman is one of the province's best restaurants in all regards—creative cooking, professional service, and faultless presentation. The setting alone is superb—a tastefully decorated room and adjacent deck, with water views from most tables. Seafood is the house specialty. For starters, the fish chowder is a delight, and the smoked char has a unique flavor. If you order lobster, your server will invite you across the road to visit the wharf and pick out your own lobster (in season). Other mains are as creative as cod baked in a Dijon mustard and garlic crust and as local as grilled caribou tenderloin brushed with red-wine glaze. At least one daily dessert is a pie crammed with local berries. The drinks menu is as notable as the food, with everything from bakeapple wine to martinis. Adding to the appeal on Tuesday and Friday evenings are local musicians performing traditional music.

Rte. 436, L'Anse aux Meadows. ✆ **877/623-2018** or 709/754-3105. www.valhalla-lodge.com/restaurant. Reservations recommended. Main courses C$16–C$38. MC, V. Late May to late Sept daily noon–9pm.

Viking Village Bed & Breakfast ★ A modern home within walking distance of L'Anse aux Meadows National Historic Site, this is as close as you can get to Viking habitation without actually sleeping in a sod hut. Its proximity to the Norsemen Restaurant is an added bonus. The Viking theme–named guest rooms all have patio doors and balconies, which is a lovely feature if you're visiting during summer.

A full breakfast and evening snack are included with the room rates, and the owners will cook you a Newfoundland-style dinner for an extra fee of C$20 per person. The owners will pick you up at St. Anthony airport or at the bus stop. The owners do not allow smoking. The same owners also run the more basic **Viking Nest B&B** with slightly lower rates, which can be reached via the same contact numbers.

Rte. 436 to Hay Cove. ✆ **877/858-2238** or 709/623-2238. www.vikingvillage.ca. 5 units. C$72–C$78 double. Rates include full breakfast and evening snack. AE, MC, V. Free parking. **Amenities:** Library; limited room service.

TERRA NOVA NATIONAL PARK

Terra Nova National Park may not get as much attention as Gros Morne, but wilderness lovers will find plenty of adventures in this more accessible park. In addition to hiking and kayaking, tour boats search out whales and other wildlife, or you can stroll the forest-lined fairways of one of the province's finest golf courses. Terra Nova ("new land") is Newfoundland's first and more accessible national park. The main visitor center is 240km (149 miles), or about a 3-hour drive, northwest of St. John's, and about 76km (47 miles) southeast of Gander.

Essentials

GETTING THERE Terra Nova National Park is conveniently located along the Trans-Canada Highway (Rte. 1), so if you're driving across the province, you'll go straight through it. It's located in the Eastern Region about 80km (50 miles) northwest of Clarenville. Along the 48km (30-mile) stretch of the Trans-Canada Highway within the park are numerous side roads leading into the park, including to small lakes, the main information center, and two campgrounds.

VISITOR INFORMATION You can obtain visitor information for the park at the **Visitor Centre** (✆ **709/533-2801**). Set on Newman Sound, this facility is the hub of Terra Nova National Park. Hours are daily 9am until 7pm in summer, and daily 10am to 5pm mid-May to late June and September to mid-October. The facility is closed mid-October to mid-May. For general information about Terra Nova, visit **Parks Canada**'s website at www.pc.gc.ca/eng/pn-np/nl/terranova/index.aspx.

FEES If you're planning to tour the park, you'll need to purchase a pass. A day pass, valid until 4pm following the day of purchase, costs C$6 for adults, C$5 for seniors 65 and over, C$3 for children 6 to 16, and free for children 5 and under. The family rate is C$15.

Exploring the Park

If you're not into hiking or formal tours, one of the park's highlights is **Blue Hill,** the highest point in the park, at 199m (653 ft.). You must take a short, somewhat washboarded, gravel road to get here, which may be difficult for RVs and low-riding vehicles. But once at the top, you'll get a lovely view of the finger fjords. If you're feeling energetic, take the short drive to Ochre Hill, the site of an ancient volcano, and climb the lookout tower for another great view of the finger peninsulas and the Visitor Centre.

The **Junior Naturalist Club** ★ makes the park a hit with families. The program is geared toward kids 5 to 13, who get a chance to learn about nature in a fun, hands-on way. Visit the Nature House at Newman Sound Campground for more information. It is open July and August 10am until 5pm.

The **Visitor Centre** ★ (✆ **709/533-2801**) is worthy not only as a stand-alone attraction, but also as the place from which you'll take a boat or kayak tour, and from where you can access the Coastal Trail. The facility has three display areas: the wet lab, the theater, and the marine exhibit. The marine exhibit is great for children, as they can learn about and touch various live marine creatures in the touch tank. There is also a children's activity center, gift shop, and cafe (with outdoor patio). Give yourself about 1½ hours to tour the complex before you head out and explore. The centre is open mid-May to late June and Sept to mid-Oct daily 10am–5pm; late June to Aug daily 9am–7pm. Admission is free once you have purchased a park pass.

One of the nicest hiking trails in the park is the 4.5km (2.8-mile) **Coastal Trail** linking the Visitor Information Marine Centre to Newman Sound Campground. Allow around 90 minutes each way. About halfway along, you'll pass by Pissing Mare Falls—not spectacular by any means, but a soothing place to listen to the water trickling down the rocks as you relax on a bench and smell the fresh air. Depending on the time of your visit, you may see the dogberry in bloom and the "old man's beard" lichen hanging from the trees. Old man's beard is also called "traveler's joy"—it's an indication of clean air in the areas where it grows. It's edible, but beware—it acts as a natural laxative!

Where to Stay & Dine

Other than park-administered campgrounds and the sites near the park gates at the southern and northern access points, there are no visitor accommodations within the expanse of the park, but as it's only 50km (31 miles) from one end of the park to the other, this shouldn't be a problem. If you are equipped, camping is the best way to really appreciate Terra Nova. Park staff members operate an excellent outdoor theater program, with nightly events at the beachside campfire circle built from natural logs.

In addition to the camping fees detailed below, a national parks pass (see "Essentials," above) is required for all campers.

Newman Sound Campground ★ This is by far the largest campground in the park, with 356 campsites, and it's my recommended destination as it has fully serviced and treed lots. Only 66 of the sites are fully serviced with electricity, so if this is a requirement, be sure to book as far in advance as possible through the **Parks Canada camping reservation system** (✆ **877/737-3783;** www.pccamping.ca); there is an additional charge of C$11 for this service. Check-in time is 1pm; checkout time is 11am. Quiet hours are enforced beginning at 11pm. You can camp here year-round, but the electricity is turned on only from May through October.

Newman Sound is 30km (19 miles) from the south entrance of the park and is linked to the Visitor Centre by a hiking trail.

Rte. 1 to Newman Sound. ✆ **709/533-2801.** 356 sites. C$26–C$30 per site. AE, MC, V. **Amenities:** Heated washrooms with showers and flush toilets; wheelchair accessible; grocery store; snack bar; laundry services; dumping station; playground; community fire pits; kitchen shelter; hiking trails; interpretive programs; kids' activity center; campfire programs.

Starfish Eatery SEAFOOD When you've finished learning about the park at the Visitor Centre, grab a free map, take a seat at this adjacent cafe, and start planning your itinerary. Perfectly located overlooking Newman Sound, this homey cafe even has a few outdoor tables. The simple cooking includes pan-fried scallops and hearty chowders.

Visitor Information Marine Centre. ✆ **709/533-9555.** Reservations not necessary. C$5–C$10. MC, V. May to mid-Oct daily 10am–6pm.

Terra Nova Resort ★★ ☺ If you love to golf and you have kids, the Terra Nova Resort is a wonderful vacation destination. Twin Rivers, the resort's 18-hole golf course, has been voted one of the top 50 in Canada. Its challenging layout and water views make the greens fees of C$57 an excellent value. Adding to the appeal for parents is the Children's Recreation Program (included with the room rates), which includes games, supervised swimming, treasure hunts, and craft-making, as well as supervised lunches. Other facilities include an outdoor heated pool, walking trails, a playground, tennis courts, a basketball court, and mini-golf.

Guest rooms are nicely furnished in a solid, rustic style and are notably soundproof, considering the number of children you'll find scurrying about. As none of the guest rooms comes with cooking facilities (even the efficiency units have just a fridge and microwave, no stove), you'll probably eat at least one meal in the on-site Clode Sound Dining Room. But don't worry, they don't take advantage of their culinary monopoly. The surroundings are business-casual elegant, with golf-course views and thick wooden beams running overhead to remind you that you're in a lodge. Mains on the wide-ranging menu are C$14 to C$27, with children's meals under C$10. It is open daily 7am to 11am and 5pm to 10pm.

Rte. 1 (3rd exit to Port Blandford, if you're arriving from the south). ✆ **709/543-2525.** Fax 709/543-2201. www.terranovagolf.com. 83 units. C$128–C$249 double. AE, DC, DISC, MC, V. **Amenities:** 2 restaurants; lounge; babysitting; 2 golf courses; pool; room service; tennis courts; playground. *In room:* A/C, TV.

BONAVISTA PENINSULA

The Bonavista Peninsula is to the north of the Trans-Canada Highway. Here, the streets of Trinity, having changed little in generations, make this village a Bonavista highlight. Continue north to the peninsula's namesake town and you'll find a charming fishing village perched on the edge of the ocean, with history brought to life in local museums. From the roadside vendors of hand-picked seasonal berries, to a singularly unique railway loop (the only one of its type in North America), to a replica of a 500-year-old sailing ship, exploring the Bonavista Peninsula will be a highlight of your time in Newfoundland. Although you can easily make the return trip in a single day, you'll really need at least 2 days to enjoy the multitude of services and attractions you'll find here. The weather of early fall (Sept to mid-Oct) is generally very favorable, requiring just a light jacket and pants. You won't want to come here after the end of October, however, as many of the attractions and even accommodations close for the winter.

Essentials

GETTING THERE The southern gateway to the Bonavista Peninsula is Clarenville, a 2-hour drive northwest of St. John's (189km/117 miles) on the Trans-Canada Highway (Rte. 1). From the Argentia ferry terminal, Clarenville is a 1½-hour drive. From Clarenville, Route 230 winds its way 114km (71 miles) along the peninsula to the town of Bonavista. The other main attraction in the area is Trinity, which lies just off Route 230, 73km (45 miles) from Clarenville.

From the west, the Trans-Canada Highway enters Terra Nova National Park 80km (50 miles) southeast of Gander. From this point, it's 48km (30 miles) south through the park to Port Blandford, where Route 233 cuts across the southern end of the peninsula to join Route 230.

VISITOR INFORMATION You'll find visitor information in Clarenville at the office of the **Discovery Trail Tourism Association,** 54 Manitoba Dr. (✆ **866/420-3255** or 709/466-3845; www.fallfordiscovery.com).

On the peninsula itself, most accommodations hand out tourist information, as does the **Trinity Interpretation Centre** in Trinity (✆ **800/563-6353** or 709/464-2042), open mid-May through late September daily 10am to 5:30pm, and the **Ryan Premises National Historic Site** in Bonavista (✆ **709/468-1600**), open mid-May through mid-October daily 10am to 6pm.

Trinity ★★★

It's sure to be love at first sight in Trinity (pop. 350), a famously picturesque village overlooking Trinity Bight, 73km (45 miles) east of Clarenville along Route 230. Here, you'll find a passionate regard for the past embodied in an almost unanimous community-wide celebration of historically accurate home restoration. From the picket fences, vertical slider windows, vegetable gardens, and distinctive signage, it's obvious that Trinity takes pride in its history. And why not? It was a crucial pioneer settlement in the province, with some of the first clergy, doctors, and professional tradesmen in Newfoundland.

Begin your Trinity Village visit at the **Trinity Interpretation Centre** (✆ **709/464-2042**). Here, you'll get a one-page map naming each of the significant sites. From there, your next stop should be the Lester-Garland Premises, located in the former general store. Take a look at the original 1896 ledger to see the names and purchases made by residents of the time. Nearby, Lester-Garland House was built in 1819, making it Newfoundland's first brick home. Hiscock House, a 1910 restoration, represents a typical merchant's household, complete with fancy furnishings. Next door to that is a craft shop that closes at 5:30pm, so try not to arrive too late in the day or you may be disappointed. At the Green Family Forge, marvel at the work of early blacksmiths, while The Cooperage is the summer home of a cooper, who creates magnificent woodturnings using restored machinery.

The various historical sites are open mid-June to September daily 10am to 5:30pm. A pass for all sites is C$7.50 for adults. Children 12 and under are free. For more information, visit the website of the Trinity Historical Society (www.trinityhistoricalsociety.com). ***Tip:*** The admission pass is valid for more than 1 day, so plan on dividing your visits up between other activities.

If you're looking for a more active adventure than you'll find at the local museum, invigorating outdoor activities are easy to find in and around Trinity. If you're into **hiking,** you'll really enjoy the network of walking trails that lace the peninsula, all of which are easily accessed from Trinity. Ask at your local lodging for a map, or visit the **Discovery Trail Tourism Association** (www.fallfordiscovery.com) for links to local hikes. **Atlantic Adventures** (✆ **709/464-2133;** www.atlanticadventures.com) offers all-in-one-yachting adventure, whale-watching tour, dinner theater, and port exploration aboard 14m (46-ft.) ketch-rigged sailing boat *Atlantic Adventurer.* The cost of this 2-hour cruise is C$104 per person for 2 passengers and C$52 per person for 3 or more.

A trip to Trinity wouldn't be complete without treating yourself to a performance of the **Rising Tide Theatre** (✆ **888/464-3377** or 709/464-3232; www.risingtidetheatre.com), a professional theater company since 1978. Between mid-June and mid-September each year, the company puts on a number of performances in an outdoor seaside venue. It costs C$24 for one of the regular plays in the program, and C$38 for the dinner theater. Rising Tide's prime offering is the **New Founde Lande**

Trinity Pageant ★, the anchor event of Trinity's Summer in the Bight Theatre Festival. Actors move from one historical site to another throughout the town, telling a story as they go. The pageant is held from early July until Labour Day on Wednesday and Saturday, departing the Interpretation Centre at 2pm. Tickets are just C$15. If you're not into live theater but love live music, put on your dancing shoes and shuffle over to **Twine Loft** (High St.; ✆ **709/464-3377**), where there's a packed program of musicians performing through summer. On Wednesday evenings at **Rocky's Place** (✆ **709/464-3400**), just up the road from the Twine Loft, fiddlers Kelly Russell and Baxter Wareham, along with folklorist Tonya Kearley get together for Dance Up (a lively mélange of folk music and step-dancing). The action starts at 10pm.

WHERE TO STAY & DINE

Lodging in Trinity is limited to a number of small inns and bed-and-breakfasts. In summer especially, make reservations well in advance.

Artisan Inn ★★ Originally from Holland, ambitious owner Tineke Gow has transformed a number of Trinity's most historic structures into tourist accommodations. Most notable of these is the Artisan Inn, a classic two-story wooden waterfront building holding two guest rooms. The Cove View Room is slightly smaller than the Trinity Room, but has water views. It's well worth the extra C$36 to upgrade to the Ocean Shore Apartment. Located adjacent to the main house, it features a full kitchen, king bed, TV/VCR combo, small library, and best of all, a private waterfront deck outfitted with a propane barbeque. All three are furnished with locally crafted furniture, which blends perfectly with the welcoming ambience throughout.

49 High St., Trinity. ✆ **877/464-7700** or 709/464-3377. www.artisaninntrinity.com. 3 units. C$119–C$155 double. Closed Nov–Apr. AE, DC, MC, V. **Amenities:** Restaurant.

Fishers' Loft Inn ★★★ It's a 5-minute road trip outside Trinity proper to the favored destination of visiting movie stars. Dame Judi Dench and Kevin Spacey stayed at Fishers' Loft during filming of *The Shipping News* (in separate rooms, of course). With good reason: On the exterior, it fits in well with the local architecture, but inside, it has the world-class flavor you'd expect from its cosmopolitan owners. John and Peggy Fisher are from England and Ottawa, Ontario, respectively. The former professional restorers brought their talents to Port Rexton in 1990, when they decided to turn their summer home into a year-round residence. Their handiwork is evident in each of the 20 distinctive guest rooms, which are scattered through eight buildings, all of which have a big-screen view of the mini islands scattered along the shore of Trinity Bay. The spacious guest rooms feature handcrafted furniture hinting at old-world austerity, but the down-filled duvets are pure luxury where it counts the most. Also notable is the original art decorating public spaces and guest rooms.

The royal treatment becomes even more evident in the dining room, where the in-house cooks create culinary artistry with seafood, berries collected locally, and vegetables and herbs from the surrounding garden. The nightly menu is several steps ahead of the fare you'll find in most inns this size: garden greens with lime vinaigrette, herb-crusted salmon and roasted vegetables, and chocolate torte with blueberry *coulis*. ***Tip:*** Plan on splurging on the meal package—this is the place you've been saving for.

Mill Rd., Port Rexton. ✆ **877/464-3240** or 709/464-3240. www.fishersloft.com. 20 units. C$112–C$206 double; modified American plan C$248–C$342 double. Discounts for multi-night stays in May and Oct. AE, DC, MC, V. Free parking. Closed Nov–Apr. **Amenities:** Restaurant; lounge. *In room:* TV.

Bonavista ★★

At the tip of the Bonavista Peninsula and the site where *continental* Europeans first touched North American soil more than 500 years ago (the Vikings were here first; see "L'Anse aux Meadows"), Bonavista is an almost full-service community. It has a hospital, pharmacy, gas station, and banking services, but little in the way of accommodations (apart from a couple of B&Bs and a small motel). That being the case, it's best to think of Bonavista as a half-day excursion from Trinity.

A leisurely 3km (1¾ miles) through the town of Bonavista is Cape Bonavista, site of a photogenic red-and-white-striped **Cape Bonavista Lighthouse ★★** (**✆ 709/468-7444**). Interpreters dressed in 1870s costume will guide you through this beautifully restored facility. From the top of the tower you can see puffins flitting around nests burrowed into various granite cliffs. The view is magnificent. Take an hour or two to explore the marshy grounds around the site itself. Climb to the hill above the parking lot, where you'll discover a miniature pond and sandpipers searching for insects in the mud while bluebells tinkle in a light breeze and a whale snorts in the distance. Turn to the left and walk across the barrens to the municipal park, where you'll find a statue of John Cabot. The lighthouse is open daily from Mid-May to September from 10am–5:30pm. Admission is C$3 for ages 13 and up.

Located on the tip of the Bonavista Peninsula near the Cape Bonavista Lighthouse is **Dungeon Provincial Park**, a natural scenic wonder. The Dungeon is a collapsed sea cave with a natural archway carved out by ocean movement. Situated on what is locally known as "Backside," on a scenic but bumpy gravel road (approximately 2km/1¼ miles off Rte. 235), complete with pasture land for horses, cows, and sheep, a trip to the Dungeon makes for a nice diversion. Day-use facilities are open June-September.

Down at the harbor, you can board (but you can't sail on) a 20th-century reconstruction of John Cabot's 15th-century ship, the ***Matthew*** (**✆ 877/468-1497** or 709/468-1493; www.matthewlegacy.com). Start your visit at the Matthew Legacy Visitor Interpretation Centre, where exhibits tell the story of Cabot's journey and the extraordinary effort that went into building the replica of his famous ship. Then, join a 30-minute tour of the ship, led by costumed interpreters who provide a fascinating insight into the trials faced by Cabot and his crew as they sailed the wild waters of the Atlantic in the very close quarters of a 19m (62-ft.), three-masted, wooden caravel. The ship is open Mid-June to late Sept daily 10am–6pm. Admission is C$7.50 adults, C$7 seniors, C$3 children 6–16, free for children 5 and under; C$17 family.

Those interested in local history should include **Ryan Premises National Historic Site ★** (**✆ 709/468-1600**; www.pc.gc.ca/lhn-nhs/nl/ryan/index.aspx) on their itinerary. There's nothing grand or ostentatious about this cluster of five historic white, red-trimmed, wooden structures on the Bonavista waterfront. The understated drama of their purpose-built design gives new life to the daily interactions of 19th-century fishermen and merchants. As you wander around the site, you'll encounter plank floors and sawdust, thick-beamed building supports, and the unmistakable scent of salt fish. You'll watch videos, read storyboards, and speak to costumed reenactors demonstrating how the fishery brought Newfoundland and Labrador into the global economy hundreds of years before e-commerce, NAFTA, or the WTO. There's a gift shop on-site and a restaurant next door. The site is open from Mid-May to mid-October daily from 10am-6pm. Admission is C$4 adults, C$3.50 seniors, C$2 children; C$10 family.

ST. JOHN'S

The historic capital of Newfoundland and Labrador, St. John's is a bustling, character-filled city that sprawls around a natural harbor on the island's east coast. The connection to the ocean is ever-present, from the sights, sounds, and smells of a busy port to attractions such as Signal Hill (now a National Historic Site), which rises abruptly from the harbor headland. The Rooms is a modern edifice, but as the province's premier museum, it is one attraction you definitely don't want to miss. The city is also home to some of the province's best accommodations—whether you're looking for the comforts of a full-service hotel or the ambience of a historic bed-and-breakfast. The city also has a plethora of restaurants to suit all tastes. And plenty of activities are available within an hour's drive of the city. As one of the oldest cities in North America, St. John's boasts a history that bursts with stories of pirate treasure, restless ghosts, and military prowess. Visit the "City of Legends" once, and I guarantee you'll find a way to return.

Essentials

GETTING THERE **St. John's International Airport** (© **866/758-8581;** www.stjohnsairport.com) is a 3-hour flight from Toronto or Boston, a 4-hour flight from New York, and a 5-hour flight from London, England. Air Canada flies direct to St. John's from Halifax, Montréal, and Toronto, with connections from cities throughout the world made through the latter two hubs. The other major Canadian airline serving St. John's is WestJet from Halifax, Toronto, and Calgary (summer only).

Continental has daily flights between St. John's and Newark. Local airlines include Air Labrador and Provincial Airlines, both providing reliable links between the capital and points throughout the province. Upon arrival in St. John's you'll be pleased to find a modern airport with desks for all major rental-car companies, a choice of eateries, currency exchange, gift shops, and an information center. The airport is just minutes (6km/3¾ miles) and a relatively inexpensive cab ride (C$22.50 for one person, plus C$2.50 per extra person) to downtown.

Taking the **ferry** from Nova Scotia to Newfoundland is cheaper than flying, but it's a much more time-consuming endeavor. The routing that gets you closest to St. John's is a full 14-hour sailing from North Sydney to Argentia, followed by a 1½-hour drive to the city. But if you have the time, you can save a considerable chunk of change by **sailing** and **driving** your own car, versus flying and then renting a car on arrival.

VISITOR INFORMATION A **visitor information center** is located on the arrival level of St. John's International Airport. The **St. John's Visitor Information Centre** is located downtown at 348 Water St. (© **709/576-8106;** www.stjohns.ca). It's open year-round Monday to Friday 9am to 4:30pm, with extended summer hours of 9am to 5pm daily. The marketing organization **Destination St. John's** (© **877/739-8899** or 709/739-8899; www.destinationstjohns.com) is a good source of trip-planning information.

GETTING AROUND St. John's has an inexpensive public bus system, **Metrobus** (© **709/570-2020;** www.metrobus.com). Adults (including seniors) ride for C$2.25. Children ages 4 to 18 pay C$1.75; children 3 and under ride for free. You may find one of the 10-ride passes (C$20 adults, C$15 seniors and children) to be a bit more economical if you're planning to use the bus a lot; purchase these from major

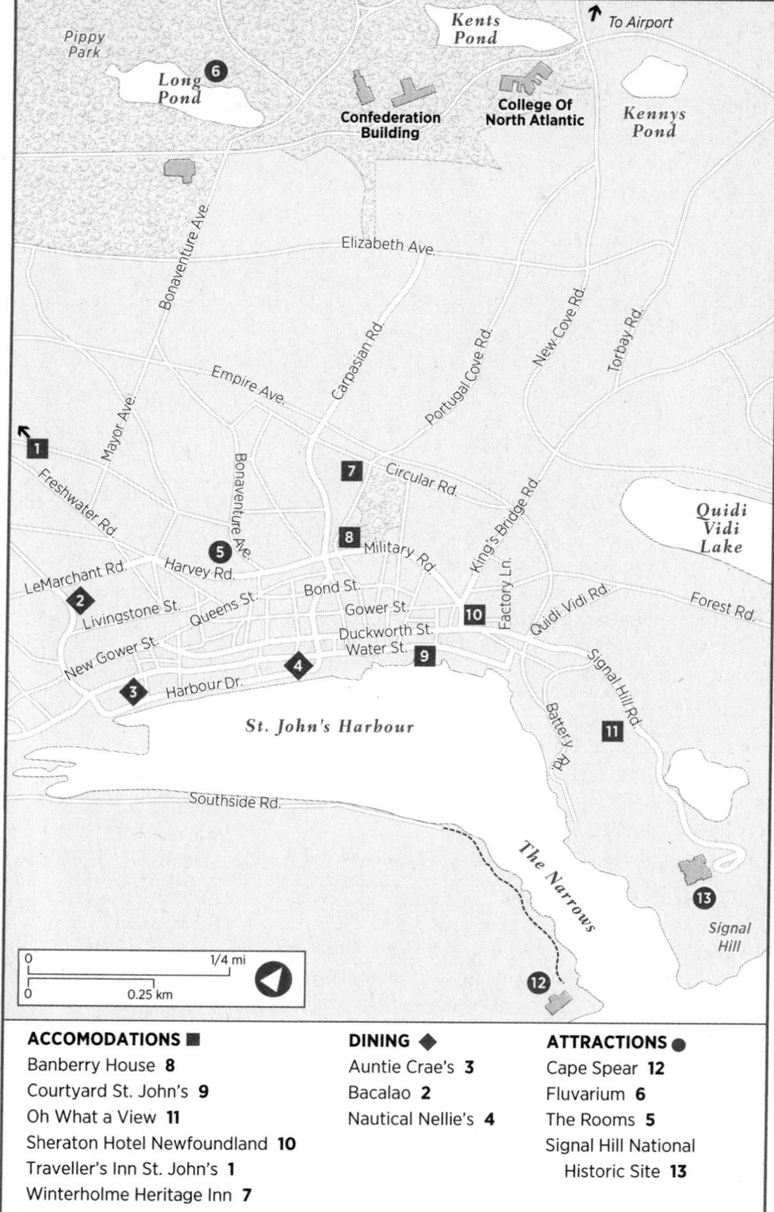
Pippy Park
Long Pond
Kents Pond
To Airport
Confederation Building
College Of North Atlantic
Kennys Pond
Bonaventure Ave.
Elizabeth Ave.
Carpasian Rd.
Portugal Cove Rd.
New Cove Rd.
Torbay Rd.
Empire Ave.
Mayor Ave.
Freshwater Rd.
Circular Rd.
Quidi Vidi Lake
Military Rd.
King's Bridge Rd.
Factory Ln.
LeMarchant Rd.
Harvey Rd.
Bond St.
Livingstone St.
Queens St.
Gower St.
Duckworth St.
Water St.
New Gower St.
Harbour Dr.
Quidi Vidi Rd.
Forest Rd.
Signal Hill Rd.
Battery Rd.
St. John's Harbour
Southside Rd.
The Narrows
Signal Hill
0
1/4 mi
0
0.25 km
ACCOMODATIONS
Banberry House 8
Courtyard St. John's 9
Oh What a View 11
Sheraton Hotel Newfoundland 10
Traveller's Inn St. John's 1
Winterholme Heritage Inn 7
DINING
Auntie Crae's 3
Bacalao 2
Nautical Nellie's 4
ATTRACTIONS
Cape Spear 12
Fluvarium 6
The Rooms 5
Signal Hill National Historic Site 13

shopping malls or the Metro Transit Centre, at 245 Freshwater Road. Metrobus operates with cash-only, exact-change fare policy. Drivers do not carry change.

Taxis in St. John's are also fairly priced. Most rides about town will cost you under C$10. The biggest company is **Bugden's Taxi** (✆ **709/726-4400**). Others include **Co-op Taxi** (✆ **709/753-5100**) and **City Wide Taxi** (✆ **709/722-0003**).

Exploring St. John's

Many of the capital city's most well-known attractions are within walking distance of downtown lodgings. Unless you have mobility problems, the best way to explore the downtown area is on foot.

Cape Spear ★★ Cape Spear is the most easterly point in North America and protected as a National Historic Site for its lighthouse, which was built in 1832. The lighthouse keeper's residence has been restored and allows a glimpse of daily life at this remote outpost in the mid-1800s. History aside, the cape is worth visiting for its naturally dramatic setting. You may be amazed at how different its weather can be from that in the city—it's situated just 15 minutes and 11km (6¾ miles) south of St. John's, but you may feel as much as a 15°C (59°F) temperature difference. Be sure to bring a sweater or jacket along with you. Allow at least 1½ hours to tour the Visitor Interpretation Centre, lighthouse, and gift shop—more if you'd like to linger and watch for whales along the coast.

Cape Spear Rd. (heading out of town, Water St. provides access to Cape Spear Rd.). ✆ **709/772-5367.** Lighthouse tour C$4 adults, C$3 seniors and children. Grounds open year-round; guided lighthouse tours mid-May to mid-Oct daily 10am–6pm. Visitor Interpretation Centre open mid-May to Aug daily 8:30am–9pm; Sept to mid-Oct daily 10am–6pm.

Fluvarium ★★ ☺ If you're interested in what's underwater in the local freshwater ponds, the Fluvarium is a great place to visit. Within this distinctive octagonal building, you'll learn about three distinct freshwater habitats and see a free-range fish habitat, a deepwater display of brown trout, and many interactive displays. You're looking through a glass wall at the underwater world outdoors, so it's best not to visit immediately after a rain, as the water will be cloudy and visibility poor. Allow no less than 1½ hours to visit, more if you'd like to enjoy the surrounding hiking trails, including one leading along Rennies River to Quidi Vidi Lake. Feeding time is at 4pm, so it's best to arrive around 3pm.

Nagle's Place, off Allandale Rd. ✆ **709/754-3474.** www.fluvarium.ca. C$5.50 adults, C$4.50 seniors and students, C$3.50 children 5 and up, free for children under 5; C$18 families. Summer daily 9am–5pm; rest of year Mon–Fri 9am–5pm, Sat–Sun noon–5pm.

The Rooms ★★★ This cultural oasis—combining the provincial museum, art gallery, and archives—is the one place you just must visit while in St. John's. Located on a hill above downtown, the design of The Rooms pays tribute to the traditional lifestyle of Newfoundland and Labrador. "Fishing rooms" were buildings along the shoreline where fish were processed and where nets and other fishing equipment were stored. While the design has historic connotations, the interior is contemporary and slick, with state-of-the-art technology used to tell the story of Newfoundland and Labrador's natural and human history.

A portion of The Rooms is devoted to the **Provincial Art Gallery,** which has the same hours as the main museum and is included in admission. It is the province's largest public gallery, housing more than 7,000 works on two floors. The emphasis is on contemporary Canadian art (but there's only a small sampling of this on display), including traditional and mixed media. The permanent collection features major works by nationally recognized artists, as well as hooked mats made by women who live in the many outport communities throughout Newfoundland and Labrador.

9 Bonaventure Ave. ✆ **709/757-8000.** www.therooms.ca. Admission C$7.50 adults, C$5 seniors and students, C$4 children 6–16, free for children 5 and under; free admission for everyone Wed 6–9pm and Nov–May on the first Sat of every month. June to mid-Oct Mon–Tues and Thurs–Sat 10am–5pm, Wed 10am–9pm, Sun noon–5pm; mid-Oct to May Tues–Sat 10am–5pm, Sun noon–5pm.

Signal Hill National Historic Site ★★★ Rising 183m (600 ft.) above the entrance to St. John's Harbour, this is the city's granite guardian. The harbor and city views alone make a drive to the top worthwhile, but as a National Historic Site, it also has much significance as a lookout post. The military history of this site is well explained at the informative Interpretive Centre halfway up the hill. You'd be wise to stop here and learn about the site before you head to the next level. Between the Interpretive Centre and the top of Signal Hill, you'll find a restored cannon battery pointed seaward, much as it was when it was necessary to protect the settlement from marauding pirates or warring nations.

At the top of the hill is Cabot Tower, a stone tower built in 1897 to commemorate the 400th anniversary of John Cabot's landing at St. John's. Inside, displays tell the story of the site, including that of Guglielmo Marconi, who received the first transatlantic wireless message from the hill in 1901. On the tower's second floor, ham-radio enthusiasts operate a small station through summer. While visitors can access the roof of the Tower, it's not advisable on windy days—particularly not with children. The winds here can get very high and could literally pull a small child out of your arms.

Try to time your visit to take in the Signal Hill Tattoo, held below Cabot Tower 4 days a week during the summer (Wed, Thurs, Sat, and Sun) at 11am and 3pm. The colorful artillery and military drumming display takes you back to the days when this site was of paramount importance to the safety of St. John's.

Outdoor Pursuits

Bowring Park Bowring Park is the city's preeminent green space. It has a river and brook running through it, ducks swimming happily about, and pigeons doing their best to make a mess of the lovely bronze statues. There's a whimsical statue of Peter Pan (it's a replica of the same statue that stands in the Kensington Gardens of London) alongside the pond that, while beautiful to look at, has a melancholy history. It's actually a memorial for a little girl who had loved the park, but who, along with her father, was tragically shipwrecked. The park also contains a tribute to St. John's military history, with a number of commemorative war plaques to read. Bowring Park also offers a large adventure playground, an outdoor swimming pool, tennis courts, picnic grounds, walking trails, and cross-country ski trails and tobogganing in the winter.

Southwest of downtown on Waterford Bridge Rd. ✆ **709/576-6134.** Free admission. Daily 9am–10pm.

Pippy Park Northwest of downtown, adjacent to the Memorial University of Newfoundland, this park features a peaceful pond where you can rent canoes or kayaks. There's a playground and mini-golf for the kids, two golf courses, camping, picnic grounds, hiking trails, a botanical garden, and the Fluvarium (see "Exploring St. John's," earlier in this chapter). Locals regard Long Pond as excellent for city bird-watching, and the occasional moose has even been sighted in the park. You'll pass the expansive park many times on your travels in and around the city.

Take Kenmount Rd. to Thorburn Rd. or Prince Philip Dr. ✆ **709/737-3655.** www.pippypark.com. Free admission. Daily dawn–dusk.

Where to Stay

EXPENSIVE

Courtyard St. John's ★★ Affiliated with the Marriott chain, the Courtyard offers smart and stylish guest rooms, with plenty of room to move around and as comfortable as those at the Sheraton. Request a room on the upper floors for harbor views. At the time of writing, Wi-Fi was only available in public areas of the hotel; guest rooms, however, have dataports.

131 Duckworth St., St. John's. ✆ **866/727-6636** or 709/722-6636. Fax 709/738-3775. www.marriott.com. 81 units. C$199–C$229 double. AE, DC, DISC, MC, V. Free parking; valet parking available for C$15 per day. **Amenities:** Restaurant; concierge; room service; Wi-Fi. *In room:* A/C, TV w/pay movies, fridge, hair dryer.

Sheraton Hotel Newfoundland ★★ Still referred to as the "Hotel Newfoundland" among locals because of its longtime history under that name, the Sheraton Hotel Newfoundland stands alone as the best full-service hotel in town. Positives include everything from one of the city's best restaurants; a luxurious spa and fitness center; an art gallery; and Club Level executive rooms where guests that pay a little more enjoy the Sheraton Club Lounge, complete with complimentary breakfast and evening snacks, and a massive flat-screen TV. The only negatives are its lack of traditional charm and windows that don't open up and provide you with a whiff of that fresh sea air.

With more than 300 guest rooms on seven floors, the Sheraton is where royalty and other dignitaries stay while in St. John's. Traditional rooms have city views, while deluxe rooms face the harbor. For these and other rooms, check the Starwood website for specials, especially on weekends and outside of summer.

115 Cavendish Sq., St. John's. ✆ **800/325-3535** or 709/726-4980. Fax 709/726-2025. www.starwoodhotels.com. 301 units. C$289–C$429 double. AE, DC, DISC, MC, V. Free parking and valet parking available. **Amenities:** 2 restaurants; lounge; babysitting; concierge; executive rooms; health club; pool; room service; spa. *In room:* A/C, TV, hair dryer, minibar, Wi-Fi.

Winterholme Heritage Inn ★★★ Anyone who appreciates fine craftsmanship and has a sense of history would enjoy staying at Winterholme, built in 1905 for the delightfully named Marmaduke Winter, who was a wealthy merchant. Sitting across the road from Bannerman Park, the property is now designated a National Historic Site—a wonderful example of Queen Anne Revival architecture, which was popular in Canadian house construction from the 1880s until about 1914, and truly breathtaking inside and out. The intricate woodwork, the lovely stained glass, and the spacious rooms are all special touches, but it's the English oak staircase that will leave you in awe. It's a piece of artwork in itself. Every guest room is different and offers its own charm. The six top-floor Attic Suites are built under the sloped roofline, but all are extremely spacious and equipped with luxuries such as a double Jacuzzi and fireplace, as are the larger suites on lower levels. A delicious full breakfast and parking are included in the rates; an on-site spa provides facials, massages, and pedicures.

79 Rennies Mill Rd., St. John's. ✆ **800/599-7829** or 709/739-7979. Fax 709/753-9411. www.winterholme.com. 11 units. C$159–C$249 double. AE, DC, MC, V. Free parking. **Amenities:** Spa. *In room:* TV/DVD player, hair dryer, Wi-Fi.

MODERATE

Banberry House ★★ One of the best things about Banberry House is its location. When staying here, just a stone's throw from Bannerman Park, where the Folk Festival is held each summer, you can actually sit on the patio amid the potted plants and enjoy the music without ever leaving the yard. Built in 1892, immediately following the Great Fire, Banberry House boasts wonderful stained glass by the same craftsman whose work adorns the nearby Catholic Basilica of St. John the Baptist.

The guest rooms at the Banberry exhibit carefully preserved historical authenticity. One of the rooms has a four-poster bed and wood-burning fireplace. Some have the old-fashioned footed tubs, as well as shower stalls. The main-floor "Labrador Room" has an especially rugged feel to it, as well as a fireplace and views across the private garden. Upon rising in the morning, you are bound to be pleased with such local breakfast delicacies as *toutons* (fried bread dough that tastes much better than it sounds, especially topped with molasses), salt cod cakes, and bread-stuffed bologna. Everything is made on-site, and guests are guaranteed not to get the same breakfast twice if they're staying for a week or less, as a different specialty is featured each morning.

116 Military Rd., St. John's. ✆ **877/579-8226** or 709/579-8006. Fax 709/579-3443. www.banberryhouse.com. 6 units. C$139–C$169 double; off-season rates from C$99. AE, DC, MC, V. Free street parking. *In room:* TV.

Oh What a View! 🎁 A simple Newfoundland home has been converted to this welcoming bed-and-breakfast that is central to the attractions of Signal Hill and the restaurants you find within the Battery Hotel and Sheraton Hotel Newfoundland. A full breakfast is included, and the most expensive room has harbor views. The same owners rent out the nearby Harbour View Cottage, a two-bedroom home with a full kitchen and views that extend across the harbor to downtown, for C$150.

184 Signal Hill Rd., St. John's. ✆ **709/576-7063.** Fax 709/753-6934. www.ohwhataview.com. 4 units. C$75–C$150 double. MC, V. Free parking. Closed Dec–Mar. *In room:* TV/DVD player, Wi-Fi.

Traveller's Inn St. John's Moderately priced, reliably clean, and uncomplicated accommodations that are perfect for the budget-conscious visitor. Because it's situated on one of the busiest streets in St. John's, you'll want to ask for a room at the back of the building, where the noise of passing traffic is less likely to keep you awake at night. The guest rooms are bright, spacious, and comfortably appointed. It also has one of the province's few outdoor pools, and as a bonus for families, children 18 and under stay free, and those 12 and younger eat free.

199 Kenmount Rd., St. John's. ✆ **800/261-5540** or 709/722-5540. Fax 709/722-1025. www.greatcanadianhotels.com. 99 units. C$89–C$119 double. AE, DC, MC, V. Free parking. **Amenities:** Restaurant; lounge; pool. *In room:* TV w/pay movies, hair dryer.

Where to Dine

For such a small city, St. John's has some wonderful restaurants and a great variety of culinary adventures to choose from. One of the most appealing things about dining in the capital is that you can enjoy local favorites—especially seafood—on all budgets.

EXPENSIVE

Bacalao ★★★ NEWFOUNDLAND Meaning "salt cod" in Spanish, Bacalao is a gem of a restaurant that does a wonderful job of bringing the best out of Newfoundland's best known export, cod. And they do so using local ingredients as much as possible, including vegetables from organic farms scattered around the capital and seafood from local suppliers. The homegrown theme extends through all ingredients—mussels are steamed open in Quidi Vidi beer, and the caribou salad is drizzled with blueberry wine from the province's only winery. Even the bathroom hand soap is made by a St. John's company. As a dinner main, the cod au gratin topped with a creamy sauce and melted cheddar cheese is hard to fault. Other notable mains include seafood risotto and medallions of caribou with partridgeberry sauce. If you love fancy desserts, it's hard to choose between the Republic Mousse, which comes in the three colors of the Newfoundland flag, and the gooseberry Pavlova.

65 Lemarchant Rd. ✆ **709/579-6565.** www.bacalaocuisine.ca. Reservations recommended. Main courses C$21–C$34. AE, MC, V. Mon 6–10pm; Tues–Fri noon–2:30pm and 6–10pm; Sat–Sun 11am–2:30pm and 6–10pm.

MODERATE

Nautical Nellies ★ PUB FARE From the road, this pub looks rather nondescript. But once inside, your eyes will quickly become accustomed to the dim lighting, and the friendly bar staff will welcome you with a choice of draft beers and a menu of traditional Newfoundland cooking. It's always crowded—especially from the start of Friday happy hour until closing. And, as you can tell from a quick conversation with any of those with Scottish, British, or Australian accents seated at the bar, it's the preferred hangout of visiting oil industry personnel. Why? Because it's the ideal place to have an ale and unwind, a true pub where staff know the regulars by name and drink preference. The food is excellently prepared and generously portioned—even at lunch, when one meal is probably enough for two people. Their pan-fried cod with sides of pork scrunchions and rice is delicious. The seafood chowder and crab spring roll appetizers are similarly tasty. ***Note:*** The pub gets so busy during happy hour that meals aren't served then.

201 Water St. ✆ **709/738-1120.** Reservations not accepted. Main courses C$12–C$18. AE, DC, MC, V. Meals served: Mon–Thurs and Sat 11:30am–3pm and 5–9pm; Fri 11:30am–3pm; Sun 11am–3pm.

INEXPENSIVE

Auntie Crae's ★★ NEWFOUNDLAND Step back in time while immersing yourself completely in Newfoundland culture at this unique establishment that combines a grocery store with Fishhook Neyle's Common Room. The former is filled with nostalgic provincial delicacies, such as canned meats, jams and preserves, and "nunny bags" (picnic baskets), as well as modern treats such as freshly ground coffee; muffins and savory bakery items fresh from the upstairs bakery; and cod chowder with two other daily soup choices. The adjacent common room is exactly as the name suggests—a room with two long tables where you can eat and socialize, and not necessarily in that order. Visitors are even allowed to bring their own food!

272 Water St. ✆ **709/754-0661.** www.auntiecraes.com. Reservations not accepted. Light meals and snacks C$2–C$7. MC, V. Tues–Sat 8am–7pm.

St. John's After Dark

St. John's has a vibrant nightlife. You'll find great live music playing everywhere, as well as a good selection of dinner theaters and other cultural offerings.

Within a 2-block stretch of **George Street**, you'll find about 20 establishments eager to draw you a pint. Very welcoming to visitors is **Trapper John's** (2 George St.; ✆ **709/579-9630**), a pub well known for its "screeching-in" ceremony, which allows you to become an honorary Newfoundlander. **Bridie Molloy's** (5 George St.; ✆ **709/576-5990**) has a great outdoor patio and traditional Irish music.

If you're looking for a quieter atmosphere, try the aviation-themed **Windsock Lounge** (161 Water St.; ✆ **709/722-5001**). This downtown piano bar features local performers Thursday to Saturday.

The **Ship Inn** on Solomon's Lane (access from 265 Duckworth St.; ✆ **709/753-3870**) is the most famous drinking establishment in the city. Its history boasts many well-known writers and artists as frequent customers. Expect live jazz, blues, reggae, rock, or folk Thursday through Saturday and poetry readings on Monday.

The **Resource Centre for the Arts** presents entertaining comedy and alternative theater at the newly renovated LSPU Hall (3 Victoria St. at Duckworth St.; ✆ **709/753-4531;** www.rca.nf.ca). The building itself has been designated a registered heritage structure, and you'll find an art gallery downstairs.

If you like classical music, see if the **Newfoundland Symphony Orchestra** is playing while you're in town. Call ✆ **709/722-4441** or visit **www.nso-music.com** for an online schedule of performances and corresponding ticket prices. The season runs mid-September through early April, with most performances at either the Arts & Culture Centre on Prince Philip Drive or Cook Recital Hall on the university campus.

THE AVALON PENINSULA

If your visit to Newfoundland allows for a mere week or so, you really have time to see only one region of the province—St. John's and the surrounding Avalon Peninsula. Adventure abounds on the Avalon Peninsula. Wildlife is a major attraction throughout Newfoundland and Labrador, but nowhere is it as accessible and as concentrated as it is here. **Witless Bay,** immediately south of St. John's, is the summer playground of more than 5,000 humpback and minke whales, as well tens of thousands of entertaining puffins. Farther south, and seemingly perched at the edge of the world, is **Cape St. Mary's Ecological Reserve,** where an offshore sea stack provides a summer home for 60,000 seabirds. Meanwhile, back on the mainland, herds of caribou migrate through the interior.

Most of the population lives in historic coastal communities, with **Ferryland,** first settled in 1621, the oldest of them all. It's an easy day trip from St. John's south to Witless Bay and Ferryland, but there are many reasons to travel farther, none more inviting than the wild coastal scenery that changes at every turn.

Essentials

GETTING THERE Most of the Peninsula can most easily be reached by driving south from St. John's along the **Irish Loop**. Take Route 2 (Pitts Memorial Dr.) out of town, and then head south via Route 3, which will lead you to Route 10, forming the first section of the Irish Loop.

VISITOR INFORMATION The **Visitor Information Centre** at St. John's Airport has information on the Avalon Peninsula. It's open from 10am to midnight, 7 days a week. For pre-trip planning, you can contact **Destination St. John's** (✆ **877/739-8899** or 709/739-8899; www.destinationstjohns.com). The websites **www.southernavalontourism.ca** and **www.northernavalon.com** are also useful.

Witless Bay Ecological Reserve ★★★

Extending from **Bay Bulls** in the north to **Bauline East** in the south, Witless Bay Ecological Reserve was established to protect North America's largest puffin colony, which is at its peak April through mid-August. In addition to 520,000 of the province's official bird, the reserve provides a summer home for over two million other seabirds, as well as humpback and minke whales. If you're visiting in spring, icebergs are a spectacular bonus. The actual reserve is offshore, protecting coastal water and four uninhabited islands. Access to the reserve is by tour boat from the village of Bay Bulls, although island landings are not permitted.

Gatherall's Puffin & Whale Watch (✆ **800/419-4253** or 709/334-2887; www.gatheralls.com) operates a high-speed catamaran that departs one to seven times daily from Bay Bulls. Cost is C$56 adults, C$49 seniors, C$19 children 9 to 17, and C$8 children 8 and under. Also departing from the Bay Bulls waterfront, **O'Brien's** (✆ **877/639-4253** or 709/753-4850; www.obriensboattours.com) is justifiably popular. It's like getting two events for the price of one: a world-class marine adventure and a heck of a party, too. During the 2-hour tour, you'll hear—and sing along to—lively Irish Newfoundland folk music; drink screech; have lots of fun; and get to see whales, puffins, and icebergs. Prices are similar to Gatherall's. O'Brien's also offers a zippy 2-hour Zodiac trip that will get you close to the Spout, sea caves, sea stacks, and more. These trips are C$85 per person. This trip is not recommended for really young kids. Transfers from downtown St. John's hotels are C$25 per person.

For general information on the reserve, visit **www.env.gov.nl.ca/parks/wer/r_wbe.**

WHERE TO STAY

Bears Cove Inn ★★ Guests at this oceanfront lodging have a choice of comfortable rooms in a modern home. Some rooms face the garden, others offer a sweeping ocean panorama; or choose an apartment with a small but well-stocked kitchen. Unlike many bed-and-breakfasts in Newfoundland, Bears Cove has a delightful contemporary ambience, which extends from the en suite bathrooms to polished hardwood floors. Rates include a gourmet breakfast.

15 Bears Cove Rd., Witless Bay. ✆ **866/634-1171** or 709/334-3909. www.bearscoveinn.com. 7 units. C$129–C$179 double. MC, V. *In room:* TV/DVD player, Wi-Fi.

Ferryland

With almost 400 years of European settlement to its credit, Ferryland, 75km (47 miles) south of St. John's, is one of the oldest communities in North America.

Colony of Avalon ★★ The reason you'll want to visit Ferryland is for the opportunity to immerse yourself in the history of this living archaeological dig. Located in the heart of the village, the site is composed of two parts—the modern Interpretation Centre and the actual dig site. Start at the interpretation center. Watch the short documentary and then view artifacts from the first successful planned colony in Newfoundland. Visitors are welcome to view the second-floor Conservation Laboratory, where the cataloging and reconstruction of artifacts takes place (weekdays 8am–4:30pm). You're then ready to take a 1½-hour guided tour (or a more leisurely self-guided tour) of the village settled in 1621 by Sir George Calvert (who later became Lord Baltimore). On the guided tour, you'll learn about the world's first flushable toilet (we have clogs to thank for artifacts found in the "pipe") and walk on the oldest cobblestone street in British North America.

Rte. 10, Ferryland. ✆ **877/326-5669** or 709/432-3200. www.colonyofavalon.ca. Admission C$7.50 adults, C$5.50 seniors and students; C$15 families. Mid-May to June and Sept to early Oct daily 8:30am–4:30pm, July and Aug daily 8:30am–7pm.

WHERE TO STAY & DINE

Hagan's Hospitality Home B&B The house isn't an architectural masterpiece, nor will the decorating scheme win any awards, but everything beyond that is extraordinary. Both in portion and flavor, the generous cooked breakfast epitomizes homemade perfection. But even that pales in comparison to the warmth and friendliness of your host, the delightful Rita Hagan. Her perpetual smile and musical brogue more than make up for any splendor lacking from her listed amenities. With a mug of tea in your hand and one of her timeless stories in your ear, you'll feel as privileged as royalty.

Rte. 10, 8km (5 miles) southwest of Ferryland in Aquaforte. ✆ **709/363-2688.** 2 units. C$60 double; 10% discount for seniors. Rate includes lunch and full breakfast. No credit cards. Free parking. **Amenities:** Room service; TV lounge. *In room:* No phone.

Lighthouse Picnics ★★★ LIGHT FARE From the archaeological dig, walk up onto the headland, and Ferryland Lighthouse will soon come into view. Built in 1870, this classic red-and-white lighthouse was abandoned until 2004, when enterprising locals spruced up the exterior and began using it as a store, providing picnic baskets for visitors. You can order goodies as simple as muffins baked in-house, or as extravagant as gourmet sandwiches, imported cheeses, crab cakes, and salad. The strawberry shortcake is an absolute must. Picnic baskets come with thoughtful extras, such as blankets and books, which encourage visitors to linger longer on the surrounding grassy headland.

Ferryland Lighthouse, Ferryland. ✆ **709/363-7456.** www.lighthousepicnics.ca. Picnic baskets C$12–C$35. MC, V. Mid-June to late Sept Tues–Sun 11:30am–5pm.

Cape Shore

Circling the extreme southwest corner of the Avalon Peninsula, the Cape Shore provides access to **Cape St. Mary's Ecological Reserve,** the province's best birdwatching spot. In fact, the symbol for the Cape Shore Route is one of our fine feathered friends because this region is a birder's paradise.

Cape St. Mary's Ecological Reserve ★★★ Even if you're not a keen birder, visiting Cape St. Mary's is a must. The reserve protects the breeding ground of 24,000 northern gannets, 20,000 common murres, 2,000 thick-billed murres, 20,000 black-legged kittiwakes, and more than 200 northern razorbills. The birds are only part of the attraction—the cliff-top setting is also spectacular. Upon arriving at the cape, just east of St. Bride's and a 3-hour drive from St. John's, your first stop should be the Interpretive Centre, where you can familiarize yourself with the types of birds you'll be seeing.

From the center, it's a 1km (½-mile) walk across subarctic tundra to the lookout point for **Bird Rock.** It will take you 15 minutes if you're a fast walker, 30 minutes if you take the time to appreciate the sights along the way. This 100m-high (328-ft.) sandstone sea stack is separated from the mainland by only a few meters. You'll be standing high atop a rock roughly equivalent in height to Bird Rock itself, where thousands of northern gannets can be seen courting, nesting, and feeding.

Tip: Be sure to bring a weatherproof jacket and nonslip footwear for the walk. And remember that this is a site to protect wildlife—not humans—so be sure to hang on to children when you are hiking near the edge of the cliff. You'll also want to be extra cautious when the fog rolls in, which happens around 200 days each year (May and June are particularly foggy).

15km/9¼ miles east, then south off Rte. 100 from St. Bride's. ✆ **709/277-1666.** www.env.gov.nl.ca/parks/wer/r_csme. Free admission; 1½-hour guided tour to Bird Rock C$7. Trail to Bird Rock open year-round; Interpretive Centre mid-May to early Oct daily 9am–5pm.

WHERE TO STAY

Rosedale Manor B&B ★★ One of the finest bed-and-breakfasts to be found on the Avalon Peninsula, Rosedale Manor is a restored heritage home with well-manicured gardens overlooking the ocean. Located a short drive from Argentia, it's also a handy overnight stop for arriving or departing ferry passengers. The stylish rooms are outfitted with handcrafted Newfoundland-made furniture, and some (such as the Osprey Room) enjoy water views. Instead of in-room televisions, guests congregate in the living room. But it is the breakfast that is most memorable. Unusual for the province, the emphasis is on ingredients such as free-range eggs and bread made daily with organic whole grains. Even the jams and preserves are made with berries grown in the surrounding garden.

40 Orcan Dr., Placentia. ✆ **877/999-3613** or 709/227-3613. www.rosedalemanor.ca. 5 units. C$79–C$99 double. MC, V. Free parking. *In room:* Wi-Fi.

East Coast Trail

For the avid hiker, the East Coast Trail will be the Avalon Peninsula's most magnetic attraction. The trail takes you 220km (137 miles) along North America's easternmost coastline. You can see whales and seabirds close to shore, and parts of the trail are easy enough for the beginner. Some sections are difficult, requiring overnight excursions. It's divided into sections, so you can do as much or as little as you like, tailoring your hike(s) to your time frame and fitness level. The trail is open year-round. There is no fee for walking the East Coast Trail, nor do you need to book a time for your journey.

Serious hikers use the services operators affiliated with **Trail Connections** (✆ **709/335-8315;** www.trailconnections.ca) to arrange accommodations and transportation, allowing overnight excursions. But most visitors are content to walk a short length of trail as a day hike. Your best resource is the **East Coast Trail Association** (✆ **709/738-4453;** www.eastcoasttrail.com). They can advise you about renting hiking equipment from any number of outfitters in the St. John's area if you don't want to bring (or don't have) your own. They also sell two volumes of comprehensive guidebooks covering the main trail. Alternatively, for C$33 you can purchase a set of 19 waterproof topographic maps—also available through the ECTA website. The association also organizes guided day hikes; check the website for a schedule and other helpful information such as carpool arrangements from St. John's. If you plan to hike the East Coast Trail and want to do a little kayaking at the same time, get in touch with **Stan Cook Sea Kayak Adventures** (✆ **888/747-6353** or 709/579-6353; www.wildnfld.ca), which is based out of a converted general store at Cape Broyle. Guided kayaking is C$59 for 2½ hours, C$89 for 4 hours, and C$129 for a full day of kayaking and hiking. The company also offers the opportunity to paddle with whales for C$129 for 4 hours.

LABRADOR

Labrador is Canada's last undiscovered frontier and North America's most pristine wilderness. In a word association game, it would likely be coupled with "cold," "vast," and "remote." The slightly more enlightened might add "fjords," "bakeapples," and "permafrost." All of which are true, but just barely hint at the complexity that is Labrador.

Its nickname is **The Big Land**—a moniker it well deserves. Physically, it dwarfs the island of Newfoundland by a ratio of two to one. It covers a distance of more than 1,080km (671 miles) from north to south and 839km (521 miles) from east to west, for a total landmass of 294,330 sq. km (113,641 sq. miles). Looking at it another way, it's almost identical in size to the U.S. state of Arizona but has a population of just 27,000 people (compared to Arizona's 6.1 million).

Within that epic terrain are natural and man-made wonders of immense proportion: the **highest mountain range** east of the Rockies, one of the **world's longest airport runways,** 7,800km (4,847 miles) of coastline, world-class nickel and iron-ore deposits, the **largest caribou herd** in the world, and the world's largest underground hydroelectric project at **Churchill Falls.**

It is simultaneously simple and mysterious, a place of ancient civilizations but few people, a land of glacial conditions and temperate breezes. Here, engineers have achieved numerous record-setting feats, but paved highways are few and far between.

The Labrador Straits

In the southeastern corner of Labrador, an 80km (50-mile) paved highway extends northeast along the Strait of Belle Isle from Blanc Sablon, where ferries from St. Barbe, Newfoundland, dock. At Red Bay, the road turns to gravel and extends 238km (148 miles) north to Cartwright Junction. From this point, it's 87km (54 miles) northeast to the coastal community of Cartwright and 250km (155 miles) west to Happy Valley–Goose Bay along a remote stretch of the Trans-Labrador Highway. The route north to Cartwright is known as the Labrador Coastal Drive. Most attractions are concentrated along the paved road, where approximately 2,200 people inhabit nine small coastal communities. Each of the communities is so close to the next one, you really won't know when you're leaving one and entering another until you see a sign with a different town's name! This is the section of Labrador you'll be most likely to visit if you're planning a Newfoundland *and* Labrador vacation.

Tip: Public transportation is nonexistent along the Labrador Straits. Those planning to arrive by ferry or air without a vehicle should make arrangements well in advance with **Eagle River Rent-a-Car** (✆ **709/931-2352**) in L'Anse au Clair.

Information about the Labrador Straits can be obtained in L'Anse au Clair at the **Gateway to Labrador Visitor Centre** (✆ **709/931-2013**), located in a restored building formerly occupied by St. Andrew's Anglican Church. It's right on Route 510 and open mid-June through early October, daily 9:30am to 5:30pm. A helpful online resource for this region is the website for **Labrador Coastal Drive** (**www.labradorcoastaldrive.com**).

EXPLORING THE LABRADOR STRAITS

Drive the "slow road" that connects the villages of the Labrador Straits. Traveling southwest to northeast, here's some of what you'll find along the way.

In L'Anse au Clair, **Moores Handicrafts,** 8 Country Rd., just off Route 510 (✆ **709/931-2186**), sells handmade summer and winter coats, traditional cassocks, moccasins, knitted items, handmade jewelry, and other crafts, as well as homemade jams. They also do traditional embroidery on Labrador cassocks and coats, and if you stop on the way north and choose your design, they'll finish it by the time you return to the ferry—even the same day. Prices are quite reasonable. The shop, run by the Moores family, is open daily in season from 9am to as late as 10pm.

The **Point Amour Lighthouse ★★** (✆ **709/927-5825**), at the western entrance to the Strait of Belle Isle, is the tallest lighthouse in the Atlantic provinces and the second tallest in all of Canada. The walls of this slightly tapered, circular tower (built in 1858) are 2m (6½-ft.) thick at the base; the dioptric lens up top was imported from Europe for the princely sum of C$10,000—a lot at the time. This light kept watch for submarines during World War II, and is still in use; in fact, it was maintained by a resident lightkeeper right up until 1995. Remember to climb the 122 steps to reach good views from the top. The lighthouse is open to the public daily from mid-May to September 10:30am to 5:30pm, with an admission fee of C$3 adults, free for children 12 and under. This is about a 3km (2-mile) detour off the main road.

After you pass the fishing settlements of **L'Anse-au-Loup** ("Wolf's Cove") and West St. Modeste, the road follows the scenic Pinware River, where the trees start becoming noticeably taller. Along this stretch of road, you'll also see glacial erratics—big odd boulders deposited by the melting ice cap. **Pinware River Provincial Park ★** (✆ **709/927-5516**), open June through mid-September, is about 42km (26 miles) from L'Anse au Clair and offers a picnic area, hiking trails, and 15 simple campsites with neither flush toilets nor showers for C$10 per night. There's a C$5 fee per car to enter the park. The 81km-long (50-mile) Pinware River, which passes through the park, is known for its trout and salmon fishing; it is mandatory for anglers from outside the province to be accompanied by a local fishing guide. For complete and current information on fishing regulations, licenses, fees, and outfitter information, contact the **Newfoundland & Labrador Department of Conservation** (✆ **709/927-5580;** www.env.gov.nl.ca).

The highway ends in **Red Bay.** Here, the interesting **Red Bay National Historic Site ★★** (✆ **709/920-2142**) showcases artifacts from the late 1500s, when Basque whalers came here in numbers to hunt right and bowhead whales. Beginning in 1977, excavations began turning up whaling implements, pottery, glassware, and even partially preserved seamen's clothing. If you're really gung-ho about this sort of thing, you can arrange tours of sites on **Saddle Island ★**, the home of Basque whaling stations in the 16th century. Or you can simply scope out the island from afar: the observation deck on the third floor of the visitor center has a good view of it. Admission to the historic site complex is C$8 adults, C$7 seniors, C$4 ages 6 to 16, C$20 family. The site is open daily from 9am to 6pm early June through end of September, closed the rest of the year.

WHERE TO STAY & DINE

Basinview Bed & Breakfast The best place to stay in Red Bay, this modern home is the residence of Wade and Blanche Earle. It's an inviting waterfront property beside Route 510 on the south side of town. The home has a large sitting room with a great view where guests can enjoy satellite TV and have access to the telephone. Blanche will even cook you a real Labrador-style dinner, such as caribou stew or pan-fried cod, for an additional C$18. The three basement rooms share a bathroom but have the most privacy. The upstairs bedroom has a private bathroom and water views, but is directly off the living room.

145 Main Hwy. (Rte. 510), Red Bay. ✆ **866/920-2001** or 709/920-2002. 4 units. C$58–C$75 double. MC. Rates include continental breakfast (C$7 extra for a cooked breakfast). *In room:* No phone.

Grenfell Louie A. Hall Bed & Breakfast ☺ A Registered Heritage Structure 1 block from the harbor, this inn is in a former nursing station started by Dr. Grenfell and named after the Rochester, New York, woman who, in 1946, donated the funds to build it. Unlike some heritage sites (those with atmospheres as welcoming as a mausoleum), this is an enchantingly nostalgic building filled with curious antiques, old-fashioned radiators, and a resident dog. It's an ideal place for families because the upstairs attic has been converted into a guest unit with two double beds and lots of playroom for the kids. All guest rooms are comfortable (they're each named for a different nurse who once worked here) but share bathrooms. ***Hint:*** Be careful getting in and out of bed: The charmingly sloped bedroom ceilings can give you a nasty bump if you're not careful. Guests can order full breakfasts and other meals in the dining room for an additional charge.

3 Willow Lane, Forteau. ✆ **709/931-2916.** www.grenfellbandb.ca. 5 units. C$65 double. Rates include continental breakfast. MC, V. Free parking. Closed Nov–Apr. *In room:* No phone.

Lighthouse Cove Bed & Breakfast ★ The ferry was delayed and the other guests had finished dinner by the time I knocked on the door. But welcoming owners Rita and Cecil Davis were more than happy to make sure I was well fed before turning in for the night at Lighthouse Cove—one of only four homes set around a picturesque cove. Cecil is a retired fisherman with simultaneously funny and poignant stories of how he made his living from the sea. His ancestors were granted this cove from the king of England back in 1922, so in effect, L'Anse Amour is a private cove—and very special to the Davis family that today inhabits all four homes.

Rita is the shining light of the home. From the moment you enter the door, you'll feel like your visit is the highlight of her day. With a little encouragement, she'll tell you about life in L'Anse Amour—including the story of how, in 1922, the family was able to retrieve six mahogany dining-room chairs and a piano from the HMS *Raleigh*—hung up on a sandbar just offshore—before it broke up and sank. A continental breakfast is included with your room rate. With advance notice, dinner is available at an additional charge (keep your fingers crossed that Rita makes you her delicious chocolate brownies). The three guest rooms are fairly compact, but completely spotless and very tidy. There are no private bathrooms.

L'Anse-Amour Rd., L'Anse-Amour. ✆ **709/927-5690.** http://lighthousecovebb.labradorstraits.net. 3 units. C$45 double. Rates include continental breakfast. MC, V. 1km (½ mile) from Point Amour Lighthouse; 3km (1¾ miles) off Rte. 510 on a gravel road. *In room:* No phone.

Northern Light Inn ★ With 49 standard hotel rooms, five suites, five housekeeping cottages, and 10 fully serviced RV sites, the Northern Light Inn is the largest accommodations option along the Labrador Straits. This clean, cozy, and cheerful place has facilities not found at local bed-and-breakfasts: wake-up service, in-room phone, coffee shop, licensed lounge, craft shop, and ATM. A nearby indoor swimming pool makes it a perfect location for water recreation. It has no elevator, however, so be prepared to struggle up stairs with your suitcase to the upper-floor rooms.

Even if you don't stay overnight at the Northern Light Inn, you may find yourself dining at the hotel's Basque Dining Room, which is open daily 7am to 10pm. Standard Canadian favorites are served, along with local specialties such as pan-fried cod tongues. No main meal is over C$24.

58 Main St., L'Anse au Clair. ✆ **800/563-3188** or 709/931-2332. www.northernlightinn.com. 59 units, 10 campsites. C$89–C$159 double; C$20 campsites. Weekly rates and senior discounts available. AE, MC, V. Free parking. **Amenities:** Restaurant; cafe; lounge; room service. *In room:* A/C, TV.

MONTRÉAL

by Leslie Brokaw

7

Montréal and Québec City are the twin cities of the province of Québec. Just 3 hours apart by car, they have a stronger European flavor than Canada's other municipalities. Most residents' first language is French, and a strong affiliation with France continues to be a central facet of the region's personality.

The defining dialectics of Canadian life are culture and language, and they're thorny issues that have long threatened to tear the country apart. Many Québécois have long believed that making Québec province a separate, independent state is the only way to maintain their rich French culture in the face of the Anglophone (English-speaking) ocean that surrounds them. Québec's role within the Canadian federation has been the most debated and volatile topic of conversation in Canadian politics.

There are reasons for these beliefs, of course—about 250 years' worth. Québec was an outpost of "New France," but after France lost power to the British in the 18th century a linguistic exclusionism developed, with wealthy Scottish and English bankers and merchants denying French-Canadians access to upper levels of business and government. This bias continued into the 20th century.

Many in Québec have stayed committed to the French language and culture. It is that tenacious French connection that gives the province its special cultural and linguistic character.

Two cultural phenomena have become signifiers of the province in recent years. The first is an institutional and cultural acceptance of homosexuality. By changing the definition of "spouse" in 39 laws and regulations in 1999, Québec's government eliminated all legal distinctions between same-sex and heterosexual couples. It was Canada's first province to recognize the legal status of same-sex civil unions (gay marriage became legal in all of Canada's provinces and territories in 2005). Montréal in particular has transformed into one of North America's most welcoming cities for gay people.

The second phenomenon is an influx of even more immigrants into the province's melting pot. "Québec is at a turning point," declared a 2008 report about the province's accommodation of minority religious practices. "The identity inherited from the French-Canadian past is perfectly legitimate and it must survive," the report said, "but it can no longer occupy alone the Québec identity space." Together with 70,000 aboriginal people from 11 First Nation tribes who live in the province, immigrants help make the region as vibrant and alive as any on the continent.

The blending of cultures and languages occurs in particularly intense fashion in Montréal, the province's largest city. While the first language of the majority of residents is French (making them Francophones) and most of the remaining population speaks English primarily (Anglophones), a growing number of residents have another primary tongue. Residents blend French and English phrases into their conversation, for a unique regional patois.

Much of what makes Montréal special is either very old or very new. The city's gleaming skyscrapers come in unexpected shapes and noncorporate colors. A highly practical underground city, a labyrinth of shops, restaurants, and offices where an entire winter can be avoided in coatless comfort, dates from the 1960s. The renaissance of much of the oldest part of the city, Vieux-Montréal, blossomed in the 1990s. Meanwhile, the city's creative inhabitants provide zest to the ever-changing Plateau Mont-Royal and Mile End, large neighborhoods of artists' lofts, boutiques, and cafes, and miles of restaurants—many of which are unabashedly clever and stylish.

Travelers will likely find Montréal an urban near-paradise. The subway system, called the Métro, is modern and swift, and streets are safe.

Montréal is terrific for walking and has miles of bike paths. And not many cities have a mountain at their core. Montréal is named for Mont-Royal—the "Royal Mountain"—and the park that surrounds it is a soothing urban pleasure. Stroll through it or, for a more romantic trip, take a horse-drawn calèche to the top for a sunset view of the city and St. Lawrence River.

Note: Like the Québecois themselves, chapters 7 and 8 go back and forth between using the French names and the English names for areas and attractions. Most often, we use French. Québec's state-mandated language is French, and most signs, brochures, and maps in the region appear in French. However, we use the English name or translation, as well, if that makes the meaning clearer. *Bon voyage!*

ESSENTIALS

Getting There

BY PLANE Most of the world's major airlines fly into the **Aéroport International Pierre-Elliott-Trudeau de Montréal** (airport code YUL; ✆ **800/465-1213** or 514/394-7377; www.admtl.com), more commonly known as Montréal-Trudeau Airport. It used to be called Montréal-Dorval, which you'll find on older maps. The airport is 23km (14 miles) from downtown.

Montréal-Trudeau is served by **Express Bus 747,** which debuted in March 2010. It operates 24 hours a day, 7 days a week, and runs between the airport and the Berri-UQAM Métro station (the city's main bus terminal). It has about half a dozen designated stops along boulevard René-Lévesque. A trip takes about 35 minutes, and buses leave every 20 to 30 minutes. One-way tickets are sold for C$7 at the currency exchange (ICE) location on the airport's international arrivals level, and downtown at the Berri-UQAM station and the Infotourist Centre, 1255 rue Peel (✆ **877/266-5687** or 514/873-2015; Métro: Peel). Details are at **www.stm.info/info/747.htm.** Hotels that offer shuttles are listed on the airport's website under "access and parking."

A taxi trip to downtown Montréal costs a flat fare of C$38, plus tip. Call ✆ **514/394-7377** for more information.

Greater Montréal

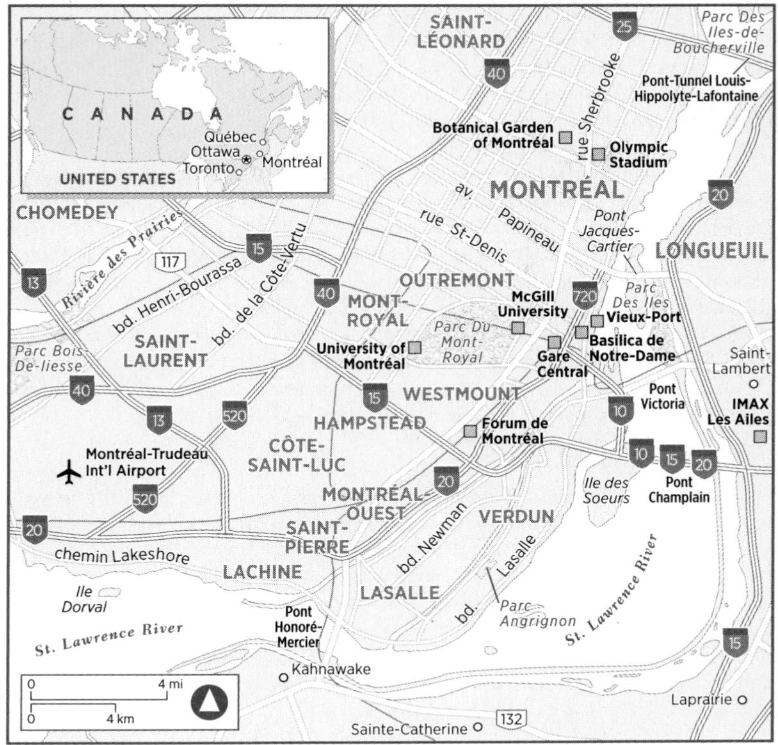

BY TRAIN Montréal is a major terminus on Canada's **VIA Rail** network (✆ **888/842-7245** or 514/989-2626; www.viarail.ca). Its station, **Gare Centrale,** at 895 rue de la Gauchetière ouest (✆ **514/989-2626**), is centrally located downtown. The station is connected to the Métro subway system at **Bonaventure Station.** VIA Rail trains are comfortable—all major routes have Wi-Fi, and some trains are equipped with dining cars and sleeping cars. (Gare Windsor, which you might see on some maps, is the city's former train station. It's a castle-like building now used for offices.)

BY BUS Montréal's central bus station, called **Station Centrale d'Autobus** (✆ **514/842-2281**), is at 505 bd. de Maisonneuve est. It has a restaurant and an information booth. Beneath the terminal is **Berri-UQAM Station,** the junction of several Métro lines. (UQAM—pronounced "*Oo*-kahm"—stands for Université de Québec à Montréal.) **Taxis** usually line up outside the terminal building,

BY CAR All international drivers must carry a **valid driver's license** from their country of residence. A U.S. license is sufficient as long as you are a visitor and actually are a U.S. resident. A U.K. license is sufficient, as well. If the driver's license is in a language other than French or English, an additional **International Driver's Permit** is required.

Driving north to Montréal from the U.S., the entire journey is on expressways. From New York City, all but about the last 64km (40 miles) of the 603km (375-mile) trip are within New York state on Interstate 87. I-87 links up with Canada's Autoroute 15 at the border, which goes straight to Montréal.

Throughout Canada, highway distances and speed limits are given in kilometers (km). The speed limit on the autoroutes is 100kmph (62 mph). There's a stiff penalty for neglecting to wear your seatbelt, and all passengers must be buckled up.

Note on radar detectors: Radar detectors are prohibited in the province of Québec. They can be confiscated, even if they're not being used.

It is illegal to turn right on a red light on the island of Montréal. It is permitted in the rest of Québec and Canada.

Cellphone use is restricted to hands-free only while driving.

In 2008, Québec became the first province to mandate that residents have **radial snow tires** on their cars in winter. Visitors and their cars are exempt, but the law does give an indication of how seriously rough the winter driving can be. Consider using snow tires when traveling in the region from December through March.

Visitor Information

The main tourist center for visitors in downtown Montréal is the large **Infotouriste Centre,** at 1255 rue Peel (© **877/266-5687** or 514/873-2015; Métro: Peel). It's open daily, and the bilingual staff can provide suggestions for accommodations, dining, car rentals, and attractions. Paper copies of the Montréal Official Tourist Guide are available here. A PDF of the guide is available at **www.octgm.com/guide.**

In Vieux-Montréal, there's a teeny **Tourist Welcome Office** at 174 rue Notre-Dame est, at the corner of Place Jacques-Cartier (Métro: Champ-de-Mars). It's open April to October daily and November to March Wednesday through Sunday 10am to 6pm, and it has brochures, maps, and a helpful staff.

Montréal: Clarifying North and South—And East and West

For the duration of your visit to Montréal, you'll need to accept local directional conventions, strange as they may seem. The city borders the St. Lawrence River, and as far as locals are concerned, that's south, with the U.S. not far off on the other side. Never mind that the river, in fact, runs almost north and south at this section. (For this reason, Montréal is the only city in the world where the sun rises in the "south".) Don't fight it: Face the river. That's south. Turn around. That's north.

When examining a map of the city, note that horizontal streets, such as rue Ste-Catherine and boulevard René-Lévesque, are said to run either "east" or "west." The dividing line is boulevard St-Laurent, which runs "north" and "south." For east-west streets, the numbers start at St-Laurent and then go in *both directions*. They're labeled either *est*, for east, or *ouest*, for west. That means, for instance, that the restaurants Chez l'Epicier, at 311 rue St-Paul est, and Marché de la Villette, at 324 rue St-Paul ouest, are 1km (about a half mile, or 13 short blocks) from each other—not directly across the street.

The city of Montréal maintains a terrific website at **www.tourisme-montreal.org**, and the Québec province an equally good one at **www.bonjourquebec.com.**

City Layout

MAIN ARTERIES & STREETS In **downtown Montréal**, the principal east-west streets include boulevard René-Lévesque, rue Ste-Catherine (*rue* is the French word for "street"), boulevard de Maisonneuve, and rue Sherbrooke. The north-south arteries include rue Crescent, rue McGill, rue St-Denis, and boulevard St-Laurent, which serves as the line of demarcation between east and west Montréal. Most of the downtown areas featured in this book lie west of boulevard St-Laurent.

In **Vieux-Montréal**, the main thoroughfares are rue St-Jacques, rue Notre-Dame, and rue St-Paul. Rue de la Commune is the waterfront road that hugs the promenade bordering the St. Lawrence River.

In **Plateau Mont-Royal**, northeast of the downtown area, major streets are avenue du Mont-Royal and avenue Laurier.

In addition to the maps in this book, neighborhood street plans are available online at www.tourisme-montreal.org and from the information centers listed above.

FINDING AN ADDRESS As explained in the sidebar "Montréal: Clarifying North and South—and East and West," above, boulevard St-Laurent is the dividing point between the east and west (*est* and *ouest*) sides of Montréal. There's no equivalent division for north and south (*nord* and *sud*)—the numbers start at the river and climb from there, just as the topography does. Make sure you know if an address is est or ouest, and confirm the cross street.

Montréal used to be split geographically along cultural lines. Those who spoke English lived predominantly west of boulevard St-Laurent, while French speakers were concentrated to the east. Things still do sound more French as you walk east, as street names and Métro stations change from Peel and Atwater to Papineau and Beaudry.

The Neighborhoods in Brief

Centre Ville/Downtown This area contains most of the city's large luxury and first-class hotels, principal museums, corporate headquarters, main transportation hubs, and department stores.

The district is loosely bounded by rue Sherbrooke to the north, boulevard René-Lévesque to the south, boulevard St-Laurent to the east, and rue Drummond to the west.

Within this neighborhood is the area often called "the Golden Square Mile," an Anglophone (English-speaking) district once characterized by dozens of mansions erected by the wealthy Scottish and English merchants and industrialists who dominated the city's political and social life well into the 20th century. Many of those stately homes were torn down to make way for skyscrapers, but some remain.

At downtown's northern edge is the urban campus of prestigious McGill University. Further west, rue Crescent and the nearby streets is one of the city's major dining and nightlife districts, with dozens of restaurants, bars, and clubs of all styles.

The party atmosphere builds to crescendos as weekends approach, especially in warm weather when the area's 20- and 30-something denizens take over sidewalk cafes and balcony terraces.

Vieux-Montréal The city was born here in 1642. Today, especially in summer, many people converge around Place Jacques-Cartier, where cafe tables line narrow terraces. This is where street performers, strolling locals, and tourists congregate.

The neighborhood is larger than it might seem at first. It's bounded on the north by rue St-Antoine, once the "Wall Street" of Montréal and still home to some banks. Its southern boundary is the Vieux-Port (Old Port), now dominated by a well-used waterfront promenade that provides welcome breathing room for cyclists, in-line skaters, and picnickers. To the east, Vieux-Montréal is bordered by rue Berri, and to the west, by rue McGill.

Several small but intriguing museums are housed in historic buildings here, and the district's architectural heritage has been substantially preserved. Restored 18th- and 19th-century structures have been adapted for use as shops, boutique hotels, galleries, bars, offices, and apartments. In the summer, sections of rue St-Paul and rue Notre-Dame turn into pedestrian-only lanes. The neighborhood's official website is **www.vieux.montreal.qc.ca.** The site usually has a live video feed from a webcam on Place Jacques-Cartier.

Plateau Mont-Royal "The Plateau" is where many Montréalers feel most at home—it's where locals come to dine, shop, and play.

Bounded roughly by rue Sherbrooke to the south, boulevard St-Joseph to the north, avenue Papineau to the east, and rue St-Urbain to the west, the Plateau has a vibrant ethnic atmosphere.

Rue St-Denis runs the length of the district from south to north and is the heart of the neighborhood, as central to French-speaking Montréal as boulevard St-Germain is to Paris. It is thick with cafes, bistros, offbeat shops, and lively nightspots. Its southern end is near the concrete campus of the Université du Québec à Montréal (UQAM) in the Latin Quarter (in French, *Quartier Latin*) neighborhood. Farther north, above rue Sherbrooke, a raffish quality persists along the rows of three- and four-story Victorian houses, but the average age of residents and visitors nudges past 30. Prices are higher, and some of the city's better restaurants are here.

Boulevard St-Laurent, running parallel to rue St-Denis, is known as "the Main." Without its gumbo of languages and cultures, St-Laurent would be something of an urban eyesore. It's not pretty in the conventional sense. But its ground-floor windows are filled with glistening golden chickens, collages of shoes and pastries and aluminum cookware, curtains of sausages, and the daringly far-fetched garments of designers on the forward edge of Montréal's active fashion industry.

Many warehouses and former tenements in the Plateau have been converted to house this panoply of shops, bars, and high- and low-cost eateries.

The Village Also known as the Gay Village, Montréal's gay and lesbian enclave is one of North America's largest. This compact but vibrant district is filled with clothing stores, antiques shops, dance clubs, and cafes.

It runs along rue Ste-Catherine from rue St-Hubert to rue Papineau and onto side streets.

In recent years, the city has made the length of rue Ste-Catherine in the Village pedestrian-only for the entire summer. Bars and restaurants build ad-hoc terraces into the street, and a summer-resort atmosphere pervades.

A rainbow, the symbol of the gay community, marks the Beaudry Métro station, which is on rue Ste-Catherine in the heart of the neighborhood.

The Underground City During Montréal's long winters, life slows on the streets of downtown as people escape into *la ville souterraine,* a parallel subterranean universe. Here, in a controlled climate that recalls an eternal spring, there are more than 1,000 retailers and eateries in or connected to the network.

The city has begun rebranding it as the "underground pedestrian network," but most people still call it the underground city. It was built in fits and starts, and with no master plan, so it's a mazes of corridors, tunnels, and plazas. It covers a vast area without the convenience of a logical street grid, and it can be confusing. There are plenty of signs, but it's wise to make careful note of landmarks at key corners along your route if you want to return to where you started. Expect to get lost, but consider it part of the fun of exploring.

Mile End Adjoining Plateau Mont-Royal at its northwest corner, this blossoming neighborhood is contained by boulevard St-Joseph on the south, rue Bernard in the north, rue St-Laurent on the east, and avenue Du Parc on the west. It's outside of the usual tourist orbit but has many worthwhile restaurants and a growing number of designer clothing boutiques and shops specializing in household goods.

Mile End has pockets of many ethnic mini-neighborhoods, including Italian, Hassidic, Portuguese, and Greek. The area some still call Greektown, for instance, runs along avenue du Parc and is thick with restaurants and taverns.

Parc Jean-Drapeau: Ile Ste-Hélène & Ile Notre-Dame Ile Ste-Hélène is home to an amusement park, La Ronde, and the Casino de Montréal (p. 264). Ile Notre-Dame, created from the earth and rock dredged from the bottom of the St. Lawrence during the excavations for the Métro and the Décarie Expressway, is connected by two bridges to Ile Ste-Hélène. The islands make up Parc Jean-Drapeau, which is almost entirely car-free and accessible by Métro. The park has its own website: www.parcjeandrapeau.com.

Quartier International When Route 720 was constructed in the early 1970s, it left behind a desolate swath of derelict buildings, parking lots, and empty spaces on either side of it, smack-dab between downtown and Vieux-Montréal.

This former no-man's land has been spruced up with new parks and office buildings (notably agencies or businesses with an international focus, hence the name "International Quarter").

Also here is the recently expanded **Palais des Congrès (Convention Center).** The convention center is a design triumph, with transparent glass exterior walls that are a crazy quilt of pink, yellow, blue, green, red, and purple rectangles. You can step into the inside hallway for the full effect—when the sun streams in, it's like being inside a huge children's kaleidoscope. The walls are the vision of Montréal architect Mario Saia.

GETTING AROUND

Montréal is a terrific walking city. One thing to keep in mind when strolling is to cross only at street corners and only when you have a green light or a walk sign. City police began cracking down on jaywalkers in 2007 in an attempt to cut down on the number of accidents involving pedestrians, and newspapers continue to carry stories of fines being issued to people who cross in the middle of the street.

By Metro or Bus

For speed and economy, nothing beats Montréal's **Métro system.** The stations are marked on the street by blue-and-white signs that show a circle enclosing a down-pointing arrow. The Métro is relatively clean, and quiet trains whisk passengers through a decent network. It runs from about 5:30am to 1am 6 days a week, and until 1:30am on Saturday night/Sunday morning. Information is available online at **www.stm.info** or by phone at ✆ **514/786-4636.**

Fare prices are by the ride, not by distance. Single rides cost C$2.75 with a paper ticket. A set of six paper tickets costs C$13.25. You can buy single-trip tickets, known as à la carte tickets, or a set of six tickets, from the booth attendant in any station (cash only). Also, there are automatic vending machines that take credit cards. They charge C$2.75 for a single ticket and C$11 for a set of four paper tickets. Single-trip tickets serve as proof of payment, and travelers need to keep the ticket for the duration of the trip—transit police sometimes check at transfer points or as you're exiting the station for proof that you've paid, and if you've thrown out the ticket the fine can run as high as C$215.

One-day and three-day passes are a good deal if you plan to use the Métro more than two times a day. You get unlimited access to the Métro and bus network for 1 day for C$7 or 3 consecutive days for C$14. The front of the card has scratch-off sections like a lottery card—you scratch out the month and day (or 3 consecutive days) on which you're using the card. They're available at select stations; find the list at www.stm.info.

You'll see locals using the plastic OPUS card, on which fares can be loaded from automated machines. The Métro is pushing the use of the new cards, which create less trash and whose purchase can be automated. Using the OPUS card provides reduced fares for seniors, children, and students. But blank OPUS cards must first be purchased for C$3.50 plus C$10 for non-residents before any value is loaded onto them, so unless you're a frequent traveler to the city, the paper tickets and 1- or 3-day passes are your best options.

Bus fares are the same as fares for Métro trains, and Métro tickets are good on buses, too. Exact change is required if you want to pay in cash. Although they run throughout the city and give tourists the advantage of traveling aboveground, buses don't run as frequently or as swiftly as the Métro. Only 1- or 3-day pass holders or those with OPUS cards can get a free transfer between the bus and the subway.

By Taxi

There are plenty of taxis run by many different companies. Cabs come in a variety of colors and styles, so their principal distinguishing feature is the plastic sign on the roof. At night, the sign is illuminated when the cab is available. The initial charge is C$3.30. Each additional kilometer (½ mile) adds C$1.60, and each minute of waiting adds C60¢. A short ride from one point to another downtown usually costs about C$7. Tip about 10% to 15%. Members of hotel and restaurant staffs can call cabs, many of which are dispatched by radio. They line up outside most large hotels or can be hailed on the street.

Montréal taxi drivers range in temperament from unstoppably loquacious to sullen and cranky. Some know their city well; others have sketchy geographical knowledge and poor language skills. It's a good idea to have your destination written down—with the cross street—to show your driver.

By Car

Montréal is an easy city to navigate by car, although traffic during morning and late-afternoon rush hour can be horrendous.

It can be difficult to park for free on downtown Montréal's heavily trafficked streets, but there are plenty of metered spaces. Traditional meters are set well back from the curb so they won't be buried by plowed snow in winter. Computerized Pay 'N Go stations are in use in many neighborhoods, too. Look for the black metal kiosks, columns about 1.8m (6 ft.) tall with a white "P" in a blue circle. Press the "English" button, enter the letter from the space where you are parked, and then pay with cash or a credit card, following the onscreen instructions. Parking costs C$3 per hour, and meters are in effect weekdays until 9pm and weekends until 6pm. Be sure to check for signs noting parking restrictions, usually showing a red circle with a diagonal slash. The words LIVRAISON SEULEMENT mean "delivery only."

Montréal Métro

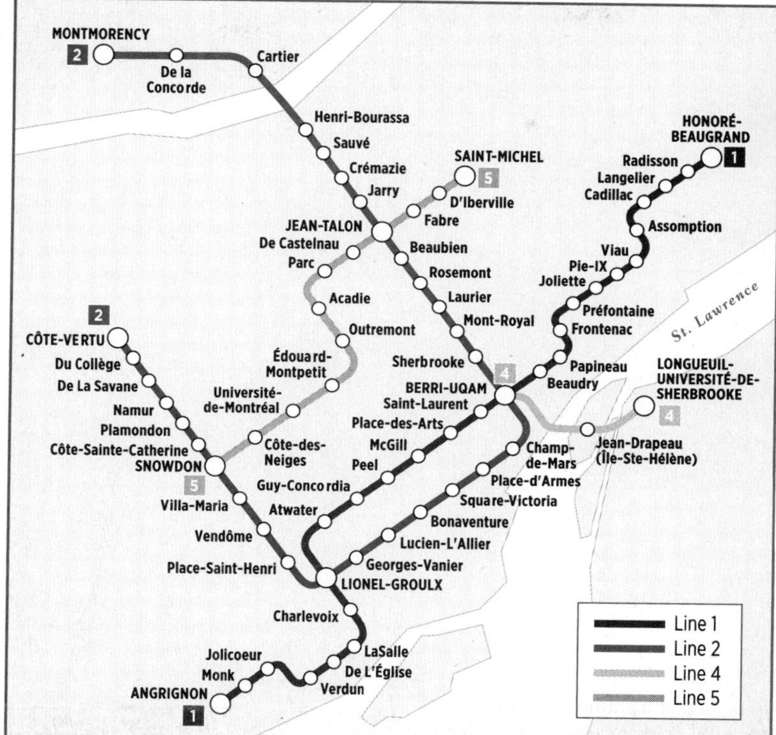

Most downtown shopping complexes have underground parking lots, as do the big downtown hotels. Some hotels offer in and out privileges, letting you take your car in and out of the garage without a fee—useful if you plan to do some sightseeing by car.

Because French is the province's official language, most road signs are only in French, though Montréal's autoroutes and bridges often bear dual-language signs.

One traffic signal function often confuses newcomers: Should you wish to make a turn and you know that the street runs in the correct direction, you may be surprised to initially see a green arrow pointing straight ahead instead of a green light permitting the turn. The arrow gives pedestrians time to cross the intersection. After a few moments, the light will turn from an arrow to a regular green light and you can proceed with your turn.

A blinking green light means that oncoming traffic still has a red light, making it safe to make a left turn.

Turning right on a red light is prohibited on the island of Montréal, except where specifically allowed by an additional green arrow. Off the island, it is legal to turn right after stopping at red lights, except where there's a sign specifically prohibiting that move.

Drivers using cellphones are required to have "hands free" devices. Radar detectors are illegal in Québec. Even if it's off, you can be fined for having one in sight.

Gasoline and diesel fuel are sold by the liter, and are significantly more expensive than in the United States (visitors from other countries are likely to find the prices less of a shock).

By Bike

Montréal has an exceptionally great system of bike paths, and bicycling is common not just for recreation, but for transportation, as well.

Since 2009, a self-service bicycle rental program called BIXI (**www.bixi.com**) has become a big presence in the city. A combination of the words *bicyclette* and *taxi,* BIXI is similar to programs in Paris, Barcelona, and Minneapolis, where users pick up bikes from designated stands throughout the city and drop them off at any other stand, for a small fee. Some 3,000 bikes are in operation and available at 300 stations in Montréal's central boroughs. While 1-year and 30-day subscriptions are available, visitors can buy a 24-hour access pass for C$5. During those 24 hours, you can borrow bikes as many times as you want, and for each trip, the first 30 minutes are free. Trips longer than 30 minutes incur additional charges, which are added onto the initial C$5 fee. Depending on your needs, zipping on and off BIXI bikes throughout the day can be both an economical and a fun way to get around the city.

If you want a helmet and lock, which are not included with BIXI, or if you want a bike for a half-day or longer, rent from a shop. One of the most centrally located is **Ça Roule/Montréal on Wheels** (✆ **877/866-0633** or 514/866-0633; www.caroule montreal.com), at 27 rue de la Commune est, the waterfront road in Vieux-Port.

The nonprofit biking organization **Vélo Québec** (✆ **800/567-8356** or 514/521-8356; www.velo.qc.ca) has the most up-to-date information on the state of bike paths and offers guided tours throughout the province (*vélo* means "bicycle" in French).

Several taxi companies participate in the **Taxi+Vélo** program. You call, specify that you have a bike to transport, and a cab with a specially designed rack arrives. Up to three bikes can be carried for an extra fee of C$3 each. The companies are listed in a PDF file at www.velo.qc.ca (search for *Taxi+Vélo*). They include **Taxi Diamond** (✆ **514/273-6331**).

[FastFACTS] MONTRÉAL

American Automobile Association (AAA) Members of **AAA** are covered by the **Canadian Automobile Association (CAA)** while traveling in Canada. Bring your membership card and proof of insurance. The 24-hour hot line for emergency road service is ✆ **800/222-4357.** The AAA card also provides discounts at a wide variety of hotels and restaurants in the province of Québec. Visit **www.caaquebec.com** for more information.

Drinking Laws The legal drinking age in the province is 18. All hard liquor and spirits in Québec are sold through official government stores operated by the Québec Société des Alcools (look for maroon signs with the acronym SAQ). Wine and beer are available in grocery stores and convenience stores, called *dépanneurs*. Bars can pour drinks as late as 3am, but often stay open later. Penalties for drunk driving in Canada are heavy. Provisions instituted in 2008 include higher mandatory penalties, such as a minimum fine of C$1,000 for a convicted first offense, and for a second offense, a minimum of 30 days in jail.

Drivers caught under the influence face a maximum life sentence if they cause death, and a maximum 10-year sentence if they cause bodily harm. Learn more at **www.mto.gov.on.ca.**

Embassies & Consulates Embassies are located in Ottawa, Canada's capital. There are consulate offices throughout the Canadian provinces, including Québec. The U.S. Embassy information line ✆ **888/840-0032** costs C$1.59 per minute. The U.S. has a consulate in Montréal at 1155 rue St-Alexandre (✆ **514/398-9695**) where nonemergency American citizen services are provided by appointment only. The U.K. consulate in Montréal is at 1000 rue de la Gauchetière ouest, Ste. 4200 (✆ **514/866-5863**). For contact information for other embassies and consulates, search for "Foreign Representatives in Canada" at **www.international.gc.ca.**

Emergencies Dial ✆ **911** for police, firefighters, or an ambulance.

Gasoline (Petrol) Gasoline in Canada is sold by the liter; 3.78 liters equals 1 gallon. At C$1.15 a liter, that's the equivalent of about US$4.35 per gallon.

Hospitals In Montréal, hospitals with emergency rooms include **Hôpital Général de Montréal** (1650 rue Cedar; ✆ **514/934-1934**) and **Hôpital Royal Victoria** (687 av. des Pins ouest; ✆ **514/934-1934**). **Hôpital de Montréal pour Enfants** (2300 rue Tupper; ✆ **514/412-4400**) is a children's hospital. All three are associated with McGill University.

Insurance Medical treatment in Canada is not free for foreigners, and hospitals and doctors will make you pay your bills at the time of service. Check whether your insurance policy covers you while traveling in Canada, especially for hospitalization abroad. Most policies require you to pay for services upfront and, if they reimburse you at all, will only do so after you return home. Carry details of your insurance plan with you and leave a copy with a friend at home.

Language Canada is officially bilingual, but the province of Québec has laws that make French mandatory in signage. About 65% of Montréal's population has French as its first language (about 95% of Québec City's population does). An estimated four out of five Francophones (French speakers) speak at least some English. Hotel desk staff, sales clerks, and telephone operators nearly always greet people initially in French, but usually switch to English quickly, if necessary. Outside of Montréal, visitors are more likely to encounter residents who don't speak English. If smiles and sign language don't work, look around for a young person—most of them study English in school.

Newspapers & Magazines ***The Globe and Mail*** (www.theglobeandmail.com) is the national English-language paper. Montréal's primary English-language newspaper is the ***Montréal Gazette*** (www.montrealgazette.com). The most extensive list of arts and entertainment happenings appears in print on Friday. The Sunday paper is web-only. Most large newsstands and shops in larger hotels carry the ***New York Times, Wall Street Journal,*** and ***International Herald Tribune.***

Smoking Smoking was banned in the province's bars, restaurants, clubs, casinos, and some other public spaces in 2006. Most small inns and many larger hotels have become entirely smoke-free over the past few years as well. Check before you book if you're looking for a room in which you can smoke.

Taxes Most goods and services in Canada are taxed 5% by the federal government (the TPS) and 7.5% by the province of Québec (the TVQ). Confusingly—and, once you figure it out, maddeningly—the provincial tax comes out to 7.88% because the federal tax is added to the cost of the good or service *before* the provincial tax is calculated. In Montréal, hotel bills have an additional 3% accommodations tax.

Time Montréal, the Laurentians, and Québec City are on Eastern Standard

Time. Daylight Saving Time (summer time) is observed by moving clocks ahead an hour on the second Sunday in March. Clocks move back an hour on the first Sunday in November.

Visitor Information

The terrific website **www.tourisme-montreal.org** offers a broad range of information for Montréal visitors. The equally good **www.bonjourquebec.com** is run by the province of Québec's tourism department and covers the entire province. In Montréal, the main tourist center in downtown is the large **Infotouriste Centre** (1255 rue Peel; ✆ **877/266-5687** or 514/873-2015; Métro: Peel). It's open daily, and the bilingual staff can provide suggestions for accommodations, dining, car rentals, and attractions. In Vieux-Montréal, there's a small **Tourist Information Office** at 174 rue Notre-Dame est, at the corner of Place Jacques-Cartier (Métro: Champ-de-Mars). It's open daily in warmer months, Wednesday through Sunday in winter.

WHERE TO STAY

Accommodations in Montréal range from skyscrapers on grand boulevards, to converted row houses, to stylish inns and boutique luxury hotels—the latter of which are found in ever-increasing numbers in Vieux-Montréal.

Nearly all hotel staff members are reassuringly bilingual. The busiest times are July and August, especially during the frequent summer festivals, during holiday periods (Canadian or American), and during winter carnival.

Most goods and services in Canada have a federal tax of 5% (the TPS). On top of that, the province of Québec adds a tax that comes out to 7.88% (the TVQ). An additional accommodations tax of 3.5% is in effect on hotel bills in Montréal. Prices listed in this book do not include taxes.

The tourist authorities in the province of Québec apply a six-level rating system (zero to five stars) to seven categories of establishments that host travelers. A shield bearing the assigned rating is posted near the entrance to most hotels and inns. The Québec system is based on quantitative measures such as the range of services and amenities. Most of the recommendations below have gotten at least three stars from the state system. The stars in this book are based on Frommer's own rating system, which assigns between zero and three stars. The Frommer's ratings are more subjective than the state's, taking into account such considerations as price-to-value ratios, quality of service, ambience, location, helpfulness of staff, and the presence of such facilities as spas and exercise rooms.

All rooms in properties listed here have private bathrooms unless otherwise noted. Most hotels provide Wi-Fi in either part or all of their facilities, although this continues to be a work in progress for some properties. Most Montréal hotels are entirely nonsmoking. Those that aren't have a limited number of smoking rooms available.

Centre Ville/Downtown

EXPENSIVE

Fairmont the Queen Elizabeth (Le Reine Elizabeth) ★★ ☺ Montréal's largest hotel—it has more than 1,000 rooms—stacks its 21 floors atop VIA Rail's Gare Centrale, the main train station, with the Métro and popular shopping areas such as Place Ville-Marie and Place Bonaventure accessible through underground arcades. This desirable location makes "the Queen E" a frequent choice for heads of state and touring celebrities, even though other hotels in town offer more luxurious pampering. The Fairmont Gold 18th and 19th floors are the best choice, offering a private concierge lounge with complimentary breakfasts and cocktail-hour canapés. Other rooms are satisfactory, with traditional furnishings, easy chairs, ottomans, and bright reading lamps. Most rooms have windows that open, a rarity in this city.

900 bd. René-Lévesque ouest (at rue Mansfield), Montréal, PQ H3B 4A5. ✆ **866/540-4483** or 514/861-3511. Fax 514/954-2296. www.fairmont.com/queenelizabeth. 1,037 units. C$189–C$359 double, from C$289 suite. Children 17 & under stay free in parent's room. Packages available. AE, DC, MC, V. Valet parking C$28. Métro: Bonaventure. Pets accepted for fee. **Amenities:** 3 restaurants; 2 bars; babysitting; concierge; executive-level rooms; health club; Jacuzzi; pool (indoor); room service; Wi-Fi (C$14/day, in lobby). *In room:* A/C, TV, hair dryer, Internet (C$14/day), minibar.

Hôtel Le Germain ★★★ Since 1999, this undertaking by the owner of Québec City's equally desirable boutique hotel **Hôtel Le Germain-Dominion** (p. 282) has added a shot of panache to the downtown lodging scene. The hotel vibe is stylish loft, with white Asian minimalist decor accented by candy-pink and lime-green accessories. Bedrooms have super-comfy bedding, marshmallowy-plush reading chairs, ergonomic work areas with eye-level plugs and ports, windows that open, and a useful variety of lighting options. A glass partition between the bed and the shower is standard (the modest can lower a shade). Self-serve breakfasts include perfect croissants and café au lait, and there's a free espresso machine in the lobby. Its in-house **Laurie Raphaël Montréal** is an offshoot of the esteemed Québec City restaurant. Near-constant renovations and sprucing of paint, bedding, and amenities keeps the Germain at the top of its game.

2050 rue Mansfield (at av. du President-Kennedy), Montréal, PQ H3A 1Y9. ✆ **877/333-2050** or 514/849-2050. Fax 514/849-1437. www.hotelgermain.com. 101 units. C$230–C$475 double. Rates include breakfast. Packages available. AE, DC, MC, V. Valet parking C$25. Métro: Peel. Pets accepted (C$30 per day). **Amenities:** Restaurant; bar; babysitting; concierge; exercise room; room service. *In room:* A/C, TV, hair dryer, minibar, MP3 docking station, Wi-Fi (free).

Le Centre Sheraton Montréal Hotel ★ Ever-bustling, this branch of the familiar brand goes about its business with efficiency and surety of purpose. That figures, since earnest people in suits make up most of the clientele. They gravitate toward the Club Rooms, which include a free breakfast and a private lounge with expansive views and evening hors d'oeuvres. Recently renovated regular guest rooms are decorated in modest corporate style but are clean and have good beds. The health club includes an indoor pool, sauna, whirlpool, a fully equipped fitness center with skylights, a massage studio, and summer terrace. True to its name, this hotel has a central downtown location that's near Dorchester Square, Gare Centrale (the main train station), and the high-stepping rue Crescent dining and nightlife district.

1201 bd. René-Lévesque ouest (btw. rue Drummond & rue Stanley), Montréal, PQ H3B 2L7. ✆ **800/325-3535** or 514/878-2000. Fax 514/878-3958. www.sheraton.com/lecentre. 825 units. C$169–C$319 double, from C$300 suite. Packages available. AE, DC, DISC, MC, V. Valet parking C$30, self-parking C$20. Métro: Bonaventure. Pets accepted (free). **Amenities:** Restaurant; bar; babysitting; concierge; executive-level rooms; health club; pool (indoor w/whirlpool); room service; sauna; spa. *In room:* A/C, TV, hair dryer, Wi-Fi (C$15/day).

Loews Hôtel Vogue ★★ ☺ Open since 1990, the Vogue sits at the top tier of the local luxury-hotel pantheon. Confidence and capability resonate from every member of the staff, and luxury permeates the hotel from the lobby to the well-appointed guest rooms. Feather pillows and duvets dress oversize beds, and huge marble bathrooms are fitted with Jacuzzis—double-size in suites—and separate shower stalls.

Downtown Montréal

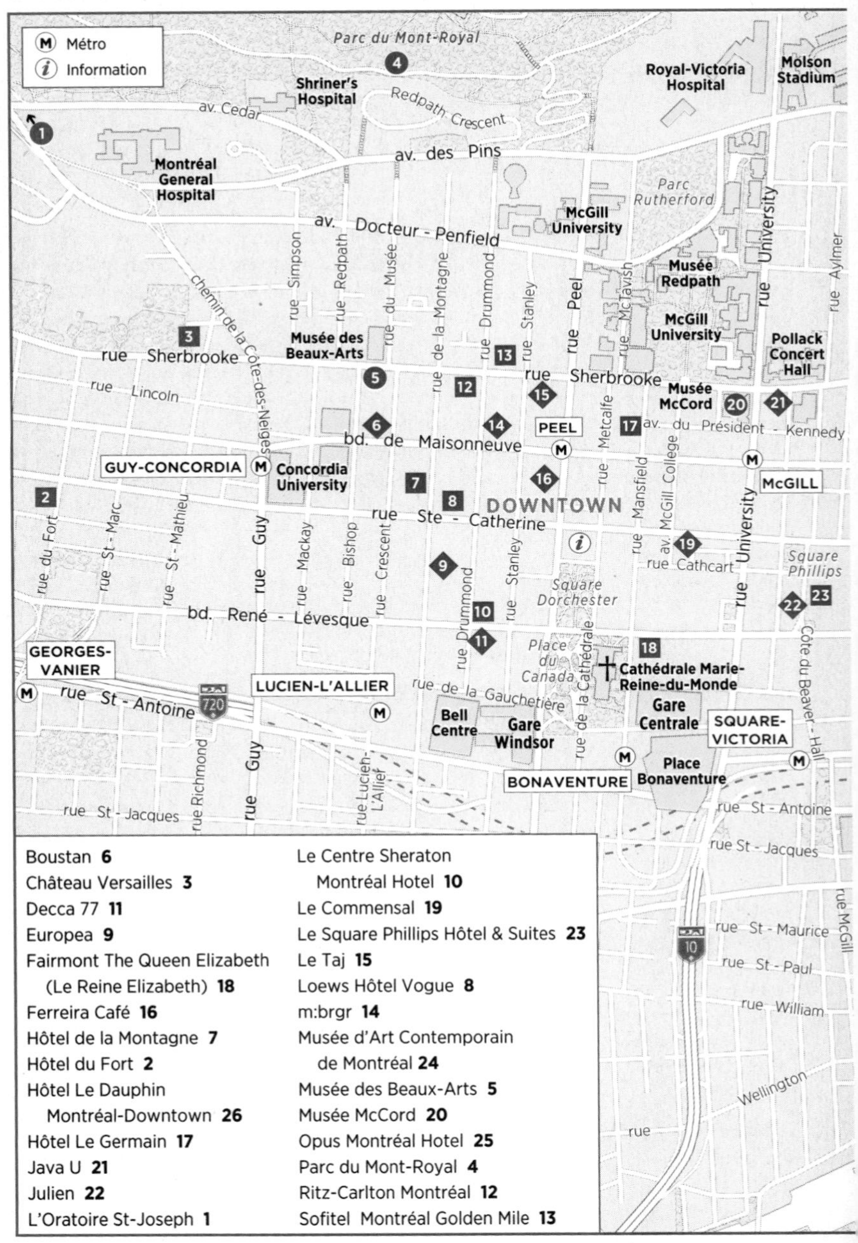

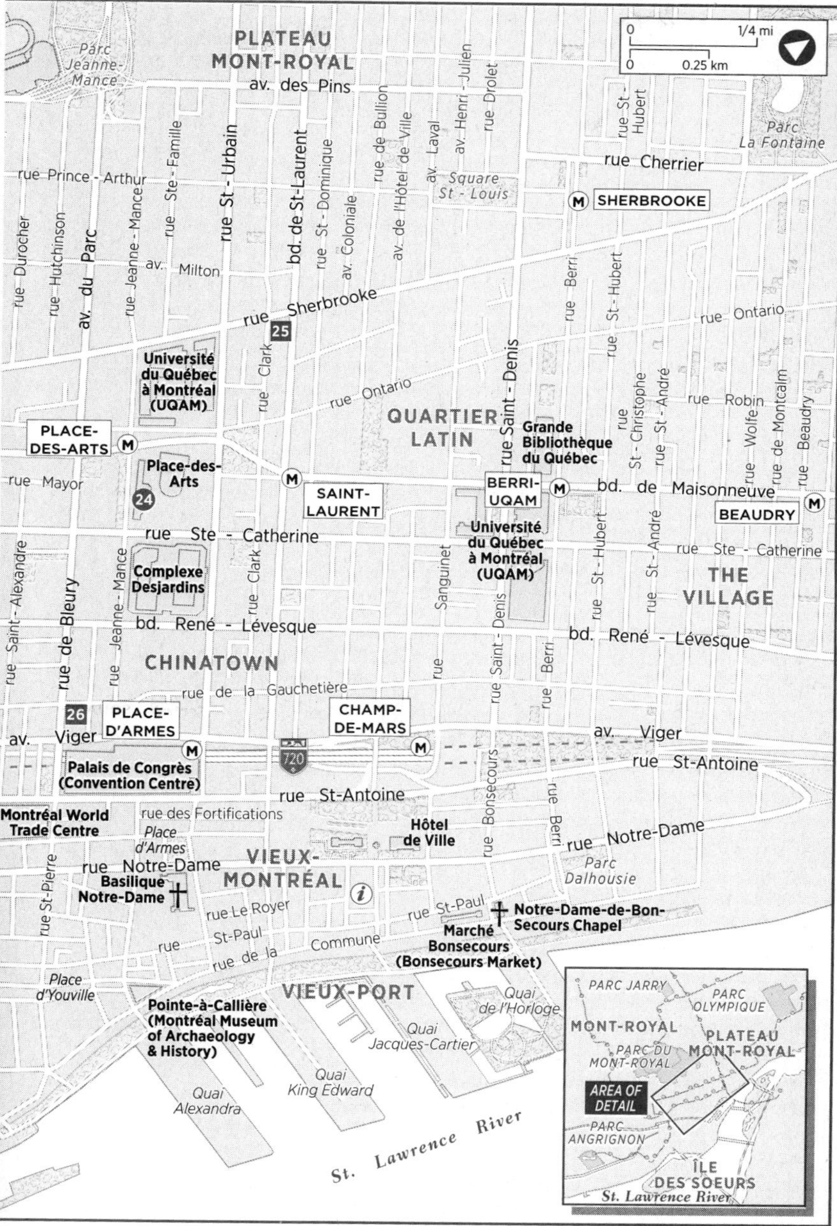

PLATEAU MONT-ROYAL
Parc Jeanne-Mance
av. des Pins
Parc La Fontaine
rue Cherrier
Square St-Louis
SHERBROOKE
rue Prince-Arthur
av. Milton
rue Sherbrooke
rue Ontario
Université du Québec à Montréal (UQAM)
QUARTIER LATIN
Grande Bibliothèque du Québec
PLACE-DES-ARTS
Place-des-Arts
SAINT-LAURENT
BERRI-UQAM
bd. de Maisonneuve
BEAUDRY
rue Mayor
rue Ste-Catherine
Complexe Desjardins
THE VILLAGE
bd. René-Lévesque
CHINATOWN
rue de la Gauchetière
PLACE-D'ARMES
CHAMP-DE-MARS
av. Viger
rue St-Antoine
Palais de Congrès (Convention Centre)
Montréal World Trade Centre
rue des Fortifications
Place d'Armes
Hôtel de Ville
rue Notre-Dame
Parc Dalhousie
VIEUX-MONTRÉAL
Basilique Notre-Dame
rue Le Royer
rue St-Paul
rue de la Commune
Notre-Dame-de-Bon-Secours Chapel
Marché Bonsecours (Bonsecours Market)
Place d'Youville
VIEUX-PORT
Pointe-à-Callière (Montréal Museum of Archaeology & History)
Quai de l'Horloge
Quai Jacques-Cartier
Quai King Edward
Quai Alexandra
St. Lawrence River
PARC JARRY
PARC OLYMPIQUE
MONT-ROYAL
PLATEAU MONT-ROYAL
PARC DU MONT-ROYAL
AREA OF DETAIL
PARC ANGRIGNON
ÎLE DES SOEURS
St. Lawrence River

Rooms all have consistent decor, so what you see on the website is what you'll get when you arrive. The hotel's **L'Opéra Bar** is a two-story nook off the lobby with floor-to-ceiling windows and is open until 2am.

1425 rue de la Montagne (near rue Ste-Catherine), Montréal, PQ H3G 1Z3. ✆ **800/465-6654** or 514/285-5555. Fax 514/849-8903. www.loewshotels.com. 142 units. C$229–C$329 double, C$429 suite. Children 17 & under stay free in parent's room. Packages available. AE, DC, DISC, MC, V. Valet parking C$32. Métro: Peel. Pets accepted (for fee). **Amenities:** Restaurant; 2 bars; babysitting; children's programs; concierge; exercise room & discounted access to Club Sportif MAA gym & pool; room service. *In room:* A/C, TV/DVD player, CD player, hair dryer, minibar, MP3 docking station, Wi-Fi (C$15/day).

Opus Montréal Hotel ★ One of Montréal's nightlife epicenters is the Opus's restaurant and bar, **Koko** (p. 263), which boasts the city's most expansive terrace. Hotel guests can cut its notoriously long lines and sip neon drinks among the clubbing elite, where heel height regularly exceeds 5 inches. Bedrooms are designed for this crowd: The concrete ceilings and sugarplum walls look better in evening light, showers are lit from below, and linens are silky soft. Guests often need the earplugs found on every nightstand. The structure began life in 1914 as the first poured concrete building in North America and was a boutique hotel named for its architect, Joseph-Arthur Godin, until the Opus group purchased it in 2007. Though technically downtown, the hotel borders Plateau Mont-Royal, where city dwellers both live and party.

10 Sherbrooke ouest (near rue St-Laurent), Montréal, PQ H2X 4C9. ✆ **866/744-6346** or 514/843-6000. Fax 514/843-6810. www.opushotel.com. 136 units. C$199–C$249 double, C$399–C$599 suite. Children 17 & under stay free in parent's room. Packages available. AE, MC, V. Valet parking C$26 (indoor garage). Pets accepted (C$50/stay). Métro: St-Laurent. **Amenities:** Restaurant; bar; babysitting; concierge; health club; room service; Wi-Fi (free, in lobby). *In room:* A/C, TV, CD player, hair dryer, Internet (C$15/day), minibar.

Ritz-Carlton Montréal The Ritz and its restaurants were closed for all of 2009 and 2010, and expected to reopen in 2011. The C$100-million renovation project will convert some of the property to private condominiums and hopefully retain the grandeur of the hotel accommodations and public spaces. Since its launch in 1912, the luxe hotel has been a favorite, with **Café de Paris** favored for high tea and **Le Jardin du Ritz** for its duck pond and ducklings. Fingers crossed that both will be part of the new operation. Check the hotel's website for updates and pricing details.

1228 rue Sherbrooke ouest (at rue Drummond), Montréal, PQ H3G 1H6. ✆ **800/363-0366** or 514/842-4212. www.ritzmontreal.com.

Sofitel Montréal Golden Mile ★★ In 2002, the French luxury hotel chain transformed a bland 1970s downtown office tower into this coveted destination for visiting celebrities and the power elite. It wows from the moment of arrival, from the light-filled stone-and-wood lobby to the universally warm welcome visitors get from the staff. The 100 standard rooms (called Superior) have floor-to-ceiling windows, furnishings made from Québec-grown cherry wood, down duvets, and a soothing oatmeal-cream decor. Desks jut out from the wall and are comfortable to use. Bathrooms have rain showers. In-room spa services such as facials and massages were added in 2010, to better compete with hotels with on-site spas. The ambitious **Renoir** restaurant is in a bright, airy room and features an upscale bar and outdoor terrace. Catering to the international and business guests whose bodies are still operating on different time zones, the exercise room is open 24 hours per day.

1155 rue Sherbrooke ouest (at rue Stanley), Montréal, PQ H3A 2N3. ✆ **514/285-9000.** Fax 514/289-1155. www.sofitel.com. 258 units. C$195–C$325 double, from C$295 suite. Packages available. AE, DC, MC, V. Valet parking C$30. Métro: Peel. Pets accepted (free). **Amenities:** Restaurant; bar; babysitting; concierge; executive-level rooms; exercise room; room service; sauna; in-room spa services. *In room:* TV, DVD player (by request), CD player (by request), hair dryer, minibar, MP3 docking station, Wi-Fi (C$15/day).

MODERATE

Château Versailles One of the official lodging sites for the **Musée des Beaux-Arts** (p. 241) and McGill University, the Versailles is near the museum but outside most of the tourist orbit. It began as a European-style pension in 1958 and expanded into adjacent pre-WWI town houses. The most spacious rooms have modern furnishings with Deco and Second Empire touches. Some have fireplaces. Loyal guests return for just this reason—every room is different. A buffet breakfast is served in the main living room, where you can sit at a small table or in an easy chair in front of a fireplace. One obstacle: the lack of an elevator by which to deal with the three floors. As well, at the time of our last visit, some bedding needed an upgrade. Across the street is sister property Le Meridien Versailles (1808 rue Sherbrooke ouest; ✆ **888/933-8111** or 514/933-8111; www.lemeridienversailleshotel.com).

1659 rue Sherbrooke ouest (at rue St-Mathieu), Montréal, PQ H3H 1E3. ✆ **888/933-8111** or 514/933-8111. Fax 514/933-6967. www.versailleshotels.com. 65 units. C$185–C$375 double, from C$275 suite. Rates include breakfast. Packages available. AE, DC, DISC, MC, V. Valet parking C$24. Métro: Guy-Concordia. Pets accepted (C$17/day). **Amenities:** Babysitting; concierge; exercise room; room service; sauna. *In room:* A/C, TV, hair dryer, minibar, Wi-Fi (free).

Hôtel de la Montagne Eras collide at this hotel, where an Art Deco lobby with giant tusked elephants and a fountain topped by a nude figure with stained-glass butterfly wings opens onto a jazz piano cabaret lounge. Just a few steps further, and you're in the giant singles watering hole **Thursday's** (p. 262), which has a terrace opening onto lively rue Crescent. In warmer months, patrons from all over the city stand in line for the hotel's rooftop pool and bar (both open till 3am). Factor in the trio of slot machines and the discothèque, and you could be in Vegas, baby! After that, the relatively serene bedrooms, all with balconies, seem downright bland, but they're clean and include good-size bathrooms and high-end bedding. Some rooms have benefited from a sleek update in the last few years (they cost more). All in all, the hotel offers a competent staff and bit of old-fashioned pizzazz.

1430 rue de la Montagne (north of rue Ste-Catherine), Montréal, PQ H3G 1Z5. ✆ **800/361-6262** or 514/288-5656. Fax 514/288-9658. www.hoteldelamontagne.com. 147 units. C$175–C$225 double. Packages available. AE, DC, DISC, MC, V. Valet parking C$16, for SUV C$32. Métro: Peel. Pets accepted (for fee). **Amenities:** 2 restaurants; 3 bars; babysitting; concierge; pool (heated, outdoor); room service. *In room:* A/C, TV, hair dryer, minibar, Wi-Fi (free).

Hôtel du Fort ☺ This reliable hotel takes as its primary duty providing lodging to longer-term business travelers, although because all rooms are a good size and many have sofas with hide-a-beds, they're good for small families or persons who use wheelchairs, too. Details include a fitness room sufficient enough for a thorough workout, basic kitchenettes with fridges and microwave ovens in every room (the concierge can have groceries delivered), and a wheelchair-accessible underground parking garage. A buffet breakfast is served in the lounge. In a nod toward sustainability, kitchenettes feature energy-efficient appliances with Energy Star designation. The hotel also bills itself as "Shabbat-friendly," offering special accommodation for Jewish guests observing the Sabbath. Kosher breakfasts, manual locks, and a Shabbat elevator service can all be provided upon request.

1390 rue du Fort (at rue Ste-Catherine), Montréal, PQ H3H 2R7. ✆ **800/565-6333** or 514/938-8333. www.hoteldufort.com. 124 units. C$159–C$225 double, C$219–C$395 suite. Children 12 & under stay free in parent's room. Packages available. AE, DC, MC, V. Self-parking C$21. Métro: Guy-Concordia. **Amenities:** Babysitting; concierge; exercise room; room service. *In room:* A/C, TV, hair dryer, kitchenette, Wi-Fi (C$11/day).

Le Square Phillips Hôtel & Suites ★ 🏷 ☺ The advantages here are space, livability, and locale. Originally designed as a warehouse by the noted Québec architect Ernest Cormier (1885–1980), the building was converted to its present function in 2003. The vaguely cathedral-like spaces were largely retained (some rooms have columns and arches), and they make for capacious studio bedrooms and suites fully equipped for long stays. Full kitchens in every unit come with all essential appliances—toasters, fridges, stoves, dishwashers, crockery, and pots and pans. Rooms got new mattresses in 2009, and new couches and sofa beds in 2010. There's a rooftop pool with a downtown view and an exercise room, and a laundry room is also available for guest use. The location, at the edge of the downtown shopping district, is central, and an easy walk to Vieux-Montréal and the rue Crescent nightlife district. Because it gets a lot of business travelers, weekends tend to be cheaper than weekdays.

1193 Square Phillips (south of rue Ste-Catherine), Montréal, PQ H3B 3C9. ✆ **866/393-1193** or 514/393-1193. Fax 514/393-1192. www.squarephillips.com. 160 units. C$162–C$202 double, C$259–C$358 suite. Rates include breakfast. Discount for stays of 7 or more nights. AE, DC, DISC, MC, V. Valet parking C$20. Métro: McGill. Pets accepted (free). **Amenities:** Babysitting; concierge; exercise room; pool (heated, indoor, rooftop). *In room:* A/C, TV, hair dryer, kitchen, Wi-Fi (free).

INEXPENSIVE

Hôtel Le Dauphin Montréal-Downtown 🏷 This member of the small Dauphin hotel chain presents a terrific option for travelers on a budget. Room furnishings are simple and clean, if blandly dorm-room functional. On the other hand, bathrooms are sleek (black counters, slate floors, and glass-walled shower stalls), beds are comfy, and all units have—get this—a computer terminal and free Internet access. There also are bigger-hotel touches: flat-screen TVs, in-room safes, large refrigerators (unstocked), and morning newspaper delivery. The location, next to the convention center on the northern end of Vieux-Montréal, is central, though the immediate surroundings are nondescript. A key is required to access the elevator, for extra safety.

1025 rue de Bleury (near av. Viger), Montréal, PQ H2Z 1M7. ✆ **888/784-3888** or 514/788-3888. Fax 514/788-3889. www.hoteldauphin.ca. 80 units. C$129–C$195 double. Rates include breakfast. AE, MC, V. Parking C$19 at convention center. Métro: Place d'Armes. **Amenities:** Exercise room. *In room:* A/C, TV/DVD player, fridge, hair dryer, Wi-Fi (free), in-room computer w/free Internet.

Vieux-Montréal (Old Montréal)

VERY EXPENSIVE

Hôtel Le St-James ★★★ In a word, gorgeous. Montréal's surge of designer hotels spans the spectrum from minimalist to ornate, and Le St-James sits squarely at the ornate end of the range. It began life as a merchant's bank in 1870, and the opulence of that station has been retained. The grand hall, with Corinthian columns and balconies with gilded metal balustrades, houses **XO Le Restaurant** and a chic bar area—the result of a complete overhaul of the space, making it more easygoing but still off-the-charts glamorous. Come for gastronomic cocktails and appetizers or weekend brunch, stay for chef Michele Mercur's tasting menu. Sumptuous rooms are furnished with antiques and impeccable reproductions, and bathrooms are a sea of white marble. The stone-walled, candlelit **Le Spa** specializes in full-body water therapy. A member of the Leading Small Hotels of the World, Le St-James represents a triumph of design and preservation for visiting royalty—or those who want to be treated like it.

355 rue St-Jacques ouest (near rue St-Pierre), Montréal, PQ H2Y 1N9. ✆ **866/841-3111** or 514/841-3111. Fax 514/841-1232. www.hotellestjames.com. 61 units. From C$400 double, from C$525 suite. Packages available. AE, DC, DISC, MC, V. Valet parking C$33. Métro: Square Victoria. Pets accepted (C$40/day). **Amenities:** Restaurant; bar; babysitting; concierge; exercise room; room service; spa. *In room:* A/C, TV, CD player, hair dryer, minibar, MP3 docking station, Wi-Fi (free).

Le Saint-Sulpice Hôtel ★★ ☺ Open since 2002 and part of the wave of high-style boutique hotels that has washed across Vieux-Montréal, Le Saint-Sulpice impresses with an all-suites configuration, an ambitious eatery called **S Le Restaurant,** and courtly service. Though independently owned and operated, the hotel is a member of Hotels & Preference and easily meets that brand's demanding, sophisticated standards. Three levels of suites come with myriad conveniences and gadgets, including mini-kitchens with microwave ovens, stoves, and fridges. Some have fireplaces or private balconies. The largest suites, at the executive level, are often taken by film crews in town for movie productions. There's an outdoor terrace where lunch, dinner, and drinks are served facing the gardens of the Sulpician Seminary. Children's services include gaming consoles in every room, board games, kid-friendly TV programming, a children's menu, and day care.

414 rue St-Sulpice (next to the Basilique Notre-Dame), Montréal, PQ H2Y 2V5. ✆ **877/785-7423** or 514/288-1000. Fax 514/288-0077. www.lesaintsulpice.com. 108 units. Summer C$239–C$269 suite; winter from C$159 suite. Rates include full breakfast. Children 11 & under stay free in parent's room. Packages available. AE, DISC, MC, V. Valet parking C$25, for SUV C$32. Métro: Place d'Armes. Pets accepted (C$50/stay). **Amenities:** Restaurant; bar; babysitting; children's programs; concierge; health club; room service; sauna; spa. *In room:* A/C, TV, kitchenette, minibar, Wi-Fi (free).

EXPENSIVE

Auberge du Vieux-Port ★★ Terrifically romantic, this tidy luxury inn is housed in an 1882 building facing the waterfront, and many of the rooms, as well as a rooftop terrace, offer unobstructed views of Vieux-Port—a particular treat on summer nights when there are fireworks on the river or in winter when it's snowing. Exposed brick and stone walls, massive beams, polished hardwood floors, and windows that open define the hideaway bedrooms; number 403, for instance, has expansive views, space to stretch out, and a king bed. For each stay, guests receive a complimentary glass of wine in **Narcisse,** the small, sophisticated wine bar off the lobby, with live jazz adding to the mood Thursday through Saturday starting at 6:30pm.

97 rue de la Commune est (near rue St-Gabriel), Montréal, PQ H2Y 1J1. ✆ **888/660-7678** or 514/876-0081. Fax 514/876-8923. www.aubergeduvieuxport.com. 27 units. C$230–C$285 double. Rates include full breakfast & 1 glass of wine per stay. Children 11 & under stay free in parent's room. AE, MC, V. Valet parking C$24. Métro: Place-d'Armes or Champs-de-Mars. **Amenities:** Bar; babysitting; concierge; exercise room at sister hotel; room service. *In room:* A/C, TV, CD player, CD library, hair dryer, minibar, Wi-Fi (free).

Embassy Suites ★ ☺ Along with the **W Montréal** (p. 226), the **InterContinental Montréal** (see below), and the new **Le Westin Montréal,** this recent entry from the Hilton empire helps constitute an expanding hotel row opposite the

Palais des Congrès (Convention Center). While it is the most moderately priced and least flashy of the four—don't expect 600-count Egyptian cotton sheets or complimentary limo service—it is as welcoming a place for families as it is for executive road warriors. As befits an establishment in the area on the northern edge of Vieux Montréal that tourism authorities call the "Quartier Internationale," guests range widely over diverse nationalities and ethnicities. Cooked-to-order breakfasts are free, as are evening cocktails, which can add up to a significant savings. All but 20 of the units are bona fide suites, with pull-out sofas, big-screen TVs, and kitchenettes with microwave ovens, fridges, and (in pricier suites) ranges.

208 rue St-Antoine ouest (at rue St-François-Xavier), Montréal, PQ H2Y 0A6. © **877/601-7666** or 514/288-8886. Fax 514/288-8899. www.embassysuitesmontreal.com. 210 units. C$209–C$269 double. Rates include full breakfast. Children 18 & under stay free in parent's room. Packages available. AE, DC, DISC, MC, V. Parking C$25. Métro: Place-d'Armes. Pets up to 25 lb. accepted (C$35/stay). **Amenities:** Restaurant; bar; babysitting; concierge; exercise room. *In room:* A/C, TV, fridge, hair dryer, kitchenette (in some suites), Wi-Fi (C$10/day).

Hostellerie Pierre du Calvet ★ Step from cobblestone streets into an 18th-century home boasting velvet curtains, gold-leafed writing desks, and four-poster beds of teak mahogany. The wildly atmospheric public spaces are furnished with original antiques—not reproductions. Likewise, the voluptuous dining room, **Les Filles du Roy,** suggests a 19th-century hunting lodge. (*Masterpiece Theatre* fans, this hotel is for you.) Most of the nine bedrooms sport fireplaces, and rooms 1 and 6 even have showers with stone walls. Door locks, which used to look like they could be kicked in by a baby, have been updated. In warm months, a walled-in outdoor courtyard with a small fountain is a hideaway dining terrace. There's also an intimate veranda just outside rooms 8, 9, and 10. Gaëten Trottier, whose family began the establishment in 1962, has converted a space here into the **Musée du Bronze de Montréal.** It contains his sculpture and is well worth a look.

405 rue Bonsecours (at rue St-Paul), Montréal, PQ H2Y 3C3. © **866/544-1725** or 514/282-1725. Fax 514/282-0456. www.pierreducalvet.ca. 9 units. C$265–C$295 double; about C$100 less in low season. Rates include breakfast. Packages available. AE, MC, V. Parking C$15. Métro: Champ-de-Mars. **Amenities:** Restaurant. *In room:* A/C, TV, hair dryer, Wi-Fi (free).

Hotel Gault ★★ The Gault explores the edges of minimalism; design aficionados will likely love it. Raw, monumental concrete walls and brushed-steel work surfaces have been softened in recent years with a few more rugs and some lollipop-colored mod furniture, cutting down on what used to be a looming sense of austerity. Bedrooms are large, and the color and tone of their design shifts on each floor. Even with just 30 rooms, there are eight styles and shapes. Terra room #170, for instance, has brick walls, a snazzy bathtub, and heated floors, while all rooms on the fifth floor have balconies—a rare treat in Montréal. The sleek lobby, where a complimentary breakfast is served, has massive arched windows and comfortable chairs for lounging, and a small library offers a mass of design magazines to browse through. Painting and photos in public spaces are by local artists and change every 6 to 8 weeks.

449 rue Ste-Hélène (near rue Notre-Dame), Montréal, PQ H2Y 2K9. © **866/904-1616** or 514/904-1616. Fax 866/904-1717. www.hotelgault.com. 30 units. C$187–C$279 double, C$225–C$589 suite. Rates include full breakfast. Packages available. AE, DISC, MC, V. Valet parking outdoor C$19, indoor C$25. Métro: Square Victoria. Pets accepted (C$25/day). **Amenities:** Cafe; bar; babysitting; concierge; exercise room; room service; spa. *In room:* A/C, TV/DVD player, movie library, hair dryer, minibar, MP3 docking station, Wi-Fi (most rooms; free).

Hôtel Nelligan ★ Occupying adjoining 1850 buildings, the Nelligan opened in 2002 and expanded in 2007 from 63 to 105 units. More than half of the accommodations are now suites. Many of the bedrooms are dark-wooded, masculine retreats, with puffy duvets, heaps of pillows, and quality mattresses. The staff performs its duties admirably, and the building maintains beautiful public spaces, including **Verses Restaurant** on the ground floor and Verses Sky Terrace, where drinks and light meals are served until 11pm. One distraction is that the hotel's indoor atrium can sometimes pull noise from the downstairs bar up to rooms. Still, claiming an enveloping lobby chair facing the open front to the street, with a book and a cold drink at hand, is one definition of utter contentment. The hotel is named for the 19th-century Québécois poet Emile Nelligan (1879–1941), whose lines are excerpted on the bedroom walls.

106 rue St-Paul ouest (at rue St-Sulpice), Montréal, PQ H2Y 1Z3. © **877/788-2040** or 514/788-2040. Fax 514/788-2041. www.hotelnelligan.com. 105 units. From C$265 double, from C$315 suite. Rates include breakfast & 1 cocktail per stay. Packages available. AE, DISC, MC, V. Valet parking C$24. Métro: Place d'Armes. **Amenities:** 2 restaurants; bar; babysitting; concierge; exercise room; room service. *In room:* A/C, TV, DVD player (on request), CD player, hair dryer, Wi-Fi (free).

Hôtel St. Paul ★★ The St. Paul has been a star to design and architecture aficionados since it opened a decade ago, and it ranks among the most worthwhile of old buildings converted to hotels. Minimalism pervades, with simple lines and muted colors. Hallways are hushed and dark (truth be told, they border on pitch black), and they open into bright rooms with furnishings in grounded tones. This being Canada, pops of texture come from pelt rugs. In the bathroom, marble sinks are square, and clear plastic cubes cover the toiletries. Locally-made chocolates are delivered with turndown service. Many rooms face Vieux-Montréal's less touristed far western edge, with its mixture of stone and brick buildings (although the rumble of rue McGill's morning buses and commuters may keep you from sleeping in). A splashy restaurant, **Vauvert,** offers locally inspired French cuisine with a Mediterranean flair and attracts the cocktail crowd when the DJ arrives on Thursday and Saturday nights.

355 rue McGill (at rue St-Paul), Montréal, PQ H2Y 2E8. © **866/380-2202** or 514/380-2222. Fax 514/380-2200. www.hotelstpaul.com. 120 units. C$209–C$339 double, C$351–C$439 suite. Rates include breakfast. Children 11 & under stay free in parent's room. Packages available. AE, MC, V. Valet parking C$22. Métro: Square Victoria. Pets under 30 lb. accepted (C$75/stay). **Amenities:** Restaurant; bar; babysitting; concierge; exercise room; room service. *In room:* A/C, TV, CD player, hair dryer, minibar, MP3 player, Wi-Fi (free).

InterContinental Montréal ★ Across the street from the convention center, the InterContinental completed a floor-to-ceiling renovation in 2009 of its rooms, lobby, bar, restaurant, and reception area, all to better compete with the new Le Westin Montréal and **Embassy Suites** (p. 223), both down the block. Guest rooms fall under four confusing categories—"irresistible," "inspiring," "iconic," and "illustrious"—but are spacious, quiet, and outfitted with marble bathrooms, low-slung wingback chairs, and comfortable beds. An upscale buffet breakfast in the new Provençal restaurant, **Osco!**, includes plump, ripe fruit and omelets made to order. But what really sets the InterContinental apart is its absinthe bar, the **Sarah B.,** named after actress Sarah Bernhardt (1844–1923), whose spirit is said to roam the adjacent 1888 Nordheimer building. In-hotel posters promise a night of "Pure sexytude, where the green fairy may be met in a suave and relaxed atmosphere." Perhaps what's lost in translation can, after a glass of absinthe, be found.

360 rue St-Antoine ouest (near rue de Bleury), Montréal, PQ H2Y 3X4. ✆ **800/361-3600** or 514/987-9900. Fax 514/847-8730. www.montreal.intercontinental.com. 360 units. C$129–C$299 double, from C$277 suite. Children 17 & under stay free in parent's room. Packages available. AE, DC, DISC, MC, V. Valet parking C$29, self-parking C$22. Métro: Square Victoria. Pets accepted (C$35/stay). **Amenities:** Restaurant; bar; babysitting; concierge; executive-level rooms; health club w/steam rooms; pool (w/ whirlpool); room service; sauna. *In room:* A/C, TV, DVD player (on request), hair dryer, minibar, Wi-Fi (C$15/day).

Place d'Armes Hôtel & Suites ★★ Three adjoining buildings make up this romantic hotel, with their elaborate architectural details of the late-19th and early-20th centuries in abundant evidence. Many bedrooms have richly carved capitals and moldings, high ceilings, or original brick walls, and all are decorated in contemporary fashion: deluxe bedding, slate floors in the bathrooms, spotlight lighting. (That spotlight lighting can be pretty dim in some rooms, especially suites—ask for a bright room if you prefer lots of sun.) Many bathrooms have disc-shaped rain-shower nozzles in the showers. The hushed **Rainspa** has a *hammam*—a traditional Middle-Eastern steam bath—and offers massages and facials. There are two terrific in-house dining options: the hushed and high-end **Aix Cuisine du Terroir**, where meals are created around Québec ingredients, and the airy, tall-ceilinged **Suite 701** (p. 263), where guests are served breakfast and the *cinq-à-sept* (5-to-7) after-work crowd gathers to eat and drink.

55 rue St-Jacques ouest, Montréal, PQ H2Y 3X2. ✆ **888/450-1887** or 514/842-1887. Fax 514/842-6469. www.hotelplacedarmes.com. 131 units. C$188–C$255 double, from C$268 suite. Rates include one cocktail per stay. Packages available. AE, DISC, MC, V. Valet parking C$24. Métro: Place d'Armes. **Amenities:** 2 restaurants; bar; babysitting; concierge; exercise room; room service; spa. *In room:* A/C, TV, hair dryer, minibar, Wi-Fi (free).

W Montréal ★★★ Combining contemporary decor with in-house nightlife and attentive service, the W brand is unique on the hotel landscape, and the Montréal property follows suit. A dance-club tone greets guests upon entry: neon lights around the doorway, a red glow in the front lobby. The hotel's **Ristorante Otto** attracts a sleek crowd of models, people who date models, and people who wish they were one or the other. So too does the intimate **W Café/Bartini,** which concocts specialty martinis and is often open until 3am, and the **Wunderbar,** which picks up the pace with beat-spinning DJs, also until 3am. Bedrooms follow through, with pillow-top mattresses, goose-down comforters, and 350-count Egyptian cotton sheets. Flat-screen TVs and DVD players are standard in even the basic (called Cozy) rooms, which is only to be expected. Open since 2004, the W is located where Vieux-Montréal meets downtown, both literally and figuratively.

901 Square-Victoria (at rue St-Antoine), Montréal, PQ H2Z 1R1. ✆ **877/W-HOTELS** (877/946-8357) or 514/395-3100. Fax 514/395-3150. www.whotels.com/montreal. 152 units. C$179–C$720 double. Packages available. AE, DC, DISC, MC, V. Valet parking C$30. Métro: Square Victoria. Pets accepted (C$25/day, plus C$100 cleaning fee). **Amenities:** Restaurant; 3 bars; concierge; executive-level rooms; exercise room; room service; spa. *In room:* A/C, TV/DVD player, hair dryer, MP3 docking station, Wi-Fi (C$15/day).

MODERATE

Auberge Bonaparte ★ Even the smallest rooms in this fashionable urban inn are gracefully presented—they're sizeable, with comfortable, firm beds and bright decor. About half feature whirlpool tubs with separate showers. Guests can spend time on the rooftop terrace, which overlooks the Basilique Notre-Dame; one suite, on the top floor, offers superb views of the basilica's cloistered gardens. **Bonaparte** restaurant (p. 232) on the ground floor—romantic in a Left Bank sort of way—has long been one of our Vieux-Montréal favorites. Generous gourmet breakfasts are included in the cost of the room and served here. Sitting at one of the restaurant's elegant window tables with a newspaper, a croissant, coffee, and an omelet feels like an especially civilized way to start the day.

447 rue St-François-Xavier (just north of rue St-Paul), Montréal, PQ H2Y 2T1. © **514/844-1448.** Fax 514/844-0272. www.bonaparte.com. 30 units. C$180–C$230 double, C$355 suite. Rates include full breakfast. AE, DC, MC, V. Parking C$15 per calendar day. Métro: Place d'Armes. **Amenities:** Restaurant; babysitting; concierge; access to nearby health club; room service. *In room:* A/C, TV, hair dryer, Wi-Fi (free).

Auberge Les Passants du Sans Soucy ★ This cheery inn in the heart of Vieux-Montréal is a gracefully converted former 1723 fur warehouse. The nine romantic rooms feature mortared stone walls, beamed ceilings, wrought-iron or brass beds, lace curtains, buffed wood floors, jet tubs, flat-screen TVs, and electric fireplaces. Renovations in 2008 knocked out some walls and brought in sleeker furnishings to make four smaller rooms larger. Breakfast is a special selling point: A sky-lit dining nook features communal tables on either side of a fireplace imported from Bordeaux. The substantial morning meals include chocolate croissants and made-to-order omelets. The marble-floored front entry immediately sets a relaxed, urbane tone.

171 rue St-Paul ouest (at rue St-François-Xavier), Montréal, PQ H2Y 1Z5. © **514/842-2634.** Fax 514/842-2912. www.lesanssoucy.com. 9 units. C$160–C$190 double, C$225 suite. Rates include full breakfast. AE, MC, V. Parking C$17 per calendar day. Métro: Place d'Armes. *In room:* A/C, TV, hair dryer, Wi-Fi (free).

Lhotel Hotel Montréal ★ Formerly Hotel XIXe Siècle, with stately interiors that echoed the building's Second Empire exterior (it began life in 1870 as a bank), the new Lhotel is in the midst of change. One step into the oddly juxtaposed lobby—at once Victorian library, neon bar, and pop art emporium—and you'll see what we mean. Still, this tidy little hotel is worth seeking out for its central location and spacious, faintly aristocratic guest rooms, with 4.5m (15-ft.) ceilings, large windows, and functional work desks. Rooms facing the nondescript inner courtyard may not be scenic, but they're nearly silent—perfect for light sleepers. And who can complain when original Andy Warhols and Roy Lichtensteins from the hotel's new owner's personal collection line the hallways? One of the original LOVE sculptures by Robert Indiana stands sentry next to the front door, too.

262 rue St-Jacques ouest (at rue St-Jean), Montréal, PQ H2Y 1N1. © **877/553-0019** or 514/985-0019. Fax 514/985-0059. www.lhotelmontreal.com. 59 units. C$170–C$190 double, from C$200 suite. Rates include breakfast. Children 12 & under stay free in parent's room. AE, MC, V. Valet parking C$22. Métro: Place d'Armes. **Amenities:** Bar; concierge; exercise room; room service. *In room:* A/C, TV, DVD player (on request), hair dryer, Wi-Fi (free).

Le Petit Hôtel ★ This picturesque section of rue St-Paul in Old Montréal has long housed some favorite small hotels—Auberge Les Passants du Sans Soucy (above), just across the narrow street, and Auberge Bonaparte (above) around the corner. Le Petit Hôtel opened in 2009 and is a variation on the same theme: A renovated industrial building from 1885, with original stone and brick walls exposed throughout. Rooms range from extra large (#208, with a long stone wall, floor-to-ceiling arched windows overlooking the street, and a flat screen TV equipped with a Wii workout system) to the medium-cozy (#306) to the small (#303). Continental breakfast features high-end muesli, great croissants, and espresso drinks with soy milk as an option. Front staff are competent and friendly, and the overall vibe is chic. A noisy bar down the block makes rooms on the side or back preferable on warm nights.

168 rue St-Paul ouest (at rue St-François-Xavier), Montréal, PQ H2Y 1Z7. © **877/530-0360** or 514/940-0360. Fax 514/940-0363. www.petithotelmontreal.com. 24 units. C$188–C$268 double. Rates include breakfast. Packages available. AE, MC, V. Valet parking C$24. Métro: Place d'Armes. **Amenities**: Cafe; concierge; access to exercise rooms at sister hotels Hôtel Nelligan & Place d'Armes Hôtel & Suites. *In room:* A/C, TV, DVD rental, hair dryer, minibar, MP3 docking station, Wi-Fi (free).

Plateau Mont-Royal

MODERATE

Auberge de La Fontaine ★ Colorful, quirky, and eminently competent, La Fontaine has the feel of a cheerful hostel. It's located directly on the lovely Parc de La Fontaine and one of the city's central bike paths. Bedrooms are done up in bright, funky colors, and beds are comfortable. The downstairs kitchen, in addition to being stocked with free tea, juices, cookies, and cheese, also has a microwave and a refrigerator for guest use. The front desk sells beer and wine. A third-floor terrace faces the park and is open during the day, and one suite has a private park-side patio. For visitors who plan to spend time at the restaurants and bars of Plateau Mont-Royal and who are looking for a casual option, Auberge de La Fontaine can't be beat.

1301 rue Rachel est (at rue Chambord), Montréal, PQ H2J 2K1. © **800/597-0597** or 514/597-0166. Fax 514/597-0496. www.aubergedelafontaine.com. 21 units. C$179–C$207 double, C$235–C$259 suite; Nov–Apr from C$119 double, from C$153 suite. Rates include breakfast. Packages available. AE, DC, MC, V. 3 parking spots; free street parking. Métro: Mont-Royal. **Amenities:** Bikes can be delivered; kitchen. *In room:* A/C, TV, hair dryer, Wi-Fi (free).

WHERE TO DINE

There was a time not so long ago when eating out in the province of Québec meant dining on French food, and that was that. Over the last 15 years, however, this has changed dramatically. Partly, this is because of immigration: As the population diversified, an intermingling of styles, ingredients, and techniques was inevitable. Montréal is now as cosmopolitan in its offerings as any city on the continent. Indeed, in some eyes, it has taken Canada's lead role in gastronomy. Montréalers now routinely indulge in Portuguese, Indian, Moroccan, Thai, Turkish, Mexican, and Japanese cuisines, and a meal here can equal the best offered anywhere.

Restaurants are colloquially called "restos." Many moderately priced bistros offer outstanding food, congenial surroundings, and amiable service at reasonable prices. Nearly all have menus posted outside, making it easy to do a little comparison shopping.

Always look for table d'hôte meals. These fixed-price menus with three or four courses usually cost just a little more than the price of a single à la carte main course. Restaurants at all price ranges offer them, and they represent the best value around. If you want to try many of the top restaurants, schedule some for noon-time meals if they offer table d'hôte menus at lunch. You'll get your best deal that way.

Keep in mind that the midday meal is called *dîner* (dinner) and the evening meal is *souper* (supper). An *entrée* is an appetizer, and a *plat principal* is a main course.

Insider websites featuring reviews and observations about the Montréal dining scene include **www.midnightpoutine.ca/food** and **www.endlessbanquet.blogspot.com.** Montréal Gazette restaurant critic Lesley Chesterman has a terrific blog at **www.lesleychesterman.com** about the city's food scene.

The restaurants recommended here are categorized by neighborhood and then by the cost of the main courses. Prices listed are for dinner unless otherwise indicated (lunch prices are usually lower) and do not include the cost of wine, tip, or the 5% federal tax and 7.88% provincial tax that are tacked on the restaurant bill. Montréalers consider 15% of the check (before taxes) to be a fair tip, increased only for exceptional food and service. In all, count on taxes and tip to add another 30% to the bill.

Make a reservation if you wish to dine at one of the city's top restaurants, especially on a weekend evening. A day or two in advance is sufficient for most places on most days. A hotel concierge can make the reservation, though nearly all restaurant hosts will switch immediately into English when they sense that a caller doesn't speak French.

Except in a handful of luxury restaurants, dress codes are all but nonexistent. But Montréalers are a fashionable lot and manage to look smart, even in casual clothes.

Centre Ville/Downtown

VERY EXPENSIVE

Europea ★★★ CONTEMPORARY FRENCH From the outside, Europea looks like many of the city's low-brow brownstone eateries. But once inside—after either ascending the spiral staircase or tucking into a cozy table in the cellar—you'll see why chef Jérôme Ferrer was named "Chef of the Year" by the Société des Chefs, Cuisiniers et Pâtissiers du Québec, in 2007, and why *Debeur,* the French-language guidebook for Québec gourmands, named Europea the 2010 restaurant of the year. An *amuse* might arrive in a three-segment dish with foam-topped nibbles, or as a demitasse of lobster-cream cappuccino with truffle shavings. For the main event, consider the roasted U10 scallops in beurre blanc emulsion. Gaps in the procession are short. Be sure to leave room for dessert, which comes in small, delectable servings. For the full treatment, order the 10-course *menu dégustation.* For a bargain, come at lunch, when the table d'hôte starts at C$24.

1227 rue de la Montagne (near rue Ste-Catherine). ✆ **514/398-9229.** www.europea.ca. Reservations strongly recommended. Main courses C$30–C$44; table d'hôte lunch C$24–C$30, dinner C$60; 10-course *menu dégustation* C$87. AE, MC, V. Tues–Fri noon–2pm, daily 6–10pm. Métro: Peel.

EXPENSIVE

Decca 77 ★★ CONTEMPORARY FRENCH The food is stunning, presented with both flair and perfection, yet it's difficult to see past this restaurant's drab setting in the lower corner of an office tower, even with the swaths of raspberry- and cappuccino-colored fabrics and high-design intent. Being steps from the Centre Bell presents a similar conundrum: handy location (with valet parking some nights—ask when reserving) but not atmospherically rewarding. But darn if the *pâté en croute* with marinated beets and asparagus milk emulsion wasn't divine. The same can be said of the bone-marrow soup, the smoked trout with sweet corn, and the olive cake for dessert. *Magnifique!* Prix-fixe options for both lunch and dinner are good value.

1077 rue Drummond (at Réné-Lévesque). © **514/934-1077.** www.decca77.com. Reservations recommended. Main courses C$24–C$42; table d'hôte lunch C$25, dinner C$35. AE, DC, MC, V. Mon–Fri 11:30am–2:30pm, Mon–Sat 5:30–10:30pm. Métro: Bonaventure or Lucien L'Aller.

Ferreira Café ★★★ SEAFOOD/PORTUGUESE You'll feel transported to Portugal at this popular downtown spot, where walls are embedded with a mosaic of broken cobalt and white ceramic plates. At lunch, customers are mostly dressed in business suits; at night, more festive diners come out to play. One highlight: *Cataplana,* which is the name of both a venerated Portuguese recipe and the hinged copper clamshell-style pot in which it is cooked. The dish is a fragrant stew of mussels, clams, potatoes, shrimp, *chouriço* sausage, and chunks of cod and salmon. A smaller late-night menu for C$24 is available from 10pm. As *Montréal Gazette* food critic Lesley Chesterman has noted, "Downtown Montréal may not be the coolest dining destination anymore, but at Ferreira on a sunny Friday night, I can think of few restaurants more impressive."

1446 rue Peel (near bd. de Maisonnueve). © **514/848-0988.** www.ferreiracafe.com. Reservations recommended. Main courses C$26–C$42. AE, MC, V. Mon–Fri 11:45am–3pm, Sun–Wed 5:30–11pm, Thurs–Sat 5:30pm–midnight. Closed Sun in winter. Métro: Peel.

MODERATE

Julien TRADITIONAL FRENCH A quiet downtown block in the financial district has been home to this relaxed Parisian-style bistro for years, hosting businesspeople at lunch and after-work cocktails, and mostly tourists from nearby hotels in the evening. Much of the year, diners have the option of sitting at tables on the heated terrace. The menu offers generous-sized portions without any pyrotechnics and features classics such as grilled steak in Béarnaise sauce or mussels with frites. There's always a vegetarian option, too. Service is friendly and attentive.

1191 av. Union (at bd. René-Lévesque). © **514/871-1581.** www.restaurantjulien.com. Reservations recommended. Main courses C$18–C$24. AE, MC, V. Mon–Fri 11:30am–3pm & 5–11pm, Sat 5:30–11pm. Métro: McGill.

Le Taj ★ INDIAN Still one of downtown's tastiest bargains. The price of the lunch buffet (C$14) has barely changed since the restaurant opened in 1985, and it's a real treat. The kitchen specializes in the Mughlai cuisine of the Indian subcontinent, and seasonings tend more toward the tangy than the incendiary. Dishes are perfumed with turmeric, saffron, ginger, cumin, mango powder, and *garam masala* (a spice combination that usually includes cloves, cardamom, and cinnamon). Vegetarians have ample choices, with the chickpea-based *channa masala* among the most complex. Evenings are quiet, and lunchtimes are busy but not hectic.

2077 rue Stanley (near rue Sherbrooke). © **514/845-9015.** www.restaurantletaj.com. Main courses C$10–C$27; lunch buffet C$14; table d'hôte dinner C$36. AE, DC, MC, V. Mon–Fri 11:30am–2:30pm & 5–10:30pm, Sat 5–11pm, Sun noon–2:30pm & 5–10:30pm. Métro: Peel.

m:brgr LIGHT FARE The hype would have it that m:brgr is *the* spot in the city for burgers, when really it's just fine, no better no worse. It's kitschy for sure, with options for what it candidly terms "crazy expensive toppings" such as black truffle carpaccio. The menu makes a big production about "building your own burger," but choosing cheese and toppings is not revolutionary. The basic burger itself is okay (be sure to specify how you want it cooked). The scene is festive and the staff friendly, and there's a big drink menu with mojitos and margaritas.

2025 rue Drummond. © **514/906-2747.** www.mbrgr.com. Main courses C$8.75–C$39 (most under C$15). AE, MC, V. Mon–Thurs 11:30am–11pm, Fri–Sat 11:30am–midnight, Sun noon–9pm. Métro: Peel.

INEXPENSIVE

Boustan LEBANESE In the middle of the hubbub among the bars and clubs on rue Crescent, this Lebanese eat-in or take-out spot is completely nondescript and consistently popular. It's full at 2pm (office workers) and again at 2am (late-night partiers), all jonesing for its famed falafel, *shish taouk,* or *shawarma* sandwiches.

2020A rue Crescent (at bd. de Maisonneuve). © **514/843-3576.** Most items cost less than C$10. MC, V. Mon–Sat 11am–4am, Sun 5pm–4am. Métro: Peel.

Java U LIGHT FARE A small local chain. This particular outpost is right across from the McGill campus, ensuring that you'll likely be next to college kids tapping away on MacBooks or looking over music scores. Options are fresh and healthy: sandwiches, quiche, fresh fruit. The atmosphere is on the sophisticated side for what's essentially fast food. It's open daily from at least 8am to at least 9pm.

626 rue Sherbrooke (at av. Union). © **514/286-1991.** www.java-u.com. Most items cost less than C$8. AE, MC, V. Mon–Fri 7am–9pm, Sat & Sun 8am–10pm. Métro: McGill.

Le Commensal VEGETARIAN Vegetarian fare is presented buffet-style here, and you pay the cashier by the weight of your plate—about C$8 for an ample portion (the restaurant has a "maximum price or less!" policy of C$13 at lunchtime and $16 in the evening). Dishes include quinoa, garbanzo curry, several types of salads, a large variety of hot dishes, tofu with ginger sauce, and so on. Even avowed meat eaters are likely to not feel deprived. Beer and wine are available, too. With white tablecloths and a second-floor location overlooking rue Ste-Catherine, this is a satisfying spot to keep in mind when you're downtown. There's another branch at 1720 rue St-Denis (© **514/845-2627**).

1204 av. McGill College (at rue Ste-Catherine). © **514/871-1480.** www.commensal.com. Most meals cost less than C$10. A, MC, V. Daily 11:30am–10pm. Métro: McGill.

Vieux-Montreal

VERY EXPENSIVE

Toqué! ★★★ CONTEMPORARY FRENCH Toqué! is the gem that single-handedly raised the entire city's gastronomic expectations. A meal here has long been obligatory for anyone who admires superb, dazzlingly presented food. "Post-nouvelle" might be an apt description for chef Normand Laprise's creations. A short menu and top-of-the-bin ingredients, some of them rarely seen together—for example, cauliflower soup with foie gras shavings and milk foam, or smoked suckling pig cheek with maple-water sponge toffee—ensure a unique tasting experience. The decor is 1960s loungey, with bulbous lamps hanging from the ceiling and low-back chairs. In 2010, Laprise opened a moderately-priced restaurant, **Brasserie T** (1425 rue Jeanne-Mance, © **514/282-0808,** www.brasserie-t.com) in front of Place des Arts and the Musée d'Art Contemporain.

900 Place Jean-Paul-Riopelle (at rue St-Antoine). © **514/499-2084.** www.restaurant-toque.com. Reservations required. Main courses C$40–C$44; tasting menu C$92. AE, DC, MC, V. Tues–Sat 5:30–10:30pm. Métro: Square-Victoria.

EXPENSIVE

Bonaparte ★ TRADITIONAL FRENCH In a city brimming with accomplished French restaurants, this is a personal favorite. The dining rooms run through the ground floors of two old row houses, with rich decorative details suggestive of the namesake's era. Adroit service is provided by schooled pros who manage to be knowledgeable without being stuffy. Highlights have included snails and oyster mushrooms in phyllo dough, Dover sole filet with fresh herbs, and mushroom ravioli seasoned with fresh sage. The seven-course tasting menu, reasonably priced at C$62, lets you try out a large variety of the chef's special creations. Lunches cater to an upscale business crowd, and the restaurant offers an early evening menu for theatergoers. The clean and bright 30-room **Auberge Bonaparte** (p. 226) is upstairs.

447 rue St-François-Xavier (north of rue St-Paul). ✆ **514/844-4368.** www.bonaparte.com. Main courses C$23–C$37; table d'hôte lunch C$16–C$23, dinner C$29; 7-course tasting menu C$62. AE, DC, MC, V. Mon–Fri noon–2:30pm, daily 5:30–10:30pm. Métro: Place d'Armes.

Chez l'Epicier ★ CONTEMPORARY QUEBECOIS The self-assuredness of this bright corner eatery beckons from the street, where the menu, handwritten on a blackboard (as well as *produits du terroir,* developed by the chef and sold to go), can be glimpsed through large, arched windows. It's not a restaurant you stumble into; it draws you in. You'll find creative interpretations of the pork chop, served over a mushroom tart with shoestring sweet potatoes in a molasses emulsion, or crispy-skinned trout with lobster-infused risotto. Global ingredients and techniques are part of the mix, as are witty surprises, like a chocolate club sandwich with pineapple fries for dessert. Dinner is on the steep side, but lunch can be had for under C$30, tip included.

311 rue St-Paul est (at rue St-Claude). ✆ **514/878-2232.** www.chezlepicier.com. Main courses C$27–C$40; table d'hôte lunch C$15–C$25; 7-course tasting menu C$80. AE, MC, V. Thurs & Fri 11:30am–2pm, daily 5:30–10pm. Métro: Champ-de-Mars.

DNA ★★ CONTEMPORARY QUEBECOIS Open since 2008, DNA suffuses concept dining with affable, expert service. Glass slabs divide the restaurant into nooks that allow the excitement of a packed house to bubble over without sacrificing intimacy or views of the building's architectural elements. Wondering about the origin of the fiddleheads or nettles? Servers will carry a basket of fresh and locally-grown ingredients to your table. This gesture adds charm to an evening out and can prompt gastronomic dialogue—so don't hesitate to ask questions. Since the chef buys whole animals, veal-heart tartar mixed with foie gras is always on the menu, as are inventive recipes with ingredients like pork brain. The wine list, which earned a 2009 *Wine Spectator* award of excellence, overflows with Canadian options.

355 rue Marguerite D'Youville (at rue St-Pierre). ✆ **514/287-3362.** www.dnarestaurant.com. Main courses C$24–C$36; table d'hôte lunch C$20; 5-course tasting menu C$85. AE, MC, V. Tues–Fri 11:30am–2:30pm, Tues–Sat 6–10:30pm. Métro: Square Victoria.

Le Club Chasse et Pêche ★ CONTEMPORARY QUEBECOIS The name "Hunting and Fishing Club" doesn't suggest fine dining, but here *chasse et pêche* more accurately means "new-school surf and turf." The contrast is apparent the moment you open the upholstered leather door—slate-blue stucco walls and stuffed seating feel both retro and mod, cozy and sleek. The food follows suit:

Chilled sweet pea soup is garnished with fried oysters; a boar chop is drizzled with corn purée. The restaurant's website includes a quirky blog of reviews, YouTube films, and other stuff the staff likes, and hints at the establishment's loyal, hip following.

423 rue St-Claude (btw. rue St-Paul & rue Notre-Dame). © **514/861-1112.** www.leclubchasseetpeche.com. Reservations recommended. Main courses C$29–C$35. AE, MC, V. May–Sept daily 11:30am–2pm (lunch served in garden of nearby Musée du Château Ramezay); year-round Tues–Sat 6–10:30pm. Métro: Champ-de-Mars.

Le Garde Manger SEAFOOD From the dark roadhouse decor to the rowdy slip of a bar, this giddy resto is a smackdown to its Vieux-Montréal neighbors. The menu changes nightly, but options might include spicy jerk snow crab, lobster *poutine,* or beef short ribs over arugula. You'll need a lead stomach to survive a whole portion of the signature dessert, a fried Mars bar, unless deafening rock music helps you digest. There's no sign outside, just a blank, white cube that glows pink when there's action inside. If the restaurant looks closed, they could be shooting episodes of "Chuck's Day Off" for Canadian Food Network, a reality show starring owner Chuck Hughes.

408 rue St-François-Xavier (north of rue St-Paul). © **514/678-5044.** Reservations recommended. Main courses C$25–C$35. AE, MC, V. Tues–Sun 6–11pm; bar open until 3am. Métro: Place d'Armes.

Le Local ★★ CONTEMPORARY FRENCH Whereas many of its counterparts have exquisite food but predictably styled atmosphere, or vice versa, Le Local musters originality in both arenas. The kitchen breathes new life into standards like surf and turf (theirs has BBQ ribs), and the concrete, wood, and glass interior feels remarkably current. Chef Charles-Emmanuel Pariseau trained locally before opening these doors in 2008, and sommelier Elyse Lambert has received regional and national recognition for her skills. The *chiogga* beet salad with bacon, tomatoes, and truffle oil stood out as a starter; so, too, did the main course of a puff pastry tart with roasted scallops, chorizo, and blood pudding with pan-seared foie gras. But truly, you can roam anywhere on the menu with great satisfaction. For a more casual night out or to sample highlights without the steep check, check out the bar and its lower-priced offerings.

740 rue William (at rue Prince). © **514/397-7737.** www.resto-lelocal.com. Reservations recommended. Main courses C$18–C$35; bar menu C$5–C$14. MC, V. Mon–Fri 11:30am–midnight, Sat 5:30pm–midnight, Sun 5:30–11:30pm. Métro: Square Victoria.

Modavie ★ MEDITERRANEAN A highly visible location directly on the main pedestrian street no doubt helps keep this restaurant and wine bar full, but the management leaves little to chance. Live jazz is presented nightly during the early evening, making this a comfortable place for singles, as well as couples and groups. On summer nights, candles flicker in river breezes that flow in through the tall front and side windows, while ceiling fans twirl gently overhead. A handsome horseshoe-shaped bar faces walls stacked with bottles of wine and single-malt scotches. Food is put together well and generously portioned. Lamb is the house specialty and comes in five iterations, or try wild boar chop, tiger shrimp in Grand Marnier sauce, or ravioli stuffed with goat cheese in a roasted pepper sauce.

1 rue St-Paul ouest (corner of rue St-Laurent). © **514/287-9582.** www.modavie.com. Reservations recommended. Main courses C$16–C$49; table d'hôte lunch C$13–C$16, dinner C$27–C$31. AE, MC, V. Sun–Thurs 11:30am–10pm, Fri & Sat 11:30am–11pm. Métro: Place d'Armes.

MODERATE

Boris Bistro ★★ BISTRO Boris attracts a smartly-dressed crowd of business folk, couples, and groups. It does big volume, but service is fast and efficient. The outdoor space here is especially pretty: In warm months, the restaurant opens its side doors to what feels like an adjacent vacant lot (the facade of a building that once stood here remains at one end), but leafy trees, large umbrellas, and subtle lighting make it an oasis. Some standout menu options include meltingly buttery cod served over a basil-citrus risotto; an escargot "lasagna" layered in large potato chips; and a sublime sage risotto with pine nut emulsion. French fries cooked in duck fat are a signature dish, and there's a choice of about a half-dozen *fromages du terroir,* local cheeses, along with sweet treats, to close a meal. A fun evening option allows you to pick three, four, or five appetizers for a fixed price.

465 rue McGill (1 block south of rue Notre-Dame). ✆ **514/848-9575.** www.borisbistro.com. Main courses C$16–C$23; table d'hôte of 3, 4, or 5 appetizers C$23, C$29, or C$35. AE, MC, V. Summer Mon–Fri 11:30am–11pm, Sat & Sun noon–11pm; winter Mon–Fri 11:30am–2pm, Tues–Fri 5–9pm, Sat 6–9pm. Métro: Square-Victoria.

Gandhi ★ INDIAN Classy but inexpensive enough to accommodate student and retiree budgets, Gandhi got so busy that the owners expanded into the adjacent building a few years ago, doubling their seating space. The contiguous dining rooms are bright, and service is brisk but polite. Cooking is mostly to order and arrives fresh from the pot, pan, or oven. Biriyani and curry specialties are delicate and subtle, but the kitchen will oblige requests for spicier levels. Tandoori duck and lamb and chicken *tikka* are popular, and vegetarian dishes fill a large section of the card.

230 rue St-Paul ouest (near rue St-Nicolas). ✆ **514/845-5866.** www.restaurantgandhi.com. Main courses C$12–C$27; table d'hôte lunch C$23–C$27. AE, MC, V. Mon–Fri noon–2:30pm, daily 5:30–10:30pm. Métro: Place d'Armes.

Vieux-Port Steakhouse STEAK There are a couple good options for steak clustered on rue St-Paul, including **Le Steak Frites** (12 rue St-Paul ouest; ✆ **514/842-0972;** www.steakfrites.ca) and **The Keg Steakhouse & Bar** (25 St-Paul est; ✆ **514/871-9093;** www.kegsteakhouse.com). But it's hard to go wrong at Vieux-Port Steakhouse. For one thing, you can nearly always get a spot: If all the tables in the pleasant first floor corner room overlooking St-Paul are full, there are two more floors, plus a 300-seat back terrace in summer, for a capacity of *1,200*. With that kind of space, the restaurant packs in large groups, as well as solo diners. Another draw are the value deals, like the C$13 table d'hôte lunch of soup or salad, an appetizer, a main course, and coffee (dessert just C$2 extra). The food is executed well, and even with the heavy volume, the atmosphere mixes "proper" and "casual" in good balance.

39 rue St-Paul est (at rue St-Gabriel). ✆ **514/866-3175.** www.vieuxportsteakhouse.com. Main courses C$16–C$41; table d'hôte lunch $13, dinner C$20–C$38. AE, MC, V. Daily 11:30am–10pm. Métro: Place d'Armes.

INEXPENSIVE

Cluny ArtBar LIGHT FARE Artists and high-tech businesses have repopulated the loft-and-factory district west of avenue McGill, at the edge of Vieux-Montréal, though the streets are still very quiet here. Among the pioneers is the Darling Foundry, an avant-garde exhibition space in a vast, raw, former industrial space. Room is provided for Cluny, which serves coffee, croissants, and lunch, with options such as stuffed leg of lamb, vegetarian antipasto, and macaroni and cheese. Though it's called a bar, it's open only during daylight hours, when the sun streams in through mammoth industrial windows. Still, wine by the glass and other adult beverages are available. Tables are topped with recycled bowling alley floors, just so you know.

257 rue Prince (near rue William). ✆ **514/866-1213.** www.fonderiedarling.org/louer_e/cluny.html. Main courses C$4–C$19. AE, MC, V. Mon–Fri 8am–5pm. Métro: Square Victoria.

Eggspectation ☺ BREAKFAST/BRUNCH Let the punny-funny name deter you and you'll miss a meal that may constitute one of your fondest food memories of Montréal, especially if you love big breakfasts. The atmosphere and food here are funky and creative, and prices are fair for the large portions. What's more, the kitchen knows how to deal with volume and turns out good meals in nearly lightning speed, even on packed weekend mornings. There are eight variations of eggs Benedict alone, as well as sandwiches, burgers, and pasta options. Dishes are tagged with names like "Eggiliration" and "Oy Vegg." This is a chain ("constantly eggspanding," as they put it), with eight locations in Greater Montréal.

201 rue St-Jacques ouest (at rue St-François-Xavier). ✆ **514/282-0119.** www.eggspectation.ca. Most items cost less than C$12. AE, MC, V. Mon–Fri 6am–3pm, Sat & Sun 7am–4pm. Métro: Place d'Armes.

Olive et Gourmando ★ BAKERY/LIGHT FARE A local favorite, this started out as an earthy bakery painted in reds, pinks, and gold curlicues, then added table service and transformed itself into a full-fledged healthy-foods cafe with extraordinary baked goods. Sample the croissants, scones, biscuits, brioche, or exemplary "morning glory muffin" (featuring shaved carrot and chunks of pineapple). As for lunch, come early or late—it gets jammed. Interesting sandwich compositions include smoked trout with capers, sun-dried tomatoes, spinach, and herbed cream cheese on grilled bread; or caramelized onions, goat cheese, and homemade ketchup on panini. The only pity is that this eminently appealing spot is not open Sunday, Monday, or evenings.

351 rue St-Paul ouest (at rue St-Pierre). ✆ **514/350-1083.** www.oliveetgourmando.com. Most items cost less than C$10. No credit cards. Tues–Sat 8am–6pm. Métro: Square-Victoria.

Stash Café POLISH At this site for more than 30 years, this *restauracja polska* continues to draw throngs of enthusiastic returnees for its abundant offerings and low prices. The interior is composed of brick-and-stone walls, red-satin-dome hanging lamps, wood refractory tables, and pews salvaged from an old convent. Roast wild boar has long been featured, along with *bigos* (a cabbage-and-meat stew) and *pierogis* (dumplings stuffed with meat, cheese, or cabbage)—as to be expected in a Polish restaurant. Filling options and sides include potato pancakes and borscht with sour cream. A jolly tone prevails, with animated patrons and such menu admonitions as "anything tastes better with wodka, even wodka."

200 rue St-Paul ouest (at rue St-François-Xavier). ✆ **514/845-6611.** www.stashcafe.com. Main courses C$11–C$17; table d'hôte dinner C$29–C$39. AE, DISC, DC, MC, V. Mon–Fri 11:30am–10pm, Sat & Sun noon–10pm. Métro: Place d'Armes.

Plateau Mont-Royal

VERY EXPENSIVE

Moishes STEAKHOUSE Those who care to spend serious money for a slab of beef should bring their platinum cards here. Positioned as a home for delicious classics, the menu features T-bones, chopped liver, and herring in cream sauce. Patrons include the trim new breed of up-and-coming executives (who are likely to go for the chicken teriyaki or arctic char), as well as those members of the older generation who didn't know about triglycerides until it was too late. The wine list is substantial, and the restaurant offers tasting evenings.

3961 bd. St-Laurent (north of rue Prince Arthur). ✆ **514/845-3509.** www.moishes.ca. Reservations recommended. Main courses C$28–C$54. AE, DC, MC, V. Mon–Fri 5:30–11pm, Sat & Sun 5–11pm. Métro: Sherbrooke.

EXPENSIVE

Au Pied de Cochon ★★ QUEBECOIS Packed to the walls 6 nights per week, this Plateau restaurant is a cult favorite, and I've drunk the Kool-Aid, too. As the name—which means "the pig's foot"—suggests, the menu here is mostly about slabs of meat, especially pork. The PDC's Cut, weighing in at more than a pound, is emblematic. Meats are roasted to the point of falling off the bone in a brick oven, and there's a grand selection of seafood, from oysters to lobster to soft-shell crab. Chef Martin Picard gets particularly clever with one pervasive product: foie gras. It comes in as many as 10 combinations, including as a tart, with *poutine,* and in a goofy creation called Duck in a Can which does, indeed, come to the table with a can opener. When you feel like another bite will send you into a cholesterol-induced coma, sugar pie is the only fitting finish.

536 rue Duluth est (near rue St-Hubert). ✆ **514/281-1114.** www.restaurantaupieddecochon.ca. Reservations strongly recommended. Main courses C$17–C$51. AE, MC, V. Tues–Sun 5pm–midnight. Métro: Sherbrooke.

Maestro S.V.P. SEAFOOD Smaller and more relaxed than other restaurants in the 2 blocks of the Main north of Sherbrooke, the highlight of this storefront bistro is its oysters—get them raw, baked, or in a vodka shooter. The staff is happy to help you pick a few to taste: the PEI Raspberry Point, for instance, is particularly salty when contrasted with the smooth and creamy BC Kusshi (who knew?). The Maestro Platter, an extravagant medley of clams, mussels, calamari, a half-lobster, *and* king crab, can be shared by the table. A 40-item tapas menu available Tuesday through Friday from 11am until 5pm, as well as all night on Tuesday and Wednesday, makes this a fun spot to kick off an evening or to break for shrimp cocktail and a martini. An all-you-can-eat mussel special is available on Sunday and Monday nights for C$13 per person.

3615 bd. St-Laurent (at rue Prince Arthur). ✆ **514/842-6447.** www.maestrosvp.com. Reservations recommended. Main courses C$20–C$43. AE, DC, MC, V. Mon 5–10pm, Tues & Wed 11am–10pm, Thurs & Fri 11am–11pm, Sat 4pm–midnight, Sun 4–10pm. Métro: Sherbrooke.

MODERATE

L'Express ★ BISTRO No obvious sign announces L'Express, with its name only spelled out discreetly in white tiles in the sidewalk. There's no need to call attention to itself, since *tout* Montréal knows exactly where this most classic of Parisian-style bistros is. Eternally busy and open until 3am, the bistro's atmosphere hits all the right notes, from checkered floor to high ceiling to mirrored walls. Popular dishes include the ravioli *maison* (round pasta pockets filled with a flavorful mixture of beef, pork, and veal), the *soupe de poisson,* and the *croque-monsieur*—and kids will love the crepes. Though reservations are often necessary for tables, single diners and walk-ins can often find a seat at the zinc-topped bar, where full meals also are served. Service is usually good, although be prepared for long waits during brunch hours.

3927 rue St-Denis (just north of rue Roy). ✆ **514/845-5333.** Reservations recommended. Main courses C$10–C$23. AE, DC, MC, V. Daily 8am–3am. Métro: Sherbrooke.

Pintxo ★★ SPANISH Pronounced "Peent-choo," the Basque word for tapas, this jovial resto draws from the Spanish Basque tradition, offering exquisitely composed dishes at fair prices in pleasant surroundings. Cooking happens in an open kitchen in a room with antique wood floors and brick walls. Each *pintxo* is true tapa size, only three or four bites, so order recklessly. Some of our favorites include the braised beef cheek, the seared foie gras on a bed of lentils, and the white asparagus with Serrano ham and fried onion cut so fine it looks like tinsel. Dinners aren't confined to meals composed solely of tapas presented on 4-inch tiles or slates, although that isn't a bad way to go. For C$30, the *menu dégustation* provides four chef's-choice *pintxos* and a main dish of your choice, in a considerably larger proportion.

256 rue Roy est (2 blocks west of St-Denis). ✆ **514/844-0222.** www.pintxo.ca. Main courses C$14–C$21; tapas C$6 or less; *menu dégustation* C$30. MC, V. Wed–Fri noon–2pm, Mon–Sat 6–11pm, Sun 6–10pm. Métro: Sherbrooke.

INEXPENSIVE

Chez Schwartz Charcuterie Hébraïque de Montréal ★ DELI French-first language laws turned the name of this old-time delicatessen into a linguistic mouthful, but it's still known simply as Schwartz's to its ardent fans. Many are convinced it's the only place to indulge in the guilty treat of *viande fumée*—a kind of brisket that's called, simply, smoked meat. Housed in a long, narrow storefront, with a lunch counter, and simple tables and chairs crammed impossibly close to each other, this is as nondescript a culinary landmark as you'll find. Any empty seat is up for grabs. Sandwich plates come heaped with smoked meat and piles of rye bread. Most people also order sides of fries and mammoth garlicky pickles. There are a handful of alternative edibles, but leafy green vegetables aren't among them. Schwartz's has no liquor license, but it's open late. It now has a take-out window, opened in 2008 in honor of its 80th birthday.

3895 bd. St-Laurent (just north of rue Roy). ✆ **514/842-4813.** www.schwartzsdeli.com. Sandwiches & meat plates C$5.50–C$17. No credit cards. Sun–Thurs 8am–12:30am, Fri 8am–1:30am, Sat 8am–2:30am. Métro: Sherbrooke.

La Banquise ☺ LIGHT FARE Open 24 hours a day in the heart of the Plateau on Parc La Fontaine's north end, this friendly, funky, hippie-meets-hipster diner is a city landmark for its *poutine:* La Banquise offers some two dozen variations on the standard French fries with gravy and cheese curds, with add-ons ranging from smoked sausage to hot peppers to smoked meat to bacon. "Regular" size is huge and enough for two. Also on the menu are steamed hot dogs ("steamies") served with hot cabbage coleslaw, burgers, omelets, and club sandwiches. Everything is best washed down with a local brew like Belle Gueule or Boréale. In warm weather, there's an outside terrace.

994 rue Rachel est (near rue Boyer). ✆ **514/525-2415.** www.restolabanquise.com. *Poutine* plates C$6.50–C$9.50; most other items less than C$11. No credit cards. Daily 24-hr. Métro: Mont-Royal.

POUTINE, smoked meat & OTHER COMFORT FOODS

While you're in Montréal, indulge in at least a couple of Québec staples. Though you'll find them dolled up on some menus, these are generally thought of as the region's basic comfort foods:

- ***Poutine:*** French fries doused with gravy and cheese curds. Its profile has risen outside of the province in recent years, and a four-page essay in *The New Yorker* magazine in 2009 posited that the "national joke" may be becoming a national dish. It's a perfect symbol, wrote Calvin Trillin, "for a country that prides itself on lumpy multiculturalism—whatever impact it has on another point of pride, the national health-care system."
- **Smoked meat:** A maddeningly tasty sandwich component particular to Montréal whose taste is similar to pastrami and corned beef.
- ***Tourtière:*** A meat pie of spiced ground pork, often served with tomato chutney.
- ***Queues de Castor:*** A deep-fried pastry the size of a man's footprint served with melted chocolate or cinnamon. The name means "beaver tails."
- ***Tarte au sucre:*** Maple-sugar pie, like pecan pie without the pecans.

Mile End/Avenue Laurier

EXPENSIVE

Leméac ★ BISTRO On a recent Saturday night, there was a jovial din among the well-heeled crowd at this bustling, sprightly restaurant on the far western end of the avenue-Laurier scene. With a long, tin-topped bar along one side, well-spaced tables, and a crew of cheerful wait-staff, the atmosphere is Parisian-elegant. There's a serious wine list, with over 350 options. The food is different—but not startlingly so—and is served in an atmosphere that invites lingering. Weekend brunch is popular, and on a spring morning, a plate of *oeufs pochés, blinis, saumen fumé, et caviar d'Espagne*, served on a street-level terrace, is an affordable slice of decadence. Save room for the homemade donuts, too. Or come late at night: a C$22 appetizer-plus-main menu kicks in at 10pm.

1045 av. Laurier ouest (corner of av. Durocher). ✆ **514/270-0999.** www.restaurantlemeac.com. Reservations recommended. Main courses C$19–C$38; late-night menu C$22; weekend brunch C$7.50–C$16. AE, DC, MC, V. Mon–Fri noon–midnight, Sat & Sun 10am–midnight. Métro: Laurier.

MODERATE

Chao Phraya ☺ THAI Still a contender for the title of best Thai in town, Chao Phraya has a panache that sets it a few notches above most of its rivals, and it gets packed most evenings (reserve or arrive early). Named for a river in Thailand, Chao Phraya brightens its corner of the fashionable Laurier Avenue with white table linens, and the atmosphere is warm and cozy. While the peanut sauce is heavy-duty—it's a tasty combo that includes crispy spinach with tofu—the red curry is a lovely, lighter option. Sides of sticky rice come in small woven baskets. One to three hot-pepper symbols grade hotness, and one or two peppers are fine for milder palates. There is a good selection of vegetarian options on the 12-page menu.

50 av. Laurier ouest (1 block west of bd. St-Laurent). ✆ **514/272-5339.** www.chao-phraya.com. Reservations recommended. Main courses C$12–C$20. AE, DC, MC, V. Thurs–Sat 5–11pm; Sun, Tues & Wed 5–10pm. Métro: Laurier.

INEXPENSIVE

Aux Vivres ★ ☺ VEGAN In business since 1997, this bright restaurant with white Formica tables, raw blonde walls, and pink Chinese lanterns hums with activity at all hours of the day. A large menu includes bowls of chili with guacamole, and bok choy with grilled tofu and peanut sauce. Other options include salads, sandwiches, desserts, and a daily chef's special. All foods are vegan, all vegetables are organic, and all tofu and tempeh are local and organic. In addition to inside tables, there is a juice bar off to one side and a back terrace.

4631 bd. St-Laurent (north of av. du Mont-Royal). ✆ **514/842-3479.** Most items less than C$12. No credit cards. Daily 11am–11pm. Métro: Mont-Royal.

Fairmont Bagel ★ BAKERY Bagels in these parts of North America are thinner, smaller, and crustier than the cottony monsters found south of the border. Here, they're hand-rolled, twist-flipped into circles, and baked in big wood-fired ovens right on the premises. Fairmont was founded in 1919 and now offers 20 types, including trendy options like muesli and (shudder) blueberry, but why opt for oddball tastes when you can get a perfect sesame version? A teeny shop, Fairmont sells its bagels and accoutrements (such as lox and cream cheese) to go only. It's open 24 hours a day, 7 days a week—even on Jewish holidays.

74 av. Fairmont ouest (near rue St-Urbain). ✆ **514/272-0667.** www.fairmountbagel.com. Most bagels less than C$1. No credit cards. Daily 24-hr. Métro: Laurier.

Wilensky Light Lunch DINER Wilensky's has been a Montréal tradition since 1932 and has its share of regular pilgrims nostalgic for its grilled-meat sandwiches, low prices, curt service, and utter lack of decor. Ambience can best be described as Early Jewish Immigrant. There are nine counter stools, no tables. The house special is grilled salami and bologna, with mustard, thrown on a bun and squashed on a grill, and never, for whatever reason, cut in two. You can wash it down with an egg cream or Cherry Coke jerked from the rank of syrups—this place has drinks typical of the old-time soda fountain that it still is. Enter Wilensky's to take a step back in time; we're talking tradition here, not cuisine.

34 rue Fairmount ouest (1 block west of bd. St-Laurent). ✆ **514/271-0247.** All items less than C$5. No credit cards. Mon–Fri 9am–4pm. Métro: Laurier.

Outer Districts

EXPENSIVE

Joe Beef ★ SEAFOOD/STEAK In 2005, a group of folks who used to run glamorous resto-clubs in downtown Montréal opened this 28-seat steaks-n-seafood joint far west of Vieux-Montréal, on a bland street near Atwater Market. The atmosphere is moneyed roadhouse, with diners elbow to elbow. In 2007 and 2008, the owners added two adjacent restaurants—**Liverpool House** (at no. 2501), an Italian gastropub, and **McKiernan** (no. 2485), a luncheonette (see below)—and suddenly the block was a go-to destination for people serious about food. Mains often include suckling pig, cabbage stuffed with veal cheeks, and *steak au poivre*.

2491 rue Notre-Dame ouest (near rue Vinet). ✆ **514/935-6504.** www.joebeef.com. Reservations required. Main courses C$21–C$50. MC, V. Tues–Sat 6:30pm–"close." Métro: Lionel-Groulx.

INEXPENSIVE

McKiernan DINER Even the tragically hip must eat, and when they do, they head to the McKiernan luncheonette and wine bar, where a giant bait lure provides the decor and the wine chills in a stainless steel tub. This cramped (12-seat) outcropping by the proprietors of **Joe Beef** (above) may feel inhospitable to persons not dressed like rock stars (and the waitstaff don't do much to warm up the welcome), but the food is inventive and reasonably priced. The *poulet rôti tikka* sandwich with two chutneys married all the right flavors and textures. Even the asparagus salad, with shaved pecorino and a hard-boiled egg, tasted like an extreme version of itself, like veggies pulled fresh from the garden. McKiernan is especially popular for Saturday brunch.

2485 rue Notre-Dame ouest (near rue Vinet). ✆ **514/759-6677.** Most items less than C$13. MC, V. Tues–Sat 11am–3pm, Wed–Sat 6:30pm–"close." Métro: Lionel-Groulx.

SEEING THE SIGHTS

Montréal offers a feast of choices, able to satisfy the desires of both physically active and culturally curious visitors. Walk up the city's small mountain, Mont-Royal, in the middle of the city; cycle for miles beside 19th-century warehouses and locks on the Lachine Canal; take in artworks and ephemera at museums and historic buildings; party until dawn on rue Crescent and The Main; or soak up the concrete and spiritual results of some 400 years of conquest and immigration: It's all here for the taking.

Montréal has an efficient Métro system, a logical street grid, wide boulevards, a vehicle-free underground city, and an innovative bike-share program that all aid in the swift, largely uncomplicated movement of people from place to place.

For families, few cities assure children will have as good a time as this one does. There are riverboat rides, Olympic Park and the fascinating Biodôme, the Centre des Sciences de Montréal by the water, and magical circus performances by the many troupes that come through this circus-centric city. We've flagged attractions that are recommended for children with the ☺ icon.

Centre Ville/Downtown & Parc Mont-Royal

L'Oratoire St-Joseph ★ This huge Catholic church—dominating Mont-Royal's north slope—is seen by some as inspiring, by others as forbidding. It's Montréal's highest point, with an enormous dome 97m (318 ft.) high. Consecrated as a basilica in 2004, it came into being through the efforts of Brother André, a lay brother in the Holy Cross order who earned a reputation as a healer. By the time he had built a small wooden chapel in 1904 on the mountain, he was said to have performed hundreds of cures. His powers attracted supplicants from great distances, and he performed his work until his death in 1937. His dream of building a shrine to honor St. Joseph, patron saint of Canada, became a completed reality in 1967. In 1982, he was beatified by the pope—a status one step below sainthood—and on October 17, 2010, he earned the distinction of sainthood, too. Montréalers and pilgrims gathered in the Olympic Stadium at 4am to celebrate while the ceremony unfolded in Rome. A new exhibit is being planned to commemorate this honor.

The church is largely Italian Renaissance in style, its giant copper dome recalling the shape of the Duomo in Florence, but of greater size and lesser grace. Inside is a sanctuary and exhibit that displays Brother André's actual heart in a formalin-filled urn. His original wooden chapel, with its tiny bedroom, is on the grounds and open to the public. Two million pilgrims visit annually, many of whom seek intercession from St. Joseph and Brother André by climbing the middle set of 99 steps on their knees. The 56-bell carillon plays Wednesday to Friday at noon and 3pm, and Saturday and Sunday at 12:15 and 2:30pm. Also on site is an oratory museum featuring 264 nativity scenes from 111 countries.

A modest 14-room hostel on the grounds is called the **Jean XXIII Pavilion.** Single rooms with shared bathroom start at C$50 and include breakfast. Details are at www.saint-joseph.org/en_1060_index.php.

In 2002, the oratory embarked on a 10-year renovation project to improve overall accessibility for the ever-increasing number of visitors. Most recent completions include an elevator to the basilica and a new vehicle entrance. In coming years, visitors will have unprecedented 360-degree views of Montréal from the basilica's dome.

3800 chemin Queen Mary (on the north slope of Mont-Royal). ✆ **877/672-8647** or 514/733-8211. www.saint-joseph.org. Free admission to most sights, donations requested; oratory museum C$4 adults, C$3 seniors & students, C$2 children 6–17. Crypt & votive chapel daily 6am–9:30pm; basilica & exhibition on Brother André daily 7am–9pm; oratory museum Tues–Sun 10am–4:30pm. C$5 suggested donation for parking. Métro: Côtes-des-Neiges or Snowdon. Bus: 165 or 51.

Musée d'Art Contemporain de Montréal Montréal's Museum of Contemporary Art is the country's only museum devoted exclusively to the avant-garde. Its focus is works created since 1939, and much of the permanent collection is by Québécois artists such as Jean-Paul Riopelle (1923–2002) and Betty Goodwin (1923–2008). Also represented are international artists Richard Serra (1939–), Bruce Nauman (1941–), Sam Taylor-Wood (1967–), and Nan Goldin (1953–). No single style prevails, so expect to see installations, video displays, and examples of pop, op, and abstract expressionism. On Friday Nocturnes—the first Friday of most months—the museum stays open until 9pm with live music, bar service, and tours of the exhibition galleries. A mélange of fun videos are online at www.youtube.com/macmvideos. The museum's glass-walled restaurant, **La Rotonde,** has a summer dining terrace.

185 rue Ste-Catherine ouest. ✆ **514/847-6226.** www.macm.org. Admission C$10 adults, C$8 seniors, C$6 students, free for children 11 & under; free admission Wed 6–9pm. Tues & Thurs–Sun 11am–6pm, Wed & Friday Nocturnes 11am–9pm. Métro: Place des Arts.

Musée des Beaux-Arts ★★★ Montréal's grand Museum of Fine Arts, the city's most prominent museum, is made up of several buildings, including the original neoclassical pavilion on the north side of Sherbrooke, a striking annex built in 1991 directly across the street, and (new in 2011) the adjacent Erskine and American Church, which features the new pavilion of Canadian art behind it. The 1894 church is a designated National Historic Site and will be a destination in its own right, with 20 stained-glass windows created by Louis Comfort Tiffany (1848–1933). The entire complex will be linked through underground galleries.

Art on display is dramatically mounted, carefully lit, and diligently explained in both French and English. In addition to Canadian and international contemporary art created after 1960, the museum features European painting, sculpture, and decorative art from the Middle Ages to the 19th century. Among the collection's gems are paintings by Bruegel (ca. 1525–1569), El Greco (1541–1614), and Hogarth (1697–1764)—and illustrative, if not world-class, works by Renoir (1841–1919), Monet (1840–1926), Cézanne (1839–1906), and Picasso (1881–1973).

Temporary exhibitions can be dazzling. Recent shows have focused on the 40-year career of fashion designer Yves Saint Laurent (1936–2008) and the music of Miles Davis (1926-1991). The life-sized terracotta soldiers of Chinese Emperor Qin will be on display in winter 2011.

The museum's street-level store sells an impressive selection of quality books, games, and folk art. The museum's quite good restaurant, **Café des Beaux-Arts,** is above the store and has an entrance adjacent to the boutique.

1339–1380 rue Sherbrooke ouest (at rue Crescent). © **514/285-2000.** www.mmfa.qc.ca. Free admission to the permanent collection; donations accepted. Admission to temporary exhibitions C$15 adults, C$10 seniors (Wed 5–8:30pm C$7.50 adults & seniors), C$7.50 students, free for children 12 & under; C$30 families (1 adult & 3 children 16 & under, or 2 adults & 2 children 16 & under; C$15 families Wed 5–8:30pm). Tues 11am–5pm, Wed–Fri 11am–9pm, Sat & Sun 10am–5pm. Métro: Guy-Corcordia.

Musée McCord ★ The permanent exhibition "Simply Montréal: Glimpses of a Unique History" justifies a trip here all on its own. The show steeps visitors in what city life was like over the centuries, and even includes a substantial section about how Montréal handles the massive amounts of snow and ice it receives each year. Associated with McGill University, McCord showcases the eclectic—and, not infrequently, the eccentric—collections of scores of benefactors from the 19th century through today. More than 16,600 costumes, 65,000 paintings, and 1.25 million historical photographs documenting Canada's history are rotated in and out of storage to be displayed. A First Nations room has portions of the museum's extensive collection of objects from Canada's native population, including meticulous beadwork, baby carriers, and fishing implements. Exhibits are intelligently mounted, with texts in English and French. There's a small cafe near the front entrance and a shop that sells Canadian arts and crafts, pottery, and more.

690 rue Sherbrooke ouest (at rue University). © **514/398-7100.** www.mccord-museum.qc.ca. Admission C$13 adults, C$10 seniors, C$7 students, C$5 children 6–12, free for children 5 & under; free admission on the first Sat of the month 10am–noon. Tues–Fri 10am–6pm, Sat & Sun 10am–5pm; Mon 10am–5pm June 24 to Sept 7 & holiday weekends. Métro: McGill.

Parc du Mont-Royal Montréal is named for this 232m (761-ft.) hill that rises at its heart—the "Royal Mountain." Walkers, joggers, cyclists, dog owners, and skaters all use this largest of the city's green spaces throughout the year. In summer, **Lac des Castors (Beaver Lake)** is surrounded by sunbathers and picnickers (no swimming allowed, however). In winter, cross-country skiers and snowshoers follow miles of paths and trails laid out for their use through the park's 200 hectares (494 acres). **Chalet du Mont-Royal** near the crest of the hill is a popular destination, providing a sweeping view of the city from its terrace. Up the hill behind the chalet is the spot where, legend says, Paul de Chomedey, Sieur de Maisonneuve (1612–1676), erected a wooden cross after the colony sidestepped the threat of a flood in 1643. The present incarnation of the steel **Croix du Mont-Royal** was installed in 1924 and is lit at night. It usually glows white, though it was purple in 2005 after the death of Pope John Paul II. Use the interactive online map at www.lemontroyal.qc.ca/carte/en for a suggested walking route.

Downtown (entrances include one at rue Peel and av. des Pins). © **514/843-8240** (the Maison Smith information center in the park's center). www.lemontroyal.qc.ca. Métro: Mont-Royal. Bus: 11.

SIGHTSEEING savings

- **Buy the Montréal Museums Pass.** Good for 3 consecutive days, this pass grants entry to 34 museums and attractions, including most of those mentioned in this chapter. The C$50 pass includes unlimited access to public transportation (including the airport shuttle, bus #747) along with the museums. The C$45 pass covers just the museums, without the transportation. There are no separate rates for seniors or children. The pass is available at all participating museums, many hotels, the tourist offices at 1255 rue Peel (downtown) and 174 rue Notre-Dame (in Vieux-Montréal), and online at www.montrealmuseums.org.
- **Visit Vitrine Culturelle de Montréal for last-minute ticket deals.** The discount ticket office for Montréal cultural events is at 145 rue Ste-Catherine ouest at the Place des Arts, ✆ **866/924-5538** or 514/285-4545. The website (www.vitrineculturelle.com) lists the events on sale.
- **Flash your AAA card.** Members of the American Automobile Association (AAA) get the same discounts as members of its Canadian sister organization, the CAA. That includes reduced rates at many museums, hotels, and restaurants (and C$2 off the Montréal Museums Pass).

Vieux-Montreal (Old Montreal)

Vieux-Montréal's central plaza is **Place Jacques-Cartier,** the focus of much activity in the warm months. The plaza consists of two repaved streets bracketing a center promenade that slopes down from rue Notre-Dame to Old Port, with venerable stone buildings from the 1700s along both sides. Horse-drawn carriages gather at the plaza's base, and outdoor cafes, street performers, and flower sellers recall a Montréal of a century ago. Locals insist they would never go to a place so overrun by tourists—which makes one wonder why so many of them do, in fact, congregate here. They take the sun and sip sangria on the bordering terraces just as much as visitors do, enjoying the unfolding pageant.

Montréal's Old Port, at the edge of Vieux-Montréal, was transformed in 1992 from a dreary commercial wharf area into a 2km-long (1¼-mile), 53-hectare (131-acre) promenade and public park with bicycle paths, exhibition halls, and a variety of family activities, including the **Centre des Sciences de Montréal** (see below). The area is most active from mid-May to October, when harbor cruises set out from here and bicycles, in-line skates, and family-friendly quadricycle carts are available for rent. In the winter, things are quieter, but an outside ice-skating rink brings people out. There's an information booth at the Centre des Sciences. The Vieux-Port stretches along the waterfront parallel to rue de la Commune.

Basilique Notre-Dame ★★★ Breathtaking in the richness of its interior furnishings and big enough to hold 4,000 worshipers, this magnificent structure was designed in 1824 by James O'Donnell (1774–1830), an Irish-American Protestant architect from New York—who was so profoundly moved by the experience that he converted to Catholicism after its completion. The impact is understandable. Of Montréal's hundreds of churches, Notre-Dame's interior is the most stunning, with a wealth of exquisite details, most of it carved from rare woods that have been delicately gilded and painted. O'Donnell, clearly a proponent of the Gothic Revival style, is the only person honored by burial in the crypt.

The main altar was carved from linden wood, the work of Québécois architect Victor Bourgeau (1809–1888). Behind it is the **Chapelle Sacré-Coeur (Sacred Heart Chapel),** much of which was destroyed by an arsonist in 1978; it was rebuilt and rededicated in 1982. The altar displays 32 bronze panels representing birth, life, and death, cast by a Montréal artist named Charles Daudelin (1920–2001). A 10-bell carillon resides in the east tower, while the west tower contains a single massive bell, nicknamed **"Le Gros Bourdon,"** which weighs more than 12 tons and emanates a low, resonant rumble that vibrates right up through your feet.

A sound-and-light show called "Et la lumière fut" ("And Then There Was Light") is presented nightly Tuesday through Saturday.

110 rue Notre-Dame ouest (on Place d'Armes). ✆ **514/842-2925.** www.basiliquenddm.org. Basilica C$5 adults, C$4 children 7–17, free for children 6 & under; includes 20-min. guided tour. Light show C$10 adults, C$9 seniors, C$5 children 17 & younger. Basilica Mon–Fri 9am–4pm, Sat 9am–3:30pm, Sun 12:30–3:30pm; light show Tues–Thurs 6:30pm, Fri 6:30 & 8:30pm, Sat 7 & 8:30pm. Métro: Place d'Armes.

Centre des Sciences de Montréal ★★ ☺ Running the length of a central pier in Vieux-Port (Old Port), this ambitious complex (in English, the Montréal Science Centre) focuses on science and technology. Its attractions include interactive displays and a popular IMAX theater, and the extensive use of computers makes it particularly appealing to youngsters (the whole place is designed for 9- to 14-year-olds). One temporary exhibit guided kids in making television news reports using a combination of pre-recorded interview clips and video of themselves. Another bold exhibit focused on the human body and sexuality, and addressed in a frank and straightforward way every—and we mean every—question adolescents might have. Admission fees vary according to the combination of exhibits and movie showings you choose. To avoid long lines, preorder tickets for special exhibits. Indoor and outdoor cafes sell sandwiches, salads, and sweets.

Quai King Edward, Vieux-Port. ✆ **877/496-4724** or 514/496-4724. www.montrealsciencecentre.com. Admission for exhibitions C$12 adults, C$11 seniors & children 13–17, C$9 children 4–12, free for children 3 & under. Movie tickets C$12 adults, C$11 seniors & children 13–17, C$9 children 4–12, free for children 3 & under. Mon–Fri 9am–4pm, Sat & Sun 10am–5pm. Métro: Place d'Armes or Champ-de-Mars.

Fantômes Ghost Walks ☺ Evenings at 8:30pm, join with other intrepid souls for a ghost walk of Vieux-Montréal. The 90-minute tour heads down back alleys to places where gruesome events occurred and actors appear as phantoms to tell about the historical crimes of the city. Because their stories include tales of sorcery, hangings, and being burned and tortured, it's probably too scary for children under 10.

360 rue St-François-Xavier. ✆ **800/363-4021** or 514/844-4021. www.fantommontreal.com. Admission C$22 adults, C$19 students, C$13 children 12 & under. July–Oct various evenings at 8:30pm; call or go online for exact days. Métro: Place d'Armes.

Pointe-à-Callière (Montréal Museum of Archaeology and History) ★★★ A first visit to Montréal might best begin here. Built on the very site where the original colony (called Pointe-à-Callière) was established in 1642, this modern museum engages visitors in rare, beguiling ways. The triangular new building echoes the Royal Insurance building (1861) that stood here for many years.

Go first to the 16-minute multimedia show in an auditorium that stands above the actual exposed ruins of the earlier city. Music and a playful bilingual narration keep the history slick and painless, if a little chamber-of-commerce upbeat. Children 11 and younger may find it a snooze.

Evidence of the area's many inhabitants—from Amerindians to French trappers to Scottish merchants—was unearthed during archaeological digs that took more than a decade. Artifacts are on view in display cases set among the ancient building foundations and burial grounds below street level. Wind your way on the self-guided tour through the subterranean complex until you find yourself in the former customhouse, where there are more exhibits and a well-stocked gift shop. Allow 1½ hours to visit this museum.

L'Arrivage Café is open daily for lunch and presents a fine view of Vieux-Montréal and Vieux-Port. Food here is terrific.

350 Place Royale (at rue de la Commune). ✆ **514/872-9150.** www.pacmuseum.qc.ca. Admission C$15 adults, C$10 seniors, C$8 students, C$6 children 6–12, free for children 5 & under. Late June to early Sept Mon–Fri 10am–6pm, Sat & Sun 11am–6pm; Sept to mid-June Tues–Fri 10am–5pm, Sat & Sun 11am–5pm. L'Arrivage Café Mon 11:30am–2pm, Tues–Sun 11:30am–3pm. Métro: Place d'Armes.

Plateau Mont-Royal & Olympic Park

A 20-minute drive east on rue Sherbrooke or an easy Métro ride from downtown is **Olympic Park**. It has four attractions: Stade Olympique (Olympic Stadium), Biodôme de Montréal, Jardin Botanique (Botanical Garden), and Insectarium de Montréal, all described below. All are walking distance from each other. Combination ticket packages are available, and the Biodôme, Jardin, and Insectarium are all included in the **Montréal Museums Pass** (see the "Sightseeing Savings" box on p. 243). Underground parking at the Olympic Stadium is C$12 per day, with additional parking at the Jardin Botanique and Insectarium.

Biodôme de Montréal ★★ ☺ A terrifically engaging attraction for children of nearly any age, the delightful Biodôme houses replications of four ecosystems: a tropical rainforest, a Laurentian forest, the St. Lawrence marine system, and a polar environment. Visitors walk through each and hear the animals, smell the flora, and (except in the polar region, which is behind glass) feel the changes in temperature. The rainforest area is the most engrossing (the subsequent rooms increasingly less so), so take your time here. It's a kind of "Where's Waldo" challenge to find all the critters, from the capybara, which looks like a large guinea pig, to the golden lion tamarin monkeys that swing on branches only an arm's length away. Only the bats, fish, penguins, and puffins are behind glass. The open-air space features hundreds of shore birds whose shrieks can transport you to the beach. A continual schedule of temporary exhibits and new programs keeps things fresh. The building was originally the velodrome for cycling during the 1976 Olympics. The facility also has a hands-on activity room called Naturalia, a shop, a bistro, and a cafeteria.

4777 av. Pierre-de-Coubertin (next to Stade Olympique). ✆ **514/868-3000.** www.biodome.qc.ca. Admission C$17 adults, C$13 seniors & students, C$8.25 children 5–17, C$2.50 children 2–4. Daily Aug to late June 9am–5pm, late June to Aug 9am–6pm. Closed most Mon Sept–Dec. Métro: Viau.

Insectarium de Montréal ☺ Live exhibits featuring scorpions, tarantulas, honeybees, ants, hissing cockroaches, and assassin bugs are displayed in this two-level structure near the rue Sherbrooke gate of the **Jardin Botanique** (**Botanical Garden,** below). Alongside the live creepy critters are thousands of mounted ones, including butterflies, beetles, scarabs, maggots, locusts, and giraffe weevils. It closed for the first half of 2011 for renovations.

4581 rue Sherbrooke est. ✆ **514/872-1400.** www.ville.montreal.qc.ca/insectarium. Mid-May to Nov C$17 adults, C$13 seniors & students, C$8.25 children 5–17, C$2.50 children 2–4. Nov to mid-May rates drop about 15%. Admission includes access to the Botanical Garden next door. Combination tickets with the Stade Olympique & Biodôme are available. Mid-May to mid-Sept daily 9am–6pm; mid-Sept to Nov daily 9am–9pm; Nov to mid-May Tues–Sun 9am–5pm. Métro: Pie-IX or Viau.

Jardin Botanique ★★★ Spread across 75 hectares (185 acres), Montréal's Botanical Garden is a fragrant oasis 12 months a year. Ten large exhibition greenhouses each have a theme: one houses orchids; another has tropical food and spice plants, including coffee, cashews, and vanilla; another features rainforest flora. In a special exhibit each spring, live butterflies flutter among the nectar-bearing plants, occasionally landing on visitors. In September, visitors can watch monarch butterflies being tagged and released for their annual migration to Mexico.

Outdoors, spring is when things really kick in: lilacs in May, lilies in June, and roses from mid-June until the first frost. The **Chinese Garden,** a joint project of Montréal and Shanghai, evokes the 14th- to 17th-century era of the Ming Dynasty and was built according to the landscape principles of yin and yang. It incorporates pavilions, inner courtyards, ponds, and plants indigenous to China. A serene **Japanese Garden** fills 2.5 hectares (6¼ acres) and has a cultural pavilion with an art gallery, a tearoom where ancient ceremonies are performed, a stunning bonsai collection, and a Zen garden. A small train runs through the gardens from mid-May to October and is included in the entrance fee.

The grounds are also home to the **Insectarium** (above), which displays some of the world's most beautiful and sinister insects (both mounted and live). Exhibits acquaint young and old with honey bees, cockroaches, beetles, and hundreds of other "misunderstood" creatures.

4101 rue Sherbrooke est (opposite Olympic Stadium). ✆ **514/872-1400.** www.ville.montreal.qc.ca/jardin. Mid-May to Nov C$17 adults, C$13 seniors & students, C$8.25 children 5–17, C$2.50 children 2–4. Nov to mid-May rates drop about 15% & free admission to outdoor gardens. Admission includes access to the Insectarium. Mid-May to mid-Sept daily 9am–6pm; mid-Sept to Nov daily 9am–9pm; Nov to mid-May Tues–Sun 9am–5pm. No bicycles or dogs. Métro: Pie-IX, Viau (w/free shuttle from Olympic Park).

Parc La Fontaine The European-style park in Plateau Mont-Royal is one of the city's oldest and most popular. Illustrating the traditional dual identities of the city's populace, half the park is landscaped in the formal French manner, the other in the more casual English style. A central lake is used for ice-skating in winter, when snowshoe and cross-country trails wind through trees. In summer, these trails become bike paths, and tennis courts become active. An open amphitheater, the **Théâtre de Verdure** (p. 259), features free outdoor theater, music, and tango dancing. The northern end of the park is more pleasant than the southern end (along rue Sherbrooke), which attracts a seedier crowd.

Bounded by rue Sherbrooke, rue Rachel, av. Parc LaFontaine & av. Papineau. ✆ **514/872-3948** for park, ✆ 514/872-3626 for tennis reservations. www.ville.montreal.qc.ca. Free admission; C$9 an hour for use of tennis courts. Park daily 6am–midnight; tennis courts weekdays 9am–11pm, weekends 9am–9pm. Métro: Sherbrooke.

Stade Olympique Montréal's space-age Olympic Stadium, the centerpiece of the 1976 Olympic Games, looks like a giant stapler. The main event is the 175m (574-ft.) inclined tower, which leans at a 45-degree angle and does duty as an observation deck, with a funicular that whisks passengers to the top in 95 seconds. On a clear day, the deck bestows an expansive view over Montréal and into the neighboring Laurentian mountains. At C$15, though, the admission price is as steep as the tower.

The complex includes a stadium that seats up to 56,000 for sporting events and music concerts and seven swimming pools open for public swimming and classes, including one deep enough for scuba diving. Thirty-minute guided tours that describe the 1976 Olympic Games and use of the center today are available daily for C$8.

4141 av. Pierre-de-Coubertin. ✆ **877/997-0919** or 514/252-4141. www.rio.gouv.qc.ca. Tower admission C$15 adults, C$11 seniors & students, C$7.50 children 5–17. Public swimming admission C$5.50 adults, C$4.65 students & seniors, C$4.10 children 15 & under. Tower daily summer 9am–7pm, winter 9am–5pm. See website for pool hours. Closed mid-Jan to mid-Feb. Métro: Viau.

CIRQUE DU SOLEIL: MONTRÉAL'S hometown CIRCUS

The whimsical, talented band of artists that became Cirque du Soleil began as street performers in Baie-St-Paul, a river town an hour north of Québec City. Stilt-walkers, fire-breathers, and musicians, they had one pure intention: to entertain. The troupe formally founded as Cirque du Soleil (Circus of the Sun) in 1984.

It has matured into a spectacle like no other. Using human-size gyroscopes, trampoline beds, trapezes suspended from massive chandeliers, and the like (but no animals), Cirque creates worlds that are spooky, sensual, otherworldly, and beautifully ambiguous.

More than 1,000 of the company's acrobats, contortionists, jugglers, clowns, and dancers tour the world. Resident shows are established in Las Vegas, Macau, New York, Orlando, and Tokyo. The company's offices are in Montréal in the northern Saint-Michel district, not far beyond the Mile End neighborhood.

And they're not just offices. Cirque has been developing a small campus of buildings in this industrial zone since 1997. All new artists come here to train for a few weeks to a few months and live in residences on-site. The complex has acrobatic training rooms, a dance studio, workshops in which the elaborate costumes and props are made, and a space large enough to erect a circus tent indoors. Some 1,800 people are employed at the Montréal facility, including more than 400 who work on costumes alone.

The company doesn't have regular performances in Montréal, alas, although they do put on a free show most nights in the summer in Québec City (see p. 296). Information about where to find a show is at **www.cirquedusoleil.com.**

SPECIAL EVENTS & FESTIVALS

La Fête des Neiges (Snow Festival) (www. parcjeandrapeau.com) is Montréal's winter carnival, with outdoor events such as dog-sled runs, a mock survival camp, street hockey, and tobogganing. It's held during the last 2 weekends in January and the beginning of February at Parc Jean-Drapeau. Also in February, **Festival Montréal en Lumière (Montréal High Lights Festival)** (www.montrealhighlights.com) offers up an array of cultural events, including culinary competitions, wine tastings, multimedia light shows, classical and pop concerts, and an All-Nighter that ends with a free breakfast at dawn.

In April, the **Bal en Blanc Party Week** (www.balenblanc.com) draws some 15,000 people for a 5-day rave/dance party. It's one of the biggest such events in the world.

Late May into June, the **Montréal Bike Fest** (www.velo.qc.ca) puts on cycling competitions that include a nocturnal bike ride (Tour la Nuit) and the grueling Tour de l'Île, a 52km (32-mile) race around the island's rim, which gets 30,000 cyclists, shuts down roads, and attracts more than 100,000 spectators.

On nearly a dozen Saturdays from June to August, **L'International des Feux Loto-Québec (International Fireworks Competition)** (www.internationaldesfeuxloto-quebec.com) pits the pyrotechnics of different countries against each other. Tickets are sold to watch from the open-air theater at La Ronde amusement park (✆ **514/397-2000;** www.laronde.com) on Ile Ste-Hélène, although the fireworks can be enjoyed for free from almost anywhere overlooking the river (tickets do include entrance to the amusement park).

In July, the **Festival International de Jazz de Montréal ★★** (www.montrealjazzfest.com) is one of the monster events on the city's calendar, with some 450 free outdoor performances in addition to the ticketed events. Montréal has a long tradition in jazz, and this enormously successful festival has been celebrating America's art form since 1979. See p. 261.

In October, the **Black & Blue Festival** (www.bbcm.org) is one of the biggest gay festivals on the planet, with dance parties, sports events, and more. The 20th anniversary edition in 2010 was held at the Palais des congrès de Montréal (Convention Center).

OUTDOOR ACTIVITIES & SPECTATOR SPORTS

Even if you come to Montréal without your outdoor gear, it's easy to get outside and join the fun.

Outdoor Activities

BICYCLING & IN-LINE SKATING

Bicycling and rollerblading are hugely popular in Montréal, and the city helps people indulge these passions. It boasts an expanding network of more than 560km (348 miles) of cycling paths and year-round bike lanes. In warm months, car lanes in heavily biked areas are blocked off with concrete barriers, creating protected bike-only lanes. A self-service bicycle rental program called BIXI, where users pick up bikes from designated bike stands in the city and drop them off at other stands for a small fee, launched in 2009 and is wildly popular; see p. 214 for details.

If you're serious about cycling, get in touch with the nonprofit biking organization **Vélo Québec** (© **800/567-8356** or 514/521-8356; www.velo.qc.ca). Vélo (which means bicycle) was behind the development of a 4,000km (2,485-mile) bike network called **Route Verte (Green Route)** that stretches from one end of the province of Québec to the other. The route was officially inaugurated in summer 2007. The Vélo website has the most up-to-date information on the state of the paths, the Montréal Bike Fest, road races, new bike lanes, and more. It also offers guided tours throughout the province. ***Tip:*** Several taxi companies provide bike racks and charge C$3 extra for each bike.

The shop **Ça Roule/Montréal on Wheels** (© **877/866-0633** or 514/866-0633; www.caroulemontreal.com) at 27 rue de la Commune est, the waterfront road in Vieux-Port, rents bikes and skates from March to November. Rentals are C$5 to C$9 per hour and C$30 per day on the weekend, with a deposit required. Helmets and locks are included. The staff will set you up with a map (also downloadable from their website) and likely point you toward the peaceful **Lachine Canal,** a nearly flat 11km (6¾-mile) bicycle path, open year-round and maintained by Parks Canada from mid-April through October, that travels alongside locks and over small bridges. The canal starts just a few blocks away.

Guidatour (© **514/844-4021;** www.guidatour.qc.ca) offers a 3-hour bicycling tour in conjunction with Ça Roule/Montréal on Wheels that goes from Vieux-Port through the Latin Quarter, to Parc La Fontaine and then west to Parc du Mont-Royal, south through the business district, and back into Vieux-Montréal. The C$49 fee includes rental of a bike, helmet, and lock for the day. Tours are available daily from late June to early September, and Saturday and Sunday mid-May to mid-October. Tours start at 9am at the bike shop at 27 rue de la Commune est in Vieux-Port. Reservations are required.

BOAT TOURS

Le Bateau-Mouche (© **800/361-9952** or 514/849-9952; www.bateau-mouche.com) offers an air-conditioned, glass-enclosed vessel reminiscent of those on the Seine in Paris. It plies the St. Lawrence River from mid-May to mid-October with 1-, 1½-, and 3½-hour cruises. The shallow-draft boat takes passengers on a route inaccessible by traditional vessels, passing under several bridges, and providing sweeping views of the city, Mont Royal, and the St. Lawrence and its islands. Prices start at C$23 for an adult on a 1-hour trip to C$153 for the most expansive dinner cruises. Tours depart from the Jacques-Cartier Pier, opposite Place Jacques-Cartier.

Croisières AML Cruises (© **800/563-4643** or 514/842-3871; www.croisieresaml.com) also travels the harbor and the St. Lawrence, with similar options as Le Bateau-Mouche. Boats depart from the King Edward Pier, in Vieux-Port.

Les Sautes-Moutons (also known as Lachine Rapids Tours; © **514/284-9607**; www.jetboatingmontreal.com) provides an exciting—and wet—experience. Its wave-jumper powerboats take on the St. Lawrence River's roiling Lachine Rapids, which has 2.4m to 3.7m (8- to 12-ft.) waves. The streamlined jet boat operates from May to mid-October daily. Reservations are required. Plan to arrive 45 minutes early to obtain and don rain gear and a life jacket. Bring a towel and change of clothes, as you almost certainly will get splashed or even soaked. Fares are C$65 adults. The jet boats depart from the Clock Tower Pier (quai de l'Horlage) in Vieux-Port.

CROSS-COUNTRY SKIING

Parc du Mont-Royal has an extensive cross-country course, as do many of the other city parks, though skiers have to supply their own equipment. Just an hour from the city, north in the Laurentides and east in the Cantons de l'Est, there are numerous options for skiing and rentals; see p. 264 for more information.

HIKING

The most popular hike is to the top of **Mont Royal.** There are a web of options for trekking the small mountain, from using the broad and handsome pedestrian-only **chemin Olmsted** (a bridle path named for Frederick Law Olmsted, the park's landscape architect), to following smaller paths and sets of stairs. The park is well-marked and small enough that you can wander without getting too lost.

ICE SKATING

In the winter, outdoor skating rinks are set up in Vieux-Port, Lac des Castors (Beaver Lake), and other spots around the city; check tourist offices for your best options. One of the most agreeable venues for skating any time of the year is **Atrium Le 1000** in the downtown skyscraper at 1000 rue de la Gauchetière ouest. It's indoors and warm, and it's surrounded by cafes at which to relax after twirling around the big rink. And yes, it's even open in the summer.

KAYAKING

It's fun to rent kayaks, large Rabaska canoes, pedal boats, or small eco-friendly electric boats on the quiet **Lachine Canal,** just to the west of Vieux-Port. **H2O Adventures** (© **877/935-2925** or 514/842-1306; www.h2oadventures.com) won a Grand Prix du Tourisme Québécois award for being a standout operation. Their rentals start at C$8 per half-hour. Two-hour introductory kayak lessons, on Wednesday nights and Sunday afternoons, start at C$35. From June to August, the shop is open daily from 9am to 9pm. Cross the footbridge past Marché Atwater (p. 254), where you can also pick up lunch from the inside *boulangerie* and *fromagerie,* adjacent to the canal. Métro: Lionel-Groulx.

SAUNA

Bath complexes are common throughout Scandinavia, but less so in North America. **Scandinave Les Bains** ★ (71 rue de la Commune ouest, © **514/288-2009,** www.scandinave.com), which opened in 2009, aims to bring Euro-style relaxation-through-water to Montréal's locals and guests. Visitors check in, change into bathing suits, and then have the run of the complex for the visit. There's a warm bath the size of a small swimming pool with jets and a waterfall, a steam room thick with the scent of eucalyptus oil, and a Finnish-style dry sauna. Peppered throughout the hallways are sling-back chairs, and one room is set aside just for relaxing or having a drink from the juice bar. The recommended routine is to heat your body for about 15 minutes, cool down in one of the icy rinse stations, and relax for 15 minutes—and then repeat the circuit a few times. Admission is C$46. Guests must be 16 or older.

Spectator Sports

Montréalers are as devoted to ice hockey as other Canadians are, with plenty of enthusiasm left over for soccer, U.S.-style football, and the other distinctive national sport, curling. They liked baseball too, but not enough: In 2005, the Montréal Expos, plagued by poor attendance, left for Washington, D.C., where they became the

Nationals. (Fun fact: Pioneering black athlete **Jackie Robinson** played for the Montréal Royals in 1946, and there's a sculpture of him outside of Olympic Stadium.)

The biggest single event on the Montréal sports calendar is the Grand Prix car race that roars into town for 3 days each summer.

AUTO RACING: GRAND PRIX

The **Grand Prix** came back to Montréal in 2010 after a 1-year hiatus (the result of contract negotiations between the city and Formula One, which puts on the race), and the international auto race is slated to return to the city each summer through at least 2014. The event attracts more than 100,000 people to the city's track (and to hotels and restaurants), bringing in as much as C$100 million in tourism dollars and making it the single biggest tourism event of the year. In 2010, it took place from June 11 to 13. Tickets range from C$45 to C$113 for general admission, C$286 to C$617 for grandstand seats, and C$4,436 for a 1-day pass for the Formula One Paddock Club. Details are at **www.formula1.com.**

Auto-race aficionados can also sate their needs with **NASCAR** (www.circuitgilles villeneuve.ca), which comes to Montréal for 2 days in late August, bringing more than 40 top drivers and race cars. One-day general-admission tickets cost C$30 to C$40, with 2-day tickets ranging from C$55 to C$165.

FOOTBALL (BOTH KINDS)

What Americans call soccer most of the rest of the world calls football, and there's a big fan base for *that* kind of football in Montréal—not surprising, given the city's wide and varied immigrant population. Montréal doesn't have a team in the Major League Soccer network, but the **Montréal Impact** (**© 514/328-3668;** www.montrealimpact.com) is part of the United Soccer League's First Division and plays at Saputo Stadium, rue 4750 Sherbrooke est, near the Olympic Stadium. Tickets are C$10 to C$30.

Meanwhile, there's also U.S.-style professional football in Canada. The **Montréal Alouettes** (French for "larks") play at McGill University's Percival-Molson Memorial Stadium from June to November. The "Als," as they're fondly known, enjoy considerable success, frequently appearing in the Grey Cup, the Canadian Football League's version of the U.S. Super Bowl. Tickets start at C$25. Details are at **© 514/871-2255** and www.montrealalouettes.com.

HOCKEY

The beloved **Montréal Canadiens** play downtown at the Centre Bell arena. The team has won 24 Stanley Cups (the last one in 1992–93), and the season runs from October to April, with playoff games potentially continuing into June. Tickets are C$25 to C$225. Check www.canadiens.com for schedules and ticketing, or call **© 877/668-8269** or 514/790-2525.

TENNIS

The **Rogers Cup** tournament (**© 514/273-1515;** www.rogerscup.com) comes each August to the Uniprix Stadium, which is near the De Castelnau and the Jarry Métro stops, with singles and doubles matches. Men's and women's tournaments are played in two different locations, alternating between Montréal and Toronto. The stadium's Centre Court holds more than 11,000. Tickets cost between C$10 and C$158, with up to four matches included. To make the tournament more green, the stadium provides 175 bike-rack slots and 24-hour bike surveillance, free public transit tickets to all spectators, and a downtown shuttle service.

SHOPPING

You can shop in Montréal until your feet swell and your eyes cross. Whether you view shopping as a focus of your travels or simply as a diversion, you won't be disappointed. Among natives, shopping ranks right up there with dining out as a prime activity.

Best buys include **Canadian Inuit sculptures** and quilts, drawings, and carvings by Amerindian and other folk artists. The province's daring **clothing designers** produce appealing fashions at prices that are often reasonable. And while demand has diminished, superbly constructed **furs and leather goods** are high-ticket items.

Ice cider (*cidre de glace*) and **ice wines** made in Québec province from apples and grapes left out after the first frost are inexpensive regional foods to bring home. They are sold in duty-free shops at the border in addition to the provincial **Société des Alcools du Québec (SAQ)** stories throughout the region.

For fashion, art, and luxury items, head to **rue Sherbrooke** in downtown. Also downtown, **rue Ste-Catherine** is home to the city's top department stores and myriad satellite shops, although you may recognize most of the names of the chain stores (Tommy Hilfiger, Kiehl's, Banana Republic, Mango, H&M, Apple, etc.).

In Vieux-Montréal, the western end of **rue St-Paul** has a growing number of art galleries, clothing boutiques, and jewelry shops.

In Plateau Mont-Royal, the funkier **boulevard St-Laurent** sells everything from budget practicalities to off-the-wall handmade fashions. In Mile End, **avenue Laurier** between boulevard St-Laurent and avenue de l'Epée, is where to head for French boutiques, furniture and accessories shops, and products from the ateliers of young Québécois designers. This is a vibrant, upscale street, with a rich selection of restaurants, too.

When you're making purchases with a credit card, the charges are automatically converted at the going bank rate before appearing on your monthly statement. In most cases, this is the best deal of all for visitors. Visa and MasterCard are the most popular credit cards in this part of Canada.

Most stores are open from 9 or 10am to 6pm Monday through Wednesday, until 9pm on Thursday and Friday, and until at least 5pm on Saturday. Many stores are now also open on Sunday from noon to at least 5pm.

Antiques

Some of the city's quirkier antiques shops have disappeared in recent years, but there are still tempting shops along **"Antique Alley,"** as it's nicknamed, on rue Notre-Dame west of Vieux-Montréal. They're especially concentrated between rue Guy and avenue Atwater, near the restaurant Joe Beef (p. 239), about 3km (2 miles) from the heart of Vieux-Montréal. Antiques can also be found in the Village (the gay neighborhood described on p. 210) on rue Amherst.

Arts, Crafts & Galleries

Some of the best shops for crafts are found in city museums. Tops among them are shops in **Pointe-à-Callière** (the Montréal Museum of Archaeology and History), in Vieux-Montréal; shops in the **Musée des Beaux-Arts** and the **Musée McCord,** both on rue Sherbrooke in downtown; and the shop at the **Musée d'Art Contemporain** in the Place-des-Arts, on rue Ste-Catherine ouest, also downtown.

Atelier Entre-Peaux This company specializes in lightweight bags made in Québec from recycled billboards—all products, in fact, are produced from 75% to 95% recycled material, earning the business recognition on Recyc-Québec, the official government recycling industry website. The company is officially appointed by the city of Montréal to transform all the banners posted on the city's street lamps. The bags are super-cool looking, too. Bike bags run about C$69 and grocery bags about C$17. They can be found at **Galerie Zone Orange** (see below) or the company website (www.entre-peaux-ecodesign.com).

Galerie Le Chariot Galleries that feature Inuit art are found throughout the city, but few are as accessibly located as Le Chariot, whose showroom is directly on the Place Jacques-Cartier, in the heart of Vieux-Montréal. Here, shoppers can find handmade pieces by Inuk artists from Cape Dorset, Lake Harbour, and Baffin Island—carved bears, seals, owls, and tableaus of mothers and children. Pieces range in price from about C$150 to C$25,000 and are certified by the Canadian government. Think of it as a museum where you can buy the art. 446 Place Jacques-Cartier (in the center of the plaza), Vieux-Montréal. ✆ **514/875-4994.**

Galerie Zone Orange Angry sock monkeys, creative jewelry, and colorful ceramics from regional artists are on display at the small Zone Orange, which also has a teeny espresso bar in its center. Perhaps the coolest products are the lightweight bags made from recycled billboards and street lamp banners by the eco-focused Atelier Entre-Peaux, a Montréal company (see above). There are sweet dolls for infants made from organic cotton. 410 rue St-Pierre (near rue St-Paul), Vieux-Montréal. ✆ **514/510-5809.** http://shop.galeriezoneorange.com.

Guilde Canadienne des Métiers d'Art ★ In English, it's called the Canadian Guild of Crafts. A small but choice collection of items is displayed in a meticulously arranged gallery setting. Among the objects are blown glass, silk paintings, pewter, tapestries, wooden bowls, and ceramics. The store is particularly strong in avant-garde jewelry and Inuk sculpture. A small carving might be had for C$100 to C$300, while larger, more important pieces go for thousands more. 1460 rue Sherbrooke ouest (near rue Mackay), downtown. ✆ **866/477-6091.** www.canadianguild.com.

Bath & Body

Fruits & Passion Started in Candiac, Québec, in 1992, this popular chain features "personal care and ambience products"—fruity lotions, hand soaps, bubble bath, home cleaning agents, and more. There are nearly 160 Fruits & Passion boutiques throughout the world. 4159 rue St-Denis (at rue Rachel), Plateau Mont-Royal. ✆ **514/840-0778.** www.fruits-passion.com.

Department Stores

Montréal's major downtown shopping emporia stretch along rue Ste-Catherine from avenue Union westward to rue Guy. Most of the big department stores here were founded when Scottish, Irish, and English families dominated the city's mercantile class, so most of their names are identifiably English, albeit shorn of their apostrophes. The principal exception is La Baie, French for "the Bay," itself a shortened reference to an earlier name, the Hudson's Bay Company.

Henry Birks et Fils ★ A highly regarded jeweler since 1879. This beautiful old store has marble pillars and an ornamental ceiling, and is a living part of Montréal's Victorian heritage. The expensive products on display go beyond jewelry to encompass pens, desk accessories, watches, belts, glassware, and china. 1240 Phillips Square (at rue Ste-Catherine), downtown. ✆ **514/397-2511.** www.birks.com.

Holt Renfrew ★ One of the best known department stores in the city began as a furrier in 1837 and is now a showcase for the best in international style. A young Montréal clothier recently praised it as hip for "both grandmother and granddaughter." Wares are displayed in mini-boutiques and focus on fashion for men and women. Brands, including Armani, Dolce & Gabbana, Eileen Fisher, and Stella McCartney, are displayed with a tastefulness bordering on solemnity. 1300 rue Sherbrooke ouest (at rue de la Montagne), downtown. ✆ **514/842-5111.** www.holtrenfrew.com.

La Baie ★ No retailer has an older or more celebrated pedigree than the Hudson's Bay Company, whose name was shortened to "the Bay" and then transformed into "La Baie" by Québec language laws that decreed French the lingua franca. The company was incorporated in Canada in 1670. Its main store focuses on clothing, but also offers crystal, china, Inuit carvings, and its famous Hudson's Bay "point blanket." The company is the official outfitter of the Canadian Olympic teams in 2012. 585 rue Ste-Catherine ouest (at rue Aylmer), downtown. ✆ **514/281-4422.** www.hbc.com.

Ogilvy ★★ The most vibrant of a classy breed of department store that appears to be fading from the scene. Ogilvy was established in 1866 and has been at this location since 1912. A bagpiper still announces the noon hour (a favorite sight for tourists), and special events, glowing chandeliers, and wide aisles enhance the shopping experience. Ogilvy has always had a reputation for quality merchandise and now contains more than 60 boutiques, including Louis Vuitton, Anne Klein, and Burberry. It's also known for its eagerly awaited Christmas windows. The basement-level **Café Romy** sells quality sandwiches, salads, and desserts. 1307 rue Ste-Catherine ouest (at rue de la Montagne), downtown. ✆ **514/842-7711.** www.ogilvycanada.com.

Edibles

Canadian Maple Delights ☺ Everything maple-y is presented here by a consortium of Québec producers: pastries, gift baskets, truffles, and every grade of syrup. A wee little cafe serves sweets and gelato; on any day, a cone of maple-raspberry gelato is a good thing. For a taste, the mini-cone costs just C$1.60. 84 rue St-Paul est (near Place Jacques-Cartier), Vieux-Montréal. ✆ **514/765-3456.** www.mapledelights.com.

Le Canard Libéré, Espace Gourmand World-famous Lac Brome ducks, found on many of Montréal's finest gastronomic menus, are raised near Lac Brome, just 109km (68 miles) southeast the city. This shop sells take-home duck products and has a cafe area for sampling on the spot, such as duck-fat French fries. 4396 bd. St-Laurent (near av. Mont-Royal), Plateau Mont-Royal. ✆ **514/286-1286.** www.canardsdulacbrome.com.

Marché Atwater ★ The Atwater market, west of Vieux-Montréal, is an indoor-outdoor farmer's market that's open daily. French in flavor, it features fresh fruits, vegetables, and flowers; *boulangeries* and *fromageries;* and shops with easy-to-travel-with food. There are also specialty boutiques like Chocolats Geneviève Grandbois. You can walk to the market from Vieux-Montréal by heading down rue Notre-Dame, where you'll pass Antique Alley (p. 252), or taking the Métro to Lionel-Groulx. 138 av. Atwater (at rue Notre-Dame ouest), west of Vieux-Montréal. www.marche-atwater.com.

Marché Jean-Talon ★ Gourmands will want to make a pilgrimage to the north part of the city to this market. Many locals prefer it over the Atwater market (above), perhaps because it's surrounded on all sides by the buzz and energy of the city. It's full of fresh fruits and vegetables and a host of gourmet shops. One, for instance, is the spice shop Olives & Épices, which *Food & Wine* magazine named the best of Montréal in 2010, citing its *ras el hanout,* "which contains 24 ingredients, including saffron and three kinds of dried roses." The market isn't near any of the sites, restaurants, or hotels listed in this guidebook, but it's an easy ride on the Métro—just head north to the Jean-Talon stop. 7070 av. Henri-Julien (at rue Jean-Talon est), north of Mile End. ✆ **514/277-1588.** www.marche-jean-talon.com.

Suite 88 Chocolatier ★ Fancy chocolates are displayed in cases like fine jewelry, in flavors that include jalapeño, chili-cayenne, ouzo, sake, and *mojito.* Small bars start at C$3.75. There's a cafe, too, with gelato. And on cold days, be sure to try the hot chocolate—made with cayenne. There's another location at 1225 bd. de Maisonneuve, downtown. 3957 rue St-Denis (near rue Roy), Plateau Mont-Royal. ✆ **514/844-3488.** www.suite88.com.

Fashion For Men

Eccetera & Co. Favoring ready-to-wear attire from such higher-end manufacturers as Baldessarini and Canali, this store lays out its stock in a soothing setting with personalized service. Its motto, posted at the front window: GOOD CLOTHES OPEN ALL DOORS. 2021 rue Peel (near bd. de Maisonneuve), downtown. ✆ **514/845-9181.** www.eccetera.ca.

Harry Rosen ★★ For more than 50 years, this well-known retailer of designer suits and accessories has been making men look good in Armani, Dolce & Gabbana, and its own Harry Rosen Made in Italy line. The store's website features a nifty timeline of the shop's evolution from Toronto made-to-measure store to national leader in men's fashion. Les Cours Mont-Royal, 1455 rue Peel (at bd. de Maisonneuve), downtown. ✆ **514/284-3315.** www.harryrosen.com.

L'Uomo Montréal ★ Another top men's clothing boutique on rue Peel, this one was founded in 1980. L'Uomo mostly deals in Italian and other European menswear by such forward-thinking designers as Ermenegildo Zegna, Kiton, Prada, and Borrelli. 1452 rue Peel (near rue Ste-Catherine), downtown. ✆ **514/844-1008.** www.luomo-montreal.com.

Fashion For Women

Montréal Fashion Week happens every March. The 2010 event took place at the **Marché Bonsecours** and featured 24 Canadian designers including **Harricana** (below). Photos are at www.montrealfashionweek.ca. The **Montréal Fashion & Design Festival** happens on avenue de McGill College in August; see www.festivalmodedesign.com.

Aime Com Moi If you're heading to the northern end of the Plateau to the hipster bar Bílý Kůň (p. 263), build in time to stroll avenue du Mont-Royal, which is chock-full of new and used clothing. Among the shops is this one, which features fabulously funky dresses by Québécois designers. 150 av. du Mont-Royal est (3 blocks from bd. St-Laurent), Plateau Mont-Royal. ✆ **514/982-0088.**

Harricana ★ One designer taking a unique cue from the city's long history with the fur trade is Mariouche Gagné. Her company recycles old fur into funky patchwork garments and uses the slogan "Made from your mother's old coat." A leader in the ecoluxe movement, Gagné also recycles silk scarves, turning them into tops and skirts. Her workshop-boutique is close to the Marché Atwater (p. 254) and the Lionel-Groulx Métro station. 3000 rue St-Antoine ouest (at av. Atwater), west of Vieux-Montréal. ✆ **877/894-9919** or 514/287-6517. www.harricana.qc.ca.

Kaliyana ★ Vaguely Japanese and certainly minimalist, the free-flowing garments sold here are largely asymmetrical separates. Made by a Canadian designer, they come in muted tones of solid colors. Ask for "the kit," and you'll get six of Kaliyana's most popular pieces, apt foundation for a new wardrobe. Simple complementary necklaces and comfy but über-cool shoes are available, too. 4107 rue St-Denis (near rue Rachel), Plateau Mont-Royal. ✆ **514/844-0633.** www.kaliyana.com.

Fashion For Men & Women

Henri Henri As the porkpie makes a comeback, so may Henri Henri, a Montréal haberdasher since 1932. Step in and be outfitted with a classic Stetson or any number of styles that come in wool, felt, fur, leather, suede, cotton, or straw. Wondering how you look? Three-way oak mirrors abound, or the gentleman behind the counter will give you his honest assessment. Shop includes a hint of a women's section and accessories like umbrellas with hardwood handles. 189 rue Ste-Catherine est (at Hôtel-de-Ville), downtown. ✆ **888/388-0109** or 514/288-0109. www.henrihenri.ca.

Kanuk ★ One of the top Canadian manufacturers of high-end winter jackets makes its clothes right in Montréal and has a warehouse-like factory store in the heart of Plateau Mont-Royal. Like L.L.Bean in the U.S., Kanuk's first customers for the heavy parkas were outdoor enthusiasts. Today, its clientele includes the general public. The jackets aren't cheap—the heavy-duty ones cost upwards of C$600—but they're extremely popular. The more modestly priced winter caps make nice (and cozy) souvenirs. Look, too, for end-of-season sales. 485 rue Rachel est (near rue St-Denis), Plateau Mont-Royal. ✆ **514/284-4494.** www.kanuk.com.

Housewares

Arthur Quentin ★ Doling out household products of quiet taste and discernment for more than 25 years, this St-Denis stalwart sells tableware, kitchen gadgets, and home decor. That means lamps and Limoges china, terrines and tea towels, and cake molds and copper pots. Clay jugs for making vinegar? *Naturellement.* 3960 rue St-Denis (south of av. Duluth), Plateau Mont-Royal. ✆ **514/843-7513.** www.arthurquentin.com.

Kitsch 'n Swell From oil paintings on black velvet to leopard print rugs, this reseller of vintage home collectibles takes the pineapple upside-down cake. There are also fur coats and jewelry, and, with two other vintage stores right in the neighborhood, this is definitely worth a trip if you like collectable kitsch. 3968 bd. St-Laurent (near av. Duluth), Plateau Mont-Royal. ✆ **514/845-6789.** www.kitschnswell.ca.

Option D Option D sells high-end housewares, candy-colored and steel, in the heart of Old Town. Brands include Alessi, Guzzini, Iittala, and Bodum. 50 rue St-Paul ouest (near rue St-Sulpice), Vieux-Montréal. ✆ **514/842-7117.** www.optiond.ca.

Zone This housewares stores features colorful bowls and plates, clocks and frames, furnishings, and vases at several outposts throughout the province. 4246 rue St-Denis (at rue Rachel), Plateau Mont-Royal. ✆ **514/845-3530.** www.zonemaison.com.

MONTRÉAL AFTER DARK

Montréal's reputation for effervescent nightlife reaches back to the Roaring Twenties—specifically to the United States' 13-year experiment with Prohibition from 1920 to 1933. Americans streamed across the border for temporary relief from alcohol deprivation (while Canadian distillers and brewers made fortunes—few of them with meticulous regard for legalistic niceties). Montréal already enjoyed a sophisticated and slightly naughty reputation as the Paris of North America, which added to the allure.

Nearly a century later, packs of Americans still travel across the border to go to the city's bars and strip clubs (as do Canadians from other provinces). Clubbing and barhopping are hugely popular activities, and nightspots stay open until 3am—much later hours than in many U.S. and Canadian cities, which still heed Calvinist notions of propriety and early bedtimes.

Nocturnal pursuits are often as cultural as they are social. The city boasts its own outstanding symphony and dozens of French- and English-language theater companies. It's also on the standard concert circuit that includes Chicago and New York.

A ticket office for Montréal cultural events is centrally located at the Place des Arts. **Vitrine Culturelle de Montréal** (Cultural Window of Montréal; ✆ **866/924-5538** or 514/285-4545; www.vitrineculturelle.com) is at 145 rue Ste-Catherine ouest and sells last-minute deals, as well as full-price tickets.

The Performing Arts

CIRCUS

The extraordinary, internationally-renowned circus company **Cirque du Soleil** is based in Montréal. Each show is a celebration of pure skill and nothing less than magical, with acrobats, clowns, trapeze artists, and performers costumed to look like creatures not of this world—iguanas crossed with goblins, or peacocks born of trolls. There are as many as 20 shows playing across the globe simultaneously. Although there isn't a permanent show in Montréal, the troupe often comes to town in late spring and sets up its signature blue-and-yellow-striped tents in Vieux-Port. In 2010,

Resources: Checking What's on in Montréal Nightlife

For details about performances or special events when you're in town, pick up a free copy of ***Montréal Scope*** (www.montrealscope.com), a monthly ads-and-events booklet usually available in hotel lobbies, or the free weekly papers ***Mirror*** (www.montrealmirror.com) and ***Hour*** (www.hour.ca), both in English. ***Fugues*** (www.fugues.com) provides news and views of gay and lesbian events, clubs, restaurants, and activities. One particularly fun source for city happenings, and a regular at the top of the *Mirror*'s annual ranking of best blogs, is **Midnight Poutine** (www.midnightpoutine.ca), a self-described "delicious high-fat source of rants, raves and musings." Listings of mainstream cultural and entertainment events are posted at **www.canada.com** and **www.montrealplus.ca.**

the company was in town from April through July. Check **www.cirquedusoleil.com** for the schedule.

CLASSICAL MUSIC & OPERA

Many churches have exemplary music programs. At **Cathédrale Christ Church** (635 rue Ste-Catherine ouest; ✆ **514/843-6577,** ext. 369; www.montrealcathedral.ca), a top-notch choir sings Sundays at 10am and 4pm with programs that often include modernists such as Benjamin Britten and David Lord.

Opéra de Montréal ★★★ Founded in 1980, this outstanding opera company mounts six productions per year in Montréal, with artists from Québec and abroad participating in such shows as Mozart's *The Magic Flute* and Puccini's *Tosca.* Video translations are provided from the original languages into French and English. Performances are held from September to June at Place des Arts. Place des Arts, 175 rue Ste-Catherine ouest (main entrance), downtown. ✆ **514/985-2258** for tickets. www.operademontreal.com. Tickets from C$46. Métro: Place des Arts.

Orchestre Métropolitain du Grand Montréal The orchestra performs during its regular season at Place des Arts. Its 2010 schedule included an assorted program *Airs de jeunesse* and Mahler's Symphony No. 8. In summer, it presents free outdoor concerts at Théâtre de Verdure in Parc La Fontaine. Place des Arts, 175 rue Ste-Catherine ouest (main entrance), downtown. ✆ **866/842-2112** or 514/842-2112. www.orchestremetropolitain.com. Tickets from C$30. Métro: Place des Arts.

Orchestre Symphonique de Montréal (OSM) ★★ Kent Nagano, who has been the music director here since 2005, focuses the symphony's repertoire on programs featuring works by Beethoven, Bach, Brahms, Mahler, and Messiaen. The orchestra performs at Place des Arts and occasionally at the Notre-Dame Basilica, and offers a few free concerts in regional parks each summer. Place des Arts, 175 rue Ste-Catherine ouest (main entrance), downtown. ✆ **514/842-9951** for tickets. www.osm.ca. Tickets from C$28; discounts available for people under 30. Métro: Place des Arts.

CONCERT HALLS & AUDITORIUMS

Centre Bell Seating up to 22,500, Centre Bell is the home of the Montréal Canadiens hockey team and host to the biggest international rock and pop stars traveling through the city, including Montréal native Céline Dion (1968–), Beyoncé Knowles (1981–), and Coldplay, as well as shows like Disney On Ice. Check the website for information about guided tours and the newly-minted 929-sq.-m (10,000-sq.-ft.) Montréal Canadiens Hall of Fame. 1260 rue de la Gauchetière ouest, downtown. ✆ **800/663-6786** or 514/989-2841. www.centrebell.ca. Métro: Bonaventure.

Métropolis After starting life as a skating rink in 1884, the Métropolis is now a prime showplace for traveling rock groups, especially for bands on the way up or retracing their steps down. It has recently hosted The Flaming Lips, Cyndi Lauper, Kool and the Gang, and the "The Ethnic Show" comedy tour. There's also a small attached lounge, **Le Savoy.** 59 rue Ste-Catherine est, downtown. ✆ **514/844-3500.** www.montrealmetropolis.ca/metropolis. Métro: St-Laurent or Berri-UQAM.

Place des Arts ★★ Since 1992, Place des Arts has been the city's central entertainment complex, presenting performances of musical concerts, opera, dance, and theater in five halls: **Salle Wilfrid-Pelletier** (2,990 seats), where the Orchestre Symphonique de Montréal (see above) and Les Grands Ballets Canadiens (see below) often perform; **Théâtre Maisonneuve** (1,458 seats), where the Orchestre Métropolitain du Grand Montréal (see above) performs; **Théâtre Jean-Duceppe** (765 seats); **Cinquième Salle** (417 seats); and the small **Studio-Théâtre Stella Artois** (138 seats). Portions of the city's many arts festivals are staged in the halls and outdoor plaza here, as are traveling productions of Broadway shows. ***Note:*** In 2011, portions of the Place des Arts plaza may be under construction. Consult the website for current parking information and updates about temporary entrances. Place des Arts, 175 rue Ste-Catherine ouest (ticket office), downtown. ✆ **866/842-2112** or 514/842-2112 for information & tickets. www.pda.qc.ca. Métro: Place des Arts.

Théâtre de Verdure Tango nights in July are especially popular at the open-air theater nestled in a popular park in Plateau Mont-Royal. Everything is free: music, dance, and theater, often with well-known artists and performers. Many in the audience pack picnics. Performances are held from June to August. Check with the tourism office (p. 208) for days and times. Parc La Fontaine, Plateau Mont-Royal. ✆ **514/872-4041.** Métro: Sherbrooke.

DANCE

Montréal hosts frequent appearances by notable dancers and troupes from other parts of Canada and the world—among them Hofesh Shechter Company, National Ballet of Cuba, Balé de Rua, and Toronto's Le Ballet National du Canada—and has accomplished resident companies, too.

Les Grands Ballets Canadiens ★★ The prestigious touring company, performing both a classical and a modern repertoire, has developed a following far beyond national borders in its 50-plus years (it was founded in 1957). In the process, it has brought prominence to many gifted Canadian choreographers and composers. The troupe's production of *The Nutcracker* is always a big event each winter. Performances are held October through May. Place des Arts, 175 rue Ste-Catherine ouest (main entrance), downtown. ✆ **514/842-2112.** www.grandsballets.qc.ca. Tickets from C$35; discounts available for people under 30. Métro: Place des Arts.

THEATER

Centaur Theatre The city's principal English-language theater is housed in a former stock-exchange building (1903). Presented here are a mix of classics, foreign adaptations, and works by Canadian playwrights. It was here that famed playwright Michel Tremblay's (1942–) *Forever Yours, Marie-Lou* received its first English-language staging in 2008. Slated for 2011 are *Schwartz's: The Musical* (the restaurant Schwartz's; see p. 237), and a satire about the financial crash, coproduced with Toronto's Crow's Theatre. 453 rue St-François-Xavier (near rue Notre-Dame), Vieux-Montréal. ✆ **514/288-3161.** www.centaurtheatre.com. Tickets from C$44. Métro: Place d'Armes.

MUSIC & DANCE CLUBS

A note to clubbers: This city is *serious* about partying. Regular bars stay open until 3am, and still others keep the fire burning after-hours. Popular clubs can be exclusive—waiting in line is an unfortunate reality, and dress codes are observed. You can increase your chances for entry at the most exclusive spots by making advance reservations or guaranteeing a table by "buying a bottle." Frequent clubbers get cover charge discounts and avoid lines by registering with **www.montrealguestlist.com.** Once on the list, you may have to arrive early or within a small window of time.

Cabaret Mado The glint of the sequins can be blinding! Inspired by 1920s cabaret theater, this determinedly trendy place in the Village has nightly performances and a dance floor, and is considered a premiere venue these days. Friday and Saturday feature festive drag shows, which, on a given night, may honor the likes of Tina Turner (1939–) or Céline Dion. Look for the pink-haired drag queen on the retro marquee. 1115 rue Ste-Catherine est (near rue Amherst), the Village. ✆ **514/525-7566.** www.mado.qc.ca. Cover C$5–C$10. Métro: Beaudry.

Piknic Electronik 🎁 From May to October on sunny Sunday afternoons and into the evenings, a DJ starts spinning or live acts amp up, and the electronica begins at Parc Jean-Drapeau. Hipster kids, families, and dancing queens who just didn't get enough on Saturday night gather and shake it outdoors under the Alexander Calder (1898–1976) sculpture, *Man and His World,* located on the Belvedere on the north shore of Ile Sainte-Hélène, facing the river. (The website suggests getting off at the Métro and just following the rhythms!) Music starts by 1 or 2pm and runs until about 8pm, sometimes 10:30pm. From 2010 on, all materials used at the Piknic Electronik site will be recyclable or compostable. Belvedere in Parc Jean-Drapeau (Ile Ste-Hélène). ✆ **514/904-1247.** www.piknicelectronik.com. Admission C$10 adults, free for children 12 & under. May–Oct Sun. Métro: Jean-Drapeau.

Sky Club & Pub ★ A complex that includes drag performances in the cabaret room, a pub serving dinner daily from 4 to 9pm, a hip-hop room, a spacious dance floor that's often set to house music, and a popular roof terrace, Sky is thought by many to be the city's hottest spot for the gay, young, and fabulous. It's got spiffy decor and pounding music. Did we mention there's also a pool? And a spa? 1474 rue Ste-Catherine est (near rue Plessis), the Village. ✆ **514/529-6969.** www.complexesky.com. Métro: Beaudry.

Tokyo Bar It's all about the rooftop terrace at this dance club, which draws well-dressed 20-somethings and tourists, rain or shine, 10pm to 3am. There's indoor space, too, for live music or DJs, hip-hop to disco. 3709 bd. St-Laurent (near av. des Pins), Plateau Mont-Royal. ✆ **514/842-6838.** www.tokyobar.com. Cover C$7–C$10. Métro: Sherbrooke.

ROCK, POP & FOLK

Casa del Popolo ★ The heart of the Montréal indie music scene. Set in a scruffy storefront, Casa del Popolo serves vegetarian food, operates a laid-back bar, and has a small first-floor stage. Across the street is a sister performance space, La Sala Rosa (below). 4873 bd. St-Laurent (near bd. St-Joseph), Plateau Mont-Royal. ✆ **514/284-3804.** www.casadelpopolo.com. Cover C$5–C$15. Métro: Laurier.

Club Soda The long-established rock club in a seedy part of the Latin Quarter remains one of the prime destinations for performers just below the star level—Queensryche, Mara Tremblay, and Pauly Shore have all come through recently—and also hosts several of the city's comedy festivals and acts for the annual jazz festival. Montréaler Antoine Gratton is slated for early 2011. 1225 bd. St-Laurent (at rue Ste-Catherine), west of the Village. ✆ **514/286-1010.** www.clubsoda.ca. Tickets from C$17. Métro: St-Laurent.

La Sala Rosa ★★ A bigger venue than its sister performance space Casa del Popolo (above), La Sala Rosa has a full calendar of interesting rock, experimental, and jazz music, and is probably the premiere indie-rock club in the city. The attached **Sala Rosa Restaurant** serves hearty Spanish food with a big card of tapas and paella—and, every Thursday, live flamenco music with dancing and singing. Reserve your spot a week or more in advance. 4848 bd. St-Laurent (near bd. St-Joseph), Plateau Mont-Royal. ✆ **514/844-4227.** www.casadelpopolo.com. Cover C$5–C$30. Métro: Laurier.

JAZZ & BLUES

Montréal's major **Festival International de Jazz ★★** is held every summer for 11 days and caters to the huge interest in this original American art form. The 2010 edition featured performances by Lionel Richie, Cassandra Wilson, the Steve Miller Band, and Paolo Fresu. It costs serious money to hear stars of such magnitude, and tickets often sell out months in advance. Fortunately, hundreds of free outdoor performances also take place during the late-June/early July party, many right on downtown's streets and plazas. "Jazz" is broadly interpreted to include everything from Dixieland to reggae, world beat, and the unclassifiable experimental. For information call ✆ **888/515-0515** or 514/871-1881, or visit **www.montrealjazzfest.com.**

Maison de Jazz ★ Right downtown, this New Orleans–style jazz venue has been on the scene for decades. Lovers of barbecued ribs and jazz arrive early to fill the room, which is decorated in mock–Art Nouveau style with tiered levels. Live music starts around 8pm most nights and continues until closing time. The ribs are okay, and the jazz is of the swinging mainstream variety, with occasional digressions into more esoteric forms. 2060 rue Aylmer (south of rue Sherbrooke), downtown. ✆ **514/842-8656.** www.houseofjazz.ca. Cover C$5. Métro: McGill.

Modavie Set aside an evening for dinner with jazz at this popular Vieux-Montréal bistro (p. 233) and wine bar. Music is usually mainstream jazz by duos or trios, and there's no fee for the show. In addition to tables, there are about a dozen seats at a handsome horseshoe-shaped bar just inside the door. There's a long list of scotches, wine, cognacs, grappas, and ports. It's a friendly place, and the food is good, too. 1 rue St-Paul ouest (corner of rue St-Laurent), Plateau Mont-Royal. ✆ **514/287-9582.** www.modavie.com. Métro: Place d'Armes.

Upstairs Jazz Bar & Grill ★ The Upstairs Jazz Bar, decidedly *down* a few steps from the street, has been hosting live jazz music nightly for years. Big names are infrequent, but the groups are more than competent. Sets begin as at 8:30pm, and there are three a night, 7 days a week. Decor includes record-album covers and fish tanks. Pretty good food ranges from bar snacks to more substantial meals. Most patrons are edging toward their middle-age years. 1254 rue Mackay (near rue Ste-Catherine), downtown. ✆ **514/931-6808.** www.upstairsjazz.com. Cover usually C$5–C$30. Métro: Guy-Concordia.

Bars

There are four main drags to keep in mind for a night on the town. Downtown's **rue Crescent** hums with activity from late afternoon until far into the evening, especially on summer weekend nights, when the street swarms with people careening from bar to restaurant to club. It's young and noisy. In the Plateau Mont-Royal neighborhood, **boulevard St-Laurent**—or the Main, as it's known—has blocks and blocks of bars and clubs, most with a distinctive French personality, as opposed to rue Crescent's Anglo flavor. In Vieux-Montréal, **rue St-Paul** west of Place Jacques-Cartier falls somewhere in the middle on the Anglophone-Francophone spectrum. And in the Village, **rue Catherine** closes in summer to cars and becomes flush with people as the cafes and bars that line the street build temporary terraces that fill in the afternoons and evenings.

Most bars tend to open around 11:30am and stay open until 2 or 3am. Many have *heures joyeuses* (happy hours) from as early as 3pm to as late as 9pm, but usually for a shorter period within those hours.

CENTRE VILLE/DOWNTOWN & RUE CRESCENT

Brutopia ★ This pub pulls endless pints of its own microbrews, which might include maple cream, IPA, or java stout on a given day. With several rooms on three levels, a terrace in back, and a street-side balcony, it draws a mix of ages, students with laptops, and old friends just hanging out. Unlike other spots on rue Crescent, where the sound levels can be deafening, here you can actually have a conversation. The snacking menu spans the globe. Bands perform, too, with an open-mic night on Sunday. 1219 rue Crescent (north of bd. René-Lévesque). ✆ **514/393-9277.** www.brutopia.net. Métro: Lucien L'Allier.

Dominion Square Tavern Located just steps away from the central tourist office on Square Dorchester, the tavern got an overhaul in early 2010. It is visually arresting, done up in 1920s grandeur, with original tiles, lead mirrors, and an amber glow. The menu includes *moules et frites* (mussels and French fries) and a Ploughman's Lunch, featuring either meat or fish. Mains run from C$11 to C$23. It's open 11:30am to midnight weekdays and 5pm to midnight Saturday. 1248 Metcalfe (south of rue Ste-Catherine). ✆ **514/564-5056.** www.tavernedominion.com. Métro: Peel.

Pullman A sleek wine bar that offers either 60mL or 120mL (2- or 4-oz.) pours, so you can sample a number of vintages. A competent tapas menu with standards like charcuterie and grilled cheese bedazzled with port are prepared with the precision of a sushi chef. The smartly designed multilevel space creates pockets of ambience, from cozy corners to tables drenched in natural light. Open daily from 4:30pm to 1am. 3424 av. du Parc (north of Sherbrooke). ✆ **514/288-7779.** www.pullman-mtl.com. Métro: Place des Arts.

Sir Winston Churchill Pub ★ The three levels of bars and cafes here are rue Crescent landmarks, and the New Orleans–style sidewalk and first-floor terraces (open in warm months) make perfect vantage points from which to check out the pedestrian traffic. Inside and down the stairs, the pub, with English ales on tap, attempts to imitate a British public house and gets a mixed crowd of young professionals. Open daily to 3am, with DJs every day. 1459 rue Crescent (near rue Ste-Catherine). ✆ **514/288-3814.** www.swcpc.com. Métro: Guy-Concordia.

Thursday's A prime watering hole for Montréal's young, professional set. The pubby bar spills out onto a terrace that hangs over the street, and there's a glittery disco in back. Voted "Best Pick-Up Spot" year after year by the *Montréal Mirror,* which quips that Thursday's "gets more people laid than Craigslist." In L'Hôtel de la Montagne, 1430 rue de la Montagne (north of rue Ste-Catherine). ✆ **514/288-5656.** www.thursdaysbar.com. Métro: Guy-Concordia.

Tour de Ville Memorable and breathtaking. We're talking about the view from Montréal's only revolving restaurant and bar, up on the 30th floor of the Delta Centre Ville (the bar part doesn't revolve, but you still get a great view). The best time to go is when the sun is setting and the city lights are beginning to blink on. Open Friday and Saturday from 5:30 to 11pm (and Sunday brunch for two seatings: 10:30am–12:30pm and 1–3pm). In the Delta Centre-Ville Hôtel, 777 rue University (at rue St-Jecques). ✆ **514/879-4777.** Métro: Square Victoria.

VIEUX-MONTREAL

Le Jardin Nelson Tuck into the large tree-shaded garden court in back, which sits behind a stone building dating from 1812. A pleasant hour or two can be spent listening to live jazz, played every afternoon and evening. The kitchen does well with its pizzas and crepes, with crepe options both sweet and savory (including lobster). There are heaters outdoors to cut the chill and a few indoor tables, too. When the weather's nice, it's open until 2am. Closed November through mid-April. 407 Place Jacques-Cartier (at rue St-Paul). ✆ **514/861-5731.** www.jardinnelson.com. Métro: Place d'Armes or Champ-de-Mars.

Suite 701 When Le Place d'Armes Hôtel (p. 226) converted its lobby and wine bar into this spiffy lounge, young professionals got the word fast. The so-called *cinq-à-sept* (5-to-7) after-work crowd fills the space evenings, especially on Thursdays. Upscale bar food comes from the same kitchen as the restaurant's high-end operation, **Aix Cuisine du Terroir** (p. 226), with snacks for C$8 to C$14 and main courses for C$21 to C$25. 711 Côte de la Place d'Armes (at rue St-Jacques). ✆ **514/904-1201.** Métro: Place d'Armes.

Verses Sky Terrace When the weather is warm enough, ascend to this rooftop restaurant/bar inside the snazzy **Hôtel Nelligan** (p. 225). It's open from 11am to 11pm, with food available all day. 100 rue St-Paul ouest (at St-Sulpice). ✆ **514/788-4000.** www.hotelnelligan.com. Métro: Place d'Armes.

PLATEAU MONT-ROYAL & MILE END

Bílý Kůň ★★ Pronounced "Billy Coon," this popular bar is a bit of Prague right in Montréal, from the avant-garde decor (mounted ostrich heads ring the room) to the full line of Czech beers, local microbrews, and dozen-plus scotches. Martini specials include the Absinthe Aux Pommes. Students and professionals jam in for the relaxed candle-lit atmosphere, which includes twirling ceiling fans and picture windows that open to the street. There's live jazz from 6 to 8pm daily and DJs spinning upbeat pop most nights from 8pm to 3am. Get here early to do a little shopping in the hipster boutiques along the street. 354 av. Mont-Royal est (near rue St-Denis). ✆ **514/845-5392.** www.bilykun.com. Métro: Mont-Royal.

Champs Montréalers are no less enthusiastic about sports, especially hockey, than other Canadians, and fans both avid and casual drop by this three-story sports emporium to catch up with their teams and hoist a few. Games from around the world are fed to walls of TVs; more than a dozen athletic events might be showing at any given time. Food is what you'd expect—burgers, steaks, and such. 3956 bd. St-Laurent (near rue Duluth). ✆ **514/987-6444.** Métro: Sherbrooke.

Dieu Du Ciel ★★ This appealing neighborhood artisanal brewpub offers an alternating selection of some dozen beers, including house brews and exotic imports. The place buzzes, even midweek. With good conversation and some friends to sample the array, what more do you need? If it's guidance on where to begin, how about starting with the Première Communion (First Communion), a Scottish ale; moving on to the Rosée d'Hibiscus, which is less sweet than feared; and finishing with the Rigor Mortis ABT. Dieu du Ciel beers are also bottled and sold throughout the province. 29 rue Laurier ouest (near St. Laurent). ✆ **514/490-9555.** www.dieuduciel.com. Métro: Laurier.

Koko One of *the* chicest bars of the city. Koko is a prime reason to visit, if not stay at, the **Opus Hotel** (p. 220). The bar includes a spectacular terrace and an Asian-influenced menu, and it's open "until late"—1am Sunday through Wednesday and 3am Thursday through Saturday. As befits its positioning as a premier venue for urban glamour, a bouncer often stands watch at the door. Try the C$12

Wilde Child cocktail, with Prosecco and candied wild hibiscus flower. 8 rue Sherbrooke ouest (at bd. St-Laurent). ✆ **514/657-5656.** www.kokomontreal.com. Métro: Saint-Laurent.

Gambling & Cabaret

The **Casino de Montréal** (✆ **800/665-2274** or 514/392-2746; www.casinosduquebec.com), Québec's first, is housed in recycled space: The complex reuses what were the French and Québec pavilions during the 1967 Word's Fair. Asymmetrical and groovy, the buildings provide a dramatic setting for games of chance. Four floors contain more than 120 game tables, including roulette, craps, blackjack, baccarat, and varieties of poker, and there are more than 3,000 slot machines. It has four restaurants, including the elegant **Nuances**, one of the top restaurants in the city.

No alcoholic beverages are served in the gambling areas, and patrons must be at least 18 years old and dressed neatly (beachwear and clothing depicting violence are prohibited). The casino is entirely smoke-free, with outside smoking areas. It's open 24 hours a day, 7 days a week, with overnight packages available at nearby hotels.

The casino is on Parc Jean-Drapeau. You can drive there, or take the Métro to the Parc Jean-Drapeau stop and then walk or take the casino shuttle bus (no. 167, labeled CASINO). From June through October, a free shuttle bus *(navette)* leaves on the hour from the downtown Infotouriste Centre at 1001 rue du Square Dorchester (it makes other stops downtown, too). Shuttles depart from the Infotouriste Centre starting at 10am and ending at 7pm; the last shuttle leaves the casino for downtown at 7:45pm. Call ✆ **514/392-2746** with questions.

THE LAURENTIAN MOUNTAINS

You don't have to travel far from Montréal to get to ski mountains, parks, or bike trails; just 30 minutes north, for instance, gets you to the base of the resort region of the Laurentian mountain range. You won't find spiked peaks—the rolling hills and rounded mountains of the Laurentian Shield average between 300m and 520m (984 ft. and 1,706 ft.) in height. Nearer to Montréal, the terrain resembles a rumpled quilt, its folds and hollows cupping a multitude of lakes large and small. Farther north the summits are higher and craggier.

The pearl of the Laurentians (also called the Laurentides) is **Mont-Tremblant**, the highest peak in eastern Canada at 875m (2,871 ft.). It's a mecca in the winter for skiers and snowboarders from all over North America. Development has been heavy in the resort village at the base of the mountain, an Aspen-meets-Disneyland development that is just 1½ hours from Montréal. This pedestrian village has the prefabricated look of a theme park, but at least planners used the Québécois architectural style of pitched or mansard roofs in bright colors, not ersatz Bavarian Alpine flourishes. Trails for those with advanced skills typically have short pitches and challenging moguls, with broad, hard-packed avenues for beginners and the less experienced. Skiers can usually expect reliable snow from early December to late March.

Skiing, though, is only half the story. As transportation to the region improved, people took advantage of the obvious warm-weather opportunities for watersports, golf (courses in the area now total nearly 30), mountain biking, and hiking.

The busiest times are February and March for skiing, July and August for summer vacation, and during the Christmas-to-New Year's holiday period.

In March and April, the maple trees are tapped, and *cabanes à sucre* (sugar shacks) open up everywhere, some selling just maple syrup and candies, others serving full meals and even staging entertainment. May is often characterized by warm days, cool nights, and just enough people that the streets don't seem deserted. September is the same way, and in the last 2 weeks of that month, the leaves put on a stunning show of autumnal color.

In May and June, it must be said, the indigenous black flies and mosquitoes can seem as big and as ill-tempered as buzzards. Some of the resorts and inns close down for a couple of weeks in spring and fall, so check ahead if you're traveling then.

A few words of clarification about the abundant use of the name Tremblant: There is Mont-Tremblant, the mountain. At the base of its slope is Tremblant, the resort village that is sometimes called Mont-Tremblant Station or the pedestrian village. Just adjacent is Lac (Lake) Tremblant. And there is the small former village of Mont-Tremblant, known today as the old village, about 5km (3 miles) northwest of the resort.

Getting There

BY CAR The fast and scenic **Autoroute des Laurentides,** also known as **Autoroute 15,** goes straight from Montréal to the Laurentians. Leaving Montréal, follow the signs to St-Jérôme. About 103km (64 miles) north of Montréal, the autoroute ends and **Route 117** becomes the major artery for the region.

Exit numbers represent the distance in kilometers from Montréal. There are four exits to the Mont-Tremblant area. Exit 113 takes visitors through Centre-Ville Mont-Tremblant (formerly known as the village of St-Jovite). The main street, rue de St-Jovite, is lined with cafes and shops. Exit 119 goes directly to the mountain and most of the hotels listed here.

BY BUS From Montréal, **Galland** buses (✆ **514/333-9555;** www.galland-bus.com) stop in the larger Laurentian towns, including Mont-Tremblant. The ride to Mont-Tremblant takes about 3 hours.

BY PLANE **Mont-Tremblant International Airport** (airport code YTM; ✆ **819/275-9099**; www.mtia.ca), 39km (24 miles) northwest of Mont-Tremblant, receives direct flights from Toronto through Porter Airlines (www.flyporter.com) and from Newark, New Jersey, through Continental Airlines (www.continental.com) in winter months only. Car rentals are available from Hertz and Discount by reservation only. An airport shuttle bus delivers guests directly to many of the hotels in Mont-Tremblant and to the ski mountain, and taxis are available. The ride takes about 40 minutes. **Aéroport International Pierre-Elliott-Trudeau de Montréal** (see p. 206) is about 60 minutes south of Mont-Tremblant.

Cold-Weather Activities

DOWNHILL SKIING

The **Mont-Tremblant ski resort** (www.tremblant.ca) draws the biggest downhill crowds in the Laurentians and is repeatedly ranked as the top ski resort in eastern North America by *Ski Magazine.* Founded in 1939 by a Philadelphia millionaire named Joe Ryan, it's one of the oldest in North America. It pioneered creating trails on both sides of a mountain and was the second mountain in the world to install a chairlift. The vertical drop is 645m (2,116 ft.).

When the snow is deep, skiers here like to follow the sun around the mountain, making the run down slopes with an eastern exposure in the morning and down the western-facing ones in the afternoon. The resort has snowmaking capability to cover almost three-quarters of its skiable terrain (265 hectares/655 acres). Of its 95 downhill runs and trails, half are expert terrain, about a third are intermediate, and the rest beginner. The longest trail, Nansen, is 6km (3¾ miles).

CROSS-COUNTRY SKIING

Parc National du Mont-Tremblant boasts 10 loops (53km/33 miles) of groomed cross-country track in the Diable sector, including 12km (7½ miles) for skate skiing. The Pimbina sector is designated exclusively for snowshoeing and backcountry skiing. Visit www.sepaq.com to locate visitor centers and information kiosks, or to check availability of the sector's five new yurts, which sleep four in any season.

Many enthusiasts maintain that some of the best trails are on the grounds **of Domaine Saint-Bernard,** formerly a congregation of the Brothers of Christian Instruction and now managed by a land trust (545 chemin St-Bernard; ✆ **819/425-3588;** www.domainesaintbernard.org). It's also common for hotels adjacent to golf courses to have trails leading directly from their property.

ADDITIONAL SNOW SPORTS

Ice skating, dog-sledding, snowmobiling, curling, ice fishing, tubing, and **acrobranche**—a series of zip lines that allow you to swing from tree to tree at heights exceeding 22m (72 ft.)—are also available in the Mont-Tremblant region. For a truly unique aerial view, try acrobranche at night; make reservations through the **Tremblant Activity Center** (✆ **819/681-4848;** www.tremblantactivities.com).

Warm-Weather Activities

BIKING

Parc Linéaire le P'Tit Train du Nord (1000 rue Saint Georges; ✆ **450-227-3313;** www.laurentides.com), a bike trail on a former rail bed. The route runs through Mont-Tremblant.

BOATING, CANOEING & KAYAKING

From June until October, **Croisières Mont-Tremblant** (2810 chemin du Village; ✆ **819/425-1045;** www.croisierestremblant.com) offers a 60-minute narrated cruise of Lac Tremblant, focusing on its history, nature, and legends. Fares are C$18 for adults, C$15 for seniors, C$5 for children ages 6 to 15, and free for children 5 and younger.

Centre Nautique Pierre Plouffe Tremblant (2900 chemin du Village; ✆ **888/681-5634** or 819/681-5634; www.tremblantnautique.com) has boats for hire, as well as waterskiing and wakeboarding lessons.

Guided and self-guided canoe and kayak trips along the Diable or Rogue rivers can be planned through the **Tremblant Activity Centre** on Place Saint-Bernard in the pedestrian village (✆ **888/736-2526** or 819/681-4848; www.tremblantactivities.com). Reservations are required. Maps and guides are also available through the **Fédération québécoise du canot et du kayak** (✆ **514/252-3001;** www.canot-kayak.qc.ca).

GOLFING

One could golf a fresh 18 holes every day for a month in this region. Options include the renowned **Le Diable** and **Le Géant** courses, which are operated by the Tremblant ski resort. Le Diable (*the devil*) is the trickier, more challenging course, while Le Géant is the "gentler giant." Virtual tours are at **www.tremblant.ca/golf.**

HORSEBACK RIDING

About 10 minutes from the mountain, **Le Ranch de la Rivière Rouge** (3377 chemin du Moulin, Labelle; ✆ **819/686-2280;** www.ranchdelariviererouge.com) leads year-round horseback experiences for persons of all ages and skill levels.

SWIMMING

In warm months, watersports are almost as popular as the ski slopes are in winter. **Lac Tremblant** is a gorgeous stretch of lake, and another dozen lakes, as well as rivers and streams, are accessible through **Parc National du Mont-Tremblant** (www.sepaq.com). **Crémaillère beach** and **Lac-Provost beach,** both in Parc National, have lifeguards and bathrooms.

SOMETHING DIFFERENT

Right on the ski mountain at the pedestrian village, there's a downhill dry-land alpine **luge run** in summer. The engineless sleds are gravity-propelled, reaching speeds of up to 48kmph (30mph), if you so choose (it's easy to go down as a slowpoke, too). Rides are priced by number of descents, starting at C$13 for one ride. The village has other games and attractions, such as **dune buggy tours, bungee trampoline, paintball,** and **outdoor climbing walls.**

No matter the season, the lucky (or brave) can hold 'em or fold 'em at **Casino de Mont-Tremblant** (✆ **800/665-2274** or 514/499-5180; www.casinosduquebec.com/mont-tremblant), which opened its doors in summer 2009. Table games include

WITH apologies TO MONTY PYTHON: "SPA, SPA, SPA, SPA . . ."

Spas are big business around here: They're the most popular new features at hotels, especially in the Mont-Tremblant area, where guests are looking for new ways to pamper themselves beyond dropping a lot of money on skiing.

At some hotels, innkeepers might say they have a "spa" on-site when what they've got is an outdoor hot tub. What we're talking about here, though, is a complex that features therapeutic services—particularly, ones that involve water.

If you've never experienced a European-style Nordic spa before, set aside 3 hours for a visit to **Le Scandinave Spa** (4280 Montée Ryan, Mont-Tremblant; ✆ **888/537-2263** or 819/425-5524; www.scandinave.com). It's a rustic-chic complex of small buildings among evergreen trees on the Diable River shore. For C$45, visitors (18 and older only) have run of the facility. Options include outdoor hot tubs designed to look like natural pools (one is set under a manmade waterfall); a Norwegian steam bath thick with the scent of eucalyptus oil; indoor relaxation areas with supercomfortable, low-slung chairs; and the river itself, which the heartiest of folk dip into even on frigid days. (A heat lamp keeps a small square of river open during the iciest part of winter.) The idea is to move from hot to cold to hot, which supposedly purges toxins and invigorates your skin. Bathing suits are required, and men and women share all spaces except the changing rooms.

Couples, mothers and daughters, groups of friends, and people on their own all come to "take the waters." The spa is year-round.

poker, baccarat, blackjack, craps, roulette, and 500 slot machines. Admittance is free but restricted to persons over 18. Located on the newly-developing side of the mountain called Versant Soleil at 300 chemin des Pléiades and connected to the pedestrian village by a gondola, getting there may be half the fun—unless of course, you win big.

Where to Stay

There are abundant options for housing in the area. In addition to the listings below, **B&Bs** are listed at **www.bbtremblant.com.** About 30 **campgrounds** dot the Laurentians, some operating through national or regional parks, others privately-run. **Tourisme Laurentides** (www.laurentians.com) has an online directory with services listed for each campground. Also keep in mind the cabins and recently-added yurts in the national park, available year-round.

Of the accommodations listed below, the following are at or just adjacent to the base of the mountain: Ermitage du Lac, Fairmont Tremblant, Homewood Suites by Hilton, and Quintessence. The following are a short driving distance from the mountain: Auberge La Porte Rouge, Château Beauvallon, and Le Grand Lodge.

Many mountain-side hotels are booked 9 months in advance for holidays, such as the week between Christmas and New Year's or for school vacation week. Be prepared for and inquire about strict cancellation policies and 2- to 4-night minimum stays. Likewise, some hotels offer discounts for booking and paying in advance.

Auberge La Porte Rouge An unusual motel-inn, run by a third-generation owner, located in the old village of Mont-Tremblant right on a public beach. Wake to a view of Lake Mercier through your picture window (every unit has one), or take in the vista from a little balcony. Some rooms have both fireplaces and whirlpool tubs. There is a terrace facing the lake and a small cocktail lounge. Rooms accommodate 2 to 3 people, while cottages have space for 10. Rowboats, canoes, and pedal boats are all available, and the motel is directly on the regional bike and cross-country ski linear park, Le P'tit Train du Nord.

1874 chemin du Village, Mont-Tremblant, PQ J8E 1K4. ✆ **800/665-3505** or 819/425-3505. Fax 819/425-6700. www.aubergelaporterouge.com. 26 units. C$174–C$224 double. Rates include breakfast & dinner. Packages available. C$30 additional children 6–17; children 5 & under stay free. AE, MC, V. **Amenities:** Restaurant; bike rental; pool (heated outdoor); watersports equipment. *In room:* A/C, TV, hair dryer, Wi-Fi (free).

Château Beauvallon ★★ ☺ Since opening in 2005, Château Beauvallon has become the region's premiere property for families who want to stay off the mountain. A member of Small Luxury Hotels of the World, the 70-suite, three-story hotel has positioned itself as an affordable luxury retreat for seasoned travelers, and it delivers with a relaxed elegance. Every suite has two bathrooms, a small bedroom with a plush California-king-size bed, a queen-size Murphy bed, a pullout couch, a balcony, a gas fireplace, a 32-inch high-definition flat-screen TV (with a smaller TV in the bedroom), and an equipped kitchenette. All rooms face the pool or the lake behind the property, which sits between two holes on La Diable golf course. A large central fireplace lounge provides a warm gathering place, and the staff is friendly and competent. Both hotel and restaurant adhere to eco-friendly guidelines set by regional and national associations.

6385 Montée Ryan, Mont-Tremblant, PQ J8E 1S5. ✆ **888/681-6611** or 819/681-6611. Fax 819/681-1941. www.chateaubeauvallon.com. 70 units. C$229–C$289 suite. Children 17 & under stay free in parent's room. Packages available. AE, DC, MC, V. Free parking. **Amenities:** Restaurant; bar; babysitting; children's programs (high-season); concierge; golf adjacent; exercise room; hot tub (all-year outdoor); 2 pools (outdoor heated pool w/terrace, indoor heated); room service. *In room:* A/C, TV, DVD player (on request), hair dryer, kitchenette, MP3 docking station, Wi-Fi (free).

Ermitage du Lac ☺ Convenient to the ski mountain and the pedestrian village without being directly upon either, this boutique hotel offers a little more peace and quiet than larger properties closer to the action. It's also agreeably close to Parc Plage, the beach on Lac Tremblant, which makes for an enjoyable summer stay. All units are large studios or one- to three-bedroom suites, with kitchenettes or full kitchens equipped with oven ranges, microwaves, unstocked fridges, and necessary cookware and crockery (not all have dishwashers, though). Most have fireplaces and balconies, too. There is a secure underground parking garage.

150 chemin du Curé-Deslauriers, Mont-Tremblant, PQ J8E 1C9. ✆ **800/461-8711** or 819/681-2222. Fax 819/681-2223. www.tremblant.ca. 69 units. C$245 double, from C$335 suite. Rates include breakfast. Packages available. Children 17 & under stay free in parent's room. AE, MC, V. Parking C$10. **Amenities:** Breakfast room; children's activity room; concierge; exercise room; hot tub (outdoor, year-round); pool (outdoor, in summer). *In room:* A/C, TV, CD player, hair dryer, kitchenette or kitchen, Wi-Fi (C$10/day).

Fairmont Tremblant ★★ ☺ The high-end resort for families who want to stay directly on the mountain was built in 1996, and a renovation of its slope-side bar and restaurant was completed in 2010. The luxury property stands on a crest above the pedestrian village, as befits its stature among the Tremblant hostelries. Thirteen levels of rooms include the appealing Fairmont View, which overlooks the ski runs and the fairy-tale resort, and Fairmont Gold, which offers access to a private lounge. Families can take advantage of arts-and-crafts programs, year-round outdoor and indoor pools, the 38-person outdoor Jacuzzi, and ski-in-ski-out accessibility to the chairlifts. Couples looking for a quiet break or the attention to detail normally paid at a Fairmont may want to avoid school vacation weeks. An on-site **Amerispa** offers body wraps, facials, and massages. Even vacationers staying elsewhere come for the C$56 surf, turf, and sushi dinner buffet of in-house restaurant **Windigo.**

3045 chemin de la Chapelle, Mont-Tremblant, PQ J8E 1E1. ✆ **800/257-7544** or 819/681-7000. Fax 819/681-7099. www.fairmont.com/tremblant. 314 units. C$249–C$609 double. Children 17 & under stay free in parent's room. Packages available. AE, DC, DISC, MC, V. Valet parking C$20, free self-parking (10-min. walk). Pets accepted (C$25 per pet per day). **Amenities:** Restaurant; bar; cafe (in ski season); babysitting; bike rental; children's programs; concierge; executive-level rooms; exercise room; pools (indoor & heated outdoor); room service; sauna; spa; access to watersports equipment; Wi-Fi (in lobby, C$14/day). *In room:* A/C, TV, hair dryer, Internet (C$14/day), minibar.

Homewood Suites by Hilton ★ Of the hotels that offer ski-in-ski-out access to the mountain's slopes, which are just across the plaza, the Hilton offers the best relative value. Directly on the pedestrian village at Place St-Bernard, a central gathering space, the resort's restaurants, bars, and shops are all within walking distance. An outdoor pool was added in 2008, and in-suite upgrades in 2010 brought in new appliances, granite counters, and new carpeting. The hotel is made up of several buildings decorated on the outside to look like candy-colored row houses, and all accommodations are crisply furnished suites with fireplaces and fully outfitted kitchens—useful when you want to avoid the village's expensive food venues. Suites range in size from studios to two-bedroom units. Laundry facilities and free grocery delivery are added conveniences, and ski lockers are free for guests.

3035 chemin de la Chapelle, Mont-Tremblant, PQ J8E 1E1. ✆ **888/288-2988** or 819/681-0808. Fax 819/681-0331. www.hiltontremblant.com. 103 units. C$200–C$399 suite. Rates include breakfast, afternoon snack & beverages every Mon–Thurs. Children 18 & under stay free in parent's room. Packages available. AE, MC, V. Parking C$10. **Amenities:** Babysitting; hot tub (outdoor year-round); pool (outdoor seasonal); room service; sauna; Wi-Fi (in dining room, free). *In room:* A/C, TV, DVD player (for rent), hair dryer, Internet (free), kitchen.

Le Grand Lodge ★★ ☺ At a quiet distance from the main resort's frequent clamor, this handsome hotel, which consists mostly of suites, is on the shore of Lake Ouimet and draws families, small conventions, and weddings. It was built in 1998 with the palatial log construction of the north country and units leave little to be desired—what with full kitchens, gas fireplaces, and balconies. Dog sledding directly from the hotel and snowshoeing flesh out the more obvious winter pursuits (for example, skiing), and in summer, guests partake in tennis, mountain biking, and canoeing and kayaking from a private beach on the lake. There are events for kids every night in the height of the summer and winter ski seasons. A big bar area overlooks the lake, and inside, you'll find what the hotel claims is Mont-Tremblant's largest pool.

2396 rue Labelle (Rte. 327), Mont-Tremblant, PQ J8E 1T8. ✆ **800/567-6763** or 819/425-2734. Fax 819/425-9725. www.legrandlodge.com. 112 units. C$189–C$299 studio or suite. Children 17 & under stay free in parent's room. Packages available. AE, DC, DISC, MC, V. Valet parking C$10, free self-parking. Pets accepted (C$25/day). **Amenities:** Restaurant; bar; babysitting; bike rental; children's programs; concierge; exercise room; whirlpools (indoor & outdoor); pool (indoor); sauna; spa; 4 tennis courts; watersports equipment. *In room:* A/C, TV, hair dryer, kitchen, Wi-Fi (free).

Quintessence ★★★ The region's most luxurious property. All units have views of Lake Tremblant, and guests have access to a private beach. Go assuming that virtually every service you might find in a larger deluxe hotel will be available to you—then concentrate on the extras. Comfortable beds have thick feather mattress covers. Bathroom floors are heated, showers are of the drenching rainforest variety, and every unit has a wood-burning fireplace and balcony. If it's warm, you can book a ride on the hotel's 1910 mahogany motorboat. There's an outdoor infinity pool and a spa (hotel guests only) that limits the number of visitors to ensure an unhurried atmosphere. Lavish dinners can be taken in the La Quintessence dining room or the intimate Jardin des Saveurs, and there's a 5,000-bottle wine cellar to draw from. Nature fans will want to consider the one rustic cabin, which has a four-poster bed.

3004 chemin de la Chapelle, Mont-Tremblant, PQ J8E 1E1. ✆ **866/425-3400** or 819/425-3400. Fax 819/425-3480. www.hotelquintessence.com. 31 units. C$460–C$1,625 suite, C$380–C$545 cabin. Rates include breakfast. Children 5 & under stay free in parent's room. Packages available. AE, MC, V. Free valet parking. **Amenities:** Restaurant; wine bar; babysitting; concierge; health club; hot tub; pool (heated outdoor); room service; sauna; spa; Wi-Fi (free). *In room:* A/C, TV (on request), CD player, hair dryer, minibar.

Where to Dine

Many Laurentian resorts have their own dining facilities and may require that guests use them (especially in winter), but the area does have some good independent dining options for casual lunches or the odd night out. Also keep in mind **La Quintessence** in Quintessence (see above).

Right within the pedestrian village, **Au Grain de Café**, tucked into a corner of the upper village just off Place St-Bernard, is a favorite for coffee and sandwiches. It's open daily from 7:30am until 11pm during ski season, 8am until 9pm the rest of the year. Baked goods and specialty chocolates are also available at **La Chouquetterie**, 116 chemin Kandahar, and **Brûlerie Saint-Denis**, just left of the base of the main gondola.

As with most ski mountains, beer is abundant. There are always crowds at the slope-side drink palaces **Le Shack** or **La Forge**. If you're in the mood for a cocktail, head to **Avalanche Bistro,** 127 chemin Kandahar (✆ **819/681-4727;** www.avalanchebistro.com), where you can choose from more than 25 martinis.

Aux Truffes ★★ FRENCH CONTEMPORARY The management and kitchen here are more ambitious than just about any on the mountain, evidenced by a wine cellar that sails through Canadian, Californian, Argentine, Australian, Spanish, and many admirable French bottlings (for 9 years running, *Wine Spectator* magazine gave Aux Truffes its award of excellence for its wine list). Put yourself in the hands of the knowledgeable sommelier and go from there. Seared duck foie gras from the region is a steadfast opener. Imaginative mains include a roasted rack of caribou served shepherd's-pie-style with *chicoutai* berries sauce and braised veal cheek "profiteroles" with grilled apricot sauce and bleu cheese from Québec. Close with selections from the *plateau* of raw-milk Québec cheeses. The service is impeccable.

Place Saint-Bernard, 3035 chemin de la Chapelle (in the pedestrian village). ✆ **819/681-4544.** www.auxtruffes.com. Lunch main courses C$15–C$17, dinner main courses C$32–C$47; chef's tasting from C$100. AE, MC, V. High season (summer & winter) daily 11:30am–10pm; low season Wed–Sun 6–10pm. Call to confirm hours.

Crêperie Catherine BREAKFAST/BRUNCH This is the spot for those who long for a hot breakfast and bottomless cup of coffee before venturing onto the ski slopes. In addition to both savory and sweet crepes made before your eyes, Crêperie Catherine has cultivated something neighboring restaurants can lack—cozy ambience. A collection of chef figurines can be found in every nook of the wood paneled interior, and each comes with a personal story tied to the restaurant's origins. Don't hesitate to smother your crepe with the house specialty, *sucre a la crème* (a concoction of brown sugar and butter). You can order from any part of the menu any time of day.

113 chemin Kandahar (in the pedestrian village). ✆ **819/681-4888.** www.creperiecatherine.ca. Main courses C$12–C$17, dessert crepes from C$4.95. Daily 8am–9pm.

Microbrasserie La Diable BREW PUB Though the microbrewery craze has come and gone, it's hard to kill the craving for beer after a day on the slopes (or the links), so why not go local? You're in surprisingly good hands here, for both food and drink. Burgers and ribs are fine options, but we suggest choosing two of four styles of sausage (Smoked Swiss, Ocktoberfest, Toulouse, or Louisiana) with sauerkraut, fries, and side salad for C$14. The six frothy house beers have been brewed on site since 1995. A pitcher sets you back just C$20, which, after a couple nights in this pricey village, feels like a steal. Be warned that it's a bit of a walk down chemin Kandahar from the base of the ski mountain, especially in those clunky boots, but the location makes it easier to find a table.

117 chemin Kandahar (in the pedestrian village). ✆ **819/681-4546.** www.microladiable.com. Main courses C$12–C$24. MC, V. Daily 11:30am–2am.

QUÉBEC CITY & THE GASPÉ PENINSULA

by Leslie Brokaw

8

Few municipalities are as breathtaking as Québec City. Situated along the majestic St. Lawrence River, much of the oldest part of the city—Vieux-Québec—sits atop Cap Diamant, a rock bluff that once provided military defense. Fortress walls still encase the upper portion of the old city, and the soaring Château Frontenac, a hotel with castlelike turrets, dominates the landscape. Hauntingly evocative of a coastal town in the motherland of France, the tableau is as romantic as any in Europe.

Québec City is the soul of New France and holds that history dear. It was the first significant settlement in Canada, founded in 1608, by Samuel de Champlain. The city got a significant sprucing up for its 400th anniversary celebrations in 2008, adding more access to the waterfront.

The city is almost entirely French in feeling, spirit, and language, and 95% of the population is Francophone, or French-speaking. But many people know some English, especially those who work in hotels, restaurants, and shops. Although it is more difficult in Québec City than in Montréal to get by without French, the average Québécois goes out of his or her way to communicate—in halting English, sign language, simplified French, or a combination of all three. Most of the Québécois are uncommonly gracious, even with the city being the capital of the politically prickly Québec province.

A stroll through Québec is comparable to walking in similar *quartiers* in northern European cities. Stone houses come right to the edge of sidewalks; carriage wheels creak behind muscular horses; sunlight filters through leafy canopies; and drinkers and diners lounge in sidewalk cafes on cobblestone streets.

High season in Québec City is from June 24 (Jean-Baptiste Day) through Labour Day (the first Mon in Sept, as in the U.S.). For those 11 weeks, the city is in highest gear. Tourist offices, museums, and restaurants all expand their operating hours, and hotels charge top dollar.

Ile d'Orléans, an agricultural island within sight of Vieux-Québec, is less than a half-hour by car and an easy day trip. Consider, too, a visit a few hours up the northern coast of the St. Lawrence to the shrine of **Ste-Anne-de-Beaupré,** the waterfalls inside a canyon near **Mont Ste-Anne,**

and on to pastoral **Charlevoix** and the Saguenay River, where **whales** come to play. The province ends at the eastern most tip of Canada on the **Gaspé Peninsula,** where you'll find **Rocher Percé**—Percé Rock, in English—a monumental butte that rises from the sea.

ESSENTIALS

Getting There

BY PLANE **Jean-Lesage International Airport** (airport code YQB; ✆ **418/640-2600;** www.aeroportdequebec.com) is served by a number of major airlines. Most air traffic comes by way of Montréal, although there are some direct flights from U.S. cities, including Chicago and Washington, D.C. (on United Airlines), Cleveland and New York (on Continental Airlines), and Detroit (on Delta Airlines). Some direct flights are seasonal only.

A taxi to downtown is a fixed-rate C$33. There is a public bus, #78 (✆ **418/627-2511** or visit **www.rtcquebec.ca**), but it runs only to the Les Saules bus terminal, at the corner of boulevard Massona and rue Michelet, which is well outside the tourist area.

BY TRAIN The handsome train station in Québec City, **Gare du Palais,** 450 rue de la Gare-du-Palais, was designed by Bruce Price, who is also responsible for the Château Frontenac. Many of the hotels listed in this book are up an incline from the station, so a short cab ride might be necessary.

BY BUS The bus terminal, at 320 rue Abraham-Martin (✆ **418/525-3000**), is just next to the train station. As from the train station, it is an uphill climb or quick cab ride to the Upper Town or other parts of the Lower Town.

BY CAR See p. 212 in the Montréal chapter for general driving advice within the Québec province.

Driving north from the U.S., the entire ride is on expressways. Québec City is 867km (539 miles) from New York and about 3 hours northeast from Montréal. From New York, follow the directions on p. 208. From Autoroute 15, pick up Autoroute 20 to Québec.

Coming into Québec City, follow signs for the bridge Pont Pierre-Laporte. Shortly after crossing the bridge, turn right onto boulevard Wilfrid-Laurier (Rte. 175). It changes names first to boulevard Laurier and then to Grande-Allée, the grand boulevard that leads directly into the central Parliament Hill area and the old city.

Another appealing option when you're approaching from the south is to follow Route 132 to the town of Lévis. A car-ferry there, **Traverse Québec-Lévis** (✆ **418/644-3704**), provides a 10-minute ride across the river and a dramatic introduction to the city. Although the schedule varies substantially according to time of day, week, and season, the ferry leaves at least once an hour from 6am to 2am. One-way costs C$5.95 for the car and driver, and C$2.65 for each additional adult. It's cash only; if you arrive without Canadian dollars, there's an ATM in the small transport terminal next door.

Visitor Information

The most central tourist information center is in Upper Town, across from the Château Frontenac and directly on Place d'Armes. **Centre Infotouriste de Québec** (12 rue Ste-Anne; ✆ **877/266-5687;** www.bonjourquebec.com) is run by the province

Québec City

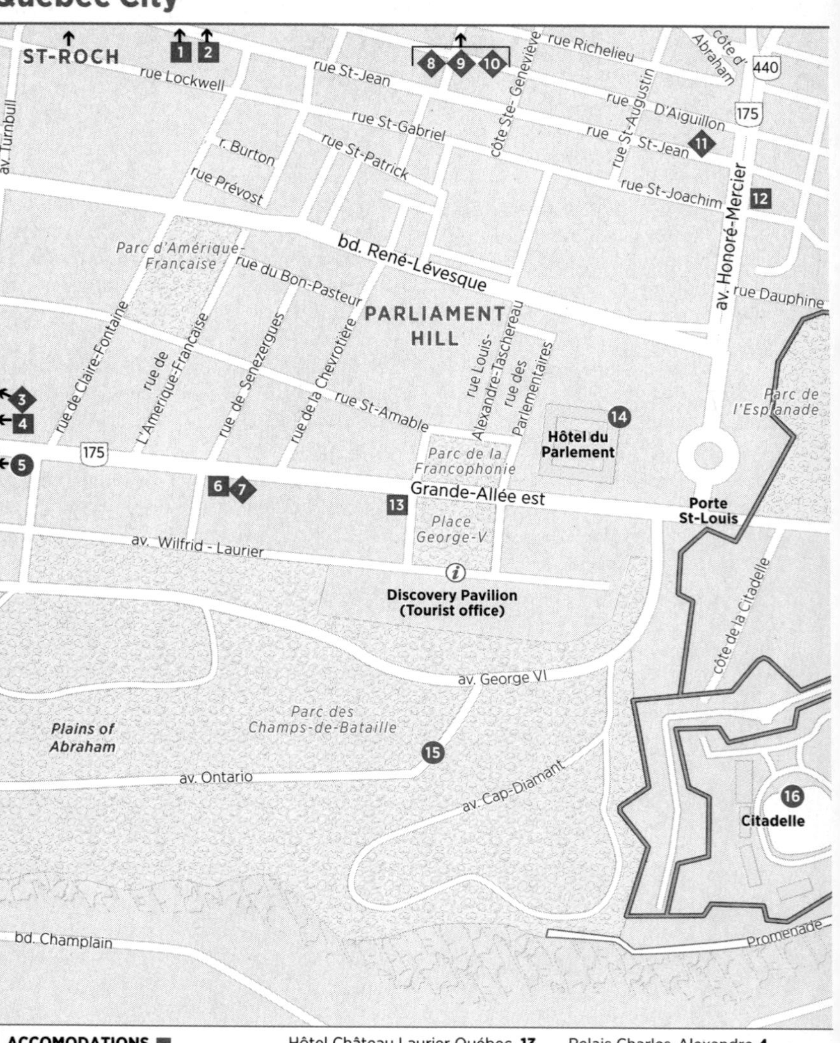

ACCOMODATIONS ■
Auberge Le Vincent **1**
Auberge Place d'Armes **27**
Auberge Saint-Antoine **47**
Cap Díamant **34**
Courtyard Marriott Québec **12**
Fairmont Le Château Frontenac **38**
Hôtel Champlain Vieux-Québec **21**
Hôtel Château Bellevue **35**
Hôtel Château Laurier Québec **13**
Hôtel des Coutellier **19**
Hôtel Le Germain-Dominion 1912 **31**
Hôtel Manoir Victoria **23**
Hôtel PUR **2**
Hôtel 71 **42**
Le Saint-Pierre **41**
Loews Le Concorde Hotel **6**
Relais Charles-Alexandre **4**

DINING ◆
Aux Anciens Canadiens **36**
Bistro Les Bossus **10**
Café Krieghoff **3**
Initiale **45**
Laurie Raphaël **32**
L'Astral **7**

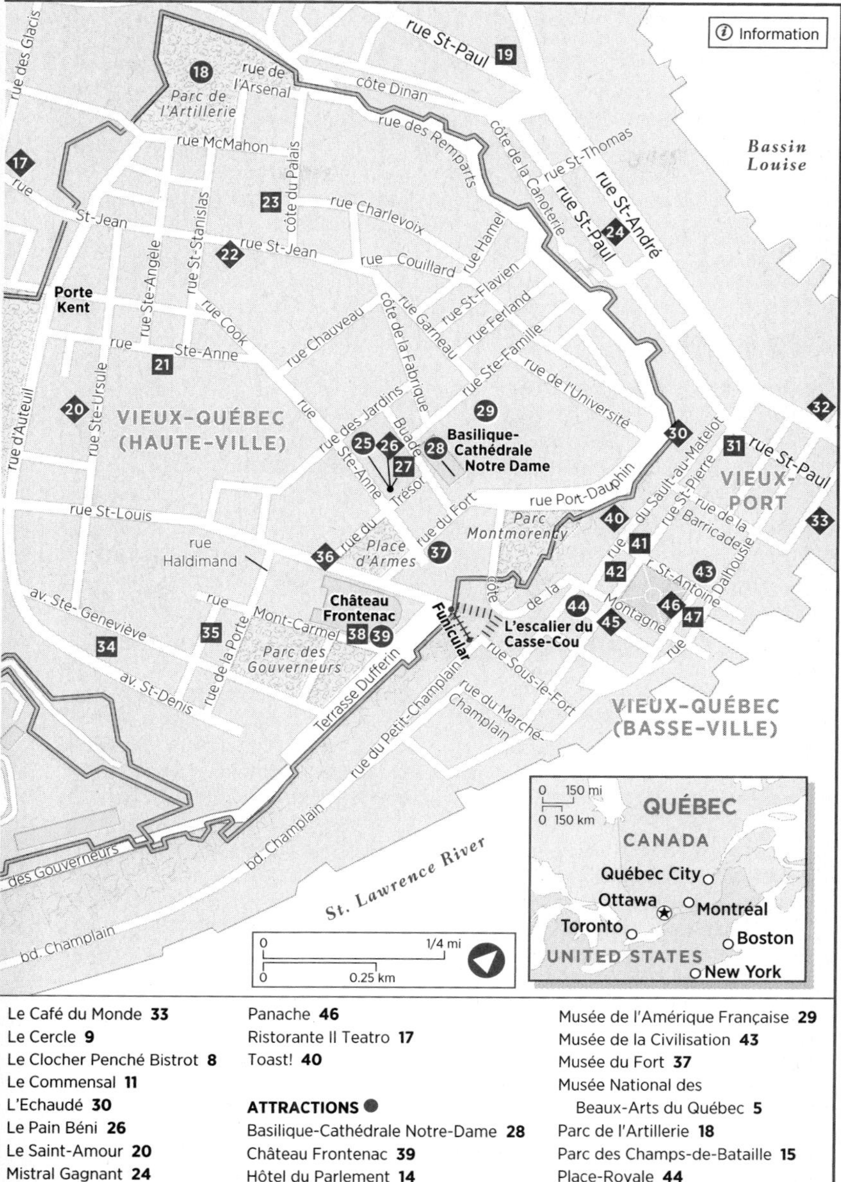

Le Café du Monde **33**
Le Cercle **9**
Le Clocher Penché Bistrot **8**
Le Commensal **11**
L'Echaudé **30**
Le Pain Béni **26**
Le Saint-Amour **20**
Mistral Gagnant **24**
Paillard **22**
Panache **46**
Ristorante Il Teatro **17**
Toast! **40**

ATTRACTIONS ●
Basilique-Cathédrale Notre-Dame **28**
Château Frontenac **39**
Hôtel du Parlement **14**
La Citadelle **16**
Musée de l'Amérique Française **29**
Musée de la Civilisation **43**
Musée du Fort **37**
Musée National des Beaux-Arts du Québec **5**
Parc de l'Artillerie **18**
Parc des Champs-de-Bataille **15**
Place-Royale **44**
Québec Expérience **25**

of Québec's tourism department and is open from 8:30am to 7pm daily from June 21 to August 31 and from 9am to 5pm daily the rest of the year. It has brochures, a lodging reservation service, a currency-exchange office, and information about tours by foot, bus, or boat.

Just outside the Old City walls on Parc des Champs-de-Bataille's northern edge, **Québec City Tourism** has an information office in the Discovery Pavilion (835 av. Wilfrid-Laurier; © **877/783-1608** or 418/641-6290; www.quebecregion.com). You'll find rack after rack of brochures, as well as attendants who can answer questions and make hotel reservations. It's open daily throughout the year, from 8:30am to 7:30pm from June 24 to Labour Day and somewhat shorter hours the rest of the year. The building is marked with a large, blue question mark.

From early June to early September, the city tourist office puts service agents on motor scooters throughout the tourist district. They are bilingual and can answer any questions you have. Their blue mopeds bear flags with a large question mark.

City Layout

MAIN AVENUES & STREETS Within the walls of Haute-Ville (Upper Town), the principal streets are **St-Louis** (which becomes **Grande-Allée** outside the city walls), **Ste-Anne,** and **St-Jean.** In Basse-Ville (Lower Town), major streets are **St-Pierre, Dalhousie, St-Paul,** and (parallel to St-Paul) **St-André.** Detailed maps of Upper and Lower Towns and the metropolitan area are available at the tourist offices.

FINDING AN ADDRESS If it were larger, the historic district's winding and plunging streets might be confusing to negotiate. However, the area is very compact. Most streets are only a few blocks long, making navigation and finding a specific address fairly easy.

The Neighborhoods in Brief

VIEUX-QUÉBEC

Haute-Ville Old Québec's Upper Town, surrounded by thick ramparts, occupies the crest of Cap Diamant and overlooks the Fleuve Saint-Laurent (St. Lawrence River). It includes many of the sites for which the city is famous, among them the **Château Frontenac** and the **Basilica of Notre-Dame. Terrasse Dufferin** is a pedestrian promenade at cliffs' edge that attracts crowds in all seasons for its magnificent views of the river and its water traffic. Also along the river is the **Citadelle,** a military fortress built by the French in the 18th century and augmented by the English (after their 1759 capture of the city) well into the 19th century.

With most buildings at least 100 years old and made of granite in similar styles, Haute-Ville is visually harmonious, with few jarring modern intrusions.

Basse-Ville and Vieux-Port Old Québec's Lower Town encompasses **Vieux-Port,** the old port district; the impressive **Museum of Civilization,** a highlight of any visit; **Place Royale,** perhaps the most attractive of the city's many small squares; and the pedestrian-only **rue du Petit-Champlain,** which is undeniably touristy, but not unpleasantly so, and has many agreeable shops. Visitors travel between Lower and Upper towns by the cliff-side elevator *(funiculaire)* at the north end of rue du Petit-Champlain, or by the adjacent stairway.

PARLIAMENT HILL

Once you pass through the walls at St-Louis Gate, you're still in Haute-Ville (Upper Town), but no longer in Vieux-Québec. Rue St-Louis becomes **Grande-Allée,** a wide boulevard that passes the stately Parliament building and runs parallel to the broad expanse of the Plains of Abraham, where one of the most important battles in the history of North America took place between the French and the British for control of the city. This is also where the lively Carnaval de Québec is held each winter. Two blocks after Parliament, Grande-Allée becomes lined on both sides with terraced restaurants and cafes. The city's large modern hotels are in this area, too, and the **Musée National des Beaux-Arts** is a pleasant 20-minute walk up the Allée from the Parliament. Here, the neighborhood becomes more residential.

ST-ROCH

Northwest of Parliament Hill, this newly revitalized neighborhood has some of the city's trendiest restaurants and bars. Much of St-Roch, including what's referred to as Québec's "downtown" shopping district, remains nondescript and a little grubby. But along the main strolling street, **rue St-Joseph est,** sidewalks have been widened, new benches added, and there are exciting new cafes and restaurants. An influx of new technology and media companies has brought a hip pop to the neighborhood. Neighborhood information is online at **www.quartiersaintroch.com.**

GETTING AROUND

Once you're within or near the walls of the Haute-Ville, virtually no hotel, restaurant, or place of interest is beyond walking distance. In bad weather, or when you're traversing between opposite ends of Lower and Upper towns, a taxi or the C$1 Ecolobus (see below) might be necessary. In general, though, walking is the best way to explore the city.

By Funicular

To get between Upper and Lower towns, you can take streets, staircases, or a cliffside elevator, known as the funicular, which has long operated along an inclined 64m (210-ft.) track. The upper station is near the front of the city's visual center—Château Frontenac and Place d'Armes—while the lower station is at the northern end of the teeny rue du Petit-Champlain, a pedestrian-only shopping street. The elevator offers excellent aerial views of the historic Lower Town on the short trip and runs daily from 7:30am until 11pm all year and until midnight in high season. Wheelchairs and strollers are accommodated. The one-way fare is C$2. Read about its history at **www.funiculaire-quebec.com.**

By Taxi

Taxis are everywhere: cruising, parked in front of the big hotels, and in some of Upper Town's larger squares. In theory, they can be hailed, but they are best obtained by locating one of their stands, as in the Place d'Armes or in front of the Hôtel-de-Ville (City Hall). Restaurant managers and hotel bell captains will also summon them upon request. The starting rate is C$3.30, each kilometer costs C$1.45, and each minute of waiting adds C55¢. Tip 10% to 15%. Companies include **Taxi Coop** (✆ **418/525-5191**) and **Taxi Québec** (✆ **418/525-8123**). Some take credit cards, but ask first.

By Bus

For travel within the most touristed areas, consider the C$1 **Ecolobus** (www.rtcquebec.ca), which makes a loop through the city. The buses run on electricity, so they're quiet and eco-friendly.

City bus routes are listed online at **www.rtcquebec.ca.** Buses in Upper Town include no. 7, which travels up and down rue St-Jean, and nos. 10 and 11, which shuttle along Grande-Allée/rue St-Louis. Bus stops have signs that state the bus numbers and direction of travel. Flag down the bus as it approaches so the driver knows to stop. The fare is C$2.60 in exact change. One-day passes cost C$6.70.

By Car

Québec City is compact, but driving is tricky because there are so few roads between Upper and Lower Town, and because many streets are one-way. See p. 212 for province-wide driving rules.

On-street parking is very difficult in Québec City's old, cramped quarters. When you find a rare space on the street, be sure to check the signs for hours when parking is permissible. Meters cost C50¢ per 15 minutes, and some meters accept payment for up to 5 hours. Meters are generally in effect Monday through Saturday from 9am to 9pm and Sunday 10am to 9pm. But be sure to double-check: Spots along Parc des Champs-de-Bataille (Battlefields Park) have to be paid for 24 hours a day.

Many of the smaller hotels and B&Bs that don't have their own parking lots maintain special arrangements with local garages, with discounts for guests of a few dollars off the usual C$14 or more per day. Check with your hotel.

Public lots include, in Upper Town, the lot beneath Hôtel-de-Ville (City Hall), with entrances on rue Ste-Anne and Côte de la Fabrique; and, in Lower Town, the lot across the street from the Musée de la Civilisation, on rue Dalhousie.

Budget and Hertz **rental-car** agencies both have offices in Upper Town on Côte du Palais at rue St-Jean.

By Bicycle

Given Vieux-Québec's hilly topography and tight quarters, cycling isn't a particularly attractive option either within the walls or in Lower Town. But beyond the walls is another story. Québec has a great network of cycling paths—nearly 400km (249 miles) in the Greater Québec Area alone. Downloadable maps are online at www.quebecregion.com/cycling. For longer treks, look into the province's **Route Verte (Green Route)**—see p. 249. Day trips and longer tours are listed at **www.routeverte.com.**

Bicycles rentals are available in Lower Town, near the train station, at **Cyclo Services** (289 rue St-Paul; ✆ **418/692-4052;** www.cycloservices.net), for C$25 for 4 hours, with other increments available. Tandem bikes and kids bikes are also available. The shop is open daily 8am to 8pm.

[FastFACTS] QUÉBEC CITY

American Automobile Association (AAA) See p. 43.

Drinking Laws See p. 214.

Embassies & Consulates Embassies are located in Ottawa, Canada's capital. There are consulate offices throughout the Canadian provinces, including Québec. The U.S. Embassy information line ✆ **888/840-0032** costs C$1.59 per minute. The U.S. has a consulate in Québec City, on Jardin des Gouverneurs at 2 rue de la Terrasse-Dufferin (✆ **418/692-2095**). The U.K. consulate in Québec City is in the St-Amable Complex, 1150 Claire-Fontaine, Ste. 700 (✆ **418/521-3000**). For contact information for other embassies and consulates, search for "Foreign

Representatives in Canada" at **www.international.gc.ca.**

Emergencies Dial ✆ **911** for police, firefighters, or an ambulance.

Gasoline (Petrol) Gasoline in Canada is sold by the liter; 3.78 liters equals 1 gallon. At C$1.15 a liter, that's the equivalent of about US$4.35 per gallon.

Hospitals In Québec City, go to the **Centre Hospitalier Hôtel-Dieu de Québec** (11 Côte du Palais; ✆ **418/525-4444**). The hospital is in Upper Town inside the city walls.

Insurance See p. 25.

Language See p. 215.

Newspapers & Magazines ***The Globe and Mail*** (www.theglobeandmail.com) is the national English-language paper. ***Le Soleil*** (www.cyberpresse.ca/le-soleil), is published in Québec City. Large newsstands and shops in larger hotels carry the *New York Times, Wall Street Journal*, and *International Herald Tribune*.

Smoking See p. 215.

Taxes See p. 215.

Time See p. 215.

Visitor Information The terrific website **www.quebecregion.com** serves Québec City travelers. The equally good **www.bonjourquebec.com** is run by the province of Québec's tourism department and covers the entire province. In Québec City, there's a tourist office in Upper Town, across from the Château Frontenac and directly on Place d'Armes. It's French name is **Centre Infotouriste de Québec** (12 rue Ste-Anne; ✆ **877/266-5687;** www.bonjourquebec.com), and it's open from 8:30am to 7pm daily from late June to early September and from 9am to 5pm daily the rest of the year. It has brochures, a lodging reservation service, a currency-exchange office, and information about tours by foot, bus, or boat trips.

WHERE TO STAY

A stay in one of the many excellent boutique hotels or small inns in Vieux-Québec might be one of your trip's most memorable experiences. Be aware that standards of amenities and prices fluctuate wildly from one small hotel to another, and even from one room to another within a single establishment. It is wise to examine any room offered before booking it.

If you prefer the conveniences of large chain hotels, there are good ones just outside the ancient walls, in Parliament Hill. Those high-rise hotels are still in walking distance from the attractions in the old city. Campers have a choice of 23 campgrounds in the greater Québec City area; for a list of sites and their specs, go to **www.quebecregion.com** and search for "camping."

Prices drop significantly from October to May, with the exception of the Christmas holiday and winter carnival in February. Many hotels offer special deals through their websites or AAA discounts.

Note: Prices listed here are rack rates for a double-occupancy room in high season (which includes the warm months, Christmastime, and Carnaval), unless otherwise noted. See p. xii for information about the Frommer's star-rating system, price rankings, categories, and taxes.

Vieux-Quebec: Haute-Ville (Upper Town)

VERY EXPENSIVE

Fairmont Le Château Frontenac ★★★ ☺ Québec's magical "castle" opened in 1893 and has been wowing guests ever since. Many of the rooms are full-on luxurious, outfitted with elegant château furnishings and marble bathrooms. More than 500 (of 618) rooms were renovated in a 3-year project that finished in 2008. Prices depend on size, location, and view, with river views garnering top dollar. Lower-priced rooms overlooking the inner courtyard are appealing, too: The gabled roofs they face are quite romantic, and children might imagine Harry Potter swooping by. Anyone can stay on the more princely (and pricey) Fairmont Gold floors, which have a separate concierge and a lounge with an honor bar in the afternoons and breakfast in the mornings. Known locally as "the Château," the hotel was built in phases, following the landline, so the wide halls take crooked paths. The **St-Laurent Bar et Lounge** (p. 304) and Café de la Terrasse both look down on the St-Lawrence River.

1 rue des Carrières (at Place d'Armes), Québec City, PQ G1R 4P5. ✆ **866/540-4460** or 418/692-3861. Fax 418/692-1751. www.fairmont.com/frontenac. 618 units. C$259–C$549 double; from C$499 suite. Packages available. AE, DC, DISC, MC, V. Valet parking C$31, self-parking C$26; hybrid vehicles free. Pets accepted (C$30 per day per pet). **Amenities:** 3 restaurants; bar; babysitting; children's programs; concierge; executive-level rooms; health club; pools (indoor & kiddie pool w/outdoor terrace); room service; spa; Wi-Fi (public areas, C$19/day). *In room:* A/C, TV, hair dryer, Internet (C$19/day), minibar.

EXPENSIVE

Hôtel Manoir Victoria ★ With an air of a grand old-timer, Manoir Victoria is formal and proper, from a lobby that features elegant Old World decor to an elaborate formal dining room. Over half the comfortable bedrooms were renovated in 2009, with everything from new mattresses to rugs and curtains, and some now feature gas fireplaces and whirlpool tubs. The hotel has some special touches not normally found in midsize properties: a small indoor pool, a full-service spa that offers massages and Canadian specials such as maple body scrubs, and a pub/bistro in addition to the main restaurant. It's located around the corner from the busy rue St-Jean restaurant-and-bar scene. Note that there's a steep staircase from the front door to the lobby, although elevators make the trip to most guest rooms.

44 Côte du Palais (at rue St-Jean), Québec City, PQ G1R 4H8. ✆ **800/463-6283** or 418/692-1030. Fax 418/692-3822. www.manoir-victoria.com. 156 units. C$175–C$400 double. Packages available. AE, DC, MC, V. Valet parking C$20. **Amenities:** 2 restaurants; bar; babysitting; concierge; exercise room; pool (indoor); room service; spa. *In room:* A/C, TV, hair dryer, minibar, Wi-Fi (free).

MODERATE

Auberge Place d'Armes ★ Renovated with care in 2008, this high-end *auberge* offers 21 sumptuous rooms with stone walls that date from 1640 and handmade artisanal furniture—at surprisingly moderate prices. The *auberge* swallowed up a museum that had been here previously, and the most eye-popping unit, the Marie Antoinette suite, has actual 17th-century decor from Versailles. A portion of the rooms are done up in blue-and-white French décor; others have red-and-white British touches. Rooms have high-end flourishes, such as heated bathroom floors and flat-screen TVs. Meals are served in the very good in-house restaurant **Le Pain Béni** (p. 286).

24 rue Ste-Anne (at Place d'Armes), Québec City, PQ G1R 3X3. ✆ **866/333-9485** or 418/694-9485. Fax 418/694-9899. www.aubergeplacedarmes.com. 21 units. Summer C$159–C$219 double; fall–spring from C$90 double. Rates include continental breakfast. Packages available. AE, MC, V. Pets accepted (C$25/day). **Amenities:** Restaurant; babysitting; concierge; room service. *In room:* A/C, CD player, fridge, hair dryer, MP3 docking station, Wi-Fi (free).

Cap Díamant There are lots of B&Bs in the quiet, pretty corner of Vieux-Québec behind the Château Frontenac. Owner Florence Guillot has turned this 1826 home into a Victoriana showpiece, with antiques and old photos richly decorating common areas and bedrooms. The whole thing is quite grand and romantic. Many rooms feature ornate fireplaces, mantles, heavy gold-edged mirrors, oriental rugs, and glass lamps. There's a small all-season back porch where breakfast is served, and a summer garden. Although it's a B&B, all rooms have private baths.

39 av. Ste-Geneviève (at Ste-Ursule), Québec City, PQ G1R 4B3. ✆ **888/694-0303** or 418/694-0303. www.hotelcapdiamant.com. 9 units. Mid-May to mid-Oct C$164–C$174 double; mid-Oct to mid-May from C$114 double. Rates include continental breakfast. Packages available. AE, MC, V. Parking C$16. *In room:* A/C, TV, fridge, hair dryer, Wi-Fi (free).

Hôtel Champlain Vieux-Québec ★ A total overhaul by new owners in 2006 made this an elegant, cozy, modern new option. All rooms have king or queen beds, 300-count cotton sheets, flat-screen TVs, and silk curtains, and most units are quite roomy. A mid-priced room, no. 13, has views of stone buildings across the street and feels very French, while guests in no. 47 can see the Château Frontenac from their bed. Windows open, an unusual feature in this city. A self-serve espresso machine by the front desk provides free cappuccinos any time of day or night. It's centrally located but not on a main thoroughfare, so it's quiet at night.

115 rue Ste-Anne (near rue Ste-Ursule), Québec City, PQ G1R 3X6. ✆ **800/567-2106** or 418/694-0106. Fax 418/692-1959. www.champlainhotel.com. 50 units. Summer C$179–C$209 double; fall–spring C$109–C$149 double. Rates include continental breakfast. AE, DISC, MC, V. Limited on-site parking. **Amenities:** Concierge. *In room:* A/C, TV/DVD player, fridge, hair dryer, MP3 docking station, Wi-Fi (free).

Hôtel Château Bellevue Occupying several row houses at the top of the Jardin des Gouverneurs in one of Vieux-Québec's prettiest areas, this 52-room hotel has a helpful staff, as well as some of the creature comforts typical of larger facilities. Renovations knocked out walls and combined rooms to make fewer, bigger units. Higher-priced rooms overlook the park, and all rooms are quiet and bright. The lobby features an unusual wine machine that dispenses selections by the glass. A sister hotel, **Château Laurier** (p. 284), is outside the walls on Parliament Hill.

16 rue de la Porte (at av. Ste-Geneviève), Québec City, PQ G1R 4M9. ✆ **800/463-2617** or 418/692-2573. Fax 418/692-4876. www.hotelchateaubellevue.com. 52 units. July–Oct C$139–C$245 double; Nov–June from C$89 double. Rates include continental breakfast for reservations made directly through the hotel. Packages available. AE, DC, DISC, MC, V. Valet parking C$15. *In room:* A/C, TV, hair dryer, Wi-Fi (free).

Vieux-Quebec: Basse-Ville (Lower Town)/ Vieux-Port

VERY EXPENSIVE

Auberge Saint-Antoine ★★★ This hotel is a knockout. The *auberge* began life as an 1830 maritime warehouse. It kept the soaring ceilings, dark beams, and stone floors, and is now one of the city's landmark luxury boutique hotels (and a member of the prestigious Relais & Châteaux luxury group). Ancient walls remain in view, and artifacts unearthed during the development are on display with curatorial care—in public areas, at the door to each room, and bedside, lit with an underwater-blue glow. Bedrooms are modern and sleek with luxury linens, plush robes, Bose sound systems, heated bathroom floors, and bathing nooks with rain-shower nozzles directly overhead. Many rooms have balconies, terraces, fireplaces, or kitchenettes; ask when booking if you want to ensure having any of these features in your room. A striking lounge serves breakfast, lunch, snacks, and drinks, and its high-end restaurant, **Panache** (p. 288), has become one of the best in town.

8 rue St-Antoine (next to the Musée de la Civilisation), Québec City, PQ G1K 4C9. ✆ **888/692-2211** or 418/692-2211. Fax 418/692-1177. www.saint-antoine.com. 95 units. C$149–C$299 double, from C$299 suite. Packages available. AE, DC, MC, V. Valet parking C$25. Pets accepted (C$150/visit). **Amenities:** 2 restaurants; 2 bars; babysitting; concierge; exercise room; room service. *In room:* TV, hair dryer, minibar, Wi-Fi (free).

Hôtel Le Germain-Dominion ★★★ Old Québec meets new in the most romantic of the city's boutique hotels. The owners stripped the 1912 building down to the studs and started over, keeping the angular lines and adding soft touches. Forty rooms got a complete overhaul in 2010 and each now features a huge black and white photo of the building's curlicue cornices as a headboard, white walls, and charcoal-black ceilings and trim. Urban modernism is tempered by beds that are exceptionally comfortable: mattresses are deep and enveloping, heaped with pillows and feather duvets. About two-thirds of rooms have both tubs and showers, and bathrooms are well-lit and elegant. A hearty continental breakfast is set out, along with morning newspapers, near the fireplace in the handsome lobby, and a machine that dispenses free espresso is available round the clock. Intimate and chic.

126 rue St-Pierre (at rue St-Paul), Québec City, PQ G1K 4A8. ✆ **888/833-5253** or 418/692-2224. Fax 418/692-4403. www.germaindominion.com. 60 units. C$169–C$425 double. Rates include breakfast. AE, DC, MC, V. Parking C$19. Pets accepted (C$30/day). **Amenities:** Espresso bar; babysitting; concierge; exercise room; room service. *In room:* A/C, TV, CD player, fridge, hair dryer, Wi-Fi (free).

Hôtel 71 ★★ Owned by the same people as the adjacent **Le Saint-Pierre** (see below), the two properties share a bar, but Hôtel 71 is slicker and ultra-contemporary. Room no. 620 is typical, with 4.5m-high (15-ft.) cream-colored walls and curtains that extend nearly floor to ceiling, warmed up with deep-red velveteen chairs and cloth panels that serve as closet doors. Bathrooms are in the open style common to the area's boutique hotels. Rooms are on floors four to seven and many feature bird's-eye views of the tops of the 19th-century buildings of Old Québec, the St. Lawrence River, or the ramparts of the fortress wall. Major renovations in 2009 and 2010 made room for **Il Matto,** the new Italian restaurant on the first floor.

71 rue St-Pierre (near rue St-Antoine), Québec City, PQ G1K 4A4. ✆ **888/692-1171** or 418/692-1171. Fax 418/692-0669. www.hotel71.ca. 40 units. C$199–C$290 double. Packages available. AE, DC, MC, V. Valet parking C$20. **Amenities:** Restaurant; bar; babysitting; concierge; exercise room; room service. *In room:* A/C, TV/DVD player, CD player, hair dryer, Wi-Fi (free).

MODERATE

Hôtel des Coutellier ★ In a quiet nook across from the city's market and down the block from the train station, Coutellier does lots of small things right. As a result, it boasts of having one of the highest occupancy rates in the city. It gets lots of repeat business travelers, but also caters to vacationers who appreciate the personal touch that can come with a 24-room operation. Breakfasts of croissant, yogurt, and orange juice are delivered each morning in a basket that hangs from the front doorknob. For bicyclists, the hotel offers free indoor bike storage. Charmingly, a *pétanque* pit (similar to boule and boccie) in front of the hotel brings out local players in the afternoons. All rooms require use of stairs. Upgrades are slated for 2011.

253 rue St-Paul (at Quai St-André), Québec City, PQ G1K 3W5. ✆ **888/523-9696** or 418/692-9696. Fax 418/692-4050. www.hoteldescoutellier.com. 24 units. C$185–C$275 double. Rates include breakfast delivered in basket to door. AE, MC, V. Parking C$9. **Amenities:** Room service (from adjacent restaurant Môss). *In room:* A/C, TV, hair dryer, minibar, MP3 docking station, Wi-Fi (free).

QUÉBEC'S ice hotel: THE COLDEST RECEPTION IN TOWN

Québec's **Ice Hotel** (✆ **877/505-0423;** www.icehotel-canada.com) is built each winter just outside of Québec City. It celebrated its 10th anniversary in 2010. For C$16 you can visit, but for C$219 per person (and up), you can have dinner and spend the night. Tempted?

The *Hôtel de Glace* is crafted each year from 500 tons of ice, and nearly everything is ice, from the ice chandelier in the 5.4m (18-ft.) vaulted main hall, to the thick-ice shot glasses in which vodka is served, to the pillars and arches and furniture. That includes the frozen slabs they call beds; deer skins and sleeping bags provide insulation.

Nighttime guests get their rooms at 9pm, after the last tours, and have to clear out before the next morning's visitors. Some rooms are themed and vaguely grand: One year there was a Chess Room featuring solid-ice chess pieces the size of small children at each corner of the bed. Other rooms bring the words "monastic" or "cell block" to mind.

Bear in mind that, except for in the hot tub, temperatures everywhere hover between 23° and 27°F (–5° and –3°C). Refrigerators are used not to keep sodas cold, but to *keep them from freezing.*

There are 36 rooms and suites, a wedding chapel, and a disco for guests to shake the chill from their booties. Open each January, it takes guests until late March—after that, it's destroyed.

Le Saint-Pierre ★ Rooms here are surprisingly spacious, and the even larger suites are a luxury on a longer visit, especially since they have modest kitchen facilities. Made-to-order furnishings suggest traditional Québec style, and units have wood floors and original brick or stone walls. All rooms are on the fourth to seventh floors, and some have a river view. Most rooms also have whirlpool baths. The full breakfasts, included, are cooked to order.

79 rue St-Pierre (behind the Musée de la Civilisation), Québec City, PQ G1K 4A3. ✆ **888/268-1017** or 418/694-7981. Fax 418/694-0406. www.le-saint-pierre.ca. 41 units. C$149–C$219 double, C$195–C$299 suite. Rates include full breakfast. Packages available. AE, DC, MC, V. Valet parking C$20. **Amenities:** Bar; babysitting; concierge. *In room:* A/C, TV, hair dryer, Wi-Fi (free).

Parliament Hill/On or Near the Grande-Allée

EXPENSIVE

Courtyard Marriott Québec ★★ The Courtyard Marriott has become a hot property in recent years, due in part to across-the-board raves on online posting boards for its friendly staff, comfortable rooms, and fair prices. Someone here is paying attention to the right details. Beds have been given the deluxe treatment and are piled with five pillows and sheet-cover duvets. All rooms have either a sofa bed or an oversized chair that pulls out into a single bed, and ergonomic chairs at the desks. The in-house restaurant, **Que Sera Sera,** is well regarded. The hotel is right on the central Place d'Youville, where there's a small ice rink in winter.

850 Place d'Youville (near rue St-Jean), Québec City, PQ G1R 3P6. ✆ **866/694-4004** or 418/694-4004. Fax 418/694-4007. www.marriott.com. 111 units. C$199–C$299 double. Packages available. AE, DC, MC, V. Valet parking C$20, self-parking C$17. **Amenities:** Restaurant; bar; exercise room; whirlpool; room service. *In room:* A/C, TV, fridge, hair dryer, Internet (free).

Loews Le Concorde Hotel ★ ☺ The skyscraper that houses this hotel rises discordantly from a neighborhood of late-Victorian town houses. But for guests, no matter: With all rooms on the fifth floor and above, the hotel offers spectacular views of the river and the Old City, and some rooms even have outdoor terraces. It's also adjacent to the Grande-Allée restaurant and party scene on one side and the pristine Joan of Arc garden in Parc des Champs-de-Bataille on the other. **L'Astral** (p. 289), the hotel's revolving rooftop restaurant with a bar and live piano music on weekends, is definitely worth a stop. For kids, there's a lending library of toys. There's a fee for pets, but they get the royal treatment.

1225 Cours du Géneral de Montcalm (at Grande-Allée), Québec City, PQ G1R 4W6. ✆ **800/463-5256** or 418/647-2222. Fax 418/647-4710. www.loewsleconcorde.com. 406 units. C$229–C$369 double. Packages available. AE, DC, DISC, MC, V. Valet parking C$28, self-parking C$23. Pets accepted (C$25/stay). **Amenities:** Restaurant; bar; babysitting; concierge; health club; pool (outdoor heated); room service; sauna. *In room:* A/C, TV, hair dryer, minibar, Wi-Fi (C$12/day).

MODERATE

Hôtel Château Laurier Québec ★ Sprawling along a broad strip of the action-packed Grande-Allée on one side and the quiet Plains of Abraham on the other, the Château Laurier is the largest non-chain hotel in the city. It takes pride in both its "eco-responsibility" and its "Franco-responsibility," with artwork and music of French and Québécois artists featured in hallways. Keep in mind when booking that the hotel has five categories of rooms of varying age, style, and price. "Prestige" rooms in the new section are the most stylish and enveloping, with king-size beds and goose-down duvets. Prestige floors are accessible only by room key, and they feature a nifty wine-by-the-glass vending machine. Rooms in the older section are way plainer, although some on the higher floors have views of the Citadelle and the St. Lawrence River. A courtyard has an igloo in winter and barbeque in the summer.

1220 Place Georges-V ouest (at Grande-Allée), Québec City, PQ G1R 5B8. ✆ **877/522-8108** or 418/522-8108. Fax 418/524-8768. www.hotelchateaulaurier.com. 289 units. C$129–C$409 double. Packages available. AE, DC, MC, V. Parking C$19. **Amenities:** Restaurant; bar; concierge; executive-level floors; exercise room; Jacuzzis (indoor & outdoor); pool (indoor, saltwater); room service; Finnish sauna; spa. *In room:* A/C, TV, hair dryer, Wi-Fi (free).

INEXPENSIVE

Relais Charles-Alexandre This little hotel is close to the Musée des Beaux-Arts du Québec and the pleasant shopping street avenue Cartier. The first floor houses a mini art gallery, while its proximity to the Plains of Abraham makes it a good choice, if you're visiting for one of the festivals held there. Rooms are very basic but crisply maintained. Spend the extra C$10 for one of the superior units, which are bigger and/or have better views. Call to inquire before bringing children.

91 Grande-Allée est (2 blocks east of av. Cartier), Québec City, PQ G1R 2H5. ✆ **418/523-1220.** Fax 418/523-9556. www.quebecweb.com/rca. 23 units. May–Oct & Carnaval C$134–C$144 double; Nov–Apr C$89–C$99 double. Rates include breakfast. MC, V. Parking C$9. **Amenities:** Breakfast room. *In room:* A/C, TV, hair dryer, Wi-Fi (free).

St-Roch

MODERATE

Hôtel PUR ★★ Step into the severely white lobby of this ultra-mod hotel tower, and you'll either love it or hate it. Either way, it'll snap you to attention. The rooms above are much cozier, with top-of-the-line linens, plush robes, spa-like bathrooms, and a desk area for getting some work done. From room #1807, the views overlooking the curved steps of Église Saint-Roch down below are stunning. Along with one of the nicest fitness rooms in the area, PUR also claims to have the largest pool in Québec City. The owners converted a Holiday Inn into this boutique accommodation and accompanying ground-floor restaurant, **Table;** one more example of the St-Roch neighborhood's gentrification. Though nothing in Québec City is too far apart, the hotel is a good walk from the more touristy Vieux-Québec.

390 rue de la Couronne (at rue St-Joseph), Québec City, PQ G1K 7X4. ✆ **800/267-2002** or 418/647-2611. Fax 418/640-0666. www.hotelpur.com. 242 units. C$199–C$249 double. Packages available. AE, DC, DISC, MC, V. Pets accepted (free w/restrictions). Valet parking C$17. **Amenities:** Restaurant; fitness center; pool (indoor, heated); sauna. *In room:* A/C, TV, hair dryer, minibar, MP3 docking station, Wi-Fi (free).

Auberge Le Vincent ★ ☺ Tucked in among the restaurants, bistros, tech companies, skateboard punks, and well-heeled hipsters of the St-Roch neighborhood is the Van Gogh–inspired Le Vincent. Housed in a renovated 100-year-old building, the sophisticated accommodations represent a terrific value, considering all the luxe features: goose duvets, 400-thread-count sheets, custom-made dark cherry-wood furniture, generous lighting options, and local art. Breakfast, which is included, is served in a brick-walled seating area off the lobby. Bike storage is available. Rooms are up either one or two flights of stairs. A significant upgrade to the windows has reduced ambient noise from the streets below.

295 rue St-Vallier est (corner of rue Dorchester), Québec City, PQ G1K 3P5. ✆ **888/523-5005** or 418/523-5000. Fax 418/523-5999. www.aubergelevincent.com. 10 units. C$199–C$279 double. Rates include full breakfast. Packages available. AE, MC, V. Parking C$15. *In room:* A/C, TV/DVD player, CD player, fridge, hair dryer, Wi-Fi (free).

WHERE TO DINE

With a little research, it's possible to eat extraordinarily well in Québec City. It used to be that this gloriously scenic town had few temples de cuisine comparable to those of Montréal. That has changed. There are now restaurants equal in every way to the most honored establishments of any North American city, with surprising numbers of creative, ambitious young chefs and restaurateurs bidding to achieve similar status.

Game is popular, including caribou, wapiti (North American deer), and quail. Many menus feature emu and lamb raised just north of the city in Charlevoix. Mussels and salmon are also standard.

There are blatantly touristy restaurants along rue St-Louis in Upper Town and around the Place d'Armes, many of them with hawkers outside, and accordion players and showy tableside presentations inside. They can produce decent meals and are entirely satisfactory for lunch.

At the better places, reservations are essential during holidays and festivals. Other times, it's necessary to book ahead only for weekend evenings. Dress codes are rarely stipulated, but "dressy-casual" works almost everywhere.

Remember that for the Québécois, *dîner* (dinner) is lunch, and *souper* (supper) is the evening meal. The word "dinner" is used below in the common American sense. Also note that an *entrée* in Québec is an appetizer, while a *plat principal* is a main course.

The evening meal tends to be served earlier in Québec City than in Montréal, at 7pm rather than 8pm. In the winter months, when tourist traffic slows, restaurants can close early or cut down on their days, so confirm before heading out.

FOR A bargain, LOOK FOR THE TABLE D'HÔTE

The best dining deals in Québec are table d'hôte, fixed-priced, meals. Nearly all full-service restaurants offer them. Generally, these meals include at least soup or salad, a main course, and a dessert. Some places add an extra appetizer and/or a beverage. The total price ends up being approximately what you'd pay for the main course alone. At lunchtime, table d'hôte meals are even cheaper (and you have more time to walk off the big meal).

Vieux-Quebec: Haute-Ville (Upper Town)

VERY EXPENSIVE

Le Saint-Amour ★ CONTEMPORARY QUEBECOIS Perhaps the most impressive cuisine in the city, in terms of gastronomic dining. The otherwise formal wait-staff heartily boasts of visits from rock stars Paul McCartney and Sting, whose menu from a visit July 2009 is online at the restaurant's website. While many diners take advantage of dishes like red deer and foie gras seven ways, we asked for a vegetarian course on chef's whim. Though not revolutionary, the rosette of beets stuffed with asparagus was fresh and sophisticated. The Valrhona Grand Cru dessert, crème brûlée, and macaroons were ridiculous—in a good way. Atmosphere has a dated feel, especially the glassed-in atrium and the foliage in the main dining room, yet the staff here pulls it off in the same way that a fashionista can pull off stirrup pants.

48 Rue Sainte-Ursule (near rue St-Louis). ✆ **418/694-0667.** www.saint-amour.com. Reservations recommended. Main courses C$39–C$53; table d'hôte lunch C$14–C$26; discovery dinner C$110. AE, DC, MC, V. Mon–Fri 11:30am–2pm; daily 6–10:30pm.

EXPENSIVE

Aux Anciens Canadiens ★ TRADITIONAL QUEBECOIS Inundated by travelers during peak months, this venerable restaurant with costumed servers is in what's probably the city's oldest house (1677); its front windows are small because their original glass came over from France, packed in barrels of molasses. Surprisingly, it's one of the best places in La Belle Province at which to sample cooking that has its roots in New France's earliest years. Traditional Québécois recipes are done well here, and servings are large enough to ward off hunger for a week. Caribou figures into many of the dishes, as does maple syrup, which goes into, for example, the duckling, goat-cheese salad, and luscious sugar pie. Prices are high except for the restaurant's afternoon special, from noon to 5:45pm, which is a terrific bargain: soup, a main course, a dessert, and a glass of beer or wine for C$20.

34 rue St-Louis (at rue des Jardins). ✆ **418/692-1627.** www.auxancienscanadiens.qc.ca. Reservations recommended. Main courses C$22–C$68; table d'hôte lunch C$20, dinner C$37–C$79. AE, DC, MC, V. Daily noon–9pm.

MODERATE

Le Pain Béni ★★ CONTEMPORARY QUEBECOIS This popular restaurant in the touristic heart of Upper Town was stylishly renovated in 2010 and has a few more private nooks than before. The vibe remains warm and casually romantic, with stone and brick walls from the 1600s. The menu is wildly innovative—hello, shiitake ice cream and shrimp with ras el hanout spices—and the lamb ravioli is a must. There are pizza options, too. Le Pain Béni is in the **Auberge Place d'Armes** (p. 280).

24 rue Ste-Anne (at rue du Trésor). ✆ **866/333-9485** or 418/694-9485. www.aubergeplacedarmes.com. Main courses C$16–C$38; table d'hôte cost of main, plus C$10. AE, MC, V. May–Oct daily 11:30am–10:30pm; Nov–Apr daily 11:30am–2:30pm and 5:30–10:30pm.

Ristorante Il Teatro ★ ITALIAN There's so much to like about this convivial Italian. There's the huge menu (20 types of pasta, for instance). There are the generous portions and fair prices (most main courses are under C$20). There's the large sidewalk cafe, directly on the hopping Place d'Youville. And there's the general ambiance: friendly, bustling, and never snooty.

972 rue St-Jean (at Place d'Youville). ✆ **418/694-9996.** www.lecapitole.com/en/restaurant.php. Main courses C$15–C$36; table d'hôte C$27–C$33. AE, DC, MC, V. Daily 7am to midnight or later.

INEXPENSIVE

In addition to **Paillard**, below, children may like **Casse-Crêpe Breton** ☺ (1136 rue St-Jean; ✆ **418/692-0438**; www.cassecrepebreton.com). Its savory and sweet crêpes run C$6 to C$9. Centrally located in the heart of Upper Town, it's usually packed at lunch. Go a little early or a little late if you don't want to wait.

Paillard LIGHT FARE ☺ Keep this bright, cavernous sandwich shop in mind when you're looking for healthy, fast food to eat in or take out. Hot and cold sandwiches on hearty *ciabatta*, baguettes, or croissants are the main event, and natural sodas, satisfying espresso drinks, and a yummy selection of pastries and gelato fill out the menu. There are small tables, as well as communal seating at large tables.

1097 rue St-Jean (near rue St-Stanislas). ✆ **418/692-1221.** www.paillard.ca. All items less than C$10. MC, V. Winter daily 7:30am–6pm; summer daily 7:30am–10pm.

Vieux-Quebec: Basse-Ville (Lower Town)/ Vieux-Port

VERY EXPENSIVE

Initiale ★★★ CONTEMPORARY QUEBECOIS Initiale is not only one of the elite restaurants of Québec City, but one of the best in the entire province. The palatial setting of tall windows, columns, and a deeply recessed ceiling sets a gracious tone, and the welcome is both cordial and correct. Lighting is subdued and the buzz barely above a murmur. This is a good place to cast economy to the winds and go with one of the prix-fixe menus. Dinner might start with a buckwheat crêpe folded around an artichoke, a round of crabmeat with a creamy purée of onions, and a flash-fried leaf of baby spinach all arrayed on the plate as on an artist's palette. It might continue with grilled tuna supported by sweet garlic, salsify, and lemon marmalade, and a swirl of pasta with marguerite leaves. Québec cheeses are an impressive topper. Men should wear jackets, and women can pull out the stops.

54 rue St-Pierre (corner of Côte de la Montagne). ✆ **418/694-1818.** www.restaurantinitiale.com. Reservations recommended on weekends. Table d'hôte dinners C$59–C$69, tasting menu C$125. AE, DC, MC, V. Thurs & Fri 11:30am–2pm; Tues–Sat 6–9pm.

Laurie Raphaël ★★ CONTEMPORARY QUEBECOIS The owners of this creative restaurant, long one of the city's most accomplished, tinker relentlessly with their handiwork. If the prices scare you off, come at lunch, when carrot soup is topped with lemon oil and orange zest, lamb with pistachio crust, and quinoa with smoked boar and *ras el hanout*, all for C$23. We still dream about chef/owner Daniel

Vézina's Willy Wonka–style dinner concoctions from years ago—silky-smooth foie gras on a teeny ice cream paddle drizzled with port-and-maple-syrup reduction, and Alaskan snow crab accompanied by a bright-pink pomegranate terrine. Service is friendly and correct, and the meal's pace spot-on. Sophisticated decor is tempered by dashes of eye-popping red and electric purple.

117 rue Dalhousie (at rue St-André). ✆ **418/692-4555.** www.laurieraphael.com. Reservations recommended. Main courses C$35–C$48; 3-course chef's inspiration lunch C$23, dinner C$60; gourmet dinner C$94. AE, DC, DISC, MC, V. Tues–Fri 11:30am–2pm; Tues–Sat 6–10pm.

Panache ★★★ CONTEMPORARY QUEBECOIS The restaurant of the superb **Auberge Saint-Antoine** (p. 281) is housed in a former 19th-century warehouse delineated by massive wood beams and rough stone walls. A wrought-iron staircase winds up to a second dining level, where tables feel like they're tucked into the eaves of a secret attic. A center fireplace, velvet couches, generous space between tables, and good acoustics enhance the inherent romantic aura, and service is flawless. Aiming to serve *cuisine Québécoise revisitée*—French-Canadian cuisine with a twist—the frequently changing menu is heavy on locally sourced game, duck, fish, and vegetables. A slip of a bar seats about a dozen. **Café Artefact,** a separate lounge just off the hotel's main lobby, provides a casual and cozy pre-meal meeting spot. At lunch, main courses start at C$14.

10 rue St-Antoine (in Auberge Saint-Antoine). ✆ **418/692-1022.** www.saint-antoine.com. Reservations recommended. Main courses lunch C$14, dinner C$36–C$49; 7-course signature menu C$95. AE, DC, MC, V. Mon–Fri 6:30–10:30am, Sat & Sun 7–11am; Wed–Fri noon–2pm; daily 6–10pm.

EXPENSIVE

L'Echaudé ★★ BISTRO The most polished of the necklace of restaurants adorning this Vieux-Port corner, L'Echaudé is like a well-worn cashmere sweater—it goes well with both silk trousers and your favorite pair of jeans. Grilled meats and fishes, and the seafood stews, are an excellent value. Among classics on the menu are steak *frites,* duck confit, and salmon *tartare.* Less expected are the calf sweet breads in a prosciutto envelope or the Cornish hen with lobster juice and ginger. The owner keeps an important cellar with hundreds of wines, with the full list posted online. The bistro is frequented mostly by locals of almost all ages (although the very young are rarely seen), and visitors are attended to by a highly efficient staff. In summer, the small street in front of the patio becomes pedestrian only.

73 rue Sault-au-Matelot (near rue St-Paul). ✆ **418/692-1299.** www.echaude.com. Reservations suggested on weekends. Main courses C$26–C$42; table d'hôte dinner cost of main course, plus C$18. AE, DC, MC, V. Mon–Sat 11:30am–2:30pm; Sun 10:30am–2:30pm; daily 5:30–10pm.

Toast! ★ CONTEMPORARY QUEBECOIS The kitchen for the zesty Toast! has its base in the French idiom but takes off in many directions. There's a poached quail egg with a truffled poultry emulsion, and goose breast served over spaghetti squash treated like risotto. For dessert, maybe hot and cold apple with cheese from nearby L'Isle-aux-Grues? Dishes are like that: sprightly, with joined tastes and textures, often from local sources. Outdoor dining, on a secluded terrace in back of the restaurant with big leafy trees overhead, is an oasis. In 2009, the owners opened the dialed-down but volume-up **SSS** (see p. 304), where small plates can be nibbled in a dining room or under blue lights and the thumping beat of the lounge.

17 rue Sault-au-Matelot (at rue St-Antoine). ✆ **418/692-1334.** www.restauranttoast.com. Reservations recommended on weekends. Table d'hôte C$65, C$75, or C$85. AE, MC, V. Sun–Wed 6–10:30pm; Thurs–Sat 6–11pm.

MODERATE

Le Café du Monde ★ TRADITIONAL FRENCH A longtime and entirely convivial eating venue, Café du Monde is a large, Parisian-style space, seating more than 100 inside and nearly that number on a terrace overlooking the St. Lawrence River. At night, the glass walls on the northern side look out on Robert Lepage's light installation, which bathes a huge stand of grain silos in an ever-changing wash of color (see p. 296). The staff is amiable, and the food creative but still within bistro conventions. The long menu features classic French preparations of pâtés, duck confit, onion soup, smoked salmon *tartare,* and mussels with *frites.* The signature house salad features duck three ways: confit (duck leg), foie gras, and shaved duck breast.

84 rue Dalhousie (next to the cruise terminal). ✆ **418/692-4455.** www.lecafedumonde.com. Reservations recommended. Main courses C$14–C$30, table d'hôte C$30–C$34. AE, DC, MC, V. Mon–Fri 11:30am–11pm; Sat, Sun & holidays 9:30am–11pm.

Mistral Gagnant ★ BISTRO This "restaurant Provençal" channels the spirit of a modest village cafe in France, in both its sunny decor and its friendly atmosphere. Better yet, the food is fairly priced and tasty. The Bouillabaisse à la Provençale is a rich broth with big chunks of salmon, flakey white fish, mussels, scallop, and shrimp, served with rounds of bread and a porcelain spoon with tangy rouille. Lunch here, with soup to start and a desert such as sublime lemon pie, can be had for less than C$16 and is the best bargain in the area.

160 rue St. Paul (near rue Rioux). ✆ **418/692-4260.** www.mistralgagnant.ca. Main courses C$15–C$31, table d'hôte dinner C$24–C$37, lunch & 3-course early-bird special (5:30–6:30pm) C$11–C$16. AE, MC, V. Summer Mon–Sat 8am–2pm & 5:30–9pm; winter Tues–Sat 11:30am–2pm & 5:30–9pm. Closed Jan.

Parliament Hill/On or Near the Grande-Allée

EXPENSIVE

L'Astral TRADITIONAL QUEBECOIS On the 29th floor of the **Hôtel Loews le Concorde** (p. 284), L'Astral is a round, slowly-revolving restaurant. All tables hug the windows, and over the course of a meal, visitors get a phenomenal 360-degree view of the city and river below. Dinner is pricey, but lunchtime table d'hôte is as low as C$14. For dessert, ask if they have their delectable version of the classic French-Canadian *pudding chômeur,* a pound cake soaked with maple syrup and brown sugar. Or order up a selection of regional cheeses, such as the nutty semi-soft Migneron de Charlevoix or Le Cendrillon, a Québec-made goat cheese that was named best in the world in 2009. Although not an obvious choice for families, the restaurant does have a children's menu, and kids will be enthralled by the view.

1225 Cours du Général de Montcalm (at Grande-Allée). ✆ **877/821-5520.** www.loewsleconcorde.com. Reservations recommended on weekends. Main courses C$24–C$40; table d'hôte lunch C$14–C$19, dinner C$35. AE, DC, DISC, M, V. Mon–Sat 6:30–10:30am & noon–3pm; Sun 9am–3pm; daily 6–10:45pm.

INEXPENSIVE

For a quick snack, **Al Wadi** (615 Grande-Allée est; ✆ **418/649-8345**) is in the heart of the Grande-Allée party district and open 24 hours a day, 7 days a week. Gyros, *shawarma,* falafel, and other veggie options are on tap.

Café Krieghoff ★ LIGHT FARE Walk down Grande-Allée about 10 minutes from the Parliament building and turn right on avenue Cartier. The 5-block street is the heart of the Montcalm residential neighborhood, with bakeries, boutiques, and a mini-mall of food shops. In the middle of the hubbub is the cheerful Krieghoff, which features an outdoor terrace a few steps up from the sidewalk. On weekend mornings, it's packed with artsy locals of all ages, whose tables get piled high with bowls of café au lait and huge plates of egg dishes, sweet pastries, or steak *frites*. Service is efficient and good-natured.

1091 av. Cartier (north of Grande-Allée). ✆ **418/522-3711.** www.cafekrieghoff.qc.ca. Most items less than C$14. MC, V. Daily 8am–10pm.

Le Commensal VEGETARIAN Like its sister outpost in Montréal (p. 231), Commensal is a vegetarian buffet, where you pay for your food by weight. Options include stir-fries, Chinese *seitan*, hazelnut cake, and sugar pie.

860 rue St-Jean (at av. Honoré-Mercier). ✆ **418/647-3733.** www.commensal.com. Pay by weight; most meals less than C$10. AE, MC, V. Sun–Wed 11am–9pm; Thurs–Sat 11am–10pm.

St-Roch

MODERATE

Bistro Les Bossus ★ BISTRO Both menu and atmosphere are urban and simple at this newer addition to the St. Roch neighborhood. One tall booth lines an exposed brick wall opposite the long bar, and a center row of square tables completes the symmetry. Typical bistro options include *quiche du moment* with a flaky crust and creamy but firm filling. With fries and salad for C$11, it's a value. There's also French onion soup, mussels and fries, and salad with grilled vegetables and goat cheese, dressed with the lightest touch. Wear jeans or spruce yourself up, the vibe here will accommodate. The large windows open when the weather warms.

620 rue St-Joseph est (near rue de la Chappelle). ✆ **418/522-5501.** www.lesbossus.com. Main courses lunch C$10–C$23, dinner C$13–C$26. AE, MC, V. Mon–Fri 11am–10pm; Sat & Sun 9am–10pm.

Le Cercle ★★ FUSION Le Cercle started as a modish tapas and wine bar with live music and art happenings, kid sister to an adjacent restaurant, the esteemed Utopie. When Utopie shut down in 2009, Le Cercle started edging into its space, and now it has performance on one side, and food and drink on the other. The fun chef's whim "tapas mania" can be ordered at whatever price you name. Wine pairing is a separate journey, best left in the capable hands of co-owner and sommelier Fréderic Gauthier. The spirit here is to bring great wine and food to anyone who wanders in. Food is served until midnight daily, with a popular weekend brunch.

226½ rue St-Joseph est (near rue Caron). ✆ **418/948-8648.** www.le-cercle.ca. Reservations recommended on weekends. Tapas C$3.50–C$9; main courses C$12–C$20; table d'hôte cost of main course, plus C$7. AE, MC, V. Mon–Fri 11am–3am; Sat 10am–3am; Sun 10am—10pm.

Le Clocher Penché Bistrot ★★ BISTRO Open since 2000, the development of this unpretentious neighborhood bistro parallels the polishing up of the overall neighborhood during the same period. With its caramel-toned woods, tall ceilings, and walls serving as gallery space for local artists, Clocher Penché has a laid-back European sophistication. There's a huge wine list, with the majority of the bottles organic or "biodynamic." The short menu changes regularly and can include duck confit or a terrific blood sausage *(boudin noir)*, which we had with a delicate pastry, caramelized onions, and yellow beets. The menu touts that nearly everything is sourced locally. Service reflects the food—amiable and without flourishes.

203 rue St-Joseph est (at rue Caron). ✆ **418/640-0597.** www.clocherpenche.ca. Reservations recommended. Main courses C$19–C$26, table d'hôte lunch & weekend brunch C$16. MC, V. Tues–Fri 11:30am–2pm; Sat & Sun 9am–2pm; Tues–Sat 5–10pm.

SEEING THE SIGHTS

Almost all of a visit to Québec City can be spent on foot in the old Lower Town—which hugs the river below the bluff—and in the old Upper Town—atop the Cap Diamant (Cape Diamond). The Old City is so compact that it's hardly necessary to plan precise sightseeing itineraries.

Wandering here, in fact, is a singular pleasure, comparable to exploring a provincial capital in Europe. You can happen upon an ancient convent, blocks of gabled houses with steeply pitched roofs, a battery of 18th-century cannons in a leafy park, or a bistro with a blazing fireplace on a wintry day. If rain or ice discourages exploration on foot, tour buses and horse-drawn calèches are options.

Vieux-Quebec: Basse-Ville (Lower Town)/ Vieux-Port

Musée de la Civilisation ★★★ ☺ Try to set aside at least 2 hours for a visit to this terrifically engrossing museum. Open since 1988, it's an innovative presence on the waterfront of historic Basse-Ville. Its precise mission has never been entirely clear: Recent temporary exhibits, for example, have focused on extraterrestrials (the 10-ft. Alien Queen from the movie *Aliens* greeted visitors) and the concept of free time. No matter. Through imaginative display techniques, hands-on devices, and holograms, curators ensure that visitors will be so enthralled by the experience that they won't pause to question its intent.

A dramatic atrium-lobby sets the tone with a representation of the St. Lawrence River with an ancient ship beached on the shore. If nothing else, definitely take in "People of Québec . . . Then and Now," a permanent exhibit that is a sprawling examination of Québec history, moving from the province's roots as a fur-trading colony to the turbulent movement for independence from the 1960s to the present, providing visitors with a rich sense of Québec's daily life over the generations. Another permanent exhibition, "Encounter with the First Nations," examines the culture of the aboriginal tribes that inhabited the region before the Europeans arrived and still live in Québec today. A show on the music of Africa runs through March 13, 2011. Exhibit texts are in French and English. There's a cafe and a museum shop, which is located in an attached house that dates from 1752.

85 rue Dalhousie (at rue St-Antoine). ✆ **866/710-8031** or 418/643-2158. www.mcq.org. Admission C$12 adults, C$11 seniors, C$9 students, C$4 children 12–16, free for children 11 & under; free to all Nov–May Tues, Jan & Feb Sat 10am–noon. Late June to mid Oct daily 9:30am–6:30pm; mid Oct to late June Tues–Sun 10am–5pm.

Place-Royale ★★★ ☺ This small but picturesque plaza is considered by Québécois to be the literal and spiritual heart of Basse-Ville—in grander terms, the birthplace of French America. There's a **bust of Louis XIV** (1643–1715) in the center. In the 17th and 18th centuries, Place-Royal, or "Royal Square," was the town marketplace, and the center of business and industry.

Eglise Notre-Dame-des-Victoires dominates the plaza. It's Québec's oldest stone church, built in 1688 after a massive fire in Lower Town destroyed 55 homes in 1682. The church was restored in 1763 and again in 1969. Its paintings, altar, and large model boat suspended from the ceiling were votive offerings brought by early settlers to ensure safe voyages. The church is open daily to visitors May through September, and admission is free. Sunday Masses are held at 10:30am and noon.

Commercial activity here began to stagnate around 1860, and by 1950, this was a poor, rundown district. Rehabilitation began in 1960, and all the buildings on the square have now been restored, though only some of the walls are original.

For years, there was an empty lot behind the stone facade on the west side. Today, there is a whole building housing the **Centre d'Interprétation de Place-Royale** on the ground floor. A 20-minute multimedia show and other exhibitions detail the city's 400-year history. When you exit, turn left and, at the end of the block, turn around to view a *trompe l'oeil* mural depicting citizens of the early city.

Centre d'Interprétation de Place-Royale, 27 rue Notre-Dame. ✆ **866/710-8031** or 418/646-3167. www.mcq.org. Centre admission C$7 adults, C$6 seniors, C$5 students, C$2 children 12–16, free for children 11 & under; free to all Nov–May Tues. Free admission to the Place-Royale & Eglise Notre-Dame-des-Victoires. Centre hours late June to early Sept daily 9:30am–5pm; early Sept to late June Tues–Sun 10am–5pm.

Vieux-Quebec: Haute-Ville (Upper Town)

Basilique Cathédrale Notre-Dame de Québec ★ Notre-Dame Basilica, representing the oldest Christian parish north of Mexico, has weathered a tumultuous history of bombardment, reconstruction, and restoration. Parts of the existing basilica date from the original 1647 structure, including the bell tower and portions of the walls, but most of today's exterior is from the reconstruction completed in 1771. The interior, a re-creation undertaken after a fire in 1922, is flamboyantly neo-baroque, with glinting yellow gold leaf and shadows wavering by the fluttering light of votive candles. It's beautifully maintained, with pews buffed to a shine. Paintings and ecclesiastical treasures still remain from the time of the French regime, including a chancel lamp given by Louis XIV. More than 900 people are buried in the crypt, including four governors of New France.

20 rue Buade (at Côte de la Fabrique). ✆ **418/694-0665.** www.patrimoine-religieux.com. Free admission for worshippers; donations encouraged. Crypt tour C$2 adults, C$1 children 16 & under. Cathedral daily 8am–4pm; a variety of thematic guided tours are available, including of cathedral & crypt May–Oct daily, check website or ask in person for details.

Château Frontenac Tour ★ ☺ Visitors curious about the interior of Québec City's emblem, its Eiffel Tower, can take a 50-minute guided tour. Tours are led by 19th-century-costumed guides—maybe a "chambermaid," maybe a "wealthy guest." Designed as a version of a Loire Valley palace, the hotel opened in 1893 to house railroad passengers and encourage tourism. It's visible from almost every quarter of the city, commanding its majestic position atop Cap Diamant, the rock bluff that once provided military defense. Reservations required. See p. 279 for hotel information.

1 rue des Carrières, at Place d'Armes. ✆ **418/691-2166.** www.tourschateau.ca. Tours C$8.50 adults, C$8 seniors, C$6 children 6–16, free for children 5 & under. Tours start on the hour (reservations required). May to mid-Oct daily 10am–6pm; mid-Oct to Apr Sat & Sun noon–5pm.

La Citadelle ★★ The duke of Wellington had this partially star-shaped fortress built at the south end of the city walls in anticipation of renewed American attacks after the War of 1812. Some remnants of earlier French military structures were incorporated into the Citadelle, including a 1750 magazine. Dug into the Plains of Abraham high above Cap Diamant (Cape Diamond), the rock bluff adjacent to the St. Lawrence River, the fort has a low profile that keeps it all but invisible until walkers are actually upon it. The facility has never actually exchanged fire with an invader but still continues its vigil for the state. It's now a national historic site and, since 1950, has been home to Québec's **Royal 22e Régiment,** the only fully Francophone unit in Canada's armed forces. That makes it North America's largest fortified group of buildings still occupied by troops.

You can enter only by guided tour, which provides access to the Citadelle and its 25 buildings, including the small regimental museums in the former powder house and prison. The hour-long walk is likely to test the patience of younger visitors and the legs of many older people, though. For them, it might be better simply to attend the 45-minute choreographed ceremony of the **Changing of the Guard** (late July to early Sept daily at 10am). It's an elaborate ritual inspired by the Changing of the Royal Guard in London and is included in the regular admission fee. Note that it can be cancelled if the weather's bad.

1 Côte de la Citadelle (at rue St-Louis). ✆ **418/694-2815.** www.lacitadelle.qc.ca. Admission C$10 adults, C$9 seniors & students, C$5.50 children 8–17, free for children 7 & under; families C$22. Apr daily 10am–4pm; May–Sept daily 9am–5pm; Oct daily 10am–3pm; Nov–Mar 1 bilingual tour a day at 1:30pm.

Musée de l'Amérique Française ★ Located on the site of the Québec Seminary, which dates from 1663, the "Museum of French America" highlights the evolution of French culture in Canada and the U.S. It reopened in October 2008 after a year of renovation, and exhibits are a touch more high-tech, accompanied by clever photo montages, atmospheric lighting, and a few interactive displays. The complex includes the chapel of the seminary, which has beautiful *trompe l'oeil* ornamentation, and an exhibition pavilion a short walk away. Shows there have focused on the Huguenots (French Protestants) of New France and the settling of French Americans in New England, and there's a permanent exhibit on the heritage of the seminary and its founding of Laval University in 1852.

Even if you don't plan to visit the museum, walk down the driveway to the right of the entrance to see the inner courtyard of the complex. It's a wash of all-white walls, four stories high. It's a quiet, peaceful spot and one of the most photographed nooks in the city.

2 Côte de la Fabrique (next to Basilique Notre-Dame). ✆ **866/710-8031** or 418/692-2843. www.mcq.org. Admission C$8 adults, C$7 seniors, C$5.50 students, C$2 children 12–16, free for children 11 & under; free to all Nov–May Tues. Late June to early Sept daily 9:30am–5pm; early Sept to late June Tues–Sun 10am–5pm.

Musée du Fort ☺ Built by a history teacher in the 1960s and updated some in the 1980s, this floor-sized diorama depicts the French, British, and U.S. battles for control of Québec. As a voice-over tells the tales, teeny boats rock, wee red lights blink to depict firefights, and wisps of smoke replicate burning buildings. It's charmingly old-fashioned and especially fun for history buffs, but the 20-minute show is not likely to seem like a good value to most other visitors. The gift shop has a good selection of Québec maps from the 17th through 19th centuries.

10 rue Ste-Anne (at Place d'Armes). ✆ **418/692-2175.** www.museedufort.com. Admission C$8 adults, C$6 seniors, C$5 students. Apr–Oct daily 10am–5pm; Feb–Mar & Nov Thurs–Sun 11am–4pm. Closed Dec & Jan.

Parc de l'Artillerie A complex of defensive buildings erected by the French in the 17th and 18th centuries make up Artillery Park. They include an ammunition factory that was functional until 1964. An iron foundry, officers' mess and quarters, and a scale model of the city created in 1806 are on view. It may be a blow to romantics and history buffs to learn that the nearby St-Jean Gate in the city wall was built in 1940, the fourth in a series that began with the original 1693 entrance, which was replaced in 1747, and then replaced again in 1867.

2 rue d'Auteuil (near Porte St-Jean). ✆ **888/773-8888** or 418/648-7016. www.pc.gc.ca/artillerie. Admission C$3.90 adults, C$3.40 seniors, C$1.90 children 6–16, free for children 5 & under. Additional fees for audio guide, tea ceremony & special activities. Early May to early Sept daily 10am–6pm; early Sept to early Oct 10am–5pm. Closed early Oct to early May.

Québec Expérience ☺ A 3D show that re-creates the grand, but more often grim, realities of the evolution of the city—the difficult weather conditions endured by the European explorers in the 17th century, the disease and fire that plagued immigrant workers in Old Port in the 18th century, the wars between French and British troops in the 19th century, and modern construction disasters in the 20th century. Guns and cannons point at audiences, a simulated bridge comes crashing down, and faux flames and screams fill the hall. All in all, it's quite vivid. Take a padded bench seat at least half way back to get the full experience, and prepare to leave expecting an anvil or piano to land on your head.

8 rue du Trésor. ✆ **418/694-4000.** www.quebecexperience.com. Admission C$7.50 adults, C$5 seniors & students, free for children 5 & under. Mid-May to Sept daily 10am–10pm; Oct to mid-May daily 10am–5pm. English- & French-language shows alternate throughout the day.

Parliament Hill/On or Near the Grande-Allée

Hôtel du Parlement Since 1968, what the Québécois call their "National Assembly" has occupied this imposing Second-Empire château constructed in 1886. Twenty-two bronze statues of some of the most prominent figures in the province's tumultuous history grace the facade. Inside, highlights include the Assembly Chamber and the Legislative Council Chamber, where parliamentary committees meet. Throughout the building, representations of the fleur-de-lis and the initials VR (for Victoria Regina) remind visitors of Québec's dual heritage. Thirty-minute guided tours are available weekdays year-round from 9am to 4:30pm, and weekends in summer from 10am to 4:30pm. Tours start at the Parliament building visitor center; enter at door no. 3. Note that during summer hours, tours of the gardens are also available.

The grand Beaux Arts style restaurant **Le Parlementaire** (✆ **418/643-6640**) is open to the public, as well as parliamentarians and visiting dignitaries. Featuring Québec products and cuisine, it serves breakfast and lunch (C$14–C$26) Monday through Friday most of the year.

The massive fountain in front of the building, **La Fontaine de Tourny,** was commissioned by the mayor of Bordeaux, France, in 1857. It was installed in 2007 as a gift from the Simons department store to the city for its 400th anniversary. Also outdoors, to the right of the main entrance as you're facing it, is a large **Inuksuk** statue.

Entrance at corner of Grande-Allée est & av. Honoré-Mercier. ✆ **866/337-8837** or 418/643-7239. www.assnat.qc.ca. Free admission. Guided tours late June to Labour Day Mon–Fri 9am–4:30pm; Sat, Sun & holidays 10am–4:30pm; rest of the year Mon–Fri 9am–4:30pm. Reservations recommended.

Musée National des Beaux-Arts du Québec ★★★ Toward the southwestern end of Parc des Champs-de-Bataille (Battlefields Park) and a half-hour walk from

Upper Town is the city's major art museum. Musée du Québec, as it's known, occupies a former prison and includes a soaring glass-roofed Grand Hall.

A central reason to visit is to see the Inuit art assembled over the years by Québécois Raymond Brousseau and acquired by the museum in 2005. Much of the 2,635-piece collection was produced in the 1980s and 1990s, and some 285 works are on display. Look for the small, whimsical statue called *Woman Pulling out Grey Hairs.*

The 1933 **Gérard-Morisset Pavilion** houses much of the rest of the museum's permanent collection, North America's largest aggregation of Québécois art. The museum tilts toward the modern, as well as the indigenous, with a permanent exhibition of works by famed Québec abstract expressionist and surrealist Jean-Paul Riopelle (1923–2002). Included is his *L'Hommage à Rosa Luxemburg,* a triptych made up of 30 individual paintings.

The museum hosts some splashy temporary exhibitions, such as 2010's eye-popping show on haute couture of Paris and London from 1947 to 1957.

An 1867 section of the museum is a former prison (one cellblock has been left intact as an exhibit). The watchtower room at the top of the pavilion is worth making your way to: It's accessible only by spiral staircase, and the petite space holds a massive wooden sculpture of a body in motion by Irish artist David Moore. There are also expansive views of the city in every direction from here.

Parc des Champs-de-Bataille (near where av. Wolfe-Montcalm meets Grande-Allée). ✆ **866/220-2150** or 418/643-2150. www.mnba.qc.ca. Free admission to permanent collection; admission for special exhibitions C$15 adults, C$12 seniors, C$7 students, C$4 children 12–17, free for children 11 & under. June–Labour Day Thurs–Tues 9am–6pm, Wed 9am–9pm; day after Labour Day to May Tues & Thurs–Sun 10am–5pm, Wed 10am–9pm. Bus: 11.

Parc des Champs-de-Bataille ★★ ☺ Covering 108 hectares (267 acres) of grassy hills, sunken gardens, monuments, fountains, and trees, Québec's Battlefields Park was Canada's first national urban park. A section called the **Plains of Abraham** is where Britain's General James Wolfe and France's Louis-Joseph, marquis de Montcalm, engaged in their short but crucial battle in 1759, which resulted in the British defeat of the French troops. It's also where the national anthem, "O Canada," was first performed. Today, the park is a favorite place for Québécois when they want sunshine or a bit of exercise.

From spring through fall, visit the **Jardin Jeanne d'Arc (Joan of Arc Garden),** just off avenue Wilfrid-Laurier, near the Loews le Concorde Hotel. This spectacular garden combines French classical design with British-style flower beds. In the rest of the park, nearly 6,000 trees of more than 80 species blanket the fields and include the sugar maple, Norway maple, American elm, and American ash. Also in the park are two Martello towers, cylindrical stone defensive structures built between 1808 and 1812 when Québec feared an American invasion.

On the eastern end of the park, the **Discovery Pavilion of the Plains of Abraham** (835 av. Wilfrid-Laurier; ✆ **418/648-4071**) has a tourist office and a multimedia exhibit called "Odyssey: A Journey through History on the Plains of Abraham." It's presented in English, French, Spanish, and Japanese.

Parc des Champs-de-Bataille. www.ccbn-nbc.gc.ca. Odyssey show C$10 adults, C$8 seniors & children 13–17, C$3 children 12 & under; discount prices mid-Sept to late Mar. Pavilion open late June to mid-Sept daily 8:30am–5:30pm; mid-Sept to late June Mon–Fri 8:30am–5pm, Sat 9am–5pm & Sun 10am–5pm.

SPECIAL EVENTS & FESTIVALS

The big event on the city calendar is the **Carnaval de Québec ★★☺**, held for 17 days at the end of January and early February. Never mind that temperatures in Québec regularly plummet in winter to well below freezing. Canadians are extraordinarily good-natured about the cold and happily pack the family up to come out and play. The mascot is a snowman called Bonhomme (Good Fellow) who presides over the merriment. Revelers descend upon the city to eddy around a monumental ice palace erected in front of the Parliament Building, watch a dog-sledding race on Old Town's narrow streets, play foosball on a human-size scale, fly over crowds on a zip line, ride down snowy hills in rubber tubes, and dance at outdoor concerts.

The party is family-friendly, even considering the wide availability of plastic trumpets filled with a nasty concoction called caribou—cheap liquor and sweet red wine. Try not to miss the canoe race that has teams rowing, dragging, and stumbling with canoes across the St. Lawrence's treacherous ice floes. It's homage to how the city used to break up the ice to keep a path open to Lévis, the town across the river.

A C$12 pass provides access to most activities over the 17 days. Hotel reservations must be made well in advance. Call ✆ **866/422-7628** or 418/621-5555, or visit www.carnaval.qc.ca for details.

The ever-innovative **Cirque du Soleil ★★★☺**, which got its start just north of Québéc City and now is an internationally known circus company, puts on free—yes, free—performances every Tuesday through Saturday evening from June 24 to Labour Day. The show takes place in a no-mans-land-turned-theater under a highway where Vieux Québéc meets the St-Roch. It's all very cool and an extraordinary coup for the city. The program got started in 2008 as part of Québéc City's 400th anniversary celebrations and will be continuing each summer through at least 2013. Check the city tourist office for details about starting times for the 1-hour event (the times change throughout the summer). A small set of bleachers offers standing room with better sight lines for C$15, with advance tickets available at www.billetech.com.

The **Image Mill Light Installation ★★★** is something entirely unique to Québéc City. In 2008, as part of the city's 400th anniversary celebrations, installation artist Robert LePage (1957–) created a massive, outdoor multimedia show of photos of city history called Image Mill. It was projected in Vieux-Port along 600 meters (over a third of a mile) of industrial grain silos and produced an outdoor community event, akin to nightly fireworks displays. Like the free Cirque du Soleil show (above), the project was a highlight of the 2008 festivities and is being extended summers through 2013. The 50-minute show takes place Tuesday through Saturday evenings from June 24 to Labour Day, with music broadcast from speakers by the water. During the other evening hours from dusk to 11:30pm, the silos are bathed in a light show called Aurora Borealis, inspired by the Technicolor of the real Northern Lights. For a taste of the whole thing, check out photos at LePage's website, www.lacaserne.net/index2.php/other_projects.

Honoring St. John the Baptist, the patron saint of French Canadians, **Jean-Baptiste Day** on June 24 is a day of festivities (and celebrated throughout Québec province with far more enthusiasm than Canada Day on July 1). It's Québec's own "national" holiday *(fête nationale)* and features fireworks, music in parks, and parades.

The Festival d'Eté (Summer Festival) ★★ is what organizers say is the largest Francophone music festival. It's held for about 10 days each July. More than 400 performances of rock, jazz, reggae, and classical take place at both indoor and outdoor venues. Call ✆ **888/992-5200** or 418/523-4540, or check www.infofestival.com.

OUTDOOR ACTIVITIES & SPECTATOR SPORTS

Outdoor activities

BICYCLING & IN-LINE SKATING

Parc des Champs-de-Bataille (Battlefields Park) is the most popular park for bicycling and strolling. See p. 295. There's lots of good biking on marked paths along the river as well. The path was new in 2008 and is well-maintained. Tourist information centers provide bicycle-trail maps and can point out a variety of routes. See p. 273 for rental information.

Mountain bikers head to **Mont Ste-Anne** (www.mont-sainte-anne.com), 42km (26 miles) northeast of Québec City. It has the most well-known mountain bike network in eastern Canada and was host to the 2010 Mountain Bike and Trial World Championships.

BUS TOURS

Buses are convenient if extensive walking is difficult, especially in hilly Upper Town. Among the established tour operators, **Dupont,** which also goes by the name **Old Québec Tours** (✆ **800/267-8687** or 418/664-0460; www.tourdupont.com), offers English-only tours (preferable to bilingual tours since you get twice as much information in the same amount of time). The company's city tours are in small coaches, while day trips out of the city are in full-size buses. The company also offers a **whale-watching excursion** hours north into the Charlevoix region (see p. 318). The 10-hour day includes a 3-hour cruise among the belugas.

CROSS-COUNTRY SKIING

Parc des Champs-de-Bataille (Battlefields Park), where Carnaval de Québec establishes its winter playground during February, has a network of groomed cross-country trails in winter. Equipment can be rented at the **Discovery Pavilion** (p. 295), near the Citadelle.

DOG SLEDDING

Aventure Inukshuk ☺ (✆ **418/875-0770;** www.aventureinukshuk.qc.ca), is located in Station touristique Duchesnay, in the town of Ste-Catherine-de-la-Jacques-Cartier, about a half hour from the city. Guides show you how to lead a sled pulled by six dogs. Even on the shortest trip, you go deep into a hushed world of snow and thick woods, past rows of evergreens, and over a beaver pond. Overnight camping trips are available. The 1-hour trip, which includes an additional half-hour of training, costs C$95 in December, January, and March, and C$104 in February. Children 6 to 12 are half-price, and children 2 to 5 go free (children younger than 2 aren't allowed).

FIREWORKS

Les Grands Feux Loto-Québec ★ ☺ uses the highly scenic Montmorency Falls 15 minutes north of the city center as its setting. Pyrotechnical teams are invited from countries around the world to put on shows Wednesdays and Saturdays, late July to mid-August. Tickets get you admission to the base of the waterfalls, where there are 5,500 reserved bleacher seats and 30,000 general-admission spots. Call ✆ **888/934-3473** or 418/523-3389, or go to www.quebecfireworks.com, for details.

HORSE-DRAWN CARRIAGE RIDES

A romantic, if somewhat expensive, way to see the city at a genial pace is in a horse-drawn carriage, called a calèche. Carriages will pick you up or can be hired from locations throughout the city, including at Place d'Armes. A 40- to 45-minute ride costs C$80, plus tip, for four people maximum. Carriages operate year-round, rain or shine. Companies include **Calèches du Vieux-Québec** (✆ **418/683-9222;** www.calecheduvieuxquebec.com) and **Calèches de la Nouvelle-France** (✆ **418/692-0068;** www.calechesquebec.com).

RIVER CRUISES

Croisières AML (✆ **800/563-4643** or 418/692-1159 in late-spring to mid-fall season; www.croisieresaml.com) offers a variety of cruises. Its *Louis Jolliet* is a three-decked 1930s ferry boat–turned–excursion vessel, which carries 1,000 passengers and is stocked with bilingual guides, full dining facilities, and a bar. The company offers brunch and dinner cruises, as well as jaunts that take in the fireworks or the Image Mill presentation. The boats dock at quai Chouinard, at 10 rue Dalhousie, in Vieux-Port. Similar cruises are offered by **Groupe Dufour** (✆ **800-463-5250** or 418-692-0222; www.dufour.ca).

TOBOGGANING

An old-fashioned toboggan run called **Les Glissades de la Terrasse** (✆ **418/829-9898**) ☺ is set up on the steep wooden staircase at Terrasse Dufferin's south end in winter. The slide extends almost to the Château Frontenac. Next to the ticket booth, a little sugar shack sells sweet treats. Cost is C$2 per person.

WALKING TOURS

Times and points of departure for walking tours change, so get up-to-date information at any tourist office (addresses are listed on p. 273). Many tours leave from the Place d'Armes in Upper Town, just in front of the **Château Frontenac.**

Tours Voir Québec (✆ **877/266-0206** or 418/266-0206; www.toursvoirquebec.com) specializes in English-only guided tours of the Old City. "The Grand Tour," which is available year-round, is a 2-hour stroll that covers the architecture, events, and cultural history of the city. Tours are limited to 15 people. Cost is C$23 adults, C$20 students (ISIC card required), C$11 children 6 to 12, and free for children 5 and under. The company also offers private tours.

One way to split the difference between being out on your own and being on a guided tour is to use **Map Old Québec** (www.oldquebecmap.com), a website that offers a beautifully designed map and MP3 files. After you purchase the map and audio files, you can download a tour onto your MP3 player and go at your own pace.

WATERPARK

Village Vacances Valcartier ☺ (✆ **888/384-5524;** www.valcartier.com) in St-Gabriel-de-Valcartier, about a half-hour northwest of the city, is a major manmade water park. In summer, it boasts 35 slides, a gigantic wave pool, a huge pirate ship, and a faux Amazon River to go tubing down. In winter, the same facilities are put to use for "snow rafting" on inner tubes and skating. In the summer of 2010, it introduced a fingerprint-reading technology called Money at My Fingertip. Instead of carrying cash or credit cards in their bathing suits, visitors can register their credit cards and then pay for food and other services simply by pressing a finger to a screen.

Spectator Sports

Québec has not had a team in any of the major professional leagues since the NHL Nordiques left in 1995. Since 1999, though, it has been represented by **Les Capitales de Québec** (www.capitalesdequebec.com), a baseball club in the Can-Am League. Home games take place at Stade Municipal (Municipal Stadium), 100 rue du Cardinal Maurice-Roy (© **877/521-2244** or 418/521-2255), not far beyond the St-Roch neighborhood. Tickets cost C$8 to C$16.

There's also a local fan base for Québec City's junior hockey team (with players 16 to 20 years old), **Les Remparts de Québec** (www.remparts.ca). They play at the Colisée Pepsi from September to March. Tickets are C$6 to C$13.

SHOPPING

The compact size of Vieux-Québec makes it especially convenient for browsing and shopping. Much of the merchandise is of high quality.

Indigenous crafts, handmade sweaters, and **Inuit art** are among the desirable items specific to Québec. An official igloo trademark identifies authentic Inuit (Eskimo) art, though the differences between the real thing and the manufactured variety become apparent with a little careful study. Inuit artwork, which is usually in the form of carvings in stone or bone, is an excellent purchase not for its low price, but for its high quality. Expect to pay hundreds of dollars for even a relatively small piece.

Maple syrup products make sweet gifts, as do **regional wines** and **jams.** Look for Québec **cheeses, chocolate,** and products made from local crops such as **cranberries** or **black currants.** Be sure to double-check customs policies before crossing the border with perishables.

Vieux-Québec's Lower Town, particularly the area known as **Quartier du Petit-Champlain,** offers many possibilities—clothing, souvenirs, gifts, household items, collectibles—and is avoiding the trashiness that can afflict heavily touristed neighborhoods with an up-swell of shops that feature locally made products. The area is just around the corner from the funicular entrance.

In Upper Town, wander along **rue St-Jean,** both within and outside the city walls, and on **rue Garneau** and **Côte de la Fabrique,** which branch off the east end of St-Jean. For T-shirts, postcards, and other souvenirs, check out the myriad shops that line **rue St-Louis.**

If you're heading to St-Roch to eat, build in a little time to stroll **rue St-Joseph,** which, for a few blocks, has new boutiques alongside cafes and restaurants.

Antiques

About a dozen antiques shops line rue St-Paul in Lower Town. They're filled with knickknacks, Québec country furniture, candlesticks, old clocks, Victoriana, Art Deco and Art Moderne objects, and the increasingly sought-after kitsch and housewares of the early post–World War II period. **Machin Chouette** (225 rue Saint-Paul; © **418/525-9898;** www.machinchouette.com) hand selects antiques for homes with a modern flair and also makes custom storage units out of album covers, vinyl records, and wood butter boxes.

Arts & Crafts

Boutique Métiers d'Art In a stone building at the corner of Place-Royale, this carefully arranged store displays works by scores of Québécois craftspeople, at least some of which are likely to appeal to almost any customer. Among these objects are wooden boxes, jewelry, graphics, and a variety of gifts. 29 rue Notre-Dame, Lower Town. ✆ **418/694-0267.** www.metiers-d-art.qc.ca.

Galerie Brousseau et Brousseau In 2005, the important Inuit art collection assembled over 30 years by Québécois Raymond Brousseau was acquired by the Musée des Beaux-Arts du Québec, and 285 works from the 2,635-piece collection are on display at that museum. Here, you can buy Native Canadian carvings selected by the same family to take home. This is the most prominent of the city's art dealers, and it offers certificates of authenticity. Prices are high but competitive for merchandise of similar quality. The shop is set up like a gallery, so feel free just to browse. 35 rue St-Louis (at rue des Jardins), Upper Town. ✆ **418/694-1828.** www.sculpture.artinuit.ca.

Rue du Trésor Outdoor Gallery Sooner or later, everyone walks down alley near the Place d'Armes. Artists gather along outdoors here much of the year to exhibit and sell their work. Most of the prints on view are of Québec scenes and can make attractive souvenirs. The artists seem to enjoy chatting with interested passersby. Rue du Trésor (btw. rues Ste-Anne & Buade), Upper Town.

Vert Tuyau Coop The fused glass jewelry, turned-wood bowls, and felted wool garments on offer here are all 100% Québec-made. Everything is created by one of this artist collective's members, which was founded to offer tourists an alternative to T-shirts and trinkets manufactured then shipped from the other side of the globe. 6 rue Cul-de-Sac, Lower Town. ✆ **418/692-1111.** www.verttuyau.com.

Bath & Body

Fruits & Passion Outposts of this Québec-based chain are found throughout the region. They all carry lotions, shampoos, candles, and foods. The Cuchina hand-care line uses olive-leaf extract with scents ranging from fig to lime zest. 75 rue du Petit-Champlain, Lower Town. ✆ **418/692-2859.** www.fruits-passion.com.

Clothing

Harricana ★ Montréal designer Mariouche Gagné, who was born on Ile d'Orléans in 1971, is a leader of the so-called ecoluxe movement. Her company recycles old fur, silk scarves, and even wedding dresses to create new coats, winter hats, tops, and skirts. One favorite on a recent visit: a white aviator hat of recycled fur and scraps of a lace wedding gown, for C$250. 44 Côte de la Fabrique, Upper Town. ✆ **418/204-5340.** www.harricana.qc.ca.

La Maison Darlington The popular emporium in this historic house (it was built in 1775) comes on strong with both tony and traditional clothing for men and women produced by such makers as Dale of Norway, Geiger, and Ballantyne. Inventory includes high-quality and tasteful men's and women's hats, scarves, and sweaters, especially in cashmere and other wools. As appealing are the hand-smocked, locally made dresses for little girls. 7 rue de Buade (near Place d'Armes), Upper Town. ✆ **418/692-2268.**

Simons ☺ Old Québec's only department store opened here in 1840. Small by modern standards, Simons has two floors for men's and women's clothing, emphasizing sportswear for adults and teens. Most of it is pretty basic. 20 Côte de la Fabrique (near the Hôtel-de-Ville), Upper Town. ✆ **418/692-3630.** www.simons.ca.

Food

Marché du Vieux-Port By the water near the train station, this market is a year-round operation that blossoms in spring and summer with farmers' bounty from Ile d'Orléans and beyond. In addition to fresh fruits and vegetables, you'll find relishes, jams, honey, wines, meats, cheeses, and handicrafts. 160 quai Saint-André (near the train station), Lower Town. ✆ **418/692-2517.** www.marchevieuxport.com.

Newspapers & Magazines

Maison de la Presse Internationale As its name implies, this large store in the midst of the St-Jean shopping-and-nightlife bustle offers up racks and racks of magazines and a good assortment of newspapers from around the world, in many languages. It also has adapter plugs and converters. It's open Monday to Saturday from 7am (Sun from 8am) until 11pm. 1050 rue St-Jean (at the corner of rue Ste-Angèle), Upper Town. ✆ **418/694-1511.**

Wines & Spirits

Société des Alcools du Québec Liquor and other spirits can be sold only in stores operated by this provincial agency. SAQ outlets are supermarkets of wines and spirits, with thousands of bottles in stock. Most feature large sections with Québec products, including the unique ice cider *(cidre de glace)*, made from apples left on trees after the first frost, for around C$25. 1 rue des Carrières, in the Château Frontenac, Upper Town. ✆ **418/692-1712.** www.saq.com.

QUÉBEC CITY AFTER DARK

There are two terrifically innovative events to plan summer evenings around: free outdoor performances by **Cirque du Soleil** and the Image Mill Light Installation**.** See p. 296 for details on both. On Wednesdays and Saturdays from late July to mid-Aug, the city hosts a grand fireworks competition, **Les Grands Feux Loto-Québec,** too. See p. 297.

Most bars and clubs stay open until 2 or 3am. Cover charges and drink minimums are rare in the bars and clubs that provide live entertainment.

The Performing Arts

CLASSICAL MUSIC, OPERA & DANCE

The region's premier classical groups are **Orchestre Symphonique de Québec** (**✆ 418/643-8486;** www.osq.org), Canada's oldest symphony, which performs at the Grand Théâtre de Québec (see below), and **Les Violons du Roy** (**✆ 418/692-3026;** www.violonsduroy.com), a string orchestra that recently celebrated its 25th year. It features musicians in the early stages of their careers and performs at the centrally located Palais Montcalm (p. 302).

CONCERT HALLS & PERFORMANCE VENUES

Many of the city's churches host sacred and secular music concerts, as well as special Christmas festivities. Look for posters on outdoor kiosks around the city and check with the tourist office (p. 273) for listings.

Only in Québec City

An after-dinner stroll and a lounge on a bench on Terrasse Dufferin, the boardwalk next to the Château Frontenac, are gorgeously atmospheric. Ferries glide across the river below burnished by moon glow, and the stars haven't seemed this close since childhood.

Colisée Pepsi This 15,300-seat arena is home to the Remparts, a popular junior hockey team. The stadium also hosts events such as monster truck extravaganzas, boxing matches, and occasional rock shows. It's a 10-minute drive northwest of Parliament Hill. 250 bd. Wilfrid-Hamel (ExpoCité), north of St-Roch. ✆ **418/691-7110.** www.expocite.com.

Grand Théâtre de Québec ★★★ Classical music concerts, opera, dance, jazz, klezmer, and theatrical productions are presented in two halls. Visiting conductors, orchestras, and dance companies perform here, in addition to resident companies such as the Orchestre Symphonique de Québec. 269 bd. René-Lévesque est (near av. Turnbull), Parliament Hill. ✆ **877/643-8131** or 418/643-8131. www.grandtheatre.qc.ca.

Le Capitole Big musical productions such as *The Beatles Story* and *Cats,* along with live musical performances, keep this historic 1,262-seat theater on Place d'Youville buzzing along (productions are in French). More intimate shows, such as an homage to Johnny Cash, are put on in the attached Le Cabaret du Capitole. 972 rue St-Jean (at Place d'Youville), Parliament Hill. ✆ **800/261-9903** or 418/694-4444. www.lecapitole.com.

Palais Montcalm ★ Recent renovations made this venue bigger and more modern, and it's now a hub of the city's cultural community. The main performance space seats 979 and presents a mix of dance programs, plays, and classical music concerts. More intimate recitals happen in a 125-seat cafe-theater. 995 Place d'Youville (near Porte Saint-Jean), Parliament Hill. ✆ **418/641-6040.** www.palaismontcalm.ca.

The Club & Music Scene

If you want to stroll around and take in the nightlife options, there are three principal streets to choose from: **rue St-Jean** inside and outside the walls, **Grande-Allée** outside the walls, and **rue St-Joseph est** in the St-Roch neighborhood.

BOITES À CHANSONS & OTHER MUSIC CLUBS

Boîtes à chansons (literally, "boxes with songs") are small clubs for a casual evening of music from singer-songwriters. They're popular throughout Québec.

Largo Resto-Club An attractive restaurant and jazz club, Largo is one of a growing number of businesses sprucing up a blocks-long strip of rue St-Joseph in the St-Roch district. High ceilings and chandeliers give it old-time class, while blond-wood floors, clean angles, and contemporary art make it modern. There's jazz on Fridays, Saturdays, usually free for diners. Main courses range from C$17 to C$27. 643 rue St-Joseph est, St-Roch. ✆ **418/529-3111.** www.largorestoclub.com.

Le Pape-Georges A cozy wine bar in a 343-year-old stone-and-beamed room that features *chanson* (a French-cabaret singing style), along with other music, Friday through Sunday at 10pm (and Thurs in summer). Light fare is available, along with up to 15 choices of wine by the glass (the bar's motto: "Save water; drink wine!"). 8 rue Cul-de-Sac (near bd. Champlain), Lower Town. ✆ **418/692-1320.** www.papegeorges.com.

Théâtre Petit-Champlain Québécois and French singers alternate with jazz and blues groups in this roomy cafe and theater in Lower Town. Performances take place most Wednesdays through Saturdays at 8pm. Tickets run about C$20 to C$40. There's a pretty outdoor patio for pre-show drinks. 68 rue du Petit-Champlain (near the funicular), Lower Town. ✆ **418/692-2631.** www.theatrepetitchamplain.com.

DANCE CLUBS

Boudoir Lounge ★ The hottest club in St-Roch, Boudoir is open daily from noon until 3am, with DJs working sound systems from 10pm on Thursdays, Fridays, and Saturdays. Live music is occasionally featured. In warm weather, there's a terrace on the pedestrian street in front. The seasonal cocktail menu keeps up with trends from herbal infusions to locally-inspired mix-ins of ice wine or maple syrup. 441 rue du Parvis (at bd. Charest est), St-Roch. ✆ **418/524-2777.** www.boudoirlounge.com.

Le Drague Cabaret Club Catering mostly to gay and lesbian clientele, "the Drag" has been around since 1983 and features two dance rooms and a cabaret with drag shows on Sunday nights. Other nights bring live shows, karaoke, and country-music dancing. 815 rue St-Augustin (just off rue St-Jean), Parliament Hill. ✆ **418/649-7212.** www.ledrague.com.

Maurice Find this club in the converted mansion at the thumping heart of the Grande-Allée scene. It includes a surprisingly good restaurant (**VooDoo Grill**), a couple of bars, and music that tilts heavily toward Latin. In winter, it has been known to set up a sidewalk-level "Icecothèque" with a bar made completely of ice, ice sculptures, and roaring music. Theme nights are frequent, and large crowds are not unusual. 575 Grande-Allée est, Parliament Hill. ✆ **418/647-2000.** www.mauricenightclub.com.

Bars

If you're young and looking for fun, keep in mind the **Grande-Allée** strip just past Place George-V, where a beery collegiate atmosphere can sometimes rule as the evening wears on. The bars listed here are removed from Grande-Allée's melee.

Fou Bar No matter what your age, you'll feel welcome and comfortable sipping on a draught pulled at Fou Bar. Old stone walls, an abandoned fireplace, and walls with local art make the place feel homey. It's a great pre-dinner warm up. Or stay to catch a night of reggae, jazz, bluegrass, or acoustic live performance. Open Monday to Friday from 2:30pm, and Saturday and Sunday from noon, to 3am. 525 rue St-Jean (near rue Ste-Claire), just outside walls of Upper Town. ✆ **418/522-1987.** www.foubar.ca.

L'Astral ★ Spinning slowly above the city, this restaurant and bar atop the **Hôtel Loews le Concorde** (p. 284) unveils a breathtaking 360-degree panorama. The restaurant is high-quality (see p. 289), but you can also come just for drinks and the sunset view. 1225 Cours du Général de Montcalm (at Grande-Allée), Parliament Hill. ✆ **418/647-2222.**

Saint Alexandre Pub ★ Roomy and sophisticated, this is one of the best-looking bars in town. It's done in British-pub style: polished mahogany, exposed brick, and a working fireplace that's particularly comforting during the 8 cold months of the year. Bartenders serve more than 40 single-malt scotches and 250 beers, along with hearty bar food (*croque-monsieur,* steak-and-kidney pie, fish and chips). Check the schedule for the occasional live music—rock, blues, jazz, or Irish. 1087 rue St-Jean (near rue St-Stanislas), Upper Town. ✆ **418/694-0015.** www.pubstalexandre.com.

Savini This self-dubbed "vinothèque" had the trappings of a red-hot addition to Québec: When we visited, we found a 2-hour wait for dinner, booming sound system, hostesses in teeny dresses, and nightly DJs. A big menu offers a variety of Italian food options, and a short menu of pizza and salad is available until 1am, too. 680 Grande-Allée (near rue D'Artigny), Parliament Hill. ✆ **418/647-4747.** www.savini.ca.

SSS SSS may be the only lounge and restaurant in Vieux-Québec that adopts the sleek, bigger-city approach of sounding its techno beats onto the sidewalk to lure cocktail seekers. The most recent experiment of chefs Christian Lemelin and Stéphan D'Anjou, co-owners of the highly regarded restaurant **Toast!** (see p. 288), brings French flair to American comfort foods—ribs, hot dogs, onion rings. Best example: *beignet de morue*, or cod donuts, with lemon aioli. Guests can opt for entrées or apps, dining room or bar. On busy nights, a snack menu kicks in after 10:30pm. 71 rue St-Paul (near rue Sault-au-Matelot), Lower Town. ✆ **418/694-0015.** www.restaurantsss.com.

St-Laurent Bar et Lounge A swank little room inside Québec's magical castle, the Château Frontenac. Dark wood and marble lend an air of elegance, and a bank of windows overlooks the river. The crowd is older and well-heeled, reflected in the drink options: 19 types of single malt; 15 wines by the glass; and 30 mixed drinks, including the signature St-Laurent Club, with muddled blueberries, Tanqueray #10 Gin, and lemon juice. There's a small food menu. Château Frontenac, 1 rue des Carrières, Upper Town. ✆ **418/692-3861.** www.fairmont.com/frontenac.

DAY TRIPS FROM QUÉBEC CITY: ILE D'ORLÉANS, STE-ANNE FALLS & MORE

Ile d'Orléans: 16km (10 miles) NE of Québec City; Montmorency Falls: 11km (6¾ miles) NE of Québec City; Ste-Anne-de-Beaupré: 33km (21 miles) NE of Québec City; Canyon Ste-Anne & Parc Mont Ste-Anne: 42km (26 miles) NE of Québec City

An excursion to Ile d'Orléans, Montmorency Falls, Ste-Anne-de-Beaupré, and Canyon Ste-Anne and its waterfalls can be completed in a day, although it will admittedly be a sunrise–to–after-dark undertaking without much time to catch your breath. Most visitors will probably want to focus on a day trip to two of the suggested destinations listed here.

Bucolic Ile d'Orléans, an island within sight of Québec City, is an unspoiled mini-oasis with orchards, farms, and 18th- and 19th-century houses. The waterfalls at both Montmorency and Canyon Ste-Anne are dazzling fun. The shrine of Ste-Anne-de-Beaupré is a religious destination, attracting some million and a half pilgrims each year to its complex—a church, hillside station of the cross, chapel, and museum.

Although driving on your own provides the most flexibility, tour buses go to Montmorency Falls and the shrine of Ste-Anne-de-Beaupré, and circle Ile d'Orléans. For more information, go to **www.quebecregion.com.**

Québec City Environs

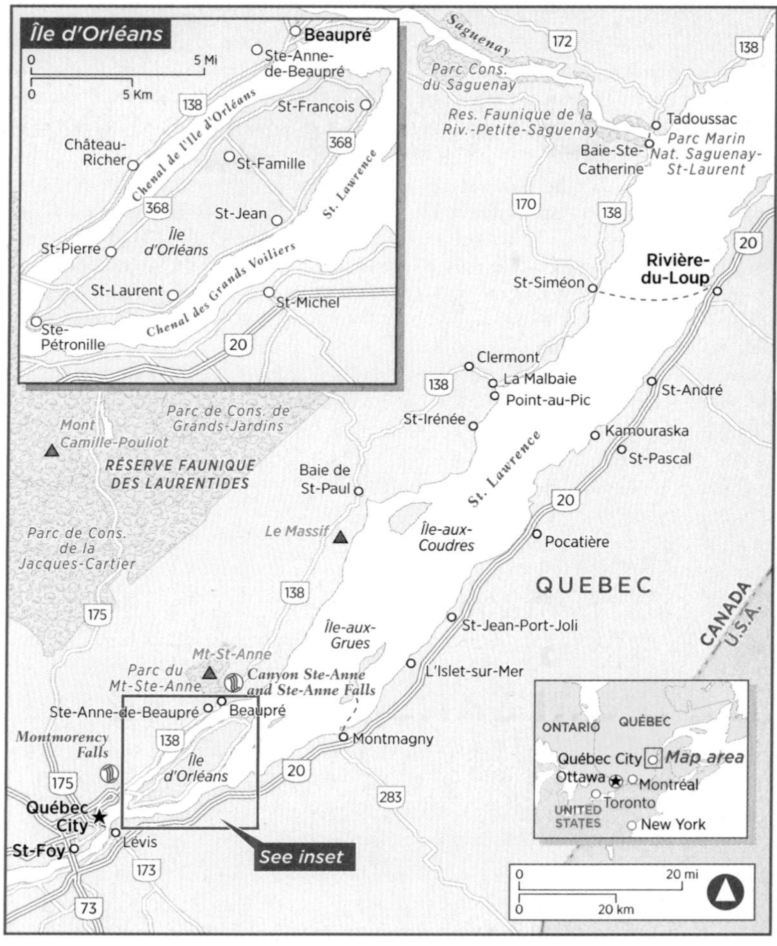

Ile d'Orleans ★★

Ile d'Orléans was long inhabited by Native Indians and then settled by the French as one of the first outposts of New France in the 17th century. Long isolated from the mainland, the island's 7,000 residents keep a firm resistance to development, so far preventing it from becoming just another sprawling bedroom community. The island remains a largely rural farming area. Many of the island's oldest houses are intact, and many also sport the island's signature bright red roofs, which made for better visibility from the river, especially when traveling through rain or snow.

AN IMPORTANT navigational NOTE

Street numbers on the ring road called "chemin Royal" start anew in each village. That means you could pass a no. 1000 chemin Royal in one stretch and another no. 1000 chemin Royal a few minutes later. Be sure that you know not just the street number of your destination, but also which village it's in.

Until 1935, the only way to get to Ile d'Orléans was by boat (in summer) or over the ice in sleighs (in winter). The highway bridge that was built that year has allowed the island's fertile fields to become Québec City's primary source of fresh foods. During harvest periods, fruits and vegetables are trucked into the city daily. In mid-July, hand-painted signs posted by the main road announce FRAISES: CUEILLIR VOUS-MEME (STRAWBERRIES: YOU PICK 'EM). The same invitation is made during apple season, August through October.

Other seasonal highlights include the visit of thousands of migrating snow geese, ducks, and Canada geese in April and May, and again in late October. It's a spectacular sight when they launch in flapping hordes so thick that they almost blot out the sun. Late May also brings the blooming of the many apple trees on the island.

Look for the bilingual cookbook *Farmers in Chef Hats* (www.farmersinchefhats.com), which features 50 recipes from the island, as well as an agro-tourism map.

It's a short drive from Québec City to the island. Take Autoroute 440 east, in the direction of Ste-Anne-de-Beaupré. In about 15 minutes, the Ile d'Orléans bridge will be on the right. If you'd like a guide, **Maple Leaf Guide Services** (✆ **877/622-3677** or 418/622-3677; www.mapleleafservices.com) can provide one in your car or theirs. Do not plan to bike over the bridge; the sidewalk is narrow and precarious. Cyclists with cars can park at the tourist office or any of the island's churches.

After the bridge, turn right on Route 368 East. The **Bureau d'Accueil Touristique,** or Tourist Information Center (✆ **866/941-9411** or 418/828-9411; www.iledorleans.com), is in the house on the right corner. Pick up the useful map that has most of the restaurants, farms, and accommodations marked. The bureau is open daily from about 9am to 5pm, with longer hours in the peak summer months and somewhat shorter hours in winter. Note that there are a limited number of restrooms on the island.

A coast-hugging road—Route 368, also called chemin Royal and, in a few stretches, chemin de Bout-de-l'Ile—circles the island, which is 34km (21 miles) long and 8km (5 miles) wide. Another couple of roads bisect the island. Farms and picturesque houses dot its east side, and abundant apple orchards enliven the west side.

The island has six tiny villages, originally established as parishes, and each has a church as its focal point. Some are **stone churches ★** that date from the days of the French regime, and with fewer than a dozen such churches left in all of Québec province, this is a particular point of pride for the islanders.

It's possible to make a circuit of Ile d'Orléans in half a day, but you can justify a full day if you stop for a good meal, visit a sugar shack, or do a little gallery hopping. If you're strapped for time, loop around as far as St-Jean, then drive across the island on Route du Mitan ("middle road"). You'll get to the bridge by turning left onto Route 368 West.

economuseums: A LOCAL (TOURISM) TRADITION

Québec is enamored with mini-museums, especially museums of food products. Called *économusées* or interpretation centers, they're often simply a room or two attached to a store. Usually, they display tools used in production and feature photographs and explanatory text in French and (usually) English. Examples on Ile d'Orléans include Chocolaterie de l'Ile d'Orléans in Ste-Pétronille (see above) and Cassis Monna et Filles in St-Pierre (see below). Designed to both educate and provide tourist oomph, they're rarely worth a visit on their own but usually provide a few minutes of interesting reading if you've stopped to shop. Many are listed at www.economusee.com.

For much of the year, you can meander at 40kmph (25 mph), pulling over only occasionally to let a car pass. There is no bike path, which means bikers share the narrow rural roads. Both drivers and cyclists need to move with care in the busy summer months.

Many island attractions and restaurants are closed or have limited hours from October through May. Check before making a special trip for any one place.

STE-PETRONILLE

If you've taken a right turn off the bridge, the first village reached on the counterclockwise tour is Ste-Pétronille. When the British occupied the island in 1759, General James Wolfe had his headquarters here before launching his successful attack on Québec City. The village is best known for its Victorian inn, **La Goéliche** (see below), and claims the northernmost stand of **red oaks** in North America, dazzling in autumn. Houses here were once the summer homes of wealthy English in the 1800s, and the church dates from 1871. Drive down to the water's edge at the inn, where there's a small public area with benches and views of Québec City.

For a light snack, the **Chocolaterie de l'Ile d'Orléans** (148 chemin du Bout-de-l'Ile; ✆ **418/828-2252**) sells soups, sandwiches, and pizza-like *tartes flambées* (the *saumon fumé,* smoked salmon, is good), along with homemade chocolates and ice cream. It's open May through early October daily, with variable hours.

Where to Stay & Dine

La Goéliche ★ On a rocky point of land at the southern tip of Ile d'Orléans stands this country inn and restaurant with a wraparound porch. The building is a virtual replica of the 1880 Victorian house that burned to the ground in 1996. The new building re-creates the period flavor with tufted chairs, Tiffany-style lamps, and antiques. All bedrooms face the water, and first-floor units have small terraces. The river slaps at the foundation of the glass-enclosed terrace dining room, which is a grand observation point from which to watch the river. Non-guests can come for breakfast, lunch, or dinner. Main courses cost C$12 to C$26 at lunch, C$35 to C$52 at dinner, and C$12 to C$18 for the fancy Sunday brunch. The inn is open year-round.

22 chemin du Quai, Ste-Pétronille, QC G0A 4C0. ✆ **888/511-2248** or 418/828-2248. Fax 418/828-2745. www.goeliche.ca. 16 units. C$188–$333 double. Rates include breakfast. Packages available. AE, DC, MC, V. Free parking. **Amenities:** Restaurant; bar; babysitting; pool (heated outdoor). *In room:* Hair dryer, minibar (in some rooms), Wi-Fi (free).

ST-LAURENT

From Ste-Pétronille, continue on Route 368, which continues to be called chemin du Bout-de-l'Ile in this village. There are a few restaurants and art galleries in this stretch, and bicycle rentals at **Ecolocyclo** (1979 chemin Royal; © **418/828-0370;** www.ecolocyclo.net). After 7km (4¼ miles), you'll arrive at St-Laurent, founded in 1679, once a boat-building center turning out ships that could carry up to 5,300 tons for Glasgow ship owners. To learn more about the town's maritime history, visit **Le Parc Maritime de St-Laurent** (© **418/828-9672;** www.parcmaritime.ca), an active boatyard from 1908 to 1967. Before the bridge was built, islanders journeyed across the river to Québec City by boat from here. The park offers demonstrations of the art of building flat-bottomed schooners. It's open mid-June through mid-October daily from 10am to 5pm. Admission is C$3.50 adults, free for children 12 and under.

From May to October, lunches, dinners, and accommodations are available at **Le Moulin de Saint-Laurent ★** (754 chemin Royal; © **888/629-3888** or 418/829-3888; www.moulinstlaurent.qc.ca). Outdoor dining is available on a shaded terrace beside a small waterfall.

ST-JEAN

St-Jean, 6km (3¾ miles) from St-Laurent, was home to sea captains. That might be why the houses in the village appear more luxurious than others on the island. The creamy yellow "Scottish brick" in the facades of several of the homes were ballast in boats that came over from Europe. The village **church** was built in 1734, and the walled **cemetery** is the final resting place of many fishermen and seafarers.

On the left as you enter St-Jean is **Manoir Mauvide-Genest** (1451 chemin Royal; © **418/829-2630;** www.manoirmauvidegenest.com). It was the manor home of a French surgeon who settled here in 1720 and went on to acquire much of the western part of the island, becoming one of New France's leading figures in the process. Jean Mauvide built this small estate in 1752, and the building is unlike any other on the island. It's filled with authentic and reproduction furnishings from Mauvide's era and is classified as an historic monument. It's open from mid-May to mid-October daily 10am to 5pm. Admission is C$6 for adults, C$2 for children 6 to 12, with an additional C$2 per person for a guided tour.

If you're pressed for time, cross the island here to Ste-Famille, back near the bridge. Route du Mitan is marked (barely) with a small sign on the left just past the church in St-Jean. Even if you're continuing the full island loop, you might want to make a short detour to see the inland farmland and forest. To continue the tour, return to St-Jean and proceed east on Route 368.

St-François is at the island's most northeastern tip. Potatoes and leeks are grown on this part of the island, which lead some to dub this "the village of vichyssoise." The 9km (5½-mile) drive from St-Jean to St-François exposes vistas of the Laurentian Mountains on the mainland. **Mont Ste-Anne** is in the far distance, its slopes scored by ski trails. The St. Lawrence River, a constant and mighty presence, is 10 times wider here than when it flows past Québec City and can be viewed especially well from the town's **observation tower,** which will come up on your right. You can park here and climb for a view.

After you've looped around the northern edge of the island, the road stops being Route 368 East and becomes Route 368 West.

STE-FAMILLE

Founded in 1661, Ste-Famille is the oldest parish on the island and 8km (5 miles) from St-François. Across the road from the triple-spired church (1743) is the convent of **Notre-Dame Congregation,** founded in 1685 by Marguerite Bourgeoys, one of Montréal's prominent early citizens.

Parc des Ancêtres is a riverside green space with picnic tables. Sharing the same parking lot is **Pub le Mitan** (3887 chemin Royal; ✆ **418/829-0408**), a microbrewery with a deck that overlooks the river.

Other potential Ste-Famille stopping points in warm months are **Les Fromages de l'Isle d'Orléans** (4696 chemin Royal; ✆ **418/829-0177**), an artisanal dairy that makes a 17th-century-style cheese called Paillasson, and the adjacent **Maison Drouin** (4700 chemin Royal; ✆ **418/829-0330;** www.fondationfrancoislamy.org), a beautifully preserved home from the 1730s that has never been modernized.

ST-PIERRE

When you reach St-Pierre, you're nearly back to where you started. If you haven't stopped at any orchards yet, consider popping into **Bilodeau** (2200 chemin Royal; ✆ **418/828-9316;** www.cidreriebilodeau.qc.ca). It's open year-round daily 9am to 5pm. It produces some of Ile d'Orléans's regular ciders and *cidre de glace,* a sweet wine made from apples left on the trees until after the first frost. Visitors can sample products such as the yummy hazelnut–and–apple-syrup mustard, and guided tours are available. Apple-picking is an option mid-August to mid-October.

Another wine option is the appealing **Cassis Monna et Filles ★** (721 chemin Royal; ✆ **418/828-2525;** www.cassismonna.com). Black currants, or *gadelle noire,* are grown here, and a chic shop features a display on how the berries are harvested and transformed into Crème de Cassis, the key element to a Kir. A variety of wines are available for tasting or purchase. Open May to November daily 10am to 6pm.

St-Pierre's church is the island's oldest (1717). Services are no longer held here, but there's a **handicraft shop** in the back, behind the altar. Look for the stone church on your right (followed immediately by a larger, newer church) and a small blue and white sign for "Corporation des artisans" at 1249 chemin Royal. Although the church's front doors are locked, you can get inside for a viewing from an entrance at the shop. The shop is open most days May to October.

Montmorency Falls ★★

Back on the mainland, the impressive **Montmorency Falls** are visible from Autoroute 440. At 83m (272 ft.) tall, they're 30m (98 ft.) higher than Niagara Falls—a boast no visitor is spared. (These falls, however, are far narrower.) They were named by Samuel de Champlain for his patron, the duke of Montmorency, to whom he dedicated his voyage of 1603.

GETTING THERE

BY BUS **Dupont,** which also goes by the name **Old Québec Tours** (✆ **800/267-8687** or 418/664-0460; www.tourdupont.com), offers tours to the falls.

BY CAR Take Autoroute 440 east out of Québec City. After 10 minutes, watch for exit 325 for the falls and the parking lot. If you miss the exit, you'll see the falls on your left and will be able to make a legal U-turn.

VIEWING THE FALLS

The falls are surrounded by the provincial **Parc de la Chute-Montmorency** (✆ **800/665-6527** or 418/663-3330; www.sepaq.com/montmorency), where visitors can take in the view and have a picnic. The grounds are accessible year-round.

A path from the lower parking area leads to the base of the falls, where the water comes crashing down. The view is spectacular from here in all four seasons. Stairs ascend from here to the top, with viewing platforms along the way. At the top, a footbridge spans the water where it flows over the cliff.

If you don't want to walk, a cable car runs from the parking lot to a terminal alongside the falls, with a pathway that leads close the water's edge. At that top terminal is **Manoir Montmorency,** a villa that contains an interpretation center, a cafe, and a restaurant. The dining room and porch have a side view of the falls; reservations are suggested (call the park phone listed above). Parking is available at the top of the falls by the villa, too.

On summer nights, the plunging water is illuminated, and from late July to mid-August, there is an international fireworks competition overhead 2 nights a week, **Les Grands Feux Loto-Québec** (p. 297). In winter, the freezing spray sent up by crashing water builds a mountain of white ice at the base, nicknamed *pain de sucre* (sugarloaf). It grows as high as 30m (98 ft.) and attracts ice climbers. The yellow cast of the falls comes from the high iron content of the riverbed.

Admission to the grounds is free, although parking costs C$9.50. Round-trip fares on the cable car cost C$9.75 for adults, C$4.45 for children 6 to 17, free for children 5 and under. The cable car operates from mid-April to October and late December to early January daily, and February to mid-April on weekends. The cable car is closed in November and is only available for group reservations in early December.

Ste-Anne-de-Beaupre

The village of Ste-Anne-de-Beaupré is a religious destination, centered around a two-spired basilica that is one of Canada's most famous shrines. Some 1.5 million people make the pilgrimage each year to the complex.

Legend has it that French mariners were sailing up the St. Lawrence River in the 1650s when they ran into a terrifying storm. They prayed to their patroness, St. Anne, to save them, and when they survived, they dedicated a wooden chapel to her on the north shore of the St. Lawrence, near the site of their perils. Not long afterward, a chapel laborer was said to have been cured of lumbago, the first of many documented miracles. Since that time, believers have made their way here to pay their respects to St. Anne, the mother of the Virgin Mary and grandmother of Jesus.

The route to the town is along the St. Lawrence River, which is tidal. At low tide, the beach is sometimes speckled with hundreds of birds, such as purple sandpipers, pecking for food. You can see them behind the houses, gas stations, and garages that pepper the road.

GETTING THERE

BY BUS **Dupont,** also called **Old Québec Tours** (✆ **800/267-8687** or 418/664-0460; www.tourdupont.com), offers a country tour that includes a visit to Ste-Anne-de-Beaupré.

BY CAR Autoroute 440 turns into Autoroute 40 at Montmorency Falls, and then becomes Route 138 almost immediately. Continue on Route 138 to Ste-Anne-de-Beaupré. The church and exit are visible from the road.

EXPLORING THE BASILICA

The towering **basilica** that dominates this small village is the most recent building raised here in St. Anne's honor. After the French sailors' first modest wooden chapel (1658) was swept away by a flood, another chapel was built on higher ground. Floods, fires, and the ravages of time dispatched later buildings, until a larger structure was erected in 1887. In 1926, it too lay in ruins, gutted by fire. The present basilica is constructed in stone, following an essentially neo-Romanesque scheme, and was consecrated on July 4, 1976.

Inside the front doors, look for the two columns dressed with racks of canes—presumably from people cured of their ailments and no longer in need of assistance—that go 9m (30 ft.) high. There are several Masses per day and, in the summer, daily outdoor candlelight processions at 8:15pm.

Other parts of the shrine complex include the **Scala Santa Chapel** (1891); the **Memorial Chapel** (1878), with a bell tower and altar from the late 17th and early 18th centuries, respectively; and the **Way of the Cross,** which is lined with life-size bronze figures depicting Christ's life. There's also a church store and the **Musée Sainte-Anne,** a small facility housing paintings and sculptures. The church runs the **Auberge de La Basilique** for visiting pilgrims. Double-occupancy rooms cost C$60.

The basilica and town are particularly busy on Ste-Anne's Novena (July 17–25) and Ste-Anne's Feast Day (July 26), days of saintly significance.

You can get information about the complex by calling © **418/827-3781** or visiting www.ssadb.qc.ca. Admission to the basilica and chapels is free; admission to the museum is C$3 adults, free for children 5 and under. The basilica is open year-round daily 7am–8pm; the museum is open May to mid-October daily 9:30am–4:30pm, mid-October to May only to groups by reservation.

Canyon Ste-Anne, Ste-Anne Falls & Parc du Mont Ste-Anne ★★

After Ste-Anne-de-Beaupré, Route 138 enters thick evergreen woods, and the busyness of urban life begins to slip away. A short drive off Route 138 is the deep gorge and powerful waterfall created by the Ste-Anne-du-Nord River. Unseen from the main road, the Canyon Ste-Anne and its falls are an exhilarating sight to experience. Nearby is the Parc Mont Ste-Anne, which surrounds an 800m-high (2,625-ft.) peak. Summertime invites camping, hiking, and biking (rentals available), while wintertime turns it into Québec City's busiest ski area.

Birders will want to visit the **Cap Tourmente National Wildlife Area** (© **418/827-4591;** www.followthegeese.com), on the coast of the St. Lawrence River. Over 300 species of birds have been seen here, but it's the great snow geese who are the stars. During migration season, usually late April to mid-May and early October into mid-November, tens of thousands of geese stop at the cape, making it an important ornithological site. Naturalists lead walks through the marshes. It's open daily mid-April through October and January to mid-March. Watch for the sign on Route 138.

GETTING THERE

BY BUS From mid-November until late April, the **Taxi Coop Québec** (© **418/525-5191;** www.taxicoop-quebec.com) shuttle service picks up passengers at Québec City hotels in the morning to take them to Parc Mont Ste-Anne, returning them to Québec City in the late afternoon.

BY CAR Continue along Route 138 from Ste-Anne-de-Beaupré. To get to the waterfalls, stay on Route 138. A marked entrance will be on your left. To get to the park and ski mountain, exit onto Route 360 east. Château Mont Sainte-Anne (see below) will be on your left, with the entrance to the park directly after it.

VIEWING THE STE-ANNE FALLS ★★★

A nondescript road from Route 360 leads through forest to a parking lot, picnic grounds, and a building containing a cafeteria, a shop, and the ticket booth. The **Canyon Ste-Anne Waterfalls** (206 Rte. 138 E., Beaupré; ✆ **418/827-4057;** www.canyonsa.qc.ca) are a 10-minute walk from the entrance, with an open-sided shuttle bus available if you'd rather ride. The path ends at the top of the falls. There are trails that go down both sides and three footbridges that go directly across the falls. The first is over the narrow river just before the water starts to drop. The second crosses right over the middle of the canyon—the proximity to the unending thunder of water crashing over massive rocks is likely to induce vertigo in even the most stable of nerves. The final bridge is at the base of the gorge, just 9m (30 ft.) above the water, where it starts to flatten out again, and ends at an observation platform. The very, very brave-hearted can ride a zip-line or walk a rope bridge across the canyon harnessed onto a cable wire. Trails have platforms that jut over the water and well-written information plaques.

The falls are 74m (243 ft.) high and at their most spectacular in the spring, when melting winter snows bloat the rivers above and send 100,000L (26,417 gal.) of water over *per second.* (The volume drops to 10,000L/2,642 gal. Aug–Sept.) From 1904 to 1965, the river was used to float logs from lumbering operations, and part of the dramatic gorge was created by dynamiting in 1917, to cut down on the literal logjams. So voluminous is the mist coming from the crashing water that it creates a wall of mini-waterfalls on the side of the gorge.

Visitors who have difficulty walking can see the falls without going too far from the bus. Those with a fear of heights can stay on the side trails, strolling amid the poplar trees and away from the bridges altogether.

Admission is C$12 adults, C$8.50 children 13 to 17, C$5.50 children 6 to 12, free for children 5 and under. Open daily May through late October. Hours are 9am to 4:30pm, with an extra hour to 5:30pm from June 24 to Labour Day. Closed the rest of the year. Hours are subject to change due to weather, so call to confirm.

PARC DU MONT STE-ANNE ★

Parc du Mont Ste-Anne (✆ **888/827-4579** or 418/827-4561; www.mont-sainte-anne.com) is a wilderness resort surrounding an 800m-high (2,625-ft.) peak and an outdoor enthusiast's dream. In summer and early fall, it is especially well known for its huge network of trails for both hard-core **mountain biking** and milder day-tripping (bikes can be rented). It has grown to be the most prominent network of mountain bike trails in eastern Canada, hosting the UCI Mountain Bike and Trials World Championships in 2010. The park also offers **camping, hiking,** and **golfing** in summer. A panoramic **gondola** operates daily from late June to early September, weather permitting.

In winter, **downhill skiing** is terrifically popular. Just 40 minutes from Québec City, this is the region's largest and busiest mountain. There are 66 trails on three sides, and about a third of the resort is expert terrain. At night, 17 trails are lit. Lift tickets cost C$65 adults, C$54 seniors, C$51 children 13 to 17, and C$35 children

7 to 12. Also in the winter, the park offers Canada's largest network of **cross-country skiing** trails—208km (129 miles) of them. A day ticket is C$21 adults, C$16 seniors, C$15 children 13 to 17, C$10 children 7 to 12, and free for children 6 and under. There are seven heated shelters along trails, including three for overnight stops. (The "rustic cabin" shelters have propane heat but you need to bring your own sleeping bag; the C$41 cost per person includes 1 night accommodation and 2 days of skiing. You can arrange to have your luggage shuttled in. Reservations are necessary: call ✆ **800/463-1568**). Other winter options include **snowshoeing, dog-sledding, ice canyoning,** and **winter paragliding.**

Details about all activities are listed seasonally on the Mont Ste-Anne website.

WHERE TO STAY & DINE

Château Mont Sainte-Anne ★ ☺ Set into the base of its namesake mountain and Parc du Mont Ste-Anne, this resort provides the closest lodging for all mountain activities. In the winter, it has ski-in-ski-out accessibility at the base of the gondola lift. In summer, the mountain's internationally regarded network of mountain biking trails and 18-hole, par-72 golf course bring brisk business. Units have either kitchenettes or full kitchens. The older units are called "standard," while the newer, sleek ones go by the name "Nordik."

500 bd. Beau-Pré, Beaupré, QC G0A 1E0. ✆ **800/463-4467** or 418/827-5211. Fax 418/827-5072. www.chateaumsa.ca. 239 units. C$119–C$219 double. Packages available. AE, DC, DISC, MC, V. Free parking. Pets accepted (in some units). **Amenities:** 2 restaurants; bar; exercise room; golf courses; Jacuzzis; pools (large outdoor, small indoor); sauna. *In room:* A/C, TV, hair dryer, kitchenette, Wi-Fi (free).

CENTRAL CHARLEVOIX: BAIE-ST-PAUL, ST-IRÉNÉE & LA MALBAIE

Baie-St-Paul: 93km (58 miles) NE of Québec City; St-Irénée: 125km (78 miles) NE of Québec City; La Malbaie: 140km (87 miles) NE of Québec City

The Laurentian mountains move closer to the shore of the St. Lawrence River as they approach what used to be called Murray Bay. U.S. President William Howard Taft, who had a summer residence in the area, once said the air here was "as intoxicating as champagne, but without the morning-after headache."

Grand vistas over the St. Lawrence abound, and there are many farms in the area. Moose sightings are not uncommon, and the rolling, dark green mountains with their white ski slope scars offer numerous places to hike and bike in the warm months and ski when there's snow. (It's not unheard of, by the way, for it to snow in May.) In 1988, Charlevoix was named a UNESCO World Biosphere Reserve, a protected area for cross-disciplinary research into conservation. This was one of the first designated areas with a human population and means development here is balanced against environmental concerns.

Baie-St-Paul is an artists' colony, and good-to-memorable country inns dot the countryside up to La Malbaie. A group of entrepreneurs has been developing an "anti-resort" in the area, a year-round destination that will hold large international events and become what they've termed "a type of Davos of sustainable tourism development." It's led by Daniel Gauthier, a co-founder of Cirque du Soleil and owner since 2002 of the ski resort Le Massif (see below).

Essentials

GETTING THERE

BY CAR Take Route 138 as far as Baie-St-Paul. Turn onto Route 362 to go into downtown Baie. To continue northeast, take either Route 138 or Route 362. Route 362 is smaller and more scenic, running closer to the water. It's the road to take to get to St-Irénée.

VISITOR INFORMATION

Baie-St-Paul has a year-round **tourist office** directly on Route 138 (© **800/667-2276** or 418/665-4454) that's open daily from 9am to 4pm, and until 7pm in the summer. It's on a dramatic hill approaching the village and well marked from the highway. (Beware, though: It's an extremely sharp turnoff.) Stop here for one of the grandest vistas of the river and town below. There are two other tourism offices: in downtown Baie-St-Paul, at 6 rue St-Jean-Baptiste, and in La Malbaie, on the water at 495 bd. de Comporté (Rte. 362). Regional information is also available at **www.tourisme-charlevoix.com**.

Baie-St-Paul ★

The main town in Charlevoix is Baie-St-Paul, an attractive, funky community of 7,317 that continues to earn its century-old reputation as an artists' retreat. Some two dozen boutiques and galleries, and a couple of small museums, show the works of local painters and artisans. Given the setting, it isn't surprising that many of the artists are landscapists, but other styles and subjects are represented, too. Work runs the gamut, from hobbyist to highly professional. Options include the **Maison de René Richard** (58 rue St-Jean-Baptiste; © **418/435-5571**), which celebrates the Swiss-born artist who made Baie-St-Paul his home until his 1982 death. Richard painted many of his well-regarded semi-abstract landscapes here.

During July and August, downtown can get thick with tourists, filling the main street with bumper-to-bumper traffic. Try to avoid driving in mid-day. Or pop off the mainland entirely to the small island of Isle-aux-Coudres ("island of hazelnuts") for some **bicycling.** The island is accessible by a free 15-minute car ferry. Popular paths offer a 23km (14-mile) island loop. From May to October, single bikes, tandems, and quadri-cycles for up to six adults and two small children can be rented from **Vélo-Coudres** (© **418/438-2118;** www.charlevoix.qc.ca/velocoudres). The island also has a smattering of boutiques and hotels. The ferry leaves from the town of St. Joseph-de-la-Rive, along Route 362 just east of Baie-St-Paul.

Gourmands should consider visits to some of the region's unique food producers. **La Ferme Basque de Charlevoix** (813 rue St-Edouard, St-Urbain [just west of Baie-St-Paul]; © **418/639-2246;** www.lafermebasque.ca) is a small-scale family farm that raises ducks and makes foie gras sold throughout the province. Tours are C$4 adults. **La Maison d'Affinage Maurice Dufour** (1339 bd. Mgr-de-Lavel/Rte. 138, Baie-St-Paul; © **418/435-5692;** www.fromagefin.com), is a *fromagerie* that makes Le Ciel de Charlevoix, an artisanal cheese that is a highlight of the region (and 2009 champion in the *Grand prix des fromages Canadiens,* or Canadian Cheese Grand Prix).

In winter, the area's largest ski mountain is **Le Massif** (© **877/536-2774** or 418/632-5876; www.lemassif.com). Located in Petite-Rivière-Saint-François, about 23km (14 miles) south of Baie-St-Paul, it's a growing powerhouse. Its fans wax rhapsodic over its Zen qualities, including quiet ski lifts and runs that give the illusion of heading directly into the adjacent St. Lawrence river. It has 48 trails, including one that's 4.8km (3 miles) long. A day ticket is C$61 adults, C$51 seniors, C$43 children 13 to 17, C$34 children 7 to 12, and free for children 6 and under. There's a daily shuttle bus from Québec City to the mountain.

Cirque du Soleil co-founder Daniel Gauthier owns Le Massif and has been working for years to develop both the ski operations and the outlying area. Marketing materials for his *Groupe Le Massif* call "Massif de Charlevoix" the largest tourism project in the province. The plan is to build a 150-room hotel (in partnership with Groupe Germain, the boutique hotel company that runs the wonderful Hôtel Le Germain-Dominion in Québec City [see p. 282]), a 500-seat multipurpose venue, and a train station in Baie-St-Paul, and to refurbish an existing railroad track and railroad cars to connect Baie-St-Paul and the ski mountain to Québec City. The budget for the project is C$230 million. Trains are scheduled to start carrying passengers in the summer of 2011.

WHERE TO STAY & DINE

La Maison Otis Right in the heart of Baie-St-Paul, with a long porch that fronts the colorful main street, Otis is a rambling collection of connecting buildings with rooms that offer cozy combinations of fireplaces, whirlpools, and four-poster beds. In the hotel is Mon Ami Alex, **a bistro** that serves regional fare. Attached to the hotel is a **spa** with a large offering of massage services and facials, a cafe with exceptional pizza, and downstairs, a **cabaret** (www.lecafedesartistes.com/cabaret.htm) that's open occasional Fridays and Saturdays.

23 rue St-Jean-Baptiste, Baie-St-Paul, QC G3Z 1M2. ✆ **800/267-2254** or 418/435-2255. Fax 418/435-2464. www.maisonotis.com. 30 units. C$122–C$207 double; C$237–C$262 suite. Packages available. MC, V. Free parking. **Amenities:** 2 restaurants; bar; pool (small indoor); spa. *In room:* A/C, TV/DVD player, hair dryer, MP3 docking station, Wi-Fi (free).

Le Saint-Pub BISTRO A casual restaurant that's part of the town's *microbrasserie,* or microbrewery. There's always a selection of over a dozen brews made on-site, and visitors sometimes get to test beverages. The kitchen serves up solid renditions of bar food, Québécois-style, and specialties include barbecue chicken and concoctions cooked with beer (beer-and-onion soup, wild-boar burger marinated in beer, chocolate-and-stout pudding, sugar pie with beer). There's a patio in summer.

2 rue Racine, Baie-St-Paul. ✆ **418/240-2332.** Main courses C$11–C$25; table d'hôte C$23–C$35. MC, V. Daily 11:30am–8pm.

St-Irénée

From Baie-St-Paul, take Route 362 northeast toward La Malbaie. The air is scented by sea salt and rent by the shrieks of gulls, and the road roller-coasters over bluffs above the river, with wooded hills and well-kept villages. This stretch, from Baie-St-Paul to La Malbaie, is one of the most scenic in the entire region and is dubbed the ***Route du Fleuve,*** which means "river route." It can be treacherous in ice, though, so in colder months, opt for the flatter Route 138.

In 32km (about 20 miles) is St-Irénée, a cliff-top hamlet of just 704 year-round residents. Apart from the setting, the best reason for dawdling here is the 60-hectare (148-acre) property and estate of **Domaine Forget** (✆ **888/336-7438** or 418/452-3535; www.domaineforget.com). The facility is a performing-arts center for music and dance, and offers an **International Festival** from mid-June through early September. Concerts are staged in a 604-seat concert hall, with **Sunday musical**

brunches on an outdoor terrace that has spectacular views of the river. The program emphasizes classical music with solo instrumentalists and chamber groups, but is peppered with jazz and dance. Most tickets are C$20 to C$40. From September to May, Domaine rents its **student dorms** to the general public. They're clean and well-appointed studios, with cooking areas and beds for two to five people. They start at C$65 for double occupancy, with discounts for longer stays.

Kayaking eco-tours, from a half-day to 5 days, can be arranged through several companies in the area. **Katabatik** (✆ **800/453-4850** or 418/665-2332; www.katabatik.ca), based in La Malbaie, offers trips that combine kayaking with education about the bays of the St-Lawrence estuary. A half-day tour costs C$55 adults, C$44 children 12 to 15, and C$36 children 5 to 11. Tours start at various spots along the coast and are in operation from March to October.

La Malbaie

From St-Irénée, Route 362 starts to bend west after 10km (6¼ miles), as the mouth of the Malbaie River starts to form. La Malbaie (or "Murray Bay," as it was called by the wealthy Anglophones who made this their resort of choice from the Gilded Age through the 1950s) is the collective name of five former municipalities: Pointe-au-Pic, Cap-à-l'Aigle, Rivière-Malbaie, Sainte-Agnès, and Saint-Fidèle. At its center is a small, scenic bay. The 8,930 inhabitants of the region justifiably wax poetic about their wildlife, and hills and trees, the place where the sea meets the sky. La Malbaie is also home to two special hotels, both listed below.

A CASINO & A MUSEUM

Casino de Charlevoix Established in 1994, the casino's cherry-wood paneling and granite floors enclose about 950 slot machines and two dozen tables, including Texas hold 'em, blackjack, and baccarat. Poker tournaments are held regularly. A 200-seat bar has live pop music on Friday and Saturday nights. Visitors must be 18 years old. The casino is just steps from the **Fairmont Le Manoir Richelieu** hotel (see below).

183 av. Richelieu (follow the many signs). ✆ **800/665-2274** or 418/665-5300. www.casino-de-charlevoix.com. Free admission (18 & over only). Daily 11am–midnight; extended hours in summer & on weekends.

Musée de Charlevoix ★ A terrific little museum. One of the three gallery spaces is devoted to a marvelous permanent exhibition called *Appartenances* ("Belonging") about the history and culture of Charlevoix. Included are photographs from the 1930s of beluga whale-hunting and frontierswomen skinning eels, artifacts from the Manoir Richelieu before its major fire in 1928, and folk art from the 1930s and '40s. Descriptive text in English and French is engaging and thorough.

10 chemin du Havre (at the corner of Rte. 362). ✆ **418/665-4411.** www.museedecharlevoix.qc.ca. C$7 adults, C$5 seniors & students, free for children 11 & under. June to mid-Oct daily 9am–5pm; mid-Oct to May Mon–Fri 10am–5pm, Sat & Sun 1–5pm.

WHERE TO STAY & DINE

The Fairmont Le Manoir Richelieu ★★★ ☺ The region's grand resort. Since 1899, there has been a hotel at the river's edge here, first serving the swells who summered in this aristocratic haven with spectacular views of the St. Lawrence River. After waves of renovations, the decor of the hotel long ago dubbed "the castle on the cliff" is reminiscent of its posh heritage, and many rooms meet deluxe standards. The golf course is a glorious 27-hole expanse overlooking the river on one side and Charlevoix's hills and mountains on the other. In winter, snowmobile rentals are available to use on the area's extensive network of "ski-doo" trails. Guests run the gamut, from young couples and families drawn to the resort's many sporting activities for children to gamers from the casino next door and older folks who have been coming here forever.

181 rue Richelieu, La Malbaie, QC G5A 1X7. ✆ **866/540-4464** or 418/665-3703. Fax 418/665-8131. www.fairmont.com/richelieu. 405 units. June–Oct from C$179 double; Nov–May from C$159 double; year-round from C$379 suite. Packages available. AE, DC, DISC, MC, V. Valet parking C$19, free self-parking. Pets accepted (C$25/pet/day). **Amenities:** 4 restaurants (confirm in off-season); bar; babysitting; children's programs; concierge; executive-level rooms; golf club; health club; pools (indoor & outdoor); room service; spa; watersports equipment. *In room:* A/C, TV, hair dryer, minibar, W-Fi (C$15/day).

La Pinsonnière ★★★ Romance with a princely touch are on offer at this understated, intimate hideaway. The six deluxe rooms of this Relais & Châteaux inn are the most spectacular, with stunning vistas of the St. Lawrence River. They deliver a serious "wow" factor and offer the most transporting visit, with private terraces and bathrooms with oversized whirlpools, private saunas, and/or steam showers. These new rooms have a contemporary, clean decor. Older rooms are classic Queen Anne and face gardens and the front driveway. An indoor pool, unspoiled river beach at the base of the property, small on-site spa, and attentive service make this tiny resort a regional star. Dinners featuring local products are extravagant, with a la carte options and three discovery menus. Wines are a particular point of pride, with 750 labels in the 12,000-bottle cellar.

124 rue St-Raphaël, La Malbaie, QC G5A 1X9. ✆ **800/387-4431** or 418/665-4431. Fax 418/665-7156. www.lapinsonniere.com. 18 units. May–Oct & holiday season C$345–C$495 double, rest of year C$295–C$445 double. Packages available. Minimum 2-night stay on weekends, 3 nights on holiday weekends. AE, MC, V. Free parking. Pets accepted (free). **Amenities:** Restaurant; bar; babysitting; concierge; health club nearby; pool (heated indoor); room service; spa. *In room:* A/C, TV, hair dryer, minibar, Wi-Fi (free).

UPPER CHARLEVOIX: BAIE STE-CATHERINE & TADOUSSAC

Baie Ste-Catherine: 207km (129 miles) NE of Québec City; Tadoussac: 214km (133 miles) NE of Québec City.

Baie Ste-Catherine, at the northern end of Charlevoix, is marked by the confluence of the Saguenay River and the St. Lawrence, and these waters attract a half-dozen species of whales, many of which can be seen from shore mid-June through late October. **Whale-watching** cruises are popular. Tadoussac is just across the Saguenay River and is the southernmost point of the tourist region called Manicouagan. The small number of accommodations and restaurants are in Tadoussac.

Essentials

GETTING THERE

BY CAR Route 138 leads to the northern end of Charlevoix, at Baie Ste-Catherine. The highway dead-ends at the dramatic Saguenay River, with the town of Tadoussac just across the way. There is a free car ferry for the 10-minute passage. In summer, there are departures every 13 minutes between 8am and 8pm, and every 20, 40, or 60 minutes the other 12 hours and in low season. The ferry is the reason that trucks travel in convoys on the highway—they pour out in groups after each ferry crossing.

Note: In winter and spring, when the whales are gone and the temperatures are lower, most of the very few establishments in this area are closed. If you're driving, pack some snacks and water, take bathroom breaks when they're available, and make sure you've got enough gasoline.

VISITOR INFORMATION

Information about the area is online at **www.tourisme-charlevoix.com.** The town of St-Siméon, which you'll pass through on your way north, has a year-round **tourist office** at 494 rue St-Laurent, open daily between late June and Labour Day.

Baie Ste-Catherine & Tadoussac

Here, at the northern end of Charlevoix, is one of the world's richest areas for **whale-watching ★★**. The confluence of the St. Lawrence and Saguenay rivers attracts 10 to 12 species each summer—as many as 1,500 minke, humpback, finback, and blue whales, who join the 1,000 or so sweet-faced beluga (or white) whales who are here year-round. Add to that the harbor porpoises who visit, and there can be 5,000 creatures diving and playing in the waters. Many can be seen from land mid-June through late October, and up close by boat or kayak.

Teeny Baie Ste-Catherine (pop. 211) sits at the meeting point of the St. Lawrence River and the Saguenay River, which comes down from the northwest. Tadoussac (pop. 850) is just across the Saguenay. The vista on the car-ferry crossing is dramatic and nearly worth a trip to Tadoussac on its own. Palisades with evergreens poking out of rock walls rise sharply from both shores. So extreme is the natural architecture, in fact, that the area is often referred to as a fjord.

Tadoussac is known as "the Cradle of New France." Established in the 1600s, it's the oldest permanent European settlement north of Florida and became a stop on the fur-trading route. Missionaries stayed until the middle of the 19th century. The hamlet might have vanished soon after had a resort hotel, now called **Hôtel Tadoussac** (see below), not been built in 1864. In those days, a steamship line brought wealthy vacationers from Montréal and points west, and deposited them here for stays that often lasted all summer.

Apart from the hotel, there's not much in Tadoussac besides a **whaling educational center** (see below), a boardwalk, and some small motels. This is raw country, where the sight of a beaver waddling up the hill from the ferry terminal is met with only mild interest.

WHALE WATCHING

From mid-May to mid-October, there are many options to see whales or cruise the majestic Saguenay river. Companies use different sizes and types of watercraft, from stately catamarans and cruisers that carry up to 500 to powered inflatables called Zodiacs that carry 10 to 25 passengers. The larger boats have snack bars and naturalists onboard to describe the action and options to sit at tables inside or ride the observation bowsprit, high above the waves. Zodiacs are more maneuverable, darting about at each sighting to get closer to the rolling and breaching behemoths. Zodiac passengers are issued life jackets and waterproof overalls, but expect to get wet. It's cold out there, so layers and gloves are a good idea.

Two of the biggest companies are **Croisières AML** (**✆ 800/856-4643;** www.croisieresaml.com) and **Group Dufour** (**✆ 800/463-5250;** www.dufour.ca). Both offer departures from wharves in both Baie Ste-Catherine and Tadoussac (other companies send tours out of St-Siméon, to the south). In high season, each offers about three daily whale-watching trips. Fares are comparable: 3-hour tours on the larger boats cost C$64 adults, C$59 seniors and students, C$29 children 6 to 12, and free for children 5 and under. Two-hour Zodiac trips cost C$59 adults, C$54 seniors and students, and C$44 children 8 to 12; children younger than 8 and/or shorter than 1.4m (4½ ft.) are not permitted. Check with each company for exact times, prices, and trip options. Children may also like Group Dufour's interactive **online Blue Museum,** at **www.museebleu.ca/en.**

Kayak trips that search out whales are available from **Mer et Monde Ecotours** (✆ **866/637-6663** or 418/232-6779; www.mer-et-monde.qc.ca). Visitors report that they *felt* the whales before they saw them—imagine being out from the shore and feeling a vibration under the kayak hull! The company is based in Les Bergeronnes, a coastal town 20km (12 miles) north of Tadoussac, and offers tours in summer that start at the bay of Tadoussac just beyond Hôtel Tadoussac's lawn. A 3-hour trip costs C$52 adults, C$40 children 15 and under.

Although the St. Lawrence is, of course, a river, it's tidal and often called the "sea" (you'll see references to "sea-kayaking"). The waters here are in a marine park, which was designated as a conservation area to protect the whales and their habitat.

Centre d'Interprétation des Mammifères Marins ☺ Start here to learn why Tadoussac is such a paradise for whale researchers. At this interpretation center directly on the Saguenay River's edge, there's a small exhibition room (plaques are in French with English booklets for translation), an exhilarating 15-minute video about the whales who visit each summer (in French, with English translation by headphone), and a bilingual expert who answers questions and explains what the team who works upstairs—as many as 50 people in summer—are up to. There's also a shop with books, cuddly toys, and clothing. The center is run by the nonprofit GREMM, a scientific research group that studies the St. Lawrence's marine mammals.

108 rue de la Cale Sèche (on the waterfront), Tadoussac. ✆ **418/235-4701.** C$9 adults, C$6.75 seniors, C$4.50 children 6–12, free for children 5 & under. Daily summer 9am–8pm; spring & fall noon–5pm. Closed in winter.

WHERE TO STAY & DINE

Hôtel Tadoussac ☺ Established in 1864 and now in a building from 1942, this handsome old-time hotel is king of the (small) hill that is Tadoussac. Public spaces and bedrooms have a shambling, country-cottage appearance—there's zero pretense of luxury. Since you're probably traveling a distance to get here, pay the premium for a river-view bedroom. They're simple, with overhead fans and no air conditioning. Meals are resort-pricey (C$36 for buffet dinner, for instance) and okay, though short of impressive. A large front lawn overlooks the river, which is wide enough here to feel like an ocean. If you're planning to whale-watch or kayak, consider a package deal.

165 rue Bord de l'Eau, Tadoussac, QC G0T 2A0. ✆ **800/561-0718** or 418/235-4421. Fax 418/235-4607. www.hoteltadoussac.com. 149 units. C$155–C$249 double. Packages available. AE, DC, MC, V. Free parking. Closed mid-Oct to early May. **Amenities:** 3 restaurants when busy, 2 restaurants when slow; bar; babysitting; children's programs (in peak months); pool (heated outdoor); spa; Wi-Fi (in lobby, free). *In room:* Overhead fan, TV, hair dryer.

Café Bohème Just a few steps from Hôtel Tadoussac is a cheery 1892 house with a white picket fence and mansard roof. It's a dependable stop for healthy food, homemade ice cream (*mmm* chocolate-cardamom), and groovy world music.

239 rue des Pionniers, Tadoussac. ✆ **418/235-1180.** Main courses C$7.50–C$15; table d'hôte C$15–C$22. MC, V.

THE GASPÉ PENINSULA

by Benoit Legault

Rivière-du-Loup: 209km (130 miles) NE of Québec City; Grand Métis: 358km (222 miles) NE of Québec City; Matane: 411km (255 miles) NE of Québec City; Percé: 765km (475 miles) NE of Québec City.

The southern bank of the St. Lawrence River sweeps north, then eastward, and then back in towards itself, creating a large thumb of land called the Gaspé Peninsula—*la Gaspésie* in French. The Gaspésie is where Jacques Cartier landed in 1534 (officially "discovering" Canada) and planted a flag in the name of the King of France. The wind-swept region holds a special place in the hearts of the Québécois; it is heaped with aged, blunt hills covered with hundreds of square miles of woodlands. Over much of its northern perimeter, slopes fall directly into the sea.

The fishing villages in the coves cut from the coast are sparsely populated, with eagles and some caribou in the high grounds. Winter here is long and harsh; but sunny winter days are very rewarding, and winter tourism has been increasing steadily in recent years. Yet tourism peaks in the precious crystal days of summer. All that makes it the perfect place for hiking, biking, bird-watching, whale-watching, and fishing in legendary salmon streams.

A trip here will be a complete escape from the cities, and for most, the final destination is the village of **Percé,** at the easternmost edge of the province, along the Gulf of St. Lawrence. It's here that you'll find **Rocher Percé**—Percé Rock, in English—the famed 470m-long (1,542-ft.) butte rising from the sea. It's an astounding sight that you should walk up to at low tide.

Essentials

GETTING THERE

BY TRAIN **VIA Rail** (✆ **888/842-7245;** www.viarail.ca) travels to the Gaspé region. The slow train goes along the St. Lawrence River, and then cuts inland and on to the southern shore of the peninsula. The train makes the overnight trip three times a week (it departs at 6:25pm and arrives at 12:25pm the following day), on Wednesdays, Fridays, and Sundays, and returns on Mondays, Thursdays, and Saturdays (it departs at 3pm and arrives at 9am the following day). A Comfort Supersaver seat, with 5 days advance booking, costs C$109 one way; a berth or cabin costs between C$259 and C$339 one way. Early booking discounts are available but very much sought after, so reserve as soon as your plans are confirmed. Rental cars in Gaspé can be arranged with **National** (✆ **418/368-1541**) or **Budget** (✆ **418/368-1610**).

BY CAR From Québec City, it's 765km (475 miles) to Percé, the furthest point on the peninsula, via the coastal *route provinciale* 132 on the northern shore. This "north tour" is the most scenic route. Leave Québec City by crossing to the southern side of the St. Lawrence River and picking up Route 20 East. Route 20 (a four-lane divided expressway) turns into Route 132 in the Gaspé region. The underside of the peninsula, which you'll travel on if you continue on Route 132 after leaving Percé, is largely a flat coastal plain beside a regular shoreline.

BY BUS **Orléans Express** intercity bus lines (✆ **888/999-3977;** www.orleans express.com) provide excellent daily, year-round service two to three times a day from

Montréal and Québec City to Rimouski, Matane, Gaspé, and every town in between. Buses take 3½ hours to go from Québec City to Rimouski, 1½ hours from Rimouski to Matane, 2 hours from Matane to Ste-Anne-des-Monts, and 3 hours from Ste-Anne-des-Monts to Gaspé. Québec City to Gaspé regular fares are C$115 adults, C$87 students and seniors. Orléans Express buses are generally more comfortable than buses in the United States (with elegant soft-leather seats, cup and laptop holders), and the drivers are polite, pleasant, and helpful.

VISITOR INFORMATION

The Québec Government's tourism office's website, **www.bonjourquebec.com,** is thorough and up-to-date. Click on "Explore" and then go to "Tourist Regions" and select Gaspésie. Gaspé's regional tourism association (**www.tourisme-gaspesie.com**) has a number of brochures that they'll mail to you. Note that as you move farther away from Québec City, the more difficult it becomes to find people who speak English, although there are Anglophone communities in the Chaleur Bay area, near the New Brunswick border. For a map of this region, see the "New Brunswick & the Gaspé Peninsula" map, on p. 107.

Grand Métis

After Rivière-du-Loup, 209km (130 miles) from Québec City, the country slowly grows more typically Gaspésien: bogs on the river side of the road yield bales of peat moss, which are shipped to gardeners throughout the continent, while low rolling hills and fenced fields house dairy cattle. Along the roadside, hand-painted signs advertise ***pain de ménage*** (homemade bread) and other baked goods for sale. At this point, the expressway turns into the slower, more scenic 132 EST (east).

The region's largest city, Rimouski, is 108km (67 miles) past Rivière-du-Loup. Travelers not there on business are likely to pass on through. However, in the town of **Grand Métis,** 41km (25 miles) past Rimouski, you'll find the north shore's stellar attraction: the former Reford estate, known under both its French and English names, **Jardins de Métis** and **Reford Gardens.**

Jardins de Métis/Reford Gardens ★ These 16 hectares (40 acres) near the Métis and St. Lawrence rivers are home to over 3,000 species and varieties of native and exotic plants. The gardens were originally cultivated by Elsie Reford, an English-Canadian woman of such passion that even in Gaspé's relatively severe climate, she was able to create a wonderland. Sections are laid out in the informal English manner and include a Blue Poppy Glade, Crabapple Garden, and Woodland Walk. There are shops, a small museum, and a busy garden cafe. Since 2000, an international garden festival has been hosted here each summer. It has a special focus on avant-garde design and runs June through September with gourmet dinners, art exhibitions, literary teas, musical brunches, and of course, temporary gardens by contemporary international designers.

200 Rte. 132. ✆ **418/775-2222.** Fax 418/775-6201. www.refordgardens.com. C$16 adults, C$15 seniors, C$14 students, C$8 children 14–17, free for children 13 & under. June 4 to Oct 2 daily 8:30am–6pm; July & Aug 8:30am–8pm (last entrance at 6pm).

Vignoble Carpinteri About 40km (25 miles) past Grand-Métis, in the village of St-Ulric, you will find the northernmost winery in the Americas. This labor of love is called **Vignoble Carpinteri.** Wines produced here will not compete anytime soon with the Tuscany wines that inspired the establishment, yet the new, free *curiosité* is a hit with locals and tourists alike. A former strawberry field located in a sheltered microclimate area has allowed for the growing of wine grapes. There is a picnic area. Free guided tours and tastings take place every day mid-May to mid-October from 10am to 6pm, and Sat-Sun the rest of the year from 10am to 6pm.

3141 chemin du Pont Couvert, Saint-Ulric. © **418/737-4305.** www.vignoblecarpinteri.com.

Matane

About 55km (34 miles) past Grand Métis, Highway 132 enters commercial **Matane.** This is about the halfway point to Percé and a logical place to stop for the night if you're trying to make the trip in 2 days. There are many motels and modest B&Bs called *gîtes*. The town's focal point is the Matane River, a thoroughfare for the **annual migration of spawning Atlantic salmon.** They begin their swim up the Matane in June through a specially designed dam that facilitates their passage, continuing to September. Near the lighthouse is a seasonal **information bureau** (© **877/762-8263**).

WHERE TO STAY

Riôtel Matane Directly on the beach, this property is part of a reliable, small Gaspé chain. The best guest rooms are on the third floor and have sea views, minibars, Internet access, and other big-city conveniences. Overlooking the beach, the refined, licensed dining room serves three meals a day year round; *crevettes de Matane* (Matane shrimp) is the house specialty.

250 av. du Phare Est, Matane, QC G4W 3N4. © **877/566-2651** or 418/566-2651. Fax 418/562-7365. www.riotel.com. 96 units. C$79–C$299 double. Packages & Sept–May discounts available. AE, DC, MC, V. Free parking. **Amenities:** 2 restaurants; bar; exercise room; heated outdoor whirlpool; heated outdoor pool (in summer); limited room service; sauna; tennis courts. *In room:* TV, fridge, hair dryer, Wi-Fi (free).

Ste-Anne-des-Monts & Parc de la Gaspésie

It takes 5 nonstop driving hours to get from Matane to Percé. There are frequent picnic grounds (look for signs announcing *Halte Municipale*), a couple of large nature preserves, and ample opportunities to sit by the water and collect driftwood. While towns along the way are smaller and more spread out, simple sustenance isn't a problem. Look for *casse-croûtes,* simple roadside snack stands that always serve *poutine* and sometimes more refined light fare like lobster rolls.

Ste-Anne-des-Monts is a fishing village 87km (54 miles) past Matane, with a seasonal **tourist booth** (© **418/763-7633**) on Route 132, 1km (½ mile) past the bridge, operating only from mid-June to late-September. The town also has stores, gas stations, and other necessary services. Scenic views of the St. Lawrence River are outstanding here.

Rising higher inland are the spectacular Chic-Choc Mountains, the northernmost end of the Appalachian range. Most of them are contained by the **Parc national de la Gaspésie** (© **418/763-7494,** after the start of the recorded message, you must press 9 for the English message; www.sepaq.com/pq/gas/en) and adjoining preserves just off Route 132. For a scenic detour, turn south onto Route 299 in Ste-Anne-des-Monts. The road climbs into the mountains, some of which are naked rock at the summits, displaying rare artic-alpine flora and the only caribou south of the St-Lawrence. After about 24km (15 miles), a welcome station provides information about the wilderness park. Back here, the rivers brim with baby salmon and speckled trout, and the forests and meadows sustain herds of moose, caribou, and deer. Return on Route 299 the way you came and continue on Route 132.

Mont-St-Pierre

After Ste-Anne, the highway becomes a narrow band crowded up to water's edge by sheer rock walls. Waterfalls spill along the cliffs alongside the road. Around a rocky point and down a slope, **Mont-St-Pierre,** 55km (34 miles) past Ste-Anne, is much like other Gaspésien villages except for the eye-catching striations in the rock of the mountain east of town. Due to its favorable updrafts, the site is regarded as nearly perfect for hang-gliders and paragliders, and for 10 days (at the end of July and the beginning of August), the town hosts the **Fête du Vol-Libre** (Hang-Gliding Festival). Colorful gliders that loop and curve on air currents fill the sky, landing on sports grounds behind city hall. For more information, visit the village website at **www.mont-saint-pierre.ca.**

In winter, the Mont-St-Pierre area remains a hub for outdoor enthusiasts. Nearby, skiers go down a wild, 550m (1,804-ft.) vertical drop, and then they go back up . . . with snowmobiles! Such is the off-trail skiing thrill of the **Vallée Taconique** (**© 418/797-2177** or 866/797-2177; www.valleetaconique.ca), a new ski area where at least 6m (20 ft.) of snow falls every winter and does not thaw until spring. This is a true snow Eden.

Parc National Forillon ★

Soon the road winds up through the mountains, down into valleys, and up again to the next rise. The settlements get smaller, but there are still roadside stands advertising fresh and smoked fish. Approaching the eastern edge of Quebec, this is the part of the country known as Land's End.

About 120km (75 miles) past Mont-St-Pierre, there's an option to turn off Route 132 onto Route 197. This option goes to Gaspé and Percé more directly, skipping the very eastern-most tip of the peninsula that you'll have to pay to drive through.

If you stay on Route 132, you'll soon reach the reception center for the beautiful **Parc National du Canada Forillon** (**© 418/368-5505;** www.pc.gc.ca/forillon). Bilingual attendants advise on park activities and regulations. Route 132 continues around the park, whose 244 sq. km (94 sq. miles) of headlands capture a surprising number of the features characteristic of eastern Canada: rugged coastline, dense forests, colonies of seabirds, and abundance of wildlife. On the northern shore are sheer rock cliffs carved from the mountains by the sea, and on the south is the broad Bay of Gaspé. Hikers and campers from all over North America come for nature walks, beaches, picnicking, and overnight stays. The daily entrance fee in season is C$7.80 adults, with reduced fees for seniors and children, and a family rate of $20. Prices are lower in the off season. There are 367 campsites; some are open year-round, with others open mid-May through mid-October. Serviced camp sites cost C$30.

From within the park, you can pick up whale-watching cruises and sea kayaking excursions. **Croisières Baie de Gaspé** (**© 418/892-5500** or 866/617-5500; www.baleines-forillon.com) has 2½-hour boat cruises to get relatively close to the seven species of whales in the area. Fares are C$60 adults, C$55 seniors and students, and C$35 children, and park entrance fees are in addition to fares. Reserve in advance.

Gaspé

Shortly after the exit from the park is the town of Gaspé, protected from the gulf of St. Lawrence by the long, narrow Baie de Gaspé. In 1534, Jacques Cartier stepped ashore here to claim the land for the king of France, erecting a wooden cross to mark the spot. Today, the port is important economically because of the salmon rivers that empty into it. The principal attraction is the **Musée de la Gaspésie,** at Jacques Cartier Point on Route 132 (✆ **418/368-1534;** www.museedelagaspesie.ca), which tells the story of Cartier's landing. It's open June through October daily, November to May Monday to Saturday. Admission is C$7 adults, C$5 seniors and students.

Percé ★

About 62km (39 miles) past Gaspé, you'll wind around the hills southbound toward Percé. From Route 132, you'll see **Percé Rock**—Rocher Percé—and just farther in the sea, **Bonaventure Island.**

The town of Percé isn't large, and except for a few quiet inland residential streets, it's confined to the main road running along the shore. The souvenir shops, snack bars, and motels that serve the summer tourists start to open by late May, and in high season, there's a family-oriented beach-party ambience. People are so friendly and attentive, in fact, that you might wonder if you've grown a really cute second head.

Fishing was once the primary enterprise, with tourism as a sideline. With fish stocks dangerously depleted and with ever-harsher government restrictions, that relationship is reversed. A vibrant artists' community has also recently brought a special, refined feel and flair to Percé. The **Percé Information Touristique** office, at 142 Rte. 132 (www.perce.info), is open daily in the summer season.

EXPLORING PERCÉ ROCK

Percé Rock ★ is a massive butte that sits off the coast of Percé and is one of the natural icons of the Québec province. Made of limestone, it is 470m (1,542 ft.) long and nearly 88m (289 ft.) tall at its highest point. It gets its name ("pierced rock") from an arch on its southern end that looks as if a giant needle has cut right through. At low tide, the rock can be reached by foot. Be careful, though: Percé authorities advise that, because of falling rock, you should avoid walking directly alongside the monolith.

Just beyond the rock is **Parc national de l'Ile-Bonaventure-et-du-Rocher-Percé ★** (✆ **418/782-2240;** www.sepaq.com/pq/bon/en), a bird sanctuary whose lure is its nearly 300,000 nesting birds. On the island are gannets, puffins, razorbills, black guillemots, kittiwakes, and over 200 other species. There are four trails totaling 15km (9.3 miles), observation decks, and in warm months, an interpretation center staffed with naturalists. The center also has a modest cafe open June through September. The park is open year-round, although the visitor center is open only from May 28 to October 12. Entrance is C$3.50 adults, C$1.50 children 6 to 17, or free with a Parcs Québec card.

To get to the island, 75-minute boat tours take visitors around Percé Rock and then on to the bird colony. Park wardens are often on board to answer questions, and the boats stop at the island to drop off and pick up visitors. Tours are available from **Les Bateliers de Percé** (✆ **877/782-2974**), **Les bateaux de croisières Julien Cloutier Enr** (✆ **877/782-2161**), and **Croisières Les Traversiers de l'Ile** (✆ **866/782-5526**). Trips are C$25 adults, C$15 students and seniors, and C$6 children 6 to 12. The boat operators also offer more expensive whale-watching and sea-fishing cruises. They operate from mid-May to late October.

WHERE TO STAY & DINE

Most hotels and restaurants are open in season, generally mid-May to mid-October. Business starts to tail off in mid-August, making it easier to find lodgings in the fall.

La Maison du Pêcheur ★ ☺ SEAFOOD It's close to sacrilegious to eat anything but fish here, within sight of the most important fishing grounds in the North Atlantic. *L'assiette du Pêcheur* is a combination of fresh lobster, crab, scallops, and catch of the day. There are 15 choices of pizza, including options with squid or salmon. A cafe below the main room is open from 7:30am to midnight during the busiest months. Find the restaurant next to the town pier, behind the shops of the main street.

End of quai de Percé. ✆ **418/782-5331.** Table d'hôte dinner C$18–C$40. AE, MC, V. June to mid-Oct daily 11:30am–2:30pm & 5:30–9:30pm.

La Normandie ★ This small downtown hotel facing Percé Rock is the class act of the town in style, service, dining, and facilities. All guest rooms have small sitting areas, and those facing the water have decks. The kitchen is open for a buffet breakfast and lunch in season, and is fairly ambitious, sending table d'hôte dinners (C$24–C$49) into a dining room with unobstructed views of the rock from every chair. Lobster, deep-sea scallops, cod, and trout are always à la carte. Reserve ahead.

221 Rte. 132 ouest, C.P. 129, Percé, QC G0C 2L0. ✆ **800/463-0820** or 418/782-2112. Fax 418/782-2337. www.normandieperce.com. 45 units. C$79–C$239 double. Packages available. AE, DC, MC, V. Closed mid-Oct to mid-May. **Amenities:** Restaurant; bar. *In room:* A/C, TV, hair dryer.

OTTAWA & EASTERN ONTARIO

by James Hale & Pamela Cuthbert

9

As a native of Ottawa, I've seen this city evolve over the past 5 decades from a sleepy civil-service town to a national capital that can proudly hold its own with any city of comparable size.

The official population is more than 800,000, but the central core is compact and its skyline relatively short. Most Ottawans live in suburban, or even rural, communities. The buses are packed twice a day with government workers who live in communities like Kanata, Nepean, Gloucester, and Orleans, which were individually incorporated cities until municipal amalgamation in 2001. Although there are a number of residential neighborhoods close to downtown, you won't find the kind of towering condominiums that line the downtown streets of Toronto or Vancouver. As a result, Ottawa is not the kind of city where the downtown sidewalks are bustling with people after dark, with the exception of the ByWard Market and Elgin Street.

One could make the case that Ottawa would be very dull indeed were it not for Queen Victoria's decision to anoint it capital of the newly minted Dominion of Canada. Thanks to her choice, tourists flock to the Parliament Buildings, five major national museums, a handful of government-funded festivals, and the Rideau Canal. Increasingly, tourists are spreading out beyond the well-established attractions to discover the burgeoning urban neighborhoods like Wellington West and the Glebe, and venturing into the nearby countryside.

For visitors, Ottawa is an ideal walking city. Most of the major attractions—and since this is a national capital, there are many—are within easy walking distance of the major hotels.

After visiting Ottawa, you may wish to explore eastern Ontario for a few more days. **Kingston,** an appealing lakefront town, is the principal gateway to the **Thousand Islands** district of the St. Lawrence River. East from there is **Prince Edward County**—a tranquil region of farms, orchards, quaint villages, and a burgeoning wine and culinary scene.

ESSENTIALS

Getting There

BY PLANE The **Ottawa Macdonald-Cartier International Airport (YOW; www.ottawa-airport.com)** is Ottawa's only public airport, located about 15 minutes by car from the downtown core. Within Canada, the city receives direct flights from **Air Canada** (✆ **888/247-2262;** www.aircanada.com), **WestJet** (✆ **888/937-8538;** www.westjet.com) and **Porter Airlines** (✆ **888/619-8622;** www.flyporter.com).

Air Canada operates year-round, nonstop flights from Las Vegas; Chicago; New York (LaGuardia); Washington, D.C. (Dulles and Reagan); and Boston, and seasonal nonstop flights from Fort Lauderdale and Orlando. **American Airlines** (✆ **800/433-7300;** www.aa.com) and **United Express** (✆ **800/864-8331;** www.united.com) fly nonstop to Ottawa from Chicago. **Delta** (✆ **800/221-1212;** www.delta.com) operates nonstop flights from Atlanta. **Continental Express** (✆ **800/523-3273;** www.continental.com) flies nonstop from Cleveland and Newark (Liberty). **Northwest** (✆ **800/225-2525;** www.nwa.com) offers nonstop service from Detroit. **US Airways** (✆ **800/428-4322;** www.usairways.com) operates nonstop flights from Philadelphia. From November to May, **WestJet** flies nonstop from Tampa and Orlando.

YOW Airporter (✆ **613/260-2359;** www.yowshuttle.com) shuttle service departs for major hotels from Arrivals Level 1, Post 10, every half-hour from 5am to 11:55pm. The one-way fare is C$15, round-trip is C$25. An airport limo can be summoned by calling ✆ **613/523-1560.** You can also hop into a regular cab; the fare will be around C$25 to downtown. If you wish to use the public transit system, OC Transpo provides high-frequency rapid service along the scenic Transitway, a roadway built specifically for buses. Rte. 97 departs the terminal at the curb outside the arrivals area. Adult cash fare (exact change only) is C$3.25.

BY TRAIN **VIA Rail** (✆ **888/842-7245;** www.viarail.ca) trains arrive at the Ottawa Station at 200 Tremblay Rd. (at blvd. St-Laurent), in the southeastern quadrant of the city. From here, buses and taxis connect to downtown.

BY BUS Buses arrive at the **Ottawa Bus Terminal,** 265 Catherine St., between Kent and Lyon. **Greyhound Canada** (✆ **800/661-8747;** www.greyhound.ca) provides coast-to-coast service with connections to Ottawa from most cities and Montreal's Pierre Trudeau International Airport.

BY CAR Driving from New York, take Interstate 81 to Canada's Route 401 east, then continue to the new Route 416 north, which leads directly into the city. Coming from the west, come via Toronto on Route 401 east to Route 416 north. From Montréal, follow Route 17 west to Route 417.

Visitor Information

TOURIST OFFICES The most convenient place to gather answers and pick up maps and brochures is the **Capital Infocentre,** 90 Wellington St., across from Parliament Hill (✆ **800/465-1867** or 613/239-5000; www.canadascapital.gc.ca); it's open daily 9am to 9pm in summer and 9am to 5pm daily in winter.

The **Ottawa Tourism and Convention Authority** (OTCA; 130 Albert St., Ste. 1800, Ottawa, ON K1P 5G4) maintains a comprehensive website with visitor information at **www.ottawatourism.ca.** The **OTCA** publishes an annual visitor guide, which includes maps and listings of cultural sites, things to see and do, accommodations, places to dine and shop, and services. You can obtain a free printed copy of the guide by phoning the **Capital Infocentre** (✆ **800/465-1867**).

City Layout

The **Ottawa River**—Canada's second longest, at more than 1,125km (700 miles) in length—curves around the northern edge of city. The compact downtown, where most of the major attractions are clustered, lies just south of the river.

The **Rideau Canal** sweeps past the National Arts Centre, cleaving downtown into two parts: Centretown and Lowertown. In **Centretown** are Parliament Hill, the Supreme Court, and the National Museum of Natural Sciences. In **Lowertown,** on the east side of the canal, are the National Gallery of Canada, ByWard Market, and (along Sussex Drive) the prime minister's residence, diplomats' row, and Rockcliffe Park. The area lying south of the Queensway, stretching west to Bronson and east to the canal, is known as the **Glebe,** and it harbors a number of popular restaurants and clubs, especially along Bank Street. North across the river, in the province of Québec, lies the city of **Gatineau,** the result of a recent merger that consolidated the city of Hull (where many national government offices are located) and four other suburban communities. It's reached via the Macdonald-Cartier and Alexandra bridges from the eastern end of town, or the Portage and Chaudière bridges from the western end of the city. At the end of the Alexandra Bridge stands the curvaceous Museum of Civilization, and nearby are some of the city's best French restaurants and liveliest nightlife action. North and east of Hull stretch the Gatineau Hills, with acres of parklands and ski country.

Getting Around

Ottawa is a walker's paradise. Its compact size, relatively flat setting, and numerous parks make it easy to get around, and with most of the major national sites in the downtown core, you can leave the car in the hotel parking lot for most of your visit. You can readily find your way around the city without a car, using one only if you have time for a few day trips to outlying attractions.

Public transit in Ottawa is provided by **OC Transpo.** This is an economical and efficient way to get around, since buses can bypass rush-hour traffic through the Transitway, a rapid-transit system of roadways reserved exclusively for buses. Routes 94, 95, 96, 97, 101, and 102 are the main Transitway routes, operating 22 hours a day. For transit information, call ✆ **613/741-4390** or visit www.octranspo.com. The regular exact-cash fare is C$3.25 for an adult and C$1.60 for a child. It's cheaper to use tickets, at C$1.25 each, since the adult fare is two tickets and the child fare (ages 6–11) is one ticket. The exception is during weekday rush hours, when some express routes charge C$4.25 or a three-ticket fare. DayPasses are available at C$7.50 on the bus for unlimited rides. And on Sunday and statutory holidays, a single DayPass entitles families, comprising up to two adults and four children ages 11 and under, to unlimited same-day travel—a great bargain. You can buy bus passes and tickets at more than 300 vendor locations across the city.

Public transit throughout the city of **Gatineau** and the **Outaouais region** on the Québec side of the Ottawa River is provided by **Société de transport de l'Outaouais** (**STO;** ✆ **819/770-3242;** www.sto.ca).

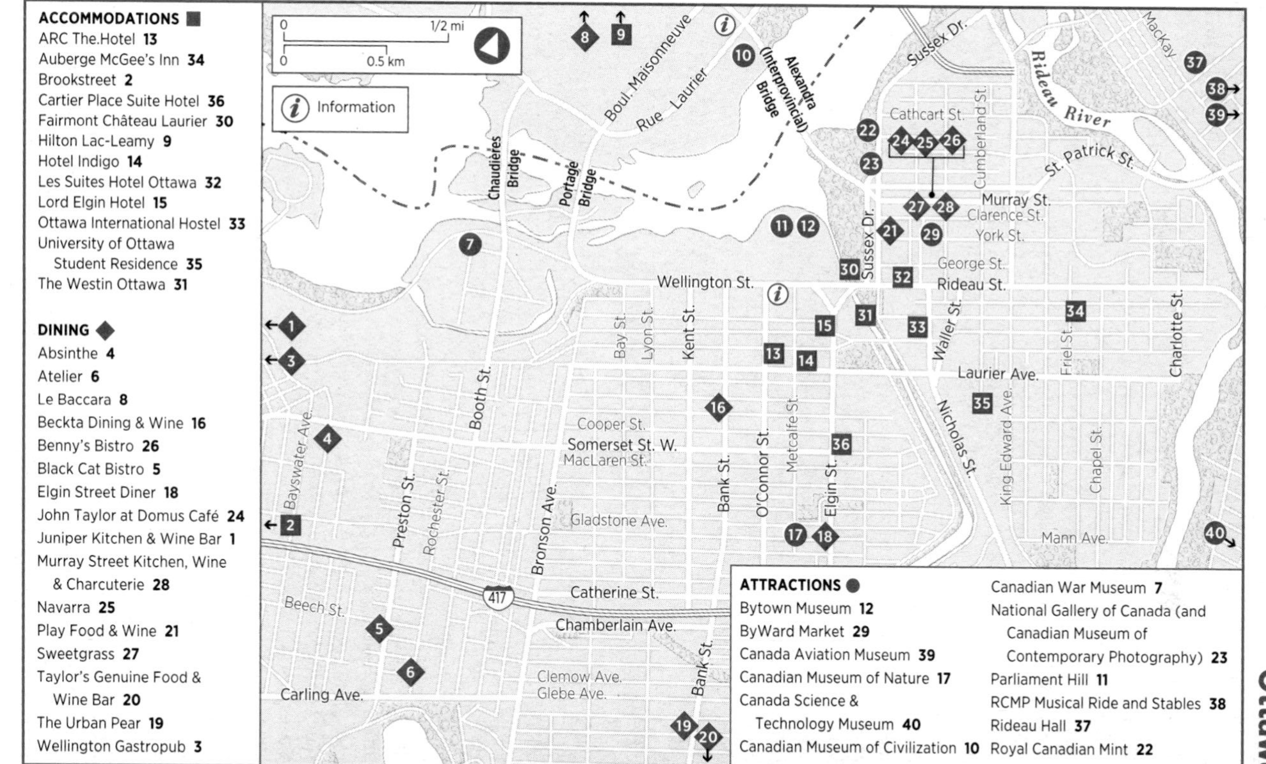
ACCOMMODATIONS
ARC The.Hotel 13
Auberge McGee's Inn 34
Brookstreet 2
Cartier Place Suite Hotel 36
Fairmont Château Laurier 30
Hilton Lac-Leamy 9
Hotel Indigo 14
Les Suites Hotel Ottawa 32
Lord Elgin Hotel 15
Ottawa International Hostel 33
University of Ottawa Student Residence 35
The Westin Ottawa 31
DINING
Absinthe 4
Atelier 6
Le Baccara 8
Beckta Dining & Wine 16
Benny's Bistro 26
Black Cat Bistro 5
Elgin Street Diner 18
John Taylor at Domus Café 24
Juniper Kitchen & Wine Bar 1
Murray Street Kitchen, Wine & Charcuterie 28
Navarra 25
Play Food & Wine 21
Sweetgrass 27
Taylor's Genuine Food & Wine Bar 20
The Urban Pear 19
Wellington Gastropub 3
ATTRACTIONS
Bytown Museum 12
ByWard Market 29
Canada Aviation Museum 39
Canadian Museum of Nature 17
Canada Science & Technology Museum 40
Canadian Museum of Civilization 10
Canadian War Museum 7
National Gallery of Canada (and Canadian Museum of Contemporary Photography) 23
Parliament Hill 11
RCMP Musical Ride and Stables 38
Rideau Hall 37
Royal Canadian Mint 22
0
1/2 mi
0
0.5 km
Information
Boul. Maisonneuve
Rue Laurier
Alexandra (Interprovincial) Bridge
Chaudières Bridge
Portage Bridge
Sussex Dr.
Rideau River
MacKay
Cathcart St.
Cumberland St.
St. Patrick St.
Murray St.
Clarence St.
York St.
George St.
Rideau St.
Wellington St.
Bay St.
Lyon St.
Kent St.
Waller St.
Friel St.
Charlotte St.
Laurier Ave.
Booth St.
Bayswater Ave.
Cooper St.
Somerset St. W.
MacLaren St.
Metcalfe St.
O'Connor St.
Bank St.
Elgin St.
Nicholas St.
King Edward Ave.
Chapel St.
Preston St.
Rochester St.
Bronson Ave.
Gladstone Ave.
Mann Ave.
417
Catherine St.
Chamberlain Ave.
Beech St.
Clemow Ave.
Glebe Ave.
Carling Ave.

You can hail a taxi on the street, but you'll find one more readily at taxi stands in front of most hotels, many government buildings, and some museums. You can also summon a taxi by phone. The drop charge for Ottawa taxis is C$3.30, and the mileage charge is C16¢ for every 93m (305 ft.). In the Ottawa area, 24-hour cab companies include **Blue Line** (✆ **613/238-1111**), with a fleet of more than 500 cabs, and **Capital Taxi** (✆ **613/744-3333**). **West-Way Taxi** (✆ **613/727-0101**) has drivers who have been trained to transport people with disabilities.

The scale of Ottawa makes driving your vehicle unnecessary for most sightseeing, although it will come in handy if you want to visit outlying attractions, such as the Canada Aviation Museum, the Diefenbunker, or Gatineau Park.

Generally, short-term parking rates downtown are C50¢ for 12 minutes. Your best bet is to use a municipal parking lot, marked with a large white "P" in a green circle. On weekends, parking is free in city lots and at meters in the area bounded by the Rideau Canal and Bronson Avenue, and by Wellington and Catherine streets.

In Ontario, a right turn on a red light is permitted after coming to a complete stop unless the intersection is posted otherwise, provided you yield to oncoming traffic and pedestrians. Be aware that once you cross the Ottawa River, you enter the province of Québec, where the rules are different, and vary from municipality to municipality. In Gatineau, you can turn right on a red light when it is safe to do so and only if there is no signage indicating that right-hand turns on a red light are not allowed. Throughout Québec, some street signs prohibit right turns on a red during specific periods. Wearing your seat belt is compulsory; fines for riding without a seat belt are substantial.

[FastFACTS] OTTAWA

Area Codes The telephone area code for Ottawa is **613;** for Gatineau and surrounding areas it's **819.** The area codes must be used for all local calls, although there is no charge for calls between Ottawa and Gatineau.

Drinking Laws You must be **19 years of age or older** to consume or purchase alcohol in Ontario. Bars and retail stores are strict about enforcing the law and will ask for proof of age if they consider it necessary. The **Liquor Control Board of Ontario (LCBO)** sells wine, spirits, and beer.

Across the Ottawa River **in Quebec, the drinking age is 18.** Quebec has traditionally had more liberal liquor laws than Ontario, and while hard liquor and imported wine is sold through provincially controlled outlets run by the **Société des alcools du Québec (SAQ),** beer and less-expensive domestic wines can be purchased at convenience and grocery stores.

Embassies & High Commissions As the nation's capital, Ottawa is the home to embassies and high commissions representing almost every country in the world. If your country isn't listed below, call for directory information in Ottawa (✆ **613/555-1212**) or check **www.ottawakiosk.com/embass.html.**

The embassy of the **United States** is at 490 Sussex Dr., Ottawa, ON K1N 1G8 (✆ **613/238-5335;** http://ottawa.usembassy.gov).

The high commission of **Australia** is at 50 O'Connor St., Ste. 710, Ottawa, ON K1P 6L2 (✆ **613/236-0841;** www.canada.embassy.gov.au/otwa/home.html).

The embassy of **Ireland** is at 130 Albert St., Ste. 1105, Ottawa, ON K1P 5G4 (✆ **613/233-6281;** www.embassyofireland.ca).

The high commission of **New Zealand** is at 99 Bank St., Ste. 727, Ottawa, ON K1P 6G3 (✆ **613/238-5991;** www.nzembassy.com/canada).

The high commission of the **United Kingdom** is at 80 Elgin St., Ottawa, ON K1G 5K7 (✆ **613/237-1530;** ukincanada.fco.gov.uk/en/).

Emergencies Call ✆ **911** emergency services for fire, police, or ambulance. For Poison Control, call ✆ **800/267-1373** or 613/737-1100.

Hospitals The **Children's Hospital of Eastern Ontario (CHEO)** (401 Smyth Rd.; ✆ **613/737-7600**), is a pediatric teaching hospital affiliated with the University of Ottawa that services a broad geographical area, including Eastern Ontario and Western Quebec. The hospital has an emergency department. For adult care, the **Ottawa Hospital** is a large multi-campus academic health sciences center with emergency departments at two sites: the **Civic** campus at 1053 Carling Ave. (✆ **613/722-7000**) and the **General** campus at 501 Smyth Rd. (✆ **613/722-7000**). Ontario emergency rooms are extremely busy, and wait times for non-urgent cases are typically several hours.

Newspapers & Magazines The daily newspapers are the ***Ottawa Citizen,*** the ***Ottawa Sun,*** and ***Le Droit,*** Ottawa's French-language newspaper. Keep an eye out for ***Capital Parent,*** a local free publication that advertises family-friendly events. ***Where Ottawa*** is a free monthly guide to shopping, dining, entertainment, and other tourist information. You can find it at most hotels and at some restaurants and retail stores. ***Ottawa Magazine*** and ***Ottawa Life*** are city monthlies. Arts and entertainment newspapers include the English-language ***Xpress*** and the French-language ***Voir.*** Gays and lesbians should check out ***Capital Xtra!*** For a great variety of international publications, visit **Mags and Fags,** at 254 Elgin St. (✆ **613/233-9651**), or **Planet News,** at 143 Sparks St. (✆ **613/232-5500**).

Police In a life-threatening emergency, or to report a crime in progress or a traffic accident that involves injuries or a vehicle that cannot be driven, call ✆ **911.** For other emergencies (a serious crime or a break-and-enter), call ✆ **613/230-6211.** For all other inquiries, call ✆ **613/236-1222.**

Smoking Ontario has among the most stringent nonsmoking legislation in the world. Smoking is prohibited in any enclosed, public place in Ottawa, and within several meters of most public buildings. There is no smoking in any restaurants or bars, and smoking is permitted only in designated rooms in hotels.

Time Ontario and Québec are in the eastern time zone, the same as New York City. **Daylight Saving Time** is in effect from 1am on the second Sunday in March to 1am on the first Sunday in November.

WHERE TO STAY

What characterizes the city's hotel scene are the unusually high percentage of suite hotels—a reflection of the number of expense-conscious people who come to town on long-term government business—and B&Bs, which cater to the large number of summer tourists on a budget. You can find some very chic rooms at Ottawa's top hotels—particularly at Brookstreet, Hilton Lac-Leamy, and ARC The.Hotel—but this is not a city that aims to wow you with over-the-top accommodations.

What you will find in Ottawa are some great views—especially from higher, north-facing rooms at the Fairmont Château Laurier, the Westin Hotel, and the Delta Ottawa Hotel & Suites—and hotels that are within walking distance to all the major downtown attractions. If you're used to paying in excess of C$200 a night in large cities, you may be pleasantly surprised at Ottawa's hotel rates; it's quite possible to find comfortable accommodations for much less than you'll pay in other cities of comparable size and interest.

Downtown

VERY EXPENSIVE

ARC The.Hotel ★★ Aiming to blend efficiency with luxury, this is one of the few properties in Ottawa to have adopted the boutique approach. Rooms are in neutral, earthy tones and are uniformly sized. Popular amenities include down-filled duvets, oversize pillows, Frette bathrobes, luxury toiletries (guests with allergies can request non-allergenic bedding and toiletries), and nightly turn-down service that includes cold spring water, Belgian chocolates, and a fresh Granny Smith apple—the hotel's trademark. Six pricier rooms feature extra-large tubs and fresh-cut flowers. Sip a complimentary glass of sparkling wine (served after 3pm daily), browse the original artwork by local artists, or catch up on your reading in the attractive library just off the lobby. If you wish to customize your return visit, make your preferences known to the front desk staff, and on your next trip, you'll feel even more at home. The ARC lounge serves signature martinis at cocktail hour, and the fine-dining ARC Lounge Restaurant (p. 356) features the best hotel dining in the city's core. Chef Jason Duffy is a proponent of buying local meats and produce, and his menu accentuates bistro-style specialties like duck breast and seasonal pastas.

140 Slater St., Ottawa, ON K1P 5H6. ✆ **800/699-2516** or 613/238-2888. Fax 613/235-8421. www.arcthehotel.com. 112 units. C$300 double; C$375 junior suite; C$425 executive 1-bedroom suite. Children 17 & under stay free in parent's room. AE, DC, DISC, MC, V. Valet parking C$25. **Amenities:** Restaurant/lounge; babysitting; concierge; executive suites; exercise room; limited room service. *In room:* A/C, TV w/pay movies, CD player, hair dryer, Internet (C$9.95/day), minibar.

Fairmont Château Laurier ★★★ One of Ottawa's premier landmarks, this grand hotel, built in 1912 in the same Loire Valley Renaissance style as Quebec City's Château Frontenac, has an imposing stone facade and a copper-paneled roof. If you're looking for luxury, tradition, and attentive service, this is the place to stay—royalty and celebrities have always been attracted to the Château Laurier's graceful beauty. You'll pay for the pleasure, but the surroundings are exceptional. The spacious public areas display the grandeur of another era, having been refurnished with the hotel's original furniture, rescued from a storeroom and meticulously restored. The less-expensive rooms are rather small but just as elegant as the larger rooms and suites; nine rooms are equipped for guests with disabilities. The upper floors offer impressive views over the Ottawa River toward the Gatineau Hills. The extensive health club and pool area, built in 1929 in Art Deco style, has been admirably preserved. The two dining rooms, Wilfrid's and Zoë's—named for former prime minister Sir Wilfrid Laurier and his wife, who were the first guests at the hotel—offer a sumptuous dining experience. This is a world-class hotel in every detail.

1 Rideau St., Ottawa, ON K1N 8S7. ✆ **800/441-1414** or 613/241-1414. Fax 613/562-7032. www.fairmont.com. 429 units. Low season C$219–C$289 double, C$469 suite; high season C$300–C$420 double, C$550 suite. Children 17 & under stay free in parent's room. AE, DC, DISC, MC, V. Valet parking C$29; self-parking C$23. Small pets (C$25/day). **Amenities:** Restaurant; bar/tearoom; babysitting; concierge; executive floor; exercise room; large indoor pool; 24-hr. room service; sauna. *In room:* A/C, TV w/pay movies, hair dryer, Internet (C$14.93/day), minibar.

The Westin Ottawa ★★★ A contemporary alternative to the Fairmont Château Laurier, the newly refurbished Westin Ottawa is attractively perched by the canal. All rooms have floor-to-ceiling windows to provide the best possible views of the city, and canal views are available for a premium. As with any hotel in this price range, you can expect a full array of amenities, including 24-hour room service, in-room safes, and high-speed Internet access—and, of course, the Westin chain is renowned for the quality of its bedding and bath accessories. When you're ready for exercise, go for a challenging game of squash on one of the three international standard courts or take a dip in the indoor pool, which has an adjacent outdoor sun deck. The exercise facilities are contained in a branded "WestinWORKOUT" gym, and the plate-glass windows offer great views. For those who live to shop, the third floor of the hotel provides direct access to the stores and services of the Rideau Centre. The high-end Shore Club restaurant is on the hotel's ground floor.

11 Colonel By Dr., Ottawa, ON K1N 9H4. ✆ **888/625-5144** or 613/560-7000. Fax 613/560-2707. www.starwoodhotels.com. 496 units. C$290–C$350 double; C$465–C$565 suite. Children 18 & under stay free in parent's room. AE, DC, DISC, MC, V. Valet parking C$25; self-parking C$14. Pets accepted (free). **Amenities:** Restaurant; concierge; executive floors; health club; hot tub; indoor pool; 24-hr. room service; sauna; spa. *In room:* A/C, LCD TV w/pay movies, hair dryer, minibar, Wi-Fi (C$15.99/day).

EXPENSIVE

Brookstreet ★★★ Built with high-tech money to service the adjacent high-tech community, Brookstreet exudes contemporary luxury at every turn. Signature guest-room colors are raspberry and gray, and a minimalist approach gives a boutique-hotel feel to rooms and suites. Although surrounded by low-rise office buildings, Brookstreet nestles on the edge of green space, overlooking the award-winning Marshes Golf Club, as well as cycling and walking paths and cross-country ski trails. With a full spa on-site; indoor and outdoor swimming pools; children's wading pool; skating rink; putting green; and 9-hole, par 3 MarchWood golf course, in addition to the 18-hole championship course, you will never wonder what to do with your time. The dining facilities are top class; Brookstreet's restaurant, Perspectives, has been awarded accolades for its cuisine, and features Food & Wine Raves on the first Friday of each month, allowing guests to participate in preparing and discussing the meal and wine selections. Options bar has live music on Thursday, Friday, and Saturday. Check the website for packages, ranging from romantic getaways to golf and spa weekends.

525 Legget Dr., Ottawa, ON K2K 2W2. ✆ **888/826-2220** or 613/271-1800. Fax 613/271-1850. www.brookstreet.ca. 276 units. C$189–C$219 double; C$250 junior suite; C$299–C$499 master suite. Children 17 & under stay free in parent's room. AE, DC, DISC, MC, V. Underground parking C$10; free parking above ground. Pets C$25/day. **Amenities:** Restaurant; bar/lounge; concierge; 2 golf courses; health club; Jacuzzi; 24-hr. room service; steam room; spa. *In room:* A/C, TV w/pay movies, hair dryer, kitchenette (in some), minibar, Wi-Fi (C$12.95/day).

Hotel Indigo ★ The boutique hotel chain's first Canadian property occupies one of Ottawa's busiest street corners and is the only downtown hotel to be retrofitted into a heritage building. The renovation was of major proportions—opening the center of the structure into a spectacular atrium. The light that floods the lobby and exposed upper corridors is symbolic of the chain's emphasis on nature and renewal. The corporate philosophy of the Indigo chain—which espouses belief in the power of Fibonacci numbers to define everything in nature—can seem a bit cultish, but look past the hotel's branding mumbo jumbo, and you'll find a restful hotel with some pleasant designer touches. The beds are large and sumptuous, and the dark hardwood flooring is a welcome change from ubiquitous industrial-strength broadloom, as are the operational windows. Thirteen of the hotel's rooms have Jacuzzis, and all are equipped with ergonomically pleasing glass-and-tile shower stalls. Spa-quality Aveda products abound. The in-room electronics—including CD/MP3 players and flat-screen TVs—are contemporary, but the nature of the building means that Wi-Fi is accessible only in the lobby; however, the wired Internet service in the rooms is complimentary. Indigo prides itself on exceptional service, but there are some compromises in this location: While the fitness center is open 24/365, room service operates only during the hours of the in-house restaurant, Phi.

123 Metcalfe St., Ottawa, ON K1P 5L9. ✆ **866/246-3446** or 613/231-6555. Fax 613/231-7555. www.ottawadowntownhotel.com. 106 units. C$149–C$219 double; C$209 deluxe double; C$229 suite. AE, DC, DISC, MC, V. Parking C$19. Pets C$75/stay. **Amenities:** Restaurant; executive suites; 24-hour fitness room; whirlpool; indoor pool; limited room service; sauna; Wi-Fi. *In-room:* A/C, LCD flat-screen TV w/pay movies, CD/MP3 player, hair dryer, Internet (free).

Les Suites Hotel Ottawa ★ Les Suites was originally built as a condominium complex in 1989. As a result, the traditional one- and two-bedroom suites are spacious and well equipped, with a full kitchen and washer/dryer in each. Renovated Premiere rooms are somewhat smaller and don't have laundry appliances. Elevators are situated away from the rooms, and bedrooms are located at the back of the suites, away from potential hallway noise. For an even quieter environment, ask for a suite overlooking the garden courtyard. The 24-hour health club and the indoor pool on the fifth floor have a panoramic city view and are shared with guests of Novotel Ottawa. The Rideau Centre and the ByWard Market area are on the hotel's doorstep. Many rooms have private balconies, and the windows can be opened.

130 Besserer St., Ottawa, ON K1N 9M9. ✆ **800/267-1989** or 613/232-2000. Fax 613/232-1242. www.les-suites.com. 241 units. C$155–C$235 1-bedroom suite; C$205–C$285 2-bedroom suite. Children 17 & under stay free in parent's room. AE, DC, DISC, MC, V. Parking C$17. Pets accepted in traditional suites (C$35). **Amenities:** Restaurant; babysitting; concierge; executive suites; 24-hr. health club; hot tub; indoor pool; limited room service; sauna. *In room:* A/C, TV w/pay movies, hair dryer, kitchen, Wi-Fi (free).

MODERATE

Auberge McGee's Inn ★ Nestled on a quiet tree-lined avenue, the inn was built in 1886 as a residence for influential politician John J. McGee, and the current owners have furnished the inn with some nice touches, including a 1901 player piano and antique telephone and camera collections. The guest rooms are individually decorated, and amenities vary. Some rooms have fireplaces; others have private balconies. There are two suites designed with romantic couples in mind: the Egyptian Room and the Victorian Roses Suite, both with fireplaces and double Jacuzzis. The Windsor Room was renovated in 2008 to include a double Jacuzzi, and a steam shower body spa that includes a TV and hands-free phone. The second floor has an ironing board and iron, in-room coffeemakers are available on request, and Wi-Fi is complimentary. The entire inn is nonsmoking. Special packages are often available; check the website or call for details.

185 Daly Ave., Ottawa, ON K1N 6E8. ✆ **800/262-4337** or 613/237-6089. Fax 613/237-6201. www.mcgeesinn.com. 14 units. C$108–C$120 double; C$198 suite. Rates include breakfast. Children 11 & under stay free in parent's room. AE, MC, V. Free parking. *In room*: A/C, TV, fridge, hair dryer, Wi-Fi (free).

Cartier Place Suite Hotel ★ ☺ This suite hotel has wonderful amenities for children, making it an attractive choice for families. In addition to the indoor pool, bathed in natural light streaming through glass doors (which are thrown open in the summer and lead onto a sun deck), there is a well-equipped children's playroom and even a preschool-size play structure in the pool area. An outdoor courtyard features a climbing gym and children's play equipment in summer. Redecoration and replacement of kitchen appliances has been ongoing for the past few years, a couple of floors at a time, so many of the suites are fresh and bright. All units have full kitchens and private balconies with garden chairs.

180 Cooper St., Ottawa, ON K2P 2L5. ✆ **800/236-8399** or 613/236-5000. Fax 613/238-3842. www.suitedreams.com. 250 units. C$119–C$169 1-bedroom suite; C$189–C$250 2-bedroom suite. Children 16 & under stay free in parent's room. AE, DC, MC, V. Parking C$15. Small pets accepted (C$15/day). **Amenities:** Restaurant/lounge; babysitting; children's playroom; exercise room; Jacuzzi; indoor pool; limited room service; sauna. *In room:* A/C, TV w/pay movies, hair dryer, kitchen, Wi-Fi (free).

Lord Elgin Hotel ★ One of Ottawa's landmark properties, this hotel is in an elegant, château-inspired building that has been preserved and restored with attention to 1940s interior detail. The location could not be better as a base for visitors to Ottawa. Directly across the street is Confederation Park, a small but pretty city park that provides a peaceful respite from the dense metropolis of skyscrapers crowding the business district behind the hotel. Two new guest-room wings have been seamlessly added to the property, and all of the hotel's original rooms were renovated in the past 5 years. The massive renovation and expansion included upgrades to the health club and a new indoor lap pool. Room sizes vary, with larger units found in the new wings. Bathrooms have been fitted with dark granite countertops and polished nickel accents. Executive rooms on the top two floors have upgraded amenities from Gilchrist & Soames, in-room safes, bathrobes and slippers, and complimentary high-speed Internet and phone calls. The premium for these upgraded rooms is only C$45. Rooms at the back are quieter, but you lose the view of the park. One nice architectural feature is that all of the windows open. The staff is formal, courteous, and efficient.

100 Elgin St., Ottawa, ON K1P 5K8. ✆ **800/267-4298** or 613/235-3333. Fax 613/235-3223. www.lordelgin.ca. 355 units. C$140–C$240 double; C$185–C$285 suite. Children 17 & under stay free in parent's room. AE, DC, DISC, MC, V. Valet parking C$23. Pets free. **Amenities:** Restaurant; lounge; Starbucks coffee shop; babysitting; bicycle rental nearby; concierge; executive floors; health club; hot tub; indoor pool; limited room service; sauna. *In room:* A/C, TV w/pay movies, fridge (in most), hair dryer, Internet (C$11.24/day, free in Executive rooms).

INEXPENSIVE

Ottawa International Hostel ☺ Before becoming a hostel, this building was the Carleton County Gaol (1862–1972). Guided tours of the former prison are available. Your bed for the night is a bunk in a jail cell or one of the dorms. Enjoy a quiet night's sleep behind bars—if the ghost of the last prisoner to be publicly hanged in Canada doesn't disturb you. The cozy TV lounge has leather couches and a big-screen TV. The communal kitchen recently received new appliances, tables, and chairs. Lockers for storing food are available for guests. The dining room is housed in the former prison chapel, and in the summer, guests may use the barbecue in the garden. Washroom facilities, with washbasins, toilets, and showers, are unisex (except in single-sex dorm areas). Families may opt for a private room with bunk beds, which accommodates up to five people, but most likely, your kids will want to sleep in the jail cells. Although the space is cramped and the beds are narrow, the experience will be authentic. Hostelling International members receive a discounted rate.

75 Nicholas St., Ottawa, ON K1N 7B9. ✆ **866/299-1478** or 613/235-2595. Fax 613/235-9202. www.hihostels.ca. 110 units. C$32 dorm bed (members), C$37 dorm bed (nonmembers); C$85 private room (members), C$97 private room (nonmembers). Children 9 & under stay free. AE, MC, V. Parking C$5. **Amenities:** Lounge. *In room:* No phone, Wi-Fi (free).

University of Ottawa Student Residence Although availability is limited to May through August, this is prime tourist time, so for many visitors, staying here will work out just fine. Rooms are available in a variety of student residences, but the one I recommend is the building at 90 rue Université, a recently built, all-suite residence. Each unit has two bedrooms with double beds; a kitchenette with fridge, microwave, sink, and storage; and an en suite bathroom. The location is perfect for visiting downtown attractions.

90 rue Université, Ottawa, ON K1N 1H3. ✆ **613/564-5400.** Fax 613/654-6530. www.uottawa.ca. 300 units. C$135 double w/shared bathroom; C$105 2-bedroom suite. MC, V. Parking C$13. **Amenities:** Exercise room (fee); pool (fee). *In room:* A/C, TV, Internet (free), kitchenette.

In Gatineau

VERY EXPENSIVE

Hilton Lac-Leamy ★★★ To say that the Hilton Lac-Leamy is the closest the Ottawa area comes to Las Vegas is to refer to more than its close proximity to a luxury casino; it's really a case of doing so much more than any other area hotel, and doing it all well. There is a sense of whimsy about this place—which begins with the spectacular blown-glass sculptures that hang in the lobby—that makes it easy to forgive how over the top the place can seem when stacked up against any of its competitors. Little wonder, then, that Celine Dion and her husband stayed in the his-and-hers luxury suites on the top floor; I'm sure she felt that she'd never left the Nevada desert. Of course, not every guest room in the hotel has a grand piano and full-service butler's pantry, but the spectacular views of Lac Leamy and Lac de la Carrière are shared throughout. All the rooms are larger than standard, and every bathroom features extensive marble and woodwork, huge soaker tubs, large glass shower enclosures, and an array of bath products. The 24-hour gym and spa facilities are substantial, and a three-floor executive area—which houses 35 large guest rooms, six suites, and the aforementioned "presidential" apartments—has a private lounge where a buffet breakfast is served. In addition, there is the Arôme Seafood and Grill restaurant, which has a terrific 100-seat heated patio; the Bacchus bar and cigar lounge; and a poolside cocktail terrace. Beyond the sense of effortlessness the staff exudes and the plethora of first-class amenities, what makes Hilton Lac-Leamy so different is its setting: on one side the wilderness of the Gatineau Hills, on the other the capital city—somehow it manages to sum up Canadian history perfectly.

3 boulevard du Casino, Gatineau, QC J8Y 6X4. ✆ **866/488-7888** or 819/790-6444. Fax 819/790-6408. www.hiltonlacleamy.com. 349 units. C$300 double; C$450–C$2,500 suite. Children 18 & under stay free in parent's room. AE, DC, DISC, MC, V. Valet parking C$22; self-parking free. Pets accepted on 2 floors (C$50/stay). **Amenities:** 2 restaurants; bar; babysitting; bike/in-line skate rental nearby; children's center; concierge; executive floors; health club; hot tub; indoor & outdoor pools; 24-hr. room service; sauna; spa; tennis courts. *In room:* A/C, flat-screen LCD TV w/pay movies, CD player, hair dryer, minibar, MP3 player, Internet (C$7.95/day).

WHERE TO DINE

In recent years, Ottawa's restaurant scene has been characterized—and greatly enlivened—by the arrival of a number of very good, young chefs. Following the example of local mainstays Richard Nigro (of Juniper Kitchen & Wine Bar) and John Taylor (of John Taylor at Domus and Taylor's Genuine Food & Wine Bar), these young chefs have embraced the local produce movement, pushing Ottawa into the forefront of this trend. All this activity on the local restaurant scene reached some sort of critical mass in 2008, when suddenly half a dozen of the city's most interesting chefs were on the move, starting new restaurants or spicing up the menus and food presentation at existing places.

In addition to pushing local produce and meats (with its close proximity to farmland, Ottawa is ideally suited for this), a number of these young chefs have designed their menus to cater to contemporary tastes, with smaller plates that lend themselves to trying more dishes and flavor, and custom pairings with wine. Tasting menus—a great chance to sample a wide variety of a chef's offerings at a reasonable price—are popular at a number of the leading spots.

Downtown

EXPENSIVE

Beckta Dining & Wine ★★★ CONTEMPORARY CANADIAN No Ottawa restaurant has ever garnered as much press as Beckta has since opening in 2003 (much of which is posted in the front hall of its heritage house). Owner Stephen Beckta—who serves as the restaurant's sommelier—swept back into his hometown from New York City's Café Boulud as something of a savior to the capital's stale cuisine. So, is the hype deserved? My wife and I considered that question as we marveled at the tenderness and flavor of my wife's pan-roasted chicken breast, served with black truffles and lemon thyme on a cloud of chanterelle and corn risotto. The bird's skin alone was a thing of beauty—succulent and lightly crisped. My charred leg of lamb was perfectly cooked, and its full, rich flavor played against the *maitake* mushrooms and piquant jus. The organic string beans and small potatoes were exceptionally fresh. The waitstaff knowledgeably handled questions about Beckta's extensive and distinctive wine list. While Beckta has gone through several chefs since its debut, subsequent visits have shown no slippage in quality or imagination. Mark us down as believers: Beckta is a gem. The restaurant also offers a tasting menu, which can be paired with cheese- and wine-tasting selections, as well. On Sunday and Monday, diners may bring their own bottles of wine for a C$20 corkage fee.

226 Nepean St. ✆ **613/238-7063.** www.beckta.com. Reservations recommended. Main courses C$27–C$39; tasting menus (5–6 courses) C$79; wine selection C$42. AE, DC, MC, V. Daily 5:30–9:45pm.

John Taylor at Domus Café ★★★ CONTEMPORARY CANADIAN Named to reflect the growing fame of co-owner and chef John Taylor, the restaurant exudes freshness, from the butter-yellow walls and high ceilings to the locally grown produce that Taylor uses extensively on his all-Canadian menu. An Ottawa favorite for many years, the restaurant is an ideal place to dine if you want to sample the country's diversity of cuisine and wine. The selection changes frequently, but main courses often include quail, Arctic char, and venison. On our most recent visit, we enjoyed a summery risotto with chanterelle mushrooms and peas, and a surprisingly piquant corn bisque. A warm salad featured more fresh, local corn, crisped prosciutto, and a sunny-side-up quail's egg. Sommelier Sylvia Taylor's specialty is finding distinctive Canadian wines that are perfect matches for her husband's creations, and the restaurant works directly with a number of the leading wineries in Ontario's Niagara region to find distinctive new offerings. Service is friendly and efficient.

87 Murray St. ✆ **613/241-6007.** www.domuscafe.ca. Main courses C$26–C$34. AE, MC, V. Mon–Sat 11:30am–2pm & 5:30–10pm; Sun 10:30am–2:30pm. Closed Sun during summer.

Navarra ★★★ BASQUE The narrow wooden house in the center of Murray Street's "Gastro Alley" is one of the oldest in Ottawa, and over the past decade, it has established the reputation as housing one of the city's best kitchens. Ottawa native René Rodriguez has been responsible for that twice, now; first as chef—for 3 years—of the Black Cat Café, and currently at the helm of his own Basque-influenced restaurant. My wife and I had just returned from the heart of Spain's Basque region when we first dined at Navarra in 2008, and my lobster *pil pil* took me right back to Vitoria-Gasteiz and Bilbao. More recently, Rodriguez has adopted a small-plates approach and broadened his menu to include a wide range of regional specialties, including a beef *tartare* with pepper aioli and octopus confit. One of the joys of Navarra—aside from the service, which just may be the most knowledgeable and pleasant in the city—is that Rodriguez seems to be constantly creating new combinations. On our last visit, we gave ourselves over to the tasting menu that was on offer, the highlight of which was a barbecued pork cheek that re-defines the concept of food that melts in your mouth. The wine pairing was also imaginative and delightful.

93 Murray St. ✆ **613/241-5500.** www.navarrarestaurant.com. Reservations recommended. Main courses C$22–C$30. MC, V. Mon–Fri 11:30am–2pm; Mon–Sat 5:30–10pm.

Sweetgrass ★★★ 🎁 ABORIGINAL CANADIAN Among bistros that tout "fusion" cuisine, few offer blends as unique as those served up by Phoebe Sutherland, a James Bay Cree, and her husband Warren, who's Jamaican by birth. Since opening in the ByWard Market area in late 2003, this 57-seat restaurant has attracted a growing number of devotees to its serene atmosphere and the chefs' clever interpretations of Native American cuisine. Earth tones dominate the main room of the small heritage house, and the walls display a changing assortment of aboriginal art. The menus shift with the seasons in keeping with Native tradition, but game dishes are always plentiful. My favorites on the spring menu are the grilled *tatonka* (buffalo) and the crispy leg of duck, which is accompanied by spicy corn crepes stuffed with a variety of spring beans and drizzled with a garlic-ginger sauce. Grilled caribou from Canada's Nunavut territory nestles on a bed of spinach with a side of mushroom-potato ragout. Arctic char is spiced mildly with a cucumber-cilantro sauce. Vegetarians aren't forgotten, with at least one main and a variety of salads that feature original dressings. Appetizers include smoked British Columbia salmon with peppered crème fraîche and pan-fried rabbit dumplings topped with a honey-mustard sauce. Sweetgrass excels at the small touches that create a memorable experience, like the wide variety of Native teas on offer, the understated, attentive service, and the warmth that exudes from Phoebe and Warren in their welcoming, open kitchen.

108 Murray St. ✆ **613/562-3683.** www.sweetgrassbistro.ca. Reservations recommended. Main courses C$20–C$36. MC, V. Mon–Fri 11:30am–2pm; daily 5:30–10pm.

MODERATE

Benny's Bistro ★★ 🎁 BISTRO Tucked away down a narrow hallway behind a French bakery and open only for breakfast and lunch, this unpretentious little jewel is easy to miss. Build it into your agenda, along with a tour of the ByWard Market or the National Gallery of Canada, and you won't be disappointed. Maged Kamal's design—combining primary colors on the walls; a checkered floor; a high-pressed, tin ceiling; and open kitchen—is simple but creative, and chef Scott Adams' menu follows that lead. What he does with duck is a perfect example. The slices of duck breast are straightforward enough—tender, moist, and perfectly pan-fried—but to this, Adams adds his version of French toast, served with roasted rhubarb from his garden and a vanilla bean compote. Or, consider his risotto, which is actually made from pearl barley and served with delicious wild mushrooms and grilled asparagus with a salad of radicchio and baby arugula. For smaller lunchtime appetites, Adams also has a daily sandwich and green salad combination for C$13. Needless to say, the bread from the front of the house is oven-fresh.

119 Murray St. ✆ **613/789-6797.** www.bennysbistro.ca. Main courses C$15–C$19. AE, MC, V. Daily 8am–2:30pm.

Murray Street Kitchen, Wine & Charcuterie ★★ BISTRO This creation by high-profile Ottawa restaurateurs Steve Mitton and Paddy Whelan addresses what they see as the need for high-quality Canadian comfort food. Their idea of comfort comes in the form of top-notch meats and cheeses, and a small but select menu of Old and New World wines. At the bar, you can sample hand-cut slices of meats and a few pâtés, or you can take a table and tuck into something more substantial. An appetizer of *poutine* made with sheep-yogurt spaetzle—substituting for French fries—and shredded duck confit and gravy might be deemed almost too much comfort; it redefines the phrase *over the top,* but it's so good! Chef Mitton's braised shortrib is beyond tender—the result of 2 days' processing in its red-wine reduction. Despite the obvious care taken in dishes like this, Murray Street exudes a rustic air—a feeling that's reflected in the rough-hewn wooden floors, the artisan bread that arrives at your table in a small brown bag, and the casual grace of the serving staff. Set in an old house, Murray Street is a deceptively large place with an inviting patio in the back.

110 Murray St. ✆ **613/562-7244.** www.murraystreet.ca. Main courses C$24–C$29. AE, MC, V. Daily 11:30am–midnight.

Play Food & Wine ★★ BISTRO If Stephen Beckta's eponymous fine-dining establishment west of the Rideau Canal (see p. 328) can elicit a certain amount of sticker shock from some patrons, his newer ByWard Market entry fits just about every budget. Indeed, you'll find everyone from texting teenagers—who seem more interested in their iPhones than their dining companions—to silver-haired seniors at Play. That's the beauty of small plates; they fit all comers. If you're looking for a light repast, you can part with as little as C$17 for some soft-shell crab and a side of fries. Arrive with a couple of friends and share seven or eight dishes, and you could find yourself parting with well over C$100. If you're in the Market during lunch, the C$20 special, which allows you to choose any two dishes, is particularly attractive. Whether you opt for wild trout with anchovy butter and capers, or quail on a tiny cushion of polenta with salsa *verde* and onions, the quality is exceptionally high, and Beckta's insistence on attention to detail is always present. As at the parent eatery, the staff displays effortless good humor and product knowledge, and the wine list—Beckta's specialty—is varied and informed.

1 York St. ✆ **613/667-9207.** www.playfood.ca. Reservations recommended. Main courses C$12–C$19. AE, MC, V. Mon–Fri noon–2pm; Mon 5:30–10pm, Tues–Thurs 5:30–11pm, Fri 5:30pm–midnight; Sat noon–midnight.

INEXPENSIVE

Elgin Street Diner DINER Make no mistake, Ottawa is a far cry from New York City. That said, there are those who do party—or work—late into the night, and the Elgin Street Diner meets their needs for a place that never closes. This is an unpretentious, neighborhood kind of place, and if home-style comfort food is your thing, this will be heaven for you. I have a friend who comes here just for the club sandwiches, made with grilled chicken, and another who thinks that the *poutine*—a distinctive French-Canadian dish made with fried potatoes, cheese curds, and gravy—is the best anywhere. You can also cure what ails you with the Hangover Breakfast of two eggs, *poutine,* and baked beans, or make like it's the 1950s with the homemade macaroni and cheese. For those who like fewer carbs in their diet, there are salads, a veggie burger, and a grilled vegetable club.

374 Elgin St. ✆ **613/237-9700.** www.elginstreetdiner.com. Most items under C$15. AE, DC, MC, V. Daily 24 hr.

The Glebe/Ottawa South

EXPENSIVE

The Urban Pear ★★ CONTEMPORARY CANADIAN Quality trumps location at the Urban Pear, which is tucked away on a quiet side street in the Glebe. While the views are mostly of parking lots, the long, bright room—which features exhibitions of original artwork—quickly makes you forget the external environment. Owner-chef Ben Baird brings so much passion for food to the game that people come to this place in droves. Baird believes in using only fresh, local, seasonal ingredients. He also believes in staying in touch with his community and frequently hosts special dinners to showcase new recipes and wine pairings. Often, he invites an estate owner along, as well, to discuss the finer points of his or her wines. An ideal spot for lunch if you're perusing the Glebe's shopping options, the restaurant has a menu that changes daily. My last visit yielded an exceptionally light-yet-bold frittata, spiked with organic oyster mushrooms, chard, goat cheese, and fingerling potatoes. Baird's menus also frequently feature at least one fowl and beef main, pasta, and often a concoction based around a stuffed, open-face apple or Anjou pear. Freshness and variety rule here.

151 2nd Ave. ✆ **613/569-9305.** www.theurbanpear.com. Reservations recommended. Main courses C$23–C$32. AE, DC, MC, V. Mon–Fri 11:30am–2pm, Sun 11am–2pm; daily 5:30–9pm.

MODERATE

Taylor's Genuine Food and Wine Bar ★★ WINE BAR John and Sylvia Taylor were so far ahead of the curve on the local food and wine movement that the rest of the crowd still hasn't caught up to them. Rather than resting on their laurels (their home base in the ByWard Market—John Taylor at Domus—is consistently ranked among the best restaurants in the region), the pair has expanded south and transformed a former coffee shop into a neighborhood hot spot. Dominated by a bar and a highly visible service area, the small restaurant was already filled to capacity on many nights just months after opening in 2010. I squeezed in with a friend on a sultry evening and was immediately cooled off by a crisp glass of *viognier* and a beet and ginger soup that struck a perfect balance between sweet and tart. My main was an extremely good fillet of pickerel, nicely crisped and plated very simply. As expected, food comes first here, just as it does at the Taylors's other restaurant. The menu is small, with only four or five entrees, and changes at least twice a week. My only beef was a somewhat watery cup of coffee, but with food this fresh and service this attentive, that's a minor quibble.

1091 Bank St. ✆ **613/730-5672.** Reservations recommended. Main courses C$15–C$27. AE, MC, V. Daily 11:30am–2pm & 5–10pm.

Wellington Street West/Westboro

EXPENSIVE

Absinthe ★★ BISTRO Directly across Wellington Street from the Irving Greenberg Theatre Centre, Absinthe aims to evoke a hip, casual mood set in a Parisian bistro of the mind. While there's little mistaking this for the real Paris, chef-owner Patrick Garland does a good job at creating a faux-French experience—right down to the noisy atmosphere and the slightly arrogant stance of refusing to cook his signature hanger steak beyond medium rare. That suits me okay; in fact, I lean the other way and it's just fine—nicely marinated and with the edges perfectly seared. A pricier cut of Black Angus is just so, as well, as is pork tenderloin that's stuffed with apple and topped with a combination of cauliflower, goat cheese, and cranberries. With its sponged pumpkin-colored walls, extensive use of mirrors, and bare wooden floor, Absinthe is a beautiful room, and Garland's waitstaff strikes just the right note of knowledge about the menu and cheeky playfulness. On Friday and Saturday, a DJ takes over after the food service ends, and the place stays open well past midnight.

1208 Wellington St. ✆ **613/761-1138.** www.absinthecafe.ca. Reservations recommended. Main courses C$20–C$32. AE, MC, V. Mon–Fri 11am–2pm; daily 5:30–10pm.

Juniper Kitchen & Wine Bar ★★ CONTEMPORARY CANADIAN Richard Nigro was one of the first Ottawa chefs to gain quasi-celebrity status, back when he worked at the original Domus. Now, in partnership with chef Norm Aitken, he is a strong proponent of fresh, local produce and distinctive new Canadian cuisine. Juniper specializes in unusual combinations of flavors, which was evident in my exceptionally tender piece of Angus tenderloin with its jus of port and figs. We also sampled a lamb shank rubbed with Indonesian spices, which was complemented by tomato-mint chutney and a sweet and spicy coconut sauce, and served with corn cakes. At C$30, a chunk of wild salmon seemed a bargain—and tasty, too, topped with a gooseberry and red pepper vinaigrette. In keeping with its Canadian focus, Juniper has a good selection of domestic wines from boutique wineries.

245 Richmond Rd. ✆ **613/728-0220.** www.juniperdining.ca. Reservations recommended. Main courses C$27–C$39. AE, MC, V. Mon–Fri 11:30am–2pm; Mon–Thurs & Sun 5:30–10pm, Fri & Sat 5:30–11pm.

MODERATE

Wellington Gastropub ★★ BISTRO Up one flight of stairs from a small courtyard on busy Wellington Street, this restaurant is divided into two rooms that flank a small bar. The jean-clad, bearded, and tattooed waiters might make you think you've mistakenly entered a diner, but this is a place that mixes first-rate, big-flavored food with a casual atmosphere. A larger-than-average by-the-glass wine list and several local microbrews are welcome, as is the attractive offering of artisan breads. Chef Chris Deraiche changes his menu daily; a sucker for risotto, I couldn't resist one that was filled with a variety of mushrooms, and I was rewarded with a large portion and expertly balanced flavors. I cadged a sizeable forkful of my companion's Arctic char and immediately wished I'd forsaken my Italian rice fixation for the night; it was one of the best pieces of fish I've tasted. Equally fine was a creamy vanilla crème brûlée embedded with fresh blueberries and one succulent strawberry.

1325 Wellington St. W. © **613/729-1315.** www.thewellingtongastropub.com. Reservations recommended. Main courses C$18–C$26. AE, MC, V. Mon–Fri 11:30am–2pm; Mon–Sat 5:30–10pm.

Corso Italia (Little Italy)

VERY EXPENSIVE

Atelier ★★★ MODERN CANADIAN I knew something special was up with chef Marc Lepine when he served me an amazing olive oil ice cream when he ran the kitchen at the Courtyard restaurant. After leaving Courtyard in 2008 all was revealed; Lepine planned to expose Ottawans to his own take on molecular gastronomy. Atelier has no sign, and looks like nothing more than an anonymous single-family house on an anonymous street that is dominated by a federal government building. Inside, the narrow living quarters have been converted to a luxurious lounge environment, with cream leather chairs and dark banquettes. A 12-course tasting menu (C$88) is the sole selection, and a staff member will call you in advance to discuss any potential food-related issues. A large, interesting selection of wine is available, or you can put yourself in the capable hands of sommelier Steve Robinson for a wine pairing (C$55). While some of Lepine's concepts—an array of sea plants and an oyster served on a rock, a plate of silky raw tuna named "Jessica Albacore" and a "Back to School" special served on a slab of blackboard—can seem a bit too cute, the parade of tastes and textures passing your lips is nothing short of stunning. While there are a few "foams" that are the earmark of molecular gastronomy, Lepine seems more interested in exploring the wide range of what's edible in the world and how tastes can complement each other. One dish had no fewer than 40 different ingredients—from a single, small flower to powdered olive oil. A spoon holding a square of pork belly enhanced by caramel, hot peppers, and a burning stick of cinnamon was other-worldly. Is the Atelier experience worth the price? The proof is in the liquid nitrogen-enhanced "Subterranean Homesick Alien" pudding.

540 Rochester St. © **613/321-3537.** www.atelierrestaurant.ca. Reservations required. Fixed price menu (12 courses) C$88. AE, MC, V. Tues–Sat 5–10pm.

MODERATE

Black Cat Bistro ★★ BISTRO The Black Cat name and distinctive feline logo have been around Ottawa longer than just about any other dining establishment, and since 1979, owner Richard Urquhart has stayed one step ahead of restaurant trends. In 2008, he opened this sleek, high-ceilinged, split-level spot with the creative Patricia Larkin in the kitchen. The results are nothing short of marvelous. While the menu tempted us with a pan-roasted wild king salmon served with olives and asparagus, and a grilled loin of lamb with *rapini*, we put ourselves in the care of our low-key waiter, who recommended a maple-glazed pork belly and the chicken breast. Served with spaetzle and oyster mushrooms, and hit with a generous shot of truffle oil, the incredibly moist chicken had exactly the right blend of crisp crust and moist flesh. The pork belly was equally superb, with maple syrup infusing the crisped fat. Urquhart's wine list also held its share of pleasures, featuring a number of small California producers who are rare in these parts. A "classic French" lemon tart was just the right finishing touch.

428 Preston St. ✆ **613/569-9998.** www.blackcatbistro.ca. Reservations recommended. Main courses C$19–C$30. AE, MC, V. Tues–Sat 5–10pm.

Gatineau

VERY EXPENSIVE

Le Baccara ★★★ FRENCH Easily the most-honored restaurant in the Ottawa region, the 70-seat Le Baccara makes you wonder why anyone would bother stopping off in the gaming rooms of the Casino du Lac-Leamy (see p. 354) on the way in. There's absolutely no gambling here; you are guaranteed delightful food, carefully prepared and served with utmost professionalism. Despite the steep price and quality of service, Le Baccara picks up on the easygoing atmosphere that's evident throughout the casino-hotel complex. Even with its cherry-wood paneling and rich fabrics, the restaurant is anything but stuffy; within 5 minutes of being seated, the sommelier was telling me about his recent multistage marathon run in the Sahara. We opted for the eight-course Gastronomic Menu with our marathon man's recommendations from the restaurant's 13,000-bottle cellar. The menu changes with the season but always features fresh local game, meat, and vegetables, as well as imaginatively prepared seafood. Whether you've just lined your pockets at the blackjack table or simply feel like splurging on a meal you'll remember from your vacation, Le Baccara offers exceptional dining experiences.

1 boulevard du Casino, Gatineau. ✆ **800/665-2274** or 819/772-6210. Main courses C$29–C$58; table d'hôte (5–8 courses) C$65–C$120; wine selection C$65–C$75. AE, DC, MC, V. Wed–Sun 5:30–11pm.

SEEING THE SIGHTS

Ottawa is defined by two factors: its role as Canada's capital, and its proximity to nature. As a result, there is a wealth of major attractions—such as the national museums, Parliament Buildings, and cultural festivals—and an abundance of opportunities to explore the historic Rideau Canal, bike, in-line skate, or ski in the nearby Gatineau Hills.

You could build a jam-packed itinerary for each day of your vacation and still not see and do everything, so take the time to plan well and create a mix of activities that will allow you to sample the best the city has to offer.

If you're in Ottawa for only a short break, concentrate your sightseeing in and around the downtown area. You'll find that many of the major attractions are within walking distance of one another along Wellington Street and Sussex Drive, or on streets leading off these two roads. Visit **www.virtualmuseum.ca** for a listing and brief description of some of Ottawa's museums and heritage attractions.

Don't forget that Ottawa is a year-round destination, despite the harsh winters. Officially recognized as the world's largest skating rink, the Ottawa portion of the Rideau Canal becomes a focal point for outdoor activities in winter, especially during Winterlude in February. Once spring comes, each week brings a new festival or cultural celebration.

If this is a family vacation, keep in mind that many museums put on special programs and workshops for children and families on weekends and during school holidays (1 week in mid-Mar, the months of July and Aug, and 2 weeks surrounding Christmas and New Year's Day). Call the **Capital Infocentre** (✆ **800/465-1867** or 613/239-5000) for exact dates, as they vary from year to year.

The Top Attractions

Parliament Hill ★★★ ☺ The dominant site in downtown Ottawa, **Parliament Hill** is the focal point for most of Canada's national celebrations, including day-long events and spectacular fireworks on July 1, Canada Day. The **Parliament Buildings,** with their grand sandstone-block construction, steeply pitched copper roofs, and multiple towers are an impressive sight. In 1860, Prince Edward (later King Edward VII) laid the cornerstone for the original buildings, which were finished in time to host the inaugural session of the first Parliament of the new Dominion of Canada in 1867. As you enter through the main gates on Wellington Street and approach the **Centre Block** with its stately central **Peace Tower,** you'll pass the Centennial Flame, lit by then–prime minister Lester B. Pearson on New Year's Eve 1966 to mark the start of Canada's centennial year. In June, July, and August, you can meet the **Royal Canadian Mounted Police** (affectionately called Mounties) on Parliament Hill. They're friendly—and love to have their photo taken.

If you're visiting the capital between mid-May and early September, your first stop on Parliament Hill should be the **Info-Tent,** where you can pick up free information on the Hill and **free same-day tickets for tours of the Parliament Buildings.** Between September and May, get same-day tickets from the **Visitor Welcome Centre,** at the foot of the Peace Tower. Tickets are limited, though, and there is no guarantee in the busy summer months or on weekends in spring and fall that you will get tickets for your first choice of time, or even day. If you're visiting in summer and are adverse to lines, try to book your tour for one of the evening sessions. During the busy summer months, drop by the information tent on the lawn in front of the Parliament Buildings between 9 and 10am. You can reserve a spot on the free tour of the Centre Block for later in the day, including some evening bookings, and avoid the long lines.

Tours of the Parliament Buildings last from 20 minutes to an hour, depending on whether Parliament is in session. Allow at least 2 hours for a full tour of Parliament Hill. The Parliament Buildings consist of 3 blocks of buildings—the **Centre Block,** with its central **Peace Tower,** and the flanking **West Block** and **East Block.** This is the heart of Canadian political life—the workplace of the House of Commons and the Senate. When the House of Commons is sitting, you can visit the public gallery and observe the 308 elected members debating in their grand green chamber with its tall stained-glass windows. Parliament is in recess usually from late June until early September and occasionally between September and June, including the Easter and Christmas holidays. Otherwise, the House usually sits on weekdays. The 105 appointed members of the Senate sit in a stately red chamber. The West Block, containing parliamentary offices, is closed to the public. You can tour the East Block, which has four historic rooms restored for public viewing: the original governor-general's office, restored to the period of Lord Dufferin (1872–1878); the offices of Sir John A. Macdonald and Sir Georges-Étienne Cartier (the principal fathers of Confederation); and the Privy Council Chamber with anteroom.

The **Centre Block** is considered to be one of the world's best examples of Gothic revival architecture, complete with the pointed arches, prominent buttresses, and contrasting stonework that characterize the style. Free guided tours of the Centre Block, which may include the **House of Commons,** the **Senate,** the richly ornamented **Hall of Honour,** and the **Library of Parliament,** are available in English and French all year. Guides tell animated stories and interesting anecdotes about the buildings and the people who have worked there. When Parliament is in session, the tours do not visit the House of Commons or the Senate, but visitors are invited to take a seat in the public galleries and watch the proceedings. Centre Block tour times vary throughout the year and can change without prior notice; call the **Capital Infocentre** at ✆ **800/465-1867** or 613/239-5000 for information.

The imposing 92m (302-ft.) campanile of the Peace Tower is one of the most easily recognizable Canadian landmarks and dominates the Centre Block's facade. It houses a 53-bell carillon, a huge clock, an observation deck, and the Memorial Chamber, commemorating Canada's war dead. A 11m (36-ft.) bronze mast flying a Canadian flag tops the tower. When Parliament is in session, the tower is lit. One-hour concerts of the 53-bell carillon of the Peace Tower are presented weekdays in July and August at 2pm. From September to June, there is a 15-minute noon concert most weekdays.

Also in the Centre Block, the Library of Parliament is a glorious 16-sided dome hewn from Nepean sandstone, supported outside by flying buttresses and paneled inside with Canadian white pine. Designed in Gothic revival style, the library was opened in 1876. The center of the room is dominated by a white marble statue of a young Queen Victoria, created in 1871.

Between late June and early September, you can get free same-day tickets at the Info-Tent for a guided tour of the Parliament Hill grounds. Visitors will enjoy an introduction to some of the historical figures who have shaped Canada's past and present. Otherwise, you can wander around Parliament Hill and explore the monuments, grounds, and exterior of the buildings on your own with the help of a 24-page outdoor self-guiding booklet called ***Discover the Hill,*** available from the **Capital Infocentre** across the street from the Parliament Buildings. Stroll the grounds clockwise around the Centre Block—they're dotted with statues honoring such prominent historical figures as Queen Victoria, Sir George-Étienne Cartier, William Lyon Mackenzie King, and Sir Wilfrid Laurier. Behind the building is a promenade with sweeping views of the Ottawa River.

One last attraction for summer visitors to the Parliament Buildings is **Sound and Light on the Hill.** Every evening between early July and early September, Canada's history unfolds and the country's spirit is revealed through music, lights, and giant images projected on the Parliament Buildings. This half-hour display of sound and light is free of charge, and limited bleacher seating is available.

Wellington St., just west of the Rideau Canal. ✆ **800/465-1867** or 613/239-5000. www2.parl.gc.ca/Sites/LOP/Visitors/index-e.asp. Free admission. Daily from 9am (subject to change without notice). Centre Block closed Christmas Day, New Year's Day & July 1.

MORE MUST-SEES

Canadian Museum of Civilization ★★★ ☺ The largest of Canada's cultural institutions, the Canadian Museum of Civilization (CMC) is a combination of permanent and temporary exhibits that explore human history with special, although not exclusive, reference to Canada. Along with Parliament Hill, this is Ottawa's must-see attraction for visitors. The building is the work of Canadian architect Douglas Cardinal, whose Native heritage is frequently reflected in his designs. Added attractions within the building are the Canadian Children's Museum, the Canadian Postal Museum, and the IMAX theater. You could easily spend the whole day here, especially if you take in an IMAX show, but even a cursory visit will take at least 2 hours.

From the street-level lobby, descend the escalator to the museum's showpiece—the magnificent **Grand Hall ★★**. This enormous exhibition hall features a display of more than 40 totem poles, representing the culture of the Native peoples of Canada's Pacific Northwest coast. Six Native house facades have been constructed in the hall, based on architectural styles of different coastal nations over the past 150 years.

Set under a dramatically lit 17m-high (56-ft.) dome, **Canada Hall ★★★** takes visitors on a journey through 1,000 years of Canada's social and cultural history. The Canada Hall is a presentation of full-scale tableaux and buildings that have been constructed in the architectural style of specific historical periods using materials and methods in use at the time. **First Peoples Hall** showcases the cultural, historical, and artistic accomplishments of aboriginal peoples in Canada, and contains more than 2,000 artifacts.

100 Laurier St., Gatineau, QC. ✆ **800/555-5621** or 819/776-7000 for museum, 819/776-7010 for IMAX Theatre. www.civilization.ca. C$12 adults, C$10 seniors & students, C$8 children 3–12, free for children 2 & under; C$30 families. Free admission year-round Thurs 4–8pm, July 1 & Nov 11. IMAX tickets C$12 adults, C$10 seniors & students, C$8 children 3–12, free for children 2 & under; C$38 families. May & June Mon–Wed 9am–6pm, Thurs 9am–8pm (children's museum until 6pm), Sat & Sun 9:30am–6pm; July to Sept 6 Mon–Wed 9am–6pm, Thurs & Fri 9am–8pm, Sat & Sun 9:30am–6pm; Sept 7 to Oct 11 Mon–Wed 9am–6pm, Thurs 9am–8pm (children's museum until 6pm), Sat & Sun 9:30am–6pm; Oct 12 to Apr Tues–Wed & Fri 9am–5pm, Thurs 9am–8pm (children's museum until 5pm), Sat & Sun 9:30am–5pm. IMAX Theatre hours may differ from museum hours. From the Ottawa River Pkwy. or Wellington St. downtown, take the Portage Bridge to Gatineau & turn right onto rue Laurier. The museum is on the right. From the east side of the canal, take Sussex Dr. & cross the Royal Alexandra Bridge. The museum is on the immediate left as you exit the bridge.

Canadian War Museum ★★ The Canadian War Museum, which opened on May 8, 2005—the 60th anniversary of V-E (Victory in Europe) Day and the 125th anniversary of the Canadian War Museum as an institution—delivers an unforgettable visitor experience. The **permanent galleries** have made full use of leading-edge museum-design theories and techniques to bring to life Canada's role in conflicts and war, emphasizing how military events have affected Canadians at a personal, national, and international level. The story of war and its consequences is told through the stories, artifacts, and memories of ordinary Canadians, with a view to presenting the human story, rather than simply a display of objects and artifacts, although there is an extensive collection of weaponry, trucks, and tanks. In addition to eight permanent exhibit galleries, which trace conflict involving Canada from the European settlement to the present, there are spaces for **special exhibitions,** an **art gallery** featuring a fine collection of **war art,** and two special halls: **Memorial Hall** and **Regeneration Hall.** The museum is located at **Lebreton Flats,** a green-space area about 2km (1¼ miles) west of **Parliament Hill.** Allow 3 hours for a full tour of the museum, and be aware that children under 12 will likely tire quickly here.

1 Vimy Place, Ottawa. ✆ **800/555-5621** or 819/776-8600. www.warmuseum.ca. C$12 adults, C$10 seniors & students, C$8 children 3–12, free for children 2 & under; C$30 families. Free admission year-round Thurs 4–8pm, July 1 & Nov 11. May & June Mon–Wed 9am–6pm; Thurs 9am–8pm; Sat & Sun 9:30am–6pm. July to Sept 6 Mon–Wed 9am–6pm; Thurs & Fri 9am–8pm; Sat & Sun 9:30am–6pm. Sept 7 to Oct 11 Mon–Wed 9am–6pm; Thurs 9am–8pm; Sat & Sun 9:30am–6pm. Oct 12 to Apr Tues, Wed & Fri 9am–5pm; Thurs 9am–8pm; Sat & Sun 9:30am–5pm. Closed 1 week early to mid-Jan. From Wellington St. in downtown Ottawa, head west past Booth St. traffic lights until you reach Vimy Place. Turn right into the museum. There is no access to the museum when heading north on Booth St. toward Québec.

National Gallery of Canada ★★ One of the most attractive buildings in the city, the National Gallery, designed by architect Moshe Safdie, glitters and gleams from a promontory overlooking the Ottawa River. Regularly on display are more than 800 paintings, sculptures, and decorative works by Canadian artists, a sampling of the 10,000 works in the permanent collection. Among the highlights are a comprehensive collection of works by Tom Thomson and the Group of Seven, early Québécois artists, and Montreal *automatistes*. European masters are also represented, from Corot and Turner to Chagall and Picasso, and contemporary galleries feature pop art and minimalism, plus abstract works from Canadian and American artists. Budget at least 2 hours of viewing time, and if you're like me, you'll want to take a break at some point to revive your senses. Advance tickets may be purchased for some exhibitions—if you particularly want to see a certain one, avoid disappointment by getting tickets ahead of time. Visit **www.national.gallery.ca** for a full calendar of events and ticket information.

380 Sussex Dr. ✆ **800/319-2787** or 613/990-1985. www.national.gallery.ca. C$9 adults, C$7 seniors & students, C$4 children 12–19, free for children 11 & under; C$18 families. Free admission Thurs 5–8pm. Admission for special exhibitions varies. May–Sept Fri–Wed 10am–5pm, Thurs 10am–8pm; Oct–Apr Tues, Wed & Fri–Sun 10am–5pm, Thurs 10am–8pm.

Canadian Museum of Nature ★★★ ☺ The wonders of the natural world are featured at the Canadian Museum of Nature, housed in the 100-year-old Victoria Memorial Museum building, which was officially recognized for its national historical significance in 2004. The architecture of the building is remarkable. Built of local sandstone, the Tudor-Gothic revival design includes towers, arched windows, a crenellated roofline, magnificent stained-glass windows, and a grand central staircase.

In 2004, a massive rebuilding project began, with a new design that included a spectacular glass "Lantern" at the front of the building, which replaces the original tower. The renovation was unveiled in May 2010.

Parts of western Canada have yielded exceptional finds of dinosaur skeletons, and the museum has some particularly good specimens. Canada's mammals are featured on the second floor, many of them showcased to great effect in dioramas painted by famed Manitoba landscape artist Clarence Tillenius in the 1950s.

The second floor also houses the **Blue Water Gallery,** which contains one of just two massive blue whales on display in Canada. A number of hands-on exhibits are already proving to be very popular with young visitors. The **Earth Gallery** dominates the museum's third floor and features more than 800 rock and mineral specimens, as well as a high-definition digital globe that illustrates how the Earth evolved. The **Bird Gallery** on the fourth floor displays hundreds of species and is one of the world's largest collections of Canadian birds. This gallery is highly interactive, with touchscreen computer displays and a wild-bird play area for younger children.

Victoria Memorial Museum bldg., 240 McLeod St. ✆ **800/263-4433** or 613/566-4700. www.nature.ca. C$10 adults, free for children 2 & under; C$25 families. Free admission Thurs 5–8pm. Sat–Wed 9am–6pm, Thurs & Fri 9am–8pm. Located at the corner of Metcalfe & McLeod sts., 1 block west of Elgin St.

Canada Science and Technology Museum ★★ ☺ Easy to overlook because it is located outside the downtown core, this excellent museum has eye-catching interactive exhibits at every turn. Plan a half-day visit here if you or your kids enjoy applied science. One of the most intriguing long-term exhibits is **Canada in Space.** A space flight simulator will take you on a virtual voyage in a six-seat cinema pod that moves to the action on the huge screen. A separate ticket at a cost of C$3 is required.

The **Locomotive Hall** holds four huge steam locomotives, meticulously restored and maintained. You can climb in the cabs of some of them and you can also see a caboose, business car, and old number boards, and hear sound effects that give you the feel of riding in a live locomotive. Lively, short demonstrations on various science and technology topics are held frequently during the day; ask for show times and topics when you arrive, and take in an entertaining show or two during your visit.

1867 St. Laurent Blvd. ✆ **866/442-4416** or 613/991-3044. www.sciencetech.technomuses.ca. C$9 adults, C$6 seniors & students, C$4 children 4–14, free for children 3 & under; C$20 families. Simulator ride ticket C$3. May to Labour Day daily 9am–5pm; after Labour Day to Apr Tues–Sun 9am–5pm. From the Queensway (Hwy. 417), take the St. Laurent Blvd. South exit. Go south on St. Laurent Blvd. to Lancaster Rd. & turn left. The museum entrance is on the left.

Canada Aviation Museum ★★ One of the world's best collections of vintage aircraft is on display here, with the emphasis on Canada's significant role in aviation history. Whether you're young or old, you'll find something to catch your interest as you stroll through the huge exhibition hall and trace the history of aviation from its beginning to the jet age. You can come close (but not close enough to touch) to more than 50 aircraft inside the building and a number of others displayed outside in the summer months; the total number of aircraft in the collection is approximately 130. Several interactive displays designed to teach the principles of flight are simple enough for children to operate and understand.

If you're looking for something a little different, try an evening program with scheduled events and dinner, or an overnight stay, where you can explore the museum by flashlight and sleep under the wings of an airplane. If you are an aviation buff or just love to fly, take advantage of a rare opportunity and splurge on a vintage aircraft flight, available from May to autumn. A 15-minute ride in an open-cockpit Waco UPF-7 biplane costs C$75 for a tour of Parliament Hill and downtown Ottawa or C$110 for a flight that also includes the Gatineau Hills. Prices are per person, based on two passengers per flight.

11 Aviation Pkwy. ✆ **800/463-2038** or 613/993-2010. www.aviation.technomuses.ca. C$9 adults, C$6 seniors & students, C$5 children 4–15, free for children 3 & under; C$18 families. Free admission daily 4–5pm. May to Labour Day daily 9am–5pm; after Labor Day to Apr Wed–Sun 10am–5pm. Closed Mon & Tues in winter, except holidays & school breaks. From downtown, travel northeast on Sussex Dr. (changes name to Rockcliffe Pkwy.) to Aviation Pkwy. Follow signs; museum is on the left.

RCMP Musical Ride Centre at Rockcliffe Stables The Mounties are one of the most recognizable symbols of Canada throughout the world, and the police force's Musical Ride—which features mounted riders on highly trained horses—is its highest-profile public element. Free tours of the training school and stables of the RCMP Musical Ride are available year-round. In the summer months, you'll find greater numbers of visitors and more frequent tour schedules. In the winter, it's advisable to call ahead and set up a time with the coordinator, although it's not essential. If you happen to visit on a day when the riders aren't practicing, or if the ride is away on tour across Canada (which happens often during the summer—check the Musical Ride website for an updated tour schedule), try to get tickets to one of their shows.

Northeast corner of Sandridge Rd. & St. Laurent Blvd. ✆ **613/741-4285.** www.rcmp-grc.gc.ca/mr-ce/centre-eng.htm. Free admission (donations accepted). May–Aug daily 9am–3:30pm; Sept–Apr Mon–Fri 10am–2pm. From downtown, follow Sussex Dr. (changes name to Rockcliffe Pkwy.) to Aviation Pkwy; follow the signs.

More Museums & Galleries

Bytown Museum ★ Housed in Ottawa's oldest stone building (1827), which served as the commissariat during the construction of the Rideau Canal, this museum is operated by the Historical Society of Ottawa. Articles belonging to Lieutenant Colonel John By, the canal's builder and one of Ottawa's (then known as Bytown) most influential citizens, are on display. In addition, artifacts reflect the social history of local pioneer families in four period rooms and a number of changing exhibits. The rooms depict an 1850s Bytown kitchen, a French-Canadian lumber camp shanty, a Victorian parlor, and an early toy store. In 2008, the museum introduced a new audio tour that is available in six different languages and included in the price of admission. The museum is situated beside the Ottawa Locks, sandwiched between Parliament Hill and the Fairmont Château Laurier Hotel, and is worth a brief visit.

Beside Ottawa Locks. ✆ **613/234-4570.** www.bytownmuseum.com. C$6 adults, C$4 seniors & children 13–18, C$3 children 5–12, free for children 4 & under; C$15 families. Free admission Mid-May to mid-Oct Thurs 5–9pm. Mid-May to mid-Oct Fri–Wed 10am–5pm, Thurs 10am–9pm; mid-Oct to mid-May daily 11am–4pm.

Royal Canadian Mint ★ Established in 1908 to produce Canada's circulation coins, the Royal Canadian Mint is the oldest and one of the largest gold refineries in the Western Hemisphere. The mint also enjoys an excellent reputation around the world for producing high-quality coins. Since 1976, this facility has concentrated on producing numismatic (commemorative) coins. As you might expect, security is exceptionally high; double gates and watchful guards ensure that nothing valuable leaves the building. When you enter the stone "castle," you find yourself in a foyer with a set of stairs leading upward on your left and an elevator straight ahead. Both will take you to the boutique, which displays the many coins and souvenirs available for purchase in well-lit glass showcases around the room. When it's time for the tour, you're ushered into a small theater to watch a short film on a selected aspect of the mint's activities. Next your guide accompanies you to the viewing gallery, which winds its way through the factory. There is a lot to see here, and the tour guide outlines the process of manufacturing coins as you move along the corridor above the factory floor. The process is fascinating, from the rollers that transform the cast bars into flattened strips, to tubs of blanks that have been punched from the strips, to workers hand-drying the blanks after washing, right to the final inspection and hand packaging of the finished coins.

320 Sussex Dr. ✆ **800/276-7714** or 613/993-8990. www.mint.ca. C$5 adults, C$4 seniors, C$3 children 5–17, free for children 4 & under, C$13 families Mon–Fri; C$3.50 adults, C$2.80 seniors, C$2 children 5–17, free for children 4 & under, C$10 families Sat & Sun. Victoria Day (third Mon in May) to Labour Day Mon–Fri 9am–6pm, Sat & Sun 9am–4:30pm; rest of the year daily 9am–4pm. Call for reservations for guided tours.

Heritage Attractions

ByWard Market ★ For many Ottawans, the heart and soul of the city is the ByWard Market. It's where they go for fresh produce early in the morning and to let their hair down late into the night. I love it at both times—particularly the smells and general bustle surrounding the open-air stalls early in the day and the beautifully lit courtyards just east of Sussex Drive after dark. In the center of the area, 1 block east of Sussex Drive between York and George streets, lies the ByWard Market building and the outdoor stalls of the farmers' market, where you can buy outstanding fresh local produce, flowers, and other products, such as maple syrup. To complement the produce, you'll find gourmet food vendors inside the market building, as well as dozens of excellent food retailers in the district. Increasingly, the ByWard Market has also attracted independent boutiques, specializing in everything from designer clothing to high-end paper products. At night, the ByWard Market throbs with activity due to its large concentration of bars and restaurants. At night, the east end of the market tends to be dominated by college-age partiers, while the west end is home to upscale restaurants such as **Social**, **Kinki**, and **E18hteen**. One exception to the rule is Murray Street, which tends to be relatively sedate all along its length and is the site of so many first-rate restaurants—including **John Taylor at Domus**, **Navarra**, and **Sweetgrass**—that it has picked up the sobriquet "Gastro Alley."

Between Sussex Dr. & King Edward Ave., Rideau & St. Patrick sts. www.byward-market.com. Outdoor vendors open daily 7am–6pm or later.

Rideau Hall ★★ Rideau Hall has been the official residence and workplace of Canada's governor-general since 1867 and is considered to be the symbolic home of all Canadians. The public is welcome to wander the 32 hectares (79 acres) of beautiful gardens and forested areas, and visit the greenhouse—and for that reason alone, the place is worth a visit; the grounds are exceptional. Outdoor concerts and cricket matches are held in the summer, and there's ice skating on the pond in winter. Free guided tours of the staterooms of the residence are offered; hours vary throughout the year, although in peak tourist season in the summer, there are self-guided tours every

GATINEAU park ★★

One of the star attractions in an Ottawa visit is **Gatineau Park,** which is across the river in Québec. It begins just 3km (2 miles) from Parliament, yet holds some 35,000 hectares (86,486 acres) of woodland and lakes, all named after the Québec notary-turned-explorer Nicolas Gatineau. This park was inaugurated in 1938, when the federal government bought up large tracts of land in the Gatineau Hills to put a halt to logging, development, and forest destruction in the region. Black bear, timber wolf, otter, marten, and raccoon are joined by white-tailed deer, beaver, and more than 100 species of birds.

The park's facilities include 145km (90 miles) of **hiking trails** and supervised **swimming beaches** at Meech Lake, Lac Philippe, and Lac la Pêche. Canoes, kayaks, and rowboats can be rented at Lac Philippe and Lac la Pêche. Motorboats are only permitted on Lac la Pêche, where motors up to 10 horsepower may be used for fishing. Most of the park's lakes can be fished (if it's not allowed, it will be posted), too—a Québec license is required, and can be obtained at many of the convenience stores around the park.

Camping facilities are at or near Lac Philippe, accessible by highways 5, 105, and 366; there are also 35 canoe camping sites at Lac la Pêche. For details on camping facilities, contact the **Gatineau Park Visitor Centre,** 33 Scott Rd., Chelsea, PQ J9B 1R5 (✆ **800/465-1867** or 819/827-2020; www.capitaleducanada.gc.ca/gatineau), or the **National Capital Commission,** 40 Elgin St., Suite 202, Ottawa, ON K1P 1C7. Reservations are vital.

morning and guided tours in the afternoons, approximately 45 minutes long. The Governor General's Awards are presented here annually, honoring Canadians for extraordinary accomplishments, courage, and contributions to science, the arts, and humanity. Two major events are held annually for the public—the Garden Party in June or July and the Winter Celebration. The Ceremonial Guard is on duty at Rideau Hall during July and August. The first Changing of the Guard Ceremony, held in late June, features a colorful parade led by a marching band. Relief of the Sentries is a ceremony performed hourly during the summer, 9am to 5pm, and is always popular with young children. The visitor center, operating daily between May and October, has family activities, a play structure, and hands-on activities for children.

1 Sussex Dr. ✆ **866/842-4422** or 613/991-4422. www.gg.ca. Free admission (including tours & activities). Grounds daily 8am to 1 hr. before sunset (subject to change without notice). From the Queensway, take the Nicholas St. exit (exit 118), turn left on Rideau St., then right on Sussex Dr. The entrance to Rideau Hall is on the right, just after crossing the Rideau River.

Parks & Gardens

One of the first things you'll notice about Ottawa is how much green space there is within the city's core. In fact, two parks dominate the downtown area, providing terrific sites for outdoor festivals. **Confederation Park,** on Elgin Street, is home to **Winterlude** and the **Ottawa International Jazz Festival.** There are memorials to Canadian history here, including a fountain that originally stood in Trafalgar Square in London and has been dedicated to **Lieutenant Colonel John By,** the British engineer who supervised the building of the Rideau Canal. The lieutenant colonel was a major influence in establishing Bytown, as Ottawa was formerly known. **Major's Hill Park,** Ottawa's oldest park, established in 1874, is tucked in behind the Fairmont Château Laurier. A statue of Lieutenant Colonel By stands close to the site of his house, which was destroyed by fire. This park offers outstanding views of the Parliament Buildings, the Rideau Canal, the Ottawa River, the city of Gatineau and the hills beyond, and the National Gallery of Canada. It's also a major site for many festivals and events, including the **Canadian Tulip Festival.** At the tip of the park, just north of the National Gallery of Canada, you'll find **Nepean Point.** You can share the view with a statue of **Samuel de Champlain,** who first explored the Ottawa River in 1613. The **Astrolabe Theatre,** a venue for summer concerts and events, is located here.

Hog's Back Park is situated at the point where the Rideau Canal meets the Rideau River. A refreshment pavilion, parking, and restrooms are available. Immediately south is **Mooney's Bay Park,** which has a supervised, sandy swimming beach, a playground, shade trees, a refreshment pavilion, and public restrooms. Cross-country skiing is available in the winter, on 5km (3 miles) of groomed, well-lit trails. In the same vicinity, on Heron Road, west of Riverside Drive and just north of Hog's Back Park, is **Vincent Massey Park,** a popular place for family celebrations and other large gatherings. Amenities include ball diamonds, horseshoe pits, a bandstand, picnic tables, fireplaces, a refreshment pavilion, playing fields, recreational pathways, drinking fountains, and public restrooms. A parking fee is charged from May to October.

When it's time to let off some steam, there's **canoeing** or **boating** at Dow's Lake, **biking** along the canal or **ice skating** on it, plus activities outside the city in Gatineau Park.

SPECIAL EVENTS & FESTIVALS

In a city that gets as cold as Ottawa does, there are only two ways you can approach winter: hibernate or celebrate. On the first three weekends each February, **Winterlude** (✆ **800/465-1867;** www.canadascapital.gc.ca/winterlude) takes over the city of Ottawa with parades, family winter fun in the snow and ice. Sites on both sides of the Ottawa River are transformed into winter wonderlands filled with gigantic snow sculptures, glittering ice sculptures, and a Snowflake Kingdom especially for kids. Children's entertainment, craft workshops, horse-drawn sleigh rides, snowboarding demonstrations, dogsled rides, and more are on offer for little ones.

But Ottawa's *biggest* annual event, surprisingly, is the **Canadian Tulip Festival** (✆ **613/567-5757** or 800/66-TULIP; www.tulipfestival.ca), which takes places over 2 weeks in mid-May. Ottawa blooms with millions of tulips every spring, courtesy of an annual gift of bulbs from the Netherlands, given in gratitude for Canada's sheltering of the Dutch royal family during World War II. Visitors can view the blooms at sites along a 15km (9¼-mile) Tulip Route, explore the Tulip Explosion floral design show, or catch concerts and a craft show in Major's Hill Park.

Mid-June brings the **Festival Franco-Ontarien** (✆ **613/321-0102;** www.ffo.ca), a 3-day celebration of Francophone Canada, featuring classical and other musical concerts, fashion shows, street performers, games and competitions, crafts, and French cuisine. Also in mid-June, the city is filled with the sounds of the **Ottawa International Jazz Festival** (✆ **613/241-2633** or 888/226-4495; www.ottawajazzfestival.com). Local, national, and international artists give more than 125 performances at more than 20 venues.

Each July 1, hundreds of thousands of Canadians gather in Ottawa to celebrate **Canada Day** (✆ **800/465-1867;** www.capcan.ca/canadaday)—activities center around Parliament Hill, Majors Hill Park, and Jacques-Cartier Park in Hull. Shows, street performers, and concerts mark the event. Don't miss the spectacular nighttime fireworks display over the Ottawa River. The 2-week **Ottawa Chamber Music Festival** (✆ **613/234-8008;** www.chamberfest.com), the world's largest, brings dozens of concerts to the city's most beautiful churches in late July and early August.

On Labour Day weekend (early Sept), about 150 brilliantly colored balloons fill the skies over Ottawa, while on the ground, people flock to musical events and midway rides during the **Gatineau Hot Air Balloon Festival** (✆ **819/243-2331;** www.balloongatineau.com).

OUTDOOR ACTIVITIES & SPECTATOR SPORTS

BIKING Ottawans are enthusiastic cyclists, fully utilizing the more than 370km (230 miles) of major bike routes and 273km (170 miles) of minor routes in the City of Ottawa. Designated recreational pathways in the National Capital Region account for 170km (106 miles) of this total. If you didn't bring your own equipment, **Rent-A-Bike** (on the east side of the Rideau Canal at Plaza Bridge, next to Paul's Boat Lines; ✆ **613/241-4140;** www.rentabike.ca) has all kinds of bikes, including standard hybrid bikes designed for comfortable, leisurely touring; standard light-trail mountain bikes; on- and off-road performance bikes; and on-road tandems. Bikes and in-line skates can also be rented at **Dow's Lake Marina Pavilion** (✆ **613/232-5278**), located on the Rideau Canal at 1001 Queen Elizabeth Dr. **OC Transpo,** Ottawa's public transit system, has installed bike racks on more than 300 buses—most buses on routes 12, 85, 95, 96, 97, 99, 101, 106, and 118 have racks. There's no cost to use the rack, other than regular bus fare. The program runs from spring through fall.

BOATING/CANOEING If you want to spend a lazy summer afternoon drifting around in a boat, visit **Dow's Lake Pavilion** (1001 Queen Elizabeth Dr.; ✆ **613/232-1001**). A fully operational marina at the pavilion site on Dow's Lake rents out paddle-boats, canoes, kayaks, and rowboats. Dow's Lake is an artificial lake that provides a quiet place for water recreation away from the main traffic in the Rideau Canal. In **Gatineau Park,** boat rentals are available at **Philippe Lake** and **La Pêche Lake.** Call ✆ **819/827-2020** to check opening hours for the rental booths.

GOLF The Ottawa metro region offers more than 60 courses in all, including the one on the premises of the **Château Montebello** in Québec (✆ **819/423-6341**). Greens fees for 18 holes generally run C$30 to C$50, but are more expensive at resorts.

HIKING & NATURE WALKS As well as checking out the pathways and trails through many of Ottawa's **city parks** and the **greenbelt** area, you might wish to explore **Gatineau Park,** the **Rideau Trail,** and parts of the **Trans Canada Trail,** particularly if you're looking for more challenging, longer routes.

The **Rideau Trail** is a cleared and marked hiking trail approximately 380km (236 miles) long that links Ottawa with the city of Kingston, on the shores of Lake Ontario. The trail path is indicated by orange triangular markers. To distinguish the two directions, Kingston-bound markers have yellow tips. The trail is designated for walking, cross-country skiing, and snowshoeing. You can pick up a comprehensive guide book with maps and a description of the trail for C$40 from the **Rideau Trail Association** (P.O. Box 15, Kingston, ON K7L 4V6; ✆ **613/545-0823**) or order one online at www.rideautrail.org.

SKATING The number-one place to skate in the nation's capital is the world-famous **Rideau Canal Skateway.** If you visit Ottawa during the skating season, you must take everyone for a glide along the canal—it's an experience not to be missed. The Skateway is the world's largest outdoor skating rink, offering almost 8km (5 miles) of continuous skating surface. The ice is usually ready in early January, and the season lasts until early March. Skating is free. Heated shelters, skate and sled rentals, boot-check and skate-sharpening services, rest areas, food concessions, and toilets are located at various points along the Skateway. There are many access points along the canal for skating, so it's easy to get on the ice. To find out about ice conditions on the Rideau Canal, call the Skateway hotline at ✆ **613/239-5234.**

SKIING You're spoiled with choice for cross-country skiing in the Ottawa area. If you want to use the trails throughout the extensive **greenbelt,** consult the **"Greenbelt All Seasons Trail Map."** All trails are suitable for beginner and family outings. Many of the trails pass through wooded areas. Or go to **Mooney's Bay Cross-country Ski Centre** (2960 Riverside Dr.; ✆ **613/247-4883**) and ski on 5km (3.1 miles) of groomed and well-lit trails. Classic and skate skiing are available at a nominal fee. Across the Ottawa River in the city of **Gatineau,** you'll find **Parc du Lac Beauchamp** at 745 boul. Maloney (✆ **819/669-2548**). Winter activities in the park include outdoor ice skating and 15km (9.3 miles) of cross-country ski trails. Equipment rental is available.

For the ultimate cross-country ski experience, visit **Gatineau Park.** The park has earned a reputation as one of the best ski-trail networks in North America due to its remarkable 200km (124 miles) of trails. Both skiing styles are accommodated throughout the park, so you can glide along in classic Nordic fashion or burn up energy with the skate-skiing technique. There are eight heated shelters where you can stop to rest and refuel with a snack from your backpack. Gatineau Park ski patrollers are on watch to assist skiers in difficulty. When you arrive at the park, you can buy a day pass at any of the 16 parking lots, which give direct access to the ski trails, or at the **Gatineau Park Visitor Centre** (33 Scott Rd., Chelsea, QC; ✆ **819/827-2020**), open throughout the year daily from 9am to 5pm. Daily pass prices for cross-country ski trails are C$13 adults; C$9 seniors, students, and children 13 to 17; free for children 12 and under; and C$27 for families.

SWIMMING Pools open to the public include those at **Carleton University** on Colonel By Drive, the University of Ottawa at 125 University Dr., and the YMCA-YWCA at 180 Argyle Dr. Lake swimming is available in **Gatineau Park, Meech Lake, Lac la Pêche,** and at **Lac Philippe.**

WHITE-WATER RAFTING Enjoy the exhilaration of a day of white-water rafting and be back in your hotel bed that night. Outings are available from mid-May to September, depending on the river. **Owl Rafting** (✆ **613/646-2263** in summer, or 613/238-7238 in winter; www.owlrafting.com) offers white-water rafting trips within 90 minutes of the city, pounding over extensive rapids for the fit and adventurous and floating on gentler stretches for families. Prices start at around C$100 per person per day during the week, more on the weekends, meals included. Shorter trips of 2 hours are intended for families and are more cost effective.

Spectator Sports

The **Ottawa Senators** (✆ **800/444-7367** or 613/599-0200; www.capitaltickets.ca) won the NHL's Eastern Conference in 2007, but that success is starting to become a distant memory; nonetheless, their fans are devoted and there's not a bad seat in the arena for watching hockey. The team plays at Scotiabank Place, west of the city center. Tickets mostly cost from C$30 to C$80; call ✆ **613/599-3267.**

OTTAWA AFTER DARK

Ottawa has many things going for it, but a dynamic, year-round cultural scene and thriving nightlife are not among them. True, the city has seen an upswing in high-end restaurants, and there have always been bars that cater to students from the three main postsecondary schools, but Ottawa will never be mistaken for Toronto, Vancouver, or San Francisco. Fortunately, the fact that the city is the national capital means government money subsidizes some major cultural institutions and annual festivals that might not otherwise exist without more grassroots arts infrastructure.

Most of the after-dark action is centered around the ByWard Market, although Hull (now the Hull sector of Gatineau) has long held the reputation as the city where Ottawans go to play at night. Today, most of that action happens at the **Casino du Lac-Leamy.**

FINDING OUT WHAT'S ON For current live music, theater, and film—particularly aimed at young audiences—your best bet for finding out what's happening and where is to pick up a copy of ***Ottawa Xpress,*** a free publication distributed each Thursday, or read it online at www.ottawaxpress.ca. ***Where Ottawa/Gatineau,*** a free monthly tourist guide listing entertainment, shopping, and dining, is available at hotels and stores in the city. ***Voir*** is a French-language weekly arts-and-entertainment paper that lists some venues and events in Gatineau, as well as Ottawa.

Visiting families should keep an eye out for ***Capital Parent,*** a free monthly newspaper that's available at 400 outlets. The ***Ottawa Citizen*** has a comprehensive Arts section on Friday with an emphasis on films and a special "Going Out" section on Saturday, which lists upcoming live entertainment events.

The Performing Arts

Canadian and international musical, dance, and theater artists—including the resident NAC Orchestra—perform at the expansive **National Arts Centre,** located at 53 Elgin St. at Confederation Square (✆ **613/947-7000**; www.nac-cna.ca). The building, created by architect Fred Lebensold, is made of three interlocking hexagons beside the Rideau Canal, its terraces tendering views of Parliament Hill and the Ottawa River. There are three auditoriums: the European-style **Opera;** a 950-seat **Theatre** with an innovative apron stage; and the **Studio,** used for experimental works. The **National Arts Centre Orchestra** performs in seven or eight main concert series here each year. The center also offers classic and modern drama in English and French, and guided tours are also available. Ask for the free monthly *Calendar of NAC Events.*

Augmenting the main events at the National Arts Centre, the ensemble at the **Great Canadian Theatre Company** (✆ **613/236-5196;** www.gctc.ca) has been providing bold, innovative, and thought-provoking theater for more than a quarter of a century. Featuring predominantly Canadian playwrights and local actors, the season runs from September to March in a sparkling theater facility known as the **Irving Greenberg Theatre Centre.** It's located at 1233 Wellington St. W. (at Holland Ave.).

Music Clubs

It is the era of the DJ, the sports bar, and the high-end martini place. Consequently, Ottawa's popular music scene has seen better times, and likely will again. These things tend to go in cycles, and clubs come and go. A good example of these trends is **Barrymore's Music Hall** (323 Bank St.; ✆ **613/233-0307**). In its heyday, it regularly featured top-name performers and became somewhat legendary for playing host to the likes of U2 and Tina Turner just before they hit the big time. The place has changed hands several times in recent years and now only sporadically features live music.

Supplanting Barrymore's as the city's main venue for live music is **Capital Music Hall** (128 York St.; ✆ **613/789-9922**), which features rock, punk, and hip-hop artists who are on the international tour circuit.

Zaphod Beeblebrox (27 York St.; ✆ **613/562-1010**) is another club that has suffered somewhat from changing musical tastes and the shifting economics of the music business, yet it continues to feature live acts on a regular basis. It is best known for figuring prominently in a video the Rolling Stones shot in Ottawa in 2005.

Some of the most interesting independent acts on the road, particularly American roots and folk musicians, perform at the **Blacksheep Inn** (753 Riverside Dr., Wakefield, QC; ✆ **819/459-3228**), which is located in a picturesque village on the Gatineau River, a 20-minute drive from downtown Ottawa. Still a working-class tavern by day, the Blacksheep gained a higher profile when it became the launching pad for singer-songwriter Kathleen Edwards, who still performs here between world tours.

One genre of music that has always thrived in Ottawa is blues, and although it, too, has fallen on hard times, it continues to rule at the **Rainbow Bistro** (76 Murray St.; ✆ **613/241-5123**). An oddly shaped room (patrons must climb a staircase beside the stage to access the restrooms), the Rainbow has hosted the biggest names in the business and helped launch the careers of Ottawa musicians like Sue Foley. Live music is featured 7 nights a week.

Café Paradiso (199 Bank St.; ✆ **613/565-0657**) features local acts on weekends and occasionally books New York City–based jazz musicians like saxophonist Dave Liebman and singer Sheila Jordan.

The Bar Scene

With three postsecondary institutions and Parliament Hill, you *know* Ottawa must have its share of drinking establishments. In fact, there are now so many bars in the ByWard Market/Lowertown area that the city council has twice issued a moratorium on new liquor licenses there. Elgin Street is also chockablock with bars, and you can find one on almost every block in the Glebe and Ottawa South, too. The trick, as always, is finding the *right* bar. In Ottawa, it's usually a good idea to avoid any bar with a name that sounds like a double entendre or a tawdry pickup line—this is a three-college town, after all. Usually, that means staying away from the area of the ByWard Market east of William Street, especially on York Street, and from Elgin Street south of Somerset Street West (with the exception of the Manx and a couple of others). The recommendations here attempt to cover all the bases, including places where the only wines sold are either house red or white, and some where martinis come in every color of the rainbow.

ARC Lounge The lounge bar at ARC The.Hotel (p. 332) is sleek, minimalist, and sophisticated. Try their signature martini, the Arctini. An upscale destination. 140 Slater St. (in ARC The.Hotel). ✆ **613/238-9998.** www.arclounge.ca.

The Barley Mow Cask-conditioned ales and about 18 microbrews and imported beers on tap, plus an extensive selection of single-malt Scotch, earns this pub a nod from beer and whiskey lovers. 1060 Bank St. ✆ **613/730-1279.**

Earl of Sussex Located right on the tourist track, the Earl of Sussex is an English-style pub, with wing chairs, a fireplace, and a dartboard. The atmosphere is friendly and cozy, as tourists mix with regulars and businesspeople. There are more than 30 beers on tap, including European and domestic. The sunny rear patio is popular in warm weather. 431 Sussex Dr. ✆ **613/562-5544.**

The Irish Village In the heart of the ByWard Market, four distinct pubs have come together to make a small "Irish village." The first, the **Heart & Crown,** opened in 1992. A few years later, the **Snug Pub** was added with a fireplace and cozy corners for small groups. **Mother McGintey's** and **Roisin Dubh** (the Black Rose) are the most recent additions. All have a good range of beer. Live Celtic music is offered at Heart & Crown and Mother McGintey's several nights a week. Favorite pub fare is served, including fish 'n' chips. 67 Clarence St. ✆ **613/562-0674.** www.irishvillage.ca.

Métropolitain Brasserie & Restaurant This sprawling, Parisian-style bar is located on the ground floor of the city's hottest condominium, and it just oozes style. From the zinc-covered bar to the great jazz that's always playing, this place really does have a European feel to it, but it has yet to catch on with many people. The bar features a wide selection of cocktails and a better-than-average choice of single malts. 700 Sussex Dr. ✆ **613/562-1160.** www.metropolitainbrasserie.com.

Royal Oak You'll bump into Royal Oaks all over town—downtown, east end, west end, the Glebe; there are 13 in total. All locations have a good selection of British and Irish beers on draft. 318 Bank St. ✆ **613/236-0190.** www.royaloakpubs.com.

Gay & Lesbian Bars

Social life and entertainment for the gay and lesbian community in Ottawa is clustered around Bank Street in the vicinity of Frank Street, Somerset Street West, and Lisgar Street. There are also a couple of venues in the ByWard Market district. A free monthly paper, ***Capital Xtra,*** serves the gay and lesbian community and has extensive entertainment listings. You can find it at vendor boxes throughout the downtown core.

CellBlock For those that like an edge to their entertainment, this place draws Ottawa's leather and denim crowd. Part of the **Centretown Pub,** which is located in a three-story Victorian house, the Cell Block is comfortable and friendly and frequented by regulars, mostly men. It has been described as a "gay Cheers." 340 Somerset St. W. ✆ **613/594-0233.**

Lookout This bar attracts a diverse crowd of gays, lesbians, and straights of all ages. The balcony is popular in the summer. On DJ nights, tables are moved back to make room for dancing. Latin music is featured on Sunday. 41 York St. (upstairs). ✆ **613/789-1624.** www.thelookoutbar.com.

EASTERN ONTARIO

By Pamela Cuthbert

From the quiet village of **Port Hope,** 105km (65 miles) east of Toronto, the coast of Lake Ontario takes in the **Bay of Quinte** and **Quinte's Isle.** Once off the speedy main highway (Hwy. 401), you'll discover a tranquil stretch of farmland and waterways that were mostly settled by United Empire Loyalists—British sympathizers who fled the impudent new republic to the south during and after the American Revolution. This region remains off the beaten track today, except to those in the know who come to explore attractive villages; troll for antiques; or enjoy the beaches, dunes, and waterfront activities of the area's provincial parks. **Kingston,** an appealing lakefront city with a regular flea-and-farmers' market, is intriguing both architecturally and historically, and is the gateway to the mighty St. Lawrence River, the **Thousand Islands** region, and **St. Lawrence National Park.**

Kingston ★

A 2-hour drive from Ottawa and about 3 hours from Toronto (172km/107 miles southwest of Ottawa, 255km/158 miles northeast of Toronto), Kingston draws on more than 300 years of history—a history that includes a brief tenure as Canada's capital city. That rich heritage lingers in grand old limestone public buildings and private residences lining downtown's streets; the city has a gracious air. It's a university town, which makes for some lively culture—small galleries, good restaurants—and it's also home to one of the country's biggest jails, the Kingston Penitentiary.

The city is at the confluence of Lake Ontario, the Rideau Canal, and the St. Lawrence Seaway. This position makes for remarkable scenery, best viewed by taking the free ferry to **Wolfe Island.** Ferries leave at frequent intervals for the sparsely populated island that doubles as a quiet offshore retreat. (See the box "A Journey into the Thousand Islands," below, for details about other seagoing sightseeing voyages.) A

A JOURNEY INTO THE thousand ISLANDS

The beautiful St. Lawrence River, which runs some 1,200km (746 miles), was a significant trade route in New France and, to this day, remains Canada's most important commercial waterway. Traveled by explorers, fur traders, and missionaries in the 17th century and later by settlers en route to Ontario and the plains west, the river is still a magnificent sight. In some stretches, the river swells to more than 19km (12 miles) wide.

Along this stretch at Kingston, the St. Lawrence is known primarily for its **Thousand Islands** region. The Thousand Islands are nationally administrated as the **St. Lawrence Islands National Park,** headquartered at 2 C.R. 5 in Mallorytown (✆ **613/923-5261;** www.pc.gc.ca). Canada's smallest national park is a beauty, encompassing an 80km (50-mile) stretch of the St. Lawrence from Kingston to Brockville. Along that stretch, you'll find a good supply of motels, cabin colonies, campgrounds, RV sites, and boat-launching sites, but development has mostly been contained. The park's visitor center and headquarters are on the mainland, where you'll find a picnic area, beach, and nature trail; access to the park's island facilities is via boat only. Most of the islands have docking and picnicking facilities, available on a first-come, first-served basis; primitive campsites cost about C$16 per day. Three consecutive days is the docking limit at each island.

Kingston is a good jumping-off point for touring the Thousand Islands. In summer, **cruise boats** navigate the channels, past such extraordinary sights as **Boldt Castle ★**, built on Heart Island in the early 1900s by millionaire George Boldt as a gift for his wife. (When she died suddenly, the work was abandoned, and it stands as a symbol of loss.) From Kingston Harbour at City Hall, in May to mid-October, you can take a 3-hour cruise for C$32 adults, C$16 children 4 to 12, on the ***Island Queen,*** a triple-deck paddle wheeler; a lunch on the boat during the cruise costs extra. The 90-minute cruises (about C$24 adults, C$12 children 4–12) aboard its sister boat, the ***Island Belle,*** take in the Kingston Harbour and waterfront. Both boats are used for 2-hour sunset cruises. Sunset dinner cruises of 3½ hours are also available. For details, call ✆ **613/549-5544** or check the website **www.1000islandscruises.ca.**

Eastern Ontario

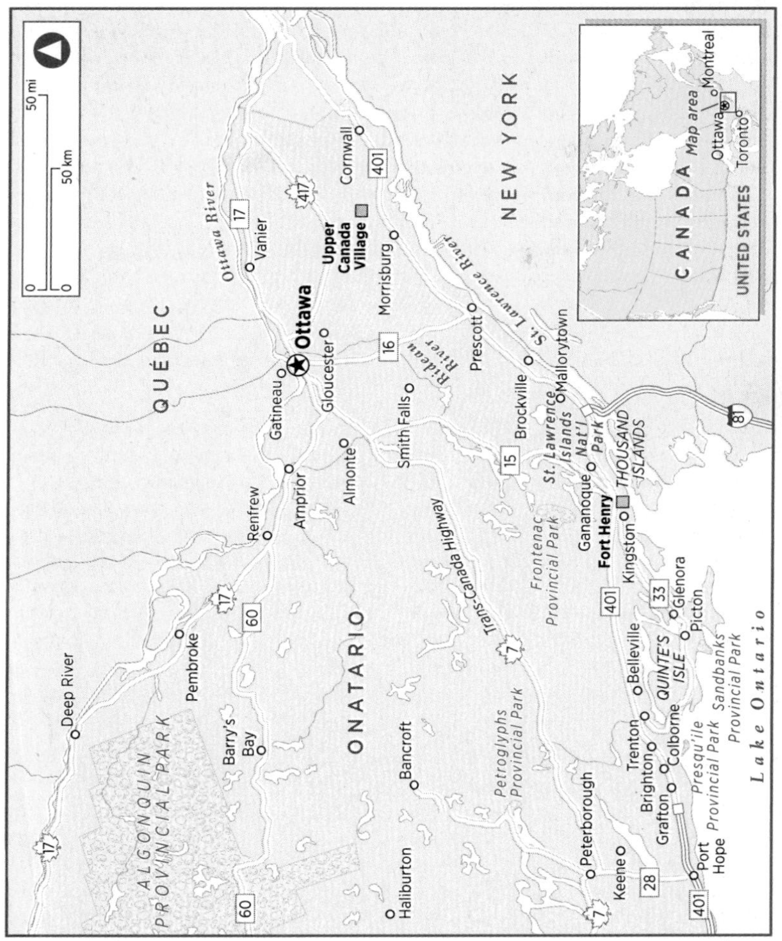

stroll along Kingston's waterfront is a must; there are many hotels and restaurants here, as well as marinas, pocket parks, gardens, and a maritime museum.

During the summer, **Confederation Park,** at the harbor, is the site of blues and buskers festivals, as well as frequent free concerts; in winter, you might catch a local hockey game. Three times a week, a farmers' market assembles behind City Hall in the refurbished **Market Square.** On Sundays, this space is transformed into a flea market with a few lingering produce stalls. It's all worth exploring at your leisure.

Essentials

GETTING THERE If you're driving from Ottawa, take Highway 416 south to Highway 401 (the Trans-Canada Hwy.), then drive west to Kingston. Or, with a little more time, take scenic Route 2 instead. Highway 401 is an expressway, heavily trafficked and good if you want to get from A to B in a hurry. But if you're looking for relaxation, it's best avoided. From Toronto, you have little choice but to take Highway 401 directly east to the Kingston exits.

If you want to take public transit, several comfortable daily **VIA Rail** (✆ **888/VIA-RAIL;** www.viarail.ca) trains run through Kingston coming from Ottawa, Toronto, and Montréal.

VISITOR INFORMATION Stop by the handsome **Kingston Tourist Information Office** at 209 Ontario St. (✆ **888/855-4555** or 613/548-4415), housed inside the old railroad station on the waterfront across from City Hall. Its attendants can help you find lodging and sell tickets for the bus tours that start out front. Also consult the city's tourism website at **http://tourism.kingstoncanada.com.**

EXPLORING THE TOWN

Get a street map as soon as you arrive; this isn't one of those cities where a handy sign is available on every corner. A good way to get acquainted with the town is aboard the **Confederation Tour Trolley** (✆ **613/548-4415**), a bus made to look like a streetcar. It leaves from in front of the Tourist Information Office (see above) every hour on the hour from mid-May to Labour Day 10am to 5pm (July and Aug 10am–7pm). The tour lasts 50 minutes and costs C$15 adults, C$10 seniors and children ages 6 and up. If you want to explore **Wolfe Island,** there's a free 25-minute trip aboard the **car ferry** from downtown Kingston; it departs frequently from the dock near the intersection of Queen and Ontario streets. Or, if you want to do some serious hiking, the **Rideau Trail** runs 390km (242 miles) along the Rideau Canal from Kingston all the way to Ottawa. For details, contact the **Rideau Trail Association** at ✆ **613/545-0823.**

Kingston was built for defense. The attack never came, however, which is why there are walls, forts, and other strategic structures in good condition. You can view some of these along the waterfront, where **Confederation Park** stretches from the front of the old 19th-century town hall down to the yacht basin. Several blocks west of the park is one of the city's finest Martello towers, built during the Oregon Crisis of 1846 to withstand naval bombardments. The moated, cylindrical **Murney Tower** (✆ **613/544-9925**) is now a museum where you can see the basement storage rooms, the barracks room, and the gun platform. Mid-May to Labour Day, it's open daily 10am to 5pm, charging C$4 adults; admission is free for kids.

While exploring downtown or ambling along the waterfront, visit **City Hall** at 216 Ontario St. (✆ **613/546-4291**); free guided tours are offered weekdays from 10am to 4pm, weekends from 11am to 3pm. If there isn't enough time, at least take a look at the stained-glass windows upstairs in Memorial Hall, each one commemorating a World War I battle. It's open weekdays from around 8:30am until 4:30pm.

Agnes Etherington Art Centre ★ On the campus of Queen's University, the center displays a good collection in seven galleries. The emphasis is Canadian, though there are also African sculpture and 16th- to 19th-century European masters.

The center's heart is in the original 19th-century home of benefactor Agnes Richardson Etherington, and three rooms are furnished in period style.

University Ave. (at Bader Lane). ✆ **613/533-2190.** C$4 adults, C$2.50 seniors, free for students & children; free admission Thurs. Tues–Fri 10am–4:30pm; Sat & Sun 1–5pm.

Bellevue House On July 1, 1867, Canada was officially born; the Canadian Confederation was proclaimed in Kingston's Market Square. One of the chief architects of that great political construction was Canada's first prime minister, Sir John A. Macdonald. Kingston was his home for most of his life, where he lived at Bellevue House as a young lawyer and as a rising member of Parliament. Now a National Historic Site, the building is a stucco-faced, vaguely Italianate villa with green trim and a red roof, jokingly referred to as the "Pekoe Pagoda" or the "Tea Caddy Castle" by some locals. Apple trees and hollyhocks fill the front yard, and costumed docents greet visitors. It has been restored to the period of 1848 to 1849, and afternoon tea is served here. Reservations recommended.

35 Centre St. ✆ **613/545-8666.** www.pc.gc.ca. C$3.90 adults, C$3.40 seniors, C$1.90 children 6–15; C$9.90 families. Apr, May & day after Labour Day to Oct daily 10am–5pm; June to Labour Day daily 9am–6pm.

Fort Henry ★ Fort Henry, erected in 1812 and largely unchanged since its reconstruction in the 1830s, commands a high promontory overlooking the harbor and town. From Victoria Day (mid-May) until the end of August, the Fort Henry Guard and their goat mascot, David, perform 19th-century drills, musters, and parades. Regular programming includes music and marching displays by the fife-and-drum band, exhibitions of infantry drill, and mock battles of tall ships, many of them brought to a close with the firing of the garrison artillery and the lowering of the Union Jack. Parts of the fort—the officers' quarters, men's barracks, kitchens, and artisans' shops—have been restored to show the military way of life as it was around the year 1867. The most impressive events are the Sunset Ceremonies, elaborate military maneuvers with martial music performed Wednesdays at 7:30pm in July and August. On those nights, a three-course dinner (starting at C$65) is served in the officers' dining room before the Ceremonies.

On Rte. 2, just east of Kingston. ✆ **613/542-9127.** www.forthenry.com. C$11 adults, C$9.75 seniors, C$8.50 children 13–18, C$5.50 children 5–12, C$2 children 2–4; slight discounts in Sept. Sunset Ceremonies C$17 adults, C$16 seniors, C$14 children 13–18, C$11 children 5–12, C$2 children 2–4. Late May to Sept daily 10am–5pm, 7:30pm during Sunset Ceremony days.

Marine Museum of the Great Lakes ★ Stop by the Marine Museum to get a handle on the importance of shipping on the Great Lakes, which were critical in the development of central Canada. With model boats, memorabilia, vintage photos, and salvaged engines, the museum outlines the evolution from sailing in the 17th century to steamships in the 19th century, from the great schooners of the 1870s to today's bulk freighter carriers that still ply these waters. Moored at the far end of the museum is the 64m (210-ft.) ***Alexander Henry.*** A retired Coast Guard icebreaker, it can be toured, and it also functions as an offbeat **bed and breakfast ★** with 25 simple, compact cabins available from around mid-May until Labour Day; double rates are C$95 to C$125 per cabin, with many single bunks in shared rooms also available. Breakfast and museum admission are included.

55 Ontario St. ✆ **613/542-2261.** www.marmuseum.ca. C$6.50 adults, C$6 seniors & students; C$13 families. May–Sept daily 10am–4pm; off-season by appointment only.

Side Trips to Frontenac Provincial Park & Upper Canada Village

Frontenac Provincial Park (✆ **613/376-3489**), near Sydenham, about 143km (89 miles) from Kingston and 72km (45 miles) from Ottawa, is a wilderness park with more than 182km (113 miles) of hiking trails exploring Moulton Gorge, the Arkon Lake bogs, and the Connor-Daly mine.

There are also terrific opportunities here to combine camping with water journeys; an adventure might include sea kayaking among the Thousand Islands, for instance, with equipment supplied by a local outfitter. **Frontenac Outfitters** (✆ **613/376-6220,** or 800/250-3174 from Ontario) rents canoes, kayaks, paddles, life jackets, and car-top carriers for relatively modest fees, starting from C$25 per person per day. Both wooded and waterfront campsites are also available through the same outfitter, for C$25 per day (maximum of four campers per site). A program of guided tours through the region runs from about April to November.

About 50km (31 miles) east of Brockville along Route 2, just east of Morrisburg, is **Upper Canada Village** ★ (✆ **800/437-2233** or 613/543-4328; www.uppercanadavillage.com). This is Ontario's effort to preserve its pre-Dominion past, and the sprawling riverfront museum village represents frontier life in the 1860s, with some 40 brick-and-stone structures and interiors that have been accurately restored using hand-forged nails and wooden pegs. They appear as if they could still serve their purpose today, and they're occupied by costumed bilingual docents who answer questions while performing the chores and crafts of the day—sewing quilts, milling lumber, fashioning tin-ware, conducting church services, and the like. In the woolen mill, a waterwheel turns old machinery weaving wool into blankets; bellows wheeze and hammers clang against anvils in the blacksmith's shop; and the heady aroma of fresh bread drifts from a bake shop near the Willard's Hotel (which serves lunch and high tea, C$5.99-C$29.99). "True Canadian" draft horses draw both tour wagons and a barge. A good spot for history buffs and kids.

Admission to the village is C$20 adults, C$18 seniors, C$12 children 5 to 18, and C$3.95 children 2 to 4; families traveling together get a 10% discount. It's open daily 9:30am to 5pm from mid-May to early October.

Where to Stay

Several chain-style business hotels commandeer prime positions beside the harbor—the **Holiday Inn** (2 Princess St.; ✆ **800/465-4329** or 613/549-8400), the **Confederation Place Hotel** (a former Howard Johnson; 237 Ontario St.; ✆ **888/825-4656** or 613/549-6300), and the **Radisson Kingston Harbourfront** (1 Johnson St.; ✆ **800/333-3333** or 613/549-8100). There's also a **Comfort Inn** at 1454 Princess St. (✆ **800/228-5150** or 613/549-5550).

Best Western Fireside Inn ★ This is an unusually charming Best Western with a cozy lounge off the lobby, rooms with gas fireplaces, and some with Jacuzzis. Some people come for the fantasy suites—beds whimsically placed inside a Rolls-Royce (the Lord and Lady suite) or the basket of a 2½-story hot air balloon, or on a simulated Tranquility Moon Base. The standard rooms are equipped with four-poster canopy beds, marble bathrooms, puffy quilts, sofas, and shelves of old books. The hotel's Bistro Stefan is unexpectedly capable.

1217 Princess St., Kingston, ON K7M 3E1. ✆ **800/567-8800** or 613/549-2211. Fax 613/549-4523. www.bestwestern.kingston.on.ca. 77 units. C$155–C$174 double; from C$220 suite. Suite rates include full breakfast on weekdays. AE, DC, MC, V. **Amenities:** Restaurant; lounge; heated outdoor pool; room service. *In room:* A/C, TV, fridge, hair dryer, Internet (free).

Four Points by Sheraton Hotel & Suites ★ One of the youngest hotels in the city, Kingston's Four Points has an excellent location with great unobstructed views of the town and the lake from the upper floors. The staff is professional and helpful. The 47 suites have fridges and microwaves, and all have PlayStations and high-speed Internet access. Parking in the underground garage is complimentary.

285 King St. E., Kingston, ON K7L 3B1. ✆ **888/478-4333** or 613/544-4434. Fax 613/548-1782. www.fourpoints.com. 171 units. C$159–C$225 double; from C$259 suite. AE, DC, MC, V. **Amenities:** Restaurant; bar; exercise room; whirlpool; heated indoor pool; limited room service. *In room:* A/C, TV, fridge (in some units), hair dryer, Internet (free).

Frontenac Club Inn ★★ On one of the most attractive streets in town, lined with handsome 19th-century houses, this limestone building was originally a bank (built in 1845). Later, it was made a private men's club (in 1903) and, a century later, became a fine bed-and-breakfast. The large common rooms on the ground floor are furnished with oversize leather sofas and chairs, and the breakfast area stretches onto a deck in summer. Bedrooms are on the second and third floors (though there is no elevator); they're spacious and tastefully furnished. Some have gas fireplaces or Jacuzzis.

225 King St. E., Kingston, ON K7L 3A7. ✆ **613/547-6167.** www.frontenacclub.com. 13 units. C$149–C$209 double. Rates include full breakfast. AE, MC, V. *In room:* A/C.

Hochelaga Inn & Spa ★ All the guest rooms are distinctively furnished in this 1870s Victorian, which has recently gone more upscale with the addition of a spa and Jacuzzis in more of the rooms. One favorite is no. 301, an oddly shaped space with a love seat and a bed set on a diagonal, a large armoire, steps leading to an 11-sided tower with windows, and a stepladder reaching a tiny sitting area. Other rooms are furnished with oak pieces and wing chairs. Enjoy the sitting room with its carved ebony fireplace or take a seat on the veranda facing the garden. The day spa features aromatherapy, massage, manicures, facials, and body treatments.

24 Sydenham St., Kingston, ON K7L 3G9. ✆ **877/933-9433** or ✆/fax 613/549-5534. www.hochelagainn.com. 21 units. C$115–C$205 double. Rates include buffet breakfast. AE, MC, V. **Amenities:** Spa. *In room:* A/C, TV, hair dryer, Internet (free).

Where to Dine

Kingston is a university town, so there are plenty of pizzerias—including some with wood-burning ovens—and coffee shops. The city is short on fine dining, but there are lots of casual, unpretentious, and pretty good spots that satisfy a range of budgets.

Casa Dominico ★★ ITALIAN The front windows open in summer, a fireplace blazes in winter, and this upscale downtown rendezvous is busy almost every night of the year. Renovations make for a more sophisticated ambience than its previous look, and it has a menu to match. Standards include a generous Caesar salad, eggplant Parmigiana, and many pasta dishes. Main courses might run to free-range chicken in a mushroom sauce, roasted salmon, tiger shrimp in a lobster sauce, an oven-roasted pork chop with saltimbocca sauce, or a grilled steak in mushrooms and Madeira, paired with Gorgonzola-flavored fries. Popular with large parties, as well as romantic couples, it's noisy (in a happy way), and the food is worth it.

35 Brock St. ✆ **613/542-0870.** Reservations recommended. Main courses lunch C$10–C$18, dinner C$15–C$34. AE, MC, V. Mon–Sat 11:30am–2:30pm; Mon–Thurs & Sun 5–10pm, Fri & Sat 5–11pm.

Chez Piggy ★★ ECLECTIC Just off Princess Street in a complex of renovated 19th-century buildings, this remains one of Kingston's favorite restaurants. Out front is a paved dining courtyard, and inside are a long bar and an upstairs dining room. Dinner possibilities include rack of venison, rib steaks, duck-leg confit, or any one of the half-dozen pastas; daily specials could include teriyaki salmon or fried chorizo with black-bean cakes and eggs. This is also a good place to put together a meal of several appetizers; try the Vietnamese salad, heaping antipasto platter, or Calabrese salad with sausage and grilled asparagus. Prix-fixe meals are offered nightly.

68 Princess St. ✆ **613/549-7673.** Reservations recommended on weekends. Main courses lunch C$9–C$18, dinner C$14–C$30. AE, DC, MC, V. Mon–Sat 11:30am–midnight; Sun 11am–midnight.

Kingston Brewing Company PUB FARE Peer through the window behind the bar at the huge brewing tanks in this, one of Ontario's first microbrew pubs. Lagers, ales, and specialty brews are produced here, including the popular Dragon's Breath Ale—so rich it's almost syrupy. Locals come here for substantial fare: monster burgers, fat onion rings, pizzas, smoked chicken and ribs, and charbroiled chicken wings with fiery barbecue sauce, as well as daily specials that include curries and pastas. All is served at polished wood tables, in a rear courtyard, or on the covered sidewalk terrace. A couple of TVs in the bar keep track of whatever games are on.

34 Clarence St. ✆ **613/542-4978.** Most items under C$15. AE, DC, MC, V. Mon–Sat 11am–2am; Sun 11:30am–1am.

Le Chien Noir ★ BISTRO/WINE BAR Diners gather at this busy bar at the door, where more than 20 wines are available by the glass. Tables for dining are in back or out on a courtyard terrace with an awning. Some of the menu is traditional bistro fare: think onion soup, steak frites, mussels, and duck confit. There's also red snapper paired with ratatouille and chorizo, PEI mussels in white wine, a rack of lamb in a crust of cumin and garlic, or filet of salmon with a bright green purée of mint and peas. They sometimes do an upscale version of *poutine,* an over-the-top take on that irrepressible Québécois comfort food, with the fries scattered among shredded duck confit, brie, and a peppercorn-and-cognac sauce. All yummy.

69 Brock St. ✆ **613/549-5635.** Reservations recommended. Main courses C$17–C$34. AE, DC, MC, V. Mon–Wed 11:30am–2pm & 5–10pm; Thurs–Sat 11:30am–11pm; Sun 11:30am–10pm.

Pan Chancho ★ ECLECTIC There's no better way to ease into a Kingston day than with a big glass of orange juice, fresh chocolate croissant, and a bowl of cafe au lait, served beneath the trees on the terrace of this cafe/bakery/gourmet food store. Put together a picnic lunch from offerings in the cold cases packed with appetizing selections of prepared foods and add some pastries, focaccia, baguettes, scones, or sourdough *batards,* all baked on the premises. Or eat in, choosing from plates of imported and domestic cheeses or full meals that might start with *frites aioli,* taco salads, or mussels in butter sauce, and continue on to smoked wild salmon with roasted beets or a Vietnamese shrimp cake with dragon noodles.

44 Princess St. ✆ **613/544-7790.** Main courses C$10–C$17. AE, DC, MC, V. Mon–Sat 7am–7pm; Sun 7am–5pm.

PRINCE EDWARD COUNTY

75km (47 miles) SW of Toronto

Culinary tourism is on the rise everywhere, and Ontario is definitely in on the game. The trend has turned Prince Edward County (PEC), a once-remote island on Lake Ontario a couple of hours' drive east of Toronto, into a very hot spot.

Originally settled by Mohawk Indians, the United Empire Loyalists moved into the area known as "the County" and soon turned it into a wealthy region rich in barley. As demand for beer grew across North America, so did the County's barley-baron mansions. Today, a handful of these beauties have been transformed into luxury inns. For most of the past century, PEC was a quiet, sometimes poor, agricultural area with just one small town, the struggling Picton. It still has one main town, but now Picton is thriving. And a number of smaller towns and villages—such as Bloomfield, Wellington, Milford, and Waupoos—have distinguished themselves with food-related attractions such as a craft brewery, a stellar ice-cream shop, or a unique cheese dairy.

A couple of decades ago, a back-to-the-land movement started attracting painters, artisans, glass blowers, and organic-minded farmers. Now, the place is a hot culinary spot, especially for Torontonians. Given the pristine sand dunes, inland lakes, the Sandbanks Provincial Park, and a mysterious lake that sits perched 62m (203 ft.) *above* Lake Ontario, the County is worth a day or two to take in the sights. Keep in mind that it's best explored during warm months, from spring through fall. A number of shops, galleries, and restaurants close, or seriously cut back hours, during the winter months.

Essentials

VISITOR INFORMATION **Prince Edward County Chamber of Tourism & Commerce** is at 116 Main St., Picton (✆ **613/476-2421** or 800/640-4717; www.pecchamber.com). It has a wealth of information about what to see and do, as well as where to dine and sleep. Hours change with the seasons, but it's generally open 9am to 5pm, with some added hours in summer and through autumn.

To help you choose from the range of culinary vacations, visit the **Savour Ontario** website (www.savourontario.ca; the site is a bit obtuse—start by clicking "Find a Restaurant," and you're on your way). There's also the **Ontario Culinary Tourism Alliance** website (www.ontarioculinary.com); although the organization serves people who work in the industry, the site has a lot of useful information for tourists.

GETTING THERE Prince Edward County is easy to reach by car. From Toronto, take Highway 401 east to exit 5252 (before Trenton), then take Highway 33 to Picton. The drive takes about 2½ hours.

What to See & Do

The County is best explored by car, although it's also a great place to bike once you've arrived. You can visit wineries and restaurants on cycling tours or map your own itinerary. In fact, most of the tours in the region, from art to wine, are self-directed. It's in keeping with the region's independent, off-the-beaten-path character.

Arts Trail The County is a busy community of artists, in addition to food and wine pros, and this initiative equips visitors with the information and routes they need to discover more than 30 artists, artisans, and galleries. You can expect to find beautiful paintings, sculpture, contemporary photography, pottery, blown glass, handcrafted jewelry, and more. There are eight galleries that represent multiple artists, as well; the Oeno is particularly cutting-edge. Like most things in the County, this is a seasonal program; the 2010 kick-off was late May and ran through autumn.

✆ **866/845-6644.** www.artstrail.ca.

Lake on the Mountain It's a small, sometimes turquoise-hued lake perched 62m (203 ft.) above the great Lake Ontario and a local legend because its source remains a mystery to this day. Surrounded by a pretty park, a popular pub, some lovely country homes, and a small inn, the lake offers a grand view across the Bay of Quinte. Bring a picnic lunch and watch the ferries below as they cross the 1km (½-mile) channel to the mainland. It's a great place to bid farewell to the County before hopping aboard the car ferry below at Glenora.

C.R. 7 (off Hwy. 33, near Glenora). www.ontarioparks.com/english/lakem.html. Daily vehicle permit C$10–C$18. Daily 9:30am–dusk. From Hwy. 401, take Hwy. 49 south to Picton.

Sandbanks National Park ★ It's a short drive to this spectacular provincial park that includes the West Lake formation, claimed to be the largest freshwater baymouth sand-dune system in the world. In other words: It's an amazing beach. The water is shallow, the sand clean, and the dunes—many between 12 and 25m (39–82 ft.) high—provide a bit of topography that's good for hiking and also for sheltered picnic areas on blistering days. In fact, this camping ground and natural water park features plenty of picnic areas and day-use programs. So, you can come for the day or stay overnight—but the latter only if you've planned well ahead since these campground sites are booked months in advance.

R.R. 1, Picton. ✆ **613/393-3319.** www.ontarioparks.com/english/sand.html. Daily vehicle permit C$10–C$18. Daily 9:30am–dusk.

Taste Trail If you're interested in exploring wineries, cafes, restaurants, breweries, and more, this self-guided route through the County has a lot to offer. There's a free booklet that lists 31 participating businesses, as well as route maps and brief listings on each destination. Once on the road, you'll find there are signs identifying the Taste Trail, too. Along the way, there are plenty of tastings and tours to consider. Take your time; this is slow food—anything but fast.

✆ **866/845-6644.** www.tastetrail.ca.

sipping SPOTS

Barley Days Brewery With a nod to the County's barley-rich past, this craft brewery is an entirely modern enterprise. Stop by for a taste and a tour. 13730 Loyalist Pkwy., Picton. ✆ **613/476-7468.** www.barleydaysbrewery.com.

Norman Hardie Wines This small estate makes excellent wines from grapes grown in the area and in Niagara. The acclaimed results are putting the County on the wine map. Stop by for a tasting: There are a handful of vintages to choose from and always someone on hand to guide you through the experience. A little taste of Burgundy in Ontario. 1152 Greer Rd., Wellington. ✆ **613/399-5297.**

More Cheese, Please

Fifth Town Artisan Cheese (4309 C.R. 8, Picton; ✆ **613/476-5755**; www.fifthtown.ca) is the world's first LEED-certified dairy, meaning it has outstanding eco-practices. It's worth a visit and tour just to see the process, which includes recycling clean water for the property's wetlands, and to check out the ultra-modern building design. All very new. More importantly, the cheeses are works of art—and definitely good enough to eat. They also offer wine and cheese tastings from June to September. Call ahead to check on hours and tours.

Where to Stay

There are many good options for staying a night or two, from homey B&Bs to lakeside self-catering cottages to very pretty inns. The County's inns are some of the best choices if you're looking for good dining and lodging all in one locale.

Angéline's Restaurant Inn ★★ ☺ The heart of this modest but pretty property is the original Victorian house, where the dining room serves up local ingredients with sophisticated flare under the guidance of chef Sebastien Schwab. There are three dining areas, including the Victorian Room for small private parties. The cozy rooms are mostly situated in a separate building; a new suite has been added to the main house. There are gardens and public rooms for all to enjoy, too. Angéline's is known also for its workshops, which range from on-site pottery classes to well-being seminars (think: feng shui and numerology).

433 Main St. (Hwy. 33), Bloomfield, ON K0K 1G0. ✆ **613/393-3301** or 877/391-3301. www.angelinesrestaurantinn.com. 10 units. C$80–C$135 double. AE, DC, DISC, MC, V. Free parking. Take Hwy. 401 E. & take exit 522. Proceed south on Wooler Rd. to Hwy. 33 S. (Loyalist Pkwy.).Turn left on C.R. 1 (Prince Edward Rd. 1), then turn right on Hwy. 62 S. & drive directly to Bloomfield. **Amenities:** Restaurant; cafe. *In room:* TV, DVD player, Wi-Fi (free).

isaiah tubbs This is the biggest resort around these parts, with acres of gardens and woodlands very close to Sandbanks Park. The rooms range from simple ones in the restored 1820s home to more spacious suites in outlying lodges; best of all are the Beach House Suites, which give you a taste of the exceptional location. The food is pretty standard but better than many family-style resorts.

1642 C.R. 12, Picton. ✆ **800/724-2393.** www.isaiahtubbs.com. 88 units. From C$169 double. AE, DC, MC, V. Take Hwy. 401 E. to exit 522 (Wooler Rd.), then go south on Wooler Rd. to Hwy. 33. Turn right onto Hwy. 33, then turn right at C.R. 32 in Bloomfield. Turn right onto C.R. 12 & follow it for approximately 9km (5½ miles). **Amenities:** 2 restaurants; bar; fitness center; heated pool (seasonal); sauna; tennis courts. *In room:* A/C, TV, fridge, hair dryer, Wi-Fi (free).

Merrill Inn ★ Simply one of the nicest inns in the area, the Merrill has a great location in the center of Picton. Housed in an impressive Victorian manse, the rooms are elegant yet comfortable, and attention to detail is evident throughout, from the good linens to tasteful antique decorations and pretty bathrooms. The food is another top draw, whether you're staying the night or not. The stellar dining room led by chef Michael Sullivan is a leader in regional cuisine. There's also a good wine bar and a sunny patio. In between hot breakfasts with homemade breads, a picnic lunch, and a three-course a la carte dinner, there's time for one of the Merrill's 1-hour walking tours of Picton. Choose between the "Graveyards and Gallows" tour or the less grim option of the town's historic architecture. Either way, a good way for a little exercise in between meals.

343 Main St., Picton. ✆ **866/567-5969** or 613/476-7451. www.merrillinn.com. 13 units. From C$179 double. Rates include breakfast. AE, MC, V. Free parking. **Amenities:** Restaurant; wine bar; spa. *In room:* A/C, TV, Wi-Fi (free).

Where to Dine

Food is a major attraction here, so unless you stay for quite a while, there are more places to feast than your belt can comfortably accommodate. Road trips around the region will lead you to discoveries like a beautiful little winery, or you can opt for staying in Picton, where you can choose from the many cafes, restaurants, and specialty shops. For a more complete list of what's on offer, visit www.pec.on.ca.

The Bean Counter Coffee Co. & Gelaterie LIGHT FARE/ICE CREAM One of the many good choices on Picton's main street, this open and airy cafe serves fair-trade coffee, homemade cakes, light lunch fare, and more than 20 flavors of ice cream made in-house. A perfect spot for refueling after a day on the dunes.

172 Main St., Unit 101, Picton. ✆ **613/476-1718.** www.beancountercafe.com. Sandwiches from C$5. AE, DC, MC, V. Mon–Fri 8am–9pm; Sat & Sun 9am–9pm.

Buddha Dog LIGHT FARE Healthy hot dogs: The concept might be hard to swallow, but in fact, these tasty little dogs—more like sausages, really—are made using local, small-scale farm goods. Since starting out in the County, the owners have also opened shops in Toronto. Expect to eat at least two. There are a number of excellent sauces to pile on, too.

172 Main St., Picton. ✆ **613/476-3814.** www.buddhafoodha.com. Hot dogs from C$2.50. AE, DC, MC V. Mon–Fri 11am–4pm; Sat & Sun 11am–5pm.

Harvest Restaurant ★ CANADIAN/ECLECTIC Probably the County's top gourmet destination, this friendly, stylish restaurant is a favorite for locals, as well as food-focused travelers. Chef Michael Potters is a fine craftsman, and his passion for supporting local farmers means that you get a virtual tour of the County's best produce, meats, dairy, and wines in dishes such as Wild BC red spring salmon with sauce a la *Grecque,* or chicken and dumplings in a wild mushroom and chive flower broth.

106 Bridge St., Picton. ✆ **613/476-6763.** www.harvestrestaurant.ca. Main courses C$13–C$30. AE, MC, V. Wed–Sun 5–10pm.

Slickers ICE CREAM The County is known for a healthy sense of pride in local foods, and even the ice-cream shops are in on the trend. This small spot with a pretty patio in Bloomfield serves up an eclectic collection of flavors, each one inspired by what's in season. Flavors include rhubarb ginger, local cantaloupe, apple pie, and even a maple walnut made with local syrup. They're all delicious. Open in summer only.

271 Main St., Bloomfield. No phone. www.slickersicecream.com. Single scoop from C$3. No credit cards. Summer daily 11am–9pm.

TORONTO

by Pamela Cuthbert

I grew up in downtown Toronto, and it's where I still choose to live with my family. It's an ever-evolving version of the multicultural city I remember from childhood: an interlocking collection of neighborhoods that change every year with new arrivals. Toronto is friendly in a somewhat reserved way, a generally safe place to explore, and it has plenty to discover, from restaurants to museums, festivals to towers, arts to shopping, with loads of green spaces throughout. Sure, times have changed since I was kid, and crime has risen along with traffic, but it's still relatively safe for a metropolis with a 5 million-plus population. It also, happily, ranks as one of the world's most diverse cities.

Toronto has a sprawling layout and miles of suburbs, but if you stay focused on its core, the density of attractions and vibrant communities makes it an incredibly approachable place to explore. For example, just stepping out my front door leads me to great cafes for people watching; lip-smacking charcuterie; the Art Gallery of Ontario, MOCCA, the Cinematheque, and assorted galleries for inspiration; funky pubs with great live music; *and* a handful of parks.

Exploring Toronto is easy. Hop on a red-rocket streetcar and ride with the locals. Get your bearings from the top of the CN Tower or from a rooftop lounge. Take a ferry ride if the weather is good or opt for a bracing walk along the waterfront. Look up to see the city's great architecture. Look down to navigate the city's mazelike underground. Be prepared to shop until you drop. Eat till you're stuffed. Dance till dawn. Walk, and then walk some more. The reward: In just a few days, you can tour the town and leave with the feeling that you've got the hang of the place. A great, and lasting, souvenir.

ESSENTIALS

Getting There

BY PLANE **Pearson International Airport** (YYZ) is the busiest airport in Canada, and its terminals are massive (particularly Terminal 1). Almost all flights into Toronto arrive here. Expect a long walk to the Immigration and Customs area, which you will have to clear in Toronto, even if you're flying on to another Canadian destination. (There are maps of both terminals online at www.gtaa.com.) There are tourism information booths at both terminals.

Downtown Toronto

Harbord St.
University of Toronto Art Centre
Barnicke Gallery
Queen's Park
Queen's Park Crescent E
Dupont St.
Bloor St. W
Yonge St.
Avenue Rd.
Bathurst St.
Spadina Ave.
University Ave.
Dufferin St.
Ossington Ave.
College St.
Dundas St. E
Queen St. W
King St. W
AREA OF DETAIL
Ulster St.
Willcocks St.
Lippincott St.
Brunswick Ave.
Major St.
Spadina Crescent
St. George St.
Provincial Legislature
QUEEN'S PARK
College St.
KENSINGTON
DISCOVERY DISTRICT
Henderson Ave.
Mansfield Ave.
Oxford St.
Nassau St.
Spadina Ave.
Huron St.
Cecil St.
Henry St.
McCaul St.
Murray St.
University Ave.
Bellevue Ave.
Augusta Ave.
Baldwin St.
Beverley St.
Dundas St. W
Wales Ave.
D'Arcy St.
CHINATOWN
Dundas St. W
Manning Ave.
Claremont St.
Euclid Ave.
Bellwoods Ave.
ALEXANDRA PARK
Alexandra Park
Grange Ave.
Grange Pl.
Grange Park
ST. PATRICK
Centre Ave.
Simcoe St.
St. Patrick St.
Carr St.
Robinson St.
Augusta Ave.
Cameron St.
Sullivan St.
Phoebe St.
Soho St.
GRANGE PARK
Wolseley St.
Bulwer St.
Queen St. W
THEATRE DISTRICT
OSGOODE
Richmond St. W
Camden St.
Niagara St.
Palmerston Ave.
Bathurst St.
Adelaide St. W
Walnut Ave.
Portland St.
Brant St.
Spadina Ave.
Peter St.
Widmer St.
John St.
Duncan St.
Simcoe St.
ST. ANDREW
York St.
King St. W
ENTERTAINMENT DISTRICT
Stanley Park
Wellington St. W
Clarence Square
Blue Jays Wy.
Wellington St. W
University Ave.
Victoria Mem. Sq.
Niagara St.
Front St. W
Convention Center
Station St.
Rogers Centre
Bremner Blvd.
Gardiner Expy.
Roundhouse Park
Simpson Ave.
Gerrard St. E
Pape Ave.
Galt Ave.
Lake Shore Blvd. W
York St.
Munro St.
Queens Quay W
HTO Park
Dundas St. E
Broadview Ave
Boulton Ave.
Jimmie Simpson Park
Logan Ave.
Carlaw Ave
Boston Ave.
Jones Ave
Leslie St.
Alton Ave.
HARBOURFRONT
Maple Leaf Quays
York Quay
Inner Harbour
Queen St. E
Booth Ave.
Eastern Ave.
0 1/4 mi
0 0.25 km

10 Essentials | TORONTO

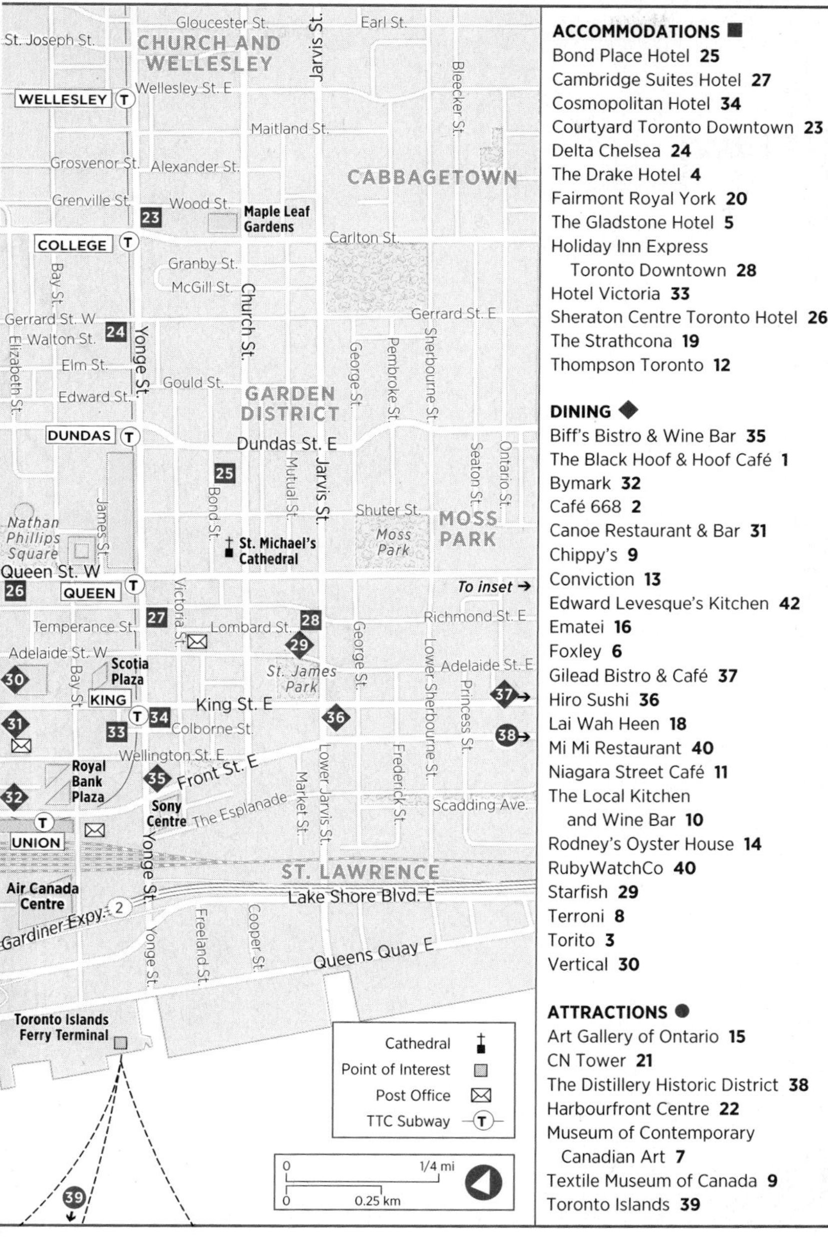

ACCOMMODATIONS ■

Bond Place Hotel **25**
Cambridge Suites Hotel **27**
Cosmopolitan Hotel **34**
Courtyard Toronto Downtown **23**
Delta Chelsea **24**
The Drake Hotel **4**
Fairmont Royal York **20**
The Gladstone Hotel **5**
Holiday Inn Express Toronto Downtown **28**
Hotel Victoria **33**
Sheraton Centre Toronto Hotel **26**
The Strathcona **19**
Thompson Toronto **12**

DINING ◆

Biff's Bistro & Wine Bar **35**
The Black Hoof & Hoof Café **1**
Bymark **32**
Café 668 **2**
Canoe Restaurant & Bar **31**
Chippy's **9**
Conviction **13**
Edward Levesque's Kitchen **42**
Ematei **16**
Foxley **6**
Gilead Bistro & Café **37**
Hiro Sushi **36**
Lai Wah Heen **18**
Mi Mi Restaurant **40**
Niagara Street Café **11**
The Local Kitchen and Wine Bar **10**
Rodney's Oyster House **14**
RubyWatchCo **40**
Starfish **29**
Terroni **8**
Torito **3**
Vertical **30**

ATTRACTIONS ●

Art Gallery of Ontario **15**
CN Tower **21**
The Distillery Historic District **38**
Harbourfront Centre **22**
Museum of Contemporary Canadian Art **7**
Textile Museum of Canada **9**
Toronto Islands **39**

Midtown Toronto

ACCOMMODATIONS ■

Clarion Hotel & Suites Selby **18**
Four Seasons Hotel Toronto **10**
Holiday Inn Toronto Midtown **7**
Howard Johnson Yorkville **9**
Park Hyatt Toronto **11**
The Sutton Place Hotel **17**

DINING ◆

Bar Mercurio **5**
C5 **12**
earth **15**
Lalibela **1**
Loire **3**
Messis **4**
Nataraj **2**
Pangaea **16**

ATTRACTIONS ●

Bata Shoe Museum **6**
George R. Gardiner Museum of Ceramic Art **14**
Royal Ontario Museum (ROM) **13**
University of Toronto Art Centre **8**

Davenport Rd.
Rathnelly Ave.
Macpherson Ave.
Dupont St.
DUPONT
Chicora Ave.
Pears Ave.
Walmer Rd.
Davenport Rd.
Bernard Ave.
Webster Ave.
Tranby Ave.
Spadina Ave.
Madison Ave.
Huron St.
St. George St.
Admiral Rd.
Bedford Rd.
Elgin Ave.
Avenue Rd.
Hazelton Ave.
ANNEX
Yorkville Ave.
Prince Arthur Ave.
Cumberland St.
BATHURST
SPADINA
Bloor St. W
ST. GEORGE
Lennox St.
Huron St.
Devonshire Pl.
MUSEUM
Charles St. W
Sussex Ave.
Palmerston Ave.
Herrick St.
Glen Morris St.
University Of Toronto
Hoskin Ave.
Harbord St.
Brunswick Ave.
Robert St.
Sussex Mews
St. George St.
Queen's Park Crescent E
Ulster St.
Willcocks St.
Markham St.
Bathurst St.
Lippincott St.
Howland Ave.
Spadina Crescent
Russell St.
King's College Rd.
QUEEN'S PARK
College St.
College St.
KENSINGTON
Huron St.
Henry St.
DISCOVERY DISTRICT
Oxford St.
Orde St.
Cecil St.

10
Essentials
TORONTO

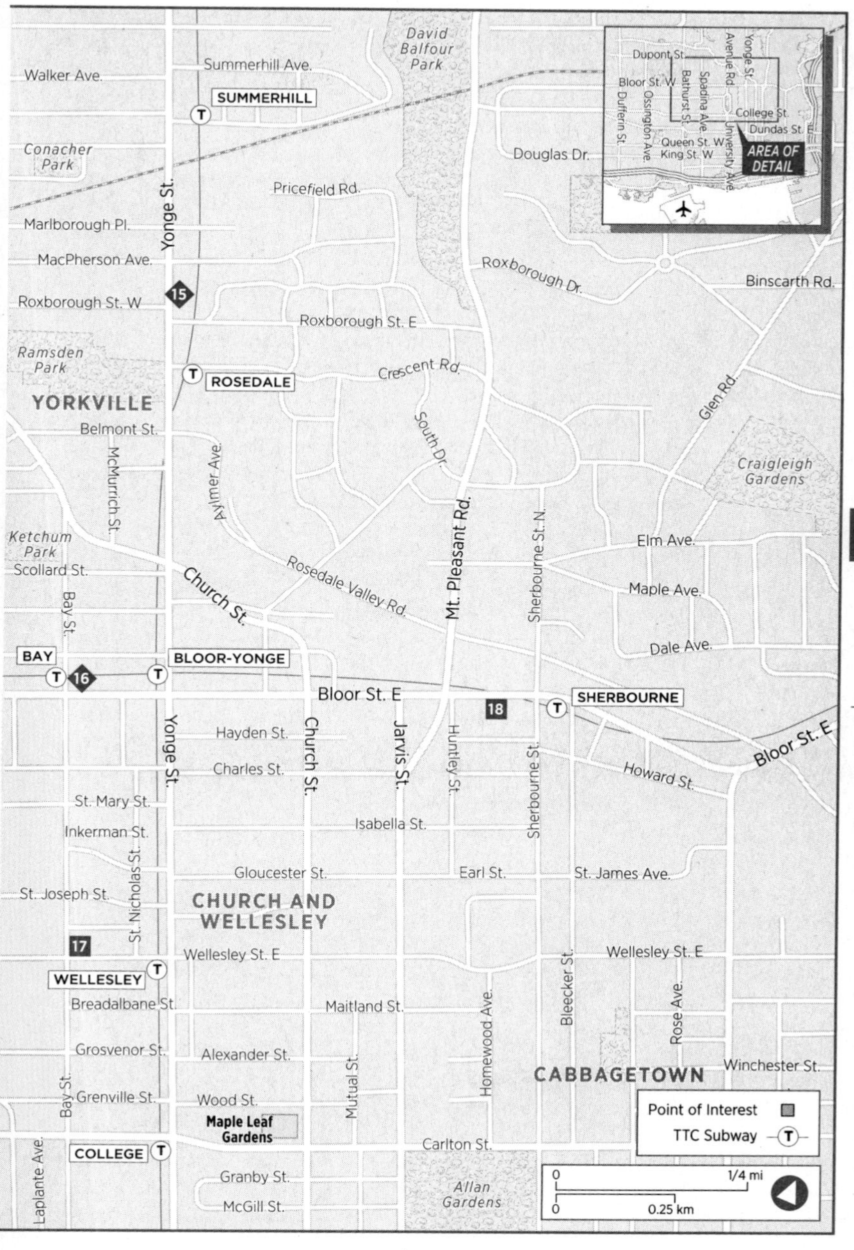

10

TORONTO | Essentials

Canada's only national airline, **Air Canada** (✆ **888/247-2262;** www.aircanada.ca), operates direct flights to Toronto from most major American cities and many smaller ones. It also flies from major cities around the world and operates connecting flights from other U.S. cities. It is based in Pearson's Terminal 1. **WestJet** (✆ **888/937-8538;** www.westjet.com), based in Calgary, has become an increasingly popular choice for anyone coming to Toronto from the United States, as well as some locations in the Caribbean and Mexico.

Upstart **Porter Airlines** (✆ **888/619-8622** or 416/619-8622; www.flyporter.com) has gained a great reputation for service and flies to **Toronto City Centre Airport** from four U.S. locations—Newark, Chicago, Boston, and Myrtle Beach—as well as a rapidly increasing number of Canadian cities, including Halifax, Montréal, Québec City, St. John's, and Ottawa. Porter, along with a handful of commuter flight services, is the only airline that flies to the Toronto City Centre Airport, which is located on the western side of the Toronto Islands.

To get from the airport to downtown, take Highway 427 south to the Gardiner Expressway East. A **taxi** costs about C$50 if you're going downtown (it's higher if you're heading to north or east Toronto).

The convenient **Airport Express bus** (✆ **905/564-6333;** www.torontoairportexpress.com) travels between the airport, the bus terminal, and major downtown hotels—the Westin Harbour Castle, Fairmont Royal York, Sheraton Centre Toronto, and Delta Chelsea—every 20 to 30 minutes, from 4:55am to 12:55am. The fare is C$20 one-way, C$33 round-trip.

The cheapest way to go is by **bus and subway,** which takes about an hour. During the day, you have three options: the no. 192 "Airport Rocket" bus to Kipling station, the no. 58A bus to Lawrence West station, or the no. 307 bus to Eglinton West station. In the middle of the night, you can take the no. 300A bus to Yonge and Bloor streets. The fare of C$3 includes free transfer to the subway (which is available till 1:30am). All buses make stops at both airport terminals 1 and 3. It doesn't matter which bus you use; they all take roughly the same amount of time. (The Airport Rocket reaches the subway fastest, but the subway ride to downtown is twice as long as from the other stations.) For more information, call the **Toronto Transit Commission,** or TTC (✆ **416/393-4636;** www3.ttc.ca).

BY CAR Crossing the border between Canada and the U.S. by car gives you a lot of options—the U.S. highway system leads directly into Canada at 13 points. If you're driving from Michigan, you'll enter at Detroit-Windsor (I-75 and the Ambassador Bridge) or Port Huron–Sarnia (I-94 and the Bluewater Bridge). If you're coming from New York, you have more options. On I-190, you can enter at Buffalo–Fort Erie; Niagara Falls, New York–Niagara Falls, Ontario; or Niagara Falls, New York–Lewiston. On I-81, you'll cross the Canadian border at Hill Island; on Route 37, you'll enter at either Ogdensburg-Johnstown or Rooseveltown-Cornwall.

From the United States, you are most likely to enter Toronto from the west on Highway 401 or Highway 2 and the Queen Elizabeth Way. If you come from the east, via Montréal, you'll also use highways 401 and 2.

Here are approximate driving distances to Toronto: from Boston, 911km (566 miles); Buffalo, 155km (96 miles); Chicago, 859km (534 miles); Cincinnati, 806km (501 miles); Detroit, 379km (235 miles); Minneapolis, 1,564km (972 miles); Montréal, 545km (339 miles); New York, 797km (495 miles); Ottawa, 453km (281 miles); and Québec City, 790km (491 miles).

BY TRAIN **Amtrak**'s (**©800/USA-RAIL** or 800/872-7245; www.amtrak.com) "Maple Leaf" service links New York City and Toronto via Albany, Buffalo, and Niagara Falls. It departs daily from Penn Station. The journey takes 12½ hours. Note that the lengthy schedule allows for extended stops at Customs and Immigration checkpoints at the border. **VIA Rail Canada** (**©888/VIA-RAIL** or ©888/842-7245; www.viarail.ca) is the nation's top rail line and offers many routes and generally pleasant service. Trains arrive in Toronto at Union Station on Front Street, 1 block west of Yonge Street, opposite the Fairmont Royal York Hotel (see p. 381). The station has direct access to the subway.

BY BUS **Greyhound** (**© 800/231-2222;** www.greyhound.com) is the best-known bus company that crosses the U.S. border. You can travel from almost anywhere in the United States and Canada. You'll arrive at the Metro Coach Terminal downtown at 610 Bay St., near the corner of Dundas Street. Another option is **Coach Canada** (www.coachcanada.com), which travels from many places in the United States, as well as from Québec, to Ontario.

Visitor Information

TOURIST OFFICES The best source for Toronto-specific information is **Tourism Toronto,** 207 Queens Quay W., Suite 590, Toronto, ON M5J 1A7 (**© 800/499-2514** from North America, or 416/203-2600; www.torontotourism.com). Call before you leave and ask for the free information package, which includes sections on accommodations, sights, and dining. Better yet, visit the website, which provides all of the above plus up-to-the-minute events information.

For information about traveling in the province of Ontario, contact **Ontario Tourism** (**© 800/ONTARIO;** www.ontariotravel.net), or visit its information center in the **Atrium on Bay** (street level) at 20 Dundas St. W.—it's just across Dundas from the Sears store at the northern edge of the Eaton Centre. (The Atrium's mailing address is 595 Bay St., but since the information booth is on the south side of the complex, they use a different street address for the same building.) It's open daily from 8:30am to 5pm; hours are extended during the summer, often to 8pm.

To pick up brochures and a map before you leave **Pearson International Airport,** stop by the **Transport Canada Information Centre** (**© 905/676-3506** or 416/247-7678). There's one in each terminal. A staff fluent in a dozen languages can answer questions about tourist attractions, ground transportation, and more.

WEBSITES **Toronto.com** (www.toronto.com), operated by the *Toronto Star,* offers extensive restaurant reviews, events listings, and feature articles. A couple of other great sources for local goings-on and news: the **Torontoist** blog (www.torontoist.com) and **blogTO** (www.blogto.com). If you love to shop, check out **SweetSpot** (www.sweetspot.ca) for its extensive Toronto coverage of local designers and boutiques. The **Gridskipper** blog (www.gridskipper.com) covers some Toronto news, too.

City Layout

Toronto is laid out in a grid . . . with a few interesting exceptions. **Yonge Street** (pronounced *young*) is the main north-south artery, stretching from Lake Ontario in the south well beyond Highway 401 in the north. Yonge Street divides western cross streets from eastern cross streets. The main east-west artery is **Bloor Street,** which cuts through the heart of downtown.

"Downtown" usually refers to the area from Eglinton Avenue south to the lake, between Spadina Avenue in the west and Jarvis Street in the east. Because this is such a large area, it's been divided here into five sections. **Downtown West** runs from the lake north to College Street; the eastern boundary is Yonge Street. **Downtown East** goes from the lake north to Carlton Street (once College St. reaches Yonge St., it becomes Carlton St.); the western boundary is Yonge Street. **Midtown** extends from College Street north to Davenport Road; the eastern boundary is Jarvis Street. **The Danforth/the East End** runs east to Danforth Avenue; the western boundary is Broadview Avenue. **Uptown** is the area north of Davenport Road.

In Downtown West, you'll find many of the lakeshore attractions: Harbourfront, Ontario Place, Fort York, Exhibition Place, and the Toronto Islands. It also boasts the CN Tower, City Hall, the Four Seasons Centre for the Performing Arts, the Rogers Centre (formerly known as SkyDome), Chinatown, the Art Gallery of Ontario, and the Eaton Centre. Downtown East includes the Distillery District, the St. Lawrence Market, the Sony Centre (formerly the Hummingbird Centre), the St. Lawrence Centre for the Arts, and St. James's Cathedral. Midtown contains the Royal Ontario Museum; the Gardiner Museum; the University of Toronto; Markham Village; and chic Yorkville, a prime area for shopping and dining. The Danforth/the East End features Riverdale Farm, the historic Necropolis, and Greektown. Uptown has traditionally been a residential area, but it's now a fast-growing entertainment area, too. Its attractions include the Sunnybrook park system and the Ontario Science Centre.

GETTING AROUND

By Public Transportation

The **Toronto Transit Commission,** or TTC (© **416/393-4636** for 24-hr. information; recordings available in 18 languages; www3.ttc.ca), operates the subway, bus, streetcar, and light rapid transit (LRT) system.

Fares, including transfers to buses or streetcars, are C$3 or 5 tokens for C$13 for adults. Seniors and students ages 13 to 19 with valid ID pay C$2, or 10 tickets for C$17; children 12 and under pay C$0.75, or 10 tickets for C$5.50. You can buy a special day pass for C$10 that's good for unlimited travel for one adult on weekdays and for up to two adults and four children on weekends.

For surface transportation, you need a token, a ticket (for seniors or kids), or exact change. You can buy tokens and tickets at subway entrances and at authorized stores that display the sign TTC TICKETS MAY BE PURCHASED HERE. Bus drivers do not sell tickets, nor will they make change. Always obtain a free transfer where you board the train or bus, in case you need it. In the subways, use the push-button machine just inside the entrance. On streetcars and buses, ask the driver for a transfer.

THE SUBWAY The TTC faced some serious public-relations issues in 2010, including a drunken bus driver, but it nonetheless remains fast (especially compared with snarled surface traffic), clean, and very simple to use. There are two major lines—Bloor-Danforth and Yonge-University-Spadina—and one smaller line, Sheppard, in the northern part of the city. The Bloor Street east-west line runs from Kipling Avenue in the west to Kennedy Road in the east (where it connects with Scarborough Rapid Transit to Scarborough Centre and McCowan Rd.). The Yonge Street north-south line runs from Finch Avenue in the north to Union Station (Front St.) in the south. From

The TTC Subway System

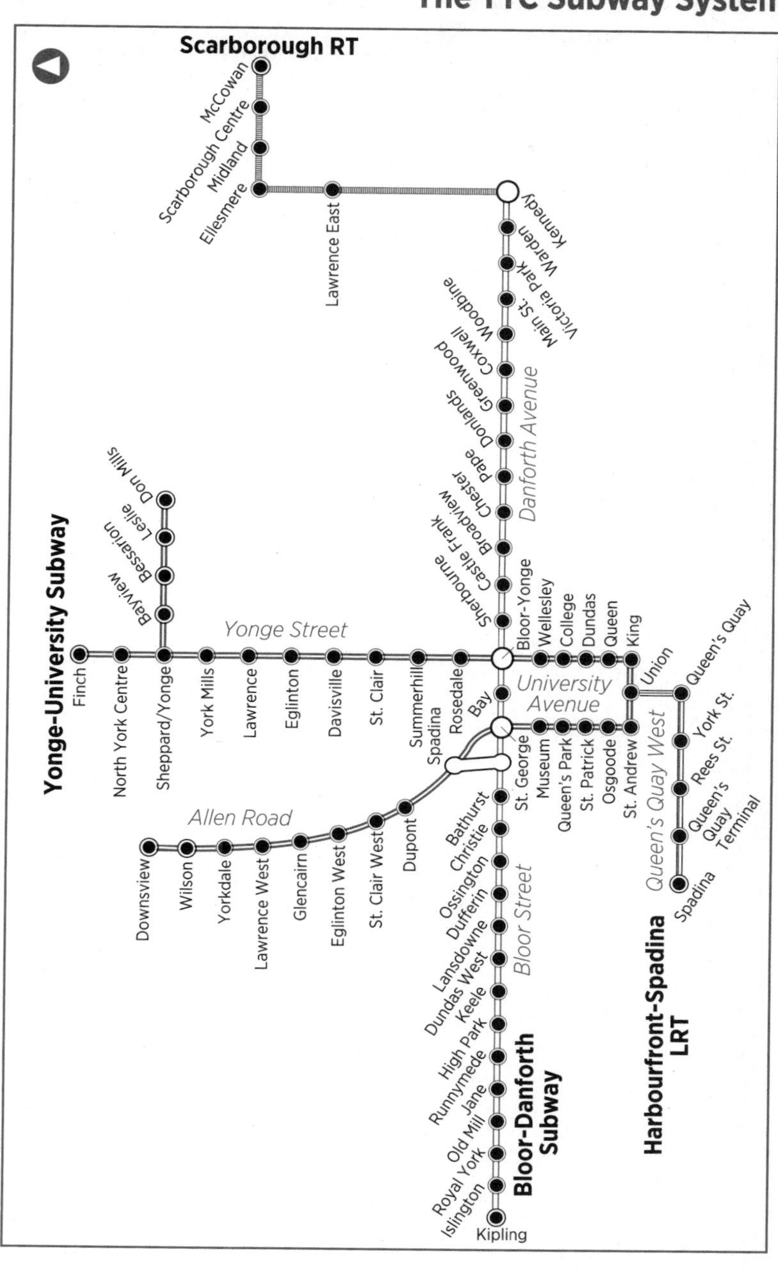

there, it loops north along University Avenue and connects with the Bloor line at the St. George station. A Spadina extension runs north from St. George to Downsview station at Sheppard Avenue. The Sheppard line connects only with the Yonge line at Sheppard Station and runs east through north Toronto for just 6km (3¾ miles).

The LRT system connects downtown to Harbourfront. The fare is one ticket or token. It runs from Union Station along Queens Quay to Spadina Avenue, with stops at Queens Quay ferry docks, York Street, Simcoe Street, and Rees Street; then it continues up Spadina to the Spadina subway station. The transfer from the subway to the LRT (and vice versa) at Union Station is free.

The subway operates Monday to Saturday from 6am to 1:30am and Sunday from 9am to 1:30am. From 1am to 5:30am, the Blue Night Network operates on basic surface routes. It runs about every 30 minutes. For route information, pick up a *Ride Guide* at subway entrances or call © **416/393-4636.** Multilingual information is available.

BUSES & STREETCARS Where the subway leaves off, buses and streetcars take over. They run east-west and north-south along the city's arteries. When you pay your fare (on bus, streetcar, or subway), always pick up a transfer so that you won't have to pay again if you want to transfer to another mode of transportation.

TAXIS In many cities, taxis are an expensive mode of transportation, but this is especially true of Toronto. In 2008, rates were raised (again) because of the high cost of fuel. It's C$4 the minute you step in and C$0.25 for each additional 155m (509 ft.). Fares can quickly mount up. You can hail a cab on the street, find one in line in front of a big hotel, or call one of the major companies—**Diamond** (© **416/366-6868**), **Royal** (© **416/777-9222**), or **Metro** (© **416/504-8294**). If you experience problems with cab service, call the **Metro Licensing Commission** (© **416/392-3082**).

FERRY SERVICE Toronto Parks and Recreation operates ferries that travel to the Toronto Islands. Call © **416/392-8193** for schedules and information. Round-trip fares are C$6.50 adults, C$4 seniors and children 15 to 19, C$3 children under 15.

By Car

Toronto is a rambling city, but that doesn't mean the best way to get around is by car. There are long traffic jams, especially during morning and afternoon rush hours. A reputation for "two seasons: winter and construction" means the warmer months are especially busy with road work. And to make matters worse, there is an escalating turf war between the numerous cyclists and motorists sharing the road.

Parking can be very expensive, too, and the city's meter maids are notoriously aggressive in issuing pricey parking tickets at any opportunity. Generally speaking, the city-owned lots, marked with a big green "P," are the most affordable. They charge about C$2 per half-hour. After 6pm and on Sunday, there is usually a maximum rate of C$12. Observe the parking restrictions—otherwise, the city will tow your car away, and it'll cost more than C$100 to get it back.

[FastFACTS] TORONTO

Area Codes Toronto's area codes are **416** and **647;** outside the city, the code is **905** or **289.** You must dial all 10 digits for all local phone numbers.

Business Hours Banks are generally open Monday through Thursday from 10am to 3pm, Friday 10am to 6pm. Most stores are open Monday through

Wednesday from 10am to 6pm, and Saturday and Sunday from 10am to 5pm, with extended hours (until 8 or 9:30pm) on Thursday and often on Friday.

Drinking Laws The legal age for purchase and consumption of alcoholic beverages is 19 throughout Ontario; proof of age is required and often requested at bars, nightclubs, and restaurants, so it's always a good idea to bring ID when you go out.

Bars are usually open until 2am in Toronto, except during special events like the Toronto International Film Festival, when many venues are open later. A government monopoly runs liquor sales: **Liquor Control Board of Ontario (LCBO)** stores sell liquor, wine, and some beers. Most are open daily from 10am to 6pm (some have extended evening hours). The nicest shop is the **LCBO Summerhill** (10 Scrivener Sq.; ✆ **416/922-0403;** subway: Summerhill). Built in a former train station, this outpost hosts cooking classes, wine and spirit tastings, and party-planning seminars. See **www.lcbo.com** for information about products and special in-store events.

Do not carry open containers of alcohol in your car or any public area that isn't zoned for alcohol consumption. The police can fine you on the spot.

Embassies & Consulates All embassies are in Ottawa, but local consulates include the **Australian Consulate-General** (175 Bloor St. E., Ste. 314, at Church St.; ✆ **416/323-1155**), the **British Consulate-General** (777 Bay St., Ste. 2800, at College St.; ✆ **416/593-1290**), and the **U.S. Consulate** (360 University Ave.; ✆ **416/595-1700**).

Emergencies Call ✆ **911** for fire, police, or ambulance.

Hospitals In the downtown core, the **University Health Network** (UHN) manages three hospitals: **Toronto General,** at 200 Elizabeth St.; **Princess Margaret,** at 610 University Ave.; and **Toronto Western,** at 399 Bathurst St. The UHN has a central switchboard for all three (✆ **416/340-3111**). Other hospitals include **St. Michael's** (30 Bond St.; ✆ **416/360-4000**) and **Mount Sinai** (600 University Ave.; ✆ **416/596-4200**). Also downtown is the **Hospital for Sick Children** (555 University Ave.; ✆ **416/813-1500**). Uptown, there's **Sunnybrook Hospital** (2075 Bayview Ave., north of Eglinton Ave. E.; ✆ **416/480-6100**). In the eastern part of the city, go to **Toronto East General Hospital** (825 Coxwell Ave.; ✆ **416/461-8272**).

Hotlines **Poison Information Centre** (✆ **800/267-1373**), **Distress Centre** suicide-prevention line (✆ **416/408-4357**), **Toronto Rape Crisis Centre** (✆ **416/597-8808**), **Assaulted Women's Helpline** (✆ **416/863-0511**), and **AIDS & Sexual Health InfoLine** (✆ **416/392-2437**). For kids or teens in distress, there's **Kids Help Phone** (✆ **800/668-6868**).

Lost & Found If you leave something on a TTC bus, a streetcar, or the subway, call the **TTC Lost Articles Office** (✆ **416/393-4100**), at the Bay Street subway station. It's open Monday through Friday from 8am to 5pm.

You can also contact the **Toronto Police Service** about lost or found items at ✆ **416/808-2222.**

Newspapers & Magazines The four daily newspapers are the *Globe and Mail,* the *National Post,* the *Toronto Star,* and the *Toronto Sun. Eye* and *Now* are free arts-and-entertainment weeklies. *Xtra!* is a free weekly targeted at the gay and lesbian community. In addition, many English-language ethnic newspapers serve Toronto's Portuguese, Hungarian, Italian, East Indian, Korean, Chinese, and Caribbean communities. *Toronto Life* is the major monthly city magazine. *Where Toronto* magazine is usually free at hotels and some Theater District restaurants.

Police In a life-threatening emergency, call ✆ **911.** For all other matters, contact the Toronto Police Service (40 College St.; ✆ **416/808-2222**).

Smoking The Smoke-Free Ontario Act, which came into effect in 2006, is one of the most stringent in North America. It bans smoking in all workplaces and in all enclosed public spaces. It's all but impossible to smoke at Ontario restaurants because the law banned designated smoking areas; even patios that have any sort of covering have also had to go smoke-free.

Taxes As of July 1, 2010, the Ontario government implemented a "harmonized" tax system, with a 13% sales tax on virtually everything for sale. (Previously, the federal GST was 5% and the Ontario sales tax was 8%, but the Ontario sales tax was not applied to purchases such as fast-food meals.) Taxes are added when you purchase an item, rather than being included in the original price as is common in much of Europe. The Canadian government suspended the GST Visitors' Rebate Program in 2007. Within the city of Toronto, there is a new bylaw, introduced in 2009, that obliges retailers to charge a minimum of 5¢ per plastic bag. There are no exceptions to this rule.

Time Toronto is on Eastern Standard Time. When it's noon in Toronto, it's 9am in Los Angeles (PST), it's 7am in Honolulu (HST), 10am in Denver (MST), 11am in Chicago (CST), noon in New York City (also on EST), 5pm in London (GMT), and 2am the next day in Sydney (UTC).

Daylight Saving Time is in effect from 1am on the second Sunday in March to 1am on the first Sunday in November. Daylight Saving Time moves the clock 1 hour ahead of standard time.

Toilets You won't find public toilets or "restrooms" on the streets in Toronto, but they can be found in hotel lobbies, bars, restaurants, museums, department stores, railway and bus stations, and service stations. Large hotels and fast-food restaurants are often the best bet for clean facilities. Restaurants and bars in resorts or heavily visited areas may reserve their restrooms for patrons. There are also restrooms throughout the underground PATH system near the various food courts. There are restrooms at major subway stations, such as Yonge-Bloor which are best used in the daytime when the subways are busy.

WHERE TO STAY

Toronto's hotel landscape offers plenty of choice, from idiosyncratic inns to homey B&Bs, conventional hotels to deluxe boutiques properties. The biggest news of late is the long-overdue arrival of a slate of five-star hotels: The city is midway through a rich development of luxury properties, including a Ritz Carlton, a groovy Thompson boutique, and a new Four Seasons in the city where the renowned chain is based. Chances are good, especially given the economic climate, that there will be deals at the high end as the newbies compete for heads on beds. While proximity to central attractions such as the CN Tower, Harbourfront, Rogers Centre, and Eaton Centre can drive up the cost of a stay, there are some great budget-priced downtown options, too.

Downtown West

VERY EXPENSIVE

Thompson Toronto ★★★ This swank downtown property, part of the quite perfect New York–based boutique chain, opened this, their first Canadian outpost, last year amid much hype and expectation. And the news is good: It delivers. The luxe rooms are chic yet comfortable; the service attentive but not cloying; the location a welcome launching point for seeing the groovier parts of the city, but also convenient to the theater district and beyond. The rooftop infinity swimming pool with its breathtaking views along with the rooftop's cozy fireplace lounge—pick your season—together offer a unique destination on the city's hotel scene. Ditto for the dining options, which range from a diner (very good fare; open 24/7) to an outpost of Scott Conant's upscale, and much praised, Scarpetta restaurant. Expect high-end fitness facilities, including a yoga studio; a 40-seat screening room; SFERRA linens on your bed and Carrera marble in the bathroom; floor-to-ceiling windows for a bright, open aspect onto the street life; and a serene, white-toned backdrop with wooden touches and creative flare.

550 Wellington St. W., Toronto, ON M5V 2V4. ✆ **416/640-7778** or 888/550-8368. www.thompsonhotels.com. 102 units. From C$245 double. AE, DC, MC, V. Valet parking C$35. Subway: St. Patrick, then streetcar west to Bathurst St. **Amenities:** 2 restaurants; bar; fireplace lounge; concierge; babysitting; health club; outdoor pool; room service. *In room:* A/C, TV/DVD player, CD player, hair dryer, minibar, Wi-Fi ($10 per day).

EXPENSIVE

The Drake Hotel ★ An early convert to the boutique phenomenon, which came late to Toronto, The Drake is better known for its bars and restaurants than the tiny (from 14 to 36 sq. m [151–388 sq. ft.]) guest rooms that give it its name. However, the rooms *are* cleverly designed and have good amenities (CD/DVD players and lovely linens, for example) and it makes an ideal place to rest your head after a long night's indulgence in the hotel's public rooms. The Drake is something of a trend-setter and attracts a stylish and fashionable crowd to its restaurant and bar, rooftop lounge, and cafe. There is an exercise studio for yoga classes and a performance venue, the Underground, that features live music. An artist-in-residence program keeps the wall art changing. You're far more likely to meet city residents here than visitors.

1150 Queen St. W. (at Beaconsfield Ave.), Toronto, ON M6J 1J3. ✆ **800/372-5386** or 416/531-5042. Fax 416/531-9493. www.thedrakehotel.ca. 19 units. From C$219 double. AE, MC, V. Subway: Osgoode, then streetcar west to Beaconsfield Ave. **Amenities:** 2 restaurants; cafe; 2 bars; access to local health club. *In room:* A/C, TV/DVD player, CD player, hair dryer, Internet (free), MP3 docking station.

Fairmont Royal York ★★ Built by the Canadian Pacific Railroad in 1929, this massive hotel has 1,365 guest rooms and suites, and 35 meeting and banquet rooms. Just sitting on a plush couch in the magnificent old-fashioned lobby and watching the crowd is an event. Still, you have to decide whether you want to stay under the same roof with countless business travelers, tour groups, and conventioneers. Service is efficient, if impersonal. Located across from Union Station, the hotel pays particular attention to accessibility, and some guest rooms are specially designed for wheelchair users, the hearing impaired, and the visually impaired. The hotel is also a leader in eco-friendly initiatives. The restaurants are also a good bet and eco-minded, as well, with an award for sustainable seafood and beehives on the roof that supply honey for the kitchens and your toast. Other special features include the Elizabeth Milan Day Spa, Epic restaurant, and the leather-lined Library Bar. ***Tip:*** Watch the website for specials.

100 Front St. W. (at York St.), Toronto, ON M5J 1E3. ✆ **800/441-1414.** Fax 416/368-9040. www.fairmont.com/royalyork. 1,365 units. From C$205 double. Packages available. AE, DC, DISC, MC, V. Parking C$40. Subway: Union. Pets accepted. **Amenities:** 5 restaurants; 2 bars/lounges; babysitting; concierge; health club; Jacuzzi; sky-lit indoor pool; room service; sauna; spa. *In room:* A/C, TV, hair dryer, Internet, minibar.

MODERATE

Delta Chelsea ★★ ☺ Though it doesn't look the part, the Delta Chelsea is the city's biggest hotel, based on number of rooms. Guest rooms are bright and cheery; a few have kitchenettes. Business travelers should consider a room on the Signature Club floor, which comes with many in-room comforts like cordless speakerphones, well-stocked desks, and ergonomic chairs. The hotel boasts a four-story indoor waterslide, plus grown-up amenities, such as Deck 27, a lounge with a panoramic view of

Toronto. The pool and awesome slide, combined with a children's center and babysitting, make this a particularly attractive option for families. Weekend packages often combine tickets to the city's top attractions and theaters.

33 Gerrard St. W. (just west of Yonge St.), Toronto, ON M5G 1Z4. ✆ **800/243-5732** or 416/595-1975. Fax 416/585-4362. www.deltahotels.com. 1,590 units. From C$179 double. Additional adult C$20. Children 17 & under stay free in parent's room. Multi-night packages available. AE, DC, DISC, MC, V. Parking C$29. Subway: College. **Amenities:** 3 restaurants; 3 bars; babysitting; children's center; concierge; health club; Jacuzzi; 2 pools (1 for adults only); sauna. *In room:* A/C, TV, hair dryer, Internet, MP3 docking station.

The Gladstone Hotel ★ This lovely Victorian redbrick hotel is the longest continually operating hotel in the city. Those first guests of the old railroad hotel probably wouldn't know what to make of the arty offerings of the Gladstone today, where each room is decorated—some quite extravagantly—by artists. Since it opened in 1889, "The Gladdy," as it's affectionately known, has seen its share of ups and downs, but artist Christina Zeidler and her architecturally-inclined family (her father, Eb, designed The Eaton Centre and Ontario Place; her sister Margie redesigned the art space 401 Richmond St. W.) took over in 2005, transforming the place while preserving its heritage features, including the birdcage elevator. The hip public rooms are now a hive of cultural activity, with offerings ranging from burlesque shows to indie bands, and the Melody Bar hosts the city's most colorful weekend karaoke. The 37 rooms are featured on the website, so you can choose decor according to your taste and mood, with everything from lumberjack chic (a four-poster bed anchored by tree trunks) to a teen-idol theme, where the walls are plastered with retro posters, on offer. ***Note:*** If you're a light sleeper, this may not be the place for you.

1214 Queen St. W. (at Gladstone Ave.), Toronto, ON M6J 1J6. ✆ **416/531-4635.** Fax 416/539-0953. www.gladstonehotel.com. 51 units. From C$195 double. AE, MC, V. Parking C$15. Subway: Osgoode, then streetcar west to Gladstone Ave. **Amenities:** Restaurant; cafe; bar. *In room:* A/C, TV/DVD player, CD player, hair dryer, Wi-Fi (free).

Sheraton Centre Toronto Hotel ☺ It's entirely possible to stay at this hotel and never venture outside—the Sheraton complex includes restaurants, bars, and a huge pool, and the building connects to Toronto's underground city. If you long for a patch of green, the hotel provides that, too: The south side of the lobby contains a manicured garden with a waterfall. It's also a good option for families due to its central location and extensive list of child-friendly features, including a children's center. Most of the guest rooms in this skyscraper-heavy neighborhood lack a serious view, though as you near the top of the 46-story complex, the sights are inspiring indeed, especially on the north side with a clear view of City Hall. Designed for business travelers, the Club Level rooms come with a fax/printer/copier and two-line speakerphone.

123 Queen St. W., Toronto, ON M5H 2M9. ✆ **800/325-3535** or 416/361-1000. Fax 416/947-4854. www.sheratontoronto.com. 1,377 units. From C$249 double. Additional adult C$20. 2 children 17 & under stay free in parent's room. Packages available. AE, DC, MC, V. Parking C$33. Subway: Osgoode. **Amenities:** 2 restaurants; bar; babysitting; children's center; concierge; health club; Jacuzzi; gigantic heated indoor/outdoor pool; room service; sauna; spa. *In room:* A/C, TV, hair dryer, Internet.

The Strathcona ★★ If you want to be in the Financial District but don't want to pay a bundle, this is a great option. For years, the Strathcona has been one of the best buys in the city, and a recent renovation has made it more attractive. It sits in the shadow of the Fairmont Royal York, a short walk from all major downtown attractions. The trade-offs aren't as extensive as you might think. The Strathcona's rooms are on the small side but are no less comfortable for their compact design. Lately, the hotel has taken some green initiatives, changing its lighting, reducing water usage, and becoming entirely smoke-free.

60 York St., (btw. Front St. W. & Wellington St. W.), Toronto, ON M5J 1S8. ✆ **800/268-8304** or 416/363-3321. Fax 416/363-4679. www.thestrathconahotel.com. 194 units. From C$155 double. AE, DC, MC, V. Subway: Union. Private paid parking nearby C$16–C$38. **Amenities:** Cafe; bar; babysitting; bike rental; children's center; concierge; access to nearby health club; room service. *In room:* A/C, TV, hair dryer, Wi-Fi ($10 per day).

INEXPENSIVE

Hotel Victoria ★ In a landmark downtown building near the Hockey Hall of Fame, the Victoria retains the glamorous touches of an earlier age, such as crown moldings and marble columns in the lobby. It's Toronto's second-oldest hotel (built in 1909), but the facilities are upgraded annually. Because of its small size, the hotel offers an unusually high level of personal service and attention, which you normally wouldn't expect in budget accommodations. Standard rooms are on the small side but are nicely put together; deluxe rooms are larger, with coffeemakers and mini-fridges.

56 Yonge St. (at Wellington St.), Toronto, ON M5E 1G5. ✆ **800/363-8228** or 416/363-1666. Fax 416/363-7327. www.hotelvictoria-toronto.com. 56 units. From C$160 double. Additional adult C$15. Rates include continental breakfast. AE, DC, MC, V. Parking in nearby garage C$14. Subway: King. **Amenities:** Restaurant; babysitting; access to nearby health club. *In room:* A/C, TV, hair dryer, Internet (free).

Downtown East

EXPENSIVE

Cambridge Suites Hotel ★★ The emphasis at this all-suite hotel is comfortable home-away-from-home luxury, which makes it popular for extended stays. The smallest suite is a generous 51 sq. m (550 sq. ft.) and moves up to deluxe duplexes. The amenities for business travelers are solid. If you can drag yourself away from the cozy desk area, which has two two-line telephones and a fax, you can enjoy some of the comforts of home: fridge, microwave, and dining ware, plus coffee, tea, and snacks. And if you hand over your shopping list, the staff will stock the fridge, too. Penthouse suites come complete with Jacuzzi and breathtaking views.

15 Richmond St. E. (near Yonge St.), Toronto, ON M5C 1N2. ✆ **800/463-1990** or 416/368-1990. Fax 416/601-3751. www.cambridgesuitestoronto.com. 229 units. From C$240 suite. Rates include continental breakfast. AE, DC, DISC, MC, V. Parking C$25. Subway: Queen. **Amenities:** Restaurant; bar; babysitting; concierge; small health club; access to much larger health club nearby; Jacuzzi; room service; sauna; spa. *In room:* A/C, TV, fax, fridge, hair dryer, minibar, Wi-Fi ($11.95/day).

Cosmopolitan Hotel ★★ This discrete, all-suite boutique property is tucked away on quiet Colborne Street, just off Yonge Street. No surprise then to discover it caters to a Zen sensibility of serenity in all aspects of its service, from decor to turndown service (a gemstone is placed on the pillow, not a mint). Yoga mats, incense sticks, and a guided relaxation CD round out the room experience. If you're not blissed out by all this, head for Shizen Spa for more serious soothing of the soul.

8 Colborne St., Toronto, ON M5E 1E1. ✆ **416/350-2000**. Fax 416/350-2460. www.cosmotoronto.com. 80 suites. From C$229. Rates include continental breakfast. AE, DC, DISC, MC, V. Valet parking C$33. Subway: King. **Amenities:** Wine bar; concierge; gym; room service; spa. *In room:* A/C, TV, DVD player, kitchen, Wi-Fi.

MODERATE

Courtyard Toronto Downtown ★ Most Courtyard-brand properties in the Marriott chain are usually out of the city center. This one near Yonge and College streets is an exception, as it's on the subway line and a convenient base to get around from. The lobby, with its double-sided fireplace, has a surprisingly intimate feel, given the size of the 575-room hotel. Tour groups, which often book here, have a separate reception area. The guest rooms aren't big, but they are comfortable, with smart features such as windows that open and additional sinks outside the bathrooms. Ongoing refurbishments keep guest rooms looking fresh rather than lived in. While Courtyards are generally regarded as business hotels, this one has family-friendly facilities such as a children's wading pool.

475 Yonge St. (1 block north of College St.), Toronto, ON M4Y 1X7. ✆ **800/847-5075** or 416/924-0611. Fax 416/924-8692. www.courtyard.com/yyzcy. 575 units. From C$149 double. AE, DC, MC, V. Parking C$30. Subway: College. **Amenities:** 2 restaurants; bar; health club; children's wading pool; room service. *In room:* A/C, TV, hair dryer, minibar, Wi-Fi (free).

INEXPENSIVE

Bond Place Hotel ★ The location is right—a block from the Eaton Centre, around the corner from the Canon and Elgin theaters—and so is the price. Perhaps that's why this hotel tends to be popular with tour groups. The rooms are on the small side. Book as far in advance as you can; the hotel is usually packed, especially in summer. ***Note:*** This hotel has partnerships with many Toronto hospitals, so if you're coming to the city to visit a sick relative, Bond Place will give you an especially low rate.

65 Dundas St. E. (at Bond St.), Toronto, ON M5B 2G8. ✆ **800/268-9390** or 416/362-6061. Fax 416/360-6406. www.bondplace.ca. 287 units. From C$119 double. Additional adult C$15. Multi-night packages available. AE, DC, DISC, MC, V. Off-site parking C$25. Subway: Dundas. **Amenities:** Restaurant; bar; concierge; room service. *In room:* A/C, TV, hair dryer, Wi-Fi ($12.95/day).

Holiday Inn Express Toronto Downtown The main selling point of this no-frills hotel is its location, close to the Financial District and the Eaton Centre. It often offers special promotions, so be sure to ask. Rooms tend to be small, with standard amenities.

111 Lombard St. (btw. Adelaide & Richmond sts.), Toronto, ON M5C 2T9. ✆ **800/228-5151** or 416/367-5555. Fax 416/367-3470. www.ichotelsgroup.com. 196 units. From C$139 double. Rates include continental breakfast. AE, DC, DISC, MC, V. Parking C$20. Subway: King or Queen. **Amenities:** Breakfast bar. *In room:* A/C, TV, hair dryer, Wi-Fi (free).

Midtown

VERY EXPENSIVE

Four Seasons Hotel Toronto ★★ ☺ Although its days are numbered in this location, the legend lives on. The Rolling Stones call the Four Seasons home in Toronto, and during the Toronto International Film Festival, you can't get in for love or money. The hotel, in the ritzy Yorkville district, has earned a reputation for offering fine service and complete comfort. Despite the high rollers who frequent the place, this is a family-friendly hotel that really takes care of kids. Rooms tend to be on the small side (a standard is only about 30 sq. m/323 sq. ft.), but they're well designed and easy on the eye. Corner rooms have charming balconies offering great views of the street scene below. Take a window seat at the Avenue bar off the lobby for the serious sport of people-watching. You never know who might walk by. When The Four Seasons' new location is ready in 2013, at the other end of Yorkville on Bay Street, the in-crowd scene will no doubt move right along with it.

21 Avenue Rd. (at Yorkville Ave.), Toronto, ON M5R 2G1. ✆ **800/268-6282** or 416/964-0411. Fax 416/964-2301. www.fourseasons.com/toronto. 380 units. From C$305 double. Multi-night discounts & packages available. AE, DC, DISC, MC, V. Parking C$30. Subway: Bay. **Amenities:** 2 restaurants; 2 bars/lounges; babysitting; bike rental; concierge; health club; Jacuzzi; indoor/outdoor pool; room service. *In room:* A/C, TV/DVD player, CD player, hair dryer, minibar, Wi-Fi ($15/day).

Park Hyatt Toronto ★★★ This venerable hotel commands a prime location opposite the Royal Ontario Museum at the corner of Bloor Street West and Avenue Road. It's glamorous and grown up, and boasts the best hotel bar in town (author Mordecai Richler famously called its 18th-floor Roof Lounge the only civilized place in Toronto). The Park Hyatt's two towers are linked by a lobby dotted with Eastern-inspired objets d'art. The guest rooms in the newer North Tower are among the most generously proportioned in town—the *smallest* is 46 sq. m (495 sq. ft.). The older, but frequently refurbished, rooms in the South Tower have spectacular, unobstructed views of downtown Toronto. The ground-floor restaurant **Annona** is a treat, as is the Stillwater Spa, which is a popular destination for locals.

4 Avenue Rd. (at Bloor St. W.), Toronto, ON M5R 2E8. ✆ **800/233-1234** or 416/925-1234. Fax 416/924-6693. www.parktoronto.hyatt.com. 346 units. From C$289 double. Multi-night packages available. AE, DC, DISC, MC, V. Valet parking C$34. Subway: Museum or Bay. No pets accepted. **Amenities:** Restaurant; 2 bars; concierge; health club; Jacuzzi; room service; sauna; spa. *In room:* A/C, TV, fax, hair dryer, Internet (free), minibar.

EXPENSIVE

The Sutton Place Hotel ★ The Sutton Place boasts the advantage of a small hotel, with detail-oriented, personalized service not often found in a 300-plus room property. In addition to hosting a galaxy of stars, the hotel draws sophisticated business and leisure travelers in search of serious pampering. Guest rooms are spacious, and a few suites have full kitchens. Not that you'd want to cook while you're here—the ground-floor **Accents** restaurant serves continental fare, and across the street, the star-studded Bistro 990 produces impeccable French cuisine. One downside is that The Sutton Place stands alone in its neighborhood. It's about a 10- to 15-minute walk to attractions such as the Royal Ontario Museum (see p. 398) and the Yorkville shopping district.

955 Bay St. (at Wellesley St.), Toronto, ON M5S 2A2. ✆ **866/378-8866** or 416/924-9221. Fax 416/924-1778. www.toronto.suttonplace.com. 311 units. From C$189 double. Additional adult C$29. Children 17 & under stay free in parent's room. AE, DC, MC, V. Parking C$25. Subway: Wellesley. **Amenities:** Restaurant; bar; babysitting; concierge; health club; indoor pool; room service; sauna. *In room:* A/C, TV, hair dryer, minibar, Wi-Fi ($16/day).

MODERATE

Clarion Hotel & Suites Selby ★ Ornate chandeliers, stucco moldings, and high ceilings make this 1890s Victorian building a charming character property. In a predominantly gay neighborhood, the Selby attracts gay and straight couples, as well as seniors (they get special discounts). All of the rooms have private bathrooms, but only a few have old-fashioned claw-foot tubs. While there's no concierge, the staff is very friendly and will provide plenty of recommendations for what to see and do. History buffs will love the fact that Ernest Hemingway lived here for a couple of years while he was on staff at the *Toronto Star* newspaper (and yes, there is a Hemingway suite).

592 Sherbourne St. (1 block south of Bloor St. E.), Toronto, ON M4X 1L4. ✆ **800/4-CHOICE** (800/424-6423) or 416/921-3142. Fax 416/923-3177. www.choicehotels.ca. 82 units. From C$155 double. Rates include continental breakfast. AE, DISC, MC, V. Parking C$20. Subway: Sherbourne. **Amenities:** Access to nearby health club. *In room:* A/C, TV, hair dryer, Wi-Fi (free).

Holiday Inn Toronto Midtown Considering this hotel's tony location—steps from Yorkville and several museums, including the Royal Ontario Museum (see p. 398)—the price is hard to beat. The rooms are small but comfortable, and outfitted with well-lit worktables. All rooms have free high-speed Internet access, but there aren't many other amenities or services. This is a good home base for a leisure traveler who prizes location over other considerations. If you're not planning to hang out a lot in your hotel room, it's a small trade-off for the price.

280 Bloor St. W. (at St. George St.), Toronto, ON M5S 1V8. ✆ **888/HOLIDAY** (888/465-4329) or 416/968-0010. Fax 416/968-7765. www.ichotelsgroup.com. 209 units. From C$150 double. Multi-night & other packages available. AE, DC, DISC, MC, V. Parking C$22. Subway: St. George. **Amenities:** Restaurant; coffee shop; babysitting; health club; room service. *In room:* A/C, TV, hair dryer, Wi-Fi (free).

Howard Johnson Yorkville This hotel is a bargain in a very expensive neighborhood. The Yorkville location is excellent, which compensates for small rooms (you're probably not going to want to spend much time there, as is the case with many value-priced hotels).

89 Avenue Rd. (btw. Yorkville & Webster aves.), Toronto, ON M5R 2G3. ✆ **800/446-4656** or 416/964-1220. Fax 416/964-8692. www.hojoyorkville.com. 69 units. From C$150 double. Rates include continental breakfast. AE, DC, MC, V. Parking C$22. Subway: Bay or Museum. **Amenities:** Concierge; Wi-Fi (free). *In room:* A/C, TV, hair dryer.

WHERE TO DINE

Toronto is a good place to eat. In keeping with the city's overall character—generally agreeable, occasionally inventive, sometimes brilliant—you can expect to find plenty of decent food, as well as some truly memorable fare (fine or rustic). Lately, there's glamour in the air: Chef-driven openings and no-reservation hot-spots draw eager crowds, and there is a proliferation of restaurant-related books, shows, stars, and blogs.

The city's multicultural makeup ensures a rich banquet, and fusion here goes well beyond the realm of Asian: Many of the city's best cooks and chefs reinvent as they go, inspired by culinary cultures from around the globe or down the street. Other things Toronto's foodies love: the local movement, all manner of meat (and offal), pretty bakeries, Italian *trattorias,* bistros, thin-crust pizza, super-fresh seafood, a good cup of joe, and a lively pub scene. The only thing that's in short supply is fine dining on par with the world's great restaurants. However, hungry citizens do engage in a bit of adventure, like molecular gastronomy, new ways to savor brains, eating in the dark, wild foods like pickled spruce tips, and serious gourmet happenings such as Japanese, nine-course set menus at C$300 per person.

Downtown West

This is where you will find Toronto's highest concentration of great restaurants. **Little Italy,** which runs along College Street, generally has better bars and cafes than restaurants; the streets of **Chinatown,** which radiate from Spadina Avenue, are lined with brightly lit, busy eateries; and lately, **West Queen West, Dundas West,** and **Ossington Avenue** are all proving to be enticing destinations for dining.

VERY EXPENSIVE

Canoe Restaurant & Bar ★★★ CANADIAN Some come for the panoramic view offered at this modern, chic dining room, but the top-quality service, sophisticated food, and fine wine cellar are what keep them coming back. Simply put, this is one of the city's—and perhaps country's—best restaurants. Executives are the main clientele at lunchtime, when the place can feel corporate; dinner, with the twinkling cityscape backdrop, is more romantic. Thanks to the passion of executive chef Anthony Walsh, menus are seasonal and offer a selection of top ingredients from local purveyors. The flavor is Canadian cuisine with rarities such as Nunavut caribou and Québec foie gras, all handled with delicacy and brilliant technique. If you're ready to splurge, tasting menus, at C$100 per person (add C$50 for paired wines), are impressive and generous. If you're on a budget, drop in at the bar for a glass of Niagara wine and a nibble.

54th floor, Toronto Dominion Tower, 66 Wellington St. W. ✆ **416/364-0054.** www.canoerestaurant.com. Reservations required. Main courses C$39–C$44. AE, DC, MC, V. Mon–Fri 11:45am–2:30pm & 5–10:30pm. Subway: King.

Lai Wah Heen ★★★ CANTONESE This is one hotel dining room where you'll find more locals than visitors. The interior is vintage Art Deco; spare pictograms dominate the walls of the two-level space. The extensive menu is mainly Cantonese, and regulars come for the excellent Peking Duck, dim sum (especially the Sunday brunch tasting menu), and delicacies such as alligator loin dumplings. There's a midtown location, too: Lai Toh Heen (629 Mount Pleasant Rd.; ✆ **416/489-8922**).

In the Metropolitan Hotel, 110 Chestnut St. ✆ **416/977-9899.** www.metropolitan.com/lwh. Reservations recommended. Main courses C$22–C$48. AE, DC, MC, V. Daily 11:30am–3pm; Sun–Thurs 5:30–10:30pm; Fri & Sat 5:30–11pm. Subway: St. Patrick.

EXPENSIVE

Bymark ★★ AMERICAN/ BISTRO In the heart of the financial district sits the most corporate of the Mark McEwan empire of swanky restaurants. Think burgers, onion rings, steaks, and snazzy seafood—all top-grade. The kitchen delivers consistently fine, if uninspired, fare. The extensive wine list, which was a draw for big expense accounts before the recession hit, now offers good value, especially with a fine selection of wines by the glass.

66 Wellington St. W. (at Bay St.). ✆ **416/777-1144.** www.bymarkdowntown.com. Reservations recommended. Main courses C$32–C$47. AE, DC, MC, V. Mon–Fri 11:30am–2:30pm; Mon–Sat 5–11pm. Subway: King, then walk west to Bay St.

Conviction ★★ FRENCH/PIZZA If you've visited Toronto before, you may have sampled some of Marc Thuet's excellent cooking at Centro, Bite Me, or Thuet. His new spot, Conviction, started with a gimmick: All of the kitchen and serving staff has served time in jail. The risk has paid off: The quality of the food and service is excellent. The concept even attracted a film crew for a reality show, "Conviction Kitchen." The restaurant has inspired the chef to return to his Alsatian roots, a welcome move for all who love Thuet's generous and rich treats such as the hearty soups, slow-braised stews, and excellent pizzas which are made with his signature dough (his family has been in the baking business for 200 years). For a sample of Thuet's irresistible baked goods, try one of the handful of Petite Thuet *boulangeries* around town (www.petitethuet.com).

609 King St. W. ✆ **416/603-2777.** www.convictionrestaurant.com. Reservations required. Main courses C$23–C$37. AE, DC, MC, V. Tues–Sat 6pm–midnight; Sun 11am–2pm. Subway: St. Andrew, then a streetcar west to Portland St.

Foxley ★★ FUSION/BISTRO It was just four years ago that this unpretentious bistro opened on Ossington Avenue, unknowingly leading a brigade of new eateries to what is now the city's must-visit strip for foodies. Chef/owner Tom Thai, long known as a top sushi chef, creates beautiful small-plate dishes such as plump dumplings, steamed (often sustainable) fish dishes, smoked pork belly, and more. The flavor is fusion: pan-Asian with European and Mexican influences. Eat what you please since there's a fresh note to this cooking—light on salt and fat—and the reasonable prices are equally encouraging. The only drawback, really, is that they don't accept reservations. So arrive early, put your name on the list, and then trundle off for a drink while you wait.

207 Ossington Ave. ✆ **416/534-8520.** Reservations not accepted. Main courses C$7–C$24. Mon–Sat 5–11pm. Subway: Dundas St., then a streetcar west to Ossington Ave.; or Ossington Ave. (on Bloor line), then a bus south to Foxley St.

Niagara Street Café ★★ BISTRO Owner Anton Potvin has flare, as does accomplished chef Nick Liu, and together they have created a lovely little bistro with an emphasis on local, organic, and artisanal ingredients. Don't worry, there's nothing righteous or even dutiful about the experience; it's pure pleasure, from the crispy snail and lettuce salad to the duck confit, the daily wild fish special, or the bison *bavette*. Desserts, made in-house, are worth saving room for; service-with-a-smile adds another positive note. Brunch is a neighborhood draw.

169 Niagara St. (at King St.). ✆ **416/703-4222.** www.niagarastreetcafe.com. Main courses C$19–C$27. AE, DC, MC, V. Wed–Sun 6–10:30pm. Subway: St. Patrick & then King St. streetcar west to Niagara St.

Vertical ★★ MEDITERRANEAN The prime location of Vertical in First Canadian Place is secondary to the refined cooking from chef Tawfik Shehata. The local-loving chef combines Mediterranean flavors with local sources and often organic ingredients. The look, and clientele, are somewhat corporate, but the mainstream menu with a seasonal bent is treated with a surprising degree of culinary passion. Don't miss the daily seafood specials. Service is smooth, and the wine list offers plenty of excellent pairings.

In First Canadian Place, 100 King St. W. ✆ **416/214-2252.** www.verticalrestaurant.ca. Reservations recommended. Main courses C$18–C$39. AE, DC, MC, V. Mon–Fri 11:30am–midnight. Subway: King.

MODERATE

The Black Hoof & Hoof Café ★★★ BISTRO Nose-to-tail eating is taken to extremes, and to truly tasty heights, at this brilliant restaurant-bar and its sister brunch-and-bar bistro right across the street. Co-owner/chef Grant van Gameren's in-house charcuterie is the star, with the tongue sandwich drawing raves, but the pastas and soups are equally inspired. At the Café, brunch dishes include standouts like pancakes topped with rabbit confit and little bone-marrow doughnuts, all daring and beautiful. Be prepared to wait: The buzz around these two spots is deafening.

928 & 923 Dundas St. W. ✆ **416/551-8854** or 416/792-7511. Reservations not accepted. Main courses C$10–C$24. No credit cards. Restaurant Sun–Wed 6–11:30pm, Thurs–Sat 6pm–1am; cafe Thurs–Mon 10am–2pm & 6pm–2am. Subway: St. Patrick, then a streetcar west to Grace St.

Ematei ★★ JAPANESE/SUSHI One of Toronto's most authentic sushi and *izakaya* spots, this place attracts regulars looking for fine fare who don't mind the drab decor. Don't miss the hot pots, grilled fish, tantalizing tempura, and hand-rolls. The best values are the three-course menus. Service is no-nonsense.

30 St Patrick St. ✆ **416/340-0472.** Main courses C$9–C$29. AE, DC, MC, V. Mon–Fri noon–2:30pm; daily 5pm–midnight. Subway: Osgoode.

The Local Kitchen and Wine Bar ★★ ITALIAN Parkdale's latest hot number is part authentic Italian *trattoria,* part contemporary Toronto. The crowded, convivial room is idiosyncratic, the service pro yet friendly, and the food absolutely fantastic. Chef Fabio Bondi arrives pre-dawn each morning to make stunning fresh pasta like smoked gnocchi with creamy Taleggio cheese. Vegetables, fish, and meats are often on par with the noodles. The wine list is simple yet good, and each evening, there's an interesting wine highlighted, whether a rare Sicilian white or a new local vintage.

1710 Queen St. W. ✆ **416/534-6700.** Reservations not accepted. Main courses C$15–C$25. AE, DC, MC, V. Tues & Wed 5:30–10pm; Thurs–Sat 5:30–11pm. Subway: Osgoode, then a streetcar west to Triller Ave.

Rodney's Oyster House ★★ SEAFOOD Rodney is Toronto's original "Oysterman," one of only a handful left now. This spot is a favorite with nearby condo dwellers and office workers, but is also a draw as a destination. The Maritime-inspired setting is unpretentious and includes whimsical touches such as fishing paraphernalia. The main draw is the super-fresh oysters, but chowders and pastas are very good, too. There's a new locale at 56 Temperance St. (✆ **416/703-5111**).

469 King St. W. ✆ **416/363-8105.** www.rodneysoysterhouse.com. Reservations recommended (reservations cannot be made for the patio except for groups of 10 or more). Main courses C$10–C$29. AE, DC, MC, V. Mon–Sat 11am–1am. Subway: St. Andrew.

Terroni ★★ ITALIAN/PIZZA This was Toronto's first serious venture into true Southern Italian pizza. It's since grown to be something of a mini-empire and a tried-and-true place for fine, thin-crust pies; good pastas; traditional salads made with beans, greens, and sausage (yum!); and other traditional dishes and desserts made with nonna's kitchen in mind. Great value and always popular. There are other locations at 1 Balmoral Ave. (✆ **416/925-4020**) and 106 Victoria St., Dundas Square (✆ **416/955-0258**).

720 Queen St. W. (at Claremont St.). ✆ **416/504-0320.** www.terroni.ca. Main courses C$10–C$23. AE, MC, V. Mon–Wed & Sun 9am–10pm; Thurs–Sat 9am–11pm. Subway: Osgoode, then a streetcar west to Claremont.

INEXPENSIVE

Café 668 ★ ASIAN FUSION This vegetarian restaurant used to be a dingy spot at 668 Dundas West, but it has been reinvented as a sleek cafe/bistro offering the same Asian-fusion fare it won acclaim for, but in a much prettier room. Soups are a standout, as are the wide selection of noodles. Mock meats are, well, a poor stand-in. Salad rolls are fresh and worth a try. Overall, spicing can be through the roof, so take note from the friendly guide on the menu.

885 Dundas St. W. (at Claremont St.). ✆ **416/703-0668.** www.cafe668.com. Main courses C$11–C$14. No credit cards. Tues–Fri 12:30–4pm & 6–9pm; Sat & Sun 1:30–9pm. Subway: St. Patrick, then a streetcar west to Claremont St.

Chippy's ★ FISH AND CHIPS Great, non-greasy fish and chips are hard to find, so little wonder this shoe-box spot on Queen West is a hit with its signature light batter (Guinness beer is a key ingredient) and chunky, home-cut fries. There's halibut, cod, and haddock for frying, and an assortment of garnishes, most of them in fact not any improvement over a bit of ketchup or malt vinegar. The location, across the street from the beautiful and sprawling Trinity Bellwoods Park, calls out for a good-weather picnic. A second location is at 490 Bloor St. W., at Bathurst St. (✆ **416/516-7776**).

893 Queen St. W. (at Strachan Ave.). ✆ **416/866-7474.** Sun–Wed 11:30am–8pm; Thurs–Sat 11:30am–9pm. Main courses C$9–C$13. No credit cards. Subway: Osgoode, then a streetcar west to Strachan Ave.

Torito ★★ SPANISH/TAPAS Kensington Market—and Augusta Avenue, in particular—is filled with eateries, but this one is a little gem that serves small-plate, Spanish-rooted fare that is fun and fine, like roasted quail with a pomegranate glaze, smoked trout with potato salad, and "tongue in cheek": braised tongue beside seared-and-braised cheek in a red-wine sauce. The wine list offers plenty of sherry and cava (sparkling Spanish wine), plus sangria for pairing.

276 Augusta Ave. ✆ **647/436-5874.** www.toritotapasbar.com. Reservations not accepted. Tapas plates C$5–C$11. Mon–Sat 5:30–11pm. MC, V. Subway: Spadina, then a streetcar south to College St.

Downtown East

EXPENSIVE

Biff's Bistro & Wine Bar ★★ BISTRO The Oliver-Bonacini team that created a number of top-notch Toronto restaurants (Jump, Canoe, and Auberge du Pommier, among others) also invented this good-value, classic bistro. The setting is cozy but chic, and the menu features fine fare like pan-fried halibut covered with thinly sliced potatoes and traditional roast leg of lamb. The three-course dinner is a steal at C$33, with many choices for appetizers and mains. The good wine list focuses on Ontario. If you're heading to a Canadian Stage Company show or to the Sony Centre, you could not pick a better place to dine.

4 Front St. E. (at Yonge St.). ✆ **416/860-0086.** www.oliverbonacini.com. Reservations strongly recommended. Main courses C$18–C$35. AE, DC, MC, V. Mon–Fri noon–2:30pm; Mon–Sat 5–10pm. Subway: Union or King.

Hiro Sushi SUSHI Take a seat at the bar, as many sushi aficionados do, and enjoy the spectacle of watching star chef Hiro Yoshida create beauty in front of your eyes. Pick from the master chef's selection of sushi and sashimi for a memorable experience. Soups are also inspired, and tempura is light as air.

171 King St. St. E. (at Jarvis St.). ✆ **416/304-0550.** Main courses C$20–C$30. AE, DC, MC, V. Mon–Fri noon–2:30pm; Mon–Sat 6:30–10:30pm. Subway: King.

RubyWatchCo ★★★ BISTRO Star chef Lynn Crawford, formerly of Four Seasons in Toronto and New York, teamed with Michelin-starred chef Lola Kirk to create a unique dining experience: There's one prix-fixe dinner offered nightly with four courses—no choices—and the main ingredients are supplied by local purveyors. At C$49 a head, the price might seem high, but given that the food is stellar, the atmosphere convivial, and the chefs work attentively on all details, the risky venture is proving a hit. Don't try to visit without a reservation.

730 Queen St. E. (at Broadview Ave.) ✆ **416/465-0100.** www.rubywatchco.ca. Reservations essential. Prix-fixe menu C$49. AE, MC, V. Tues–Sat 6–11pm. Subway: Broadview, then a streetcar south to Queen St. E.

MODERATE

Gilead Bistro & Café ★★★ CAFE/BISTRO After years of building a restaurant empire and then recently scaling back, star chef Jamie Kennedy is behind the stove at this exceptional, small, beautiful bistro. In other words, the food is sublime. Menus change daily and draw inspiration from local and seasonal ingredients. (Kennedy is a pioneering locavore.) Come for a light breakfast of fresh baked pastries and organic yogurt; at lunch, try the chef's famous, thyme-scented frites alongside impossibly light battered whitefish. At dinner, the more sophisticated menu is a showcase for Kennedy's classical French training: *gallantine* of chicken, pork confit, perfect duck breast, delicately handled vegetables, soups that sing, and fine desserts. Wines are local, including some from Kennedy's vineyard. Finding your way can be tricky: It's in a tiny alley in Corktown.

4 Gilead Place. ✆ **647/288-0680.** www.gileadcafe.ca. Reservations accepted for dinner & for parties of 6 or more at brunch. Main courses C$6–C$26. AE, DC, MC, V. Mon 8am–5:30pm; Tues–Sat 8am–11pm; Sun 10am–3pm. Subway: King, then a streetcar east to Trinity St. & walk 1 block east to Gilead Place.

Edward Levesque's Kitchen ★★ BISTRO An early arrival to the now-popular, once-empty Leslieville, this casual diner and bistro emphasizes local and organic products that up the quality overall. The burgers are good and are made fresh as are the generous salads; breakfasts are excellent, including eggs poached in tomato sauce and fine frittatas. Bistro fare includes succulent leg of lamb, veggie risotto, and lovely desserts, including house-made pies.

1290 Queen St. E. ✆ **416/465-3600.** www.edwardlevesque.ca. Reservations accepted for dinner. Main courses C$15–C$24. AE, MC, V. Sat & Sun 9am–3pm; Thurs & Fri 11:30am–2:30pm; Tues–Sat 5:30–10pm. Subway: Queen, then a streetcar east to Leslie St.

Starfish SEAFOOD Toronto has a thing for bivalves: There's a wealth of excellent oyster houses around town. Owner Patrick McMurray is a world-champion oyster-shucker, and he knows his goods. Stop by for some beautiful oysters or sample the excellent fish and chips, perfect prawns, or more substantial fare like poached and grilled fish and seafood. Beers and wines are well selected, and the ambiance is cheerful.

100 Adelaide St. E. (at Church St.). ✆ **416/366-7827.** www.starfishoysterbed.com. Main courses C$18–C$35. AE, DC, MC, V. Mon–Fri noon–3pm; Mon–Sat 5–11pm. Subway: King.

INEXPENSIVE

Mi Mi Restaurant VIETNAMESE Authentic Vietnamese is the name of the game at this family-run spot, where locals go for fine barbecued meats, delicate seafood, well-done rice and noodle dishes, fine *pho* soups, and inspired rice rolls. The vibe is fun and relaxed; it may take a while to get a seat or for dishes to arrive, but it's worth it.

688 Gerrard St. E. (at Broadview Ave.). ✆ **416/778-5948.** Main courses C$5–C$17. No credit cards. Mon, Tues, Thurs & Fri 10am–10pm; Wed noon–10pm; Sat & Sun 10am–10:30pm. Subway: Broadview, then a streetcar south to Gerrard St.

Midtown

VERY EXPENSIVE

C5 ★★★ BISTRO/CANADIAN The renovation of the Royal Ontario Museum remains controversial, but there's little argument that this beautiful restaurant, located on the top level and headed by chef Ted Corrado, is worth a visit. The skylights and crisscrossing window segments provide a gorgeous view of the city. More importantly, the modern dining room is host to fine dining with a distinct local flavor.

At the Royal Ontario Museum, 100 Queen's Park. ✆ **416/586-7928.** www.c5restaurant.ca. Reservations recommended for dinner. Main courses C$26–C$45. AE, DC, MC, V. Tues–Sat 11:30am–2:30pm; Thurs–Sat 5:30–10pm. Subway: Museum or Bay.

EXPENSIVE

earth ★★★ 🎁 BISTRO Globe Bistro's (see p. 393) team has moved to Rosedale, and the news is good: Prices are trimmed, and the attractive dining room and lounge are hopping with locals who love chef Kevin McKenna's culinary talent and owner Ed Ho's gracious touch. Together, they share a serious commitment to local foods, so produce is local and seasonal. Meats are sourced from nearby farms and butchered on-site, and you can order your flesh by the ounce. Smart. The wood-burning oven is used to cook beautiful flatbreads and more, including a scrumptious suckling pig. A long list of wines by the glass, some local, and homey desserts round out the experience.

1055 Yonge St. (at Roxborough St. E.). ✆ **416/551-9890.** www.globeearth.ca. Reservations essential. Main courses C$17–C$25. AE, DC, MC, V. Mon–Fri 11:30am–11pm; Sat & Sun 11am–11pm. Subway: Rosedale.

Pangaea ★★★ INTERNATIONAL In a neighborhood with few good places to eat—it's all about work or shopping here—this truly delightful, high-end restaurant hops with chic regulars at lunch and dinner. Open for 15 years, the chef/co-owner team of Martin Kouprie and Peter Geary deliver consistent elegance with fine food, attentive service, and a stellar cellar. The tone of the place is muted, even conservative, but behind the scenes, Kouprie's adventurous streak makes for an unusual selection of wild foods; think wild-caught fish (the restaurant is certified by Ocean Wise for its sustainable practices), wild mushrooms, wild berries—whatever is in season and inspires the chef.

1221 Bay St. ✆ **416/920-2323.** www.pangaearestaurant.com. Reservations recommended. Main courses C$29–C$44. AE, DC, MC, V. Mon–Sat 11:30am–11:30pm. Subway: Bay.

MODERATE

Bar Mercurio ★★ ITALIAN There's something quintessentially Italian about this casual *trattoria* (it's not a bar) that stays open from breakfast through to late suppers. You can come for an espresso and brioche, return for excellent pizzas made in the wood-burning oven at lunch and—why not?—stroll back for dinner and sample the signature beef medallion with crab or some fine pastas and salads. Whatever time of day, linger on the noisy patio or inside (often equally boisterous); take your time. Across the street is the stylish (and more subdued) L'Espresso, good for brunch and a great deal for lunch.

270 Bloor St. W. (at St. George St.). ✆ **416/960-38770.** Main courses C$22–C$32. AE, MC, V. Mon–Sat 7am–11pm. Subway: St. George.

Loire ★★★ FRENCH For awhile, this pretty bistro was too hot to handle: It was tough to get in, and sometimes service came with an attitude. But things have lightened up, and it's now a convivial spot for fine and sometimes inventive French fare. Chef Jean-Charles Dupoire and top sommelier Sylvain Brissonet are clearly enjoying their hard-earned accolades. Both hail from the Loire region, so expect French classics and plenty of beautiful wines and perfect pairings. Dupoire is stretching a bit, adding fusion touches to standards, and to good ends. Lake Erie whitefish comes with a chili-cornmeal crust and a garlic confit, lemon polenta, and salsa *verde*. Regulars opt for the burgers, lamb, or beef.

119 Harbord St. ✆ **416/850-8330.** www.loirerestaurant.ca. Reservations recommended. Main courses C$17–C$27. AE, MC, V. Tues–Fri noon–2:30pm; Tues–Sat 5:30–10pm. Subway: Spadina, then the LRT south to Harbord St.

Messis ★★ BISTRO/INTERNATIONAL Nearly 20 years old, this simple bistro is Eugene Shewchuk's vision realized: he wanted to create an accessible and pleasant spot with good food and fair prices, a place where cooks can happily eat. The menu changes frequently, keeping as its mainstays Italian pastas and Mediterranean meat dishes, and ranging into Asia, too. Thin-crust pizzas are kept simple, and mains tend to stick to a small selection of two meats, one fish. It's all very good. To boot, it was one of the first fine restaurants along the Harbord Street strip, which now has good options from one block to the next. The California-dominated wine list is as reasonably priced as the food.

97 Harbord St. ✆ **416/920-2186.** www.messis.ca. Reservations accepted. Main courses C$13–C$25. AE, MC, V. Sun–Thurs 5:30–10pm; Fri & Sat 5:30–11pm. Subway: Spadina, then the LRT south to Harbord St.

INEXPENSIVE

Caplansky's ☺ DELICATESSEN Montréal's smoked meat is rightfully famous. Now, Toronto has a fantastic version to call its own. Zane Caplansky's fatty, um, marbled pastrami-on-rye is the main attraction: The hand-cut slices of pink, salty goodness are also featured in hash browns, with eggs, in a burger, and numerous other worthy ways. Choose your fat content: lean, medium, or full-on. Students and profs, foodies and families all make pilgrimages. There are other deli delights at this spacious new spot with a great patio. Try the pickled tongue, the lox, or if you're feeling sanctimonious, the salad (protein provided by only chick peas). The kids menu includes kosher hot dogs.

356 College St. W. ✆ **416/500-3852.** http://caplanskys.com. Main courses C$10–C$13. V. Sun–Tues 10am–10pm; Wed–Sat 10am–11pm. Subway: Osgoode, then the College streetcar west to Brunswick Ave.

Lalibela ☺ ETHIOPIAN This is delicious Ethiopian cuisine with plenty of vegetarian options, rich with flavor and a friendly vibe, too. It's a winning combination; little wonder a second location has opened up (1405 Danforth Ave.; ✆ **416/645-0486**). If you don't know your *yemiser wat* from your *asa gulashe,* have no fear: The staff will guide you to what you're looking for and prepare custom tasting platters. It's great for kids, too, with a special menu of small tasting portions or, for fussy eaters, mac-and-cheese and fries.

869 Bloor St. W. ✆ **416/535-6615.** www.lalibelaethiopianrestaurant.com. Main courses C$5–C$12. V. Daily 10am–2am. Subway: Ossington, then walk 1 block east.

Nataraj ★ INDIAN There's usually a bit of a wait for a table, especially at dinnertime—Nataraj's cuisine is popular with Annex residents and university students given its good value and better-than-fair Northern Indian menus. The decor is tired, but this isn't a place to linger anyway. Line up, sit down, order curries, tandoori chicken, rich veggie dishes such as the *chana masala* (chickpeas cooked with potatoes, tomatoes, onions, and spices), and the *saag paneer* (house-made cottage cheese cooked in onion and spinach), and be on your merry way. The tandoor-baked breads are good for scooping up the special relishes, such as the *kachumbor* (cucumber, tomato, and onion marinated in lime juice).

394 Bloor St. W. ✆ **416/928-2925.** Reservations not accepted. Main courses C$9–C$13. AE, DC, MC, V. Mon–Fri noon–2:30pm; daily 5–10:30pm. Subway: Spadina.

The Danforth/The East End

The general theme along the Danforth has long been Greek, although today there is more variety: good pubs, bars, restaurants, and lounges line the busy thoroughfare. You can still come for good and middling (but cheap) Greek, too.

EXPENSIVE

Globe Bistro ★★ BISTRO There's a chic dining room, a cool bar, a breezy patio, and some very fine cooking at this popular neighborhood bistro. Owner Ed Ho and chef Kevin McKenna have created a go-to destination with staying power, in part due to a great wine cellar and generous deals, such as half-price bottles on Sunday. The vibe is fun, the dishes sometimes stellar, such as the Muscovy duck breast and elk loin. You can also make a meal of the many tantalizing starters. There is a definite local-and-seasonal bent that is genuine.

24 Danforth Ave. ✆ **416/466-2000.** www.globebistro.com. Reservations recommended. Main courses C$19–C$29. AE, DC, MC, V. Mon–Fri 11:30am–2pm; Sun 11am–2pm; daily 6–11pm. Subway: Broadview.

MODERATE

Allen's ★★ AMERICAN This time-honored pub, burger joint, and casual dining room takes its name and inspiration from the institution in New York City. Take note of the excellent beef, lamb, and pork—the heart of any great burger—which is sourced from local farms and then butchered and ground on-site. Pastas, salads, and mains are all consistently good. Brunch, especially when the lovely patio is open, is a treat. Desserts are comfort food: pies and homey sweets. The selection of beers—on tap and in bottles—is another draw. The fine wine list is focused on local.

143 Danforth Ave. (at Broadview Ave.). ✆ **416/463-3086.** www.allens.to. Main courses C$10–C$26. AE, DC, MC, V. Mon–Fri 11:30am–1am; Sat & Sun 11am–1am. Subway: Broadview.

Pan on the Danforth ★ GREEK Pan feels like a spot for a celebration: Staff are friendly; weekend nights, in particular, are busy and humming; and the vibe is all Mediterranean warmth. This long-established eatery serves Greek classics—dips and starters are especially conventional—but the quality is good and often a notch above competitors on the strip. Portions are generous, and fish and lamb dominate. The well-chosen wine list favors the New World. The crowd is fairly sophisticated, which may explain the cryptic message over the bar: YOU'VE DONE IT ALREADY. On weekend evenings, diners are treated to live music: traditional Greek bouzouki on Fridays and jazz piano on Saturdays (there's also a belly dancer who turns up for performances on other evenings, too).

516 Danforth Ave. ✆ **416/466-8158.** www.panonthedanforth.com. Reservations recommended. Main courses C$16–C$25. AE, MC, V. Sun–Thurs noon–11pm; Fri & Sat noon–midnight. Subway: Chester or Pape.

Uptown

This area is too large to be considered a neighborhood, stretching as it does from north of Davenport Road to Steeles Avenue. While it doesn't have the concentration of restaurants that the downtown area enjoys, a number of stellar options make the trip north worthwhile.

VERY EXPENSIVE

Auberge du Pommier ★★★ FRENCH Don't have time to drop by your French country house this weekend? Then this cozy, fine-dining room that exudes Provençal-style charm is a ready alternative. Chef Jason Bartenger combines classical French technique with the best of Canadian ingredients. Service is equally refined, as is the extensive wine list. Creamy lobster and white-bean soup, and baked artichokes stuffed with French goat cheese are lovely starters. Entrees, such as pan-seared scallops with braised oxtail in a cabernet *jus,* keep up the pace. Crème brûlée isn't always on the dessert menu (which changes with the season, just like the regular menu), but be sure to order it when available.

4150 Yonge St. ✆ **416/222-2220.** www.oliverbonacini.com. Reservations strongly recommended. Main courses C$36–C$44. AE, DC, DISC, MC, V. Mon–Fri 11:45am–2:30pm; Mon–Thurs 5–9pm; Fri & Sat 5:30–9:30pm. Subway: York Mills.

Scaramouche ★★★ INTERNATIONAL Tucked into a tony midtown apartment building with beautiful views over the city, Scaramouche isn't easy to find. But it's worth the effort. Chef Keith Froggett and maitre d' Carl Corte have been quietly perfecting one of the city's finest restaurants for more than 25 years. Understated and elegant, the menus are laden with luxe ingredients like caviar, foie gras, truffles, and oysters; main dishes include venison loin wrapped in smoked bacon and a rich, red-wine glaze. Top pastry chef Joanne Yolles has returned after years at Pangaea (see p. 391), so the sweets are equally stunning. The wine list has a broad reach, and there's a nice selection of cognacs. The formal dining room, which is best for special occasions, is complemented by the adjoining casual pasta bar and grill.

1 Benvenuto Place (off Avenue Rd.). ✆ **416/961-8011.** www.scaramoucherestaurant.com. Reservations required. Main courses C$34–C$47. AE, DC, MC, V. Dining room Mon–Sat 5:30–10pm; pasta bar Mon–Fri 5:30–10:30pm, Sat 5:30–11pm. Subway: St. Clair, then a streetcar west to Avenue Rd. & walk 4 blocks south to Edmund Ave.

EXPENSIVE

Cava ★★★ SPANISH/TAPAS Chef Chris McDonald is a local legend for his culinary prowess, which was honed at his formal (and former) Avalon restaurant. Now with partner and chef Doug Penfold, he is the driving force at Cava, where inventive, small-plate dishes—sometimes daring, but always delicious—offer Iberian-inspired menus with salt cod cakes, beef cheeks, and more. House-cured charcuterie is not to be missed: think smoky chorizo and dried salamis, plus Iberico ham hand-cut to order (a skill in itself). There are more than 20 well-selected wines offered by the glass for pairing. The vibe is delightfully low-key, although professionalism informs everything from service to sweets. And speaking of desserts, Xococava, next door, is worth a visit on its own for rich, artisan chocolates, silken ice creams, and more, all made on-site.
1560 Yonge St. ✆ **416/979-9918.** www.cavarestaurant.ca. Reservations strongly recommended. Tapas plates C$3.50–C$18. AE, DC, MC, V. Daily 5–10pm. Subway: St. Clair.

SEEING THE SIGHTS

Toronto presents a wealth of attractions, so it's best to pick a focus and stick with it. If it's simply getting to know the city, you're off to the races: There are plenty of things to do, see, and taste in the downtown core and beyond, all within reasonable reach. Many major museums, art galleries, and top attractions are downtown and situated in neighborhoods worth exploring. There's plenty in the heart of the city to keep all ages engaged, but there are day trips to consider, too: pristine waters, sublime beaches, a massive theme park, and spectacular stretches of wine country. There are lots of new things to visit for returnees as well: the recently renovated and expanded Art Gallery of Ontario, new five-star hotels, added attractions lakeside, and more. The Royal Ontario Museum, the Gardiner Museum, and the Ontario Science Centre have also recently completed renovations.

Some attractions can easily take up an entire day, such as the Ontario Science Centre, Harbourfront, the Toronto Islands, and Canada's Wonderland. For less ambitious outings, explore the many parks, the thriving arts scene, or the shopping possibilities. And pack a good pair of walking shoes because the best way to appreciate Toronto is on foot.

The Top Attractions

Art Gallery of Ontario ★★★ If you go to only one major attraction while you're in Toronto, let it be the AGO. Fresh from a top-to-bottom renovation—and reinvention—by Toronto son Frank Gehry, it is a wonder. Gehry's vision is throughout; the fabulously twisted floating staircase is especially impressive. There are skylights in some rooms, adjusted every day to best display the works (to spectacular effect with Lawren Harris's paintings of the arctic). Gorgeous Galleria Italia lets you view the scene on Dundas Street down below while you take a rest from the art. Most of all, there's a dramatic increase in the amount of viewing space. Gehry's work is inspired yet practical, a tough act to follow.

Local media magnate the late Ken Thomson gave his beautiful and extensive collection of paintings, carved miniatures, medieval triptychs, and model ships to the AGO. The Thomson Collection, which includes an unparalleled collection of great Canadian art and international drawings such as Peter Paul Reubens' masterpiece, *The Massacre of the Innocents,* is a must. (The late Lord Thomson believed that art should be allowed to speak for itself, in other words, unencumbered by the usual identifying labels. For some, this is an irritant, but for others, it improves the experience.)

And there's far more to see. The AGO's European collection ranges from the 14th century to the French Impressionists and beyond. The Canadian collection is strong, particularly the paintings by the Group of Seven and the extensive collection of Inuit art. The AGO is also famous for its collection of Henry Moore sculptures, which number more than 800. (The artist gave them to Toronto as a tribute to local citizens' enthusiasm for his work: Public donations brought his sculpture *The Archer* to decorate Nathan Phillips Square after politicians refused to support it.) In one room, 14 or so of his large works are displayed, while some of Moore's largest sculptures sit outside the museum, where everyone can appreciate them.

317 Dundas St. W. (btw. McCaul & Beverley sts.). ✆ **416/977-0414.** www.ago.net. Admission C$20 adults, C$16 seniors, C$11 students (w/ID) & children 6–17, free for children 5 & under; free admission Wed 6–8:30pm. Tues & Thurs–Sun 10am–5:30pm; Wed 10am–8:30pm. Closed Jan 1 & Dec 25. Subway: St. Patrick.

CN Tower ★ ☺ The CN Tower may no longer be the world's tallest freestanding structure (thanks, Burj Dubai), but Torontonians, who have long disparaged the tower, have come to admire it, partly because the new LED lights on it look glorious after sundown. However you approach Toronto, the first thing you see is this slender structure. Glass-walled elevators glide up the 553m (1,814-ft.) tower, first stopping at the 346m-high (1,135-ft.) Look Out level. (The truly fearless can ride up in the vertiginous glass-*floored* elevator, which the CN Tower opened in 2008.) Walk down one level to experience the Glass Floor, which is great for a dizzying face-plant: Through it, you can see all the way down to street level. Take comfort: The floor won't break. The glass can withstand the weight of 14 adult hippos.

Above the Look Out is the world's highest public observation gallery, the Skypod, 447m (1,467 ft.) above the ground. From here, on a clear day, the sweeping vista stretches to Niagara Falls, 161km (100 miles) south, and to Lake Simcoe, 193km (120 miles) north. Atop the tower sits a 102m (335-ft.) antenna mast erected over 31 weeks with the aid of a giant Sikorsky helicopter. It took 55 lifts to complete the operation.

The tower attractions are often revamped. Some perennial draws are the IMAX Theatre and the flight simulators. A series of interactive displays showcases the CN Tower, along with such forerunners as the Eiffel Tower and the Empire State Building.

301 Front St. W. ✆ **416/868-6937.** www.cntower.ca. Look Out & Glass Floor C$23 adults, C$21 seniors, C$15 children 4–12; Total Tower Experience (Look Out, Glass Floor, Skypod, IMAX & 2 rides) C$35 all ages. Daily 9am–11pm (shorter hours in winter). Closed Dec 25. Subway: Union, then walk west on Front St.

The Distillery District ★★★ Although founded in 1832, it wasn't until 2003 that this 45-building complex was reinvented as an historic district. This was once home to the Gooderham-Worts Distillery, which was Canada's largest distilling company in the 19th century. A miller named James Worts, who emigrated from Scotland in 1831, built the first building on the site: a windmill intended to power a grain mill (the millstone he brought with him is still on display). His brother-in-law, William Gooderham, soon joined him in the business. In 1834, Worts's wife died in childbirth, and in despair, Worts drowned himself in the mill's well. Gooderham took over the business and adopted Worts's son, who eventually joined the business.

The complex is an outstanding example of industrial design from the 19th century. Much of the construction here was done with Toronto's own red brick; you'll see it in everything from the buildings to the streets themselves. One exception is the mill building, which was built out of stone.

The Distillery District has launched an ambitious program of events throughout the year, including a blues festival, a jazz festival, and an outdoor art exhibition; also, a farmers' market takes place on summer Sundays.

55 Mill St. ✆ **416/367-1800.** www.thedistillerydistrict.com. Free admission. Subway: King, then a streetcar east to Parliament St.

Harbourfront Centre ★ ☺ This cultural center encompasses a 38-hectare (94-acre) strip of waterfront land, once-abandoned warehouses, charming piers, and an old smoke stack. The center, which opened in 1974, is a stunning urban playground and one of the most popular destinations for locals and visitors alike—a great place to spend time strolling, picnicking, gallery-hopping, biking, shopping, and sailing.

Queen's Quay, at the foot of York Street, is the first stop on the LRT line from Union Station (you can also get there in 5 min. on foot, walking south from Front St., but that requires you to go under the Gardiner Expwy.). From here, boats depart for harbor tours and ferries leave for the Toronto Islands. In this renovated warehouse, you'll find the Premiere Dance Theatre and two floors of shops. To get something to eat, you can stay at Queen's Quay's casual Boathouse Grill or walk west to **York Quay**'s Lakeside Terrace restaurant. York Quay also has a decent art gallery with rotating art installations. There's an information booth with a calendar of events, also available online (www.harbourfrontcentre.com).

Harbourfront has several venues devoted to the arts. The **Power Plant** is a contemporary art gallery with some excellent and often edgy shows; behind it is the **Du Maurier Theatre Centre.** At the **Craft Studio,** you can watch artisans blow glass, throw pots, and make silk-screen prints. You can buy their works at **Bounty Contemporary Canadian Craft Shop.** The **Artists' Gardens** features outdoor gardens created by local and visiting landscape architects, designers, and other artists.

More than 4,000 events take place annually at Harbourfront, the biggest of which are two literary gems: the **Harbourfront Reading Series** in June and the **International Festival of Authors** in October. Other happenings include films, dance, theater, music, children's events, multicultural festivals, and marine events. Harbourfront is best in the summer but a great destination year-round, especially with the pretty skating rink and other activities for wintertime fun. In midwinter, the winds blowing off Lake Ontario can be wicked, so dress appropriately.

235 Queens Quay W. ✆ **416/973-4000.** www.harbourfrontcentre.com. Subway: Union, then LRT to Queen's Quay or York Quay.

Ontario Science Centre ★★★ ☺ Since this pioneering interactive science museum opened in 1969, generations of Toronto's kids, and their offspring, have proven loyal fans. It's not surprising: The hands-on approach to exploring the wide world of science is absolutely thrilling. With more than 800 exhibits, there is an abundance of things to touch, push, pull, or crank. Test your reflexes, or balance, or heart rate, or grip strength; watch frozen-solid liquid nitrogen shatter into thousands of icy shards; study slides of butterfly wings, bedbugs, fish scales, or feathers under a microscope; land a spaceship on the moon; see how many lights you can turn on or how high you can elevate a balloon using pedal power. The fun goes on and on.

In addition, the city's only planetarium, an Omnimax cinema, and a collection of small theaters showing assorted documentaries and slide shows are located here. A recent addition is the C$40-million Weston Family Innovation Centre, with new exhibit halls and a focus on interactive learning and problem-solving. There are also some outdoor improvements, including a music-making water garden. The food is much less exciting: Spots for hungry visitors are Galileo's Bistro, a buffet-style restaurant, and Valley Marketplace, a cafeteria. The on-site gift shop, a Mastermind outlet, has a good collection of educational toys and games. This is one Toronto attraction that always seems to be busy (blame school groups), so arrive at 10am to see everything. Make no mistake: The OSC provides a full day's entertainment.

770 Don Mills Rd. (at Eglinton Ave. E.). ✆ **416/696-3127,** or 416/696-1000 for Omnimax tickets. www.ontariosciencecentre.ca. OSC C$18 adults, C$14 seniors & children 13–17, C$11 children 4–12, free for children 3 & under; Omnimax C$12 adults, C$9 seniors & children 13–17, C$8 children 4–12, free for children 3 & under. Combination discounts available. Daily fall–spring 10am–5pm, summer 10am–7pm. Closed Dec 25. Subway: Yonge St. line to Eglinton Ave., then 34 Eglinton bus east to Don Mills Rd. By car: From downtown, take Don Valley Pkwy. to Don Mills Rd. exit & follow signs.

Royal Ontario Museum ★★ ☺ This is Canada's largest museum, with 6 million objects in its collections. Now that the massive and controversial renovation designed by star-chitect Daniel Libeskind is complete, visitors can appreciate the results, or decry them, as many Torontonians do. The new crystal wing, which houses six galleries, hangs out over Bloor Street, hiding the main entrance. (Finding your way in is just one of the inconveniences of the design.) From the interior of the crystal, there are peek-a-boo views to the street below, but it's best to focus on the content here, rather than the playful and often irritating renovation. Fortunately, there's plenty to see, with particular strengths in natural history and world cultures.

Don't miss the Chinese galleries, which feature an intact Ming tomb, as well as the Bishop White Gallery of Chinese Temple Art, wonderful galleries exploring the ancient world (Egypt, Greece, Cyprus, and Bronze Age Aegean are standouts), dazzling dinosaurs for days, a newly improved Bat Cave (a very popular draw for kids), and galleries devoted to birds and mammals. Hands-on galleries invite children to play educational games such as the Discovery Gallery's "dinosaur dig" (a hit with would-be paleontologists). The totem poles are remarkable, too, as are the mummies.

You can easily spend a day here, especially if you include a meal at either the refined C5 (one of the city's top restaurants) or at the humble but delicious Food Studio in the basement.

100 Queen's Park. ✆ **416/586-8000.** www.rom.on.ca. C$24 adults, C$21 seniors & students (w/ID), C$16 children 4–14, free for children 3 & under; free admission Wed 4:30–5:30pm; half-price admission Fri 4:30–9:30pm. Sat–Thurs 10am–5:30pm; Fri 10am–9:30pm. Closed Dec 25. Subway: Museum.

The Toronto Islands ★★★ ☺ In only 7 minutes, an 800-passenger ferry takes you to 245 hectares (605 acres) of island parkland crisscrossed by shaded paths and quiet waterways—a glorious spot to walk, play tennis, bike, feed the ducks, putter around in boats, picnic, or soak up the sun. Of the 14 islands, the 2 major ones are **Centre Island** and **Ward's Island.** The first is the most popular with tourists; Ward's is more residential (about 600 people live on the islands). Originally, the land was a peninsula, but in the 1800s, storms shattered the finger of land into islands.

On Centre Island, families enjoy **Centreville** (✆ **416/203-0405;** www.centreisland.ca), an old-fashioned amusement park that's been in business since 1966. You won't see the usual neon signs, shrill hawkers, and greasy hotdog stands. Instead, you'll find a turn-of-the-20th-century village complete with a Main Street; tiny shops; a firehouse; and the Far Enough Farm, where the kids can pet lambs, chicks, and other barnyard animals. The kids will also love trying out the antique cars, fire

SAVING ON admission costs

The major museums are pricey in Toronto, especially when compared with the smart and progressive freebie programs in cities like London. The ROM is particularly expensive, with a C$24 admission for adults and additional charges for special exhibitions. The list below will help you save on admission fees. Just keep in mind that these free or discounted times do change, so check before you visit.

- **Art Gallery of Ontario:** Free admission every Wednesday from 6 to 8:30pm.
- **Bata Shoe Museum:** Pay-what-you-can admission every Thursday from 5 to 8pm (suggested donation is C$5).
- **Royal Ontario Museum:** Free admission every Wednesday from 4:30 to 5:30pm; half-price admission every Friday from 4:30 to 9:30pm (note that these policies do not apply to special exhibitions, which are always ticketed at the full price).
- **Textile Museum of Canada:** Pay-what-you-can admission every Wednesday from 5 to 8pm; also, the website often offers coupons for C$1 off regular-priced admissions.

engines, old-fashioned train, authentic 1890s carousel, flume ride, and aerial cars. All-day rides pass costs C$21 for those 4 feet tall and under, C$30 for those taller than 4 feet; a family pass for four is C$90. Centreville is open from 10:30am to 6pm daily from mid-May to Labour Day, and weekends in early May and September.

Centreville Amusement Park 84 Advance Road, Centre Island. ✆ **416/392-8193.** www.toronto.ca/parks/island/summerschedule.htm. Round-trip fare C$6.50 adults, C$4 seniors & students 15–19, C$3 children 3–14, free for children 2 & under. Ferries leave from docks at the bottom of Bay St. Subway: Union Station, then the LRT to Queen's Quay.

Toronto Zoo ★★ ☺ Covering 284 hectares (702 acres) of parkland, this unique zoological garden contains some 5,000 animals, plus an extensive botanical collection. Pavilions—including Africa, Indomalaya, Australasia, and the Americas—and outdoor paddocks house the plants and animals.

One popular zoo attraction is at the **African Savanna** project. It re-creates a market bazaar and safari through Kesho (Swahili for "tomorrow") National Park, past such special features as a bush camp, rhino midden, elephant highway, and several watering holes. It also includes the **Gorilla Rainforest,** one of the most popular sights at the zoo and the largest indoor gorilla exhibit in North America. Another hit is Splash Island, a kids-only water park that includes a replica of a Canadian Coast Guard ship.

Ten kilometers (6¼ miles) of walkways offer access to all areas of the zoo. Be prepared to walk long distances, but during the warmer months, the Zoomobile takes visitors around the major walkways to view the animals in the outdoor paddocks. The zoo has restaurants, a gift shop, first aid, and a family center. Visitors can rent strollers and wagons, and borrow wheelchairs. The African pavilion has an elevator for strollers and wheelchairs. There are several parking areas and plenty of picnic tables.

361A Old Finch Avenue, Scarborough, ON. (north of Hwy. 401 & Sheppard Ave.), Scarborough. ✆ **416/392-5900.** www.torontozoo.com. C$23 adults, C$17 seniors, C$13 children 4–12, free for children 3 & under. Summer daily 9am–7:30pm; spring & fall daily 9am–6pm; winter daily 9:30am–4:30pm. Last admission 1 hr. before closing. Closed Dec 25. Subway: Bloor-Danforth line to Kennedy, then bus no. 86A north. By car: From downtown, take Don Valley Pkwy. to Hwy. 401 east, exit on Meadowvale Rd. & follow signs.

More Museums

Bata Shoe Museum ★★ Imelda Marcos—and anyone else obsessed with shoes—would love this museum, which houses the Bata family's 10,000-item collection. The building, designed by Raymond Moriyama, looks like a whimsical shoebox. The main gallery, "All About Shoes," traces the history of footwear. It begins with a plaster cast of some of the earliest known human footprints, which date to 4 million B.C. You'll come across such specialty shoes as spiked clogs used to crush chestnuts in 17th-century France, Elton John's 12-inch-plus platforms, and Prime Minister Pierre Trudeau's well-worn sandals. One display focuses on Canadian footwear fashioned by the Inuit, while another highlights 19th-century ladies' footwear. The second-story galleries house changing exhibits, which have taken on some serious topics, such as a history of foot binding in China.

327 Bloor St. W. (at St. George St.). ✆ **416/979-7799.** www.batashoemuseum.ca. C$14 adults, C$12 seniors, C$8 students (w/ID), C$5 children 5–17, free for children 4 & under. Tues, Wed, Fri & Sat 10am–5pm; Thurs 10am–8pm; Sun noon–5pm. Subway: St. George.

Black Creek Pioneer Village ★ ☺ In this quaint reconstruction of a Victorian-era village, costumed interpreters happily answer questions about life in the 19th century. Dress casually because you'll be spending most of your time here outside. Life at Black Creek moves at the gentle pace of rural Ontario as it was more than a century ago. The original pioneers on this land were Daniel and Elizabeth Strong, a newlywed couple in 1816 who cleared 40 hectares (99 acres) of wilderness for farming and built a log house in their spare time. Eventually, a village developed around this site, and many of the existing buildings date from the 1860s. Every day is different here, so depending on when you visit, you might find "villagers" spinning, sewing, rail splitting, sheep shearing, or threshing. You can count on sampling the villagers' cooking, wandering through the cozily furnished homesteads, visiting the working mill, shopping at the general store, and rumbling past the farm animals in a horse-drawn wagon. The beautifully landscaped village has more than 30 restored buildings.

1000 Murray Ross Pkwy. (at Steeles Ave. & Jane St.), Downsview. ✆ **416/736-1733.** www.blackcreek.ca. C$15 adults, C$14 seniors & students, C$11 children 5–15, free for children 4 & under. May & June Mon–Fri 9:30am–4pm; Sat, Sun & holidays 11am–5pm. July to Labour Day Mon–Fri 10am–5pm; Sat, Sun & holidays 11am–5pm. Sept–Dec Mon–Fri 9:30am–4pm; Sat, Sun & holidays 11am–4:30pm. Closed Jan–Apr, Dec 25 & 26. Subway: Finch, then bus no. 60 west to Murray Ross Pkwy.

George R. Gardiner Museum of Ceramic Art ★★ It's a rarity: a museum dedicated to the ceramic arts. Plus, since its renovation that expanded it from 1,765 sq. m (19,000 sq. ft.) to 2,694 sq. m (29,000 sq. ft.), it is quite simply a beautiful and tranquil space to explore. Located across the street from the Royal Ontario Museum, there's plenty to see here, from pre-Columbian relics including Olmec and Maya figures, to objects from Ecuador, Colombia, and Peru. It's clearly a collection curated with passion. The majolica collection includes spectacular 16th- and 17th-century salvers and other pieces from Italy, and the Delftware collection includes fine 17th-century chargers. The 18th century is represented by Continental and English porcelain: Meissen, Sèvres, Worcester, Chelsea, Derby, and other great names. Among the highlights are objects from the Swan Service—a 2,200-piece set that took 4 years (1737–1741) to make—and a collection of commedia dell'arte figures. There are free guided tours on Tuesday, Thursday, and Sunday at noon. Popular chef Jamie Kennedy runs a pretty cafe above, so you can stay for lunch.

111 Queen's Park. ✆ **416/586-8080.** www.gardinermuseum.on.ca. C$12 adults, C$8 seniors, C$6 students (w/ID), free for children 12 & under. Mon–Thurs 10am–6pm; Fri 10am–9pm; Sat & Sun 10am–5pm. Closed Jan 1 & Dec 25. Subway: Museum.

Museum of Contemporary Canadian Art ★ MOCCA has relocated to the very hot Art & Design District on Queen Street West. The ever-growing collection includes works by Stephen Andrews, Genevieve Cadieux, Ivan Eyre, Betty Goodwin, Micah Lexier, Arnaud Maggs, and Roland Poulin, among many others. MOCCA's mandate has been widening in recent years, and that has made this gallery increasingly a must-visit. Some of the temporary exhibits, such as 2009's collection of pulp-fiction-themed art and the 2010 exhibit on the Andy Warhol transsexual star Candy Darling, have proven show-stoppers. There is an air of irreverence and playfulness that make this museum a delight to visit.

952 Queen St. W. ✆ **416/395-7430.** www.mocca.ca. Free admission; donation requested. Tues–Sun 11am–6pm. Closed all statutory holidays. Subway: Osgoode, then a streetcar west to Shaw St.

Textile Museum of Canada ★ This museum is internationally recognized for its collection of historic and ethnographic textiles and related artifacts; although due to its specialized nature, it's best for those with an interest in the wide world of fabrics. There are fine Oriental rugs and tapestries from all over the world, a gallery that presents the work of contemporary artists, and the museum, which is so small only a fraction of the collection is on display at once. The space is vibrant and interesting.

55 Centre Ave. ✆ **416/599-5321.** www.textilemuseum.ca. C$15 adults, C$10 seniors, C$6 students & children 5–14, free for children 4 & under. Thurs–Tues 11am–5pm; Wed 11am–8pm. Closed Jan 1 & Dec 25. Subway: St. Patrick.

University of Toronto Art Centre ★ This is a real find—and one that very few people outside the Toronto university community know about. You enter the center from the University College quad, an Oxford-style cloistered garden that itself is a work of art. Inside, you'll find a gallery housing the Malcove Collection, which consists mainly of Byzantine art dating from the 14th to the 18th centuries. There are early stone reliefs and numerous icons from different periods. One of the Malcove's gems was painted by a German master in 1538: Lucas Cranach the Elder's *Adam and Eve*. The rest of the Art Centre is devoted to temporary exhibitions, which may display University College's collection of Canadian art or other special exhibits.

15 King's College Circle. ✆ **416/978-1838.** www.utac.utoronto.ca. Free admission. Tues–Fri noon–5pm; Sat noon–4pm. Closed all statutory holidays. Subway: St. George or Museum.

Architectural Highlights

Toronto is a beautiful city in spite of itself—or, rather, in spite of some of the city planners and developers who have torn down valuable parts of the city's architectural legacy in the name of progress. The good news here and now: Toronto is in the throes of an impressive architectural renaissance, from Gehry's AGO to Libeskind's ROM (love it or hate it), Alsop's quirky OCAD building to the Four Seasons Hotel stunner, and much, much more.

Casa Loma ★★★ ☺ A kitschy glitch in the city's skyline to locals, this castle on a hill offers an inspiring view of the sweep of the city (you'll see a lot more of Toronto from here than you did from the CN Tower). But while you can admire the view for free, it's worth visiting the interior of the castle, too. The elegant rooms and period furniture are appropriately grand, though most interesting is perhaps climbing the towers (one Norman, one Scottish, both great).

Sir Henry Pellatt, who built it between 1911 and 1914, had a lifelong fascination with castles. He studied medieval palaces, and gathered materials and furnishings from around the world, bringing marble, glass, and paneling from Europe; teak from Asia; and oak and walnut from North America. He imported Scottish stonemasons to build the massive walls that surround the 2.5-hectare (6¼-acre) site.

Wander through the majestic Great Hall, with its 18m-high (59-ft.) hammer-beam ceiling; the Oak Room, where three artisans took 3 years to fashion the paneling; and the Conservatory, with its elegant bronze doors, stained-glass dome, and pink-and-green marble. The castle encompasses battlements and a tower; Peacock Alley, designed after Windsor Castle; and a 1,800-bottle wine cellar. A 244m (801-ft.) tunnel runs to the stables, where Spanish tile and mahogany surrounded the horses.

The tour is self-guided; pick up an audiocassette, available in eight languages, upon arrival (it's included in the price of admission). From May to October, the gardens are open, too. There's also a Druxy's deli (part of a local chain) on-site, which is good to know, as there aren't many dining options nearby.

1 Austin Terrace. ✆ **416/923-1171.** www.casaloma.org. C$20 adults, C$14 seniors & children 14–17, C$11 children 4–13, free for children 3 & under. Daily 9:30am–5pm (last entry at 4pm). Closed Dec 25. Subway: Dupont, then walk 2 blocks north.

City Hall ★ An architectural spectacle, city hall houses the mayor's office and the city's administrative offices. Daringly designed in the late 1950s by Finnish architect Viljo Revell, it consists of a low podium topped by the flying-saucer-shaped Council Chamber, enfolded between two curved towers. Its interior is as dramatic as its exterior. A free brochure detailing a self-guided tour of city hall is available from its information desk; the tour can also be printed from the website below in French, Chinese, German, Italian, Japanese, Korean, Portuguese, and Spanish.

In front stretches **Nathan Phillips Square** (named after the mayor who initiated the project). In summer, you can sit and contemplate the flower gardens, fountains, and reflecting pool (which doubles as a skating rink in winter), as well as listen to concerts. Here, you'll find Henry Moore's *The Archer* (formally, *Three-Way Piece No. 2*), purchased through a public subscription fund, and the Peace Garden, which commemorates Toronto's sesquicentennial in 1984. In contrast, to the east stands the **old city hall,** a green-copper-roofed Victorian Romanesque–style building.

Looking Sharp

No building in Toronto is more distinctive than the Sharp Centre for Design. While it doesn't dominate Toronto's skyline the way that the CN Tower does, it's a work of stark originality. Designed by renowned architect Will Alsop, it opened in 2004 to near-universal shock—and acclaim—including a Worldwide Architecture Award from the Royal Institute of British Architects. The upper portion of the structure is referred to as the "table top," and its white-and-black checkerboard body stands 26m (85 ft.) above the street on 12 spindly, colorful legs. It's most dramatic at night, when it's lit by 16 large metal lights with blue bulbs. Sadly, it's open only to students of the Ontario College of Art & Design, not the public, on McCaul Street just south of Dundas Street West.

100 Queen St. W. ✆ **416/338-0338.** www.toronto.ca/city_hall_tour/nps.htm. Free admission. Self-guided tours Mon–Fri 8:30am–4:30pm. Subway: Queen, then walk west to Bay Street.

Ontario Legislature ★ At the northern end of University Avenue, with University of Toronto buildings to the east and west, lies Queen's Park, a lovely green place in the heart of the city. Embedded in its center is the rose-tinted sandstone-and-granite Ontario Legislature, which has stood here since 1893. Its stately domes, arches, and porte-cocheres are the work of English architect Richard Waite, who was influenced by the Richardson Romanesque style. Be sure to call ahead before you visit to make sure that the building will be open to the public that day. Try to take the Friday afternoon "Art & Architecture" tour that runs between 2 and 3:30pm (it's free, but advance reservations are required to participate). If you're interested in observing the Ontario Legislature in session, consult its schedule on the website.

111 Wellesley St. W. (at University Ave.). ✆ **416/325-7500.** www.ontla.on.ca. Free admission. Early Sept to late May Mon–Fri; late May to early Sept daily. Call for tour information & reservations. Subway: Queen's Park.

St. Michael's Cathedral ★★★ The principal seat of the Catholic archdiocese of Toronto, St. Michael's is another 19th-century neo-Gothic structure. Built between 1845 and 1848, it originally had a plain interior design with clear-glass windows and white walls. That changed in 1850, when Armand de Charbonnel became the second Bishop of Toronto. Charbonnel was a Frenchman who lived in Montréal, and at first, he was so opposed to his new position that he actually traveled to Rome to beg Pope Pius IX not to make him take it. The pope had other ideas and used Charbonnel's visit to consecrate him in the Sistine Chapel. However, when the new bishop finally arrived in Toronto in September 1850, he threw himself into beautifying St. Michael's. He sold lands that he owned in France and donated the proceeds to the cathedral. He bought dazzling stained-glass windows from France, built interior chapels, and commissioned paintings; he also imported the Stations of the Cross from France (that's why they're in French). While improvements and additions have been made since Charbonnel's time, no one did more to make St. Michael's the masterpiece it is.

St. Michael's is particularly venerated for its musical tradition. It has its own boys' choir—which has won awards internationally—and of the four Masses they sing weekly, three are on Sunday.

65 Bond St. ✆ **416/364-0234.** www.stmichaelscathedral.com. Free admission. Mon–Sat 6am–6pm; Sun 6am–10pm. Subway: Queen or Dundas.

Historic Buildings

Fort York ★ ☺ For those interested in history—especially military history—this is a treat. This historic base was established by Lt. Gov. John Graves Simcoe in 1793 to defend "little muddy York," as Toronto was then known. Americans sacked it in April 1813, but the British rebuilt that same summer. Fort York was used by the military until 1880 and was pressed back into service during both world wars.

You can tour the soldiers' and officers' quarters; clamber over the ramparts; and in summer, view demonstrations of drills, music, and cooking. If you can, try to visit on Victoria Day, Canada Day, or Simcoe Day, when there are plenty of special events. These include the popular Kids' Drill, in which kids take part in a military exercise.

100 Garrison Rd. (off Fleet St., btw. Bathurst St. & Strachan Ave.). ✆ **416/392-6907.** www.fortyork.ca. C$8 adults, C$4 seniors & children 13–18, C$3 children 6–12, free for children 5 & under. Mid-May to early Sept daily 10am–5pm; early Sept to mid-May Mon–Fri 10am–4pm, Sat & Sun 10am–5pm. Subway: Bathurst, then streetcar no. 911 south.

Spadina Museum Historic House & Garden ★ How do you pronounce "Spadina"? In the case of the avenue, it's Spa-*dye*-na; for this lovely landmark, it's Spa-*dee*-na. Why? Who knows! But if you want to see how the leading lights of the city lived in days gone by, visit the historic home of financier James Austin. The exterior is beautiful; the interior, even more impressive. Spadina House contains a remarkable collection of art, furniture, and decorative objects. The Austin family occupied the house from 1866 to 1980, and successive generations modified and added to the house and its decor. ***Note:*** At press time, the museum was undergoing a restoration, but the impressive gardens remain open while work continues inside.

285 Spadina Rd. ✆ **416/392-6910.** www.toronto.ca/spadinamuseum. Free admission. Gardens Mon-Fri 9am–4pm. Subway: Dupont.

For Sports Fans

Air Canada Centre ★ This sports and entertainment complex is home to the Maple Leafs (hockey) and the Raptors (basketball). Longtime fans were crushed when the Leafs moved here in 1999 from Maple Leaf Gardens—the arena that had housed the team since 1931—but the Air Canada Centre has quickly become a fan favorite; the center was designed with comfort in mind (the seats are wide and upholstered). Seating is on a steeper-than-usual grade; even the "nosebleed" sections have decent sightlines.

40 Bay St. (at Lakeshore Blvd.). ✆ **416/815-5500.** www.theaircanadacentre.com. Subway: Union, then the LRT to Queen's Quay.

Hockey Hall of Fame ★ ☺ Ice hockey fans will be thrilled by the artifacts collected here. They include the original Stanley Cup, a replica of the Montréal Canadiens' locker room, Terry Sawchuck's goalie gear, Newsy Lalonde's skates, and the stick Max Bentley used. You'll also see photographs of the personalities and great moments in hockey history. Most fun are the shooting and goalkeeping interactive displays, where you can take a whack at targets with a puck or don goalie gear and face down flying video pucks or sponge pucks.

In Brookfield Place, 30 Yonge St. (at Front St.). ✆ **416/360-7765.** www.hhof.com. C$15 adults, C$12 seniors, C$10 children 4–18, free for children 3 & under. Mon–Fri 10am–5pm; Sat 9:30am–6pm; Sun 10:30am–5pm. Closed Jan 1 & Dec 25. Subway: Union.

Rogers Centre ★ This is home to the Toronto Blue Jays baseball team and the Toronto Argonauts football team. In 1989, the opening of this stadium, then known as SkyDome, was a gala event. The stadium represents an engineering feat, featuring the world's first fully retractable roof and a gigantic video scoreboard. It is so large that a 31-story building would fit inside the complex when the roof is closed.

1 Blue Jays Way. ✆ **416/341-2770.** www.rogerscentre.com. Subway: Union, then follow the signs & walkway.

Parks & Gardens

High Park ★ ☺ This 161-hectare (398-acre) park in the far west of Midtown was architect John G. Howard's gift to the city. He lived in Colborne Lodge, which still stands in the park. The grounds contain a large lake called Grenadier Pond (great for ice skating in wintertime); a small zoo; a swimming pool; tennis courts; sports fields; bowling greens; and vast expanses of green for baseball, jogging, picnicking, bicycling, and more. The Dream in High Park, an annual Shakespearean offering in the open air, is staged each summer and draws crowds who often picnic on-site.

1873 Bloor St. W. (south to the Gardiner Expwy.). No phone. www.toronto.ca/parks. Free admission. Daily dawn–dusk. Subway: High Park.

Necropolis ★ If you have a fascination with historic cemeteries, definitely make a stop here. Located in Midtown East, this is one of the city's oldest cemeteries, dating to 1850. Some of the remains were originally buried in Potters Field, where Yorkville stands today. Before strolling through the cemetery, pick up a History Tour brochure at the office. You'll find the graves of William Lyon Mackenzie, leader of the 1837 rebellion, as well as those of his followers Samuel Lount and Peter Matthews, who were hanged for their parts in the rebellion. (Mackenzie himself went on to become a member of Parliament. Go figure.) Other notables buried in the 7.2-hectare (18-acre) cemetery include George Brown, one of the fathers of Confederation; Anderson Ruffin Abbot, the first Canadian-born black surgeon; Joseph Tyrrell, who unearthed dinosaurs in Alberta; and world-champion oarsman Ned Hanlan. Henry Langley, who designed the Necropolis' porte-cochere and the Gothic Revival chapel—as well as the spires of St. James' and St. Michael's cathedrals (p. 403)—is also buried here.

200 Winchester St. (at Sumach St.). ✆ **416/923-7911.** www.mountpleasantgroupofcemeteries.ca. Free admission. Daily 8am–dusk. Subway: Castle Frank, then bus no. 65 south on Parliament St. to Wellesley St. & walk 3 blocks east to Sumach St.

Scarborough Bluffs ★★ On the eastern edge of Toronto is a natural wonder that's well worth a half-day visit. The Scarborough Bluffs are unique in North America, and their layers of sand and clay offer a remarkable geological record of the great ice age. Rising up to 105m (345 ft.) above Lake Ontario, they stretch out over 14km (8¾ miles). The first 45m (148 ft.) contains fossil plants and animals that were deposited by the advancing Wisconsin Glacier 70,000 years ago. The bluffs were given their name in 1793 by Lady Elizabeth Simcoe, wife of the first Lieutenant Governor of Upper Canada (Ontario); as she sailed to York, as Toronto was then known, she was reminded of the cliffs of Yorkshire.

South of Kingston Rd. No phone. www.toronto.ca/parks. Free admission. Daily dawn–dusk. Subway: Victoria Park, then no. 12 Kingston Rd. bus to Brimley Rd. & about a 15-min. walk south along Brimley Rd. By car: From downtown, take Don Valley Pkwy. to Hwy. 401 east, exit on Brimley Rd. & drive south.

Toronto Music Garden ★★★ Toronto is a city of gardens, but this one along Toronto's waterfront is a favorite of mine. Cellist Yo-Yo Ma and landscape designer Julie Moir Messervy created the Toronto Music Garden to invoke Bach's First Suite for Unaccompanied Cello. The prelude is represented by the undulating curves of a river-scape; the allemande by a forest grove that's filled with wandering trails; the courante by a swirling path through wildflowers; the *menuett* by a pavilion of formally arranged flowerbeds; and finally the gigue, with its giant grass steps that lead you back to the real world. It's tough to translate the experience into words, but the music garden is a don't-miss spot if you visit Toronto in warm weather.

475 Queens Quay W. ✆ **416/338-0338.** Free admission. Daily dawn–dusk. Subway: Union, then the LRT to Spadina.

Especially for Kids

The city puts on a fabulous array of special events for children at **Harbourfront.** In February, there's **ALOUD: A Celebration for Young Readers.** Come April, **Spring Fever** welcomes the season with egg decorating, puppet shows, and more; on Saturday mornings in April, the 5-to-12 set enjoys **cushion concerts.** For information, call ✆ **416/973-4000** or visit **www.harbourfrontcentre.com**.

For more than 30 years, the **Lorraine Kimsa Theatre for Young People** (165 Front St. E., at Sherbourne St.; ✆ **416/862-2222** for box office or 416/363-5131 for administration) has been entertaining youngsters. Its season runs from August to May.

Help! We've Got Kids is an all-in-one print and online directory for attractions, events, shops, and services appropriate for kids younger than 13 in the greater Toronto area. It doesn't provide a lot of detail about most of the entries, but the listings make a great starting point. Visit **www.helpwevegotkids.com**.

Ontario Place ☺ For all its Space Age looks, this is really just a fun amusement park, more thrilling than Centreville on Centre Island (p. 398) but nowhere near as cool as Paramount Canada's Wonderland (see below). From a distance, you'll see five steel-and-glass pods suspended on columns 32m (105 ft.) above the lake, three artificial islands, and a huge geodesic dome. The five pods contain a multimedia theater, a children's theater, a high-technology exhibit, and displays that tell the story of Ontario in vivid kaleidoscopic detail. The dome houses Cinesphere, where specially made IMAX movies are shown year-round.

Ontario Place has many attractions targeted at kids, starting with the **H2O Generation Station,** a gigantic "soft play" structure with twisting slides, towers, and walkways. The **Atom Blaster**—which claims to be Canada's largest foam-ball free-for-all—is fun for the whole family. Younger children will enjoy the **MicroKids** play area with its ball pit, climbing platforms, and other tot-appropriate draws.

At night, the **Molson Amphitheatre** accommodates concert-goers in the reserved seating area under the canopy and on the surrounding grass. For concert information, call ✆ **416/260-5600;** for tickets, call **Ticketmaster** (✆ **416/870-8000**).

955 Lakeshore Blvd. W. ✆ **416/314-9811,** or 416/314-9900 for recorded info. www.ontarioplace.com. Grounds only C$18 adults, C$12 seniors & children 4–5, free for children 3 & under, separate fees for rides & events (pricing varies by month); Play All Day pass C$34 adults, C$18 seniors & children 4–5, free for children 3 & under. Park open mid-May to Labour Day daily 10am–dusk; evening events end & dining spots close later. Closed (except Cinesphere) early Sept to early May. Subway: Bathurst, then Bathurst St. streetcar south.

Paramount Canada's Wonderland ★ ☺ An hour north of Toronto lies Canada's answer to Disney World. The 120-hectare (297-acre) park features more than 200 attractions, including 65 rides, a water park, a play area for tiny tots (KidZville), and live shows. Because the park relies on a local audience for most of its business, it introduces new attractions every year. Some of the most popular have been the Behemoth, Canada's biggest, fastest, and tallest rollercoaster; the Fly, a roller coaster designed to make every seat feel as though it's in the front car (the faint of heart can't hide at the back of this one!); Sledge Hammer, a "menacing mechanical giant" that stands 24m (80 ft.) tall and hurls riders through accelerated jumps and free-falls; Cliffhanger, a "super swing" that executes 360-degree turns and makes riders feel immune to gravity; and the Xtreme Skyflyer, a hang-gliding and skydiving hybrid that plunges riders 46m (151 ft.) in a free-fall. The roller coasters range from the looping, inverted Top Gun to the track-free suspended Vortex.

The Splash Works water park offers a huge wave pool and water rides spread over 8.1 hectares (20 acres), from speed slides and tube rides to special scaled-down slides and a kids' play area. You'll also find Hanna-Barbera characters, including Scooby-Doo, strolling around the park (and ready to get their picture taken with the kids). Additional attractions include Wonder Mountain and its high divers (they take the 20m/66-ft. plunge down Victoria Falls to the mountain's base), restaurants, and shops.

9580 Jane St., Vaughan. ✆ **905/832-7000** or 905/832-8131. www.canadaswonderland.com. Pay-One-Price Passport (includes unlimited rides & shows, but not special attractions or Kingswood Music Theater) C$45 adults and children, free for children 2 & under; check website for specials. June 1 to June 25 Mon–Fri 10am–8pm, Fri & Sat 10am–10pm; June 26 to Labour Day daily 10am–10pm; late May & early Sept to early Oct Sat & Sun 10am–8pm. Closed mid-Oct to mid-May. Subway: Yorkdale or York Mills, then GO Express Bus to Wonderland. By car: From downtown, take Yonge St. north to Hwy. 401 & go west to Hwy. 400. Go north on Hwy. 400 to Rutherford Rd. exit & follow signs. From the north, exit at Major Mackenzie Dr.

Riverdale Farm ★★ Situated on the edge of the Don Valley Ravine, this working farm located on 3 hectares (7½ acres) right in the city is a favorite with small tots. They enjoy watching the cows, pigs, turkeys, and ducks—and can get close enough to pet many animals, such as the rabbits. Because this really is a farm, you'll see all of the chores of daily life, such as horse grooming, cow and goat milking, egg collecting, and animal feeding. Adults should note that the farm shop has some seasonal produce and baked goods, and that there's a farmers' market on Tuesdays from May to October.

201 Winchester St. (at Sumach St.). ✆ **416/392-6794.** Free admission. Daily 9am–5pm. Subway: Castle Frank, then bus no. 65 south on Parliament St. to Wellesley St. & walk 3 blocks east to Sumach St.

OUTDOOR ACTIVITIES

Toronto residents love the great outdoors, whatever the time of year. In summer, you'll see people cycling, boating, and hiking; in winter, they are skating, skiing, and snowboarding.

For additional information on facilities in the parks, golf courses, tennis courts, swimming pools, beaches, and picnic areas, contact **Toronto Parks and Recreation** (✆ **416/392-8186;** www.toronto.ca/parks). Also, see "Parks & Gardens," earlier in this chapter.

Beaches

The Beaches is the neighborhood along Queen Street East from Coxwell Avenue to Victoria Park. It has a charming boardwalk that connects the beaches, starting at **Ashbridge's Bay Park,** which has a sizable marina. **Woodbine Beach** connects to **Kew Gardens Park** and is a favorite with sunbathers and volleyball players. Woodbine also boasts the **Donald D. Summerville Olympic Pool.** Snack bars and trinket sellers line the length of the boardwalk.

Many locals prefer the beaches on the **Toronto Islands.** The ones on **Centre Island,** always the busiest, are favorites with families because of such nearby attractions as **Centreville.** The beaches on **Wards Island** are much more secluded. They're connected by the loveliest boardwalk in the city, with masses of fragrant flowers and raspberry bushes along its edges. **Hanlan's Point,** also in the Islands, is Toronto's only nude beach.

Canoeing & Kayaking

The **Harbourfront Canoe and Kayak School** (283A Queens Quay W.; ✆ **800/960-8886** or 416/203-2277; www.paddletoronto.com) rents canoes and kayaks; call ahead if you are interested in taking private instruction.

You can also rent canoes, rowboats, and pedal boats on the **Toronto Islands** just south of Centreville.

Cross-Country Skiing

Just about every park in Toronto becomes potential cross-country skiing territory as soon as snow falls. Best bets are Sunnybrook Park and Ross Lord Park, both in North York. For more information, contact **Toronto Parks and Recreation** (✆ **416/392-8186;** www.toronto.ca/parks). Serious skiers interested in day trips to excellent out-of-town sites such as Horseshoe Valley can contact **Trakkers Cross Country Ski Club** (✆ **416/763-0173;** www.trakkers.ca), which also rents equipment.

Cycling

With biking trails through most of the city's parks and more than 29km (18 miles) of street bike routes, it's not surprising that Toronto has been called one of the best cycling cities in North America. Favorite pathways include the **Martin Goodman Trail** (from The Beaches to the Humber River along the waterfront); the **Lower Don Valley** bike trail (from the east end of the city north to Riverdale Park); **High Park** (with winding trails over 160 hectares/395 acres); and the **Toronto Islands,** where bikers ride without fear of cars. For advice, call the **Ontario Cycling Association** (✆ **416/426-7416**), contact **Toronto Parks and Recreation** (✆ **416/392-8186;** www.toronto.ca/parks), or visit www.toronto.ca/livegreen/greenlife_onthego_cycling.htm. Bike lanes are marked on College/Carlton streets, the Bloor Street Viaduct leading to the Danforth, Beverly/St. George streets, Jarvis Street, and Davenport Road.

For a list of bike rental shops, contact the **Toronto Bicycling Network** (✆ **416/766-1985;** www.tbn.ca). One sure bet is **Wheel Excitement** (249 Queens Quay W., Unit 110; ✆ **416/260-9000;** www.wheelexcitement.ca). If you're interested in cycling with a group or want information about daily excursions and weekend trips, contact the Toronto Bicycling Network.

Be forewarned: Like many other North American cities, the tensions between cyclists and car drivers are mounting, so be on your guard and take it easy.

Fitness Centers

The **Metro Central YMCA** (20 Grosvenor St.; ✆ **416/975-9622;** www.ymcatoronto.org) has excellent facilities, including a 25m (82-ft.) swimming pool, all kinds of cardiovascular machines, Nautilus equipment, an indoor track, squash and racquetball courts, and aerobics classes. The **University of Toronto Athletic Centre** (55 Harbord St., at Spadina Ave.; ✆ **416/978-3436;** www.ac-fpeh.com) offers similar facilities. Guest passes to both centers are C$25 per day.

For yoga aficionados, there's no better place to stretch than **Yoga Plus** (40 Eglinton Ave. E., 8th Floor; ✆ **416/322-9936;** www.yogaplustoronto.com). A single class costs C$20; there's also a pay-what-you-can "Karma" class available. For a listing of all of Toronto's yoga studios, visit **www.yogatoronto.ca**, which covers the city and the Greater Toronto Area.

Golf

Toronto is obsessed with golf: There are more than 75 public courses within an hour's drive of downtown. Here's information on some of the best.

- **Don Valley.** 4200 Yonge St., south of Highway 401 (✆ **416/392-2465**). Designed by Howard Watson, this is a scenic par-71 course with some challenging elevated tees. The par-3 13th hole is nicknamed the Hallelujah Corner (it takes a miracle to make par). It's considered a good place to start your kids. Greens fees are C$30 to C$63.

- **Humber Valley.** 40 Beattie Ave., at Albion Road (✆ **416/392-2488**). The relatively flat par-70 course is easy to walk, with lots of shade from towering trees. The three final holes require major concentration (the 16th and 17th are par-5s). Greens fees are C$44 to C$52.
- The **Glen Abbey Golf Club.** 1333 Dorval Dr., Oakville (✆ **905/844-1800;** www.glenabbey.ca). The championship course is one of the most famous in Canada. Designed by Jack Nicklaus, the par-73 layout traditionally plays host to the Canadian Open. Greens fees are C$135 to C$265.

Travelers who are really into golf might want to consider a side trip to the **Muskoka Lakes** (see chapter 12). This area, just 90 minutes north, has some of the best golfing in the country at courses such as **Taboo** and the **Deerhurst Highlands.**

Ice Skating & In-Line Skating

Nathan Phillips Square in front of city hall becomes a free ice rink in winter, as does an area at Harbourfront Centre. Rentals are available on-site. More than 25 parks contain artificial rinks (also free), including Grenadier Pond in High Park—a romantic spot, with a bonfire and vendors selling roasted chestnuts. They're open from November to March.

In summer, in-line skaters pack Toronto's streets (and sidewalks). Go with the flow and rent some blades from **Wheel Excitement** (see "Cycling," above).

Jogging

Downtown routes might include **Harbourfront** and along the lakefront, or through **Queen's Park** and the University. The **Martin Goodman Trail** runs 20km (12 miles) along the waterfront from the Beaches in the east to the Humber River in the west. It's ideal for jogging, walking, or cycling. It links to the **Tommy Thompson Trail,** which travels the parks from the lakefront along the Humber River. Near the Ontario Science Centre in the Central Don Valley, **Ernest Thompson Seton Park** is also good for jogging. Parking is available at the Thorncliffe Drive and Wilket Creek entrances.

These areas are generally quite safe, but you should take the same precautions you would in any large city.

Rock Climbing

Toronto has several climbing gyms, including **Joe Rockhead's** (29 Fraser Ave.; ✆ **416/538-7670;** www.joerockheads.com) and the **Toronto Climbing Academy** (100 Broadview Ave.; ✆ **416/406-5900;** www.climbingacademy.com). You can pick up the finer points of knot tying and belaying. Both gyms also rent equipment.

Snowboarding & Skiing

The snowboard craze shows no sign of abating, at least from January to March (or anytime there's enough snow on the ground). One popular site is the **Earl Bales Park** (4169 Bathurst St., just south of Sheppard Ave.), which offers rentals. The park also has an alpine ski center, which offers both equipment rentals and coaching. Call ✆ **416/395-7931** for more information.

Swimming

The municipal parks, including High and Rosedale parks, offer a dozen or so outdoor pools (open June–Sept). Several community recreation centers have indoor pools. For **pool information,** call ✆ **416/338-7665.**

Visitors may buy a day pass to use the pools at the **YMCA** (20 Grosvenor St.; ✆ **416/975-9622**) and the **University of Toronto Athletic Centre** (55 Harbord St., at Spadina Ave.; ✆ **416/978-4680**).

Tennis

There are 200 municipal parks across Toronto with tennis facilities. The most convenient are the courts in High, Rosedale, and Jonathan Ashridge parks. They are open from April to October only. Call **Toronto Parks** (✆ **416/392-1111**) for information. The Toronto Parks website also has a brochure you can download; visit www.toronto.ca/parks.

SPECTATOR SPORTS

AUTO RACING **The Grand Prix of Toronto** (formerly the Molson Indy; ✆ **416/588-7223;** www.grandprixtoronto.com) takes place in July at the Exhibition Place Street circuit. Check the website for 2011 updates.

BASEBALL **Rogers Centre** (1 Blue Jays Way, on Front St., beside the CN Tower) is the home of the **Toronto Blue Jays.** For tickets, contact the Toronto Blue Jays at ✆ **888/OK-GO-JAY** (888/654-6529) or 416/341-1234, or http://toronto.bluejays.mlb.com.

BASKETBALL Toronto's basketball team, the **Raptors,** has its home ground in the **Air Canada Centre** (40 Bay St., at Lakeshore Blvd.). The NBA schedule runs from October to April. The arena seats 19,500 for basketball. For information, contact the **Raptors Basketball Club** (40 Bay St.; ✆ **416/815-5600;** www.nba.com/raptors). For tickets, call **Ticketmaster** (✆ **416/870-8000**).

FOOTBALL Remember Kramer on *Seinfeld?* He would watch only Canadian football. If you're not familiar with it, here's your chance to catch a game. **Rogers Centre** (1 Blue Jays Way) is home to the **Argonauts** of the Canadian Football League. They play between June and November. For information, contact the club at ✆ **416/341-2700** or visit www.argonauts.on.ca. For tickets, call **Ticketmaster** (✆ **416/870-8000**).

GOLF TOURNAMENTS Canada's national golf tournament, the **Bell Canadian Open,** usually takes place at the **Glen Abbey Golf Club** (✆ **905/844-1800**) in Oakville, about 40 minutes from the city. Most years, it runs over the Labour Day weekend.

HOCKEY Hockey isn't Canada's national sport, believe it or not (that's lacrosse), but it's undoubtedly the most popular. The **Air Canada Centre** (40 Bay St., at Lakeshore Blvd.) is the home of the **Toronto Maple Leafs** (http://mapleleafs.nhl.com). The team hasn't won a Stanley Cup since 1967, but droves of fans stick with the franchise nonetheless. Though the arena seats 18,700 for hockey, tickets are not easy to come by because many are sold by subscription. The rest are available through **Ticketmaster** (✆ **416/870-8000**).

HORSE RACING Thoroughbred racing takes place at **Woodbine Racetrack** (Rexdale Blvd. and Hwy. 427, Etobicoke; ✆ **416/675-6110** or 416/675-7223). It's famous for the Queen's Plate (usually contested on the third Sun in June); the Canadian International, a classic turf race (Sept or Oct); and the North America Cup (mid-June). Woodbine also hosts harness racing in spring and fall.

SOCCER Toronto's new soccer club, the **Toronto FC** (http://toronto.fc.mlsnet.com), is beloved by Torontonians. It's the first non-U.S. team in Major League Soccer. They play at BMO Field at Exhibition Place; it was built for the FC, and holds 20,195 spectators. For tickets, call **Ticketmaster** (✆ **416/870-8000**).

TENNIS TOURNAMENTS Canada's international tennis championship, the **Rogers Cup,** takes place in Toronto *and* Montréal every August (the men's and women's championships alternate cities each year). In 2011, the women play in Toronto, the men in Montréal. For more information, call ✆ **877/283-6647** or check www.lovemeansnothing.ca.

SHOPPING

While you may want to investigate the impressive array of international retailers, don't forget the local talent. If your passion is fashion, there are great Canadian labels such as Anne Hung, Mercy, Lida Baday, Lydia K, Ross Mayerand, and Comrags, for starters.

Stores usually open around 10am from Monday to Saturday. Closing hours change depending on the day. From Monday to Wednesday, most stores close at 6pm; on Thursday and Friday, hours run to 8 or 9pm; on Saturday, closing is quite early, usually around 6pm. Most stores are open on Sunday, though the hours may be restricted—11am or noon to 5pm is the norm.

Antiques

Decorum Decorative Finds If you're going on an ocean voyage, can you resist a vintage Louis Vuitton trunk? The wares here range from tables and chaise lounges to oil paintings and old books. Wares are expensive, but also top of the line. 1210 Yonge St. ✆ **416/966-6829.** Subway: Summerhill.

L'Atelier This is all about glamour. Napoleon III side tables share space with chrome bar stools and rococo Italian lamps. Many of the price tags hit four digits, but there are lovely accoutrements for moderate budgets, too. 1224 Yonge St. ✆ **416/966-0200.** Subway: Summerhill.

Zig Zag ★ This shop stocks a mélange of styles, but the specialty is early Modernist pieces. The names to watch out for are Eames, Saarinen, Arne Jacobsen, and Warren Platner. This is one store that's popular with some uptown antiques dealers. 985 Queen St. E. ✆ **416/778-6495.** Subway: Queen, then any streetcar east to Carlaw Ave.

Art

Sandra Ainsley Gallery ★★ Specializing in glass sculpture, this renowned gallery represents Canadian, American, and international artists, including Dale Chihuly, Jon Kuhn, Peter Powning, Tom Scoon, Susan Edgerley, and David Bennett. The one-of-a-kind pieces have big price tags, but you can also find some affordable items, such as paperweights, vases, and jewelry. In the Distillery District, 55 Mill St. ✆ **416/214-9490.** www.sandraainsleygallery.com. Subway: King, then a streetcar east to Parliament St.

Stephen Bulger Gallery ★★ If you're interested in fine-art photography, especially in the documentary tradition, this is the place to go in Toronto. The Gallery displays Canadian and international photography, both by established artists and up-and-comers, from Ruth Orkin to Pete Doherty. It is one of the driving forces behind

CONTACT, Toronto's Annual Celebration of Photography, which has helped launch many careers. Artists represented include Robert Burley, Ruth Kaplan, Vincenzo Pietropaolo, and Alex Webb. This is also a place locals go for some of the city's best photography exhibits. 1026 Queen St. W. ✆ **416/504-0575.** www.bulgergallery.com. Subway: Osgoode, then a streetcar west to Ossington Ave.

Ydessa Hendeles Art Foundation ★ This is one of the most interesting contemporary art collections in the city. Hendeles features installations by international artists. Works on display include paintings, photography, and multimedia projects. Hours are limited, so call ahead to see if they're open when you're in town. 778 King St. W. ✆ **416/603-2227.** Subway: St. Andrew, then any streetcar west to Bathurst St.

Books

The Cookbook Store ★ In a world where neighborhood bookstores are too often on life support, this gem, 20-plus years and running, stands out for its fine selection of cookbooks, food memoirs, and the best in food writing. If you're lucky enough to be in town for one of their many book launches, book the date—Julia Child, for one, was once here. 850 Yonge St. ✆ **416/920-2665.** www.cook-book.com. Subway: Yonge/Bloor.

Indigo Books Music & More ★★ ☺ This Canadian-owned chain offers an excellent selection of books, magazines, and a smaller selection of music. Like its sister brand Chapters, Indigo comes complete with coffee shops and comfy seating. A favorite with night owls, they're open until 11pm or midnight every day. You'll find branches at the Eaton Centre (✆ **416/591-3622**) and at 2300 Yonge St., at Eglinton Ave. (✆ **416/544-0049**). Manulife Centre, 55 Bloor St. W. ✆ **416/925-3536.** www.chapters.indigo.ca. Subway: Yonge/Bloor or Bay.

Type Books ★ 🎁 This small, smart bookstore is run by a couple of English literature grads. Hip but not too cool, the selection includes serious fiction, fine books on food and art, a healthy collection of poetry, traditional and contemporary children's literature, and a lot of indie stuff that you'd have a hard time finding elsewhere. The mix proved so popular, there is now a second location on Spadina north of St. Clair Avenue (427 Spadina Rd.). 883 Queen St. W. ✆ **416/366-8973.** Subway: Osgoode, then a streetcar west to Trinity-Bellwoods.

The World's Biggest Bookstore ★ Whether or not it is indeed the world's biggest, the 27km (17 miles) of bookshelves do contain a broad selection, as you'd expect, and a lot of remaindered stuff, too. The magazine racks alone seem endless. There's a lot to peruse, but the overly bright, bare-bones space doesn't make for a pleasant browse. 20 Edward St. ✆ **416/977-7009.** Subway: Dundas.

Department Stores

The Bay The Hudson's Bay Company started out as a fur-trading business when the first French-speaking settlers came to Canada. Today, the Bay boasts excellent midrange selections of clothing and housewares. Of the several Toronto locations, here are the two best. 176 Yonge St. (at Queen St.). ✆ **416/861-9111.** www.thebay.com. Subway: Queen. 2nd location at 2 Bloor St. E. (at Yonge St.). ✆ **416/972-3333.** Subway: Yonge/Bloor.

Sears If you visited Toronto before 2000, you'll remember the gorgeous Eaton's department store, which anchored the Eaton Centre complex. Sears Canada bought the Eaton's name and opened this department store in its place. It's more upscale than your average Sears. Eaton Centre. ✆ **416/343-2111.** www.sears.ca. Subway: Dundas.

Fashion

Delphic Don't like trendy? Then don't shop here. If you do, you'll be confronted by fashion favorites such as Evisu Jeans, which are imported from Japan. 706 Queen St. W. ✆ **416/603-3334.** Subway: Osgoode, then a streetcar west to Manning Ave.

Fashion Crimes ★ Toronto designer Pam Chorley's store looks like a princess's dressing room, complete with Venetian glass and ornate chandeliers. There are clothes for women here, too, but her Misdemeanors line makes gossamer gowns and ruby slippers for little girls who dream they're really princesses. 322½ Queen St. W. ✆ **416/351-8758.** Subway: Osgoode.

Fresh Baked Goods ★ 🎁 Surprise—this *isn't* a bakery. Owner Laura Jean, "the knitting queen," features a line of flirty knitwear made of cotton, mohair, wool, or lace. The staff is friendly and incredibly helpful; if you like a sweater but not its buttons, they'll sew on different ones from their sizeable collection free of charge. They also do custom orders. 274 Augusta Ave. ✆ **416/966-0123.** www.freshbakedgoods.com. Subway: Spadina, then the LRT to Baldwin St. & walk 2 blocks west to Augusta Ave.

Girl Friday ★★ 🎁 Local designer Rebecca Nixon creates feminine dresses, suits, and separates for her shop under the name Girl Friday. The store also carries pieces from hip labels Nougat and Dish, but many come for Nixon's elegant yet affordable pieces. 740 Queen St. W. ✆ **416/364-2511.** www.girlfridayclothing.com. Subway: Osgoode, then a streetcar west to Claremont St.

Harry Rosen ★ Designed like a mini–department store, Harry Rosen carries the crème de la crème of menswear designers, including Hugo Boss, Brioni, and Versace. There are also a good selection of work-worthy footwear and a famous "Great Wall of Shirts." Now the flagship store also claims Canada's only Tod's Place, the luxe international brand of shoes and leather accessories. 82 Bloor St. W. ✆ **416/972-0556.** www.harryrosen.com. Subway: Bay.

Preloved ★★ The original Toronto boutique was destroyed by a fire in 2008. Since then, Preloved has reopened in a storefront across from Trinity-Bellwoods Park. The store's pieces really *are* one of a kind: The shop's owners breathe new life into vintage clothing and cast-off jeans and T-shirts by changing the shapes and adding details such as vintage lace. The roster of celeb fans includes Alanis Morissette. 881 Queen St. W. ✆ **416/504-8704.** Subway: Osgoode, then a streetcar west to Trinity-Bellwoods Park.

Roots ★ This is one Canadian retailer that seems to be universally loved. The clothes are casual, from hooded sweats to fleece jackets, and there's a good selection of leather footwear. Don't overlook the tykes' department, which has the same stuff in tiny sizes. Other locations include the Eaton Centre (✆ **416/593-9640**). 95A Bloor St. W. ✆ **416/323-9512.** www.roots.ca. Subway: Bay.

Secrets From Your Sister ★ 🎁 Thanks to Oprah, we know that the vast majority of women in North America are wearing the wrong bra size. That won't be true of you if you visit this store, which carries a terrific selection of bras to suit figures as dissimilar as Audrey Hepburn and Jayne Mansfield, and everything in between. 560 Bloor St. W. ✆ **416/538-1234.** www.secretsfromyoursister.com. Subway: Bathurst.

Food

House of Tea Visitors to this shop can drink in the heady scent of more than 150 loose teas. And the selection of cups, mugs, and tea caddies runs from chic to comical. 1017 Yonge St. ✆ **416/922-1226.** Subway: Rosedale.

Senses Bakery ★★★ The pastries and chocolates here are simply exquisite. The bottles of maple syrup come from an Ontario family-run operation, so they're a particularly good souvenir. In the Maritime Life Tower, 2 Queen St. E. ✆ **416/364-7303.** www.senses.ca. Subway: Queen.

Soma Chocolatemaker ★★★ There are a mere handful of great chocolatiers in the world that compare with this artisan shop. Co-owners Cynthia Leung and David Castellan source cocoa beans from around the world and make their chocolate on-site. The open-lab design of the place allows you to watch the process, from bean to bar, and it's also an inviting place to hang out and savor one of the house specialties, like the warm coffee-and-chocolate drink *bicerin* (bee-cha-reen) or a cool, rich gelato. Don't forget to buy some to take home. In the Distillery District, 55 Mill St. ✆ **416/815-7662.** www.somachocolate.com. Subway: King, then a streetcar east to Parliament St.

Markets

Kensington Market ★★★ This neighborhood has changed dramatically over the years. Originally a Jewish community, it became home to Portuguese and other European immigrants, and then evolved into a community bordering Chinatown with shopkeepers who hail from the Caribbean, the Middle East, and elsewhere. There are several Asian herbalists and grocers, as well as West Indian and Middle Eastern shops. Kensington Avenue has the greatest concentration of vintage clothing stores in the city, as well as some good grub and excellent cafes for refueling. Along Baldwin, Kensington & Augusta aves. No phone. Subway: Spadina, then the LRT to Baldwin St. or Dundas St. W.

St. Lawrence Market ★ This market is a local favorite for fresh produce, and it even draws people who live a good distance away. The peameal-bacon sandwiches are famous. Check out the gallery on the second floor, a quiet retreat from the busy market, where exhibits about the city are mounted, with free admission. Hours are Tuesday through Thursday from 8am to 6pm, Friday from 8am to 7pm, and Saturday from 8am to 5pm. On Saturday, there is also the farmers market from 5am, when the farmers arrive, to 1pm. 92 Front St. E. ✆ **416/392-7219.** www.stlawrencemarket.com. Subway: Union.

Toys

Mastermind Toys ☺ This Canadian-owned chain stocks toys for all ages, sizes, and quirks. The stores are well laid out and staff is helpful. With dozens of major brands and some of the top lines—like Playmobil, Plan Toys, and Lamaze—it's one of the best options in Toronto, especially if you want to avoid the big-box stores. There are many locations, although they tend to be on the city's outskirts. There's also a location in the Ontario Science Centre. 2134 Queen St. ✆ **416/699-3797.** www.mastermindtoys.com. Subway: Queen, then a streetcar east to Glen Manor.

Science City ★★ ☺ Kids and adults alike will love this tiny store filled with games, puzzles, models, kits, and books—all related to science. Whether your interest is astronomy, biology, chemistry, archaeology, or physics, you'll find something here. Holt Renfrew Centre, 50 Bloor St. W. ✆ **416/968-2627.** www.sciencecity.ca. Subway: Yonge/Bloor.

TORONTO AFTER DARK

You're not going to lack for things to do after the sun goes down in Toronto. The city is a genuine Mecca for top-notch theater, with some acclaimed productions actually premiering in Toronto before heading to Broadway or London's West End. Notable local performing arts organizations include the Canadian Stage Company, the Canadian Opera Company, the National Ballet of Canada, Soulpepper (which has a reputation as one of North America's most creative theater companies), the Tafelmusik Baroque Orchestra and Chamber Choir, and the Toronto Symphony Orchestra.

Toronto's many dance and music venues also host the crème de la crème of Canadian and international performers. Some of the best entertainment is in Toronto's comedy clubs, which have served as training grounds for stars such as Jim Carrey, Mike Myers, Dan Aykroyd, and John Candy.

The Sony Centre for the Performing Arts—formerly known as the Hummingbird Centre—reopened in October 2010 after a major renovation and restoration. There's plenty going on at the Four Seasons Centre, Roy Thomson Hall, Massey Hall, the new and impressive Koerner Hall, and at other theaters around town.

The hottest news on the nightlife front is Ossington Avenue. This used to be a quiet stretch, but it's now *the* place to go for the coolest watering holes. The action has spilled onto the adjacent Dundas Street West strip, too. Some spots to look for: The Communist's Daughter, Dakota Tavern, Watusi, Reposado, and Sweaty Betty's.

The Performing Arts

Canadian Opera Company ★★★ Canada's largest opera company, the sixth-largest in North America, was founded in 1950. Performances take place at the Four Seasons Centre for the Performing Arts (p. 416), a venue built with opera aficionados in mind. To give you an idea of how popular the Canadian Opera Company is, its performances have been at 99% capacity for the past four years. More than three-quarters of the tickets are held by subscribers, making this a tough "get" for visitors, so plan ahead. The COC is now headed by music director Johannes Debus. Their 2010–2011 season includes productions of *Aida* and *The Magic Flute*. 145 Queen St. W. ✆ **416/363-8231** for tickets or 416/363-6671 for administration. www.coc.ca. Tickets C$62–C$292. Subway: Osgoode.

Canadian Stage ★★★ Formerly known as CanStage, this company performs an eclectic variety of Canadian (from the likes of Michel Tremblay and Robert Lepage) and international plays. Their productions are often ground-breaking. They perform at the Bluma Appel Theatre, which seats 875, and the Berkeley Theatre, a more avant-garde, intimate (240-seat) space. Bluma Appel Theatre (St. Lawrence Centre): 27 Front St. E.; Berkeley Theatre: 26 Berkeley St. ✆ **416/368-3110.** www.canadianstage.com. Tickets C$30–C$75; Mon free admission (donation required). Senior & student discounts may be available 30 min. before performance. Subway for St. Lawrence Centre: Union; for Berkeley Theatre: King, then any streetcar east to Berkeley St.

Distillery District ★★★ This was once the home of the Gooderham-Worts Distillery, Canada's largest distilling company in the 19th century. The 45-building complex is an outstanding example of industrial design from the Victorian age. In 2003, it was reinvented as the Distillery District, which includes galleries, restaurants, and shops. The district also houses several performing-arts venues, including the Case Goods Theatre and the state-of-the-art Young Centre for the Performing Arts. The Dancemakers, Soulpepper, and Native Earth troupes now perform here. 55 Mill St. ✆ **416/367-1800.** www.thedistillerydistrict.com. Subway: King, then a streetcar east to Parliament St.

The Elgin and Winter Garden Theatre Centre ★ These landmark theaters first opened their doors in 1913, and the Centre is now a designated National Historic Site, owned and operated by the Ontario Heritage Trust. Both the Elgin and the Winter Garden have been restored to their Edwardian gilded glory and the theaters vie with the Royal Alexandra and the Princess of Wales Theatre for major shows and attention. The Centre has been termed the last operating double-decker theater in the world. The downstairs Elgin is larger, seating 1,500 and featuring a lavish domed ceiling and gilded decoration on the boxes and proscenium. Hand-painted frescoes adorn the striking interior of the 1,000-seat Winter Garden. Both theaters offer everything from Broadway musicals and dramas to concerts and opera performances, with the Toronto International Film Festival utilizing the Elgin as a cinema. 189 Yonge St. ✆ **416/872-5555** for tickets or 416/314-2901 for administration. Subway: Queen.

Four Seasons Centre for the Performing Arts ★★★ Toronto's opera house, which opened in 2006, is a stunner. Designed by architect Jack Diamond of the renowned Toronto firm, Diamond and Schmitt, it has a simple exterior, resembling a house of glass. Inside, in the tradition of truly grand opera houses, there are three stages: main, rear, and side. But the masterstroke in the Four Seasons Centre's design is its perfect acoustics. No small feat given that the structure is set on not one but two major thoroughfares, and a subway line rumbles beneath it. This is home to the Canadian Opera Company and the National Ballet of Canada. 145 Queen St. W. ✆ **416/363-8231** for tickets or 416/363-6671 for administration. www.fourseasonscentre.ca. Subway: Osgoode.

Koerner Hall Opened in 2009, this is a new jewel on Toronto's performing arts scene. Designed by the renowned KPMB Architects group, the concert hall seats 1,135 patrons. The centerpiece of The Royal Conservatory of Music's TELUS Centre for Performance and Learning, it has received rave reviews for its acoustics and has attracted such international stars as Steve Reich, Frederica von Stade, Ravi Shankar, and Baaba Maal in genres ranging from jazz to blues to world music to classical. 273 Bloor St. W. ✆ **416/408-2825.** www.rcmusic.ca.Subway: St. George or Museum.

Lorraine Kimsa Theatre for Young People ★★ ☺ Toronto's such a theater town that even tiny tots (and the rest of the family) get their own performance center. For more than 30 years, the always-enjoyable Lorraine Kimsa Theatre (formerly known as the Young People's Theatre) has mounted whimsical productions such as *Jacob Two-Two Meets the Hooded Fang* (by the late, great Mordecai Richler) and children's classics like *You're a Good Man, Charlie Brown*. This theater company is particularly committed to diversity in its programming and in its artists. 165 Front St. E. ✆ **416/862-2222** for tickets or 416/363-5131 for administration. www.lktyp.ca. Tickets C$15–C$30. Subway: Union, then a streetcar east to Jarvis St.

Massey Hall This landmark 1892 building is one of Canada's premier music venues. Its 2,753 seats are not the most comfortable in town, but the flawless acoustics will make you stop squirming. It has hosted now-legendary concerts from the likes of Charlie Parker and Neil Young, and its programming runs the gamut from classical to pop to rock to jazz. Recent visitors have included Norah Jones, Diana Krall, Jimmy Cliff, and Pat Metheny. This is also a popular stop for lectures. 178 Victoria St. ✆ **416/872-4255** for tickets or 416/593-4822 for administration. www.masseyhall.com. Subway: King.

National Ballet of Canada ★★★ Perhaps the most beloved and famous of Toronto's cultural icons is the National Ballet of Canada. English ballerina Celia Franca launched the company in Toronto in 1951 and served as director, principal dancer, choreographer, and teacher. Over the years, the company has achieved great renown. The legendary Canadian ballerina Karen Kain became its artistic director in 2005. The company shares the Four Seasons Centre for the Performing Arts with the Canadian Opera Company. Its repertoire includes the classics and works by luminaries such as George Balanchine, as well as from some Canadian choreographers. 145

discount TICKETS

Want to take in a show, but don't want to spend a bundle? Drop by the T.O. Tix booth ★ (✆ **416/536-6468,** ext. 40), which sells half-price day-of-performance tickets. The booth is in Yonge-Dundas Square, just across the street from the Eaton Centre. T.O. Tix accepts cash, debit cards, Visa, and MasterCard, and all sales are final. The booth is open Tuesday to Saturday from noon to 6:30pm; it's closed Sunday and Monday (tickets for performances on those days are sold on Sat). You can also buy tickets via the website www.totix.ca, but be warned that not all tickets are available online. Also available on the website are hipTIX, where students between the ages of 15 and 29 can score C$5 tickets for certain shows.

Queen St. W. ✆ **866/345-9595** or 416/345-9595 for tickets, or 416/345-9686 for administration. www.national.ballet.ca. Tickets from C$45–C$200. Subway: Osgoode.

Royal Alexandra Theatre ★★ The 1,495-seat Royal Alex is a magnificent spectacle, never mind the show! Constructed in 1907, it owes its current health to discount-store czar and impresario Ed Mirvish, who refurbished it (as well as the surrounding area) in the 1960s. Inside, it's a riot of plush reds, gold brocade, and baroque ornamentation. Recent productions here have included *Dirty Dancing,* a musical based on the movie, and *Rock of Ages.* Avoid the vertigo-inducing second balcony and the seats "under the circle," which don't have the greatest sight lines. Be forewarned that legroom is very limited here. 260 King St. W. ✆ **416/872-1212.** www.mirvish.com. Subway: St. Andrew.

Roy Thomson Hall ★★★ This important concert hall is home to the Toronto Symphony Orchestra, which performs here from September to June, and to the Toronto Mendelssohn Choir. Since it opened in 1982, it has also hosted an array of international musical artists, including Yo-Yo Ma, Jessye Norman, and Kiri Te Kanawa. The hall was designed to give the audience a feeling of unusual intimacy with the performers—none of the 2,812 seats is more than 33m (108 ft.) from the stage. This is one of the few venues where you can feel happy in the "nosebleed" seats. With Roy Thomson's perfect acoustics, who cares about sightlines? 60 Simcoe St. ✆ **416/872-4255** for tickets or 416/593-4822 for administration. www.roythomson.com. Subway: St. Andrew.

Soulpepper ★★ Founded in 1997, this artist-created classical repertory company presents theatrical masterpieces of the 20th century, under the able artistic direction of Albert Schultz Theatre. Education and youth outreach are key parts of their mandate. The highly respected—and award-winning—group recently staged *Glengarry Glen Ross* and the Canadian classic *Billy Bishop Goes To War.* Performing at the Young Centre in the Distillery District, 55 Mill St. ✆ **416/866-8666.** www.soulpepper.ca. Tickets C$40–C$75; C$20–C$22 for ages 21–30 available through www.stageplay.ca. Subway: King, then a streetcar east to Parliament St.

Toronto Symphony Orchestra ★★★ The TSO has been revitalized under the direction of Peter Oundjian and the improved acoustics of their home venue. They perform anything from classics to jazzy Broadway tunes to new Canadian works at Roy Thomson Hall from September to June. 60 Simcoe St. ✆ **416/593-4828.** www.tso.on.ca. Tickets C$33–C$99. Subway: St. Andrew.

Comedy Clubs

Toronto must be one heck of a funny place. How else to explain why a disproportionate number of comedians, including Jim Carrey and Mike Myers, hail from here. The annual Just For Laughs festival delivers laughs every July, and the city's comedy clubs are thriving.

Comedy Bar This new kid on the comedy block has quickly proved popular. It stresses sketch and improv comedy over stand-up (it's co-owned by Gary Rideout of sketch troupe the Sketchersons). 945 Bloor St. W. ✆ **416/238-7337.** www.comedybar.ca. Cover: free to C$12. Subway: Ossington.

Second City ★ This was where Mike Myers received his formal—and improvisational—comic training. Over the years, the legendary Second City nurtured the likes of John Candy, Dan Aykroyd, Bill Murray, Martin Short, Andrea Martin, and Eugene Levy. It continues to turn out talented young actors. The shows are always funny and topical, though the outrageous post-show improvs usually get the biggest laughs. 51 Mercer St. ✆ **800/263-4485** or 416/343-0011. www.secondcity.com. Show only C$24–C$29; dinner & show C$39–C$56. Reservations required. Subway: St. Andrew.

Live Music Venues

El Mocambo ★ This world-renowned rock-'n'-roll institution hosted an infamous Rolling Stones show in the '70s, while the likes of U2 and Elvis Costello graced its stage in their early years. Its famous neon sign blinked no more when the club closed for a few years, but the venue is now back. A top-to-toe renovation has resulted in quite a different look, and it now welcomes acts from genres as diverse as indie rock, hip-hop, and roots. 464 Spadina Ave. ✆ **416/777-1777.** Cover C$5–C$20. Subway: Spadina, then a streetcar south to College St.

The Garrison Since opening in 2009, this club has quickly become a valued member of Toronto's live music scene. A mid-sized venue (capacity 350), it sports good sightlines and sound, and has a separate bar area up front if your ears need a break. It is co-owned and booked by scene veteran (Sneaky Dee's) and former rocker Shaun Bowring, and concentrates on local and visiting indie rock bands. 1197 Dundas St. W. ✆ **416/519-9439.** Cover free to C$20. Subway: St. Patrick, then a streetcar west to Ossington Ave.

The Horseshoe Tavern Since 1947, this much-loved honky-tonk has played a crucial role in Toronto's music community. The country and blues sounds it showcased in the '60s and early '70s gave way to punk and new wave, while its current booking policy primarily concentrates on modern rock and roots music styles. The Stones had a secret gig here in 1997, and the likes of Los Lobos, Wilco, and local heroes Blue Rodeo have also graced its stage. For 16 years, the free Nu Music Night every Tuesday has presented some real gems. The expanded room now holds 520, and a friendly and unpretentious atmosphere has remained constant. 368 Queen St. W. ✆ **416/598-4753.** www.horseshoetavern.com. Cover free to C$25. Subway: Osgoode.

Hugh's Room Call this a folk supper club for baby boomers. Around since 2001, the 200 seat venue has good sound and sightlines (except at the bar) and decent food. The booking policy ranges from folk legends like Judy Collins and the Strawbs to emerging roots singer/songwriters. 2261 Dundas St. W. ✆ **416/531-6604.** Cover C$10–C$50 Subway: Dundas W.

The Melody Bar ★★ This is Toronto's favorite karaoke bar, and sessions moderated by Peter Styles pack the place Friday and Saturday nights. During the rest of the week, you'll find local musicians (roots music is prominent), DJs, and open-mic events. Wednesday is queer night. At the Gladstone Hotel, 1214 Queen St. W. ✆ **416/531-4635.** www.gladstonehotel.com. No cover. Subway: Osgoode, then a streetcar west to Gladstone Ave.

The Mod Club Theatre ★★ One of Toronto's best mid-sized live-music venues, it's co-owned by Mark Holmes, former frontman of '80s rock faves Platinum Blonde. The Killers, Amy Winehouse, and Canadian favorites like Metric and Stars have all performed here; the concert hall morphs into a dance club later at night. 722 College St. ✆ **416/588-4MOD (416/588-4663).** www.themodclub.com. Cover up to C$15; higher prices for major concerts. Subway: Queen's Park, then a streetcar west to Crawford St.

The Rex Hotel Jazz & Blues Bar ★ The busiest jazz club in the city, it presents two or even three different acts daily, 7 days a week. A casual watering hole lacking the pretensions of some jazz joints, it has been drawing jazz fans since it opened in 1951. The decor hasn't changed much since the old days, but the sounds here range from the traditional to the cutting edge. The Rex features the city's best players and sometimes attracts international talent. 194 Queen St. W. ✆ **416/598-2475.** www.therex.ca. Cover up to C$12. Subway: Osgoode.

Dance Clubs

Dance clubs come and go at an alarming pace in Toronto. Be sure to check out the club listings in the free weeklies *Now* (www.nowtoronto.com) and *Eye* (www.eyeweekly.com), or at www.martiniboys.com or www.torontolife.com, to keep up with the currently cool (or hot) spots.

The Social The first dance club to make a mark on the west Queen West strip, it continues to draw large crowds on the weekend. An eclectic mix of music styles is played, and a rotating cast of international star DJs is featured on Saturday nights. 1100 Queen St. W. ✆ **416/532-4474**. Cover from C$10. Subway: Osgoode, then a streetcar west to Dovercourt Ave.

This Is London ★ This club is more sophisticated and less frenzied than most of its peers—you might even manage a conversation. It is reminiscent of an old-fashioned gentlemen's club with its Oriental rugs and comfortable armchairs, though the dance floor is pretty hot. The music ranges from house to R&B to Top 40 and rock, and the dress code can be strict. The club's amazing ladies room features a makeup artist and hairstylist to help femmes fatales primp. 364 Richmond St. W. ✆ **416/351-1100.** Cover C$15–$20. Subway: Osgoode.

The Bar Scene

Allen's Allen's sports a great bar that offers more than 150 beer selections and 278 single malts. Guinness is the drink of choice on Tuesday and Saturday nights, when folks reel and jig to the Celtic entertainment. 143 Danforth Ave. ✆ **416/463-3086.** Subway: Broadview.

The Drake Lounge ★ The bar at the Drake Hotel (see p. 381) is a perfect perch for sipping martinis and envisioning yourself in a glamorous bygone era. The Lounge is designed to evoke a mid-20th-century feel. It's dressed-up, grown-up fun, and it attracts a crowd of devoted locals and suburbanites. At the Drake Hotel, 1150 Queen St. W. ✆ **416/531-5042.** Subway: Osgoode, then a streetcar west to Beaconsfield Ave.

El Convento Rico ★★ The Latin beat beckons one and all—straight, gay, and otherwise—to this lively club. It has welcomed a diverse crowd for nearly 20 years now. If you don't know how to salsa, meringue, or cha-cha, you can pick up the basics at the

Friday night dance lessons, but if you don't learn, no one on the jam-packed dance floor will notice. There's a substantial hetero contingent that comes out just to watch the fabulous drag queens—and don't be surprised if you encounter a bachelorette party in progress. Post-midnight shows, Friday and Saturday, are big draws. 750 College St. ✆ **416/588-7800.** www.elconventorico.com. Subway: Queen's Park, then a streetcar west to Shaw Ave.

Mill Street Brew Pub ★ Situated in the historic site of an old brewery, this pub features an award-winning array of beers brewed in small batches (some are available only seasonally). The Tankhouse Pale Ale is a constant, with its five malts blended for a particularly complex flavor. It's a top pick of local hipsters. In the Distillery District, 55 Mill St. ✆ **416/681-0338.** Subway: King, then a streetcar east to Parliament St.

Reposado The increased fashionableness of premium tequila is reflected in this chic little tequila bar on the scorching hot Ossington strip. It sports a relaxed vibe, the largest selection of tequilas in the city, and cool music from local combos and guest DJs on some nights. 136 Ossington Ave. ✆ **416/532-6474.** Subway: Osgoode, then a streetcar west to Ossington Ave.

The Roof ★★★ Author Mordecai Richler called this the only civilized spot in Toronto. It's an old literary haunt, with comfortable couches in front of a fireplace and excellent drinks. The walls sport caricatures of members of Canada's literary establishment. The James Bond martini—vodka with a drop of Lillet—is a popular choice. The south-facing view from the outdoor terrace is one of the best in the city. At the Park Hyatt Toronto, 4 Avenue Rd. ✆ **416/924-5471.** Subway: Museum or Bay.

Watusi ★★ The popularity of "Mad Men" has been well-timed for Watusi, a swanky cocktail lounge exuding retro '60s cool. Located on the now hip Ossington Avenue, the place is littered with pop art, and as the clock ticks toward midnight, furniture is swept aside to make way for a long, lean dance floor. 11 Ossington Ave. ✆ **416/533-1800.** Subway: Osgoode, then a streetcar west to Ossington Ave.

SOUTHWESTERN ONTARIO

11

by Pamela Cuthbert

This lush, temperate region is bordered by three Great Lakes, making for some of the best farmland in Canada. A mix of Carolinian forests, rolling hills, and fertile plains, the Niagara area is rich with rare flora and fauna, and is home to the one of the country's biggest wine-producing regions. And it's home to several of Canada's award-winning vintners, as well as a few burgeoning culinary trails that lure hungry travelers. Niagara-on-the-Lake is famed for its excellent theater festival, the Shaw, and Niagara Falls, a honeymoon capital, is one of the natural wonders of the world.

Southwestern Ontario attracted many of Canada's early pioneers. Different ethnic groups built their own towns, and these early influences are still felt today in local traditions and celebrations. Scots built towns such as Elora, Fergus, and St. Marys; the Germans, Kitchener-Waterloo; the Mennonites, Elmira and St. Jacobs; and the English Loyalists, Stratford and London. This cultural heritage inspires popular festivals such as Oktoberfest, the Highland Games, and the Mennonite quilt sale, but the biggest cultural draw is the world-famous theater festival at Stratford. This region is also home to Hamilton, Ontario's third-largest city, which offers historic sites, an up-and-coming arts community, and spectacular botanical gardens.

EXPLORING THE REGION

The main attractions of the southwestern Ontario region—Niagara-on-the-Lake, Niagara Falls, and Stratford—are all within a 2-hour drive from Toronto. But if you're driving across the Canada-U.S. border, you can see some of the sights on the way to the big city.

Essentials

VISITOR INFORMATION Contact **Ontario Tourism** (© **800/ONTARIO** [800/668-2746]; www.ontariotravel.net) or visit its Toronto travel information center in the Atrium on Bay (street level) at 20 Dundas St. W.—it's just across Dundas from the Sears store at the northern edge of the Eaton Centre. (The Atrium's mailing address is 595 Bay St., but since the information booth is on the south side of the complex, they use a different street address for the same building.) It's open daily from 8:30am to 5pm; hours are extended during the summer, often to 8pm.

Another good resource is the **Southern Ontario Tourism Organization** (✆ **800/267-3399;** http://soto.on.ca), which has a travel-planning booklet, an e-mail newsletter, and an informative website.

TOURIST OFFICES In addition to the Atrium on Bay location, you can find a **Travel Information Centre** in **Niagara Falls** (5355 Stanley Ave.; ✆ **905/358-3221**) and in **St. Catharines,** on the QEW as you head north from Niagara Falls (✆ **905/684-6354**). There are two information centers in **Windsor:** One is just east of the Ambassador Bridge at 1235 Huron Church Rd. (✆ **519/973-1310**) and the other by the Detroit/Windsor Tunnel at 110 Park St. E. (✆ **519/973-1338**).

Getting There

The Rainbow Bridge connects Niagara Falls with its New York State counterpart. Niagara-on-the-Lake is easily accessible from the QEW heading north out of Niagara Falls, and it's a scenic drive on the QEW around Lake Ontario on the way up to Toronto. This route also takes you past the city of Hamilton, which is well worth a stop for its botanical gardens and historic castle.

Windsor sits across from Detroit on the Canadian side of the border. From here, visitors can travel along either Highway 401 east or the more scenic Highway 3 (called the Talbot Trail, which runs from Windsor to Fort Erie), stopping along the way to visit some major attractions on the Lake Erie shore. Northeast of Windsor lies London, and from London, it's an easy drive to Stratford. From Stratford, visitors can turn west to Goderich and Bayfield on the shores of Lake Huron or east to Kitchener-Waterloo and then north to Elmira, Elora, and Fergus.

The Great Outdoors

Ontario's extensive provincial parks system includes over 330 parks that cover 9 million hectares (22 million acres) of land and attract some 10 million visitors each year. If you've visited before 2005, keep in mind that the regulations have since changed and you'll do well to familiarize yourself with the new rules at www.ontarioparks.com. One of the main changes is that all Ontario parks are now classified as either premium, middle, or low—a reference to a park's level of popularity, and to the fees it charges. Staying 1 night in a premium park can cost C$46 per person, whereas a low park would be more in the C$22 range (there are discounts for seniors and people with disabilities in all parks). The daily in-season entry fee for a vehicle starts at C$9.50. To make a park reservation, contact **Ontario Parks Reservations** (370 Stone Rd. W., Guelph; ✆ **888/668-7275;** www.ontarioparks.com); a reservation in any provincial park costs C$12.

BIKING The South Point and Marsh trails in **Rondeau Provincial Park,** near Blenheim (✆ **519/674-1750**), are great for cycling.

BIRD-WATCHING **Point Pelee National Park,** southeast of Windsor (✆ **519/322-2365;** www.pc.gc.ca), is one of the continent's premier bird-watching centers. The spring and fall migrations are spectacular; more than 300 species of birds can be spotted here. In late summer, it's also the gathering place for flocks of monarch butterflies, which cover the trees before taking off for their migratory flight down south. Located at the southernmost tip of Canada, which juts down into Lake Erie at the same latitude as northern California, it's a charming and often overlooked destination.

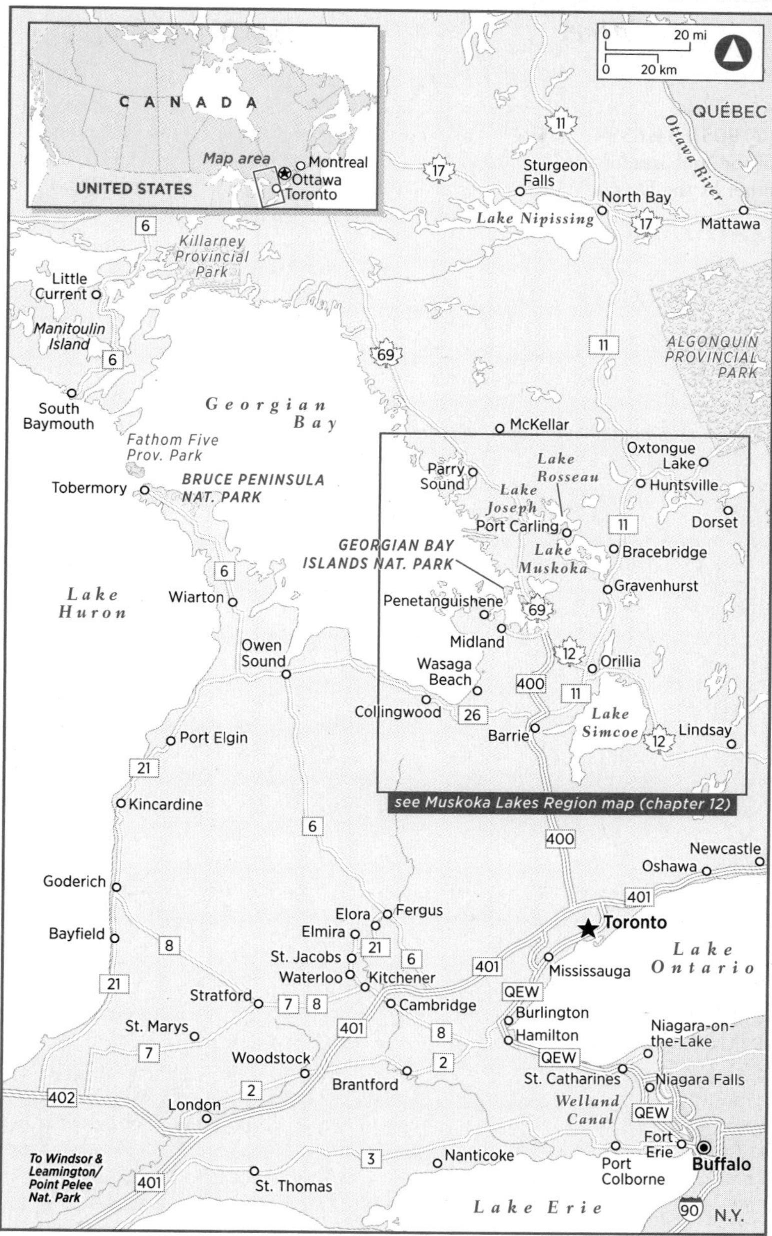
CANADA
UNITED STATES
Map area
Montreal
Ottawa
Toronto
0 20 mi
0 20 km
QUÉBEC
Ottawa River
Sturgeon Falls
North Bay
Lake Nipissing
Mattawa
Killarney Provincial Park
Little Current
Manitoulin Island
South Baymouth
Georgian Bay
ALGONQUIN PROVINCIAL PARK
McKellar
Fathom Five Prov. Park
Tobermory
BRUCE PENINSULA NAT. PARK
Parry Sound
Lake Rosseau
Lake Joseph
Oxtongue Lake
Huntsville
Dorset
Port Carling
Lake Muskoka
Bracebridge
Gravenhurst
GEORGIAN BAY ISLANDS NAT. PARK
Lake Huron
Wiarton
Penetanguishene
Midland
Owen Sound
Wasaga Beach
Orillia
Collingwood
Lake Simcoe
Barrie
Lindsay
Port Elgin
Kincardine
see Muskoka Lakes Region map (chapter 12)
Newcastle
Oshawa
Goderich
Elora
Fergus
Elmira
Toronto
Bayfield
St. Jacobs
Lake Ontario
Waterloo
Kitchener
Mississauga
Stratford
Cambridge
Burlington
St. Marys
Hamilton
Niagara-on-the-Lake
Woodstock
Brantford
St. Catharines
Niagara Falls
Welland Canal
London
Fort Erie
Port Colborne
Buffalo
Nanticoke
To Windsor & Leamington/ Point Pelee Nat. Park
St. Thomas
Lake Erie
N.Y.
6
11
17
69
12
26
400
21
8
7
2
3
401
402
QEW
90

Another good bird-watching outpost is the **Jack Miner Bird Sanctuary** (Rd. 3 W., 3km/1¾ miles north of Kingsville off Division Rd.; ✆ **877/289-8328** or 519/733-4034; www.jackminer.com). The famed naturalist established the sanctuary to protect migrating Canada geese, and the best time to visit is late October and November, when thousands of migrating waterfowl stop over.

BOATING, CANOEING & KAYAKING Companies offering trips on the Grand River include the **Heritage River Canoe & Kayak Company** (73 Oakhill Dr., Brantford; ✆ **866/462-2663** or 519/758-0761; www.heritageriver.com) and **Canoeing the Grand** (3734 King St. E., Kitchener; ✆ **877/896-0290** or 519/896-0290; www.canoeingthegrand.com). There are also canoe rentals in **Point Pelee National Park** (✆ **519/322-2371**).

GOLF Golf is a major pastime in this part of the country; check out the Ontario listings and reviews on Golf Canada (www.golfcanada.com) to get some sense of the diversity of the offerings, both in terms of design and difficulty. There are more than 650 courses to choose from and plenty of post-game attractions. In southwestern Ontario, you can't go wrong with golfing in the Niagara region. The **Royal Niagara Golf Club** in Niagara-on-the-Lake (✆ **905/685-9501;** www.royalniagara.com) features three 9-hole courses, and south of Niagara Falls off the Niagara Parkway, **Legends on the Niagara** (✆ **866/465-3642;** www.niagaralegends.com) also has three courses, including two 18-hole courses.

HIKING Canada's oldest and most famous hiking trail, the **Bruce Trail,** starts in Queenston in Niagara-on-the-Lake and runs 885km (550 miles) up north to Tobermory at the top of the Bruce Peninsula. A favorite section runs along the Niagara Escarpment. The **Bruce Trail Association** (✆ **800/665-4453** or 905/529-6821; www.brucetrail.org) has 40 hiking routes on its website, all of which can be downloaded as PDFs free of charge. Ontario Tourism's website contains a wealth of information about different sections of the mighty trail (www.ontariotravel.net).

The 130km (81-mile) **Thames Valley Trail** follows the Thames River through London, past the University of Western Ontario and into farmlands all the way to St. Mary's. For information, contact **Thames Valley Trail Association** (✆ **519/645-2845;** www.thamesvalleytrail.org).

The 275km (171-mile) **Grand Valley Trail** is a footpath that runs from Rock Point Provincial Park on Lake Erie to the town of Alton, where it connects with the **Bruce Trail.** It follows the Grand River from Dunnville, north through Brantford, Paris, and farmlands around Kitchener-Waterloo to the Elora Gorge (see "Elora & Fergus," later in this chapter). For information, contact the Grand Valley Trails Association (✆ **519/576-6156;** www.gvta.on.ca).

SWIMMING The Elora Gorge is a favorite swimming spot; the conservation area includes a 1-hectare (2½-acre) lake with two beach areas; contact the Grand River Conservation Authority (✆ **866/900-4722** or 519/846-9742; www.grandriver.ca) for details. Swimming is also very popular at **Rondeau Provincial Park** (✆ **519/674-1750**), which is located on Lake Erie (off Hwy. 21 near Blenheim); lots of other watersports are available here, as well.

ACCOMMODATIONS ■
Harbour House **15**
Moffat Inn **20**
Oban Inn **1**
The Old Bank House **2**
Prince of Wales Hotel & Spa **19**

DINING ◆
Angel Inn **11**
Epicurean **5**
Niagara Home Bakery **8**
Shaw Café and Wine Bar **3**
Stagecoach Family Restaurant **10**

ATTRACTIONS & SHOPPING ●
Court House Theatre **12**
Festival Theatre **21**
Fort George National
  Historic Site **22**
Greaves Jam **9**
Irish Design **7**
Maple Leaf Fudge **17**
Niagara Apothecary **18**
Niagara Historical
  Society Museum **16**
The Owl & the Pussycat **13**
Royal George Theatre **4**
Scottish Loft **14**
Shaw Shop **6**
Studio Theatre **21**

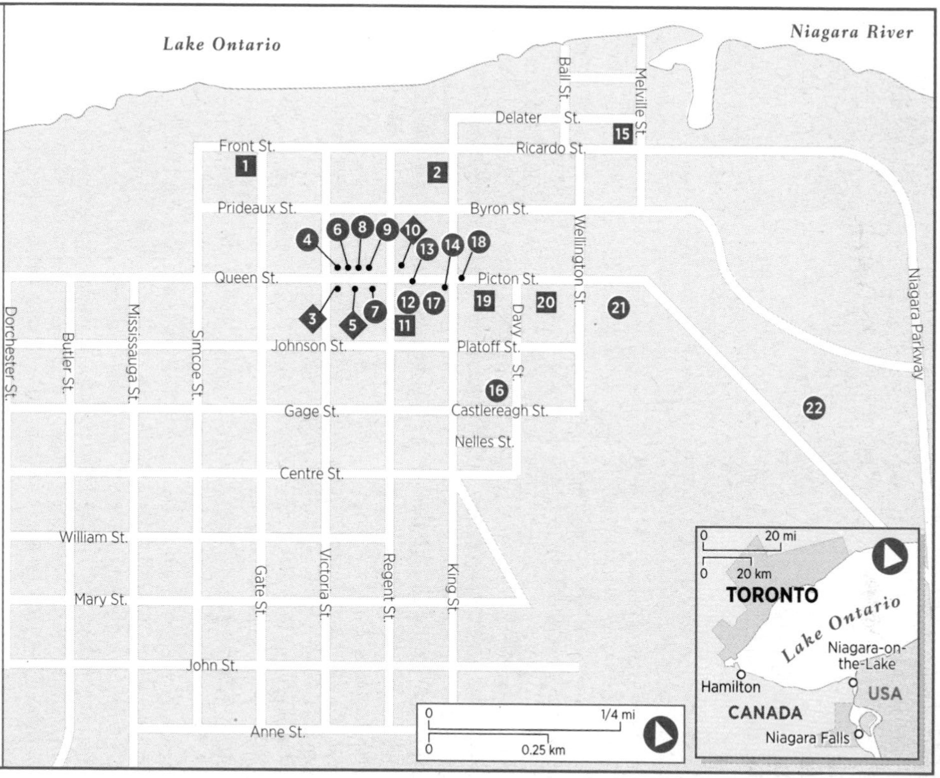

Lake Ontario
Niagara River
Ball St.
Melville St.
Delater St.
Front St.
Ricardo St.
Prideaux St.
Byron St.
Queen St.
Picton St.
Wellington St.
Niagara Parkway
Dorchester St.
Butler St.
Mississauga St.
Simcoe St.
Johnson St.
Platoff St.
Davy St.
Gage St.
Castlereagh St.
Nelles St.
Centre St.
William St.
Gate St.
Victoria St.
Regent St.
King St.
Mary St.
John St.
Anne St.
0 1/4 mi
0 0.25 km
0 20 mi
0 20 km
TORONTO
Lake Ontario
Niagara-on-the-Lake
Hamilton
USA
CANADA
Niagara Falls

NIAGARA-ON-THE-LAKE & NIAGARA FALLS

130km (81 miles) SE of Toronto

Never mind that Oscar Wilde called it "a bride's second great disappointment," the honeymoon capital of Niagara Falls is worth the 2-hour drive from Toronto just to witness the majesty of the falls themselves. The tacky shops, motels, and attractions—it's an unabashed tourist trap—can either be ignored or enjoyed, depending on your sensibility. Then, take a scenic drive about a half-hour back toward Toronto, along the **Niagara Parkway** (p. 431), to Niagara-on-the-Lake (NOTL), a quiet and pretty 19th-century village that offers a welcome retreat after the carnival atmosphere of Niagara Falls. Many travelers prefer to stay at NOTL, where the food and wine offerings go well beyond the fast-food chains of the Falls and can be quite sophisticated for a tourist region. (You're now in the heart of Niagara wine country.) This is also home to the **Shaw Festival,** a theater event on par with Stratford's festival and another reason to visit, or even stay for a day or two.

Essentials

VISITOR INFORMATION The **Niagara-on-the-Lake Chamber of Commerce** (26 Queen St., Niagara-on-the-Lake; ✆ **905/468-1950;** www.niagaraonthelake.com) provides information and can help you find accommodations. It's open April through October daily from 9am to 7:30pm and the rest of the year daily from 10am to 5pm.

For Niagara Falls travel information, contact **Niagara Falls Tourism** (5515 Stanley Ave., Niagara Falls; ✆ **800/56-FALLS** [800/563-2557] or 519/356-6061; www.niagarafallstourism.com) or the **Niagara Parks Commission** (✆ **877/NIA-PARK** [877/642-7275]; www.niagaraparks.com).

GETTING THERE Niagara-on-the-Lake is best seen by **car.** From Toronto, take the Queen Elizabeth Way (signs read QEW) to Niagara via the cities of Hamilton and St. Catharine's, and exit at Highway 55. The trip takes about 1½ hours.

Amtrak and **VIA Rail** (✆ **416/366-8411**) operate **trains** between Toronto and New York, but they stop only in Niagara Falls and St. Catharine's, not in Niagara-on-the-Lake. Call ✆ **800/361-1235** in Canada or **800/USA-RAIL** (800/872-7245) in the United States. From either place, you'll need to rent a car. Rental outlets in St. Catharine's include **Hertz** (350 Ontario St.; ✆ **905/682-8695**). In Niagara Falls, **Avis** is at 5734 Valley Way (✆ **905/357-2847**).

The Shaw Festival

Founded in 1962, the Shaw was known for many years for presenting the dramatic and comedic works of George Bernard Shaw and his contemporaries. However, since Jackie Maxwell became artistic director, the mandate has changed: The Shaw now features forgotten plays from Shaw's era (often penned by women writers), as well as classics and new works by Canadian playwrights. As impressive a destination for theater-goers as Stratford, it runs from April until the first weekend of November and plays in the historic **Court House Theatre,** the exquisite **Shaw Festival Theatre,** the **Royal George Theatre,** and the **Studio Theatre.** Recent performances have included *Born Yesterday, Star Chamber,* and Shaw's *In Good King Charles's Golden Days.*

Free chamber concerts take place Sunday at 11am. Chats introduce performances on Friday evenings in July and August, and question-and-answer sessions follow Tuesday-evening performances.

The Shaw announces its festival program in mid-January. Prices range from C$30 to C$110; there are some "special matinees" that offer tickets for C$40 seniors and C$25 students. For more information, contact the **Shaw Festival** (✆ **800/511-7429** or 905/468-2172; www.shawfest.com).

Exploring the Town

Niagara-on-the Lake is small, and most of its attractions are along one main street, making it easy to explore on foot. In 1792, it briefly served as the capital of Upper Canada (though the town was then called Newark). The town was burned down during the War of 1812 but quickly rebuilt afterwards.

SIGHTS

Fort George National Historic Site ★ ☺ The fort played a central role in the War of 1812: It was headquarters for the British Army's Centre Division. The division was comprised of British regulars, local militia, Runchey's corps of former slaves, and aboriginal forces. The fort was destroyed by American artillery fire in May 1813. After the war, it was partially rebuilt, but it was abandoned in 1828 and not reconstructed until the 1930s. You can view the guardroom (with its hard plank beds), the officers' quarters, the enlisted men's quarters, and the sentry posts. The self-guided tour includes interpretive films. The fort is one of Ontario's favorite "haunted" sites (ghost-hunting tours are available throughout the summer and in October).

26 Queen St., Niagara Pkwy. ✆ **905/468-4257.** www.parkscanada.ca or www.friendsoffortgeorge.ca. C$12 adults, C$10 seniors, C$6 children 6–16, free for children 5 & under. Apr–Oct daily 10am–5pm; Nov–Mar Sat & Sun 10am–5pm.

Niagara Historical Society Museum For history buffs, this museum has more than 8,000 artifacts pertaining to local history. The collection includes possessions of United Empire Loyalists who first settled the area at the end of the American Revolution. So, if branding irons, portraits, maps, and other artifacts are your thing, take a few hours to peruse the museum.

43 Castlereagh St. (at Davy). ✆ **905/468-3912.** C$5 adults, C$3 seniors, C$2 students (w/ID), C$1 children 5–12, free for children 4 & under. May–Oct daily 10am–5pm; Nov–Apr daily 1–5pm.

A SHOPPING STROLL

It's a pleasant pastime to stroll along the town's main artery, Queen Street, and check out some entertaining, albeit touristy, shops. The **Niagara Apothecary,** at no. 5 (✆ **905/468-3845**), dates to 1866 and is a store and also a bit of a museum, with the original, gold-leaf and black-walnut counters, and glass and ceramic apothecary ware, on display. At no. 13 is the **Scottish Loft** (✆ **905/468-0965**), which is filled with tartans, Celtic memorabilia, candy, books, and other assorted Scottish-themed notions. **Maple Leaf Fudge** (no. 14; ✆ **905/468-2211**) is a tooth-aching stop: You can watch as the aproned staff makes 20-plus flavors on marble slabs. At no. 16 is a charming toy store, the **Owl and the Pussycat** (✆ **905/468-3081**). At no. 35 is **Greaves Jam** (✆ **905/468-7331**), run by fourth-generation jam makers—truly good stuff. **Irish Design,** at no. 38 (✆ **905/468-7233**), sells hand-knit sweaters, traditional gold and silver jewelry, and other treasures from the Emerald Isle. The **Shaw Shop** (✆ **800/511-7429**), no. 79, next to the Royal George Theatre, carries

TOURING NIAGARA-ON-THE-LAKE wineries

Visiting a local winery is one of the most delicious ways to pass an hour or two in this region. You'll also see some of the best in new and innovative wine design, architecture, and viticulture. As with any major wine region, there are the big, commercial enterprises and the small, artisan ones. Lately, celebrities have joined the club (here, as elsewhere), so you can try wines with names such as Mike Weir, Wayne Gretzky, or Dan Aykroyd; mostly for the novelty, not the nose. Look for the VQA label: It identifies wines made with locally grown grapes. For maps of the area and information about vintners, contact the **Wine Council of Ontario** (✆ **905/684-8070;** www.winesofontario.org). The wineries listed below are close to the town of Niagara-on-the-Lake. Tours are free. Prices for tastings vary with the winery and the wine you're sampling, but are usually about C$10.

If you turn off Highway 55 and go down York Road, you'll reach **Château des Charmes** (✆ **905/262-4219;** www.chateaudescharmes.com), west of the town of St. David's. The winery was built to resemble a French manor house, and its architecture is unique in the region. One-hour tours are given daily. It's open from 10am to 6pm year-round.

To reach **Stratus** (2059 Niagara Stone Rd.; ✆ **905/468-1806;** www.konzelmann.ca), one of the region's more cutting-edge wineries with a focus on sustainable practices and eco-design, take Niagara Stone Road out of Niagara-on-the-Lake. This vintner is famous for its award-winning blends. Reservations are not required for tastings, but if you're traveling in a group of six or more, it's best to call in advance. Tours of the modern winery are by appointment only.

GBS memorabilia and more. A Dansk outlet and several galleries selling contemporary Canadian and ethnic crafts round-out the mix.

JET-BOATING THRILLS

Jet-boat excursions leave from the dock across from 61 Melville St., at the King George III Inn. Don a rain suit, poncho, and life jacket, and climb aboard. The boat takes you out onto the Niagara River for a trip along the stonewalled canyon to the whirlpool downriver. The ride starts slow but gets into turbulent water. Trips, which operate from May to October, last an hour and cost C$57 adults and C$48 children 13 and under. Reservations are required, and if you make your booking online, you'll get a discount of C$5 per ticket. Call the **Whirlpool Jet Boat Company** at ✆ **888/438-4444** or 905/468-4800, or visit **www.whirlpooljet.com.**

Where to Stay In Niagara-on-the-Lake

In summer, hotel space is in high demand. If you're having trouble nailing down a room, contact the **Niagara-on-the-Lake Chamber of Commerce** (✆ **905/468-1950;** www.niagaraonthelake.com), which provides information about accommodations, from luxurious hotels to charming bed-and-breakfasts. B&Bs can also be located and booked via **www.bbcanada.com.** The prices listed below are for the peak summer season; deep discounts are available at all of these properties in early spring, late fall, and winter.

IN TOWN

Harbour House ★★★ Tucked away on a quiet street that's close to the marina, this hotel offers serenity and tranquility from the moment you step through the front door. The focus is on comfort with understated luxury, from the Frette robes to the flickering fireplaces. The beds are particularly cozy, with king-sized mattresses topped by a layer of hypoallergenic duck feathers. (For those with allergies, alternative bedding is available). Service is thoughtful and efficient, and guests are treated to lavish breakfasts and late afternoon wine-and-cheese receptions. The hotel is entirely nonsmoking.

85 Melville St., Niagara-on-the-Lake, ON L0S 1J0. ✆ **866/277-6677** or 905/468-4683. Fax 905/468-0366. www.harbourhousehotel.ca. 31 units. From C$299 double. Rates include breakfast. AE, DC, MC, V. Free parking. **Amenities:** Bike rental; concierge; room service. *In room:* A/C, TV/DVD player, CD player, hair dryer, minibar, Wi-Fi (free).

Moffat Inn This is a fine budget-conscious choice in a convenient location. Most rooms have brass-framed beds, and eight have fireplaces. Guests tend to congregate on the patio, which is set in a beautiful flower garden. But if you have trouble climbing stairs, this hotel is not a good choice since most of the guest rooms are on the second floor, and there's no elevator and no porter to handle luggage.

60 Picton St. (at Queen St.), Niagara-on-the-Lake, ON L0S 1J0. ✆ **905/468-4116.** www.moffatinn.com. 24 units. From C$125 double. AE, MC, V. Free parking. **Amenities:** Restaurant. *In room:* A/C, TV, hair dryer, Wi-Fi (free).

Oban Inn ★ In a prime location overlooking the lake, the Oban Inn is a lovely place to stay. The town's first real country inn, it's in a charming, sizeable white Victorian house with a large veranda. The gorgeous gardens provide the fragrant bouquets throughout the house. A complete renovation updated the pretty rooms with modern amenities, including LCD plasma televisions, Bose sound systems, and individual temperature controls in all rooms. The spa is also a popular attraction.

160 Front St. (at Gate St.), Niagara-on-the-Lake, ON L0S 1J0. ✆ **866/359-6226** or 905/468-2165. www.obaninn.ca. 26 units. From C$260 double. AE, DC, DISC, MC, V. Free parking. **Amenities:** Restaurant; lounge; babysitting; bike rental; concierge; room service; spa. *In room:* A/C, TV, CD player, hair dryer, Internet (fee).

The Old Bank House ★ Beautifully situated down by the river, this two-story Georgian was built in 1817 as the first branch of the Bank of Canada. In 1902, it hosted the Prince and Princess of Wales, and today, it's a charming bed-and-breakfast inn. Several tastefully decorated units have private entrances, and one also has a private trellised deck. If you're planning a romantic weekend away, you'll love the Rose Suite, with its cathedral ceiling and private balcony.

10 Front St., Niagara-on-the-Lake, ON L0S 1J0. ✆ **877-468-7136** or 905/468-7136. www.oldbankhouse.com. 9 units. From C$189 double. Rates include breakfast. AE, MC, V. Free parking. **Amenities:** Restaurant (in high season); Jacuzzi. *In room:* A/C, TV, Wi-Fi (free).

Prince of Wales ★★ This is one of Niagara-on-the-Lake's most luxurious hotels, and you could say it has it all: a central location across from the lovely gardens of Simcoe Park; recreational facilities, including an indoor pool; a full-service spa; lounges, bars, and restaurants; and conference facilities. If you're adverse to floral fabrics and overstuffed furniture, this is not the place for you. However, if you're looking to be seriously pampered in a faux-Victorian setting, it's a good bet. Also, it's one of the rare hotels in town with a wheelchair-accessible room. Pets are welcome. This is a smoke-free hotel.

6 Picton St., Niagara-on-the-Lake, ON L0S 1J0. ✆ **888/669-5566** or 905/468-3246. www.vintage-hotels.com. 110 units. From C$275 double. AE, DC, DISC, MC, V. Free parking. Small pets accepted ($35). **Amenities:** Dining room; cafe; bar; lounge; bike rental; concierge; health club; Jacuzzi; indoor pool; room service; spa. *In room:* A/C, TV, CD player, hair dryer, Wi-Fi ($10/day).

ALONG THE WINE ROUTE

Inn on the Twenty and the Vintage House ★ Across the street from Cave Spring Cellars, one of Niagara's best known wineries, the inn offers modern, well-equipped, and generous suites. Each one has an elegantly furnished living room with a fireplace and a Jacuzzi in the bathroom. Seven are duplexes—one of them, the deluxe loft, has two double beds on the second level—and five are single-level suites with high ceilings. All of the suites are nonsmoking. The inn's eatery, On the Twenty Restaurant & Wine Bar (below), is also across the street and is a great place to dine. The inn's spa offers a full range of services for men and women, and has special packages for couples. Next door is the **Vintage House,** an 1840 Georgian mansion with three suites, all with private entrances. All rooms are nonsmoking.

3845 Main St., Jordan, ON L0R 1S0. ✆ **800/701-8074** or 905/562-5336. www.innonthetwenty.com. 30 units. From C$259 suite. MC, V. Free parking. From QEW, take the Jordan Rd. exit south; at the 1st intersection, turn right onto 4th Ave., then right onto Main St. **Amenities:** Restaurant; concierge; nearby golf course; health club; spa. *In room:* A/C, TV, hair dryer, Internet (free).

Where to Dine

IN TOWN

The stylish **Shaw Cafe and Wine Bar** (92 Queen St.; ✆ **905/468-4772**) serves lunch and light meals, and has a patio. The **Epicurean** (84 Queen St.; ✆ **905/468-3408**) offers hearty soups, quiches, sandwiches, and other fine dishes in a sunny, Provence-inspired dining room. Service is cafeteria style. Half a block off Queen Street, the **Angel Inn** (224 Regent St.; ✆ **905/468-3411**) is a delightfully authentic English pub. For an inexpensive down-home breakfast, go to the **Stagecoach Family Restaurant** (45 Queen St.; ✆ **905/468-3133**). It also serves basic family fare, such as burgers, fries, and meatloaf, but it doesn't accept credit cards. **Niagara Home Bakery** (66 Queen St.; ✆ **905/468-3431**) is the place to stop for sweet treats like chocolate-date squares and pastries, and savories such as individual quiches.

ALONG THE WINE ROAD

Hillebrand Estates Winery Restaurant ★ CANADIAN/CONTINENTAL This dining room is light and airy, and its floor-to-ceiling windows offer sweeping views over the vineyards to the distant Niagara Escarpment and more intimate peeks into wine cellars that bulge with oak barrels. The seasonal menus feature such dishes as poached Arctic char with shellfish ragout, or prosciutto-wrapped pheasant breast atop linguine tossed with mushrooms, roasted eggplant, and shallot. The starters are equally luxurious. In case the food isn't enticing enough (and it should be), the restaurant also hosts special events throughout the year, many featuring jazz musicians.

Hwy. 55, btw. Niagara-on-the-Lake & Virgil. ✆ **905/468-7123.** www.hillebrand.com. Reservations strongly recommended. Main courses C$36–C$40. AE, MC, V. Spring–fall daily noon–11pm (closes earlier in winter).

On the Twenty Restaurant & Wine Bar ★ CANADIAN This warm and friendly restaurant is a favorite among foodies for good service, and a small but well-chosen selection of Ontario wines (with a few international additions)—but mostly for the cuisine that features ingredients from many local producers. There's the added advantage that the food is created with wine pairings in mind; especially rich desserts are made to enjoy with ice wines and late-harvest wines. On the Twenty Restaurant is associated with **Inn on the Twenty** (p. 430), across the street.

At Cave Spring Cellars, 3836 Main St., Jordan. ✆ **905/562-7313.** www.innonthetwenty.com. Reservations recommended. Main courses C$22–C$35. MC, V. Daily 11:30am–3pm & 5–10pm.

The Restaurant at Vineland Estates ★★★ CANADIAN/CONTINENTAL Situated in a renovated 1845 farmhouse with a sprawling patio that offers beautiful views, this restaurant serves some of the most innovative food along the wine trail. Start with a plate of mussels in a ginger broth. Follow with Canadian Angus tenderloin with a risotto of truffles and morel mushrooms; or pan-seared sweetbreads with a celeriac and potato mash, and confit of mushrooms glazed with ice wine. For dessert, try the tasting plate of Canadian farm cheeses, including Abbey St. Benoit blue Ermite; sweet-tooths can indulge in the maple-walnut cheesecake in a biscotti crust.

3620 Moyer Rd., Vineland. ✆ **888/846-3526** or 905/562-7088. www.vineland.com. Reservations strongly recommended. Main courses C$32–C$38. AE, MC, V. Daily noon–2:30pm & 5–9pm.

Along the Niagara Parkway ★★

The Niagara Parkway, on the Canadian side of the falls, is a lovely, scenic drive. Unlike the American side, there is plenty of natural beauty, including vast tracks of parkland. You can drive along the 56km (35-mile) parkway all the way from Niagara-on-the-Lake to Niagara Falls, taking in attractions en route. Here are the major ones, listed in the order in which you'll encounter them:

- **The White Water Walk** (4330 River Rd.; ✆ **905/374-1221**): The boardwalk runs beside the raging white waters of the Great Gorge Rapids. Stroll along and wonder at your leisure how it must feel to challenge this mighty torrent, where the river rushes through the narrow channel at an average speed of 35kmph (22 mph). Admission is C$8.75 adults, C$5.15 children 6 to 12, free for children 5 and under. Open daily from 9am to 5pm (closes at 7 or 8pm from mid-May to Labour Day).
- **The Whirlpool Aero Car** (✆ **905/354-5711**): This red-and-yellow cable-car contraption whisks you on a 1,097m (3,599-ft.) jaunt between two points on the Canadian side of the Falls. High above the Niagara Whirlpool, you'll enjoy excellent views of the surrounding landscape. Admission is C$12 adults, C$6.80 children 6 to 12, free for kids 5 and under. Open daily May to the third Sunday in October. Hours are from 10am to 5pm (closes at 7 or 8pm from mid-May to Labour Day).
- **The Niagara Parks Botanical Gardens & School of Horticulture** (✆ **905/356-8119**): Stop here for a free view of the vast gardens and a look at the 12m-diameter (39-ft.) **Floral Clock,** made up of 25,000 plants. The gorgeous **Butterfly Conservatory** is also in the gardens. In this lush tropical setting, more than 2,000 butterflies (50 international species) float and flutter among such nectar-producing flowers as lantanas and *pentas.* The large, bright-blue, luminescent Morpho butterflies from Central and South America are particularly gorgeous. Interpretive programs and other presentations take place in the auditorium and two smaller theaters. The native butterfly garden outside attracts the more common swallowtails, fritillaries, and painted ladies. Visitors are encouraged to wear brightly colored clothing to attract the butterflies. Admission is C$12 adults, C$6.80 children 6 to 12, free for children 5 and under. Open daily September to June 9am to 5pm, July and August 9am to 7pm.

- **Queenston Heights Park:** This is the site of a famous War of 1812 battle, and you can take a walking tour of the battlefield. Picnic or play tennis in the shaded arbor before moving to the **Laura Secord Homestead** (Partition St., Queenston; ✆ **905/262-4851**). This heroic woman threaded enemy lines to alert British authorities to a surprise attack by American soldiers during the War of 1812. Her home contains a fine collection of Upper Canada furniture from the period, plus artifacts recovered from an archaeological dig. Stop at the candy shop and ice-cream parlor. Tours run every half-hour. Admission is C$4.75 adults, C$3.65 children 6 to 12, free for children age 5 and under. It's open summer daily 11am to 5pm, fall to spring Wednesday to Sunday 11am to 5pm.
- **Fruit Farms & Wineries:** This is home to some of Canada's best stone fruit and other orchards, so you'll find peaches, apples, pears, nectarines, cherries, plums, and strawberries at **Kurtz Orchards** (✆ **905/468-2937**) and elsewhere; you can tour the 32 hectares (79 acres) at Kurtz on a tractor-pulled tram. **Inniskillin Winery** (Line 3, Service Rd. 66; ✆ **905/468-3554** or 905/468-2187), the pioneering winery behind Canada's famous ice wine, is open June to October daily from 10am to 6pm, November through May Monday through Saturday from 10am to 5pm. The self-guided free tour has 20 stops that explain the winemaking process. A free guided tour, offered daily in summer and Saturdays only in winter, begins at 2:30pm.
- **Old Fort Erie** (350 Lakeshore Rd., Fort Erie; ✆ **905/871-0540**): It's a reconstruction of the fort that was seized by the Americans in July 1814, besieged later by the British, and finally blown up as the Americans retreated across the river to Buffalo. Guards in period costume stand sentry duty, fire the cannons, and demonstrate drill and musket practice. Open from the first Saturday in May to mid-September daily from 10am to 5pm, and weekends only mid-September to Canadian Thanksgiving (U.S. Columbus Day). Admission is C$9.25 adults, C$5.15 children 6 to 12, free for children 5 and under.

Seeing Niagara Falls

You simply cannot come this far and not see the falls, which are one of the seven *natural* wonders of the world. When you arrive, step up to the low railing that runs along the road and take in the spectacular view over Horseshoe Falls. Then consider climbing aboard the ***Maid of the Mist*** ★★ (5920 River Rd.; ✆ **905/358-5781;** www.maidofthemist.com). The sturdy boat takes you right in to the basin—through the turbulent waters around the American Falls; past the Rock of Ages; and to the foot of the Horseshoe Falls, where 159 million L (42 million gal.) of water tumble over the 54m-high (177-ft.) cataract each minute. You'll get wet, and your glasses will mist—but that just adds to the thrill. Boats leave from the dock on the parkway just down from the Rainbow Bridge. Trips operate daily from mid-May to mid-October. Fares are C$15 adults, C$8.90 children 6 to 12, free for children 5 and under.

Go down under the falls using the elevator at the **Table Rock Centre,** which drops you 46m (151 ft.) through solid rock to the tunnels and viewing portals of the **Journey Behind the Falls** (✆ **905/354-1551**). You'll receive—and appreciate—a rain poncho. Admission is C$13 adults, C$7.50 children 6 to 12, free for children 5 and under. Another attraction at the Table Rock Centre (which has just completed a C$32-million renovation) is **Niagara's Fury.** Visitors "experience" the creation of the falls in a chamber that swirls visual images over a 360-degree screen. It's a sense-surround ride, complete with shaking ground underfoot, an enveloping blizzard, and a temperature drop in the room from 75° to 40°F degrees (24°–4°C) in 3 seconds.

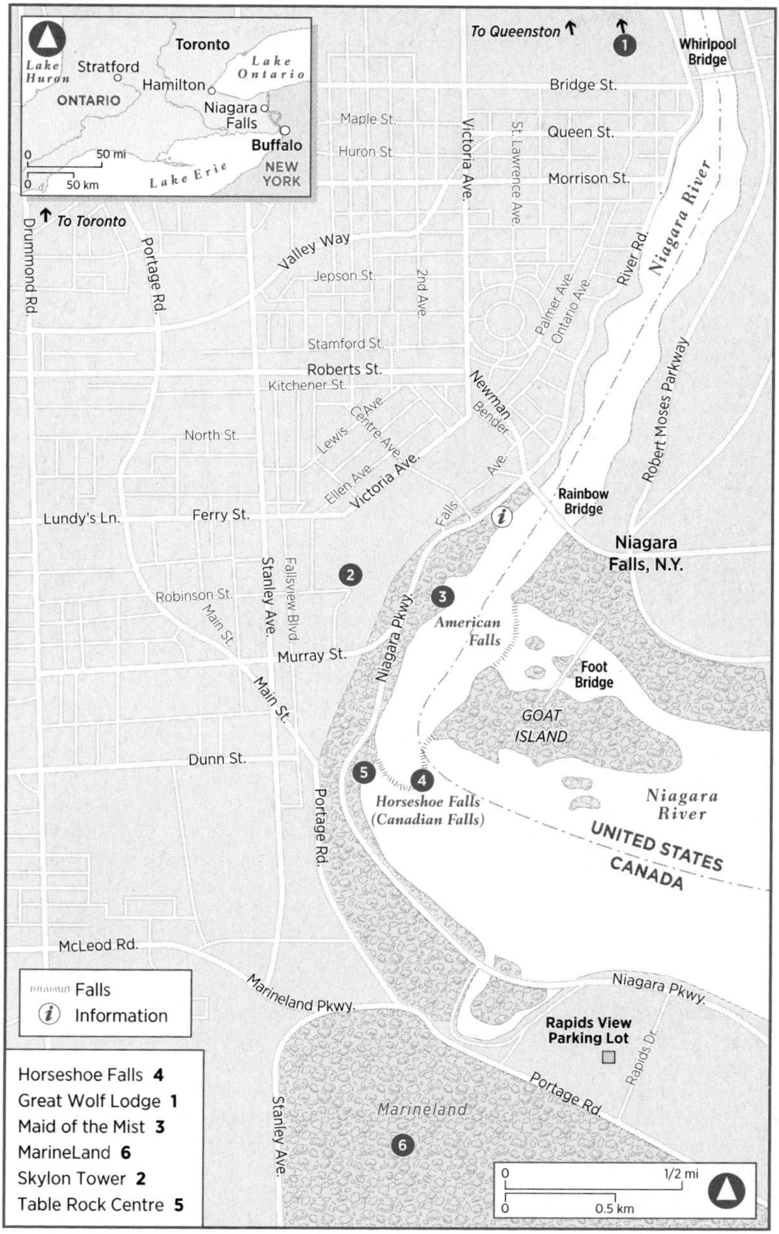

Toronto
Lake Huron
Stratford
Hamilton
ONTARIO
Lake Ontario
Niagara Falls
Buffalo
0 50 mi
0 50 km
Lake Erie
NEW YORK

To Queenston
To Toronto
Whirlpool Bridge
Bridge St.
Maple St.
Queen St.
Huron St.
Morrison St.
Victoria Ave.
St. Lawrence Ave.
Niagara River
River Rd.
Valley Way
Drummond Rd.
Portage Rd.
Jepson St.
2nd Ave.
Palmer Ave.
Ontario Ave.
Stamford St.
Roberts St.
Kitchener St.
Robert Moses Parkway
Newman
Bender
Lewis Ave.
Centre Ave.
North St.
Ellen Ave.
Victoria Ave.
Ave.
Rainbow Bridge
Lundy's Ln.
Ferry St.
Falls
Niagara Falls, N.Y.
Stanley Ave.
Fallsview Blvd.
Robinson St.
Main St.
Niagara Pkwy.
American Falls
Murray St.
Foot Bridge
Main St.
GOAT ISLAND
Dunn St.
Horseshoe Falls (Canadian Falls)
Portage Rd.
Niagara River
UNITED STATES
CANADA
McLeod Rd.
Marineland Pkwy.
Niagara Pkwy.
Rapids View Parking Lot
Rapids Dr.
Portage Rd.
Stanley Ave.
Marineland
0 1/2 mi
0 0.5 km

Falls
Information

Horseshoe Falls 4
Great Wolf Lodge 1
Maid of the Mist 3
MarineLand 6
Skylon Tower 2
Table Rock Centre 5

It's an intense experience and not appropriate for young children. Fares are C$15 adults, C$9 children 6 to 12, free for children 5 and under. (***Warning:*** The operators advise that Niagara's Fury may not be appropriate for children 6 and under, as they might find it too scary. Also, adults with a history of heart disease or back/neck injuries may want to pass on this attraction.) Open daily 9am to 9pm.

If you can't get enough of the falls, ride the external glass-fronted elevators 159m (522 ft.) to the top of the **Skylon Tower Observation Deck** (5200 Robinson St.; ✆ **905/356-2651;** www.skylon.com). The observation deck is open from June to Labour Day daily from 8am to midnight; hours vary the rest of the year, so call ahead. Adults pay C$13, children 12 and under C$7.55. It's pricey for an elevator ride.

The falls are equally dramatic in winter, when ice formations add a certain beauty to it all and the crowds of high summer are wonderfully absent.

WHERE TO STAY & DINE NEAR THE FALLS

My honest recommendation is for visitors to stay in scenic and charming Niagara-on-the-Lake and take in the carnival-like Niagara Falls during the day. But I know some people will enjoy the bright lights—and the casino scene—of Niagara Falls after dark. If you do, one high-end hotel is the **Niagara Fallsview Casino Resort** (6380 Fallsview Blvd.; ✆ **888/325-5788;** www.fallsviewcasinoresort.com), which opened in 2004. It has its own 18,580-sq.-m (199,993-sq.-ft.) casino, a performing-arts theater, a spa, and 10 dining spots. Another good hotel bet is the **Sheraton on the Falls** (5875 Falls Ave.; ✆ **888/234-8410** or 905/374-4445), which offers rooms with a truly gorgeous view of the falls; many have balconies. There's also the **Skyline Inn** (5685 Falls Ave.; ✆ **800/263-7135** or 905/374-4444), which is right by Casino Niagara.

Niagara Falls likes to boast about its newly invigorated dining scene, but it's a challenge to find good food that doesn't cost a small fortune. The **Pinnacle Restaurant** (6732 Fallsview Blvd.; ✆ **905/356-1501**) offers a continental menu and a remarkable view from the top of the Konica Minolta Tower. **The Keg** (5950 Victoria Ave.;

A family ADVENTURE

Niagara Falls has plenty of family attractions. A popular choice is **MarineLand ★** (7657 Portage Rd.; ✆ **905/356-9565;** www.marinelandcanada.com). Its multiple aquariums have a walrus mascot, dolphins, sea lions, and freshwater fish. Friendship Cove, a 17-million-L (4.5-million-gal.) breeding and observation tank, lets the little ones see killer whales up close.

MarineLand also has rides, including a Tivoli wheel (a fancy Ferris wheel), Dragon Boat rides, and Dragon Mountain, a roller coaster that loops, double-loops, and spirals through 305m (1,001 ft.) of tunnels. Admission is C$40 adults and children 10 and over, C$33 children 5 to 9, free for children 4 and under. It's open daily mid-May to June and September to mid-October 10am to 5pm, July and August 9am to 6pm; it's closed mid-October through mid-May.

A new attraction at the falls is Canada's first **Great Wolf Lodge** (3950 Victoria Ave.; ✆ **905/354-4888** or 800/605-9653; www.greatwolf.com). Part of an American chain of family resorts known for the quality of services, rooms, and activities, Great Wolf is probably best known for its massive indoor water park. But there's more, including a four-story interactive tree-house water fort.

NIAGARA PARKWAY COMMISSION restaurants

The Niagara Parkway Commission has commandeered the most spectacular scenic spots for its restaurants. These used to be reasonably priced places serving lunch and dinner, but recent renovations have focused on creating more upscale settings, with prices to match. **Table Rock Centre,** right across from the falls, has had a complete renovation, and its new restaurant, **Elements on the Falls** (✆ **905/354-3631**) is expensive but delicious. Also close to the falls is **Edgewaters Tap & Grill** (✆ **905/356-2217**), a more casual restaurant that's appropriate for the whole family (there's a special menu for kids). **Whirlpool Restaurant** (✆ **905/356-7221**), at the Whirlpool Golf Course near Queenston, is open to the public while the course is open (May–Dec). A favorite is the **Queenston Heights Restaurant** (14184 Niagara Pkwy.; ✆ **905/262-4274**). Set in the park among firs, cypresses, silver birches, and maples, the restaurant affords a magnificent view of the lower Niagara River and the lush, abundant land through which it flows. The restaurant also serves up a fine duck confit and has a great wine list.

✆ **905/353-4022**) is a reliable steakhouse chain. Over at Casino Niagara, **Lucky's** (5705 Falls Ave.; ✆ **888/946-3255**) serves up hearty portions of prime rib, as well as burgers and pizza. The **Rainforest Café** (5875 Falls Ave.; ✆ **905/374-2233**) is a family favorite with its animatronic gorillas and serpents, and its tried-and-true menu of pizzas, burgers, and sandwiches. The **Skylon Tower** (✆ **905/356-2651**) revolving restaurant is the top choice in town at 236m (774 ft.) above the ground and overlooking the falls, with menus featuring Caesar salads, filet mignon, lobster tails, and more fancy classics.

IN NEARBY ST. CATHARINES

Café Garibaldi ★ ITALIAN This relaxed spot is a favorite among locals. It serves Italian classics such as *zuppa di pesce* and veal scaloppine; homemade lasagne is the most requested dish. The wine list features the local vintners' goods and some fine bottles from Italy.

375 St. Paul St., St. Catharines. ✆ **905/988-9033.** Reservations recommended for dinner. Main courses C$18–C$28. AE, DC, MC, V. Tues–Sat 11:30am–2:30pm & 5:30–10pm. From QEW, exit at Ontario St., follow DOWNTOWN sign to St. Paul St. & turn left.

Wellington Court ★★ CONTINENTAL In an Edwardian town house with a flower trellis, the three candlelit dining rooms here are adorned with mirrors, lithographs, and photographs. The menu features daily specials along with such items as beef tenderloin in shallot-and-red-wine reduction; roast capon with a bacon, leek, and goat-cheese tart; and grilled sea bass with cranberry vinaigrette. Not surprisingly, given the location, the wine list is filled with excellent Niagara bottles.

11 Wellington St., St. Catharines. ✆ **905/682-5518.** www.wellington-court.com. Reservations recommended. Main courses C$22–C$30. MC, V. Tues–Sat 11:30am–2:30pm & 5–9:30pm. From QEW, exit at Lake St., turn left, follow to Wellington Ave., turn left, follow for 1 block, turn right.

HAMILTON

75km (47 miles) SW of Toronto

Hamilton may be Ontario's most-overlooked city, and it's a shame. Situated on a landlocked harbor spanned by the Burlington Skyway's dramatic sweep, Hamilton has long been nicknamed "Steeltown" for its industrial roots. Since the early 1990s, however, Hamilton has been making a name for itself with its ever-expanding list of attractions and lately has become an arts community of note. It takes roughly an hour to drive here from Toronto, and a day trip here is time well spent for the whole family.

Essentials

GETTING THERE Hamilton is easy to reach by car. From Toronto, take the Queen Elizabeth Way (signs read QEW) to Hamilton. The drive will take about an hour. **GO (Government of Ontario) Transit** has a commuter train that connects Toronto and Hamilton. Call ✆ **800/438-6646** or 416/869-3200 for information, or check out www.gotransit.com. The **John C. Munro Hamilton International Airport** (✆ **905/679-8359;** www.hamiltonairport.com) has long been popular with cargo carriers and is now a hub for WestJet. In 2007, **flyglobespan** airlines began service to Hamilton, connecting the city to 13 U.K. destinations, including London (via Gatwick), Birmingham, Liverpool, Manchester, Belfast, Edinburgh, and Glasgow; visit **www.flyglobespan.ca** for details.

VISITOR INFORMATION The **Tourism Hamilton Visitor Information Centre** is at 2 King St. W., Unit 234 (✆ **800/263-8590** or 905/546-2666; www.tourismhamilton.com). It has a wealth of information about what to see and do, as well as where to dine and sleep. Its year-round hours run Monday to Friday 9am to 5pm.

Exploring Hamilton

Hamilton's downtown core is best explored on foot, but you will need a car to visit attractions in the outlying areas (such as the African Lion Safari).

African Lion Safari ★★ ☺ Just a half-hour drive northwest of Hamilton, you'll find a mirror image of a traditional zoo: At the African Lion Safari, visitors remain caged in their cars or in a tour bus while the animals roam wild and free. The 300-hectare (741-acre) wildlife park contains rhinos, cheetahs, lions, tigers, giraffes, zebras, vultures, and many other species. In addition to the safari, the cost of admission covers other attractions, like the cruise aboard the *African Queen,* during which a tour guide will take you around the lake and point out local inhabitants like spider monkeys, crested macaques, and ring-tailed lemurs. A train will take you through a forest populated by snapping turtles and other captured wildlife.

The park has several baby Asian elephants, and the elephant-bathing event, which occurs daily, never fails to fascinate the kids. The Pets' Corner is filled with frisky otters and pot-bellied pigs. There are several play areas for children, including the Misumu Bay water park (bring bathing suits!).

Safari Rd., Cambridge. ✆ **800/461-WILD** (800/461-9453) or 519/623-2620. www.lionsafari.com. C$27 adults, C$24 seniors, C$22 children 3–12, free for children 2 & under; rates are discounted in spring & fall. Late June to Labour Day daily 10am–5:30pm; mid-Apr to late June & early Sept to mid-Oct daily 9am–4pm. Closed mid-Oct to mid-Apr.

Art Gallery of Hamilton ★ This art gallery first opened in 1914, but it was only when it reopened in 2005 that it became one of Hamilton's greatest attractions. The

AGH has gained a reputation as a fine place to visit, with one of the most comprehensive collections of Canadian art in the country and some notable holdings of European and American works—all thanks to one of the largest bequests in Canadian history, the Joey and Toby Tannenbaum Collection that includes 211 works of 19th-century art from Europe. The renovation also helped shape areas such as the open-air Irving Zucker Sculpture Garden, a green, serene space that can also be viewed from the Sculpture Atrium inside the gallery.

123 King St. W. ✆ **905/527-6610.** www.artgalleryofhamilton.com. C$12 adults, C$10 students & seniors, C$5 children 6–17, free for children 5 & under. Tues & Wed noon–7pm; Thurs & Fri noon–9pm; Sat & Sun noon–5pm. Closed Mon except on most civic holidays, Jan 1, Dec 25 & 26.

Canadian Warplane Heritage Museum If you're an aircraft buff, you'll love this interactive museum that charts the course of Canadian aviation from the beginning of World War II to the present. Visitors can climb into the cockpits of World War II trainer crafts or a CF-100 jet fighter. The most popular attractions are the flight simulators, which allow aspiring pilots to test their skills. There are also short documentary films, photographs, and other memorabilia. The aircraft on display include rarities like the Avro Lancaster bomber and the deHavilland Vampire fighter jet.

9280 Airport Rd. (at the John C. Munro Hamilton International Airport), Mount Hope. ✆ **877/347-3359** or 905/670-3347. www.warplane.com. C$10 adults, C$9 seniors & children 13–17, C$6 children 6–12, free for children 5 & under. Daily 9am–5pm. Closed Jan 1 & Dec 25.

Dundurn National Historic Site ★★ Here, you'll find two key attractions: **Dundurn Castle** and the **Hamilton Military Museum.** Dundurn, in fact a very grand manor house and not a castle, does afford a glimpse into daily life for the opulent in southern Ontario in the mid–19th century. Costumed interpreters "living" in 1855 guide you through the house and tell vivid stories of what life was like there—for both the aristocrats and the servants.

Sir Allan Napier MacNab, premier of the United Canadas in the mid-1850s and a founder of the Great Western Railway, built Dundurn between 1832 and 1835; Queen Victoria knighted him for the part he played in the Rebellion of 1837. The 35-plus-room mansion has been restored and furnished in the style of 1855. The gray stucco exterior, with its classical Greek portico, is impressive enough, but inside, from the formal dining rooms to Lady MacNab's boudoir, the furnishings are rich. The museum contains a fascinating collection of Victoriana. In December, the castle is decorated splendidly for a Victorian Christmas.

The Hamilton Military Museum is on the grounds of Dundurn Castle. For those who are interested, it traces Canadian military history from the War of 1812 through World War I. Admission is included when you buy a ticket for Dundurn Castle.

Dundurn Park, York Blvd. ✆ **905/546-2872.** C$11 adults, C$9 seniors & students w/ID, C$5.50 children 6–14, free for children 5 & under. Victoria Day to Labour Day daily 10am–4pm; the rest of the year Tues–Sun noon–4pm. Closed Jan 1, Dec 25 & 26.

Hamilton Museum of Steam and Technology ☺ This city takes pride in its industrial roots, and this museum is a case in point. It explains—and celebrates—the technology that made urban life possible in the Victorian age. Don't miss the two 14m-tall (46-ft.), 63,503kg (70-ton) steam engines that first pumped clean water to Hamilton, or the stone-and-cast-iron Romanesque building that houses them, which is a nice example of 19th-century public-works architecture. The waterworks were built to protect Hamilton from the deadly cholera outbreaks and fires that destroyed so many cities in that era. The museum also hosts a series of exhibits and special events, which let you do things like ride on a mini-version of a steam-powered train.

900 Woodward Ave (at the QEW). ✆ **905/546-4797.** C$6.50 adults, C$5.50 seniors & children 13–17, C$4.50 children 6–12, free for children 5 & under. June to Labour Day Tues–Sun 11am–4pm; the rest of the year Tues–Sun noon–4pm. Closed Jan 1, Dec 25 & 26.

Royal Botanical Gardens ★ Situated just north of the city, the Royal Botanical Gardens spread over 1,214 glorious hectares (3,000 acres) with a variety of gardens and landscapes, both tamed and wild, to attract anyone with an interest in botany or simply beautiful gardens. The range of activities includes biodiversity programs and casual tours that take visitors through the multiple marshes, sanctuaries, and parks.

The gardens host many festivals during the year, including the Mediterranean Food & Wine Festival in February, the popular Ontario Garden Show in early April, the Tulip Festival in May, the Rose Society Show in June, and the Japanese Flower Society Show in September.

Should you work up an appetite while strolling the grounds, the on-site dining options include the Gardens Café, which is open year-round, and the Rock Garden Tea House or the Turner Pavilion (both open throughout the summer).

680 Plains Rd. W., Burlington. ✆ **905/527-1158.** www.rbg.ca. C$8 adults, C$6 seniors & children 13–18, C$3 children 5–12, free for children 4 & under. Daily 9:30am–dusk. Closed Jan 1 & Dec 25.

Where to Stay

Because Hamilton is so close to Toronto, it's easy to make a day trip here and back, rather than pulling up stakes and spending the night here. However, if you do want to stay in the area, several well-known chains have hotels here, including **Sheraton** (✆ **800/514-7101** or 905/529-5515), **Ramada** (✆ **800/2RAMADA** or 905/528-3451), and **Comfort Inn** (✆ **877/424-6423** or 905/560-4500).

Where to Dine

The suggested restaurants in St. Catharines and Welland, such as **Café Garibaldi** and **Wellington Court** (p. 435 and 435), are just a short drive away from Hamilton. However, Hamilton has a few restaurants worth checking out, too.

Ancaster Old Mill Located in the neighboring town of Ancaster, which is no more than a 10-minute drive, this popular and very pretty destination offers delicious fare a good cut above the rest in the area. To boot, it's a favorite for those seeking local and seasonal cuisine. Chefs Jeff Crump and Bettina Schormann promise a delightful culinary experience that is worth the drive if you love good food.

548 Old Dundas Rd., Ancaster. ✆ **905/648-1828.** www.ancastermill.com. Reservations recommended. Main courses C$18–C$40. AE, MC, V. Tues–Sat 11:30am–10pm; Sun 9:30am–2:30pm & 5–9pm.

La Cantina ★ ITALIAN This is really two restaurants in one. A dining room serves up plates of veal scaloppini in a dry Marsala sauce and seared ostrich medallions cooked with pinot noir. The casual pizzeria features more than 20 varieties of pizza, including the traditional Quattro Stagione (four seasons) with prosciutto, artichokes, olives, and mozzarella. This is a very popular spot, so try to make a reservation or arrive early, especially at lunch. If you're very lucky, you might just secure a seat in the restaurant's garden patio.

60 Walnut St. S. ✆ **905/521-8989.** Reservations recommended. Main courses C$12–C$26. AE, MC, V. Tues–Thurs 11:30am–10pm; Fri 11:30am–11pm; Sat 5–11pm.

LONDON ★

195km (121 miles) SW of Toronto

If you're driving into Canada from the U.S. Midwest, consider stopping in this pretty university town that sits on the Thames River—particularly if you have kids in tow.

Essentials

GETTING THERE If you're driving, London is about 192km (119 miles) from Detroit via Highway 401; 110km (68 miles) from Kitchener via Highway 401; 195km (121 miles) from Niagara Falls via QEW, and highways 403 and 401; and 65km (40 miles) from Stratford via highways 7 and 4. Direct flights from Toronto, Ottawa, and Detroit arrive at **London International Airport** (**✆ 519/452-4015;** www.londonairport.on.ca). **VIA Rail** (**✆ 888/VIA-RAIL** [888/842-7245] or 416/366-8411; www.viarail.ca) operates a Toronto-Brantford-London-Windsor route and also, in conjunction with **Amtrak** (**✆ 800/USA-RAIL** [800/872-7245]; www.amtrak.com), a Toronto-Kitchener-Stratford-London-Sarnia-Chicago route. Both offer several trains a day. The VIA Rail station in London is at 197 York St. (**✆ 519/434-2149**). **Greyhound** (**✆ 800/231-2222;** www.greyhound.ca) provides service from Toronto, Detroit, Buffalo, and other Canadian and American destinations.

VISITOR INFORMATION Contact **Tourism London** (**✆ 800/265-2602** or 519/661-5000; www.londontourism.ca). There are two information centers in London, one at 696 Wellington Rd. S. and the other one downtown at 267 Dundas St. Both are open 8:30am to 4:30pm on weekdays and from 10am to 5pm on Saturdays, but only the downtown location is open Sunday (10am–5pm).

SPECIAL EVENTS & FESTIVALS The 10-day **Western Fair** (**✆ 800/619-4629** or 519/438-7203; www.westernfair.com), held in September, is a major draw for the whole family.

Exploring London

London Regional Children's Museum ★ ☺ This interactive museum for kids occupies several floors of an old school building. In every room, children can explore, experiment, and generally have fun—like on "The Street Where You Live," where they can dress up in firefighters' uniforms, slip on a pair of workmen's overalls, or assume the role of a dentist or a doctor. Some rooms contrast daily life from long ago with today's world.

21 Wharncliffe Rd. S. **✆ 519/434-5726.** www.londonchildrensmuseum.ca. C$5 adults, C$2 children 1–2; free for children under 1. Sept–May Tues–Sun 10am–5pm; June–Aug & holidays daily 10am–5pm. Closed Jan 1, Dec 25 & 26.

Museum of Ontario Archaeology ★ Affiliated with the University of Western Ontario, the museum contains artifacts from various periods of Native Canadian history—projectiles, pottery shards, effigies, turtle rattles, and more. The most evocative exhibit is the on-site reconstruction of a 500-year-old Attawandaron village. Behind the elm palisades, longhouses built according to original specifications and techniques have been erected on the 2 hectares (5 acres) where archaeological excavations are taking place.

1600 Attawandaron Rd. (off Wonderland Rd. N., just south of Hwy. 22). **✆ 519/473-1360.** www.uwo.ca/museum. C$4 adults, C$3.25 seniors & students, C$2 children 5–12, free for children 4 & under; C$10 families. May to Labour Day daily 10am–4:30pm; day after Labour Day to Dec Tues–Sun 10am–4:30pm; Jan–Apr Sat & Sun 1–4pm.

Storybook Gardens ★ ☺ The Storybook Gardens started out as a park with a storybook theme but has become a more interesting destination, with the Slippery's Great Escape water park, Pirate's Island (complete with towers, slides, and lookout points), and Storybook Valley with its seals and otters. Special daily events include the seal feeding at 3:30pm and live entertainment. There's also a conservation area that is currently being developed.

Off Commissioners Rd. W. ✆ **519/661-5770.** www.storybook.london.ca. C$7.50 adults, C$6.50 seniors, C$5 children 2–17, free for children 2 & under. May to Labour Day daily 10am–8pm; day after Labour Day to early Oct Mon–Fri noon–6pm, Sat & Sun 11am–6pm; early Oct to Apr hours vary greatly, so call ahead.

Where to Stay

London is less than a half-hour's drive away from Stratford, so it's easy to stay there for the theater festival and detour into London for a day. But you might want to make an exception for the property below.

Delta London Armouries Hotel Built into the facade of a castle-like armory, this hotel is an impressive example of architectural conservation and conversion. The armory's 3.5m-thick (11-ft.) walls, built in 1905, form the building's main floor and base, and above the crenellated turrets and ramparts soars a modern glass tower. Inside, the well-equipped rooms are furnished with Federal reproductions. A recent renovation has freshened up both the guest rooms and the fitness facilities.

325 Dundas St., London, ON N6B 1T9. ✆ **877/814-7706** or 519/679-6111. www.deltahotels.com. 245 units. From C$140 double. Additional adult C$15. Children 17 & under stay free in parent's room. AE, DC, DISC, MC, V. Valet parking C$12; self-parking C$10. **Amenities:** Restaurant; lounge; children's activity center; exercise room; pool; squash court. *In room:* A/C, TV, minibar.

Where to Dine

Mostly, there's an assortment of child-friendly restaurants with thoughtful waitstaffs. But if you're looking for something gourmet, head to Stratford.

Mongolian Grill ☺ ASIAN This is cooking as performance art. Diners assemble their own meal-in-a-bowl with raw ingredients ranging from chicken to shrimp, broccoli to bok choy, and ginger to coriander. The bowl is presented to the cooks, who labor at a huge wheel-shaped grill that sizzles and steams. The young cooks know how to put on a good show, but don't expect a dish that is more than the sum of its parts. There is a separate menu for children.

645 Richmond St. **519/645-6400.** Main courses $8–$12. AE, DC, MC, V. Daily noon–2:30pm & 5–10:30pm.

GODERICH & BAYFIELD

220km (137 miles) W of Toronto

Goderich bills itself as Canada's prettiest town, which is open to question—although it is postcard perfect. The town's most striking feature is the central octagonal space with the Huron County Courthouse at its hub. Another highlight is the **Historic Huron Gaol,** with walls 5.5m (18 ft.) high and .5m (1¾ ft.) thick. Goderich has won numerous prizes for its flower gardens, a local point of pride. **Goderich Tourism** (✆ **800/280-7637** or 519/524-6600; www.goderich.ca) operates a visitor center at 91 Hamilton St., which is open daily. For information about the town's lovely architecture—and efforts to preserve it—contact **Heritage Goderich** (✆ **519/524-8344;** www.goderich.ca/en/communitylife/heritage.asp).

Bayfield is no slouch in the beauty stakes, either. This lovely, well-preserved 19th-century town is about 20km (12 miles) from Goderich and 65km (40 miles) from Stratford. Once a major grain-shipping port, it became a quiet backwater when the railroad passed it by. Today, the main square, High Street, and Elgin Place are part of a Heritage Conservation District. Bayfield's Chamber of Commerce (✆ **866/565-2499** or 519/565-2499; www.villageofbayfield.com) handles tourism inquiries.

Where to Stay & Dine

Benmiller Inn & Spa ★★ The heart of the inn is the original wool mill, which dates from 1877, and now contains the dining room, bar, reception, and 12 guest rooms. When it became an inn in 1974, many mechanical parts were refashioned into decorative objects—mirrors made from pulley wheels, lamps from gears. Rooms feature barn-board siding, desks, floor lamps, heated ceramic tile in the bathrooms, and handmade quilts. The 18 rooms in Gledhill House, the original mill-owner's home, are generously proportioned, while the four suites have fireplaces and Jacuzzis. There are more rooms in the River Mill, which is attached to the building containing the swimming pool, whirlpool, and running track. The brick patio overlooking the gardens is a pleasant place to sit and look at the totem pole, brought from British Columbia. Spa day packages start at C$165. The elegant yet comfy dining room serves up dishes such as teriyaki-glazed Atlantic salmon and rack of New Zealand lamb. It's open daily for lunch and dinner.

R.R. 4, Goderich, ON N7A 3Y1. ✆ **800/265-1711** or 519/524-2191. www.benmiller.on.ca. 57 units. From C$169 double. Rates include breakfast. Some packages include dinner. AE, DC, MC, V. **Amenities:** Restaurant; indoor pool; sauna; spa. *In room:* A/C, TV.

The Little Inn at Bayfield ★ The inn, originally built in 1832, has been completely modernized while still retaining its traditional charm. The older rooms in the main building are small and have only showers, but they are comfortably furnished with oak or sleigh beds. Rooms in the newer section are larger and feature platform beds and modern furnishings. The suites are located across the street in the old carriage house; they have platform beds and pine hutches, and feature whirlpool bathrooms, propane-gas fireplaces, and verandas. Also in the carriage house is the new Sapphire Spa, which offers everything from sports massage to a chocolate body wrap.

The Little Inn's popular restaurant is open for lunch and dinner 7 days a week. The innovative menu includes the likes of smoked pork tenderloin in a walnut-horseradish-ale cream sauce.

Main St., Bayfield, ON N0M 1G0. ✆ **800/565-1832** or 519/565-2611. www.littleinn.com. 28 units. From C$195 double. Special packages available. AE, DC, MC, V. **Amenities:** Restaurant; babysitting; concierge; room service; spa. *In room:* A/C, TV, hair dryer.

STRATFORD & THE STRATFORD FESTIVAL ★★

145km (90 miles) SW of Toronto

For those who care: This is the hometown of Justin Bieber. But its real claim to fame is the great Stratford Festival. Plus, it's a charming, friendly, and very pretty place to amble before and after taking in a show. The grand Stratford Festival has humble roots. The idea of a theater was launched in 1953, when director Tyrone Guthrie lured the great Sir Alec Guinness to the stage. Whether Sir Alec knew the "stage" was set up in a makeshift tent is another question, but his acclaimed performance gave the festival the push—and press—it needed to become an annual tradition. Since then, the Stratford Festival has grown to become one of the most famous in North America, and its four theaters have put this scenic town on the cultural map. It's also a lovely place to eat, cycle, walk, and relax. Even the local library is lovely.

Essentials

VISITOR INFORMATION For first-rate visitor information, go to the **Visitors' Information Centre** by the river, on York Street at Erie. From May to early November, it's open Sunday through Wednesday 9am to 5pm and Thursday through Saturday 9am to 8pm. At other times, contact **Tourism Stratford** (✆ **800/561-SWAN** [800/561-7926] or 519/271-5140; www.welcometostratford.com).

GETTING THERE Driving from Toronto, take Highway 401 west to Interchange 278 at Kitchener. Follow Highway 8 west onto Highway 7/8 to Stratford. (Hwy. 7/8 turns into Ontario St., Stratford's main drag, once you enter city limits.)

For me, nothing beats the train, and Stratford is a small and very walkable town, so unless you're planning to tour the surrounding area, call **VIA Rail** (✆ **800/VIA-RAIL** [800/842-7245] or 416/366-8411; www.viarail.ca). Canada's national rail company operates several trains daily along the Toronto-Kitchener-Stratford route. The toll-free number works within North America; if you're traveling from overseas, you can book your rail travel in advance through one of VIA's general sales agents (there's a long list of local agents on www.viarail.ca).

The Stratford Festival ★★★

On July 13, 1953, *Richard III,* starring Sir Alec Guinness, was staged in a huge tent. From that modest start, Stratford's artistic directors have built on the radical, but faithfully classic, base established by Tyrone Guthrie to create a repertory theater with a glowing international reputation.

Stratford has four theaters. The **Festival Theatre** (55 Queen St.) has a dynamic thrust stage (a modern re-creation of an Elizabethan stage). The **Avon Theatre** (99 Downie St.) has a classic proscenium. The **Tom Patterson Theatre** (111 Lakeside Dr.) is an intimate 500-seat theater. The **Studio Theatre** (34 George St. E.) is a 278-seat space used for new and experimental works.

World-famous for its Shakespearean productions, the festival also offers classic and modern theatrical masterpieces. Recent productions have included *West Side Story, Cyrano de Bergerac,* and *Three Sisters;* from the Bard, there's an encyclopedia of productions, including *Macbeth* and *A Midsummer Night's Dream.* The bill always presents an impressive line-up that is designed to suit tastes from the contemporary to the historic, the comedic to the tragic.

The season usually begins in early May and continues through mid-November, with performances Tuesday through Sunday. Ticket prices range from C$25 to C$120, with special deals for students and seniors. For tickets, call ✆ **800/567-1600** or 519/273-1600, or visit **www.stratfordfestival.ca.** Tickets are also available in the United States and Canada at Ticketmaster outlets. The box office opens for the new season in mid-January.

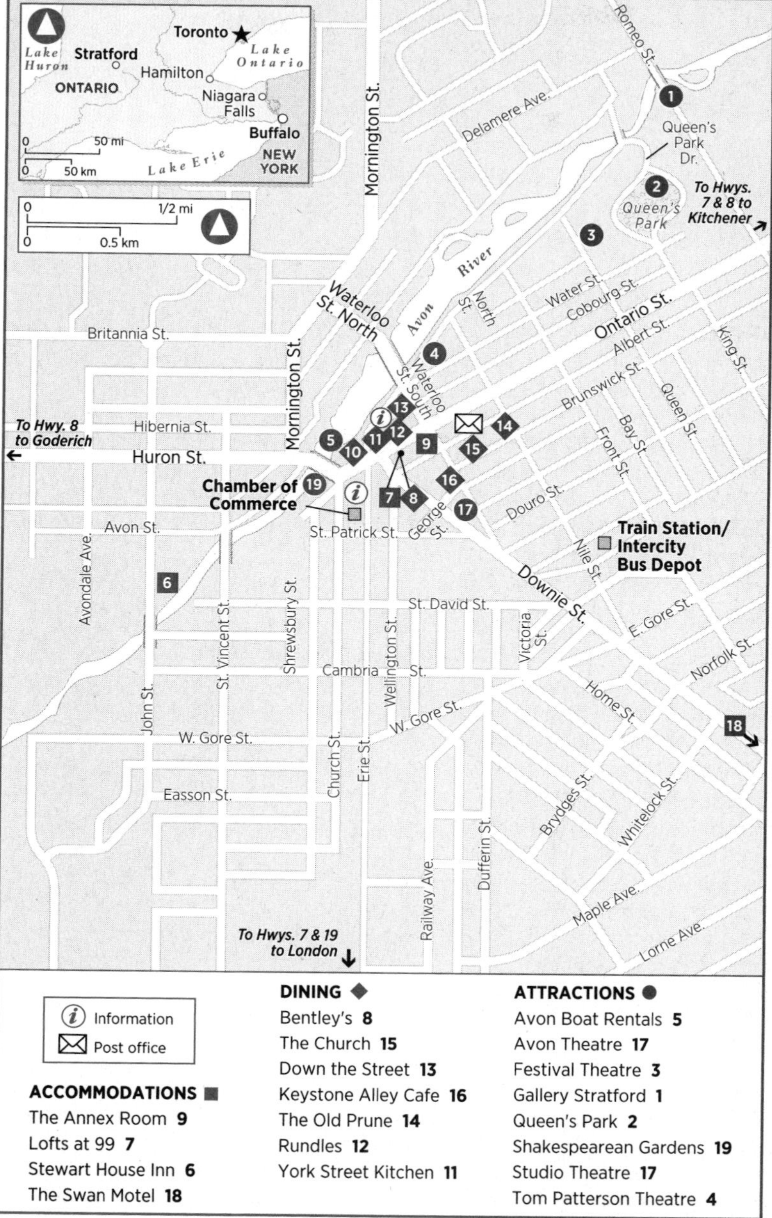
Toronto
Lake Ontario
Lake Huron
Stratford
Hamilton
ONTARIO
Niagara Falls
Buffalo
NEW YORK
Lake Erie
0 50 mi
0 50 km
0 1/2 mi
0 0.5 km
Romeo St.
Delamere Ave.
Queen's Park Dr.
Queen's Park
To Hwys. 7 & 8 to Kitchener
Mornington St.
Avon River
Waterloo St. North
North St.
Water St.
Cobourg St.
Ontario St.
Albert St.
King St.
Britannia St.
Waterloo St. South
Brunswick St.
Queen St.
To Hwy. 8 to Goderich
Hibernia St.
Huron St.
Bay St.
Front St.
Chamber of Commerce
Douro St.
George St.
St. Patrick St.
Avon St.
Train Station/ Intercity Bus Depot
Nile St.
Downie St.
Avondale Ave.
Shrewsbury St.
St. David St.
St. Vincent St.
Wellington St.
Victoria St.
E. Gore St.
Cambria St.
Norfolk St.
Home St.
John St.
W. Gore St.
Church St.
Erie St.
Easson St.
Brydges St.
Whitelock St.
Railway Ave.
Dufferin St.
Maple Ave.
To Hwys. 7 & 19 to London
Lorne Ave.
Information
Post office
ACCOMMODATIONS
The Annex Room 9
Lofts at 99 7
Stewart House Inn 6
The Swan Motel 18
DINING
Bentley's 8
The Church 15
Down the Street 13
Keystone Alley Cafe 16
The Old Prune 14
Rundles 12
York Street Kitchen 11
ATTRACTIONS
Avon Boat Rentals 5
Avon Theatre 17
Festival Theatre 3
Gallery Stratford 1
Queen's Park 2
Shakespearean Gardens 19
Studio Theatre 17
Tom Patterson Theatre 4

Behind the Festival Curtain ★

The Stratford Festival offers several behind-the-scenes tours that will thrill theater buffs. There are **backstage tours of the Festival Theatre,** which take about an hour, and tours of the **costume and props warehouse** at 350 Douro St., which run roughly 45 minutes. Tours cost C$8 adults, C$6 seniors and students, and should be scheduled in advance by calling the box office at ✆ **800/567-1600** or 519/273-1600.

Some performances have preshow lectures or post-performance discussions. These are free of charge but need to be reserved in advance via the box office. There are also free "Meet the Festival" events with members of the acting company and a series of special lectures about the major plays of the season. For details, dates, and times, check out **www.stratfordfestival.ca.**

Exploring the Town

Stratford was founded in 1832, and much of its historic heart has been preserved. Wandering through its pristine residential streets—lined with historic homes decorated with turrets, wraparound verandas, and stained-glass windows—is a little like stepping back in time. The Visitors' Information Centre by the Avon River has maps for self-guided tours. You can also download several free audio-tour podcasts about Stratford's gardens, landmarks, and downtown from **www.welcometostratford.com.**

Paddleboat, kayak, and canoe rentals are available at the **Boathouse,** behind the information center. In summer, it's open daily from 9am until dusk. Contact **Avon Boat Rentals** (40 York St.; ✆ **519/271-7739**). There's also a boat, the ***Juliet III,*** that offers scenic half-hour tours.

The **Shakespearean Gardens**—a pretty, formal English garden—is a great place to relax and contemplate the flowerbeds and tranquil river lagoon, and muse on a bust of Shakespeare by Toronto sculptor Cleeve Horne. For a picnic-friendly patch of green, visit **Queen's Park,** a stone's throw from the Festival Theatre.

And speaking of picnics, Stratford is in the heart of an agricultural belt, and the abundant food options reflect the city's pride in its regional culinary riches. There are farmers markets; big seasonal food fares such as Savour Stratford in September; loads of restaurant, farm, and dairy tours; and more. Check out www.welcometostratford.com/savour-stratford.php.

Stratford also has a good art museum, the **Gallery Stratford** (54 Romeo St.; ✆ **519/271-5271;** www.gallerystratford.on.ca). Located in an historic building on the fringes of Confederation Park, the museum exhibits contemporary and historical works by Canadian artists. Its hours change with the seasons, but mid-May through late September, it's open Tuesday through Sunday from 10am to 5pm (call ahead for hours Oct to mid-May).

A Couple of Excursions from Stratford

Only half an hour or so from Stratford, the twin cities of **Kitchener** and **Waterloo** have two drawing cards: the **Farmers' Market** and the famous 9-day **Oktoberfest** (✆ **888/294-HANS** [888/294-4267] or 519/570-HANS [519/570-4267]; www.oktoberfest.ca). The cities still have a large population of descendents of German settlers, and many are also Mennonites. On Saturday, starting at 6am, you can sample shoofly pie, apple butter, birch beer, summer sausage, and other Mennonite specialties at the market in the Market Square complex, at Duke and Frederick streets in Kitchener. For additional information, contact the **Kitchener-Waterloo Area Visitors and**

Convention Bureau (2848 King St. E., Kitchener; ✆ **519/748-0800;** www.explorewaterlooregion.com). It's open in winter weekdays from 9am to 5pm, in summer daily from 9am to 5pm.

Eight kilometers (5 miles) north of Kitchener is the town of **St. Jacobs.** It has close to 100 shops in venues such as a converted mill, silo, and other factory buildings. The **Meetingplace** (33 King St.; ✆ **519/664-3518**) runs a short film about the Amish-Mennonite way of life (daily in summer, weekends only in winter). There's also the **St. Jacobs Outlet Mall** at 25 Benjamin Rd. E.; its offerings include Levi's, Lego, Reebok, Corningware, Liz Claiborne, and Paderno. The mall is open Monday through Friday 9:30am to 9pm, Saturday 8:30am to 6pm, and Sunday noon to 5pm (closed Jan 1 and Dec 25). Call ✆ **519/888-0138** for more information.

Where to Stay

When you book your theater tickets, you can book your accommodations at no extra charge. Options range from guest homes for as little as C$75 to first-class hotels charging more than C$200. Call the **Stratford Tourism Alliance** at ✆ **800/561-7926** for information (note that some accommodations are open only to festival-goers, and these can be booked only through the Accommodation Bureau). You can also book a room via **Tourism Stratford's website** (www.welcometostratford.com); for extensive bed-and-breakfast listings, check out **www.bbcanada.com.** Rooms in Stratford are most expensive in June, July, and August; it's easier to get a discount from fall to spring. In winter, even the most opulent properties deeply discount their rates. Keep in mind that most accommodations here are smoke-free.

The Annex Room ★ This small, centrally located hotel is quaint, yet luxurious: Each room has a whirlpool tub and a fireplace. The rooms are airy and bright, and elegantly decorated. Because of the hotel's tiny size, you can count on personal, considerate service. The one drawback is that there is no elevator, so guests need to be able to climb stairs.

38 Albert St., Stratford, ON N5A 3K3. ✆ **800/361-5322** or 519/271-1407. Fax 519/272-1853. www.bentleys-annex.com. 6 units. In season C$225 double; off-season C$125 double. Additional adult C$25. AE, DC, MC, V. Free parking. **Amenities:** Restaurant. *In room:* A/C, TV, fridge, hair dryer, minibar, Wi-Fi (free).

Lofts at 99 ★★ For convenience, you can't beat this spot at the center of town formerly known as Bentley's (the on-site restaurant still goes by that name; see p. 447). Recent renovations have turned it into a modern, chic inn with a streamlined look. The rooms are elegant duplex suites with kitchenettes; five units have skylights. The split-level feature makes it great for families with young children. Like most Stratford accommodations, Lofts at 99 doesn't have an elevator. This is a smoke-free hotel.

99 Ontario St., Stratford, ON N5A 3H1. ✆ **800/361-5322** or 519/271-1121. www.bentleys-annex.com. 12 units. From C$295 double. Additional adult C$25. Children 11 & under stay free in parent's room. AE, DC, MC, V. Free parking. **Amenities:** Restaurant. *In room:* A/C, TV, fridge, hair dryer, minibar, Wi-Fi (free).

Stewart House Inn ★ 🎁 This house was built in 1870, and the owners have decorated it with a suitably opulent Victorian style. There's also old-fashioned guest service: In the morning, coffee is delivered to your room; if you want to swim in the backyard saltwater pool, you'll be supplied with robes, towels, and tumblers for drinks. A full breakfast is served every morning between 8 and 10am in what used to be the ballroom. The guest rooms are nicely appointed, with each one themed to play up the romantic atmosphere. Still, the modern conveniences (flat-screen TVs, DVD players, and Wi-Fi) aren't spared. House policies are no smoking, no children, and no pets (there are, however, two small dogs in residence).

62 John St. N., Stratford, ON N5A 6K7. ✆ **866/826-7772** or 519/271-4576. Fax 519/273-1746. www.stewarthouseinn.com. 7 units. From C$199 double. Rates include full breakfast. MC, V. Street parking. No children allowed. **Amenities:** Outdoor pool. *In room:* A/C, TV/DVD player, CD player, hair dryer, Wi-Fi (free).

The Swan Motel The simple rooms here are typical, if high-end, motel fare, but the grounds are more like a small estate garden. Located 3km (1¾ miles) from downtown Stratford, the setting offers a tranquil escape. The property has been run by the same family for more than 40 years, and it has a warm, gracious atmosphere. The rooms are simple and clean. The grounds are the real drawing card, with a sweet Victorian gazebo, beds of perennial flowers, and an outdoor pool. This is a smoke-free hotel.

960 Downie St. S., Stratford, ON N5A 6S3. ✆ **519/271-6376.** Fax 519/271-0682. www.swanmotel.ca. 24 units. From C$102 double. Rates include continental breakfast. Additional adult C$15. MC, V. Free parking. **Amenities:** Outdoor pool. *In room:* A/C, TV, fridge, hair dryer, Wi-Fi (free).

A NEARBY PLACE TO STAY & DINE

Langdon Hall ★★ Less than an hour's drive from Stratford, this elegant house stands at the head of a curving, tree-lined drive. Eugene Langdon Wilks, a great-grandson of John Jacob Astor, completed it in 1902. It remained in the family until 1987, when it was transformed into a beautiful country-house hotel. Today, Langdon Hall is a Relais & Châteaux property with Ontario's first restaurant to earn the much-vaunted Relais Gourmands status (a title held by the French Laundry and Fat Duck, among others). Its 81 hectares (200 acres) is a pleasing mix of manicured lawns, English gardens, and rustic woodlands. What's more, there's a balance of comfort and refinement that, combined with top-notch service, puts it on a par with Canada's truly great inns. You can choose to stay in the original house, in the converted stable suites, or in one of the rooms surrounding the cloister garden. There is an on-site spa, a small swimming pool, a network of cross-country ski trails, and a small billiards room. The generous public rooms are great gathering places, with wood-burning fires in winter and lush garden views in summer. Many come for the dining alone: Seasonal ingredients are turned into exquisite fare under the direction of chef Jonathan Gushue, and the wine list is extensive. Tea is served on the canopied veranda.

R.R. 3, Cambridge, ON N3H 4R8. ✆ **800/268-1898** or 519/740-2100. www.langdonhall.ca. 52 units. From C$329 double. Rates include full breakfast. AE, DC, MC, V. Free parking. From Hwy. 401, take exit 275 south, turn right onto Blair Rd. & follow signs. Pets accepted (free). **Amenities:** Dining room; bar; babysitting; bike rental; concierge; health club; Jacuzzi; outdoor pool; room service; sauna; spa; tennis courts. *In room:* A/C, TV, CD player, hair dryer, Wi-Fi (free).

Where to Dine

EXPENSIVE

The Church ★★ FRENCH The Church is simply stunning. The organ pipes and the altar of the 1873 structure are intact, along with the vaulted roof, carved woodwork, and stained-glass windows. You can sit in the nave or the side aisles, and dine to appropriate music—usually Bach. Appetizers might include asparagus served hot with black morels in their juices, white wine, and cream; or sauté of duck foie gras with leeks and citron, mango, and ginger sauce. The menu is brief and to the point: classic meats with Canadian twists, such as caribou with port-and-blackberry sauce and cream-braised cabbage with shallots and glazed chestnuts; or lobster salad with green beans, new potatoes, and truffles scented with caraway. Desserts are equally dramatic. The upstairs Belfry, a more modest affair, is a popular pre- and post-theater gathering place and is open for lunch and dinner. To dine here during the festival, make reservations as soon as you buy your tickets.

70 Brunswick St. (at Waterloo St.). ✆ **519/273-3424.** www.churchrestaurant.com. Reservations required. Main courses C$38–C$44. AE, DC, MC, V. The Church: Tues–Sat 5–8:30pm, Sun 11:30am–1:30pm & 5–8pm; off-season hours vary; closed Dec to mid-Apr. The Belfry: Tues–Sat 11:30am–midnight; off-season hours vary.

The Old Prune ★ CONTINENTAL Situated in a lovely Edwardian home, the Old Prune has three dining rooms and an enclosed garden patio. Former Montréalers, the proprietors demonstrate Québec flair in both decor and menu. The menu changes based on what's fresh and what's in season (much of the produce comes from the region's organic farms). Goods from local dairies, cheese makers, and other artisans are prominent on the menu. Among the main courses, you might find Perth County pork loin grilled with tamari and honey glaze, and served with shiitake mushrooms, pickled cucumbers, and sunflower sprouts; steamed bass in Napa cabbage with curry broth and lime leaves; or rack of Ontario lamb with smoky tomatillo-chipotle pepper sauce. Desserts, such as rhubarb strawberry Napoleon, are inspired.

151 Albert St. ✆ **519/271-5052.** www.oldprune.on.ca. Reservations required. 3-course prix-fixe menu C$66. AE, MC, V. Fri–Sun 11:30am–1pm, Tues–Sun 5–9pm; call for winter hours.

Rundles ★ INTERNATIONAL Rundles provides a premier dining experience in a serene dining room overlooking the river. Proprietor James Morris eats, sleeps, thinks, and dreams food. The prix-fixe dinner offers palate-pleasing flavor combinations. Appetizers might include shaved fennel, arugula, artichoke and Parmesan salad, or warm seared Québec foie gras. Typical main dishes include poached Atlantic salmon garnished with Jerusalem artichokes, wilted arugula, and yellow peppers in a light carrot sauce; or pink roast rib-eye of lamb with ratatouille and rosemary aioli. For dessert, try glazed lemon tart and orange sorbet, or hot mango tart with pineapple sorbet. In 2008, Rundles opened the Sophisto-Bistro, a more casual dining room, with a less-expensive (yet incredibly delicious) prix-fixe menu.

9 Cobourg St. ✆ **519/271-6442.** www.rundlesrestaurant.com. Reservations required. Rundles 3-course prix-fixe dinner C$80; Sophisto-Bistro 3-course prix-fixe menu C$50. AE, DC, MC, V. Apr–Oct Sat & Sun 11:30am–1:15pm; Tues & Sat 5–7pm, Wed–Fri 5–8:30pm. Closed Nov–Mar.

MODERATE

Bentley's CANADIAN/ENGLISH Located in the Lofts at 99 hotel (see p. 445), Bentley's is *the* local watering hole and a favorite theater-company gathering spot. In summer, you can sit on the garden terrace and enjoy the light fare—grilled shrimp, burgers, pizza, fish and chips, shepherd's pie, and pastas. The dinner menu features more substantial stuff, including lamb curry, sirloin steak, and salmon baked in white wine with peppercorn-dill butter. The bar offers 15 drafts on tap.

99 Ontario St. ✆ **519/271-1121.** www.bentleys-annex.com. Reservations not accepted. Main courses C$15–C$18. AE, DC, MC, V. Daily 11:30am–1am.

Down the Street ★ INTERNATIONAL This charming bohemian spot is a welcome sight, given Stratford's delicious but often pricey food scene. The menu offers selections from around the globe: Mexican guacamole and corn tortillas, Vietnamese-style pork chops in a spicy chili-honey glaze, French Dijon chicken supreme. The dessert list is short but good; try the bittersweet chocolate tart with raspberry sorbet.

30 Ontario St. ✆ **519/273-5886.** Reservations recommended. Main courses C$18–C$28. AE, DC, MC, V. Tues–Sat 11:30am–3pm & 5–9pm (bar open till 1am).

Keystone Alley Cafe ★ ASIAN/CONTINENTAL The food here is better than at some pricier competitors. Working thespians often stop in for lunch options that may include a maple-grilled chicken-and-avocado club or a cornmeal-crusted Mediterranean tart. At dinner, entrees include breast of Muscovy duck with stir-fried Asian vegetables and egg noodles in honey-ginger sauce, as well as escallops of calf's liver with garlic potato purée and creamed Savoy cabbage with bacon. The short wine list is reasonably priced.

34 Brunswick St. ✆ **519/271-5645.** Reservations recommended. Main courses C$15–C$27. AE, DC, MC, V. Mon–Sat 11:30am–2:30pm; Tues–Sat 5–9pm.

INEXPENSIVE

York Street Kitchen ECLECTIC This small restaurant is a fun, funky spot that serves reasonably priced, high-quality food. It's a favorite with locals, especially the arts and media set. Grub is up all day, from breakfast burritos and other morning fare to build-your-own sandwiches at lunch and, in the evenings, good comfort foods such as meatloaf and mashed potatoes, or barbecued chicken and ribs.

41 York St. ✆ **519/273-7041.** www.yorkstreetkitchen.com. Main courses C$14–C$16. AE, V. Apr to early Oct daily 8am–8pm; early Oct to Mar daily 8am–3pm. Closed Dec 24 to Jan 5.

ELORA & FERGUS

115km (71 miles) W of Toronto

If you're driving from Toronto, take Highway 401 West to Highway 6, drive north to Highway 7 East, then get back on Highway 6 North and take it into Fergus. From Fergus, take Highway 18 West to Elora.

Elora has always been a special place. To the aboriginals, the gorge was a sacred site, home of spirits who dwelt within the great cliffs, and early explorers and Jesuit missionaries also wondered at the natural spectacle. Scotsman William Gilkinson put the town on the map in 1832 when he purchased 5,700 hectares (14,085 acres) on both sides of the Grand River and built a mill and a general store, and named it Elora, after the Ellora Caves in India.

Most of the houses that the settlers built in the 1850s stand today. You'll want to browse the stores along picturesque Mill Street. For real insight into the town's history, pick up a walking-tour brochure from the tourist booth on Mill Street.

The **Elora Gorge** is a 140-hectare (346-acre) park on both sides of the 20m (66-ft.) limestone gorge. Nature trails wind through it. Overhanging rock ledges, small caves, a waterfall, and the evergreen forest on its rim are some of the gorge's scenic delights. The park (✆ **519/846-9742**) has camping and swimming facilities, plus picnic areas and playing fields. It's a favorite with rock climbers. Located just west of Elora at the junction of the Grand and Irvine rivers, it is open from May 1 to October 15 from 10am to sunset. For information, contact the **Grand River Conservation Authority** (✆ **866/900-4722** or 519/846-9742; www.grandriver.ca).

An additional summer attraction is the **Elora Festival,** a 3-week music celebration held from mid-July to early August. For more information, contact the **Elora Festival** (✆ **888/747-7550** or 519/846-0331; www.elorafestival.com).

Fergus (pop. 7,500) was founded by Scottish immigrant Adam Ferguson. There are more than 250 fine old 1850s buildings to see—examples of Scottish limestone architecture—including the foundry, which now houses the Fergus market. The most noteworthy Fergus event is the **Fergus Scottish Festival,** which includes Highland

Games, featuring pipe-band competitions, caber tossing, tug-of-war contests, Highland dancing, and the North American Scottish Heavy Events, held usually on the second weekend in August. For more information on the games, contact the **Fergus Scottish Festival and Highland Games** (✆ **866/871-9442** or 519/787-0099; www.fergusscottishfestival.com).

Where to Stay & Dine

Breadalbane Inn ★★ Located in the heart of Fergus, the inn's main house is an excellent example of 1860s architecture. The stone imported from Scotland is complemented by intricate ironwork, walnut banisters, and newel posts. It was built by the Honorable Admiral Ferguson as a residence, but also served as a nursing home and rooming house before it was converted into a charming country hotel. Guest rooms are all extremely comfortable and elegantly furnished with early Canadian–style furniture. The deluxe suites (four of which are located in the Coach House) have fireplaces and Jacuzzi tubs. This is a romantic spot, and there are several romantic-getaway packages. Also on offer is a learn-to-fly-fish package.

The Breadalbane dining room is formal, with polished dark-wood tables set with Royal Doulton china. The cooking—think venison with a lingonberry sauce, or beef strip loin with a shallot-mushroom marmalade—is traditional and very good. Prices range from C$26 to C$32. There's also the Fergusson Room for true Scottish pub fare.

487 St. Andrew St. W., Fergus, ON N1M 1P2. ✆ **888/842-2825** or 519/843-4770. www.breadalbaneinn.com. 13 units. From C$185 double. Rates include continental breakfast. AE, MC, V. **Amenities:** Restaurant; bar.

Elora Mill Inn This inn is located in a former gristmill that was built in 1870 and operated until 1974. This explains both its rustic charm and its idyllic view of the Grand River and the Elora Gorge itself. Each guest room is uniquely furnished with a mix of antiques and pieces by local artisans. (Modern conveniences—such as televisions—are hidden from view in armoires.) Some rooms in adjacent buildings are duplexes and have decks and river views. Many inn rooms have gorge views, and some units have fireplaces. All rooms are designated nonsmoking.

The dining room is a treat: While the menu is relatively short, it features tasty entrees like the shellfish *pot-au-feu*. It's open daily for lunch and dinner.

77 Mill St. W., Elora, ON N0B 1S0. ✆ **866/713-5672** or 519/846-9118. www.eloramill.com. 32 units. From C$190 double. Rates include breakfast. AE, DC, MC, V. **Amenities:** Restaurant. *In room:* A/C, TV.

12

NORTH TO ONTARIO'S LAKELANDS & BEYOND

by Pamela Cuthbert

If southern Ontario is marked by its sprawling cities and picturesque towns, the northern part of the province is remarkable for its vast wilderness. You'll be struck by the rugged beauty of the landscape, the forests of old-growth pine, and the thousands of lakes in the region. The most popular destinations are Georgian Bay, Algonquin Provincial Park, and the cottage country of Huronia and the Muskoka Lakes.

EXPLORING THE REGION

On weekends, many Torontonians head north to the cottage or to a resort to unwind. But if you want to explore the whole region, drive out from Toronto via Highway 400 north to Barrie. At Barrie, you can either turn west to explore Georgian Bay, the Bruce Peninsula, and Manitoulin Island, or continue due north to the Muskoka Lakes, Algonquin Provincial Park, and points farther north.

Essentials

VISITOR INFORMATION Contact **Ontario Tourism** (© **800/ONTARIO** [800/668-2746]; www.ontariotravel.net), which operates 18 Travel Information Centres throughout Ontario. If you're beginning your trip in Toronto, visit the information center at the Atrium on Bay (street level) at 20 Dundas St. W.—it's just across Dundas from the Sears store at the northern edge of the Eaton Centre. (The Atrium's mailing address is 595 Bay St., but since the information booth is on the south side of the complex, they use a different street address for the same building.) It's open daily from 8:30am to 5pm; hours are extended during the summer, often to 8pm.

There are also Ontario Tourism **Travel Information Centres** in Barrie (21 Mapleview Dr., at Hwy. 400; © **705/725-7280**), Sault Ste.

Marie (261 Queen St. W.; ✆ **705/945-6941**), and Fort Frances (400 Central Ave.; ✆ **807/274-7566**).

Those who are interested in exploring Northern Ontario's rich Native culture should contact the **Northern Ontario Native Tourism Association** (✆ **866/844-0497** or 807/623-0497).

The Great Outdoors

In the parts of northern Ontario covered by this chapter, you'll find plenty of terrific places to canoe, hike, bike, or fish. Some 330 provincial parks in Ontario, which cover 9 million hectares (22 million acres) of land and attract some 10 million visitors each year, offer ample opportunities for outdoor recreation.

Ontario Parks uses Google maps on its website. Detailed topographic maps (vital for extended canoeing or hiking trips) can be downloaded from the **Canada Map Office;** the government bureau also lists on its website more than 900 outlets in Canada, the U.S., and overseas where the printed maps can be purchased. See http://maps.nrcan.gc.ca for details.

BIKING You'll find networks of biking and hiking trails in the national and provincial parks. Contact the individual parks directly for more information. One good route is the **Georgian Cycle and Ski Trail,** running 32km (20 miles) along the southern shore of Georgian Bay from Collingwood via Thornbury to Meaford. The **Bruce Peninsula** and **Manitoulin Island** also offer good cycling opportunities. In the Burk's Falls–Magnetawan area, the **Forgotten Trail** has been organized along old logging roads and railroad tracks. For details, contact the **Georgian Triangle Tourist Association** (30 Mountain Rd., Collingwood; ✆ **888/227-8667** or 705/445-7722; www.visitsouthgeorgianbay.ca).

CANOEING & KAYAKING Northern Ontario is a canoeist's paradise. You can enjoy exceptional canoeing in **Algonquin, Killarney,** and **Quetico provincial parks;** along the rivers in the **Temagami** (Lady Evelyn Smoothwater Provincial Park) and **Wabakimi** regions; along the **Route of the Voyageurs** in Algoma Country (Lake Superior Provincial Park); and along the rivers leading into James Bay, such as the **Missinaibi. Killbear Provincial Park, Georgian Bay,** and **Pukaskwa National Park** also are good places to paddle.

Around Parry Sound and Georgian Bay, canoeing and kayaking trips can be arranged by the **White Squall Paddling Centre** (53 Carling Bay Rd., Nobel; ✆ **705/342-5324;** www.whitesquall.com). There's a range of packages, from half-day paddling programs to 4-day trips. In Algonquin Provincial Park, several outfitters serve park visitors, including **Algonquin Outfitters** (Oxtongue Lake [R.R. 1], Dwight; ✆ **705/635-2243;** www.algonquinoutfitters.com) and **Opeongo Outfitters** (P.O. Box 123, Whitney; ✆ **800/790-1864** or 613/637-5470; www.opeongooutfitters.com). In the Georgian Bay area, **Killarney Outfitters** (✆ **800/461-1117** or 705/287-2828; www.killarneyoutfitters.com), on Highway 637, 5km (3 miles) east of Killarney, offers canoe and kayak rentals. Around the Quetico area, contact **Canoe Canada Outfitters** (300 O'Brien St., Atikokan; ✆ **807/597-6418;** www.canoecanada.com).

North of Thunder Bay is excellent terrain for camping, fishing, hunting, and canoeing in the **Wabakimi Wilderness Park,** with plenty of scope for beginners, intermediates, and advanced paddlers. Contact **Mattice Lake Outfitters** (✆ **800/411-0334** or 807/583-2483; www.matticelake.com) for excursions that run from 3 to 9 days. For other outfitters, call the **Northern Ontario Tourist Outfitters Association** (✆ **705/472-5552;** www.noto.net).

Note: In most provincial parks, you must register with park authorities and provide them with your route.

FISHING Ontario is one of the world's biggest freshwater fishing grounds, with more than 250,000 lakes and 96,000km (59,652 miles) of rivers supporting more than 140 species. The northern area covered in this chapter is the province's best fishing region. Before you go, check out the **Fish Ontario!** website (www.fishontario.com) for the latest information. In summer, on **Manitoulin Island,** fishing for Chinook and coho salmon, rainbow and lake trout, perch, and bass is excellent in Georgian Bay or any of the island lakes—**Mindenmoya, Manitou, Kagawong,** and **Tobacco,** to name a few. Trips can be arranged through **Timberlane Lodge** (✆ **800/890-4177** or 705/377-4078; www.timberlane.ca).

Around **Nipissing** and **North Bay,** there's great fishing, as well as around the **Temagami** region. You can find more remote fishing in the **Chapleau** and **Algoma** regions, the **James Bay Frontier,** and north of **Lake Superior.**

Some outfitters will rent lakeside log cabins, each equipped with a propane stove and refrigerator, and a motorboat to go along with it. One outfitter to contact is **Mattice Lake Outfitters** (see above). For additional suggestions, contact **Ontario Tourism** or the **Northern Ontario Tourist Outfitters Association** (see above).

Note: You must follow fishing limits and regulations. Canadian residents need to acquire an Outdoors Card before they can get a fishing license; contact the **Ministry of Natural Resources** (✆ **800/387-7011;** www.mnr.gov.on.ca). Residents of other countries can obtain a fishing license without this added requirement; call ✆ **800/667-1940** for information.

GOLF For a golf getaway, Muskoka is a popular destination. The greens here truly are unique: Muskoka is located on the **Canadian Shield,** a bedrock layer just a few feet below the surface. The same granite that thwarted farmers who tried and failed over centuries to work the land makes an excellent setting for golfers. The landscape is filled with natural rock outcroppings, and the golf courses take full advantage. Not only does the locale make for a stunning landscape, but it heightens the challenge. Some of the area's top-rated golf courses—such as **Taboo** and the Mark O'Meara Course at **Grandview**—have banded together to create the **Muskoka Golf Trail,** with design-your-own-package plans that allow you to stay at one resort but golf at the others (otherwise, competition for tee times can be tough). Call ✆ **800/465-3034** or 905/755-0999, or visit www.ultimategolf.ca, for details. For general information about all of the courses in Muskoka, including the spectacular **Deerhurst Highlands,** visit www.teeingitup.com/ontario.

Barrie has two exceptional courses—the **National Pines Golf and Country Club** (✆ **800/663-1549** or 705/431-7000) and the **Horseshoe Resort** golf course (✆ **800/461-5627** or 705/835-2790; www.horseshoeresort.com). Collingwood offers the scenic **Cranberry Resort** course (✆ **800/465-9077**). In the Huronia region, there's the **Bonaire Golf and Country Club** (✆ **888/266-2473** or 705/835-3125; www.bonairegolf.com), in the town of Coldwater.

HIKING The region is a hiker's paradise. Canada's oldest and most famous hiking trail, the **Bruce Trail,** starts in Queenston in Niagara-on-the-Lake and runs 885km (550 miles) up north to Tobermory at the top of the Bruce Peninsula. A favorite section runs along the Niagara Escarpment. The **Bruce Trail Association** (© **800/665-4453** or 905/529-6821; www.brucetrail.org) has 40 hiking routes on its website, some of which can be downloaded as PDFs free of charge. In the Bruce Peninsula National Park are four trails, three linked to the Bruce Trail. There's also a hiking trail around Flowerpot Island in Fathom Five National Park.

Manitoulin Island is popular with hikers, particularly the **Cup and Saucer Trail.** South of Parry Sound, hikers can follow the 66km (41-mile) **Seguin Trail,** which meanders around several lakes. In the Muskoka region, trails abound in **Arrowhead Provincial Park** at Huntsville and the Resource Management Area on Highway 11, north of Bracebridge, and in **Algonquin Park.** Algonquin is a great choice for an extended backpacking trip, along the Highland Trail or the Western Uplands Hiking Trail, which combines three loops for a total of 170km (106 miles).

You can do a memorable 7- to 10-day backpacking trip in **Killarney Provincial Park** on the 97km (60-mile) La Cloche Silhouette Trail, which takes in some stunning scenery. **Sleeping Giant Provincial Park** has more than 81km (50 miles) of trails. The Kabeyun Trail provides great views of Lake Superior and the 245m-high (804-ft.) cliffs of the Sleeping Giant. And the **Pukaskwa National Park** offers a coastal hiking trail between the Pic and Pukaskwa rivers along the northern shore of Lake Superior.

For additional hiking information, see the park entries in "Some Northern Ontario Highlights: Driving along Highways 11 & 17," later in this chapter.

HORSEBACK RIDING On Manitoulin Island, **Honora Bay Riding Stables** (R.R. 1, Little Current; © **705/368-2669;** www.hbrstable.com) offers riding lessons, trail rides, and overnight excursions. Near Sault Ste. Marie, **Cedar Rail Ranch** (428 Wharncliffe Rd., Thessalon; © **705/842-2021**), offers both hourly and overnight trail rides with stops for swimming breaks along the route.

SKIING & SNOWMOBILING Ontario's largest downhill-skiing area is the **Blue Mountain Resorts** (© **877/445-0231**) in Collingwood. In Huronia, there are several good resorts, including **Horseshoe Valley** (© **800/461-5627**) and **Mount St. Louis Moonstone** (© **877/835-2112**). In the Muskoka region, there's downhill skiing at **Hidden Valley Highlands** (© **800/398-9555** or 705/789-1773; www.skihiddenvalley.on.ca). Up north around Thunder Bay, try **Loch Lomond** (© **807/475-7787**) or **Mount Baldy** (© **807/683-8441**).

You can cross-country ski at **Kamview Nordic Centre** (© **807/625-5075**) and in provincial parks such as **Sleeping Giant** and **Kakabeka Falls.**

One of the top destinations is the **Parry Sound** area, which has an extensive network of cross-country ski trails and more than 1,047km (651 miles) of well-groomed snowmobiling trails. There are nine snowmobiling clubs in the area, and the **Chamber of Commerce** (© **705/746-4213**) can put you in touch with them. For details on cross-country skiing, contact the **Georgian Nordic Ski and Canoe Club** (© **888/866-4447** or 705/746-5067; www.georgiannordic.com), which permits day use of its ski trails.

You'll also find groomed cross-country trails at **Sauble Beach** on the Bruce Peninsula and in many of the provincial parks farther north. Along the mining frontier, contact the **Porcupine Ski Runners** at © **705/360-1444** (www.porcupineski runners.com) in Timmins.

For a complete listing of alpine and cross-country ski resorts by area, visit www.skiontario.ca.

FROM COLLINGWOOD TO TOBERMORY

Nestled at the base of Blue Mountain, **Collingwood** is the town closest to Ontario's biggest skiing area. Collingwood first achieved prosperity as a Great Lakes port and shipbuilding town. Many mansions and the Victorian main street are reminders of the glory days. And just east of Blue Mountain sweep 14km (8¾ miles) of golden sands at **Wasaga Beach.**

North beyond Collingwood stretches the **Bruce Peninsula National Park,** known for its limestone cliffs, wetlands, and forest. From **Tobermory,** you can visit an underwater national park.

Essentials

GETTING THERE If you head west from Barrie, northwest from Toronto, you'll go along the west Georgian Bay coast from Collingwood up to the Bruce Peninsula. Driving from Toronto, take Highway 400 to Highway 26 West.

VISITOR INFORMATION For information, contact the **Georgian Triangle Tourist Association** (✆ **888/227-8667** or 705/445-7722; www.visitsouthgeorgian bay.ca).

Blue Mountain Ski Trails, Slides, Rides & More

In winter, skiers flock to **Blue Mountain Resort,** at R.R. 3, Collingwood (✆ **705/ 445-0231;** www.bluemountain.ca). Ontario's largest resort has 15 lifts, 98% snowmaking coverage on 36 trails, and three base lodges. In addition, there are three repair, rental, and ski shops, a ski school, and day care. Lift rates start at C$34 per day.

In summer, you can take advantage of the so-called "Green Season" attractions. These include tennis, golfing, and mountain biking; there's also a private beach on the shores of Georgian Bay that's a 10-minute ride by shuttle from the resort. Blue Mountain offers many programs for kids, ranging from tennis camp to weekend scavenger hunts on the beach.

A popular spot in Collingwood is the **Scenic Caves Nature Adventures** (260 Scenic Caves Rd., Collingwood; ✆ **705/446-0256;** www.sceniccaves.com). The area was carved out by glaciers during the Ice Age and today is a UNESCO World Biosphere Reserve. The caves are set into limestone cliffs and offer unique sights—including the "chilling" Ice Cave, a natural refrigerator that boasts icicles, even on the hottest days of summer.

Bruce Peninsula National Park

Bruce Peninsula National Park (P.O. Box 189, Tobermory; ✆ **519/596-2233** or 519/596-2263; www.pc.gc.ca) features limestone cliffs, abundant wetlands, quiet beaches, and forest sheltering many species of orchids, ferns, and several insectivorous plants. About 100 species of bird also inhabit the park. Three campgrounds (one trailer, two tent) offer 242 campsites (no electricity).

The **Bruce Trail** winds along the Georgian Bay Coastline, while Highway 6 cuts across the peninsula; both end in Tobermory. The Bruce Trail is one of Ontario's best-known trails, stretching 885km (550 miles) from Queenston in Niagara Falls to Tobermory. The most rugged part of the trail passes through the park along the Georgian Bay shoreline. **Cypress Lake trails,** from the north end of the Cyprus Lake campground, provide access to the Bruce Trail and lead to cliffs overlooking the bay. You can use canoes and manpowered craft on Cyprus Lake. The best swimming is at **Singing Sands Beach** and **Dorcas Bay,** both on Lake Huron on the west side of the peninsula. Winter activities include cross-country skiing, snowshoeing, and snowmobiling.

An Underwater National Park

From Tobermory, you can visit the underwater national park. The **Fathom Five National Marine Park** (P.O. Box 189, Tobermory; ✆ **519/596-2233;** www.pc.gc.ca) features a good 20 shipwrecks that lie in wait for divers who want to explore the 19-odd islands in the park. The most accessible is **Flowerpot Island,** which you can visit by tour boat to view the weird and wonderful rock pillar formations. Go for a few hours to hike and picnic. Six campsites are available on the island on a first-come, first-served basis. Boats leave from Tobermory harbor.

Where to Stay

Beild House Country Inn & Spa ★ *Beild* is the Scottish word for shelter, but this charming inn is anything but basic. The stately Edwardian house dates from 1909. The public rooms are warmed by two wood-burning fireplaces and decorated with folk art, quill boxes from Manitoulin, and sculptures. Guest rooms are individually furnished with elegant pieces (one contains a bed once owned by the duke and duchess of Windsor). The five third-floor rooms have canopied beds and fireplaces. The hotel offers a generous breakfast. There's also a fine five-course dinner, with such dishes as Georgian Bay trout on spinach with herbed beurre blanc, and pork tenderloin with grilled apples and a port wine glaze.

64 3rd St., Collingwood, ON L9Y 1K5. ✆ **888/322-3453** or 705/444-1522. Fax 705/444-2394. www.beildhouse.com. 11 units. From C$280 double. Rates include breakfast. AE, MC, V. **Amenities:** Restaurant; spa. *In room:* A/C.

Blue Mountain Resort ★ ☺ Stay here, right at the mountain base, and you can beat the winter lift lines. In summer, the resort offers access to a private beach, which is 10 minutes away by shuttle. The real reason to stay at Blue Mountain is the wealth of activities—it's impossible to be bored here. Guest rooms are on the smallish side and are simply furnished in a country style. You can also rent one- to three-bedroom condos, either slope-side or overlooking the fairway. This is an excellent choice for families—Blue Mountain has a great deal to offer kids.

R.R. 3, Collingwood, ON L9Y 3Z2. ✆ **705/445-0231.** www.bluemountain.ca. 95 units. From C$149 double; from C$179 suite. Special packages available. AE, MC, V. **Amenities:** Dining room; 2 lounges; mountain-bike rental; children's programs; fitness center; 18-hole golf course; outdoor & indoor pools; spa; 12 tennis courts; squash courts; kayak rental. *In room:* A/C, TV.

Where to Dine

Alphorn Restaurant ☺ SWISS Bratwurst, Wiener schnitzel, chicken Ticino, and cheese fondue are just some of the favorites served at this casual, Alpine-style restaurant. It's popular with families. Best to go early, as the place is crowded winter and summer. Save room for the Swiss crepes with chocolate and almonds.

Hwy. 26 W., Collingwood. ✆ **705/445-8882.** Reservations not accepted. Main courses C$14–C$22. AE, MC, V. Year-round Mon–Fri 4–10pm, Sat & Sun 4–10:30pm; summer also daily 11:30am–3pm.

Spike & Spoon Bistro & Gallery ★ CONTINENTAL This longtime favorite is under new management, and the few changes are an improvement. The Spike &

Spoon's menu is shorter than it used to be, and an art gallery has been added to the second floor (a charming addition). The setting is still grand—the restaurant is in an elegant mid–19th-century redbrick house that once belonged to a Chicago millionaire—and seasonal dishes are prepared with fresh ingredients and garnished herbs grown out back in the restaurant garden.

637 Hurontario St. ✆ **705/446-1629.** Reservations recommended. Main courses C$16–C$26. MC, V. Tues–Sat noon–2:30pm; Tues–Sun 6–10pm.

MANITOULIN ISLAND

Manitoulin Island, named after the Great Indian Spirit Gitchi Manitou, is for those who seek a quiet, remote, and spiritual place, where life is slow.

Essentials

GETTING THERE By road, you can cross over the swing bridge connecting Little Current to Great Cloche Island and via Highway 6 to Espanola. You can also reach the island via the **Chi-Cheemaun ferry,** which transports people and cars from Tobermory to South Baymouth on a 1¾- to 2-hour trip. Ferries operate early May to mid-October, with four departures a day in summer. One-way fare is C$14 adults and C$7.05 children 5 to 11; an average-size car costs C$31 one-way, and bicycles cost C$6.10. For information, contact the **Owen Sound Transportation Company** (✆ **800/265-3163** or 519/376-6601; www.ontarioferries.com) or the **Tobermory Terminal** (✆ **519/596-2510**). Reservations are strongly recommended during the summer, but plan carefully: You can make a reservation on the first and last ferries of the day for no fee, but there is an additional C$20 charge for the two ferry trips in the middle of the day.

VISITOR INFORMATION Contact the **Manitoulin Tourism Association** (✆ **705/368-3021;** www.manitoulintourism.com), open daily late April to late October 10am to 4pm, or stop by the **information center** just past the swing bridge in Little Current, which is open daily May through September 10am to 4pm.

Exploring the Island

Native peoples have lived on this land for centuries, and you can visit the **Ojibwa Indian Reserve,** occupying the large peninsula on the island's eastern end. It's home to about 2,500 people of Odawa, Ojibwa, and Potawotami descent; the area was never ceded to the government. The reserve isn't a tourist attraction but may appeal to anyone genuinely interested in modern life on a reservation. Summer weekends are busy with powwows, with the **Wikwemikong Annual Competition Powwow** in early August being one of the biggest draws. The island has long been a haven for artists, and you can visit some in their studios, such as jewelry designer **Ursula Hettmann** (3 Dominion Rd., Spring Bay; ✆ **705/377-4265;** www.hettmannstudio.com). One gallery worth a visit is the **Perivale Gallery** (1320 Perivale Rd. E., Spring Bay; ✆ **705/377-4847**), open the May Victoria Day holiday to mid-September daily 10am to 6pm. Owners Sheila and Bob McMullan scour the country in search of remarkable artists and craftspeople to display their works in the log-cabin gallery overlooking Lake Kagawong. Glass, sculpture, paintings, engravings, fabrics, and ceramics fill the space. From Spring Bay, follow Perivale Road east for about 3km (1¾ miles); turn right at the lake and keep following the road until you see the gallery on the right.

Although there are several communities on the island, the highlights are scenic and mostly outside their perimeters, such as the **Mississagi Lighthouse,** at the western end outside Meldrun Bay. Follow the signs that'll take you about 6km (3¾ miles) down a dirt road past the limestone/dolomite quarry entrance (from which materials are still shipped across the Great Lakes) to the lighthouse. From late May through Labour Day, you can see how the light keeper lived in this isolated area before the advent of electricity. Its dining room—the Foghorn—is also open in summer. From the lighthouse, several short trails lead along the shoreline.

The island is great for hiking, biking, bird-watching, boating, cross-country skiing, and just plain relaxing. Charters also operate from Meldrun Bay. You'll find golf courses in Mindemoya and Gore Bay. Fishing is excellent either in Georgian Bay or in the island's lakes and streams. You can arrange trips through **Timberlane Lodge** (**© 800/890-4177** or 705/377-4078; www.timberlane.ca). May through October, **Honora Bay Riding Stables** (R.R. 1, Little Current; **© 705/368-2669;** www.hbrstable.com), 27km (17 miles) west of Little Current on Highway 540, offers trail rides.

There are several nature trails on the island. Among the more spectacular is the **Cup and Saucer Trail,** starting 18km (11 miles) west of Little Current, at the junction of Highway 540 and Bidwell Road. Also off Highway 540 lies the trail to **Bridal Veil Falls** as you enter the village of Kagawong. Halfway between Little Current and Manitowaning, stop at **Ten Mile Point** for the view over the North Channel, dotted with 20,000 islands. The best beach with facilities is at **Providence Bay** on the island's south side.

Where to Stay

Your best bet is to seek out one of the island's bed-and-breakfasts, which will most likely be plain and simple, but clean. Contact **Manitoulin Tourism Association** (P.O. Box 119, Little Current; **© 705/368-3021;** www.manitoulintourism.com). One standout is the **Queen's Inn,** a B&B located in a grand 1880 house that is filled with Victorian antiques (19 Water St., Gore Bay; **© 705/282-0665;** www.thequeensinn.ca).

Rockgarden Terrace Resort and the Shaftesbury Inn The Rockgarden Terrace, long known for its Bavarian flare, is a family resort on the rocks above Lake Mindemoya. Accommodations are mostly motel-style units furnished in contemporary style, but there are also four log-cabin–style suites. The dining room seems like an Austrian hunting lodge, with trophies displayed on the oak-paneled walls and a cuisine featuring German-Austrian specialties such as Wiener schnitzel, sauerbraten, goulash, and beef *rolladen*. The Shaftesbury Inn is a different experience altogether: nine very romantic guest rooms are in a sprawling house that dates back to 1884.

R.R. 1, Spring Bay, ON P0P 2B0. **© 705/377-4652.** www.rockgardenresort.on.ca. 18 motel units, 4 chalet suites, 9 guest rooms. From C$102/person. Rates include breakfast & dinner. Weekend & weekly packages available. MC, V. **Amenities:** 3 restaurants; lounge; bike rental; nearby golf course; Jacuzzi; outdoor pool; sauna. *In room:* TV.

Where to Dine

The food on the island is simple and homey. In summer, the **Foghorn Restaurant** at the **Mississagi Lighthouse** overlooking Meldrun Bay is arguably the most scenic spot (note that it's open only from late May through Labour Day). For more sophisticated palate-pleasers, go to the **Rockgarden Terrace Resort** (**© 705/377-4642**) near Spring Bay (see above). In Little Current, one of the nicest casual spots on the island for breakfast, lunch, or dinner is the **Anchor Inn Bar & Grill** (1 Water St.;

(✆ **705/368-2023**). While the menu carries a wide range of dishes, the specialty here is local seafood, so you'll find plenty of whitefish, rainbow trout, and arctic char. Open year-round (except for the patio, which is open June–Sept), the Anchor Inn serves meals daily from 7am to 11pm.

ALONG GEORGIAN BAY: MIDLAND & PARRY SOUND

Midland

Midland is the center for cruising through the thousands of beautifully scenic Georgian Islands, and **30,000 Island Cruises** (✆ **705/549-7795;** www.georgianbaycruises.com) offers 3-hour cruises following the route of Brele, Champlain, and La Salle up through the inside passage to Georgian Bay. May to Canadian Thanksgiving (U.S. Columbus Day), boats usually leave the town dock twice a day. Fares are C$18 adults, C$16 seniors, C$8 children ages 5 to 14, and free for children 4 and under.

THE tragic tale OF SAINTE-MARIE AMONG THE HURONS

Midland's history dates from 1639, when Jesuits established a fortified mission, **Sainte-Marie Among the Hurons,** to bring Christianity to the Huron tribe. However, the mission retreat lasted only a decade, for the Iroquois, jealous of the Huron-French trading relationship, stepped up their attacks in the area. By the late 1640s, the Iroquois had killed thousands of Hurons and several priests, and had destroyed two villages within 10km (6¼ miles) of Sainte-Marie. Ultimately, the Jesuits burned down their own mission and fled with the Hurons to Christian Island, about 32km (20 miles) away. But the winter of 1649 was harsh, and thousands of Hurons died. In the end, only a few Jesuits and 300 Hurons were able to make the journey back to the relative safety of Québec. The Jesuits' mission had ended in martyrdom and murder. It was 100 years before the Native Canadians in the region saw Europeans again, and those newcomers spoke a different language.

Today, local history is recaptured at the **mission** (✆ **705/526-7838**), 8km (5 miles) east of Midland on Highway 12 (follow the HURONIA HERITAGE signs). The blacksmith stokes his forge, the carpenter squares a beam with a broadaxe, and the ringing church bell calls the missionaries to prayer, while a canoe enters the fortified water gate. A film depicts the life of the missionaries. Special programs given in July and August include candlelight tours and a 1½-hour canoeing trip (at extra cost). Admission is C$11 adults, C$9.75 seniors and students, C$8.50 children 6-12, and free for children 5 and under (all prices are slightly discounted in early May and in the fall after Labour Day). From April 30 to November 2, it's open daily 10am to 5pm.

Just east of Midland on Highway 12 rise the twin spires of the **Martyrs' Shrine** (✆ **705/526-3788**), a memorial to the eight North American martyr saints. As six were missionaries at Sainte-Marie, this imposing church was built on the hill overlooking the mission, and thousands make pilgrimages here each year. The bronzed outdoor stations of the cross were imported from France. Admission is C$3 adults, free for children 9 and under.

Bright Lights in the Wilderness

While most visitors to northern Ontario are drawn by the peaceful expanses of wilderness, less sporty travelers are gravitating to the Casino Rama (5899 Rama Rd., Orillia; © 888/817-7262 or 705/329-3325; www.casinorama.com), the 18,000-sq.-m (193,750-sq.-ft.) state-of-the-art casino just east of Orillia. Open 24 hours, the casino boasts more than 2,100 slot machines and 109 gaming tables. There are also three full-service restaurants, a food arcade, and a lounge with live entertainment (headliners include Michael Bolton, Jewel, the Barenaked Ladies, and that Vegas perennial Wayne Newton). So, when all that peace and quiet starts getting to you, you know where to turn.

Midland lies 53km (33 miles) east of Barrie and 145km (90 miles) north of Toronto. If you're driving from Barrie, take Highway 400 to Highway 12 West to Midland.

EXPLORING THE AREA

See the box below for details on **Sainte-Marie Among the Hurons.** Across from the Martyrs' Shrine, the **Wye Marsh Wildlife Centre** (© **705/526-7809;** www.wyemarsh.com) is a 60-hectare (148-acre) wetland/woodland site offering wildlife viewing, guided and self-guided walks, and canoe excursions in the marsh. A floating boardwalk cuts through the marsh, fields, and woods, where trumpeter swans have been reintroduced into the environment and now number 40 strong. Reservations are needed for the canoe trips (call the number above) offered in July and August and occasionally September. In winter, cross-country skiing and snowshoeing are available. For information, visit the website. Admission is C$11 adults; C$8.50 students, seniors, and children 6 to 12; and free for children 5 and under. The center is open daily 9am to 5pm, but is closed on December 25.

In town, **Freda's,** in an elegant home at 342 King St. (© **705/526-4851**), serves excellent Continental cuisine. Just down the street at 249 King St. is **Riv Bistro** (© **705/526-9432**), which offers Mediterranean cooking and plenty of seafood.

EN ROUTE TO THE MUSKOKA LAKES: ORILLIA

Traveling to the Muskoka Lakeland region, you'll probably pass through **Orillia** (from Barrie, take Hwy. 11). Here, you can visit Canadian author/humorist **Stephen Leacock's** summer home (50 Museum Dr.; © **705/329-1908;** www.leacockmuseum.com), a green-and-white mansard-roofed and turreted structure with a central balcony overlooking the beautiful lawns and garden sweeping down to the lake. The interior is filled with heavy Victorian furniture and mementos of this Canadian Mark Twain, author of 35 volumes of humor, including *Sunshine Sketches of a Little Town* (New Canadian Library), which caricatured many of the residents of Mariposa, a barely fictionalized version of Orillia. Admission is C$5 adults, C$4 seniors, C$3 students, and C$2 children ages 3 to 12. It's open weekdays from 9am to 5pm; closed on legal holidays.

GEORGIAN BAY ISLANDS NATIONAL PARK

The park consists of 59 islands in Georgian Bay and can be reached by water taxi from Honey Harbour, a town north of Midland right on the shore. (As you're taking Hwy. 400 north, branch off to the west at Port Severn to reach Honey Harbour.) Hiking, swimming, fishing, and boating are the name of the game in the park. In summer, and on weekends and holidays, the boaters really do take over—but it's a quiet retreat weekdays, late August, and off-season. The park's center is on the largest island, **Beausoleil,** with camping and other facilities. For more information, contact **Georgian Bay Islands National Park** (✆ **705/756-2415;** www.pc.gc.ca).

The Parry Sound Area

Only 225km (140 miles) north of Toronto and 161km (100 miles) south of Sudbury, the Parry Sound area is the place for active vacations. For details, contact the **Parry Sound Area Chamber of Commerce** (70 Church St.; ✆ **705/746-4213;** www.parrysoundchamber.ca), which is open daily from 10am to 4pm.

There's excellent canoeing and kayaking; if you need an outfitter, contact **White Squall Paddling Centre** (53 Carling Bay Rd., Nobel; ✆ **705/342-5324;** www.whitesquall.com), which offers both day trips and multiday excursions. Run by **30,000 Island Cruise Lines** (9 Bay St., Parry Sound; ✆ **705/549-3388;** www.georgianbaycruises.com), the *Island Queen* cruises through the 30,000 islands for 3 hours. It leaves the town dock once or twice a day; fares are C$18 adults, C$16 seniors, C$8 children ages 5 to 14, and free for children 4 and under.

And there are many winter diversions, as well—loads of cross-country ski trails and more than 1,000km (621 miles) of well-groomed snowmobiling trails. For details on cross-country skiing, contact the **Georgian Nordic Ski and Canoe Club** (✆ **888/866-4447** or 705/746-5067; www.georgiannordic.com), which permits day use of their ski trails.

Nature lovers will head for **Killbear Provincial Park** (✆ **705/342-5492,** or 705/342-5227 for reservations), farther north up Highway 69; it offers 1,600 hectares (3,954 acres) set in the middle of 30,000 islands. There are plenty of watersports—swimming at a 3km (1¾-mile) beach on Georgian Bay, snorkeling or diving off Harold Point, and fishing for lake trout, walleye, perch, pike, and bass. The climate is moderated by the bay, which explains why trillium, wild leek, and hepatica bloom. Among the more unusual fauna are the Blandings and Map turtles that inhabit the bogs, swamps, and marshes.

There are three **hiking trails,** including 3.5km (2.2-mile) Lookout Point, leading to a commanding view over Blind Bay to Parry Sound; and the Lighthouse Point Trail, crossing rocks and pebble beaches to the lighthouse at the peninsula's southern tip. There's also **camping** at 883 sites in seven campgrounds.

WHERE TO STAY

Since the recent closure of the stunning and long-established Inn at Manitou, the area is short on destination resorts. Still, this remains a great place to explore for the remarkable landscapes and abundant outdoor activities. For where to lay your head, there are a handful of small inns and B&Bs like the charming and clean **Little Lake Inn** (669 Yonge St., Midland; ✆ **888/297-6130**; www.littlelakeinn.com; C$119-C$169) and the newly refurbished and upscale **Glenn Burney Lodge** (49 Glenn Burney Rd., Seguin; ✆ **705/746-5943**; www.glennburneylodge.ca; C$129-C$199) that fully reopened in 2010. Alternatively, it's a safe bet to choose from one of the many chains that operate here, like the **Best Western** in Midland (924 King St.; ✆ **705/526-9307**; www.bestwestern.com; C$109-C$139) or the **Comfort Inn** in Parry Sound (120 Bowes St.; ✆ 705/746-6221; www.comfortinn.com; C$79-C$114). The **Microtel Inn** (292 Louisa St.; ✆ **705/746-2700**; www.microtelinn.com; C$89-C$119) in Parry Sound is popular for its affordability, good service, and basic comforts.

THE MUSKOKA LAKES ★

Just a 2-hour drive north of Toronto, the Muskoka region has been a magnet for visitors since the 19th century. Though the area proved futile for farming (it's located on the Canadian Shield, where you need dig only a foot or two in some places to come up against sheets of granite), its more than 1,600 lakes, unspoiled wilderness, and laid-back attitude made it an excellent place for a retreat. In recent years, Muskoka's charms have expanded to include excellent golf courses, soothing spas, and top-notch restaurants. While the region is most popular in summer, when families congregate at the resorts and Hollywood celebrities such as Goldie Hawn and Tom Hanks lounge at their lakefront "cottages," this is a great area to visit at any time of the year.

Once accessible only by water, Muskoka is still a boater's dream. The region also has several towns of note: Gravenhurst, Bracebridge, Port Carling, Huntsville, and Bala. It's well worth devoting a day or two to explore the area, the quaint towns, and, most of all, the dazzling waterways. Be forewarned: This is not the Great White North. Particularly in summer, the area is busy with crowds. If you're looking for wide open wilderness, you have to travel further north to Algonquin Park or to some of the more remote stretches of Georgian Bay.

Essentials

GETTING THERE You can drive from the south via Highway 400 to Highway 11, from the east via highways 12 and 169 to Highway 11, and from the north via Highway 11. It's about 160km (99 miles) from Toronto to Gravenhurst, 15km (9¼ miles) from Gravenhurst to Bracebridge, 25km (16 miles) from Bracebridge to Port Carling, and 34km (21 miles) from Bracebridge to Huntsville. **VIA Rail** (✆ **416/366-8411;** www.viarail.ca) services Gravenhurst, Bracebridge, and Huntsville from Toronto's Union Station. An airport about 18km (11 miles) from Gravenhurst is used mainly for small aircraft. Several other landing strips and a helicopter landing pad are at the Deerhurst Resort in Huntsville.

VISITOR INFORMATION For information on the region, contact **Muskoka Tourism** (✆ **800/267-9700** or 705/689-0660; www.discovermuskoka.ca).

GETTING AROUND While you won't need a car if you plan to stay close to your resort while you're here (an entirely reasonable proposition), you will need a car if you're planning to do a lot of sightseeing in the area. You could take the train to Bracebridge and then rent a car at **Budget** (1 Robert Dollar Dr.; ✆ **705/645-2755**). Huntsville has an **Enterprise** car rental center at 197 Main St. W. (✆ **705/789-1834**).

Exploring the Towns

Gravenhurst and Huntsville are scenic, and they also have enough shops, restaurants, parks, and public squares to make them worth a visit. Unless you have kids and plan to visit Santa's Village (see below), there's not much of a reason to linger in Bracebridge.

GRAVENHURST

Gravenhurst is Muskoka's first town—the first you reach if you're driving from Toronto and the first to achieve town status.

The **Norman Bethune Memorial House** (235 John St. N.; ✆ **705/687-4261**) is the restored 1890 birthplace of Dr. Norman Bethune. In 1939, this surgeon, inventor, and humanitarian died tending the sick in China during the Chinese Revolution. Tours of the historic house include a modern exhibit on Bethune's life. In summer,

The Muskoka Lakes Region

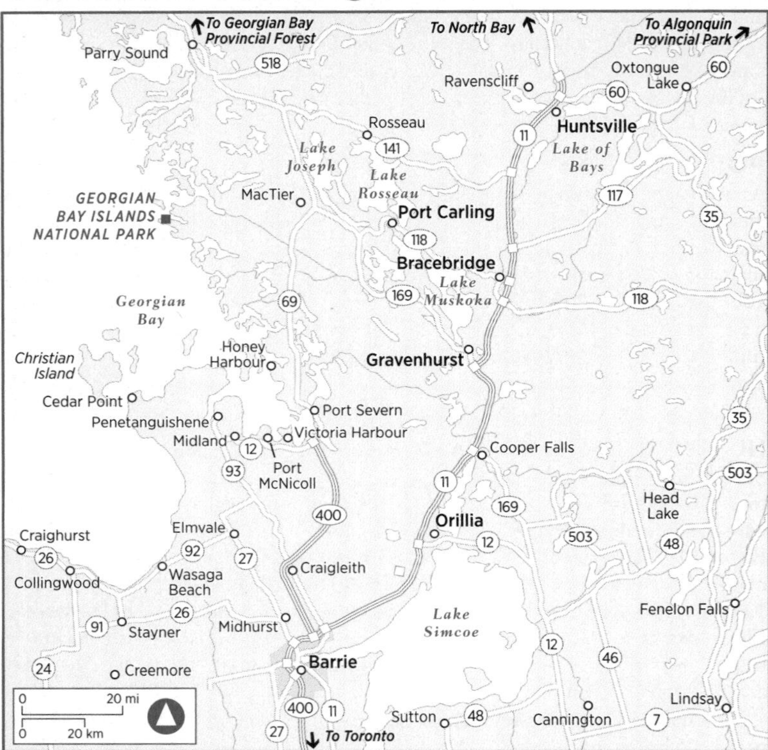

the house is open June through October daily from 10am to 4pm, November through May weekdays only from 1 to 4pm. Admission is C$4 adults, C$2.50 children 6 to 16, free for children 5 and under.

Sailing is one of Muskoka's greatest summer pastimes. Gravenhurst is home to the Muskoka Fleet, which includes a lovingly restored coal-powered 1887 steamship, the **RMS *Segwun*.** There are many options for cruising, such as a 1-hour tour; a 2½-hour lunch cruise; and a 4-hour late-afternoon tour of **Millionaire's Row,** where the real estate is as dazzling as the natural beauty. Reservations are required for all tours; call ✆ **866/687-6667** or 705/687-6667, or visit **www.realmuskoka.com** for more information. Tour prices start at C$18 adults, C$11 children 12 and under.

Year-round, there are theater performances at the **Gravenhurst Opera House** (295 Muskoka Rd. S., Gravenhurst; ✆ **705/687-5550**), which celebrated its 109th anniversary in 2010. In summer, there are shows at the **Port Carling Community Hall** (3 Bailey St., Port Carling; ✆ **705/765-5221**).

BRACEBRIDGE: SANTA'S WORKSHOP

Halfway between the equator and the North Pole, **Bracebridge** bills itself as Santa's summer home, and **Santa's Village** (✆ **705/645-2512;** www.santasvillage.ca) is an imaginatively designed fantasyland full of kiddie delights: pedal boats and bumper boats on the lagoon, a roller-coaster sleigh ride, a Candy Cane Express, a carousel, and a Ferris wheel. At Elves' Island, children can crawl on a suspended net, and over or through various modules—the Lunch Bag Forest, Cave Crawl, and Snake Tube Crawl. Mid-June through Labour Day, it's open daily from 10am to 6pm. Admission is C$27 adults and children 5 and older, C$22 seniors and children 2 to 4, and free for children under 2.

PORT CARLING

As waterways became the main means of transportation in the region, **Port Carling** grew into the hub of the lakes. It became a boat-building center when a lock was installed connecting Lakes Muskoka and Rosseau, and a canal between Lakes Rosseau and Joseph opened all three to navigation. The **Muskoka Lakes Museum,** at 100 Joseph St. (✆ **705/765-5367**), captures the flavor of this era. July and August, it's open Monday through Saturday from 10am to 5pm and Sunday noon to 4pm; June, September, and October, hours are Tuesday through Saturday from 10am to 4pm and Sunday from noon to 4pm. Closed Nov–May. Admission is by donation, with a suggested C$2 minimum.

HUNTSVILLE

Starting in the late 1800s, lumber was the name of the game in Huntsville, which is today Muskoka's biggest town. You can see some of the region's early history at the **Muskoka Heritage Place,** which includes **Muskoka Pioneer Village** (88 Brunel Rd.; ✆ **705/789-7576;** www.muskokaheritageplace.org). It's open from mid-May to mid-October daily from 11am to 4pm. Admission is C$10 adults, C$7 children 3 to 12, free for children 2 and under. Muskoka Heritage Place also features the **Portage Flyer Steam Train.** Once part of the world's smallest commercial railway (running from 1904–1958), it's been reborn as a tourist attraction and reopened in 2010 after a thorough renovation.

Robinson's General Store on Main Street in Dorset (✆ **705/766-2415**) is so popular, it was voted Canada's best country store. Wood stoves, dry goods, hardware, pine goods, and moccasins—you name it, it's here.

Where to Stay

Muskoka is famous for its lakes, and also for its resorts. Bed-and-breakfast and country-inn choices also abound. Contact **Muskoka Tourism** (✆ **800/267-9700** or 705/689-0660; www.discovermuskoka.ca). The prices listed below are for the peak summer season; deep discounts are available at all of these properties in early spring, late fall, and winter.

RESORTS

Deerhurst Resort ★★★ ☺ The Deerhurst is a perfect spot for a family vacation. This stunning resort complex rambles over 320 hectares (791 acres), and it offers everything from two 18-hole golf courses (part of the Muskoka Golf Trail) to a golf academy; a full-service Aveda spa; endless kilometers of nature trails for hiking (or snowmobiling or cross-country skiing in winter); canoeing, kayaking, and all manner of watersports; an ambitious musical revue that runs all summer; and horseback riding. The accommodations here are spread out among several buildings on the property and range from high-ceilinged hotel rooms in the Terrace and Bayshore buildings to fully appointed one-, two-, or three-bedroom suites, many with fireplaces and/or whirlpools.

The Shania Connection

The Deerhurst has many charms to recommend it, and whether or not you stay there, you must check out the pro song-and-dance stage show. Now in its 28th year, it's famous in part because Shania Twain performed in it for 3 years (1988–1990). Twain has kept up her connection with the Deerhurst since, even having her wedding there. In 2002, she brought Katie Couric and a NBC film crew to reminisce about her days here on stage. Twain continues to visit the resort—and rumor has it that when she does, she always checks out the show.

1235 Deerhurst Dr., Huntsville, ON P1H 2E8. © **800/461-4393** or 705/789-6411. Fax 705/789-2431. www.deerhurstresort.com. 388 units. From C$197 double. AE, DC, DISC, MC, V. Free parking. Take Canal Rd. off Hwy. 60 to Deerhurst Rd. **Amenities:** 2 restaurants; 2 bars; children's programs; concierge; 2 18-hole golf courses; 11 Jacuzzis; 5 pools (2 indoor, 3 outdoor); room service; sauna; spa; tennis courts; 3 squash courts; racquetball court. *In room:* A/C, TV, hair dryer, Internet (free), minibar.

Taboo Resort ★★★ ☺ Near Gravenhurst in the southern Muskoka region, Taboo stands out for sleek sophistication in a leafy setting. Known until May 2003 as Muskoka Sands, the resort's new name may suggest a hedonistic adults-only retreat. The truth is anything but: Taboo is a family-friendly zone, with a kids' club that schedules activities for every day of the week during the high season in summer. And the fact that the resort is so willing to take care of the children means that many adults can soak up spa treatments or dine at one of the on-site restaurants without a second thought. One of my favorite things about Taboo is that every single room, large and small alike, has its own deck or balcony. While all of the sophisticated offerings at the resort are excellent, nothing beats taking in the utterly serene setting it enjoys. The hotel is entirely nonsmoking.

1209 Muskoka Beach Rd., Gravenhurst, ON P1P 1R1. © **800/461-0236** or 705/687-2233. www.tabooresort.com. 157 units. From C$229 double. AE, DC, MC, V. Free parking. **Amenities:** 2 restaurants; bar; children's programs; concierge; 2 golf courses (18-hole & 9-hole); health club; Jacuzzi; 4 pools (3 outdoor, 1 indoor); room service; sauna; spa; 5 tennis courts; squash court. *In room:* A/C, TV, fridge, hair dryer, Wi-Fi (free).

Windermere House Resort ★ This traditional lakeside resort was destroyed by fire in 1996 but was rebuilt according to the original 1870s design. Well-manicured lawns sweep down to the lovely Lake Rosseau, while a broad veranda furnished with Adirondack chairs sets the leisurely mood. You can take in the water sports or just kick back with a book and a beverage. Rebuilding post-fire allowed the guest rooms to incorporate modern conveniences (including air-conditioning) while retaining old-fashioned charm. Most of the rooms have gorgeous views (the best ones overlook the lake), and a few have balconies or decks. This is a smoke-free hotel.

Off Muskoka Rte. 4 (P.O. Box 68), Windermere, ON P0B 1P0. © **888/946-3376** or 705/769-3611. Fax 705/769-2168. www.windermerehouse.com. 70 units. From C$220 double. Rates include breakfast. Weekly rates available. AE, MC, V. Free parking. **Amenities:** Restaurant; lounge; children's programs; golf course; outdoor pool; room service; tennis courts. *In room:* A/C, TV, Internet (free), minibar.

A COUNTRY INN

Inn at the Falls ★ This attractive "inn" is actually a group of seven Victorian houses on a quiet cul-de-sac overlooking Bracebridge Falls and the Muskoka River. Inviting floral gardens surround an outdoor heated pool, patios, and lawns for relaxing. Some units have fireplaces, Jacuzzis, and balconies; others have views of the falls. The Fox & Hounds is a popular local gathering place. In winter, the fire crackles and snaps; in summer, the terrace is filled with umbrella-shaded tables. The more elegant Carriage Room serves upscale continental fare. Quite the perfect get-away-from-it-all spot, and easy on the budget, too. This is a smoke-free hotel.

1 Dominion St., Bracebridge, ON P1L 1V3. ✆ **877/645-9212** or 705/645-2245. www.innatthefalls.net. 39 units. From C$155 double. Rates include breakfast. Additional adult C$16. AE, DC, MC, V. Free parking. **Amenities:** 2 restaurants; nearby golf course; outdoor pool; Wi-Fi (free). *In room:* TV.

Where to Dine

Blondie's ★ COMFORT FOOD/DELI/SEAFOOD This family-run restaurant is a rare find in Muskoka: a mix of the area's typical comfort foods—fish and chips, prime rib, eggs Benedict, smoked-meat sandwiches—plus more exotic fare, such as sushi. Blondie's is also the official caterer to the Gravenhurst Opera House. The setting is like a country kitchen, with round wooden tables and cheery decorations, and the service is just as warm.

151 Brock St., Gravenhurst. ✆ **705/687-7756.** Reservations recommended for dinner. Main courses C$12–C$21. MC, V. Mon & Tues 9:30am–3pm; Wed–Sat 9:30am–8pm.

Eclipse ★★ CANADIAN/INTERNATIONAL The spacious dining room with a soaring ceiling of Douglas fir beams offers an expansive view over hills and lakes. The lengthy dinner menu has plenty of vegetarian options and fare for carnivores, too. A favorite appetizer is the baked phyllo pastry filled with forest mushrooms and goat cheese. The Sizzle—the signature dish—is tiger shrimp sautéed in garlic, dried chilies, and white wine, and baked under mozzarella. Filling stuff. Entrees include breast of pheasant filled with wild rice and cranberries, and a rack of lamb rubbed with fresh herbs and served with an apple-maple compote. The wine list, with 300-plus selections, offers plenty of pairings.

1235 Deerhurst Dr., Huntsville. ✆ **705/789-6411.** www.deerhurstresort.com. Reservations recommended. Main courses C$24–C$45. AE, DC, MC, V. Daily 5–11pm.

Elements Restaurant, Culinary Theatre & Lounge ★★★ CANADIAN The fact that the chefs here have cooked at some of Toronto's most famous kitchens draws gourmets from far and wide. The restaurant's floor-to-ceiling windows face west, so that you can take in the glorious sunset over the lake. The a la carte menu includes Nova Scotia lobster with charred-corn-and-crab bread pudding.

The Culinary Theatre offers another kind of dining experience. Only 18 seats are available at a time for this culinary school/live cooking show mix. Guests participate by selecting ingredients. Each meal—a tasting menu of three, five, or seven courses—is cooked as you watch and learn.

At Taboo Resort, 1209 Muskoka Beach Rd., Gravenhurst. ✆ **705/687-2233.** www.tabooresort.com. Reservations required. Main courses C$21–C$41; Culinary Theatre menu C$90, higher for special events. AE, DC, MC, V. Daily 6–10pm.

3 Guys and a Stove ★★ ☺ INTERNATIONAL This is a family restaurant with a special menu for kids. But don't let the unpretentious atmosphere and the casual name fool you—the cooking is *very* fine. The curried pumpkin-and-sweet-potato soup is an absolute must when it's on the menu; the spicy chicken stew is another winner. This restaurant is also a terrific choice for vegetarians: The list of pasta and rice main-course dishes is substantial.

143 Hwy. 60, Huntsville. © **705/789-1815.** www.3guysandastove.com. Main courses C$20–C$38. AE, MC, V. Daily 11am–9:30pm.

ALGONQUIN PROVINCIAL PARK

Immediately east of Muskoka lie **Algonquin Provincial Park**'s 7,770 sq. km (3,000 sq. miles) of wilderness—a haven for the naturalist, camper, and fishing and sports enthusiast.

Essentials

GETTING THERE The main access points (West Gate and East Gate) are on Highway 60, east of Huntsville.

VISITOR INFORMATION Algonquin's excellent **Visitor Centre** on Highway 60 (© **705/633-5572**), at Km 0.0, is open daily from 9am to 9pm from late June through Labour Day, and from 10am to 4 or 6pm during the rest of the year. The center features exhibits about the park's history, a bookstore, a restaurant, and a gallery of Algonquin art. Inside the East Gate, at Km 54.5, is the **Algonquin Logging Museum.** It's open daily from 9am to 5pm from mid-May through early October; during the rest of the year, only its outdoor exhibits along an easy-to-walk 1.3km (.8-mile) trail are accessible.

FEES lTo familiarize yourself with regulations about stays in provincial parks visit **www.ontarioparks.com.** Day-use fees are C$16 per vehicle, but camping and other fees vary depending on the date you're visiting, the ages of the people in your group, and other factors. You can call © **888/ONT-PARK** (888/668-7275) to make a reservation (reservation fee of C$12 required).

Exploring the Park

Algonquin Park is an especially memorable destination for the canoeist, with more than 1,610km (1,000 miles) of **canoe routes** for paddling. One of Canada's largest provincial parks, it served as a source of inspiration for the famous Group of Seven artists. Algonquin Park is a sanctuary for moose, beaver, bear, and deer, and offers camping, canoeing, backpacking trails, and plenty of fishing for speckled, rainbow, and lake trout and smallmouth black bass (more than 230 lakes have native brook trout and 149 have lake trout).

Among the **hiking trails** is the 2.4km (1.5-mile) self-guided trail to the 100m-deep (328-ft.) Barron Canyon on the park's east side. In addition, there are 16 day trails. The shortest is the 1km (.6-mile) **Hardwood Lookout Trail,** which goes through forest to a fine view of Smoke Lake and the surrounding hills. Other short walks are the 1.5km (.9-mile) **Spruce Bog Boardwalk** and the **Beaver Pond Trail,** a 2km (1.2-mile) walk with good views of two beaver ponds.

For longer backpacking trips, the **Highland Trail** extends from Pewee Lake to Head, Harness, and Mosquito lakes for a round-trip of 35km (22 miles). The **Western Uplands Hiking Trail** combines three loops for a total of 169km (105 miles), beginning at the Oxtongue River Picnic Grounds on Highway 60. The first 32km (20-mile) loop will take 3 days; the second and third loops take longer. There's also a **mountain bike trail.**

Fall is a great time to visit—the maples usually peak in the last week of September. Winter is wonderful, too; you can **cross-country ski** on 80km (50 miles) of trails.

Three trails lie along the Highway 60 corridor with loops ranging from 5km (3.1 miles) to 24km (15 miles). Mew Lake Campground is open in winter, and you can rent skis at the west gate. Spring offers the best **trout fishing** and great **moose viewing** in May and June. During summer, the park is most crowded, but it's also when park staff lead expeditions to hear the timber wolves howling in response to naturalists' imitations. More than 250 **bird species** have been recorded in the park, including the rare gray jay, spruce grouse, and many varieties of warbler. The most famous bird is the common loon, found nesting on nearly every lake.

Where to Stay & Dine

There are eight **campgrounds** along Highway 60. The most secluded sites are at **Canisbay** (248 sites) and **Pog Lake** (281 sites). **Two Rivers** and **Rock Lake** have the least secluded sites; the rest are average. Four remote wilderness campgrounds are set back in the interior: **Rain Lake** with only 10 sites; **Kiosk** (17 sites) on Lake Kioshkokwi; **Brent** (28 sites) on Cedar Lake, great for pickerel fishing; and **Achray** (39 sites), the most remote site on Grand Lake, where Tom Thomson painted many of his great landscapes (the scene that inspired his Jack Pine is a short walk south of the campground). Call the **Visitor Centre** (✆ **705/633-5572**) for details.

Arowhon Pines ★ Located 8km (5 miles) off Highway 60 down a dirt road, Arowhon guarantees you total seclusion and serenity. The cabins are dotted around the pine forests surrounding the lake, and each is furnished uniquely with assorted Canadian pine antiques; they vary in layout, but all have bedrooms with private bathrooms and sitting rooms with fireplaces. You can opt for a private cottage or one containing anywhere from 2 to 12 bedrooms and sharing a communal sitting room with a stone fireplace. Sliding doors lead onto a deck. There are no TVs or phones—just the sound of the loons, the gentle lap of the water, the croaking of the frogs, and the sound of paddles cutting the smooth surface of the lake. You can swim in the lake or canoe, sail, row, or windsurf. At the heart of the resort is a hexagonal dining room beside the lake with a spacious veranda. A huge fireplace is at the room's center. The food is good, with fresh ingredients, and there's plenty of it. No alcohol is sold in the park, so if you wish to have wine with dinner, you'll need to bring your own (the staff will uncork it free of charge).

Algonquin Park, ON P1H 2G5. ✆ **866/633-5661,** or 705/633-5661 in summer or 416/483-4393 in winter. www.arowhonpines.ca. 50 units. From C$189/person. Rates include all meals. A 15% service charge is automatically added to the bill. MC, V. **Amenities:** Dining room; sauna; 2 tennis courts; free use of canoes, sailboats & kayaks. *In room:* Hair dryer, no phone.

Killarney Lodge The Killarney isn't as secluded as Arowhon (the highway is still visible and audible), but it too has charm. The pine-log cabins, with decks, stand on a peninsula jutting out into the Lake of Two Rivers. Furnishings include old rockers, country house–style beds, desks, chests, and braided rugs. A canoe comes with every cabin. Home-style meals are served in an attractive rustic log dining room. You can relax in the log cabin lounge, warmed by a woodstove.

Algonquin Park, ON P1H 2G9. ✆ **866/473-5551,** or 705/633-5551 in summer or 416/482-5254 in winter. www.killarneylodge.com. 26 units. From C$159/person. Rates include all meals. MC, V. Closed mid-Oct to mid-May. Enter the park on Hwy. 60 from either Dwight or Whitney. **Amenities:** Dining room; lounge; watersports equipment rental.

SOME NORTHERN ONTARIO HIGHLIGHTS: DRIVING ALONG HIGHWAYS 11 & 17

From the Muskoka region, **Highway 11** winds up toward the province's northernmost frontier via North Bay, Kirkland Lake, Timmins (using Rte. 101), and Cochrane before sweeping west to Nipigon. There, it links up briefly with **Highway 17,** the route traveling the northern perimeters of the Great Lakes from North Bay via Sudbury, Sault Ste. Marie, and Wawa, to Nipigon. At Nipigon, highways 11 and 17 combine and lead into Thunder Bay. They split again west of Thunder Bay, with Highway 17 taking a more northerly route to Dryden and Kenora, and Highway 11 proceeding via Atikokan to Fort Frances and Rainy River.

Highway 11 from Huntsville to North Bay, Cobalt & Timmins

From Huntsville, Highway 11 travels north past **Arrowhead Provincial Park** (**© 705/789-5105**), which has close to 400 campsites. The road heads through the town of Burk's Falls, at the head of the Magnetawan River, and the town of South River, the access point for **Mikisew Provincial Park** (**© 705/386-7762**), with sandy beaches on the shore of Eagle Lake. There is also an access point to Alongquin Park east of the town.

From South River, the road continues to **Powassan,** famous for its excellent cedar-strip boats. Stop in at B. Giesler and Sons to check out these reliable specimens. The next stop is **North Bay,** on the northeast shore of Lake Nipissing. The town originated on the northern *voyageurs* route traveled by fur traders, explorers, and missionaries. Noted for its nearby hunting and fishing, North Bay became world famous in 1934, when the Dionne quintuplets were born in nearby Corbeil; their original home is now a local museum.

From North Bay, Highway 11 continues north toward New Liskeard. Along the route, you'll pass **Temagami,** at the center of a superb canoeing region. Its name is Ojibwa for "deep waters by the shore." The region is also associated with the legendary figure Grey Owl, who first arrived from Scotland in 1906 as 17-year-old Archie Belaney and later became a famous author under his assumed Ojibwa identity. In this unspoiled region, Archie realized his long-held dream of living in the wilderness among the Indians: He learned to speak Ojibwa, became an expert in wilderness living, married an Ojibwa woman, and became accepted as a Native trapper. He subsequently published a series of books that quickly made him a celebrity.

Finlayson Point Provincial Park (**© 705/569-3205**) is on Lake Temagami. The small park—only 94 hectares (232 acres)—is a great base for exploring the lake and the many waterways. The landscape is rugged: steep cliffs; deep, clear waters dotted with 1,300 islands; and magnificent stands of tall pines. The park offers 113 secluded campsites (many on the lakeshore), plus canoeing, boating, swimming, fishing, hiking, and biking.

Lady Evelyn Smoothwater Provincial Park is 45km (28 miles) northwest of Temagami and encompasses the highest point of land in Ontario: Maple Mountain and Ishpatina Ridge. There are plenty of waterfalls along the Lady Evelyn River, with Helen Falls cascading more than 24m (79 ft.). White-water skills are required for river travel. There are no facilities. For details, contact District Manager, **Temagami District,** Ministry of Natural Resources, Temagami (✆ **705/569-3205**).

The next stop is **Cobalt,** where silver mines were discovered in 1903. Legend has it that blacksmith Fred LaRose threw his hammer at what he thought were fox's eyes, but he hit one of the world's richest silver veins. Cobalt was also in the ore; hence the name of the town. By 1905, a mining stampede extended to Gowganda, Kirkland Lake, and Porcupine. A little farther north, **New Liskeard** is at the northern end of Lake Timikaming and at the mouth of the Wabi River. Strangely, this is a dairy center, thanks to the "Little Clay Belt," a glacial lake bed that explains the acres of farmland among the rock and forest.

Even farther north, **Kap-kig-iwan Provincial Park** (✆ **705/544-2050**) lies just outside **Englehart,** also the name of the river that rushes through the park, and is famous for its "high falls," or *kap-kig-iwan*. Recreational facilities are limited to 64 campsites and self-guided trails. Further along Highway 11, **Kirkland Lake** is the source for more than a fifth of Canada's gold. At **Iroquois Falls,** a town on the Abitibi River, you can take Route 101 southwest to **Timmins.** Along the way, you'll pass the access road to **Kettle Lakes Provincial Park** (896 Riverside Dr.; ✆ **705/363-3511**), named for the glacial depressions that dot the landscape. It has 137 camping sites, five trails, three small beaches, and 22 lakes to fish and enjoy.

In Timmins, you can take the **Timmins Underground Gold Mine Tour** (James Reid Rd.; ✆ **800/387-8466** or 705/360-8500; www.timminsgoldminetour.com). Discovered by Benny Hollinger in 1909, it produced hundreds of millions of dollars of gold in its day. You put on helmets, overalls, and boots, and grab a torch before walking down into the mine to observe a scaling bar, slusher, mucking machine, and furnace—all at work. At the surface is a panoramic view from the Jupiter Headframe and ore samples along the Prospector's Trail. Admission is C$19 adults, C$17 students, and C$8 for surface tours only. In July and August, tours are offered daily at 9:30, 11:30am, 1:30, and 3pm. For the rest of the year, two tours are offered each day, though it's essential to call ahead, as the center isn't open every day.

Adjacent to the gold mine is a center dedicated to a more recent—but just as valuable—Timmins export: Shania Twain. The country-pop singer's hometown has dedicated a **Shania Twain Centre** (220 Algonquin Blvd. E.; ✆ **800/387-8466** or 705/360-8510; www.shaniatwaincentre.com), which opened in June 2001. Filled with memorabilia detailing the star's climb, this is really just for devoted fans—particularly those willing to shell out good money to see displays such as Shania's suede parka. Admission is C$9 adults, C$7 students and seniors. A combined ticket with the gold mine is C$23 adults, C$20 students and seniors. It is open daily 10am to 5pm.

For additional city information, contact the **Tourism Timmins** (220 Algonquin Blvd. E.; ✆ **800/387-8466** or 705/360-2619; www.tourismtimmins.com). June through August, hours are daily from 10am to 4pm, and noon to 3pm during the rest of the year.

Cochrane: Starting Point of the Polar Bear Express

Back on Highway 11, the next stop is **Cochrane,** at the junction of the Canadian National Railway and the Ontario Northland Railway. From here, the famous ***Polar Bear Express*** ★ departs to Moosonee and Moose Factory, making one of the world's great railroad/nature excursions. The train travels 4½ hours, 300km (186 miles) from Cochrane along the Abitibi and Moose rivers to Moosonee on James Bay, gateway to the Arctic.

Northern Ontario

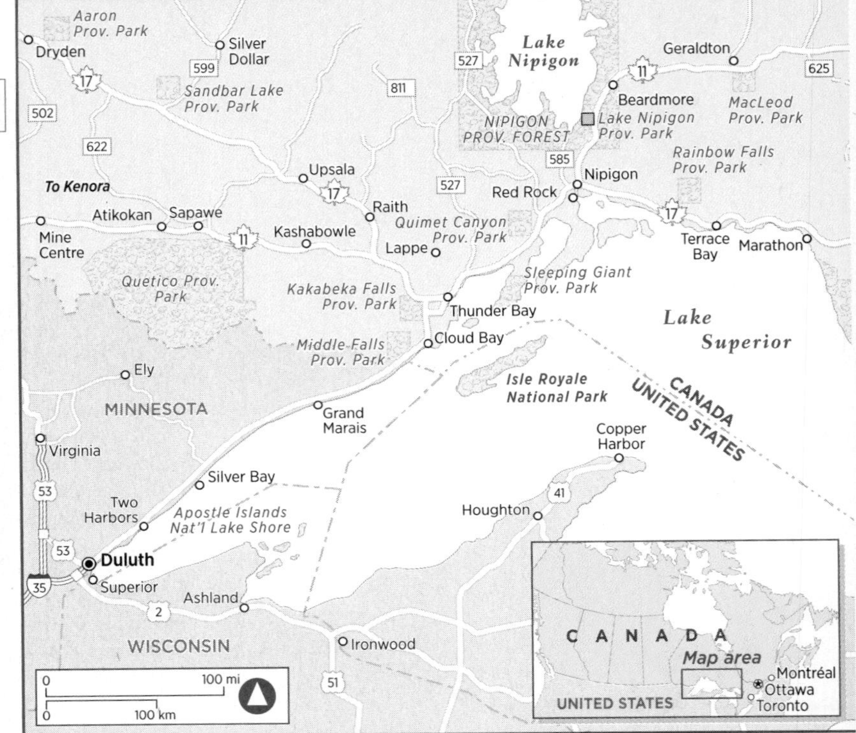

Your destination, **Moosonee** and **Moose Factory,** on an island in the river, will introduce you to frontier life—still challenging, though it's easier today than when Native Cree and fur traders traveled the rivers and wrenched a living from the land hundreds of years ago. You can take the cruiser ***Polar Princess*** or a freighter-canoe across to Moose Factory (site of the Hudson's Bay Company, founded in 1673) and see the 17th-century Anglican church and other sights. If you stay over, you can also visit **Fossil Island,** where you can see 350-million-year-old fossils in the rocks, and the **Shipsands Waterfowl Sanctuary,** where you might spot some rare birds.

Trains operate the end of June to Labour Day, but tickets are limited (priority is given to the excursion passengers). Round-trip fares are C$105 adults, C$53 children 2 to 11. Various 3-day/2-night and 4-day/3-night packages are also offered from North Bay and Toronto. Contact **Ontario Northland** (✆ **800/268-9281** or 705/272-5338, ext. 28; www.ontarionorthland.ca). From June to Labour Day, you'll need to make lodging reservations well in advance.

For information, contact the **Corporation of the Town of Cochrane** (✆ **705/272-4361;** www.town.cochrane.on.ca).

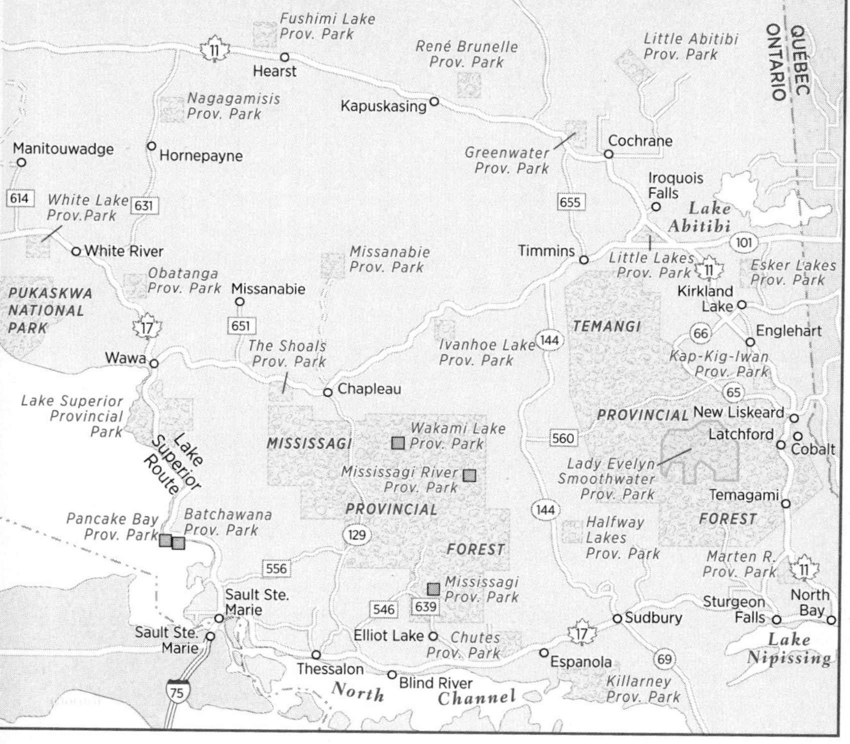

WHERE TO STAY

The accommodations in this area are low-key—think motels and B&Bs. To see what's available, contact the **James Bay Frontier Travel Association** (✆ **800/461-3766** or 705/360-1989; www.jamesbayfrontier.com).

En Route from Cochrane to Nipigon

From Cochrane, Highway 11 loops farther north past the turnoff to **Greenwater Provincial Park** (✆ **705/272-6335**). This 5,350-hectare (13,220-acre) park has good camping (90 sites in three campgrounds), swimming, boating (rentals available), hiking, and fishing on 26 lakes. If you're looking for a challenging hike, try the trail that goes along Commando Lake, and if you're there at the right time of year, watch for the spectacular northern lights.

Highway 11 continues west past **Rene Brunelle Provincial Park** (✆ **705/367-2692**) and **Kapuskasing,** where General Motors has a cold-weather testing facility, to **Hearst.** Canada's "Moose Capital" is situated at the northern terminus of the Algoma Central railway, which continues all the way to **Lake Nipigon Provincial**

Park (© **807/887-5000**) on the shores of Lake Nipigon, famous for black-sand beaches. Facilities include 60 camping sites, boat rentals, and self-guided trails.

The nearby town of **Nipigon** stands on Lake Superior at the mouth of the Nipigon River. It's where the world-record brook trout, weighing 6.5kg (14 lb.), was caught. At this point, highways 17 and 11 join and head to Thunder Bay.

Traveling Highway 17 Along the Perimeter of the Great Lakes

Instead of traveling north from North Bay up Highway 11 to explore the northern mining frontier, you could choose to take Highway 17 along the perimeter of the Great Lakes—the more scenic and interesting route.

SUDBURY

The road travels past Lake Nipissing through Sturgeon Falls to **Sudbury,** a nickel-mining center. With a population of 160,000, this is northern Ontario's largest metro area, a rough-and-ready mining town with a landscape so barren that U.S. astronauts were trained here for lunar landings.

Sudbury's two major attractions are **Science North** (100 Ramsey Lake Rd.; © **705/522-3701,** or 705/522-3700 for recorded info; www.sciencenorth.ca) and the **Dynamic Earth** (formerly the Big Nickel Mine; 122 Big Nickel Rd.; © **705/522-3701;** www.dynamicearth.ca). The more impressive of the two is **Science North,** which occupies two giant stainless-steel snowflake-shaped buildings dramatically cut into a rock outcrop overlooking Lake Ramsey. You can conduct experiments such as simulating a hurricane, monitoring earthquakes on a seismograph, or observing the sun through a solar telescope. In addition to the exhibits, a 3-D film/laser experience, *Shooting Star,* takes you on a journey 5 billion years into the past, charting the formation of the Sudbury Basin. A performance in another theater tells the story of the naturalist Grey Owl. There's also a water playground (kids can play, and adults can build a sailboat), space-exploration and weather command centers, and a fossil-identification workshop. It's open daily May and June 9am to 5pm and July to Canadian Thanksgiving (U.S. Columbus Day) 9am to 6pm; call ahead for winter hours (usually 10am–4pm). **Dynamic Earth** explores life under the surface of our planet. The 9m (30-ft.) replica of a Canadian nickel remains from this destination's former life as the Big Nickel Mine. It's open daily March and April 10am to 4pm, May and June 9am to 5pm, July through Labour Day 9am to 6pm, mid-September to mid-December 10am to 4pm, and closed January and February. Admission to both Science North and Dynamic Earth is C$40 adults, C$30 seniors and children. Admission to Science North only is C$18 adults, C$15 students and seniors. Admission to Dynamic Earth only is C$16 adults, C$13 seniors and children. (The dual admission is more expensive because it also includes admission to an IMAX film and some other promotions.)

For further information on Sudbury, contact **Sudbury Tourism** (© **877/304-8222** or 705/523-5587; www.sudburytourism.ca).

Where to Stay

Your best bets for lodgings are the chains—**Best Western** (151 Larch St.; © **705/673-7801**); the **Comfort Inn,** which has two locations in town: 2171 Regent St. S. (© **705/522-1101**) and 440 Second St. (© **705-560-45022**); or **Howard Johnson** (50 Brady St.; © **705/675-5602**).

KILLARNEY PROVINCIAL PARK

Less than an hour's drive southwest of Sudbury is **Killarney Provincial Park** (**✆ 705/287-2900**), called the "crown jewel" of the province's park system. This 48,479-hectare (119,794-acre) park on the north shore of Georgian Bay can be explored only on foot or by canoe. It features numerous lakes and a fabulous range of quartzite ridges. More than 100 species of birds breed here, including kingfishers and loons on the lakes in summer. Four members of the Group of Seven painted in the region: Frank Carmichael, Arthur Lismer, A. Y. Jackson, and A. J. Casson. The park has 122 campsites at the George Lake campground near the entrance.

Killarney is a paradise for the canoeist (rentals are available in the park). Compared to Algonquin Park, it's much quieter and smaller—you have to cross only one lake to find total privacy at Killarney, while at Algonquin, you may have to canoe across three or more. Three hiking trails loop from the campground and can be finished in 3 hours.

For a more ambitious backpacking tour, the park's **La Cloche Silhouette Trail** winds for more than 97km (60 miles) through forest and beaver meadows past crystal-clear lakes. The trail's main attraction is Silver Peak, towering 370m (1,214 ft.) above Georgian Bay and offering views of 80km (50 miles) on a clear day. This is a serious undertaking; it'll take 7 to 10 days to complete the entire trail.

DRIVING WEST FROM SUDBURY

From Sudbury, it's 305km (190 miles) west along Highway 17 to Sault Ste. Marie, or the Soo, as it's affectionately called. At Serpent River, you can turn off north to the town of Elliot Lake, which is near **Mississagi Provincial Park** (**✆ 705/848-2806**) and the river of the same name. The park has 90 campsites and swimming, and offers some fine canoeing. Hikers will find short, self-guided trails, as well as trails from 6 to 16km long (3.7–9.9 miles).

Continuing along Highway 17, bordering the North Channel, will bring you past the access point to **Fort St. Joseph National Park** (**✆ 705/941-6203**) on St. Joseph Island (between Michigan and Ontario) and into the Soo, 305km (190 miles) west of Sudbury.

SAULT STE. MARIE

The highlights of any visit to **Sault Ste. Marie** are the **Soo locks,** the **Agawa Canyon Train,** and the **Bon Soo,** one of North America's biggest winter carnivals, which is celebrated in late January and early February. There's an **Ontario Tourism Information Centre** at 261 Queen St. W. (**✆ 705/945-6941**).

The **Soo,** at the junction of lakes Superior and Huron, straddles the border. The twin cities, one in Ontario and the other in Michigan, are separated by the St. Marys River rapids and are now joined by an international bridge. The Northwest Fur Trading Company founded a post here in 1783, building a canal to bypass the rapids from 1797 to 1799. That canal was replaced later by the famous **Soo locks**—four on the American side and one on the Canadian. The locks are part of the St. Lawrence Seaway system, enabling large international cargo ships to navigate from the Atlantic Ocean to the St. Lawrence River and into the Great Lakes. Lake Superior is about 7m (23 ft.) higher than Lake Huron, and the locks raise and lower the ships. You'll find a viewing station at both sets of locks.

The Algoma Central Railway, which operates the **Agawa Canyon Tour Train ★**, was established in 1899. The Group of Seven shunted up and down the track in a converted boxcar that they used as a base camp for canoe excursions into the wilderness. Today, the tour train takes you on a 184km (114-mile) trip from the Soo to the Agawa Canyon, where you can enjoy a 2-hour stop to view the waterfalls, walk the nature trails, or enjoy a picnic. The train snakes through a vista of deep ravines and lakes, hugging the hillsides and crossing gorges on skeletal trestle bridges. The most spectacular time to take the trip is mid-September to mid-October, when the fall foliage is at its best, but it's a magical trip any time of year. In the fall, fares are at their highest—C$85 adults, C$53 children 5 to 18, and C$28 children 4 and under. In other seasons, there are substantial discounts, though in some cases, there are also changes to the schedule (the winter train stops for only a few minutes in the canyon, so it's a shorter voyage). For information, contact the **Algoma Central Railway** (✆ **800/242-9287** or 705/946-7300; www.agawacanyontourtrain.com).

The surrounding area offers great fishing, snowmobiling, cross-country skiing, and other sports opportunities. Contact **Tourism Sault Ste. Marie** (✆ **800/461-6020** or 705/759-5432; www.saulttourism.com) for information.

Where to Stay

Whatever you do, make your reservations in advance. If you're taking the Algoma Train, the most convenient hotel is the **Quality Inn Bay Front** (180 Bay St.; ✆ **705/945-9264**), across from the train station. You can also try the other chains: the **Holiday Inn** (208 St. Marys River Dr., on the downtown waterfront; ✆ **705/949-0611**) or **Comfort Inn** (333 Great Northern Rd.; ✆ **705/759-8000**). The **Best Western** (229 Great Northern Rd.; ✆ **705/942-2500**), has great facilities for families—a waterslide, bowling, indoor golf, and more.

LAKE SUPERIOR PROVINCIAL PARK

Alona and Agawa bays are in **Lake Superior Provincial Park ★** (✆ **705/856-2284**). The 1,550-sq.-km (598-sq.-mile) park, one of Ontario's largest, offers the haunting shoreline and open waters of Longfellow's "Shining Big-Sea Water," cobble beaches, rugged rocks, and limitless forests. Dramatic highlights include rock formations such as Lac Mijinemungshing, the Devil's Chair, and Old Woman Bay. At the park's east end, the Algoma Central Railway provides access to the park along the Agawa River. At Agawa Rock, you can still see traces of the early Ojibwa—there are centuries-old paintings depicting animals and scenes from their legends.

The magnificent scenery has attracted artists for years, and some of the most famous paintings inspired by the park include Frank Johnston's *Canyon and Agawa,* Lawren Harris's *Montreal River,* A. Y. Jackson's *First Snows,* and J. E. H. MacDonald's *Algoma Waterfall and Agawa Canyon*. As for wildlife, you might see moose and caribou, which once were common here and have been reintroduced along the coast areas and offshore islands. More than 250 bird species have been identified here; about 120 types nest in the area.

Some 269 camping sites are available at three **campgrounds.** The largest, at Agawa Bay, has a 3km (1¾-mile) beach. Crescent Lake, at the southern boundary, is the most basic, while Rabbit Blanket Lake is well located for exploring the park's interior.

The park has eight canoe routes, from 3 to 56km (1¾–35 miles) and ranging in difficulty from easy to challenging, with steep portages and white water. Rentals are available at the campgrounds, but outfitter services are limited. Contact **Township of Wawa Tourism** (✆ **800/367-9292,** ext. 260, or 705/856-2244, ext. 260; www.wawa.cc/tourism).

Where Winnie-the-Pooh Was Born

On Highway 17, 98km (61 miles) from Wawa, is White River, birthplace of Winnie-the-Pooh. In 1916, Winnipeg soldier Harry Colebourne, on his way to Europe from his hometown, bought a mascot for his regiment here and named it Winnie. When he shipped out from London, he couldn't take the bear cub, so it went to the London Zoo, where it became the inspiration for A. A. Milne's classic character. Just outside White River are the spectacular Magpie High Falls.

The 11 **hiking trails** offer short interpretive trails and rugged overnight trails up to 55km (34 miles) long. The most accessible is the **Trapper's Trail,** featuring a wetlands boardwalk from which you can watch beaver, moose, and great blue heron. The 16km (9.9-mile) **Peat Mountain Trail** leads to a panoramic view close to 150m (492 ft.) above the surrounding lakes and forests. The 26km (16-mile) **Toawab Trail** takes you through the Agawa Valley to the 25m (82-ft.) Agawa Falls. The **Orphan Lake Trail** is popular due to its moderate length and difficulty, plus the panoramic views over the Orphan and Superior lakes, a pebble beach, and Baldhead Falls. The **Coastal Trail,** along the shoreline, is the longest at 55km (34 miles), stretching from Sinclair Cove to Chalfant Cove, and will take 5 to 7 days to complete. The fall is the best time to hike, when the colors are amazing and the insects are few.

In winter, though there are no formal facilities or services provided, you can cross-country ski, snowshoe, and ice-fish at your own risk.

WAWA & THE CHAPLEAU GAME RESERVE

From the park, it's a short trip into **Wawa,** 230km (143 miles) north of the Soo, the site of the famous salmon derby. Wawa serves as a supply center for canoeists, fishermen, and other sports folks.

East of Wawa is some of Ontario's best canoeing and wildlife viewing (especially moose and waterfowl) in **Chapleau-Nemegosenda River Provincial Park**—200km (124 miles) northeast of the Soo and 100km (62 miles) west of Timmins. It's accessible from Chapleau or by Emerald Lake on Highway 101 to Nemegosenda Lake. There are no facilities, and hunting is not permitted. Nonresidents need a permit to camp, costing C$10 per person per night. For additional info, contact the **Ministry of Natural Resources Northeast Zone** (190 Cherry St., Chapleau; ✆ **705/864-1710,** ext. 214; www.ontarioparks.com).

PUKASKWA NATIONAL PARK

Southwest of White River on the shores of Lake Superior is Ontario's only wilderness national park, **Pukaskwa National Park** (Hattie Cove, Heron Bay; ✆ **807/229-0801;** www.pc.gc.ca/pukaskwa), reached via Highway 627 from Highway 17. The interior is accessible only on foot or by boat.

In this 1,878-sq.-km (725-sq.-mile) park survives the most southerly herd of **woodland caribou**—only dozens of them. Lake Superior is extremely cold, and for this reason, rare arctic plants are also found here. **Hattie Cove** is the center of most park activities and services, including a 67-site campground, a series of short walking trails, access to three sand beaches, parking facilities, and a visitor center.

The 60km (37-mile) **Coastal Hiking Trail** winds from Hattie Cove south to the North Swallow River and requires proper planning and equipment (camping areas are half- to a full-day's hike apart). A 15km (9.3-mile) day hike along this trail can be taken to the White River Suspension Bridge. There are also backcountry trails. In winter, cross-country skiers can use 6km (3.7 miles) of groomed trails or hazard the fast slopes and sharp turns created by the topography. Snowshoers are welcome, too.

CANOEING THE WHITE & PUKASKWA RIVERS

The White and Pukaskwa rivers offer white-water adventures. You can paddle the easily accessed **White River** any time during the open-water season. Many wilderness adventurers start from nearby **White Lake Provincial Park** and travel 4 to 6 days to the mouth of the White River, and then paddle about an hour north on Lake Superior to Hattie Cove.

The **Pukaskwa River** is more remote, more difficult (with rugged and long portages and a 260m/853-ft. drop between the headwaters at Gibson Lake and the river mouth at Lake Superior), and navigable only during the spring runoff. The best place to start is where the river crosses Highway 17 near Sagina Lake and paddle to Gibson Lake via Pokei Lake, Pokei Creek, and Soulier Lake. Otherwise, you'll have to fly in from White River or Wawa.

Outfitters include **Naturally Superior Adventures** (R.R. 1 Lake Superior, Wawa; ✆ **800/203-9092** or 705/856-2939; www.naturallysuperior.com).

MORE PROVINCIAL PARKS

From White River, it's 270km (168 miles) to **Nipigon** and **Nipigon Bay,** where there are fine rock, pine, and lake vistas. It's another 12km (7½ miles) to **Ouimet Canyon Provincial Park** (✆ **807/977-2526**), at the location of a spectacular canyon 100m (328 ft.) deep, 150m (492 ft.) wide, and 1.5km (1 mile) long. When you stand on the edge of the canyon and gaze out over the expanse of rock and forest below, you can sense the power of the forces that shaped, built, and split the Earth's crust, and then gouged and chiseled this crevasse—one of eastern Canada's most striking canyons. The park is for day use only.

About 25km (16 miles) on, the next stop is **Sleeping Giant Provincial Park** (✆ **807/977-2526**), named after the rock formation the Ojibwa Indians say is Nanabosho (the Giant), turned to stone after disobeying the Great Spirit. Take Route 587 south along the Sibley Peninsula, which juts into the lake. Among the park's natural splendors are bald eagles, wild orchids, moose, and more than 190 species of birds. Facilities include 168 campsites at Marie Louise Campground, plus about 40 interior sites. There's a beach at the campground.

The trail system consists of three self-guided nature trails, three walking trails, and a network of about 70km (43 miles) of hiking trails, including the 2-day Kabeyun Trail, which originates at the Thunder Bay lookout and follows the shoreline south to Sawyer Bay. The park has great cross-country skiing with 30km (19 miles) of trails.

THUNDER BAY

Just before you enter Thunder Bay, stop and honor Terry Fox at the **Monument and Scenic Lookout.** Not far from this spot, he was forced to abandon his heroic cross-Canada journey to raise money for cancer research. To access the remote **Wabakimi region,** take Route 527 north just east of Thunder Bay. It'll take you to Armstrong, the supply center for this wilderness region.

From the port city of **Thunder Bay**—an amalgam of Fort William and Port Arthur—wheat and other commodities from the prairie provinces to the west are shipped out from the Great Lakes to destinations all over the world. Fifteen grain elevators still dominate the skyline. You can't really grasp the city's role and its geography unless you take the **Harbor Cruise.** Other highlights include **Fort William Historical Park** (✆ **807/473-2344;** www.fwhp.ca), about 16km (10 miles) outside the city on the Kaministiquia River. From 1803 to 1821, this reconstructed fort was the headquarters of the North West Fur-Trading Company, which was later absorbed by the Hudson's Bay Company.

Where to Stay

For hotel, motel, and B&B accommodations, contact the **North of Superior Tourism Association** at ✆ **800/265-3951** or visit www.nosta.on.ca. Your best bets are the chains: **Best Western** (655 Arthur. St. W.; ✆ **807/577-4241**), **Super 8 Motel** (439 Memorial Ave.; ✆ **807/344-2612**), and the **Valhalla Inn** (1 Valhalla Inn Rd.; ✆ **807/577-1121;** www.valhallainn.com).

From Thunder Bay to Fort Frances/Rainy River

From Thunder Bay, it's 480km (298 miles) along the Trans-Canada Highway to **Kenora.** Several provincial parks line the route.

Kakabeka Falls Provincial Park (435 James St. S., Suite 221, Thunder Bay; ✆ **807/473-9231**), with its fantastic 40m-high (131-ft.) waterfall, is 29km (18 miles) along the Trans-Canada Highway. The gorge was carved out of the Precambrian Shield when the last glaciers melted, and fossils dating back 1.6 billion years have been found here. The park has several nature trails, plus safe swimming at a roped-off area above the falls. Two campgrounds provide 166 sites. In winter, there are 13km (8 miles) of groomed cross-country ski trails.

Atikokan is the gateway to **Quetico Provincial Park** ★ (✆ **807/597-2737**), a wilderness canoeing park. The 4,662-sq.-km (1,800-sq.-mile) park has absolutely no roads, and only two of the six entrance stations are accessible by car (those at French Lake and Nym Lake, both west of Thunder Bay). Instead, there are miles of interconnecting lakes, streams, and rivers with roaring white water dashing against granite cliffs. It's one of North America's finest canoeing areas. **Dawson Trail Campgrounds,** with 133 sites at French Lake, is the only accessible site for car camping. Extended hikes are limited to the 13km (8-mile) trip to Pickerel Lake; there are also six short trails in the French Lake area (three interpretive). The park can be skied, but there are no groomed trails. Also in the park, on some rocks near Lac la Croix, you can see 30 ancient pictographs representing moose, caribou, and other animals, as well as hunters in canoes.

Fort Frances is an important border crossing to the United States and the site of a paper mill. Here, you'll find an **Ontario Travel Information Centre** at 400 Central Ave. (✆ **807/274-7566**) at the Minnesota border. Another 90km (56 miles) will bring you to **Rainy River** at the extreme western point of Ontario across from Minnesota. The district abounds in lake-land scenery, much of it in **Lake of the Woods Provincial Park** (R.R. 1, Sleeman; ✆ **807/488-5531**), 43km (27 miles) north of Rainy River. This shallow lake has a 169m-long (554-ft.) beach and is good for swimming and water-skiing. In spring, you can fish for walleye, northern pike, and large- and smallmouth bass. You can rent canoes and boats in nearby Morson. The park has 100 campsites, as well as a couple of easy nature trails to hike.

Almost due north of Thunder Bay via Route 527 lies **Wabakimi Provincial Park** (www.ontarioparks.com/english/waba.html), which has some fine canoeing and fishing. It's accessible from Armstrong.

From Thunder Bay to Kenora

Instead of taking Highway 11 west from Thunder Bay (as described above), you can take Highway 17, which follows a more northerly route. Just follow Highway 17 where it branches off at Shabaqua Corners, about 56km (35 miles) from Thunder Bay. Continue northwest to **Ignace,** the access point for two provincial parks.

At Ignace, turn off onto Highway 599 to **Sandbar Lake** (**© 807/934-2995,** or 807/934-2233 for local Natural Resources office), which offers more than 5,000 hectares (12,355 acres) of forest with nine smaller lakes, plus its larger, namesake lake. The park's most notable inhabitants are the painted turtle (whose tracks you can often see in the sand), the spotted sandpiper, the loon, the common merganser, and several species of woodpecker. The campground has 75 sites; the beach has safe swimming; and there are several short and long canoe routes, plus several hiking trails, including the 2km (1.2-mile) **Lookout Trail,** which begins on the beach.

Turtle River Provincial Park is a 120km (75-mile) long waterway from Ignace to Mine Centre. The canoe route begins on Agimak Lake at Ignace and follows a series of lakes into the Turtle River, ending on Turtle Lake just north of Mine Centre. The park also includes the famous log castle built by Jimmy McQuat in the early 1900s on White Otter Lake. Follow Highway 599 farther north to the remote Albany and Apawapiskat rivers, which drain into James Bay.

Back on Highway 17 from Ignace, it's another 40km (25 miles) to the turnoff on Highway 72 to **Ojibway Provincial Park** (**© 807/737-2033**), which has only 45 campsites but offers swimming, boating, and self-guided trails. Back on Highway 17, it's only a short way beyond Highway 72 to **Aaron Provincial Park** (**© 807/938-6534,** or 807/223-3341 for Natural Resources office), where you'll find close to 100 campsites, facilities for boating and swimming, and some short nature trails. Nearby Dryden is the supply center for Aaron.

From Dryden, it's about 43km (27 miles) to Vermilion Bay, where Route 105 branches off north to Red Lake, the closest point to one of the province's most remote provincial parks, **Woodland Caribou** (**© 807/727-2253**). Offering superb fishing, the 450,000-hectare (1.1-million-acre) park has no facilities except picnic tables and boat rentals nearby. It's home to one of the largest herds of woodland caribou south of the Hudson Bay lowlands. It's also inhabited by black bears, great blue heron, osprey, and bald eagles. There are 1,600km (994 miles) of canoe routes. Contact the **Northern Ontario Tourist Outfitters Association** (**© 705/472-5552;** www.noto.net) for details on fly-in camps. Back on Highway 17 from Vermilion Bay, it's only 72km (45 miles) until the road links up with Highway 71 outside Kenora, just shy of the Manitoba border. West of Kenora, there's a **Visitors Information Centre** on Highway 17 at the Manitoba border.

WHERE TO STAY & DINE NEAR KENORA

Totem Lodge At the end of Long Bay on Lake of the Woods, this lodge caters to outdoor enthusiasts and families who come for the fishing and hunting. The main lodge is an A-frame featuring a dining room, a lounge, and decks with umbrella-shaded tables overlooking the water. The timber-and-stone decor is appropriately rustic. The cabins have full modern bathrooms, beds with Hudson's Bay blankets, fireplaces, and screened-in porches or outdoor decks, plus cooking facilities. Rooms above the boathouse lack cooking facilities but do have refrigerators. Management will arrange fly-out fishing trips for guests. Fish-cleaning facilities and freezer service are available.

P.O. Box 180, Sioux Narrows, ON P0X 1N0. ✆ **800/668-6836** or 807/226-5275. www.totemresorts.com/totem.html. 27 cabins, 3 units. C$180/person. Rate includes all meals. Weekly & special packages available. MC, V. Access is off Hwy. 71, 2km (1¼ mile) north of Sioux Narrows. **Amenities:** Dining room; fishing boats; canoes; windsurfers. *In room:* A/C, TV.

Wiley Point Lodge This lodge is accessible only by boat and therefore offers more of a wilderness experience. This is a fishing lodge, offering trout, walleye, bass, and muskie as the principal lures for visitors. (Spring and fall bear hunts are also offered, as well as more traditional hunting.) The main lodge has eight suites, plus there are seven cabins (two- or three-bedroom), all with full bathroom, refrigerator, and screened-in porch. The lodge contains a dining room, lounge, and deck overlooking the lake.

P.O. Box 180, Sioux Narrows, ON P0X 1N0. ✆ **800/668-6836** or 807/226-5275. www.totemresorts.com/wiley.html. 8 units, 7 cabins. Fishing packages C$220/person (based on 2 people/boat). Rate includes boat, gas & bait. Hunting packages also available. MC, V. **Amenities:** Dining room; lounge; exercise room; hot tub; sauna; paddleboats; windsurfers.

MANITOBA & SASKATCHEWAN

by Andrew Hempstead

13

Visitors don't exactly flock to Manitoba and Saskatchewan, but that can be a plus if you like unpopulated, wide-open spaces. Located where the northern Great Plains meet the southern reaches of the subarctic boreal forests, these two provinces boast miles of fertile farmland, beautiful wilderness and parkland, and an almost infinite chain of lakes, making them terrific choices for fishing, canoeing, wildlife-watching, and more.

Manitoba is famous for its friendly people, who not only brave long, harsh winters but also till the southern prairie lands in summer, making the region a breadbasket for the nation and the world. Along the southern border outside Winnipeg, wheat, barley, canola, sunflowers, and flax wave at the roadside, the horizon is limitless, and grain elevators pierce the skyline. The province's northern half, punctuated by Lake Winnipeg and Lake Manitoba, is one of North America's last wilderness frontiers, a paradise for anglers and outdoors enthusiasts of all sorts. Here, you'll find many of the province's thousands of lakes, which cover about 20% of Manitoba (the province is sometimes claimed to have 100,000 lakes). In the far north, Churchill is a legendary destination for viewing beluga whales (in summer) and is one of the world's most accessible places to see polar bears (during the fall).

Five times the size of New York State, with a population of a little over a million, **Saskatchewan,** like neighboring Manitoba to the east, is an outdoor adventurers paradise. Hiking, fishing, camping, cross-country skiing, and wildlife viewing draw visitors to the province's two national parks and 33 provincial parks. The two major cities are the capital, Regina, which is home to one of North America's largest urban parks, and Saskatoon, a progressive university city.

EXPLORING THE PROVINCES

The **Trans-Canada Highway** (Hwy. 1) cuts across the southern part of both provinces. In Manitoba, you can stop along Highway 1 at Whiteshell Provincial Park in the east. You can return to the highway or visit the shores of Lake Winnipeg at Grand Beach Provincial Park, and then head

Manitoba

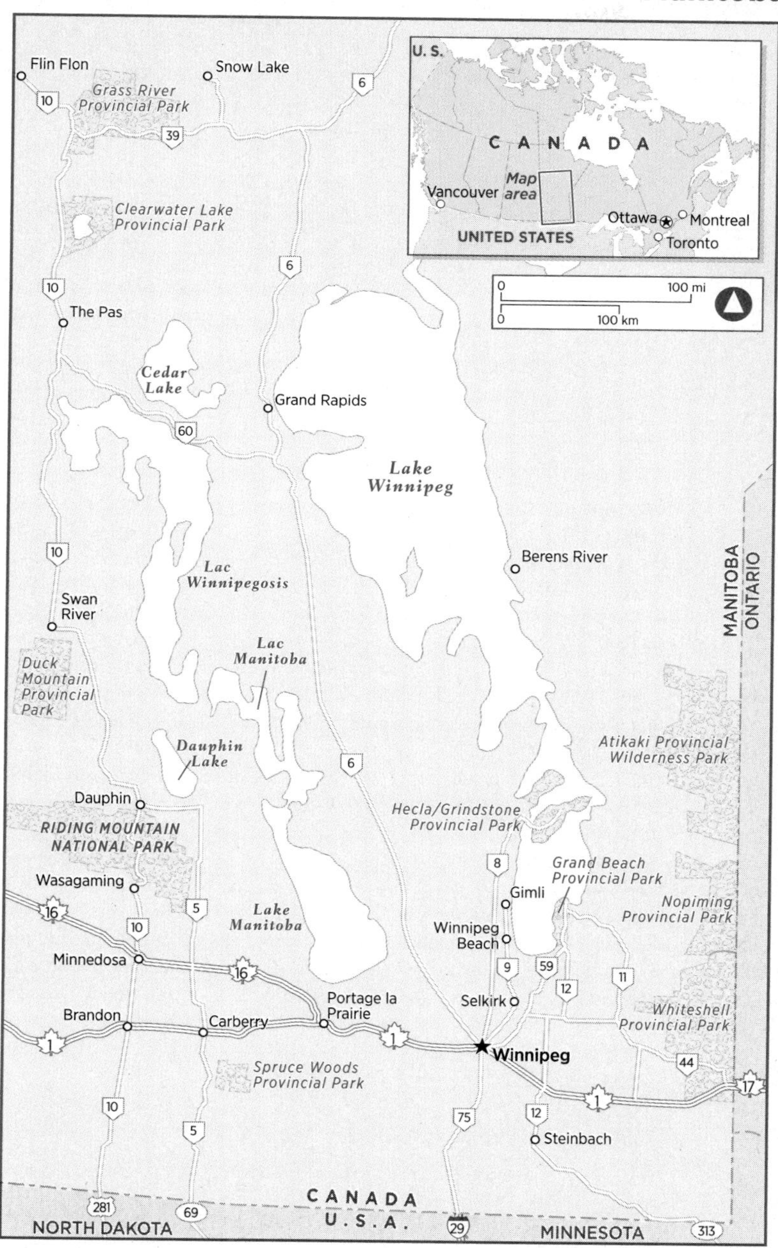

13 MANITOBA & SASKATCHEWAN | Exploring the Provinces

south via Selkirk and Lower Fort Garry to Winnipeg, the provincial capital. From Winnipeg, you can pick up Highway 1 again and drive west across the province, stopping for a detour to Riding Mountain National Park or to Spruce Woods Provincial Park before exiting into Saskatchewan. The only way to reach Churchill and its unique wildlife viewing opportunities is by plane or train. Winnipeg is the main gateway, with both scheduled rail service and flights departing regularly from the provincial capital.

Highway 1 leads west from Manitoba to Saskatchewan's capital, Regina, with a stop perhaps at Moose Mountain Provincial Park along the way. From Regina, it's a 2½-hour or so drive to Saskatoon, and about another 2½-hour drive further north to Prince Albert National Park (Batoche is a worthwhile stop en route). From Prince Albert, you can return via Fort Battleford National Historic Site to Saskatoon and then take Highway 1 to Swift Current, or you can take Highway 4 directly from Battleford to Swift Current. From here, the Trans-Canada Highway heads west to the Alberta border. From Winnipeg, the other driving option for westbound travelers is the more northerly Yellowhead Highway (Hwy. 16), which runs through Saskatoon to Edmonton (Alberta), reaching the Pacific coast at Prince Rupert (British Columbia).

Visitor Information

In advance of your visit, contact **Travel Manitoba** (✆ **800/665-0040** or 204/927-7800; www.travelmanitoba.com). Provincial visitor centers are located at all major provincial border crossings, including Highway 1 (east and west), Highway 16, and highways 10 and 75 from the U.S. Once you've arrived in Winnipeg, plan on stopping by the **Explore Manitoba Centre** at 21 Forks Market Rd., open daily 9am to 6pm mid-May to early September.

For Saskatchewan information, contact **Tourism Saskatchewan** (✆ **877/237-2273** or 306/787-9600; www.sasktourism.com) or drop by a **Visitor Reception Centre** (located where highways enter the province, at Lloydminster [Hwy. 16] and where Highway 39 crosses into Canada from the U.S.).

The Great Outdoors

Manitoba's major wilderness playground is **Riding Mountain National Park,** renowned for abundant wildlife, including bears and bison. Provincial parks of note include **Whiteshell,** which is blessed with an abundance of lakes and waterfalls; **Duck Mountain,** protecting Manitoba's highest peak; and **Grand Beach,** where white sand beaches attract hordes of summer vacationers. For information on Manitoba parks, contact **Manitoba Conservation** (✆ **800/214-6497** or 204/945-6784; www.manitobaparks.com). Manitoba provincial parks camping fees range from C$10 to C$25 per day. For camping reservations, call ✆ **888/482-2267** or 204/948-3333.

Saskatchewan boasts 80,290 sq. km (31,000 sq. miles) of water, and 1.2 million hectares (3 million acres) of land are given over to parks—nearly 400,000 hectares (988,422 acres) alone constitute **Prince Albert National Park,** a glacially carved wilderness laced with hiking trails and dotted with lakes. Don't let the name put you off—**Grasslands National Park** is a surprisingly interesting prairie wilderness, with colorful wildflowers and lots of wildlife. In addition, there are 34 provincial parks. The two best known are **Cypress Hills,** a high point of the prairies that attracts visitors with outdoor activities and well-serviced campgrounds, as well as Buffalo Pound, where a herd of bison are the main attraction; and **Moose Mountain,** renowned for its abundant and varied birdlife. For information about the province's

Saskatchewan

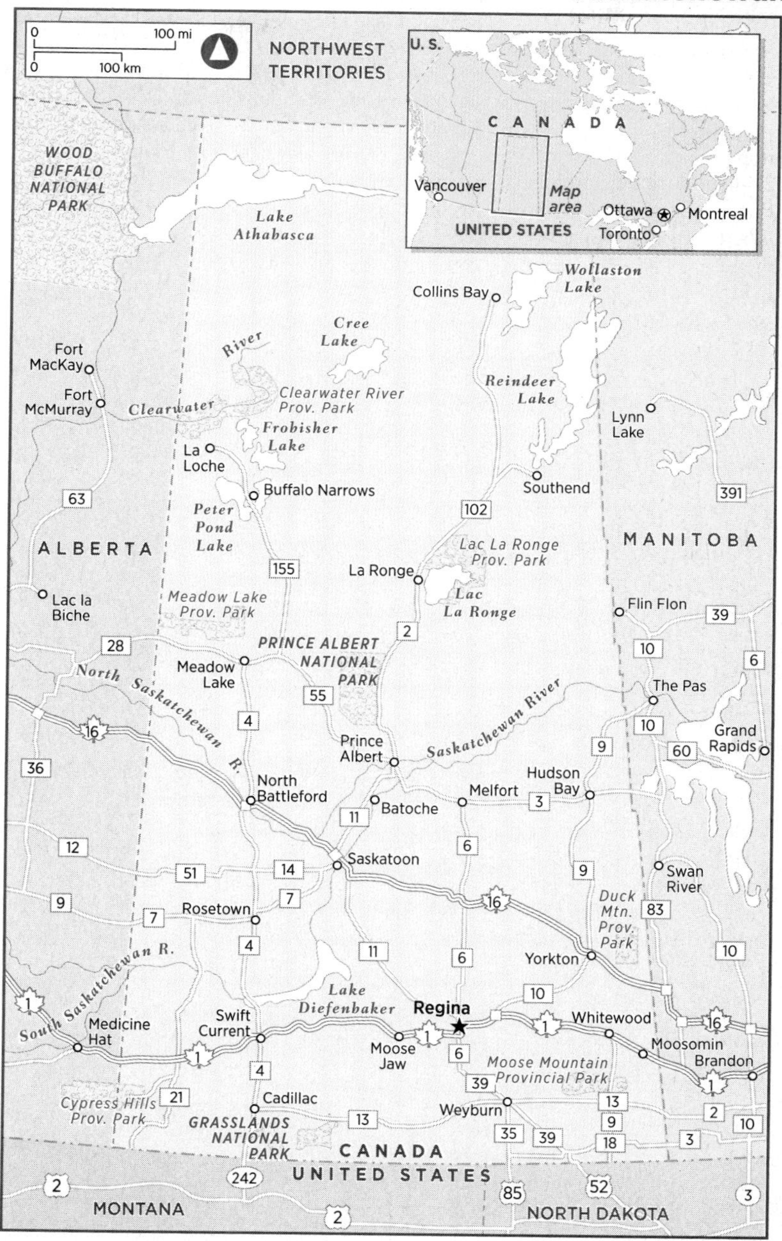

provincial parks, contact the **Department of Tourism, Parks, and Culture** (✆ **800/667-2757** or 306/787-2700; www.tpcs.gov.sk.ca/Parks).

At the parks, you can camp for C$17 to C$32, plus a C$7 daily entry fee for vehicles, or pay C$25 for a 7-day pass. Some parks, such as Cypress Hills, also have cabins and lodge rooms that rent for anywhere from C$65 to C$135 a day.

Summers in both provinces can be simply magnificent, with warm, sunny days and cool, refreshing evenings and nights. Winter temperatures are pretty harsh, with highs usually well below freezing, but that doesn't stop winter-sports enthusiasts.

BIRD-WATCHING In Manitoba, you'll find a goose sanctuary at **Whiteshell Provincial Park.** Gull Harbour's **Hecla/Grindstone Provincial Park,** on Lake Winnipeg, has a wildlife-viewing tower; the Grassy Narrows Marsh there is home to a wide variety of waterfowl. More than 200 species of birds have been recorded at **Riding Mountain National Park.** And many varieties stop near **Churchill** on their annual migrations.

In Saskatchewan, **Moose Mountain Provincial Park** is home to many waterfowl and songbirds, including the magnificent blue heron and the red-tailed hawk. As you may expect, **Prince Albert National Park** has a wide variety of bird life; the highlight is an enormous colony of white pelicans at Lavallee Lake. Finally, the Wascana Centre in the middle of downtown **Regina** is a wide expanse of urban marshland where over 60 bird species have been sighted.

CANOEING In Manitoba, the best places to canoe are Riding Mountain National Park, Whiteshell Provincial Park, Woodland Caribou Provincial Park, Atikaki Provincial Park (on the Bloodvein River), and the chain of lakes around Flin Flon, which is right on the border between the two provinces.

Saskatchewan is one of the world's great wilderness canoe areas. Half of the province is covered by forest, and one-eighth is water. The Precambrian Shield in northern Saskatchewan provides the setting for an adventurer's paradise. **Prince Albert National Park** has some fine canoeing, and plenty of other northern water routes offer a challenge to both novice and expert. Some 55 canoe routes have been mapped, traversing terrain that hasn't changed since the era of explorers and fur traders. You can get to all but three of the routes by road. Various outfitters will supply tents, camping equipment, and canoes; look after your car; and transport you to your trip's starting point. Most are in either Flin Flon, in the remote northwest, or Lac La Ronge, 400km (249 miles) north of Saskatoon.

Churchill River Canoe Outfitters in Missinipe, near La Ronge, Saskatchewan (✆ **877/511-2726** or 306/635-4420; www.churchillrivercanoe.com), offers a selection of packages. Canoes and kayaks rent for C$40 to C$60 per day, or they can outfit you for a multiday wilderness expedition. You can also rent cabins from C$45 per person per day, with a C$125 to C$225 per-cabin daily minimum. The **Canoe Ski Discovery Company** (✆ **306/653-5693;** www.canoeski.com) offers several canoeing and cross-country skiing wilderness eco-tours in Prince Albert National Park, in Lac La Ronge Provincial Park, and along the Churchill and Saskatchewan rivers. The trips last 2 to 12 days. Prince Albert National Park canoe packages include 2-day, 1-night trips from C$375 per person, to 4-day, 3-night excursions for C$850, and are led by qualified eco-interpreters. For additional information on canoeing in the province, contact **Tourism Saskatchewan** (✆ **877/237-2273** or 306/787-9600; www.sasktourism.com) or **Canoe Saskatchewan** (www.canoesaskatchewan.rkc.ca).

FISHING The same clear, cold northern lakes that draw experienced paddlers hold out the chance of catching walleye, northern pike, four species of trout, and arctic grayling. Licenses are required in both provinces.

Since Manitoba has strong catch-and-release and barbless-hook programs, the number of trophy fish is high. The province is also known as one of the best places in Canada to hook a monster channel catfish, particularly along the Red and Bloodvein rivers. Good fishing abounds in **Whiteshell** and **Duck Mountain provincial parks,** the lake chains around the **Pas** and **Flin Flon,** and in fly-in areas up north. For a selection of outfitters, visit the **Manitoba Lodges and Outfitters Association** website (www.mloa.com).

In Saskatchewan, **La Ronge, Wollaston,** and **Reindeer** are just a few of the lakes so densely inhabited by northern pike and walleye that you can practically pluck them from the clear waters. More than 300 northern outfitters—both fly-in and drive-in camps—offer equipment, accommodations, and experienced guides to take you to the best fishing spots. Rates for packages vary—commonly in the range of C$1,400 to C$3,800 per person per week, including transportation, meals, boat, guide, and accommodations. Contact the **Saskatchewan Outfitters Association** (✆ **306/763-5434;** www.soa.ca). A motorboat rental will cost about C$120 to C$250 per day, and guide services run about C$100 to C$250 per day.

WILDLIFE VIEWING Manitoba's **Riding Mountain National Park** is a prime destination for wildlife enthusiasts, who may be able to spot moose, coyote, wolf, lynx, black bear, beaver, and more—even a bison herd. **Grass River Provincial Park** is home to moose and woodland caribou. **Churchill,** in the far northern part of the province, is a fantastic place for viewing polar bears. During the summer, you can use Churchill as a base for day trips to see beluga whales in the mouth of the Churchill River.

In Saskatchewan, **Prince Albert National Park** is the place to be; you'll be able to spot and photograph moose, elk, caribou, bison, black bears, and more. It'll come as no surprise that moose live in **Moose Mountain Provincial Park,** where their neighbors include deer, elk, beaver, muskrat, and coyote. You can also spot adorable black-tailed prairie dogs in **Grasslands National Park.**

WINNIPEG ★★

572km (355 miles) E of Regina, 697km (433 miles) NW of Minneapolis, 235km (146 miles) N of Grand Forks

Tough, sturdy, muscular, Midwestern—that's Winnipeg, Manitoba's capital. The history of its rich architecture—brick warehouses, quarried stone banks, railroad depots, and grain elevators—all testify to its historical role as a distribution-and-supply center, first for furs and then for agricultural products. It's a toiling city where about 650,000 inhabitants sizzle in summer and shovel in winter.

That's one side. The other is a city and populace that have produced a symphony orchestra that triumphed in New York, the first Royal ballet company in the British Commonwealth, and a theater-and-arts complex worthy of any national capital.

As a hard-working city in the midst of the prairies, Winnipeg has a lot in common with Chicago. Although a smaller city, Winnipeg also has a long history of immigrant assimilation and, due to its cultural mix, an extremely rich restaurant scene.

Essentials

GETTING THERE **Winnipeg International Airport** (✆ **204/987-9402;** www.waa.ca) is a 20-minute drive west-northwest of the city center (allow 30–40 min. in rush hours). You can get from the airport to downtown by taxi for C$18 to C$25, or by city bus on **Winnipeg Transit** (✆ **877/311-4974;** www.winnipegtransit.com) for C$2.35. Buses run from the south corner of the main terminal to Portage Avenue about every 15 minutes during the day, and then every 22 minutes until 12:50am.

The **VIA Rail** train depot is at 123 Main St., where Main Street intersects Broadway Avenue. For VIA Rail information, call ✆ **888/842-7245** or 204/943-3578, or go online to www.viarail.ca.

VISITOR INFORMATION Contact **Travel Manitoba** (✆ **800/665-0040** or 204/927-7800; www.travelmanitoba.com). You can also visit the **Explore Manitoba Centre** at 21 Forks Market Rd., open daily 9am to 6pm mid-May to early September. For specific Winnipeg information, contact **Tourism Winnipeg** (259 Portage Ave.; ✆ **800/665-0204** or 204/943-1970; www.tourismwinnipeg.com), open Monday through Friday 8:30am to 4:30pm, or stop by the information kiosk at Winnipeg International Airport (✆ **204/982-7543**), open daily 8am to 9:45pm.

CITY LAYOUT A native Winnipegger once said to me, "I still can't get used to the confined and narrow streets in the east." When you see Portage Avenue and Main Street, each 40m (131 ft.) wide (that's 9m/30 ft. off the width of a football field), and the eerie flatness that means no matter where you go, you can see where you're going, you'll understand why.

The Forks—the site of the original Winnipeg settlement, at the junction of the Red and Assiniboine rivers—remains a hub of the city, with its historic warehouses converted to shops and restaurants, and the ample riverside green space dedicated to festivals and concerts. Northwest of the Forks is the city's most famous corner, **Portage Avenue and Main Street**—the focus of the city's high-rise commercial district. This intersection is also known as the historic site of the 1919 General Strike and has the reputation as the windiest spot in Canada (it has to do with the way the business towers funnel the prevailing winds).

The Red River runs north-south, as does Main Street; the Assiniboine River and Portage Avenue run east-west. Going north on Main Street from the Portage Avenue-Main Street junction will bring you to City Hall, the Exchange District, the Manitoba Centennial Centre (including the Manitoba Theatre Centre), the Manitoba Museum, and on into the North End, once a mosaic of cultures and still dotted with bulbous Ukrainian church domes and authentic delis.

From Portage Avenue and Main Street, if you go 6 blocks west along Portage Avenue (a major shopping district) and 2 blocks south, you'll hit the Convention Centre. From here, going 1 block south and 2 blocks west brings you to the Legislative Building, the art gallery, and south, just across the Assiniboine River, trendy Osborne Village.

On the east side of the Red River, across the Provencher Bridge, is the old French-Canadian settlement of St. Boniface. Boulevarde Provencher is the main commercial street through St. Boniface, while avenue Taché runs along the riverfront and past the ruined facade of the Roman Catholic cathedral.

GETTING AROUND **Winnipeg Transit** (421 Osborne St.; ✆ **877/311-4974;** www.winnipegtransit.com) offers daily bus transport throughout the entire metro area. Also operated by Winnipeg Transit are Downtown Spirit buses, part of a free service along three downtown routes that link popular tourist areas. A brochure

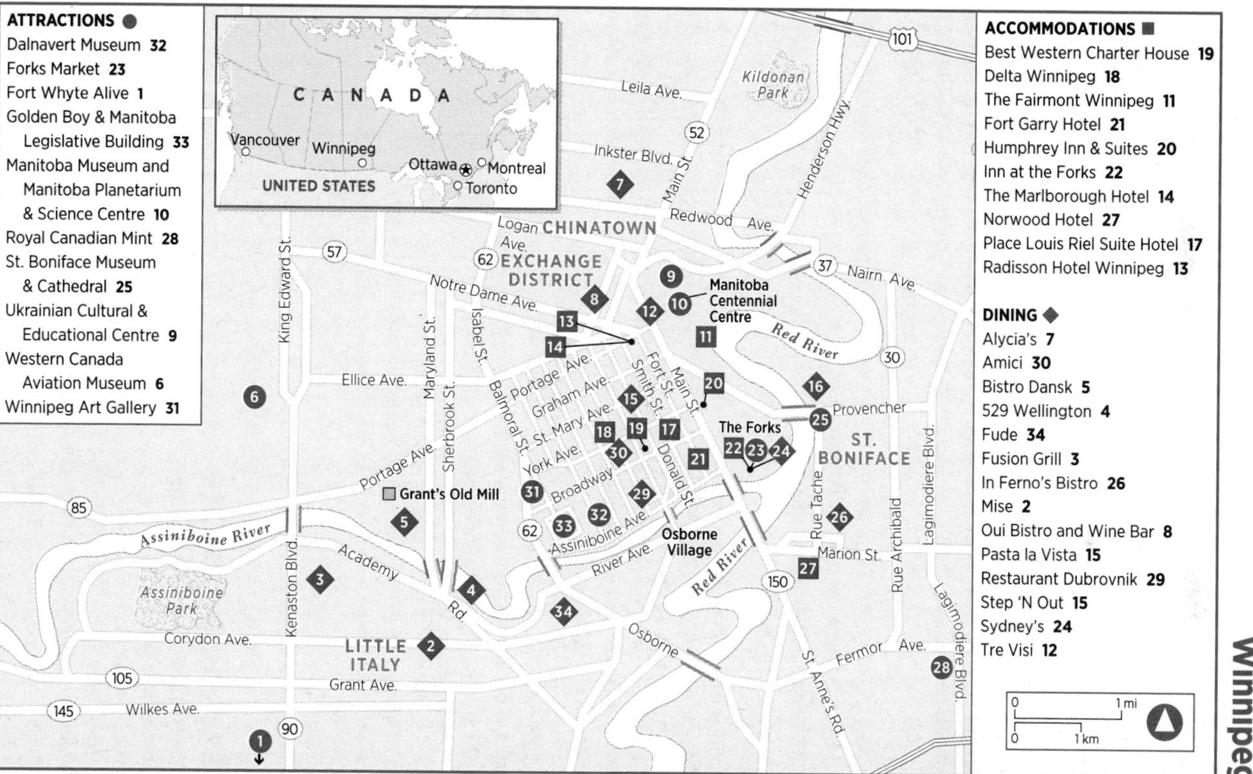
ATTRACTIONS
Dalnavert Museum 32
Forks Market 23
Fort Whyte Alive 1
Golden Boy & Manitoba Legislative Building 33
Manitoba Museum and Manitoba Planetarium & Science Centre 10
Royal Canadian Mint 28
St. Boniface Museum & Cathedral 25
Ukrainian Cultural & Educational Centre 9
Western Canada Aviation Museum 6
Winnipeg Art Gallery 31
ACCOMMODATIONS
Best Western Charter House 19
Delta Winnipeg 18
The Fairmont Winnipeg 11
Fort Garry Hotel 21
Humphrey Inn & Suites 20
Inn at the Forks 22
The Marlborough Hotel 14
Norwood Hotel 27
Place Louis Riel Suite Hotel 17
Radisson Hotel Winnipeg 13
DINING
Alycia's 7
Amici 30
Bistro Dansk 5
529 Wellington 4
Fude 34
Fusion Grill 3
In Ferno's Bistro 26
Mise 2
Oui Bistro and Wine Bar 8
Pasta la Vista 15
Restaurant Dubrovnik 29
Step 'N Out 15
Sydney's 24
Tre Visi 12
CANADA
Vancouver
Winnipeg
Ottawa
Montreal
Toronto
UNITED STATES
0 1 mi
0 1 km
CHINATOWN
EXCHANGE DISTRICT
ST. BONIFACE
The Forks
Manitoba Centennial Centre
Osborne Village
Grant's Old Mill
LITTLE ITALY
Red River
Assiniboine River
Kildonan Park
Assiniboine Park
Henderson Hwy.
Main St.
Nairn Ave.
Redwood Ave.
Leila Ave.
Inkster Blvd.
Logan Ave.
Notre Dame Ave.
Isabel St.
Sherbrook St.
Maryland St.
Ellice Ave.
Portage Ave.
Academy Rd.
King Edward St.
Kenaston Blvd.
Corydon Ave.
Grant Ave.
Wilkes Ave.
Osborne
Provencher
Rue Archibald
Lagimodiere Blvd.
Rue Tache
Marion St.
Fermor Ave.
St. Anne's Rd.
Fort St.
Smith St.
Donald St.
Graham Ave.
St. Mary Ave.
York Ave.
Broadway
Balmoral St.
Assiniboine Ave.
River Ave.

detailing the service is readily available, and your hotel concierge can also help you navigate the system. For regular buses, adults need C$2.35 in exact change (C$1.75 for seniors and children). Call for route and schedule info, or visit the Transit Service Centre in the Portage-and-Main concourse, open daily 8:15am to 4:45pm.

In addition, in summer and early fall, **River Spirit** water taxis (✆ **204/783-6633**) ply the waters of the Red and the Assiniboine rivers. Departing every 15 minutes or so, the covered boats link 11 riverside tourist and business areas, including the Exchange District, Taché Dock (for St. Boniface), the Forks, and Hugo Dock, within easy walking distance of the trendy Corydon and Osborne districts. Tickets are C$3, or pay $15 for a day pass. These water taxis are the easiest way to get to St. Boniface from the Forks, which is otherwise rather a challenge on public transport.

The five car-rental companies based at Winnipeg International Airport are **Avis** (✆ **204/956-2847**), **Budget** (✆ **204/989-8510**), **Enterprise** (✆ **204/779-2422**), **Hertz** (✆ **204/925-6625**), and **National** (✆ **204/925-3529**). Each of these companies also has downtown locations.

You can find taxis at major downtown hotels. Try **Duffy's Taxi** (✆ **204/925-0101**) or **Unicity Taxi** (✆ **204/925-3131**).

SPECIAL EVENTS & FESTIVALS The Winnipeg International Children's Festival (✆ **204/958-4730;** www.kidsfest.ca), hosted at the Forks in mid-June, is a kids' paradise, with plays, storytelling, puppetry, competitions, and live music.

The **Red River Exhibition** (3977 Portage Ave.; ✆ **204/888-6990;** www.redriverex.com), at Red River Exhibition Park, usually starting the third week of June, celebrates the city's history, showcasing agricultural, horticultural, commercial, and industrial achievements. There are also the rural-themed Prairie Town Adventures for kids, a midway, a photography show, live entertainment, and other themed features such as a lumberjack show.

The **Winnipeg Folk Festival** (✆ **204/231-0096;** www.winnipegfolkfestival.ca) is held the first weekend of July at Bird's Hill Provincial Park, north of the city. It is the world's oldest and largest folk-music festival. Over 85 acts perform on five daytime stages and one main stage each evening.

Folklorama is a 2-week multicultural festival in early August featuring more than 40 pavilions celebrating ethnic culture, with traditional food, dancing, music, costumes, entertainment, and crafts. It attracts more than 400,000 guests yearly. For more information, contact the Folk Arts Council of Winnipeg (✆ **800/665-0234** or 204/982-6210; www.folklorama.ca).The 10-day **Festival du Voyageur** (✆ **204/237-7692;** www.festivalvoyageur.mb.ca), held in mid-February in St. Boniface, celebrates the adventures of the original French *voyageurs,* or fur traders, the first Europeans to settle in Canada, as well as French Métis culture.

Exploring the City

THE TOP ATTRACTIONS

Exchange District Just north of the famous corner of Portage Avenue and Main Street is the historic Exchange District, the best-preserved turn-of-the-20th-century district in North America. Now protected from development as a National Historic Site, the area encompasses 20 city blocks and 150 heritage buildings, featuring unparalleled examples of terra-cotta and cut-stone architecture. In recent years, the area has been in great demand as a backdrop for movie production by filmmakers from across the continent. The Exchange District is also home to many of Winnipeg's best art galleries. Check out the **Artspace Inc.** (425–100

Arthur St.; ✆ **204/947-0984**), a six-story building housing numerous arts organizations, including several galleries, publishers, and art studios. For a unique gift, stop by **Botanical Paperworks** (111 Pacific Ave.; ✆ **204/956-7393**), where you can pick up "seed paper" cards that can be planted to grow wildflowers. For more information on things to do and places to go in the Exchange District, pick up the widely available and free Exchange District visitors guide from any tourist office.

The **Exchange District Business Improvement Zone** or **BIZ** (for contact information, see below) offers guided walking tours of historic sites in the Exchange District—including the interiors of some buildings—from June to Labour Day, weather permitting. Tours begin at the Exchange District Info Centre in Old Market Square (King St. and Bannatyne Ave.), daily at 10am and 2pm, lasting roughly 1½ to 2 hours each. The cost is C$7 adults, C$6 seniors and students.

Bounded by Portage, Main, Bannatyne & Princess sts. ✆ **204/942-6716** for Exchange District Business Improvement Zone (BIZ). www.exchangedistrict.org. Free admission.

The Forks ★★ At the junction of the Red and Assiniboine rivers is the Forks National Historic Site, which has been a trade and meeting place for over 6,000 years. First Natives, then fur traders and settlers, found this river confluence a propitious place for settlement. The area was redeveloped in the late 1980s when the old Canadian National rail yard was redeveloped into the bustling **Forks Market** (✆ **888/942-6302** or 204/957-7618; www.theforks.com). A major draw is the fresh-food market and inexpensive market restaurants in the historic rail warehouses—this is a good spot to come for lunch or a light supper. A number of shops and boutiques offer gifts and housewares, while street musicians and magicians entertain.

Other Forks attractions include the **Oodena Celebration Circle,** a shallow, bowl-like platform surrounded by a set of astronomically arranged metal structures that look like fanciful sci-fi creatures, commemorating the region's First Nations people; **Prairie Garden,** which is filled with regional plants; and **Festival Park,** the site of summer concerts such as Folklorama and Canada Day celebrations. The **Manitoba Children's Museum** (✆ **204/924-4000**) and the **Manitoba Theatre for Young People** (✆ **204/947-0394**) are both here at the Forks, as well. In summer, you can stroll on the river walks along the Red and Assiniboine rivers, picnic by the riverside, and catch water taxis to other parts of the city; in winter, there's free skating on outdoor artificial ice or along groomed river trails. Free Downtown Spirit buses connect the Forks to the rest of downtown Winnipeg from beside Forks Market.

123 Main St. (at the confluence of the Red & Assinboine rivers). ✆ **204/942-6302.** www.theforks.com. Free admission. Forks Market open July to Labour Day Mon–Sat 9:30am–9pm, Sun 9:30am–6:30pm; day after Labour Day to June Sat–Thurs 9:30am–6:30pm, Fri 9:30am–9pm.

Manitoba Museum ★ ☺ This museum is a fascinating place, with galleries depicting local history, culture, and geology through life-size exhibits such as a buffalo hunt, prehistoric creatures, pioneer life, pronghorn antelope, tepees, sod huts, and log cabins. In the Urban Gallery, you can walk down a 1920s Winnipeg street past typical homes and businesses of the era. The Boreal Forest Gallery depicts Manitoba's most northerly forested region, while the Grasslands Gallery depicts the surprisingly varied life forms of the prairies. You can climb aboard the *Nonsuch,* a full-size replica of the 17th-century ketch that returned to England in 1669 with the first cargo of furs out of Hudson Bay. One wing is dedicated to the Hudson's Bay Company—with over 10,000 artifacts and artworks that the company began amassing in 1920.

190 Rupert Ave. (in the Manitoba Centennial Centre). ✆ **204/956-2830.** www.manitobamuseum.ca. C$8.50 adults; C$7 seniors, students & children 3–17; C$29 families. AE, MC, V. Victoria Day to Labour Day daily 10am–6pm. The rest of the year Tues–Fri 10am–4pm; Sat, Sun & holidays 11am–5pm.

Manitoba Planetarium & Science Gallery ☺ The planetarium, part of the Manitoba Museum (see above), offers shows in its 280-seat Star Theatre, exploring everything from cosmic catastrophes to the reality of UFOs. The Science Gallery is a hands-on museum containing close to 100 interactive exhibits explaining a gamut of scientific phenomena, ranging from the world's waterways to forensics.

190 Rupert Ave. (in the Manitoba Centennial Centre). ✆ **204/943-2830.** www.manitobamuseum.ca. Planetarium or Science Gallery C$7 adults; C$5.50 seniors, students & children 3–17; free for children under 3; C$22 families; combined admission for museum, planetarium, and science gallery C$19 adults, C$13.50 seniors, students & children. AE, MC, V. Planetarium shows mid-May to Labour Day Thurs, Sat, Sun & holidays four to six times daily; the rest of the year, call for show times. Science Gallery Victoria Day to Labour Day daily 10am–6pm. The rest of the year Tues–Fri 10am–4pm; Sat, Sun & holidays 11am–5pm.

Royal Canadian Mint Canada's original mint, in Ottawa, now produces only commemorative coins, while the Winnipeg facility, which opened in 1976, produces all of Canada's regular coins, as well as currency for countries worldwide (it is claimed that one in four people in the world carry coins made in Winnipeg's mint). The process of making money is mind-boggling, and the tour offered here will prove it to you. Dies are produced; a roof crane lifts 1,818kg (4,008-lb.) strips of bronze and nickel; three 150-ton presses stamp out up to 8,800 coin blanks per minute; and coining presses turn out up to 18,000 coins per hour to the telling machines that count the number for bagging. The whole process represents an extraordinary engineering feat streamlined by conveyor belts and an overhead monorail.

520 Lagimodière Blvd. ✆ **204/983-6429.** www.mint.ca. Weekday tours C$5 adults, C$4 seniors, C$3 children 4–15, C$13 families; weekend tours C$3.50 adults, C$2.50 seniors, C$2 children 4–15, C$10 families. Tours Victoria Day to Labour Day daily 9am–4pm, the rest of the year Tues–Sat 9am–4pm. Take Main St. south over the Assiniboine/Red rivers, turn left onto Marion St. & then right onto Lagimodière. You'll see the mint rise up just beyond the Trans-Canada Hwy. (Rte. 135).

Ukrainian Cultural & Educational Centre (Oseredok) The Oseredok, or Ukrainian Centre, one of the largest such institutions in North America, conserves the artifacts and heritage of the Ukrainian people. The art gallery and museum feature changing Ukrainian exhibits on such subjects as 18th-century icons, embroidery, weaving, painted eggs, woodcarving, ceramics, clothing, and other folk arts. The gift shop stocks traditional and contemporary folk arts and crafts. There's also an extensive library, and guided tours of the museum are available on request.

184 Alexander Ave. E. (at the corner of Main St. & the Disraeli Fwy.). ✆ **204/942-0218.** www.oseredok.org. Free admission (donations required). Sept–June Mon–Sat 10am–4pm; July & Aug Mon–Sat 10am–4pm, Sun 1pm–4pm.

Winnipeg Art Gallery ★★ A distinctive triangular building of local Tyndall stone, the Winnipeg Art Gallery houses one of the world's largest collections of contemporary Inuit art. Other collections focus on historic and contemporary Canadian art, as well as British and European artists such as Eugene-Loius Boudin. The decorative art collections feature works by Canadian silversmiths and studio potters, while the photography collection contains large-scale works by Edward Burtynsky and represents other 20th-century photographers, such as Diane Arbus and Ian Wallace. You'll always find a number of interesting rotating exhibits on display, as well. The Storm Restaurant overlooks the fountain and flowers in the sculpture court. It's open daily except Monday for lunch.

TASTE OF FRANCE ACROSS THE RIVER: THE historic district OF ST. BONIFACE

Across the Red River from downtown in **St. Boniface,** a street becomes a *rue* and a hello becomes *bonjour.* Here, you'll find the largest French-speaking community in western Canada, dating from 1783, when Pierre Gaultier de Varennes established Fort Rouge at the junction of the Red and Assiniboine rivers. The junction became the center of a thriving fur trade for the North West Company, which rivaled and challenged the Hudson's Bay Company. A basilica built in 1819 was dedicated to Boniface, and in 1846, four Grey Nuns arrived and began their ministry by establishing the area's first hospital.

300 Memorial Blvd. ✆ **204/786-6641.** www.wag.ca. C$9 adults, C$7 seniors & students, C$3 children 6–12; C$22 families. Tues, Wed & Fri–Sun 11am–5pm; Thurs 11am–9pm.

MORE ATTRACTIONS

Dalnavert Museum Just 2 blocks east of the Legislative Building (see below) stands the Queen Anne–revival home built in 1895 for Hugh John Macdonald, the only son of Canada's first prime minister and one of Manitoba's premiers. Now a National Historic Site, it's a fine example of a late-Victorian gingerbread house with a wraparound veranda and the latest innovations of the time—electric lighting, indoor plumbing, central hot-water heating, and walk-in closets—opulently decorated and full of heirloom objects. The new "green" visitors center offers a well-stocked gift shop.

61 Carlton St. (btw. Broadway & Assiniboine aves.). ✆ **204/943-2835.** www.mhs.mb.ca. C$5 adults, C$4 seniors, C$3 children 5–17, free for children 4 & under; C$12 families. MC, V. Wed–Fri 10am–5pm; Sat 11am–6pm; Sun noon–4pm.

FortWhyte Alive About 15 minutes from downtown, old cement quarries have been converted into lakes at FortWhyte Alive and now serve as the focal point of a feature-packed environmental educational facility. A 929-sq.-m (10,000-sq.-ft.) interpretive center houses Manitoba's largest indoor aquarium, which displays local freshwater species such as the northern pike and walleye. Outside, you can view a herd of 25 bison on a 28-hectare (69-acre) section of fenced prairie, as well as a prairie-dog town. There are also self-guided nature trails, floating boardwalks, bird-feeding stations, bike paths, waterfowl gardens, a restaurant, and a gift shop.

1961 McCreary Rd., Fort Whyte. ✆ **204/989-8355.** www.fortwhyte.org. C$6 adults, C$5 seniors, C$4 students & children 3–17. MC, V. Mon–Fri 9am–5pm; Sat & Sun 10am–5pm.

Golden Boy & Manitoba Legislative Building There he stands, 73m (240 ft.) above ground, atop the Legislative Building's dome, clutching a sheaf of wheat under his left arm and holding aloft in his right arm an eternally lit torch symbolizing the spirit of progress. French sculptor Charles Gardet created his 5-ton, 4m (13-ft.) bronze statue during World War I. The building, a magnificent classical Greek structure, was designed in 1919 by British architect Frank Worthington Simon. The building's focal point is the Legislative Chamber, where the 57 members of Manitoba's legislative assembly meet. Outside are well-tended gardens and the 23-room Government House, home to the province's Lieutenant Governor since 1883.

450 Broadway Ave. ✆ **204/945-5813.** Free admission. July to Labour Day free tours given hourly daily 9am–6pm, by reservation at other times of the year.

St. Boniface Museum & Cathedral ★ The religious, historic, and cultural home to many of western Canada's French-speaking Catholics was St. Boniface (see "Taste of France Across the River," above), established in 1818. The museum in the old convent house of the Grey Nuns is Winnipeg's oldest building and one of the oldest oak log structures in North America, and it tells the story of the region's early Francophone settlers, with a sharp focus on the story of Louis Riel, the messianic Métis leader who was instrumental in the establishment of both Manitoba and Saskatchewan. Also on the grounds is St. Boniface Cathedral. All that remains of the historic stone structure are portions of the walls and the noble facade—a fire in 1968 destroyed the rest of the structure. The current cathedral was rebuilt within the original walls.

494 Taché Ave. ✆ **204/237-4500.** C$5 adults, C$4 seniors & children 6–17, free for children 5 & under; C$15 families. Mon–Fri 9am–5pm; Sat & Sun noon–4pm. Closed major holidays.

Western Canada Aviation Museum ☺ Among the dozens of historic flying treasures at the Western Canada Aviation Museum is Canada's first helicopter, designed and test flown between 1935 and 1939. There's also a plane-flight simulator, and the Spaceways exhibit, which includes a space-flight simulator, is a great kid's favorite. Housed in a passenger terminal once used by Trans-Canada Airlines, the museum is both fun and educational, as you are able to interact with real airplanes and learn about the history and technology of flight, from early plane designs to spacecraft and everything in between. Children love the Skyways Discovery Zone, where they can sit in a cockpit and learn about gravity through interactive displays.

958 Ferry Rd. ✆ **204/786-5503.** www.wcam.mb.ca. C$7.50 adults, C$5 seniors & students, C$3 children 3–12; C$18 families. Mon–Fri 9:30am–4:30pm; Sat 10am–5pm; Sun noon–5pm. Closed Dec 25 & 26, Jan 1 & Good Friday.

PARKS & GARDENS

Comprising 160 hectares (395 acres) for playing, picnicking, or biking, **Assiniboine Park,** at 2355 Corydon Ave., contains a miniature railway, duck pond, English garden (June to late September), and conservatory. In winter, you can go skating on the pond or tobogganing. The park also contains a zoo (see "Especially for Kids," below). Art lovers will also want to visit the **Leo Mol Sculpture Garden** (✆ **204/986-6531**) to see around 300 works of this renowned Winnipeg sculptor. Assiniboine Park is open daily dawn to dusk. The elegant **Terrace Fifty-Five** (✆ **204/938-7275**) is within a grand pavilion. Tuesday through Sunday, it offers lunch 11:30am to 2:30pm (C$9–C$16) and dinner 5 to 9:30pm (C$17–C$36). Reservations are suggested. In the same building, the **Pavilion Gallery** (✆ **204/888-5466**) houses a permanent collection of works by Manitoba artists. And the outdoor **Lyric Theatre** (✆ **204/888-5466,** ext. 5) provides free entertainment in summer with performances by the Winnipeg Symphony, the Royal Winnipeg Ballet, and local jazz combos, and it also hosts a Canada Day picnic.

Beside the Red River north of downtown, century-old **Kildonan Park** is quite delightful, with landscaped gardens, picnic spots, biking paths, outdoor swimming, and wading pools, as well as a golf course. Also look for the Witch's Hut from *Hansel and Gretel* in the park. In winter, the park is popular for its outdoor skating rink and toboggan hill.

CRUISES & A STEAM-TRAIN EXCURSION

During summer, the cruise boats **MS *River Rouge*** and **MS *Paddlewheel Queen*** depart from their dock at the east end of Alexander Avenue on a variety of cruises, including a sunset dinner-dance cruise beginning at 7pm and a moonlight version on weekends leaving at 10pm. Both cost C$19 adults, C$17 seniors. Two-hour sightseeing trips costing C$18 adults, C$16 seniors, and C$9.50 children 10 and under, depart at 1pm and provide fine views of the city from the Red and Assiniboine rivers. Fares cover the cruises only; drinks and meals are extra. For details, contact **Paddlewheel River Boats** (✆ **204/944-8000;** www.paddlewheelcruises.com). The ticket office is 2 blocks from the dock at 78 George Ave.

A 1900 steam-era train, the ***Prairie Dog Central,*** takes you on a 2½-hour, 58km (36-mile) round-trip from Winnipeg's Inkster Junction station north on the Oak Point line. En route, you get a feel for the prairie and what the late-19th-century immigrants might've seen when they arrived. The train operates every weekend from June to September, plus special days such as Canada Day, Mother's Day, and Halloween. Basic fares range from C$26 adults, C$18 children on the regular steam train schedule to C$28 adults, C$23 children for special events such as Halloween. For details, contact the **Vintage Locomotive Society** (✆ **866/751-2348** or 204/832-5259; www.pdcrailway.com); for tickets, call Ticketmaster (✆ **204/253-2787;** www.ticketmaster.ca).

ESPECIALLY FOR KIDS

At the Forks, the **Manitoba Children's Museum** (45 Forks Market Rd.; ✆ **204/924-4000;** www.childrensmuseum.com) was scheduled to reopen in spring 2011 after major renovations. There are 12 themed galleries, including the water-themed Splash Lab; Tot Spot for toddlers; Lasagna Lookout, a food-oriented playroom; and Engine House, where children can explore the insides of a train. Admission is C$7.50 adults, C$6.50 seniors, C$7 children 2 to 17, and free for children under 2. The museum is open Sunday through Thursday from 9:30am to 4:30pm, Friday and Saturday 9:30am to 6pm. The museum is closed for major holidays.

Assiniboine Park (2355 Corydon Ave.) is a great place to picnic or play. Its top attraction, however, is the 40-hectare (99-acre) **Assiniboine Park Zoo** (✆ **204/927-6000;** www.zoosociety.com), where 1,700 animals of 325 species—including bears, lions, tigers, zebras, bison, and monkeys—are kept in as natural an environment as possible. Some exotic species on display are snow leopards, ruffed lemurs, and Irkutsk lynx. Many spectacular birds live and breed in the Tropical House. A Discovery Centre with a barnful of young farm animals is fun. March through October, admission is C$4.60 adults, C$4.30 seniors, C$3 children 13 to 17, and C$2.45 children 2 to 12; November through February, it's C$4 adults, C$3.75 seniors, C$2.25 children 13 to 17, and C$1.80 children 2 to 12. The park is open daily dawn to dusk, with the zoo open daily 10am to dusk (July and Aug from 9am). To get there, take Portage Avenue west, exit onto Route 90 south, and then turn right onto Corydon.

The **Manitoba Theatre for Young People** (2 Forks Market Rd.; ✆ **877/871-6897** or 204/942-8898; www.mtyp.ca) presents plays for children and teens. The season runs October through May, and tickets start at C$14 for both adults and children.

SHOPPING & ROAMING

Several areas in Winnipeg are known for their shops, galleries, and cafes, and make good destinations for those spending a few days in town to get a better feel for the city and its diversity. These areas are **Academy Road,** in River Heights, trending toward upscale shops and appealing to a middle-aged and older crowd; **Corydon**

WINNIPEG THE bear

When Canadian Army lieutenant Harry Colebourn purchased an orphaned bear cub and took it with him to Europe during the First World War, little did he know that naming it after his home town of Winnipeg would lead its name to be immortalized as one of the world's best known fictional characters. By 1919, the bear had been donated to the London Zoo, where it became known as "Winnie" to hordes of admiring visitors. One frequent zoo visitor was Christopher Robin Milne, son of author A. A. Milne. Learning of his son's love of the bear, Milne was inspired to write a book of short fictional stories about Winnie, Christopher Robin, and their friends. First published in 1926, the stories of **Winnie the Pooh** are known throughout the world by young and old. The bear's link with Winnipeg is celebrated by a bronze statue of Colebourn and Winnie in Assiniboine Park.

Avenue, or Little Italy, known for its restaurants, as well as plenty of boutiques, second-hand and curio shops, and galleries; **Osborne Village,** on Osborne Street, the city's most densely populated precinct, catering to the young and fashion-minded with an almost bohemian vibe and lots of outdoor patios; the **Exchange District** (as described in the section "The Top Attractions," earlier in this chapter), the most historic part of town, with many shops, galleries, restaurants, and clubs; the **Wolseley** (aka the "Granola Belt"), particularly along Westminster Avenue, with shops catering to ecological and spiritual interests, plus bakeries, cafes, and organic grocery stores; and **Chinatown,** between James and Logan avenues west of Main Street, where you can find excellent restaurants, visit herbalists and import shops, and view some beautiful architecture at the Chinese Cultural Centre.

SPAS

Ten Spa (222 Broadway Ave.; ✆ **204/946-6520;** www.tenspa.ca) provides a world-class spa experience atop the Fort Garry Hotel (see p. 495). The C$3-million, 929-sq-m (10,000-sq.-ft.) facility is the result of 3 years of research at many of the world's foremost spas. Ten Spa offers a full range of aesthetic treatments and state-of-the-art steam rooms, with aroma- and light therapy, a variety of mud baths, scrubs, and massage and body treatments, as well as a *hamam,* a modern reinterpretation of the traditional Turkish bath. The full *hamam* treatment (C$219) is a 3-hour journey that includes a salt scrub, steam bath on a marble slab with foot and scalp massage, full body exfoliation, and olive-oil soap scrub-down, finished with a flexibility massage. The entire Ten Spa is beautifully designed, its tasteful modern aesthetic in distinction to the Victorian splendor found in the rest of the Fort Garry Hotel.

Where to Stay

EXPENSIVE

Delta Winnipeg ★ ☺ The massive 17-story Delta Winnipeg, right downtown, is connected by a skywalk to the Convention Centre. This reliable property focuses on corporate business travelers but offers lots of extras for families. Delta's Premier rooms, all with king-size beds, are great for business travelers or for anyone who needs to keep in touch while traveling, with wireless Internet access, wireless phones, and the option of in-room printers. Two secure Signature floors offer concierge service plus other luxuries such as a private lounge with breakfast buffet, afternoon hors d'oeuvres, and honor bar. Standard rooms are large and beautifully furnished—all rooms have balconies. Family suites sleep six comfortably. Throughout, deep rich colors and quality furniture make your stay restful and comfortable. The Delta also offers access to a private health club with full fitness facilities and a large indoor pool. The **Elephant and Castle Pub** is open for all-day dining, as well as billiards, the **Blaze Bistro and Lounge** offers notable contemporary cuisine based on Manitoba-produced ingredients, while **Urban Bean** is the place for a morning coffee.

350 St. Mary Ave., Winnipeg, MB R3C 3J2. ✆ **888/311-4990** or 204/942-0551. Fax 204/943-8702. www.deltahotels.com. 393 units. C$149–C$269 double, C$329–C$569 suite. Children 17 & under stay free in parent's room & eat free in hotel restaurants. AE, DC, DISC, MC, V. Valet parking C$18; heated self-parking C$12. **Amenities:** Restaurant; bar; lounge; babysitting; concierge; executive-level rooms; fitness center; Jacuzzi; indoor, outdoor & wading pools; 24-hr. room service; sauna. *In room:* A/C, TV, hair dryer, Wi-Fi (free).

The Fairmont Winnipeg ★ Don't let looks deceive—at the corner of Portage Avenue and Main Street rises the Fairmont, whose graceless concrete facade disguises a stylish luxury hotel: The lobby is a study in understated chic, a savvy aesthetic that extends to many of the hotel guest rooms. If it's in the budget, step up to the Fairmont Gold rooms. Stocked with lots of extras (the two-room suites have five phones and two TVs), these rooms feature upgraded furniture with walls and upholstery in muted, restful colors. Standard rooms are also comfortable (though they march to a different aesthetic) and offer a choice of two doubles or one queen-size bed. Wheelchair-accessible rooms are also available. An unexpected bonus is the rooftop saltwater swimming pool and affiliated fitness room. The Fairmont is attached to an underground arcade with shops and services such as a hairdresser. The opulent **Velvet Glove** restaurant features luxurious dining amid gilt-framed portraits, wood paneling, and brass torchieres.

2 Lombard Place, Winnipeg, MB R3B 0Y3. ✆ **866/540-4466** or 204/957-1350. Fax 204/956-1791. www.fairmont.com. 340 units. C$229–C$649 double. Additional adult C$20. Weekend packages available. AE, DC, DISC, MC, V. Valet parking C$22; self-parking C$17. Small pets allowed (C$25 per pet per night). **Amenities:** Restaurant; lounge; babysitting; concierge; fitness center; hot tub; outdoor pool; 24-hr. room service; steam room. *In room:* A/C, TV w/pay movies, hair dryer, minibar, Wi-Fi (free).

Fort Garry Hotel ★★ If you love grand historic hotels, the Fort Garry is the lodging for you. Built in 1913 for the Canadian Pacific Railway, the Fort Garry was for decades the city's most opulent hotel. With its towering château style, it was designed to mirror New York's Plaza Hotel. The Fort Garry boasts an elegant lobby and handsome dining rooms and lounges, and the ballrooms are classics of early-20th-century grandeur. For a hotel of this vintage, rooms are spacious and exquisitely furnished with top-flight linens, feather-top beds and pillows, and luxury soaps and lotions. Forget the cheap coffeemaker and stale coffee usually found in hotel rooms; the Fort Garry offers complimentary (and freshly brewed) coffee, tea, cookies, apples, and newspapers delivered to guest rooms whenever required. The quality amenities, exemplary service, and the overall sense of elegance make this a memorable stay. The luxurious **Ten Spa** (see p. 494) sprawls over the entire 10th floor of the hotel and, in addition to treatments and massage, offers a *hamam* (traditional Turkish bath).

222 Broadway Ave., Winnipeg, MB R3C 0R3. ✆ **800/665-8088** or 204/942-8251. Fax 204/956-2351. www.fortgarryhotel.com. 246 units. C$159–C$229 double. Parking C$12. **Amenities:** Restaurant; lounge; concierge; fitness center; whirlpool; indoor pool; 24-hr. room service; steam room; spa. *In room:* A/C, TV w/pay movies, hair dryer, Wi-Fi.

Inn at the Forks ★ This newer hotel overlooks the Forks (see p. 489), the confluence of the Assiniboine and Red rivers, once the heart of a fur-trading community and now a lively market and arts venue. The Inn at the Forks is not just new, it's modern—the decor is sleekly contemporary with light earth-tone colors and lively carpets. Guest rooms are thoughtfully furnished, with high-end linens and works by local artists, which add warmth and focus. The bathrooms feature glass countertops and upscale amenities. If you're here to work, guest rooms have large desks and leather office chairs. For more room, step up to a Deluxe Room—for C$40 or so extra, you'll get a second TV, three-piece bathroom with rain shower, and upgraded amenities such as a Bose Wave radio. The **Riverstone Spa** offers upscale pampering and aesthetic treatments, plus massage, hydrotherapy, and a menu of treatments for men. The **Current Restaurant,** open for three meals daily, serves innovative Canadian cuisine.

75 Forks Market Rd., Winnipeg, MB, R3C 0A2. ✆ **877/377-4100** or 204/942-6555. Fax 204/942-6979. www.innforks.com. 117 units. From C$164 double; from C$284 suite. Free parking. **Amenities:** Restaurant; lounge; limited room service; full spa. *In room:* A/C, TV w/pay movie channels, hair dryer, Wi-Fi.

Radisson Hotel Winnipeg ★ Winnipeg's tallest hotel, the 29-story Radisson, offers very pleasant and thoughtfully equipped guest rooms with great views over the city. The King Suites and business-class rooms are especially nice, with king-size beds, large desks, and ergonomic office chairs. In addition to a full business center, the 13th floor has a large tiled pool, fitness room, two saunas, and an open-air patio. **12 resto** is a contemporary dining room offering three meals a day, or you can grab a coffee from the lobby Starbucks. The Radisson is the most centrally located hotel in Winnipeg—within easy walking distance of most tourist and business destinations.

288 Portage Ave. (at Smith St.), Winnipeg, MB R3C 0B8. ✆ **800/395-7046** or 204/956-0410. Fax 204/947-1129. www.radisson.com. 272 units. C$144–C$164 double; from C$244 suite. Weekend packages available. AE, DC, DISC, MC, V. Valet or self-parking up to C$15. **Amenities:** Restaurant; lounge; babysitting; children's center; concierge; exercise room; Jacuzzi; indoor pool; 24-hr. room service; sauna. *In room:* A/C, TV, hair dryer, Wi-Fi (free).

MODERATE

In addition to the following choices, you may want to look at any of seven **Canad Inns** (✆ **888/332-2623** or 204/269-9090; www.canadinns.com) hotels, a locally owned chain with 12 properties across the province and beyond. Many of their hotels tend toward a Las Vegas–like atmosphere, with casinos in the lobbies, theme rooms, and common areas.

Best Western Charter House Centrally located a block from the Convention Centre, the five-story Charter House was last renovated in 2002. A third of the rooms are designed for business travelers, with king-size beds, lots of work space and large desks, and separate sitting areas. Rooms are comfortably outfitted, and some have balconies. In-house dining is at the **Rib Room** steakhouse, a lively pub with pool tables and well-priced food.

330 York Ave. (at Hargrave St.), Winnipeg, MB R3C 0N9. ✆ **800/782-0175** or 204/942-0101. Fax 204/956-0665. www.bwcharterhouse.com. 86 units. C$119–C$179 double. Additional adult C$10. Children 16 & under stay free in parent's room. Weekend rates, senior & AAA discounts available. AE, DC, DISC, MC, V. Parking C$8. **Amenities:** Restaurant; lounge & gaming room; free airport shuttle; executive-level rooms; exercise room; room service (7am–11pm). *In room:* A/C, TV w/pay movies, hair dryer, Wi-Fi (free).

Humphry Inn & Suites ★ Built as a Hampton Inn and now independent, this modern hotel provides excellent value halfway between the heart of downtown and the Forks, and is within walking distance of both. Even the standard rooms are very spacious, and each has a work desk and comfortable office chair. Another bonus is the free breakfast, which is a hot buffet complete with eggs, bacon, and waffles.

260 Main St., Winnipeg, MB R3C 1A9. ✆ **877/486-7479** or 204/942-4222. Fax 204/480-4612. www.humphryinn.com. 128 units. C$134–C$166 double. Rates include breakfast. Additional adult C$10. Children 17 & under stay free in parent's room. AAA & corporate discounts available. AE, DC, MC, V. **Amenities:** Cafe; fitness room. *In room:* A/C, TV w/pay movies, hair dryer, Wi-Fi (free).

The Marlborough Hotel Opened in 1914 as the Olympia Hotel, the Marlborough today retains its grandiose Gothic Revival vaulted ceilings, Tiffany chandeliers, English stained-glass windows, and exquisite walnut-paneled dining room from a more opulent era. The standard rooms are on the small side, although several have been expanded into very large suites. All rooms boast new beds, comfortable pillow-top mattresses, and 27-inch flat-screen TVs. The most recent renovation also converted an adjoining building into a conference center, making the Marlborough the largest convention hotel facility in Winnipeg, though the moderate prices make this an attractive lodging for the general traveler. The Marlborough also features an indoor pool with small waterslide and a fitness center. Dining options include the faux-medieval Joanna's Café, the English-style Royal Beagle Pub, and the sumptuous Churchill's Dining Room, where the British prime minister indeed once dined. The latter is open only for brunch Sunday 10:30am to 2pm (C$17 adults, C$13 seniors, and C$7 children).

331 Smith St. (at Portage Ave.), Winnipeg, MB R3B 2G9. ✆ **800/667-7666** or 204/942-6411. Fax 204/942-2017. www.themarlborough.ca. 148 units. C$99–C$175 double; from C$320 suite. Children 17 & under stay free in parent's room. Weekend rates, senior & AAA discounts available. AE, MC, V. Parking $8. Pets accepted. **Amenities:** Restaurant; pub; fitness facility; hot tub; indoor pool w/waterslide; limited room service. *In room:* A/C, TV w/pay-per-view movies, hair dryer, Wi-Fi (free).

Norwood Hotel Although you can't tell by looking at this large, modern building across the Red River from the Forks district in St. Boniface, the Norwood is Manitoba's oldest family-owned and -operated hotel, dating from 1885. Bearing no resemblance to its original wooden structure, this is a comfortable and clean hotel with plenty of standard amenities, including free Wi-Fi in even its least expensive rooms. Executive suites add full living rooms, dining tables, refrigerators, and bathrobes. For dining, you can choose between the Jolly Friar Cafe and the Wood Tavern & Grill pub.

112 Marion St. (at Taché Ave.), Winnipeg MB R2H 0T1. ✆ **888/888-1878** or 204/233-4475. Fax 204/231-1910. www.norwood-hotel.com. 52 units. From C$115 double; from C$154 suite. Senior & AAA discounts available. AE, DC, MC, V. Free parking. **Amenities:** Restaurant; bar; room service (7am–9pm). *In room:* A/C, TV, hair dryer, Wi-Fi (free).

Place Louis Riel Suite Hotel ★★ ☺ In the heart of downtown is a friendly, all-suite hotel with excellent, personalized service. Always a top hotel pick, the PLR, as it's known by locals, was practically rebuilt in 2008. Guests may not notice the new room configurations, but they will notice the sumptuous new fixtures, luxury linens, and granite and leather accents. Built as an apartment building, the Place Louis Riel has a great many room types, ranging from studios to one- and two-bedroom suites, all with full kitchens equipped with stainless steel appliances. Courtesy of the new renovation and communicating doors, corner units can expand to include two kitchens, four TVs, two bathrooms and five beds—perfect for a large family traveling together. All rooms feature original Canadian art. The Ground Floor Urban Diner dishes up tasty, inexpensive cooking, with no dinner main course over C$25. This is a pet- and kid-friendly hotel.

190 Smith St. (at St. Mary Ave.), Winnipeg, MB R3C 1J8. ✆ **800/665-0569** or 204/947-6961. Fax 204/947-3029. www.placelouisriel.com. 294 units. C$89–C$150 standard double; C$140–C$175 premier-floor double.

Additional adult C$10. Children 16 & under stay free in parent's room. Weekend rates, senior & AAA discounts available. AE, DC, MC, V. Parking C$7. Pets accepted (C$10/day). **Amenities:** Restaurant; executive-level rooms; fitness room; room service (6:30am–10:30pm). *In room:* A/C, TV w/pay movies, fridge, hair dryer, kitchen, Wi-Fi (free).

Where to Dine

An excellent place for a good Mediterranean restaurant (or a funky bar or eclectic shopping) is along **Corydon Avenue,** south of downtown across the Assiniboine River. Known as **Little Italy,** the area was settled by Italian immigrants and still has a continental feel, with lots of cafes and good people-watching, although the cuisine has expanded to include a number of Japanese restaurants. Many of the restaurants have outdoor courtyard seating in summer. Likewise, the **Osborne Village** area, just south of the Assiniboine River on Osborne Street, is another nucleus of pubs and trendy, casual restaurants, many with patios. Note that most independent chef-owned restaurants are closed on Sundays, and many are closed on Mondays.

EXPENSIVE

Amici ★★ ITALIAN Although very traditional, Amici is at the pinnacle of sublime northern Italian cuisine. You have your choice of 20 or more antipasti (appetizers); try gnocchi with herbed-brie cream sauce and carpaccio (thinly sliced beef tenderloin) for a wonderful combination of flavor and texture. Entrees include traditional but highly refined Italian classics such as veal scaloppini stuffed with asparagus and *bocconcini,* and other richly flavored meat, chicken, and fish classics, plus more innovative Italian-influenced dishes such as grilled duck breast with sweet and sour sauce. The menu changes regularly, but the ingredients are always fresh and the preparations top-notch. For a casual pre-dinner drink, or maybe a less formal meal, visit Bombolini, a wine bar below the main restaurant.

326 Broadway Ave. ✆ **204/943-4997.** www.amiciwpg.com. Reservations recommended. Main courses C$19–C$48. AE, MC, V. Mon–Fri 11:30am–2pm; Mon–Sat 5pm–10pm.

529 Wellington STEAKS/SEAFOOD Situated in a lushly renovated, grand old stone-faced mansion—once home to the family of Winnipeg businessman and mayor, James H. Ashdown—529 Wellington serves up steak and seafood in an elegant setting. Worthy starters include maple-smoked Atlantic salmon or a salad of fire-roasted peppers with shaved garlic, herbs, and goat cheese. Entrees include a massive 28-oz. prime rib, bison, beef tenderloin, or any of a number of fresh seafood choices, ranging from Atlantic salmon or whole Prince Edward Island lobster to sushi-grade ahi tuna. To top things off, the award-winning wine list features about 400 selections.

529 Wellington Crescent. ✆ **204/487-8325.** www.wowhospitality.ca. Reservations recommended. Main courses C$30–C$47. Mon–Fri 11:30am–11pm; Sat 5–11pm; Sun 5–10pm. Take Broadway/Hwy. 1 west, then go left/south on Maryland St., cross the Assiniboine River & turn left on Wellington Crescent.

Fusion Grill ★ CANADIAN This is a hip and fun place serving up some cuisine that takes full advantage of local produce and game. Begin by getting into a different mindset with the "Soup of Tomorrow," featured daily. Then the fusion experience begins. Tantalizing starters may include crispy tiger prawn dumplings with garlic-sesame noodles and sweet soy dipping sauce, or white-truffle pierogies with duck sausage and walnut cream. Daily changing entrees may include seared duck breast with wild-rice potato latkes or slow roasted Manitoba bison back ribs. Fusion Grill is a fun and exciting place—prepare to be wowed.

550 Academy Rd. (near Lanark St.). ✆ **204/489-6963.** www.fusiongrill.mb.ca. Reservations recommended. Main courses C$30–C$43. AE, DC, V, MC. Tues–Sat 11:30am–2pm & 5:30–10pm.

Mise ★★ CANADIAN Very much Winnipeg's restaurant of the moment, Mise is a contemporary two-story dining room where the chefs do an excellent job of sourcing top-quality local ingredients to create a mix of traditional and creative dishes. Choose between mushroom bruschetta and candied salmon watermelon salad for a starter, then get serious with slow roasted pork back ribs and cornmeal-crusted pickerel. Save room for a generous slab of mint cheesecake. In summer, the most sought-after tables are out on the patio.

842 Corydon Ave. ✆ **204/284-7916.** www.miserestaurant.com. Reservations recommended. Main courses C$27–C$30. AE, MC, V. Tues–Sat 11:30am–midnight; Sun 3pm–midnight.

Restaurant Dubrovnik ★ CONTINENTAL Dubrovnik offers a romantic setting for fine continental cuisine and Eastern European specialties. It occupies a beautiful Victorian brick town house with working fireplaces, leaded-glass windows, and an enclosed veranda. Each dining area is decorated tastefully with plants and colorful *gusle* (beautifully carved musical instruments, often inlaid with mother-of-pearl). Start with hearty borscht topped with sour cream, or scallops seared in a curry-lobster sauce. Main courses are very refined—Muscovy duck breast is served with sour cherries and pomegranate glaze, while baked bison filet comes with parsnip puree. Finish with crepes suzette, prepared for two tableside. Rounding out the fine-dining experience is a thoughtful wine list dominated by French bottles.

390 Assiniboine Ave. ✆ **204/944-0594.** www.restaurantdubrovnik.com. Reservations recommended. Main courses C$26–C$49. AE, MC, V. Mon–Fri 11am–2pm; Mon–Sat 5–11pm.

Step 'N Out ECLECTIC Located in St. Boniface, at the end of the Provencher Bridge, this classy but campy restaurant is noted for its unique setting—it's just the spot for an upbeat dinner with someone special. The smallish restaurant is richly decorated, with a huge collection of vintage miniature shoes, photos of Hollywood stars, and lots of plants and twinkling lights, all the better to highlight the superlative food. The handwritten menu, brought to diners on chalkboards, changes regularly to ensure that seasonal products take center stage. Everything served here is handcrafted, from appetizers such as escargot and spinach-stuffed prawns to Moroccan-spiced beef over chilled asparagus. The chef's Australian roots show through in grilled fish dishes and the abundance of pumpkin.

157 Provencher Blvd. ✆ **204/956-7837.** www.stepnout.ca. Reservations required. Main courses C$25–C$42. AE, DC, MC, V. Tues–Fri 11am–2pm; Tues–Sat 5–9pm.

Sydney's ECLECTIC Not so long ago, going out for a multicourse dinner meant out-of-control portions and formal dining according to rules laid down 200 years ago in Paris. However, the prix-fixe menu at Sydney's approaches multicourse dining from the perspective of an upscale, very global tapas bar. For a single price, diners choose a sequence of five courses from an ambitiously large and international menu. Menus change seasonally and to reflect what's cutting edge (the kitchen is very responsive to the latest food trends). Because portions are tapas-size, you won't end up stuffed (and the table buried in plates), and you are able to devise your own formula to assemble a unique series of flavors.

For starters, a Napoleon of candied pears with brie drizzled with cognac syrup awakens the palate. After a palate-cleansing sorbet, the main course may be rosemary-and-black-mustard-crusted rack of lamb with cabernet and espresso sauce, or Greek lamb kebabs with mango salsa. The red-brick warehouse at the Forks serves as historic backdrop for this very up-to-date cuisine. The lunch menu is served a la carte, with all main courses under C$20.

1 Forks Market Rd., 2nd floor. ✆ **204/942-6075.** www.sydneysattheforks.com. Reservations recommended. 5-course menu C$51. AE, DC, MC, V. Tues–Fri 11:30am–2pm; Mon–Sat 5pm–midnight.

MODERATE

Fude ★ REGIONAL/CONTEMPORARY A restaurant with a stated philosophy is usually to be avoided, but when your server summarizes the culinary thinking behind Fude, it's encouraging. As much as possible, all food is made in-house (for instance, all the breads and desserts), and ingredients are sourced in Manitoba. Beyond this, the philosophy goes, eating Fude ought to be fun! Fude's culinary zing comes from its sophisticated forays into world cuisine. The house specialty, grilled chicken breast with chocolate-chili sauce, is available as both a starter and a main course. In summer, diners can sit on the second-floor deck above bustling Osborne Street, just south of downtown. Fude is a splendid example of the cuisine alchemy popular in Winnipeg.

99 Osborne St. (upstairs). ✆ **204/284-3833.** www.fude.ca. Reservations recommended. Main courses C$21–C$33. AE, DC, MC, V. Tues–Thurs 5–10pm; Fri & Sat 5–11pm.

In Ferno's Bistro ★ FRENCH In Ferno's Bistro is a popular and bustling restaurant—with lots of patio seating—in the heart of St. Boniface. While the menu preserves the hallmarks of classic French and French-Canadian bistro cooking—five preparations of mussels, onion soup *grantinee,* and a creamy veal *grandmère* fricassee—it's the more contemporary dishes that truly stand out. Stylized but not precious, an appetizer such as bison spring rolls with sweet chili sauce and a salad robed in mango-chutney dressing is an explosion of flavors and textures, as is salmon ceviche with thin slices of white onion and lemon. The house specialty, braised lamb shank with maple syrup and maple-balsamic reduction, is another great combo of flavors. However, it's the extensive list of seasonal specials that should guide your choice of main courses. For food of this quality, the prices are very reasonable.

312 Des Meurons St. ✆ **204/262-7400.** www.infernosbistro.com. Reservations recommended. Main courses C$15–C$25. AE, MC, V. Mon–Thurs 11am–11pm; Fri & Sat 11am–midnight.

Peasant Cookery ★ EUROPEAN Formerly Oui, a classic French bistro, Peasant Cookery retains the refined ambiance of its predecessor while offering a less-expensive menu of rustic European fare. In an historic Exchange District storefront, Peasant Cookery is stylish room with high ceilings, Belle Epoque mirrors, and golden drapes. Chef Tristan Foucault dusts off classic recipes to rediscover the simple tastes and textures behind the great standards of European cooking. For appetizers, roasted beets and goat cheese are served on a bed of spinach, seared foie gras appears with chicken liver terrine, and escargot is drizzled with brandy. Main courses include beef bourguignon, roasted lamb shank, cassoulet with house-made duck confit and garlic sausages—all enlivened with the best of local ingredients.

283 Bannatyne Ave. ✆ **204/989-7700.** www.peasantcookery.com. Reservations recommended. Main courses C$17–C$29. AE, MC, V. Tues–Fri 11:30am–2:30pm; Tues–Sat 5–11pm.

Tre Visi ITALIAN This Exchange District restaurant has a tiny dining room but a big reputation for serving the city's best traditional Italian food. Tre Visi seems like a transplant from New York, with studied, expert service and a menu that doesn't expand the boundaries of Italian cooking, but instead delivers expertly prepared classics. All the details are exactly right: Spaghetti *puttanesca* is pungent with a touch of heat; *vitello boscaiola,* a traditional veal scaloppini topped with mushrooms and Marsala wine, is both moist and crispy. Gnocchi is one of the house specialties, served with either creamy pesto or deep, rich tomato sauce. The walls glow with creamy golden colors, the better to display the mural-like paintings that flank the always-bustling dining room.

173 McDermot Ave. ✆ **204/949-9032.** www.trevisirestaurant.com. Reservations required. Main courses C$16–C$29. AE, MC, V. Mon–Fri 11:30am–2:30pm; Mon–Wed 5–9pm, Thurs–Sat 5–10pm.

INEXPENSIVE

The **Forks Market** area is filled with inexpensive food stalls and places for a quick bite to eat. Also, both the **Portage Place** (on Portage Ave., btw. Vaughan and Carlton sts.) and **cityplace** shopping centers (at Graham Ave. and Donald St., and linked to the convention center by a skywalk) have large food courts.

Alycia's UKRAINIAN Famed as one of the late comedian John Candy's favorite restaurants, Alycia's is the ultimate place for comfort food and lets you sample Winnipeg's Ukrainian culture gastronomically. The atmosphere is homey and warm, bedecked with Ukrainian knickknacks and art, and the place is often full of Ukrainian diners. The menu prominently features pierogies, potato-and-cheese stuffed dumplings, which can be pan-fried or boiled (Alycia's pumps out 12,000 a day!), as well as cabbage rolls and pickled herring. Alycia's menu also features many North American standards, including plenty of sandwiches on the lunch menu. Prices are extremely reasonable, and the service is quick and friendly.

559 Cathedral Ave. (at McGregor St.). ✆ **204/582-8789.** Reservations not required. Main courses C$7–C$13. AE, MC, V. Mon–Fri 8am–8pm; Sat 9am–8pm. Go north on Hwy. 52 to Cathedral Ave. & turn left.

Winnipeg after Dark

THE PERFORMING ARTS Winnipeg's most important performing arts venue is the **Centennial Concert Hall** (555 Main St.; ✆ **204/956-1360;** www.centennialconcerthall.com), which is home to the Royal Winnipeg Ballet, the Winnipeg Symphony Orchestra, and the Manitoba Opera. The world-renowned **Royal Winnipeg Ballet** ★ (380 Graham Ave., at Edmonton St.; ✆ **204/956-2792** for the box office; www.rwb.org) was founded in 1939 by two British immigrant ballet teachers, making it North America's oldest continuously operating ballet company. By 1949, it was a professional troupe, and in 1953, it was granted a royal charter. Today, its repertoire includes both contemporary and classical works, such as Ashton's *Thais, Giselle,* and *Sleeping Beauty.* The company performs at the Centennial Concert Hall, usually for a week in each October, November, December, March, and May. Tickets are C$28 to C$84, with discounts for students, seniors, and children.

Established in 1947, **Winnipeg Symphony Orchestra** (555 Main St.; ✆ **204/949-3950,** or 204/949-3999 for the box office; www.wso.ca) performs at the Centennial Concert Hall. The orchestra's prestige has attracted guest artists such as Manitoba's own James Ehnes, as well as Itzhak Perlman, Isaac Stern, Tracy Dahl, and Maureen Forrester. The season usually runs September to mid-May, and tickets are C$28 to C$55.

The **Manitoba Opera** (555 Main St.; ✆ **204/942-7479,** or 204/944-8824 for the box office; www.manitobaopera.mb.ca), features a season of two or three operas each year at the Centennial Concert Hall, with performances throughout the winter months. Tickets range from C$35 to C$129.

THEATER You can enjoy theater in the park at the **Rainbow Stage,** in Kildonan Park at 2021 Main St. (✆ **204/989-5261,** or 204/989-0888 for tickets; www.rainbowstage.net), Canada's largest and oldest continuously operating outdoor theater. The theater group actually presents two musical classics, running about 3 weeks each, one in the summer at Kildonan and one in mid-winter at the Pantages Playhouse (180 Market St.). On the banks of the Red River, the outdoor Rainbow Stage is easily accessible by public transport.

The **Manitoba Theatre Centre** (140 Rupert Ave., at Lily St.; ✆ **204/956-1340,** or 204/942-6537 for the box office; www.mtc.mb.ca) presents more cutting-edge, controversial plays in an intimate 300-seat theater. Its four-play season generally runs mid-October to mid-May, and tickets are C$15 to C$65.

The **Prairie Theatre Exchange** (Portage Place, 393 Portage Ave.; ✆ **204/942-7291,** or 204/942-5483 for the box office; www.pte.mb.ca) offers about six productions from October to April and provides the most serious alternative to MTC shows. Standard ticket prices are C$32 to C$42 adults, C$25 to C$32 seniors and students. Some less-expensive shows run on Wednesdays.

CASINOS The tropical-themed **Club Regent Casino** (1425 Regent Ave. W.; ✆ **800/265-3912** or 204/957-2500; www.clubregent.com) offers slots, electronic blackjack, bingo, poker, and keno, plus traditional bingo and the Fountain of Fortune, a series of progressive slot machines. Huge, walk-through aquariums and two live music stages add to the diversions. The club is open Monday through Saturday 9:30am to 3am and Sunday 11:30am to 3am.

The Grand Railway Hotel–themed **McPhillips Station Casino** (484 McPhillips St.; ✆ **800/265-3912** or 204/957-2500; www.mcphillipsstation.com) is your other major casino option in town, featuring many of the same gaming choices as at the Club Regent (both are operated and regulated by the Manitoba Lotteries Corporation). The side show here is the indoor re-creation of an historic railway village, taking you back into Manitoba's past. McPhillips Station operates during the same hours as its sister casino, and both have restaurants and gift shops.

DANCE CLUBS Country-western dance bars used to be a large part of the nightlife in Winnipeg, but the scene is rapidly changing. Even the **Palomino Club** (1133 Portage Ave.; ✆ **204/722-0454**), once the best place to sample line dancing, mostly features classic rock. **Silverado's** (2100 McPhillips St., in the Canad Inn Destination Centre Garden City; ✆ **204/633-0024**) has three floors of dancing to country bands and rock acts, plus DJ-spun dance-floor hits.

Winnipeg's dance club scene mirrors that of similar-sized cities across Canada. **The Empire,** at 436 Main St., near Portage Avenue (✆ **204/943-3979**), features a Roman-themed dance floor in an historic bank building. In the Exchange District, **Alive** (140 Bannatyne Ave.; ✆ **204/989-8080**) has both DJs and live bands, and attracts an older crowd—it allows entry only to those over 21. As dance clubs can be ephemeral, you may want to check out the latest news when you visit town; see *Uptown Magazine*'s website at **www.uptownmag.com** to search the latest club information and listings.

Side Trips from Winnipeg

Lower Fort Garry National Historic Site The oldest intact stone fur-trading post in North America is **Lower Fort Garry** (✆ **888/773-8888** or 204/785-6050; www.pc.gc.ca), in St. Andrews, 32km (20 miles) north of Winnipeg on Highway 9. Built in the 1830s, Lower Fort Garry was an important Hudson's Bay Company transshipment and provisioning post. Within the walls of the compound are the governor's residence; several warehouses, including the fur loft; and the Men's House, where male employees lived. Outside the compound are company buildings—a blacksmith's shop, the farm manager's home, and so on. The fort is staffed by costumed volunteers who make candles and soap; forge horseshoes, locks, and bolts; and generally demonstrate the ways of life of the 1850s. In a lean-to beside the fur-loft building stands an original York boat; hundreds of these once traveled the waterways from Hudson Bay to the Rockies and from the Red River to the Arctic carrying furs and trading goods. Mid-May to September, the site is open daily from 9am to 5pm, although there are no interpreters after Labour Day. Admission is C$7.80 adults, C$6.55 seniors, C$3.90 children 6 to 16, free for children 5 & under, and C$20 families.

Steinbach Mennonite Heritage Village About 48km (30 miles) southeast of Winnipeg is the **Mennonite Heritage Village** ★ (✆ **204/326-9661;** www.mennoniteheritagevillage.com), 2.5km (1½ miles) north of Steinbach on Highway 12, south of the Trans-Canada Highway, east from town. This 16-hectare (40-acre) museum complex is worth a detour. Between 1874 and 1880, about 7,000 Mennonites migrated here from the Ukraine, establishing settlements such as Kleefeld, Steinbach, Blumenort, and others. Between 1922 and 1926, many moved to Mexico and Uruguay when Manitoba closed all unregistered schools, but they were replaced by another surge of emigrants fleeing the Russian Revolution. Their community life is portrayed here in a complex of about 20 buildings. In the museum, dioramas display daily life and community artifacts, such as woodworking and sewing tools, sausage makers, clothes, medicines, and furnishings. Elsewhere in the complex, you can view a windmill grinding grain, ride in an ox-drawn wagon, watch a blacksmith at work, or view any number of homes, agricultural machines, and more. In summer, a restaurant serves Mennonite food at reasonable prices—a full meal of borscht, thick-sliced homemade brown bread, coleslaw, *vereniki* (pierogies), and *foarma worscht* (pork sausage), plus rhubarb crumble is just C$12.

The village is open May and September 10am to 5pm; hours during June, July, and August are 10am to 6pm. On Sunday, the gates don't open until noon. October to April, the museum is open Monday through Friday 10am to 4pm. Admission is C$10 adults, C$7 seniors and students, C$2 children 6 to 12, and C$20 for families.

WHITESHELL PROVINCIAL PARK & LAKE WINNIPEG

Whiteshell Provincial Park ★

Less than a 2-hour drive east of Winnipeg (144km/89 miles) lies a network of a dozen rivers and more than 200 lakes in the 2,590-sq.-km (1,000-sq.-mile) **Whiteshell**

Provincial Park (✆ **204/369-5246**). Among the park's natural features are Rainbow and Whitemouth falls; a lovely lily pond west of Caddy Lake; West Hawk Lake, Manitoba's deepest lake, created by a meteorite; and a goose sanctuary (best seen mid-May to July, when the goslings are about). You can also view petroforms, stone arrangements fashioned by an Algonquin-speaking people to communicate with the spirits. In fall, you can witness an ancient ritual—First Nations Canadians harvesting wild rice. One person poles a canoe through the rice field while another bends the stalks into the canoe and knocks the ripe grains off with a picking stick.

There are six signed interpretive trails, plus several hiking trails you can complete in less than 2 hours. From the visitor center, a 30-minute trail leads to the **Alf Hole Goose Sanctuary,** where Canada geese are often sighted. For serious backpackers, the **Mantario Trail** is a 3- to 6-day hike over 60km (37 miles) of rugged terrain. There are also all-terrain biking trails. You can choose among one of several canoe routes, including the Frances Lake route, which covers 18km (11 miles) of pleasant paddling with 12 beaver-dam hauls and three portages, and takes about 6 hours. There is swimming at Falcon Beach; scuba diving in West Hawk Lake; and sailing, windsurfing, water-skiing, and fishing in other places. **Nature Manitoba** (✆ **204/943-9029;** www.manitobanature.ca) operates wilderness programs and other workshops at their wilderness education center on Lake Mantario.

Horseback riding is offered at **Falcon Beach Ranch** (✆ **877/949-2410** or 204/349-2410; www.falconbeachranch.com). In winter, there is downhill skiing, cross-country skiing, snowmobiling, snowshoeing, and skating. Most recreational equipment, including skis, canoes, snowshoes, and fishing gear, is available from the **Falcon Trails Resort** (✆ **204/349-8273;** www.falcontrails.mb.ca), which also rents lakeside cabins.

Within the park, Falcon Lake is the center of one of Canada's most modern recreational developments, including various resorts with tennis courts, an 18-hole par-72 golf course, hiking trails, horseback riding, fishing, canoeing, and skiing. Most park resorts and lodges charge C$125 to C$225 for a double. Most resorts offer recreational equipment rentals. Camping facilities abound. For more information, contact **Manitoba Conservation** (✆ **204/349-2201;** www.gov.mb.ca/conservation).

Lake Winnipeg

The continent's seventh largest lake, **Lake Winnipeg** is 425km (264 miles) long, and its shores shelter some interesting communities and attractive natural areas. At its southeast end, **Grand Beach Provincial Park** has beautiful white-sand beaches backed by 12m-high (39-ft.) dunes in some places. This is a good place to relax on the beach, swim, hike, or camp.

About 97km (60 miles) north of Winnipeg, on the western shore, the farming-and-fishing community of **Gimli** is the hub of Icelandic culture in Manitoba. Established over a century ago as the capital of New Iceland, it had its own government, school, and newspapers for many years. It still celebrates an Icelandic festival known as Islendingadagurinn on the first long weekend in August (✆ **204/642-7417;** www.icelandicfestival.com).

Linked to the mainland by a bridge, **Hecla Island,** 165km (103 miles) north of Winnipeg, was once a part of the Republic of New Iceland and home to a small Icelandic-Canadian farming-and-fishing community. Today, the island and its surrounds are protected by **Hecla/Grindstone Provincial Park.** Open year-round, it's an excellent place to hike (with five short trails), golf, fish, camp, bird-watch, canoe, swim, windsurf, play tennis, cross-country ski, snowshoe, or snowmobile and toboggan. Photographers and wildlife enthusiasts appreciate the park's wildlife-viewing tower and the **Grassy Narrow Marsh,** which shelters many species of waterfowl. A campground and 17 cabins are available. For campground and cabin reservations at all provincial parks, call ✆ **888/482-2267** or 204/948-3333, or go to http://prssya.gov.mb.ca. Another option is Hecla Oasis Resort (see below).

WHERE TO STAY AROUND LAKE WINNIPEG

Hecla Oasis Resort Within Hecla/Grindstone Provincial Park, Hecla Oasis Resort is a grand old property that underwent extensive renovations in 2008. In addition to updating the entire resort, the remodel introduced a family water park with both indoor and outdoor slides, a full-service day spa and wellness center, biologist-led eco- and adventure tours, a pet spa and culinary studio, and the Hecla Oasis Learning Centre. These join the resort's two restaurants, comfortable rooms, and one of Manitoba's best golf courses, along with hiking and biking trails, beaches, and tennis courts. There are plenty of wintertime activities also, including cross-country skiing, snowmobiling, snowshoeing, and kite-boarding, with plans for an Icelandic Family Winter Park.

Hwy. 8, Hecla Provincial Park. ✆ **800/267-6700** or 204/279-2041. www.heclaoasis.com. 90 units. C$189–C$450 double. Additional adult C$30. Children 11 & under stay free in parent's room. Specials, packages & AAA/CAA discounts available. AE, DC, MC, V. **Amenities:** 2 restaurants; lounge; bike rental; golf course; fitness center; indoor & outdoor water park; day spa; sports equipment rental. *In room:* A/C, TV, fridge, Internet (free).

SPRUCE WOODS PROVINCIAL PARK & BRANDON

About 67km (42 miles) west of Portage la Prairie, before reaching Carberry, turn south on Highway 5 to **Spruce Woods Provincial Park.** The park's unique and most fragile feature is **Spirit Sands,** a 5-sq.-km (2-sq.-mile) tract of open, blowing sand dunes that are all that remain of a massive delta at the edge of the ancient Lake Agassiz. Only a few hardy creatures—including the prairie skink (Manitoba's only lizard), hognose snake, Bembix wasp, and one type of wolf spider—live here. The rest of the park is forest and prairie grasslands inhabited by herds of elk.

The park is on the Assiniboine River canoe route, which starts in Brandon and ends north of the town of Holland. You can rent canoes at Pine Fort IV in the park. The park's longest hiking trail is the 40km (25-mile) **Epinette Trail,** but its most fascinating is the **Spirit Sands/Devil's Punch Bowl,** accessible from Highway 5 on the north side of the river. A network of trails loop through the dunes and lead to Devil's Punch Bowl, a deep sandy depression carved by underground streams. There are also bike and mountain-bike trails; river swimming; camping at the park's Kiche Manitou Campground (for reservations, call ✆ **888/482-2267** or 204/948-3333, or go to http://prssya.gov.mb.ca); and in winter, cross-country skiing, skating, and tobogganing.

Around 200km (124 miles) west of Winnipeg is **Brandon,** Manitoba's second-largest city (population 46,000). This university town features the **Art Gallery of Southwestern Manitoba,** at 710 Rosser Ave. (✆ **204/727-1036;** www.agsm.ca), and the **B.J. Hales Museum of Natural History,** in McMaster Hall on the Brandon University campus, Hwy. 10 (✆ **204/727-7307;** http://flinflon.brandonu.ca/bjhales), with mounted specimens of birds and mammals. Another worthy attraction is the **Commonwealth Air Training Plan Museum,** along Hwy. 10 out at the airport (✆ **204/727-2444;** www.airmuseum.ca), with historical aircraft and artifacts from Royal Canadian Air Force training schools of World War II.

RIDING MOUNTAIN NATIONAL PARK ★★

About 248km (154 miles) northwest of Winnipeg, **Riding Mountain National Park** (✆ **204/848-7275;** www.pc.gc.ca) is set in the highlands atop a giant wooded escarpment sheltering more than 260 species of birds, plus moose, wolf, coyote, lynx, beaver, black bear, and a bison herd at Lake Audy.

The park has more than 400km (249 miles) of **hiking trails.** Twenty are short, easily accessible, and easy to moderate in difficulty; another 20 are long backcountry trails. Call the number above for more info. You can ride many trails on mountain bike and horseback, and can rent both bikes and horses in Wasagaming.

You can rent canoes and other watercraft, or take a lake cruise, from the **Marina at Clear Lake** (✆ **204/848-1770**). As for **fishing,** northern pike is the main game fish, and specimens up to 14kg (31 lb.) have been taken from Clear Lake. Rainbow and brook trout populate Lake Katherine and Deep Lake. The park also has one of the province's best **golf courses** (✆ **204/848-4653;** www.clearlakegolfcourse.com); greens fees are C$50. In winter, there's **ice fishing** and **cross-country skiing** (call the park for permits and information).

The **visitor center** is open daily in summer 9:30am to 8pm, and in spring and fall daily 9:30am to 5pm. For information, contact the park (see above). To get to the park from Brandon, head north about 95km (59 miles) along Highway 10. Entry is C$7.80 adults, C$6.55 seniors, C$3.90 children, and C$20 families.

Where to Stay

In Wasagaming, you can stay at five park **campgrounds,** or in motel and cabin accommodations for anywhere from about C$75 to C$200 for a double. Wasagaming also has six tennis courts, lawn-bowling greens, a children's playground, and a log-cabin movie theater in the **Wasagaming Visitor Centre** beside Clear Lake. There are also picnic areas with stoves and a band shell down by the lake for Sunday-afternoon concerts. At the lake itself, you can rent boats and swim at the main beach.

Wasagaming Campground, within walking distance of town services, has more than 500 sites, most of which are unserviced. Facilities include showers and toilets, kitchen shelters, and a sewage-disposal station nearby. Rates range from C$28 to C$39 for full service. Advance reservations (✆ **877/737-3783** or 450/505-8302; www.pccamping.ca) are strongly recommended, especially on summer weekends.

Elkhorn Resort This lodge is on the edge of Wasagaming, with easy access to Riding Mountain, overlooking quiet fields and forest. Guest rooms are large, comfortable, and nicely appointed with modern pine furnishings; some have fireplaces and private balconies. Facilities include a riding stable, indoor playground, and indoor pool, and there's a lake nearby for water activities. Winter pleasures include sleigh rides, cross-country skiing, outdoor skating, and tobogganing. Also on the property are several fully equipped two- and three-bedroom chalets (with fireplaces, toasters, dishwashers, microwaves, and balconies with barbecues) designed after Quonsets.

Mooswa Dr. E., Clear Lake, MB R0J 1N0. © **866/355-4676** or 204/848-2802. Fax 204/848-2109. www.elkhornresort.mb.ca. 57 units. C$150–C$215 double, C$325–C$725 chalet. Additional adult in lodge C$20. Children 16 & under stay free in parent's room. AE, DC, DISC, MC, V. **Amenities:** Restaurant; babysitting; bike rental; children's center; golf course; exercise room; Jacuzzi; indoor pool; room service; sauna; day spa; tennis courts. *In room:* TV/DVD player, fridge, hair dryer, Wi-Fi (free, not available in chalets).

DUCK MOUNTAIN PROVINCIAL PARK

Northwest of Riding Mountain via Highway 10, off Route 367, **Duck Mountain Provincial Park** is popular for fishing, camping, boating, hiking, horseback riding, and biking. Accessible by road, **Baldy Mountain,** near the park's southeast entrance, is the province's highest point at 831m (2,726 ft.). **East Blue Lake** is so clear the bottom is visible at 9 to 12m (30–39 ft.).

For accommodations in Duck Mountain, the place to stay is **Wellman Lake Lodge** on Hwy. 366 (© **888/525-5896** or 204/525-4422; www.wellmanlakelodge.com), which has cabins starting at C$125 for two. All are modern and winterized, with full bathrooms and well-equipped kitchenettes, plus a covered deck with picnic table. Two have fireplaces or pellet stoves. There's also a beach for swimming. There are three campgrounds in Duck Mountain that offer various levels of service. For reservations, call © **888/482-2267** or 204/948-3333, or visit http://prssya.gov.mb.ca.

CHURCHILL, THE WORLD'S POLAR BEAR CAPITAL ★★

Best known as the self-proclaimed polar bear capital of the world, Churchill is a long way from anywhere. Still, thousands of wildlife enthusiasts visit each summer to watch up to 2,000 beluga whales gathering around the mouth of the Churchill River and, in fall, to see polar bears from specially developed "bear buggies."

East of town, the **Churchill Wildlife Management Area** and **Wapusk National Park** combine to protect one of the world's largest polar bear denning sites. Visit early October to mid-November to see these awesome creatures as they congregate along the shore of Hudson Bay, waiting for sea ice to form before heading out for the winter to hunt seals. In summer, beluga whales frolic in the mouth of the Churchill River. You can often see the whales from the shore, but a number of tour operators offer whale-watching cruises, some with unique options such as snorkeling with the whales. The tundra and boreal forest around Churchill is also vital habitat for hundreds of thousands of waterfowl and shorebirds. More than 200 species, including the rare Ross Gull, nest or pass through on their annual migration, and you can often sight seals and caribou along the coast.

Essentials

GETTING THERE The only ways to reach Churchill are by plane or train. VIA Rail's *Hudson Bay* train makes the 1,700km (1,056-mile) trip between Winnipeg and Churchill twice weekly. (You can also drive 764km/465 miles north from Winnipeg to Thompson and take the train from there.) Passing through a remote region covered with lakes, forests, and frozen tundra, the one-way trip takes over 40 hours. The train leaves Winnipeg every Tuesday and Sunday at 12:05pm. Prices vary considerably depending on time of year and the type of seat or cabin booked. If you don't mind sleeping in reclining seats or a multi-berth cabin, the trip can cost as little as C$330 each way, 7-day advance purchase, in economy class any time of year. A single cabin costs around C$780 one way and a cabin that sleeps two (on bunk beds) is C$1,200. For more information, contact **VIA Rail** (✆ **888/VIA-RAIL** or 800/561-8630; www.viarail.ca). You can also fly into Churchill on **Calm Air** (✆ **800/839-2256;** www.calmair.com), with fares costing around C$1,100 roundtrip from Winnipeg.

VISITOR INFORMATION The **Churchill Visitor Centre,** at 211 Kelsey Blvd. (✆ **888/389-2327** or 204/675-2022), is open from July to late November Monday to Saturday 11am to 3pm. Another source of information is the **Town of Churchill** website (www.townofchurchill.ca). For information on Wapusk National Park, contact **Parks Canada** (✆ **888/773-8888** or 204/675-8863; www.pc.gc.ca).

Exploring the Area

Although the vast majority of visitors who travel this far north do so for wildlife viewing, there are a few other sights in and around town. From an industrial perspective, most impressive are the towering grain terminals along the waterfront. Grain is transported by train from the prairies to Churchill, where it is loaded onto ships bound for European markets. You can watch the grain being unloaded from grain cars onto ships—25 million bushels of wheat and barley clear the port in only 12 to 14 weeks of frantic nonstop operation through summer. Also in town, the **Eskimo Museum** (242 Laverendrye St.; ✆ **204/675-2030**) has a collection of fine Inuit carvings and artifacts. In the summer (June to mid-Nov), it's open Monday from 1 to 5pm and Tuesday through Saturday from 9am to noon and 1 to 5pm, and in winter (mid-Nov to May), the hours are Monday through Saturday from 1 to 4:30pm. Admission is by donation. Within walking distance from town is **Cape Merry,** at the mouth of the Churchill River. This is an excellent vantage point for getting a layout of the town and surrounding wilderness, as well as for viewing beluga whales and seabirds.

You can also take a boat ride to the **Prince of Wales Fort** (✆ **204/675-8863;** www.pc.gc.ca). Construction of this partially restored, large stone fort was started in 1730 by the Hudson's Bay Company and took 40 years to complete. Yet after all that effort, Governor Samuel Hearne and 39 clerks and tradesmen surrendered the fort to the French without resistance in 1782, when faced with a possible attack by three French ships. July to October, the fort is open daily 1 to 5pm and 6 to 9pm. Admission to the grounds is free, though there is a C$8 per person charge for a guided tour. Access is by boat from Churchill and is usually combined with a whale-watching tour.

WILDLIFE VIEWING

From Churchill, a number of outfitters offer polar bear tours (Oct and Nov) and whale-watching boat tours (July and Aug), most of which combine accommodations and airfares from Winnipeg. The polar bear tours take place east of town in specially designed "buggies" (one company calls them "Polar Rovers"), with large wheels and outdoor viewing decks to take you out onto the tundra to safely watch and photograph these magnificent creatures. You may also see other tundra wildlife such as foxes, caribou, and snowy owls.

A week-long tour, beginning and ending in Winnipeg and inclusive of lodging and airfare, costs between C$5,500 and C$10,000 per person, depending on the types of activities and accommodation. One local Churchill outfitter with an excellent reputation, and one of the few to offer polar-bear-viewing day trips, is **Great White Bear**

Tours (✆ **866/765-8344** or 204/675-2781; www.greatwhitebeartours.com). This company charges C$350 per person, including motel pickups in Churchill, although availability is often limited as most seats are booked by tour companies. Great White Bear Tours works with **Natural Habitat Adventures** (✆ **800/543-8917;** www.nathab.com) to provide packages that include airfares from Winnipeg. Accommodations on these tours are at downtown motels or at Great White Bear's Tundra Lodge, comprising mobile platforms parked within the Churchill Wildlife Management Area. Bathrooms here are shared and beds are bunk-style, but the opportunity to stay overnight out amongst polar bears is unequalled. Away from city lights, this is also a great place to view the northern lights. The lodge has a dedicated dining car, a lounge car, and satellite Internet access.

Frontiers North (✆ **800/663-9832** or 204/949-2050; www.tundrabuggy.com) also offer the option of motel- or lodge-based tours. For those with limited time, this company operates a 3-night, 2-day tour for C$2,500 per person, inclusive of airfares from Winnipeg. **Lazy Bear Lodge** (✆ **866/687-2327** or 204/663-9377; www.lazybearlodge.com) offers its own package tours, charging from C$3,700 per person for airfare from Winnipeg, 3 nights' accommodation, and meals, with 2 days spent out on the tundra viewing the bears.

While polar bears get most of the attention in Churchill, in the last decade, during July and August, the beluga whales that congregate around the mouth of the Churchill River have become a major attraction for nature-loving visitors. During summer, daily boat tours offered by **Sea North Tours** (✆ **888/348-7591** or 204/675-2195; www.seanorthtours.com) focus on these magnificent white whales. The cost is C$96 per person for a 2½-hour tour. For a truly unique experience, Sea North supplies wetsuits for those looking to try snorkeling with beluga whales (C$175 per person), with up to an hour spent in the water.

Where to Stay

The majority of visitors to Churchill, especially during the polar-bear-viewing season, arrive in town as part of package put together by local tour companies or accommodations.

The **Aurora Inn** (24 Bernier St.; ✆ **888/840-1344** or 204/675-2071; www.aurora-inn.mb.ca) is one of Churchill's newest hotels, featuring 19 spacious, split-level loft suites with fully equipped kitchens, plus three smaller standard rooms. Doubles go for C$235 during peak polar-bear-viewing season (Oct and Nov), and C$155 or C$125 in shoulder or off seasons, respectively. The **Polar Inn & Suites** (153 Kelsey Blvd.; ✆ **877/765-2733** or 204/675-8878; www.polarinn.com) offers standard rooms, plus one-bedroom apartments and kitchenette suites with fridges and coffeemakers for C$135 to C$245.

Lazy Bear Lodge (313 Kelsey Blvd.; ✆ **866/687-2327** or 204/663-9377; www.lazybearlodge.com) is a log cabin–type hotel with 33 rooms, each with an en suite bathroom and cable TV. The in-house restaurant has a distinctive northern-rustic ambience, with a menu of game to match. Rates range from C$150 to C$280, although in polar-bear-viewing season, most guests are staying as part of a package (C$3,700 per person, including airfare from Winnipeg, 3 nights' accommodation, meals, and 2-day tours). In summer, a 2-night package, inclusive of airfares and a boat tour, is a reasonable C$1,485 per person.

REGINA

257km (160 miles) SE of Saskatoon, 572km (355 miles) W of Winnipeg, 788km (490 miles) E of Calgary

Originally named "Pile O' Bones" after the heap of buffalo skeletons the first settlers found (Native Canadians had amassed the bones in the belief they would lure the vanished buffalo back again), the city of **Regina** (pronounced Re-*jeye*-na) has Princess Louise, daughter of Queen Victoria, to thank for its more regal name. She named the city in her mother's honor in 1882 when it became the capital of the Northwest Territories. Despite the barren prairie landscape and the infamous Regina mud, the town grew.

Today, the provincial capital of Saskatchewan has a population of about 200,000 and remains true to its agrarian roots, but has developed a sophisticated veneer, with creative restaurants, interesting attractions, and a sprawling urban park.

Essentials

GETTING THERE There is no passenger rail service to Regina. The closest rail connections are in Saskatoon.

Regina Airport (www.yqr.ca) is west of the city, only 15 minutes from downtown. It is served by **Air Canada** (✆ **888/247-2262;** www.aircanada.com) and **WestJet** (✆ **800/538-5696;** www.westjet.com) from destinations throughout Canada, as well as by **Delta** (✆ **800/441-1818;** www.delta.com) from the U.S. **Express Air** (✆ **877/392-2582** or 306/757-2582; www.expressairclub.ca) has scheduled flights between Saskatoon and Regina.

The Regina **bus station** is downtown, at 2041 Hamilton St. (✆ **306/787-3340**). Greyhound, as well as Saskatchewan Transportation Company (www.stcbus.com), buses—the dominant public transport services in the province—use the station.

If you're **driving,** the Trans-Canada Highway passes just south of Regina.

VISITOR INFORMATION Contact **Tourism Saskatchewan** (✆ **877/237-2273** or 306/787-9600; www.sasktourism.com) or the **Regina Regional Opportunities Commission** (✆ **800/661-5099** or 306/789-5099; www.reginaroc.com).

CITY LAYOUT The two main streets are **Victoria Avenue,** which runs east-west, and **Albert Street,** which runs north-south. South of the intersection lies the **Wascana Centre.** Most of the downtown hotels stretch along Victoria Avenue between Albert Street on the west and Broad Street on the east. The RCMP barracks are to the north and west of the downtown. **Lewvan Drive** and **Ring Road** together encircle the city.

GETTING AROUND **Regina Transit** (333 Winnipeg St.; ✆ **306/777-7433;** www.regina.ca) operates nine bus routes that make it easy to get around. For schedules and maps, go to the **Transit Information Centre** at 2124 11th Ave., at the Cornwall Centre, open weekdays 7am to 9pm and Saturday 9am to 4pm. Fares are C$2.50 per sector, or you can pay C$7 for a day pass. Exact fare is required.

Each of the following car-rental agencies also has a bureau at the airport: **Avis** (✆ **306/751-5460**), **Budget** (✆ **306/791-6814**), **Enterprise** (✆ **306/359-3535**), **Hertz** (✆ **306/791-9131**), **National** (✆ **306/757-5757**), and **Thrifty** (✆ **306/525-1000**).

You can most easily find **taxis** at downtown hotels. From downtown to the airport, the cost is about C$15. **Capital Cab** (✆ **306/791-2222**) is the most-used service.

SPECIAL EVENTS & FESTIVALS During the first week of June, **Mosaic: A Festival of Cultures** (✆ **306/757-5990;** www.reginamulticulturalcouncil.ca) celebrates the city's multiethnic population. Festival passports entitle you to enter pavilions and experience the food, crafts, customs, and culture of each group. Regina's **Buffalo Days** (✆ **888/734-3975** or 306/781-9200; www.buffalodays.ca), held the end of July into the first week in August, recalls the time when this noble beast roamed the West. Throughout the city, businesses and individuals dress in Old West style, while the fairgrounds sparkle with a midway, grandstand shows, big-name entertainers, livestock competitions, and much more.

Top Sights

While **Casino Regina** is described below as a gaming destination (see "Regina after Dark," below), even non-gamblers will be interested in this impressive gambling establishment. Right downtown, it incorporates Regina's original Canadian National rail terminal from 1911 and features antique rail cars in its dining room and a Vegas-style show lounge; admission is free.

Government House This elegant structure was built in 1891 as home to the British lieutenant governor, the queen's representative who served as head of government for the entire Northwest Territories—which at the time included all of western and northern Canada except British Columbia. Visitors are free to explore the manicured gardens, as well as visit the modern Interpretive Centre, which describes the building and its history, as well as the intriguing role of the British monarchy in Canada today.

4607 Dewdney Ave. ✆ **306/787-5773.** www.governmenthouse.gov.sk.ca. Free admission. Summer daily 9am–5pm; fall–spring Tues–Sun 9am–4pm.

Legislative Building This splendid, stately edifice, built from 1908 to 1912, boasts 30 kinds of marble in the interior. Check out the mural *Before the White Man Came,* depicting Native people in the Qu'Appelle Valley preparing to attack a herd of buffalo on the opposite shore. See also the Legislative Assembly Chamber, the 400,000-volume library, and the art galleries in the basement and on the first floor.

2405 Legislative Dr. ✆ **306/787-5357.** www.legassembly.sk.ca. Free admission. Tours every half-hour daily 8am–5pm; extended tour hours of 8am–9pm Victoria Day to Labour Day. Tours can be arranged through the visitor services office.

RCMP Training Academy & Heritage Centre ★★ This is the primary training facility for the Royal Canadian Mounted Police, or the Mounties, who function as both Canada's national police and the country's version of the FBI. Tours of the training grounds and academy are offered Monday to Friday at 1:30pm. In addition to visiting the **chapel**—the oldest building in Regina—you can watch fledgling Mounties strut their stuff during **Sergeant Major's Parade,** which normally takes place around 12:45pm Monday, Wednesday, and Friday. The schedule is tentative, so call before you go. From July through mid-August, the **Sunset-Retreat Ceremony**—an event that dates from the RCMP's roots—takes place on Tuesdays just after 6:45pm; it's an exciting 45-minute display of horsemanship by the Mounties accompanied by pipe and bugle bands.

In addition to these activities, the RCMP Heritage Centre traces the fascinating history of the Royal Canadian Mounted Police since 1874, when they began the

Great March West to stop liquor traffic and enforce the law in the Northwest Territories. In six different galleries, the museum documents the lives of the early Mounties and pioneers using replicas, newspaper articles, artifacts, uniforms, weaponry, and mementos to illustrate the Mounties' role in the 1885 Riel Rebellion, the Klondike Gold Rush, the Prohibition era, World Wars I and II, the 1935 Regina labor riot, the capture of the mad trapper (who was pursued in arctic temperatures for 54 days in 1931–1932), and modern policing techniques. In addition to the main exhibits, the RCMP Heritage Centre offers an impressive 27-minute multimedia presentation called "Tour of Duty"—it's definitely worth seeing.

5907 Dewdney Ave. W. ✆ **306/780-5838.** www.rcmpheritagecentre.com. RCMP Heritage Centre C$12 adults, C$10 seniors & children 13–17, C$6 children 6–12, C$3 children 3–5. Free admission to the Sunset Retreat Ceremony. Heritage Centre daily 9am–6pm (until 8pm on Sunset Retreat Ceremony nights).

Royal Saskatchewan Museum ☺ This museum focuses on the province's anthropological and natural history, displaying a life-size mastodon and "Megamunch," a robotic dinosaur that comes roaring to life, plus other specimens. The museum is organized into three main galleries: Life Sciences; Earth Sciences, which features Saskatchewan geologic history; and First Nations, which tells the stories of the province's indigenous peoples. A video cave, a sand table, and dinosaur-size board games are all found in the interactive Paleo Pit. The Apperley Place gift shop offers, among other things, traditional Native art and Saskatchewan crafts.

2445 Albert St. ✆ **306/787-2815.** www.royalsaskmuseum.ca. Free admission (suggested donations C$6 adults, C$5 seniors, C$3 children; C$15 families). May to Labour Day daily 9am–5:30pm; day after Labour Day to Apr daily 9am–4:30pm. Closed Dec 25.

Saskatchewan Science Centre ☺ Ensconced inside a 1914 power plant beside Wascana Lake, the Saskatchewan Science Centre is home to the Powerhouse of Discovery and the Kramer IMAX Theatre. The first houses more than 80 thought-provoking and fun hands-on exhibits demonstrating basic scientific principles, ranging from a hot-air balloon that rises three stories in the central mezzanine to exhibits where you can test your strength, reaction time, and balance. Displays of local farming practices encourage participation. The Kramer IMAX Theatre shows films on a five-story screen with thrilling six-channel surround-sound. Call for show times.

Winnipeg St. & Wascana Dr. ✆ **800/667-6300** or 306/522-4629. www.sasksciencecentre.com. Powerhouse of Discovery C$8 adults, C$6 seniors & children 6–13, C$3.75 children 3–5, free for children 2 & under. IMAX theater C$7.50 adults, C$5.50 seniors & children 6–13, C$3.75 children 5 & under. Combination tickets C$13 adults, C$9.50 seniors & children 6–13, C$6.50 children 3–5. MC, V. Tues–Fri 9am–5pm; Sat & Sun noon–6pm.

Wascana Centre This 930-hectare (2,298-acre) park in the city center—one of the largest urban parks in North America—contains its own **waterfowl park,** frequented by 60 or more species of marsh and water birds. There's a naturalist on duty Monday to Friday 9am to 4pm. Another delightful spot is **Willow Island,** a man-made island reached by a small ferry from the overlook west of Broad Street on Wascana Drive. Other highlights include a fountain that once stood in London's Trafalgar Square, a totem pole, and a war memorial. In winter, ice skaters take to the park's central lake, and cross-country skiers navigate its snowy trails.

The center also contains the domed Saskatchewan Legislative Building, the University of Regina, the Royal Saskatchewan Museum, the MacKenzie Art Gallery, and the Saskatchewan Centre of the Arts.

Wascana Place, headquarters for the **Wascana Centre Authority** (✆ **306/522-3661;** www.wascana.sk.ca), provides public information. You can get a fine view from its fourth-level observation deck. Victoria Day through Labour Day, it's open daily 9am to 6pm; winter hours are Monday to Saturday 9:30am to 5:30pm.

Where to Stay

EXPENSIVE

Delta Regina Location, location, location. Conveniently located downtown in the Saskatchewan Trade and Convention Centre, the Delta Regina is linked by skyways to the shops of the Cornwall Centre and the Casino Regina. Premier rooms offer lots of light, plus plenty of living and working space, while Signature Club rooms offer luxury touches such as granite-tiled bathrooms, king-size beds, and Jacuzzi tubs, plus access to a private lounge. Standard guest rooms are nicely appointed with a choice of two double or one queen-size bed, an easy chair, and a small work desk. The hotel also has a massive indoor water park, with a three-story indoor waterslide and whirlpool. Also on-site are the contemporary Indigo Dining Room, a cafe, and a lounge.

1919 Saskatchewan Dr., Regina, SK S4P 4H2. ✆ **888/890-3222** or 306/525-5255. Fax 306/781-7188. www.deltahotels.com. 274 units. C$160–C$210 double. Additional adult C$15. Children 17 & under stay free in parent's room. Weekend, senior & package rates available. AE, DC, DISC, MC, V. Adjacent parking C$7. **Amenities:** Restaurant; lounge; fitness center; indoor pool w/3-story waterslide; limited room service; day spa. *In room:* A/C, TV, hair dryer, Wi-Fi (free).

Hotel Saskatchewan ★★ The historic hotel's elegant Old World lobby and solid limestone exterior look as if they belong in London—except the Hotel Saskatchewan is more beautifully maintained and comfortable than many of the classic hotels it resembles. Built as a regal railroad hotel in 1927, the hotel is filled with opulence, from the gilt moldings and luxury carpets to the spacious specialty suites literally designed for royalty. Standard guest rooms are large for a hotel of this vintage—most have walk-in closets—and have quality furnishings. Business-class rooms—on corners for extra light—are even larger and outfitted with king-size beds, large business desks, and ergonomic chairs. Plaza Club guests have extra amenities such as feather duvets and luxury-level furniture, plus access to the wonderful Plaza Club Room, a fantastic sitting room and private lounge that looks like a drawing room for Edwardian aristocrats. The Essence Organic Day Spa (✆ **306/522-7272**) offers a selection of massage and beauty treatments.

Needless to say, there aren't many hotels like this in Regina, and even if you don't stay here, consider stopping by for a meal—Sunday brunch is C$25—or a drink in Monarch's Lounge, a lovely formal room with a fireplace and carved beams. On Friday and Saturday, the Victoria Tea Room is open for traditional afternoon tea.

2125 Victoria Ave. (at Scarth St.), Regina, SK S4P 0S3. ✆ **800/967-9033** or 306/522-7691. Fax 306/757-5521. www.hotelsask.com. 224 units. C$149–C$319 double. Additional adult C$15. Children 11 & under stay free in parent's room. Group, senior & package rates available. AE, DC, MC, V. **Amenities:** Restaurant; lounge; executive-level rooms; fitness center; whirlpool; room service; steam room; day spa. *In room:* A/C, TV, hair dryer, minibar, Wi-Fi (free).

Ramada Hotel & Convention Centre ★ With its lobby and atrium completely renovated in 2010, the Ramada offers very comfortable rooms, conference facilities, and lots of extras for both corporate and leisure travelers. Standard rooms come with two double beds and a full range of amenities, while the business-class rooms occupy the hotel's top two floors, both secured. These rooms offer king-size beds, large work desks, and adjustable office chairs, plus a sitting area with overstuffed easy chairs. The suites at the Ramada are exceptional—junior suites are very large, light filled, and homelike, while seven executive suites are practically apartments. The spa area features cascading multilevel pools, exercise equipment, and a deck.

1818 Victoria Ave., Regina, SK S4P 0R1. ✆ **800/667-6500** or 306/569-1666. Fax 306/352-6339. www.saskramada.com. 233 units. C$120–C$160 double; from C$220 suite. Children 17 & under stay free in parent's room. Weekend packages, senior & AAA discounts available. AE, DC, MC, V. Parking C$8. **Amenities:** Restaurant; lounge; children's center; exercise room; Jacuzzi; indoor pool; room service; sauna. *In room:* A/C, TV w/pay movies, hair dryer, Wi-Fi (free).

Regina Inn ★ The Regina Inn provides stylish and comfortable rooms at moderate prices, right in the center of the city. The Superior Queen and Business Class rooms were renovated in 2010; both come in contemporary beige colors, with the latter having multiple phones and other perks for business travelers, such as granite-countered bathrooms. Additionally, there are Jacuzzi suites. Standard rooms are simpler, but still very pleasant and spacious. Nearly all rooms have balconies, with either city or lake views. All in all, a good value for very high quality. The hotel offers the botaniCa all-day cafe and drinks in a stone-flanked lounge, complete with waterfall.

1975 Broad St., Regina, SK S4P 1Y2. ✆ **800/667-8162** in Canada or 306/525-6767. Fax 306/352-1858. www.reginainn.com. 235 units. C$128–C$185 double; from $215 suite. Additional adult C$10. Children 17 & under stay free in parent's room. Weekend & other packages, group & senior rates available. AE, DC, DISC, MC, V. Parking C$6. **Amenities:** Restaurant; lounge; fitness center; room service. *In room:* A/C, TV w/cable & pay movies, hair dryer, Wi-Fi (free).

INEXPENSIVE

HI-Regina ★ Also known as Turgeon International Hostel, HI-Regina is a welcoming facility located in a handsome 1907 town house adjacent to the Wascana Centre. Accommodations range from dorms with three or four bunks to private rooms; the top floor has two larger dorms, and each dorm has access to a deck. Downstairs is a comfortable sitting room worthy of any inn, with couches in front of the oak fireplace and plenty of magazines and books in the library. The basement contains an impeccably clean dining and cooking area. Picnic tables and a barbeque are available in the backyard.

2310 McIntyre St., Regina, SK S4P 2S2. ✆ **306/791-8165.** Fax 306/721-2667. www.hihostels.ca. 30 beds. Dorm beds C$28 members, C$33 nonmembers; private rooms C$45–C$65 members, C$55–C$75 nonmembers. Limited street parking. Closed Dec 24 to Jan. **Amenities:** Wi-Fi (free). *In room:* A/C, no phone.

Where to Dine

In addition to the places below, try **Afghan Cuisine Family Restaurant** (832 Albert St.; ✆ **306/949-0800**) for traditional Afghan food; it's open Monday through Saturday 11:30am to 9pm, with a buffet offered at lunch. Although this is beef country, **Green Spot Cafe** (1838 Hamilton St.; ✆ **306/757-7899**) serves good vegetarian dishes such as quiche, salads, pasta salads, and sushi. It's open Monday through Friday 7am to 5pm and Saturday 8am to 3pm.

Cathedral Freehouse PUB This spacious and atmospheric pub features a number of local ales and also serves exceptional pub fare. In addition to standards such as burgers and wood-fired pizza, this popular institution offers specialties such as fire-roasted chicken with a choice of three sauces and local pickerel with lemon sauce. Just the spot for a drink and a casual meal.

2062 Albert St. ✆ **306/359-1661.** www.thefreehouse.com. Reservations not accepted. Main courses C$14–C$23. AE, MC, V. Mon–Sat 11am–midnight; Sun noon–midnight.

Crave Kitchen + Wine Bar ★ INTERNATIONAL Located downtown in the historic, once-private Assiniboia Club, Crave updates the ornate 1925 setting with excellent modern cuisine, wild colors, and moody neon lights. The extensive menu boils down to a selection of multicultural tapas, with main courses featuring local game and produce prepared with aspirations toward Europe and Asia. As starters, the Caesar salad is very tasty, and the duck confit spring rolls with a side of Asian slaw is a delight. For a main course, you can choose from pesto and crab flatbread pizza, a classic East Indian butter chicken, a New York strip loin with a Cognac-and-mushroom demi-glace, or roast chicken with risotto. In warm weather, you can dine on the outdoor patio; wireless Internet is free; and on weekends, there's frequently live music and DJs.

1925 Victoria Ave. ✆ **306/525-8777.** www.cravekwb.com. Reservations recommended. Main courses C$13–C$29. AE, MC, V. Mon–Thurs 11am–midnight; Fri 11am–1am; Sat 4pm–1am.

Creek in Cathedral Bistro ★★ CONTINENTAL The Cathedral neighborhood of Regina, west of the downtown core, has the reputation of being the city's most artsy enclave. Therefore, it's not surprising to find one of the city's most noteworthy and innovative restaurants here. The Creek's frequently changing menu is a bit hard to characterize, but it generally features up-to-date preparations of prairie foods (and fresh seafood) dressed in French and continental preparations. A roast chicken breast is dressed with Saskatoon berry–Calvados reduction and served with local wild-mushroom risotto, and pan-seared sable fish comes with fennel confit. In good weather, the outdoor patio here is one of the most popular see-and-be-seen spots in the city.

3414 13th Ave. ✆ **306/352-4448.** Reservations recommended. Main courses C$27–C$30. MC, V. Mon–Fri 11am–2pm & 5–9pm; Sat 10am–2pm & 5–10pm.

Diplomat Steakhouse CANADIAN You wouldn't know from the nondescript exterior, but this old-style steakhouse is a longtime favorite of Regina movers and shakers. Inside, the Diplomat has the well-aged patina of a London club. At each booth hang original oil paintings of eminent-looking Canadian prime ministers, with lots of dark wood and a fireplace and lounge upfront. The sizable menu's main attractions are the steaks—16-oz. filet mignon, 18-oz. T-bone, a chateaubriand for 2, and more, all cut from AAA Canadian Angus Pride beef—along with bison, lamb, and ribs. Tableside preparations are another specialty—this is your chance for a perfectly prepared steak Diane. In addition, you'll find such specialties as seafood casserole; Chicken Neptune, grilled chicken breast topped with crabmeat, asparagus, and a tarragon sauce; and a single choice for vegetarians. The Diplomat has over 200 wines to complement your meal. If you're planning on splurging on a classy steak dinner, this is the place to do it.

2032 Broad St. ✆ **306/359-3366.** www.thediplomatsteakhouse.com. Reservations recommended. Main courses C$19–C$54. AE, DC, MC, V. Mon–Fri 11am–2pm; Mon–Sat 4pm–midnight.

Willow on Wascana ★★ CANADIAN A combination of creative cooking and sweeping views across Wascana Lake, this bright yet elegant room is one of Regina's most popular restaurants. The kitchen does an unbelievable job of carefully selecting local ingredients. These are highlighted in the Taste of Saskatchewan four-course prix fixe menu (C$67), which takes from the al a carte choices. As a starter, look for creamy Willow's Land chowder, filled with caramelized leek and honey-glazed pork belly, or something a little lighter such as the tomato basil salad. Mains include a coffee-crusted, triple-smoked beef rib-eye and handmade ravioli stuffed with beef pâté. Save room for the chocolate ganache tart.

3000 Wascana Dr. ✆ **306/585-3663.** www.willowonwascana.ca. Reservations recommended. Main courses C$27–C$34. AE, MC, V. Tues–Sat 11:30am–11pm; Sun & Mon 4:30–11pm.

Regina After Dark

The focus of the city's cultural life is the Conexus Arts Centre, on the southern shore of Wascana Lake, at 200 Lakeshore Dr. (✆ **800/667-8497,** or 306/525-9999 for the box office; www.conexusartscentre.ca). With two theaters and a 2,000-seat concert hall, the center is home to the **Regina Symphony Orchestra** (www.reginasymphony.com) and features many other performance companies. The box office is open Monday through Saturday 10am to 6pm.

Late September to early May, the **Globe Theatre** (Old City Hall, 1801 Scarth St.; ✆ **866/954-5623** or 306/525-6400; www.globetheatrelive.com) performs as a theater-in-the-round within a restored building that was built as Regina's original city hall. The company presents six plays annually. Productions run the gamut from classics (Shakespeare, Molière, Shaw, and others) to modern dramas, musicals, and comedies. Tickets are C$35 to C$45. Box office hours are Monday through Saturday 10am to 5pm.

Casino Regina (1880 Saskatchewan Dr., at Broad St.; ✆ **800/555-3189** or 306/565-3000; www.casinoregina.com) is very impressive. Seven blocks long and incorporating the city's original rail station, Casino Regina has over 35 gaming tables to go with its more than 600 slots, as well as a restaurant and Vegas-style live shows, and is open daily 9am to 4am (closed Christmas). The top live-music venue in Regina is **The Distrikt** (1326 Hamilton St.; ✆ **306/359-8223**), offering national and local bands, three bars, a large dance floor, and three outdoor decks.

Across the tracks from downtown is the old railway warehouse district, now being revived as an arts and clubs area. Centering on Dewdney Avenue, between Albert and Broad streets, this district offers travelers a number of pubs and nightclubs. **Envy Nightclub** downstairs at 2300 Dewdney Ave. (✆ **306/757-3689**) is as trendy as it gets in Regina. The room has a lively dance-club atmosphere, while on weekends, DJs give the club an electric vibe. Of the many pubs in the area, check out **Bushwakker Pub and Brewing Company** (2206 Dewdney Ave.; ✆ **360/359-7276;** www.bushwakker.com), with a wide selection of beers and ales brewed on-site to go with well-priced pub fare.

A couple of other pubs with an Irish flavor popular in Regina are **O'Hanlon's** (1947 Scarth St.; ✆ **306/566-4094**) and **McNally's,** at 2226 Dewdney Ave. (✆ **306/522-4774;** www.mcnallystavern.ca), which also features live music.

HIGHLIGHTS ALONG THE TRANS-CANADA HIGHWAY

Moose Mountain Provincial Park & West to Regina

About 106km (66 miles) southeast of Regina, south down Highway 9 from Whitewood, is **Moose Mountain Provincial Park** (✆ **306/577-2600;** www.tpcs.gov.sk.ca). This 388-sq.-km (150-sq.-mile) forested wilderness is dotted with lakes and marshes. The park harbors a variety of waterfowl and songbirds—blue-winged teal, red-necked duck, blue heron, red-tailed hawk, ovenbird, rose-breasted grosbeak, and Baltimore oriole—and animals, including deer, elk, moose, beaver, muskrat, and coyote. The Beaver Lake Peninsula trails take a little over 1 hour each and are easy to follow. You can also bike along the **nature trails,** swim at the **beach** south of the visitor center, and camp in the treed campground. In winter, the park has more than 56km (35 miles) of **cross-country ski trails** and more than 120km (75 miles) of **snowmobiling trails.**

At the park entrance is the summer village of **Kenosee Lake.** Here, you can cool off at the super-fun **Kenosee Superslides** (✆ **306/577-4422**), which include an eight-story freefall slide; play **golf** at the 18-hole course; go **horseback riding;** or play **tennis.**

The modern, comfortable **Kenosee Inn** off Hwy. 9 (✆ **306/577-2099;** www.kenoseeinn.com), offers 30 guest rooms and 23 cabins overlooking Kenosee Lake. Facilities include a restaurant, bar, indoor pool, and hot tub. High-season rates are C$111 to C$141 for a double, C$99 for a one-bedroom cabin, and C$140 to C$170 for a two-bedroom cabin. Outside of summer, discounted rates are available. The park also has two **campgrounds.**

Moose Jaw

Moose Jaw gained notoriety as Canada's rum-running capital; it was known as "Little Chicago" in the 1920s. Today, some restored buildings still retain the underground tunnels used for the illicit trade. **The Tunnels of Moose Jaw** (18 Main St.; ✆ **306/693-5261;** www.tunnelsofmoosejaw.com) provides two guided tours of the tunnels, one detailing the "Chicago Connection"—including stories of Al Capone beating the heat up north—and the other, "Passage to Fortune," telling the story of Chinese immigrants who came to Moose Jaw looking for economic opportunity through work in the tunnels. There's also a small museum archive of documents and pictures from Moose Jaw's heyday. Individual tours cost C$14 adults, C$11 seniors and children 13 to 18, and C$7.50 children 6 to 12; there are discounts if you take both tours on the same day. Tours last around 50 minutes and are generally offered every half-hour Monday to Friday 10am to 4:30pm, Saturday 10am to 5:30pm, and Sunday noon to 4:30pm.

Moose Jaw Museum and Art Gallery (461 Langdon Crescent, in Crescent Park; ✆ **306/692-4471;** www.mjmag.ca) has a fine collection of Cree and Sioux beadwork and clothing, plus plenty of contemporary art and history exhibits. It's open daily noon to 5pm; admission is by donation. Moose Jaw is also known for its 46 outdoor murals depicting aspects of the city's heritage. Visit www.moosejaw.ca for a detailed list of the murals and a downloadable map.

The **Western Development Museum's History of Transportation** branch, at 50 Diefenbaker Dr., by the intersection of highways 1 and 2 (✆ **306/693-5989;** www.wdm.ca), showcases the roles that air, rail, land, and water transportation played in opening up the West. The highlight is the Snowbirds Gallery, which pays tribute to the Snowbirds, Canada's famous aerobatic squadron. Another exhibit lays out the various threads of history that led to the founding of Saskatchewan, using dioramas. It's open daily 9am to 5pm. Admission is C$8.50 adults, C$7.50 seniors, C$5.75 students, C$2 children 6 to 12, and C$19 families; free admission for preschoolers.

Wakamow Valley (✆ **306/692-2717;** www.wakamow.ca), which follows the course of the river through town, includes six parks with 14km (8.7 miles) of walking and biking trails, 6 picnic areas, canoeing, and skating facilities.

If you stop overnight in Moose Jaw, the place to stay is **Temple Gardens Mineral Spa** (24 Fairford St. E.; ✆ **800/718-7727** or 306/694-5055; www.templegardens.sk.ca), offering 179 rooms, including Signature Suites with mineral-water Jacuzzis. It's a full-facility resort with an expansive indoor and outdoor mineral pool complex where guests enjoy complimentary access. The spa offers a full range of body treatments. Rates are C$139 to C$159 for a double and from C$199 for a Signature Suite.

For more information, stop by the **Moose Jaw Visitor Centre** (450 Diefenbaker Dr.; ✆ **866/693-8097;** www.moosejaw.org), on the south side of the Trans-Canada Highway as it passes through town (look for the giant moose out front).

Swift Current

Swift Current (pop. 15,000), Saskatchewan's base for western oil exploration and a regional trading center for livestock and grain, is 167km (104 miles) west along the Trans-Canada Highway from Moose Jaw. It's known for its **Frontier Days,** on the first weekend of July, which is anchored by one of Canada's largest rodeos. For more information about Swift Current, visit the **Swift Current Visitor Centre** (44 Robert St. W.; ✆ **306/778-9174;** www.tourismswiftcurrent.ca).

From Swift Current, it's a further 201km (125 miles) west to the Alberta border along the Trans-Canada Highway, with the following two very different parks well worth visiting.

Grasslands National Park

About 121km (75 miles) south of Swift Current along the U.S. border stretches **Grasslands National Park** (✆ **360/298-2257;** www.pc.gc.ca)—two areas of protected land separated by about 27km (17 miles). On this mixed prairie and grassland, there's no escape from the sun and the wind. The **Frenchman River** cuts deep into the West Block, where you can spot pronghorn antelope and bison. Black-tailed **prairie dogs,** which bark warnings at intruders and reassure each other with kisses and hugs, also make their home here. In the East Block, the open prairie is broken with coulees and the adobe hills of the Killdeer Badlands, so called because of their poor soil.

Although the park doesn't have facilities, there are two self-guided **nature trails,** and you can also climb to the summit of **70 Mile Butte** and practice no-trace camping. The **Visitor Reception Centre** (✆ **306/298-2257**) is in Val Marie, at the junction of Highway 4 and Centre Street. It's open mid-May to early September daily 8am to 5pm, early September to mid-May Monday to Friday 8am to noon and 1 to 4:30pm.

Cypress Hills Interprovincial Park & Fort Walsh

Straddling the Saskatchewan/Alberta border is **Cypress Hills Interprovincial Park** (✆ **306/662-5411;** www.cypresshills.com). En route to Cypress Hills, off the Trans-Canada Highway, is **Maple Creek,** a thoroughly Western cow town with many heritage storefronts on the main street. On the park's Saskatchewan side, it's divided into a Centre Block, off Route 21, and a West Block, off Route 271. Both blocks are joined by Gap Road, which is impassable when wet. The park's core is in the Centre Block, where there are six campgrounds; an outdoor pool; canoe, row/paddleboat, and bike rentals; a 9-hole golf course; tennis courts; a riding stable; and swimming at the beach on Loch Leven. In winter, there are 24km (15 miles) of **cross-country skiing trails.** Entry to the park costs C$7 per vehicle per day, or C$17 for 3 days. Camping costs C$13 to C$26 per day, or you can stay at **Cypress Park Resort Inn** (✆ **306/662-4477;** www.cypressresortinn.com). Off Highway 221, this largish resort offers nice hotel-style rooms for C$115 to C$175, cabins with one to three bedrooms for C$115 to C$160, and condominium accommodations from C$125. Resort amenities include an indoor pool and a pleasant restaurant with a wide-ranging, well-priced menu.

In the park's southern reaches, **Fort Walsh National Historic Site** (© **306/662-3590;** www.pc.gc.ca) can be accessed from Route 271 or directly from the park's West Block via an unpaved road. Built in 1875, the fort's soldiers tried to contain local Native tribes and the many Sioux who sought refuge after the Battle of Little Bighorn in 1876, as well as keep out American criminals seeking sanctuary. It was dismantled in 1883. Today, the reconstruction consists of five buildings and a trading post staffed with folks in period costume. Victoria Day to Labour Day, it's open daily 9:30am to 5:30pm. Admission is C$9.80 adults, C$8.30 seniors, C$4.90 children 6 to 16, free for children 5 and under, and C$22 for families.

SASKATOON

257km (160 miles) NW of Regina, 524km (326 miles) SE of Edmonton

Saskatoon (pop. 210,000) retains a distinctly Western air, with cowboys and horse trailers as numerous as flame-haired University of Saskatchewan students on its downtown streets. It's not a glitzy place, but there's a lot more going on here than you'd think from the surface.

The university provides Saskatoon with its economic clout, as it is one of North America's top bioscience research centers. This seemingly remote city on the edge of Canadian prairies is at the center of today's world of agribusiness. In addition, much of the city's recent wealth has come from the Athabasca Basin, which yields potash, uranium, diamonds, petroleum, gas, and gold; Key Lake, in northern Saskatchewan, is one of the world's richest uranium deposits.

Scenically, Saskatoon possesses some distinct natural advantages. The South Saskatchewan River cuts a swath through the city. Spanned by several graceful bridges, its park-lined banks are great for strolling, biking, and jogging.

Essentials

GETTING THERE **Saskatoon John G. Diefenbaker Airport** (© **306/975-8900;** www.yxe.ca) is served by **Air Canada** (© **888/247-2262**) and **WestJet** (© **877/937-8538**) from across Canada, while the city is linked to the U.S. by **Delta** (© **800/441-1818**).

VIA Rail (© **888/842-7245;** www.viarail.ca) trains arrive in the west end of the city at 1701 Chappell Dr.

If you're **driving,** Highway 16 (the Yellowhead Hwy.) leads to Saskatoon from the east or west. From Regina, Route 11 leads northwest to Saskatoon.

VISITOR INFORMATION From mid-May to the end of August, a booth is open at Avenue C North at 47th Street. Otherwise, contact **Tourism Saskatoon** (202 4th Ave. N.; © **800/567-2444** or 306/242-1206; www.tourismsaskatoon.com). Summer hours for both are Monday to Friday 8:15am to 5pm and Saturday and Sunday 8:30am to 5:30pm; winter hours for the Tourism Saskatoon office are Monday through Friday 8:15am to 5pm.

CITY LAYOUT The South Saskatchewan River cuts a diagonal north-south swath through the city. The main downtown area lies on the west bank; the **University of**

Saskatchewan and the long neon sign–crazed **8th Street** dominate the east bank. Streets are laid out in a numbered grid system—22nd Street divides north- and south-designated streets; **Idylwyld Drive** divides, in a similar fashion, east from west. **1st Street** through **18th Street** lie on the river's east side; **19th Street** and up are situated on the west bank in the downtown area. **Spadina Crescent** runs along the river's west bank, where you'll find such landmarks as the Delta Bessborough, the Ukrainian Museum, and the art gallery.

GETTING AROUND You may need to use transportation only when you visit the University of Saskatchewan and the Western Development Museum. **Saskatoon Transit** (✆ **306/975-3100;** www.saskatoon.ca) operates buses to all city areas Monday through Saturday 6am to 12:30am and Sunday 9:15am to 9pm for an exact-change fare of C$2.75 adults, C$2.10 high school students, and C$1.65 grade-school students.

Car-rental companies with airport desks include **Avis** (✆ **306/652-3434**), **Budget** (✆ **306/664-0670**), **Enterprise** (✆ **306/664-4454**), **Hertz** (✆ **306/373-1161**), **National** (✆ **306/664-8771**), and **Thrifty** (✆ **306/244-8000**). For a taxi, call **United Blueline Cabs** (✆ **306/652-2222**).

SPECIAL EVENTS & FESTIVALS The 8-day **Saskatoon Exhibition** (✆ **888/931-9333** or 306/931-7149; www.saskatoonexhibition.ca), usually held the second week of August, attracts over 200,000 patrons. It provides some grand agricultural spectacles, such as the threshing competition in which steam power is pitted against gas—sometimes with unexpected results—and the tractor-pulling competition, when standard farm tractors are used to pull a steel sled weighted down with a water tank. Admission of C$13 adults, C$9 children 11 to 15 (free for children 10 and under with an adult), lets you in all the entertainments—a craft show, talent competitions, chuckwagon races, thoroughbred racing, a midway, and fireworks. Parking is C$7.

In mid-August, **Folkfest** (✆ **306/931-0100;** www.saskatoonfolkfest.ca) celebrates the city's many ethnic groups through food, displays, and performances; admission is C$14 adults, free for children 12 and under if accompanied by an adult.

Exploring the City

An excellent introduction to the city comes from exploring the **Meewasin Valley,** along the banks of the South Saskatchewan River through the downtown area. Particularly pleasant is the west bank of the river, where a riverside trail accesses viewpoints that show the massive Delta Bessborough hotel rising like a French château above parklands and the river.

The **University of Saskatchewan** (✆ **306/966-4343;** www.usask.ca) occupies a dramatic 750-hectare (1,853-acre) site overlooking the South Saskatchewan River across from downtown and is attended by some 15,000 students. The actual campus buildings are set on 200 hectares (494 acres), while the rest of the area is largely given over to the university farm and experimental plots. A good starting point for exploring the sprawling campus is the **Diefenbaker Canada Centre** (101 Diefenbaker Place; ✆ **306/966-8384**), which is named for Canada's 13th Prime Minister, who was born in Saskatchewan. Displays pertain to Diefenbaker's political accomplishments and the role of politics, in general, in Canadian society. It's open Monday through Friday 9:30am to 4:30pm, and Saturday and Sunday noon to 4:30pm. Admission is C$7 adults, C$5 seniors and children, or C$15 families. Enquire here about walking tours of the campus (minimum of four people required) that cost C$5 per person. The **University Observatory** (✆ **306/966-6429;** open Sat evenings after dusk) houses the Duncan telescope. Also worth searching out is **Victoria School House**, built in 1887, which served as the city's first school and community center. It's off College Drive near the southwest corner of the campus. To get to the campus, take bus no. 7 or 19 from downtown at 23rd Street and 2nd Avenue.

Mendel Art Gallery ★ Along the north bank of the South Saskatchewan River, just a short walk from downtown, is the Mendel Art Gallery. Housed in a striking Modernist building, the gallery has collected over 5,000 works of art in different media, including paintings, sculpture, prints, and drawings of national importance. The collection began with the acquisition of works by Canada's famed Group of Seven landscape artists, but the focus now extends to vital and very compelling works by contemporary Saskatchewan artists.

950 Spadina Crescent E. ✆ **306/975-7610.** www.mendel.ca. Free admission. Daily 9am–9pm. Closed Dec 25.

Ukrainian Museum of Canada Also on the north riverbank near downtown is this museum of Ukrainian culture. Reminiscent of an early-1900s Ukrainian home in western Canada, this museum preserves Ukrainian heritage in clothing, linens, tools, books, photographs, documents, wooden folk art, ceramics, *pysanky* (Easter eggs), and other treasures and art forms brought from the homeland by Ukrainian immigrants to Canada.

910 Spadina Crescent E. ✆ **306/244-3800.** www.umc.sk.ca. C$4 adults, C$3 seniors, C$2 children 6–12. Tues–Sat 10am–5pm; Sun 1–5pm.

Wanuskewin Heritage Park ★★ This park is built around the archaeological discovery of 19 Northern Plains peoples' pre-contact sites. Walking along its four trails, you'll see archaeological digs in progress, campsites, stone cairns, tepee rings, a medicine wheel, bison jumps, and other trace features of this ancient culture. At the amphitheater, First Nations performers present dance, theater, song, and storytelling; at the outdoor activity area, you can learn how to build a tepee, bake bannock, tan a hide, or use a travois (a transportation device). The exhibit halls feature computer-activated displays and artifacts, multimedia shows exploring the archaeology and culture of the Plains peoples, and a fascinating collection of contemporary Native Canadian art. The restaurant, open daily for breakfast and lunch, offers a menu dominated by First Nations cuisine. Try baked bannock (bread), a roast bison wrap, rabbit pot pie, and wild rice salad.

Penner Rd., 5km (3 miles) north of Saskatoon off Hwy. 11 & Warman Rd. ✆ **877/547-6546** or 306/931-6767. www.wanuskewin.com. C$8.50 adults, C$7.50 seniors, C$5 children 6–18, free for children 5 & under; C$25 families. Victoria Day to Labour Day daily 9am–8pm; the rest of the year daily 9am–4:30pm. Follow bison signs as you near the park.

Shopping

For Canadian merchandise, stop in at the **Trading Post** (226 2nd Ave. S.; ✆ **306/653-1769**), which carries Inuit soapstone carvings, small marble sculptures, First Nations paintings, Cowichan sweaters, mukluks, beadwork, and more. Other galleries showing local artists that are worth browsing include **Prairie Pottery** (150B 2nd Ave. N.; ✆ **306/242-8050**); the **Darrell Bell Gallery** (317–220 3rd Ave S.; ✆ **306/955-5701**); the **Collector's Choice Art Gallery** (625D 1st Ave. N.; ✆ **306/665-8300**); and the **Handmade House Handcraft Store** (710 Broadway Ave.; ✆ **306/665-5542**), which specializes in crafts.

Where to Stay

A hotel just north of downtown, and within walking distance of restaurants and shopping, the **Holiday Inn Express Hotel & Suites** (315 Idylwyld Dr. N.; ✆ **877/660-8550** or 306/384-8844; www.hiexpress.com) may be your hotel if you're looking for modern easy-in, easy-out rooms (C$129–C$149 double). It features an indoor pool, complimentary breakfast, and free wireless Internet.

Delta Bessborough ★★★ There are few hotels in Canada where dramatic location, superb historic architecture, and exceptional hospitality come together so magnificently as the Delta Bessborough. Built in the 1930s to resemble a French château, the towering, turreted hotel dominates the Saskatoon skyline and the parklands along the South Saskatchewan River.

The stylish decor throughout celebrates the hotel's gracious past, while thoroughly updated systems and facilities create one of western Canada's great luxury hotels. Even many of the standard Delta rooms have king-size beds, LCD TVs, and cordless phones. Upgrade to Signature Club rooms and enjoy more space, feather duvets, and handsome furniture, plus access to a private lounge. Be sure to peek inside the hotel's magnificent ballrooms on the third floor, especially the Versailles-like Adam Ballroom. Facilities also include a modern fitness center, an indoor pool, a splash pool for younger children, and a tanning booth. The Samurai Japanese Restaurant (✆ **306/683-6926**) offers delicious tableside *teppanyaki* grill preparations.

601 Spadina Crescent E., Saskatoon, SK S7K 3G8. ✆ **800/268-1133** or 306/244-5521. Fax 306/665-7262. www.deltahotels.com. 225 units. C$189–C$209 double. Additional adult C$15. Children 17 & under stay free in parent's room. AE, DC, MC, V. Valet or self-parking C$8. **Amenities:** 2 restaurants; lounge; fitness center; Jacuzzi; indoor pool; sauna. *In room:* A/C, TV w/video games, hair dryer, Wi-Fi (free).

Hilton Garden Inn Saskatoon Downtown This modern hotel has a very convenient location, right downtown opposite the Midtown Plaza shopping complex and TCU Place. Standard family rooms come with two queen-size beds or one king-size bed, while larger business rooms have a king-size bed plus a work desk; all rooms offer high-speed Internet access. A very affordable option for downtown lodging.

90 22nd St. E. (at 1st Ave.), Saskatoon, SK S7K 3X6. ✆ **877/782-9444** or 306/244-2311. Fax 306/664-2234. www.stayhgi.com. 180 units. From C$119 double. AE, MC, V. Free parking. **Amenities:** Restaurant; lounge; Jacuzzi; indoor pool; room service. *In room:* A/C, TV w/pay movies, fridge, hair dryer, Wi-Fi (free).

Radisson Hotel Saskatoon ★ Rising 19 stories above the city and the river, the Radisson is a busy corporate and convention hotel with a wide variety of room types, most recently remodeled and redecorated in 2007 (the lobby and pool were renovated in 2010) with soft earth tones, new furniture, and luxury linens. Standard rooms come with two queen-size beds—ask for a corner room, which offers more room and light. The one-bedroom suites occupy the hotel's top floors and offer lots of extras such as business desks, dining tables, couches and chairs, and super-large bathrooms with Jacuzzis. Aroma Mediterranean Resto-Bar offers fine dining and a cozy setting for a quiet drink, and guests enjoy a large indoor pool and waterslide complex.

405 20th St. E., Saskatoon, SK S7K 6X6. ✆ **800/395-7046** or 306/665-3322. Fax 306/665-5531. www.radisson.com/saskatoonca. 291 units. C$139–C$199 double; from C$239 suite. Additional adult C$15. Children 15 & under stay free in parent's room. Senior & CAA/AAA discounts available. AE, DC, MC, V. Parking C$12. **Amenities:** Restaurant; lounge; executive-level rooms; fitness center; whirlpool; indoor water park w/pool; room service; sauna. *In room:* A/C, TV, hair dryer, Internet (free).

Sheraton Cavalier ★★ ☺ This handsome hotel offers a lot in the way of luxury and facilities in an excellent downtown location overlooking the Saskatchewan River. All rooms were refurbished in 2007, with all new beds and furnishings. The rooms are stylishly decorated with a sleek contemporary look, with soft forest colors, handsome furniture, and plush upholstery and linens. The top-of-the-line suites are very cosmopolitan, some with two stories and hardwood floors. Club Level rooms come with king-size beds, granite bathroom counters, in-room printers, and telecommunication extras, plus a private lounge with complimentary hot drinks and breakfast. Traveling families will love the extensive indoor water park, with two large waterslides, swimming pool, children's wading pool, and hot tubs.

612 Spadina Crescent E., Saskatoon, SK S7K 3G9 ✆ **800/325-3535** or 306/652-6770. www.sheratoncavaliersaskatoon.com. 249 units. C$169 double; C$249 1-bedroom suite. AE, MC, V. Heated parking C$12. **Amenities:** 2 restaurants; bar; fitness center; pool complex; room service. *In room:* A/C, TV w/pay movies, hair dryer, minibar, Wi-Fi (free).

Where to Dine

Ivy's Dining & Lounge ★★ CANADIAN Located in the fast-changing warehouse area just north of the city center, Ivy's is a swank restaurant that, design-wise, manages to be industrial and warm at the same time. A stylized waterfall and fireplace take the chill off the dark and slightly formal dining room and bar, with the result that you feel you're welcomed into a very comfortable, stylish cave (you may need to ask for extra light to read the menu). The lunchtime soup-and-salad combo is just C$10; more tempting is the baguette filled with chicken breast, pear, and blue cheese. Main courses include herb-crusted rack of lamb, baked steelhead trout, and seared venison loin and cherry brandy demi-glace. Pasta and wood-fired pizza are also offered, as well as a fine selection of salads (for example, pear and blue cheese). The bar, with its atmospheric pools of light, makes a great spot for a cocktail and appetizer.

301 Ontario Ave. (at 24th St. E.). ✆ **306/384-4444.** www.ivydiningandlounge.com. Reservations recommended. Main courses C$21–C$33. AE, MC, V. Mon–Fri 11am–2pm & 4–11pm; Sat 4pm–midnight; Sun 5–9pm.

St. Tropez Bistro CONTINENTAL This little dining room is a favorite downtown spot for French- and Cajun-influenced meals at the right price and with just the right touch of cozy formality. Although the menu is small, it packs a lot of flavor. For dinner, you can choose from a variety of pastas, stir-fries, or creative dishes such as salmon poached with Saskatoon berries, lemon, and white wine. For dessert, you might try the triple-chocolate mousse pie or daily cheesecake.

238 2nd Ave. S. ✆ **306/652-1250.** www.sainttropezbistro.ca. Reservations recommended. Main courses C$23–C$30. AE, MC, V. Tues–Sun 5–10pm.

Spadina Freehouse ★ PUB FARE Bright and lively, and right on a busy downtown intersection, the Spadina Freehouse combines the best features of a youthful brewpub and a casual but exciting restaurant. The menu goes well beyond the standard brewpub fare, with baked halibut with lemon caper sauce, citrus-flavored noodle bowl, and wood-fired pizzas all standouts. Excellent, cheerful service and a welcoming outdoor patio add to the charm.

608 Spadina Crescent E. ✆ **306/668-1000.** www.thefreehouse.com. Main courses C$11–C$24. AE, DC, MC, V. Mon–Sat 11am–midnight; Sun 11:30am–10pm.

Weczeria FRENCH Although the restaurant's name is Ukrainian for "evening meal," Weczeria is renowned for its modern French cooking. You could begin with the sweet potato soup with apple and red onion marmalade, then move on to main courses such as wild boar in a red wine jus. Rounding out Weczeria is an elegant setting, professional yet unpretentious service, and a thoughtful wine list.

616 19th St. E. ✆ **306/933-9600.** www.weczeriarestaurant.ca. Reservations recommended. Main courses C$23–C$28. AE, MC, V. Mon–Sat 5–10pm.

Saskatoon After Dark

TCU Place (35 22nd St. E.; ✆ **306/975-7770,** or 306/938-7800 for tickets; www.tcuplace.com), the city's convention center, provides a superb 2,000-seat theater for much of what there is, with a range of shows. The **Saskatoon Symphony** (✆ **306/665-6414;** www.saskatoonsymphony.org) regularly performs during a September-to-April season. Tickets are C$21 to C$58.

The leading local theater company, **Persephone Theatre** (✆ **306/384-2126,** or 306/384-7727 for the box office; www.persephonetheatre.org) is based at the Remai Arts Centre, at 100 Spadina Crescent E. Persephone offers six shows per fall-to-spring season (dramas, comedies, and musicals); tickets are C$25 to C$32. **Shakespeare on the Saskatchewan** (✆ **306/653-2300,** or 306/652-9100 for the box office; www.shakespeareonthesaskatchewan.com) produces the Bard in two tents overlooking the river just south of the Mendel Art Gallery from July to mid-August. Two Shakespeare plays are performed, plus a number of guest performances during the season. Tickets are C$30 adults, C$24 seniors, and C$18 students, with discounts for previews and matinees.

For quiet drinking and conversation in a refined setting, you can't beat **Stovin's Lounge** in the **Delta Bessborough Hotel** (601 Spadina Crescent E.; ✆ **306/244-5521**). For a more pub-like atmosphere, try **O'Shea's Irish Pub** (222 2nd Ave. S.; ✆ **306/384-7444**), within easy walking distance from downtown hotels. The **Marquis Downs** racetrack, at Saskatoon Prairieland Park, at 503 Ruth St. (✆ **306/242-6100;** www.marquisdowns.com), is open for live and simulcast racing. The live season goes mid-May to mid-October. The racetrack has a lounge, cafeteria, and terrace dining overlooking the home stretch. Admission is free. The other place to wager is **Dakota Dunes Casino,** south of the city off Highway 219 (✆ **306/667-6400;** www.dakotadunescasino.com), where you can play five or so table games. It opens at 5:30pm weekdays and at 2pm weekends.

Side Trips from Saskatoon

In addition to the National Historic Sites listed below, visitors looking for a little healthful rejuvenation may want to consider a trip to **Little Manitou Lake,** near Watrous, about an hour's drive southeast of Saskatoon on Highway 16, then Highway 2. The lake is renowned for its mineral-rich waters, a composition found only here, in the Czech Republic, and in the Dead Sea. The water contains magnesium, carbonate, sulfate, potassium, mineral salts, sodium, calcium, iron, silica, and sulfur, all combining to give it a high specific gravity. This property offers increased buoyancy to swimmers so that they float in it effortlessly.

Fort Battleford National Historic Site About 138km (86 miles), a 1½-hour drive, northwest of Saskatoon on Highway 16, **Fort Battleford** (✆ **306/937-2621;**

www.pc.gc.ca) served as the headquarters for the Northwest Mounted Police from 1876 to 1924. Outside the interpretative gallery, a display relates the role of the mounted police from the fur-trading era to the events that led to the rebellion of 1885. You'll see a Red River cart, the type used to transport police supplies into the West; excerpts from the local *Saskatchewan Herald;* a typical settler's log-cabin home, which is amazingly tiny; articles of the fur trade; and an 1876 Gatling gun.

Inside the palisade, the Visitor Reception Centre shows two videos about the 1885 Uprising and the Cree People. From there, proceed to the Guardhouse (1887), containing a cell block and the sick-horse stable (1898), and the Officers Quarters (1886), with police documents, maps, and telegraph equipment.

Perhaps the most interesting building is the Commanding Officer's Residence (1877), which, even though it looks terribly comfortable today, was certainly not so in 1885 when nearly 100 women took shelter in it during the siege of Battleford. Admission is C$7.80 adults, C$6.55 seniors, C$3.90 students, and C$20 families. It's open Victoria Day through Labour Day daily from 9am to 5pm.

Batoche National Historic Site ★ In spring 1885, the Northwest Territories exploded in an armed uprising led by the Métis Louis Riel and Gabriel Dumont. Trouble had been brewing along the frontier for several years. The Métis were demanding food, equipment, and farming assistance that had been promised to them in treaties. The settlers were angry about railway development and protective tariffs that meant higher prices for the equipment and services they needed.

The Métis were the offspring of the original French fur traders, who had intermarried with the Cree and Saulteaux women. Initially, the Métis had worked for the Hudson's Bay and North West companies, but when the two companies merged, many were left without work and returned to buffalo hunting or became independent traders with the Indians in the west. When Riel was unable to obtain guarantees for the Métis in Manitoba from 1869 to 1870, even when he established a provisional government, it became clear the Métis would have to adopt the agricultural ways of the whites to survive. In 1872, they moved westward and established the settlement at **Batoche** along the South Saskatchewan River; but they had a hard time acquiring legal titles and securing scrip, a certificate that could be exchanged for a land grant or money from the British authorities. The French-speaking Métis complained to the British government but received no satisfactory response. So they called on Riel to lead them in what became known as the Northwest Rebellion.

Of the rebellion's five significant engagements, the Battle of Batoche was the only one the British government forces decisively won. From May 9 to May 12, 1885, fewer than 300 Métis and Indians led by Riel and Dumont defended the village against the Northwest Field Force commanded by Gen. Frederick Middleton and numbering 800. On the third day, Middleton succeeded in breaking through the Métis lines and occupying the village. Dumont fled to the United States but returned and is buried at the site; Riel surrendered, stood trial, and was executed.

At the site, you can view four battlefield areas and a number of buildings dating back to the 1880s. For more information, contact **Batoche National Historic Site** (**© 306/423-6227;** www.pc.gc.ca). Admission is C$7.80 adults, C$6.55 seniors, C$3.90 students, and C$20 families; special events and presentations may cost extra. Mid-May to mid-September, Batoche is open daily 9am to 5pm. The site is about an hour from Saskatoon via Highway 11 to Highway 312 to Highway 225.

PRINCE ALBERT NATIONAL PARK ★

The 400,000-hectare (988,422-acre) wilderness area of Prince Albert National Park, 240km (149 miles) north of Saskatoon and 91km (57 miles) north of the town of Prince Albert, is one of the jewels of Canada's national park system. Its terrain is astoundingly varied, since it lies at the point where the great Canadian prairie grasslands give way to the pristine boreal forests of the north. Here, you'll find clear, cold lakes, ponds, and streams created thousands of years ago as glaciers receded. It's a hilly landscape, forested with spruce, poplar, and birch.

The park offers outdoor activities, from canoeing and backpacking to nature hikes, picnicking, swimming, and great wildlife viewing. You can see and photograph moose, caribou, elk, black bear, bison, and loons. (The moose and caribou tend to wander through the forested northern part of the park, while the elk, bison, and deer graze on the southern grasslands.) Lavallee Lake is home to Canada's second-largest white-pelican colony.

In the 1930s, this park's woods and wildlife inspired famed naturalist Grey Owl, an Englishman adopted by the Ojibwe who became one of Canada's pioneering conservationists and most noted naturalists. For 7 years, he lived in a simple one-room cabin called Beaver Lodge on Ajawaan Lake; many hikers and canoeists make a pilgrimage to see his cabin and nearby grave site.

More than 30% of the park's surface is water, making a canoe or kayak a great way to navigate and explore this nearly road-less area. **Canoeing** routes wind through much of the park through a system of interconnected lakes and rivers. Canoes can be rented at three lakes, including Lake Waskesiu, where you can easily get a feel for the watery environment in an hour or so. For experienced paddlers, the two major overnight canoe trips are the Bagwa and Bladebone routes. **CanoeSki Discovery Company** (**© 306/653-5693;** www.canoeski.com) offers a selection of multiday canoe adventures into the heart of the park. The trips, some especially for families and birders, are led by naturalists and certified canoeing guides. Canoe packages include a 4-day, 3-night trip for C$850 per person. There's also terrific fishing in the park, but anglers must have a national-park fishing license, available for sale at the Visitor Centre.

The park has 10 short **hiking trails,** plus four or so longer trails ideal for overnight trips. Several easier ones begin in or near Waskesiu Lake, though the best begin farther north. From the northwest shore of Lake Kingsmere, you can pick up the 20km (12-mile) one-way trail leading to Grey Owl's cabin. This is an overnight hike.

For additional info, contact **Prince Albert National Park** (**© 306/663-4522;** www.pc.gc.ca) or stop by the Visitor Centre in the village of Waskesiu Lake. It's open mid-May through mid-September daily 8am to 8pm. A park day pass is C$7.80 adults, C$6.55 seniors, C$3.90 children 6 to 16, and C$20 families. The park is open year-round, but many campgrounds, motels, and facilities are closed after September.

Where to Stay

Prince Albert National Park has five road-accessible **campgrounds,** as well as a number of simple motel and cabin accommodations starting from C$80 for a double. Most of these lodgings are in the **village of Waskesiu Lake,** which has tennis courts, lake-front picnic areas, bowling greens, an 18-hole golf course, a playground, and a few eateries.

In the village of Waskesiu Lake, **Red Deer Campground** has 152 sites with full services and **Beaver Glen Campground** has 213 sites, many with power. Facilities at both include showers and toilets, kitchen shelters, and sewage-disposal stations. Rates range from C$26 to C$35 for a site. Both are operated by Parks Canada. Advance reservations (✆ **877/737-3783** or 450/505-8302; www.pccamping.ca) are strongly recommended. Scattered through the park are four smaller campgrounds with limited services.

Hawood Inn This charming wooden lodge is across the road from Waskesiu Lake and one of the best beaches in Prince Albert National Park. Standard guest rooms are on the sparse side, but for C$20, you can upgrade to lake views and a balcony. Also on the property are seven condos that sleep between two and eight comfortably. Each has a full kitchen, dining table, lounge chairs, and a barbeque. The resort restaurant features simple, inexpensive meals, with lake views as a bonus.

850 Lakeview Dr., Waskesiu Lake, SK S0J 2Y0. ✆ **877/441-5544** or 306/663-5911. Fax 306/663-5219. www.hawood.com. 41 units. C$129–C$185 double; C$209–C$249 condo. Additional adult in lodge C$10. Children 10 & under stay free in parent's room. MC, V. **Amenities:** Restaurant; lounge; nearby golf course; hot tub; nearby tennis courts. *In room:* TV.

ALBERTA & THE ROCKIES

by Christie Pashby

14

Alberta's fame—and international tourist reputation—is built on three pillars: mountains, cowboys, and more mountains. All right, that's two, but you get the point. This is an extravagantly gorgeous outdoor wonderland, and the Canadian Rockies are the main attraction. This is not to say all that is worthwhile is to be found at high altitudes. Calgary's growing, urbane charms are drawing more visitors every year, and in Edmonton, the second-largest Fringe Theatre Festival in the world has long been a magnet for international travelers. In the badlands, the strong pull of paleontology, anchored by the Royal Tyrrell Museum in Drumheller, draws more than half a million visitors every year.

But the mountains still receive top billing, and with good reason. A practiced mix of otherworldly natural beauty and creature comforts—the Alberta Rockies have within their midst some of the finest resorts, inns, and restaurants to be found anywhere in the world—there are few places on Earth where enjoying rugged wilderness can be so relaxing.

And if relaxing is not your idea of a good time, then take to the hills for world-class ski resorts, endless hiking trails, fly-fishing, and rock and ice climbing, to name but a few pastimes. Out here, the sky truly is the limit.

EXPLORING THE PROVINCE

It's no secret that Alberta contains some of Canada's most compelling scenery and outdoor recreation. Mid-June through August, this is a very busy place; Banff is generally acknowledged to be Canada's single most popular destination for foreign travelers. A little planning is essential, especially if you're traveling in summer or have specific destinations or lodgings in mind.

Skiers should know that heavy snowfall closes some mountain roads in winter. However, major passes are maintained and usually remain open. Highways 3, 1, and 16 are open year-round, though it's a good idea to call to check road conditions. You can inquire locally or call **Travel Alberta** (© **800/661-8888;** www.travelalberta.com) or the **Alberta Motor Association** (© **403/474-8601;** www.ama.ab.ca). If you're a member of AAA or CAA, call their information line (© **800/642-3810**). Always carry traction devices such as tire chains in your vehicle, plus plenty of warm clothes and a sleeping bag if you're planning winter car travel.

Alberta

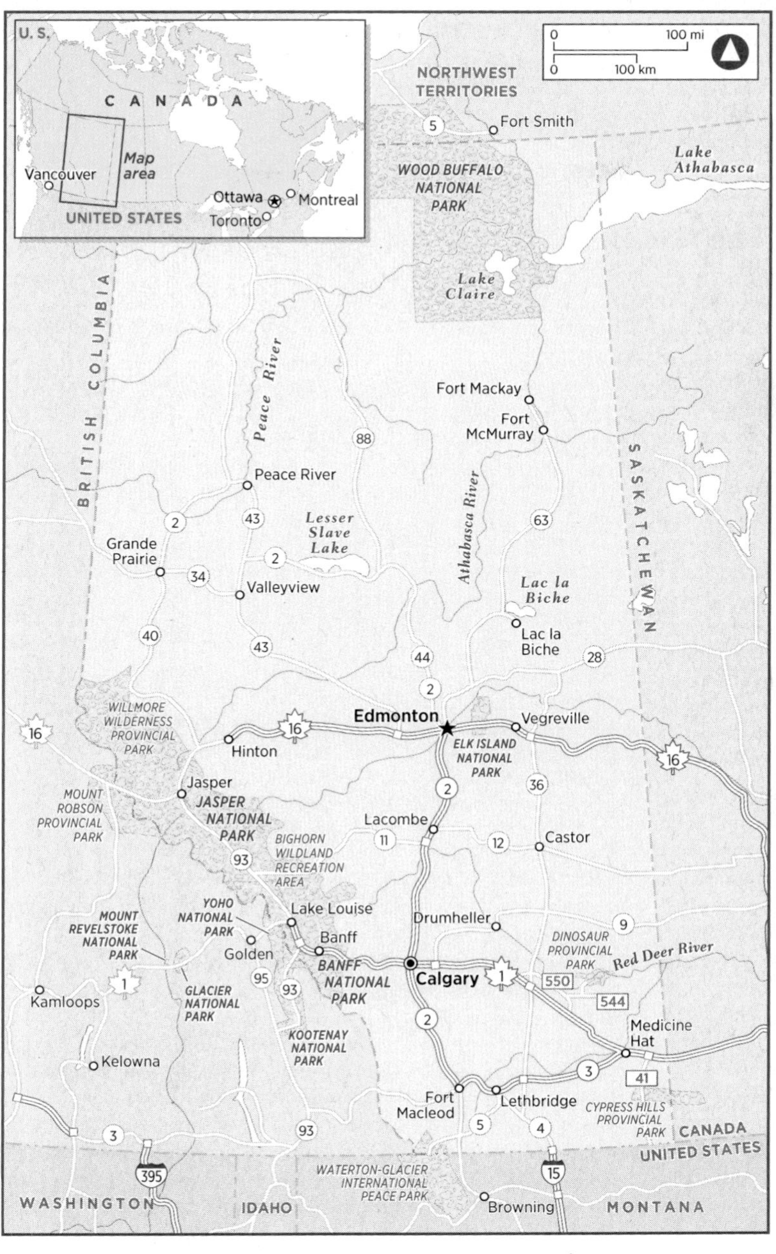

14

ALBERTA & THE ROCKIES | Exploring the Province

Visitor Information

For information about the entire province, contact **Travel Alberta,** Box 2500, Edmonton, AB T5J 2Z4 (✆ **800/252-3782;** www.travelalberta.com). Be sure to ask for a copy of the accommodations guide (**www.explorealberta.com** has many listings also), as well as the excellent *Traveler's Guide* and a road map. There's a separate guide for campers, which you should ask for if you're considering camping at any point during your trip.

Alberta has no provincial sales tax. There's only the 5% goods and services tax (GST), plus a 5% accommodations tax.

The Great Outdoors

Most people don't come to Alberta with the intention of sticking to the cities. Blessed with extraordinary mountain terrain; beautiful rolling foothills; vast prairie land; and endless, big blue sky (most of the time), the province of Alberta cries out to be seen from the outside in.

There are wildlife to glimpse and diverse ecosystems to observe, and in the far north, there's the Athabasca, the second largest river delta in the world (after the Amazon), with wetlands that cradle more than 55 species of mammals and more than 200 species of birds. The national parks of Waterton Lakes, Banff, Jasper, and Wood Buffalo are all UNESCO World Heritage Sites and offer unique opportunities to explore nature—albeit with wildly varying degrees of solitude.

Even urban Albertans often embrace the outdoors, so you'll also find plenty of opportunities for cycling in Calgary and Edmonton on an expansive and well-connected system of bicycle paths. In the winter, these paths can be used to cross-country ski, as well—always an interesting sight amid the downtown skyscrapers.

Whether you're intent on adventure or just want to try something new, this is the place to get out of the car and stretch yourself. This chapter lays out your options, from tour operators who run multi-activity packages to the best spots to visit outdoors (with listings of tour operators, guides, and outfitters that specialize in each), and provides an overview of Alberta's parks.

HIKING In a nutshell, Alberta's varied alpine terrain and transition zones offer hiking enthusiasts endless choices for all kinds of excursions, from short trips through rolling foothills and spare forest, and along swift-running alpine creeks and rivers; to multi-day excursions up and over mountain passes, past towering waterfalls and massive glaciers, through the Continental Divide—on and on and on. There is a lifetime of options.

Some regions are particularly conducive to hiking excursions (read: the mountains); read on for some guidelines, including where to find trail maps and tour operators.

In the Canmore/Kananaskis area, **Tourism Canmore** (✆ **866/CAN-MORE** [866/226-6673] or 403/678-1296; www.tourismcanmore.com) has a comprehensive guide of hiking trails near town, as well as throughout the vast Kananaskis Country to the south; here, just east of Banff, the terrain is a little more varied—a mixture of alpine and foothills. For guided tours, contact **Inside Out** (✆ **888/999-7238;** www.insideoutexperience.com) in Canmore; they can set you up with a huge variety of guided hikes in the area. Costs per person for half-day hikes are C$69 (C$59 for children, or groups of eight or more), for full-day hikes C$139 (C$129 for children or groups). All guided tours include shuttle service to the trail head. **Mahikan Trails**

(✆ **866/776-HIKE** [866/776-4453] or 403/609-2489; www.mahikan.ca) will lead you to archaeologically significant First Nations sites in the area (p. 561). Full-day rates are C$600 for a group of four people, with an additional C$124 for each extra person up to eight. Banff National Park offers an almost immeasurable number of hiking options (1,600km/994 miles' worth), from short day trips to multi-day treks. Not all of them are difficult (though many are), but be aware that the easier hikes tend to draw the most crowds in summer. It's wise to check with the park to find the right trail for you. Parks Canada's website for Banff (www.pc.gc.ca/banff) has many maps and good tips, as well as regularly updated trail reports. Or call them at ✆ **403/762-1550.** Guided hikes and overnight backpacking trips are led by a number of companies, including **WildTrips** (✆ **403/678-0929;** www.wildtrips.ca) and **Yamnuska Mountain Adventures** (✆ **866/678-4164;** www.yamnuska.ca). The **Sunshine Meadows** guided hike, run by **White Mountain Adventures** (✆ **403/762-7889**) takes you above the Sunshine Village ski area and into a gorgeous alpine meadow. Group hikes cost C$35 per person.

In Jasper, your best bet for hiking isn't the local tourist authority, **Jasper Tourism** (✆ **780/852-3858;** www.jaspercanadianrockies.com), though they are able to help with hiking guides and trail maps. The *real* hiking authority in Jasper is the *Hike Jasper* guide, a tremendous online resource run by local enthusiasts. On their website, www.hikejasper.com, you'll find their take on the best hikes summer and winter, night-time hiking, and a listing of the best guides plying the park and their offerings (a top one is a 5-day guided hike retracing the route of legendary explorer David Thompson as he pushed through the Rockies and on to the Pacific Ocean).

Waterton Lakes National Park is considerably less developed than the other national parks in Alberta—which, overall, is a good thing. At the **park office** (✆ **403/859-2252;** www.pc.gc.ca/pn-np/ab/waterton/index.aspx), you'll find all the information you need, from maps of hiking trails to weather conditions. They'll also let you know if there's been a bear sighting recently—handy info if you plan to venture forth on foot.

However, Waterton's relatively untrammeled wilderness will make finding a guide a little tougher. You can try the one outfitter in town, **Tamarack Outdoor Outfitters** (✆ **403/859-2378**), which may be able to hook you up with a game local; otherwise, follow the guidelines the parks service provides and be aware of wildlife: This is the wildest of Alberta's mountain parks.

BIKING Some of the earliest adopters in the annals of mountain biking were rabid cyclists in Alberta, and the province remains one of the hotbeds of the sport. The **Canmore Nordic Centre Provincial Park** (1988 Olympic Way, Canmore; ✆ **403/678-2400**) is probably ten times as busy in summer as in winter thanks to the adaptability of the ski trails to world-class mountain biking. More than 70km (43 miles) of trails are taken over by mountain bikers in summer, and Trail Sports (on-site) offers bike rentals, skill-building courses, and guided rides.

Mountain biking in the national parks is a little bit trickier, given the sensitive nature of the environment, not to mention the throngs of tourists that might be meandering the trails at any given time. Banff National Park has more than 190km (118 miles) of mountain-biking trails, but it's permitted on only a select number of the hiking trails. You are subject to fines if you are caught biking on a hiking-only trail. The park's website (www.pc.gc.ca/banff) has a good list of biking trails. The same is true of Jasper, where information, trail maps, and excluded areas can be found at www.explorejasper.com/recreation/biking.htm. And remember, be bear aware!

The **Bow Valley Parkway ★** between Banff and Lake Louise and **Parkway 93A ★** in Jasper Park are both good less trafficked roads for road bike touring. Bike rentals are easily available nearly everywhere in the parks.

FISHING Alberta's fast-running mountain rivers and streams, as well as its northern lakes, offer a great many opportunities for anglers. The north in particular, in the Peace-Athabasca delta, is a favorite; hundreds of remote lakes throughout the wetlands offer sport fishers ample opportunity to trawl for lake trout, northern pike, and walleye. Fly-fishers will want to cast into the Bow River and wade the rivers of the Crowsnest Pass.

Keep in mind that you need a license (C$26 for Canadians and C$71 for non-Canadians) to catch fish in Alberta. Most fishing outfitters in the province sell them, as well as many sporting goods stores. You also need a permit from Parks Canada to fish in Banff. They cost C$10 per day or C$34 for an annual pass.

In the national parks, you'll find tour operators (far too many to list here) that offer anything from hip-wading fly fishing in the rivers to trawling the mountain lakes. Be warned: Unless you're an experienced fly fisher or very familiar with the area, do not attempt to wade into the mountain rivers on your own. The water is ice-cold, and the current is unpredictable at different points in the river and at different times of the year. An imprudent wade in the wrong place or at the wrong time could easily kill you.

SKIING There are **downhill** areas at Banff, Lake Louise, Jasper, Nakiska and Golden. At its best, skiing is superb here: The snowpack is copious, the scenery is beautiful, the après-ski festivities are indulgent, and the accommodations are world-class. There's good value in an Alberta ski holiday—lift tickets here are generally cheaper than those at comparable ski areas in the United States. Lift tickets range from C$58 to C$78 per day (adults), with tickets for children a bargain at approximately one-third the cost.

Heli-skiing isn't allowed in the national parks but is popular in the adjacent mountain ranges near Golden in British Columbia. **CMH Heli-Skiing** (**✆ 800/661-0252** or 403/762-7100; www.cmhski.com) is the leader in this increasingly popular sport, which uses helicopters to deposit skiers on virgin slopes far from the lift lines and runs of ski resorts. CMH offers 4-, 5- and 7-day trips to 12 locations; prices begin at C$4,690 for 5 days, including lodging, food, and transport from Calgary.

Cross-country skiers will also find a lot to like in the Canadian Rockies. A number of snowbound mountain lodges remain open throughout winter and serve as bases for adventurous Nordic skiers. You'll also find endless pleasure in exploring the **Canmore Nordic Centre Provincial Park** (**✆ 403/678-2400**), also built for the 1988 games. More than 70km (43 miles) of trails are available to skiers all winter; Trail Sports (on-site) offers ski rentals, skill-building courses, and guided excursions.

WHITE-WATER RAFTING & CANOEING The Rockies' many glaciers and snowfields are the source of mighty rivers. Outfitters throughout the region offer white-water rafting and canoe trips of varying lengths and difficulty—you can spend a single morning on the river or plan a 5-day expedition. Jasper is central to a number of good white-water rivers; **Maligne Rafting Adventures Ltd.** (**✆ 780/852-3370;** www.mra.ab.ca) has packages for rafters of all experience levels.

WILDLIFE VIEWING If you're thrilled by seeing animals in the wild, the Rocky Mountain national parks are all teeming with wildlife—bighorn sheep, grizzly and black bears, deer, mountain goats, moose, coyotes, lynxes, wolves, and more. Aside from the Rockies, Elk Island National Park ★, just outside Edmonton, harbors the tiny pygmy shrew and the immense wood buffalo.

GETTING A taste OF THE OLD WEST AT A GUEST RANCH

Alberta has been ranch country for well over a century, and the Old West lifestyle is deeply ingrained in its culture. Indulge in a cowboy fantasy and spend a few days at one of the province's many historic guest ranches.

At Seebe, in the Kananaskis Country near the entrance to Banff National Park, are a couple of the oldest and most famous guest ranches. **Rafter Six Ranch** (✆ **888/267-2624** or 403/673-3622; www.raftersix.com), with its beautiful log lodge, can accommodate up to 60. The original Brewster homestead was transformed in 1923 into the **Brewster's Kananaskis Guest Ranch** ★ (✆ **800/691-5085** or 403/673-3737; www.kananaskisguestranch.com). Once a winter horse camp, the **Black Cat Guest Ranch** (✆ **800/859-6840** or 780/865-3084; www.blackcatguestranch.ca) near Hinton is another long-established guest ranch in beautiful surroundings.

At all these historic ranches, horseback riding and trail rides are the main focus, but other western activities, such as rodeos, barbecues, and country dancing, are usually on the docket. Gentler pursuits, such as fishing, hiking, and lolling by the hot tub, are equally possible. Meals are usually served family-style in the central lodge, while accommodations are either in cabins or in the main lodge. A night at a guest ranch usually ranges from C$110 to C$200 and includes a ranch breakfast. Full bed-and-board packages are available for longer stays. There's usually an additional hourly fee for horseback riding.

Homestays at smaller working ranches are also possible. Here you can pitch in and help your ranch-family hosts with their work or simply relax. For a stay on a real mom-and-pop farm or ranch, obtain a list of members from **Alberta Country Vacations Association** (✆ **403/722-3053;** www.albertacountryvacation.com).

CALGARY ★★

303km (188 miles) S of Edmonton, 788km (490 miles) W of Regina, 512km (318 miles) NW of Great Falls

Calgary has come a long way in a relatively short period of time: From its beginnings as Fort Calgary, an outpost of the Northwest Mounted Police, in 1876, the city has evolved in just over 130 years to a bustling, dynamic urban center of more than a million souls and a center of international commerce.

The 1988 Winter Olympic Games helped put Calgary on the international map, and its legacy has been one of enduring tourism. Visitors now associate Calgary with the mountains, even if they are still another hour's drive west.

But despite some Calgarians' protestations to the contrary, this is an oil town, first and foremost. More than 90% of the country's oil, gas, and energy business is right here, as are more than half of the coal companies. Calgary's fortunes have ever followed the price of oil, and the city is well acquainted with the boom-and-bust cycle.

Boom or bust, business rules here. People in this city are entrepreneurs and risk takers, and when the good times are rolling, they roll right along with them, flaunting their wealth and doing their best to live large. Posh restaurants and cafes are routinely jammed, and high-end retail shopping is practically a contact sport here as flush Calgarians seem hurried to spend their money as quickly as they can.

With the influx of money has come a flood of cultural facilities and awareness, too. The city is more cosmopolitan than at any time in its history, and the common phrase that seems to be gaining momentum here tells the tale: During the first oil boom, Calgary grew; in the second one, it grew up. This leaves Calgary, ever-ambitious, looking to join the top shelf of North American urban centers—if, as many Calgarians believe, it's not there already.

Essentials

GETTING THERE BY PLANE **Calgary International Airport** (© **877/254-7427;** www.calgaryairport.com) lies 16km (10 miles) northeast of the city. You can go through U.S. Customs right here if you're flying to or coming from the U. S. via Calgary. The airport is served by **Air Canada** (© **888/247-2262;** www.aircanada.com), **Delta** (© **800/221-1212;** www.delta.com), **American Airlines** (© **800/433-7300;** www.aa.com), **United** (© **800/241-6522;** www.united.com), **Continental** (© **800/525-0280;** www.continental.com), and the homegrown **WestJet** (© **800/937-8538;** www.westjet.com), a Calgary-based carrier with dozens of destinations across North America. Being a hub of international commerce, Calgary is also served by several commuter lines.

Cab fare to downtown hotels comes to around C$25. Several downtown hotels provide shuttle service from the airport; the only devoted airport shuttle is the new **Allied Downtown Shuttle Service** (© **403/299-9555;** www.airportshuttlecalgary.ca; one-way C$15 adults, C$10 children), which now runs only pre-arranged shuttle service.

GETTING THERE BY TRAIN The nearest VIA Rail station is in Edmonton. You can, however, take a scenic train ride to/from Vancouver/Calgary on the Rocky Mountaineer, operated by **Rocky Mountaineer Vacations** (© **800/665-7245** or 604/606-7245; www.rockymountaineer.com). The lowest-priced tickets begin at C$609 for 2 days of daylight travel, which includes four meals and overnight accommodation in Kamloops; many other packages are available.

GETTING THERE BY BUS **Greyhound** buses (© **800/661-8747** or 403/260-0877; www.greyhound.ca) link Calgary with most other points in Canada, including Banff and Edmonton, as well as towns in the United States. The depot is at 877 Greyhound Way SW, west of downtown near the corner of 9th Avenue SW and 16th Street SW.

GETTING THERE BY CAR From the U.S. border, Route 89 in Montana becomes Highway 2 at the Carway border crossing and runs to Calgary. It continues north to Edmonton (via Red Deer). From either Vancouver in the west or Regina in the east, take the Trans-Canada Highway.

VISITOR INFORMATION The downtown **Visitor Service Centre** (© **800/661-1678** or 403/263-8510; www.tourismcalgary.com), at the base of the Calgary Tower (101 9th Ave. SW) and at the airport near the luggage carousels, provides free literature, maps, and information. The friendly white-hatted volunteer greeters at the Calgary Airport can also point you in the right direction.

CITY LAYOUT Central Calgary lies between the Bow River in the north and the Elbow River to the south. The two rivers meet at the eastern end of the city, forming **St. George's Island,** which houses a park and the zoo. South of the island stands Fort Calgary, birthplace of the city. The Bow River makes a bend north of downtown, and in this bend nestles **Prince's Island Park** and **Eau Claire Market.** The Canadian

Calgary

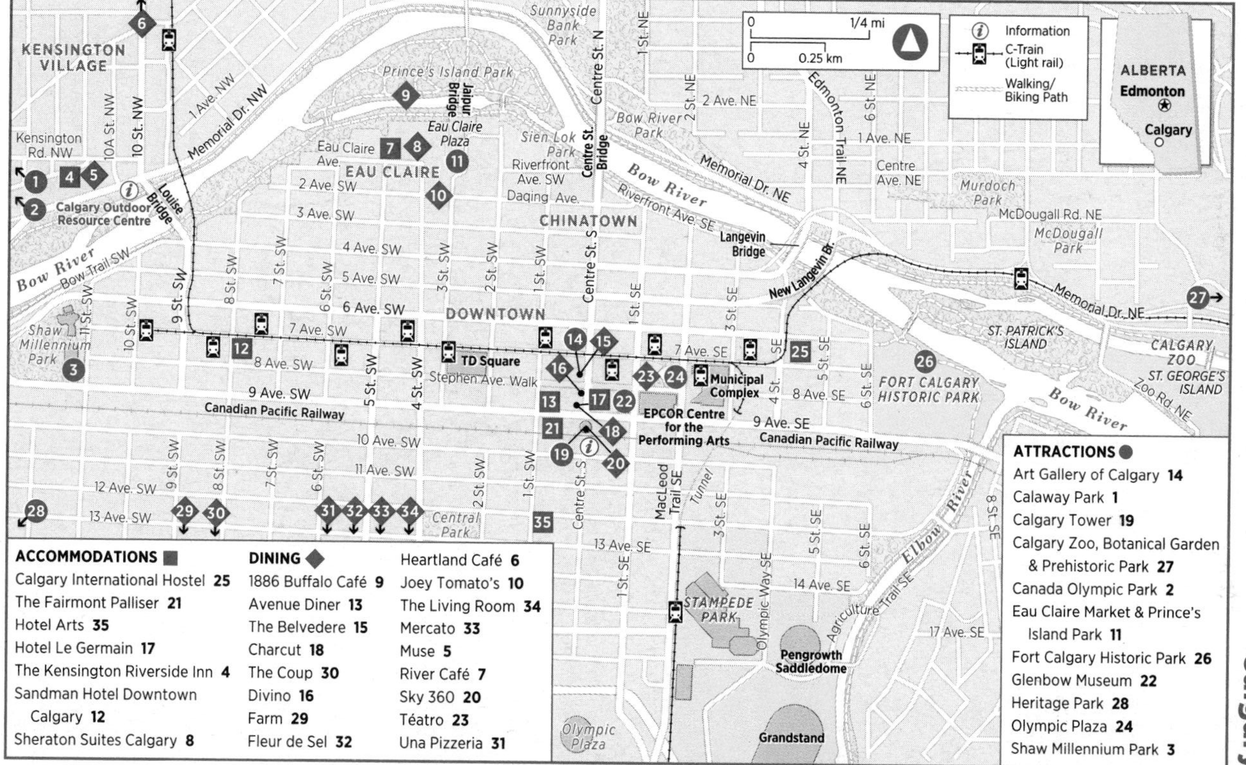
KENSINGTON VILLAGE
EAU CLAIRE
CHINATOWN
DOWNTOWN
Calgary Outdoor Resource Centre
Louise Bridge
Jaipur Bridge
Eau Claire Plaza
Centre St. Bridge
Langevin Bridge
New Langevin Br.
TD Square
Stephen Ave. Walk
Municipal Complex
EPCOR Centre for the Performing Arts
Canadian Pacific Railway
Bow River
Elbow River
Prince's Island Park
Sunnyside Bank Park
Sien Lok Park
Bow River Park
Murdoch Park
McDougall Park
ST. PATRICK'S ISLAND
FORT CALGARY HISTORIC PARK
CALGARY ZOO
ST. GEORGE'S ISLAND
STAMPEDE PARK
Pengrowth Saddledome
Grandstand
Olympic Plaza
Central Park
Shaw Millennium Park
Memorial Dr. NE
Memorial Dr. NW
Edmonton Trail NE
MacLeod Trail SE
Olympic Way SE
Agriculture Trail SE
Riverfront Ave. SE
Riverfront Ave. SW
Zoo Rd. NE
McDougall Rd. NE
Bow Trail SW
Kensington Rd. NW
Eau Claire Ave.
Daqing Ave.
Tunnel
0
1/4 mi
0
0.25 km
Information
C-Train (Light rail)
Walking/ Biking Path
ALBERTA
Edmonton
Calgary
ACCOMMODATIONS
Calgary International Hostel 25
The Fairmont Palliser 21
Hotel Arts 35
Hotel Le Germain 17
The Kensington Riverside Inn 4
Sandman Hotel Downtown Calgary 12
Sheraton Suites Calgary 8
DINING
1886 Buffalo Café 9
Avenue Diner 13
The Belvedere 15
Charcut 18
The Coup 30
Divino 16
Farm 29
Fleur de Sel 32
Heartland Café 6
Joey Tomato's 10
The Living Room 34
Mercato 33
Muse 5
River Café 7
Sky 360 20
Téatro 23
Una Pizzeria 31
ATTRACTIONS
Art Gallery of Calgary 14
Calaway Park 1
Calgary Tower 19
Calgary Zoo, Botanical Garden & Prehistoric Park 27
Canada Olympic Park 2
Eau Claire Market & Prince's Island Park 11
Fort Calgary Historic Park 26
Glenbow Museum 22
Heritage Park 28
Olympic Plaza 24
Shaw Millennium Park 3

Pacific Railway tracks run between 9th and 10th avenues, and **Central Park** and **Stampede Park,** scene of Calgary's greatest annual festival, stretch south of the tracks. Northwest, across the Bow River, is the **University of Calgary**'s lovely campus. The airport is northeast of the city.

Calgary is divided into four segments: **northeast** (NE), **southeast** (SE), **northwest** (NW), and **southwest** (SW), with avenues running east-west and streets north-south. The north and south numbers begin at Centre Avenue, the east and west numbers at Centre Street—a recipe for confusion if ever there was one.

GETTING AROUND **Calgary Transit System** (✆ **403/276-1000;** www.calgarytransit.com) operates buses and a light-rail system called the C-Train. You can transfer from the light rail to buses on the same ticket. The ride costs C$2.75 for adults and C$1.75 for children; the C-Train (a light rail train that runs above ground) is free (buses are not) in the downtown stretch between 10th Street and City Hall. Tickets are good for travel in only one direction.

Car-rental firms include **Avis,** 211 6th Ave. SW (✆ **403/269-6166**); **Budget,** 140 6th Ave. SE (✆ **403/226-0000**); and **Hertz,** 227 6th Ave. SW (✆ **403/221-1681**). Each of these has a bureau at the airport.

To summon a taxi, call **Checker Cabs** (✆ **403/299-9999**), **Red Top Cabs** (✆ **403/974-4444**), or **Yellow Cabs** (✆ **403/974-1111**).

The Calgary Stampede ★★★

The tagline is "the greatest outdoor show on Earth"; most Calgarians would agree, though most would apply the label to more than just the rodeo it ostensibly refers to. Since 1912, the Stampede has become more than a rodeo; it's a civic party. The first week in July, banks, restaurants, bars, offices, the airport, and shops pile hay bales around their front doors and erect clapboard door frames over the modern glass and steel, and button-down office workers don their boots, hats, and jeans for a hootin' hollerin' good time. For Calgarians, Stampede is not a spectator sport: By lunchtime, most offices sit vacant as the majority of the working crowd have gone in for some serious "Stampeding"—local code for going to (and staying too long in)—the city's numerous (and packed) bars.

A curious counterpoint to all the nocturnal social activity is the Stampede tradition of a "Stampede breakfast." Served daily—and early, and free!—every day of the Stampede at parking lots, shopping malls, and corporate offices all over town, it usually consists of flapjacks, sausages, orange drink (not to be confused with juice), and coffee. There may be some kind of hangover remedy embedded in this combination—heaven knows most of the indulgers could use it—but one thing's certain: If you pay for a single breakfast during Stampede, you're just not paying attention. See www.flapjackfinder.com for complete listings and reviews of the nearly 100 breakfasts offered.

The main event, of course, is the rodeo, the largest and most prestigious of its kind in North America, in which cowboys from all over the world compete in such events as bull-riding, steer-roping, and chuck-wagon races for prize money totaling more than C$1 million.

Parts of Stampede Park, just off Macleod Trail (near 25th Ave. SW), become amusement areas, whirling, spinning, and rotating with rides. Other areas are just for the kids, who romp through Kids' World and the Petting Zoo. Still other sections host livestock shows, a food fair, handicraft exhibitions, an art show, lectures, a bazaar, a casino, lotteries, and entertainment on several stages.

[FastFACTS] CALGARY

American Express The office at 421 7th Ave. SW (✆ **403/261-5982**) is open Monday through Friday 9am to 5pm.

Area Code Calgary and Southern Alberta are in the 403 area code. From anywhere in Canada and the U.S., simply add "1" to the number you're dialing, a 10-digit number. When dialing locally in-city, you must use 10-digit dialing; add "403" before every seven-digit number.

Doctors If you need non-emergency medical attention, check the phone book for the closest branch of **Medicentre,** a group of walk-in clinics open daily 7am to midnight. Also see their website, www.medicentres.com, for a list of locations.

Drugstores Check the phone book for **Shoppers Drug Mart,** which has more than a dozen stores in Calgary, most open till midnight. The branch at the Chinook Centre, 6455 Macleod Trail S. (✆ **403/253-2424**), is open 24 hours.

Emergency For medical, fire, or crime emergencies, dial ✆ **911.**

Hospitals If you need immediate attention, the following hospitals have emergency departments: **Foothills Hospital** (1403 29th St. NW; ✆ **403/670-1110**), **Alberta Children's Hospital** (1820 Richmond Rd. SW; ✆ **403/229-7211**), and **Rockyview General Hospital** (3500 26th Ave. SW; ✆ **403/541-3000**).

Newspapers Calgary's two dailies, the ***Calgary Herald*** (www.calgaryherald.com) and the ***Calgary Sun*** (www.calgarysun.com), are both morning papers. ***FFWD*** (www.ffwdweekly.com) is a youth-oriented newsweekly and a good place to look for information on the local music and arts scene.

Police The 24-hour number is ✆ **403/266-1234.** Dial ✆ **911** in emergencies.

Post Office The main post office is at 207 9th Ave. (✆ **403/974-2078**). Call ✆ 403/292-5434 to find other branches.

Time Calgary is on Mountain Standard Time, the same as Edmonton and Denver, and it observes daylight saving time.

Reserving accommodations well ahead is essential—as many months ahead of your arrival as you can possibly foresee. Some downtown watering holes even take reservations for space at the bar; that should give you an idea of how busy Calgary gets.

The same advice applies to reserving tickets for Stampede events. Park admission is C$14 adults, and tickets to the top rodeo events begin at C$25 but go up from there, depending on the event, the seats, and whether the event takes place in the afternoon or evening. A number of centennial projects are also in the works for the 100th anniversary year in 2012 (visit their website closer to the date for details), which are sure to bring Calgary major global attention and make tickets extra hard to come by. For mail-order bookings, contact the Calgary Exhibition and Stampede (P.O. Box 1060, Station M, Calgary, AB T2P 2K8; ✆ **800/661-1767;** fax 403/223-9736; www.calgarystampede.com).

Exploring Calgary

DOWNTOWN

Art Gallery of Calgary ★★ A small but mighty faction of contemporary-arts advocates here have been lobbying for years for funding to build a large-scale contemporary art gallery along the lines of the Vancouver Art Gallery or Toronto's Art Gallery of Ontario, but thus far have had no success. With Edmonton's stunning new Art Gallery of Alberta, the fight has gotten even tougher for them to see their dreams become a reality. But, knowing Calgary's limitless ambitions, they will. And in the meantime, there's the very good Art Gallery of Calgary on downtown's Stephen Avenue Mall, a mostly pedestrian stretch in the heart of the city's financial district. Housed in an historic building, the gallery's constantly changing program features prominent contemporary artists from all over the city and around the world in virtually every discipline—you will see well-curated photography (both documentary and conceptual), painting, and avant-garde sculpture, all with a smart, contemporary edge. It also offers a cafe (✆ **403/410-9358**) with a lovely sidewalk patio.

117 8th Ave. SW. ✆ **403/770-1350.** www.artgallerycalgary.org. C$5 adults, C$2.50 students, free for children 5 & under. Tues–Sat 10am–5pm; first Thurs of every month 10am–9pm. Closed Sun & Mon.

Calgary Tower ☺ Make this your first stop, for there's no better place to get your bearings. Reaching 762 steps—or 191m (627 ft.)—into the sky, this enduringly touristy landmark offers brilliant views from its observation terrace, from which you can take in the city, the mountains, the Bow River, and the prairies beyond. The elevator whisks you to the top in just 63 seconds. A stairway from the terrace leads to the rotating restaurant Sky 360 (see "Where to Dine," below). Photography from up here is fantastic.

101 9th Ave. SW (at Centre St. SW). ✆ **403/266-7171.** www.calgarytower.com. Elevator ride C$14 adults, C$12 seniors, C$10 children 6–17, C$6 children 5 & under. Sept–May daily 9am–9pm; June–Aug daily 9am–10pm. C-Train: 1st St. E.

Eau Claire Market & Prince's Island Park Eau Claire Market is part of a car-free pedestrian zone north of downtown on the banks of the Bow River; it links to lovely Prince's Island Park, a bucolic island lined with paths, shaded by cottonwood trees, and populated by hordes of Canada geese. This is where much of downtown Calgary comes to eat, drink, shop, sunbathe, jog, and hang out in good weather. The market itself no longer offers much for the traveler except a few eateries (better options are the pubs in the plaza outside the market), though it remains busy with a four-screen cinema and an IMAX theater (✆ **403/974-4629**) that has a five-story domed screen. The riverside park area and the island are your absolute best bets for a bit of outdoor urban Calgary; on a gorgeous summer day, a meander through Prince's Island, followed by a little window-shopping at the eclectic booths at the market, can't be beat.

200 Barclay Parade SW (near 2nd Ave. SW & 3rd St. SW). ✆ **403/264-6450.** Free admission. Market building Mon–Sat 9am–9pm, Sun noon–4pm; shop & restaurant hours vary. C-TRAIN: 3rd St. W.

Fort Calgary Historic Park On the occasion of the city's centennial in 1975, Fort Calgary became a public park of 16 hectares (40 acres), spread around the ruins of the original Mounted Police stronghold. In 2001, volunteers completed a replica of the 1888 barracks using traditional methods and building materials. The Interpretive Centre captures the history of Calgary, from its genesis as a military fort to its 20th-century beginnings as an agricultural and oil boomtown. Kids can do time in the 1875-era jail or dress up as a Mountie. There are a number of interesting videos and guided displays; always in focus are the adventures and hardships of the Mounties a century ago. The rigors of their westward march and the almost unbelievable isolation these pioneer troopers endured now seems incredible. If all this history whets your appetite, cross the Elbow River on 9th Avenue and head to the Deane House. This historic home was built by a Fort Calgary superintendent nearly 100 years ago and is now the Deane House Restaurant (✆ **403/269-7747**), operated by Fort Calgary.

750 9th Ave. SE. ✆ **403/290-1875.** www.fortcalgary.com. C$11 adults, C$10 students & seniors, C$7 children 7–17, C$5 children 3–6, free for children under 2. Daily 9am–5pm. C-TRAIN: Bridgeland.

Glenbow Museum ★ One of the country's finest museums, the Glenbow is a must for anyone with an interest in the history and culture of western Canada. What sets it apart from other museums chronicling the continent's Native cultures and pioneer settlement is the excellence of its interpretation. The walls and halls come alive with engaging storytelling. Especially notable is the third floor, with its vivid evocation of Native cultures—particularly of the local Blackfoot—and compelling descriptions of western Canada's exploration and settlement.

130 9th Ave. SE (at 1st St.). ✆ **403/268-4100.** www.glenbow.org. C$14 adults, C$10 seniors, C$9 students & children 7–17, free for children under 6; C$32 families. Mon–Sat 9am–5pm; Sun noon–5pm. C-TRAIN: 1st St. E.

Olympic Plaza ★★ Not to be confused with Canada Olympic Park, Olympic Plaza is a public square just across the street from Calgary's stately, sandstone Old City Hall. Plunked at the eastern end of the Stephen Avenue stroll, the plaza was built for the Winter Olympics in 1988. It served as a very public place for medal winners to receive their awards and has continued in the celebratory vein. This is now where Calgarians come to celebrate everything from hockey victories to Reggaefest. Bands play here in the summer—the regular being every Wednesday at lunch time—and a host of events play out here, as well. When it's not occupied, the summertime plaza features a wading pool for kids—and sweaty office workers—to cool off in. In the winter, the plaza is a popular public skating rink. It includes a Legacy Wall, with plaques commemorating medal winners from the Calgary Olympic Winter Games.

228 8th Ave. SE. ✆ **403/268-2489.** Free admission. Open 24 hours a day. C-TRAIN: Olympic Plaza.

Shaw Millennium Park ☺ This massive park, maintained by the City of Calgary, is the largest free, outdoor 24-hour skateboarding park in North America. There's a gnarly street course with ledges, flat bars, stairs, and trannies, an intermediate course with rails down stairs and banks, and an advanced course with a cloverleaf bowl and a large full pipe. With 6,968 sq. m (75,000 sq. ft.) of skate-able surface, basketball courts, and four sand volleyball courts, it's one of the largest skateboard parks in North America and draws skaters of all ages from all over the continent.

1220 9 Ave SW. Free admission. Open 24 hours. C-TRAIN: 10th St SW.

SOUTH OF DOWNTOWN

Heritage Park ★★ ☺ In the city's southwest, on the banks of the man-made Glenmore Reservoir—which is also Calgary's water supply—sits one of the liveliest historical re-creations to be found in Alberta. The largest historical village in all of Canada, Heritage Park, as the name suggests, offers visitors a taste of Calgary's frontier past, from its settler days in the early 19th century through its fur-trading roots in the 1860s all the way through to the construction of the railway in 1910, which linked what was, until then, an outpost to the rest of the country. Steam engines, horse-drawn carriages, and a paddlewheel on the Reservoir are all part of the attraction. The park offers costumed interpreters, street theater, and over 150 buildings and exhibits.

1900 Heritage Dr. SW. ✆ **403/268-8500.** www.heritagepark.ca. C$19 adults, C$14 children. May 22 to Labour Day daily 9am–5pm. C-TRAIN: Heritage station.

EAST OF DOWNTOWN

Calgary Zoo, Botanical Garden & Prehistoric Park ★ ☺ Calgary's large and thoughtfully designed zoo resides on St. George's Island in the Bow River. The Calgary Zoo comes as close to providing natural habitats for its denizens as is technically possible. You'll particularly want to see the troop of majestic lowland gorillas and the African warthogs. The flora and fauna of western and northern Canada are on display in the Botanical Garden, and there's an amazing year-round tropical butterfly enclosure, as well. If you're there at 10am, you can take in the official welcome and meet with a zoo professional. Call to inquire about special summer events, such as Thursday Jazz Nights and free interpretive talks called "Nature Tales."

1300 Zoo Rd. NE. ✆ **403/232-9300.** www.calgaryzoo.ab.ca. C$19 adults, C$17 seniors, C$11 children 3–12, free for children under 2. Daily 9am–5pm. C-TRAIN: Zoo station.

WEST OF DOWNTOWN

Canada Olympic Park ☺ The lasting memento of Calgary's role as host of the 1988 Winter Olympics stands in Olympic Park, which was the site for ski jumping, luge, and bobsledding during the Games. The Olympic Hall of Fame and Museum features the world's largest collection of Olympic artifacts, including the torch used to bring the flame from Greece; costumes and equipment used by the athletes; superb photographs; and a gallery of all medal winners. The reason why the park is still an exciting destination is the availability of activities and lessons. In winter, both adults and children can take downhill and cross-country ski lessons, learn to ski jump or snowboard, or get an introduction to snow skating. More exciting are the opportunities to ride a luge or bobsled. In winter, for C$165 adults, you can experience the twists and turns of the Olympic Track in a bobsled. In summer, there's mountain biking, a kid-friendly Eurobungy (a trampoline-like bungee jump), zip-lining, minigolf, and a climbing wall.

88 Canada Olympic Park Rd. SW. ✆ **403/247-5452.** www.coda.ab.ca. Daily lift ticket C$42 adults, C$36 students, C$28 seniors, C$33 children 13–17, C$26 children 5–12, C$2 children under 5; C$99 families (separate fees for activities & lessons). Museum C$6.20 adults. Tour venues year-round Fri–Mon 10am–4pm, Tues–Thurs 10am–9pm; ski hill Nov 14 to Mar 29 Mon–Fri 9am–9pm, Sat & Sun 9am–5pm.

Calaway Park ★ ☺ On the western fringes of the city, just off the Trans-Canada Highway on the way to Banff, Calgary's Calaway Park is the largest outdoor amusement park in western Canada. The park contains everything from roller coasters to the log ride and bumper cars, as well as daily live entertainment, western-themed minigolf, and a whole host of rides designed specifically for younger kids. It also regularly holds a variety of events to entice the visitor, such as the fantastically named Rad Dad day. ***Note:*** At the beginning and end of the season, the park is open only on the weekend and on public holidays.

245033 Range Rd. 33. ✆ **403/240-3822.** www.calawaypark.com. C$32 adults, C$23 seniors, C$25 children 3–6. May 17 to June 27 Sat & Sun 10am–7pm; Sept 6 to Oct 13 Sat & Sun 11am–6pm; June 28 to Sept 1 daily 10am–7pm.

Shopping

SHOPPING DISTRICTS OF NOTE

The main shopping district is downtown along **8th Avenue SW,** between 5th and 1st streets SW. The lower part of 8th Avenue is a pedestrian zone called the **Stephen Avenue Mall.** Major centers lining 8th Avenue between 1st and 4th streets include the Hudson's Bay Company and Holt Renfrew. Check out **Art Central,** 100 7th Ave.

SW, a visual-arts complex with over 30 artists' studios and galleries. A hip hangout for the young at heart, **Kensington Village** is just northwest of downtown across the Bow River, centered at 10th Street NW and Kensington Road. Crowded between the ubiquitous coffeehouses are bike shops and trendy boutiques. The stretch of **17th Avenue SW** between 4th and 10th streets SW has developed a mix of specialty shops, boutiques, cafes, and bars that makes browsing a real pleasure.

Mountain Equipment Co-op, 830 10th Ave. SW (✆ **403/269-2420;** www.mec.ca), is the largest outdoors store in Calgary, with everything from kayaks to ice axes. Come here before you head to the backcountry. If you like the look of pearl-snap shirts and the cut of Wranglers jeans, head to **Riley & McCormick,** 220 8th Ave. SW (✆ **403/262-1556**), one of Calgary's original western-apparel stores. If you're looking for cowboy boots, **Alberta Boot Company,** 614 10th Ave. SW (✆ **403/263-4605;** www.albertaboot.com), is Alberta's only remaining boot manufacturer.

The **Inglewood** neighborhood, south of downtown on 9th Avenue SE, is filled with antiques stores.

Where to Stay

A thriving hub of international commerce makes finding a cheap bed in Calgary difficult. Downtown offers a full complement of international business-class brands like Sheraton, Westin, and Delta, with few independents and little to distinguish between them, save location. Newer modern and sleek hotels like Le Germain and Hotel Arts have livened things up a bit.

Less expensive rooms, if they're available at all, tend to cluster around the motel strips: Macleod Trail S, or 16th Avenue NW, which is what the Trans-Canada Highway becomes as it passes through the city. A few deals can be found downtown at cheaper chains like **Best Western** (www.bestwestern.com), **Sandman Inn** (www.sandmanhotels.com), or **Travelodge** (www.travelodge.com). There is a dearth of accommodation outside the central financial core and motel strips, unfortunately, notably in trendy neighborhoods like the Mission.

If you like B&Bs, try the **Bed and Breakfast Association of Calgary** (www.bbcalgary.com), which has several dozen listings for the city. The many hotels in Motel Village (see below), which link to the city center via the C-Train, are another option; you can often find these rooms at discount hotel websites.

DOWNTOWN

Very Expensive & Expensive

The Fairmont Palliser ★ Opened in 1914 as one of the Canadian Pacific Railroad hotels, the Palliser remains Calgary's landmark historic hotel, its most visible expression of old-world luxury and upper-crust class. The vast marble-floored lobby, surrounded by columns and lit by gleaming chandeliers, is the very picture of Edwardian sumptuousness. You'll feel like an Alberta Cattle King in the Rimrock Dining Room, with vaulted ceilings, period murals, a massive stone fireplace, and hand-tooled leather panels on teak beams, although it's a bit grandfatherly to some. Guest rooms are large for a hotel of this vintage—the Pacific Premier rooms would be suites at most other properties—and they preserve the period charm while incorporating modern luxuries. Fairmont Gold rooms come with their own concierge and a private lounge with breakfast, drinks, and hors d'oeuvres included. In early 2010, a C$30-million renovation delivered new carpets, upholstery, and furniture throughout.

133 9th Ave. SW, Calgary T2P 2M3. ✆ **800/441-1414** or 403/262-1234. www.fairmont.com/palliser. 405 units. C$179–C$499 double; C$259–C$579 suite; C$1,800–C$2,500 suite w/multiple bedrooms. AE, DC,

DISC, MC, V. Valet parking C$30–C$37; self-parking C$25. **Amenities:** Restaurant; lounge; babysitting; concierge; concierge-level rooms; health club; indoor pool; 24-hr. room service; spa. *In room:* A/C, TV, hair dryer, minibar, Wi-Fi.

Hotel Arts ★ You can still feel the old skeletons of the Holiday Inn it once was, but ever since this hotel reopened in 2006, it's been the city's see-and-be-seen destination. Raw Bar, the hotel's lounge, is a cocktail hotspot and a popular sushi bar, while Saint Germain, its dining room, is one of the top-rated fine-dining experiences in the city. Keep your eyes peeled for one or two players from the Calgary Flames, the city's NHL hockey team, leaving their Porsches with the valet. An interior courtyard sports a nice-sized open-air pool, which in turn sports a ring of poolside tables with cocktail and dinner service. The rooms, meanwhile, do their best to be chic, with long draping curtains, large plasma screens, and faux-fur throws on their Egyptian-cotton-clad beds. All come with small balconies, as well, ideal for surveying the city's late-night skyline. Rooms, generally, are small; and the bathrooms, in particular, feel dark and tiny when compared to other hotels in new buildings. But the common spaces are vast and inspired, dotted with contemporary art and dark velvet.

119 12th Ave. SW, Calgary T2R 0G8. © **800/661-9378** or 403/266-4611. www.hotelarts.ca. 185 units. C$269 double; C$359 suite. AE, DC, MC, V. Valet parking C$30; free self-parking. **Amenities:** Restaurant; bar; concierge; pool. *In room:* A/C, TV, hair dryer, minibar, Wi-Fi.

Hotel Le Germain ★★ Calgary's newest hotel is a breath of fresh air in a brand new building right downtown. Le Germain, a chain from Montréal, brings a modern and stylish flair to their 143 rooms (too many to be called "boutique," even if they try). Guests are chic business folks and cosmopolitan travelers from places like New York and Europe. Staff, many of whom are bilingual, will go beyond the call of duty to ease your stay. Dark browns and purples mix with retro white chairs and mirrors in spacious and very comfortable rooms. There are large work spaces, a good music system, and all the bells and whistles for those with work to be done. Smart extras, like a hidden ironing board and individual climate control, hit the mark, as well. Bathrooms are all very large, with a bright separated shower and plenty of light. The gym connects with the next-door apartments, so it can be crowded. The ground level restaurant, Charcut (see p. 544), is the best in town.

899 Centre St. SW, Calgary T2G 1B3. © **877/362-8990** or 403/264-8990. www.germaincalgary.com. 143 units. C$279–C$529 superior double; C$309–C$559 deluxe double; from C$759 suite. AE, MC, V. Parking C$35. **Amenities:** Restaurant; lounge; gym; concierge. *In room:* A/C, TV, hair dryer, minibar, Wi-Fi.

The Kensington Riverside Inn ★★★ At all of two stories high and half a block from the city's vibrant—and eminently walkable—Kensington District, the Riverside Inn is a delightful surprise. A chic redo in recent years has erased its country charm, replacing it with a sleek, sophisticated aesthetic. It's private, secluded, and quiet. The large salon features a fireplace and couch-side cocktail and appetizer service from its award-winning restaurant, the Chef's Table. The 19 rooms are ample and have all the comforts, including plush down pillows and duvets. A short walk across the footbridge lands you on Prince's Island Park, perhaps the city's most appealing urban oasis, which sits in the shadow of the downtown office towers. With its just-close-enough-to-downtown location, the Riverside is Calgary's top boutique hotel, without a doubt.

1126 Memorial Dr. NW, Calgary T2N 3E3. © **877/313-3733** or 403/228-4442. Fax 403/228-9608. www.kensingtonriversideinn.com. 19 units. C$209 double; C$309 suite. Rates include breakfast. AE, DC, MC, V. Free parking. **Amenities:** Restaurant; bar; concierge. *In room:* A/C, TV, hair dryer, minibar, Wi-Fi.

Sheraton Suites Calgary The Sheraton Suites overlooks the Eau Claire Market area, just steps away from both the Bow River Greenway and downtown business towers. As an all-suite hotel, the Sheraton offers large and thoughtfully designed rooms that put luxury and business ease foremost. The decor is strikingly modern, with quality and notably comfortable furniture, plus easy access to high-tech tools to help a business traveler multitask. The built-in cabinetry makes it feel very homelike, as do the Prairie-influenced art, plants, and two TVs in every room. Corner king suites are especially nice, with huge bathrooms, tiled showers, and Jacuzzi tubs. If being near green space is important to you and you'll be staying for a few nights, this should be your top choice.

255 Barclay Parade SW, Calgary T2P 5C2. © **888/784-8370** or 403/266-7200. www.sheratonsuites.com. 323 units. C$127–C$295 suite. Additional adult C$30. AE, DC, DISC, MC, V. Valet parking Sun–Thurs C$38, Fri & Sat C$27. **Amenities:** 2 restaurants; lounge; babysitting; concierge; exercise room; Jacuzzi; indoor pool; 24-hr. room service; sauna; Wi-Fi (in public spaces). *In room:* A/C, TV w/games & movie channels, fridge, hair dryer, Internet.

Moderate & Inexpensive

Calgary International Hostel The 120 beds at the Calgary hostel are the city's most affordable lodgings—but there are reasons beyond economy to stay here. The hostel is on the edge of downtown, convenient to bars and restaurants along Stephen Avenue and theaters near the performing-arts center. There is a games room and Internet access, it has homey—if somewhat dated—common areas, and it's clean as a whistle. It's very highly rated by guests from all over the world. There are 110 dorm-style beds with two family rooms available. A small convenience store is on-site.

520 7th Ave. SE, Calgary T2G 0J6. © **866/762-4122** or 403/269-8239. www.hihostels.ca, 94 beds. Members C$26–C$30 shared room, C$69–C$100 private room; nonmembers C$30–C$35 shared room, C$77–C$110 private room. MC, V. Free parking.

Sandman Hotel Downtown Calgary ★ This hotel on the west end of downtown is one of Calgary's best deals. The Sandman is conveniently located on the free rapid-transit mall, just west of the main downtown core. The standard rooms are a good size, but the real winners are the very large corner units, which feature small kitchens and great views. Rooms may be dated, but they are clean and cared for. The Sandman is a popular place with corporate clients, due to its central location and good value. It also boasts a complete fitness facility. Its private health club, available free to guests, has a lap pool, three squash courts, and aerobics and weight-training facilities.

888 7th Ave. SW, Calgary, AB T2P 3J3. © **800/726-3626** or 403/237-8626. www.sandmanhotels.com. 301 units. C$99–C$139 double. Children under 16 stay free in parent's room. AE, DC, DISC, MC, V. Parking C$6–C$16. **Amenities:** Restaurant; bar; concierge; health club; indoor pool; limited room service. *In room:* A/C, TV, fridge, hair dryer, Wi-Fi.

MOTEL VILLAGE

Northwest of downtown, this triangle of more than 20 large motels, plus restaurants, stores, and gas stations, forms a self-contained hamlet near the University of Calgary. Enclosed by Crowchild Trail, the Trans-Canada Highway, and Highway 1A, the village's costlier establishments flank the highway, and the cheaper ones lie off Crowchild Trail. If you're driving and don't want to deal with downtown traffic, just head here to find a room; for C-Train service, use the Lions Park or Banff Park stops. Except during the Stampede, you'll be able to find a vacancy without reservations. Use a discount hotel website such as Travelocity to find deals here. Popular chain hotels and some independents are located here, including **Comfort Inn** (2369 Banff Trail NW; © **403/289-2589**), **Calgary Motel Village** (2369 Banff Trail NW; © **800/228-5150** or

403/289-2581), **Best Western Village Park Inn** (1804 Crowchild Trail NW; ✆ **888/774-7716** or 403/289-4645), **Travelodge North** (2304 16th Ave. NW; ✆ **800/578-7878** or 403/289-0211), and the **Quality Inn University** (2359 Banff Trail NW; ✆ **800/661-4667** or 403/289-1973). You can expect rates of about C$120 to C$140 for a double.

CAMPING

The **Calgary West Campground** (✆ **403/288-0411;** www.calgarycampground.com), on the Trans-Canada Highway west of the city, allows tents and pets. Facilities include washrooms, toilets, laundry, a dumping station, hot showers, groceries, and a pool. The price for full hook-up with two people is C$45 per night; tent sites are C$29 to C$32 per night.

Where to Dine

Gone are the days when the Calgarian restaurant scene offered a vast array of dishes featuring Alberta beef—generally acknowledged as some of the best in the world—and little else. Recent economic boom times and an influx of outsiders from around the country and all over the world have bestowed upon the city a vibrantly eclectic, cosmopolitan dining scene. As is the case with most things here, a fresh, contemporary take dominates most menus, and the emphasis on organic and local ingredients seems to grow by the day. Don't be shocked to find local bison and elk on a great many menus around town, if accompanied by such cutting-edge culinary trends like molecular gastronomy (ginger-celeriac foam, anyone?).

The city's most vibrant dining districts can be found either in or on the edge of the city core. Downtown, both workers on their lunch breaks and travelers lodging in the many nearby hotels have a huge variety of options, most along Stephen Avenue Mall or 9th Street. The handful of blocks around 17th Avenue SW, between about 8th Street and 2nd Street, and 4th Street SW, between 17th Avenue and 25th Avenue (also known as the Mission) are also dense with choices.

DOWNTOWN

Expensive

The Belvedere ★ CONTEMPORARY A favorite power-lunch spot for flush oilmen, the very stylish Belvedere, on Stephen Avenue Mall, is one of the most impressive of Calgary's restaurants. The dining room exudes a darkly elegant, 1930s atmosphere. The menu blends traditional favorites with stand-up-and-take-notice preparations. Foie gras frequently appears as an appetizer, perhaps seared with a brioche, chili-battered onions, and black pepper foam. Main courses feature local meats and seasonal produce; favorite main courses include an elk rack with melon salsa, Digby scallops with mango and chilies, and duck breast with black truffle chutney. The bar is a quiet and sophisticated spot for a drink. They also have what is probably Calgary's best wine list.

107 8th Ave. SW. ✆ **403/265-9595.** www.thebelvedere.ca. Reservations recommended. Main courses C$24–C$44. AE, DC, MC, V. Tues–Fri 11:30am–2pm & 5pm–midnight; Sat 5:30–10pm.

Charcut ★★ GRILL This is the evolution of the steakhouse, a gorgeous and hot new restaurant that moves beyond the typical Alberta chunk of beef (tenderloin, New York strip, T-bone) and looks at being a locavore and carnivore in a whole new light. The locally sourced menu is relaxed and simple, encouraging sharing. For example, split a butter-like bone marrow au gratin to start; then, pass around a pig's head mortadella with pistachios and truffles on house-made brioche or a lamb neck terrine with garden rhubarb. The simply prepared meat comes next, charbroiled, wood smoked, or hot off a rotisserie. There's a marbled and flavorful butcher steak, lamb leg, prime rib, or heritage chicken. Non-carnivores can enjoy the whole fish on the bone. Good value, an extensive beer list, and smart service add to the satisfying experience.

101-899 Centre St. SW. ✆ **403/836-7482.** www.charcut.com. Reservations recommended. Main courses C$19–C$29. AE, DC, MC, V. Mon & Tues 11am–11pm; Wed–Fri 11am–1am; Sat 5pm–1am; Sun 5–10pm.

River Café ★★ CONTEMPORARY If you have one meal in Calgary, it should be here. You might have a slightly better meal at, say, Téatro, but nothing touches the River Café's combo of cuisine and location. To reach the aptly named River Café, it takes a short walk through the Eau Claire Market area, then over the footbridge to pretty Prince's Island Park. On a lovely summer evening, the walk is a plus, as are the restaurant's park-side decks (no vehicles hurtling by). Wood-fired, free-range, and wild-gathered foods teamed with organic whole breads and fresh-baked desserts form the backbone of the excellent menu. There's a wide range of appetizers and light dishes—many vegetarian—as well as pizza-like flat breads topped with zippy cheese, vegetables, and fruit. Specialties from the grill include braised pheasant breast with mustard spaetzle, black-cherry oil, and roasted apple. Menus change seasonally and read like a very tasty adventure novel.

25 Prince's Island Park. ✆ **403/261-7670.** www.river-cafe.com. Reservations recommended. Main courses C$24–C$49. AE, MC, V. Mon–Fri 11am–3pm, Sat & Sun 10am–3pm; daily 5–11pm (5–10pm in winter). Closed Jan.

Sky 360 REGIONAL There's more than just spectacular views 762 steps (or a quick elevator ride) up the Calgary Tower. The menu here is now much more gourmet-focused and upscale than in years past, but it's also full of crowd-pleasers like goat cheese penne, grilled salmon, tenderloins, and strip loins. The elevator fee is included in your meal; the wine list is surprisingly good, and with the place rotating on a 45-minute schedule, you'll get a couple of full city views in with a meal.

101 9th St. (in the Calgary Tower). ✆ **403/532-7966.** www.sky360.ca. Reservations recommended. Main courses C$22–C$42. AE, MC, V. Mon–Sat 11am–2pm, Sun 10am–2pm; daily 5–10pm.

Téatro ★★ ITALIAN Located in the historic, spectacularly renovated Dominion Bank building, Téatro is about entertainment. It's just across from the Centre for the Performing Arts, and the restaurant's open kitchen and chic atmosphere offer distraction and drama. Oh, and the chef delivers the best New Italian cooking in Calgary. The high-ceilinged dining room is dominated by columns and huge panel windows, bespeaking class and elegance. The extensive menu is based on "Italian market cuisine," featuring what's seasonally best and freshest; some of the best dishes come from the wood-fired oven that dominates one wall. For lighter appetites, there's a large selection of antipasti, boutique pizzas, and salads; the entrees, featuring Alberta beef, veal, pasta, and seafood, are prepared with flair and innovation. Lobster-and-scallop ravioli is a favorite. Service is excellent.

200 8th Ave. SE. ✆ **403/290-1012.** www.teatro.ca. Reservations recommended. Main courses C$22–C$50. AE, DC, MC, V. Mon–Fri 11:30am–2pm; daily 5pm–midnight.

Moderate & Inexpensive

1886 Buffalo Café ★★★ TRADITIONAL/BREAKFAST The name means what it says: Founded in 1886 (the "Buffalo" was added in recent years) and made moderately famous by a sweet Visa ad made for the 1988 Calgary Winter Olympics, it's probably the longest-running breakfast in town, if not the whole country. With good reason—the hash browns are piled high, the bacon and sausages fresh and perfectly cooked, the flapjacks come in towers, and the array of egg dishes is dizzying. All served in the noisy din of the cafe's resoundingly authentic, pioneer-era environment (clapboard shack exterior, rough old-wood interior), it's an experience not to be missed. The cafe got here first, but the city has built up around it; 1886 is now surrounded by gleaming office towers and the condos of Eau Claire Market (which is right across the street), but its authenticity remains undiminished. Try Kenny's Special, a mountain of egg, cheese, green pepper, and mushroom; plan to skip eating the rest of the day. You can also try the Barley Mill (✆ **403/290-1500**), a large pub that is its sister property, right next door, for good, unpretentious, reasonably priced pub fare.

187 Barclay Parade SW. ✆ **403/269-9255.** Reservations not accepted. Main courses C$9–C$15. MC, V. Mon–Fri 6am–3pm; Sat & Sun 7am–3pm.

Avenue Diner Along the Stephen Avenue Mall pedestrian strip, the Avenue is a reasonably priced alternative. Their specialties are breakfasts and lunches. In fact, they're not even open in the evenings. There's a cool retro feel to the scene, and the menu has some blasts-from-the-past, as well—namely, their signature macaroni and cheese made with aged white cheddar and truffle oil. The Eggs Bennys are vegetarian-friendly; try the one with vine-ripened tomatoes, basil, and reduced balsamic. Come mid-morning on a weekday; it can be tough to get a table for weekend brunch.

105 8th St. ✆ **403/263-2673.** www.avenuediner.com. Reservations not accepted. Main courses C$6–C$18. Mon–Fri 7am–3pm; Sat & Sun 8am–3pm.

Divino ★ BISTRO This estimable bar and restaurant calls itself a "wine and cheese bistro," and while a casual spot for a drink and cheese platter is welcome on busy Stephen Avenue, Divino offers a lot more. This bustling, stylish gathering spot offers intriguing light entrees, from sandwiches (lamb confit melt with fig jam) to pasta (cannelloni filled with lobster and chanterelles), in addition to full-flavored and satisfying main courses such as roast chicken with herb mustard gnocchi. A class act.

113 8th Ave. SW. ✆ **403/234-0403.** www.crmr.com/divino. Reservations recommended. Main courses C$17–C$37. AE, DC, MC, V. Mon–Thurs 11am–10pm; Fri 11am–11pm; Sat 5–11pm; Sun 5–10pm. Closed Sun Oct–June.

Joey Tomato's ITALIAN In the popular Eau Claire Market complex, the lively Joey Tomato's serves Italian/Asian fusion cooking to throngs of appreciative Calgarians. And no wonder it's often packed with the city's young and tanned: The food is really good, the prices are moderate (by the city's standards), and there's a lively bar scene. The broad menu includes steaks, fresh fish, and stir-fried veggies. It's always a fun, high-energy place to eat.

200 Barclay Parade SW. ✆ **403/263-6336.** www.joeyrestaurants.com. Reservations not accepted. Main courses C$12–C$35. AE, MC, V. Sun–Thurs 11am–midnight; Fri & Sat 11am–1am.

17TH AVENUE & THE MISSION (4TH ST.)

Expensive

The Living Room ★ CONTEMPORARY Along the burgeoning 17th Avenue cluster of boutiques, bars, and restaurants, the Living Room offers an inventive contemporary menu in an almost cottage-like setting. Set in an old bungalow—a holdover from much earlier days in this development-mad city—the dining room is cozy and homey, with modern design flair, and the expansive street-side patio, under the cover of lush trees, is an urban oasis perfect for summer evening dining. The solid wooden fence that separates the patio from the sidewalk is a perfectly calculated height: short enough to observe the dynamic street scene, but just tall enough to feel apart from it. The restaurant features an "interactive" component (which is just a fancy way of saying it makes dishes for two, to share) and offers an array of local fare (bison, lamb, and beef) prepared in inventive ways, such as the Hamilton Farms Black Angus tenderloin, with seared Quebec foie gras, sun choke and salsify ragout with ginger cider and beet reduction. Also, an updated version of fondue can be found here—perfect for the waning, chilling days of patio season in the fall.

514 17th Ave. SW. ✆ **403/228-9830.** Reservations recommended, particularly for patio. Main courses C$26–C$39. AE, MC, V. Mon–Fri 11:30am–2pm & 5–11pm.

Mercato ★★★ ITALIAN One of Calgary's true see-and-be-seen hotspots, Mercato serves up gorgeous traditional Italian fare with outstanding flair and panache. It's a casual environment with an open kitchen and, when it fills up at lunch and dinner—as it almost always does—it's a loud, boisterous, fun affair. Attached to the restaurant is a culinary boutique, where specialty cheeses, breads, and pastas can be found; particularly appealing are the barrel-sized kegs of Uncle Luigi's olive oil and balsamic vinegar, which the staff bottle before your eyes. The menu features a sublime selection of pastas, including a killer traditional fettuccine carbonara and a linguini with fresh ricotta, arugula, and *prosciuttino* (crisped prosciutto). Adventurous diners can tuck into such dishes as braised rabbit legs in a wild mushroom, tomato, and olive *ragu,* or requisite beef and poultry dishes, served with elegance.

2224 4th St. ✆ **403/263-5535.** Reservations strongly recommended. Main courses C$16–C$40. AE, MC, V. Daily 11:30am–2pm & 5:30–11pm.

Moderate

The Coup ★ VEGETARIAN Calgary's best vegetarian food comes with a healthy, fresh, and creative fusion vibe at this hip spot on 17th Avenue. Most ingredients are organic and local. There are jam-packed salads, falafel quesadillas, and a dragon bowl that has steamed veggies, tofu, and brown rice. Flavors stem from all over the map, Latin to Asian. There's also a fun cocktail list. This place is always busy, but you can have a drink at the sister lounge next door called Meet while you wait.

924 17th Ave. SW. ✆ **403/541-1041.** www.thecoup.ca. Reservations not accepted. Main courses C$7–C$16. AE, MC, V. Tues–Fri 11:30am–3pm, Sat & Sun 9am–3pm; Tues–Thurs 5–10pm, Fri & Sat 5–11pm, Sun 5–9pm.

Farm ★ REGIONAL Owner Janice Beaton is a locavore leader in these parts. As the name suggests, this is a place to sample wholesome, simple food. Modeled after the Slow Food movement (Beaton is one of the founders of the local chapter), the food is more precious than pastoral. Small plates and platters make sampling from the outstanding cheese and cold cuts a good idea. The bubbly and mildly spicy signature mac 'n' cheese is by far the best in town. Trout and steak are larger options. The ambience is as relaxing as the countryside.

1006 17th Ave SW. ✆ **403/246-2276.** www.farm-restaurant.com. Reservations recommended for dinner. Main courses C$9–C$19. Mon–Fri 11:30am–2pm; Mon–Thurs 5–10pm, Fri 5–11pm; Sat 10:30am–11pm; Sun 10:30am–10pm.

Fleur de Sel ★★ BISTRO Locals don't get more local than this. With its rich, red walls and black-and-white tile, everything about Fleur de Sel screams "French!"—

including its boisterous owner and chef, Patrice. Like most of his staff, he knows most of the customers by name—many of them from the dense neighborhood nearby or from up the hill in tony Mount Royal—and greets them with the enthusiasm of a favorite uncle. This is not a place to observe your cholesterol intake—Fleur de Sel, with its lovely, liberal application of butter and cream, takes the credo "fat is flavor" quite literally; what it is, though, is a place to throw caution to the wind for a moment, sit back, and enjoy the ride. This is the kind of homey place where strangers at adjacent tables can quickly become friends, brought together by a love for cuisine. If you enjoy your confit with a side dish of possibility, then Fleur de Sel is the place for you.

#2-2015 4th St. SW. © **403/228-9764.** www.fleurdeselbrasserie.com. Reservations recommended. Main courses C$29–C$39. MC, V. Tues–Fri 11:30am–2pm; daily 5:30pm "'til the last guest!"

Una Pizzeria ★ PIZZERIA The best pizza in Calgary is at this chic wine bar on 17th Street. There's nothing avant-garde about a staple like the *margherita,* but the toppings—*flor di latte* mozzarella—are certainly gourmet. You can also opt for a flat-iron steak with salsa *verde* and caper berries or a stunningly simple (there's that word again) appetizer of marinated zucchini with lemon, olive oil, and Romano cheese. The wine list includes 25 to 30 wines by the glass.

618 17th Ave. SW. © **403/453-1183.** www.unapizzeria.com. Reservations not accepted. Main courses C$13–C$21. MC, V. Daily 11:30am–1am.

KENSINGTON

Expensive

Muse ★ CANADIAN/FRENCH Tucked away on a quiet side street in perhaps Calgary's most walkable district, Muse resides in an adobe-type building that evokes a modern Mediterranean experience. The building's patchwork floor plan includes several levels, some open to small patios, and tucks diners into small, intimate spaces within the larger building. The menu, which breaks down into four courses, is focused on fresh, local ingredients and modern takes on traditional French fare. The smoked Pembina pork rack, with *"primeurs"* vegetables, Yukon potato hash, and grainy mustard jus is outstanding fare, both light and hearty, while the BC halibut with quinoa and cherry tomato salad, prosciutto-wrapped asparagus, and *vierge* sauce is a field-fresh, summery delight. All in, Muse is an intimate, urbane, yet ultimately casual experience with can't-miss cuisine—a winning combination.

107 10A St. NW. © **403/670-6873.** Reservations recommended. Main courses C$15–C$38. AE, MC, V. Tues–Thurs & Sun 5–10pm; Fri & Sat 5–11pm. Closed Mon.

Inexpensive

Heartland Café ★ CAFE A little east of the main drag of 10th Street NW, this traditional Kensington spot, tucked amongst the houses, is an original and one of the best cafes in town. With counter-service sandwiches, coffee, and decadent baked goods all served in a homey general store environment, Heartland feeds the soul at the same time as the belly.

940 2nd Ave. NW. © 403/270-4541. Sandwiches from C$6. AE, MC, V. Mon–Fri 8am–8pm; Sat & Sun 8am–5pm.

ELSEWHERE

Calgary sprawls into distant suburbs in every direction, making culinary adventures in the far-flung corners a time-consuming, confusing affair. However, at least a couple of spots, new this year, are worth the geographical challenge. Near the Calgary Zoo is the acclaimed and decidedly high-brow **Rouge** (© **403/531-2767;**

www.rougecalgary.com), which was recently listed amongst the top 60 restaurants in the world by the esteemed S. Pellegrino awards. Their French-inspired cuisine is dainty and precise, and a summer meal on their patio is a perfect special-occasion splurge. On the far south side of Calgary is **The Ranche** (✆ **403/225-3939;** www.crmr.com/theranche), set inside a heritage ranch home in Fish Creek Park. The menu is heavy on meat and game. Great for weekend brunch.

Calgary After Dark

To get a read on Calgary's vibrant cultural scene, pick up a copy of *FFWD,* the local free arts and entertainment weekly. There, you'll find listings for movies, art openings, upcoming concerts, clubs, and theater.

THE PERFORMING ARTS The **Calgary Centre for the Performing Arts** (205 8th Ave. SE; ✆ **403/294-7455**)—now called the Epcor Centre, after its corporate sponsor—is the catch-all venue for live theater, symphony, and opera. Calgary has a vibrant theater scene, with three major companies: **Alberta Theatre Projects** (✆ **403/294-7402**; www.atplive.com), **Theatre Calgary** (✆ **403/294-7440;** www.theatrecalgary.com), and the avant-garde, internationally celebrated **One Yellow Rabbit** (✆ **403/264-3224**; www.oyr.org), all working out of the Epcor Centre. Epcor is also home to the excellent **Calgary Philharmonic Orchestra** (✆ **403/571-0270;** www.cpo-live.com), an international-class ensemble.

THE CLUB & BAR SCENE Cover charges at most clubs are C$5 to C$10 for live music. Eau Claire Market is the home of the **Garage** (✆ **403/262-67620**), a hip warehouse-of-a-bar for playing billiards and listening to loud indie rock. A number of pubs and late-night watering holes are just outside the market on the Barclay Parade plaza. Check out **Barleymill Neighbourhood Pub,** 201 Barclay Parade SW (✆ **403/290-1500**), an oldsy-worldsy pub plunked down in the plaza across from the Eau Claire Market.

If you're looking for dance clubs, head south of downtown. **Hi-Fi Club,** 219 10th Ave. SW (✆ **403/263-5222**), offers more alternative music and occasional live music and entertainment. **Broken City**, 613 11th Ave. SW (✆ 403/262-9976), is a hipster hangout with live local bands on Tuesdays, Thursdays, and Saturdays.

Put on your cowboy boots and swing your partner out to **Ranchman's Cookhouse and Dance Hall,** 9615 Macleod Trail S. (✆ **403/253-1100**), the best country-western dance bar in the city. Free swing and line dance lessons are usually offered on Sunday afternoons; call to confirm.

Twisted Element, 1006 11th Ave. SW (✆ **403/802-0230**), is Calgary's largest gay bar and dance club. The bar, in the city's northwest, not far from Kensington or the University of Calgary, features a cocktail lounge in the basement and a jam-packed dance club on the main floor.

CASINO Calgary has several legitimate casinos whose proceeds go wholly to charities. None impose a cover. Located across from the Stampede grounds, the **Elbow River Inn Casino** (1919 Macleod Trail S; ✆ **403/266-4355;** www.elbowrivercasino.com) is the largest and most central; it offers Las Vegas–style gaming, plus a poker variation called Red Dog. It has a 24-hour poker room.

The Alberta Badlands ★★

The Red Deer River slices through Alberta's rolling prairies east of Calgary, revealing underlying sedimentary deposits that have eroded into badlands. These expanses of desertlike hills, strange rock turrets, and banded cliffs were laid down about 75 million years ago, when this area was a low coastal plain in the heyday of the dinosaurs. Erosion has incised through these deposits spectacularly, revealing a vast cemetery of Cretaceous life. Paleontologists have excavated here since the 1880s, and the Alberta badlands have proved to be one of the most important dinosaur-fossil sites in the world. Two separate areas have been preserved and developed for research and viewing.

Royal Tyrrell Museum ★★ ☺ Just north of Drumheller, and about 145km (90 miles) northeast of Calgary, this is one of the world's best paleontology museums and educational facilities. It is also the main event here: Of the half-million visitors that come to Drumheller each year, the Tyrrell draws almost 400,000 of them.

And it offers far more than just impressive skeletons and life-size models, though it has dozens of them. The entire fossil record of the Earth is explained, era by era, with an impressive variety of media and educational tools. You can walk through a prehistoric garden, watch numerous videos, use computers to "design" dinosaurs for specific habitats, watch plate tectonics at work, and see museum technicians preparing fossils. The museum is also a renowned research facility where scientists study all forms of ancient life and give visitors a window into their work.

Kids will go crazy for the interactive displays, to say nothing of the hands-on experiences, like a bucket of fossilized T-Rex teeth there for the handling. Multiple programs for kids age 7 and up can be found here, with the Badlands Science Camp being the best: Kids from 9 to 15 can overnight in the badlands with museum staff and explore the realm of the dinosaurs for themselves. Give yourself at least 2 hours for the inside part and at least 30 minutes to walk the interpretive trail just in front.

Hwy. 838, Midland Provincial Park, Drumheller, AB T0J 0Y0. ✆ **888/440-4240** or 403/823-7707. www.tyrrellmuseum.com. Admission C$10 adults, C$8 seniors, C$6 children 7–17, free for children under 7; C$30 families. Mid-May to Sept daily 9am–9pm; Oct to mid-May Tues–Sun 10am–5pm.

Dinosaur Provincial Park ★ In Red Deer River Valley near Brooks, about 225km (140 miles) east of Calgary and 193km (120 miles) southeast of Drumheller, this park contains the world's greatest concentration of fossils from the late Cretaceous period. More than 300 complete dinosaur skeletons have been found in the area, which has been named a UNESCO World Heritage Site. Park excavations continue from early June to late August, based out of the Field Station of the Royal Tyrrell Museum. Much of the park is a natural preserve, with access restricted to guided interpretive bus tours and hikes. Space on these tours is limited, so be prepared to be flexible with your choices. "Rush" tickets are sold at 8:30am for that day's events (maximum four tickets per person). Reservations are strongly encouraged in July and August. May through August, lab tours run so that you can view fossil preparation.

Five self-guiding trails and two outdoor fossil displays are also available. Facilities at the park include a campground, a picnic area, and a service center.

P.O. Box 60, Patricia, AB T0J 2K0. ✆ **403/378-4342** or 403/378-4344 for tour reservations. Fax 403/378-4247. www.tprc.alberta.ca/parks/dinosaur. Fees for bus tours and hikes. Advance tickets C$12 adults, C$8 youths 7–17, C$34 family. Tours daily mid-May to Labour Day; weekends Labour Day to mid-Oct.

Day Trips from Calgary: The Old West

The Old West isn't very old in Alberta. If you're interested in the life and culture of the cowboy and rancher, drive through the ranch country along the foothills of the Rockies and stop at the historic Bar U Ranch. This short side trip into the Old West is just a short detour on the way from Calgary to the Rocky Mountains.

Bar U Ranch National Historic Site ★★ An hour southwest of Calgary is this well-preserved and still-operating cattle ranch, a national historic site. Some say this is where corporate ranching was born: The Bar U ran a big operation, employing thousands of cowboys and running hundreds of thousands of cattle from 1882 to 1950. As ranches modernized and herds grew, Bar U owner Patrick Burns sold off parts of the vast ranch in 1950, bringing its dominance to a close. But the original Bar U site, with its horse barns, bunkhouses, mess hall, and office, remain intact. Thirty-five buildings, all told—a slice of Alberta history, perfectly preserved.

Follow Hwy. 22 south from Calgary to the little community of Longview. ✆ **403/395-2212.** www.pc.gc.ca. Admission C$7.80 adults, C$6.90 seniors, C$3.90 for children, C$19.60 families. Late May to early Oct daily 10am–6pm.

SOUTHERN ALBERTA

South of Calgary, running through the grain fields and prairies between Medicine Hat and Crowsnest Pass in the Canadian Rockies, Highway 3 roughly parallels the U.S.-Canadian border. This rural connector links several smaller Alberta centers and remote but interesting natural and historic sites.

Medicine Hat & Cypress Hills Provincial Park

Medicine Hat, 291km (180 miles) southeast of Calgary, is at the center of Alberta's vast natural-gas fields. (Rudyard Kipling famously described it as the city with "all hell for a basement.") To be near this inexpensive source of energy, a lot of modern industry has moved to Medicine Hat, making this an unlikely factory town surrounded by grain fields. In the early 1900s, the primary industry was fashioning brick and china from the local clay deposits. Consequently, the town's old downtown is a showcase of handsome frontier-era brick buildings; take an hour and explore the historic city center, flanked by the South Saskatchewan River.

About 81km (50 miles) south of Medicine Hat lies **Cypress Hills Provincial Park**, 316 sq. km (122 sq. miles) of highlands—outliers of the Rockies—that rise 450m (1,476 ft.) above the flat prairie grasslands. In this preserve live many species of plants and animals, including elk and moose, usually found farther west in more mountainous regions.

Lethbridge

East of Fort Macleod, 105km (65 miles) north of the U.S. border and 216km (134 miles) southeast of Calgary, Lethbridge is a delightful garden city set in the deep, beautiful Old Man River Valley and a popular convention site (it gets more annual hours of sunshine than most places in Canada). Lethbridge started out as Fort Whoop-Up, a notorious trading post that bartered whiskey to the Plains Indians in return for buffalo hides and horses. The post boomed during the 1870s, until the Mounties arrived to bring order. Today, Lethbridge is a pleasant prairie city and Alberta's third largest, with a population of 66,000. For details, contact the **Lethbridge Visitor Centre** (2805 Scenic Dr.; ✆ **800/661-1222** or 403/320-1222; www.visitlethbridge.com), open daily 9am to 5pm.

Though downtown is slightly disappointing in its lack of activity (many of the storefronts are vacant), the city has much to offer. Lethbridge has two good art centers that display regional and touring art. The **Southern Alberta Art Gallery** (601 3rd Ave. S; ✆ **403/327-8770;** www.saag.ca) has a number of changing art shows throughout the year; the gift shop is a good place to go for local crafts. It's open

Tuesday to Saturday from 10am to 5pm and Sunday from 1 to 5pm. The **Bowman Arts Centre** (811 5th Ave.; ✆ **403/327-2813**) is housed in an old school and is the fine-arts hub of Lethbridge, with studios, classes, offices for arts organizations, and two galleries featuring the works of area artists; it's open Monday to Friday 9am to 9pm and Saturday 10am to 4pm.

The **Sir Alexander Galt Museum and Archives,** at the west end of 5th Ave. (502 1st St. S, ✆ **403/320-4258;** www.galtmuseum.com), is an excellent regional museum located in an historic former hospital. Exhibit galleries focus on the local Native culture, the city's coal-mining past, and the role of immigrants in the region's growth. Two galleries are devoted to the works of regional artists. The back windows of the museum overlook the impressive Oldman River Valley, with its natural park systems. It's open daily 10am to 5pm; admission is C$5 adults, C$4 seniors and students, C$3 children 7 to 17, and free for children 6 and under.

The city's heritage as a frontier whiskey-trading center is commemorated at the **Fort Whoop-Up Interpretive Centre** (✆ **403/329-0444;** www.fortwhoopup.com) in **Indian Battle Park** (follow 3rd Ave. S toward the river). A replica of the fort—the original was built by Montana-based traders of buffalo skins and whiskey in the 1870s—stands in the park, with costumed guides providing horse-drawn carriage tours, interpretive programs, and historic reenactments. During July and August, it's open daily 10am to 5pm; the rest of the year, it's open Wednesday to Sunday 10am to 4pm. Admission is C$7 adults, C$6 seniors, C$5 students, and free for children under 6.

The pride of Lethbridge is the **Nikka Yuko Japanese Garden** (✆ **403/328-3511;** www.nikkayuko.com) in Henderson Lake Park on Mayor Mangrath Drive, east of downtown. Its pavilion and dainty bell tower were built by Japanese artisans without nails or bolts. The garden is one of the largest Japanese gardens in North America; Japanese-Canadian women in kimonos give tours and explain the philosophical concepts involved in Japanese garden design. From late June to Labour Day, the garden is open daily 9am to 8pm; mid-May to late June and after Labour Day to early October, it's open daily 9am to 5pm. Admission is C$7 adults, C$5 seniors, C$4 children 6 to 17, and free for children 5 and under.

WHERE TO STAY

Ramada Lethbridge Along the city's aptly named Scenic Drive, which curls south and west from downtown along the Old Man River Valley, you'll eventually reach a cluster of commercial activity (big-box stores and chain restaurants) at the intersection with Mayor Magrath Drive S. Here, you'll find the Ramada, a pleasant, off-the-rack mid-range hotel made slightly exceptional by its excellent service. Breakfast is included here, as is access to its giant indoor waterslide—not a bad way to keep kids happy after a long day in the car.

2375 Mayor Magrath Dr. S., Lethbridge, T1K 7M1. ✆ **403/380-5050.** www.ramadalethbridge.ca. 119 units. C$95 double; C$225 suite. Rates include continental breakfast & access to all-day coffee, tea & treats. AE, DC, DISC, MC, V. **Amenities:** Restaurant; fitness center; pool w/waterslide. *In room:* TV, hair dryer, high-speed Internet.

Sandman Inn Another budget staple, the Sandman sits on a busy stretch of Mayor Magrath Drive, just south of downtown. Surrounded by fast-food joints and gas stations, it's hardly picturesque, but it is convenient. Across the street from Nikko Yuko Japanese Garden and a few blocks from Highway 3, it's a good spot from which to access what the town has to offer and then easily move on. Rooms are large, pleasant, and unremarkable; a 24-hour Denny's downstairs offers cheap and easy fare.

421 Mayor Magrath Dr. S., Lethbridge, T1J 3L8 ✆ **403/328-1111.** www.sandmanhotels.com/hotel/alberta/lethbridge.php. 139 units. C$159 double; $179 suite. AE, DC, DISC, MC, V. **Amenities:** Restaurant; fitness center; pool. *In room:* TV, hair dryer, high-speed Internet.

WHERE TO DINE

Dono Sushi JAPANESE World War II internment camps gave Lethbridge a relatively high Japanese population, and most agree the new Dono Sushi is the best place for Japanese fare in town. Sushi, sashimi, *maki, donburi*—Dono covers all the bases, and amply so. The C$42 dinner special set for two, with sushi, tempura, chicken *katsu,* beef teriyaki, house salad, and two bowls of rice, could easily feed three.

1009 Mayor Magrath Dr. S. ✆ 403-380-3308. Main courses C$10–C$15. AE, MC, V. Mon–Sat 11:30am–2pm & 5–9pm. Closed Sun & holidays.

Ric's Grill NORTH AMERICAN/STEAKHOUSE The Lethbridge branch of this popular chain is certainly unique in its location, atop what was once a 30,000-gallon water tank. Ric's rises at the axis of Mayor Magrath Drive and Highway 3, just south of downtown, and offers a commanding view of downtown and the river valley beyond. Fare here is uncomplicated, hearty, and good quality: Lots of steaks and ribs, rack of lamb, and a grilled ahi tuna steak with wasabi lime butter. Pastas, sandwiches, and stir-fries round out the extensive menu.

103 Mayor Magrath Dr. S. ✆ **403/317-7427.** www.ricsgrill.com. Main courses C$15–C$38. AE, MC, V. Daily 11am–11pm.

Fort Macleod

Fort Museum of the North West Mounted Police Forty-four kilometers (27 miles) west of Lethbridge stands what was in 1873 the western headquarters of the Northwest Mounted Police. Named after Colonel James Macleod, the redcoat commander who brought peace to Canada's west, the reconstructed Fort Macleod is now a provincial park and is still patrolled by Mounties in their traditional uniforms.

The fort is filled with fascinating material on the frontier period. Among its treasured documents is the rule sheet of the old Macleod Hotel, written in 1882: "All guests are requested to rise at 6am. This is imperative as the sheets are needed for tablecloths. Assaults on the cook are prohibited. Boarders who get killed will not be allowed to remain in the house." The fort grounds also contain the Centennial Building, a museum devoted to the history of the local Plains Indians. A highlight of visiting the fort in summer is the **Mounted Patrol Musical Ride** at 10am, 11:30am, 2pm, and 3:30pm, with eight horseback Mounties performing a choreographed equestrian program to music.

219 25th St., Fort Macleod, AB T0L 0Z0. ✆ **403/553-4703.** www.nwmpmuseum.com. Admission C$8.50 adults, C$7.50 seniors, C$6 youths 12–17, C$5 children 6–11, free for children under 6. May 1 to Victoria Day and day after Labour Day to Canadian Thanksgiving Wed–Sun 10am–4pm; Victoria Day to June 30 daily 9am–5pm; July 1 to Labour Day daily 9am–5pm.

Head-Smashed-In Buffalo Jump ★★ One of the most interesting sights in southern Alberta, and a World Heritage Site, is the curiously named Head-Smashed-In Buffalo Jump. This excellent interpretive center/museum is built into the edge of a steep cliff over which the First Nations peoples used to stampede herds of bison, the carcasses then providing them with meat, hides, and horns. The multimillion-dollar facility tells the story of these ancient harvests by means of films and First Nations guide-lecturers. Other displays illustrate and explain the traditional life of the prairie-dwelling Natives in precontact times and the ecology and natural history of the northern Great Plains. Hiking trails lead to undeveloped jump sites.

Fort Macleod, AB T0L 0Z0. ✆ **403/553-2731.** www.head-smashed-in.com. C$9 adults, C$8 seniors, C$5 children 7–17. Daily 9am–6pm in summer; 10am–5pm in winter. Spring Point Rd., 19km (12 miles) west of Fort Macleod on Hwy. 2.

WATERTON LAKES NATIONAL PARK ★

In the southwestern corner of the province, Waterton Lakes National Park is linked with Glacier National Park in neighboring Montana; together these two beautiful tracts of wilderness compose Waterton-Glacier International Peace Park. Once the hunting ground of the Blackfeet, 526-sq.-km (203-sq.-mile) Waterton Park contains superb mountain, prairie, and lake scenery and is home to abundant wildlife.

During the last ice age, the park was filled with glaciers, which deepened and straightened river valleys; those peaks that remained above the ice were carved into distinctive thin, finlike ridges. The park's famous lakes also date from the Ice Ages; all three of the Waterton Lakes nestle in glacial basins.

The park's main entrance road leads to **Waterton Townsite,** the only commercial center, with a number of hotels, restaurants, and tourist facilities. Other roads lead to more remote lakes and trail heads. Akamina Parkway leads from the townsite to Cameron Lake, glimmering beneath the crags of the Continental Divide. At the small visitor center, you can rent canoes; this is a great spot for a picnic. Red Rock Parkway follows Blackiston Creek past the park's highest peaks to Red Rock Canyon. From here, three trails lead up deep canyons to waterfalls.

The most popular activity in the park is the **Inter-Nation Shoreline Cruise** (✆ **403/859-2362;** www.watertoninfo.com/m/cruise.html), which leaves from the townsite and sails Upper Waterton Lake past looming peaks to the ranger station at Goat Haunt, Montana, in Glacier Park. The tour boat operates from June 1 through early October. In the high season, from the last weekend of June through August, there are five tour boat departures daily, with two or three daily in the shoulder seasons (check the website for exact schedules). Only during the high season does the boat land in Montana for a 15-minute stop. The cruise usually takes just over 2 hours, including the stop in Montana. The price is C$38 adults, C$18 children 13 to 17, and C$12 children 4 to 12.

For more information, contact the **Waterton Park Chamber of Commerce and Visitors Association,** P.O. Box 5599, Waterton Lakes National Park, AB T0K 2M0 (✆ **403/859-5133** summer, or 403/859-2224 winter; www.pc.gc.ca and www.discoverwaterton.com). The per-day park entry fee is C$7.80 adults, C$6.80 seniors, C$3.90 children 6 to 16, free for children 5 an under; C$20 families.

Where to Stay

Crandell Mountain Lodge A Tudor-like inn a few blocks from the lake, this lodge has rooms in all sorts of configurations. The country decor is consistent throughout, but there's charm in the old country style. Some deluxe rooms have tubs, but most have only stand-up showers in tight bathrooms. Most rooms have fireplaces. The doubles with two queen beds are the most modern. The three-room suite with one bathroom and full kitchen sleeps up to six. Ask for a quieter top-floor room.

102 Mountview Rd., Waterton Park, AB T0K 2M0. ✆ **866/859-2288** or 403/859-2288. www.crandellmountainlodge.com. 17 units. C$140–C$170 double, from C$195 suites. AE, DC, DISC, MC, V. **Amenities:** Concierge. *In room:* TV, minibar, no phone.

Prince of Wales Hotel Situated on a hillock that rises above the north end of Waterton Lake, the Prince, a National Historic Site built in 1927, is surely one of the most dramatically placed hotels in the world. From the atrium-style lobby, windows stretch from the floor to several stories above, giving visitors the entire vista to drink in. As a hotel, the Prince just barely passes muster and is much in need of a makeover. Rooms are a little weary, with a strange layout that will remind you of a cruise ship (sinks across from the bed, small windows). The beds all have new soft-top mattresses, so you'll likely get a good night's sleep. If you have mobility issues, be warned, there are a lot of stairs to climb and only one elevator that works only some of the time. But then there's that view … which is what you're paying for. It's not a bad investment when in one of the most beautiful places on Earth. The Prince serves high tea on Royal Doulton china every day at 2pm in the lobby. Another investment, at C$29 per person, but well worth it.

Waterton Lakes National Park, Waterton, AB T0K 2M0. ✆ **403/236-3400.** www.princeofwaleswaterton.com. 86 units. June 27 to Sept 21 from C$234 double; C$799 suite. AE, DC, DISC, MC, V. Closed mid-Sept to early June. **Amenities:** Restaurant; lounge; Wi-Fi. *In room:* Minibar (in some rooms).

THE CANADIAN ROCKIES

If you're a tourist in Alberta, either Banff or Jasper—and likely both—is probably why you're here. Along with Waterton to the south, and Yoho and Kootenay to the west (in British Columbia), Banff and Jasper complete a network of federal parkland that protects the majestic peaks of the Canadian Rockies in a continuous flow of staggering size and beauty. A UNESCO World Heritage Site reaching more than 20,000 sq. km (7,722 sq. miles), it's rightly one of the most famous, and most successful, nature preserves on Earth.

But if you've come here to see Banff, don't think you're alone in that idea. More than 3 million tourists pass through Banff National Park each year, meaning that that lovely, protected natural zone all along the Rockies can sometimes have the hectic feel of being in a city—albeit a particularly beautiful one. Visitors tend to cluster in a few key areas: the Banff townsite, the shores of Lake Louise, and the Columbia Icefield.

The crowds flock here for good reason: You'll rarely, if ever, see such jaw-dropping mountain splendor. But the town of Banff, plunked down in a stunningly beautiful valley, has, at times, the air of a high-priced mall or theme park; Jasper, while significantly more subdued, still draws its throngs, with ample ways to separate you from your money.

Still, both places have so much more to offer than luxury shopping and dining in a mountain setting. So, get out of the car and get into the mountains. Hiking, biking, rafting, canoeing, kayaking, and fishing, as well as pack trips on horseback, are great ways to leave the crowds behind and experience the parks as nature (and the government) intended. Many of these adventures are just steps away from your hotel. Skiing here is also world-class: the resorts of Mount Norquay, Sunshine Village, and the jewel of the parks, Lake Louise (the site of annual World Cup races), are among the largest ski areas in the world; also not to be missed is the excellent but largely under-the-radar (and thus much less crowded) Marmot Basin in Jasper.

Essentials

The Banff and Jasper parks regions are among the most rugged and wild in the world. The natural splendor is almost beyond belief: Jagged peaks soar above burbling mountain streams that link icy, emerald alpine lakes; summertime brings colorful wildflowers dotting expansive alpine meadows, walled in by mountains all around; preternatural glaciers are cradled in massive mountain bowls; and all this is populated by wildlife particular to its alpine ruggedness—cougars, grizzlies, and the like. Between them, Banff and Jasper, along with Waterton to the south, and Yoho and Kootenay National Parks to the west, preserve the entire spine of the Rockies from the U.S. border stretching north for 1,127km (700 miles).

It's best to visit the parks in the off-season if you can—September and October, or May and June for hiking; December or April for skiing. If not, be sure to plan well ahead, or you may find it difficult to secure the accommodation you want. The parks can handle only so many people, and they're usually full all summer long.

GETTING THERE The parks are traversed by one of the finest highway systems in Canada, plus innumerable nature trails leading to more remote valleys and peaks. The two "capitals," Banff and Jasper, lie 287km (178 miles) apart, connected by Highway 93, one of the most scenic routes you'll ever drive. Banff is 128km (80 miles) from Calgary via Highway 1; Jasper, 375km (233 miles) from Edmonton on Route 16, the famous Yellowhead Highway.

VISITOR INFORMATION For visitor information on Kananaskis Country, and the Banff and Jasper national parks, see the respective sections on each later in this chapter.

Yoho National Park Visitor Centre is located just off the Trans-Canada Highway, 83km (51 miles) northwest of Banff (P.O. Box 99, Field, BC V0A 1G0; ✆ **250/343-6783;** www.pc.gc.ca), and is open daily 9am to 4pm.

Kootenay National Park Visitor Centre, 7556 Main St. E., Radium Hot Springs, BC V0A 1M0 (✆ **250/347-9505;** www.pc.gc.ca), is 134km (83 miles) southwest of Banff, but you drive through the park to get to the Visitor Centre, which is open daily 9am to 5pm.

Mount Robson Provincial Park (✆ **250/566-4325**) is just across the Alberta and British Columbia border from Jasper and is open May through September daily 7am to 11pm.

FEES Admission to Banff, Jasper, Yoho, and Kootenay parks costs C$9.80 adult, C$8.30 seniors, C$4.90 youths 6–16, or C$19.60 families per day.

Tours & Excursions

The Brewster family has long been a fixture in Banff, and as such, they've become one of the titans of the local tourist trade. Brewster operates the park system's principal tour bus operation, as well as the specialized vehicles that clamber up the mountainside to the Athabasca Glacier along the Icefields Parkway.

Brewster Transportation and Tours (100 Gopher St., Banff; ✆ **866/606-6700** or 403/762-6767; www.brewster.ca) can take you to most of the main attractions in both parks, either as a package tour or one-off trios to single attractions. Their local Rockies-based adventures are operated under the brand **Explore Rockies** (✆ **800/760-6934;** www.explorerockies.com). Call for a full brochure or ask the concierge at your hotel to arrange a trip. Sample packages include

The Canadian Rockies

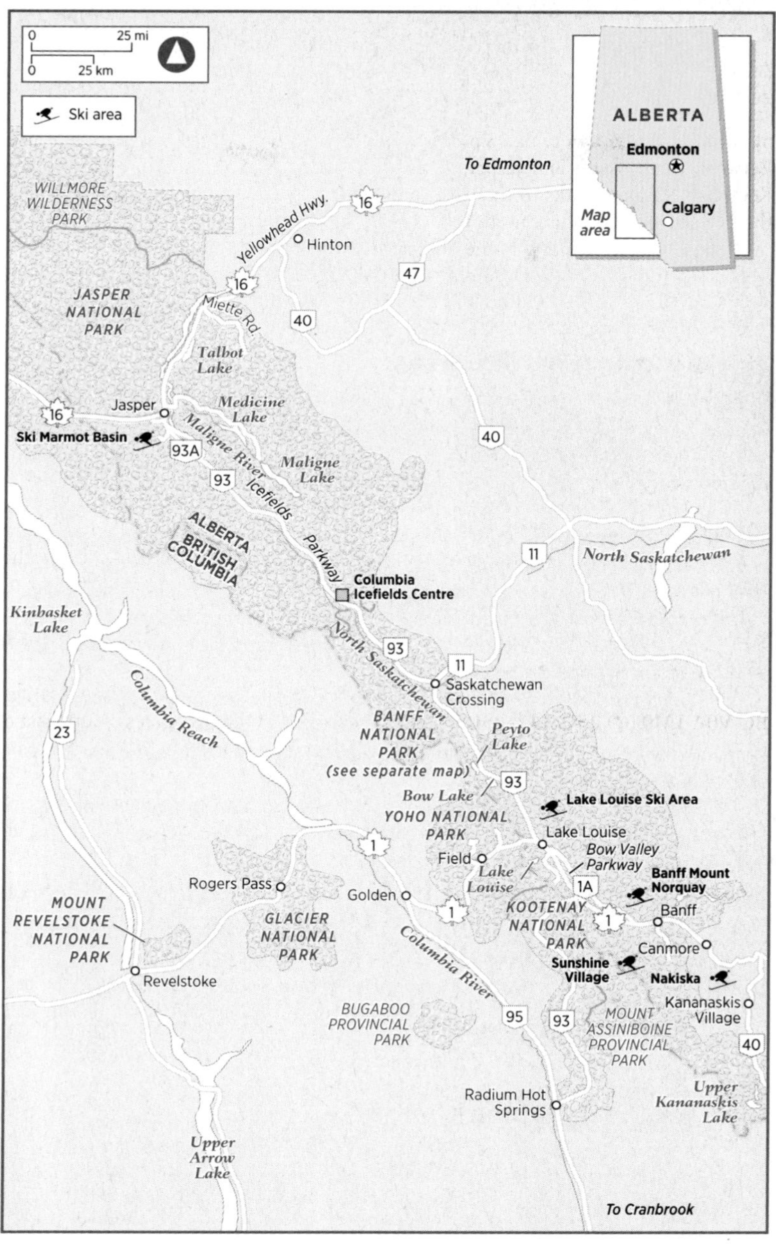

- **Banff to Jasper (or vice versa):** Some 9½ hours through unrivaled scenery, this tour takes in Lake Louise and a view of the ice field along the parkway. (The return trip requires an overnight stay, not included in the price.) In summer, the one-way fare is C$172 adults, C$82 children. If you don't want the tour, there's also a daily express bus between Banff and Jasper for C$79 one-way; kids under 15 pay half price.
- **Columbia Icefields:** On this 9-hour tour from Banff, you stop at the Icefields Centre and get time off for lunch and a Snocoach ride up the glacier. Adults pay C$151 and children pay C$75; tour prices include a trip up onto the glacier in the massive Explorer—essentially a bus on steroids with wheels the height of a pickup truck. It's open from mid-April through mid-October only.

Another local tour company offering smaller-sized tours is **Discover Banff Tours** (✆ **877/565-9372** or 403/760-5007; www.banfftours.com). They'll help you set up a self-guided driving tour with a personalized GPS, and they also have excellent wildlife-viewing safaris in the evenings.

Lodging in the Rockies

If you're in the parks in high season, you almost have to think of it as a competition or musical chairs. Both Banff and Jasper could easily add a few thousand hotel rooms and fill them without much trouble, but they can't; due to conservation regulations, development is severely restricted in the parks.

Although there are more than 5,000 tourist beds in Banff, rates can be expensive and are often under the control of big tour-bus companies that reserve huge amounts of rooms well ahead of the season. It's important to plan ahead. If you're flexible, last-minute-deal travel websites are a great alternative—try Priceline, Travelocity, or Expedia, all of which may turn last-minute cancellations into savings of as much as 50% for you. Demand in neighboring Canmore, while high, isn't quite at Banff levels, so the 20-minute drive can often pay off.

If you are have trouble finding a room or simply don't want to deal with the hassle, contact **Banff Accommodation Reservations** (✆ **877/226-3348;** www.banffinfo.com). They'll help you find available rooms and also happily give advice to help you make the most of your trip.

In the off-season, prices drop dramatically—often as much as 50%. Most hotels offer ski packages in winter, as well as other attractive getaway incentives. Ask about any special rates, especially at the larger hotels.

HOTEL ALTERNATIVES

If you're looking for a B&B, there are many options; check out www.banffbedandbreakfast.org for a complete listing.

Hostels are probably the most affordable option in Alberta's Rocky Mountain parks—at least, if you want a roof over your head and running water. **Hostelling International** runs a large network of hostels throughout the parks; to find out more about Alberta hostels, check out www.hihostels.ca.

There is a wide variety of campgrounds in Banff National Park, and you can now reserve a spot via telephone at ✆ 877/737-3783 or online at www.pccamping.ca. Many, though, remain first-come, first-served—don't expect to be able to arrive any day of the summer and find availability at your choice campground. You must plan ahead, especially if you want to be near the town of Banff. Check with Parks Canada at the **Banff Information Centre** (224 Banff Ave.; ✆ **403/762-1550**) for updated campsite availabilities.

Park Wildlife & You

While it's thrilling to see wildlife here, the parklands are no zoos! Here, animals roam free, and the natural rhythms of the wilderness are maintained. There are 53 species of wild mammals here, 13 of which are on Parks Canada's "Species at Risk" list. Some animals meander along and across highways and hiking trails, within easy camera range. However tempting, never feed the animals and don't touch them. You can be fined up to C$500 for feeding any wildlife, for one thing. For another, it's extremely dangerous.

As docile as some of these animals may seem, remember: These are wild creatures for whom the first rule is survival. If they feel threatened, they will either run or attack. And while they can seriously hurt you, you might be doing the same to them. Bighorn sheep, for one, get accustomed to summer handouts of bread, candy, potato chips, and marshmallows when they should be grazing on the high-protein vegetation that'll help them survive through the winter. Moose have taken a kindly offered snack as an invitation to join a picnic, and once a moose has decided that's what he or she wants, you won't be able to say no: They sometimes weigh well over a ton.

Then there are bears. Both black and grizzly bears call the parks home; grizzlies, at up to 2m (6½ ft.) on their hind legs, are the more threatening of the two, but don't underestimate the grizzly's smaller cousin, the black bear, which is relatively small at 1.5m (5 ft.) long. Both can be very dangerous when startled or threatened; your best bet is to make plenty of noise on the trails as you walk (singing and clapping your hands work well) to let them know you're coming.

The grizzly spends most of the summer in high alpine ranges, well away from tourist haunts. As one of North America's largest carnivores, its appearance and reputation are awesome enough to make you beat a retreat on sight. But the cuddly looks and circus antics of the black bear tend to obscure the fact that these, too, are wild animals: powerful, faster than a horse, and completely unpredictable.

Hiking in bear country (and virtually all parkland is bear country) necessitates certain precautions; ignore them at your peril. Never hike alone and never take a dog along. Dogs often yap at bears, then when the animal charges, they run toward their owners for protection, bringing the pursuer with them. Above all, never go near a cub. The mother is usually close by, and a female defending her young is the most ferocious creature you'll ever face—and possibly the last. In the Canadian Rockies, there are more "bear jams" than "traffic jams" as tourists pile up in their vehicles to snap photos of grizzlies or black bears, creating chaos on the roads. Whistling, yelling, running about . . . tourists behave strangely in the presence of a magnificent mammal, causing problems that can turn fatal for the bear and for other drivers. If you see a bear and want a closer look, slow down safely but do not stop. Give the bear space. No matter the circumstances, stay in your vehicle and do not approach the bear. Once alerted to the sighting of a bear, Parks Canada staff and often the police will appear at the scene and urge travelers to keep moving. Remember to call in a bear sighting to ✆ **403/762-1470.**

KANANASKIS COUNTRY & CANMORE

Kananaskis Country is the name given to a cluster of Alberta provincial parks on the Rocky Mountains' eastern slope, southeast of Banff National Park, including Peter Lougheed Provincial Park, Spray Valley Provincial Park, and Elbow-Sheep Wildland

Provincial Park. Together, they make up 4,250 sq. km (1,641 sq. miles) of protected Rocky Mountain wilderness.

Once considered only a gateway region to more glamorous Banff, Kananaskis has come into its own and is now a recreation destination on par with more famous brand-name resorts in the Rockies in terms of offerings, and it's quieter in terms of crowds. Kananaskis—or "K-Country," as it's called by locals—has an air of the untouched about it, especially compared to the well-trodden streets and highly maintained trails of Banff. This can be both a good and bad thing because, while it feels much less busy and picked over, Kananaskis lacks some of the amenities that a more veteran tourist region like Banff possesses. Still, it's equally spectacular in terms of its surroundings, and that's why you're here. Wildlife abounds here, from deer and moose to bighorn sheep, mountain goats, black bears, and grizzlies.

Located just west of K-Country and just outside the eastern boundary of Banff National Park, the town of Canmore is an old mining village that's grown into a resort town a la Whistler or Aspen, with real estate developments and golf courses in a dramatic location beneath the soaring peaks of Three Sisters Mountain. Only 20 minutes from Banff, the scenery here is magnificent and the accommodations generally much less expensive and less busy than those in Banff. Dining and shopping are equal to the offerings in Banff, and Canmore has a more authentic small-town feel than tourist-trodden Banff.

Also, because Kananaskis Country isn't governed by national-park restrictions, there's better road access to out-of-the-way lakeside campgrounds and trail heads, which makes this a more convenient destination for family getaways (there are more than 3,000 campsites in the area!). This provincial parkland also allows "mixed use," including some traditional (though heavily regulated) ranching. Some of the best guest ranches in Alberta operate here.

The main road through Kananaskis Country is Highway 40, which cuts south from Highway 1 at the gateway to the Rockies and follows the Kananaskis River. Kananaskis Village—a small collection of resort hotels, a golf course, and shops—is the center of activities in Kananaskis Country, with Canmore serving as the main hub, about 30 minutes from the village. Highway 40 eventually climbs up to 2,206m (7,238 ft.) at Highwood Pass, the highest pass in Alberta, before looping around to meet Highway 22 south of Calgary. Highway 40 is open only in summer, from mid-June to November, so be sure to check closures before you attempt it.

Outdoor Sports

It's the excellent access to outdoor activities that makes Canmore and the Kananaskis such a prime destination. For the outdoors-minded, from its offices in Kananaskis Village and in Canmore (at 999 Bow Valley Trail), **Inside Out Experience Tours** (✆ **877/999-7238;** www.insideoutexperience.com) represents most local outfitters. You'll find bike trips, trail rides, rafting, hiking, and sightseeing tours on offer. **Canadian Rockies Adventure Centre** (701 Bow Valley Trail; ✆ **877/226-7625** or 403/678-6535; www.canadianrockies.ca) also will help you book anything and everything.

CROSS-COUNTRY SKIING & MOUNTAIN BIKING The **Canmore Nordic Centre Provincial Park,** just south of town off Spray Lakes Road (1988 Olympic Way, Canmore; ✆ **403/678-2400;** http://tpr.alberta.ca/parks/kananaskis/parks_canmore.asp), was developed for the Olympics' cross-country skiing competition, though the facility is now open year-round. In winter, the center offers 70km (43 miles) of scenic cross-country trails, plus the on-site **Trail Sports** shop (✆ **403/678-6764**) for rentals, repairs, and sales. In summer, hikers and mountain bikers take over the trails, and Trail Sports offers bike rentals, skill-building courses, and guided rides.

DOWNHILL SKIING Kananaskis gained worldwide attention when it hosted the alpine ski events for the Winter Olympics in 1988, and skiing remains a primary attraction in the area. At **Nakiska** (✆ **800/258-7669** or 403/591-7777; www.skinakiska.com), skiers can follow in the tracks of past Winter Olympians. Very family-friendly, it offers terrain for every age and ability, and is open from early December to mid-April. Adult lift tickets cost C$52.

GOLF The Kananaskis area features four championship golf courses and one of Canada's premier golf resorts. **Kananaskis Country Golf Course** boasts two 18-hole, par-72 courses set among alpine forests and streams, and featuring water hazards on 20 holes, 140 sand traps, and four tee positions. It's rated among the top courses in Canada. For information, contact Golf Kananaskis (Kananaskis Country Golf Course, P.O. Box 1710, Kananaskis Village, AB T0L 2H0; ✆ **877/591-2525** or 403/591-7272; www.kananaskisgolf.com). Greens fees are C$90.

Near Canmore, the low-key 18-hole **Canmore Golf Course** is right along the Bow River, at 2000 Eighth Ave. (✆ **403/678-4785;** www.canmoregolf.net). Greens fees are C$80. Their clubhouse has a great patio.

The Les Furber–designed **Silver Tip Golf Course** (✆ **403/678-1600;** www.silvertipresort.com) is an 18-hole, par-72 course high above Canmore that calls itself "extreme mountain golf." You'll be eye-to-eye with the Canadian Rockies here and perhaps look wildlife in the eye, too—grizzly bears have been known to roam on the course. Boasting a length of 7,300 yards, the course has sand bunkers on all holes and water on eight. Greens fees range from C$105 to C$175. Also at Canmore is the **Stewart Creek Golf Club** (✆ **877/993-4653;** www.stewartcreekgolf.com), with 18 holes, 32 bunkers, and a beautiful location below the Three Sisters peaks. The course measures 7,150 yards and incorporates natural lakes, streams, and even historic mine entrances. Greens fees range from C$150 to C$195, including use of a golf cart.

HIKING Canmore is surrounded by mountains and, being on the doorstep of Kananaskis Country, it's an ideal base from which to explore the many, many hiking trails to be found here. You can set out for days or just a few hours, depending on your level of ambition. **Canadian Rockies Adventure Centre** (701 Bow Valley Trail; ✆ **877/226-7625** or 403/678-6535; www.canadianrockies.ca) or **Inside Out Experience** (✆ **888/999-7238;** www.insideoutexperience.com) can help set you on your way, with maps and/or guides, as you prefer; so can **Canmore's Tourism Office** (907 7th Ave., Canmore; ✆ **403/678-1295;** www.tourismcanmore.com).

A number of tour operators are happy to take you on interpretive hikes in the area. **Mahikan Trails** (✆ **403/609-2489;** www.mahikan.ca) leads half- and full-day hikes into the mountains all year long, through significant Aboriginal sites with a mind to teaching guests about the natural history of the area and its first peoples.

The **Grassi Lakes hiking trail** is one of the region's signature hikes. Rated as a moderately difficult hike, it's 3.8km (2.4 miles) round trip—a half-day outing. You reach it by driving up the Spray Lakes Road past the Nordic Centre; the trail head is just beyond where the pavement turns to gravel.

Spray Lakes in Kananaskis Country also offers some of the most iconic scenery to be found in the Rockies. Some of the best include Burstall Pass, Rummel Lake, and

Chester Lake. All trails are accessed from the **Smith Dorrien Trail/Spray Lakes Road.** The road climbs sharply south of Canmore and turns to gravel not far past the Nordic Centre. You'll see trail heads every 10 minutes or so. These are the access points to genuine alpine terrain, many of them leading to alpine meadows and mountain lakes.

As you get deeper into Kananaskis Country, you'll find yourself at Peter Lougheed Provincial Park, which is centered around the Upper and Lower Kananaskis Lakes, about 30km (19 miles) south of town along Route 742, the Spray Lakes Parkway. This is as gorgeous as Kananaskis gets. There's almost no end to trails in and around the lakes to be found here for hiking, biking, and horseback riding; try the **Kananaskis Canyon interpretive hike** at the north end of the lower lake or the **Upper Kananaskis Lake circuit,** about 10km (6¼ miles) that takes you around this gorgeous mountain lake. Those seeking altitude might choose the **Rawson Lake Trail**, a fast 4km (2.5-mile) climb up to a lovely lake beneath the cliffs of Mt. Sarrail.

HORSEBACK TRIPS The Kananaskis is noted for its dude ranches (see "Getting a Taste of the Old West at a Guest Ranch," p. 533), which offer a variety of horseback adventures from short trail rides to multiday pack trips. A 2-hour guided ride will generally cost about C$60 per person. In addition, **Boundary Ranch,** just south of Kananaskis Village on Highway 40 (© **877/591-7177** or 403/591-7171; www.boundaryranch.com), offers a variety of trail rides, including a horseback lunch excursion.

RAFTING Then there's always an old classic, white-water rafting. The Kananaskis and Bow rivers are the main draw here. In addition to a range of half-day (C$75) and full-day (C$125) white-water trips, there are excursions that combine a half-day of horseback riding with an afternoon of rafting (C$144). Inside Out Experience (see above) can provide more information. All prices are per person.

The **Canadian Rockies Rafting Company** (© **877/226-7625;** www.rafting.ca) is among the most established rafting tour companies in the area, with a range of different trips—the more gentle ride along the Kananaskis River, to the white-water rush of British Columbia's Kicking Horse River (with rapids as high as Class IV). These are mountain rivers, so bear in mind, it's cold.

Where to Stay

Kananaskis is a major camping destination for families in Calgary, and the choice of **campgrounds** is wide. There's a concentration of campgrounds at Upper and Lower Kananaskis lakes, some 32km (20 miles) south of Kananaskis Village. A few campgrounds are scattered nearer to Kananaskis Village, around Barrier Lake and Ribbon Creek. For a full-service campground with RV hookups, go to **Mount Kidd RV Park** (© **403/591-7700**) just south of the Kananaskis golf course.

KANANASKIS VILLAGE

The lodgings in Kananaskis Village were built for the Olympics, and in fact, Kananaskis was the site of the G8 Summit in 2002, so you may well stay in a room once graced by a world leader. There's no more than a stone's throw between the hotels, and to a high degree, public facilities are shared among all the hotels.

Delta Lodge at Kananaskis This resort hotel, built for the Olympics and more recently the site of a G8 Summit in 2002, consists of two separate buildings that face each other across a pond at the center of Kananaskis Village. The Lodge includes a shopping arcade and a number of drinking and dining choices. Its guest rooms are large and well furnished; many have balconies, and some have fireplaces. The hotel hosts many conferences and has a bit of an impersonal, corporate feel, as well as a slightly dated look. The Signature Club service rooms are more private and include breakfast. The Summit Spa and Fitness Centre provides health and beauty treatments for both men and women. Golf courses, bike paths, and hiking trails are right at your doorstep.

1 Centennial Dr., Kananaskis Village, AB T0L 2H0. ✆ **866/432-4322** or 403/591-7711. www.deltalodgeatkananaskis.ca. 412 units. C$249–C$319 double. Ski/golf package rates & discounts available. AE, DC, MC, V. Self-parking C$11; valet parking C$15. **Amenities**: 4 restaurants; bar; babysitting; bike rental; concierge; concierge-level rooms; golf courses nearby; health club; whirlpool; 2 pools (saltwater & indoor); room service (7am–1am); spa; tennis courts. *In room:* A/C (in Signature Club), TV/VCR w/pay movies, fridge, hair dryer, Internet, minibar.

Kananaskis Wilderness Hostel This is a great place for a recreation-loving traveler on a budget. The hostel is located at the Nakiska Ski Area, within walking distance of Kananaskis Village, and is close to 60 mountain biking, hiking, and cross-country ski trails. Area outfitters offer special discounts to hostel guests. The hostel has a common room with a fireplace and four private family rooms. Families are welcome.

1 Ribbon Creek Rd., at Nakiska Ski Area. ✆ **866/762-4122** or 403/670-7580 for reservations, or 403/591-7333 for the hostel. www.hihostels.ca. 38 beds. C$23 (members), C$27 (nonmembers) bed; C$60 (members), C$68 (nonmembers) private room. MC, V. Free parking. *In room:* No phone.

Sundance Lodges and Camp ☺ Part wilderness campground, part Tipi-lodge, this complex in Kananaskis is family-friendly and a great way to immerse yourself in the outdoors without giving up simple luxuries like hot water. Painted canvas tipis sleep four and have simple wooden-framed beds and a small kerosene heater; "trapper's tents" are more rustic but still cozy. Both have private picnic areas and fire pits. There's also laundry, hot showers, a small store, and room for RVs and personal tents. Best of all, the Kananaskis River is just steps away.

Hwy. 40 (22km/14 miles south of the Trans-Canada Hwy. in Kananaskis); Kananaskis Village, AB T0L 2H0. ✆ **403/591-7122.** www.sundancelodges.com. 60 units (18 trapper's tents, 12 tipis & 30 campsites). Trapper's tent C$79; tipi C$57–C$77; unserviced campsite C$28. Closed Sept 18 to May 23. **Amenities:** Camping equipment rental.

CANMORE

About half of the hotel development in Canmore dates from the 1988 Olympics, and the rest dates from—oh, last week or so. That said, Canmore's steam-rolling growth slowed somewhat in the last couple of years; many buildings originally set up as private condominiums have been shifted to vacation rentals and hotel-type lodging options. To a large degree, this is due to the restrictions on development within the national parks to the west: Hoteliers, outfitters, developers, larger stores, and other businesses designed to serve the needs of park visitors find Canmore, right on the park boundary, a much easier place to locate than Banff. As a result, Canmore is now a destination in its own right.

The main reason to stay in Canmore is the price of hotel rooms. Rates here are between a half and a third lower than in Banff, and the small downtown area is blossoming with interesting shops and good restaurants. Canmore hotels can represent especially good deals on discount hotel websites.

For a complete list of B&Bs, contact the **Canmore-Bow Valley B&B Association** (P.O. Box 8005, Canmore, AB T1W 2T8; www.bbcanmore.com).

Chateau Canmore ★ You can't miss this enormous red-roofed complex along the hotel strip. Like a series of 10 four-story conjoined chalets, the all-suite Chateau Canmore offers some of the largest rooms in the area. The accommodations are very nicely decorated in a comfortable rustic style, while the lobby and common rooms look like they belong in a log-style lodge. Each standard suite has a fireplace and separate bedroom, while the deluxe one- or two-bedroom suites add a living room and dining area. Just like home, but with a better view. The best rates are available on their website.

1718 Bow Valley Trail, Canmore, AB T1W 2X3. ✆ **800/261-8551** or 403/678-6699. Fax 403/678-6954. www.chateaucanmore.com. 120 units. From C$124 standard suite; from C$149 deluxe suite. AE, DC, DISC, MC, V. Free parking. **Amenities:** Dining room; lounge; health club; indoor pool; limited room service; spa. *In room:* AC, TV, fridge, hair dryer, Wi-Fi.

Grande Rockies Resort The newest and largest place in town was opened in the summer of 2010 by the luxury hotel chain Metropolitan Hotels. The design is thoroughly modern and user-friendly. You can squeeze a whole crowd into a single unit. Rooms are all suites, with one or two bedrooms (some with additional pull-out couches), and they're all equipped with full kitchens and stream showers. They're mostly decorated in creams with brown linen fabrics and contemporary Western art. Other luxury bonuses include barbecues, flat-screen TVs with Blu-Ray players, and digital safes. There's also a family-friendly indoor pool area. It's right on the highway, so ask for a south-facing unit.

901 Mountain St., Canmore, AB T1W 0C9. ✆ **877/223-3398** or 403/678-8880. www.granderockies.com. 150 units. From C$215 one-bedroom; from C$295 two-bedroom. AE, DC, MC, V. Free parking. **Amenities:** Restaurant; lounge; concierge; fitness center; hot tub; pool; Wi-Fi. *In room:* A/C, TV w/Blu-Ray player, hair dryer, kitchen.

Mount Engadine Lodge ★★★ While not in Canmore proper, this rustic lodge—set in pristine wilderness along the Spray Lakes Parkway in Kananaskis Country, where the pavement turns to gravel—is a great candidate for a true mountain getaway. It takes about half an hour to reach the lodge, but it's worth the trip. Small and cozy, the lodge is perched at 1,844m (6,050 ft.) above sea level, surrounded by the majesty of the Rockies. Just below the bluff where it sits is Moose Meadows—so named for the many moose that wander through, among countless other wildlife, as you sip wine on the deck—an expanse of mountain meadow wetland. The sense here is of a place unstuck in time, the mountains as they were before the ranchers, settlers, or tour buses ever came close. Of course, when you go back inside and enjoy home-cooked meals with some of the best fresh, local ingredients, it's hardly roughing it. Simply one of the best options to be found in the Rockies.

South of Canmore, on the Spray Lakes Pkwy., Rte. 742; P.O. Box 40025, Canmore, AB T1W 3H9. ✆ **403/678-4080.** www.mountengadine.com. 8 units. From C$390 double. Rates include breakfast and dinner. Children 6–12 C$100; children under 5 stay free in parent's room. AE, MC, V. **Amenities:** Restaurant. *In room:* No phone.

Paintbox Lodge ★ One of the few lodgings in Canmore's charming town center, the Paintbox Lodge is a cozy, small, and luxurious boutique inn that mingles rustic mountain charm and refined sophistication. The lodge offers seven guest rooms in the main building and a two-bedroom suite with a full kitchen in a separate lodge. Run by two former Olympians, the service is relaxed and friendly. Best of all, you'll be just steps from the Bow River and the lively cafes and shops of Canmore.

629 10th St., Canmore, AB T1W 2A2. ✆ **888/678-6100** or 403/609-0482. Fax 403/609-0481. www.paintboxlodge.com. 8 units. C$179–C$229 double. Rates include full breakfast. MC, V. Free parking. *In room:* TV w/movie channels, CD player, fridge, minibar, Wi-Fi.

CAMPING

Kananaskis is a major camping destination for families, and the choice of campgrounds is wide. Of the major parks that comprise Kananaskis, Peter Lougheed Provincial Park has six campgrounds, Kananaskis Valley has one, Spray Valley Provincial Park has two, Highwood/Cataract Creek (farther south, near Mountain View) has five, Elbow River Valley has six, and Sheep River Valley has seven.

There's a concentration of campgrounds at Upper and Lower Kananaskis Lakes in Peter Lougheed Park, some 32km (20 miles) south of Kananaskis Village. A few campgrounds are scattered nearer to Kananaskis Village, around Barrier Lake and Ribbon Creek. For the more intrepid wilderness seekers, the Lougheed Park campgrounds feel significantly more remote, surrounded by peaks and centered on a long, gorgeous mountain lake; closer to the village, campgrounds feel more civilized—and, therefore, usually are more crowded.

For a full-service campground with RV hook-ups, go to **Mount Kidd RV Park** (✆ **403/591-7700;** www.mountkiddrv.com), just south of the Kananaskis golf course.

For comprehensive listings of all campgrounds and their specific amenities, go to www.kananaskiscountrycampgrounds.com.

Where to Dine

Communitea Café ★★ CAFE/VEGETARIAN It's all about healthy choice at this funky corner cafe. Choose from more than 80 blends of tea; build your own lunch bowl (rice, noodles, or salad; soy-ginger, curry, or peanut satay). Breakfast panini and great nibbles, like *edamame* and salad rolls, make it a good choice throughout the day. Regular evening concerts are almost always surprisingly pleasant. Don't miss the lattes either; they're probably the best in town.

#117-1001 6th Ave. (at the corner of 10th St.). ✆ **403/678-6818.** www.thecommunitea.com. Main courses C$8–C$12. AE, MC, V. Mon–Sat 9am–5pm; Sun 10am–5pm.

Crazyweed Kitchen ★ FUSION You can't talk about food in Alberta without mentioning the ground-breaking, ever-innovative Crazyweed in Canmore. For a decade, foodies have flocked here for the cool vibe, hip wine list, and general enthusiasm for great food. They'll take a predictable Alberta rib-eye and add a chile crust. Short ribs are served with curry, lemongrass, and peanuts. A more affordable option is a flatbread pizza; try the pesto, pear, stilton, and spinach pie. Both the menu and the service are unpredictable and provocative, meaning there are occasional errors and misses. But, generally, it's worth the risk.

1600 Railway Ave. ✆ **403/609-2530.** www.crazyweed.ca. Main courses C$24–C$38. AE, MC, V. Mon–Fri 11:30am–3pm, Sat & Sun 10:30am–3pm; daily 5–10pm.

The Drake Inn and Pub ★ GASTRO PUB As the slogan goes, "If it's happening in Canmore, it's happening at the Drake." Definitely the most active pub in town, there's also hearty meals to be had here. The food is reasonable, simple, and very good, and the service friendly and familiar. Stick with staples like homemade burgers (which are excellent and can be beef or bison) and fish and chips. The Drake also has a rather stunning patio with views of the Three Sisters Mountain. The Drake also offers clean, bright, motel-style accommodations for reasonable rates, from C$129 for a basic double.

909 Railway Ave. ✆ **403/678-5131.** www.thedrakeinn.com. Main courses C$12–C$19. AE, MC, V. Mon–Fri 11am–11pm; Sat & Sun 10am–midnight.

Harvest ★ 🎁 CAFE Just off Main Street in downtown Canmore is one of the Bow Valley's best-kept secrets. Cafeteria-style counter service yields fresh, flavorful, and very reasonable foods like quiches, croque-monsieurs and mesdames, and soups. The sandwiches are a big draw, with fillings like curried chicken and pineapple, and *capicolli* ham with artichoke. The shady front patio, off the main drag, is a peaceful place to survey the gorgeous scenery. On Sunday mornings, locals line up for cinnamon buns.

718 10th St. ✆ **403/678-3747.** Sandwiches C$7–C$9. No credit cards. Mon–Fri 8am–4pm; Sun 10am–3pm. Closed Saturdays.

The Trough ★★ CONTEMPORARY Don't let the name fool you: This is no feedbag joint. Chosen as Canada's seventh-best restaurant by *enRoute* magazine in 2007, the Trough is a gastronome's delight. At only 10 tables, it's exceptionally intimate, and the menu offers powerful and intense flavors in inventive choices, from a Lebanese rack of lamb and jerk-spiced back ribs to wild BC halibut with orange coconut curry. The Trough is especially suited to the oenophile, as the sommelier goes out of his way to find small and limited releases, especially from the Canadian and American West.

725B 9th St. ✆ **403/678-2820.** www.thetrough.ca. Reservations recommended. Main courses C$22–C$38. AE, MC, V. Wed–Sun 5:30–11pm.

BANFF NATIONAL PARK ★★★

Having celebrated its 125th birthday in 2010, Banff is Canada's oldest and most famous national park, its fabulous and dramatic landscapes the first, best argument that Canada's abundant, spectacular wilderness was worthy of federal protection. Its 6,641 sq. km (2,564 sq. miles) of incredibly dramatic mountain landscape, glaciers, high moraine lakes, and rushing rivers make it clear no argument was to be made at all; this is one of the most gorgeous places on Earth.

If there's a downside, it's that everybody knows it. In the towns of Banff and nearby Lake Louise (though much less so in Louise), a walk on main street can give you the odd sensation of walking in midtown New York City at rush hour, and it's not because of the urbane sophistication the towns have cultivated; it's crowded, and the sidewalks can be shoulder to shoulder.

Happily, the wilderness is just steps away. Thanks to outstanding infrastructure, and professional guides and outfitters, it's easy in Banff National Park to get on a raft, bike, or horse and find a little solitude. Alternatively, consider visiting the park off-season, when prices are lower, the locals are friendlier, and the scenery is just as stunning.

For more information on the park, contact Banff National Park (P.O. Box 900, Banff, AB T1L 1K2; ✆ **403/762-1550;** www.pc.gc.ca).

Sports & Outdoor Activities in the Park

The town of Banff may tempt you with high-end shopping, impressive restaurants, and a seemingly endless array of fudge shops, but you owe it to yourself to step out

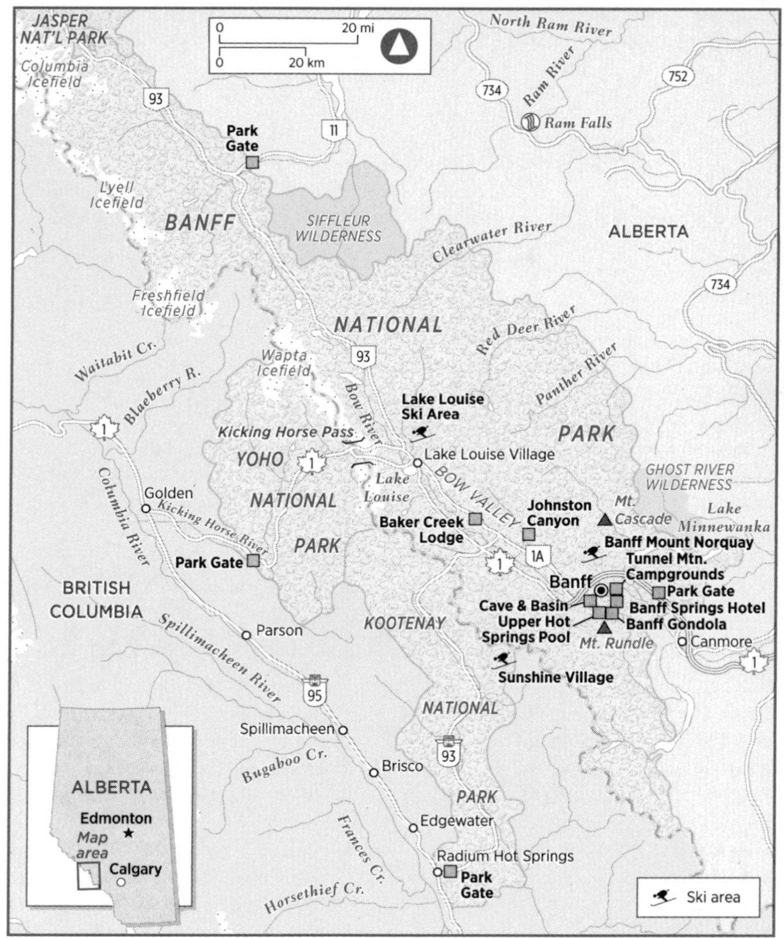

into the park's well-tended wild. From easy to extreme, there are plenty of options for everyone. If you don't know where to start, don't worry; there are many outfitters here, but the recommendations below are typical of what's available.

BIKING The most popular cycling adventure in the Canadian Rockies is the 287km (178-mile) trip between Banff and Jasper along the Icefields Parkway, possibly the most spectacular mountain drive on Earth.

You can do this on your own (bear in mind that this is a not a route for the inexperienced or out of shape), but it doesn't hurt to have an experienced bike-touring outfitter to squire you around. Give yourself at least 3 long days. Try **Rocky Mountain Cycle Tours** (✆ **800/661-2453** or 604/898-8488; www.rockymountaincycle.com) for 6-day supported trips starting at C$2,350 per person.

If you'd prefer a self-guided tour, simply rent a bike in Banff or Lake Louise, and pedal along the Bow Valley Parkway—Highway 1A—between Banff and Lake Louise; running parallel to the much busier Highway 1, the Bow Valley Parkway runs along the skirt of Castle Mountain, one of the most impressive peaks in all of Banff. It's a solid day trip for an average cyclist, with a few ups and downs.

There are more than 190km (118 miles) of mountain-biking trails in Banff National Park. Be aware that mountain biking is permitted on only a select number of trails. Families and beginners can ride the Spray River Loop. Those looking for a rush ought to try the Stoney Squaw epic downhill trail near Mt. Norquay.

FISHING You need a permit to fish in Banff National Park. Pick one up at the **Banff Information Centre** (224 Banff Ave., ✆ 403/762-1550). Vermillion Lakes is a popular spot with a limited supply of fish. Better for lake fishing is Lake Minnewanka. The Bow River is one of the finest fly-fishing rivers in the world. For the more personal touch, Big Jim Dykstra (a fair name; he's 6'5") of **Hawgwild Flyfishing** (**✆ 403/678-7980;** www.flyfishingbanff.com) specializes in fly fishing, and he'll pick you up in his vintage blue Suburban at your hotel and squire you to his rivers in the area. A catch is guaranteed, or your money back! Tours start at C$479 for two people for a full day.

Banff Fishing Unlimited (**✆ 403/762-4936;** www.banff-fishing.com) offers a number of fly-fishing expeditions on the Bow River, as well as lake fishing at Lake Minnewanka. All levels of anglers are accommodated, and packages include part- or whole-day trips.

GOLF The **Fairmont Banff Springs Golf Course** (**✆ 403/762-6801;** www.fairmont.com/banffsprings/recreation/golf) rolls out along the Bow River beneath towering Mt. Rundle. One of the most venerable courses in Canada, and one of the most expensive, it offers 27 holes of excellent golf. Although associated with the resort hotel, the course is open to the public. Greens fees for 18 holes are C$219 in summer and drop down to C$149 in spring and fall.

HIKING Banff is a hiker's dream come true. The trails are incredibly varied and rewarding, ranging from easy 1-hour strolls to demanding full-day outings. For a good listing of popular hikes, pick up the free *Banff/Lake Louise Drives and Walks* brochure from the national park information center at 224 Banff Ave. Here are a few of my favorites.

Cory Pass, at 5.8km (3.6 miles) each way and climbing 915m (3,002 ft.), is one of the most strenuous and challenging hikes in Banff, but it's also by far the most spectacular one near the town of Banff. The highlight is the 2,300m (7,546-ft.) monolithic limestone cliffs of the Sawback Range. It'll take you about 6 hours.

Johnston Canyon, 24km (15 miles) north of Banff on Highway 1A, is one of the best day hikes and also among the most popular. Round trip to the Inkpots is a good 4 hours; but budget for longer—the meadow, with a swift-running creel, is as scenic a spot as you'll find anywhere and relatively untraveled.

Lake Agnes/Beehives is a classic hike above Lake Louise into a picturesque hanging valley with a treasure-like emerald lake. An historic teahouse awaits after hiking 5.1km (3.2 miles) up a moderate and wide trail. Connect to the Beehive trail down, looping along the shores of Lake Louise. This hike is good for families.

Paradise Valley/Larch Valley, near Lake Louise, is a 17km (11-mile) hike that runs the gamut of alpine terrain, from high meadow and steep cliffs to the fringe of towering peaks, beside thundering falls, and over a majestic pass before ending at spectacular Moraine Lake. This is a difficult hike that will take you 7 or 8 hours to complete; you might not want to attempt it if you're not in good physical condition. Parks Canada often requires hikers to stay in groups of six or more due to bear activity in the area. Often, small groups of less than six gather at the trail head to join forces.

Peyto Lake/Bow Summit is a short, 20-minute stroll heading out from the Icefields Parkway (Hwy. 93); this trail takes you to a jaw-dropping viewpoint of Peyto Lake, Peyto Glacier, and the Mistaya Valley. Interpretive displays along the 1.2km (.7-mile) loop explain the basics of the subalpine and alpine landscape.

Plain of the Six Glaciers is beautiful but busy; you'll want to leave early to avoid the crowds on this glorious hike. The trail begins at the far end of Lake Louise (the lake itself, not the town) and ascends to an exposed moraine below Victoria Glacier. It offers an exceptional view of six other glaciers (hence the name). You can have lunch or just a warming cup of tea at the historic Plain of the Six Glaciers Teahouse; if you're suitably fortified, you can hike the last half hour to the Victoria Glacier Viewpoint.

To reach **Sulphur Mountain Boardwalk,** take the Sulphur Mountain Gondola, in the town of Banff, to the top, where this gentle stroll begins. Wander along an elevated boardwalk for about 1km (.6 mile) that takes you to the top of Sanson Peak, where you'll find an historical weather-monitoring station. Along the way, interpretive plaques will tell you all about the stunning vista that lies below the ridge you're now skirting from the comfort of a steady, level surface.

HORSEBACK RIDING Riding a horse in the Canadian Rockies is a classic, fun way to explore the area, which has a rich cowboy heritage and plenty of backcountry to ride. **Warner Guiding and Outfitting** (✆ **800/661-8352** or 403/762-4551; www.horseback.com) offers short day trips with a meal (breakfast in the morning or evening dinner rides) from the town of Banff for C$151 per rider. Multiday trail rides start at C$825 per person for 3 days. Minimum age is 18.

In Lake Louise, **Timberline Tours** (✆ **888/858-3388** or 403/522-3743; www.timberlinetours.ca) offers day trips to some of the most spectacular nearby spots, such as a 3-hour ride to Big Beehive, above the lake (C$105) or a 4-hour ride to the Plain of Six Glaciers (C$125). Three day trips start at C$705 per rider; you can go as long as 10 days in the back country for C$2,350 per rider.

RAFTING & CANOEING Rafting can be as easy and gentle as a 2-hour family float trip on the Bow River, just below Banff Townsite; **Canadian Rockies Rafting Company** (✆ **877/226-7625** or 403/678-6535; www.rafting.ca) offers trips from C$55 adults, C$45 children under 16 (the company allows children as young as 3 on the float). On its website, Canadian Rockies Rafting rates its various trips the way ski hills do: Green circle for beginner, blue square for intermediate, and black diamond for the rough stuff.

The gnarliest rapids in the area are just across the border on British Columbia's **Kicking Horse River,** with Class IV rapids. Canadian Rockies Rafting offers trips to Kicking Horse for C$125 adults or C$115 children 12 to 15 (children under 12 not permitted), lunch included. You can do a half-day, but it's only C$15 or C$10 less, respectively, and doesn't include lunch.

It seems only natural that you'd want to paddle a canoe on these glorious Canadian lakes. Canoe rentals are available at Moraine Lake (✆ **403/522-3733**) or at the Fairmont Chateau Lake Louise (✆ **403/522-3511**). Rates are C$50 per hour. In the town of Banff, head to **Blue Canoe Rentals** (at the end of Wolf St.; © **403/762-5465**). Rates are C$35 for the first hour and then C$21 for every hour after that.

SKIING Skiers will feel close to heaven in Banff, with so much great terrain, variety, and choice. The park has three principal ski areas (Mount Norquay, Sunshine Village, and Lake Louise), two of them huge, offering an incredible mix of terrain; as an added bonus, all are within about 45 minutes of each other and of the town of Banff along Highway 1. Their proximity has resulted in an alliance for booking and promotional purposes, which makes exploring their options a single stop online, at www.skibig3.com. You can also contact the **Ski Banff Lake Louise Sunshine** office (P.O. Box 1085, Banff, AB T0l 0C0; © **403/762-4561**). Passes are 3 out of 4 days C$240 adults, 4 out of 5 days C$320 adults, and the like. Children 13 to 17 and seniors 65 and over pay C$71 per day. Kids 6 to 12 pay C$26 per day.

The smallest of the three, **Banff Mount Norquay** (© **403/762-4421;** www.banffnorquay.com), is just above the Town of Banff, across the highway; you can see the shops and restaurants of Banff Avenue from its chairlifts. It's small, but steep, and can be challenging; its signature run, the North American, is one of the steepest runs on the continent. Norquay tends to emphasize family skiing; the resort offers day care and instruction, and is the only ski area in the region to offer night skiing. They also have afternoon-only and hourly ski passes. Full-day lift tickets are C$55 adults, C$43 children 13 to 17 and seniors, and C$17 children 12 and under.

To get to **Sunshine Village's** (© **403/762-6500;** www.skibanff.com) vast skiable area, well above the tree line, you'll take a long ride on an alpine gondola just to get to the ski area's base. There, you'll find the main lodge (an old log cabin–cum–pub), a ski and snowboard school, and the recently renovated Sunshine Mountain Lodge.

Just 15 minutes west of Banff off Highway 1, Sunshine gets more snow than any ski area in the Canadian Rockies (more than 9m/30 ft. per year!). Skiing often continues into late May. Lift tickets here are C$76 adults, C$62 seniors, C$54 for children 13 to 17, and C$26 children 12 and under. Just riding the gondola is C$26 per person.

Lake Louise Ski Area (© **800/258-SNOW** [800/258-7669] in North America or 403/552-3555; www.skilouise.com) is the largest of the three, with both the front and back sides of one mountain and the front of another. It is massive, gorgeous, and at times, extremely challenging. In addition to the main lodge at the base, there are two other lodges, one halfway up the front side and another at the bottom of the back side. The one on the back side, Temple Lodge, has a big deck for BBQing burgers; on a sunny, warm spring day, it's packed with sun-worshippers working on their goggle tans. Lake Louise has 1,680 skiable hectares (4,151 acres) and 113 runs, making it among the largest ski resorts in North America. Lift tickets are C$78 adults, C$63 seniors, C$55 children 13 to 17, and C$27 children 12 and under.

Cross-country or Nordic skiing is also a favorite winter activity in Banff. It can be relaxing, strenuous, and peaceful. There are more than 80km (50 miles) of managed ski trails in the park. Get updated trail reports at www.pc.gc.ca/banff. Beginners can try the Golf Course Loop near the Fairmont Banff Springs Hotel. More experienced skiers shouldn't miss the Pipestone Loops and track-set trails at Moraine Lake near Lake Louise.

Banff Townsite ★★★

So gorgeous is Banff townsite, it can sometimes seem surreal: quaint buildings, some of them historic, line a bustling main street, over which loom the peaks of the Rockies so close you feel like you could reach out and touch them. Mt. Rundle, the town's

Banff Town

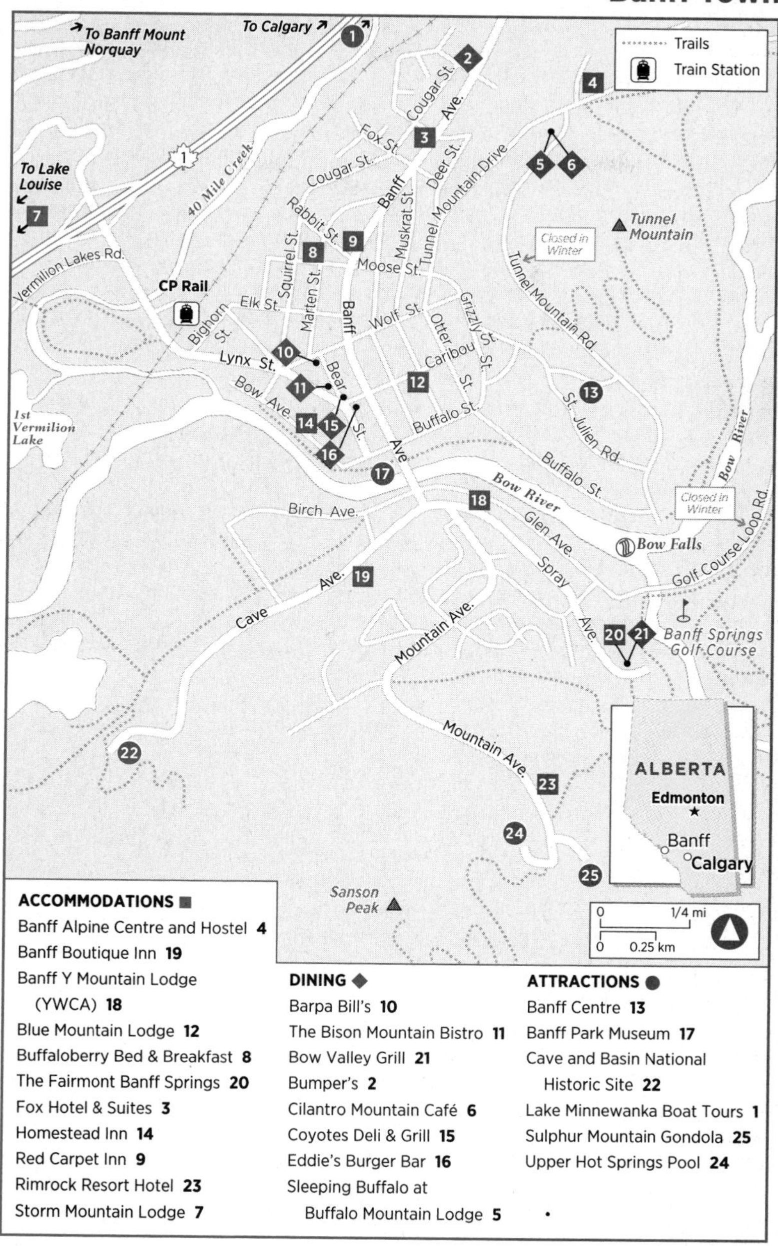

ACCOMMODATIONS ■

Banff Alpine Centre and Hostel **4**
Banff Boutique Inn **19**
Banff Y Mountain Lodge (YWCA) **18**
Blue Mountain Lodge **12**
Buffaloberry Bed & Breakfast **8**
The Fairmont Banff Springs **20**
Fox Hotel & Suites **3**
Homestead Inn **14**
Red Carpet Inn **9**
Rimrock Resort Hotel **23**
Storm Mountain Lodge **7**

DINING ◆

Barpa Bill's **10**
The Bison Mountain Bistro **11**
Bow Valley Grill **21**
Bumper's **2**
Cilantro Mountain Café **6**
Coyotes Deli & Grill **15**
Eddie's Burger Bar **16**
Sleeping Buffalo at Buffalo Mountain Lodge **5**

ATTRACTIONS ●

Banff Centre **13**
Banff Park Museum **17**
Cave and Basin National Historic Site **22**
Lake Minnewanka Boat Tours **1**
Sulphur Mountain Gondola **25**
Upper Hot Springs Pool **24**

signature peak, towers over Banff Avenue from the south; its appearance lends support to the tectonic-plate theory of mountain creation, as one side, smooth as the plains, crests at a point and gives way to a jagged underside. To the south, the Bow River Bridge traverses the fast-rushing Bow in the shadow of massive Mt. Cascade.

It's postcard perfect—exactly why the Banff Springs Hotel was built by the Canadian Pacific Railway company in 1888 (it's now owned by the luxurious Fairmont hotel chain), to draw tourists to the rugged beauty of the Rockies, providing all the comforts, including geothermally heated hot springs. The plan worked: Visitors flocked, and the town grew rapidly to accommodate.

The setting may be unreal, but in some cases, so is the town; in between the remaining historic buildings are high-end contemporary shopping malls, with luxury international brands and inflated prices. Banff also has an alarming surfeit of fudge shops—the international symbol for "tourist trap." Banff is vibrant and cosmopolitan, its sidewalks crowded with people from all over the world year-round; what it isn't, though, is peaceful—especially in summer.

ESSENTIALS

GETTING THERE If you're flying into Calgary and heading straight to Banff, call and reserve a seat on the **Banff Airporter** (✆ **403/762-3330;** www.banffairporter.com). Vans depart from Calgary Airport roughly every 2 hours; a one-way ticket costs C$53.

The closest VIA Rail train service is at Jasper, 287km (178 miles) north. **Brewster Transport** (✆ **403/762-6767**) offers an express bus between the two park centers five times weekly for C$79 one-way.

Greyhound (✆ **800/661-8747** or 403/260-0877; www.greyhound.ca) operates buses that pass through Banff on the way from Calgary to Vancouver. One-way fare between Banff and Calgary is C$26. The depot is at 100 Gopher St. (✆ **403/762-6767**).

If you're driving, the Trans-Canada Highway takes you right to Banff's main street, Banff Avenue; the town is 129km (80 miles) west of Calgary.

VISITOR INFORMATION The **Banff Information Centre,** at 224 Banff Ave. (P.O. Box 1298, Banff, AB T0L 0C0; ✆ **403/762-0270;** www.banfflakelouise.com), houses both the Banff Lake Louise Tourism Bureau and a handy and helpful national-park information center. The center is open daily June 15 to October 15 from 9am to 9pm and the rest of the year from 9am to 5pm. Ask for the Official Visitors Guide, which is packed with information about local businesses and recreation. For information on the park, go to www.pc.gc.ca.

ORIENTATION Banff's townsite is a simple place to understand; Banff Avenue is the main drag running north-south, with the Bow River Bridge at the south end. Bear Street, which has become increasingly developed as Banff has grown in recent years, parallels Banff Avenue 1 block west.

Just over the river stands the park administration building, an historical landmark, in the midst of well-kept grounds. Banff Avenue ends on the south side of the bridge, splitting into a T; to the left are the **Fairmont Banff Springs Hotel,** the **Upper Hot Springs,** and the **Banff Gondola;** turn right, and you'll be on your way to Cave and Basin Historic Site, where the park was born.

At the northwestern edge of town is the old railroad station, and a little farther northwest, the road meets the Trans-Canada Highway again, branching off to Lake Louise and Jasper. In the opposite direction, northeast, is the highway going to

Canmore and Calgary. The **Greyhound and Brewster Bus Depot** (✆ **403/760-8294**) is located at the corner of Gopher and Lynx streets, at the north end of town, about a block west of Banff Avenue.

GETTING AROUND Banff's new **ROAM** (✆ **403/760-8294**) public bus system has hybrid buses zipping all over town, with stops at all the attractions and near most hotels. One route runs from the Fairmont Banff Springs down Banff Avenue and on to Tunnel Mountain; the other runs between the north end of Banff Avenue and the Sulphur Mountain Gondola and Upper Hot Springs. The bus operates year-round. Fares are $2 adults, $1 seniors and children 6 to 12, and free for children under 6. An unlimited day pass costs $5 per person. For a taxi, call **Mountain Taxi and Tours** (✆ **403/762-3351**).

For a rental car, contact **National** at Caribou and Lynx streets (✆ **403/762-2688**) or **Budget** at the corner of Banff Avenue and Caribou Street (✆ **403/762-4565**). Reserve well in advance, as cars are frequently sold out.

SPECIAL EVENTS & FESTIVALS The **Banff Centre,** St. Julien Road (✆ **800/413-8368** or 403/762-6300; www.banffcentre.ca), is a remarkable year-round institution devoted to the arts and entertainment in the widest sense. From June to August, the center hosts the **Banff Summer Arts Festival** ★, offering a stimulating mixture of drama, opera, jazz, ballet, classical, and pop music, and the visual arts. Highlights include the International String Quartet Competition, with 10 world-class quartets vying for a cash prize and a national tour, and the Digital Playgrounds series, which brings performance artists to the stage. Tickets for some of the events cost from pay-what-you-can to C$25; a great many are absolutely free. In November, the center is home to the **Banff Mountain Film Festival.** Find out what's currently on at the Banff Tourism Bureau or by checking out the Banff Centre's website.

EXPLORING BANFF

Banff Centre ★★ A center for arts, culture, leadership, and education, this institution is known around the world as a breeding ground for creativity and innovation. Built in 1933 as a theater school, it now hosts courses, workshops, festivals, and concerts with some of the most acclaimed performing artists in the world. They come to Banff to expand their artistic horizons amid inspirational surroundings, and visitors lucky enough to nab tickets are the richer for it. Throughout the summer, there are regular events, from literary readings to jazz concerts to outdoor theater performances. There's also a great indoor pool and fabulous rooftop restaurant open to visitors, all within walking distance of Banff Avenue. Check the schedule as soon as you get to Banff and drop by the new box office in a tiny heritage cabin downtown (211a Bear St.) for more information.

107 Tunnel Mountain Dr. ✆ **403/762-6100** or 403/762-6301 Summer Arts Festival hotline. Pay-what-you-can to C$40. Main box office Tues–Sat noon–5pm; downtown box office Tues–Sat noon–3pm & 3:30–6pm.

Banff Park Museum ★ Built in 1903 by the Natural History Branch of the Geological Survey of Canada, the museum is a showcase of its growing stock of creatures preserved by taxidermy, a must for wildlife fans. Its original tally of mounted specimens was eight mammals, 259 birds, a turtle, 57 specimens of wood, 814 plants, and 201 mineral samples. John Macoun of the Natural History Branch described these as "an almost complete representation of the birds and flowering plants found within the limits of the park." The building that houses the specimens might be the best thing about the museum; the largest and most elaborate example of the early phase of park design that used decorative cross-log construction, it's a National Historic Site.

91 Banff Ave. ✆ **403/762-1558.** C$4 adults, C$3.50 seniors, C$3 children 6–16. Summer daily 10am–6pm; fall–spring daily 1–5pm.

Cave and Basin National Historic Site This little hole in the ground was the birthplace of Banff National Park. Warm natural hot springs discovered by two railway workers on their day off were soon pumped into a large pool, where dozens of people would gather to soak. The number of travelers hoping to find solace in its apparently curative waters grew. The CPR saw the opportunity for tourism and built the Banff Springs Hotel, providing a luxury destination to go along with the healing springs.

The original springs and pools haven't held up well to the heavy traffic they've received over the decades and are no longer open to the public (the Upper Springs, further up the slope of Sulphur Mountain, serve that purpose now). But the site offers a surfeit of historical background as to how and why Banff came to be, complete with interpretive displays and historical videos.

1.5km (1 mile) west of Banff (turn right at the west end of the Bow River Bridge). ✆ **403/762-1566.** C$4 adults, C$3.50 seniors, C$3 children 6–18. May 15 to Sept daily 9am–6pm; Oct to May 14 Mon–Fri 11am–4pm, Sat & Sun 9:30am–5pm.

Lake Minnewanka Boat Tours Even though some call it a giant bathtub, there's no denying the beauty of Lake Minnewanka, an aquamarine glacial lake cradled by massive peaks all around that is the largest lake in Banff National Park. It used to be called "Lake of the Water Spirits" by the Stoney Nation. Early Europeans found it equally intimidating, calling it "Devil's Lake." A 2-hour cruise is relaxing and a nice way to come to your own conclusion on the pros and cons of Minnewanka. Your boat offers 360 degrees of windows for appropriate wilderness gawking, but your boat will also likely be packed to claustrophobia-inducing capacity. Be sure to make reservations, especially in high season. There are five sailings a day in summer; buses leave from Banff every day specifically for this purpose, from the bus station and major hotels.

24km (15 miles) north of Banff. ✆ **403/762-3473.** www.minnewankaboattours.com. Tickets C$44 adults, C$19 children 5–11. Mid-May to early Oct.

Sulphur Mountain Gondola ★★ ☺ It takes 8 minutes from where you board a gondola to the top of Sulphur Mountain, the easiest summit in Banff by far. Below you, the Bow River Valley spreads out in a glorious vista of rushing water and jagged mountain peaks below. Your altitude gain from the valley floor to the summit is 698m (2,290 ft.); once you arrive, you're at 2,281m (7,484 ft.) above sea level. The summit offers a new perspective on the peaks you've been straining your neck to gawk upward at; on Sulphur Mountain, you're at their level, so you can look not only straight at them, but also beyond—to more distant peaks and valleys in almost every direction.

Follow a boardwalk along the mountain ridge as far as neighboring Sanson Peak, where you'll find an historical weather station. Just like anywhere in Banff, even at an alpine summit, there are ways to spend money: a mediocre restaurant, a pricey snack bar, and a gift shop with very typical fare are all willing to lighten your wallet. Don't bother; it's all the same stuff you'll get in town. A coffee in the snack bar is cheap rent for the amazing view, though.

The lower terminal is 2.5km (1½ miles) southeast of town on Mountain Ave. ✆ **403/762-2523.** www.explorerockies.com/banff-gondola. C$29 adults, C$14 children 6–15. May 1 to Labour Day 8:30am–9pm; check website for off-season schedule.

Upper Hot Springs Pool For more than a century, visitors have been coming to Banff to "take to the waters." Unlike the Cave and Basin (see above), the outdoor pool here is large, hygienic, warm (usually 90°F/32°C), and pleasant. It can also be very crowded. Come when it's chilly outside; it's particularly lovely on a winter's evening. A bench runs all around the pool's edge, allowing you to sit comfortably in the soothing waters. And while the pool is updated, the building, built in 1931, is actually a perfectly preserved example of mountain architecture of the era. Inside, though, it's contemporary and where you'll find the **Pleaidas Spa** (✆ **403/760-2500**), complete with steam room, massage, and aromatherapy.

At the top of Mountain Ave. (4km/2½ miles south of Banff). ✆ **403/762-1515.** Pool C$7.30 adults, C$6.30 seniors & children; C$23 families. Swimsuit & towel rentals C$1.90 each. Spring–fall daily 9am–11pm; reduced hours in winter.

SHOPPING

Alongside skiing and hiking, shopping vies for the title of Banff's most popular sport. Most shops have clerks who speak Japanese and Chinese to serve the large contingent of Asian tourists, and a handful of these stores are actually Japanese-run. There's also a large crowd of young Australians manning the shops, thanks mainly to a diplomatic agreement between the two Commonwealth countries, which offers work visas to people under 30, and to the Aussie desire to live and breathe winter during their Canadian "walkabout."

Banff shopping also offers mountain gear shops in spades; every mall (and there are at least three) has a good-sized outdoor outfitter. There's a glut of places to buy T-shirts and other tourist *tchotchkes,* but you can also buy a Rolex here or flesh out your collection of Vuittons at exclusive Banff boutiques. It's enthralling enough for some that Banff Avenue is as much of Banff as they ever see. While it's good fun, don't squander all your time here—there are malls everywhere, but there's only one Banff National Park.

WHERE TO STAY

All accommodation prices listed are for high season, normally mid-June to mid-September and over the Christmas and New Year's holidays; nearly all hotels have discounts for late fall, late winter, and spring lodging. If you're having trouble finding affordable lodgings in Banff, try properties in Canmore, located 20 minutes away (see above). If you want to camp, Banff National Park offers hundreds of campsites. See "Camping,"below, for more information.

Very Expensive

The Fairmont Banff Springs Banff wouldn't be Banff without the Springs. Literally. Credited with kick-starting the modern local tourist trade, the stately stone building, looking like the mountain retreat of some opulent monarch, was the magnet that drew tourists west in the early part of the 20th century to discover the majesty of the Canadian Rockies for themselves. When the Canadian Pacific Railway opened its crown jewel property in 1888, it was an instant hit, and it has gone on to become an iconic building. The Springs has been added to, renovated, and reconstructed more times than anyone can count, but nothing dents its majestic air; it is still the signature hotel of the Rockies, and the level of service—and the prices—reflect it. The rooms aren't huge, but expect sumptuous linens, fancy soaps and lotions, real art, and quality furniture. Bathrooms are generally small. The Gold Floor rooms are by far the nicest. With the views, the spa, the history, and the near-pageantry of service (the Springs maintains a staff of 1,200), this is an amazing testament to a bygone era of luxury.

405 Spray Ave. Banff, AB T1L 1J4. ✆ **800/441-1414** or 403/762-2211. Fax 403/762-5755. www.fairmont.com. 768 units. C$469–C$739 double; C$719–C$769 suite. Rates include full breakfast & service charges. AE, DC, DISC, MC, V. Valet parking C$33; self-parking C$25. **Amenities:** 9 restaurants; 2 lounges; babysitting; bike rental; concierge; Banff Springs golf course (considered one of the most scenic in the world); Jacuzzi; Olympic-size pool; 24-hr. room service; spa; 4 tennis courts. *In room:* A/C, TV/VCR w/pay movies & video games, hair dryer, Wi-Fi for minimal fee.

Rimrock Resort Hotel The sleek and modern Rimrock sits perched on the edge of Sulphur Mountain, removed from town. The views are outstanding. Nearly every room has a commanding view of the stunning landscape, but the main lounge—with its towering ceilings and windows that run all the way from ceiling to floor—is an extraordinary place from which to drink it all in, especially given the huge fireplace that anchors the room in the center. Everything about it suggests understated opulence, from its unpolished marble floors to the traditional—though still plump and comfortable—sofas and chairs, and excellent service. Suites offer room to roam and have wet bars and balconies. Request a room on the east face of the south wing for the choicest views (all rooms are priced according to their views—Standard, Deluxe, Premium, and Grandview). The Rimrock is peaceful and elegant, with more seclusion than its competitor the Springs. In the winter, there's also an outdoor ice rink with a fire pit. Hot chocolate and cider are served during the winter at the rink.

300 Mountain Ave. (5km/3 miles south of Banff), Banff, AB T1L 1J2. ✆ **800/661-1587** or 403/762-3356. Fax 403/762-1842. www.rimrockresort.com. 346 units. C$220–C$680 double; C$800–C$950 suite. AE, DC, DISC, MC, V. Valet parking C$10; free self-parking in heated garage. **Amenities:** 2 restaurants; 2 bars; babysitting; concierge; health club; hot tub; pool; 24-hr. room service. *In room:* A/C, TV w/pay movies & video games, hair dryer, Internet, minibar.

Expensive

Banff Boutique Inn ★ A local couple with a passion for inn-keeping have turned an old-fashioned building (original built as a European-style *pension* in 1943 and known as Pension Tannenhof) into a lovely inn, with modern decor and mountain hospitality. It's a breath of fresh air in Banff. Rooms have strange layouts, some with very small bathrooms and others with fireplaces and jetted tubs. But the vibe is relaxing and stylish. The excellent breakfast spread includes a wide variety of home-baked goodies and is served in a cozy room with contemporary works by local artists. The kitchen is available to guests for snacks and picnic preparation, although there is a permanent coffee and tea station.

121 Cave Ave., Banff, AB T1L 1B7. ✆ **403/762-4636.** www.banffboutiqueinn.com. 10 units. C$150–$310 double. Rates include breakfast. MC, V. Free parking. *In room:* TV (in most rooms), hair dryer, Wi-Fi.

Fox Hotel and Suites Not dead-center in the town of Banff, but rather a pleasant, though still walkable, remove from the hubbub, the Fox—and its sister properties the Banff Lodging Company, the Banff Caribou Lodge, the Banff Ptarmigan Inn, and Rundle Manor, among others—offer pleasant, contemporary accommodations with a good complement of amenities. The rooms are mostly suites with kitchenettes and one or two bedrooms. Loft-style second floor units have mountain views. And while the facilities qualify as luxury, it's nowhere near the price. A man-made replica "hot springs" completes the package in the basement; the faux rock walls are kind of corny, but the hot water still sooths ski-weary bones very nicely.

461 Banff Ave., Banff, AB T1L 1H8. ✆ **800/661-8310** or 403/760-8500. www.bestofbanff.com. 117 units. C$199 double; C$279–C$379 1-bedroom suite; C$404–C$429 2-bedroom suite. AE, MC, V. Free parking. **Amenities:** Restaurant; lounge; exercise room; hot pool; steam room. *In room:* TV, hair dryer, Wi-Fi.

Storm Mountain Lodge ★★ If you're weary of the relative sameness of most of the hotels in the park, Storm Mountain Lodge is a welcome respite. Built in 1922 halfway between the town of Banff and Lake Louise by the CPR as one of eight bungalow camps to encourage tourism, the lodge doesn't just feign elegant rusticity—it *is* rustic. The main building, a log structure lined with windows and a lovely outdoor veranda, is open and cozy with its thick wood walls; most of the accommodation is in a collection of old-fashioned log cabins on the property, all of them with big stone fireplaces and large, comfy tubs. Units 9 and 10 are furthest away from the often noisy Highway 93, while units 11 and 14 have great views of Castle Mountain. On the border with British Columbia and Kootenay National Park, you'll be far from any of the decent restaurants in Banff or Lake Louise (although they do have a pretty standard restaurant on-site), but close to hiking trail heads and wildlife; if you've come here to experience the wilderness, it's right outside your door.

On Hwy. 93 (just west of Castle Junction); Banff, AB T1L 1C8. ✆ **403/762-4155.** Fax 403/762-4151. www.stormmountainlodge.com. 16 units. C$239 double; C$199 pine cabin; C$289 log cabin (sleeps up to 4). Rates include breakfast. Additional adult C$20. Children under 8 stay free in parent's room. MC, V. Closed Oct 9 to Nov 9. **Amenities:** Restaurant; concierge. *In room:* Hair dryer, kitchenette (in cabins), no phone.

Moderate

Blue Mountain Lodge Just steps from Banff Avenue, this is a good choice for travelers on a budget who don't want to miss a single second of all the action. Offering simple, clean, and pleasant rooms, the owners at this little place go the extra mile, from a superb breakfast to afternoon home-baked snacks and free wireless. Rooms are decorated in local-inspired motifs, with characters like beaver trappers and cowboys. Light meals and snacks can be prepared any time of the day in the guest kitchen. It's also family-friendly.

327 Caribou St., Banff, AB. T1L 1C4. ✆ **403/762-5134.** www.bluemtnlodge.com. 10 units. C$119–C$179 double. MC, V. Rates include breakfast. Additional adult C$15. *In room:* TV, Wi-Fi.

Buffaloberry Bed and Breakfast ★ The unpretentious owners of this little inn love the outdoors, and their B&B, in a building nestled in one of downtown Banff's quieter areas, may be the best sleep in town, thanks to soundproof rooms, blackout curtains, solid-core doors, and luxurious natural linens. Bathrooms are spacious, and each room has its own heat control. Breakfasts include homemade pastries. But the best part of staying here is the chance it gives you to slip into the "real" Banff, where people actually live and work. It's a Banff that can be hard to find amidst the rows and rows of hotels and parking stalls.

417 Marten St. Banff, AB T1L 1G5. ✆ **403/762-3750.** www.buffaloberry.com. 4 units. $325 double. MC, V. No children under 10 allowed. *In room:* TV.

Homestead Inn The decor may be a little outdated, and the polyester bedspreads aren't exactly the last word in comfort, but it's clean, spacious, comfortable, and well-located in the center of town—all you can ask for in one of the best lodging deals in Banff. Factor in the free downtown parking and free wireless Internet, and this well-maintained older motel is a real winner in the budget class.

217 Lynx St., Banff, AB T1L 1A7. ✆ **800/661-1021** or 403/762-4471. www.homesteadinnbanff.com. 27 units. C$147 double. Additional adult C$10. Children under 12 stay free in parent's room. AE, MC, V. Free parking. **Amenities:** Family restaurant. *In room:* TV, hair dryer, minibar.

Red Carpet Inn Run by a long-time innkeeper family, this classic hotel is one of the best deals in Banff. Simple guest rooms are furnished with easy chairs and desks. There's an excellent restaurant right next door. The biggest rooms have a king bed and a fireplace for very reasonable prices. Freebies include free local calling, free parking, free wireless Internet, and a complimentary continental breakfast. The entire facility is very well-maintained and very clean—just the thing if you don't want to spend a fortune.

425 Banff Ave., Banff, AB T1L 1B6 ✆ **800/563-4609** or 403/762-4184. www.banffredcarpet.com. 52 units. C$140–C$150 double; C$174 double w/king bed & fireplace. Rates include continental breakfast. AE, MC, V. Free parking. **Amenities:** Jacuzzi (in winter only). *In room:* A/C, TV, fridge, hair dryer, Wi-Fi.

Inexpensive

Banff Alpine Centre and Hostel This well-known establishment is beloved by travelers and backpackers around the world. It's a fun place to stay and very reasonably priced. Dorm rooms sleep four to six people, and there are five double rooms with private baths that are a good bargain. The atmosphere here is casual yet full of energy, as so many of the guests are keen outdoors types. The pub downstairs is always lively, and the restaurant has reasonable prices for mediocre food. A good option for younger travelers and active families.

801 Hidden Ridge Way (at Tunnel Mountain Dr.), Banff, AB T1L 1B3. ✆ **403/762-4123.** Fax 403/762-3441. www.hihostels.ca/alberta. 52 units; 216 beds. Members C$36 bed, nonmembers C$40 bed; members C$120 double, nonmembers C$128 double. Children under 12 stay half-price w/parent. MC, V. **Amenities:** Restaurant; 2 lounges; Wi-Fi. *In room:* No phone.

Banff Y Mountain Lodge (YWCA) The YWCA is a bright, modern building with good amenities, just across the Bow River bridge from downtown. The Y welcomes men, women, singles, couples, and family groups, with accommodations in private or dorm rooms. Some units have private bathrooms.

102 Spray Ave., Banff, AB T1L 1C2. ✆ **800/813-4138** or 403/760-3207. www.ymountainlodge.com. 43 units; 80 beds. C$33 bunk in dorm room (bedding included); C$88–C$120 double; C$135 family room w/private bath. MC, V. Free parking. **Amenities:** Restaurant; Internet. *In room:* No phone.

Backcountry Lodges

If you aren't up for carrying a tent and gear on your back, but still want a true wilderness experience and excellent hiking, consider spending a night or two at one of Banff's historic backcountry lodges. Banff has three rustic private lodges operating in its backcountry (meaning there is no road access; they're all ski-, hike-, or bike-in). And this is not "rustic" in the sense of luxuriously appointed log cabins with private fireplaces and stone bathrooms; no, the rusticity is not a decor choice, but is utterly authentic—meaning some lack such things as electricity, phones, and (alas) indoor plumbing.

For that level of rusticity, you might expect them to be easy on the budget. They're not. But they operate on the principle that some things are worth more than a Jacuzzi tub. Like, say, a night or two in the untouched alpine wilderness, where no car will ever go. This is peace beyond peace—places where you truly realize how tiny we are in the churn of natural history.

Most include all meals, have at least a 2-night minimum stay, and are open to hikers in July and August and skiers from January through March.

A few hours' hike from the Lake Louise ski area, the revered **Skoki Lodge** (✆ **877/956-8473** or 403/522-1347; www.skoki.com) is a National Historic Site nestled next to wildflower-dotted alpine meadows. The first ski lodge in Western

Canada, the building itself is a gorgeous log structure. It is rustic—there's no running water or electricity. But there is serene beauty and warm hospitality, not to mention a soothing wood-fired sauna and gourmet meals (all included), served buffet-style. Candles and kerosene lamps light up the lodge at night, giving the lodge that unstuck-in-time sense of apartness in the wilderness. It's open to cross-country skiers in winter and hikers in summer. Rates are C$109 to C$263 per person, depending on dates.

Brewster's Shadow Lake Lodge (✆ **866/762-0114;** www.shadowlakelodge.com), on the shore of Shadow Lake in the Egypt Lakes area about four hours hike in from the highway northwest of the Town of Banff, has heated washrooms with running water, showers, and solar-powered lighting—for the backcountry, luxury indeed. Its rates are C$215 per person per night, based on double occupancy.

Just outside the park is another historic and charming gem, **Mt. Assiniboine Lodge** (✆ **403/678-2883;** www.canadianrockies.net/assiniboine). Rooms start at C$260 per person per night, including meals, guides, and lodging. For those not keen on hiking or skiing the 28km (17 miles) into the lodge, it can be accessed by helicopter for an extra $130 per person each way.

Sundance Lodge (✆ **800/661-8352;** www.xcskisundance.com) is a heritage building deep in the woods, but only a 16km (10-mile) hike or ski from the town of Banff. It's a great choice for families looking for a true wilderness experience, with the creature comfort bonus of hot showers and fresh-cooked meals. Rates are C$166 per person for the first night, with lower rates for additional nights; children 6 to 12 are welcome here, at C$85 a night (children under 6 not allowed).

CAMPING

There are a wide variety of campgrounds in Banff National Park, and you can reserve a spot online for many of them at www.pccamping.ca or via telephone at ✆ **877/737-3783**. Very few last-minute spots are available; you must plan ahead, especially if you want to be near the town of Banff. Summer is especially crowded, for obvious reasons, so don't expect a lot of privacy at any of them from June to August.

Camping Near Banff Townsite

Castle Mountain Campground This is a small, remote campground located on the Bow Valley Parkway (Hwy. 1A) about 20 minutes from the town of Banff, half way to Lake Louise. It's a good base for exploring the trails below the fabled walls of Castle Mountain, which towers just above it. It qualifies as a "rustic" campground; not many frills to be found here (i.e., no RV hook-ups and therefore no running water) but the shop at Castle Mountain Village is just a short walk away. A good family campground.

34km (21 miles) west of Banff townsite on the Bow Valley Pkwy. (Hwy.1A). 43 sites. C$22 site. Open May 18 to Sept 4.

Johnston Canyon Campground Johnston Canyon is one of the most popular day hikes in Banff, which is good news in that most of the foot traffic is gone by late afternoon. The campsite is surprisingly peaceful, nestled in the forest here just 20 minutes from Banff townsite. The best sites back onto Johnston Creek.

25km (16 miles) west of Banff townsite on the Bow Valley Pkwy. (Hwy. 1A). 132 sites. C$27 site. Open June to Sept 18.

Tunnel Mountain Village Campground This is Banff's biggest campground. It's also the closest one to the townsite—walking distance to Banff Avenue, making it also one of the busiest and, at times, rowdiest. Adding to this, perhaps, is its size, with more than 1,000 sites. It's divided into three sections: a mixed tent and RV camp 2.5km (1½ miles) east of town; an RV Mecca 4km (2½ miles) east of town; and a trailer- and tenter-friendly section to the east of the RV area. Clearly, this is not the way to get away from it all, but RVers love it; tenters wanting to walk to Banff Avenue like it, too. But this is as far from Banff wilderness as camping gets.

4km (2½ miles) east of Banff townsite on Tunnel Mountain Rd. Tunnel Mountain Village I: 618 sites; C$27 site; May 4 to Sept. Tunnel Mountain Village II: 188 sites; C$32 site w/electrical hook-up; open year-round. Tunnel Mountain Trailer Court: 321 sites; C$38 site w/full hook-up; May 4 to Sept.

Two Jack Campground On the Minnewanka Loop, Two Jack is split into two: a main, densely wooded, relatively private larger campground, and a smaller one (Lakeside). It's about 13km (8 miles) northeast of Banff townsite. The small lakeshore area is popular, with good reason: It's the most scenic and peaceful campground near the town of Banff.

12km (7½ miles) from Banff townsite on Minnewanka Loop Rd. Two Jack Main: 380 sites; C$22 site; May 18 to Sept 4. Two Jack Lakeside: 74 sites; C$27 site; May 18 to Sept 18.

Backcountry Camping

There are 50 designated backcountry campsites in Banff; their access varies greatly. Some are just a couple of hours from the trail head; others take a full day (20km/12 miles) just to reach. ***Remember:*** Most mountain hikes demand significant altitude gain, so don't budget your time and pace thinking this is a level stroll. Hiking up into Egypt Lake, for example, the first day is almost entirely uphill and strenuous until you reach the high alpine plains.

Remember: You must have a Wilderness Pass (C$9.80 per day or C$69 for an annual pass) and a campsite reserved before you hit the trail. Some campsites are legendary among hikers all over the world, and the demand is great; campsites can be booked up to 3 months prior to your dates, and the most popular ones are booked for the season within a day or two. Contact the Banff National Park backcountry reservation line (© **403/762-1556**). Don't expect much from these sites except a fire pit, an outhouse (maybe), and somewhere to hoist your food up out of reach of animals (an essential in the backcountry). Don't drink the stream or lake water to avoid Giardiasis. You'll need to either boil the water or use a water-treatment system. And you will certainly want to bring toilet paper.

Some sites can be reached from Banff townsite, by following the Spray Valley Trail. Sites at Egypt Lake, Shadow Lake, and Fish Lakes have their trail heads about a half-hour drive from town. There are also campsites along the shores of Lake Minnewanka, northeast of the townsite, which are accessible only by canoe. Families may like sites at Taylor Lake or Glacier Lake, which are accessed by relatively easy trails.

Farther up the Icefields Parkway, there are trail heads to more sites still in Banff (not yet Jasper). Consult the Banff website for full listings and maps at www.pc.gc.ca/eng/pn-np/ab/banff/activ/activ33.aspx. The Banff Information Center, listed in "Hotel Alternatives," earlier in this chapter, will also be able to help you out. A backcountry campsite costs C$10 per person per night, and there is a C$12 reservation fee. You cannot reserve backcountry sites online.

Backcountry Huts

There is a significant amount of luck involved in reaching the backcountry huts in Banff National Park, operated by the Alpine Club of Canada (ACC), as they are few (there are six), small (most accommodate about a half-dozen people, max), and very, very popular. If you get a spot reserved at one, though, you'll quickly see what all the fuss is about. These are remote places, often along a towering bluff above a remote valley, or face-on to a glacier—places you probably won't see any other way. Almost all are a good full-day hike or ski into the backcountry; as such, they're most often used by hikers on treks lasting several days or mountain climbers making an ascent of a nearby summit. And you must reserve ahead of time. If you show up without a reservation, you'll not be given a bed unless it is an emergency.

Some of the huts are comfortable cabins (the Castle Mountain Shelter, perched on a cliff called Goat Plateau, halfway up Castle Mountain, accommodates six people comfortably and has a propane stove; it's accessed by a challenging scramble up the mountain face and is closed in winter due to extreme avalanche hazard); others are just shacks. None have running water or power, and few are close to a water source—so plan to bring that with you, too.

Bow Hut, by measure of remoteness, is the "easiest" to access, though it's far from easy by anyone's measure. It's a 6-hour hike from the trail head at Bow Lake and a steady climb.

If you aren't a member of the ACC, rates are C$36 per person per night for a simple bunk and access to the facilities: some huts are subject to peak-rate pricing at certain times of the year. Rates for members are substantially lower. For more information on backcountry huts or on ACC membership, contact the **Alpine Club of Canada** (✆ **403/678-3200;** www.alpineclubofcanada.ca). The site also lists what you should bring to a hut to make your experience as comfortable as possible. Remember, you must contact the ACC before you arrive. You can't just show up at a hut and expect to find sleeping room. You'll also need a valid Wilderness Pass from Parks Canada (see "Backcountry Camping," above).

WHERE TO DINE

Going out to eat in Banff can be surprisingly entertaining. Some complain that prices are high, waiting times long, service indifferent, and entrees smallish. But if you stick to the places listed below, you'll find charm, variety, and refreshingly good food for a little mountain town of only 8,000 people. Banff Avenue has all types of restaurants, and the crowd has spilled over to neighboring Bear Street, 1 block to the north.

Expensive

The Bison Mountain Bistro ★★★ CANADIAN Casually rustic, the Bison simply is the best of Banff. It calls itself "Rocky Mountain Comfort Food," but it manages to be innovative and elegant. Try the pizza with house-made venison pepperoni, wild mushrooms, and crisped leeks, and you'll see what I mean. With a huge emphasis on local and seasonal ingredients and as much made in-house as possible (the bread here is fantastic all by itself), the Bison is casual enough that you can stop in for a snack and not break the bank (the pizzas, a trail mix and baby spinach salad, and shrimp and crab mini tacos are all outstanding), or have a full blown multi-course meal (of grilled bison tenderloin, venison, or organic chive gnocchi, to name a few) and feel like you're in a major cosmopolitan center. The decor is as adaptable and enticing as the menu; wholly contemporary—yet with its vaulted wood ceilings and floors, still cozy and homey—it's a great respite from the touristy offerings in much of the town.

Bison Courtyard, 211 Bear St. ✆ **403/762-5550.** Reservations recommended on weekends. Main courses C$19–C$45. AE, MC, V. Sat & Sun 10am–2pm; daily 5–11pm.

Bow Valley Grill ★ CANADIAN The Banffshire Club is the fanciest dining room at the Banff Springs, but the more low-key Bow Valley Grill ranks right up there with the best in town. First, it takes in the famous hotel's multi-million-dollar views of the Fairholme Mountain Range and the Bow Valley. It also offers the hotel's almost equally famous pricing—the cocktail menu lists single drinks for as much as C$25—but the food here is excellent, and if you're into scenic dining, it's worth the premium. The open kitchen delivers such lovely local fare as pan-fried Bow River trout—that's the river you can see from your table—and, of course, top-grade Alberta beef. While the cuisine isn't overly ambitious—baked potatoes remain a standard accompaniment with beef—it's hard to argue with fresh, seasonal meats and fish grilled rotisserie style, and a perfect preparation to boot. If it lacks originality, it makes up for it in quality; this is one of Banff's most-loved, consistent restaurants for just that reason. Their brunch buffet is a classic for any special Sunday morning.

In the Fairmont Banff Springs Hotel, 405 Spray Ave. ✆ **403/762-6860.** Reservations recommended June–Aug (only on weekends the rest of the year). Brunch buffet C$27; main courses C$24–C$46. AE, DC, DISC, MC, V. Daily 6:30am–2pm & 6–9pm.

Cilantro Mountain Café ★ CALIFORNIAN Part of the sprawling Buffalo Mountain Lodge complex, this is the casual choice set in the equally peaceful location of Sleeping Buffalo. An offshoot of the original Cilantro on Calgary's 17th Avenue, the Banff Cilantro has many of the same priorities: a casual, California-style cuisine—here, inflected with a mountain flair, like the wild game meats—with a wide selection of apple-wood–fired oven pizzas, the item on which the original Cilantro's enduring reputation was based. It's cozy and rustic here, with raw-log walls and everything a rough, warm wood. There's also a great patio from which to survey the lodge's private, tranquil grounds.

In the Buffalo Mountain Lodge, 700 Tunnel Mountain Rd. ✆ **403/760-2400.** Reservations recommended on weekends. Main courses C$15–C$28. AE, MC, V. June 6 to Sept 9 Wed–Sun 5–10pm; Dec 19 to June 5 Fri–Sun 5–10pm. Closed Sept 10–Dec 18.

Sleeping Buffalo at Buffalo Mountain Lodge ★ CANADIAN Just outside town, the Buffalo Mountain Lodge occupies a peaceful, treed area that provides some escape from bustling Banff. The restaurant here, Sleeping Buffalo, reflects the chilled-out vibe; set in the hotel's spectacular log cabin–style main lodge, with a huge stone fireplace at its heart, the dining room is rustic, cozy, and posh all at once. The BML reflects the major food trend in Banff (and all of Alberta, really), with its commitment to regional ingredients and reliance on incorporating game animals (though all are farmed) like venison, caribou, and bison. The chef's fusion of the trend to a bygone era of fine dining (though the menu changes seasonally, you'll always find lamb, quail, and/or pheasant somewhere) makes the BML's take on it all its own—especially when you consider many of the sauces and seasonings are spiced with herbs from the lodge's very own extensive garden.

In the Buffalo Mountain Lodge, 700 Tunnel Mountain Rd. ✆ **403/760-4484.** www.buffalomountainlodge.com. Reservations recommended on weekends. Main courses C$19–C$44. AE, DC, MC, V. Daily noon–10pm.

Moderate

Bumper's STEAKHOUSE If a place has been serving visitors Alberta beef at affordable prices since 1975, it's got to be on to something good. Simple meals star Alberta beef: Prime rib, a half-dozen cuts of steak, and baby back ribs are the usual go-to choices. They also have the best salad bar in town. While it's nothing fancy, Bumper's is a classic. As their slogan says, "If you haven't been to Bumper's, you haven't been to Banff!"

603 Banff Ave. ✆ **403/762-2622.** Main courses $10–$40. AE, MC, V. Daily 5–10pm.

Coyotes Deli & Grill ★ SOUTHWEST/MEDITERRANEAN Fresh, healthy, relaxed (when there isn't a lineup of people waiting for a table), and very popular with locals, Coyotes is one of the few places in town where you'll find more than the standard one or two options, but rather a broad array, like a spicy black bean burrito or a southwestern polenta with ratatouille. There's something for everybody here, including a healthy baked salmon and grilled meats. They also have an excellent breakfast menu. Coyotes is popular, so make a reservation.

206 Caribou St. ✆ **403/762-3963.** Reservations recommended. Main courses C$16–C$28. AE, DC, MC, V. Daily 7:30am–11pm.

Eddie's Burger Bar ★ BURGERS Build your own gourmet burgers well into the evening at this fun bar–cum–burger shop. The bison burger comes with sautéed mushrooms, double-smoked bacon, and roasted garlic aioli on an English muffin. The Red White Blue has hot buffalo sauce, bacon, and blue cheese. Kobe, Kiwi, Aussie, veggie, and chicken burgers are also options. Beef burgers are organic and pure Albertan, and a great value. Add sweet potato fries or *poutine.* Eddie also has a large cocktail menu and the best milkshakes in the Rockies, made with Mackay's ice cream.

137C Banff Ave (at Caribou St.). ✆ **403/762-2230.** Main courses $8–$16. MC, V. Daily 11:30am–3am.

Inexpensive

Banff isn't really the place for the frugal traveler, unless you want to resort to the grocery stores. Thankfully, they're readily available; a full-sized Safeway can be found at Martin and Elk streets, and if you're in a hostel, there will almost surely be a common kitchen.

The **Cascade Plaza Mall,** on Banff Avenue, has a food court, and if you get really desperate, there's always **McDonald's,** at 116 Banff Ave. But don't do that—for just a bit more, you can go to one of the three locations of the local coffee shop **Evelyn's** (201 Banff Ave., 229 Bear St., or in the Town Centre Mall). They're all crowded by folks needing a coffee fix. There's home baking, though you're not likely to make a meal of their muffins. Your best bet to stay out of the tourist-food trap is to prepare meals yourself.

Barpa Bills GREEK For something "to go," you can't beat a souvlaki in a warm pita, hot off the grill at this little Bear Street joint. It's topped with fresh *tzatziki* sauce and cooked to order. There are also gyros, burgers, and *poutine* (a French-Canadian specialty). Grab a stool at the counter if you want to eat in, but don't expect friendly chatter with the staff!

233 Bear St. ✆ **403/762-0377.** Main courses $6–$14. No credit cards. Daily 11am–9pm.

BANFF AFTER DARK

Banff's magnetic draw for young people from all over the world, most of them working in the resorts, gives Banff nightlife an overwhelming college-town feel. Almost all the hotels have bars or lounges, but they are more sedate; all along Banff Avenue in-season, you'll find something going on in the many, many pubs.

One of the old standbys is the **Rose & Crown** (202 Banff Ave.; ✆ **403/762-2121**). It's been around long enough to establish its reputation as a rowdy, fun beer-swilling joint. On a summer night, the rooftop patio is hard to beat—all big sky and stars above, and the hustle and bustle of Banff Avenue right below. Inspired by the birthplace of Guinness, selecting a draught at the **St. James's Gate** (205 Wolf St.; ✆ **403/762-9355**) is just about the toughest challenge in Banff—there are 33 beers on tap, as well as 50 single-malt scotches and 10 Irish whiskeys. Live music is almost always Celtic, and a blast. Oenophiles will do best at **The Bison Lounge** (213 Bear St.; ✆ **403/762-5550**), which has a great list of wines by the glass and snacks from the outstanding bistro upstairs. It's the most cosmopolitan hangout in town. Grab a spot at the communal table to make new friends. At **Wild Bill's Saloon** (201 Banff Ave.; ✆ **403/762-0333**), you can embrace Alberta's western heritage wholeheartedly. Wild Bill's lets the rock bands play on its least-important nights, Monday and Tuesday, but starting Wednesday and all through the weekend, the hootin' hollerin' Western pride comes to the fore. It's non-stop line dancing and hurtin' tunes, mostly by Albertan country bands passing through.

Banff also has its own urbane cocktail lounge called **Aurora** (110 Banff Ave., downstairs; ✆ **403/760-5300**), complete with an array of DJs and martinis. Its sister club, the **Hoodoo Lounge** (137 Banff Ave.; ✆ **403/760-8636**), offers nightly events ("Throw Your Panties" being one of them) and dancing to DJs, as well.

But that's nothing compared to **Outabounds** (137 Banff Ave.; ✆ **403/762-8434**), Banff's most popular dance bar. Located in a dingy basement, the four bars serve up beers and sloppily made cocktails to young patrons—most of them resort employees—while the packed dance floor is obscured in a shroud of dry-ice fog.

Lake Louise ★★★

Lake Louise is probably most famous not for the lake itself, but for the hotel named after it, the Chateau Lake Louise. One of the same family of Canadian Pacific Railway hotels that gave us the Banff Springs, the Chateau, as the name suggests, was modeled after the French building style; some find it beautiful, others not so much. The lake, though, is undeniably stunning. At the far end of the lake (perhaps an hour's hike on the Lakeshore Trail), the Victoria Glacier hangs above the blue-green waters, preternatural and spectacular.

Lake Louise, the village, is 56km (35 miles) northwest of Banff, but leaves behind the crowded, touristy feel of its neighbor. It's small, for one thing, centered around a shopping plaza nestled in trees next to the Bow River. There is no main street, and it is an overall perfectly peaceful place. It also sits next to one of the largest ski areas in North America and offers easy access to some of the most amazing trekking to be found in the park.

When you get to the Chateau, though, expect to fight for parking in summer and brave the crowds (this might be the only place in Louise you find them) heading out to take a stroll (or just take a photo) along the Lakeshore Trail.

You can reach the back of the lake quickly and easily via a flat trail. Then, decide if you want to continue up toward the Plain of Six Glaciers Trail to a teahouse with a beautiful view. The location is deeply rewarding and otherworldly.

SEEING THE SIGHTS

In the summer, the ski lifts at the Lake Louise Ski Area become a sightseeing gondola (www.lakelouisegondola.com), taking you for a 14-minute ride to an elevation of 2,088m (6,850 ft.) at the top of Mount Whitehorn, across the wide Bow Valley from the lake. There's a Wildlife Interpretive Centre, as well as guided nature walks. From May to September (in between ski seasons), gondola fees for adults are C$26; children 6 to 15 C$13. Kids under 6 can ride for free.

On the way up the long, winding road from Lake Louise Village to the Chateau and the lake is a left turnoff to **Moraine Lake.** Don't miss this rough, windy road because the end of it is spectacular! Lake Louise may be on the top of the marquee, but this supporting act is equally stunning—and much less traveled. Wild and dramatic, Moraine Lake is walled in by a chain of 10 peaks 3,000m (9,843 ft.) high.

The lake is smaller than Louise but has an oddly intimate air, closed in as it is by the mountains on one side and a massive rock slide on another. You can hike a short stretch of lakeside path to the foot of the mountains in about 10 minutes or up a rock pile in about 15 minutes to a lookout for good view. Some of the premiere hikes in Banff begin here, as well. The serenity of this place is amazing, especially if you are here before noon. The lodge also has a lovely restaurant for lakeside dining in this very special place.

WHERE TO STAY

Lake Louise, being small as it is, has few options, most of them expensive. The local HI here, the **Lake Louise Alpine Centre** (203 Village Road, Lake Louise, AB T0L 1E0; ✆ **866/762-4122** or 403/522-2202; www.hihostels.ca), is jointly owned and run by HI and the Alpine Club of Canada, and is a very reasonable option. It's huge, modern, comfortable, and conveniently located. The hostel also offers guide-led hikes daily. Linens are included in the rates: Dorm-room beds C$28 for members, C$42 for nonmembers; private rooms C$110 members, C$118 non-members.

Baker Creek Chalets ★ Off the beaten track on the gloriously scenic Bow Valley Parkway, just east of Lake Louise, Baker Creek Chalets sit on babbling Baker Creek, apart from much of the tourist bustle. The red-roofed complex is wonderfully secluded and private; as such, Baker Creek offers the Banff wilderness that many come looking for but few find. Bears, elk, and deer routinely stroll by. Cabins mainly sleep four to six and have kitchenettes and wood-burning fireplaces. It's the kind of place you want to settle in and spend an entire week exploring. It's well worth a night away if you've been mainly centered in the town of Banff. The train runs sporadically throughout the day and night right next to the property; if you are a light sleeper, ask for a quiet cabin. There are several room configurations, so call Baker Creek to find something that best suits your needs and budget. Also, the on-site Baker Creek Bistro (see below) is one of the top places to dine in this part of Alberta.

11km (6¾ miles) east of Lake Louise on Hwy. 1A; Lake Louise, AB T0L 1E0. ✆ **403/522-3761.** www.bakercreek.com. 35 units. C$290–C$335 double. AE, MC, V. Free parking. **Amenities:** Restaurant; lounge; gym; steam room; sauna. *In room:* Kitchen, no phone.

Deer Lodge Just before reaching the lake and the Chateau, you'll pass Deer Lodge, a heritage lodge with more affordable rates in a very good location, just a short stroll from the lake (and the Chateau) itself. Plus, where the Chateau often feels overrun, Deer Lodge remains oddly tranquil. Its rustic log structure is a homey, cozy option with real mountain authenticity: Built in the 1920s, the original Lodge was a teahouse for the early mountaineers who came to the area to hike (the original tearoom is now the Mount Fairview Dining Room and Bar, offering Northwest cuisine). Now owned by the same company that owns Buffalo Mountain Lodge (see above) in Banff, like there, there's an emphasis on serenity. There are rooms from three eras: small, basic rooms in the original lodge; larger rooms in the newer Tower Wing; and Heritage Rooms, the largest rooms in the newest wing, which have been completely renovated and have sunny balconies. Comfortable but not posh, this is mountain vacationing the way your grandfather might have done it, with old-fashioned plumbing and heating issues to go with it.

109 Lake Louise Dr., Lake Louise, AB T0L 1E0. © **800/661-1595** or 403/522-3747. www.deerlodgelake louise.com. 73 units. C$105–C$200 double (lodge rooms); C$190–C$300 double (Heritage Rooms). AE, MC, V. Free parking. **Amenities:** Restaurant; lounge; rooftop Jacuzzi; sauna.

The Fairmont Chateau Lake Louise ★★★ Should you decide to forget you have a budget, the Chateau Lake Louise is one of two places where you should do it (Fairmont Jasper Park Lodge, see below, is the other). The Chateau, on the shores of the emerald waters of spectacular Lake Louise, has perhaps the most picturesque location of any hotel in the country. Ancient ice hangs suspended above the lake at the far end in the Victoria Glacier; the frigid waters, just down the steps from the dining room and lounge, are plied by canoes and kayaks in warm weather and ice-skaters in winter. The massive, formal structure, blue-roofed and turreted, is furnished with Alpine-styled sumptuousness and charm.

The guest rooms, while quite modest in size, are nevertheless very elegant, warm, and comfortable, with pine and oak furniture, walls done in soft tones, and luxurious feather duvets. Each guest room has a different heritage photo of a local pioneer and a botany sketch—unique touches. Having said this, there is a large variety in size and decor, depending on which of the three wings you stay in. Rooms with lake views cost much more than those on the other side of the hall (which still have nice mountain views). None of the rooms (save the Royal and Belvedere suites) have balconies or patios, though. The new Gold Floor has superior service. The pool is nothing special, but the hotel's rich heritage, coupled with access to amazing hiking and skiing, is unmatched on the planet. This is not a peaceful place, given the throngs of visitors that storm the Chateau every day, but the guest rooms are truly sumptuous and the service top notch. Truly the best of high-end Banff.

111 Lake Louise Dr., Lake Louise, AB T0L 1E0. © **800/441-1414** or 403/522-3511. www.fairmont.com. 554 units. C$399–C$599 double. Children under 17 stay free in parent's room. Off-season rates & packages available. AE, DC, DISC, MC, V. Valet parking C$35; self-parking C$25. **Amenities:** 5 restaurants; 2 bars; babysitting; bike rental; concierge; concierge-level rooms; health club; exercise room; Jacuzzi; indoor pool; 24-hr. room service; sauna; canoe rental. *In room:* A/C, TV, hair dryer, minibar, Wi-Fi.

Moraine Lake Lodge ★ Understated and lovely, the Moraine Lake Lodge has the feeling of being apart from the world in the wilderness—even though it's only a 15-minute drive from the Fairmont Chateau Lake Louise, and the parking lot can feel like a zoo during peak hours. When the day-trippers leave, though, this lodge becomes secluded, private, and gorgeous. There are eight modern but basic rooms in the original building and six in a separate wing next door, with frills such as fireplaces. Along the shore of the lake, private cabins with fireplaces and beautiful lake-view balconies sit in seclusion. No attempt at old-world opulence is made here; the focus is on the outside, where it should rightly be. There's really no need to go anywhere else; the restaurant is top-notch, serving inventive local cuisine like game meats and fish. Room rates include continental breakfast, afternoon tea, use of canoes on the lake, and naturalist presentations and hikes.

13km (8 miles) south of Lake Louise, at Moraine Lake, Lake Louise, AB T0L 1E0. © **877/522-2777** or 403/522-3733. www.morainelake.com. 33 units. C$227–C$449 double; C$599 cabin. Rates include continental breakfast. AE, MC, V. Free parking. Closed early Oct to May. **Amenities:** 2 restaurants; bar; concierge; canoe rental; Wi-Fi. *In room:* Hair dryer, no phone.

Post Hotel ★★★ This is almost as much a Lake Louise landmark as the Chateau—albeit 1⁄20th the size. But while you may sacrifice the lakeside setting, you'll miss none of the crowds. The Post, though understated, is quietly one of very few properties in all of Western Canada that is part of the exclusive Relais & Chateaux network, a French hospitality industry designation extended to only the best of the best. The Post is certainly that: quintessential mountain style with traditional log post-and-beam construction, but the rustic structure is tricked out in pure luxurious comfort. The service is Swiss-style (exquisite and professional). Most rooms have stone fireplaces, heated slate bathroom floors, and private balconies, while the common areas, like the lobby and library, often boast a roaring fire and comfortable overstuffed sofas and chairs. The spa is the best in Lake Louise. But the real feature of the Post Hotel is the dining room (see below), which is simply one of the best anywhere in Canada. The Post has come a long way in the past 25 years; it used to be little more than a motel, though the dining room was always special—an international destination in the backwoods of old-time Lake Louise. The current Swiss-Canadian owners built around the restaurant's reputation (and structure; it still occupies its original building) and brought the entire Post Hotel up to the dining room's standard. The result is simply one of the best mountain retreats you'll find anywhere.

200 Pipestone Rd., Lake Louise, AB T0L 1E0. ✆ **800/661-1586** or 403/522-3989. www.posthotel.com. 92 units. C$345–C$455 double; from C$585 suite; C$465–C$1,400 cabin. AE, MC, V. Free parking. Closed Nov. **Amenities:** Restaurant; 2 bars; babysitting; Jacuzzi; indoor pool; sauna. *In room:* TV/VCR, hair dryer, Wi-Fi.

WHERE TO DINE

Baker Creek Bistro ★★ CANADIAN Fresh and modern food is served by warm and friendly folks inside a cozy heritage cabin about 10 minutes south of Lake Louise. It's definitely worth the drive and makes a great pit-stop on your way to the Icefields Parkway from Banff. It focuses on local ingredients simply but inventively prepared—recent menu items included blue crab and prawn cakes in coconut, curry and lime ginger aioli, aromatic smoke-roasted game hen, cedar plank wild salmon, and bison short ribs. Chef Shelley Robinson is also an expert pastry chef, so save room for dessert.

15km (9¼ miles) east of Lake Louise on Hwy. 1A. ✆ **403/522-2182.** Reservations suggested. Main courses C$25–C$32. MC, V. Daily noon–3pm & 5–9pm.

Post Hotel Dining Room ★★★ INTERNATIONAL This is the priciest place in Lake Louise by far, but it's up there with the top restaurants in North America, so your money is well spent. *Wine Spectator* magazine made it one of only four restaurants in Canada to win its Grand Award for its exhaustively fantastic 32,000-bottle wine cellar (1,800 are on the wine list at any given time); *Gourmet* magazine recently called the dining room the "third best" rustic culinary retreat on Earth. A meal here, in the hotel's original log building, is an experience hard to match: It's cozy, with a roaring fireplace; the service is unbeatable; and the food, well, hardly needs my endorsement—Google the Post's dining room, and let your mouth water at the praise handed out by taste buds far more practiced and sophisticated than mine. The menu focuses on flavorful meat and seafood, with impressive desserts a worthy follow-up. The service is first-class; diners are expected to dress appropriately (no hiking shorts, please!). Suffice it to say that, for the true foodie in the crowd, the Post simply shouldn't be missed. If there's a restaurant in the Rockies you'll regret passing up, this is the one.

200 Pipestone Rd., Lake Louise. ✆ **403/522-3989.** www.posthotel.com. Reservations required. Main courses C$36–C$52. AE, MC, V. Daily 11:30am–2pm & 6–10pm.

Walliser Stube Wine Bar ★ SWISS The Swiss have had a legendary influence on Lake Louise, mostly as mountain guides. Their cuisine and culture live on inside the Fairmont Chateau Lake Louise's Walliser Stube. A *stube* is a parlor, and this restaurant's dark wooden walls and library-sized wine cellar balances out the deep green and blue scene out the window. The Swiss invented cheese fondue, and the version you'll have here would put most of what you'd find in Switzerland to shame—it's simply excellent. Even if the Walliser Stube were just a place for a meal, it would be fantastic; an incredibly comfortable space, in one of the best hotels in the world, in one of the most majestic settings on the planet, is hard to beat.

In the Fairmont Chateau Lake Louise, 111 Lake Louise Rd., Lake Louise. ✆ **403/522-1818.** Reservations required. Main courses C$30–C$47; fondues for 2 C$35–C$47. AE, DISC, MC, V. Daily 6–9pm.

The Icefields Parkway ★★★

The 278km (173-mile) stretch of road that winds its way along the Rockies' spine from Lake Louise to Jasper is easily one of the most awe-inspiring drives you'll ever encounter. In good traffic, you could do the drive in 3 hours, but why would you? Along Highway 93 here, it's as much about the journey as the destination.

As you wind your way through mountain bowls cradling ancient glaciers high above, you can't help but be taken by a sense of the infinite; this thin ribbon of tarmac seems so insignificant next to these looming giants that you may feel like a visitor on another planet.

Above your sightline, midway between Banff and Jasper, glaciers spill down into bowls that are fragments from the Columbia Icefields, which cover these peaks for kilometers in a massive dome of prehistoric ice. This is one of the biggest non-polar ice fields in the world, and the ice fields are the source of some of the most significant rivers in the west, including the Columbia, the Athabasca, and the North Saskatchewan.

There are dozens of turn-outs along the way—picnic areas and viewpoints alongside fascinating rock formations and aquamarine lakes—to allow you a slightly deeper drink into the abundant planetary history to be found here. This is also the domain of wildlife such as the usually elusive mountain goat (often found traversing the valley from one set of peaks to the other; you'll see them frequently on the road, so watch out); bighorn sheep are common as squirrels, and you might even catch sight of a bear.

A popular and breathtaking experience is an excursion up onto the Athabasca Glacier at the Columbia Icefields in a giant purpose-built bus with wheels 6m (20 ft.) in diameter. This is as close as you can get to the ice fields themselves. The **Columbia Icefields Centre** (✆ **780/852-7032**), a giant complex with a museum, cafeteria, gift shop, restaurant, and lodge, sits across Highway 93 from the Athabasca Glacier; an excursion up onto the ice (operated by **Brewster Snocoach Tours;** ✆ **403/762-6735;** www.columbiaicefield.com) costs C$49 adults and C$24 kids. It takes about 90 minutes. You'll be warned on-site, but it's worth understanding that walking on a glacier can be very dangerous, as fissures and breakaway chunks of ice can happen any time. Implicit with buying a ticket is that you do so at your own risk.

The **Icefields Centre** also has a Parks Canada office (✆ **780/852-7030**) that answers questions about the area. It stands beside the lodge and is open May to June 14 daily from 9am to 5pm; June 15 to September 7 daily from 9am to 6pm; and September 8 to October 15 daily from 9am to 5pm. It is closed October 16 to April.

The Icefields Parkway starts just northwest of Lake Louise, where Highway 1 continues west toward Golden, British Columbia; and Highway 93 (the Icefields Pkwy.) curls north along the Bow River towards Jasper. Bow Lake, the river's source, pools at the base of Crowfoot Glacier, a worthy stop-off point. **Num-Ti-Jah Lodge** (see "Where to Stay," below), on the shores of Bow Lake, is a good place to stop for lunch (and one of the only ones). This venerable lodge sits in a spectacular spot in the valley and also offers simple accommodations.

From Bow Summit, the parkway descends into the North Saskatchewan River drainage, where you'll find the Peyto Lake Viewpoint. You can get to it only on foot, but the brief (if steep) path pays off nicely when you reach the aquamarine lake's stunning shores.

The North Saskatchewan River turns west at the junction of highways 93 and 11. Here, there's a complex with a gas station, a basic motel, a gift shop, and cafeteria called "the Crossing" (✆ **403/761-7000;** www.thecrossingresort.com), with a subpar cafeteria and a tacky gift shop. Standard rooms are C$159 a night. This is the only gas station between Lake Louise and Jasper, so be sure to fuel up.

Out of the North Saskatchewan drainage, you'll climb up into Sunwapta Pass. You'll feel like the ascent will never end, and the surrounding terrain is awesome and a little bit frightening. But the scenery is the perfect balm for anxiety.

Here, in the shadows of 3,490m (11,450-ft.) Mount Athabasca, the icy tendrils of the Columbia Icefields come into view. You've been surveying the glaciers from below; if you took the Icefields tour, you saw the lip of the fields themselves at the top of the Athabasca Glacier. But up here, you'll see that they're tiny fragments of a colossal surface. The Columbia Icefields cover nearly 518 sq. km (200 sq. miles) and are more than 760m (2,493 ft.) thick.

From the Columbia Icefields, the parkway descends steeply into the Athabasca River drainage. From the parking area for Sunwapta Falls, travelers can choose to crowd around the chain-link fence and peer at the turbulent falls or take the half-hour hike to equally impressive but less crowded Lower Sunwapta Falls. Athabasca Falls, farther north along the parkway, is another must-see. Here, the wide and powerful Athabasca River constricts into a roaring torrent before dropping 25m (82 ft.) into a narrow canyon. The parkway continues along the Athabasca River, through a landscape of meadows and lakes, before entering the Jasper townsite.

WHERE TO STAY

Hotels are scant along the parkway, but rustic hostels that are ideal for cyclists, hikers, climbers, and other rugged sightseers can be found at Mosquito Creek, Rampart Creek, Hilda Creek, Beauty Creek, Athabasca Falls, and Mount Edith Cavell (see "Backcountry Hostels" above). Reservations for all Icefields Parkway hostels can be made by calling ✆ **866/762-4122**.

Num-Ti-Jah Lodge ★ This rustic and secluded red-roofed lodge on the shores of Bow Lake sports the most scenic location of any lodging in Banff National Park. Built in 1937 by trapper and guide Jimmy Simpson, the building is pretty much as it was then, with every detail preserved. (Simpson, who left England and came to Canada at age 19, became a legendary eccentric and much-admired Banff pioneer.)

There's nothing overly fancy here, just simple comforts, an incredible view, and the pleasure of being a half-hour's drive from the next-closest accommodations—it's one of the few secluded lodges in Banff National Park, even though it's located right off the Icefields Parkway. You'll be paying for the location, not the amenities. The stairs creak as you climb them, and the walls are thin; guest rooms are furnished in a modest style, and the light flickers a bit when you switch it on. Bathrooms in all guest rooms are clean, though quite basic and small, with stand-up showers. All-inclusive packages take away any worrying about meals. The setting is full of rustic mountain ambience. Drawing an outdoor-loving crowd of people who aren't necessarily looking for luxury amenities, guests here prefer a lodge with heaps of character and history. Sometimes, that just leaves you imagining the possibilities an upgrade could do, but to love Num-Ti-Jah is to love it as it is.

40km (25 miles) north of Lake Louise on Hwy. 93, Lake Louise, AB T0L 1E0. ✆ **403/522-2167.** www.num-ti-jah.com. 25 units. C$318–C$365 double. AE, MC, V. Rates include breakfast. Additional adult C$15. Free parking. Closed mid-Oct to early Dec. **Amenities:** Restaurant; lounge w/pool table. *In room:* No phone.

JASPER NATIONAL PARK ★★

Jasper's earliest incarnation, in the 1840s, sounded less than inviting. It was described by a visiting painter as "composed of two rooms of about 14 and 15 feet square. One of them is used by all comers and goers, Indians, voyageurs and traders, men, women, and children being huddled together indiscriminately."

An inauspicious beginning. But that's hardly the Jasper of today. Established as a park in 1907, in the intervening 170 years, Jasper has expanded from such humble beginnings to become Canada's largest mountain park, with crowds flocking there for its hiking, biking, climbing, horseback riding, and rafting. Visitors will also be able to find shopping and fine dining in Jasper, but such urbane attractions are not the focus, as in Banff; Jasper's tourists seem more interested in what lies outside of town than what's in it. The result is a charming alpine village with a few fancy frills, but nothing approaching the commercial theme park vibe that has befallen Banff. For more information on the park's attractions, contact **Jasper National Park** (P.O. Box 10, Jasper, AB T0E 1E0; ✆ **780/852-6176**; www.pc.gc.ca).

Sports & Outdoor Activities in the Park

You can find much of the gear you'll need for everything from fishing to rafting at a number of local stores. **On-Line Sport and Tackle** (600 Patricia St.; ✆ **780/852-3630**) has an assortment of mountain bikes, tents, fishing gear, skis, canoes, and rafts available for rent, and the shop can also provide guides for rafting and fishing trips. At **Freewheel Cycle** (618 Patricia St.; ✆ **780/852-3898**), you'll be able to find snowboards, cross-country ski equipment, and lots of bikes. For a full selection of local guides and outfitters, a visit to the **Jasper Adventure Centre** is a must. Whitewater rafting and canoeing trips, horseback rides, guided hikes, and other activities can be arranged out of the center, located at 604 Connaught Dr. (✆ **800/565-7547** in western Canada or 780/852-5595; www.jasperadventurecentre.com), open June 1 to October 1 daily from 9am to 9pm.

FISHING Jasper-based anglers who try their luck at trout fishing tend to favor the convenience of Patricia and Pyramid lakes, located just north of the city. Visitors, on the other hand, can visit **Currie's Guiding** (✆ **780/852-5650;** www.curriesguidingjasper.com) to arrange fishing trips to beautiful Maligne Lake. The cost is C$225 per person for an 8-hour day, with tackle, bait, boat, and lunch included (a minimum of two people is required—ask about special single and group rates). If you fish on your own, a permit is C$9.80 a day, available at outfitters in town.

GOLF Golf addicts know to play a round at the 18-hole course at **Jasper Park Lodge** (✆ **780/852-6090**), east of the Jasper townsite, ranked by *Score Magazine* as the best golf course in the province. Despite being one of the most popular courses

Jasper Town & Jasper National Park

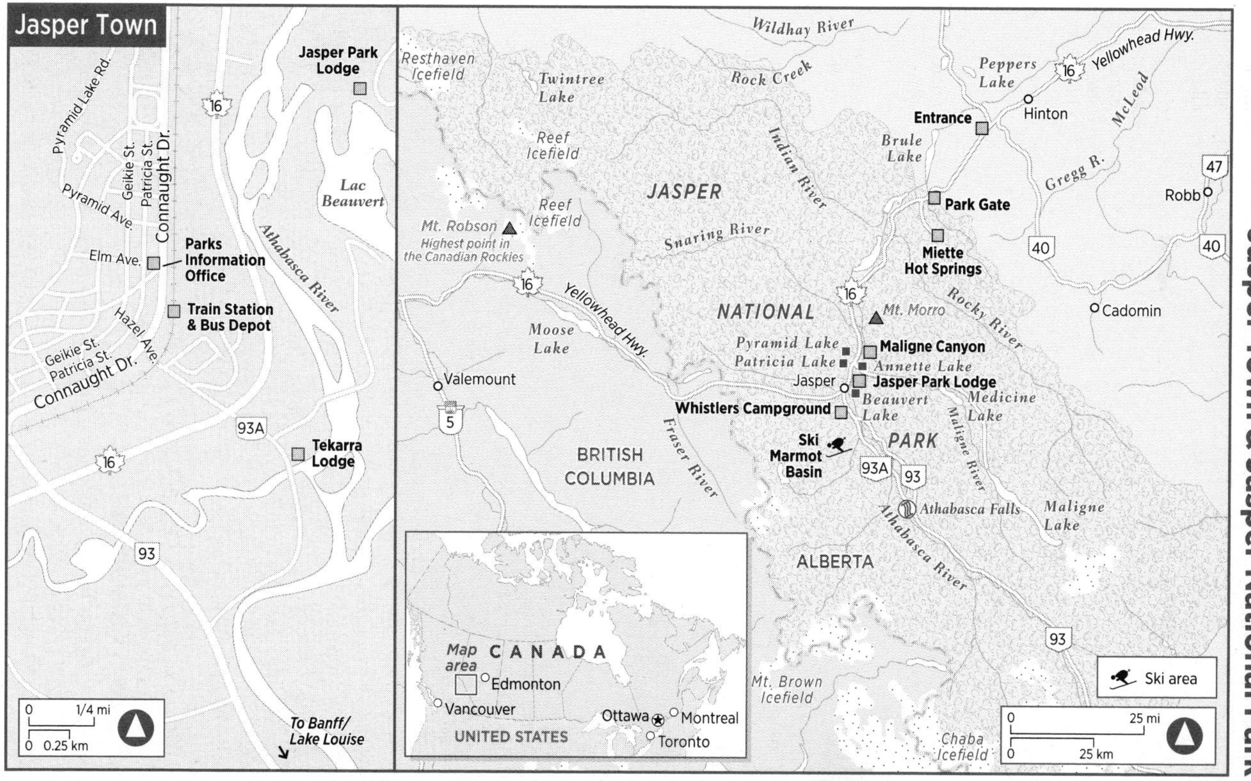

in the Rockies, it has plenty of obstacles, with 73 sand traps and even the occasional visit from curious wildlife. In high season, a round of 18 holes will cost you C$225 per person.

HIKING When selecting a day hike in Jasper, think about the weather, your own fitness level, and the trail conditions. Trails here generally involve a lot of climbing and descending. Most are open from late June to late September. Check the latest trail conditions at the **Jasper Information Centre trail conditions hotline** (✆ **780/852-6176**). The brochure *Day Hikers' Guide to Jasper National Park,* C$1 at the information center, details dozens of hikes throughout the park. For those who prefer to hike with a guide, contact **Jasper Park Lodge Mountaineering and Interpretive Hiking** (✆ **780/852-3301**) or **Walks and Talks Jasper** (✆ **780/852-4945**; www.walksntalks.com) for a selection of half- and full-day guided hikes. In general, hikers looking to spend a single, lovely day in the woods will find excellent backcountry trails around the park. For hikes that treat you to a glimpse of the most sublime scenery in the Canadian Rockies, however, multi-day and long-distance backpacking adventurers have far more options if you're willing to go the distance.

HORSEBACK RIDING For a short horseback ride, **Pyramid Stables** (✆ **780/852-7433;** www.mpljasper.com) offers 1- to 3-hour trips (as well as a day trip) that provide a stunning vista of the Athabasca River Valley. For long-distance trail rides that will take you into the backcountry, call **Skyline Trail Rides** (✆ **888/582-7787** or 780/852-4215; www.skylinetrail.com), with 3-day trips to a far-off but well-appointed lodge that include accommodation, meals, horses, and licensed guides for C$650. From early May to mid-October 1½- to 4½-hour guided rides are conducted daily, starting at C$43 for 90 minutes from both companies. Long or short, trail horseback riding is a fantastic park experience that allows you to take in views of the natural scenery. Trained guides respond to your level of riding experience in choosing the trail and use only animals that are tame, steady, and not easily spooked.

RAFTING Jasper is a good place to find float and whitewater trips down several rivers, including the Athabasca, Fraser, and Sunwapta, and the city is loaded with rafting outfitters. The mild rapids of the Athabasca River are nice for beginners and kids, with a 2-hour trip starting at C$59 adults, C$25 children under 13. Hairier trips down the Sunwapta River will appeal to those with a little more experience—or who just want a thrill. Ask your hotel concierge for assistance to find outfitters or contact **Maligne River Adventures** (✆ **780/852-3370;** www.mra.ab.ca), which offers trips down both rivers, as well as a 3-day wilderness trip on the Kakwa River (Class IV).

SKIING For the fun of Banff without the crowds, visit Marmot Basin, Jasper's exciting, underrated downhill ski region, located just 19km (12 miles) west of Jasper on Highway 93. The resort offers a chance to ski the national park's deep valleys, with their diverse wildlife, waterfalls, and carpets of thick, lush forest. Marmot has 52 runs, seven lifts, rarely any lines, and slopes with few wind gusts. Lift tickets start at C$72 during the regular season; contact ✆ **780/852-3816** or www.skimarmot.com.

Jasper Townsite

Born as a railroad division point, Jasper Townsite lacks its southern neighbor's fame, but locals—and many tourists—prefer its unpretentious air and smaller, outdoor sports–crazy crowd. Compared to Banff's amusement-park idea of alpine adventure, Jasper provides an authentic, friendly atmosphere that is refreshingly rough around the edges. Although new development can be seen on boutique strips such as Patricia

Street, with shopping malls and nightspots jostling for space, Jasper retains its small-town, lived-in charm: You can sense that real people live here.

ESSENTIALS

GETTING THERE Jasper is a significant transportation hub, with rail, highway, and bus routes all running through the town, connecting it to most major cities in western Canada. Jasper lies 287km (178 miles) northwest of Banff, on the Yellowhead Highway system that links it with Vancouver, Prince George, and Edmonton. Also connecting it to Vancouver and Edmonton are three VIA Rail trains that run weekly. At the **train station** (✆ **780/852-4102**) at the town center, along Connaught Street, you can also catch the Skeena line west to Prince George and Prince Rupert. The station is also where you can find **Greyhound buses** (✆ **780/852-3926**) and **Brewster Transportation** (✆ **780/852-3332**), which offer express service to Banff, as well as a large number of sightseeing excursions. **Sundog Tours** (✆ **888/786-3641;** www.sundogtours.com) has daily shuttles from Edmonton and Banff to Jasper. They also have various sightseeing tours, including a half-day train journey across the border into British Columbia's Mt. Robson Provincial Park.

VISITOR INFORMATION For information on the townsite, contact **Jasper Tourism and Commerce** (P.O. Box 98, Jasper, AB T0E 1E0; ✆ **780/852-3858;** www.jaspercanadianrockies.com). They can help with lodging and outfitting options, and their office is at 500 Connaught Dr. The **Jasper National Park Information Centre** (✆ **780/852-6176**) is in the same place, a heritage building in the heart of town. Get all the updates on everything Jasper here.

ORIENTATION Jasper townsite's main street, Connaught Drive, runs alongside the Canadian National Railway tracks. It plays home to many of Jasper's hotels, with another handful located at the northern end of Connaught and Geike streets, a half kilometer (¼ mile) from downtown. A block west of Connaught is Patricia Street, the center of much new development in the city, with new shops and cafes appearing each season. The post office is at the corner of Patricia and Elm streets.

GETTING AROUND For a taxi, call ✆ **780/852-5558** or 780/852-3600. For a rental car, contact **National** (607 Connaught Dr.; ✆ **780/852-1117**).

EXPLORING THE AREA

Travel just northeast of Jasper, off the Jasper Park Lodge access road, and you'll find the **Maligne River Valley,** which drops from a gorgeous alpine lake down to meet the Athabasca River, cutting a spectacular canyon into the limestone on its way. The chasm of Maligne Canyon gets up to 46m (151 ft.) deep at points, yet only 3m (9¾ ft.) across. Hikers may follow a trail down the mountainside that bridges the gorge six times and even rest in a teahouse at the top of the canyon in the summer.

According to First Nations beliefs, spirits were responsible for the way **Medicine Lake**—a natural wonder that lies downstream from Maligne Lake—appeared and disappeared regularly every year. The Maligne River flows into Medicine Lake, which comes into existence every spring, grows 8km (5 miles) long and 18m (59 ft.) deep, and then vanishes in fall, leaving only a dry gravel bed through the winter—a magic trick accomplished through a system of underground drainage caves.

Next, you'll come to the cerulean blue, alpine waters of **Maligne Lake,** ringed by towering, white-capped peaks—one of the park's great beauty spots. The glassy waters are fed by the glaciers in the mountains that surround it like icy guards; it is the second-largest lake in the world to get its water that way. Maligne is known as the "hidden lake," but that doesn't keep the tour buses away, many of them taking the wildly popular 90-minute boat cruise to **Spirit Island** in the middle of the lake. During high season, the scenic, guided tours leave every hour on the hour from below the Maligne Lake Lodge, an attractive summer-only facility with a restaurant and bar (but no lodging). Tickets for the cruise are C$55 adults and C$28 children. The site is also a popular attraction for hikers, anglers, trail riders, and rafters. All facilities at Maligne Lake—including lake cruises, fishing, trail rides, a white-water raft outfitter that offers trips down three Jasper Park rivers, and even a shuttle bus between Jasper and the lake—are operated by **Maligne Tours** (www.malignelake.com). Offices are located at the lake, as well as a second location in Jasper, at 626 Connaught Dr. (✆ **780/852-3370**). They'll also organize a shuttle to the lake from the townsite for C$20 one way.

The chilly Maligne Lake waters are too cold for swimming, but you can rent a boat, canoe, or sea kayak. The lake is also chock full of "nothin' but trout"—the rainbow and eastern brook variety. Guided fishing trips are available that include equipment, lunch, and hotel transportation, with half-day excursions starting at C$199 per person when at least two people are going (prices rise steeply for single fishers). Stop by the Maligne Lake Boathouse to purchase fishing licenses, tackle, bait, and boats.

Jasper Tramway South of Jasper, off Highway 93, lies Canada's longest and highest aerial tramway tour, Jasper Tramway. It's the fastest and easiest way to get to the high alpine environment. Starting at the foot of Whistler's Mountain, each car takes 30 passengers and hoists them 2km (1¼ miles) up to the peak (2,220m/7,283 ft.)—a beautiful, scenic midair ride. But you won't want to go back down right away. At the summit, you'll step out into an alpine tundra picnic area carpeted with mountain grass. Views of the Athabasca and Miette valleys are stunning. You can hike 45 minutes uphill to the summit of Whistler's Mountain. Dress warmly and bring good shoes. Combo tickets that include meals at the upper terminal's Treeline Restaurant are available.

Off Hwy. 93, south of Jasper. ✆ **780/852-3093.** www.jaspertramway.com. Tickets C$29 adults, C$15 children 6–15, free for children 4 & under. Lifts operate Apr 24 to May 20 & Aug 29 to Oct 11 daily 10am–5pm; May 21 to June 25 9:30am–6:30pm; June 26 to Aug 28 9am–8pm. Cars depart every 10–15 min. Call for off-season rates. Closed mid-Oct to Apr.

Miette Hot Springs The hot mineral-water pools—cooled before they are allowed to touch your skin—can be enjoyed in an expansive swimming pool or in two soaker pools, surrounded by trees and a sublime mountain skyline with a view of Ashlar Ridge. Campgrounds and a cozy lodge with food and drink are nearby. But the hot springs are only one reason to make this enjoyable side trip: There are also the elk, deer, coyotes, and moose that populate the driving route to Miette, making it one of the best places in the park to view wildlife. And the trail head for one of the best hikes in Jasper, the Sulphur Skyline, is right next door, so you can earn your soak.

Drive 60km (37 miles) northeast of Jasper off Hwy. 16. ✆ **780/866-3939.** C$6.05 adults, C$5.15 seniors & children; C$18 families. June 22 to Sept 9 daily 8:30am–10:30pm; May 11 to June 21 & Sept 10 to Oct 8 daily 10:30am–9pm.

SHOPPING

Shopping in Jasper is very particular to this mountain town. A number of galleries in the town of Jasper feature Inuit and Native arts and crafts, such as **Our Native Land** (601 Patricia St.; ✆ **780/852-5592**). Jasper's shops and boutiques are chock full of high-end outdoor and recreation gear, with Patricia Street and Connaught

Drive containing most of the quality brands such as North Face. The arcade at the Jasper Park Lodge, called the **Beauvert Promenade,** has some excellent clothing and gift shops.

WHERE TO STAY

All prices listed below are for the high season, which are typically 50% higher (or more) than the rest of the year—book before June or after September, if possible. Reserve well in advance. For off-season rates, be sure to call—they usually follow a complex structure. Lodging in Jasper can be difficult; most of the mid-range hotels were built in the same era (early 1980s) and are all owned by a single chain. If you can't find a room, contact **Rocky Mountain Reservations** (✆ **877/902-9455** or 780/852-9455; www.rockymountainreservations.com), which offers a free booking service for Jasper accommodations and activities.

Very Expensive

Fairmont Jasper Park Lodge ★★★ From the 364 hectares (900 acres) of Jasper Park Lodge's wooded, elk-inhabited grounds along Lac Beauvert to the central lodge's lofty ceilings and huge, cozy fireplaces, Jasper's most exclusive lodging lives up to its name. The Jasper Park Lodge, located about 8km (5 miles) east of Jasper proper, was built by the Canadian Pacific Railroad in 1923 and still retains a feel of woodsy gentility, a pampered wilderness experience. It's like an upscale summer camp for adults (and their kids) spread over the largest commercial property in the Canadian Rockies. There's a revered golf course, a gorgeous lake for paddling, bike trails, tennis courts, a spectacular outdoor pool, and bend-over-backward service. The decor is something of a puzzle, but an enjoyable one, as accommodations are a mix of cabins, lodge rooms, chalets, and cottages—all chosen from different eras and styles. In 2010, they finally added a full-service spa. Call and let the staff walk you through the room that will suit your budget and needs; you're certainly paying enough for the privilege. Ask about promotions and packages.

Old Lodge Road, Jasper, AB T0E 1E0. ✆ **800/441-1414** or 780/852-3301. www.fairmont.com. 446 units. C$199–C$599 double; C$399–C$829 lakefront suite; from C$1,197 cabin. AE, DC, DISC, MC, V. Free parking. **Amenities:** 8 restaurants; 2 lounges; babysitting; bike rentals; children's center; concierge; golf course; health club; heated outdoor pool; 24-hr. room service; full service spa; tennis courts; canoe & paddle-boat rentals. *In room:* TV w/pay movies, hair dryer, Wi-Fi (free).

Expensive

Alpine Village On the banks of the rushing Athabasca River, these rustic yet stylish red-roofed log cottages make a cozy, romantic base, good for keeping things quiet and simply enjoying the natural beauty of the park. They range from brand-new deluxe bedrooms suites to quaint cabins that date to 1941. Most have some form of a kitchenette. Cabins furthest from the road are quieter, but those along the river (next to the road) have the best views. The Deluxe Bedroom Suites have sweet little balconies. The one-room cabins make for great honeymooning, and the larger ones can house a large family that wants to cook its own meals. Sunshine pours into the kitchens.

2.5km (1½ miles) south of Jasper townsite (on Hwy. 93, at the junction w/Hwy. 93A); Jasper, AB. T0E 1E0. ✆ **780/852-3285.** Fax 780/852-1955. www.alpinevillagejasper.com. 41 units. C$180–C$300 double; C$210–C$230 1-bedroom cabin; C$360 family cabin. Children 6 & under stay free in parent's room. MC, V. Closed mid-Oct to mid-May. **Amenities:** Jacuzzi. *In room:* Hair dryer, kitchenette (in some).

Park Place Inn ★ Urban and friendly, this is the only place in town one could call an upscale boutique inn—with reasonable rates, to boot. The 12 spacious rooms have a cowboy heritage theme, with beautiful linens, goose-down duvets, hardwood floors, and plenty of space. Bathrooms are particularly luxurious, with huge jetted tubs (many that are claw-foot style), jetted showers, and fancy amenities. Located upstairs on Jasper's bustling Patricia Street, it feels downtown, if that's possible in Jasper.

623 Patricia St., Jasper, AB T0E 1E0. ✆ **866/852-9770** or 780/852-9770. www.parkplaceinn.com. 14 units. C$229–C$269 double. Children 13 & under stay free in parent's room. AE, MC, V. *In room:* A/C, TV, hair dryer, minibar.

Pine Bungalows A good choice if you don't need to be pampered, but want some privacy and have your own car. Cabins along the Athabasca River here are nostalgic and family-friendly. Some have been pretty much the same for 50 years, aside from a few upgrades in plumbing and heating, so it's a place that keeps families returning for generations. Most of the cabins now have fireplaces, and nearly all of them have kitchenettes. The best cabins are nos. 1 through 12, right on the river. Themed weekends, from birding to history, are offered throughout the summer.

#2 Cottonwood Creek Road, Jasper, AB T0E 1E0. ✆ **780/852-3491.** www.pinebungalows.com. 72 units. C$140–C$160 double, C$185–C$220 2-bedroom cabin. *In room:* No phone.

Moderate

Big hotels aren't your only option for staying in Jasper. In the high season, dozens of area homes become B&Bs. While they are by no means luxurious—especially compared to the classier home-stay options in Banff—they are often good value, most ranging from C$60 to C$85 for double occupancy, usually paid in cash. Get a complete list by contacting the **Jasper Home Accommodation Association** (P.O. Box 758, Jasper, AB T0E 1E0; www.stayinjasper.com). It's not a booking agency, so you'll have to contact the association's members directly to reserve.

If you're not the B&B type, Jasper also has a few motor lodges. Try the friendly but basic **Maligne Lodge** (900 Connaught Dr.; ✆ **800/661-1315** or 780/852-3143; www.malignelodge.com), a two-story motel wrapped around a kidney-shaped pool. It also has a family restaurant and bar. Rooms start at C$199 for a double.

Austrian Haven A good choice for those wishing to get away from Jasper's main strip or for longer stays, this large home on a residential street contains two generous, fully stocked suites. As a bonus, both have access to a shared sundeck with a BBQ and an impressive view of surrounding mountains. The Family suite includes a living room, kitchen, and dining area and has two queen-size beds, while the more lavish Honeymoon suite features a private sunroom and king-size bed with down duvet. Both options have a private bathroom, fridge, microwave, and TV and VCR, and include continental breakfast.

812 Patricia St., Jasper, AB T0E 1E0. ✆ **780/852-4259.** www.austrianhaven.ca. 2 units. C$140–C$160 double. Rates include continental breakfast. Cash & traveler's checks only. Free parking. *In room:* TV/VCR, fridge, kitchen (in Family suite).

Becker's Roaring River Chalets This family-run resort, dating back to the 1940s but modernized since, has a lot of things going for it that make it understandably popular: It's nestled in a stand of pine and offers stellar views of the adjacent (and, yes, roaring) Athabasca River and mountain scenery. The gourmet restaurant is one of the area's best. All accommodation is in log chalets ranging from rustic to refined. The cabins come in various sizes, from one room to four, with the largest deluxe cottages sleeping six to eight guests. Some have river views, and most include kitchens or kitchenettes, and a fireplace for huddling around on a chilly night. Rooms have televisions, but with so many natural distractions here, the TV will probably stay off. The downside is the sheer number of rooms crammed together. There's not much privacy or quiet here on a busy summer day.

Hwy. 95, 5km (3 miles) south of Jasper, Jasper, AB T0E 1E0. ✆ **780/852-3779.** www.beckerschalets.com. 118 chalets. C$160–C$190 1-bedroom cabin; C$185–C$225 2-bedroom cabin; C$400 3-bedroom cabin. AE, MC, V. Free parking. **Amenities:** Restaurant; babysitting. *In room:* TV, fridge, hair dryer, no phone.

Inexpensive

Budget travelers flock to two **Hostelling International** hostels, both reachable at P.O. Box 387, Jasper, AB T0E 1E0 (✆ **866/762-4122** or 780/852-3215; www.hihostels.ca) and open year-round. It's advisable to book well ahead in summer. The closest to town is the 80-bed **Jasper International Hostel,** on Skytram Road, 6km (4 miles) west of Jasper. It charges C$26 for members and C$29 for nonmembers. Private rooms are C$65 and C$72, respectively. Two family rooms, a barbecue area, indoor plumbing, hot showers, and bike rentals are available. In winter, ask about ski packages. A more rustic option is the **Maligne Canyon wilderness hostel,** which has no running water. It's off Maligne Lake Road, 18km (11 miles) east of Jasper, and sleeps 24; rates are C$23 for members and C$25 for nonmembers. The appeal here is immediate access to hiking, skiing, and cycling trails, since the hostel is situated above the spectacular Maligne Canyon. There's a self-catering kitchen with purified water for cooking, a refrigerator, and propane stove. More remote hostels are listed in "Backcountry Hostels," below.

In & Around Hinton

If you're willing to stay a half-hour or 45-minute drive away from downtown Jasper, you can find good accommodations with markedly lower prices in the Hinton area, which is just to the east of the park gate. Here, you will find a typical array of reliable motor hotels. The **Best Western White Wolf Inn** (828 Carmichael Lane; ✆ **800/220-7870** in Canada or 780/865-7777) has 42 air-conditioned rooms, most with kitchenettes. The **Black Bear Inn** (571 Gregg Ave.; ✆ **888/817-2888** or 780/817-2000) features an exercise room, hot tub, and restaurant. The **Crestwood Hotel** (678 Carmichael Lane; ✆ **800/661-7288** or 780/865-4001) has a pool and restaurant. Doubles at these locations range from C$95 to C$145.

Overlander Mountain Lodge It's hard to beat the views of the Rockies from the original building of this venerable lodge at the edge of Jasper National Park, which makes a good base for exploring and relaxing. The complex is expertly decorated, adding a sheen of rustic luxury, and is aided by a friendly, professional staff. Overlander features a variety of comfortable accommodations, all with private bathrooms: there are four-plex cabins with gas fireplaces and two double beds; kitchenette rooms with queen beds; large, full-featured luxury chalets; and rooms of varied amenities within the main lodge and a newer wing, each with a view of mountains or gardens. In the old building, you'll find a bar that takes full advantage of its striking mountain setting and a lounge with large stone fireplace. The Stone Peak restaurant is noted for its showcase of regional cuisines, including venison, and lamb. For a quintessential Rocky Mountain experience, Overlander offers terrific value.

1km (½ mile) from Jasper Park's east gate, Hinton, AB T0E 1E0. ✆ **877/866-2330** or 780/866-2330. www.overlandermountainlodge.com. 29 units. C$160–C$175 lodge room; C$175 cabin room; C$350 2-bedroom chalet; C$425 3-bedroom chalet. AE, MC, V. Free parking. **Amenities:** Restaurant; lounge. *In room:* Hair dryer, no phone.

Camping

If you're willing to rough it, camping is one of the best ways to get back to nature in Jasper National Park, which is home to 10 campgrounds—though only one (Wapiti) is open through the winter. Prices range from C$14 for rudimentary tenting sites to C$33 for full-service RV sites. Due to fire hazards, you need a special permit to camp anywhere in the parks outside the designated campgrounds. For a permit, contact the **parks information office** (✆ **780/852-6176**). Campgrounds in Jasper range from completely unserviced to those providing water, power, sewer connections, laundry facilities, gas, and groceries.

Columbia Icefield Campground The primary appeal of this small, no-frills campground is its proximity to the bulk of tourist activity at the Columbia Icefield Centre. It also opens earlier in the season and shuts down later than the nearby Wilcox Creek campground. It can get very cold here at night, so come prepared. Tents only.

106km (66 miles) south of Jasper townsite on the Icefields Pkwy. (Hwy. 93). 33 sites. C$16 site. Open mid-May to mid-Oct.

Honeymoon Lake Campground The most fortunate campers here are those who manage to secure one of the prime lakeside sites in this small, out-of-the-way campground.

52km (32 miles) south of Jasper townsite on the Icefields Pkwy. (Hwy. 93). 35 sites. C$16 site. Open mid-June to early Sept.

Jonas Creek Campground This is one of those rustic, heavily treed sites that almost make you forget you're in a campground. Beautiful but basic when it comes to amenities.

78km (48 miles) south of Jasper townsite on the Icefields Pkwy. (Hwy. 93). 25 sites. C$16 site. Open mid-May to early Sept.

Mount Kerkeslin Campground Another primitive setup, but a top-notch view of the mountains certainly makes waking up here easier.

36km (22 miles) south of Jasper townsite on the Icefields Pkwy. (Hwy. 93). 42 sites. C$16 site. Open mid-June to early Sept.

Pocahontas Campground This is a good place to spend the night if you're making the drive from Edmonton along the Yellowhead Highway (Hwy. 16) and are too tired to head deeper into the park. It's a large and moderately equipped campground, and the first one you'll come across as you enter Jasper National Park. Unwind at the nearby Miette Hot Springs.

44km (27 miles) east of Jasper townsite on the Yellowhead Hwy. (Hwy. 16). 140 sites. C$22 site. Open mid-May to mid-Oct.

Snaring River Campground A cheap alternative to the pricey and crowded accommodation of the Jasper townsite, Snaring River is positively idyllic in comparison. Amenities, however, are limited to dry toilets, firewood, and kitchen shelters.

13km (8 miles) east of Jasper townsite on Yellowhead Hwy. (Hwy. 16). 66 sites. C$16 site. Open mid-May to mid-Sept.

Wabasso Campground One of the more popular campgrounds—it's worth booking ahead at www.pccamping.ca—Wabasso is nestled picturesquely along the Athabasca River. Its 228 sites are well-equipped, including a sanitary station (with flush toilets), playground, wheelchair access, and a seasonal interpretive center.

16km (10 miles) from Jasper townsite on Athabasca Hwy. (Hwy. 93A). 228 sites. C$22 site. Open late June to early Sept.

Wapiti Campground Wapiti is the only campground in the park with full winter access. There are 362 sites—40 with RV hook-ups and the rest reserved for tents only—and all are accessible in the winter. But be prepared to share your camping space with meandering elk—and keep your distance. In summer, it's quieter than Whistler's (see below).

4km (2½ miles) south of Jasper townsite on the Icefields Pkwy (Hwy. 93). Victoria Day weekend (late May) & mid-June to early Sept: 362 sites; C$26 site; C$30 site w/electrical hook-up. Early Oct to early May: 93 sites; C$17 site; C$20 site w/electrical hook-up.

Whistler's Campground Whistler's may not be the most attractive or secluded place, but it's the largest campground in the park and the closest to the Jasper townsite. And its 781 campsites are often the first ones to fill up (book ahead at www.pccamping.ca). This is a camping hub, best equipped to accommodate large groups, offering interpretive programs in the high season and the most amenities for campers. There are 177 RV sites here, 77 of which offer full hook-ups. Be extra vigilant about securing your food; bears can be a problem here.

3km (1¾ miles) south of Jasper townsite on the Icefields Pkwy. (Hwy. 93). 781 sites. C$22–C$26 site; C$30 site w/electrical hook-up; C$36 site w/full hook-up. Closed early Oct to early May.

Backcountry Camping

Campers looking for pleasant backcountry campsites will find more than 100 in Jasper National Park, including well-known sites on the Skyline Trail, on the Brazeau Loop, around Maligne Lake, and in the Tonquin Valley. You need to reserve a campsite before you head out on a backcountry trip. But be sure to book early: the most popular ones book up fast in early spring—reserve 3 months before your trip if you have a favored campsite in mind. Understand that when you reserve a spot to camp at a marked campsite, you select the specific site within the camping area on a first-come, first-served basis and only once you arrive on-site. Reserve by calling the **Jasper National Park** office, at ✆ **780/852-6177**, or visit the **Jasper National Park Information Centre** (500 Connaught Dr.; same telephone number). Rates are C$10 per person per night. There is a nonrefundable reservation charge of C$12.

Backcountry Hostels

As in Banff, **Hostelling International** (✆ **877/852-0781** or 780/852-3215; www.hihostels.ca/alberta) runs a number of rustic hostels in Jasper. These are all road-accessible, however, so they're not technically "backcountry." Call the main number to make reservations or for information, as the hostels themselves don't have phones. The **Beauty Creek Hostel** on the Icefields Parkway (Hwy. 93), 17km (11 miles) north of the Icefield Information Centre (87km/54 miles south of the Jasper townsite) sleeps 24 people in 2 cabins and has wood-stove heating, propane cooking, and lamplights. It is quite austere, with an outdoor toilet and no electricity or showers—authentic backcountry. It is perfect if you're interested in getting some hiking done. Rates are C$23 per person per night for Hostelling International members and C$25 per person per night for nonmembers.

The **Mount Edith Cavell Hostel** (take Hwy. 93A south from the townsite to Cavell Road; turn west and continue 13km/8 miles to the hostel, on the east side of the road) offers basic shelter in a handful of cabins in a narrow valley in the shadow of Mount Edith Cavell. There's no running water, but purified water is available for cooking (on propane stoves). And there's a refrigerator. Rates are C$23 per person per night for Hostelling International members and C$25 per person per night for nonmembers.

WHERE TO DINE

Expensive

Andy's Bistro CONTINENTAL/CANADIAN With a creative menu that mixes Old World and New, and an intimate (40-seat) yet casual setting, Andy's is a good compromise between high-end dining and a regular night out that's been consistently successful for years. The wine list is extensive—the whole restaurant, in fact, resembles a wine cellar. Starters on the seasonal menu may include pepper bacon–wrapped scallops and mushroom ragout with sheep cheese. Mains range from a Zurich-style veal to a "vegetarian Napoleon." One communal table for six is reserved for walk-in diners.

606 Patricia St. ✆ **780/852-4559.** Reservations recommended. Main courses C$18–C$33. MC, V. Mid-May to mid-Oct daily 5–11pm; mid-Oct to mid-May Tues–Sat 5–11pm.

Cavell's Restaurant and Terrace CANADIAN The stunning former Edith Cavell Dining Room is the setting for a superb new dining option at the Jasper Park Lodge. The emphasis is on Canadian cuisine—regional meats, fish, and game paired with local vegetables, wild mushrooms, and berries. Bison, Arctic char, and Alberta beef are a restaurant specialty, plus a tandoori tofu and homemade mac & cheese for comfort food. Burgers, wraps, and flatbreads will please kids. The only thing better than the food is the view.

In the Fairmont Jasper Park Lodge, Old Lodge Road, 8km (5 miles) east of Jasper. ✆ **780/852-6052.** Reservations recommended. Main courses C$17–C$42. AE, DISC, MC, V. Daily 6–9pm.

Tekarra Restaurant ★★ STEAK/INTERNATIONAL Don't overlook this comforting space, built around a crackling fireplace in an old lodge outside town. You'll likely be very pleasantly surprised by both the sweet atmosphere and the superb food. Chef Dave Husereau's terrific menu of globetrotting cuisine has a loyal following. A playful appetizer list offers venison sliders, three tiny venison burgers, and tandoori shrimp lollipops. Mains include a macadamia nut–crusted rack of lamb and *ponzu*-marinated fish of the day. Friendly service.

Hwy. 93A, 1.6km (1 mile) east of Jasper (call for directions). ✆ **780/852-4624.** www.tekarrarestaurant.com. Reservations recommended. Main courses C$20–C$56. AE, DC, MC, V. Daily 5:30–10pm. Closed early Oct to late May.

Moderate

Evil Dave's Grill ★ CANADIAN Don't let the name scare you: The only thing sinful about Evil Dave's cuisine is how good it is. Dave himself has moved on (or better said, he's moved back to Tekarra, above), but the upbeat chef now at the helm keeps the culinary creativity on the lighter side. Entrees include Malicious Salmon (blackened with sweet curry yoghurt), Malevolent Meatloaf, Nefarious Chicken (parmesan crusted, with salsa), and Vicious Hippy (a Portobello mushroom stuffed with artichoke, served with *panko*-crusted tofu and spun root vegetables). Best on the list for spice lovers has to be Hell's Jerk Chicken, a sweat-gland-testing take on the Jamaican traditional that's as high on flavor as it is on temperature.

622 Patricia St., Jasper. ✆ **780/852-3323.** Reservations recommended on weekends. Main courses C$18–C$28. AE, DC, MC, V. June–Sept daily 4–11pm; Oct–May Mon–Fri 5–10pm, Sat 4–11pm.

Something Else INTERNATIONAL It's Greek. It's Italian. It's Creole. It's Canadian. Something Else truly aims, and largely succeeds, to be all things for all people. You want *saganaki* with your jambalaya? Pizza with moussaka? Good ol' Alberta steak?

You've come to the right place. This is the restaurant for families and large groups that tend to argue over what to have for lunch or dinner. Expect friendly service and reliable, well-prepared food without attitude.

621 Patricia St. ✆ **780/852-3850.** Main courses C$14–C$30. AE, DC, MC, V. Daily 11am–11pm.

Inexpensive

There are a number of fine options for quick foods at the table or on the go. Besides letting you check your e-mail, **Soft Rock Café** (632 Connaught Dr.; ✆ **780/852-5850**), in the Connaught Square Mall, has omelets, sandwiches, wraps, coffee, salads, Thai food, and desserts. **Coco's Café** (608 Patricia St.; ✆ **780/852-4550**) is a popular spot for breakfast. Lunches include veggie burgers, wraps, and curries. It's a great place to mingle with the young locals.

The Bear's Paw Bakery (610 Connaught Dr., ✆ **780/852-2253;** 4 Cedar Ave., ✆ **780/852-3233**) is a terrific spot to fill your knapsack before a hike. The homemade breads (sourdough, baguettes, and beyond) are served at restaurants all over town. Buy fresh sandwiches, granola, delicious fruit tarts, granny smith apple pies, and a large selection of sweet baked goods alluringly laid out under glass at the counter. There are even dog treats. Another worthy gourmet cafe and pastry shop is **Café Mondo** (inside Jasper Marketplace, at 616 Patricia St; ✆ **780/852-9676**), with bagel melts, breakfast pizzas, and sweet delectables.

Jasper Pizza Place PIZZA Thin- and thick-crust pizzas from a wood-burning oven and a lively atmosphere make this a local favorite for informal dining. The main eating area is family-friendly; there's also a rooftop patio and, downstairs, a popular pool hall. Decorate your pie with your choice of four sauces and 32 toppings—some traditional, others eyebrow-raising (escargot pizza, anyone?). In addition to pizzas, there are sandwiches, wings, ribs, and pasta offerings, all with generous portions.

402 Connaught Dr. ✆ **780/852-3225.** Reservations not accepted. Pizza C$12–C$18. MC, V. Daily 11am–11pm.

JASPER AFTER DARK

Nightlife in Jasper is largely limited to the bars and lounges found in hotels around town. By law, there is no smoking permitted at any Jasper club, even on outdoor patios.

For a post-dinner pint, head to the **Jasper Brewing Company** at 624 Connaught Dr. (✆ **780/852-4111**). Brewed on-site, there's a wide range of beers, from Union Blonde and B Hill Pilsner to Rockhopper IPA, and several others to suit your palate. There's a casually sophisticated lounge upstairs at **Earl's** (600 Patricia St, 2nd floor; ✆ **780/852-2393**), which also has the best patio in town—it's even heated!

The **Atha-B,** or just the B, is the local moniker for the Athabasca Hotel (510 Patricia St.; ✆ **780/852-3386**), home of an often crowded pool hall/sports bar (O'Shea's) and a recently renovated nightclub, which brings in DJs and live bands throughout the summer and lures a young, party-seeking crowd. With a sports-bar ambience and classic rock blaring, the **D'ed Dog Bar and Grill** (404 Connaught Dr.; ✆ **780/852-3351**) is the place you don't need to dress up to party into the night. Aptly, this is a popular spot with the summer onslaught of river and hiking guides who gather to socialize and compare notes from the trail.

Your best bet for good live music is **Pete's On Patricia,** upstairs at 614 Patricia St. (✆ **780/852-6262**), with a stream of indie rock and blues bands, as well as DJs and dancing.

Oddly enough, one of the hottest and rowdiest gathering places for the town's influx of twenty-something seasonal staffers can be found in the Fairmont Jasper Park

Lodge. The noisy **Tent City Sports Lounge,** overlooking the tennis courts, is also the hangout of choice for young JPL employees.

Finally, if it's a somewhat less youthful crowd you seek, the **Downstream Bar** (620 Connaught Dr.; ✆ **780/852-9449**), a basement dive that's far from dingy, is a welcoming spot to unwind with a pint.

EDMONTON ★

303km (188 miles) N of Calgary, 524km (326 miles) NW of Saskatoon

Edmonton, Alberta's capital city, is located on the banks of the North Saskatchewan River, straddling the deep, lush river valley that has the looks of an oasis in high summer, with its sprawling green spaces. It was a settlement in pre-European times and later a key fur trading post in the 19th century. After the arrival of the railway in 1891, it developed rapidly.

Unlike its southern counterpart, Calgary, Edmonton is a decidedly low-key metropolis, with little of the flash that is Calgary's hallmark. Where Calgary is corporate, Edmonton is a government town. More liberal, it also has a marked no-nonsense, blue-collar feel to it. In many ways, Edmonton feels like a small town that happens to have a million people living in it—and most residents you encounter would count that as one of its main attractions.

Make no mistake, though: Like much of the province, Edmonton is profiting mightily from the unprecedented oil boom, and it is geographically much closer than Calgary to the source.

Chief among Edmonton's attractions is likely the almost never-ending plethora of summer festivals that the city hosts. The main star is Edmonton's Fringe Theatre Festival, second only to Edinburgh in Scotland as the largest of the worldwide Fringe festivals. Theater troupes the world over debut their best new work in Edmonton every August, and critics and aficionados flock to the city, especially the Old Strathcona theater district, to catch top-end performers strutting their stuff. The festival is part of the reason why Old Strathcona, on the southern bank of the river, across from downtown, is perhaps the most vibrant neighborhood in the city.

Old Strathcona was once its own town, and its incorporation is telling of how Edmonton grew in spurts, following a boom-and-bust pattern as exciting as it was unreliable. During World War II, the boom came in the form of the Alaska Highway, with Edmonton as the material base and temporary home of 50,000 American troops and construction workers.

The ultimate boom, however, first gushed from the ground in 1947, when a drill at Leduc, 40km (25 miles) southwest of the city, sent a fountain of crude oil soaring skyward. Some 10,000 other wells followed, and in their wake came the petrochemical industry, and the refining and supply conglomerates. In 20 years, the population quadrupled, the skyline mushroomed with glass-and-concrete office towers, a rapid-transit system was created, and a C$150-million civic center rose.

Essentials

GETTING THERE BY PLANE **Edmonton International Airport** (✆ **800/268-7134** or 780/890-8382; www.flyeia.com) is served by **Air Canada** (✆ **800/372-9500;** www.aircanada.com); **Delta** (✆ **800/221-1212;** www.delta.com); **United** (✆ **800/864-8331;** www.united.com); and homegrown **WestJet** (✆ **800/937-8538;** www.westjet.com), a Calgary-based carrier with several destinations across

Edmonton

ACCOMMODATIONS
Courtyard by Marriott 13
Crowne Plaza Chateau Lacombe 17
Days Inn Downtown Edmonton 9
Fairmont Hotel Macdonald 14
Fantasyland Hotel 29
Glenora Bed & Breakfast 7
Hosteling International Edmonton 23
Hotel Selkirk 31
The Matrix Hotel 8
Metterra Hotel on Whyte 25
Union Bank Inn 15
University of Alberta 21
The Varscona 24
DINING
Blue Plate 5
The Blue Pear 4
Cactus Club Café 1
Chianti Café 26
Chicago's Deep Dish Pizza 10
Culina Café 22
Hardware Grill 12
Jack's Grill 34
Julio's Barrio 27
La Ronde 18
Madison's at Union Bank Inn 16
Manor Cafe 6
Packrat Louie Kitchen & Bar 28
ATTRACTIONS
Alberta Legislature 20
The Art Gallery of Alberta 11
Fort Edmonton Park 32
John Janzen Nature Centre 33
Muttart Conservatory 19
Royal Alberta Museum 3
Telus World of Science 2
The Valley Zoo 30
Information
LRT rail station
0 1/4 mi
0 0.25 km
ALBERTA
Edmonton
Calgary
Railroad Station
Citadel Theatre
Low Level Bridge
James MacDonald Bridge
105 St. Bridge
High Level Bridge
Groat Bridge
OLD STRATHCONA
UNIVERSITY OF ALBERTA
Jubilee Auditorium
Victoria Park
William Hawrelak Park
Sir Wilfrid Laurier Park
Fort Edmonton Park
North Saskatchewan River
Saskatchewan Dr.
Walterdale Hill Rd.
Bellamy Hill Rd.
River Valley Rd.
Groat Rd.
Valley View Dr.
Buena Vista Rd.
University Ave.
Belgravia Rd.
Fox Dr.
Connors Rd.
Whyte Ave.
Jasper Ave.
104 Ave.
102 Ave.
100 Ave.
110 Ave.
97 Ave.
96 Ave.
98 Ave.
95 Ave.
87 Ave.
85 Ave.
84 Ave.
83 Ave.
81 Ave.
76 Ave.
74 Ave.
72 Ave.
71 Ave.
70 Ave.
68 Ave.
66 Ave.
97 St.
99 St.
100 St.
103 St.
104 St.
105 St.
106 St.
107 St.
109 St.
111 St.
112 St.
113 St.
114 St.
116 St.
117 St.
122 St.
142 St.
145 St.
96 St.
2

North America; among other airlines. Being a hub of international commerce, Edmonton is also served by several commuter lines.

The airport lies 29km (18 miles) south of the city on Highway 2, about 45 minutes away. By cab, the trip costs about C$35; by the **Edmonton Sky Shuttle** (✆ **780/465-8515;** www.edmontonskyshuttle.com) it's C$15 per person.

GETTING THERE BY TRAIN The **VIA Rail station** (✆ **800/561-8630** or 780/422-6032; www.viarail.ca) is at 104th Avenue and 100th Street.

GETTING THERE BY BUS **Greyhound buses** (✆ **800/661-8747** or 780/413-8747; www.greyhound.ca) link Edmonton to points in Canada and the United States from the depot at 10324 103rd St.

GETTING THERE BY CAR Edmonton straddles the Yellowhead Highway, northwestern Canada's east-west interprovincial highway. Just west of Edmonton, the Yellowhead Highway is linked to the Alaska Highway. The city is 515km (320 miles) north of the U.S. border, 283km (176 miles) north of Calgary. From Calgary, take Highway 2 north; from Banff, your best bet is through Calgary on the Trans-Canada Highway East, connecting to Highway 2 North.

VISITOR INFORMATION Contact **Edmonton Tourism** (9990 Jasper Ave. NW; ✆ **800/426-4715** or 780/496-8400; www.edmonton.com). There are also visitor centers located at City Hall and at Gateway Park, both open from 9am to 6pm, and on the Calgary Trail (Hwy. 2) at the southern edge of the city, open from 9am to 9pm.

CITY LAYOUT The winding **North Saskatchewan River** flows right through the heart of the city, dividing it into roughly equal halves. Most of this steep-banked valley has been turned into public parklands.

Like Calgary, Edmonton runs on a grid system, with streets going north-south and avenues east-west. The middle of the city is downtown at 100 Avenue and 100 Street, with corresponding numbers growing to the north and west, and declining to the south and east. Edmonton's main street is **Jasper Avenue** (actually 101st Ave.), running east-west on the north side of the river. To cross the North Saskatchewan River, you'd take the pedestrian- and car-friendly High Level Bridge south or the Low Level Bridge in either direction. Beneath the downtown core stretches a network of climate-controlled pedestrian walkways—called **Pedways**—connecting hotels, restaurants, and malls with the library, City Hall, and **Citadel Theatre.**

At the northern approach to the High Level Bridge stand the buildings of the **Alberta Legislature.** Across the bridge, to the west, stretches the vast campus of the **University of Alberta.** East of the U of A is **Old Strathcona,** a bustling neighborhood of cafes, galleries, and shops that is a haven for the hip crowd. The main arterial through Old Strathcona is **Whyte Avenue,** or 82nd Avenue. Running south from here is 104th Street, which becomes the **Calgary Trail** and leads to the airport.

West of downtown, Jasper Avenue eventually becomes Stony Plain Road, which passes near the **West Edmonton Mall,** the world's largest shopping and entertainment center, before merging with Highway 16 on its way to **Jasper National Park**.

GETTING AROUND **Edmonton Transit** (✆ **780/442-5311;** www.takeets.com) operates the buses and the LRT (Light Rail Transit). This electric rail service connects downtown with **Northlands Park** to the north and the University of Alberta to the south. The LRT and buses have the same fares: C$2.75 adults and children over 5; a day pass goes for C$8.25.

In addition to the following downtown locations, **National** (10133 100A St. NW; ✆ **800/CAR-RENT** or 780/890-7700), **Budget** (4612 95th St.; ✆ **800/268-8900** or 780/448-2060), and **Hertz** (10815 Jasper Ave.; © **780/423-3431**), each have a car-rental bureau at the airport.

Call **Co-Op Taxi** (© **780/425-2525**) for a ride in a driver/owner-operated cab. **24-7 Taxi** is another option (© **780/442-4444**), as is **Edmonton Taxi** (© **780/462-3456**).

[Fast FACTS] EDMONTON

American Express The office at 10180 101st St. (at 102nd Ave.; © **780/421-0608;** LRT: Corona), is open Monday to Friday from 9am to 5pm.

Area Code Edmonton and Northern Alberta are in the 780 area code.

Business Hours Most banks are open weekdays 10am to 4pm, and Saturdays for a few hours in the morning or afternoon. Most shopping centers are open Monday to Friday 10am to 9pm, Saturday 10am to 6pm, and Sunday noon to 5pm.

Dentist Many dental clinics are open evenings and weekends. Ask your hotel to recommend one or visit the **Alberta Dental Association** website at www.abda.ab.ca to find one.

Doctors & Hospitals **Medicentres** offers walk-in medical services daily at 15 locations throughout the city; go to www.medicentres.com for the location nearest you. There is one downtown at 11087 Jasper Ave. (© **780/488-1222**). The hospital with emergency service closest to downtown Edmonton is the **Royal Alexandra Hospital** (10240 Kingsway Ave.; © **780/477-4111**; bus: 9).

Fishing Licenses If you're planning to fish, either in the city or outside of it, you need to obtain a license. They're available at most sporting goods stores, convenience stores, and gas stations at a cost of C$26. Seniors and children 16 and under don't need a license

Newspapers The ***Edmonton Journal*** (www.edmontonjournal.com) and ***Edmonton Sun*** (www.edmontonsun.com) are the local daily papers. Arts, entertainment, and nightlife listings can be found in the weekly ***See*** (www.seemagazine.com).

Police The 24-hour number is © **780/421-3333.** Dial © **911** in emergencies.

Post Office The main post office is at 103A Avenue and 99th Street (LRT: Churchill).

Special Events & Festivals

Edmonton promotes itself as "the Festival City," and in summer almost every weekend brings another celebration. The citywide **Jazz City International Festival** (© **780/432-7166;** www.edmontonjazz.com) takes over most music venues in Edmonton during the last week of June and first week of July.

The summer's biggest shindig is **Capital City Exposition,** aka Capital EX, (© **888/800-7275** or 780/471-7210; www.capitalex.ca), formerly Klondike Days. Capital EX has shed the previous event's gold-rush trappings and focuses instead on midway rides, live music performances, and shopping promotions. Most events take place at Northlands Park, northeast of the city at 75th St. and 118th Ave.

The **Edmonton Folk Music Festival** (© **780/429-1899;** www.efmf.ab.ca) is the largest folk-music festival in North America. Held in early August, it brings in musicians from around the world, from the Celtic north to Indonesia, plus major rock stars playing "unplugged." All concerts are held outdoors.

For 11 days in mid-August, Old Strathcona is transformed into a series of stages for the renowned Edmonton international **Fringe Theatre Festival** (© **780/448-9000;**

www.fringetheatreadventures.ca). Only Edinburgh's fringe festival is larger than Edmonton's—more than 150 troupes attend from around the world, as does an audience of over 600,000. The festival has 12 indoor theater stages and two outdoor stages, offering more than 1,000 individual performances; when one show ends, another begins on the same stage an hour later. In addition to the hubbub of actors and theater, the Fringe Theatre Festival also plays host to food and crafts booths, beer tents, and innumerable buskers and street performers.

Exploring the City

Alberta Legislature Perched with a view of the gorgeous river valley, Alberta's Legislature, the seat of the provincial government, is an impressive structure built between 1907 and 1913. Free 60-minute tours with engaging guides are offered daily for those interested in the building's Beaux Art–era architecture and decor. It's a stately monument brimming with the history of a frontier town made good and a province bursting with potential.

10800 97th Ave. ✆ **780/427-7362.** www.assembly.ab.ca. Free admission. May to Oct 15 daily tours every hour 9am–noon & every half-hour 12:30–4pm. Oct 16 to Apr weekday tours every hour 9am–3pm & weekend tours every hour noon–4pm.

The Art Gallery of Alberta ★★ The most exciting thing to come to Edmonton since the Stanley Cup, the stunning new AGA is the C$88-million, 2,787-sq.-m (30,000-sq.-ft.) home for revolving world-class exhibits. On any given day, you could take in Degas, Picasso, and Emily Carr; there's permanent room for Alberta's top artists, as well. It is a champion of First Nations contemporary art (think artists like Jane Ash Poitras and Carl Beam) and has been an incubator for curating talent that has gone on to larger institutions all over the country and around the world.

2 Sir Winston Churchill Sq. (at the corner of 102A Ave. & 99th St.). ✆ **780/422-6223.** www.youraga.ca. C$12 adults, C$8 seniors & students, C$8 children 7–12, free for children 6 & under. Tues–Fri 11am–7pm; Sat & Sun 10am–5pm. Closed Mon.

Fort Edmonton Park ☺ Fort Edmonton Park literally reconstructs four distinct eras of Edmonton's history. Perhaps most interesting is the complete reconstruction of the old Fort Edmonton fur trading post from the turn of the 18th century. This vast wooden structure is a warren of rooms and activities: blacksmiths, bakers, and other guides ply their trades. On 1885 Street, you'll see Frontier Edmonton, complete with saloons, general store, and Jasper House Hotel, which serves hearty pioneer meals. 1905 Street celebrates the agricultural boom years of the early 19th century, when Edmonton teemed with new immigrants and was named provincial capital. On 1920 Street, sip an old-fashioned ice-cream soda at Bill's confectionery and see the changes wrought in the rural West by World War I. You can't miss the midway, with rides for kids of all ages. If the variety of activities at Fort Edmonton appeals to your family, consider spending a night at the park's Hotel Selkirk (see "Where to Stay," below). A C$10-million expansion in 2010 brings a new replica of the Capital Theatre and more evening events.

On Whitemud Dr. (at Fox Dr.). ✆ **780/496-8787.** www.fortedmontonpark.ca. C$14 adults, C$11 seniors & youth 13-17, C$7.75 children 2-12; C$42 families. Mid-May to late June Mon–Fri 10am–4pm, Sat & Sun 10am–6pm; late June to early Sept daily 10am–6pm. Closed early Sept to mid-May, except for Christmas Dec 20-23.

Muttart Conservatory Four glass pyramids rise up from the deep snow on the south bank of the North Saskatchewan River in the depths of an Edmonton winter.

Inside, 700 species of plants, from arid to tropical, flourish despite the weather. The Muttart, a city-operated property, is an oasis for Edmontonians starving for a bit of greenery in the long, cold winter that the city's northern location always brings. Architecturally stunning and nicely curated to reflect three climatological zones—arid, temperate, and tropical—the Muttart is a welcome refuge, a place where it's moderate summer all year round.

9626 96A St. ✆ **780/442-5311.** www.muttartconservatory.ca. C$11 adults, C$8 seniors & youth 13–17, C$5.25 children 2–12; C$32 families. Sat & Sun 11am–5pm. Daily 10am–5pm.

Royal Alberta Museum ★ Expertly laid out, this 18,500-sq.-m (199,132-sq.-ft.) modern museum displays Alberta's natural and human history in three permanent galleries. Wild Alberta represents Alberta's diverse natural history with astonishingly lifelike dioramas and interactive displays utilizing computers, microscopes, and other hands-on tools. It's a good place to gain some knowledge about what you're going to see if you're heading to the Rockies. The Gallery of Aboriginal Culture tells the 11,000-year story of Alberta's First Nations inhabitants, incorporating artifacts, film, interactive media, and Native interpreters. The Natural History Gallery has fossils, minerals, and a live-bug room.

12845 102nd Ave. ✆ **780/453-9100.** www.royalalbertamuseum.ca. C$10 adults, C$8 seniors, C$7 students, C$5 children 7–17, free for children 6 & under; C$28 families. Sat & Sun half-price admission 9–11am. Daily 9am–5pm.

Telus World of Science ☺ This is one of the most advanced science centers in the world. Its wonders include an **IMAX theater,** the largest planetarium theater in Canada, high-tech exhibits (including a virtual-reality showcase and a display on robotics), and an observatory open on clear afternoons and evenings. Exhibits include a journey through the human body (including the Gallery of the Gross!) and Mystery Avenue, where young sleuths can try their hands.

11211 142nd St., Coronation Park. ✆ **780/451-3344.** www.edmontonscience.com. C$14 adults, C$12 seniors & children 13–17, C$9.50 children 3–12; C$55 families. Summer daily 10am–7pm; Sept 7–mid-June Sun–Thurs & holidays 10am–5pm, Fri & Sat 10am–7pm. Bus: 17 or 22.

The Valley Zoo ☺ Not as sprawling and impressive as the Calgary Zoo (see p. 540), Edmonton's Valley Zoo, nestled in Sir Wilfrid Laurier Park near the river, is nonetheless a diverting activity amid the lush green surroundings of the North Saskatchewan river valley. More than 100 exotic, endangered, and native animals are here, including rare red panda twins, born in May 2008.

13315 Buena Vista Rd. (87th Ave.). ✆ **780/442-5311.** www.valleyzoo.ca. May 7 to Oct 10 C$11 adults, C$8 seniors & children 12–17, C$5.25 children 11 & under; C$32 families. Oct 11 to May 36 C$8 adults, C$6 seniors & children 2-12; C$24 families. Jan 1 to May 9 9:30am–4pm; May 7 to Aug 28 9:30am–6pm; Aug 9 to Oct 10 9:30am–6pm Sat–Sun and 9:30am–4pm Mon–Fri.

Shopping

There are more shops per capita in Edmonton than in any other city in Canada. Go for it! See the **West Edmonton Mall** (p. 608).

DOWNTOWN Most of the downtown shops are in a few large mall complexes; all are linked by the Pedway system, which gives pedestrians protection from summer heat and winter cold. The largest is **Edmonton City Centre** with 170 stores; it shares the block with the Hudson's Bay Company, and is across 102nd Avenue from **Holt Renfrew** department store. All of the above face 102nd Avenue, between 103rd and 100th streets.

OLD STRATHCONA If you don't like mall shopping, then wandering the galleries and boutiques along **Whyte Avenue** (aka 82nd Ave.) may be more your style. One of the few commercial areas of Edmonton that retain historic structures, Old Strathcona is trend-central for students and bohemians. Shop for antiques, gifts, books, crystals, and crafts. Or pick up a souvenir tattoo. Be sure to stop by the **Farmers Market** at 103rd Street and 102nd Avenue.

HIGH STREET This small district, running from 102nd to 109th avenues along 124th Street, has Edmonton's greatest concentration of art galleries, housewares shops, boutiques, and bookstores. It has great restaurants, too.

WEST EDMONTON MALL It may not be the largest mall on Earth anymore, but for a time, West Edmonton Mall (8882 170th St. © **800/661-8890** or 780/444-5200. www.wem.ca), which opened in 1981, defined the enclosed, indoor shopping experience. Locals used to call it the "eighth wonder of the world." It contains 800 stores and services and 100 eateries. As a contained universe, it's fascinating; West Edmonton is the ultimate attempt to caricaturize reality, complete with themed areas—the mall has a "Europa Boulevard" with cafes mimicking the Champs d'Elysee and "Bourbon Street," an unfortunate collection of touristy big-chain restaurants with no New Orleans connection whatsoever, like the Olde Spaghetti Factory. West Edmonton Mall looks and sounds more like a theme park than a shopping center. In a space equal to 48 city blocks, it houses the world's largest indoor amusement park, including a titanic rollercoaster, bungee-jumping platform, and enclosed wave-lake, complete with a beach and enough artificial waves to bodysurf on. It has an 18-hole minigolf course, a huge ice-skating palace, 19 movie theaters, a lagoon with performing dolphins, and a submarine adventure ride to the "ocean floor." You can take it all in from 10am-9pm every day but Sunday, when it is open from 11am-5pm.

Where to Stay

For B&Bs, try **Alberta and Pacific Bed and Breakfast** (© **604/944-1793**) or the **Alberta Bed and Breakfast Association** (www.bbalberta.com). Note that unless otherwise stated, Wi-Fi service is free.

EXPENSIVE

Crowne Plaza Chateau Lacombe Centrally located downtown, the Crowne Plaza, a round 24-story tower sitting on the edge of a cliff overlooking the North Saskatchewan River, possesses some of the city's best views (best seen from La Ronde, the hotel's revolving restaurant; see p. 612). The nicely furnished standard rooms aren't huge, though the wedge-shaped design means that they are broadest toward the windows, where you'll spend time looking over the city. Riverview rooms are an extra C$18 or so; request one when booking. The Crown Plaza's Sleep Advantage program focuses on high-quality linens and pillows, plus interesting extras like relaxation CDs, "quiet floors," and aromatherapy lavender atomizers for the sheets. For just a C$30 upgrade, executive suites offer twice the square footage of standard rooms and a full living room with foldout bed—a sweet deal.

10111 Bellamy Hill NW, Edmonton, T5J 1N7. © **800/661-8801** or 780/428-6611. www.chateaulacombe.com. 307 units. From C$159 double; C$219 executive suite. Additional adult $10. Weekend packages available. AE, DC, DISC, MC, V. Parking $14. **Amenities:** Revolving restaurant; lounge; cafe; coffee bar; babysitting; exercise room; room service. *In room:* A/C, TV, CD player, hair dryer, Wi-Fi.

Fairmont Hotel Macdonald ★★ There's no denying that this lovely hotel is the best in town, from the unrivalled presence overlooking the North Saskatchewan

River to the city's most opulent rooms and historic salons. All visiting VIPs, from royalty to rock stars, stay here. Originally opened in 1915, the restored Hotel Macdonald has retained signature elements such as its deep tubs, brass door plates, and paneled doors. Everything, including the service, is absolutely top-notch. Signature rooms have the best views and include breakfast for two. If you're unable to stay here, at least come for a summer cocktail on the patio. Needless to say, there aren't many hotels like this in Edmonton—or in Canada, for that matter.

10065 100th St., Edmonton, T5J 0N6. ✆ **800/441-1414** or 780/424-5181. www.fairmont.com. 199 units. C$299–C$329 double; C$289–C$999 suite. Weekend & off-season discounts available. AE, DC, DISC, MC, V. Parking C$22. **Amenities:** Restaurant; lounge; babysitting; concierge; concierge-level rooms; health club; indoor pool; 24-hr. room service; spa; squash court. *In room*: A/C, TV/VCR w/pay movies, hair dryer, Internet, minibar.

Fantasyland Hotel ☺ With 116 theme rooms decorated in 12 different styles, it would seem impossible to get bored at Fantasyland—which is exactly the point. An active hub for visitors eager to see what locals call "the eighth wonder of the world," West Edmonton Mall, Fantasyland is all about myth-building. Theme rooms aren't just a matter of subtle touches. Take the Truck Room: Your bed is located in the back end of a real pickup; the bench seats fold down into a child's bed; and the lights on the vanity are real stoplights. In the Igloo Room, a round bed is encased in a shell of faux ice blocks; statues of sled dogs keep you company; and the walls are painted with amazingly lifelike Arctic murals. The themes continue, through the Canadian Rail Room (train berths for beds), the African Room, and more. All luxury theme rooms come with immense four-person Jacuzzis and plenty of amenities, much of it circa 1980, when the hotel was built. The hotel offers tours of the different theme types on Saturdays at 2pm. It's not all fantasy, though: 238 large, well-furnished, non-theme rooms are divided into superior rooms, with either a king-size or two queen-size beds, and executive rooms, with a king-size bed and Jacuzzi. The rooms are large and comfortable, with new flat-screen TVs. Outdoor noise is a problem in some rooms with poor windows. The hotel's new restaurant, the **L2 Grill** (✆ **780/444-5538**) is quite good; of course, you have all-weather access to the world's second largest mall and its many eateries, as well. Kids and shoppers won't find a better option.

17700 87th Ave. (at the end of the West Edmonton Mall), Edmonton, T5T 4V4. ✆ **800/737-3783** or 780/444-3000. www.fantasylandhotel.com. 355 units. C$178–C$268 double. Additional adult C$14. Weekend & off-season packages available. AE, MC, V. Free parking. **Amenities:** Restaurant; bar; babysitting; concierge; exercise room; 24-hr. room service. *In room:* A/C, TV, fax, fridge, hair dryer, Wi-Fi.

The Matrix Hotel ★★ Forgive its sci-fi name, for there's no dystopian-future theme to be found here; rather, just a stylishly contemporary hotel with all the bells and whistles. The Matrix is the modern European sister property to the cool and stylish Metterra (see below) across the river on Whyte Avenue. Downtown, the Matrix is as urbane as Edmonton can possibly get, with its grey- and neutral-stone-toned palettes, for a modern industrial feel. Some of the spacious rooms have kitchenettes. Rooms can be tight, but they are efficient, bright, and sleek. Breakfasts are served in a cocktail lounge on the second floor, and there is a Starbucks next door. There's a daily happy hour wine and cheese tasting, which is on the house. This is by far the most interesting and modern of all the downtown hotels. Get the best rates by booking via their website.

10640 100th Ave., Edmonton, T5J 3N8. ✆ **866/465-8150** or 780/429-2861. Fax 780/426-7225. www.matrixedmonton.com. 185 units. From C$195 double; from C$295 suite. Rates include local calls, continental breakfast & evening wine & cheese. Weekend packages available. AE, DC, DISC, MC, V. Free parking. **Amenities:** Lounge; babysitting; exercise room; room service. *In room:* A/C, TV, hair dryer, Wi-Fi.

Metterra Hotel on Whyte A swanky boutique hotel in the lively Old Strathcona neighborhood, filled with students and artists, great nightlife, and dining, the Metterra is where you'll want to stay if you're in town for a festival or for soaking up the city's coolest neighborhood. The lobby sets the tone with striking art, a two-story rundle-stone wall—that would be stone from Banff's Mt. Rundle—and waterfall, while the guest rooms are large, with contemporary and Indonesian art adding some style. Some rooms offer fireplaces, others feature recliners. Rates include a continental breakfast and afternoon wine and cheese. Though not a typical business hotel, Metterra offers all the features and services sophisticated business and leisure travelers require. Be warned, though: As charming as some of the outdoor decks overlooking Whyte Avenue may be, on a Saturday night, you might like to ask for a room facing north toward downtown, instead—if you plan on sleeping, that is.

10454 82nd (Whyte) Ave., Edmonton, T6E 4Z7. © **866/465-8150** or 780/465-8150. www.metterra.com. 98 units. From C$139 double; from C$249 suite. Rates include breakfast & afternoon wine & cheese. AE, MC, V. Free valet parking. **Amenities:** Fitness center; room service. *In room*: A/C, TV, fridge, hair dryer, Wi-Fi.

Union Bank Inn ★ 🎁 If you're tired of unmemorable business hotels, this is a wonderful choice. The stylish Union Bank, built in 1910, now houses an elegant restaurant and intimate boutique hotel. The owner asked Edmonton's top interior designers to each design a room; the results are charming, with each unique guest room displaying its own style, colors, furniture, and fabrics. All units, however, have the same amenities, including gas fireplaces, voicemail, feather duvets, and upscale toiletries. Joining the original inn are 20 business-class rooms in a new addition—each equally idiosyncratic and uniquely designed. The older rooms aren't incredibly big, so if you're in town with work to do, ask for one of the newer and larger units. Staff isfriendly; the guest experience is personalized. The restaurant/bar Madison's is a great place to meet friends (see "Where to Dine," below).

10053 Jasper Ave., Edmonton, T5J 1S5. © **780/423-3600.** www.unionbankinn.com. 34 units. C$209–C$299 double. Rates include full breakfast. AE, DC, MC, V. Free parking. **Amenities:** Restaurant; bar; exercise room; limited room service. *In room:* A/C, TV, fridge, hair dryer, Internet.

The Varscona Completing the three sisters sweep of boutique hotels in Edmonton—the Metterra, Varscona, and Matrix (see above) are all affiliated—is the Varscona, the oldest of the three and therefore the most traditionally appointed. With an old-world country style, including plush handmade pillows in every room, the Varscona strikes a contemporary balance with amenities like Bose CD players. Downstairs, **Murrieta's Bar and Grill** (© **780/438-4100**), with its patio open onto Whyte Avenue, is a top-notch restaurant, and an Irish pub (**O'Byrne's**, © **780/414-6766**) next door is a hopping night spot.

8208 106th St. NW, Edmonton, T6E 6R9. © **866/465-8150** or 780/434-6111. www.varscona.com. 89 units. From C$125 double. Rates include local calls, continental breakfast & evening wine & cheese. Weekend packages available. AE, DC, DISC, MC, V. Free parking. **Amenities:** Restaurant; lounge; babysitting; exercise room; room service. *In room:* A/C, TV, hair dryer, Wi-Fi.

MODERATE

Courtyard by Marriott 🎁 Don't let the name fool you; this is anything but a could-be-anywhere business hotel. Rooms are comfortable and well furnished, but it's the setting and facilities that really stand out. Edmontonians have voted the downtown bar and restaurant patio—cantilevered hundreds of feet above the North Saskatchewan River—as the city's top spot for outdoor drinks and dining. Located on the cliff-edge with vistas over the city center and the breadth of the valley, this Courtyard (formerly the Warwick) must have the best views in the entire chain. Just be sure to ask for a riverside view when booking your room.

1 Thornton Court (99th St. & Jasper Ave.), Edmonton, T5J 2E7. ✆ **866/441-7591** or 780/423-9999. www.marriott.com/hotels/travel/yegcy-courtyard-edmonton-downtown. 177 units. C$139–C$159 double. Parking C$22. **Amenities**: Restaurant; lounge. *In room*: A/C, TV, hair dryer, Wi-Fi.

Days Inn Downtown Edmonton For the price, this is one of downtown Edmonton's best deals. Located just a 5-minute walk from the city center, the former motor inn has everything you need for a pleasant stay, including comfortably furnished rooms and easy access to public transport. If all you need for a night or two is a clean and basic room in a convenient location, this is a top choice. Free parking is another bonus.

10041 106th St., Edmonton, T5J 1G3. ✆ **800/267-2191** or 780/423-1925. www.daysinn-downtown edmonton.com. 76 units. C$92–C$115 double. Senior, AAA & corporate discounts available. AE, DC, DISC, MC, V. Free parking. **Amenities:** Restaurant; bar; limited room service. *In room:* A/C, TV, hair dryer, Wi-Fi.

Glenora Bed & Breakfast Located in the heart of the artsy High Street district, just west of downtown, the Glenora occupies the upper floors of a converted 1912 heritage apartment building. While lots of care has been taken to retain the period character and charm of the rooms, the rooms have been thoroughly updated—all but three have private bathrooms, and four rooms have full kitchen facilities. Most appealing is the happy mix of unique period furnishings and snappy interior design—absolutely every room is unique. There are five styles of rooms, from simple bedroom units with shared bathrooms to one-bedroom apartment suites with kitchens. Free parking, an excellent breakfast, and access to a handsome Edwardian common room and a second-story deck are included. The Glenora is an excellent value—and fun, to boot.

12327 102nd Ave. NW, Edmonton, T5N 0L8. ✆ **877/453-6672** or 780/488-6766. www.glenorabnb.com. 25 units. C$90–C$165 double. Rates include continental breakfast. AE, MC, V. Free parking. **Amenities:** Restaurant; bar; Wi-Fi. *In room:* TV/VCR, hair dryer, minibar.

Hotel Selkirk Located inside the historic Fort Edmonton Park, this little inn manages to feel authentic and historic, yet still comfortable. While the setting is 1920, the rooms have modern furniture and plush beds. There's a two-bedroom suite on the top floor. Sit by the window and watch the trams go by. The location, right next to the river, is great for walking, biking, and running. It's quiet down here at night, and you are far from restaurants. But if you want to see the "real" history of Edmonton, you can't beat this unique inn.

1920 St., Fort Edmonton Park (on Whitemud Dr., at Fox Dr.), Edmonton, T5J 2R7. ✆ **877/496-7227** or 780/496-7227. www.hotelselkirk.com. 31 rooms. From C$141 double. Rates include breakfast & park admission. AE, DISC, MC, V. Free parking. **Amenities:** Restaurant; saloon. *In room:* A/C, Wi-Fi.

INEXPENSIVE

Hostelling International Edmonton Well-located near the University of Alberta in the lively Old Strathcona neighborhood, this pleasant hostel has a shared and newly renovated kitchen, along with spacious common rooms. Some family rooms are available, and check-in is at 3pm. Free coffee and wireless Internet, and a good location near many festival hubs, make this a good option for budget travelers and families.

10647 81st Ave., Edmonton, T6E 1Y1. ✆ **780/988-6836.** www.hihostels.ca. 88 beds. Members C$26–C$32.50 dorm bed, nonmembers C$28.60—C$35.75 dorm bed; C$83 members and C$85 non-members family room. MC, V. **Amenities:** Bike rental, Wi-Fi.

University of Alberta In May through August, two dorms are thrown open to visitors. Some are standard shared-bathroom rooms, single or twin, while others are single or twin with a private washroom. Also, the university has a number of hotel-style guest rooms with private bathrooms. U of A is on the LRT line, not far from Old Strathcona.

87th Ave. & 116th St. ✆ **780/492-4281.** www.uofaweb.ualberta.ca/residences/index.cfm. C$35 single w/shared bathroom, C$49 single w/private bathroom; C$45 twin w/shared bathroom, C$59 twin w/private bathroom; C$119 double. MC, V. Parking C$9. **Amenities:** Food service nearby.

Where to Dine

Edmonton has a vigorous dining scene, with hip new eateries joining traditional steak and seafood restaurants. In general, fine dining is found downtown and on High Street, close to the centers of politics and business. Over in Old Strathcona, south of the river, are trendy—and less expensive—cafes and bistros. For lighter meals or coffee breaks, try the very chic new **Holt's Café** downtown (10180 101st St.; ✆ **780/425-5300**) or **Leva Cafe** (11053 86th Ave.; ✆ **780/479-5362**) near the University of Alberta, which has the best espresso in Edmonton. For pastries and café au lait in the High Street area, you can't miss **La Favorite** (12431 102nd Ave.; ✆ **780/482-7024**).

DOWNTOWN

Expensive

Hardware Grill CONTEMPORARY This is easily one of western Canada's most exciting restaurants. The building may be historic (and within walking distance of most downtown hotels and theaters), but there's nothing antique about the dining room. Modern but not stark, the room is edged with glass partitions, exposed pipes, and ducts painted a smoky rose. There are as many appetizers as entrees, making it tempting to graze through a series of smaller dishes. A delicate, delicious bison carpaccio is served with Chevre Noir cheese, and a crispy duck-leg confit has sundried cranberries and sage. Entrees such as plank-roasted salmon with a crab crust, a demi-roasted lamb rack served cassoulet style, or herb-crusted venison loin with slow-braised short ribs practically leap off the plate with their inventive flavor combinations.

9698 Jasper Ave. ✆ **780/423-0969.** www.hardwaregrill.com. Reservations recommended. Main courses C$30–C$48. AE, DC, MC, V. Mon–Fri 11:30am–2pm; Mon–Thurs 5–9:30pm, Fri & Sat 5–10pm. Closed 1st week of July.

La Ronde ☺ CONTEMPORARY On the 24th floor of the Crowne Plaza, the revolving La Ronde offers the best views of any restaurant in Edmonton. The Alberta-focused menu also puts on quite a show—chef Jasmin Kobajica is passionate about local organic meats and produce. The menu is rich in locally raised beef, lamb, and game prepared with a focus on indigenous flavors. Beef-lovers can choose from a AAA tenderloin with *monchego* cheese, a AAA classic prime rib, or a 227g (8-oz.) sirloin with truffle bacon sauce. Bison, lamb, curried goat, and Arctic char round out the entree options. The intensely regional menu makes a brilliant companion to the ever-changing, revolving vista of city towers and river valley. But be warned: You're paying for the view as much as the meal, and some of the dishes fail to impress. Stick with the simple stuff, and you'll be satisfied. They also have a kids menu.

10111 Bellamy Hill. ✆ **780/428-6611.** www.chateaulacombe.com/laronde.php. Reservations required. Main courses C$28–C$33. AE, MC, V. Sun 10:30am–2pm; daily 5:30–10pm.

Madison's at Union Bank Inn CONTEMPORARY Madison's is one of the loveliest dining rooms and casual cocktail bars in Edmonton. Once an early-20th-century bank, the building's formal architectural details remain, but they now share the light-and-airy space with modern art and excellent food. The menu is contemporary, bridging continental European cuisine with regional Canadian ingredients. It features grilled and roast fish and meat, plus pasta dishes and interesting salads (one special featured smoked sablefish, watercress, avocado vinaigrette, and tomato jam). Other standouts include a pan-roasted Alberta rack of lamb and a pork tenderloin stuffed with local Saskatoon berries and gouda-stuffed pears. A six course chef's dinner runs C$85. Add wine pairings for C$50, which is a very good value. And don't miss daily breakfast and afternoon tapas menus, as well.

10053 Jasper Ave. ✆ **780/401-2222**. www.unionbankinn.com. Reservations recommended. Main courses C$34–C$39. AE, MC, V. Mon–Fri 7–10am & 11am–2pm, Sat & Sun 8–11am; Mon–Thurs 5–10pm, Fri & Sat 5–11pm, Sun 5–8pm.

Moderate & Inexpensive

Blue Plate ★★ ☺ DINER Maybe Edmonton's cozy, friendly, laid-back attitude is best represented in this vegetarian-friendly diner in the Warehouse District close to downtown. The house specialties here are burgers, including the best veggie burger in town, which is stocked with good root vegetables and served with herbed mayo and a pickle. There's also a bison burger with dried blueberries and a great steak sandwich (this is Alberta, after all). They have an impressive New World–heavy wine list. It's very popular, especially on weekends, so call ahead.

10145 104th St. ✆ **780/429-0740.** www.blueplatediner.ca. Reservations highly recommended. Main courses C$14–C$26. AE, MC, V. Mon–Fri 11am–10pm; Sat 9am–10pm.

Chicago's Deep Dish Pizza ★ ☺ PIZZA It's a long way from the Windy City to the "River City," but this joint close to the Chateau Lacombe (see "Where to Stay," above) has the best pizza in town. The Galaxy pizza is crammed with pepperoni, salami, mushrooms, bacon, shrimp, pineapple, and a few other surprises. Pastas and salads round out a very family-friendly meal.

10024 102nd St. ✆ **780/413-8866.** www.cddp.ca. Main courses C$14–C$18. AE, MC, V. Sun–Thurs 4pm–1:30am; Fri & Sat 4pm–3:30am.

HIGH STREET

The Blue Pear ★★★ CONTEMPORARY Tucked into an innocuous, petite strip mall just off the 124th Street stroll is this absolute gem of a restaurant that's my choice if you have but one night in Edmonton. A small room in muted gray and blue tones, the Blue Pear is the brainchild of a food-obsessed husband-and-wife team. He's the chef; she handles the hospitality. Over the course of a five-course meal, wonders emerge from the kitchen at perfect pace, each one leaving you breathless awaiting the next. This is simple food, with an emphasis on local ingredients, treated with respect for flavor and subtle, unique creativity: braised baby beets with Anjou pears, a goat cheese *coulis,* and candied walnuts is followed by grilled Asian marinated beef with *bulgogi* sauce and spicy cabbage puree, or a simple roasted fish of the day, with saffron-braised chickpeas, spinach, and a citrus *crostini.* Meals here are the fruits of a top-flight creative food mind whirring at full capacity.

10643 123rd St. ✆ **780/482/7178.** www.thebluepear.com. Reservations highly recommended. 5-course meal C$89, including dessert; 3-course meal C$59. AE, MC, V. Daily 5–11pm.

Manor Cafe INTERNATIONAL The Manor Cafe offers one of the most fashionable outdoor dining patios in Edmonton. This longtime Edmonton favorite offers fusion and international cuisine, from Italian pastas—Manor pasta with chicken, spinach, pancetta, goat cheese, and sundried tomato cream sauce is the signature dish—to a delicious curried chicken or beef Stroganoff. Food is eclectic but always delicious.

10109 125th St. ✆ **780/482-7577.** www.manorcafe.com. Reservations recommended on weekends. Main courses C$17–C$29. AE, MC, V. Mon–Thurs 11am–10pm; Fri & Sat 11am–midnight; Sun 11am–2pm & 5–9pm.

OLD STRATHCONA

Culina Café ★ EUROPEAN A few blocks from busy Whyte Avenue, this fresh neighborhood cafe has a leafy patio and healthy food. While the roots of the menu are in Ukrainian food, the food is really more about simple freshness. There's a duck breast on local roasted potatoes, and Alberta beef with blue cheese and chocolate sauce. For lunch, try the Persian flatbread sandwich with roasted vegetable, hummus, and quinoa salad. Many Edmontonians say this is the best breakfast in the city. There's another location just north of downtown (at 6509 112th Ave).

9914 89th Ave. ✆ **780/437-5588.** www.culinafamily.ca. Reservations recommended on weekends and for brunch. Main courses C$13–C$27. AE, MC, V. Mon–Fri 9am–3pm, Sat & Sun 10am–2pm; Mon–Sat 5–10pm.

Chianti Café ITALIAN Chianti is a rarity among Italian restaurants: very good and very inexpensive. Pasta dishes include fettuccine with scallops, smoked salmon, curry, and garlic; or try one of the veal dishes (more than a dozen are offered) or seafood specials. Chianti is located in a handsomely remodeled post-office building; the restaurant isn't a secret, so it can be a busy and fairly crowded experience.

10501 82nd Ave. ✆ **780/439-9829.** Reservations required. Main courses C$14–C$22. AE, DC, DISC, MC, V. Daily 11am–11pm.

Julio's Barrio ★ MEXICAN If you like Mexican food, it's worth a detour to Julio's. The food ranges from enchiladas and nachos to sizzling shrimp fajitas. This Mexican watering hole is a great place to snack on several light dishes while quaffing margaritas with friends. The atmosphere is youthful, high energy, and minimalist hip: no kitschy piñatas or scratchy recordings of marimba bands here.

10450 82nd Ave. ✆ **780/431-0774.** Main courses C$14–C$29. AE, MC, V. Sun–Wed 11:30am–11pm; Thurs 11:30am–midnight; Fri & Sat 11:30am–1am.

Packrat Louie Kitchen & Bar ★★ ITALIAN Bright and lively, this very popular bistro has a somewhat unlikely name, given that it's one of the best casual Italian trattoria in Edmonton. Menu choices range from specialty pizzas—from a chicken *tikka* salad to smoked salmon—to fine entree salads to grilled meats, chicken, and pasta. A stocked menu of canapés by the dozen includes phyllo tenderloin bites, lemon pizza, and buffalo meatballs. Most dishes tend toward light or healthy preparations without sacrificing complexity. A rack of lamb comes with jalapeno mint jelly, and ostrich tenderloin is served with spaetzle and sour cherry *gastrique*.

10335 83rd Ave. ✆ **780/433-0123.** www.packratlouie.com. Reservations recommended on weekends. Main courses C$12–C$42. MC, V. Mon–Fri 11:30am–10pm; Sat 11:30am–11:30pm.

ELSEWHERE

Cactus Club Café CONTEMPORARY The best food in the West Edmonton Mall is at this Western Canadian chain that's both casual and refined. It's fun to even drop in for an afternoon cocktail. Staples like pepper-sauced steak and calamari are dependable, but there's wow-factor in more creative takes—the club sandwich has duck, chicken, and carpaccio. Service can be iffy, but under the guidance of *Iron Chef* winner Rob Feenie, the kitchen here consistently puts out fine-dining–caliber meals and average-neighborhood-diner prices.

1946–8882 170th St. ✆ **780/489-1002.** www.cactusclubcafe.com. Reservations recommended for dinner. Main courses C$14–C$26. AE, MC, V. Daily 11am–midnight.

Jack's Grill ★ CONTEMPORARY Ten years ago, Jack's was *the* spot in Edmonton. Lately, it's fallen down somewhat. For one, the location is not handy, tucked away in a quiet residential area in the city's south end, near the Southgate Mall. The food, though, was a trend-setter of types, relying on simple preparation, inventive flavor combinations, and tons of fresh, local ingredients before "locavore" was a word. Try the smoked lamb carpaccio crusted in rosemary with arugula and apple salad and Dijon aioli, say, or chili-rubbed grilled beef rib-eye, aged 28 days, with smoked tomato and goat cheese tortellini and creamed spinach. Think of it, perhaps, as haute comfort food—some of the best you'll find anywhere.

5842 111th St. ✆ **780/434-1113.** www.jacksgrill.com. Reservations recommended. Main courses C$28–C$45. AE, MC, V. Mon–Sat from 5pm.

Edmonton After Dark

To get a read on what's going on in Edmonton's vibrant cultural scene, pick up a copy of ***See*** (www.seemagazine.com), the local free arts and entertainment weekly.

THE PERFORMING ARTS In the downtown cultural district, the **Winspear Centre** (4 Sir Winston Churchill Sq. NW; ✆ **780/428-1414;** www.winspearcentre.com) is home to major cultural organizations like the **Edmonton Symphony** (✆ **780/428-1414;** www.edmontonsymphony.com), the **Edmonton Opera** (✆ **780/429-4040;** www.edmontonopera.com), and many big-name traveling performers. The **Citadel Theatre** (9828 101A Ave.; ✆ **780/425-1820;** www.citadeltheatre.com) is the city's premiere live theater venue in a city known for theater, with a resident company that's generally acknowledged to be among the country's best.

Edmonton's theater scene is world-renowned, with a massive annual Fringe Festival that all but takes over the city every August. If you're not in town for the Fringe, there are a smorgasbord of local theater troupes—far too numerous to list here—to choose from year-round, performing at a variety of formal stages and informal venues, like pubs. Check your copy of *See* to see what's current.

THE CLUB & BAR SCENE Downtown, you've got to be careful not to get caught when the streets fold up at night, but Whyte Avenue, always busy during the day, kicks it up a notch after dark. **Bar Wild's** (10551 Whyte Ave; ✆ **780/504-7777**) name says it all—it's the Whyte Avenue night-time scene in a nutshell. Bar Wild draws a young crowd, many of them U of A students, bent on drowning the week's mind-expanding educational experience in beer. The **Black Dog Freehouse** (10425 Whyte Ave; ✆ **780/439-1082**) is a popular, pubby spot in the summertime, with its large rooftop patio, while **Devlin's Cocktail Lounge** (10507 Whyte Ave; ✆ **780/437-7489**) is Whyte Avenue spiffed up for the young professional set, with its look-at-me front windows out on to the Whyte Avenue stroll.

You'll find live music on weekends at some of the many, many pubs on Whyte, like the venerable **Blues on Whyte** (10329 Whyte Ave; ✆ **780/439-3981**), the **Empress Ale House** (9912 Whyte Ave; ✆ **780/758-1164**), or the **Backdraught Pub** (8307 99th St.; ✆ **780/430-9200**), whereas the **Pawn Shop** (10551 Whyte Ave, 2nd floor; ✆ **780/432-5058**) is one of the best venues for both the local and popular traveling indie bands.

And Whyte Avenue really is one-stop bar-hopping: If you're looking for dance clubs, there's a plethora of those here, too. **Suite 69** (8232 Gateway Blvd.; ✆ **780/439-6969**) is an upstairs dance club one block off Whyte Avenue, featuring popular local DJs; **Krobar** (10551 Whyte Ave; ✆ **780/916-1557**) cranks up the intensity with club music that's loud, fast, and hard.

VANCOUVER

by Donald Olson

If you really want to understand Vancouver, stand at the edge of the Inner Harbour (the Canada Place cruise-ship terminal makes a good vantage point) and look around you. To the west you'll see Stanley Park, one of the world's largest urban parks, jutting out into the waters of Burrard Inlet. To the north, just across the inlet, rise snowcapped mountains. To the east, right along the water, is the low-rise brick-faced Old Town. And almost everything else you see lining the water's edge will be a new glass-and-steel high-rise tower. As giant cruise ships glide in to berth, floatplanes buzz in and out, and your ears catch a medley of foreign tongues, you may wonder just where on earth you are. Vancouver is majestic and intimate, sophisticated and completely laid-back, a bustling, prosperous city that somehow, almost miraculously, manages to combine its contemporary, urban-centered consciousness with the free-spirited magnificence of nature on a grand scale.

15

Vancouver is probably one of the "newest" cities you'll ever visit, and certainly it's one of the most cosmopolitan. There's a youthfulness, too, a certain Pacific Northwest chic (and cheek) that comes from being used in so many movies that Vancouver is sometimes called "Hollywood North." I can guarantee you that part of your trip will be spent puzzling out what makes it so unique, so livable and lovable, what gives it such a buzz. Nature figures big in that equation, but so does enlightened city planning and the diversity of cultures. Vancouver is a place where people *want* to live. It's a place that awakens dreams and desires.

The city's history is in its topography. Thousands of years ago a giant glacier sliced along the foot of the coast range, carving out a deep trench and piling up a gigantic moraine of rock and sand. When the ice retreated, water from the Pacific flowed in and the moraine became a peninsula, flanked on one side by a deep natural harbor (on Burrard Inlet) and on the other by a river of glacial meltwater (today called the Fraser River). Vast forests of fir and cedar covered the land and wildlife flourished. The First Nations tribes that settled in the area developed rich cultures based on cedar and salmon.

Some 10,000 years later, a surveyor for the Canadian Pacific Railroad (CPR) came by, took in the peninsula, the harbor, and the river, and decided he'd found the perfect spot for the CPR's new Pacific terminus. He kept it quiet, as smart railway men tended to do, until the company had bought up most of the land around town. Then the railway moved in, set up shop, and the city of Vancouver was born.

Working indoors, Vancouverites have seemingly all fallen in love with the outdoors. And why shouldn't they? Every terrain needed for every kind of outdoor pursuit—hiking, in-line skating, mountain biking, downhill and cross-country skiing, kayaking, windsurfing, rock climbing, parasailing, snowboarding—is right there in their backyard: ocean, rivers, mountains, islands, sidewalks. The international resort town of Whistler, which took center stage during the Winter Olympics in 2010, is just 2 hours north of downtown Vancouver. And when Vancouverites aren't skiing or kayaking, they're drinking coffee or eating out. In the past decade or so, Vancouver has become one of the top restaurant cities in the world, bursting with an incredible variety of cuisines and making an international name for itself with its unique Pacific Northwest cooking.

The rest of the world has taken notice of the blessed life people in these parts lead. Surveys routinely rank Vancouver as one of the 10 best cities in the world to live. It's also one of the 10 best to visit, according to *Condé Nast Traveler.* And in 2010, Vancouver hosted the 2010 Olympic and Paralympic Winter Games. Heady stuff, particularly for a spot that less than 25 years ago was routinely derided as the world's biggest mill town.

ESSENTIALS

Getting There

BY PLANE **Vancouver International Airport** (✆ **604/207-7077;** www.yvr.ca) is 13km (8 miles) south of downtown Vancouver on uninhabited Sea Island. Daily direct flights between major U.S. cities and Vancouver are offered by **Air Canada** (✆ **888/247-2262;** www.aircanada.com); **Alaska Airlines** (✆ **800/252-7522;** www.alaskaair.com); **American Airlines** (✆ **800/433-7300;** www.aa.com); **Continental** (✆ **800/231-0856;** www.continental.com); **Frontier Airlines** (✆ **800/432-1359;** www.frontierairlines.com); **Delta Airlines** (✆ **800/447-4747;** www.delta.com); and **United Airlines** (✆ **800/241-6522;** www.united.com). Direct flights on major carriers serve 33 cities in North America, including Denver, Phoenix, Dallas, New York, Houston, Minneapolis, Reno, and San Francisco; 12 cities in Asia; and 3 cities in Europe.

For domestic travelers within Canada, there are fewer options. **Air Canada** (✆ **888/247-2262**) operates flights to Vancouver and Victoria from all major Canadian cities, connecting with some of the regional airlines. Cheaper and reaching farther all the time is the no-frills airline **WestJet** (✆ **888/WEST-JET** or 800/538-5696; www.westjet.com), which operates regular flights from Vancouver and Victoria to Prince George, Kelowna, Edmonton, Calgary, Toronto, Montréal, Ottawa, Halifax, and farther afield.

Direct flights between London and Vancouver are offered by **Air Canada** (✆ **0871/220-1111;** www.aircanada.com). Other major carriers serving London (United, Continental, British Airways) make stops in the U.S. before continuing on to Vancouver. **Air Canada** (✆ **0871/220-1111;** www.aircanada.com) also flies to Vancouver from Sydney, Australia, and Auckland, New Zealand.

Tourist information kiosks on Level 2 of the main and international arrival terminals (✆ **604/207-0953**) are open daily from 8am to 11pm. **Plaza Premium Lounges** (www.plaza-ppl.com) in the domestic and international terminals are available to all passengers regardless of airline, travel class, or membership programs. The domestic terminal lounge is located post-security and features comfortable seating,

Vancouver

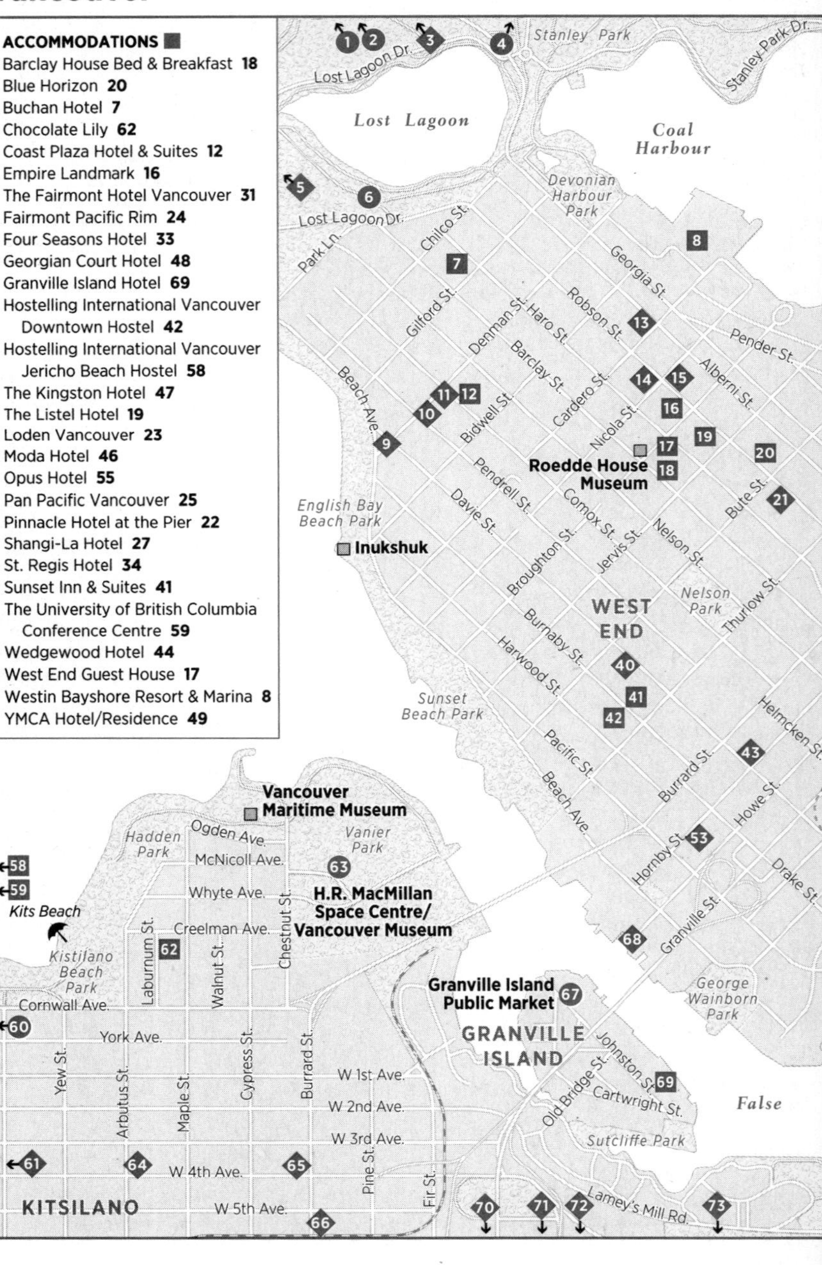
ACCOMMODATIONS
Barclay House Bed & Breakfast 18
Blue Horizon 20
Buchan Hotel 7
Chocolate Lily 62
Coast Plaza Hotel & Suites 12
Empire Landmark 16
The Fairmont Hotel Vancouver 31
Fairmont Pacific Rim 24
Four Seasons Hotel 33
Georgian Court Hotel 48
Granville Island Hotel 69
Hostelling International Vancouver Downtown Hostel 42
Hostelling International Vancouver Jericho Beach Hostel 58
The Kingston Hotel 47
The Listel Hotel 19
Loden Vancouver 23
Moda Hotel 46
Opus Hotel 55
Pan Pacific Vancouver 25
Pinnacle Hotel at the Pier 22
Shangi-La Hotel 27
St. Regis Hotel 34
Sunset Inn & Suites 41
The University of British Columbia Conference Centre 59
Wedgewood Hotel 44
West End Guest House 17
Westin Bayshore Resort & Marina 8
YMCA Hotel/Residence 49
Stanley Park
Stanley Park Dr.
Lost Lagoon Dr.
Lost Lagoon
Coal Harbour
Devonian Harbour Park
Park Ln.
Chilco St.
Gilford St.
Georgia St.
Robson St.
Denman St.
Haro St.
Barclay St.
Pender St.
Alberni St.
Beach Ave.
Bidwell St.
Cardero St.
Nicola St.
Roedde House Museum
Pendrell St.
Davie St.
Comox St.
Bute St.
English Bay Beach Park
Inukshuk
Broughton St.
Jervis St.
Nelson St.
Nelson Park
Thurlow St.
WEST END
Burnaby St.
Harwood St.
Sunset Beach Park
Helmcken St.
Pacific St.
Burrard St.
Howe St.
Hornby St.
Drake St.
Granville St.
Vancouver Maritime Museum
Hadden Park
Ogden Ave.
Vanier Park
McNicoll Ave.
Whyte Ave.
H.R. MacMillan Space Centre/ Vancouver Museum
Kits Beach
Creelman Ave.
Chestnut St.
Laburnum St.
Walnut St.
Kistilano Beach Park
Cornwall Ave.
Granville Island Public Market
George Wainborn Park
York Ave.
GRANVILLE ISLAND
Johnston St.
Yew St.
Arbutus St.
Maple St.
Cypress St.
Burrard St.
W 1st Ave.
W 2nd Ave.
W 3rd Ave.
Old Bridge St.
Cartwright St.
False
Sutcliffe Park
W 4th Ave.
Pine St.
Fir St.
Lamey's Mill Rd.
KITSILANO
W 5th Ave.

DINING ◆

Banana Leaf **11**
The Beach House at
  Dundarave Pier **3**
Bin 941 Tapas Parlour **43**
Blue Water Café and Raw Bar **56**
C **68**
Chambar Belgian Restaurant **50**
Cin Cin **21**
Coast **30**
The Fish House in Stanley Park **5**
Gyoza King **14**
Hapa Izakaya **15**
Il Giardino di Umberto Ristorante **53**
Incendio **66**
Judas Goat **37**
Jules **36**
Le Gavroche **13**
The Locus Café **74**
MARKET by Jean-Georges **28**
Memphis Blues
  Barbeque Restaurant **71**
The Naam Restaurant **61**
Park Lock Seafood
  Restaurant **52**
Pink Pearl **39**
Raincity Grill **9**
Salt **38**
Sanafir **45**
Sciué **29**
Simply Thai **54**
Sophie's Cosmic Café **64**
Stephos **40**
Sun Sui Wah **75**
Tanpopo **10**
Tojo's Restaurant **73**
Trattoria Italian Kitchen **65**
Vij **72**
West **70**

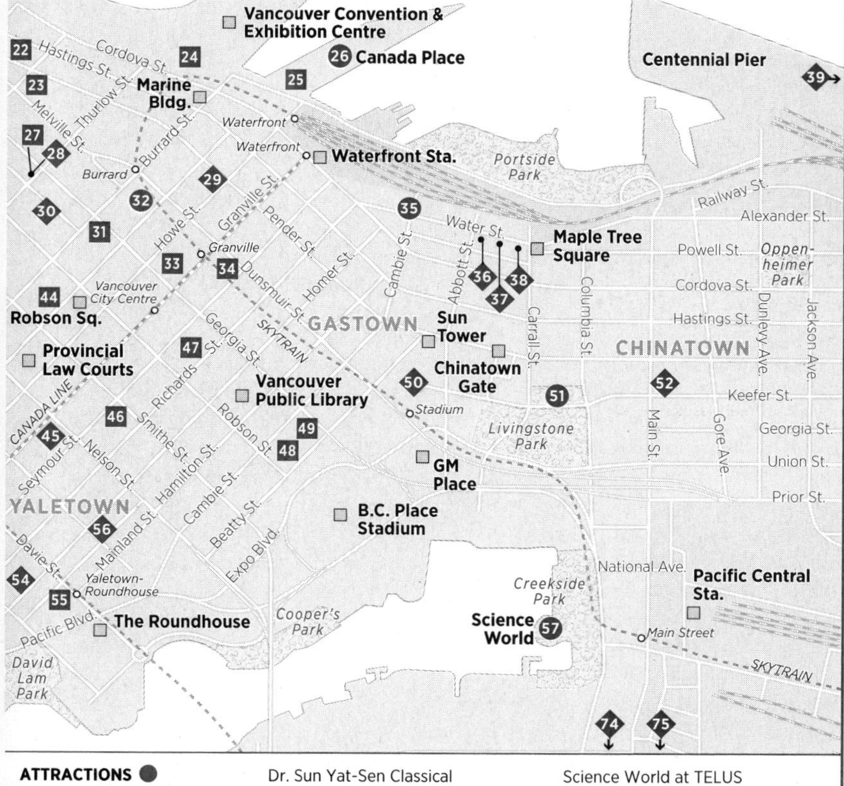

ATTRACTIONS ●

Bill Reid Gallery of
  Northwest Coast Art **32**
Canada Place **26**
Capilano Suspension Bridge
  & Park **2**
Dr. Sun Yat-Sen Classical
  Chinese Garden **51**
Granville Island **67**
Grouse Mountain **1**
H.R. MacMillan Space Centre **63**
Museum of Anthropology **60**
Science World at TELUS
  World of Science **57**
Stanley Park **6**
Steam Clock **35**
Vancouver Aquarium
  Marine Science Centre **4**
Vancouver Museum **63**

runway views, business services, Wi-Fi, and refreshments for a C$25 entrance fee; hours are 6am to 9pm. The Plaza Premium Lounge at the international terminal features all of the above, as well as napping stations and showers, for a C$30 entrance fee; the lounge is open daily from 9am to 2am.

The easiest, fastest, and cheapest way to get into Vancouver from the airport is by the brand-new **Canada Line SkyTrain** operated by **Translink** (**✆ 604/953-3333;** www.translink.ca). The train zips into Vancouver in 22 minutes, stopping at stations in Yaletown, City Centre (downtown), and Waterfront (the SeaBus Terminal, near the Canada Place cruise-ship terminal). The Canada Line costs C$8.75 for adults weekdays, C$7.50 after 6:30pm weekdays and all day on weekends. This fare includes a C$5 Airport AddOn fare which is waived if you buy your ticket in advance or use a Day Pass (see "Getting Around", below).

The average **taxi** fare from the airport to a downtown Vancouver hotel is approximately C$30, plus tip, but the fare can run up to C$40 if the cab gets stuck in traffic. **LimoJet** (**✆ 604/273-1331;** www.limojetgold.com) offers flat-rate sedan or stretch-limousine service at C$39 per trip (not per person) to the airport from any downtown location, plus tax and tip, for up to three people (C$45 for up to six passengers). The drivers accept all major credit cards; no need to reserve in advance, just look for the LimoJet Gold cars in front of the terminal. Most major **car-rental firms** have airport counters and shuttles.

BY TRAIN **VIA Rail Canada,** 1150 Station St., Vancouver (**✆ 888/842-7245;** www.viarail.ca), connects with Amtrak at Winnipeg, Manitoba. From there, you travel on a spectacular route that runs between Calgary and Vancouver. Lake Louise's beautiful alpine scenery is just part of this enjoyable journey. **Amtrak** (**✆ 800/872-7245;** www.amtrak.com) has regular service from Seattle, though buses are often substituted for trains on this line.

The main **Vancouver railway station** is at 1150 Station St., near Main Street and Terminal Avenue just south of Chinatown. You can reach downtown Vancouver from there by cab for about C$10. One block from the station is the SkyTrain Main Street Station, providing quick access to the downtown area. A one-zone SkyTrain ticket (covering the city of Vancouver) costs C$3.75 during peak hours, and C$2.50 on weekends and after 6:30pm.

BY BUS **Greyhound Canada Bus Lines** (**✆ 604/482-8747;** www.greyhound.ca) and **Pacific Coach Lines** (**✆ 604/662-8074;** www.pacificcoach.com) have their terminals at the Pacific Central Station, 1150 Station St. Pacific Coach Lines provides service between Vancouver and Victoria. The cost is C$82 round-trip, which includes the ferry ride. Pacific Coach Lines will pick up passengers from most downtown hotels; call **✆ 604/662-8074** to reserve.

BY CAR You'll probably be driving into Vancouver along one of two routes. **U.S. Interstate 5** from Seattle becomes **Highway 99** when you cross the border at the **US-BC Peace Arch border crossing.** The 210km (130-mile) drive from Seattle takes about 2½ hours. Expect to wait anywhere from 15 minutes to over an hour to get through Passport and Immigration Control. There's a **Tourist Info Centre,** 356 Hwy. 99, Surrey, located just north of the border crossing. On the Canadian side of the border you'll drive through the cities of White Rock, Delta, and Richmond, pass under the Fraser River through the George Massey Tunnel, and cross the Oak Street Bridge. The highway ends there and becomes Oak Street, a very busy urban thoroughfare heading toward downtown. Turn left at the first convenient major arterial (70th Ave., 57th Ave., 49th Ave., 41st Ave., 33rd Ave., 16th Ave., and 12th Ave. will all serve) and proceed until you hit the next major street, which will be Granville Street. Turn right on Granville Street. This street heads directly into downtown Vancouver on the Granville Street Bridge.

Trans-Canada Highway 1 is a limited-access freeway running all the way to Vancouver's eastern boundary, where it crosses the Second Narrows bridge to North Vancouver. When traveling on Highway 1 from the east, exit at Cassiar Street and turn left at the first light onto Hastings Street (Hwy. 7A), which is adjacent to Exhibition Park. Follow Hastings Street 6.4km (4 miles) into downtown. When coming to Vancouver from Whistler or parts north, take Exit 13 (the sign says TAYLOR WAY, BRIDGE TO VANCOUVER) and cross the Lions Gate Bridge into Vancouver's West End.

BY SHIP & FERRY The **Canada Place** cruise-ship terminal at the base of Burrard Street (✆ **604/665-9085;** www.portvancouver.com) is a city landmark. Topped by five eye-catching white Teflon sails, Canada Place Pier juts out into Burrard Inlet at the edge of the downtown financial district. **Princess Cruises, Holland America, Royal Caribbean, Crystal Cruises, Norwegian Cruise Lines, World Explorer Majesty Cruise Line,** and **Hanseatic, Seabourn,** and **Carnival** cruise lines dock at Canada Place and the nearby Ballantyne Pier to board passengers headed for Alaska via British Columbia's Inside Passage. They carry over 1.7 million passengers annually on their nearly 350 Vancouver-Alaska cruises. Public-transit buses and taxis greet new arrivals, but you can also easily walk to many major hotels.

BC Ferries (✆ **888/223-3779** in BC only, or 250/386-3431; www.bcferries.com) has three routes operating between Vancouver and Vancouver Island. See "Getting There" in chapter 16's Victoria section for more information.

Visitor Information

TOURIST OFFICES & PUBLICATIONS The **Vancouver Touristinfo Centre,** 200 Burrard St. (✆ **604/683-2000;** www.tourismvancouver.com), is your single-best travel information source about Vancouver and the North Shore. An incredibly helpful and well-trained staff provides information, maps, and brochures, and can help you with all your travel needs, including hotel, cruise-ship, ferry, bus, and train reservations. There's also a **half-price ticket office** (Tickets Tonight) for same-day shows and events in Vancouver. The Touristinfo Centre is open daily from 8:30am to 6pm.

If you're driving, a **Tourist Info Centre** is located just north of the **US-BC Peace Arch border crossing,** at 356 Hwy. 99, Surrey. Visitors arriving by ship will find a Tourist Info Centre at the **Canada Place Cruise Ship Terminal,** 999 Canada Place. Both of these are walk-in offices (no phone).

The free weekly tabloid ***Georgia Straight*** (✆ **604/730-7000;** www.straight.com), found all over the city in cafes, bookshops, and restaurants, provides up-to-date schedules of concerts, lectures, art exhibits, plays, recitals, and other happenings. The glossy city magazine ***Vancouver*** (✆ **604/877-7732**) is loaded with information and attitude. "VanMag," as it's also known, is available on newsstands and on the Web at **www.vanmag.com.** The free guide called ***Where Vancouver*** (✆ **604/736-5586;** www.where.ca) is available in many hotels and lists attractions, entertainment, upscale shopping, and fine dining. It also has good maps.

City Layout

With four different bodies of water lapping at its edges and mile after mile of shoreline, Vancouver's geography can seem a bit convoluted. That's part of the city's charm, of course, and visitors normally don't find it too hard to get their bearings. Think of the downtown peninsula as being like an upraised thumb on the mitten-shaped Vancouver mainland. Stanley Park, the West End, Yaletown, and Vancouver's business and financial center are located on the "thumb," which is bordered to the west by English Bay, to the north by Burrard Inlet, and to the south by False Creek. The mainland part of the city, the mitten, is mostly residential, with a sprinkling of businesses along main arterial streets. Both mainland and peninsula are covered by a simple rectilinear street pattern.

MAIN ARTERIES & STREETS

On the downtown peninsula, there are four key **east-west streets. Robson Street** starts at BC Place Stadium on Beatty Street, flows through the West End's more touristed shopping district, and ends at Stanley Park's Lost Lagoon on Lagoon Drive. **Georgia Street**—far more efficient for drivers than the pedestrian-oriented Robson—runs from the Georgia Viaduct on the eastern edge of downtown, through Vancouver's commercial core; it then carries on through Stanley Park and over the Lions Gate Bridge to the North Shore. Three blocks north of Georgia is **Hastings Street,** which begins in the West End, runs east through downtown, and then skirts Gastown's southern border as it runs eastward to the Trans-Canada Highway. **Davie Street** starts at Pacific Boulevard near the Cambie Street Bridge, travels through Yaletown into the West End's more residential shopping district, and ends at English Bay Beach.

Three **north-south downtown streets** will get you everywhere you want to go in and out of downtown. Two blocks east of Stanley Park is **Denman Street,** which runs from West Georgia Street at Coal Harbour to Beach Avenue at English Bay Beach. This main West End thoroughfare is where locals dine out. It's also the shortest north-south route between the two ends of the Stanley Park Seawall.

Eight blocks east of Denman is **Burrard Street,** which starts near the Canada Place Pier and runs south through downtown, crosses the Burrard Street Bridge, and then forks. One branch, still **Burrard Street,** continues south and intersects West 4th Avenue and Broadway Avenue before ending at West 16th Avenue on the borders of Shaughnessy. The other branch becomes **Cornwall Avenue,** which heads west through Kitsilano, changing its name to **Point Grey Road** and then **Northwest Marine Drive** before entering the University of British Columbia campus.

Granville Street starts near the Waterfront Station on Burrard Inlet and runs the entire length of downtown, crosses the Granville Bridge to Vancouver's West Side, and carries on south across the breadth of the city before crossing the Arthur-Laing Bridge to Vancouver International Airport.

On the mainland portion of Vancouver, the city's east-west roads are successively numbered from 1st Avenue at the downtown bridges to 77th Avenue by the banks of the Fraser River. By far, the most important east–west route is **Broadway** (formerly 9th Ave.), which starts a few blocks from the University of British Columbia (UBC) and extends across the length of the city to the border of neighboring Burnaby, where it becomes the **Lougheed Highway.** In Kitsilano, **West 4th Avenue** is also an important east-west shopping and commercial corridor. Intersecting with Broadway at various points are a number of important north-south commercial streets, each of which defines a particular neighborhood. The most significant of these streets are (from west to east) **Macdonald Street** in Kitsilano, **Granville Street, Cambie Street, Main Street,** and **Commercial Drive.**

What's West

The thing to keep in mind, when figuring out what's where in Vancouver, is that this is a city where property is king, and the word "west" has such positive connotations that folks have always gone to great lengths to associate it with their particular patch of real estate. Thus we have the West End and the West Side and West Vancouver, which improbably enough is located immediately beside North Vancouver. The West End is a high-rise residential neighborhood located on the downtown peninsula. The West Side is one whole half of Vancouver, from Ontario Street west to the University of British Columbia. (The more working-class East Side covers the mainland portion of the city, from Ontario St. east to Boundary Rd.) Very tony West Vancouver is a city to itself on the far side of Burrard Inlet. Together with its more middle-class neighbor, North Vancouver, it forms an area called the North Shore.

FINDING AN ADDRESS In many Vancouver addresses, the suite or room number precedes the building number. For instance, 100–1250 Robson St. is Suite 100 at 1250 Robson St.

In downtown Vancouver, Chinatown's **Carrall Street** is the east-west axis from which streets are numbered and designated. Westward, numbers increase progressively to Stanley Park; eastward, numbers increase approaching Commercial Drive. For example, 400 W. Pender would be 4 blocks from Carrall Street heading toward downtown; 400 E. Pender would be 4 blocks on the opposite side of Carrall Street. Similarly, the low numbers on north-south streets start on the Canada Place Pier side and increase southward in increments of 100 per block (the 600 block of Thurlow St. is 2 blocks from the 800 block) toward False Creek and Granville Island.

Off the peninsula the system works the same, but **Ontario Street** is the east-west axis. Also, all east-west roads are avenues (for example, 4th Ave.), while streets (for example, Main St.) run exclusively north-south.

The Neighborhoods in Brief

DOWNTOWN Most of Vancouver's commercial and office space is found in a square patch starting at Nelson Street and heading north to the harbor, with Homer Street and Burrard Street forming the east and west boundaries respectively. Many of the city's best hotels are also found in this area, clustering near Robson Square and the water's edge. The most interesting avenues for visitors are Georgia, Robson, and Granville streets. **Georgia Street** is where you'll find the Vancouver Art Gallery (p. 622), the Coliseum-shaped Vancouver Public Library, and the Pacific Centre regional shopping mall. **Robson Street** is Trend Central, crammed with designer boutiques, restaurants, and cafes. Rapidly gentrifying **Granville Street** is the home of bars, clubs, theaters, pubs, and restaurants (along with one or two remaining porn shops to add that touch of seedy authenticity).

THE WEST END This was Vancouver's first upscale neighborhood, settled in the 1890s by the city's budding class of merchant princes. All the necessities of life are contained within the West End's border, especially on **Denman** and **Robson streets:** great cafes, good nightclubs, bookshops, and some of the best restaurants in the city. That's part of what makes it such a sought-after address, but it's also the little things, like the street trees, the mix of high-rise condos and sturdy old Edwardians, and the way that, in the midst of such an urban setting, you now and again stumble on a view of the ocean or the mountains.

GASTOWN The oldest section of Vancouver, Gastown has a charm that shines through the souvenir shops and panhandlers. It can be seedy—druggies and winos hang out around its fringes—but it's recently become home to some great new restaurants and stores. It's worth visiting because it's the only section of the city that has the feel of an old Victorian town—the buildings stand shoulder to shoulder, and cobblestones line the streets. The current Gastown was built from scratch just a few months after an 1886 fire wiped out the entire city. It's the place to look for a new and experimental art gallery, a young fashion designer setting up shop, or a piece of beautiful, hand-carved First Nations art in one of the galleries along **Water** and **Hastings streets.**

CHINATOWN Even though much of Vancouver's huge Asian population has moved out to Richmond, Chinatown remains a kick because it hasn't become overtly touristy. The low-rise buildings in this lively community are painted in bright colors, and sidewalk markets abound. For the tens of thousands of Cantonese-speaking Canadians who live in the surrounding neighborhoods, Chinatown is simply the place they go to shop. For visitors, the fun is to simply wander, look, and taste.

YALETOWN & FALSE CREEK NORTH Vancouver's former meatpacking and warehouse district, Yaletown has been converted to an area of apartment lofts, nightclubs, restaurants, high-end furniture shops, and a fledgling multimedia biz. It's a relatively tiny area, and the main streets of interest are **Mainland, Hamilton,** and **Davie.** For visitors, it features some interesting cafes and patios, some high-end shops, and a kind of gritty urban feel. This old-time authenticity provides an essential anchor to the brand-new bevy of towers that has arisen in the past 10 years on **Pacific Boulevard** along the north edge of False Creek (an area called False Creek North). The two neighborhoods are slowly melding into one wonderful whole.

GRANVILLE ISLAND Part crafts fair, part farmers market, part artist's workshop, part mall, and part industrial site, Granville Island seems to have it all. Some 25 years ago, the federal government decided to try its hand at a bit of urban renewal, so they took this piece of industrial waterfront and redeveloped it into . . . well, it's hard to describe. One of the most enjoyable ways to experience the Granville Island atmosphere is to head down to the **Granville Island Public Market,** grab a latte (and perhaps a piece of cake or pie to boot), then wander outside to enjoy the view of the boats, the buskers, and the children endlessly chasing flocks of squawking seagulls.

KITSILANO Once Canada's Haight-Ashbury, with coffeehouses, head shops, and lots of incense and long hair, Kitsilano has become thoroughly yuppified. Nowadays, it's a fun place to wander. There are great bookstores and trendy furniture and housewares shops, lots of consignment clothing stores, snowboard shops, coffee everywhere, and lots of places to eat (every third storefront is a restaurant). The best parts of Kitsilano are the stretch of **West 4th Avenue** between Burrard and Balsam streets, and **West Broadway** between Macdonald and Alma streets. Oh, and **Kits Beach,** of course, with its fabulous heated saltwater swimming pool.

COMMERCIAL DRIVE Known as "The Drive" to Vancouverites, Commercial Drive is the 12-block section from Venables Street to East 6th Avenue. The Drive has a less glitzy, more down-to-earth, fading counterculture feel to it. It's an old immigrant neighborhood that, like everyplace else in Vancouver, has been rediscovered. The first wave of Italians left old-fashioned, delightfully tacky cafes such as **Calabria,** 1745 Commercial Dr. (✆ **604/253-7017**), and **Caffe Amici,** 1344 Commercial Dr. (✆ **604/255-2611**). More recent waves of Portuguese,

Hondurans, and Guatemalans have also left their mark. And lately, lesbians, vegans, and artists have moved in—the kind of folks who love to live in this kind of milieu; think Italian cafe next to the Marxist bookstore across from the vegan deli selling yeast-free Tuscan bread. After the relentless see-and-be-seen scene in the West End, it's nice to come out to The Drive for a bit of unpretentious fun.

SHAUGHNESSY Distances within Shaughnessy aren't conducive to a comfortable stroll, but Shaughnessy is a great place to drive or bike, especially in the spring when trees and gardens are blossoming. Designed in the 1920s as an enclave for Vancouver's budding elite, this is Vancouver's Westmount or Nob Hill. It takes a little bit of driving around to find your way in; it's an effort worth making, however, if only to see the stately homes and monstrous mansions. To find the neighborhood, look on the map for the area of curvy and convoluted streets between Cypress and Oak streets and 12th and 32nd avenues. The center of opulence is the Crescent, an elliptical street to the southwest of Granville and 16th Avenue.

RICHMOND Twenty years ago, Richmond was mostly farmland with a bit of sleepy suburb. Now it's Asia West, an agglomeration of shopping malls geared to the new—read: rich, educated, and successful—Chinese immigrant. The residential areas of the city are not worth visiting (unless tract homes are your thing), but malls like the **Aberdeen Mall** or the **Yao Han Centre** are something else. It's like getting into your car in Vancouver and getting out in Singapore.

STEVESTON Steveston, located at the southwest corner of Richmond by the mouth of the Fraser River, once existed for nothing but salmon. Fishermen set out from its port to catch the migrating sockeye, and returned to have the catch cleaned and canned. Much of that history is reprised in the **Gulf of Georgia Cannery National Historic Site,** near the wharf at Bayview Street and 4th Avenue (✆ **604/664-9009**). Since the fishery was automated long ago, Steveston's waterfront has been fixed up. There are public fish sales, charter trips up the river or out to the Fraser delta, and, above all, a laid-back, small-town atmosphere.

SOUTHEAST false creek: VANCOUVER'S NEW POST-OLYMPICS NEIGHBORHOOD

Where sawmills, foundries, and warehouses once stood, Vancouver's newest neighborhood has emerged. Southeast False Creek—which includes residential units, 4.5 hectares (11 acres) of park, a community center, and a boating center—was first used as the Vancouver Olympic Village to house athletes during the 2010 Winter Games. Located on the waterfront, overlooking downtown Vancouver and BC Place Stadium, the neighborhood is considered among the greenest in the world for its environmentally conscious architecture and building practices.

Southeast False Creek is easily accessed via the seawall that runs along the shores of False Creek, linking Granville Island, Science World, and Yaletown. The new seawall is great for biking or strolling, and it includes a timber boardwalk, granite seating blocks, and a kayak-shaped pedestrian bridge. Landscapers even put in a small island to increase the habitat available for local fish, plants, and birds. Come 2011, the historic Salt Building, built in the 1930s and used as the athletes' lounge during the Winter Games, will open to the public as a bakery, coffee shop, brewpub, and restaurant.

PUNJABI MARKET India imported. Most of the businesses on this 4-block stretch of Main Street, from 48th up to 52nd Avenue, are run by and cater to Indo-Canadians, primarily Punjabis. The area is best seen during business hours, when the fragrant scent of spices wafts out from food stalls, and the sound of Hindi pop songs blares from hidden speakers. Young brides hunt through sari shops or seek out suitable material in discount textile outlets. **Frontier Cloth House,** 6695 Main St. (✆ **604/325-4424**), specializes in richly colored silk saris, shawls, fabrics, and costume jewelry.

GETTING AROUND

By Public Transportation

The **Translink** (✆ **604/521-0400;** www.translink.bc.ca) system includes electric buses, SeaBus catamaran ferries, the Canada Line to and from Vancouver International Airport, and the magnetic-rail SkyTrain. It's an ecologically friendly, highly reliable, and inexpensive system that allows you to get everywhere, including the beaches and ski slopes. Regular service runs daily from 5am to 2am.

Schedules and routes are available at the Touristinfo Centre, at major hotels, online, and on buses. Pick up a copy of *Discover Vancouver on Transit* at one of the Touristinfo Centres (see "Visitor Information," above). This publication gives transit routes for many city neighborhoods, landmarks, and attractions, including numerous Victoria sites.

FARES Fares are based on the number of zones traveled and are the same for buses, the SeaBus, and the SkyTrain. One ticket allows you to transfer from one mode of transport to another, in any direction, within 90 minutes. A one-way, one-zone fare (everything in central Vancouver) costs C$2.50. A two-zone fare—C$3.75—is required to travel to nearby suburbs such as Richmond or North Vancouver, and a three-zone fare—C$5—is required for travel to the far-off city of Surrey. After 6:30pm on weekdays and all day on weekends and holidays, you can travel anywhere in all three zones for C$2.50. **DayPasses,** good on all public transit, cost C$9 for adults and C$7 for seniors, students, and children. They can be used for unlimited travel.

Keep in mind that drivers do not make change, so you need the exact fare, or a valid transit pass. Pay with cash or buy tickets and passes from ticket machines at stations, Touristinfo Centres, both SeaBus terminals, convenience stores, drugstores, and outlets displaying the FAREDEALER sign; most of these outlets also sell a transit map showing all routes.

BY SKYTRAIN The SkyTrain is a computerized, magnetic-rail train that services 20 stations along its 35-minute trip from downtown Vancouver east to Surrey through Burnaby and New Westminster. An extension, the Millennium line, opened in 2002. Not really of interest to most visitors, but those venturing off past Vancouver's Commercial Drive will find new stations at Broadway, Renfrew, and Rupert as well as new stations in New Westminster, towards Coquitlam.

BY SEABUS The SS *Beaver* and SS *Otter* catamaran ferries annually take more than 700,000 passengers, cyclists, and wheelchair riders on a scenic 12-minute commute between downtown's Waterfront Station and North Vancouver's Lonsdale Quay. On weekdays, a SeaBus leaves each stop every 15 minutes from 6:15am to 6:30pm, then every 30 minutes until 1am. SeaBuses depart on Saturdays every half-hour from 6:30am to 12:30pm, then every 15 minutes until 7:15pm, then every half-hour until 1am. On Sundays and holidays, runs depart every half-hour from 8:30am to 11pm. Note that the crossing is a two-zone fare on weekdays until 6:30pm.

BY BUS Some key routes to keep in mind if you're touring the city by bus: **no. 5** (Robson St.), **no. 2** (Kitsilano Beach–downtown), **no. 50** (Granville Island), **no. 35** or **135** (to the Stanley Park bus loop), **no. 240** (North Vancouver), **no. 250** (West Vancouver–Horseshoe Bay), and buses **no. 4** or **10** (UBC–Exhibition Park via Granville St. downtown). From June until the end of September, the **Vancouver Parks Board** operates a bus route through Stanley Park stopping at 14 points of interest. Call ✆ **604/257-8400** for details on the free service or contact ✆ **604/953-3333** for general public transportation information.

By Taxi

Cab fares start at C$2.85 and increase at a rate of C$1.66 per kilometer. In the downtown area, you can expect to travel for less than C$12, plus tip. The typical fare for the 13km (8-mile) drive from downtown to the airport is C$30.

Taxis are easy to find in front of major hotels, but flagging one down can be tricky. Most drivers are usually on radio calls. But thanks to built-in satellite positioning systems, if you call for a taxi, it usually arrives faster than if you go out and hail one. Call for a pickup from **Black Top** (✆ **604/731-1111**), **Yellow Cab** (✆ **604/681-1111**), or **MacLure's** (✆ **604/731-9211**).

By Car

Vancouver has nowhere near the almost-permanent gridlock of northwest cities such as Seattle, but the roads aren't exactly empty either. Fortunately, if you're just sightseeing around town or heading up to Whistler (a car is unnecessary in Whistler), public transit and cabs should see you through. However, if you're planning to visit the North Shore mountains or pursue other out-of-town activities, then by all means rent a car or bring your own. Gas is sold by the liter; speeds and distances are posted in kilometers. The speed limit in the city is 50kmph (31 mph); highway speed limits vary from 90kmph to 110kmph (56 mph–68 mph).

RENTALS Rates vary widely depending on demand and style of car. If you're over 25 and have a major credit card, you can rent a vehicle from **Avis,** 757 Hornby St. (✆ **800/879-2847** or 604/606-2868); **Budget,** 501 W. Georgia St. (✆ **800/472-3325** or 604/668-7000); **Enterprise,** 585 Smithe St. (✆ **800/736-8222** or 604/688-5500); **Hertz Canada,** 1128 Seymour St. (✆ **800/263-0600** or 604/606-4711); **National/Tilden,** 1130 W. Georgia St. (✆ **800/387-4747** or 604/685-6111); or **Thrifty,** 1015 Burrard St. or 1400 Robson St. (✆ **800/847-4389** or 604/606-1666). These firms all have counters and shuttle service at the airport as well. To rent a recreational vehicle, contact **Go West Campers,** 1577 Lloyd Ave., North Vancouver (✆ **800/661-8813** or 604/987-5288; www.go-west.com).

PARKING All major downtown hotels have guest parking, either in-house or at nearby lots. Secure valet parking at most hotels costs about C$25 per day. Public parking is found at **Robson Square** (enter at Smithe and Howe sts.), the **Pacific Centre** (Howe and Dunsmuir sts.), and **the Bay** department store (Richards St. near Dunsmuir St.). You'll also find larger **parking lots** at the intersections of Thurlow and Georgia, Thurlow and Alberni, and Robson and Seymour streets.

Street meters accept C$2 and C$1 coins. Rules are posted and strictly enforced; generally, downtown and in the West End, metered parking is in effect 7 days a week. (***Note:*** Drivers are given about a 2-min. grace period before their cars are towed away when the 3pm no-parking rule goes into effect on many major thoroughfares.) Unmetered parking on side streets is often subject to neighborhood residency requirements: Check the signs. If you park in such an area without the appropriate sticker on your windshield, you'll get ticketed and towed. If your car is towed away or you need a towing service and aren't a CAA or an AAA member, call **Unitow** (✆ **604/251-1255**) or **Busters** (✆ **604/685-8181**). If you are parking on the street, remove all valuables from your car; break-ins are not uncommon.

SPECIAL DRIVING RULES Canadian driving rules are similar to those in the United States. Stopping for pedestrians is required even outside crosswalks. Seat belts are required. Children under 5 must be in child restraints. Motorcyclists must wear helmets. It's legal to turn right at a red light after coming to a full stop unless posted otherwise. Unlike in the United States, however, daytime headlights are mandatory. Though photo radar is no longer in use in BC (the new government got elected partially on its pledge to eliminate the hated system), photo-monitored intersections are alive and well. If you're caught racing through a red light, fines start at C$100.

AUTO CLUB Members of the American Automobile Association (AAA) can get assistance from the **Canadian Automobile Association (CAA)** (✆ **604/268-5600** or for road service 604/293-2222; www.caa.ca).

By Bike

Vancouver's a great place to bike. There are plenty of places to rent a bike along Robson and Denman streets near Stanley Park. A trip around the **Stanley Park Seawall ★★★** is one of Vancouver's premier sightseeing experiences. Bike routes are designated throughout the city. Paved paths crisscross through parks and along beaches, and new routes are constantly being added. Helmets are mandatory and riding on sidewalks is illegal except on designated bike paths.

You can take your bike on the SeaBus anytime at no extra charge. All of the West Vancouver blue buses (including the bus to the Horseshoe Bay ferry terminal) can carry two bikes, first come, first served, and free of charge. In Vancouver, only a limited number of suburban routes allow bikes on the bus: bus no. 351 to White Rock, bus no. 601 to South Delta, bus no. 404 to the airport, and the 99 Express to UBC. For more information, see "Bicycling & Mountain Biking," later in this chapter.

By Miniferry

The **Aquabus** (✆ **604/689-5858;** www.theaquabus.com) docks at the south foot of Hornby Street, the Arts Club on Granville Island, Yaletown at Davie Street, Science World, and Stamp's Landing. Ferries operate daily from 6:40am to 10:30pm (9:30pm in winter) and run every 15 minutes to half-hour from 10am to 5pm (later in May and June). One-way fares are C$3 for adults and C$1.50 for seniors and children. A day pass is C$14 for adults and C$8 for seniors and children. You can take a 25-minute scenic boat ride (one complete circuit) for C$7 adults, C$4 seniors and children.

[FastFACTS] VANCOUVER

Area Codes The telephone area code for the lower mainland, including greater Vancouver and Whistler, is **604.** The area code for Vancouver Island, the Gulf Islands, and the interior of the province is **250.**

Business Hours Vancouver **banks** are open Monday through Thursday from 10am to 5pm and Friday from 10am to 6pm. Some banks, like Canadian Trust, are also open on Saturdays. **Stores** are generally open Monday through Saturday from 10am to 6pm. Last call at the city's **restaurant bars** and **cocktail lounges** is 2am.

Consulates The **U.S. Consulate** is at 1075 W. Pender St. (✆ **604/685-4311**). The **British Consulate** is at 800–1111 Melville St. (✆ **604/683-4421**). The **Australian Consulate** is at 1225–888 Dunsmuir St. (✆ **604/684-1177**). Check the Yellow Pages for other countries.

Dentist Most major hotels have a dentist on call. **Vancouver Centre Dental Clinic,** Vancouver Centre Mall, 11–650 W. Georgia St. (✆ **604/682-1601**), is another option. You must make an appointment. The clinic is open Monday through Wednesday 8:30am to 6pm, Thursday 8:30am to 7pm, and Friday 9am to 6pm.

Doctor Hotels usually have a doctor on call. **Vancouver Medical Clinics,** Bentall Centre, 1055 Dunsmuir St. (✆ **604/683-8138**), is a drop-in clinic open Monday through Friday 8am to 4:45pm. Another drop-in medical center, **Carepoint Medical Centre,** 1175 Denman St. (✆ **604/681-5338**), is open daily from 9am to 9pm.

Emergencies Dial ✆ **911** for fire, police, ambulance, and poison control.

Hospitals **St. Paul's Hospital,** 1081 Burrard St. (✆ **604/682-2344**), is the closest facility to downtown and the West End. West Side Vancouver hospitals include **Vancouver General Hospital Health and Sciences Centre,** 855 W. 12th Ave. (✆ **604/875-4111**), and **British Columbia's Children's Hospital,** 500 Oak St. (✆ **604/875-3163**). In North Vancouver, there's **Lions Gate Hospital,** 231 E. 15th St. (✆ **604/988-3131**).

Internet Access Most hotels have Wi-Fi hot spots, in-room Internet access, or guest computers or business centers with computer access. Free Internet access is available at the Vancouver **Public Library** Central Branch, 350 W. Georgia St. (✆ **604/331-3600**). **Cyber Space Internet Café,** 1741 Robson St. (✆ **604/684-6004**), and **Internet Coffee,** 1104 Davie St. (✆ **604/682-6668**), are both open until at least 1:30 a.m.

Liquor Laws The legal drinking age in British Columbia is 19. Spirits are sold only in government liquor stores, but beer and wine can be purchased from specially licensed, privately owned stores and pubs. LCBC (Liquor Control of British Columbia) stores are open Monday through Saturday from 10am to 6pm, but some are open to 11pm.

Newspapers & Magazines The two local papers are the *Vancouver Sun* (www.vancouversun.com), published Monday through Saturday, and *The Province* (www.canada.com/theprovince/index.html), published Sunday through Friday mornings. The free weekly entertainment paper, *The Georgia Straight* (www.straight.com), comes out on Thursday. *Where Vancouver,* a shopping/tourist guide, can be found in your hotel room or at Tourism Vancouver.

Pharmacies **Shopper's Drug Mart,** 1125 Davie St. (✆ **604/685-6445**), is open 24 hours. Several Safeway supermarket pharmacies are open late; the one on Robson and Denman is open until midnight.

Police For emergencies, dial ✆ **911.** Otherwise, the **Vancouver City Police**

can be reached at ✆ **604/717-3535.**

Post Office The **main post office** (✆ **800/267-1177**) is at West Georgia and Homer streets (349 W. Georgia St.). It's open Monday through Friday from 8am to 5:30pm. You'll also find post office outlets in Shopper's Drug Mart and 7-11 stores.

Restrooms Hotel lobbies are your best bet for downtown facilities. The shopping centers like Pacific Centre and Sinclair Centre, as well as the large department stores like the Bay, also have restrooms.

Safety Overall, Vancouver is a safe city and violent-crime rates are quite low. However, property crimes and crimes of opportunity (such as items being stolen from unlocked cars) occur frequently, particularly downtown. Vancouver's Downtown East Side, between Gastown and Chinatown, is a troubled neighborhood and should be avoided at night.

Taxes Hotel rooms, restaurant meals, and most consumer goods are subject to a 12% harmonized sales tax (HST) that went into effect in 2010 and takes the place of the provincial sales tax and goods and services tax. Motor fuels, books, and children's clothing are taxed at 5%.

Time Zone Vancouver is in the Pacific time zone, as are Seattle and San Francisco. Daylight saving time applies March through November.

Weather Call ✆ **604/664-9010** or 604/664-9032 for weather updates; dial ✆ **604/666-3655** for marine forecasts. Each local ski resort has its own snow report line. Cypress Ski area's is ✆ **604/419-7669;** Whistler/Blackcomb's is ✆ **604/687-7507** (in summer it also provides events listings for the village).

WHERE TO STAY

The past few years have seen a lot of activity in the Vancouver hotel business. The building boom associated with Expo '86 was followed by a flush of new hotel construction and renovation in the late '90s, right up to 2009, when three new hotels opened and many others upgraded and refurbished in anticipation of the 2010 Winter Olympic and Paralympic Games. There are lots of rooms and lots of choices, from world-class luxury hotels to moderately priced hotels and budget B&Bs and hostels.

Most of the hotels are in the downtown area or in the West End. Central Vancouver is small and easily walkable, so in both these neighborhoods you'll be close to major sights, services, and nightlife.

Remember that quoted prices don't include the 12% **harmonized sales tax** (HST).

If you arrive without a reservation or have trouble finding a room, call **Super Natural British Columbia's Discover British Columbia** hot line at ✆ **800/435-5622** or **Tourism Vancouver**'s hot line at ✆ **604/683-2000.** Both organizations will make free reservations using their large database of hotels, hostels, and B&Bs.

Bed & Breakfast Registries

If you prefer to stay in a B&B, **Canada-West Accommodations** (P.O. Box 86607, North Vancouver, BC V7L 4L2; ✆ **800/561-3223** or 604/990-6730; www.b-b.com) matches guests with establishments that best suit their needs.

Downtown & Yaletown

Downtown, which includes Vancouver's financial district, the area around Canada Place convention center and cruise-ship terminal, and the central shopping/business area around Robson Square, is buzzing during the day but pretty quiet at night. All downtown hotels are within 5 to 10 minutes' walking distance of shops, restaurants, and attractions. Hotels in this area lean more toward luxurious than modest, a state of affairs reflected in their prices. ***One thing to note:*** Downtown hotels on south Granville Street offer central location without the high price tag, but the area they're in is a major weekend hangout for clubgoers. It's not dangerous, but it can be crowded and loud. Yaletown, a hip area of reconverted warehouses, is loaded with clubs and restaurants and can also be noisy on weekends.

VERY EXPENSIVE

The Fairmont Hotel Vancouver ★★ ☺ A landmark in the city since it first opened in 1939, the Fairmont Hotel has been brought up to 21st-century standards but retains its traditional, old-fashioned elegance. The rooms are spacious, quiet, and comfortable, if not particularly dynamic in layout or finish. The bathrooms (with tub/shower combinations) look a bit dated when compared with other downtown hotels in this price range, but that's part of the charm. Courtyard suites feature a luxuriously furnished living room, separated from the bedroom by French doors. Guests can use the state-of-the-art gym with heated indoor pool. The hotel is family friendly and even has two resident dogs (former Seeing Eye dogs) that can be taken out for walks.

900 W. Georgia St., Vancouver, BC V6C 2W6. ✆ **866/540-4452** or 604/684-3131. Fax 604/662-1929. www.fairmont.com. 556 units. C$250–C$390 double. Children 18 & under stay free in parent's room. AE, DC, DISC, MC, V. Parking C$32. **Amenities:** 2 restaurants; bar; babysitting; concierge; executive-level rooms; health club; Jacuzzi; indoor pool; room service; sauna; spa. *In room:* A/C, TV w/pay movies, hair dryer, Internet (C$14/day), minibar.

Fairmont Pacific Rim ★★★ Fairmont's newest Vancouver property is a real show-stopper. Located across from the new addition to the Canada Place Convention Centre, the Pacific Rim is far more luxurious than the nearby Fairmont Waterfront (see below) and is as up-to-date, with all the amenities you could possibly want. The rooms are beautifully designed, especially the 18 suites with freestanding Japanese-style soaking tubs that look out over Burrard Inlet and the North Shore mountains. Some of the rooms have balconies with outdoor fireplaces. Finishes throughout are sumptuous and superbly crafted. Dining options include Giovane, the hotel's Italian-inspired cafe/bakery/deli, and Oru, a pan-Asian bistro. The signature Willow Stream Spa offers a complete menu or pampering treatments. It's hard not to feel a bit posh at this hotel, and the staff works hard to make you feel special.

1023 Canada Place Way, Vancouver, BC V6C 0B9. ✆ **877/900-5350** or 604/695-5300. Fax 604/695-5301. www.fairmont.com. 369 units. C$299–C$449 double; C$399–C$7,500 suite. Children 17 & under stay free in parent's room. AE, DC, DISC, MC, V. Valet parking C$35. SkyTrain: Waterfront Station. **Amenities:** Restaurant; cafe/deli; bar; babysitting; concierge; executive-level rooms; health club; Jacuzzi; 2 pools (1 indoor, 1 outdoor); room service; sauna; spa. *In room:* A/C, TV w/pay movies, DVD player, hair dryer, Internet (C$15/day), minibar.

Four Seasons Hotel ★★★ ☺ For over 30 years now, the Four Seasons has reigned as one of Vancouver's top hotels. From the outside, this huge high-rise hotel across from the Vancouver Art Gallery is rather unappealing. But the large, light-filled rooms are wonderfully comfortable with superb beds and interesting views of downtown with glimpses of the mountains. The marble bathrooms are on the small side but well designed. For a slightly larger room, reserve a deluxe corner room with wraparound floor-to-ceiling windows. One of the glories of this hotel is its health club with an enormous heated pool—half indoor, half outdoor—on a terrace. The Four Seasons kicked off the first stage of its top-to-bottom renovation in 2008 with the opening of its hip new bar/lounge/restaurant **Yew.**

791 W. Georgia St., Vancouver, BC V6C 2T4. © **800/819-5053** or 604/689-9333. Fax 604/684-4555. www.fourseasons.com/vancouver. 376 units. Nov–Apr C$250–C$330 double; May–Oct C$370–C$555 double. AE, DC, MC, V. Parking C$31. **Amenities:** 2 restaurants; bar; babysitting; concierge; exercise room; indoor & heated outdoor pool; room service; sauna. *In room:* A/C, TV/VCR, hair dryer, minibar, Wi-Fi (C$17/day).

Loden Vancouver ★★ This luxury boutique hotel opened in spring 2008 at the edge of Coal Harbour. The building is a narrow urban tower tucked in among other high-rise buildings just a couple of blocks from Burrard Inlet and the Seawall, and within easy walking distance of Robson Street and the West End. "Signature" (standard) rooms and one-bedroom suites are chic and comfortable at the same time, with a rich palette of fabrics, colors, and materials, and floor-to-ceiling windows that offer "view-corridor" views of the water and North Shore mountains. The bathrooms in every room have been designed to open up (if you want them to) into the bedroom area; it's like having your own private spa, with a soaker tub and a big glass-walled shower. **Voya,** the Loden's restaurant, is a lovely spot to dine.

1177 Melville St. (at Bute St.), Vancouver, BC V6E 0A3. © **877/225-6336** or 604/669-5060. www.theloden.com. 77 units. C$299–C$399 double; C$799 suite. AE, DC, MC, V. Parking C$25. **Amenities:** Restaurant; bar; babysitting; concierge; exercise room; Jacuzzi; room service; sauna. *In room:* A/C, TV/DVD, hair dryer, minibar, Wi-Fi (free).

Opus Hotel ★★★ If you want to stay in a hip, happening, luxury hotel, try the Opus—in 2005, *Condé Nast Traveler* voted it one of the world's top 100 hotels. It's the only hotel in Yaletown, the trendiest area for shopping, nightlife, and dining. Each room is furnished according to one of five "personalities," with its own layout, color, and flavor—the luscious room colors are eye candy if you're tired of blah hotel interiors. Bathrooms are fitted with high-design sinks, soaker tubs, or roomy showers (or both). The cool Opus Bar serves an international tapas menu, and on weekends becomes one of Yaletown's see-and-be-seen scenes. (Be forewarned: This area of Yaletown is "club central" and can be noisy until the wee hours; book a courtyard room if you don't want to be disturbed.) Opus's top-notch restaurant, **Elixir** serves modern French bistro food.

322 Davie St., Vancouver, BC V6B 5Z6. © **866/642-6787** or 604/642-6787. Fax 604/642-6780. www.opushotel.com. 96 units. May–Oct C$359–C$549 double, from C$815 suite; Nov–Apr C$229–C$429 double, from C$739 suite. Children 17 & under stay free in parent's room. AE, DC, MC, V. Valet parking C$29. **Amenities:** Restaurant; bar; bikes; concierge; small exercise room; room service. *In room:* A/C, TV w/pay movies, hair dryer, minibar, Wi-Fi (C$16/day).

Pan Pacific Vancouver ★★★ This 23-story luxury hotel atop Canada Place is a key landmark on the Vancouver waterfront. Despite its size, the hotel excels in comfort and service, and it provides spectacular views of the North Shore mountains, Burrard Inlet, and cruise ships arriving and departing from the terminal below. The rooms are spacious and comfortable, with contemporary furnishings and a soothing color palette. Bathrooms are large and luxurious. Guests have use of a heated outdoor pool and Jacuzzi overlooking the harbor. Spa Utopia offers a full array of pampering treatments. Café Pacifica puts on one of the best breakfast buffets in Vancouver.

300-999 Canada Place, Vancouver, BC V6C 3B5. ✆ **877/324-4856** in the U.S. or 604/662-8111. Fax 604/685-8690. www.panpacific.com. 504 units. C$240–C$540 double; C$450-C$7,500 suite. AE, DC, DISC, MC, V. Valet parking C$30. **Amenities:** 2 restaurants; bar; babysitting; concierge; health club; Jacuzzi; outdoor heated pool; room service; sauna; spa. *In room:* A/C, TV w/pay movies, hair dryer, Internet (C$15/day), minibar.

Shangri-La Hotel ★★★ For all-around luxury and excellent, unobtrusive service, the new Shangri-La, opened in 2009, can't be beat; its only rival is the Four Seasons (reviewed above). This is the first North American property for Shangri-La, and it's an impressive one, with the hotel occupying the lower 15 floors of Vancouver's tallest residential tower. Attention to detail is what sets the Shangri-La apart; everything is geared to run smoothly. The rooms are large and furnished with a quiet good taste that combines contemporary furnishings with Asian accents; over half of them have balconies (the smaller balconies are more like a glass enclosure with an open window). Bathrooms, finished in white marble, are sumptuous. Chi, the hotel's spa, offers a unique menu of treatments utilizing Asian and Tibetan techniques. And to cap it all off, the hotel's restaurant, **MARKET by Jean-Georges** (as in Vongerichten), is one of Vancouver's hottest new haute spots.

1128 W. Georgia St., Vancouver, BC V6E 0A8. ✆ **604/689-1120**. Fax 604/689-1195. www.shangri-la.com. 119 units. C$345–C$395 double. AE, DC, DISC, MC, V. Valet parking C$30. **Amenities:** Restaurant; lounge; babysitting; concierge; health club; Jacuzzi; outdoor heated pool; room service; sauna; spa. *In room:* A/C, TV w/pay movies, hair dryer, minibar, Wi-Fi (free).

Wedgewood Hotel ★★★ If you're searching for a romantic, sophisticated hotel with superb service, spacious rooms, fine detailing, a good restaurant, a full-service spa, and a central downtown location, you can't do any better than the Wedgewood. One feature that makes the award-winning Wedgewood so distinctive is that it's independently owned (by Greek-born Eleni Skalbania), and the owner's elegant personal touch is evident throughout. All 83 units are spacious and have balconies (the best views are those facing the Vancouver Art Gallery and Law Court). Furnishings and antiques are of the highest quality, and the marble-clad bathrooms with deep soaker tubs and separate walk-in Roman showers are simply the best. Bacchus, the cozy hotel restaurant, serves a fairly traditional menu of fish, pasta, and meat. In 2007, *Travel + Leisure* ranked the Wedgewood the best hotel in Vancouver. It has since become a member of the Relais & Châteaux group.

845 Hornby St., Vancouver, BC V6Z 1V1. ✆ **800/663-0666** or 604/689-7777. Fax 604/608-5349. www.wedgewoodhotel.com. 83 units. C$298–C$600 double; C$348-C$1,500 suite. AE, DC, MC, V. Valet parking C$20. **Amenities:** Restaurant; concierge; executive-level rooms; small exercise room; room service; spa; Wi-Fi (free) in common areas. *In room:* A/C, TV/VCR w/pay movies, CD player, hair dryer, minibar.

EXPENSIVE

St. Regis Hotel ★ Many hotels in downtown Vancouver occupy newer buildings, so it's a pleasure to find one—and especially one as nice as the St. Regis—in a so-called "heritage building," dating from 1913. The owners have transformed it into a unique boutique hotel that's handsome inside and out, filled with contemporary art, and wired for up-to-the-minute Wi-Fi. The redesigned rooms and suites are a bit small but have a savvy, comfy, contemporary look to them. Breakfast is included in the room rate, and there's a brewpub on the premises. You might think this part of downtown close to Gastown is a little "off," but it's convenient to everything in the commercial core of the city and is the only Vancouver hotel to offer a full breakfast with your room. The new Canada Line SkyTrain from the airport stops 1 block away at Granville and Dunsmuir. The only other heritage hotel in Vancouver to have this find of updated flair is the Moda (below).

602 Dunsmuir St., Vancouver, BC V6B 1Y6. ✆ **800/770-7929** or 604/681-1135. Fax 604/683-1126. www.stregishotel.com. 65 units. C$214–C$288 double; C$275–C$509 suite. Rates include breakfast. AE, MC, V. **Amenities:** Restaurant; bar/pub; Starbucks; concierge; executive-level rooms; access to nearby health club. *In room:* A/C, TV w/pay movies, hair dryer, minibar (in suites), MP3 docking station, Wi-Fi (free).

MODERATE

Georgian Court Hotel ★ This modern, 14-story brick hotel is extremely well located, just a block or two from BC Place Stadium, GM Place Stadium, the Queen Elizabeth Theatre, the Playhouse, and the Vancouver Public Library. You can walk to Robson Square in about 10 minutes. The guest rooms are relatively large, nicely decorated, and have good-size bathrooms. And while the big-time celebs are usually whisked off to the glamorous top hotels, their entourages often stay at the Georgian Court, as it provides all the amenities and business-friendly extras such as two phones in every room, brightly lit desks, and complimentary high-speed Internet access—a service that other hotels almost always charge for.

773 Beatty St., Vancouver, BC V6B 2M4. ✆ **800/663-1155** or 604/682-5555. Fax 604/682-8830. www.georgiancourt.com. 180 units. C$159–C$279 double. AE, DC, MC, V. Parking C$16. **Amenities:** Restaurant; bar; babysitting; exercise room; Jacuzzi; room service; sauna. *In room:* A/C, TV, fridge, hair dryer, Internet (free).

Moda Hotel ★ Situated downtown, across from the Orpheum Theatre and close to the clubs on Granville Street, the Moda offers lots of style and excellent value. Rooms and suites in this 1908 heritage building feature a sleek, tailored, European look with dramatic colors, luxury beds and linens, flat-screen TVs, nice tiled bathrooms with a tub/shower, and double-glazed windows to dampen the traffic noise. The only thing the refurbishers couldn't change was the slant in some of the old floors. Anyone with a bit of adventure and a taste for something out of the ordinary will enjoy a stay here. Suites offer an extra half-bathroom, corner locations with more light, and upgraded amenities. Other pluses include the on-site wine bar **Uva** and a very good Italian restaurant called **Cibo.**

900 Seymour St., Vancouver, BC V6B 3L9. ✆ **877/683-5522** or 604/683-4251. Fax 604/683-0611. www.modahotel.ca. 57 units. C$99–C$229 double; C$219–C$289 suite. AE, DC, MC, V. **Amenities:** 2 restaurants; bar. *In room:* A/C, TV, Internet (free).

INEXPENSIVE

Hostelling International Vancouver Downtown Hostel Located in a converted nunnery, this modern, curfew-free hostel offers a convenient base of operations for exploring downtown. The beach is a few blocks south; downtown is a 10-minute walk north. Most beds are in quad dorms, with a limited number of doubles and triples available. Except for two rooms with private bathrooms, all bathroom facilities are shared. Rooms and facilities are accessible for travelers with disabilities. There are common cooking facilities, as well as a rooftop patio and game room. The hostel is extremely busy in the summertime, so book ahead. Many organized activities such as ski packages and tours can be booked at the hostel. The hostel also provides a free shuttle service to the bus/train station and Jericho Beach.

1114 Burnaby St. (at Thurlow St.), Vancouver, BC V6E 1P1. ✆ **888/203-4302** or 604/684-4565. Fax 604/684-4540. www.hihostels.ca. 68 units (44 4-person shared dorm rooms, 24 double or triple private rooms). C$29–C$32 dorm (IYHA members), C$33–C$36 dorm (nonmembers); C$80–C$90 double (members), C$88–C$98 double (nonmembers). Rates include full breakfast. Annual adult membership C$35. MC, V. Limited free parking. **Amenities:** Bikes. *In room:* No phone, Wi-Fi (free).

The Kingston Hotel An affordable downtown hotel is a rarity for Vancouver, but if you can do without the frills, the Kingston offers a clean, safe, inexpensive place to sleep and a complimentary continental breakfast to start your day. You won't find a better deal anywhere, and the premises have far more character than you'll find in a cookie-cutter motel. The Kingston is a Vancouver version of the kind of small budget B&B hotels found all over Europe. Just 13 of the 52 rooms have private bathrooms and TVs; the rest have hand basins and shared showers and toilets on each floor. The premises are well kept, and the location is central, so you can walk everywhere. The staff is friendly and helpful, and if you're just looking for a place to sleep and stow your bags, you'll be glad you found this place.

757 Richards St., Vancouver, BC V6B 3A6. ✆ **888/713-3304** or 604/684-9024. Fax 604/684-9917. www.kingstonhotelvancouver.com. 52 units (13 w/private bathroom). C$85–C$95 double w/shared bathroom; C$105–C$175 double w/private bathroom. Additional adult C$20. Rates include continental breakfast. AE, MC, V. Parking C$20 across the street. **Amenities:** Restaurant; bar; Internet (free); sauna. *In room:* TV (in units w/private bathrooms), Wi-Fi (free).

YWCA Hotel/Residence ★ This attractive 12-story residence next door to the Georgian Court Hotel is an excellent choice for travelers on limited budgets. Bedrooms are simply furnished; some have TVs. Quite a few reasonably priced restaurants and a number of grocery stores are nearby. Three communal kitchens are available for guests' use, and all rooms have mini-fridges. The Y has three TV lounges and free access to the best gym in town, the nearby coed YWCA Fitness Centre.

733 Beatty St., Vancouver, BC V6B 2M4. ✆ **800/663-1424** or 604/895-5830. Fax 604/681-2550. www.ywcahotel.com. 155 units (53 w/private bathroom). C$70–C$86 double w/shared bathroom; C$84–C$128 double w/private bathroom. Weeklong discounts available. AE, MC, V. Parking C$14. **Amenities:** Access to YWCA facility. *In room:* A/C, TV, fridge, hair dryer, Wi-Fi (C$10/day).

The West End

The West End is green, leafy, and residential, a neighborhood of high-rise apartment houses, beautifully landscaped streets, and close proximity to Coal Harbor, Stanley Park, and the best beaches. When downtown gets quiet at night, the West End starts hopping. There are dozens of restaurants, cafes, and bars along Robson and Denman streets.

EXPENSIVE

The Listel Hotel ★★ What makes the Listel unique is its artwork. Hallways and suites on the top two Gallery floors are decorated with original pieces from the Buschlen Mowatt Gallery or, on the Museum floor, with First Nations artifacts from the UBC Anthropology Museum (see p. 653). Also unique is the fact that the Listel is the first Vancouver hotel to really go "green" with the use of solar power-generating panels. The hotel is luxurious without being flashy, and all the rooms and bathrooms feature top-quality bedding and handsome furnishings—though some bathrooms are larger than others, with separate soaker tub and shower. The roomy upper-floor suites facing Robson Street, with glimpses of the harbor and the mountains beyond, are the best bets. Rooms at the back are quieter but face the alley and nearby apartment buildings. In the evenings, you can hear live jazz at **O'Doul's,** the hotel's restaurant and bar. Downtown or Stanley Park is a 10-minute walk away.

1300 Robson St., Vancouver, BC V6E 1C5. ✆ **800/663-5491** or 604/684-8461. Fax 604/684-7092. www.thelistelhotel.com. 129 units. C$229–C$289 double; C$400–C$600 suite. AE, DC, DISC, MC, V. Parking C$26. **Amenities:** Restaurant; bar; concierge; executive-level rooms; exercise room; Jacuzzi; room service. *In room:* A/C, TV w/pay movies, hair dryer, minibar, Wi-Fi (free).

Westin Bayshore Resort & Marina ★★★ ☺ This is Vancouver's only resort hotel with its own marina, and the views from all but a handful of its rooms are stunning. The Bayshore overlooks Coal Harbour and Stanley Park on one side, and Burrard Inlet and the city on the other. The hotel is in two buildings, the original low-rise from 1961 and a newer tower, with a giant pool, restaurant, and conference center between them. All the rooms received a makeover in 2009 with comfortable, contemporary West Coast decor and floor-to-ceiling windows that open wide. In the newer tower, the rooms are a bit larger and have narrow balconies. The bathrooms in both buildings are nicely finished but fairly small. A new spa opened in October 2009. Children receive their own welcome package and love the pools.

1601 Bayshore Dr., Vancouver, BC V6G 2V4. ✆ **800/937-8461** or 604/682-3377. Fax 604/687-3102. www.westinbayshore.com. 510 units. C$460 double. Children 17 & under stay free in parent's room. AE, DC, MC, V. Self-parking C$31; valet parking C$35. **Amenities:** 2 restaurants; bar; Starbucks; babysitting; concierge; health club; Jacuzzi; 2 pools (1 indoor, 1 outdoor); room service; sauna; spa. *In room:* A/C, TV w/pay movies, hair dryer, minibar, Wi-Fi (C$15/day).

MODERATE

Barclay House Bed & Breakfast ★ The Barclay House is located on one of the West End's quiet maple-lined streets a block from historic Barclay Square. Built in 1904, this beautiful house is furnished in Victorian style; a number of the pieces are family heirlooms. The penthouse offers skylights, a fireplace, and a claw-foot tub; the south room contains a queen-size brass bed and an elegant sitting room. The parlors and dining rooms are perfect for lounging on a rainy afternoon or sipping a glass of complimentary sherry before dinner. On a summer day, the front porch, with its wooden Adirondack chairs, is a comfy spot to read and relax.

1351 Barclay St., Vancouver, BC V6E 1H6. ✆ **800/971-1351** or 604/605-1351. Fax 604/605-1382. www.barclayhouse.com. 5 units. C$155–C$295 double. Rates include breakfast. AE, MC, V. Free parking. **Amenities:** Access to nearby fitness center. *In room:* TV/VCR w/pay movies, movie library, CD player, fridge, hair dryer, Wi-Fi (free).

Blue Horizon This 31-story high-rise built in the 1960s has a great location on Robson Street, just a block from the trendier Pacific Palisades and the tonier Listel Vancouver (see above). It's cheaper than those places and has views that are just as good, if not better, but it lacks their charm and feels a bit like a high-rise motel. The rooms are fairly spacious, with a contemporary look, and every room is on a corner with wraparound windows and a small balcony; superior rooms on floors 15 to 30 offer the best views. The decor could use some updating, but overall, these rooms are a good deal for this location. The hotel uses energy-efficient lighting, low-flow showerheads, and recycling bins, and the entire hotel is nonsmoking.

1225 Robson St., Vancouver, BC V6E 1C3. ✆ **800/663-1333** or 604/688-1411. Fax 604/688-4461. www.bluehorizonhotel.com. 214 units. C$99–C$219 double; C$109–C$229 superior double; C$189–C$329 suite. Children 15 & under stay free in parent's room. AE, DC, MC, V. Parking C$14. **Amenities:** Restaurant; concierge; exercise room; Jacuzzi; indoor pool; sauna. *In room:* A/C, TV w/pay movies, fridge, hair dryer, Internet (free), minibar.

Coast Plaza Hotel & Suites ★ Built originally as an apartment building, this 35-story hotel atop Denman Place Mall attracts a wide variety of guests, from business travelers and tour groups to film and TV actors. They come for the large rooms, the affordable one- and two-bedroom suites, and great views of English Bay. The two-bedroom corner suites are bigger than most West End apartments and afford spectacular panoramas. The spacious one-bedroom suites and standard rooms feature floor-to-ceiling windows and balconies; about half the units have full kitchens, and all are nonsmoking. Furnishings are plain and comfortable. While the hotel has a good-size heated pool, it's in the not-particularly appealing basement.

1763 Comox St., Vancouver, BC V6G 1P6. ✆ **800/663-1144** or 604/688-7711. Fax 604/688-5934. www.coasthotels.com. 269 units. C$140–C$259 double; C$170–C$299 suite. AE, DC, DISC, MC, V. Self-parking C$23; valet parking C$31. **Amenities:** Restaurant; bar; babysitting; concierge; access to health club in mall below; Jacuzzi; indoor pool; room service; sauna. *In room:* A/C, TV, fridge, hair dryer, Internet (free).

Empire Landmark Originally a Sheraton, this 42-story tower hotel is the tallest building in the West End. Here's the thing about the Empire Landmark: It's a big hotel that handles a lot of tour groups and conferences, so it feels pretty anonymous. The standardized rooms, though perfectly fine, are decorated in an old-fashioned style that seems to mask instead of emphasize the spectacular views, which you can savor from a small balcony. For the best panoramas, ask for a room on floor 28 or higher. The top floor features a revolving restaurant-lounge where you can have a drink with all of Vancouver spread out before you. Also in this hotel's favor is the location, right on Robson Street, close to English Bay and Stanley Park.

1400 Robson St. (btw. Broughton & Nicola sts.), Vancouver, BC V6G 1B9. ✆ **800/830-6144** or 604/687-0511. Fax 604/687-7267. www.empirelandmarkhotel.com. 357 units. C$190–C$230 double. AE, DC, DISC, MC, V. Parking C$10/day. **Amenities:** Restaurant; bar; concierge. *In room:* A/C, TV, fridge, Wi-Fi (C$14/day).

Sunset Inn & Suites ★ ☺ Just a couple of blocks from English Bay on the edge of the residential West End, the Sunset Inn offers roomy studios or one-bedroom apartments with balconies and fully equipped kitchens. Like many other hotels in this part of town, the Sunset Inn started life as an apartment building, meaning the rooms are larger than at your average hotel. Request an upper floor since the views are better but the price remains the same. For those traveling with children, the one-bedroom suites have a separate bedroom and a pullout couch in the living room. All of the rooms were refurbished in 2008. The beds are comfy, the staff is helpful and friendly, and the location is great for this price.

1111 Burnaby St., Vancouver, BC V6E 1P4. ✆ **800/786-1997** or 604/688-2474. Fax 604/669-3340. www.sunsetinn.com. 50 units. C$159-C$229 studio, C$189-C$475 double. Additional person C$10. Children 9 & under stay free in parent's room. Rates include continental breakfast. Weekly rates available. AE, DC, MC, V. Free parking. **Amenities:** Small exercise room. *In room:* TV, kitchen, Wi-Fi (free).

West End Guest House ★ A heritage home built in 1906, the West End Guest House is a handsome example of what the neighborhood looked like before concrete towers and condos replaced the original Edwardian homes in the early 1950s. Decorated with early-20th-century antiques and a serious collection of vintage photographs of Vancouver taken by the original owners, this gay-friendly B&B is a calm, charming respite from the hustle and bustle of the West End. The seven guest rooms feature feather mattresses and down duvets; the Grand Queen Suite, an attic-level bedroom with a brass bed, fireplace, sitting area, claw-foot bathtub, and skylights, is the best and most spacious room. Owner Evan Penner and his partner, Ron Cadurette, pamper their guests with a scrumptious breakfast and serve iced tea and sherry in the afternoon.

1362 Haro St., Vancouver, BC V6E 1G2. ✆ **888/546-3327** or 604/681-2889. Fax 604/688-8812. www.westendguesthouse.com. 7 units. Oct–May C$90–C$195 double; June–Sept C$200–C$275 double. Rates include full breakfast. AE, DISC, MC, V. Free off-street parking. **Amenities:** Bikes. *In room:* TV/DVD player, hair dryer, Wi-Fi (free).

INEXPENSIVE

Buchan Hotel Built in 1926, this three-story building is tucked away on a quiet residential street in the West End, 2 blocks from Stanley Park and Denman Street. Like the Kingston (see above) downtown, this is a small European-style budget hotel that doesn't bother with frills or charming decor; unlike the Kingston, it isn't a B&B, so don't expect the second B. The standard rooms are quite plain; be prepared for cramped quarters and tiny bathrooms, half of which are shared. The best rooms are the executive rooms: four nicely furnished front-corner rooms with private bathrooms. The hotel also has in-house bike and ski storage, and a reading lounge.

1906 Haro St., Vancouver, BC V6G 1H7. ✆ **800/668-6654** or 604/685-5354. Fax 604/685-5367. www.buchanhotel.com. 60 units (30 w/private bathroom). C$50–C$86 double w/shared bathroom; C$70–C$120 double w/private bathroom; C$110–C$155 executive room. Children 12 & under stay free in parent's room. Weekly rates available. AE, DC, MC, V. Limited free street parking available. **Amenities:** Lounge. *In room:* TV, no phone.

The West Side

Right across False Creek from downtown and the West End is Vancouver's West Side. If your agenda includes a Granville Island shopping spree, exploration of the laid-back Kitsilano neighborhood, time at Kits Beach, visiting the fabulous Museum of Anthropology and famed gardens on the University of British Columbia campus, and strolls through the sunken garden at Queen Elizabeth Park, or if you require close proximity to the airport without staying in an "airport hotel," you'll find cozy B&Bs and hotels in this area of Vancouver.

EXPENSIVE

Granville Island Hotel ★ One of Vancouver's best-kept secrets, this hotel is tucked away on the edge of Granville Island in a unique waterfront setting, a short stroll from theaters, galleries, and the fabulous Granville Island public market (see p. 652). Rooms in the original wing are definitely fancier, so book these if you can, but the new wing is fine, too. Rooms are fairly spacious with traditional, unsurprising decor and large bathrooms with soaker tubs; some units have balconies and great views over False Creek. If you don't have a car, the only potential drawback to a stay here is the location. During the daytime, when the False Creek ferries are running, it's a quick ferry ride to Yaletown or the West End. After 10pm, however, you're looking at a C$15 to C$20 cab ride or an hour walk. The Island after dark is reasonably happening, and the hotel's waterside restaurant and brewpub are good-weather hang-out spots with outdoor seating.

1253 Johnston St., Vancouver, BC V6H 3R9. ✆ **800/663-1840** or 604/683-7373. Fax 604/683-3061. www.granvilleislandhotel.com. 85 units. Oct–Apr C$170 double, C$399 penthouse; May–Sept C$250 double, C$499 penthouse. AE, DC, DISC, MC, V. Parking C$12. **Amenities:** Restaurant; brewpub; babysitting; concierge; small fitness room; Jacuzzi; room service; sauna; access to nearby tennis courts. *In room:* A/C, TV w/pay movies, hair dryer, minibar, Wi-Fi (free).

MODERATE

Chocolate Lily ★ If you're looking for a self-catering place, this attractive, Craftsman-style house, just minutes from all the splash of Kits Beach and the dash of Kits shopping, is a real find. You don't need a car; public transportation can get you downtown in minutes. The two self-contained suites have private entrances and patios, and are both small but carefully designed (a sofa in each can be made into an extra bed) and furnished in a comfortable Northwest style. Both units have kitchenettes; the rear unit has only a shower. Breakfast is not served, but you're given a basket of fruit and baked goods upon arrival. In high season, a 3-day minimum stay is required; special rates apply for longer stays.

1353 Maple St., Vancouver, BC V6J 3S1. ✆ **866/903-9363** or 604/731-9363. www.chocolatelily.com. 2 suites. C$105–C$185 suite. MC, V. Free parking. *In room:* TV, DVD player (in 1 unit), Internet (free), kitchenette.

INEXPENSIVE

Hostelling International Vancouver Jericho Beach Hostel Located in a former military barracks, this hostel (open May–Sept only) is surrounded by an expansive lawn adjacent to Jericho Beach. Individuals, families with children over age 5, and groups are welcome. The 10 private rooms can accommodate up to six people each. These particular accommodations go fast, so if you want one, call far in advance. The dormitory-style arrangements are well maintained and supervised. Linens are provided. Basic, inexpensive food is served in the cafe, or you can cook for yourself in the shared kitchen. The hostel's program director operates tours and activities.

1515 Discovery St., Vancouver, BC V6R 4K5. ✆ **888/203-4303** or 604/224-3208. Fax 604/224-4852. www.hihostels.ca. 286 beds in 14 dorms; 10 private family units (w/out private bathroom). C$22–C$24 dorm (IYHA members), C$26–C$28 dorm (nonmembers); C$63–C$74 private room (members), C$71–C$82 private room (nonmembers). MC, V. Parking C$5. Bus: 4. Children 4 & under not allowed. **Amenities:** Cafe; bikes. *In room:* No phone.

The University of British Columbia Conference Centre ★ The University of British Columbia Conference Centre is in a pretty, forested setting on the tip of Point Grey, convenient to Kitsilano and the University itself. If you don't have a car, it's a half-hour bus ride from downtown. Although the on-campus accommodations are actually student dorms most of the year, rooms are usually available. The rooms are nice, but don't expect luxury. The 17-story Walter Gage Residence offers comfortable accommodations, many on the upper floors with sweeping views of the city and ocean. One-bedroom suites come equipped with private bathrooms, kitchenettes, TVs, and phones. Each studio has a twin bed; each one-bedroom features a queen-size bed; a six-bed Towers room—a particularly good deal for families—features one double bed and five twin beds. The West Coast Suites, renovated in 2007, are the most appealing and have a very reasonable price.

5961 Student Union Blvd., Vancouver, BC V6T 2C9. ✆ **888/822-1030** or 604/822-1000. Fax 604/822-1001. www.ubcconferences.com. 1,500 units. Walter Gage Residence units available May 10 to Aug 26; Pacific Spirit Hostel units available May 15 to Aug 15; West Coast Suites & Marine Drive Residence units available year-round. Walter Gage Residences & Marine Drive Residences C$39–C$53 single w/shared bathroom, C$99–C$129 studio, C$119–C$159 suite; Pacific Spirit Hostel C$33 single, C$66 double; West Coast Suites C$159–C$199 suite. AE, MC, V. Parking C$7. Bus: 4, 17, 44, or 99. **Amenities** (on campus): Restaurant; cafeteria; pub; fitness center; access to campus Olympic-size swimming pool; sauna (C$5/person); tennis courts. *In room:* TV, hair dryer, Internet (free).

The North Shore

The North Shore cities of North and West Vancouver are pleasant and lush; staying here offers easy access to the North Shore mountains and their attractions, including the Capilano Suspension Bridge and the ski slopes on Mount Seymour, Grouse Mountain, and Cypress Bowl. The disadvantage is that there is little or no nightlife, and if you want to take your car into Vancouver, there are only two bridges, and during rush hours they're painfully slow.

Pinnacle Hotel at the Pier Directly across the Burrard Inlet from the Canada Place Pier, this hotel opened in 2010 and offers comfortable rooms with great skyline views of Vancouver, modern bathrooms with glass dividing walls so you can savor the view while you soak in the tub, an indoor pool and state-of-the-art fitness center, a good restaurant, and a convenient location next to the market at Lonsdale Quay and close to several North Shore restaurants.

138 Victory Ship Way, North Vancouver V7M 3K7. ✆ **877/986-7437** or 604/986-7437. www.pinnaclehotelatthepier.com. 106 units. C$169–C$199 double. AE, DC, DISC, MC, V. Parking C$7; free on weekends and holidays. SeaBus: Lonsdale Quay. **Amenities:** Restaurant; exercise room; concierge; room service. *In room:* A/C, TV, hair dryer, iron/ironing board, Wi-Fi (free).

WHERE TO DINE

Foodies, take note: Vancouver is one of North America's top dining cities, right up there with New York, San Francisco, and any other food capital you can think of. Vancouverites dine out more frequently than residents of any other Canadian city, and outstanding meals are available in all price ranges and in many different cuisines, with a preponderance of informal Chinese, Japanese, Vietnamese, and Thai restaurants. Sushi lovers are in heaven here because superlative sushi is available all over for a fraction of what you'd pay south of the Canadian border. There are also top restaurants that for preparation, taste, and presentation of Pacific Northwest cuisine can compete with the best anywhere.

"Buy local, eat seasonal" is the mantra of all the best restaurateurs in Vancouver, and they take justifiable pride in the bounty of local produce, game, and seafood available to them. In addition, British Columbian wines are winning international acclaim to rival vintages from California, Australia, France, and Germany. The big wine-producing areas are in the Okanagan Valley (in southern British Columbia's dry interior) and on southern Vancouver Island.

The 12% harmonized sales tax (HST) is added to the cost of restaurant meals in British Columbia. Lunch is typically served from noon to 2pm; Vancouverites begin dining around 6:30pm, later in summer. Reservations are recommended at most restaurants and are essential at the city's top tables.

Downtown & Yaletown

VERY EXPENSIVE

C ★★★ SEAFOOD/PACIFIC NORTHWEST Since opening in 1997, the popularity of this award-winning trendsetter hasn't flagged. The dining room is a cool white space with painted steel and lots of glass; the waterside location on False Creek is sublime (book an outside table if the weather is fine). Ingredients make all the difference here: The chef and his highly knowledgeable staff can tell you not only where every product comes from, but also the name of the boat or farm. Expect exquisite surprises and imaginative preparations: For appetizers, sample the fresh BC oysters with tongue-tingling sauces, duck jerky, or chilled fennel consommé. Mains are artfully created and might include twice-cooked sablefish with porcini fondue or crispy trout with black truffle puree. Give chef Robert Clark a chance to show off, and order a 6-course tasting menu as you watch the sun set over the marina. Excellent wine pairings, too.

1600 Howe St. ✆ **604/681-1164.** www.crestaurant.com. Reservations recommended. Main courses C$36–C$39; tasting menu C$98; early (5–6pm) fixed-price menu C$45. AE, DC, MC, V. May to Labour Day Mon–Fri 11:30am–2:30pm; year-round daily 5:30–11pm. Valet parking C$10. Bus: 1 or 2.

EXPENSIVE

Blue Water Cafe and Raw Bar ★★★ SEAFOOD If you had to describe this busy, buzzy place in one word, it would be *fresh,* as only the best from sustainable and wild fisheries make it onto the menu. In fact, Blue Water won the top prize for "Best Seafood" at the 2008, 2009, and 2010 *Vancouver* magazine restaurant awards (in 2010 it also won "Restaurant of the Year" and "Best Chef"). If you love sushi and sashimi, the raw bar under the direction of Yoshihio Tabo offers up some of the city's finest. On the other side of the room, Frank Pabst, the restaurant's executive chef, creates his dishes in a large open kitchen. For starters, try a medley of local oysters with various toppings, a sushi platter, or smoked sockeye salmon velouté. Main courses depend on whatever is in season: It might be spring salmon, halibut, Arctic char, tuna, white sturgeon, or BC sablefish. The desserts are fabulous. A masterful wine list and an experienced sommelier assure fine wine pairings. Blue Water now offers a wonderful assortment of fixed-price menus.

1095 Hamilton St. (at Helmcken St.). ✆ **604/688-8078.** www.bluewatercafe.net. Reservations recommended. Main courses C$28–C$45; fixed-price menus C$55–C$109. AE, DC, MC, V. Daily 5–11pm. Valet parking C$10. Bus: 2.

Chambar Belgian Restaurant ★★ 🎁 BELGIAN One of Vancouver's favorite restaurants, Chambar occupies an intriguing space in a kind of no man's land on lower Beatty Street between Yaletown and Gastown. Michelin-trained chef Nico Scheuerman and his wife, Karri, have worked hard to make the place a success, and plenty of plaudits have come their way. The menu features small and large plates. Smaller choices typically include mussels cooked in white wine with bacon and cream (or with fresh tomatoes), beef or tuna carpaccio, or coquilles St. Jacques. Main dishes feature *tagine* of braised lamb shank with honey, and roasted sablefish with chickpea and zucchini salad. For dessert, try the Belgian chocolate mousse or the mocha soufflé. Chambar specializes in Belgian beers, with some 25 varieties in bottles and on tap.

562 Beatty St. ✆ **604/879-7119.** www.chambar.com. Reservations recommended. Small plates C$11–C$18; main courses C$29–C$30; 3-course set menu C$60. AE, MC, V. Daily 6pm–midnight. Bus: 5 or 17.

Coast ★★★ SEAFOOD/INTERNATIONAL This dashing restaurant moved to a new downtown location in 2009 and re-established itself as a culinary and people-watching spot of note. The concept at Coast is to offer an extensive variety of fresh and non-endangered seafood from coasts around the world. The dining room is a handsomely designed affair with a central oyster bar and seating at various levels, including a second floor that allows you to look out over the busy scene below. Coast excels at just about everything it does, and the price for top-quality seafood is actually quite reasonable. The signature seafood platter, for example, comes with BC cod, wild sea tiger prawns, sockeye salmon, Qualicum scallops, seasonal vegetables, and potato gnocchi, and costs only C$29 per person (it would cost twice that at other top seafood restaurants). Try the super sushi (the innovative sushi chef has come up with a delectable fish-and-chips hand roll), or any of the fresh fish or shellfish offerings. Service here is deft, friendly, and always on the mark. Coast also has a takeout section where you can get a wonderful lunch for under C$10.

1054 Alberni St. ✆ **604/685-5010.** www.coastrestaurant.ca. Reservations recommended. Main courses C$17–C$39. AE, DC, MC, V. Mon–Thurs 11:30am–1am; Fri 11:30am–2am; Sat 4:30pm–2am; Sun 4:30pm–1am. Bus: 1 or 22.

Il Giardino di Umberto Ristorante ★★ ITALIAN Restaurant magnate Umberto Menghi started this small restaurant, tucked away in a yellow heritage house at the bottom of Hornby Street, about 3 decades ago. It still serves some of the best Italian fare, and has one of the prettiest garden patios in town. A larger restaurant now adjoins the original house, opening up into a bright, spacious dining room that re-creates the ambience of an Italian villa. The menu leans toward Tuscany, with dishes that emphasize pasta and game. Entrees usually include classics such as *osso buco* with saffron risotto, and that Roman favorite, spaghetti carbonara. A daily list of specials makes the most of seasonal fresh ingredients, often offering outstanding seafood dishes. The wine list is comprehensive and well chosen.

1382 Hornby St. (btw. Pacific & Drake sts). ✆ **604/669-2422.** Fax 604/669-9723. www.umberto.com. Reservations recommended. Main courses C$18–C$35. AE, DC, MC, V. Mon–Fri noon–3:30pm; daily 5:30–11pm. Closed holidays. Bus: 1 or 22.

MARKET by Jean-Georges ★★★ FUSION/INTERNATIONAL Jean-Georges Vongerichten is one of the world's most famous chefs, and his first restaurant in Vancouver is a paean to his long and highly successful career. You might call the menu here "The Greatest Hits of Jean-Georges" because what's on offer are the dishes he has perfected in his score of other restaurants. Try the sablefish in a nut-and-seed crust with sweet-and-sour broth, or soy-glazed short ribs with apple-jalapeno puree. The restaurant is calmly chic and not at all fussy; you can sit in the bar, in the cafe, or on the outdoor patio, and order from the same menu. The place is usually packed, and it should be, because the fixed-price lunch and dinner menus list a selection of wonderful dishes at a remarkably reasonable price.

1115 Alberni St. (Level 3 in the Shangri-La Hotel). ✆ **604/695-1115.** Reservations recommended. Main courses C$15–C$35; fixed-price lunch C$30; tasting menu C$75. AE, DC, MC, V. Restaurant & cafe daily 7am–10:30pm; bar Mon–Sat 11:30am–1am.

MODERATE

Bin 941 Tapas Parlour ★ TAPAS/CASUAL Still booming a decade after it opened its door, Bin 941 remains the place for trendy tapas dining. True, the music's too loud and the room's too small, but the food that alights on the bar and eight tiny tables is delicious and fun, and the wine list is great. Look especially for local seafood such as scallops and tiger prawns tournedos. In this sliver of a bistro, sharing is unavoidable, so come prepared for socializing as you enjoy your "tapatizers." A second Bin, dubbed Bin 942, opened at 1521 W. Broadway (✆ **604/734-9421**). The tables start to fill up at 6:30pm at both spots, and by 8pm, the hip and hungry have already formed a long and eager line.

941 Davie St. ✆ **604/683-1246.** www.bin941.com. Reservations not accepted. All plates C$17. MC, V. Daily 5pm–1:30am. Bus: 4, 5, or 8.

Sanafir ★★ 🎁 INTERNATIONAL Influenced by the exotic dining and decor found along the Silk Road, Sanafir creates an opulent and fun dining experience that doesn't cost a fortune. The first-floor dining room is loud and buzzily exciting, but parties can also drink and dine upstairs while reclining on pillows beneath sexy harem-style draperies. The "Tapas Trio" plates come in three of five possible Silk Road variations: Asian, Mediterranean, Middle Eastern, Indian, or North African. And the trio of tastes costs only C$14. Order the chicken, for instance, and your three-dish tapas plate might contain Zatar grilled chicken kebabs, Punjuabi-style butter chicken, and drunken chicken with cucumber and chili sauce. Larger chef's specials are also available, such as the super-rich oxtail cappelletti with white truffle cream, Parmigiano-Reggiano, and shaved black truffle. There's no sign outside, so just look for the most glamorous place on gentrifying Granville Street, and you'll be there.

1026 Granville St. (at Nelson). ✆ **604/678-1049.** www.sanafir.ca. Reservations recommended. Tapas C$14; chef's specials C$17. AE, DC, MC, V. Mon–Thurs noon–1am; Fri noon–2am; Sat 4:30pm–2am; Sun 4:30pm–1am. Bus: 4 or 7.

Simply Thai ★ THAI At this small restaurant in trendy Yaletown, you can watch chef and owner Siriwan in the open kitchen as she cooks up a combination of northern and southern Thai dishes with some fusion sensations. The appetizers are perfect finger foods: *Gai* satay features succulent pieces of grilled chicken breast marinated in coconut milk and spices, and covered in a peanut sauce, while the delicious *cho muang* consists of violet-colored dumplings stuffed with minced chicken. Main courses run the gamut of Thai cuisine: noodle dishes and coconut curries with beef, chicken, or pork, as well as a good number of vegetarian options. Don't miss the *tom kha gai,* a deceptively simple-looking coconut soup with chicken, mushrooms, and lemon grass.

1211 Hamilton St. ✆ **604/642-0123.** www.simplythairestaurant.com. Reservations recommended on weekends. Main courses C$13–C$18. AE, DC, MC, V. Mon–Fri 11:30am–3pm; daily 5–10:30pm. Bus: 2.

INEXPENSIVE

Sciué ★ ITALIAN/DESSERTS/COFFEE It's hard not to like a place that serves inexpensive Italian food and wonderful coffee in an airy, close-to-authentic Italian cafe setting. Sciué (pronounced *shoe*-eh) means "good and fast" in Italian regional slang, and that's how the food comes, but you can linger as long as you want and no one will bug you. Stop in for a double-shot espresso, a glass of Italian wine, or a dish of handmade gelato. For breakfast, you can get a fresh Italian pastry or a light, healthy meal. Lunch options include *pane Romano* (thin Roman bread topped with a selection of sauces, vegetables, cheeses, meats, or seafood, and sold by weight), fresh pastas, salads, and soups.

110-800 E. Pender St. (at Howe St.). ✆ **604/602-7263.** www.sciue.ca. Main courses C$5–C$10. DC, MC, V. Mon–Fri 6:30am–8pm; Sat 9am–5pm. Bus: 2.

Gastown & Chinatown

MODERATE

Park Lock Seafood Restaurant ☺ CHINESE/DIM SUM If you've never done dim sum, this large, second-floor dining room in the heart of Chinatown is a good place to give it a try, even though you'll have to listen to schlocky Western music while you dine. From 8am to 3pm daily, waitresses wheel little carts loaded with Chinese delicacies past the tables. When you see something you like, just point and ask for it. The final bill is based upon how many little plates are left on your table. Dishes include spring rolls, *hargow* (shrimp dumplings), *shumai* (steamed shrimp, beef, or pork dumplings), prawns wrapped in fresh white noodles, small steamed buns, sticky rice cooked in banana leaves, curried squid, and lots more. Parties of four or more are best—that way, you get to try each other's food.

544 Main St. (at E. Pender St., on the 2nd floor). ✆ **604/688-1581.** Reservations recommended. Main courses C$10–C$25; dim sum C$3–C$7. AE, MC, V. Daily 7:30am–4pm; Fri–Sun 5–9:30pm. Bus: 19 or 22.

Pink Pearl ★ ☺ CHINESE/DIM SUM Opened in 1981, the Pink Pearl remains Vancouver's best spot for dim sum. The sheer volume and bustle here are astonishing, and at peak times, you may have to wait up to (or only, depending on your patience level) 15 minutes for a table. Dozens of waiters parade a cavalcade of trolleys stacked high with baskets, steamers, and bowls of dumplings, spring rolls, shrimp balls, chicken feet, and even more obscure and delightful offerings. At the tables, extended Chinese families banter, joke, and feast; towers of empty plates pile up in the middle, a tribute to the appetites of the brunchers, as well as the growing bill. Fortunately, dim sum is still a steal, perhaps the best and most fun way to sample Cantonese cooking.

1132 E. Hastings St. ✆ **604/253-4316.** www.pinkpearl.com. Main courses C$12–C$35; dim sum C$3–C$7. AE, DC, MC, V. Sun–Thurs 9am–10pm; Fri & Sat 9am–11pm. Bus: 10.

INEXPENSIVE

Judas Goat TAPAS This tiny (28-seat) tapas parlor is a cool addition to the Gastown dining scene. It's located in the scarily named but now-gentrified Blood Alley, a couple of doors down from Salt (see below). At Judas Goat, you check off what you want from a small list of tapas-style offerings that might include beef brisket meatballs, sablefish with couscous, saltimbocca, or scallop *tartare*. There's a small wine and beer list.

27 Blood Alley. ✆ **604/681-5090.** www.judasgoat.ca. Tapas C$6–C$10. AE, MC, V. Daily noon–midnight. Bus: 1 or 8.

Jules ★ FRENCH Jules is one of those places that is hard not to like. Like Salt (reviewed below), this casual French bistro is part of a mini-renaissance putting new life into Gastown. Jules can be really loud, but the staff is friendly and the food is honest, unpretentious, and reasonably priced. The menu's limited to just a few standard bistro items, all of them well prepared: steak frites (rib-eye or hanger steak with French fries), salmon Provencale, duck confit, steamed mussels, or a vegetarian offering. You can start with classics like French onion soup, escargots in garlic and herb butter, or country-style pâté. This is a good lunch spot, too.

216 Abbott St. ✆ **604/669-0033.** www.julesbistro.ca. Main courses C$14–C$24; 3-course fixed-price lunch C$23, fixed-price dinner C$26. AE, MC, V. Tues–Sat 11:30am–2:30pm & 5:30–10pm. Bus: 1 or 8.

Salt ★ CHARCUTERIE The location of this new dining spot in Gastown's Blood Alley might put some visitors off, and that's really a shame because Salt is unique and a wonderful place to get a good, inexpensive meal. The minimalistically modern room is set with communal spruce dining tables. Salt has no kitchen, per se, as it serves only cured meats and artisan cheeses plus a daily soup, a couple of salads, and grilled meat and cheese sandwiches. For the tasting plate, you mix and match three of the meats and cheeses listed on the blackboard. To drink, choose from a selection of beers, and several good wines and whiskeys, or opt for a wine flight. As Blood Alley has no apparent street numbers, look for the salt shaker flag over the doorway. Try it for lunch if you're in Gastown.

45 Blood Alley. ✆ **604/633-1912.** www.salttastingroom.com. Tasting plates C$15; lunch specials C$12. AE, MC, V. Daily noon–midnight. Bus: 1 or 8.

The West End

Cin Cin ★★★ MODERN ITALIAN Vancouverites looking for great food and a romantic atmosphere frequent this award-winning, second-floor restaurant on Robson Street. The spacious dining room, done in a rustic Italian-villa style, surrounds an open kitchen built around a huge wood-fired oven and grill; the heated terrace is an equally pleasant dining and people-watching spot. The dishes, inspired by Italy but using locally sourced ingredients, change monthly, but your meal might begin with house-made Dungeness crab sausage with herb salad and lemon vinaigrette, followed by bison-filled gnocchi or biodynamic rice with scallops. Mouthwatering main courses include local fish and meat cooked in the wood-fired oven or on the wood grill, and a delicious pizza with sautéed wild mushrooms, peppercorn pecorino, and caramelized onions. The wine list is extensive, as is the selection of wines by the glass. The service is as exemplary as the food.

1154 Robson St. ✆ **604/688-7338.** www.cincin.net. Reservations recommended. Main courses C$21–C$36; early (5–6pm) fixed-price menu C$45. AE, DC, MC, V. Mon–Fri 11:30am–2:30pm; daily 5–11pm. Bus: 5 or 22.

The Fish House in Stanley Park ★★ SEAFOOD/PACIFIC NORTHWEST/TEA Reminiscent of a more genteel era, this green clapboard clubhouse from 1929 is surrounded by lawns and old cedar trees, and looks out over English Bay (in the summer, try for a table on the veranda). Enjoy a traditional afternoon tea, Sunday brunch, or a memorable lunch or dinner of fresh BC oysters and shellfish, fresh seasonal fish, and signature dishes such as maple-glazed salmon, flaming prawns (done at your table with ouzo), and a seafood cornucopia. Chef Karen Barnaby often creates special theme menus and offers a reasonably priced three-course set dinner menu every month. The wine list is admirable; the desserts sumptuous.

8901 Stanley Park Dr. ✆ **877/681-7275** or 604/681-7275. www.fishhousestanleypark.com. Reservations recommended. Main courses C$17–C$30; 3-course set menu (until 6:15pm) C$30; afternoon tea C$24. AE, DC, DISC, MC, V. Mon–Sat 11:30am–10pm; Sun 11am–10pm. Closed Dec 24–26. Bus: 1, 35, or 135.

Le Gavroche ★★ FRENCH This charmingly intimate French restaurant located in a century-old house celebrated its 30th anniversary in 2009. It's always been a place for special occasions and celebrations, and with food and wine of this caliber, there's a lot to celebrate. The food is classical French—but with inventive overtones and underpinnings. Try one of the tasting menus with wine pairings, and you won't regret a mouthful. Start with beef tartar or crab cakes with chili *coulis,* followed by a classic Caesar salad mixed at your table (Le Gavroche is known for its personal attention). Then, try slow-braised lamb shank, a venison chop with sour cherry jus, or mustard-crusted rack of lamb. Seafood and vegetarian choices are available, as well. Finish your feast with a Grand Marnier soufflé or the incomparable "Lili" cake, a flourless merinque creation infused with almond and hazelnut liqueur.

1616 Alberni St. ✆ **604/685-3924.** www.legavroche.ca. Reservations recommended. Main courses C$19–C$39; set menus C$35–C$55. AE, DC, MC, V. Mon–Fri 11:30am–2:30pm; daily 5:30–10pm. Bus: 5.

Raincity Grill ★★★ PACIFIC NORTHWEST This top-starred restaurant on a busy, buzzy corner across from English Bay is a gem—painstaking in preparation, arty in presentation, and yet completely unfussy in atmosphere. Raincity Grill was one of the very first restaurants in Vancouver to embrace the "buy locally, eat seasonally" concept and pioneered the Ocean Wise sustainable seafood organization. The menu focuses on seafood, game, poultry, and organic vegetables from British Columbia and the Pacific Northwest. The room is long, low, and intimate. To sample a bit of everything, I recommend the seasonal "100 mile" tasting menu, a bargain at C$70, or C$97 with wine pairings. One recent tasting menu included beetroot salad, hazelnut-crusted coho salmon, seared scallops, crispy roasted duck confit, and walnut crème with fennel gelato—all of it made with ingredients found within 161km (100 miles) of the restaurant. The wine list is huge and, in keeping with the restaurant's philosophy, sticks pretty close to home. The restaurant also has a takeout window on Denman Street, where you can get delicious fish (halibut) and chips to go for C$10.

1193 Denman St. ✆ **604/685-7337.** www.raincitygrill.com. Reservations recommended. Main courses C$17–C$33; early (5–6pm) fixed-price menu C$30; tasting menu C$48. AE, DC, MC, V. Mon–Fri 11:30am–2:30pm; Sat & Sun 10:30am–2:30pm; daily 5–10:30pm. Bus: 1 or 5.

MODERATE

Hapa Izakaya ★ JAPANESE Dinner comes at almost disco decibels in Robson Street's hottest Japanese "eat-drink place" (the literal meaning of Izakaya), where chefs call out orders, servers shout acknowledgments, and the maitre d' and owner keep up a running volley to staff about the (often sizable) wait at the door. The menu features inventive nontraditional dishes such as bacon-wrapped asparagus, *negitori* (spicy tuna roll), and fresh tuna belly chopped with spring onions and served with bite-size bits of garlic bread. Inventive appetizers and meat dishes and a scrumptious Korean hot pot are also on the menu, for the non–raw fish eaters in your party. The crowd is about a third expat Japanese, a third Chinese (both local and expat), and a third Westerners. The service is fast and obliging, and the price per dish is reasonable. A second location is in Kitsilano, at 1516 Yew St. (✆ **604/738-4272**).

1479 Robson St. ✆ **604/689-4272.** www.hapa-izakaya.com. No reservations accepted 6–8pm. Main courses C$8–C$14. AE, MC, V. Sun–Thurs 5:30pm–midnight; Fri & Sat 5:30pm–1am. Bus: 5.

Tanpopo JAPANESE Occupying the second floor of a corner building on Denman Street, Tanpopo has a partial view of English Bay, a large patio, and a huge menu of hot and cold Japanese dishes. But the line of people waiting 30 minutes or more every night for a table is here for the all-you-can-eat buffet. The unlimited fare includes the standards—*makis,* tuna and salmon sashimi, California and BC rolls—as well as cooked items such as *tonkatsu,* tempura, chicken *kara-age,* and broiled oysters. The quality is okay, a bit above average for an all-you-can-eat place. A couple of secrets to getting seated: You might try to call ahead, but they take only an arbitrary number of reservations for dinner each day. Otherwise, ask to sit at the sushi bar.

1122 Denman St. ✆ **604/681-7777.** Reservations recommended for groups. Main courses C$7–C$20; all-you-can-eat buffet lunch C$14, dinner C$22. AE, DC, MC, V. Daily 11:30am–10pm. Bus: 5.

INEXPENSIVE

Banana Leaf ★ MALAYSIAN One of the city's best spots for Malaysian food, Banana Leaf is just a hop and a skip from English Bay. The menu includes inventive specials such as mango and okra salad, delicious South Asian mainstays such as *gado gado* (a salad with hot peanut sauce), *mee goreng* (fried noodles with vegetables topped by a fried egg), and occasional variations such as an Assam curry (seafood in hot-and-sour curry sauce) with okra and tomato. Must-tries are sambal green beans and a signature chili crab. For dessert, don't pass up *pisang goreng*—fried banana with ice cream. The seven-course tasting menu (C$25 per person) lets you sample a bit of everything. The small room is tastefully decorated in dark tropical woods; service is very friendly. Other locations are at 820 W. Broadway (✆ **604/731-6333**) and in Kitsilano, at 3005 W. Broadway (✆ **604/734-3005**); same prices and hours apply.

1096 Denman St. ✆ **604/683-3333.** www.bananaleaf-vancouver.com. Main courses C$13–C$20. AE, MC, V. Sun–Thurs 11:30am–10pm; Fri & Sat 11:30am–11pm. Bus: 5.

Gyoza King JAPANESE Gyoza King features an entire menu of *gyoza*—succulent Japanese dumplings filled with prawns, pork, vegetables, and other combinations—as well as Japanese noodles and staples like *katsu-don* (pork cutlet over rice) and *udon* (a rich, hearty soup). This is the gathering spot for hordes of young Japanese students and visitors looking for reasonably priced eats that approximate home cooking. The staff is very courteous and happy to explain the dishes.

1508 Robson St. ✆ **604/669-8278.** Main courses C$5–C$10. AE, MC, V. Mon–Fri 11:30am–3pm & 5:30pm–2am; Sat 11:30am–2am; Sun 11:30am–midnight. Bus: 5.

Stephos GREEK A long-time fixture on the Davie Street dining scene, Stephos offers Greek food at its simplest and cheapest. Customers line up outside for a seat amid Greek travel posters, potted ivy, and whitewashed walls (the average wait is about 10–15 min., but it could be as long as 30 min., as once you're inside, the staff will never rush you out the door). Order some pita and dip (hummus, spicy eggplant, or garlic spread) while you peruse the menu. An interesting appetizer is the *avgolemono* soup, a delicately flavored chicken broth with egg and lemon, accompanied by a plate of piping hot pita bread. When choosing a main course, keep in mind that portions are huge. The roasted lamb, lamb chops, fried calamari, and a variety of souvlaki are served with rice, roast potatoes, and Greek salad. The beef, lamb, or chicken pita come in slightly smaller portions served with fries and *tsatsiki* (a sauce made from yogurt, cucumber, and garlic).

1124 Davie St. ✆ **604/683-2555.** Reservations accepted for parties of 5 or more. Main courses C$6–C$11. AE, MC, V. Daily 11am–11:30pm. Bus: 5.

The West Side

VERY EXPENSIVE

Tojo's Restaurant ★★★ JAPANESE Tojo's is considered Vancouver's top Japanese restaurant, the place where celebs and food cognoscenti come to dine on the best sushi in town. It's expensive, but the food is absolutely fresh, inventive, and boy is it good. The dining room's main area wraps around Chef Tojo and his sushi chefs with a giant curved maple sake bar and an adjoining sushi bar. Tojo's ever-changing menu offers such specialties as sea urchin on the half shell, herring roe, lobster claws, tuna, crab, and barbecue eel. Go for the Chef's Arrangement—tell them how much you're willing to spend (per person), and let the good times roll.

1133 W. Broadway. ✆ **604/872-8050.** www.tojos.com. Reservations required. Main courses C$16–C$48; sushi/sashimi C$8–C$28; Chef's Arrangement C$70–C$200. AE, DC, MC, V. Mon–Sat 5–10pm. Closed Christmas week. Bus: 9.

West ★★★ FRENCH/PACIFIC NORTHWEST Every meal I've had at this award-winning restaurant—it was voted "Best Restaurant in Vancouver" by *Vancouver* magazine 4 years in a row—has been memorable. The credo at West is deceptively simple: "True to our region, true to the seasons." That means fresh, organic, locally harvested seafood, game, and produce are transformed into extraordinary creations. The menu changes three to four times a week, but first courses might include lightly poached BC spot prawns in a rhubarb and watermelon essence or quail tortellini with roasted sweet corn puree. For a main course, you might find fillet of smoked sablefish, seared Qualicum Bay scallops with smoked veal tongue, or crisp sliced *porchetta* with black garlic and toasted gnocchi. For the ultimate dining experience, try one of the seasonal tasting menus—a multicourse progression through the best the restaurant has to offer. A carefully chosen wine list includes a selection of affordable wines by the glass and half-bottle. If you're really into cooking, reserve one of the two "chef tables" adjacent to the bustling kitchen.

2881 Granville St. ✆ **604/738-8938.** www.westrestaurant.com. Reservations recommended. Main courses lunch C$22–C$32, dinner C$37–C$44; tasting menus C$85–C$98. AE, DC, MC, V. Mon–Fri 11:30am–2:30pm; daily 5:30–11pm. Bus: 8.

MODERATE

Memphis Blues Barbeque House ★ BARBECUE At the busy intersection of Granville and Broadway, this hole-in-the-wall barbecue pit has made a name for itself with corn-pone, Southern-boy barbecue smoked for hours over a low-heat, hardwood fire. Ribs come out tender enough to pull apart with your fingers (which is how food is eaten here; the cutlery is mostly for show), yet still sweet and firm. The beef brisket is cooked long enough that the fat is all rendered out, while the lean flesh remains juicy and tender. The pork butt is slow cooked until you can pull it apart with a fork. Those three meats (plus catfish and Cornish game hen) are essentially what's offered here. Put that meat on greens, and you've got a Southern salad. Put it on bread, and it becomes a sandwich. Serve it on a plate with beans and a potato, and it becomes a meal. Wines are sold by the glass and bottle, but what you want is the ice-cold, home-brewed beer. A second location has opened at 1342 Commercial Dr. (✆ **604/215-2599**); the same hours apply.

1465 W. Broadway. ✆ **604/738-6806.** www.memphisbluesbbq.com. Main courses C$7–C$15; complete meals C$15–C$40. AE, DC, MC, V. Mon–Thurs 11am–10pm; Fri 11am–midnight; Sat noon–midnight; Sun noon–10pm. Bus: 4, 7, or 10.

Trattoria Italian Kitchen ★ ITALIAN The group behind glowbal, Coast, Sanafir, and Italian Kitchen have scored again, this time in Kitsilano. Trattoria is Kits-friendly, meaning it's more casual than their other restaurants, but the standards remain just as high and the prices just as reasonable. You can't make a reservation here, so plan accordingly. The line begins to form at 5:30pm, and by 7pm, you may have to wait an hour or more for a table (you can order a drink while you're waiting). The menu is much the same as Italian Kitchen: excellent pizzas with delicious toppings (lamb sausage with wild mushrooms, or mascarpone and fingerling potatoes); pastas like *strozzapreti* with smoked chicken, linguine carbonara, or the sharable platter of spaghetti and meatballs (the meatballs are made of Kobe beef). Main courses are seasonal and might include seared wild spring salmon or roasted whole trout. The wine list includes all the major Italian vintages.

1850 W. 4th Ave. ✆ **604/732-1441.** www.trattoriakitchen.ca. Reservations not accepted. Main courses C$12–C$16. AE, MC, V. Mon–Thurs 11:30am–1am; Fri & Sat 11:30am–2am; Sun 10:30am–1am. Bus: 2 or 22.

Vij ★★★ INDIAN Vij doesn't take reservations, as is apparent by the line outside every night, but patrons huddled under the neon sign don't seem to mind since they're treated to tea and *papadums* (a thin bread made from lentils). Inside, the decor is as warm and subtle as the seasonings, which are all roasted, hand-ground, and used with studied delicacy. The menu changes monthly, though some of the more popular entrees remain constant. Recent offerings have included wine-marinated lamb popsicles and BC spot prawns and halibut with black chickpeas in coconut-lemon curry. Vegetarian selections abound, including vegetables and red beans in yellow mustard seed and coconut curry, and Indian lentils with naan and *raita* (yogurt-mint sauce). The wine and beer list is short but carefully selected. And for teetotalers, Vij has developed a souped-up version of the traditional Indian chai, the chaiuccino. Vij recently opened Rangoli, right next door, for lunch and takeout.

1480 W. 11th Ave. ✆ **604/736-6664.** www.vijs.ca. Reservations not accepted. Main courses C$23–C$28. AE, DC, MC, V. Daily 5:30–10pm. Closed Dec 24 to Jan 8. Bus: 8 or 10.

INEXPENSIVE

Incendio West ★ 🎁 PIZZA If you're looking for something casual and local that won't be full of other tourists, this Kitsilano pizzeria is just the spot. The 22 pizza combinations are served on fresh, crispy crusts baked in a wood-fired oven; pastas are homemade. The wine list is decent; the beer list is inspired. There's another location in Gastown, at 103 Columbia St.

2118 Burrard St. ✆ **604/736-2220.** Main courses C$14–C$24. AE, MC, V. Mon–Fri 11:30am–3pm & 5–10pm; Sat & Sun 4:30–10pm. Closed Dec 23 to Jan 3. Bus: 1 or 8.

The Naam Restaurant ★ ☺ VEGETARIAN Back in the '60s, when Kitsilano was Canada's hippie haven, the Naam was tie-dye central. Things have changed since then, but Vancouver's oldest vegetarian and natural-food restaurant still retains a pleasant granola feel, and it's open 24/7. The decor is simple, earnest, and welcoming, and includes well-worn wooden tables and chairs, plants, an assortment of local art, a nice garden patio, and live music every night. The brazenly healthy fare ranges from all-vegetarian burgers, enchiladas, and burritos to tofu teriyaki, Thai noodles, and a variety of pita pizzas. The sesame spice fries are a Vancouver institution. And though the Naam is not quite vegan, they do offer specialties like the macrobiotic Dragon Bowl of brown rice, tofu, sprouts, and steamed vegetables.

2724 W. 4th Ave. ✆ **604/738-7151.** www.thenaam.com. Reservations accepted on weekdays only. Main courses C$7–C$12. AE, MC, V. Daily 24 hr. Bus: 4 or 22.

Sophie's Cosmic Café ☺ FAMILY STYLE/AMERICAN For a fabulous home-cooked, diner-style breakfast in a laid-back but buzzy atmosphere, come to this Kitsilano landmark. On Sunday morning, get here early, or you may have to wait a half-hour or more to get in. You can also have a good, filling lunch or dinner here. Every available space in Sophie's is crammed with toys and knickknacks from the 1950s and 1960s so, understandably, children are inordinately fond of the place. Crayons and coloring paper are always on hand. The menu is simple and includes pastas, burgers and fries, great milkshakes, and a few classic Mexican and "international" dishes, but it's the breakfast menu that draws the crowds.

2095 W. 4th Ave. ✆ **604/732-6810.** www.sophiescosmiccafe.com. Main courses C$5–C$17. MC, V. Daily 8am–8pm. Bus: 4 or 7.

The East Side

EXPENSIVE

Sun Sui Wah ★★ CHINESE/DIM SUM/SEAFOOD One of the most visited and sophisticated Chinese restaurants in town, the award-winning Sun Sui Wah is well known for its seafood. Fresh and varied, the catch of the day can include fresh crab, geoduck, scallops, oyster, prawns, and more. Pick your meal from the tank or order from the menu if you'd rather not meet your food eye-to-eye before it's cooked. Dim sum is a treat, with the emphasis on seafood. Choices abound for meat lovers and vegetarians, though they will miss out on one of the best seafood feasts in town. The decor is in need of a shake-up, but don't let that stand in your way.

3888 Main St. ✆ **604/872-8822.** www.sunsuiwah.com. Main courses C$12–C$50. AE, DC, MC, V. Daily 10am–3pm & 5–10:30pm. Bus: 3.

MODERATE

The Locus Café CASUAL/SOUTHWESTERN Even if you arrive by your lonesome, you'll soon have plenty of friends because the Locus is a cheek-by-jowl kind of place, filled with a friendly, funky crowd of artsy Mount Pleasant types. The big bar is overhung with "swamp-gothic" lacquer trees and surrounded by a tier of stools with booths and tiny tables. The cuisine originated in the American Southwest and picked up an edge along the way, as demonstrated in the roasted half-chicken with a cumin-coriander crust and sambuca citrus demi-glace. Keep an eye out for fish specials, such as grilled *tomba* tuna with a grapefruit and mango glaze. If you're in the mood for a sandwich, try the smoked black cod sloppy joe. Bowen Island Brewing Company provides the beer, so quality's high. Your only real problem is catching the eye of the busy bartender.

4121 Main St. ✆ **604/708-4121.** www.locusonmain.com. Reservations recommended. Main courses C$12–C$19. MC, V. Mon–Wed 10am–midnight; Thurs & Fri 10am–1am, Sat 9am–1am; Sun 9am–midnight. Bus: 3.

The North Shore

The Beach House at Dundarave Pier ★★ PACIFIC NORTHWEST The Beach House offers a panoramic view of English Bay from its waterfront location. Diners on the heated patio get more sunshine, but they miss out on the rich interior of this restored 1912 teahouse. The food is consistently good—innovative, but not so experimental that it leaves the staid West Van burghers gasping for breath. Appetizers include fresh oysters with shaved horseradish; salmon tartare; and Dungeness crab cakes. Entrees might include linguine with wild prawns, scallops, tomatoes, and chilies; pan-roasted sablefish with clams; and a seasonal stuffed chicken breast. The wine list is award-winning. The Beach House is a favorite West Van spot for Saturday and Sunday brunch.

150 25th St., West Vancouver. ✆ **604/922-1414.** www.thebeachhouserestaurant.ca. Reservations recommended. Main courses C$20–C$38. AE, DC, MC, V. Daily 11am–10pm. Bus: 255 to Ambleside Pier.

EXPLORING VANCOUVER

A city perched on the edge of a great wilderness, Vancouver offers unmatched opportunities for exploring the outdoors. But within the city limits, Vancouver is intensely urban, with buzzy sidewalk cafes and busy shopping streets. The forest of high-rises ringing the central part of the city reminds some visitors of New York or Shanghai, and Chinatown inevitably invites comparisons to San Francisco. But comparisons with other places begin to pall as you come to realize that Vancouver is entirely its own creation: a young, self-confident, sparklingly beautiful city like no other place on earth.

The Top Attractions

DOWNTOWN & THE WEST END

Bill Reid Gallery of Northwest Coast Art ★★ Newly opened in 2008, this downtown museum-gallery showcases the work of the great Northwest coast aboriginal artist Bill Reid, who died in 1994. Permanent installations include the Raven's Trove: Gold Masterworks by Bill Reid; the monumental bronze sculpture Mythic Messengers, Reid's masterful composition of 11 intertwined figures recounting traditional Haida myths; and a monumental cedar tribute pole carved by Haida Chief 7idansuu (Jim Hart) honoring Reid. Two exhibition spaces feature rotating exhibitions of Northwest Coast art, cultural performances, and lectures. The gift shop offers a good selection of Northwest Coast Native art, books, jewelry, and museum-quality collectibles.

639 Hornby St. ✆ **604/682-3455.** www.billreidgallery.ca. Admission C$10 adults, C$7 seniors & students, C$5 children 6–17; C$25 families. Wed–Sun 11am–5pm.

Canada Place ★★ If you've never been to Vancouver, this is a good place to orient yourself and see some of what makes BC's largest city so special. (Or you may arrive here on a cruise ship, in which case, this will be your first introduction to Vancouver.) With its five tall Teflon sails and bowsprit jutting out into Burrard Inlet, Canada Place is meant to resemble a giant sailing ship. Inside, it's a convention center on one level and a giant cruise-ship terminal below, with the Pan Pacific Hotel (p. 632) perched on top. Around the perimeter is a promenade, offering wonderful views across Burrard Inlet to the North Shore peaks and toward nearby Stanley Park, with plaques explaining the sights and providing historical tidbits. Continue around the promenade, and you'll get great city views and be able to see the older, low-rise buildings of Gastown, where Vancouver began. Bus sightseeing tours begin here, there's an **IMAX Theatre** (✆ **604/682-IMAX** [604/682-4629]), and the Tourism Vancouver Touristinfo Centre (see "Visitor Information," above) is right across the street. In 2009, the new addition to the Canada Place Convention Centre opened. With its amazing "green" roof, marvelous light-filled interior spaces, and wonderful plazas and walkways, it has transformed the area adjacent to the "old" Canada Place. Canada Place (at the end of Burrard St.). Free admission. Promenade daily 24 hr. Bus: 1 or 5.

Stanley Park ★★★ ☺ The green jewel of Vancouver, Stanley Park is a 400-hectare (988-acre) rainforest jutting out into the ocean from the edge of the busy West End. Exploring the second-largest urban forest in Canada is one of Vancouver's quintessential experiences.

The park, created in 1888, is filled with towering western red cedar and Douglas fir, manicured lawns, flower gardens, placid lagoons, and countless shaded walking trails that meander through it all. The famed **seawall ★★★** runs along the waterside edge of the park, allowing cyclists and pedestrians to experience the magical interface of forest, sea, and sky. One of the most popular free attractions in the park is the **collection of totem poles ★★★** at Brockton Point, most of them carved in the 1980s to replace the original ones that were placed in the park in the 1920s and 1930s. The area around the totem poles features open-air displays on the Coast Salish First Nations and a small gift shop/visitor information center.

The park is home to lots of wildlife, including beavers, coyotes, bald eagles, blue herons, cormorants, trumpeter swans, brant geese, ducks, raccoons, skunks, and gray squirrels imported from New York's Central Park decades ago and now quite at home in the Pacific Northwest. (No, there are no bears.) For directions and maps, brochures, and exhibits on the nature and ecology of Stanley Park, visit the **Lost Lagoon Nature House** (✆ **604/257-8544;** free admission; July 1 to Labour Day daily 10am–7pm, weekends only outside this period). On Sundays at 1pm, rain or shine, they offer Discovery Walks of the park (pre-registration recommended). Equally nature-focused but with way more wow is the **Vancouver Aquarium ★★** (see below). The **Stanley Park's Children's Farm** (✆ **604/257-8531**) is a petting zoo with peacocks, rabbits, calves, donkeys, and Shetland ponies. Next to the petting zoo is **Stanley Park's Miniature Railway ★** (✆ **604/257-8531**), a diminutive steam locomotive that pulls passenger cars on a circuit through the woods.

Swimmers head to **Third Beach** and **Second Beach** (p. 661), the latter with an outdoor pool beside English Bay. For kids, there's a free **Spray Park** near Lumberman's Arch, where they can run and splash through various water-spewing fountains. Perhaps the best way to explore the park is to rent a bike (p. 662) or in-line skates, and set off along the seawall. If you decide to walk, remember the free shuttle bus that circles the park every 15 minutes, allowing passengers to alight and descend at most of the park's many attractions. The wonderful **horse-drawn carriage ride ★★★** operated by **AAA Horse & Carriage Ltd.** (✆ **604/681-5115;** www.stanleypark.com) is one of the most enjoyable ways to tour the park. Carriage tours depart every 20 minutes mid-March through October from the lower aquarium parking lot on Park

Drive near the Georgia Street park entrance. The ride lasts an hour and covers portions of the park that many locals have never seen. Rates are C$27 for adults, C$25 for seniors and students, and C$15 for children 3 to 12.

Of the three restaurants located in the park, the best is the **Fish House in Stanley Park** (p. 645), where you can have lunch, afternoon tea, or dinner.

Stanley Park. ✆ **604/257-8400.** http://vancouver.ca/parks. Free admission. Park daily 24 hr. Bus: 15. Around the Park shuttle bus July to early Sept. Parking C$2/hr, C$10/day.

Vancouver Aquarium Marine Science Centre ★★ ☺ One of North America's largest and best, the Vancouver Aquarium houses more than 8,000 marine species. From platforms above or through underwater viewing windows, you can watch the white beluga whales flashing through their pools. (One of the belugas gave birth in June 2008, and as of press time, another one is expecting.) There are also sea otters, Steller sea lions, and a Pacific white-sided dolphin. During regularly scheduled shows, the aquarium staff explains marine-mammal behavior while working with these impressive creatures. The Wild Coast area features a fascinating assortment of fish and sea creatures found in local waters, and there's always an interesting temporary exhibit or two.

For a substantial extra fee (C$150 adults, C$210 one adult and one child age 8–12), you can have a behind-the-scenes Beluga Encounter, helping to feed these giant white cetaceans, then head up to the Marine Mammal deck to take part in the belugas' regular training session. Beluga encounters are available daily from 9 to 10:30am, with extra encounters on weekends between 2 and 4pm. Other Animal Encounter tours take visitors behind the scenes to interact with beluga whales (C$135 adults, C$185 adult and child), dolphins (C$175 adults, C$240 adult and child), or help feed the Steller sea lions (C$40 adults, C$60 adult and child), sea turtles (C$40 adults, C$60 adult and child), and sea otters (C$25 adults, C$38 adult and child). Animal Encounter tours are available daily, but times vary. Call ✆ **800/931-1186** to reserve all of these programs ahead of time. Children must be 8 or older to participate.

Stanley Park. ✆ **604/659-FISH** (604/659-3474). www.vanaqua.org. Admission C$22 adults; C$17 seniors, students & children 13–18; C$14 children 4–12; free for children 3 & under. June–Sept daily 9am–7pm; Oct–May daily 9:30am–5pm. Bus: 135. Around the Park shuttle bus July–early-Sept. Parking June–Sept C$7, Oct–May C$4.

The West Side

Granville Island ★★★ ☺ Almost a city within a city, Granville Island is a good place to browse away a morning, an afternoon, or a whole day. You can wander through a busy public market jammed with food stalls, shop for crafts, pick up some fresh seafood, enjoy a great dinner, watch the latest theater performance, rent a yacht, stroll along the waterfront, or simply run through the sprinkler on a hot summer day; it's all there and more. If you have only a short period of time, make sure you spend at least part of it in the **Granville Island Public Market ★★★**, one of the best all-around markets in North America.

Once a declining industrial site, Granville Island started transforming in the late 1970s when the government encouraged new, people-friendly developments. Maintaining its original industrial look, the former warehouses and factories now house galleries, artist studios, restaurants, and theaters; the cement plant on the waterfront is the only industrial tenant left. Access to Granville Island is by Aquabus from the West End, Yaletown, or Kitsilano (see "By Mini-Ferry," above; the Aquabus drops you

360 Degrees of Vancouver

The most popular (and most touristed) spot from which to view Vancouver's skyline and surrounding topography is high atop the space needle observation deck at the Vancouver Lookout ★ (555 W. Hastings St.; ✆ 604/689-0421; www.vancouverlookout.com). It's a great place for first-time visitors who want a panorama of the city. The 360-degree view is remarkable (yes, that is Mt. Baker looming above the southeastern horizon), but the signage identifying points of interest could be a lot better. Skylift admission is C$15 adults, C$12 seniors, C$10 students and children 11 to 17, C$6 children 4 to 10, and free for children 3 and under. It's open daily June to October from 8:30am to 10:30pm and from 9am to 9pm the rest of the year. Tickets are valid for the entire day.

at the public market) or by foot, bike, or car across the bridge at Anderson Street (access from W. 2nd Ave.). Avoid driving over on weekends and holidays—you'll spend more time trying to find a parking place than in the galleries. Check the website for upcoming events or stop by the information center, behind the Kids Market.

If you can't bear to leave the island, consider staying at the **Granville Island Hotel** (p. 638). Even if you don't stay, it's worth stopping by the hotel's brewpub restaurant, the Dockside Brewery Company, for a brew with a view.

The south shore of False Creek (under the Granville St. Bridge). ✆ **604/666-5784** (information center). www.granvilleisland.com. Public market daily 9am–7pm. Bus: 50.

H. R. MacMillan Space Centre ★ ☺ In the same building as the Vancouver Museum (see below), the space center and observatory has hands-on displays and exhibits that will delight budding astronomy buffs and their parents (or older space buffs and their children). Displays are highly interactive: In the Cosmic Courtyard, you can try designing a spacecraft or maneuvering a lunar robot. Or punch a button and get a video explanation of the *Apollo 17* manned-satellite engine that stands before you. The exciting **Virtual Voyages Simulator ★★** takes you on a voyage to Mars—it's a thrilling experience for kids and adults. In the GroundStation Canada Theatre, video presentations explore space, in general, and Canada's contributions to the space program. The StarTheatre shows movies—many of them for children—on an overhead dome. The Planetarium Star Theatre features exciting laser shows in the evening.

1100 Chestnut St. (in Vanier Park). ✆ **604/738-7827.** www.hrmacmillanspacecentre.com. Admission C$15 adults; C$11 seniors, students & children 5–10; C$7 children 4 & under; C$45 families (up to 5, maximum 2 adults). Evening laser shows C$11 adults. Tues–Sun 10am–5pm; evening laser shows Fri & Sat 8, 9:15 & 10:20pm. Closed Dec 25. Bus: 22.

Museum of Anthropology ★★★ ☺ This isn't just any old museum. In 1976, BC architect Arthur Erickson created a classic native post-and-beam-style structure out of poured concrete and glass to house one of the world's finest collections of Northwest Coast Native art. A major renovation in 2009 more than doubled the gallery space and added new luster to this remarkable showplace.

Enter through doors that resemble a huge, carved, bent-cedar box. Artifacts from different coastal communities flank the ramp leading to the Great Hall's **collection of totem poles.** Haida artist Bill Reid's cedar bear and sea wolf sculptures sit at the Cross Roads; Reid's masterpiece, ***The Raven and the First Men,*** is worth the price of admission all by itself. The huge carving in glowing yellow cedar depicts a Haida creation myth, in which Raven—the trickster—coaxes humanity out into the world from its birthplace in a clamshell. Some of Reid's fabulous jewelry creations in gold and silver are also on display.

The **Masterpiece Gallery's** argillite sculptures, beaded jewelry, and hand-carved ceremonial masks lead the way to the Visible Storage Galleries, where more than 15,000 artifacts are arranged by culture. You can open the glass-topped drawers to view small treasures and stroll past larger pieces housed in tall glass cases.

Also at the museum is the somewhat incongruous Koerner Ceramics Gallery, a collection of European ceramics.

Behind the museum, overlooking Point Grey, are two **longhouses** built according to the Haida tribal style, resting on the traditional north-south axis. Ten hand-carved totem poles stand in attendance along with contemporary carvings on the longhouse facades. ***Note:*** You might want to visit the nearby UBC Botanical Garden and Nitobe Japanese Garden (see below). A number of trails also lead down to a few of Vancouver's most pristine beaches (p. 661).

6393 NW Marine Dr. (at Gate 4). ✆ **604/822-3825.** www.moa.ubc.ca. Admission C$14 adults; C$12 seniors, students & children 6–18; free for children 5 & under; C$7 for all Tues 5–9pm. Spring/summer Wed–Mon 10am–5pm, Tues 10am–9pm; fall/winter Wed–Sun 11am–5pm, Tues 1–9pm. Closed Dec 25 & Dec 26. Bus: 4 or 99 (10-min. walk from UBC bus loop).

Science World at TELUS World of Science ★ ☺ Science World is impossible to miss: It's the big blinking geodesic dome (built for Expo '86 and now partnered with TELUS, a telephone company, hence the branded name) on the eastern end of False Creek. Inside, it's a hands-on scientific discovery center where you and your kids can light up a plasma ball, walk through a 160-sq.-m (1,722-sq.-ft.) maze, wander through the interior of a camera, create a cyclone, watch a zucchini explode as it's charged with 80,000 volts, stand inside a beaver lodge, play in wrist-deep magnetic liquids, create music with a giant synthesizer, and watch mind-bending three-dimensional slide and laser shows, as well as other optical effects. Science World is loaded with first-rate adventures for kids from toddler age to early teens; you'll want to spend at least a couple of hours here. Throughout the day, special shows, many with nature themes, are presented in the OMNIMAX Theatre—a huge projecting screen equipped with surround sound.

1455 Quebec St. ✆ **604/443-7443.** www.scienceworld.ca. Admission C$19 adults, C$16 seniors & students, C$13 children 4–12, free for children 3 & under; C$66 families (up to 6 related people). OMNIMAX ticket C$5 adults. Sept–June Mon–Fri 10am–5pm, Sat & Sun 10am–6pm; July–Aug daily 10am–6pm; holidays 10am–6pm. SkyTrain: Main St.-Science World.

Vancouver Museum Located in the same building as the H. R. MacMillan Space Centre (see above), the Vancouver Museum is dedicated to the city's history, from its days as a native settlement and European outpost to its 20th-century maturation into a modern urban center. The exhibits have been remounted and revitalized to make them more interesting to the casual visitor. Of most importance here is the wonderful collection of First Nations art and artifacts. Hilarious, campy fun abounds in the 1950s Room, where a period film chronicles "Dorothy's All-Electric Home." Next to this is another fun, and socially intriguing, room devoted to Vancouver's years as a hippie capital, with film clips, commentary, and a replica hippie apartment.

1100 Chestnut St. ✆ **604/736-4431.** www.museumofvancouver.ca. Admission C$11 adults, C$9 seniors, C$7 children 4–19. Tues, Wed & Fri–Sun 10am–5pm; Thurs 10am–8pm. Bus: 22, then walk 3 blocks south on Cornwall Ave. Boat: Granville Island Ferry to Heritage Harbour.

GASTOWN & CHINATOWN

Dr. Sun Yat-Sen Classical Chinese Garden ★★ This small reproduction of a Classical Chinese scholar's garden truly is a remarkable place, but to get the full effect, it's best to take the free guided tour. Untrained eyes will only see a pretty pond surrounded by bamboo and oddly shaped rocks. The engaging guides, however, can explain this unique urban garden's Taoist yin-yang design principle, in which harmony is achieved through dynamic opposition. To foster opposition (and thus harmony) in the garden, Chinese designers place contrasting elements in juxtaposition: Soft-moving water flows across solid stone; smooth, swaying bamboo grows around gnarled immovable rocks; dark pebbles are placed next to light pebbles in the paving. Moving with the guide, you discover the symbolism of intricate carvings and marvel at the subtle, ever-changing views from covered serpentine corridors. This is one of two Classical Chinese gardens in North America (the other is in Portland, Oregon) created by master artisans from Suzhou, the garden city of China.

578 Carrall St. ✆ **604/662-3207.** www.vancouverchinesegarden.com. Admission C$12 adults, C$10 seniors, C$9 students, free for children 5 & under; C$25 families. Free guided tour included. May to June 14 & Sept daily 10am–6pm; June 15 to Aug daily 9:30am–7pm; Oct–Apr Tues–Sun 10am–4:30pm. Bus: 19 or 22.

Steam Clock ☺ The Steam Clock in Gastown is a favorite photo op for tourists, but you're not missing much if you miss it. Built by horologist Raymond Saunders in 1977 (based on an 1875 design), it's the only steam clock in the world, powered by steam from an underground system of pipes that supply heat to many downtown buildings. The clock is supposed to sound its whistles (playing "The Westminster Chimes") every quarter-hour as the steam shoots out from vents at the top. Sometimes, however, it simply steams with no musical accompaniment.

Gastown (at the intersection of Water & Cambie sts.). Free.

NORTH VANCOUVER & WEST VANCOUVER

Capilano Suspension Bridge & Park ★ Vancouver's first and oldest tourist trap (built in 1889), this attraction still works—mostly because there's still something inherently thrilling about walking across a narrow, shaky walkway 69m (226 ft.) above a canyon floor, held up by nothing but a pair of tiny cables. Set in a beautiful 8-hectare (20-acre) park about 15 minutes from downtown, the suspension bridge itself is a 135m-long (443-ft.) cedar-plank and steel-cable footbridge, which sways and bounces gently above the Capilano River. Visitors nervously cross above kayakers and salmon shooting the rapids far below. A new attraction called **"Treetops Adventure"** features more bridges and walkways, only these are attached to giant tree trunks 24m (79 ft.) above the rainforest floor.

In addition to the bridge, the park has a **carving center** where native carvers demonstrate their skill, an exhibit describing the region's natural history, guides in period costume who recount Vancouver's frontier days, and a pair of overpriced and poorly serviced restaurants. Though overall it's quite well done, it's hard to justify the exorbitant entrance fee, and the summer crowds can be off-putting. If the admission price is a roadblock, you can have a similar experience at the nearby Lynn Canyon Suspension Bridge, which is almost as high, set in a far larger forest, almost untouristed, and absolutely free (see "The *Other* Suspension Bridge," p. 656).

3735 Capilano Rd., North Vancouver. ✆ **604/985-7474.** www.capbridge.com. Admission winter/summer C$30 adults, C$28 seniors, C$24 students, C$19 children 13–16, C$10 children 7–12, free for children 6 & under. May–Sept daily 8:30am–dusk; Oct–Apr daily 9am–5pm. Hours change monthly. Closed Dec 25. Bus: 246 or 236. Car: Hwy. 99 north across Lions Gate Bridge to exit 14 on Capilano Rd.

THE OTHER suspension BRIDGE

Lynn Canyon Park, in North Vancouver between Grouse Mountain and Mount Seymour Provincial Park on Lynn Valley Road, offers a free alternative to the overpriced Capilano Suspension Bridge. True, the **Lynn Canyon Suspension Bridge ★** is both shorter and a little lower than Capilano (see above), but the waterfall and swirling whirlpools in the canyon below add both beauty and a certain fear-inducing fascination. Plus, it's free.

The park in which the bridge is located is a gorgeous 247-hectare (610-acre) rainforest of cedar and Douglas fir, laced throughout with walking trails. It's also home to an **Ecology Centre** (3663 Park Rd.; ✆ **604/981-3103**), which presents natural history films, tours, and displays that explain the local ecology. Staff members lead frequent walking tours. The center is open daily from 10am to 5pm (Oct–May Sat–Sun noon–4pm). The park itself is open from 7am to 7pm in spring and fall, 7am to 9pm in summer, and 7am to dusk in winter; it's closed December 25 and 26 and January 1. There is a cafe in the park that serves sit-down and takeout meals. To get there, take the SeaBus to Lonsdale Quay, then transfer to bus no. 229; by car, take the Trans-Canada Highway (Hwy. 1) to the Lynn Valley Road exit (about a 20-min. drive from downtown), and follow Lynn Valley Road to Peters Road, where you turn right.

Grouse Mountain ★★ ☺ Once a local ski hill, Grouse Mountain has developed into a year-round mountain recreation park that claims to be the number-one attraction in Vancouver. It's fun if you're sports minded or like the outdoors; if not, you might find it disappointing. Located only a 15-minute drive from downtown, the **SkyRide gondola ★★** transports you to the mountain's 1,110m (3,642-ft.) summit. (Hikers can take a near vertical trail called the Grouse Grind.) On a clear day, the **view ★★★** from the top is the best around: You can see the city and the entire lower mainland, from far up the Fraser Valley east across the Strait of Georgia to Vancouver Island. In the lodge, **Theater in the Sky ★** shows wildlife movies. Outside, in the winter, you can ski and snowboard (26 runs, 13 runs for night skiing/snowboarding; drop-in ski lessons available), go snowshoeing, skate on the highest outdoor rink in Canada, and take a brief "sleigh ride" (behind a huge snow-cat), and the kids can play in a special snow park. In warmer weather, you can wander forest trails, take a scenic chair ride, enjoy a lumberjack show or Birds in Motion demonstrations, visit the Refuge for Endangered Wildlife, or ride on the mountain-bike trails. Most of these activities are included in the rather exorbitant price of your SkyRide ticket; you have to pay extra for a lift ticket and equipment rentals. Casual and fine-dining options, and a Starbucks, are in the lodge.

6400 Nancy Greene Way, North Vancouver. ✆ **604/984-0661.** www.grousemountain.com. SkyRide C$40 adults, C$36 seniors, C$24 children 13–18, C$14 children 5–12, free for children 4 & under. Full-day ski-lift tickets C$55 adults, C$45 seniors & teens 13-18, C$25 children 5-12. SkyRide free with advance Observatory Restaurant reservation. Daily 9am–10pm. Bus: 232, then transfer to bus 236. SeaBus: Lonsdale Quay, then transfer to bus 236. Car: Hwy. 99 north across Lions Gate Bridge, take North Vancouver exit to Marine Dr., then up Capilano Rd. for 5km (3 miles). Parking C$3 for 2 hr. in lots below SkyRide.

Vancouver's Plazas & Parks

OUTDOOR PLAZAS

Unlike many cities, Vancouver's great urban gathering places stand not at the center but on the periphery, on two opposite sides of the **seawall** that runs around Stanley Park: **English Bay,** on the south side of Denman Street, and **Coal Harbour,** on the northern, Burrard Inlet side, are where Vancouverites go to stroll and be seen. On warm sunny days, these two areas are packed. Another waterside gathering spot is **Canada Place** (p. 650), which serves as the city's cruise-ship terminal (as well as a huge convention center with a giant hotel on top for good measure).

Designed by architect Arthur Erickson to be Vancouver's central plaza, **Robson Square**—downtown, between Hornby and Howe streets from Robson to Smithe streets—has never really worked. The square, which anchors the north end of the Provincial Law Courts complex designed by Erickson in 1972, suffers from a basic design flaw: It's sunk one story below street level, making it difficult to see and to access. The Law Courts complex, which sits on a higher level, raised above the street, is beautifully executed with shrubbery, cherry trees, sculptures, and a triple-tiered waterfall, but Robson Square below is about as appealing as a drained swimming pool. Just opposite Robson Square, however, the steps of the **Vancouver Art Gallery** are a great people place, filled with loungers, political agitators, and old men playing chess. It just goes to show you that grandiose urban theory and urban design, especially back in the 1970s, didn't always take the human element into account.

Library Square—a few blocks east from Robson Square at the corner of Robson and Homer streets—is an example of a new urban space that does work. It's been popular with locals since it opened in 1995. People sit on the steps, bask in the sunshine, read, harangue passersby with half-baked political ideas, and generally seem to enjoy themselves.

Parks & Gardens

Park and garden lovers are in heaven in Vancouver. The wet, mild climate is ideal for gardening, and come spring the city blazes with blossoming cherry trees, rhododendrons, camellias, azaleas, and spring bulbs. Roses are a favorite summer bloom. You'll see gardens everywhere, and urban gardens with fountains have been incorporated into most of the city's new development. Nature is part of the scheme here. For general information about Vancouver's parks, call ✆ **604/257-8400** or try www.parks.vancouver.bc.ca. For information on **Stanley Park,** the queen of them all, see p. 651.

The University of British Columbia on the West Side has two lovely gardens: the **UBC Botanical Garden,** one of the largest living botany collections on the west coast, and the sublime **Nitobe Japanese Garden.**

In Chinatown, the **Dr. Sun Yat-Sen Classical Chinese Garden** (p. 655) is a small, tranquil oasis in the heart of the city, built by artisans from Suzhou, China; right next to it, accessed via the Chinese Cultural Centre on Pender Street, is the pretty (and free) **Dr. Sun Yat-sen Park,** with a pond, walkways, and plantings.

On the West Side, **Queen Elizabeth Park**—at Cambie Street and West 33rd Avenue—sits atop a 150m-high (492-ft.) extinct volcano and is the highest urban vantage point south of downtown, offering panoramic views in all directions (although leafy deciduous trees now block some of the best views). Along with the Rose Garden in Stanley Park, it's Vancouver's most popular location for wedding-photo sessions, with well-manicured gardens and a profusion of colorful flora. There are areas for lawn bowling, tennis, pitch-and-putt golf, and picnicking. The **Bloedel Conservatory** (✆ **604/257-8584**) stands next to the park's huge sunken garden, an amazing reclamation of an abandoned rock quarry. A 42m-high (138-ft.) domed structure, the conservatory houses a tropical rainforest with more than 100 plant species as well as free-flying tropical birds. Admission to the conservatory is C$5 for adults, with discounts for seniors and children. Take bus no. 15 to reach the park.

VanDusen Botanical Gardens ★, 5251 Oak St., at West 37th Avenue (✆ **604/878-9274;** www.vandusengarden.org), is located just a few blocks from Queen Elizabeth Park and the Bloedel Conservatory. In contrast to the flower fetish displayed by Victoria's famous Butchart Gardens (p. 688), Vancouver's 22-hectare (54-acre) botanical garden concentrates on whole ecosystems. From trees hundreds of feet high down to the little lichens on the smallest of damp stones, the gardeners at VanDusen attempt to re-create the plant life of an enormous number of different environments. Depending on which trail you take, you may find yourself wandering through the Southern Hemisphere section, the Sino-Himalayan garden, or the northern California garden where giant sequoias reach for the sky. Should all this tree gazing finally pall, head for the farthest corner of the garden where you'll find a devilishly difficult Elizabethan garden maze. Admission April through September costs C$6.50 adults, C$5 seniors and children 13 to 18, C$3.50 children 6 to 12, and C$14 families; it's free for children 5 and under. Open daily 10am to dusk. Take bus no. 17.

Adjoining UBC on the city's west side at Point Grey, **Pacific Spirit Regional Park,** called the **Endowment Lands** by long-time Vancouver residents, is the largest green space in Vancouver. Comprising 754 hectares (1,863 acres) of temperate rainforest, marshes, and beaches, the park includes nearly 35km (22 miles) of trails ideal for hiking, riding, mountain biking, and beachcombing.

Across the Lions Gate Bridge, there are six provincial parks that delight outdoor enthusiasts year-round. Good in winter or for those averse to strenuous climbing is the publicly maintained **Capilano River Regional Park,** 4500 Capilano Rd. (✆ **604/666-1790**), surrounding the Capilano Suspension Bridge & Park (p. 655). Hikers can follow a gentle trail by the river for 7km (4¼ miles) down the well-maintained **Capilano trails** to the Burrard Inlet and the Lions Gate Bridge, or about a mile upstream to **Cleveland Dam,** which serves as the launching point for whitewater kayakers and canoeists.

The **Capilano Salmon Hatchery,** on Capilano Road (✆ **604/666-1790**), is on the river's east bank about a half a kilometer (⅓ mile) below the Cleveland Dam. Approximately two million Coho and Chinook salmon are hatched annually in glass-fronted tanks connected to the river by a series of channels. You can observe the hatching fry (baby fish) before they depart for open waters, as well as the mature salmon that return to the Capilano River to spawn. Admission is free, and the hatchery is open daily from 8am to 7pm (until 4pm in the winter). Drive across the Lions Gate Bridge and follow the signs to North Vancouver and the Capilano Suspension Bridge. Or take the SeaBus to Lonsdale Quay and transfer to bus no. 236; the trip takes less than 45 minutes.

Eight kilometers (5 miles) west of the Lions Gate Bridge on Marine Drive West, West Vancouver, is **Lighthouse Park ★★**. This 74-hectare (183-acre) rugged-terrain forest has 13km (8 miles) of groomed trails and—because it has never been clear-cut—some of the largest and oldest trees in the Vancouver area. One of the paths leads to the 18m (59-ft.) **Point Atkinson Lighthouse,** on a rocky bluff overlooking the Strait of Georgia and a fabulous view of Vancouver. It's an easy trip on bus no. 250. For information about other West Vancouver parks, call © **604/925-7200** weekdays.

Driving up-up-up the mountain from **Lighthouse Park** will eventually get you to the top of **Cypress Provincial Park.** Stop halfway at the scenic viewpoint for a sweeping vista of the Vancouver skyline, the harbor, the Gulf Islands, and Washington State's Mount Baker, which peers above the eastern horizon. The park is 12km (7½ miles) north of Cypress Bowl Road and the Highway 99 junction in West Vancouver. Cypress Provincial Park has an intricate network of trails maintained for hiking during the summer and autumn and for downhill and cross-country skiing during the winter (see "Outdoor Activities & Spectator Sports," below).

Rising 1,430m (4,692 ft.) above Indian Arm, **Mount Seymour Provincial Park,** 1700 Mt. Seymour Rd., North Vancouver (© **604/986-2261**), offers another view of the area's Coast Mountains range. The road to this park roams through stands of Douglas fir, red cedar, and hemlock. Higher than Grouse Mountain, Mount Seymour has a spectacular view of Washington State's Mount Baker on clear days. It has challenging hiking trails that go straight to the summit, where you can see Indian Arm, Vancouver's bustling commercial port, the city skyline, the Strait of Georgia, and Vancouver Island. The trails are open all summer for hiking; during the winter, the paths are maintained for skiing, snowboarding, and snowshoeing (see "Outdoor Activities & Spectator Sports," below). Mount Seymour is open daily from 7am to 10pm.

Especially for Kids

Pick up copies of the free monthly newspapers ***B.C. Parent*** (www.bcparent.com), and ***West Coast Families***; *West Coast Families'* centerfold, "Fun in the City," and event calendar, list everything currently going on, including **CN IMAX** shows at Canada Place Pier, **OMNIMAX** (© **604/443-7443**) shows at Science World at Telus World of Science, and free children's programs. Both publications are available at Granville Island's Kids Market and at neighborhood community centers throughout the city.

To give kids (and yourself) an overview of the city, you can take the fun trolley tour offered by **Vancouver Trolley Company** (© **888/451-5581** or 604/801-5515; www.vancouvertrolley.com). Gas-powered trolleys run along a route through Downtown, Chinatown, the West End, and Stanley Park.

Stanley Park ★★★ (p. 651) offers a number of attractions for children.

Also in Stanley Park, the **Vancouver Aquarium Marine Science Centre ★★** (p. 652) has sea otters, sea lions, whales, and numerous other marine creatures, as well as many exhibits geared toward children. Right in town, **Science World at Telus World of Science** (p. 654) is a hands-on kids' museum where budding scientists can get their hands into everything.

A trip to **Granville Island ★★★** by Aquabus will delight kids, and there are a couple of specific kids' places they'll really enjoy. Granville Island's **Kids Market,** 1496 Cartwright St. (© **604/689-8447**), is open daily from 10am to 6pm. Playrooms and 28 shops filled with toys, books, records, clothes, and food are all child-oriented. At **Granville Island's Water Park and Adventure Playground,** 1496 Cartwright St., kids can really let loose with movable water guns and sprinklers. They can also have fun on the water slides or in the wading pool. The facilities are open during the summer daily (weather permitting) from 10am to 6pm. Admission is free; changing facilities are nearby at the False Creek Community Centre (© **604/257-8195**).

Greater Vancouver Zoo (5048 264th St., Aldergrove; ✆ **604/856-6825;** www.gvzoo.com), located 48km (30 miles) east of downtown Vancouver (about a 45-min. drive), is a lush 48-hectare (119-acre) reserve filled with lions, tigers, ostriches, buffalo, elk, antelope, zebras, giraffes, a rhino, and camels; 124 species in all. The zoo also has food service and a playground. It's open daily 9am to 4pm from October through March, 9am to 7pm from April through September. Admission is C$18 adults, C$14 seniors and children 3 to 15, free for children 2 and under, and C$60 for families. Take the Trans-Canada Highway to Aldergrove, exit 73; parking is C$4 per day.

The prospect of walking high above the rushing waters is the main draw at the **Capilano Suspension Bridge & Park** or the **Lynn Canyon Suspension Bridge** (p. 655 and 656).

A whale-watching excursion is one of the most exciting adventures you can give a kid. See "Wildlife-Watching" in "Outdoor Activities & Spectator Sports," below, for information.

SPECIAL EVENTS & FESTIVALS

The first event of the year is the annual **New Year's Day Polar Bear Swim** at English Bay Beach; thousands of hardy citizens show up in elaborate costumes to take a dip in the icy waters of English Bay. On the second Sunday in January, the **Annual Bald Eagle Count** takes place in Brackendale, about an hour's drive north of Vancouver on the Sea to Sky Highway. The count starts at the Brackendale Art Gallery (✆ **604/898-3333**).

In late January or early February (dates change yearly), the **Chinese New Year** is celebrated with 2 weeks of firecrackers, dancing dragon parades, and other festivities. For 5 days each year, the sounds of fiddles, bagpipes, bodhrans, dancing feet, and voices resound throughout downtown Vancouver during **CelticFest** (www.celticfestvancouver.com), a celebration of Celtic culture.

The Vancouver Playhouse International Wine Festival (www.playhousewinefest.com) in late March or early April (dates change yearly) is a major wine-tasting event featuring the latest international vintages. The **Vancouver Sun Run** (www.sunrun.com), in April, is Canada's biggest 10K race, featuring 40,000 runners, joggers, and walkers who race through 10 scenic kilometers. The run starts and finishes at BC Place Stadium. On the first Sunday in May, the **Vancouver International Marathon** (www.vancouvermarathon.com) lures runners from around the world to compete here. During **Dine Out Vancouver,** which takes place over 10 days, from late April to early May, Vancouver's hottest restaurants offer three-course dinners for C$18, C$28, and C$38 per person; contact Tourism Vancouver (www.tourismvancouver.com) for details.

During the **Vancouver International Jazz Festival** (✆ **604/872-5200;** www.coastaljazz.ca) in late June and early July, more than 800 international jazz and blues players perform at 25 venues around town. Running July to September, the **Bard on the Beach Shakespeare Festival** in Vanier Park (✆ **604/739-0559;** www.bardonthebeach.org) presents Shakespeare's plays in a tent overlooking English Bay. On **Canada Day,** July 1, Canada Place Pier hosts an all-day celebration including music and dance and an evening fireworks display over the harbor to top off the entertainment. The second or third weekend in July brings the **Vancouver Folk Music Festival** (✆ **604/602-9798;** www.thefestival.bc.ca). International folk music is played outdoors at Jericho Beach Park. During the **HSBC Celebration of Light** (www.celebration-of-light.com), three international fireworks companies compete for a coveted title by launching their best displays rigged to explode in time to accompanying music over English Bay Beach. Don't miss the grand finale on the fourth night. In the last week of July and first week of August, the **Vancouver International Comedy Festival** (http://comedyfest.com) features comedians from all over Canada and the United States performing at a variety of venues around town.

On B.C. Day (the first Sun in Aug) the **Vancouver Pride Parade** (**✆ 604/687-0955;** www.vancouverpride.ca), a huge gay- and lesbian- parade, covers a route along Denman and Davie streets, beginning at noon and caps off the weeklong Pride Week festivities. In August, the **Abbottsford International Air Show (✆ 604/852-8511;** www.abbotsfordairshow.com) features barnstorming stuntmen and precision military pilots flying everything from Sopwith Camels to VTOLs and Stealth Bombers. Mid-August to Labour Day, the **Pacific National Exhibition** (**✆ 604/253-2311;** www.pne.bc.ca) offers everything from big-name entertainment to a demolition derby, livestock demonstrations, logger sports competitions, fashion shows, and North America's finest all-wooden roller coaster.

Every October, the **Vancouver International Film Festival** (**✆ 604/685-0260;** www.viff.org) features 250 new works, revivals, and retrospectives, representing filmmakers from 40 countries. All December, the **Christmas Carol Ship Parade** (www.carolships.org) lights up Vancouver Harbour; harbor cruise ships decorated with colorful Christmas lights sail around English Bay while on-board guests sip cider and sing Christmas Carols.

OUTDOOR ACTIVITIES & SPECTATOR SPORTS

Vancouver is definitely an outdoors-oriented city and just about every imaginable sport has an outlet within the city limits. Downhill and cross-country skiing, snowshoeing, sea kayaking, fly-fishing, hiking, paragliding, and mountain biking are just a few of the options. Activities that can be enjoyed in the vicinity include rock climbing, river rafting, and heli-skiing. An excellent resource for outdoor enthusiasts is **Mountain Equipment Co-op,** 130 W. Broadway (**✆ 604/872-7858;** www.mec.ca). The MEC's retail store has a knowledgeable staff, the co-op publishes an annual mail-order catalog, and you can find useful outdoor activities information on the website.

Outdoor Activities

BEACHES Only 10% of Vancouver's annual rainfall occurs during June, July, and August; 60 days of summer sunshine is not uncommon, although the Pacific never really warms up enough for a comfortable swim. Still, **English Bay Beach ★★**—at the end of Davie Street, off Denman Street and Beach Avenue—is a great place to see sunsets. The bathhouse dates to the turn of the 20th century, and a huge playground slide is mounted on a raft just off the beach every summer.

On **Stanley Park's** western rim, **Second Beach ★** is a short stroll north from English Bay Beach. A playground, a snack bar, and an immense heated ocean-side **pool ★** (**✆ 604/257-8370**), open from May through September, make this a convenient and fun spot for families. Admission to the pool is C$5.15 adults, C$3.60

seniors and children 13 to 18, and C$2.60 children 6 to 12. Farther along the seawall, due north of Stanley Park Drive, lies secluded **Third Beach.** Locals tote along grills and coolers to this spot, a popular place for summer-evening barbecues and sunset-watching.

South of English Bay Beach, near the Burrard Street Bridge, is **Sunset Beach ★**. Running along False Creek, it's actually a picturesque strip of sandy beaches filled with enormous driftwood logs that serve as windbreaks and provide a little privacy for sunbathers and picnickers. A snack bar, a soccer field, and a long, gently sloping grassy hill are available for people who prefer lawn to sand.

On the West Side, **Kitsilano Beach ★★★**, along Arbutus Drive near Ogden Street, is affectionately called Kits Beach. It's an easy walk from the Maritime Museum and the False Creek ferry dock. If you want to do a saltwater swim but can't handle the cold, head to the huge (135m/443-ft.) heated (25°C/77°F) **Kitsilano Pool ★★**. Admission is the same as for Second Beach Pool, above.

Farther west on the other side of Pioneer Park is **Jericho Beach** (Alma St. off Point Grey Rd.), another local after-work and weekend social spot. **Locarno Beach,** off Discovery Street and Marine Drive, and **Spanish Banks,** on Northwest Marine Drive, wrap around the northern point of the UBC campus and University Hill. (Be forewarned that beachside restrooms and concessions on the promontory end abruptly at Locarno Beach.) Below UBC's Museum of Anthropology is **Point Grey Beach,** a restored harbor-defense site. The next beach is **Wreck Beach ★★★**—Canada's largest nude beach. You get down to Wreck Beach by taking the very steep Trail 6 on the UBC campus near Gate 6 down to the water's edge. Extremely popular with locals and maintained by its own preservation society, Wreck Beach is also the city's most pristine and least-developed sandy stretch, bordered on three sides by towering trees.

For information on any of Vancouver's many beaches, call ✆ **604/738-8535** (summer only).

BICYCLING & MOUNTAIN BIKING Cycling in Vancouver is fun, amazingly scenic, and very popular. Cycling maps are available at most bicycle retailers and rental outlets. Some West End hotels offer guests bike storage and rentals. Hourly rentals run around C$10 to C$16 an hour for a mountain or city bike, C$30 to C$80 for a day; helmets and locks are included. Popular shops that rent city and mountain bikes, child trailers, child seats, and in-line skates (protective gear included) include **Spokes Bicycle Rentals & Espresso Bar,** 1798 W. Georgia St. (✆ **604/688-5141;** www.spokesbicyclerentals.com), at the corner of Denman Street at entrance to Stanley Park; **Alley Cat Rentals,** 1779 Robson St., in the alley (✆ **604/684-5117**); and **Bayshore Bicycle and Rollerblade Rentals,** 745 Denman St. (✆ **604/688-2453;** www.bayshorebikerentals.ca). ***Note:*** Be advised that wearing a helmet is mandatory, and one will be included in your bike rental.

The most popular cycling path in the city runs along the **seawall ★★★** around the perimeter of Stanley Park. Another popular route is the seaside bicycle route, a 15km (9⅓-mile) ride that begins at English Bay and continues around False Creek to the University of British Columbia. Serious mountain bikers also have a wealth of world-class options within a short drive from downtown Vancouver. The trails on **Grouse Mountain** (p. 656) are some of the lower mainland's best.

BOATING With thousands of miles of protected shoreline along British Columbia's west coast, boaters enjoy some of the finest cruising grounds in the world.

Explore the many inlets, passages, and islands. You can rent powerboats for a few hours or up to several weeks at **Bonnie Lee Boat Rentals** (1676 Duranleau St., Granville Island; ✆ **866/933-7447** or 604/290-7447; www.bonnielee.com), a company that has been renting boats and offering chartered fishing expeditions since 1980. Rates for a 5.8m (19-ft.) sport boat with 115-horsepower motor begin at C$65 per hour (plus C$10 insurance fee and fuel) or C$400 for an 8-hour package. **Jerry's Boat Rentals** (Granville Island; ✆ **604/696-5500**) is steps away and offers similar deals.

CANOEING & KAYAKING Both placid, urban False Creek and the incredibly beautiful 30km (19-mile) North Vancouver fjord known as Indian Arm have launching points that can be reached by car or bus. Prices range from about C$40 per 2-hour minimum rental to C$70 per 5-hour day for single kayaks and about C$60 for canoe rentals. Customized tours range from C$75 to C$150 per person.

Ecomarine Ocean Kayak Centre, 1668 Duranleau St., Granville Island (✆ **888/425-2925** or 604/689-7575; www.ecomarine.com), has 2-hour, daily and weekly kayak rentals, as well as courses and organized tours. The company also has an office at the **Jericho Sailing Centre,** 1300 Discovery St., at Jericho Beach (✆ **604/222-3565**). In North Vancouver, **Deep Cove Canoe and Kayak Rentals,** 2156 Banbury Rd. (at the foot of Gallant St.), Deep Cove (✆ **604/929-2268;** www.deepcovekayak.com), is an easy starting point for anyone planning an Indian Arm run. It offers hourly and daily rentals of canoes and kayaks, as well as lessons and customized tours.

Lotus Land Tours, 2005–1251 Cardero St. (✆ **800/528-3531** or 604/684-4922; www.lotuslandtours.com), runs guided kayak tours on Indian Arm that come with hotel pickup, a barbecue salmon lunch, and incredible scenery. The wide, stable kayaks are perfect for first-time paddlers. One-day tours cost C$180 adults, C$140 for children.

ECO-TOURS **Lotus Land Tours** runs guided kayak tours on Indian Arm (see "Canoeing & Kayaking," above). From late November to the end of January, this small local company also offers unique float trips on the Squamish River to see the large concentration of bald eagles up close. **Rockwood Adventures** (✆ **888/236-6606** or 604/741-0802; www.rockwoodadventures.com) has 4-hour **guided walks of the North Shore rainforest ★**, complete with a trained naturalist, stops in Capilano Canyon and at the Lynn Canyon Suspension Bridge (p. 656), and lunch. Cost is C$95 adults, C$85 seniors and students, and C$60 children 6 to 11.

FISHING With the Pacific Ocean to the west and an intricate river and lake system throughout the province, British Columbia has long been one of North America's best fishing destinations. Five species of salmon, rainbow and Dolly Varden trout, steelhead, and sturgeon abound in the local waters around Vancouver. To fish, anglers over the age of 16 need a **nonresident saltwater or freshwater license.** Licenses are available provincewide from more than 500 vendors, including tackle shops, sporting-goods stores, resorts, service stations, marinas, charter boat operators, and department stores. Saltwater (tidal waters) fishing licenses cost C$7.50 for 1 day, C$20 for 3 days, and C$33 for 5 days. Fly-fishing in national and provincial parks requires special permits, which you can get at any park site for a nominal fee. Permits are valid at all Canadian parks.

The *B.C. Tidal Waters Sport Fishing Guide, B.C. Sport Fishing Regulations Synopsis for Non-Tidal Waters,* and the *B.C. Fishing Directory and Atlas,* available at many tackle shops, are good sources of information. The *Vancouver Sun* prints a daily **fishing report** in the B section that details which fish are in season and where they can be found. Another good source of general information is the **Fisheries and Ocean Canada** website (www.pac.dfo-mpo.gc.ca).

Hanson's Fishing Outfitters, 102–580 Hornby St. (© **604/684-8988;** www.hansons-outfitters.com), and **Granville Island Boat Rentals,** 1696 Duranleau St. (© **604/682-6287**), are outstanding outfitters. **Bonnie Lee Fishing Charters Ltd.,** 1676 Duranleau St., Granville Island (© **604/290-7447;** www.bonnielee.com), is another reputable outfitter and also sells fishing licenses.

GOLF Golf is a year-round sport in Vancouver. With five public 18-hole courses, half a dozen pitch-and-putt courses in the city, and dozens more nearby, golfers are never far from their love. For discounts and short-notice tee times at more than 30 Vancouver-area courses, contact the **A-1 Last Minute Golf Hot Line** (© **800/684-6344** or 604/878-1833; www.lastminutegolfbc.com).

A number of excellent public golf courses, maintained by the **Vancouver Board of Parks and Recreation** (© **604/280-1818** to book tee times; http://vancouver.ca/parks), can be found throughout the city. **Langara Golf Course** (6706 Alberta St., around 49th Ave. and Cambie St.; © **604/713-1816**), built in 1926 and recently renovated and redesigned, is one of the most popular golf courses in the province. Depending on the course, summer greens fees range from C$15 to C$38 for an adult, with discounts for seniors, children, and off-season tee times.

The public **University Golf Club** (5185 University Blvd.; © **604/224-1818;** www.universitygolf.com) is a great 6,560-yard, par-71 course with a clubhouse, pro shop, locker rooms, bar and grill, and sports lounge.

Leading private clubs are situated on the North Shore and in Vancouver. Check with your club at home to see if you have reciprocal visiting memberships with one of the following: **Capilano Golf and Country Club,** 420 Southborough Dr., West Vancouver (© 604/922-9331); **Marine Drive Golf Club,** West 57th Avenue and Southwest Marine Drive (© 604/261-8111); **Seymour Golf and Country Club,** 3723 Mt. Seymour Pkwy., North Vancouver (© 604/929-2611); **Point Grey Golf and Country Club,** 3350 SW Marine Dr. (© 604/261-3108); and **Shaughnessy Golf and Country Club,** 4300 SW Marine Dr. (© 604/266-4141). Greens fees range from C$42 to C$75.

HIKING Great trails for hikers of all levels run through Vancouver's dramatic environs. Good trail maps are available from **International Travel Maps and Books,** 539 Pender St. (© **604/687-3320;** www.itmb.com), which also stocks guidebooks and topographical maps. You can pick up a local trail guide at any bookstore.

If you're looking for a challenge without a longtime commitment, hike the aptly named **Grouse Grind** from the bottom of **Grouse Mountain** (p. 656) to the top; then buy a one-way ticket down on the Grouse Mountain SkyRide gondola.

For a bit more scenery with a bit less effort, take the Grouse Mountain SkyRide up to the **Grouse chalet** and start your hike at an altitude of 1,100m (3,609 ft.). The trail north of **Goat Mountain** is well marked and takes approximately 6 hours round-trip, though you may want to build in some extra time to linger on the top of Goat and take in the spectacular 360-degree views of Vancouver, Vancouver Island, and the snowcapped peaks of the Coast Mountains.

Lynn Canyon Park, Lynn Headwaters Regional Park, Capilano River Regional Park, Mount Seymour Provincial Park, Pacific Spirit Park, and

Cypress Provincial Park (see "Exploring Vancouver," earlier in this chapter) have good, easy to challenging trails that wind up through stands of Douglas fir and cedar and contain a few serious switchbacks. Pay attention to the trail warnings posted at the parks (some have bear habitats), and always remember to sign in with the park service at the start of your chosen trail.

ICE SKATING The highest ice-skating rink in Canada is located on **Grouse Mountain** (p. 656). In the city, the **West End Community Centre,** 870 Denman St. (✆ **604/257-8333**), rents skates at its enclosed rink, open October through March. Another option is the **Kitsilano Ice Rink,** 2690 Larch St. (✆ **604/257-6983;** www.vancouverparks.ca), open from October to June. The enormous **Burnaby 8 Rinks Ice Sports Centre,** 6501 Sprott, Burnaby (✆ **604/291-0626**), is the Vancouver Canucks' official practice facility. It has eight rinks, is open year-round, and offers lessons and rentals. Call ahead to check hours for public skating at all these rinks.

IN-LINE SKATING All over Vancouver you'll find lots of locals rolling along beach paths, streets, park paths, and promenades. If you didn't bring a pair of blades, try **Bayshore Bicycle and Rollerblade Rentals,** 745 Denman St. (✆ **604/688-2453;** www.bayshorebikerentals.com). Rentals run C$5 per hour or C$20 for 8 hours. For information on in-line skating lessons and group events, visit www.inlineskatevancouver.com.

JOGGING Local runners traverse the **Stanley Park seawall ★★★** and the paths around **Lost Lagoon** and **Beaver Lake.** If you're a dawn or dusk runner, take note that this is one of the world's safer city parks. However, if you're alone, don't tempt fate—stick to open and lighted areas. Other prime jogging areas in the city are **Kitsilano Beach, Jericho Beach,** and **Spanish Banks** (for more information, see "Beaches," above); all of them offer flat, well-maintained running paths along the ocean.

The **Sun Run** in April and the **Vancouver International Marathon** in May attract runners from around the world. Contact the **Vancouver International Marathon Society,** 1601 Bayshore Dr., in the Westin Bayshore Hotel (✆ **604/872-2928;** www.vanmarathon.bc.ca), or the **Vancouver Sun Run,** 655 Burrard St. (✆ **604/689-9441;** www.sunrun.com), for information.

PARAGLIDING In Surrey, **Deimos Paragliding Flight School** (✆ **877/359-7413** or 604/418-7328; www.deimospg.com) offers tandem flights from Burnaby Mountain and other locations for C$160. No experience is necessary for this unforgettable adventure; the actual flight, controlled by an experienced instructor, takes approximately 20 minutes.

SAILING Trying to navigate a sailboat in the unfamiliar straits around Vancouver is unwise and unsafe unless you enroll in a local sailing course before attempting it. Knowing the tides, currents, and channels is essential, and you won't be able to rent a sailboat without this basic navigational and safety knowledge. Multiday instruction packages sometimes include guided Gulf Island cruises.

Cooper Boating Centre, 1620 Duranleau St. (✆ **604/687-4110;** www.cooperboating.com) offers chartered cruises, boat rentals, and sail-instruction packages.

SKIING & SNOWBOARDING World-class skiing lies outside the city at the **Whistler Blackcomb Ski Resort,** 110km (68 miles) north of Vancouver; see chapter 16. However, you don't have to leave the city to get in a few runs. It seldom snows in the city's downtown and central areas, but Vancouverites can ski before work and after dinner at the three ski resorts in the North Shore mountains. These local mountains played host to the freestyle and snowboard events in the 2010 Winter Games.

Grouse Mountain Resort (6400 Nancy Greene Way, North Vancouver; ✆ **604/984-0661,** or 604/986-6262 for a snow report; www.grousemountain.com) is about 3km (1¾ miles) from the Lions Gate Bridge and overlooks the Burrard Inlet and Vancouver skyline. Four chairs, two beginner tows, and two T-bars take you to 24 alpine runs. The resort has night skiing, special events, instruction, and a spectacular view, as well as a 90m (295-ft.) half-pipe for snowboarders. All skill levels are covered, with two beginner trails, three blue trails, and five black-diamond runs, including Coffin and Inferno, which follow the east slopes down from 1,230 to 750m (4,035–2,461 ft.). Rental packages and a full range of facilities are available. Lift tickets good for all-day skiing are C$55 adults, C$45 seniors and teens 13-18, C$25 children 5 to 12, and free for children 4 and under. Lift prices do not include your gondola ride to the summit.

Mount Seymour Provincial Park (1700 Mt. Seymour Rd., North Vancouver; ✆ **604/986-2261;** www.mountseymour.com), has the area's highest base elevation; it's accessible via four chairs and a tow. All-day lift tickets are C$44 adults, C$35 seniors, C$37 children 12 to 19, and C$22 children 6 to 11. Nighttime skiing from 4 to 10pm costs less. In addition to day and night skiing, the facility offers snowboarding, snowshoeing, and tobogganing along its 22 runs, as well as 26km (16 miles) of cross-country trails. The resort specializes in teaching first-timers. Camps for children and teenagers, and adult clinics, are available throughout the winter. Mount Seymour has one of Western Canada's largest equipment rental shops, which will keep your measurements on file for return visits. Shuttle service is available during ski season from various locations on the North Shore, including the Lonsdale Quay SeaBus. For more information, call ✆ **604/953-3333.**

Cypress Bowl (1610 Mt. Seymour Rd.; ✆ **604/926-5612,** or 604/419-7669 for a snow report; www.cypressmountain.com) was home to the 2010 Winter Olympics freestyle skiing (moguls and aerials), snowboarding (half-pipe and parallel giant slalom), and new ski-cross events. In 2008, Cypress opened nine new runs for intermediate and expert skiers and snowboarders, accessed by a new quad chairlift, and a new day lodge opened for the winter 2008/2009 season. Cypress has the area's longest vertical drop (525m/1,722 ft.), challenging ski and snowboard runs, and 16km (10 miles) of track-set cross-country ski trails (including 5km/3 miles set aside for night skiing).

SWIMMING & WATERSPORTS The **Vancouver Aquatic Centre** (1050 Beach Ave., at the foot of Thurlow St.; ✆ **604/665-3424**), has a heated, 50m (164-ft.) Olympic pool, saunas, whirlpools, weight rooms, diving tanks, locker rooms, showers, child care, and a tot pool. Admission is C$6 adults, C$3 children 2 to 12. The new, coed **YWCA Fitness Centre** (535 Hornby St.; ✆ **604/895-5800;** www.ywcavan.org), in the heart of downtown, has a 6-lane, 25m (82-ft.), ozonated (much milder than chlorinated) pool, steam room, whirlpool, conditioning gym, and aerobic studios. A day pass is C$18 adults. UBC's **Aquatic Centre** (6121 University Blvd.; ✆ **604/822-4522;** www.aquatics.ubc.ca), located next door to the Student Union Building and the bus loop, sets aside time for public use. Admission is C$5 adults, C$4 students and teens 13-18, and C$3 seniors and children 3 to 12. Vancouver's midsummer saltwater temperature rarely exceeds 65°F (18°C). If you've really got a hankering to have a saltwater swim, there are **heated outdoor pools** at both **Kitsilano Beach ★★★** and **Second Beach ★**.

TENNIS The city maintains 180 outdoor hard courts that have a 1-hour limit and accommodate patrons on a first-come, first-served basis from 8am until dusk. Local courtesy dictates that if people are waiting, you surrender the court on the hour. (Heavy usage times are evenings and weekends.) With the exception of the Beach Avenue courts, which charge a nominal fee in summer, all city courts are free.

Stanley Park has four courts near Lost Lagoon and 17 courts near the Beach Avenue entrance, next to the Fish House Restaurant. During the summer season (May–Sept), six courts are taken over for pay tennis and can be prebooked by calling **✆ 604/605-8224. Queen Elizabeth Park**'s 18 courts service the central Vancouver area, and **Kitsilano Beach Park**'s ★ 10 courts service the beach area between Vanier Park and the UBC campus.

WHITE-WATER RAFTING A 2½-hour drive from Vancouver, on the wild Nahatlatch River, **Reo Rafting** (845 Spence Way, Anmore; **✆ 800/736-7238** or 604/461-7238; www.reorafting.com) offers some of the best guided white-water trips in the province, at a very reasonable price. One-day packages—including lunch, all your gear, and 4 to 5 hours on the river—start at C$148 adults. Multiday trips and group packages are available, and they can provide transportation from Vancouver.

Only a 1½-hour drive from the city is **Chilliwack River Rafting,** 49704 Chilliwack Lake Rd. (**✆ 800/410-7238;** www.chilliwackriverrafting.com), which offers half-day trips on the Chilliwack River and in the even hairier Chilliwack Canyon. The cost is C$89 adults and C$69 children.

WILDLIFE-WATCHING Vancouver is an internationally famous stop for naturalists, eco-tourists, pods of orca whales, and thousands of migratory birds, so bring your camera, binoculars, and bird-spotting books. Salmon, bald eagles, herons, beavers, and numerous rare, indigenous marine and waterfowl species live in the metropolitan area.

Orcas, or killer whales, are the largest mammals to be seen in Vancouver's waters. Three pods (families), numbering about 80 whales, return to this area every year to feed on the salmon that spawn in the Fraser River starting in May and continuing into October. The eldest female leads the group; the head of one pod is thought to have been born in 1911. From April through October, daily excursions offered by **Vancouver Whale Watch** (12240 2nd Ave., Richmond; **✆ 604/274-9565;** www.vancouverwhalewatch.com) focus on the majestic whales, plus Dall's porpoises, sea lions, seals, eagles, herons, and other wildlife. The cost is C$125 per person. **Steveston Seabreeze Adventures** (12551 No. 1 Rd., Richmond; **✆ 604/272-7200**) also offers whale-watching tours for about the same price. Both companies offer a shuttle service from downtown Vancouver.

Thousands of migratory birds following the Pacific Flyway rest and feed in the Fraser River delta south of Vancouver, especially at the 340-hectare (840-acre) **George C. Reifel Bird Sanctuary,** 5191 Robertson Rd., Westham Island (**✆ 604/946-6980;** www.reifelbirdsanctuary.com), which was created by a former bootlegger and wetland-bird lover. The sanctuary is wheelchair accessible and open daily from 9am to 4pm. Admission is C$4 for adults and C$2 for seniors and children.

The **Richmond Nature Park,** 1185 Westminster Hwy. (**✆ 604/718-6188**), was established to preserve the Lulu Island wetlands bog. It features a nature house with educational displays and a boardwalk-encircled duck pond. On Sunday afternoons, knowledgeable guides give free tours and acquaint visitors with this unique environment. Admission is by donation.

During the winter, thousands of bald eagles—in fact, the largest number in North America—line the banks of the **Squamish, Cheakamus,** and **Mamquam** rivers to feed on spawning salmon. To get there by car, take the scenic **Sea-to-Sky Highway** (Hwy. 99) from downtown Vancouver to Squamish and Brackendale; the trip takes about an hour. Contact **Squamish & Howe Sound Visitor Info Centre** (© **604/892-9244;** www.squamishchamber.bc.ca) for more information.

The annual summer salmon runs attract more than bald eagles. Tourists also flock to coastal streams and rivers to watch the waters turn red with leaping coho and sockeye. The salmon are plentiful at the **Capilano Salmon Hatchery** (p. 658), **Goldstream Provincial Park** (p. 710), and numerous other fresh waters.

WINDSURFING Windsurfing is not allowed at the mouth of False Creek near Granville Island, but you can bring a board to **Jericho** (p.662) and **English Bay beaches** (p. 661) ★★, or rent one there. Equipment sales, rentals (including wet suits), and instruction can be found at **Windsure Windsurfing School** (1300 Discovery St., at Jericho Beach; © **604/224-0615;** www.windsure.com). Rentals start at about C$19 per hour, wet suit and life jacket included.

SPECTATOR SPORTS

Spectators and participants will find plenty of activities in Vancouver. You can get schedule information on all major events at Tourism Vancouver's **Touristinfo Centre,** 200 Burrard St. (© **604/683-2000;** www.tourismvancouver.com). You can also get information and purchase tickets from Ticketmaster at the **Vancouver Ticket Centre,** 1304 Hornby St. (© **604/280-4444;** www.ticketmaster.ca), which has 40 outlets in the greater Vancouver area. Popular events such as Canucks games and the Vancouver Indy can sell out weeks or months in advance, so it's a good idea to book ahead.

FOOTBALL The Canadian Football League's **BC Lions** (© **604/589-7627;** www.bclions.com) play their home and Grey Cup championship games (in good seasons) in the 60,000-seat **BC Place Stadium** (777 Pacific Blvd. S., at Beatty and Robson sts.). Canadian football differs from its American cousin: It's a three-down offense game on a field that's 10 yards longer and wider. Some of the plays you see will have American fans leaping out of their seats in surprise. Tickets for individual games are available from Ticketmaster (© **604/280-4639;** www.ticketmaster.ca); prices run from C$30 to C$80.

HOCKEY The National Hockey League's **Vancouver Canucks** play at **Rogers Arena** (formerly known as GM Place; 800 Griffiths Way; © **604/899-4600,** or 604/899-7444 for the event hotline; www.canucks.com). Tickets are C$55 to C$100 and, while difficult to obtain because the season tends to sell out in advance, some individual seats are made available for every home game.

HORSE RACING Thoroughbreds run at **Hastings Park Racecourse,** Exhibition Park, East Hastings and Cassiar streets (© **604/254-1631;** www.hastingspark.com), from mid-April to October. Post time varies; call ahead or check the website for the latest schedule if you want to place a wager. There is a decent restaurant there, so you can make a full evening or afternoon of dining and racing.

RUNNING The **Vancouver Sun Run** in April and the **Vancouver International Marathon** (Canada's largest) in May attract thousands of runners from around the world and even more spectators. Contact the **Vancouver International Marathon Society** (© **604/872-2928;** www.vanmarathon.bc.ca), or the **Vancouver Sun Run,** 655 Burrard St. (© **604/689-9441;** www.sunrun.com), for information.

SOCCER The American Professional Soccer League's **Vancouver Whitecaps** (✆ **604/899-9283**) play at Swangard Stadium (✆ **604/435-7121;** www.white capsfc.com) in Burnaby. Admission is normally C$22 to C$45.

SHOPPING

The Shopping Scene

Blessed with a climate that seems semitropical in comparison to the rest of Canada, Vancouverites tend to do their shopping on the street, browsing from one window to the next, on the lookout for something new. **Robson Street** is the spot for high-end fashions. The 10-block stretch of **Granville Street** from 6th Avenue up to 16th Avenue is where Vancouver's old money comes to shop for classic men's and women's fashions, housewares, and furniture. **Water Street** in **Gastown** features knick-knacks, antiques, cutting-edge furniture, First Nations art, and funky basement retro shops. **Main Street** from 19th Avenue to 27th Avenue means antiques, and lots of 'em. **Granville Island,** a rehabilitated industrial site beneath the Granville Street Bridge, is one of the best places to pick up salmon and other seafood. It's also a great place to browse for crafts and gifts.

Shopping A to Z

ANTIQUES The **Vancouver Antique Centre,** 422 Richards St. (✆ **604/669-7444**), contains 15 shops, specializing in everything from china, glass, Orientalia, and jewelry to military objects, sports, toys, and watches. **Uno Langmann Ltd.,** 2117 Granville St. (✆ **604/736-8825;** www.langmann.com), caters to upscale shoppers, specializing in European and North American paintings, furniture, and silver.

BOOKS Although this small Granville Island store tends toward general interest, **Blackberry Books,** 1663 Duranleau St. (✆ **866/685-6188;** www.bbooks.ca) has a healthy selection of books about art, architecture, and cuisine. They're right across from the public market. **Chapters**, 788 Robson St. (✆ **604/682-4066;** www.chapters.indigo.ca) stocks current titles and has a wide selection.

CAMERA **Dunne & Rundle foto source,** 595 Burard St. (✆ **604/681-9254**), located downtown in the Bentall Shopping Centre, can handle repairs for most major brands and sells parts, accessories, and film.

DEPARTMENT STORES From the establishment of its early trading posts during the 1670s to its modern coast-to-coast chain, **The Bay** (Hudson's Bay Company), 674 Granville St. (✆ **604/681-6211;** www.hbc.com), has built its reputation on quality goods. You can still buy a Hudson's Bay woolen "point" blanket (the colorful stripes originally represented how many beaver pelts each blanket was worth in trade), but you'll also find wares from Tommy Hilfiger, Polo, DKNY, Ellen Tracy, Anne Klein II, and Liz Claiborne. The high-end trend-stocker **Holt Renfrew**, 737 Dunsmuir (✆ **604/681-3121**), can be accessed through Pacific Centre shopping mall and features all the hot designers in a department store setting.

FASHION Many well-known international designers have boutiques in Vancouver, mostly scattered around Robson, Hastings, and Burrard streets. For something uniquely west coast, don't miss the one-of-a-kind First Nations designs of **Dorothy Grant,** 250–757 W. Hastings St. (✆ **604/681-0201;** www.dorothygrant.com). Grant's exquisitely detailed Haida motifs are appliquéd onto coats, leather vests, jackets, caps, and accessories. The clothes are gorgeous and collectible. **Dream,** 311

W. Cordova St. (✆ **604/683-7326**), is one of the few places to find the early collections of local designers. **Zonda Nellis Design Ltd.,** 2203 Granville St. (✆ **604/736-5668;** www.zondanellis.com), offers imaginative hand-woven separates, sweaters, vests, soft knits, and a new line of hand-painted silks.

FIRST NATIONS ART You'll find First Nations art in abundance in Vancouver. **Images for a Canadian Heritage,** 164 Water St. (✆ **604/685-7046;** www.imagesforcanada.com), is a government-licensed First Nations art gallery, featuring traditional and contemporary works. **Hill's Native Art,** 165 Water St. (✆ **504/686-4249;** www.hillsnativeart.com), established in 1946 and claiming to be North America's largest Northwest coast Native art gallery, sells moccasins, ceremonial masks, Cowichan sweaters, wood sculptures, totem poles (priced up to C$35,000), silk-screen prints, soapstone sculptures, and gold, silver, and argillite jewelry. The **Lattimer Gallery,** 1590 W. 2nd Ave. (✆ **604/732-4556;** www.leonalattimer.com), presents museum-quality displays of ceremonial masks, totem poles, argillite sculptures, and gold and silver jewelry. The newly expanded museum gift shop at the **Museum of Anthropology**, University of British Columbia, 6393 NW Marine Dr. (✆ **604/822-5087**), features excellent and elegant works by contemporary First Nations artisans, as well as books about the culture and publications on identifying and caring for Pacific Northwest crafts.

FOOD At **Chocolate Arts,** 2037 W. 4th Ave. (✆ **604/739-0475**), the works are of such exquisite craftsmanship that they're sometimes a wrench to eat. Look for the all-chocolate diorama in the window—it changes every month or so. **Murchie's Tea & Coffee,** 970 Robson St. (✆ **604/669-0783;** www.murchies.com), is a Vancouver institution. You'll find everything from Jamaican Blue Mountain and Kona coffees to Lapsing, Souchong, and Kemun teas. **The Lobsterman,** 1807 Mast Tower Rd. (✆ **604/687-4531;** www.lobsterman.com), is one of the city's best spots to pick up seafood. Salmon and other seafood can be packed for air travel. And the **Salmon Village,** 779 Thurlow St. (✆ **604/685-3378;** www.salmonvillage.com), specializes in salmon of all varieties.

GIFTS For a good range of basic souvenirs, try **Canadian Impressions at the Station,** 601 Cordova St. (✆ **604/681-3507**). The store carries lumberjack shirts, Cowichan sweaters, T-shirts, and other trinkets.

JEWELRY Opened in 1879, **Henry Birk & Sons Ltd.,** 698 W. Hastings St. (✆ **604/669-3333**), has a long tradition of designing and creating beautiful jewelry and watches and selling jewelry to international designers. On Granville Island, **The Raven and the Bear,** 1528 Duranleau St. (✆ **604/669-3990**), is a great spot to shop for west coast Native jewelry.

MALLS & SHOPPING CENTERS The **Pacific Centre Mall,** 700 W. Georgia St. (✆ **604/688-7236**), is a 3-block complex containing 200 shops and services, including Godiva, Benetton, Crabtree & Evelyn, and Eddie Bauer. For more upscale shopping, try the **Sinclair Centre,** 757 W. Hastings St. (✆ **604/659-1009;** www.sinclaircentre.com), which houses elite shops such as Armani, Leone, and Dorothy Grant, as well as smaller boutiques, art galleries, and a food court.

SHOES John Fluevog of **John Fluevog Boots & Shoes Ltd.,** 65 Water St. (✆ **604/668-6228;** www.fluevog.com), has an international following for his under-C$200 urban and funky creations. You'll find outrageous platforms and clogs, and experiments for the daring footwear fetishist.

SPORTING GOODS Everything you'll ever need for the outdoors is at **Mountain Equipment Co-op,** 130 W. Broadway (✆ **604/872-7858;** www.mec.ca).

TOYS The **Kids Only Market,** Cartwright Street, Granville Island (✆ **604/689-8447;** www.kidsmarket.ca), is a 24-shop complex that sells toys, games, computer software, and books for kids.

WINE **Marquis Wine Cellars,** 1034 Davie St. (✆ **604/684-0445;** www.marquis-wines.com), carries a full range of British Columbian wines as well as a large international selection, and has a very knowledgeable staff.

VANCOUVER AFTER DARK

For the best overview of Vancouver's nightlife, pick up a copy of the weekly tabloid, the ***Georgia Straight*** (www.georgiastraight.com). The Thursday edition of the *Vancouver Sun* contains the weekly entertainment section ***Queue.*** The monthly ***Vancouver* magazine** is filled with listings and strong views about what's really hot in the city. Check out their website at www.vanmag.com. Or get a copy of ***Xtra! West*** (www.xtra.ca), the free gay and lesbian biweekly tabloid, available in shops and restaurants throughout the West End.

The **Alliance for Arts and Culture,** 100–938 Howe St. (✆ **604/681-3535;** www.allianceforarts.com), is a great information source for all performing arts, literary events, and art films. The office is open Monday through Friday from 9am to 5pm.

Ticketmaster (Vancouver Ticket Centre), 1304 Hornby St. (✆ **604/280-3311;** www.ticketmaster.ca), has 40 outlets in the Vancouver area. Half-price tickets for same-day shows and events are available at the **Tickets Tonight** (www.tickets tonight.ca) kiosk (Tues–Sat 11am–6pm) in the **Vancouver Touristinfo Centre,** 200 Burrard St. (✆ **604/684-2787** record events info). The Touristinfo Centre is open from May to Labour Day daily from 8am to 6pm; the rest of the year, it's open Monday through Saturday from 8:30am to 5pm.

Three major Vancouver theaters regularly host touring performances: the **Orpheum Theatre,** 801 Granville St. (✆ **604/665-3050**); the **Queen Elizabeth Theatre,** 600 Hamilton St. (✆ **604/665-3050**); and the **Vancouver Playhouse,** in the Queen Elizabeth Theatre complex (✆ **604/873-3311;** www.vancouverplayhouse.com). They share a website at **www.vancouver.ca/theatres.** On the campus of UBC, the **Chan Centre for the Performing Arts,** 6265 Crescent Rd. (✆ **604/822-2697;** www.chancentre.com), hosts a winter concert series; its acoustics are the best in town.

The Performing Arts

Theater isn't only an indoor pastime here. There's an annual summertime Shakespeare series called **Bard on the Beach,** in Vanier Park (✆ **604/737-0625;** www.bardonthebeach.org). You can also bring a picnic dinner to Stanley Park and watch **Theatre Under the Stars** (✆ **604/687-0174;** www.tuts.bc.ca), which features popular musicals and light comedies. For more original fare, don't miss **Vancouver's Fringe Festival** (✆ **604/257-0350;** www.vancouverfringe.com). The Fringe features more than 500 innovative and original shows each September.

The **Arts Club Theatre Company** presents live theater in two venues, the Granville Island Stage at the Arts Club Theatre, 1585 Johnston St., and the Stanley Theatre, 2750 Granville St. For information on both theaters, call ✆ **604/687-1644** or head online to **www.artsclub.com.**

In a converted early-1900s church, the **Vancouver East Cultural Centre** (the "Cultch" to locals), 1895 Venables St. (© **604/251-1363;** www.vecc.bc.ca), hosts avant-garde theater productions, children's programs, and art exhibits.

OPERA The first-rate **Vancouver Opera,** 500–845 Cambie St. (© **604/683-0222;** www.vancouveropera.ca), alternates between less performed or new works and older, more popular favorites. English supertitles projected above the stage help audiences follow the stories.

CLASSICAL MUSIC The **Vancouver Symphony,** 601 Smithe St. (© **604/876-3434;** www.vancouversymphony.ca), presents a number of series: great classical works, light classics, modern classics and ethnic works, popular and show tunes, and music geared toward school-age children. Other classical groups in town include the **Vancouver Bach Choir,** 805–235 Keith Rd., West Vancouver (© **604/921-8012;** www.vancouverbachchoir.com); the **Vancouver Cantata Singers,** 5115 Keith Rd., West Vancouver (© **604/921-8588;** www.cantata.org); and the **Vancouver Chamber Choir,** 1254 W. 7th Ave. (© **604/738-6822;** www.vancouverchamberchoir.com).

DANCE The **Scotiabank Dance Centre,** 677 Davie St. (© **604/606-6400;** www.thedancecentre.com), provides a new focus point for the Vancouver dance community. For fans of modern and original dance, the time to be here is early July, when the **Dancing on the Edge Festival** (© **604/689-0691;** www.dancingontheedge.org) presents 60 to 80 envelope-pushing original pieces over a 10-day period. **Ballet British Columbia,** 502–68 Water St. (© **604/732-5003;** www.balletbc.com), is a young company that strives to present innovative works.

COMEDY & LIVE-MUSIC CLUBS Performers with the **Vancouver TheatreSports League** (© **604/687-1644;** www.vtsl.com) rely on a basic plot supplemented by audience suggestions the actors take and improvise on, often to hilarious results. Performances are in the Arts Club Theatre, 1585 Johnston St., Granville Island.

The old-style suspended hard-wood dance floor makes the **Commodore Ballroom,** 868 Granville St. (© **604/739-7469;** www.commodoreballroom.com), the best place in Vancouver to catch a midsize band—be it R&B, jazz, blues, hip-hop, or pop. For folk, the **WISE Hall**, 1882 Adanac (© **604/254-5858**), is the place to be. And for blues, go to the smoky, sudsy old **Yale Hotel,** 1300 Granville St. (© **604/681-9253;** www.theyale.ca).

BARS, PUBS & LOUNGES **Lift,** 333 Menchions Mews (© **604/689-5438**), built on piers behind the Westin Bayshore Resort, is one of Vancouver's nicest glamour hot spots, offering dramatic views and luxe features such as an illuminated onyx bar. Popular younger-crowd bar-lounges in hoppin' Yaletown include **Afterglow,** 350 Davie St. (© **604/642-0577**), and **Opus Bar,** 50 Davie St. (© **604/642-0577**), in the trend-setting Opus Hotel. More romantic and less noisy, with piano music instead of high-decibel rock, is **Bacchus Lounge** in the Wedgewood Hotel, 845 Hornby St. (© **604/608-5319**), a hot spot for professional powerbrokers. In Gastown, **The Irish Heather,** 210 Carrall St. (© **604/688-9779**), is a pleasant Irish pub with numerous nooks and crannies, some of the best beer in town, and a menu that does a lot with the traditional Emerald Isle spud. **The Shark Club Bar and Grill,** 180 W. Georgia St. (© **604/687-4275**), is the city's premier sports bar. If you're looking for a brew pub, **Steamworks Pub & Brewery,** 375 Water St. (© **604/689-2739**), is your best bet. Choose from a dozen in-house beers, from dark Australian-style ales to light, refreshing wheat lagers. **The Yaletown Brewing**

Company, 1111 Mainland St. (✆ **604/688-0039**), also offers good home-brewed fare. Vancouver's best spot for late-night jazz and jam sessions is **O'Douls** in the Listel Hotel, 1300 Robson St. (✆ **604/684-8461**).

DANCE CLUBS Who knows how long they will be around? At press time, these were among the hottest dance floors in Vancouver. Downtown, **Au BAR,** 674 Seymour St. (✆ **604/648-2227**), is packed with beautiful people milling from bar to dance floor to bar (there are two) and back again. **Caprice,** 965 Granville St. (✆ **604/681-2114**), has an upstairs lounge, with a fireplace, a big-screen TV showing old movies, and doors opening onto a patio; downstairs, The Nightclub is a large room with a funky semicircular glowing blue bar, big comfy wall banquettes, a secluded circular passion pit in one corner, and a medium-size dance floor.

The Cellar, 1006 Granville St. (✆ **604/605-4350**), has a small dance floor and a DJ who mostly spins Top 40, but patrons are far less interested in groovin' than they are in meeting other Cellar dwellers, a process facilitated by a wall-length message board upon which pickup lines are posted. Located in the heart of Gastown, **Fabric Nightclub**, 66 Water St. (✆ **604/683-6695**), is one of Vancouver's biggest and most legendary rooms with a 500-plus capacity, couches, a VIP balcony section that overlooks the giant dance floor, plus some of the biggest-name DJs in the world. It may be venerable, but the line of limos outside **Richard's on Richards,** 1036 Richards St. (✆ **604/687-6794**), attests to the fact that Dick's is still hot; inside there are two floors, four bars, a laser-light system, and lots of DJ'ed dance tunes and concerts.

GAY & LESBIAN BARS The "Gay Village" is in the West End, particularly on Davie and Denman streets. Many clubs feature theme nights and dance parties, drag shows are ever popular, and every year in early August, as Gay Pride nears, the scene goes into overdrive. The **Gay Lesbian Transgendered Bisexual Community Centre,** 2–1170 Bute St. (✆ **604/684-5307;** www.lgtbcentrevancouver.com), has information on the current hot spots, but to find out what's *au courant* it's easier just to pick up a free copy of ***Xtra West!,*** available in most downtown cafes.

Reflecting the graying and—gasp!—mellowing of Vancouver's boomer-age gay crowd, the hottest hangout for gays is the **Fountain Head,** 1025 Davie St. (✆ **604/687-2222**), a pub located in the heart of the city's gay ghetto on Davie Street. The Head offers excellent microbrewed draft, good pub munchies, and a pleasant humming atmosphere till the morning's wee hours.

The Lotus Hotel, 455 Abbott St. (✆ **604/685-7777**), once among the most disreputable of Gastown gay bars, was given a face-lift and is now home to three separate bars and lounges, all with a largely but not exclusively gay clientele. Downstairs, the Lotus Lounge is one of the hottest house music venues in town, particularly on Straight Up Fridays with an all-female DJ team on the turntables. Lick, on the main floor, is a hot lesbian bar. The third venue, also on the main floor, is Honey, a comfortable restaurant/lounge where a mixed crowd gathers for cocktails or beers. On most nights, the DJs keep the music on a mellow, conversational level. However, on Saturdays, decibels go up significantly when the Queen Bee review, a New York–style cabaret drag show, fills the house.

A multilevel dance club with five floors and three bars, **Numbers,** 1042 Davie St. (✆ **604/685-4077**), hasn't changed much over the years: Extroverts hog the dance floor while admirers look on from the bar above. Great sound and lights. On the second floor, carpets, wood paneling, pool tables, darts, and a lower volume of music give it a neighborhood pub feel. **The Odyssey,** 1251 Howe St. (✆ **604/689-5256**), is the hottest and hippest gay/mixed dance bar in town; shows vary depending on the night.

16

VICTORIA & BRITISH COLUMBIA

by Chris McBeath & Bill McRae

British Columbia is extravagantly scenic and quietly sophisticated. The province runs the length of Canada's west coast, from the Washington border to the Alaskan panhandle. Roughly 947,800 sq. km (365,948 sq. miles), it's more than twice the size of California, though the population (4.3 million) is less than half that of Los Angeles.

British Columbia's outstanding feature is its variety of scenery, climates, and cultures. While most residents live in the greater Vancouver and **Victoria** areas in the southwest, along a coast dotted with islands, beachfront communities, modern cities, and belts of rich farmland, just a few hours' drive to the north or east on any of BC's mostly two-lane highways, the communities are tiny, the sparse population is scattered, and the land is alternately towering forest, fields of stumps left by timber harvests, high alpine wilderness, and even desert. Between these extremes are the areas covered in this chapter.

EXPLORING THE PROVINCE

There's more to British Columbia than Vancouver's urban bustle. In fact, the other Vancouver—**Vancouver Island**—is 90 minutes from the city by ferry. On Vancouver Island is the province's capital, **Victoria.** It's a lovely seaport city that's proud of its British roots, lavish Victorian gardens, and picturesque port. It's also the ideal place to begin exploring the entire island, which stretches more than 450km (280 miles) from Victoria to the northwest tip of Cape Scott. Along the way plan to visit the island's wild west coast at Tofino and view sea life at Campbell River.

It's only a 121km (75-mile) drive from Vancouver to North America's most popular ski resorts at Whistler and Blackcomb mountains. Whistler was the site of several alpine events for the 2010 Winter Olympics, and recent years have seen lots of improvements to what several premier travel magazines have called the top ski resort in North America. Whistler is also a popular summer getaway, offering great fishing, excellent mountain-biking and hiking trails, and world-class golf.

Travel inland to interior BC and leave the maritime climate behind you. In the Okanagan and Thompson river valleys, the landscape turns more arid and mountainous—perfect for orchards and vineyards. The Okanagan is one of Canada's premier wine-growing areas, and its deep glacial lakes and warm summer temperatures provide a sunny golf-and-beach playground for visitors from across Canada.

Visitor Information

TOURIST OFFICES Contact **Tourism British Columbia** (✆ **800/HELLO-BC** or 604/683-2000; www.hellobc.com), and the **Tourism Association of Vancouver Island** (203–335 Wesley St., Nanaimo, BC V9R 2T5 (✆ **250/754-3500;** www.vancouverisland.travel) for details about travel in the province. Contact the individual regional tourism associations and Visitor Information Centres listed in this chapter for more detailed local information.

Another excellent information site online is **Tourism BC** at **www.travel.bc.ca**. And if you plan to head off to Whistler, check out the website for **Whistler and Blackcomb Resorts** at **www.whistlerblackcomb.com.**

The Great Outdoors

It's hard to believe the province's variety of sports and other outdoor activities. Even the most cosmopolitan British Columbians spend their leisure time mountain biking, windsurfing, skiing, or hiking in the surrounding mountains, rivers, and meadows. The varied and largely uninhabited terrain seems to lure visitors to get close to nature.

BIKING Throughout British Columbia are countless marked mountain-bike trails and cycling paths. Highways are also wide and well-maintained, making them well-suited to long-distance bicycle touring. In **Victoria,** the 13km (8-mile) Scenic Marine Drive has an adjacent paved path following Dallas Road and Beach Drive, then returning to downtown via Oak Bay Avenue.

The ski runs on the lower elevations of both **Whistler and Blackcomb mountains** are transformed into mountain-bike trails during summer. Bikes are permitted on the gondola ski lift, allowing you to reach the peaks where the winding marked trails begin. From here, experts, intermediates, and novices barrel down through the colorful alpine slopes. June to September, bike challenges take place regularly on both. In town, the **Valley Trail** offers 20km (12 miles) of paved paths that pass through residential areas and around alpine lakes. Next to the Chateau Whistler Golf Course, the **Lost Lake Trails** feature numerous unpaved alternative routes that fan out from the main lakeside trail.

BOATING & SAILING While you're in **Victoria,** take a leisurely cruise south to Sooke Harbour or up the Strait of Georgia in a rental boat or a skippered vessel. There are many outfitters at the **Brentwood Bay** and **Oak Bay marinas.**

In central B.C., the **Okanagan Valley** lakes lure boaters, houseboaters, and watersports enthusiasts. Whether you're into water-skiing, fishing, jet-skiing, or house- or pleasure boating, local marinas offer full-service rentals (see "The Okanagan Valley," later in this chapter).

CAMPING British Columbia's national parks, provincial parks, marine parks, and private campgrounds are generally filled during summer weekends. Most areas are first come, first served, so stake your claim early in the afternoon (for weekends, arrive by Thurs). However, April 1 to September 15 you can book a provincial park campsite up to 3 months in advance by contacting **Discover Camping** (✆ **800/689-9025** in

16 Southern British Columbia

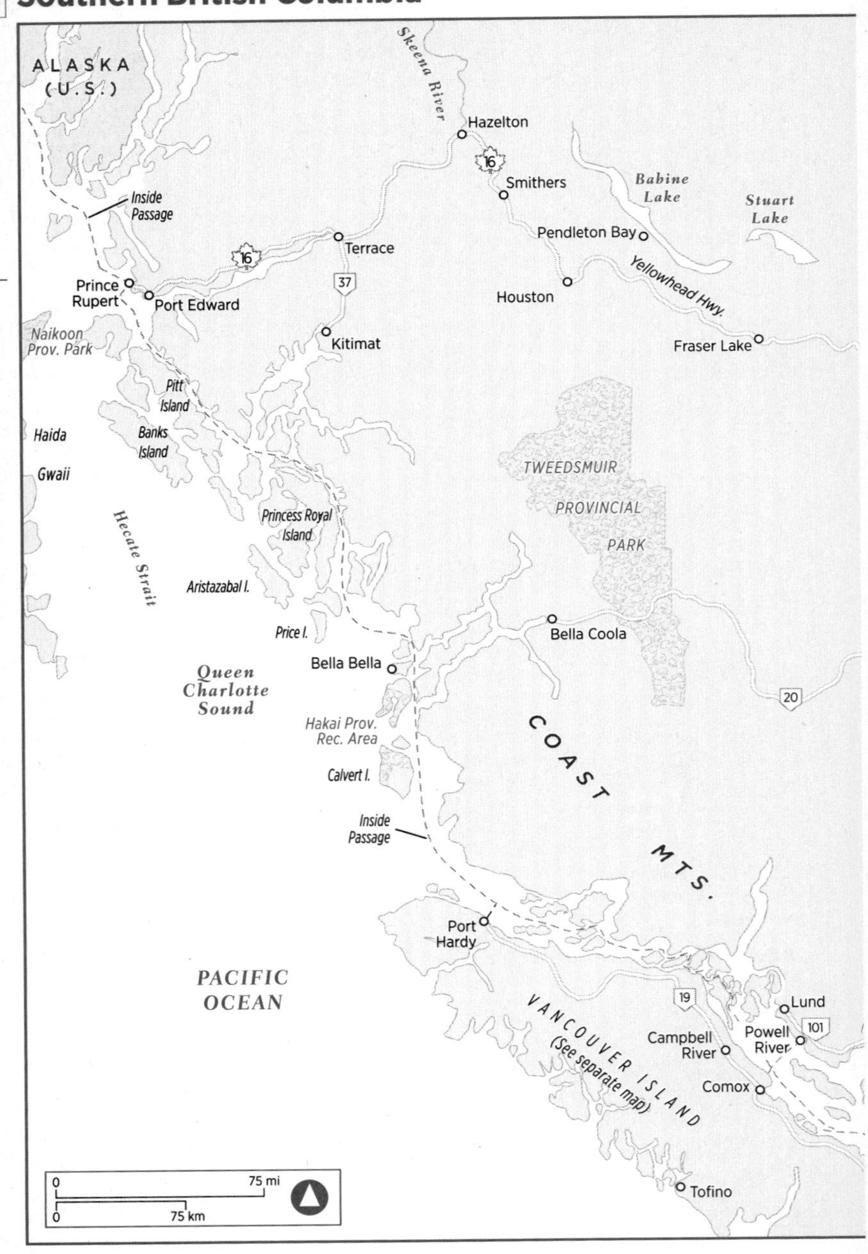

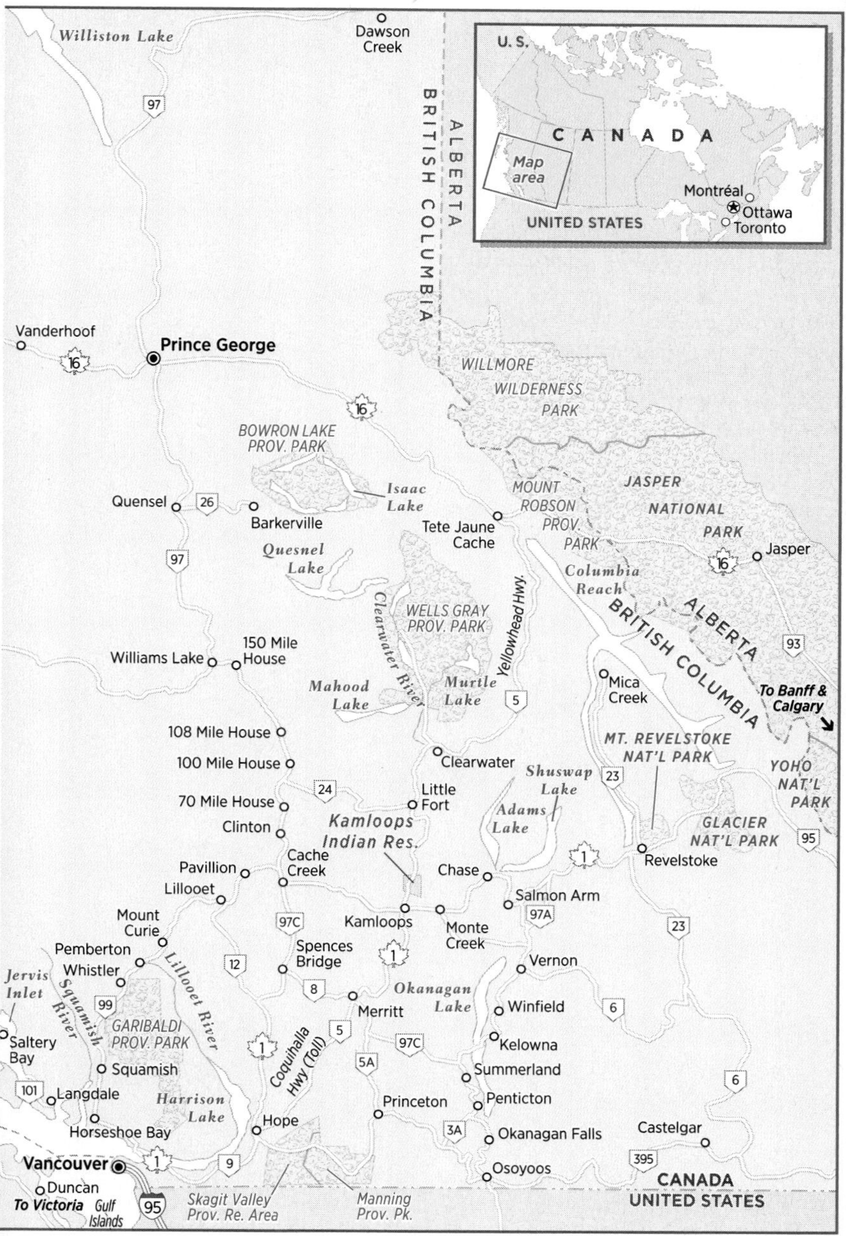
Williston Lake
Dawson Creek
ALBERTA
BRITISH COLUMBIA
U.S.
CANADA
Map area
Montréal
Ottawa
Toronto
UNITED STATES
Vanderhoof
Prince George
WILLMORE WILDERNESS PARK
BOWRON LAKE PROV. PARK
Isaac Lake
Quensel
Barkerville
Tete Jaune Cache
MOUNT ROBSON PROV. PARK
JASPER NATIONAL PARK
Jasper
Quesnel Lake
Clearwater River
WELLS GRAY PROV. PARK
Yellowhead Hwy.
Columbia Reach
Williams Lake
150 Mile House
Mahood Lake
Murtle Lake
Mica Creek
To Banff & Calgary
108 Mile House
100 Mile House
Clearwater
MT. REVELSTOKE NAT'L PARK
YOHO NAT'L PARK
Shuswap Lake
70 Mile House
Little Fort
Adams Lake
Kamloops Indian Res.
Clinton
GLACIER NAT'L PARK
Cache Creek
Pavillion
Chase
Revelstoke
Lillooet
Salmon Arm
Mount Curie
Kamloops
Monte Creek
Pemberton
Spences Bridge
Vernon
Whistler
Jervis Inlet
Squamish River
Lillooet River
Okanagan Lake
Merritt
Winfield
GARIBALDI PROV. PARK
Saltery Bay
Coquihalla Hwy (Toll)
Kelowna
Squamish
Summerland
Langdale
Harrison Lake
Princeton
Penticton
Horseshoe Bay
Hope
Okanagan Falls
Castelgar
Vancouver
Osoyoos
Duncan
To Victoria
Gulf Islands
Skagit Valley Prov. Re. Area
Manning Prov. Pk.
CANADA
UNITED STATES

North America or 604/689-9025; www.discovercamping.ca). It's open Monday through Friday 7am to 7pm and Saturday and Sunday 9am to 5pm. There's a nonrefundable service fee of C$6/night, with an additional C$5 charge for the first night if booked by phone.

The provincial park campgrounds charge C$11 to C$30 per site. There's a 2-week maximum for individual campsite stays. Facilities vary from rustic (walk-in or water-access) to basic (pit toilets and little else) to luxurious (hot showers, flush toilets, and sani-stations). All provincial drive-in campgrounds offer precut-wood piles, grill-equipped fire pits, bear-proof garbage cans, pumped well water, and well-maintained security. The rustic wilderness campgrounds provide minimal services—a covered shelter or simply a cleared patch of ground and little else.

CANOEING & KAYAKING You'll quickly discover why sea kayakers rate **Vancouver Island's west coast** one of the world's best places to paddle. Novice and intermediate paddlers launch from Tofino to explore the marine wilderness of **Clayoquot Sound.** Surf kayakers are drawn to the tidal swells that crash along the shores of **Long Beach,** part of Pacific Rim National Park. And the **Broken Island Group**'s many islands offer paddlers an excellent site for overnight expeditions amid the rugged beauty of the outer coast.

Multiday canoeing trips make popular summer and early fall expeditions; you'll see lots of wildlife and keep as gentle a pace as you like. The **Bowron Lakes** in the Cariboo Country make an excellent weeklong paddle through wilderness.

In **Whistler,** paddlers are treated to an exhilarating stretch of glacial waters that runs behind the village itself. Some kayakers and canoeists call it the "River of Dreams".

CLIMBING Off Valleyview Road, east of Penticton in the Okanagan Valley, **Skaha Bluffs** has more than 400 bolted routes set in place. For info about organized climbing trips throughout the province, contact the **Federation of Mountain Clubs of BC,** 1367 W. Broadway, Vancouver, BC V6H 4A9 (✆ **604/737-3053;** www.mountainclubs.org).

FISHING The famed salmon fisheries along the Pacific Coast face highly restricted catch limits in most areas, and outright bans on fishing in others. Not all salmon species are threatened, though, and rules governing fishing change quickly, so check locally with outfitters to find out if a season will open while you're visiting. Trout are found throughout the region, some reaching great size in the lakes in the British Columbia interior.

Fishing in Canada is regulated by local governments, and appropriate licenses are necessary. Angling for some fish is regulated by season; in some areas, catch-and-release fishing is enforced. Check with local authorities before casting your line.

Numerous fishing packages depart from the **Victoria** docks, where charters run to the southern island's best catch-and-release spots for salmon, halibut, cutthroat, and lingcod. Year-round sportfishing for salmon, steelhead, trout, Dolly Varden char, halibut, cod, and snapper lures anglers to the waters near **Port Alberni** and **Barkley Sound.** Nearby **Long Beach** is great for bottom fishing.

On Vancouver Island's east coast, **Campbell River** is the home of **Painter's Lodge.** A favorite Hollywood getaway for over 70 years, it has entertained Bob Hope, John Wayne (who was a frequent guest), and Goldie Hawn (see "Vancouver Island's East Coast," later in this chapter).

Whistler's **Green River** and nearby **Birkenhead Lake Provincial Park** have runs of steelhead, rainbow trout, Dolly Varden char, cutthroat, and salmon that attract sport anglers from around the world.

GOLFING Considering **Victoria**'s British heritage and its lush rolling landscape, it's no wonder golf is a popular pastime. The three local courses offer terrain—minus thistles—similar to Scotland's, too.

There are also a number of outstanding layouts in central **Vancouver Island,** including an 18-hole course designed by golf legend Les Furber. The **Morningstar** championship course is in Parksville. The **Storey Creek Golf Club** in Campbell River also has a challenging course design and great scenery. There are 9- and 18-hole golf courses in the **Okanagan Valley,** including the **Gallagher's Canyon Golf & Country Club** in Kelowna and **Predator Ridge** in Vernon. Visitors to **Whistler** can tee off at the **Chateau Whistler Golf Course,** at the base of Blackcomb Mountain, or at the **Nicklaus North** golf course on the shore of Green Lake.

HIKING The boardwalked **South Beach Trail** near Tofino provides a contemplative stroll through a Sitka-spruce temperate rainforest, as does the **Big Cedar Trail** on Meares Island. The trails following **Long Beach** allow hikers a close-up glimpse of the marine life that inhabits the tidal pools in the park's many quiet coves (see "Vancouver Island's West Coast," later in this chapter). At Whistler, **Lost Lake Trails**' 30km (19 miles) of marked trails around creeks, beaver dams, blueberry patches, and lush cedars are ideal for biking, Nordic skiing, or just quiet strolling and picnicking. The **Ancient Cedars** area of Cougar Mountain above Whistler's Emerald Estates is an awe-inspiring grove of towering old-growth cedars and Douglas firs.

Whistlers' **Singing Pass Trail** is a 4-hour moderately difficult hike winding from the top of Whistler Mountain down to the village via the Fitzsimmons Valley. North of Whistler, **Nairn Falls Provincial Park** features a gentle 1.5km (1-mile) trail leading to a stupendous view of the icy-cold Green River as it plunges 60m (197 ft.) over a rocky cliff into a narrow gorge. There's also an incredible view of Mount Currie peaking over the treetops.

HORSEBACK RIDING You can take an afternoon ride along a wooded trail near Victoria's Buck Mountain. In Whistler, there are riding trails along the Lillooet River near Pemberton.

RAFTING These popular trips range from daylong excursions, which demand little of a participant other than sitting tight, to long-distance trips through remote backcountry. Risk doesn't correspond to length of trip: Individual rapids and water conditions can make even a short trip a real adventure. You should be comfortable in water, and a good swimmer, if you're floating an adventurous river. Whistler's **Green River** offers novices small rapids and views of snowcapped mountains for their first rafting runs, and the Kicking Horse River near Golden, BC is another excellent destination.

SKIING & SNOWBOARDING **Whistler Mountain,** with a 1,524m (5,000-ft.) vertical and 100 marked runs, is the cream of the province's ski resorts. **Blackcomb Mountain,** which shares its base with Whistler, has a 1,600m (5,249-ft.) vertical and also has 100 marked runs. Ski passes are good for both mountains. **Helicopter skiing** makes another 100-plus runs accessible on nearby glaciers. **Lost Lakes Trails** are converted into miles of groomed cross-country trails, as are the **Valley Trail System, Singing Pass,** and **Ancient Cedars**.

Cross-country and powder skiing are the **Okanagan Valley**'s main winter attractions. **Big White Ski Resort** gets an annual average of 5.5m (18 ft.) of powder and has more than 20km (12 miles) of cross-country trails. **Apex Resort** maintains 56 downhill runs and extensive cross-country trails. Nearby **Crystal Mountain** caters to intermediate and novice downhill skiers and snowboarders.

THREE TRIPS OF A lifetime

Each of the following trips, within striking distance of Vancouver and Victoria, takes you to a place like no other on earth.

KAYAKING CLAYOQUOT SOUND ★★ In 1993, environmentalists from across the province and around the world arrived in British Columbia to protect this pristine fjord on the west coast of Vancouver Island. More than 1,000 were arrested before the government and logging companies gave in and agreed to leave Clayoquot (pronounced *Kla*-kwat) Sound's temperate old-growth rainforest intact. This trip involves paddling a kayak for 2 or 3 days through the protected waters of the sound, from the funky former fishing village of Tofino to a natural hot-springs bath near a Native village of the Hesquiaat people. Along the way, you'll see thousand-year-old trees, glaciers, whales, and bald eagles.

Three companies in Tofino can set you up with a kayak: **Pacific Kayak,** 606 Campbell St. (✆ **250/725-3232;** www.tofino-bc.com/pacifickayak); the **Tofino Sea Kayaking Company,** 320 Main St. (✆ **250/725-4222;** www.tofinokayaking.com); and **Remote Passages,** 71 Wharf St. (✆ **800/666-9833** or 250/725-3330; www.remotepassages.com). Sea kayaking isn't hard, and the great advantage of a trip on Clayoquot Sound is that it's entirely in sheltered inshore waters, though the scenery and the feeling are those of being in a wide-open wilderness. If you're tentative about kayaking on your own, many companies, like the three above, can set you up on a guided trip.

The preferred route leaves Tofino and travels through the protected waters of Clayoquot Sound up to the natural Hot Springs Cove. From there you can fly back—strapping your kayak to the floats of the plane—or retrace your route to Tofino. Whichever way you go, save some time and money for a memorable meal at The Pointe Restaurant in the Wickaninnish Inn (p. 733); after a week in the wilderness, the food here will seem sublime.

SAILING THROUGH THE GREAT BEAR RAIN FOREST ★★★ If you look at a map of British Columbia, you'll see, about halfway up the west coast, an incredibly convoluted region of mountains, fjords, bays, channels, rivers, and inlets. There are next to no roads here—the geography's too intense. Thanks to

WILDLIFE-WATCHING Whether you're in search of the 20,000 **Pacific gray whales** that migrate to **Vancouver Island**'s west coast, or the orcas and salmon off Campbell River, there are land-based observation points and numerous knowledgeable outfitters who can guide you to the best nature and bird-spotting areas on the island.

If you take the ferry cruise up the **Inside Passage,** you have a great opportunity to spot **orcas, Dall porpoises, salmon, bald eagles,** and **sea lions.**

VICTORIA ★★★

Whoever said Victoria was for the newly wed and nearly dead needs to take a second look. Although it certainly has its fair share of the blue-rinse brigade, Victoria is a romantic place and, in the past decade, has evolved into a thriving city. Described by painter Emily Carr as "more English than England," Victoria's charm is moving beyond its quaint facade. Sure, there are still plenty of double-decker buses, heritage brick buildings covered with clambering vines, English-style taverns, that isolation, this is also one of the last places in the world where grizzly bears are still found in large numbers, not to mention salmon, large trees, killer whales, otters, and porpoises. But to get there, you'll need a boat. And if you have to take a boat, why not take a 100-year-old fully rigged 28m (92-ft.) sailing schooner?

Run by an ex-park ranger, **Maple Leaf Adventures,** Box 8845, 28 Bastion Sq., Victoria, BC V8W 3Z1 (© **888/599-5323** or 250/386-7245; www.mapleleafadventures.com), runs a number of trips to this magic area. Owner Kevin Smith is extremely knowledgeable and normally brings along a trained naturalist to explain the fauna (especially the whales, dolphins, and grizzlies). The trips vary from 6 to 13 days and from C$2,180 to C$6,090, covering territory from the midcoast to the Queen Charlotte Islands (Haida Gwaii) to the coasts of Alaska. All include gourmet meals (more than you could ever eat) and comfortable but not luxurious accommodations aboard Kevin's beautiful schooner, the *Maple Leaf.*

HORSE TREKKING ON THE CHILCOTIN PLATEAU ★★ The high plateau country of the BC interior boasts some of the most impressive scenery in the west. Soaring peaks rise above deep valleys, and mountain meadows come alive with flowers that bloom for just a few weeks in high summer. The advantages to taking in this territory on horseback are that the horse's feet get sore, not yours; if you come across a grizzly, you've got some height on him; and horses can carry far more and far better food.

While dude ranches abound in both Canada and the States, there's one key difference to certain British Columbia outfits. It's called a guide-outfitter tenure—one company is granted exclusive rights to run guided tours through that section of wilderness. In BC, the territories are typically 5,000 sq. km (1,930 sq. miles), all high-country wilderness where you likely won't meet another horse team. One of the guide outfitters closest to Vancouver is the **Chilcotin Holidays Guest Ranch,** Gun Creek Road, Gold Bridge, BC V0K 1P0 (© **250/238-2274;** www.chilcotinholidays.com). Their trips run 4 to 7 days, with costs of C$989 to C$1,742, and involve encounters with wildflowers, bighorn sheep, grizzlies, and wolves.

and ever-blooming gardens, but there's also a definite zip in the air as the city's staid and sedentary pleasures give way to hipper places to shop and dine, and more active pursuits to enjoy.

In fact, Victoria is now nicknamed the "recreational capital" of British Columbia, and its range of activities reads like an exhaustive shopping list: year-round golf, whale-watching, fishing, cycling, hiking, and much more. Victoria is located around one of Canada's prettiest harbors, and the water is always busy with ships, kayaks, and so many floatplanes—sometimes as many as 120 takeoffs and landings a day—that the harbor is actually certified as the first "water aerodrome" in North America. Accommodations are first-class, many attractions are worthy of a repeat visit, shopping is varied, and restaurants are cosmopolitan and always busy. The flip side of Victoria's growth, and its balmy climate, is a marked increase in panhandlers.

You'll want to spend at least 2 days here, just to get a taste of what Victoria is becoming. It's also the ideal base from which to explore the rest of Vancouver Island. Extending more than 450km (280 miles) from Victoria to the northwest tip of Cape

Scott, the island offers some of the most dramatic stretches of coastal wilderness in the Pacific Northwest.

Essentials

GETTING THERE

BY PLANE Most visitors arrive via a connecting flight from either **Vancouver International Airport** (✆ **604/207-7077;** www.yvr.ca) or **Seatac International Airport** in Seattle (✆ **206/787-5388;** www.portseattle.org). Airlines flying into the rapidly expanding **Victoria International Airport** (✆ **250/953-7500;** www.victoria airport.com) include **Air Canada** (✆ **888/247-2262;** www.aircanada.com), **Horizon Air** (✆ **800/547-9308;** www.alaskaair.com), and **WestJet** (✆ **888/937-8538;** www.westjet.com). The Victoria International Airport is near the BC Ferries terminal in Sidney, 26km (16 miles) north of Victoria off Highway 17. Highway 17 heads south to Victoria, becoming Douglas Street as you enter downtown.

Airport bus service, operated by **AKAL Airport** (✆ **877/386-2525** or 250/386-2526; www.victoriaairporter.com), takes about 45 minutes to get into town. Buses leave from the airport daily every 30 minutes, from 4:30am to midnight. The adult fare is C$18 one-way. Drop-offs and pickups are made at most Victoria area hotels. **Yellow Cabs** (✆ **800/808-6881** or 250/381-2222), and **Blue Bird Cabs** (✆ **800/665-7055** or 250/382-2222) make airport runs. It costs about C$50 one-way, plus tip.

Several car-rental firms have desks at the Victoria International Airport, including **Avis** (✆ **800/879-2847** or 250/656-6033; www.avis.com), **Budget** (✆ **800/668-9833** or 250/953-5300; www.budgetvictoria.com), **Hertz** (✆ **800/654-3131** or 250/656-2312; www.hertz.com), and **National (Tilden)** (✆ **800/227-7368** or 250/656-2541; www.nationalcar.com). Car reservations are recommended from June to September and during peak travel times on holiday weekends.

Vintage Car Rentals (✆ **250/588-1122**) are among one of the neatest vehicle rentals around. The 1920s era Mercedes SSK100, Bugatti, and 1937 Jaguar certainly look the part, but these kit-car look-alikes are, understandably, more reliable. Rentals are geared to scenic day trips—a treat for meandering the Cowichan Valley or Saanich Peninsula. A 2-hour rental is C$99; an 8-hour rental is C$199.

BY TRAIN **VIA Rail** trains arrive at Victoria's **VIA Rail Station** (450 Pandora Ave., near the Johnson St. Bridge; ✆ **888/842-7245;** www.viarail.com).

BY BUS The **Victoria Bus Depot** is at 700 Douglas St. (behind the Fairmont Empress Hotel). **Pacific Coach Lines** (✆ **800/661-1725** within North America or 250/385-4411 in Victoria; www.pacificcoach.com) offers daily service to and from Vancouver, and it includes the ferry trip across the Georgia Strait between Tsawwassen and Sidney. **Greyhound Canada** (✆ **800/661-8747,** or 250/385-4411 in Victoria; www.greyhound.ca) provides daily service up island to Nanaimo, Port Alberni, Campbell River, and Port Hardy.

BY FERRY **BC Ferries** offers crossings from the mainland to various points on Vancouver Island (✆ **888/BCFERRY** [888/223-3779] outside the Victoria dialing area, or 250/386-3431; www.bcferries.com). **The Victoria Express** (✆ **800/633-1589**; www.victoriaexpress.com) operates a seasonal passenger-only ferry service between Port Angeles and Victoria, as does **Clipper Vacations** (✆ **800/888-2535**; www.victoriaclipper.com) between Seattle and Victoria Harbour. From the San Juan Islands, you can catch a **Washington State** passenger/car ferry (✆ **800/843-3779;**

www.wsdot.wa.gov/ferries) into Sidney, south of Victoria. **BlackBall Ferry Line** (✆ **360/457-4491** in Washington or 250/386-2202 on Vancouver Island; www.cohoferry.com) provides passenger and car service from Port Angeles into Victoria Harbour.

Visitor Information

The **Tourism Victoria Visitor Information Centre** (812 Wharf St.; ✆ **250/953-2033;** www.tourismvictoria.com) is an excellent resource for brochures, ideas for itineraries, and maps. Tourism Victoria also operates a **reservations hotline** (✆ **800/663-3883**) for last-minute bookings at hotels, inns, and B&Bs. The center is open daily September through April 9am to 5pm, May and June 8:30am to 6:30pm, and July and August 9am to 9pm. Take bus no. 1, 27, or 28 to Douglas and Courtney streets.

City Layout

Victoria was settled around the Inner Harbour in the mid-1800s and grew out from there. Because of the *curvy* shoreline, the grid system of streets doesn't kick in immediately, but there are three main **north-south arteries** that will get you almost anywhere you may want to reach in Victoria.

Government Street leads from the Inner Harbour to downtown (Wharf St. merges with Government St. in front of the Fairmont Empress Hotel); **Douglas Street** runs behind the Fairmont Empress, parallel to Government Street. It is the city's main business thoroughfare, as well as the highway north to Nanaimo and beyond. It's also the Trans-Canada Highway, Highway 1; Mile Zero is at the corner of Douglas Street and Dallas Road. **Blanshard Street,** which runs parallel to Government and Douglas streets, becomes Highway 17, the route to the Saanich Peninsula, Butchart Gardens, and the ferry terminals to Vancouver and the San Juan islands.

Three major east-west streets of note are **Johnson Street,** in Old Town/Downtown—the Johnson Street Bridge divides the Upper Harbour and the Inner Harbour. **Belleville Street** runs in front of the Parliament Buildings, along the Inner Harbour's southern edge up to Fisherman's Wharf. It then loops around to become **Dallas Road,** which follows the water's edge towards Oak Bay.

When you're looking for an address, be aware that the suite number precedes the building number, which generally speaking, goes up in increments of 100 per block as you travel north and east. Addresses for all east-west downtown streets (Fort, Yates, Johnson, and so on) start at 500 at Wharf Street. This means all buildings between Wharf and Government streets fall between 500 and 599; the next block, between Government and Douglas streets, are numbers 600 through 699, and so on. Detailed maps of downtown and farther afield are available for free at the Tourism Victoria Visitor Info Centre. Invariably, hotels have maps they will mark up with a highlighter pen, showing you the quickest, easiest, and most interesting routes.

Getting Around

BY FOOT Victoria is a great city for walking. Strolling along the Inner Harbour's pedestrian walkways and streets is a pleasant and popular activity. The terrain is predominantly flat, and, with few exceptions, Victoria's points of interest are accessible in less than 30 minutes on foot.

BY PUBLIC TRANSIT The **Victoria Regional Transit System** (BC Transit; ✆ **250/382-6161;** www.bctransit.com) operates approximately 40 bus routes throughout **Greater Victoria** and the outer suburbs of **Sooke** and **Sidney.** Regular service on the main routes runs Monday to Friday from 6am to midnight. Call for schedules on the weekends. Consult the **"Victoria Rider's Guide"** for schedules and routes, available at the **Tourism Victoria Visitor Information Centre** (see "Visitor Information," above). The guide outlines transit routes for many of the city's neighborhoods, landmarks, and attractions.

Fares are no longer based on the number of geographic zones a passenger crosses; they are a flat fare to travel from Sidney to Sooke: C$2.55 adults, C$1.65 seniors and children to grade 7, free for children 5 and under. Transfers are valid for travel in one direction with no stopovers. A **DayPass**—which costs C$7.75 adults, C$5.50 seniors and children—is available at the Tourism Victoria Visitor Information Centre, at convenience stores, and at outlets displaying the FareDealer symbol.

BY FERRY Once you're downtown, scooting across the harbor in one of the tiny, 12-passenger ferries operated by **Victoria Harbour Ferry** (✆ **250/708-0201;** www.victoriaharbourferry.com) is fun—and expedient—in getting from one part of the city to another. The squat, cartoon-style boats have big wraparound windows that allow everyone a view. Ferry connections to the Fairmont Empress, the Coast Harbourside Hotel, and the Delta Victoria Ocean Pointe Resort run May through October daily every 15 minutes from 9am to 9pm. From November to April, the ferries run only on sunny weekends from 11am to 5pm. When the weather is "iffy," call the ferry office to check whether the ferries are running that day. The cost per hop is C$5 adults, C$2.50 children 12 years and under.

BY CAR If you must bring your car (exploring downtown is really best done on foot), make sure your hotel has parking. Parking spaces around the city center are at a premium. (Hotels that have parking are identified in "Where to Stay.") For out-of-town activities, car-rental agencies include **Avis,** at 1001 Douglas St. (✆ **800/879-2847** or 250/386-8468; www.avis.com); **Budget,** at 757 Douglas St. (✆ **800/268-8900** or 250/953-5300; www.budgetvictoria.com); **Hertz Canada,** at 2634 Douglas St. (✆ **800/263-0600** or 250/385-4440; www.hertz.com); and **National (Tilden),** at 767 Douglas St. (✆ **800/387-4747** or 250/386-1213; www.nationalcar.com). Renting a car averages C$60 per day but may be less with various discounts.

BY BIKE Biking is the easiest way to get around the downtown and beach areas. There are bike lanes throughout the city and paved paths along parks and beaches. Helmets are mandatory, and riding on sidewalks is illegal, except where bike paths are indicated. You can rent bikes starting at C$7 per hour and C$24 per day (lock and helmet included) from **Cycle BC Rentals & Tours,** 950 Wharf St. (✆ **250/380-2453;** www.cyclebc.ca).

BY TAXI **Yellow Cabs** (✆ **800/808-6881** or 250/381-2222) and **Blue Bird Cabs** (✆ **800/655-7055** or 250/382-2222) are good bets. But do call ahead—very few stop for flag-downs, especially when it's raining. Rides around the downtown area cost C$7 to C$10, plus a 10% to 15% tip.

BY PEDAL-CAB You get to sit while an avid bicyclist with thighs of steel pedals you anywhere you want to go for C$1 per minute. You'll see these two- and four-seater bike cabs along the Inner Harbour, in front of the Empress Hotel, at the base of Bastion Square, or you can call **Kabuki Kabs** (✆ **250/385-4243;** www.kabukikabs.com) for 24-hour service.

Swans Hotel **16**
Villa Marco Polo **9**

DINING ◆
Azuma Sushi **17**
Blue Crab Bar & Grill **34**
Cafe Brio **12**
Camille's **19**
Foo Asian Street Food **13**
James Bay Tea Room & Restaurant **40**
The Mark **38**
rebar Modern Food **20**
Red Fish/Blue Fish **23**
Smoken Bones Cookshack **4**
Superior Restaurant **33**

ATTRACTIONS ●
Abkhazi Garden **8**
All Fun Recreation Park **2**
Art Gallery of Greater Victoria **11**
Beacon Hill Park **41**
Centre of the Universe **3**
Craigdarroch Castle **10**
Finnerty Garden **6**
Hatley Park & Museum **1**
Maritime Museum of British Columbia **18**
Miniature World **24**
Pacific Undersea Gardens **31**
Parliament Buildings **30**
Royal British Columbia Museum **29**
Victoria Bug Zoo **26**
WildPlay Elements Park **5**

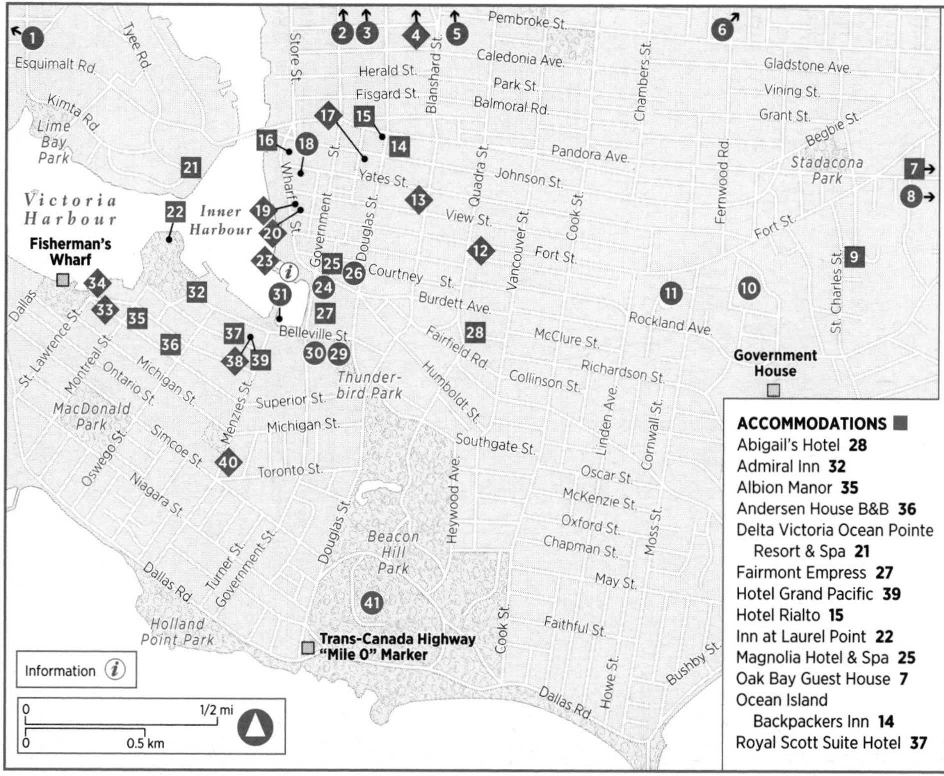

ACCOMMODATIONS ■
Abigail's Hotel **28**
Admiral Inn **32**
Albion Manor **35**
Andersen House B&B **36**
Delta Victoria Ocean Pointe Resort & Spa **21**
Fairmont Empress **27**
Hotel Grand Pacific **39**
Hotel Rialto **15**
Inn at Laurel Point **22**
Magnolia Hotel & Spa **25**
Oak Bay Guest House **7**
Ocean Island Backpackers Inn **14**
Royal Scott Suite Hotel **37**

Victoria Harbour
Inner Harbour
Fisherman's Wharf
Government House
Trans-Canada Highway "Mile 0" Marker
Beacon Hill Park
Thunderbird Park
Holland Point Park
MacDonald Park
Stadacona Park
Lime Bay Park
Information
0 1/2 mi
0 0.5 km

SPECIAL EVENTS & FESTIVALS

So many flowers bloom during the temperate month of February in Victoria and the surrounding area that the city holds an annual **Flower Count** (✆ **250/383-7191** for details). Toward the end of May, thousands of yachts sail into Victoria Harbor during the **Swiftsure Yacht Race** (✆ **250/953-2033;** www.swiftsure.org). In late June, the **Jazz Fest International** (✆ **250/388-4423;** www.vicjazz.bc.ca) brings jazz, swing, bebop, fusion, and improv artists from around the world.

The provincial capital celebrates **Canada Day** (July 1) with events centered around the Inner Harbour, including music, food, and fireworks. The August **First Peoples Festival** (✆ **250/384-3211**) highlights the culture and heritage of the Pacific Northwest First Nations tribes with dances, performances, carving demonstrations, and heritage displays at the Royal British Columbia Museum. The **Royal Victoria Marathon** (✆ **250/658-4520;** www.royalvictoriamarathon.com), an annual October race, attracts runners from around the world (half-marathon course available, too). In November, the **Great Canadian Beer Festival** (✆ **250/952-0360;** www.gcbf.com) features samples from the province's best microbreweries. And Victoria rings in the New Year with **First Night** (✆ **250/380-1211**), a family-oriented New Year's Eve celebration with free performances at many downtown venues.

[FastFACTS] VICTORIA

American Express There is no Victoria office. To report lost or stolen traveler's checks, call ✆ **800/221-7282.**

Business Hours **Banks** in Victoria are open Monday to Thursday from 10am to 3pm, Friday from 10am to 6pm. **Stores** are open Monday to Saturday from 10am to 6pm. Many stores are also open on Sunday in summers. Last call at the city's bars and cocktail lounges is 2am.

Currency Exchange The best rates of exchange are at bank ATMs. Try the **Royal Bank** (1079 Douglas St.; ✆ **250/356-4500**), in the heart of downtown. **Calforex Foreign Currency Services** (606 Humboldt St. (✆ **250/380-3711**) is open 7 days a week. **Custom House Currency Exchange** (✆ **250/389-6007**) is also open daily and has locations at 815 Wharf St. and the Bay Centre.

Dentists Most major hotels have a dentist on call. You can also visit the **Cresta Dental Centre** (28–3170 Tillicum Rd., at Burnside St., in Tillicum Mall; ✆ **250/384-7711**). Open Monday to Friday from 8am to 9pm, Saturday from 9am to 5pm, and Sunday from 11am to 5pm. Call ahead for an appointment.

Doctors Hotels usually have a doctor on call or are able to refer you to one. Clinics include the **Downtown Medical Clinic** (622 Courtney St.; ✆ **250/380-2210**), open Monday to Friday 8:30am to 5:30pm; and the **James Bay Treatment Centre** (100–230 Menzies St.; ✆ **250/388-9934**), open Monday to Friday from 9am to 6pm, Saturday 10am to 4pm. Call for an appointment.

Drugstores Pick up your allergy medication or refill your prescription at **Shoppers Drug Mart** (1222 Douglas St.; ✆ **250/381-4321**). Open Monday to Friday from 7am to 8pm, Saturday from 9am to 7pm, and Sunday from 9am to 6pm. **Rexall Drug Store** (649 Fort St.; ✆ **250/384-1195**) is open Monday to Saturday from 9am to 6pm, and Sunday and holidays from noon to 4pm.

Emergencies Dial ✆ **911** for police, fire, ambulance, and poison control.

Hospitals Local hospitals include the **Royal Jubilee Hospital** (1900 Fort St.; ✆ **250/370-8000,** or 250/370-8212 for emergencies); and **Victoria General Hospital** (1 Hospital Way; ✆ **250/727-4212,** or 250/727-4181 for emergencies).

Hotlines Emergency numbers include **Royal Canadian Mounted Police** (✆ **250/380-6261**), **Crime Stoppers** (✆ **250/386-8477**), **Emotional Crisis Centre** (✆ **250/386-6323**), **Sexual Assault Centre** (✆ **250/383-3232**), and **Poison Control Centre** (✆ **800/567-8911**).

Internet Access Nearly all hotels have either Wi-Fi or high-speed access in a public lounge or in guest bedrooms. The Greater Victoria Public Library (735 Broughton St.; ✆ **250/382-7241**) has a dozen terminals and is open Monday, Wednesday, Friday, and Saturday 9am to 6pm, Tuesday and Thursday 9am to 9pm. Or try James Bay Coffee & Books (143 Menzies St.; ✆ **250/386-4700**); it's just around the corner from the Parliament Buildings.

Police Dial ✆ **911** for emergencies. For non-emergencies, the **Victoria City Police** can be reached at ✆ **250/995-7654.**

Post Office The main **Canada Post office** is at 714 Yates St. (✆ **250/953-1352**). The **Oak Bay post office** is at 1625 Fort St. (✆ **250/595-2552**). There are also postal outlets in **Shoppers Drug Mart** (see "Drugstores," above).

Safety Crime rates are quite low in Victoria, but transients panhandle throughout the downtown and Old Town areas. Lock items in the glove compartment or trunk when you park your car, and avoid dark alleys and uninhabited areas.

Weather For local weather updates, call ✆ **250/363-6717** and follow the prompts. Or check www.theweathernetwork.com.

EXPLORING VICTORIA

If you're staying anywhere near the downtown core, trade the car for a good pair of walking shoes because virtually everything in this chapter is doable on foot. Besides, walking is by far the best way to appreciate some of Victoria's diverse architecture: heritage residences, refurbished turn-of-the-century warehouses, and assorted showpieces. Start with the attractions around the Inner Harbour and fan out from there for a refreshing walk through Beacon Hill Park, or head in the opposite direction for great shopping. The waterfront is also the departing point for most of the city's tours, whether you're off to Butchart Gardens (see below), or up for whale-watching or a kayaking excursion. Attractions that are out of Victoria Central, such as Craigdarroch Castle, Abkazi Garden, and Hatley Park, are only a 10-minute cab ride away. ***Tip:*** If you're planning to do a lot of sightseeing, invest C$20 in a **City Passport** (✆ **604/694-2489;** www.citypassports.com), a pocket-size book packed with visitor information and discounts on attractions of up to 50% at over 30 Victoria attractions.

The Top Attractions

Art Gallery of Greater Victoria Located near Craigdarroch Castle, the AGGV, as it's often called, exhibits more than 15,000 pieces of art, drawn mainly from Asia, Europe, and North America. Permanent collections include a life-size dollhouse and a Shinto shrine that is part of Canada's most extensive Japanese art collection. Most compelling is the Emily Carr exhibit, which integrates her visual and written work alongside images from the BC provincial archives, together creating an in-depth portrait of this pre-eminent Victoria artist. The Gallery organizes an annual *en plein air* every summer, an outdoor painting event for local artists.

1040 Moss St. ✆ **250/384-4101.** www.aggv.bc.ca. Admission C$12 adults, C$10 students & seniors. Fri–Wed 10am–5pm; Thurs 10am–9pm. Bus: 11, 14, or 22.

Butchart Gardens ★★★ Converted from an exhausted limestone quarry back in 1904, Butchart Gardens is an impressive place: 20 hectares (49 acres) of gardens, and not a blade of grass out of place! Just shows what having 50 gardeners can do. Every flower is grown to be a perfect match to the others in height, color, and tone, including the 300,000 bulbs that bloom in spring. On summer evenings, the gardens are illuminated with soft colored lights. Musical entertainment is provided June through September on Monday through Saturday evenings. Kids will love the new Rose Carousel, the fireworks every Saturday night through July and August, and the gi-normous displays of Christmas lights in December. An excellent lunch, dinner, and afternoon tea are offered in the **Dining Room Restaurant** (✆ **250/652-8222** for reservations); more casual fare is served in the **Blue Poppy Restaurant.** The gift shop sells seeds for some of the plants on display. If you're not traveling by car, your best bet is to take a Grayline Tour (see "Organized Tours," below) that includes admission (C$56) or a combination Garden-Grand City Tour (C$76).

Grayline Shuttle runs an hourly, summer-only shuttle (C$19 round-trip) between the gardens and downtown Victoria. Call for exact times (✆ **250/388-6539**). ***Tip:*** Plan your visit for post-3pm to avoid the more intense crowds.

800 Benvenuto Ave., Brentwood Bay. ✆ **866/652-4422** or 250/652-4422, or 250/652-8222 for dining reservations. www.butchartgardens.com. Admission C$28 adults, C$14 children 13–17, C$3 children 5–12, free for children 4 & under. Rates lower in winter. Daily 9am–sundown (call for seasonal closing time). Bus: 75. Take Blanshard St. (Hwy. 17) north toward the ferry terminal in Saanich, then turn left on Keating Crossroads, which leads directly to the gardens.

Craigdarroch Castle ★★ If you've got it, flaunt it. That's what coal baron Robert Dunsmuir (the wealthiest and most influential man in British Columbia back in the 1880s) decided to do. More than a home, this Highland-style castle rises 87 stairs through five floors of Victorian opulence—and there's not an elevator to be had! Children might think it's like something out of Disneyland. The nonprofit society that runs Craigdarroch does so with diligent care; the stained glass, Persian carpets, and intricate woodwork are treasures to behold. Visitors receive a self-guided tour booklet, and volunteers love sharing sidebars of Dunsmuir's family history. Head to the top for a view of Victoria, the Strait of Juan de Fuca, and the Olympic Mountains. Allow about an hour to tour the castle.

1050 Joan Crescent (off Fort St.). ✆ **250/592-5323.** www.craigdarrochcastle.com. Admission C$14 adults, C$13 seniors, C$8 students, C$5 children 6–12, free for children 5 & under. Mid-June to after Labour Day daily 9am–7pm; Sept to mid-June daily 10am–4:30pm. Take Fort St. out of downtown just past Pandora Ave. & turn right on Joan Crescent. Bus: 11 or 14.

Maritime Museum of British Columbia Located in a former Victoria courthouse, this museum celebrates British Columbia's seafaring history in film and exhibits, from whalers and grand ocean liners to military conflict and 20th-century explorers. Highlights include a replica of the HMS *Temeraire,* constructed entirely of beef and chicken bones by French naval prisoners captured during the Napoleonic Wars. Check out the heritage courtroom renovated by Francis Rattenbury and one of Victoria's most ornate elevators. Plan to stay 1½ hours—longer, if you have salt in your veins; the museum maintains a registry of heritage vessels and a wealth of information for maritime buffs. The gift shop has an excellent selection of nautical paraphernalia. Kids' programs include a sleepover in this purportedly haunted place!

28 Bastion Sq. ✆ **250/385-4222.** www.mmbc.bc.ca. Admission C$12 adults, C$10 seniors & students, C$5 children 6–11, free for children 5 & under; C$25 families. Daily 9:30am–4:30pm. Bus: 5 to View St.

Pacific Undersea Gardens ☺ The stark exterior looks out of place in Victoria's Inner Harbour, but descend the sloping stairway and you're in another world—below the waterline. From a glass-enclosed sunken vessel, you get to experience the harbor's marine life, which swims all around you in natural aquariums. All manner of fish—from brilliant red snapper to stonefish and octopi—swim through the kelp forest. Divers descend every hour to show the audience some of the harder-to-see creatures, like starfish tucked in rocks, wolf eels, and sharks. The observatory also cares for injured and orphaned seals, many of which prefer to stay in the area after their release. Buy a bag of herring in the gift shop and feed them a feast. Plan to stay about an hour, although feeding the seals is so captivating you may want to hang around.

490 Belleville St. ✆ **250/382-5717.** www.pacificunderseagardens.com. Admission C$10 adults, C$9 seniors, C$8 children 12–17, C$6 children 5–11, free for children 4 & under. June–Sept daily 9am–8pm; Oct–May daily 10am–5pm. Bus: 5, 27, 28, or 30.

Parliament Buildings By night, this architectural gem is lit by more than 3,300 lights so that it looks more like the Hogwarts School for Wizards than the provincial Parliament Buildings. Designed by then-25-year-old Francis Rattenbury, one of the most sought-after architects of the day, the buildings were constructed between 1893 and 1898 at a cost of nearly C$1 million. The interior is equally mystical, filled with mosaics, marble, woodwork, and stained glass. If the Legislature is sitting, head up to the visitor's gallery. There's not a lot of room there, but it's fun to watch politicians in action. British Columbia is known for its eccentric politics, and Question Period, in the early afternoon, can be very entertaining. The "been there, done that" crowd could do this in 20 minutes; guided tours (summer only) last about 40 minutes and leave every half-hour from the central lobby; they include dialogue with interpretive actors along the way.

501 Belleville St. ✆ **250/387-3046.** www.victoriabc.ca/victoria/parliamentbuildings.htm. Free admission. Daily 9am–5pm. Bus: 5, 27, 28, or 30.

Royal British Columbia Museum ★★★ ☺ As one of the best regional museums in the world, a visit to this museum is worthy of at least a half-day. The dioramas are so lifelike you'll feel as if you're stepping back in time—whether it's coming face-to-tusk with a wooly mammoth, tracking through a BC forest or to the edge of a glacier, or meandering down the cobblestone streets of a pioneer town. Feel the train rattle the timbers of the old train station each time it passes or enjoy old Charlie Chaplin movies in the movie theater. Just like an IKEA store, the museum has a route that doesn't bypass a thing, so start at the top in the Modern History Gallery (items from the early 1900s through to the power '80s highlight the lifestyles of each decade), and work your way down through the second-floor Natural History Gallery and the First Peoples Gallery, with its totems, Native longhouses, and artifacts. Once in a while, John Lennon's famous 1968 psychedelic Rolls Royce escapes its basement storage and it's displayed in the lobby. The museum also has an IMAX theater, showing an ever-changing variety of large-screen movies (✆ **250/953-IMAX** [250/953-4629]; www.imaxvictoria.com). Behind-the-scenes tours are a new addition to the summer schedule. Thunderbird Park, beside the museum, houses a cedar longhouse, where Native carvers work on new totem poles. ***Note:*** Admission rates are sometimes higher during special exhibitions.

675 Belleville St. ✆ **250/356-7226.** www.royalbcmuseum.bc.ca. Admission C$15 adults; C$9.50 seniors, students & children 6–18; free for children 5 & under; C$40 families. Museum-IMAX combination & IMAX-only tickets available. Daily 9am–5pm. Bus: 5, 28, or 30.

Victoria Bug Zoo ★★ ☺ In the heart of downtown Victoria, enter an amazing world of international insects: walking sticks, praying mantises, tarantulas, and scorpions, to name a few. Although all the creepy-crawlies are behind glass, an entomologist (bug scientist) is on hand to answer questions and show you how to handle some of the multi-legged creatures, which include a 400-leg millipede that stretches the length of your forearm. Even if you're spider-wary, this is a fascinating place. Kids will want to spend a couple of hours here.

631 Courtney St. ✆ **250/384-2847.** www.bugzoo.bc.ca. Admission C$9 adults, C$8 seniors, C$7 students, C$6 children 3–16, free for children 2 & under; C$25 annual family pass. Daily 11am–5pm. Any downtown bus.

Victoria Butterfly Gardens ★★ ☺ Hundreds of exotic species of butterflies flutter through this lush tropical greenhouse, from the tiny Central American Julia to the Southeast Asian Giant Atlas Moth (its wingspan is nearly a foot). Pick up an identification chart before you enter so you can put names to the various flying wonders around you. Then wander freely through the gardens. Along the way, you'll encounter naturalists happy to explain butterfly biology, who pepper their speech with slightly bizarre factoids, such as "Butterflies taste with their feet" and "If a human baby grew at the same rate as some caterpillars, it would weigh 8 tons in only 2 weeks." Hmm. Food for thought. Between November and February, you need a reservation to see the gardens. Combine a visit here with the Butchart Gardens nearby (see listing above) for a full day's excursion.

1461 Benvenuto Ave., Brentwood Bay. ✆ **877/722-0272** or 250/652-3822. www.butterflygardens.com. Admission C$13 adults, C$12 seniors & students, C$6.50 children 5–12, free for children 4 & under; 10% discount for families. Mar–May & Oct daily 9:30am–4pm; June–Sept daily 9am–5:30pm. Closed Nov–Feb. Bus 75.

Parks & Gardens

Victoria is famed for its garden landscapes and for its abundance of flowers. Even if there's not a horticultural bone in your body, you really can't help but appreciate the efforts that have earned the city such acclaim. Look overhead, and chances are that there'll be an overstuffed hanging basket trailing with colorful blooms. And in most of the residential neighborhoods, private homeowners take special pride in their gardens.

Among the most spectacular examples are the **Gardens at Government House** (1401 Rockland Ave.; ✆ **250/387-2080;** www.ltgov.bc.ca/gardens), the official (and private) residence of British Columbia's Lieutenant Governor. The formal gardens are free to wander from dawn to dusk, and for rose lovers in particular, they're well worth the visit. Guided tours run May through September (C$35 for groups of five or fewer) and include areas not normally open to the public.

Nearby **Abkhazi Garden** (1964 Fairfield Rd.; ✆ **250/598-8096;** www.conservancy.bc.ca—click through to heritage tabs) is a dramatic, half-hectare (1¼-acre) jewel of a garden created by Prince and Princess Nicholas Abkhazi in the 1940s. Amid the woodland, rocky slopes, and rhododendrons is a quaint tearoom and gift shop. The gardens are open March to October daily 11am to 5pm. Another once-private residence is **Hatley Park & Museum** (2005 Sooke Rd.; ✆ **250/391-2666;**

www.hatleygardens.com). A National Historic Site, the museum boasts one of the few Edwardian estates in Canada, complete with Italian, Rose, and Japanese gardens. There are hundreds of heritage trees, including 250-year-old Douglas firs, an ecologically important salt marsh estuary, and a series of natural springs. Admission is C$9 adults, with discounts for seniors and students. Children 12 and under are free; admission is half-price October through April. In summer, castle tours are offered daily for an additional C$6.

Next door, **Royal Roads University** (**© 250/391-2511**) features extensive floral gardens, which are open to the public, free of charge. The University of Victoria, too, has gardens that are free to wander: **Finnerty Gardens** (3800 Finnerty Rd.; **© 250/721-7606**) contain one of Canada's best collections of rhododendrons, many of which were started from seed from famous plant explorers. There are over 500 different varieties, as well as 1,600 trees, shrubs, companion plants, and ornamentals. The gardens cover 2.6 hectares (6½ acres) so allow an hour to tour. They are open daily from dawn to dusk, and admission is free. The entrance to the gardens is near the University Chapel, on the southwest edge of the campus. Proceed around the Ring Road to parking lot 6.

If you're staying put around the downtown core, a walk through **Beacon Hill Park** is a must. Gifted to the city by the Hudson's Bay Company in 1882, today, it stretches from just behind the Royal BC Museum to Dallas Road. Without doubt, it's the top park in Victoria—an oasis of indigenous Garry oaks, floral gardens, windswept heath, ponds, and totem poles. There's also a children's farm (see "Especially for Kids," later in this chapter), an aviary, tennis courts, a lawn-bowling green, a putting green, playgrounds, and picnic areas. En route, drop by tiny **Thunderbird Park** (at the corner of Bellevue and Douglas sts., beside the Royal BC Museum). It has several totem poles, and in summer, there's an outdoor studio for experienced carvers to create new poles. Adjacent to the park lies **Helmcken House,** the oldest house still on its original site in British Columbia.

Organized Tours

AIR TOURS **Hyack Air** (**© 250/384-2499**) offers floatplane adventures from Victoria Harbour. A 30-minute sky-view orientation of the city ranges from C$99 to C$125 per person, depending on the number of passengers. You can also fly around and above the Gulf Islands, Tofino, and Butchart Gardens. The latter includes admission.

BUS TOURS **Grayline of Victoria** (**© 800/663-8390** or 250/388-6539; www.graylinewest.com) conducts tours of the city and, notably, of **Butchart Gardens.** The 1½-hour **Grand City Tour** costs C$29 for adults, C$18 for children 2 to 11. It runs as a hop-on/hop-off loop aboard colorful trolleys and double-decker buses, as do its competitors. Tickets are valid for 48 hours, so you can make the most of visiting attractions en route. In July and August, daily tours depart every 30 minutes from 9:30am to 4:30pm. In spring and fall, tours depart hourly, and in winter, there are only three departures a day. Call ahead for exact times. Grayline also offers seasonal tours, such as Ghost Tours and Murder Mysteries.

FERRY TOURS Departing from various stops around the Inner Harbour, **Victoria Harbour Ferries** (**© 250/708-0201;** www.victoriaharbourferry.com) offers 45- and 55-minute tours of the harbor. See shipyards, wildlife, marinas, fishing boats, and floating homes from the water. Tours cost C$22 adults, C$20 seniors, and C$12 children 12 and under. For March, April, and October, they operate daily every 15 minutes from 10am to 5pm. From May through September, they run daily from 9am to 9pm. If you want to stop for food or a stroll, you can get a token that's good for reboarding at any time during the same day.

SPECIALTY TOURS In the mood for something a little different? Climb into one of the bicycle-rickshaws operated by **Kabuki Kabs** (526 Discovery St.; **© 250/385-4243;** www.kabukikabs.com). They hold up to four people, operate seasonally, and run just like regular taxis; you can flag one down or (usually) find them parked in front of the Fairmont Empress. Rates run about C$1 per minute for a two-person cab and C$1.75 per minute for a four-person cab. A typical 30-minute tour (you can set your own itinerary) runs about C$30 to C$60.

Tallyho Horse Drawn Tours (**© 866/383-5067** or 250/383-5067; www.tallyhotours.com) has conducted horse-drawn carriage and wagon tours in Victoria since 1903. Wagons hold up to 20 strangers and, as such, are by far the most affordable of the horse-drawn tours you'll find at C$15 adults, C$12 seniors, and C$7 children for a 45-minute roll around the city. In summer, tours depart daily every half-hour from 9am to dusk. By far the most romantic are the turn-of-the-20th-century two-person carriage tours, offered by several horse 'n buggy outfits. Competition keeps prices on par with one another, from a short-and-sweet 15-minute harbor tour for C$50 to a 45-minute ride through Beacon Hill Park at C$130 or a 100-minute Romance tour for C$240. All Tallyho and carriage rides start at the corner of Belleville and Menzies streets (across from the Royal London Wax Museum).

To get a bird's-eye view of Victoria, **Harbour Air Seaplanes** (950 Wharf St.; **© 800/665-0212** or 250/384-2215; www.harbour-air.com) provides 30-minute sky-tours of Victoria's panorama for C$99, as well as a romantic Fly 'n' Dine tour that combines a flight to Butchart Gardens, garden admission and dinner, and a limo ride back into town. The cost is C$239 per person.

You can also take a limousine-only tour with **Heritage Tours and Daimler Limousine Service** (713 Bexhill Rd.; **© 250/474-4332**) around Victoria; rates start at C$90 per hour. Stretch limos for 8 to 10 people are also available; hourly rates are C$90 to C$100.

WALKING TOURS Victoria is such a marvelous walking city that guided walks proliferate. Sure, there are themed, self-guided walks (maps are available at the Visitor Information Centre and at www.victoria.ca/tours), but to get the most out of what you're seeing, nothing beats hearing the history, gossip, and anecdotes that tour guides can offer. **Discover the Past** (**© 250/384-6698;** www.discoverthepast.com) is the leader of the pack, offering walks conducted by historian and entertaining storyteller John Adams. Ninety-minute tours run year-round from the Visitor Information Centre at Government and Wharf streets, and they cover eight themes or areas, from ghostly walks in Old Town to historical walks around Chinatown; starting points may vary. Tours run June through September and cost C$15, cash only.

Walkabouts Historical Tours (**© 250/592-9255;** www.walkabouts.ca) is the only company that tours the Fairmont Empress. Dressed in turn-of-the-20th-century clothes, guides are exceptionally well informed about this historical hotel (which is said to be haunted). Their knowledge adds a whole new dimension to enjoying high tea there later. The 90-minute, C$10 tour departs daily at 10am sharp; meet at the Fairmont Empress store located next to the Tea Lobby (on the Belleville St. end of the hotel).

Victoria Bobby Walking Tours (✆ **250/995-0233;** www.walkvictoria.com) offers a variety of walks around the city neighborhoods; they depart from the Visitor Information Centre May through mid-September daily at 11am. Your guide is an English ex-bobby either wearing that distinguishing helmet or brandishing an umbrella; bring along C$15.

Travel with Taste (✆ **250/385-1527;** www.travelwithtaste.com) hosts a deliciously appetizing Urban Culinary Walking Tour around central downtown, during which you can literally forage your way through hand-crafted chocolates, smoked meats, pâtés, teas, baked treats, and wine. Four-hour tours cost C$89 per person, operate seasonally, and begin at 11am near the gates of Chinatown. This is a must for foodies and for those wanting to get the low-down on the hottest eateries in town. Winery tours can also be arranged.

Another culinary tour to consider is with **Heidi Fink** (www.chefheidifink.com), an accomplished chef who takes the confusion out of the bewildering array of unfamiliar foodstuffs for sale in Chinatown. Two-hour tours run Sunday afternoons and cost C$50. Advance reservations are required for both these culinary capers.

ESPECIALLY FOR KIDS

There's no doubt that Victoria caters well to getaway travelers, whether looking for romance or simply a quality urban destination. But families with children of all ages also find much to enjoy here. There are the obvious city attractions such as the touchy-feely, creepy-crawly **Victoria Bug Zoo** (p. 690) that's bound to be a sure-fire hit and the watery kingdom of **Pacific Undersea Gardens** (p. 689). Then there's the very unstuffy **Royal BC Museum** (p. 689), which really does have something for all ages, especially when combined with a visit to the **IMAX** theater.

For youngsters, the **Beacon Hill Children's Farm** (Circle Dr., Beacon Hill Park; ✆ **250/381-2532**) is a well-established petting zoo with rabbits, goats, and other barnyard animals, which makes for a super outing, especially when coupled with some kite flying on Beacon Hill or picnicking at the wading pool and playground nearby.

Outside of the downtown core, remember to check out the **Butterfly Gardens** (p. 690); the new **Rose Carousel** in Butchart Gardens' Children's Pavilion (p. 688); **Fisgard Lighthouse** (p. 696); the amazing **Shaw Ocean Discovery Centre** in Sidney (9811 Seaport Place, Sidney, ✆ **250/665-7511**); and nearby **Mineral World & Scratch Patch** (9891 Seaport Place, Sidney; ✆ **250/655-4367;** www.mineralworld.ca), an indoor/outdoor arena containing two gold-panning pools, a pond filled with tropical shells, and mounds of semi-precious gemstones. Admission to Mineral World is free, though if you're stone-digging, you must buy a collector's bag for C$6 to C$15; anything you find, you can keep. The Patch is open daily September to June 9am to 6pm, with extended hours to 9pm in July and August.

For more kid-friendly suggestions, take a look at ***The Kids' Guide to Victoria,*** which details more than 50 places to go and things to do around Vancouver Island. You can get this guide by contacting Tourism Victoria (✆ **250/953-2033;** www.tourismvictoria.com).

All Fun Recreation Park The park has two go-kart tracks, mini-golf, and batting cages, all priced separately, so it can get expensive. For example, the cost of go-karting is C$13 per 6-minute session; mini-golf is C$6 per adult, C$4 per child; and swinging at 25 baseballs will set you back C$4. Save a few dollars and get a C$20 pass that includes a go-kart ride, 18 holes of mini-golf, and 50 balls in the batting cage.

2207 Millstream Rd. ✆ **250/474-1961.** www.allfun.bc.ca. Admission C$4–C$20; C$6 observers (including access to an 80-person hot tub & beach volleyball courts). Mid-June to Labor Day daily 11am–7pm.

Centre of the Universe The larger of the two telescopes trained to the heavens was once the largest in the world, so you know that the stargazing is good—depending on the cloud cover. Nighttime vigils for the public are offered somewhat sporadically (especially in winter), as they're scheduled between bookings by professional astronomers. The daytime 75-minute tour of the aging observatory is still a fun excursion from the downtown core.

5071 West Saanich Rd. ✆ **250/363-8262.** www.cu.hia.nrc.gc.ca. Admission 3–7pm C$9 adults, C$8 seniors & students, C$5 children 5-12 years; 7–11pm C$12 adults, C$9 seniors & students, C$7 children 5-12 years. Tues–Sat 3–11pm.

WildPlay Elements Park Located 20-minutes north of downtown, near Bear Mountain, this park offers high-flying adventure through a progressively more challenging tree-to-tree obstacle course. The course includes ziplines, bridges, scramble nets, and swing logs, many of which are 18m (59 ft.) above ground through a forest of Douglas firs. Children must be 7 years and older, and some restrictions apply to those 13 years and under. Sunset rides are especially popular.

1767 Island Hwy. ✆ **888/856-7275** or 250/590-7529. www.wildplay.com. Admission C$40 full course; C$20 kids course. Daily 9am–5pm; call ahead for special 7pm sunset rides.

Outdoor Activities

Vancouver Island, and even urban Victoria, is garnering quite a reputation for its range of outdoor activities. Hiking and biking are big pastimes for both residents and visitors, and there is an excess of whale-watching companies. And farther afield, activities include scuba diving (**Ogden Point Dive Centre,** 199 Dallas Rd.; ✆ **888/701-1177** or 250/380-9119; www.divevictoria.com) and birding (**Victoria Natural History Society;** ✆ **250/479-6622;** www.vicnhs.bc.ca).

BIKING Cycling is such a popular mode of transportation that Victoria has been nicknamed Canada's Cycling Capital. Consequently, bike paths abound, thanks largely to the Greater Victoria Cycling Coalition, a growing and influential lobby group. There's a scenic **Marine Drive bike path** that takes you around the peninsula and over to Oak Bay. The Inner Harbour also has a bike lane alongside the pedestrian pathway. The city's jewel, however, is the 60km (37-mile) **Galloping Goose Trail** (✆ **250/478-3344;** www.gallopinggoosetrail.com for maps and information). This terrific rail-to-trail conversion starts in Victoria at the south end of the Selkirk Trestle, at the foot of Alston Street in Victoria West, and travels the back roads through urban, rural, and semi-wilderness landscapes. There are access points along the entire trail route with many parking areas. It is named after a gawky and noisy 1920s gasoline-powered passenger car that operated on the abandoned CNR line between Victoria and Sooke.

Great Pacific Adventures (811 Wharf St.; ✆ **877/733-6722** or 250/386-2277; www.greatpacificadventures.com) rents bikes from C$8 per hour or C$35 per day (call ahead in winter), as does **Cycle BC,** with two locations—at 686 Humboldt St. for bikes and 950 Wharf St. for scooters and motorcycles (✆ **250/380-2453;** www.cyclebc.ca). Twenty-one-speed bicycles are C$7 per hour; off-road bikes start at C$12 per hour. Honda Scooters are C$16 per hour for a single seater (C$69/day) and

C$19 per hour for a double seater (C$79/day); and for the hard-core biker in us all, a Harley Davidson Road King rents for C$58 per hour, C$225 per day. **Eco Scooters** (✆ **250/588-1122;** www.ecoscooterentals.ca), on the wharf below the Visitor Information Centre, rents bio-fuel scooters (C$49 for 2 hours), and electric scooters (C$39 for 2 hours). Longer rentals are available, though 2 hours should suffice to follow a see-it-all downtown route. A driver's license isn't required for the electric ride.

CANOEING & KAYAKING **Ocean River Sports** (1824 Store St.; ✆ **800/909-4233** or 250/381-4233; www.oceanriver.com), on the waterfront, caters to novice and experienced paddlers alike, with rentals, equipment, dry-storage camping gear, and a number of guided tours. Beginners should opt for the 2½-hour "Explorer" around Victoria Harbour (C$125). More adventuresome kayakers can go for the multi-day, bring-your-own-tent adventure to explore the Gulf Islands (C$635, including meals). Rentals are C$25 for 2 hours, C$50 for an 8-hour day. ***Tip:*** Because of Ocean River's waterfront location, absolute beginners can rent a kayak for a try-out paddle in the harbor's protected waters. The sunset tour is a special treat.

Victoria Kayak Tours (950 Wharf St.; ✆ **250/216-5646;** www.victoriakayak.com) does 2½-hour naturalist tours to Seal Island (C$59) and a 6-hour excursion to the Strait of Juan de Fuca (C$125).

FISHING Saltwater fishing is very popular here, and guides will show you the current hot spots. **Adam's Fishing Charters** (✆ **250/370-2326;** www.adamsfishingcharters.com), **Beasleys Fishing Charters** (✆ **866/259-1111** or 250/381-8000; www.beasleysfishingcharters.com), and **Foghorn Fishing Charters** (✆ **250/658-1848;** www.foghorncharters.com) are good starting points. Rates start at C$95 an hour, for a minimum of 5 hours. Full-day charters are around C$800.

To fish, you need a **saltwater fishing license,** available at Adam's (see above) and the **Marine Adventure Centre** (950 Wharf St., ✆ **250/995-2211**). For nonresidents, a 1-day license costs C$13, a 3-day license C$25, and a 5-day license C$35. Fees are reduced for BC and Canada residents. If you're interested in taking the wheel yourself, **Great Pacific Adventures** (811 Wharf St.; ✆ **877/733-6722** or 250/386-2277; www.greatpacificadventures.com) rents watercraft, including 4.9m (16-ft.) powerboats at C$50 an hour.

For fly-fishing, **Robinson's Outdoor Store** (1307 Broad St.; ✆ **888/317-0033** or 250/385-3429; www.robinsonsoutdoors.com) is an excellent resource for information and all outdoor gear, including specialty flies for area waters, rods, reels, and resource books. They also sell **freshwater fishing licenses.** For nonresidents, a 1-day license is C$20 and an 8-day is C$50, with lower fees for BC and Canada residents.

GOLF Victoria has an enviable number of good courses. The fees are reasonable, the scenery is spectacular, and most courses are open year-round. Co-designed by Jack Nicklaus and his son Steve, the Mountain Course, which lies in the foothills of Mount Finlayson atop **Bear Mountain Golf Resort** (1999 Country Club Way; ✆ **888/533-BEAR** [888/533-2327] or 250/744-2327; www.bearmountain.ca) is a hot favorite, so book well in advance to avoid disappointment. It's Canada's only 36 holes of Nicklaus-designed golf. Rates are C$150 Monday through Thursday and C$145 Friday through Sunday. Rates include a GPS-equipped cart.

The **Olympic View Golf Club** (643 Latoria Rd.; ✆ **800/I-GOLFBC** [800/445-5322] or 250/474-3671; www.golfbc.com), is one of the top 35 golf courses in Canada, with two waterfalls and 12 lakes sharing space with the greens. The 6,414-yard course is par 72, and green fees range from C$45 in the winter season to C$80 on a summer weekend. The **Cedar Hill Municipal Golf Course,** at 1400 Derby Rd. (© **250/475-7151;** www.golfcedarhill.com), is a more modest 18-hole public course located only 3.5km (2¼ miles) from downtown Victoria. Daytime fees are C$45; twilight, junior, and winter fees are C$30. Tee-off times are first come, first served.

The website **www.vancouverisland.com/golf** lists golf courses around the island, including Arbutus Ridge at Cobble Hill and Glen Meadows Golf & Country Club in Sidney. If you're tight for time, call the **Last Minute Golf Hotline** at © **604/878-1833** for substantial discounts and short-notice tee times at courses in and around Victoria. Book online at www.lastminutegolfbc.com.

SAILING & BOATING Sailors have often remarked that the Juan de Fuca Strait is some of the best and prettiest sailing areas in the world. **Blackfish Sailing Adventures** (© **250/216-2389;** www.blackfishal.com) leaves Oak Bay Marina for 3-hour and full-day excursions aboard an 11m (35-ft.) Beneteau "oceanus" sloop. You can participate, learn to crew, or just relax. Binoculars are provided. Blackfish organizes sails around Vancouver Island, which are available to do in legs or in its entirety. It also operates the 45-foot *Aquitania,* which is modeled after an early 1900 cedar-strip Edwardian launch and motors out of Victoria's Fisherman's Wharf to Fort Rodd Hill and Fisgard Lighthouse. **Tall Ship Adventures** (© **877/788-4263** or 250/885-2311) is an even more romantic option, where you can hop aboard the 17m-tall (55-ft.) ship *Thane.* It's a 1978 vessel modeled after Joshua Slocum's *Spray,* the first vessel to circumnavigate the world single-handedly, in 1895. Departures are from the Inner Harbour; 3-hour trips are C$69 per person. If jetting around in a 4.9m (16-ft.) Double Eagle with a 50HP Honda is more your style, hourly rentals (C$50/hr.) are available through **Island Boat Rentals** (450 Swift St.; © **250/995-1211** or 250/995-1661; www.greatpacificadventures.com).

WHALE-WATCHING Orcas (killer whales), harbor seals, sea lions, porpoises, and gray whales ply these waters year-round, so whale-watching outfitters abound. Competition keeps prices in line—expect to pay about C$95 to C$115 for a 2- to 3-hour excursion—so the real choice is between riding the waves in a zippy 12-person Zodiac or in a larger, more leisurely craft. Some reputable outfits include **Orca Spirit Adventures** (© **250/383-8411;** www.orcaspirit.com), which departs from the Coast Harbourside Hotel dock; **Seafun Safaris Whale Watching** (950 Wharf St.; © **877/360-1233** or 250/360-1200; www.seafun.com); and **Prince of Whales** (812 Wharf St.; © **888/383-4884** or 250/383-4884; www.princeofwhales.com), which also offers Victoria/Vancouver one-way trips and circle runs with stopovers at Butchart Gardens and the Gulf Islands. Prince of Whales has also teamed up with **Adrena Line** (5128C Sooke Rd., ©**866/947-9145** or 250/642-1933; www.adrenalinezip.com) for adventure whale-watch and zipline packages.

Shopping

Victoria has dozens of little specialty shops that appeal to every taste and whim, and because the city is built to such a pedestrian scale, you can wander from place to place seeking out whatever treasure it is you're after. Nearly all the areas below are within a short walk of the Empress hotel.

ANTIQUES Renowned for its high-quality British collectibles, Antique Row is a 3-block stretch along Fort Street between Blanshard and Cook streets. Unfortunately, it's beginning to wane as a destination. Demand isn't what it was, and several long-time dealers are retiring. Nevertheless, it's still the best place to find the finest in estate jewelry, silverware, heritage china, and furniture, especially at the two auction houses, **Lunds** (926 Fort St.; ✆ **250/386-3308**) and **Kilshaws** (1115 Fort St.; ✆ **250/384-6441**).

In addition check out **Charles Baird** (1044A Fort St.; ✆ **250/384-8809**) for antique furniture, **Britannia & Co.** (839 Fort St.; ✆ **250/480-1954**) for porcelain figurines, and **Romanoff & Co.** (837–839 Fort St.; ✆ **250/480-1543**) for its impressive collection of coins and silverware. For the recreational antiquer looking for a bargain, the **Old Vogue Shop** (1034 Fort St.; ✆ **250/380-7751**) is a generalist shop with a hodgepodge of items and styles.

ARTS & CRAFTS **Starfish Glassworks,** 630 Yates St. (✆ **250/388-7827**), is both a glassblowing artists' studio, where you can watch pieces being created, and a gallery where contemporary glass pieces are sold. ***Note:*** Glass is blown during afternoons only, and not at all on Mondays or Tuesdays.

DEPARTMENT STORE & SHOPPING MALL **The Bay Centre,** between Government and Douglas sts., off Fort and View sts. (✆ **250/389-2228;** bus: 1, 5, or 30) formerly known as the Eaton Centre, is named after its new anchor store, the **Hudson's Bay Company** (✆ **250/385-1311**). Canada's oldest department store sells everything from housewares to fashions to cosmetics and of course the trendy Hudson's Bay woolen point blankets. The rest of the complex houses a full shopping mall, disguised as a block of heritage buildings, with three floors of shops and boutiques offering fashions, china and crystal, housewares, gourmet foods, and books.

FASHION **Breeze,** 1150 Government St. (✆ **250/383-8871**), is a high-energy fashion outlet that carries a number of affordable and trendy lines for women, plus accessories. **Hughes Clothing,** 564 Yates St. (✆ **250/381-4405**) is a local favorite for contemporary women's fashions. **The Plum Clothing Co.,** 1298 Broad St. (✆ **250/381-5005**), features quality dressy casuals. For men's fashions, try **British Importers,** 1125 Government St. (✆ **250/386-1496;** bus: 1, 5, or 30).

FOOD **Rogers' Chocolates,** 913 Government St. (✆ **250/384-7021;** http://rogerschocolates.com), is a Victoria institution housed in an appropriately old-fashioned shop loaded with tempting treats that will satisfy even a discerning chocoholic. **Murchies,** 1110 Government St. (✆ **250/383-3112**), offers many specialty teas, including the custom-made Empress blend, served at The Fairmont Empress hotel's afternoon tea.

JEWELRY Ian MacDonald of **MacDonald Jewelry,** 618 View St. (✆ **250/382-4113;** bus: 1 or 2), designs and crafts all his own jewelry, which makes for some interesting creations. At the **Jade Tree,** 606 Humboldt St. (✆ **250/388-4326;** bus: 1, 5, or 30), you'll find jewelry crafted from British Columbia jade into necklaces, bracelets, and other items.

NATIVE ART All of the First Nations are represented in the **Alcheringa Gallery,** 665 Fort St. (✆ **250/383-8224;** bus: 1 or 2), along with a significant collection of pieces from Papau New Guinea. **Cowichan Trading Ltd.,** 1328 Government St. (✆ **250/383-0321;** bus: 1, 5, or 30), sells a mix of T-shirts and gewgaws in addition to fine Cowichan sweaters, masks, and fine silver jewelry. **Hill's Native Art,** 1008 Government St. (✆ **250/385-3911;** bus: 1, 5, or 30), features traditional First Nations art, including wooden masks and carvings, Haida argillite, and silver jewelry.

OUTDOOR CLOTHES & EQUIPMENT **Ocean River Sports,** 1824 Store St. (© **250/381-4233;** bus: 6), is a good spot for outdoor clothing and camping equipment.

WHERE TO STAY

Victoria has a wide choice of fine accommodations, and all are in, or within walking distance of, the **Inner Harbour** and **downtown core.** These are the pricier neighborhoods, especially those in sight of the water in the height of summer. Generally speaking, the quality of both service and amenities is also high, or at least, is priced accordingly. Like in many cities, though, parking is an issue, so if you can get free parking, grab it, or you'll find your reasonable room rate suddenly inflated by C$10 or even C$28 per night. Thankfully, this is a walking destination, so the best advice is to leave your car at home, even if you decide to stay in a neighboring neighborhood. Further afield in Sooke, Sidney, and Brentwood Bay, there are some truly spectacular options, and transit connections make them convenient, too.

Inner Harbour & Nearby

VERY EXPENSIVE

Delta Victoria Ocean Pointe Resort and Spa ★ Huge rooms, great bathrooms, and deluxe bedding are all part of the relatively clutter-free decor, which highlights the gleaming woods and the soft, natural colors throughout. Located on the north side of the Inner Harbour, many of the guest rooms have floor-to-ceiling windows that view the Legislative Buildings and the Fairmont Empress. For a few dollars more, you get Signature perks of breakfast, evening hors d'oeuvres, and turndown service. All rooms come with the usual toiletries, down duvets, and cuddly robes. The European-style spa rivals the Fairmont's Willow Stream for top spa billing, and is a destination in itself. The hotel's sports and fitness facilities are also extensive, including racquet courts and a large, glass-walled indoor pool that feels like swimming outdoors. **Lure Seafood Restaurant and Lounge** (© **250/360-5873**), boasts the best dining-room views in the city, not to mention serving quality dishes. It's an especially romantic spot when night falls, and you can savor the very pretty night lights of the city's harbor front.

45 Songhees Rd., Victoria, BC V9A 6T3. © **800/667-4677** or 250/360-2999. www.deltahotels.com. 250 units. Apr to mid-Oct C$129–C$399 double, C$439–C$799 suite; mid-Oct to Mar C$119–C$319 double, C$329–C$629 suite. Additional adult C$30. Children 18 & under stay free in parent's room. AE, DC, DISC, MC, V. Valet parking C$15. Pets accepted (C$35 per stay). **Amenities:** Restaurant; bar; babysitting; health club; ozonated indoor swimming pool; room service; spa; 2 night-lit outdoor tennis courts; 1 indoor racquetball & squash court. *In room:* A/C, TV/DVD player, hair dryer, minibar, Wi-Fi.

Fairmont Empress ★★ It's an ivy-adorned harbor-side landmark, and staying here is the quintessential Victoria experience. Ongoing renovations maintain the old girl's elegance, but even Fairmont's magic couldn't make many of the 1908-era rooms any larger, so this still means small rooms (billed as "cozy"), narrow corridors, and a disparity of views that might just as easily include the unsightly rooftops of the hotel's working areas as the harbor. If you're slightly claustrophobic, don't even think about these. They're a lot of money for what you get, too. That said, guest rooms, as well as studio-, one-, and two-bedroom suites, are all superb, and Fairmont Gold are superb-plus, offering extra-large beds and windows that let the light pour in, as well as extras such as TVs in the bathrooms and iPod docks. Gold guests have private check-in, their own concierge, and a private lounge with an honor bar, complimentary hors d'oeuvres (often enough for a light supper), and breakfast. The **Willow Stream Spa** (✆ **250/995-4650**), still ranks as the city's finest spa retreat, and some of the services are priced accordingly. Dining choices include the Bengal Lounge (its ceiling fans and tall palms are very colonial-India), the Empress Dining Room, and Kipling's. The famous afternoon tea is served year-round in the Main Tea Lobby, spilling into surrounding areas as the number of tea drinkers dictates. Call ✆ **250/389-2727** for all dining reservations.

721 Government St., Victoria, BC V8W 1W5. ✆ **800/441-1414** or 250/384-8111. www.fairmont.com/empress. 477 units. July–Sept C$249–C$800 double, C$429–C$1,509 suite, C$399–C$1,500 Fairmont Gold; Oct–June C$199–C$479 double, C$229–C$1,269 suite, C$299–C$1,269 Fairmont Gold. Children 11 & under stay free in parent's room. Packages available. AE, DC, DISC, MC, V. Underground valet parking C$29. Bus: 5. Small pets accepted (C$25). **Amenities:** 2 restaurants; bar/lounge; tearoom; babysitting; health club; large heated indoor pool; room service; spa. *In room:* A/C, TV w/pay movies, hair dryer, minibar, iPod dock, Wi-Fi.

Hotel Grand Pacific ★★ The "grandness" begins as you approach the hotel beneath a canopy of trees—beside ducks paddling in waterfall-fed pools. Located next to the Parliament Buildings, the Grand Pacific sits right on the waterfront. Guest rooms are more sizeable and elegantly contemporary than those in the other waterfront hotels, and because of the wide range of accommodations, from standard rooms facing the Olympic Mountains and smallish bathrooms to multi-room harbor-view suites with fireplaces and lavishly large bathrooms, you might be able to afford top-notch luxury here for less than what's offered elsewhere. The hotel has a quality spa; the city's most extensive fitness facilities (with a huge ozonated indoor pool); and dining options that include the Mark (see "Where to Dine," later in this chapter), geared to high-end, romantic encounters. On weekends, a sophisticated dim sum is served in the Pacific Restaurant, paired with an extensive loose leaf tea menu.

463 Belleville St., Victoria, BC V8V 1X3. ✆ **800/663-7550** or 250/386-0450. www.hotelgrandpacific.com. 304 units. Mid-May to Sept C$199–C$389 double, from C$249 suite; Oct to mid-May C$139–C$269 double, from C$189 suite. Children 17 & under stay free in parent's room. AE, DC, DISC, MC, V. Parking C$15. Bus: 30 to Superior & Oswego sts., 27, or 28. **Amenities:** 2 restaurants; lounge; babysitting; health club; indoor ozone-filtered lap pool; room service; spa; squash court. *In room:* A/C, TV w/pay movies, hair dryer, minibar.

EXPENSIVE

Andersen House B&B ★ This small 1891 house, with its high ceilings, stained-glass windows, and ornate Queen Anne–style fireplaces, is filled with furnishings that echo the old British Empire, only to be spiced up with splashes of Art Deco paintings. The combination is very lively. Every room has a private entrance and is unique. The sun-drenched Casablanca Room has French doors and a window seat overlooking the Parliament Buildings; the Captain's Apartment comes with a claw-foot tub and an extra bedroom; and the ground level Garden Studio, the most secluded and least expensive of the three rooms, has a hot tub. Rates include a splendid breakfast.

301 Kingston St., Victoria, BC V8V 1V5. ✆ **250/388-4565.** www.andersenhouse.com. 3 units. June–Sept C$235–C$265 double; Oct–May C$135–C$195 double. Rates include full breakfast. MC, V. Free off-street parking. Bus: 30 to Superior & Oswego sts. Children 11 & under not accepted. **Amenities:** Jacuzzi. *In room:* TV/DVD player, hair dryer, Wi-Fi.

Inn at Laurel Point ★ One of the Inner Harbour's first modern hotels, the Inn at Laurel Point received a recent makeover, updating its initial simple Japanese-style design with West Coast–style slate, fresh earth-toned furnishings, and lots of windows facing the waterfront. Japanese visitors love the place. It also boasts being BC's only carbon-neutral hotel. There are two wings, and all guest rooms have balconies with views; the scene, harbor or inland, helps determine the price you'll pay. Rooms in the south wing are more spacious and have an Asian theme, including shoji-style sliding doors, down duvets, and plenty of Asian art. The exquisite Japanese Garden features a large reflecting pond and a waterfall that cascades over a whopping 21,300 kilograms (46,958 lb.) of rock. The **Aura Restaurant** is the most significant change; a veritable parade of food and views (see "Where to Dine," later in this chapter). ***Tip:*** The inn is on the waterfront pathway that links Fisherman's Wharf, BlackBall Ferry, the Parliament Buildings, and the Royal BC Museum.

680 Montreal St., Victoria, BC V8V 1Z8. ✆ **800/663-7667** or 250/386-8721. www.laurelpoint.com. 200 units (135 double, 65 suites). June to mid-Oct C$199 double, C$309 suite; mid-Oct to May C$119 double, C$189 suite. Additional adult C$25. Children 18 & under stay free in parent's room. Packages available. AE, DC, MC, V. Parking C$18. Small pets accepted (C$50). **Amenities:** Restaurant; babysitting; small heated pool; room service. *In room:* A/C, TV w/pay movies, hair dryer, iPod dock, Wi-Fi.

MODERATE

Albion Manor ★ Recent renovations have worked miracles, transforming this 1892 heritage house into an art-inspired home. The artist-owners have a background in staging international expos, so decor incorporates whimsical sculptures (sometimes edgy and always theatrical), Victorian-era antiques, and well-traveled pieces from Morocco to Papua New Guinea for an eclectic, one-of-a-kind ambiance. Guest rooms, beds, and lounges are exceptionally comfortable, with intriguing items that each have a story. The grand bed in room 6 once belonged to the Governor of Wisconsin; the 1870s bed in room 7 is from Brittany, France; and the imposing, elaborately carved four-poster in room 8 is from 1750s England. Some rooms have a private entrance, verandah, or Jacuzzi tub. Delicious breakfasts are served, family style, in the formal dining room.

224 Superior St., Victoria, BC V8V 1T3. ✆ **877/389-0012.** www.albionmanor.com. 8 units. June–Sept C$159–C$199 double; Oct to mid-Mar C$109–C$149 double; mid-Mar to May C$119–C$159 double. MC, V. Free parking. Pets accepted (C$30). **Amenities:** 2 lounges. *In room:* TV/DVD player, hair dryer, iPod dock, Wi-Fi.

The Royal Scot Suite Hotel ★ Situated a block from the Inner Harbour, this suite hotel provides excellent value if you're not hooked on a waterfront view. Converted from an apartment building, guest rooms are large with lots of cupboard space. Studios include a living/dining area and kitchen; one-bedroom suites have separate bedrooms with king-size, queen-size, or twin beds. Kitchens are fully equipped, and living areas come with sofa beds. This is an ideal home base for families; weary parents in need of a few zzz's will love having their offspring scoot off to the children's games room or the indoor pool. Jonathan's Restaurant (✆ **250/383-5103**), has a summer patio. There are nine room types, ranging from guest rooms to two-bedroom corner suites, so you're bound to find something that fits. If you didn't bring your car, the Royal Scot operates a complimentary guest shuttle to downtown. Tip: Internet specials can offer up to 40% savings, even in high season.

425 Quebec St., Victoria, BC V8V 1W7. ✆ **800/663-7515** or 250/388-5463. www.royalscot.com. 176 units. C$155–C$249 double; C$185–C$419 suite. Weekly, monthly & off-season discounts available. Children 11 & under stay free in parent's room. AE, DC, MC, V. Parking C$10. Bus: 30. **Amenities:** Restaurant; babysitting; small heated indoor pool; hydrotherapy pool; room service; sauna. *In room:* TV, hair dryer, Wi-Fi.

Downtown & Old Town

EXPENSIVE

Abigail's Hotel ★★ Tucked into a quiet residential cul-de-sac, only 3 blocks from downtown Victoria and the Inner Harbour, this European-style Tudor inn is about as chintzy and romantic as it can get. Guest rooms are resplendently decorated with antiques, wood-burning fireplaces, two-person Jacuzzis, fresh-cut flowers, and welcoming treats such as truffles and fruit. The six Coach House suites have extravagant touches such as four-poster beds, custom-made furniture, and Italian marble bathrooms with Jacuzzi tubs. Since the chef has cooked for the Queen, breakfast is fit for royalty—literally—and will be brought to your bedside on request. The small Pearl Spa offers a full range of quality spa services. Abigail's is geared to adults; children are discouraged.

906 McClure St., Victoria, BC V8V 3E7. ✆ **800/561-6565** or 250/388-5363. www.abigailshotel.com. 23 units. May–June, & Sept to mid-Oct C$219–C$379 double; July–Aug C$249–C$409 double; mid-Oct to late Apr C$189–C$259 double. Rates include full breakfast & evening hors d'oeuvres. Spa, honeymoon & wine tour packages available. AE, MC, V. Free parking. Some pets accepted (C$25). Bus: 1. **Amenities:** Spa. *In room:* TV/DVD player, hair dryer, Wi-Fi.

The Magnolia Hotel & Spa ★★ With its central downtown location, this stylishly European boutique hotel offers lots of finishing touches to make you feel immediately welcome: a huge bowl of apples, a large arrangement of fresh flowers, and crisp daily newspapers. The hotel's personalized butler service adds to this attentiveness with an array of complimentary amenities, though sadly, not a real-McCoy butler. Guest rooms are bright, with floor-to-ceiling windows, custom-designed furniture, two-poster beds, and oversize desks. Executive Diamond suites have gas fireplaces. Of special note is the excellent **Aveda concept spa** (www.spamagnolia.com), which recently expanded into new, ground-floor premises, and the hotel's **Prime Steakhouse & Lounge** (✆ **250/386-2010** reservations), a first class steak and seafood restaurant.

623 Courtney St., Victoria, BC V8W 1B8. ✆ **877/624-6654** or 250/381-0999. www.magnoliahotel.com. 64 units. July–Sept C$209–C$349 double; May & June C$189–C$229 double; Oct–Apr C$165–C$189 double. Rates include continental breakfast. Additional adult C$30. Children 11 & under stay free in parent's room. AE, DC, DISC, MC, V. Valet parking C$15. Bus: 5. Small pets accepted (C$60). **Amenities:** Restaurant; access to nearby health club; room service; spa. *In room:* A/C, TV w/pay movies, fridge, hair dryer, minibar, iPod dock, Wi-Fi.

MODERATE & INEXPENSIVE

Admiral Inn The harbor views here will more than make up for the small, motel-like rooms and bathrooms. Besides, they are comfortable and immaculately clean, and available at rates that attract couples, families, seniors, and others in search of a multimillion-dollar vista without the expense. Larger rooms have fridges, microwaves, pullout sofa beds, and balconies; the suites have full kitchens. The inn is a family-run operation, so service is empathetic and includes extras like free bicycles, cots, and cribs; free local calls; and lots of friendly advice on what to see and do. Parking is free, and that's a bonus anywhere near the city's core.

257 Belleville St., Victoria, BC V8V 1X1. ✆ **888/823-6472** or 250/388-6267. www.admiralinnhotel.com. 33 units. May & June C$129–C$179 double; July to mid-Oct C$149–C$229 double; mid-Oct to Apr C$99–C$139 double. Rates include continental breakfast. Additional adult C$10. Children 11 & under stay free in parent's room. AE, DC, MC, V. Free parking. Bus: 5 to Belleville & Government sts. Pets allowed (C$15). **Amenities:** Complimentary bikes. *In room:* A/C, TV, fridge, hair dryer, kitchen (in some units), Wi-Fi.

Hotel Rialto Like a phoenix from the ashes, the Rialto has risen out of a has-been hotel to become the city's hippest new boutique hotel. Named after the famous

Rialto Bridge in Venice, the hotel's overall decor speaks to the new owner's Italian heritage. The widespread use of marble throughout the lobby and dining areas are typical of northern Italy, though most of this marble is quarried locally. Guest rooms are modern with dark wood furnishings, granite countertops, an in-room wine bar, flat-screen plasma TVs, and superior queen or king-size beds. The lower lobby displays the building's history, including some oriental antiques. **Veneto Tapas Lounge** (✆ **250/383-7310**) has shot to the top of the "in" list for local trendies and after-work gatherings.

653 Pandora Ave., Victoria, BC V8W 1N8. ✆ **800/332-9981.** www.hotelrialto.ca. 39 units. July & Aug C$159–C$219 double; Sept–Mar C$119–C$189 double; Apr–June C$129–C$199 double. Additional adult C$25. Children 11 & under stay free in parent's room. AE, MC, V. Parking C$10. **Amenities:** Restaurant; bar. *In room:* TV w/pay movies, DVD player, fridge, hair dryer, iPod dock, Wi-Fi.

Ocean Island Backpackers Inn 🎁 This historic, four-level youth hostel–cum–apartment building attracts all age groups and families. Dorm accommodations sleep four to six people, and you can find co-ed as well as women-only rooms. If you're a twosome, the rates are reasonable enough that it's worth booking a whole dorm to yourself. Special family rooms are more hotel-like and have a private bathroom, multiple beds, and a fridge. This is not a place for shrinking violets. The lounges, bar, and dining room are magnets for lively and multilingual conversations with fellow travelers. In addition, Ocean Island operates a 1907 character house in the James Bay area that contains three self-contained, self-catering suites.

791 Pandora Ave., Victoria, BC V8W 1N9. ✆ **888/888-4180,** 866/888-4180, or 250/385-1788. www.oceanisland.com. 80 units. C$20–C$28 dorm bed; C$28–C$84 private room; C$99–C$160 family room. AE, MC, V. **Amenities:** Lounge; kitchen. *In room:* No phone, Wi-Fi.

Swans Hotel ★★ The charming Swans offers a warm welcome in an intimately comfortable modern-day tavern. But it's more than a bed-and-beer experience. One of Victoria's best-loved heritage restorations, this 1913 warehouse now provides guests with 30 distinctive—and really roomy—suites. Most of the open concept studios and one- and two-bedroom suites are two-story lofts with 3.3m (11-ft.) exposed-beam ceilings and nifty layouts that have many, if not most, of the comforts of home. The studios have king beds; the rest have queen-size. Accommodating up to six adults, they feature fully equipped kitchens, separate living and dining areas, and private patios. If you want to go for the gusto, there's even a three-level, 279-sq.-m (3,003-sq.-ft.) penthouse with its own Roy Henry Vickers totem pole. Speaking of which, the hotel has one of Canada's largest private art collections, but you only get to see what's in the lobby since many pieces are in guest rooms. The **Wild Saffron Bistro & Wine Bar** is open daily. Other facilities include **Swans Pub** and **Buckerfields' Brewery**, which offers tours by appointment.

506 Pandora Ave., Victoria, BC V8W 1N6. ✆ **800/668-7926** or 250/361-3310. www.swanshotel.com. 30 suites. Mid-June to Sept C$199 studio, C$289–C$359 suite; Oct to mid-June C$179–C$189 studio, C$219–C$259 suite. Rates include continental breakfast. Weekly & monthly rates available. Additional adult C$35. Up to 2 children 12 & under stay free in parent's room. AE, DC, MC, V. Parking C$9. Bus: 23 or 24 to Pandora Ave. **Amenities:** Restaurant; wine bar; brewpub; babysitting; access to nearby health club; room service. *In room:* TV, fridge, hair dryer, kitchen, Wi-Fi.

Outside the Central Area

EXPENSIVE

Brentwood Bay Lodge & Spa ★★ Service matches the excellent facilities at Brentwood, the region's only five-star oceanfront resort, which in 2010 Expedia rated on its *Insider Select* list. The entire place is a showcase for West Coast style with picture windows, natural finishes, and beamed, high-gabled ceilings. Each of the 33 suites has a balcony or patio view of the inlet, forested peaks, and marina; gas fireplaces; hand-crafted furnishings; and local art. The rooms' spa-like bathrooms feature hard-to-resist double-jetted tubs, and shuttered windows let you sit in the tub and bask in the views. This is only outdone by the **Essence of Life** spa itself (✆ **250/544-5111**)—a lavish affair. There's **SeaGrille** (✆ **250/544-5100**), a fine-dining restaurant that offers an ever-changing menu of primarily local seafood and regional game; a sushi-sake bar; and a marine pub that serves distinctive craft beers, upscale comfort foods and delicious brick-oven pizzas. Live entertainment, from jazz to classical guitar, runs Wednesday to Friday nights. Six oceanfront, two-bedroom villas opened in late 2010, each one including a 12m (39-ft.) boat slip. Rates were not available at press time. The hotel is a licensed PADI dive center and has an eco-marine center with kayak rentals and charters.

849 Verdier Ave. (on Brentwood Bay), Victoria, BC V8M 1C5. ✆ **888/544-2079** or 250/544-2079. www.brentwoodbaylodge.com. 39 units. Mid-June to mid-Oct C$329–C$349 double, C$549 suite; mid-Oct to mid-June C$189–C$299 double, C$389–C$499 suite. AE, MC, V. Free parking. Take Pat Bay Hwy. north to Keating Crossroads, turn left (west) to Saanich Rd., then turn right (south) to Verdier Ave. **Amenities:** Restaurant; pub; cafe; Jacuzzi; heated outdoor pool; room service; spa; 40-slip marina. *In room:* A/C, TV/DVD player, fridge, iPod dock, Wi-Fi.

Sooke Harbour House ★★★ Poised on the end of a sand spit, this little inn has an understated elegance with a friendly, yet completely unobtrusive, staff. An eclectic blend of antiques, original art, and whimsical crafts is showcased throughout the inn and comprises one of the largest public art collections on Vancouver Island. Each of the 28 guest rooms is decorated in a unique way, though they all express a Northwest theme. All have wood-burning fireplaces, exquisite views, and all but one have sundecks. Many have Jacuzzis and showers with beautiful stained-glass doors. Speaking of showers, or rather rain, rooms are well equipped with umbrellas, rubber boots, and rain jackets. If the sun is shining, take time to wander the gardens, a trove of edible wildflowers, herbs, and display blooms. And take note: This Inn was eco-conscious before it was in vogue and offers many green initiatives, including substantial water reclamation and composting programs. There's even a "green" turf parking lot. The experience wouldn't be complete without enjoying a meal at the **Sooke Harbour House** restaurant, which is the best in the region (see "Where to Dine," below). If you're not a guest at the hotel, dining here often means making a reservation weeks in advance, especially in summer. The **Sea-renity Spa** offers an excellent range of massage and aesthetic services, including seaweed treatments using Outer Coast Sooke seaweed spa products.

1528 Whiffen Spit Rd., Sooke, BC V0S 1N0. ✆ **800/889-9688** or 250/642-3421. www.sookeharbourhouse.com. 28 units. July & Aug C$399–C$589 double; Sept–June C$309–C$459 double. Rates include breakfast & picnic lunch. Children 12 & under stay free in parent's room. DC, MC, V. Free parking. Take Island Hwy. to the Sooke-Colwood turnoff (junction Hwy. 24), continue on Hwy. 14 to Sooke, turn left onto Whiffen Spit Rd. Pets accepted (C$20). **Amenities:** Restaurant; babysitting; room service; spa. *In room:* Hair dryer, Wi-Fi.

Villa Marco Polo ★★★ Just down the road from the Lieutenant Governor's residence, everything about this Italian Renaissance mansion is true to its well-traveled namesake. First are the gardens, with their ornamental statues, reflection pool, and fountains. Then there are the public lounges, filled with antiques collected from all over the world—the Chinese cabinet in the lounge, the handmade books in the library, the Italian crystal chandelier in the dining room, to mention a few. Each of the four bedrooms is thematically decorated, with plush European linens fitted to king-size beds. The Silk Road suite has vaulted ceilings and hand-painted Tuscan murals; the Persian Suite is decorated with Persian fabrics and antiques; the Zanzibar suite has French doors onto a Juliette balcony; and the most eye-catching, the Alexandria Suite, is adorned with carved Turkish wooden shutters. The top of the house has been converted into a tiny loft spa and yoga/meditation area. Breakfast is a feast for the senses. Freshly baked goods may include buttermilk 10-grain muffins or caramelized pineapple pecan cakes, while entrees run from hot lemon lavender soufflés to baked eggs Florentine with a Persian pepper hollandaise.

1524 Shasta Place, Victoria, BC V8S 1X9. ✆ **877/601-1524** or 250/370-1524. www.villamarcopolo.com. 4 units. Mid-June to mid-Sept C$145–C$295 double; mid-Sept to mid-Oct & mid-Apr to mid-Jun C$125–C$265 double; mid-Oct to mid-Apr C$105–C$225 double. Rates include breakfast, afternoon tea & hors d'oeuvres. 2-night minimum July & August. AE, MC, V. Free parking. **Amenities:** Lounge; spa. *In room:* TV/CD/DVD player, hair dryer, iPod dock.

MODERATE

Oak Bay Guest House While a nearby resort still undergoes its from-the-ground-up redevelopment, this is the only place to stay in residential Oak Bay, and it exudes old England. New owners have considerable plans for modernizing, but until those take hold, you can still step inside the 1912 Tudor-style inn and enjoy the incoherency of an older building trying to make good in the 21st century. Stairs creak, corridors are narrow, and rooms are odd shapes because each has had an en suite added as plumbing could dictate. But that's the charm of the place—and the value. It's clean, comfortable, offers the basics, and is run by a staff who really makes you feel welcome.

1052 Newport Ave., Victoria, BC V8S 5E3. ✆ **800/575-3812** or 250/598-3812. www.oakbayguesthouse.com. 11 units. May to mid-Oct C$89–C$179 double; mid-Oct to Apr C$79–C$149 double. Rates include breakfast. MC, V. Free parking. **Amenities:** TV lounge. *In room:* Hair dryer, no phone, Wi-Fi.

WHERE TO DINE

Purporting to have the second-highest number of restaurants per capita in North America (behind San Francisco), Victoria offers something for every taste and budget, and refreshingly, you don't always have to pay through the nose to get quality. And that includes one or two holes-in-the-wall. What you will pay for is the restaurant's proximity to a waterfront view. Most of the best restaurants are either in or within walking distance of downtown hotels, so you don't have to worry about who'll be the designated driver.

Vancouver Island is hugely influenced by the 100-Mile Diet and Slow Food movement, which takes full advantage of the island's extraordinary number of microclimates where fresh produce, fisheries, farms, and vineyards thrive. The collaboration between chefs is creating a very sustainable restaurant and agri-tourism economy, all of which is best showcased in locally inspired menus. An Ocean Wise logo identifies restaurateurs (and/or their dishes) that use sustainable harvest.

Inner Harbour & Nearby

EXPENSIVE

Blue Crab Bar & Grill ★★ SEAFOOD This is the best seafood spot in the city, with killer views of the harbor to boot, so naturally, it's always busy and has a tendency to get noisy. Blue Crab's seafood specials, featured on their signature blackboards, are what keep this restaurant at the top. Dishes are unpredictable inventions, such as blue crab fish pot, grilled salmon with crispy yucca-root spaetzles, or smoked Alaskan black cod poached in coconut milk with a hint of red curry. For a real treat, the platters for two include sampler morsels from several menu items. There's also a good selection of landlubber dishes for those whose tastes run away from the sea. The wine list is excellent, particularly when it comes to BC and California wines. It consistently wins awards, as do its chefs, who in 2008 garnered several accolades at Salon Culinaire at Hotelympia in London, England.

In the Coast Hotel, 146 Kingston St. ✆ **250/480-1999.** www.bluecrab.ca. Reservations required. Main courses lunch C$8–C$25, dinner C$20–C$26. AE, DC, MC, V. Daily 6:30am–10pm. Nibbles available until 1am.

The Mark ★★ CONTINENTAL The Mark has no view, preferring to create an intimate dining experience within the confines of a discreet, wood-paneled room, but it's perfect for memorable and romantic encounters—it seats only 26 diners. The upscale menu matches the high-end wine list with dishes such as long pepper–rubbed ahi tuna with cardamom-scented white bean and endive marmalade, and a truffle infused fallow venison loin. The six-course apple-tasting menu celebrates the Gulf Islands' apple heritage, which today produces more that 300 varieties. There's apple linguine, apple caviar, apples and oysters, and a mouth-watering frangipane Gala-apple pie with Tugwell honey cream and vanilla-bean gelato. Waiters are well informed on dishes, and the service has gracious finesse (extra butter arrives quietly almost before you realize it's running out), without staff hovering.

In the Hotel Grand Pacific, 450 Quebec St. ✆ **250/380-4487.** www.themark.ca. Reservations recommended. Main courses C$30–C$43; six-course tasting menu C$70, add C$40 with wine pairings. AE, DC, DISC, MC, V. Daily 5–9:30pm.

MODERATE & INEXPENSIVE

The James Bay Tea Room & Restaurant PUB FARE When these folks tried to dump the traditional British fare from the menu, it caused such an uproar that home-style bangers and mash, Welsh rarebit on toast, and roast beef with Yorkshire pudding have returned with zeal. It's one of the few places that serves kippers for breakfast, which lasts all day, alongside burgers, soups, salads, and even low-carb, Atkins-friendly items. Then there's high tea, which starts in earnest mid-morning, and represents better value than most. The decor includes Tiffany lampshades, brass knickknacks, and sepia-tinted family portraits. Tables are crowded with locals, and the atmosphere is lively, with English-accented chatter. Tarot card readings are offered on Saturday afternoons.

332 Menzies St. (behind the Parliament Buildings). ✆ **250/382-8282.** www.jamesbaytearoomandrestaurant.com. Reservations recommended. Main courses breakfast & lunch C$6–C$10, high tea & dinner C$16–C$29. AE, MC, V. Mon–Fri 7am–5pm; Sat & Sun 8am–5pm.

Red Fish/Blue Fish ★ FISH AND CHIPS This is one of the most innovative take-out fish eats concepts around: a 6.1×3m (20×9¾-ft.) gourmand's fish-and-chips cafe out of a repurposed ship's container, much like the metal freight boxes you see rolling down the highway atop 18-wheelers. This one was used to ship a Hummer and now has a rooftop garden (which also acts as roof insulation) and a conscientious green program that includes composting and recycling potato starch. It also uses only Ocean Wise seafood, some caught by the owners themselves. Here, you get wild Pacific halibut, salmon, or cod coated with a light tempura batter; twice-fried, hand-cut potatoes, some slathered in curry; grill-seared tuna; fish tacones (taco-cones); and mushy edamame, a quirky twist on mushy peas. Because tables are forbidden on the dock, the cafe provides stools for waterside dining, year-round.

1006 Wharf St. (on the pier below). ✆ **250/298-6877.** www.redfish-bluefish.com. Main courses C$10–C$17. MC, V. Daily 11:30am–7pm.

Superior Restaurant ★ REGIONAL Everything here is designed to evoke the senses and share, from its nightly, live entertainment and small plates of regional cuisine to a lovely garden patio shaded by trees and an interior of surrealist art. The building dates back to 1912 and once housed wayward sailors. Graze on dishes of bruschetta, charcuterie, pate, or a grilled Caesar salad while enjoying everything from jazz to classical to R&B. On Friday and Saturday nights, non-diners can expect a cover charge after 7:30pm; on other nights, a bucket is passed, New Orleans–style.

106 Superior St. ✆ **250/380-9515.** Reservations recommended. Main courses C$10–C$16. MC, V. Tues–Sun 11am–3pm & 5–11pm. Closed Mon.

Downtown & Old Town

EXPENSIVE

Cafe Brio ★ REGIONAL This award-winning bistro-style restaurant serves delicious Tuscan-inspired West-Coast fare (and decor), likely because its two chefs, one Canadian and one Italian, blend their styles into the ever-changing menu that's based on whatever organic produce they purchased that day. The result is a creative mix of natural flavors zinging with just the right amount of added spices. In winter, expect substantial items such as venison shank and confit of duck. In summer, items are lighter: a charcuterie menu featuring local salami, lomo, pâtés, and terrines, and served with homemade mustards and pickles; and seared scallops topped with crisp potato rösti. Service is top-notch, and the wine list is exceptional, with more than 300 wines by the bottle and 30 by the glass or half-liter. Tip: The entire menu is available in half portions.

944 Fort St. ✆ **250/383-0009.** www.cafe-brio.com. Reservations recommended. Main courses C$16–C$36. AE, MC, V. Daily 5:30–10:30pm.

Camille's ★ PACIFIC NORTHWEST The restaurant's owner was one of the founders of the Vancouver Island Farm Co-Operative, so, true to form, the ever-changing menu is seasonal and packed with locally sourced ingredients. This might mean tender fiddleheads in spring, and wild salmon and blackberry desserts in the autumn. Canadian bison, wild boar, and caribou might also be on the menu, alongside pheasant, quail, and partridge. Everything has an unexpected touch, such as prawn bisque with ginger and lemon, or fennel cakes in a champagne sauce. Camille's is a very romantic spot with cliché, crisp white linens, exposed-brick walls, stained-glass lamps, soft jazz, and candlelight. As with many Victoria restaurants, the five-course tasting menu (C$90) includes a bit of everything; add C$30 for wine pairings.

45 Bastion Sq. ✆ **250/381-3433.** www.camillesrestaurant.com. Reservations recommended. Main courses C$26–C$37. AE, MC, V. Tues–Sat 5:30–10pm.

MODERATE & INEXPENSIVE

Azuma Sushi SUSHI This modern, busy, and bright restaurant has the best-value sushi in town. Rumor has it that at his previous restaurant, Azuma's chef developed quite the following for his special rice sauce, the secret of which he has brought with him. The seafood is top quality (not an imitation crab in sight), and the *unagi*

THE tea EXPERIENCE

When the Duchess of Bedford complained about a "sinking feeling" in the late afternoon, she invented afternoon tea to keep her going until dinner. Today, however, tea has come to mean everything from a genteel cup of Earl Grey to a full-blown meal in itself with scones with whipped cream, savory crust-less sandwiches, sweet tartlets, and home-baked biscuits. Among the top choices are:

- The Fairmont Empress (721 Government St.; ✆ **250/389-2727**): Serves its famed epicurean feast in the Tea Lobby and elsewhere as the throngs of tea-takers dictate. It's expensive (C$44–$C55 per person in high season) and, quite frankly, overrated, although the inflated price does include a keepsake of nicely packaged Empress tea.
- The Blethering Place Tearoom (2250 Oak Bay Ave., Oak Bay; ✆ **250/598-1413**): Slightly less pretentious and has the art of tea down pat. Tea menus start at C$20 and are what a quintessential Victorian teahouse is all about.
- White Heather Tea Room (1885 Oak Bay Ave., Oak Bay; ✆ **250/595-8020**): A local favorite just down the road from the Blethering Place Tearoom. Small, bright, and exceptionally friendly, the Big Muckle Giant Tea for Two (C$40) is the grand slam of all teas. Smaller options are available.
- Point Ellice House (2616 Pleasant St.; ✆ **250/380-6506**): Where Victoria's social elite gathered in early 1900s. Take a 5-minute ferry ride across the Inner Harbour and enjoy tea (summer only) near the water on carefully mowed lawns. The cost of C$23 per person includes a half-hour tour of the mansion and gardens.
- Murchie's Tea and Coffee (1110 Government St.; ✆ **250-383-3112**): Has purveyed tea since 1894 and offers one of the best selections of teas in the city, plus good coffee and everything from snacks to full-blown sandwiches and salads (C$5–C$14).
- Dutch Bakery (718 Fort St.; ✆ **250/385-1012**): Where to go for a quick pick-me-up, as well as a one-of-a-kind baked treat and European-style sugared confection. This is a fourth-generation Victoria institution that still feels a part of the '50s era. Try the dollar, a sponge roll and marzipan.
- The Butchart Gardens Dining Room (800 Benvenuto Ave.; ✆ **250/652-4422**): Although farther afield, taking tea here is worth the drive, although you can only enjoy the experience if you've also paid for admission to the gardens. A full tea is C$27.
- Silk Road Tea (1624 Government St.; ✆ **250/704-2688**): For something entirely differently, tea tasting here is like sampling flights of wine. A 30-minute revelation of exotic infusions from all over the world is C$10 per person. Silk Road also pairs its teas to the Hotel Grand Pacific's weekend dim sums for some inspired combinations.

nigiri and spicy tuna sashimi are especially good. The daily two-for-one bento boxes are a real bargain for hungry appetites.

615 Yates St. (btw. Broad & Government Sts.). ✆ **250/382-8768.** Reservations recommended. Main courses C$10–C$20. Daily 11am–10pm.

Foo Asian Street Food ★★ ASIAN Superlative Asian food served in a take-away box off a street corner just about sums up one of Victoria's hottest concepts. By avoiding fine-dining overheads such as linens and wait staff, the restaurant devotes its creativity and effort into a menu inspired by the multiple food carts found around various regions in Asia: Thai red coconut curry, Indian butter chicken, Vietnamese Ginger caramel chicken, as well as a fabulous green papaya salad, prawn and pork lettuce cups, crispy pakoras and *paneer* cheese dumplings. Pull up a chair, sit at the bar to watch the chefs create their magic, or join others on the patio, sitting around a repurposed university lab table, complete with student etchings. Inside seats about 8; outside about 12; most orders, however, are take out.

769 Yates St. ✆ **250/383-3111.** www.foofood.ca. Main courses C$9–$12. Mon–Fri 11:30am–10pm; Sat & Sun 5–9:30pm.

rebar Modern Food ★ ☺ VEGETARIAN This bright and busy basement restaurant is likely the best vegetarian cafe on the west coast. The juice bar alone boasts more than 80 varieties of deliciously healthful smoothies, shakes, wheatgrass drinks, and power tonics. The stress-busting Soul Change—a blend of carrot, apple, celery, ginger, and Siberian ginseng—is a winner. The menu is geared to vegetarian and vegan diners (though not exclusively), featuring international cuisine, from Thai curries and pastas to hummus and fresh shrimp quesadillas. The homemade muesli is dynamite, and the Cascadia Bakery produces everything from decadent vegan Belgian chocolate fudge cake to hand-shaped whole-grain specialty breads. The small wine list offers predominately BC wines, and even when it's really busy (which is most of the time), the service remains fast and friendly.

50 Bastion Sq. (downstairs). ✆ **250/361-9223.** www.rebarmodernfood.com. Reservations not accepted. Main courses C$8–C$16. AE, MC, V. Mon–Thurs 8:30am–9pm; Fri & Sat 8:30am–10pm; Sun 8:30am–3:30pm. Reduced hours in winter.

Outside the Central Area

VERY EXPENSIVE

Sooke Harbour House ★★★ REGIONAL The cuisine has seduced thousands of palates, and the restaurant's award-winning wine cellar is regarded as one of the best on the West Coast. Chef Edward Tuson's imaginative menu focuses on local seafood and organically grown produce, much of it harvested from the over 200 herbs, greens, flowers, and vegetables grown on the premises. Their culinary transformation creates predominately seafood dishes such as creamy broccoli soup with smoked sablefish and daylily oil, or yellow split pea–crusted lingcod with a carrot-and-mint emulsion. Even the sorbets are a cornucopia of flavors served together: green apple and mint; yellow plum and Anjou pear black currant. The food is so good here that you should probably opt for the multi-course gastronomic adventure tasting menu. These are C$120; add C$80 or more if you choose the wine pairings. The four-course set menu is an excellent value at C$75 and includes a vegetarian option. Dinner is by reservation only, at least 3 days in advance (but you'd be better off calling 3 weeks in advance in the summer). Breakfast and lunch are served for hotel guests only.

In Sooke Harbour House, 1528 Whiffen Spit Rd., Sooke. ✆ **250/642-3421.** Reservations required. Main courses C$35; prix-fixe menu C$47–C$75. DC, MC, V. Mid June–mid Sept daily 5–9:30pm; mid Sept–mid

June Thurs–Mon 5–9:30pm. Take Island Hwy. to the Sooke-Colwood turnoff (junction w/Hwy. 24), continue on Hwy. 14 to Sooke & turn left onto Whiffen Spit Rd.

MODERATE

Smoken Bones Cookshack ★★★ CAJUN/CREOLE Chef/owner Ken Hueston is high up in the food chain of the island's Chefs Collaborative. This box-like restaurant lies in a small strip mall and positively pulsates with activity every minute it's open. Here's why: The southern BBQ and Cajun-Creole–influenced dishes are phenomenal, the result of natural wood-smoking techniques that see pork ribs spending hours in the smoker. The restaurant goes through about 20,000kg (44,092 lb.) of pork ribs a month! Because the island would soon be pig-less with this kind of ongoing volume, Hueston buys about 20% of his products from the mainland. But for everything else—for the spicy Gumbo, fresh-baked cornbread, braised collard greens, and butter-fried cabbage—it's backyard shopping. The portions are generous, so it's a real find for families, with lots of opportunity for sharing plates and eat-all-you-can buffets to satiate hearty appetites.

101-721 Station St. ✆ **250/391-6328.** www.smokenbones.ca. Reservations recommended. Main courses C$12–C$18. MC, V. Mon–Sat 11:30am–9pm; Sun noon–9pm.

VICTORIA AFTER DARK

As vibrant as Victoria is by day, once the hour hand passes 10pm, city activity just seems to fade into the darkness. Granted, the pubs and the Yates Street area remain pretty busy, especially on weekends, but all in all, when the theaters, concert venues, and movie houses close up shop, so does downtown.

Monday magazine (**www.mondaymag.com**) covers everything going on in town, from nightclubs and the performing arts to films and poetry readings. You name it, *Monday's* got it. You can also call the **Community Arts Council of Greater Victoria's** events hotline at ✆ **250/381-ARTS** (250/381-2787). Tickets and schedules are also available at the **Tourism Victoria Travel Visitor Information Centre** (812 Wharf St.; ✆ **250/953-2033**).

THE PERFORMING ARTS The **Royal Theatre,** 805 Broughton St. (✆ **250/361-0820;** box office 250/386-6121; www.rmts.bc.ca; bus: 5 or 30), hosts events such as Victoria Symphony concerts, dance recitals, and touring stage plays. The box office is at the **McPherson Playhouse,** 3 Centennial Sq., at Pandora Avenue and Government Street (✆ **250/386-6121;** bus: 5 or 30), which is also home to Victoria's Pacific Opera and the Victoria Operatic Society. The box office is open Monday through Saturday from 9:30am to 5:30pm.

The **Belfry Theatre,** 1291 Gladstone St. (✆ **250/385-6815;** www.belfry.bc.ca; bus: 1 or 2), is a nationally acclaimed theatrical group that stages four productions October to April and a summer show in August. The **Victoria Fringe Festival** (✆ **888/FRINGE-2** or 250/383-2663; www.victoriafringe.com) presents short, inexpensive original fare at various venues from late August to mid-September.

The **Pacific Opera Victoria,** 1316B Government St. (✆ **250/385-0222,** box office 250/386-6121; www.pov.bc.ca; bus: 5 or 30), presents productions in October, February, and April. Performances are normally at the McPherson Playhouse and Royal Theatre. **The Victoria Operatic Society,** 798 Fairview Rd. (✆ **250/381-1021;** www.vos.bc.ca), stages old-time Broadway musicals and other popular fare year-round at the McPherson Playhouse.

The **Victoria Symphony Orchestra,** 846 Broughton St. (✆ **250/385-9771;** www.victoriasymphony.bc.ca; bus: 5 or 30), kicks off its season on the first Sunday of August with Symphony Splash, a free concert performed on a barge in the Inner Harbour. Regular performances begin in September and last to May.

LIVE-MUSIC CLUBS **Herman's Jazz Club,** 753 View St. (✆ **250/388-9166;** www.hermansjazz.com) has delivered Victoria's best live jazz and Dixieland. Martinis are named after famous musicians such as Duke Ellington and Ella Fitzgerald. **The Lucky Bar,** 517 Yates St. (✆ **250/382-5825;** www.luckybar.ca), is currently the hottest spot in Victoria. This low cavernous space has a pleasantly grungy feel like Seattle's Pioneer Square. Lucky's DJs spin on the weekends, with bands often showing up earlier in the week. **Touch Lounge,** 751 View St. (✆ **250/384-2582;** www.touchlounge.com), is one of the city's hottest lounge bars. The place is geared to the under-30s crowd; you'll want to dress to impress and express. The DJs spin mainly Top 40, retro, hip-hop, funk, and R&B.

LOUNGES, BARS & PUBS A truly unique experience, the **Bengal Lounge** in the Empress hotel, 721 Government St. (✆ **250/384-8111**), is one of the last outposts of the old Empire, except the martinis are ice cold and jazz plays in the background (on weekends it's live in the foreground). A restaurant by day, **The Reef** (533 Yates St.; ✆ **250/388-5375;** www.thereefrestaurant.com) transforms into a funky reggae lounge after dark, with great martinis, good tunes, and a DJ thrown in now and again just to spice things up. **Harbour Canoe Club,** 450 Swift St. (✆ **250/361-1940**), is one of the most pleasant spots to go to hoist a pint after a long day's sightseeing. **Big Bad John's,** 919 Douglas St., in the Strathcona Hotel (✆ **250/383-7137**), is Victoria's only hillbilly bar—a low, dark warren of a place, with inches of discarded peanut shells on the plank floor and a crowd of drunk and happy rowdies.

Overlooking Victoria Harbour on the west side of the Songhees Point Development, **Spinnakers Brewpub,** 308 Catherine St. (✆ **250/386-BREW** or 250/386-2739), has one of the best views and some of the best beer in town. The same ownership team runs **Sips Artisan Bistro,** 425 Simcoe St. (✆ **250/590-3519**), dedicated to tasting, especially when they're serving limited edition wines from Vancouver Island, the Okanagan, or elsewhere in the province. Customized flights of 59mL (2-oz.) pourings average C$3.50 per pour. **Swans Butterfield Brewpub,** 506 Pandora Ave. (✆ **250/361-3310**), is an enjoyable and convivial drinking spot in Swans Hotel, with a collection of Pacific Northwest and First Nations art and beer brewed on-site; there's live entertainment every night.

GAY & LESBIAN BARS **Hush,** 1325 Government St. (✆ **250/385-0566;** www.hushnightclub.ca), a gay but straight-friendly space, features top-end touring DJs. Loud music (usually live) and electronica pack the place on weekends.

A SIDE TRIP FROM VICTORIA: GOLDSTREAM PROVINCIAL PARK

The tranquil arboreal setting of Goldstream Provincial Park overflowed with prospectors during the 1860s gold-rush days. Trails take you past abandoned mine shafts and tunnels, as well as 600-year-old stands of towering Douglas fir, lodgepole pine, red cedar, indigenous yew, and arbutus trees. The **Gold Mine Trail** leads to Niagara

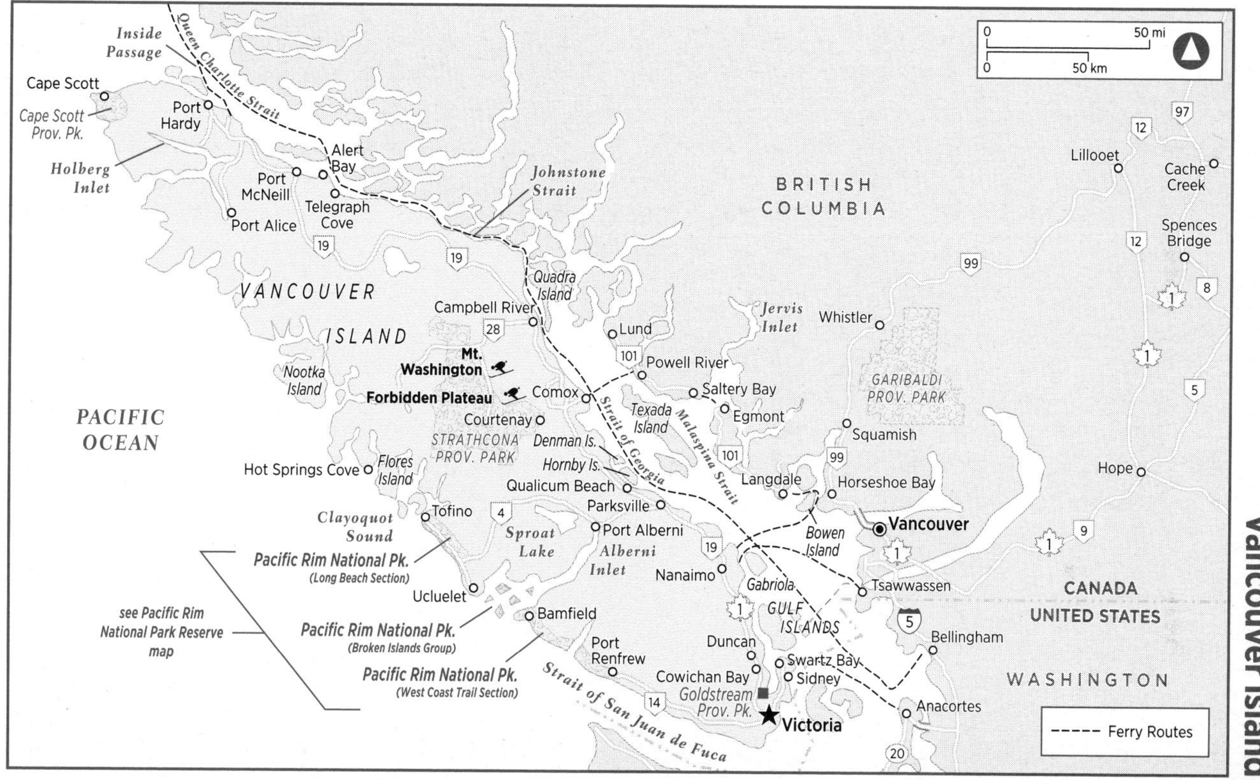

VICTORIA & BRITISH COLUMBIA | A Side Trip from Victoria: Goldstream Provincial Park

Creek and the abandoned mine that was operated by Lt. Peter Leech, a Royal Engineer who discovered gold in the creek in 1858. The **Goldstream Trail** leads to the salmon spawning areas. (You might also catch sight of mink and river otters racing along this path.)

The park is 20km (12 miles) west of downtown Victoria along Highway 1; the drive takes about half an hour. For general information on this and all the other provincial parks on the South Island, contact **BC Parks** at **© 250/391-2300.** Throughout the year, Goldstream Park's **Freeman King Visitor Centre** (**© 250/478-9414**) offers guided walks, talks, displays, and programs geared toward kids but interesting for adults, too. It's open daily 9:30am to 4:30pm.

From mid-October through November, thousands come to Goldstream Provincial Park to watch salmon spawn, while in December and January, they come for the Bald Eagle Count. Many areas of the park are wheelchair accessible. For information on Goldstream Provincial Park and all other provincial parks on the South Island, contact BC Parks (www.env.gov.bc.ca/bcparks). Interested in camping in the park? Choose from among 173 sites. Reserve through **Discover Camping** (**© 800/689-9025** or 604/689-9025; www.discovercamping.ca).

THE GULF ISLANDS

Clustered between Vancouver Island and the mainland, the Gulf Islands are pastoral havens. Their protected waterways provide some of the finest cruising in the world, and their semi-Mediterranean climate is enviable, even by West Coast standards. Add to this sweeping scenes of woods and water, pebble and shell beaches, and placid lakes stocked with bass and rainbow trout ideal for fly-fishing, and you can understand why the Gulf Islands have been described as "fragments of paradise."

The raggedly beautiful archipelago, the northern extension of Washington's San Juan Islands, is made up of more than 200 islands. The five larger islands, off the southeastern tip of Vancouver Island—Salt Spring Island, the Pender Islands, and Galiano, Mayne, and Saturna islands—are home to about 15,000 permanent residents and are served by a regularly scheduled ferry service.

The Gulf Islands are a heavenly place to hike, kayak, and canoe, or simply enjoy a glass of wine from the deck of a cottage. Families usually choose cabins or hotels because many of the islands' inns and B&Bs are geared to adults. When a hotel does welcome children, however, this information is included in the review in this chapter. The islands may lack many urban amenities such as ATMs and laundromats, but they do have a wealth of quirky features that will make your visit memorable. One example is the "honesty stands" that dot the roadsides. You drop your money in the box provided and walk away with honey, flowers, veggies, jams, and whatever else local folk have for sale.

Of all the islands, Salt Spring is the most dynamic and the easiest to get to from Vancouver Island, especially if you have only a day to spare. Once on a Gulf Island, it is easy to hop to another, arriving in the early morning and departing late afternoon. You're best to incorporate at least one night on each island—it's the only way to experience the very different personality of each.

Getting There

BY PLANE Seaplanes crisscross the skies above the Gulf Islands at regular intervals, between Vancouver Island, Vancouver on the mainland, and Seattle. **Seair Seaplanes** (**© 800/447-3247** or 604/273-8900; www.seairseaplanes.com) and **Harbour Air**

(✆ **800/665-0212** or 604/274-1277; www.harbour-air.com) offer daily flights. One-way fares average C$95. **Kenmore Air** (✆ **866/435-9524,** or 425/486-1257 in Seattle; www.kenmoreair.com) flies from Seattle May through September. One-way fares are US$200 each way, with slight round-trip discounts. Prices are fluctuating, however, with fuel surcharges. There are no areas on the islands that accommodate commercial flights, although some islands have small, grassy airstrips for private aircraft.

BY FERRY Juggling your schedule with ferry departures is an art that requires patience, if not a master's degree in reading timetables. **BC Ferries** (✆ **888/223-3779** or 250/386-3431; www.bcferries.com) provides good basic service to the Gulf Islands, with at least two sailings a day from **Tsawwassen,** a 22km (14-mile) drive south of Vancouver on the mainland, and from **Swartz Bay,** 32km (20 miles) north of Victoria on Vancouver Island. Ferries also run frequently between islands. Schedules are available from BC Ferries. One-way fares from Tsawwassen to the Gulf Islands average C$16 adults, C$58 for a standard-size vehicle. One-way fares from Swartz Bay to the islands average C$11 adults; C$32 for a standard-size vehicle. Return fares to Tsawwassen are less, and vary according to which island you are returning from. Return fares to Swartz Bay are free. Inter-island trips average C$5 adults, C$11 for a standard-size vehicle.

Note: Ferry travel can be costly if you're taking a vehicle, and long boarding waits are not uncommon. Ticket prices vary seasonally; mid-week travel is slightly less expensive than that on weekends and holidays, when reservations are essential. During these peak periods, book at least 3 weeks in advance to avoid disappointment. Reservations can be made with BC Ferries by phone or online. **Washington State Ferries** (✆ **800/843-3779** in Washington, 888/808-7977 in Canada, or 206/464-6400; www.wsdot.wa.gov/ferries) provides daily service from **Anacortes to Sidney,** a short distance from Swartz Bay. From Swartz Bay, you can transfer to a BC Ferries ferry to the Gulf Islands. There is only one Anacortes-Sidney crossing daily fall through spring; two in summer, during which vehicle reservations are strongly recommended. Reservations must be made by 5:30pm the day prior to travel. From May to early October, one-way fares are C$16 adults, C$8 seniors, C$13 children 6 to 18, and C$55 for a standard-size vehicle and driver. From mid-October to April, fares remain the same for adults, seniors, and children, but drop to C$50 for a standard-size vehicle and driver. Crossing time is 3 hours.

Gulf Islands Water Taxi (✆ **250/537-2510**) is a local inter-island service that operates June through August on Saturdays. When school is in session, September through June, it operates as a weekday school boat, and adults often hitch a ride for day excursions. The one-way fare between any two points is C$15 adults. Round-trips are C$25 adults. People often transport kayaks for C$5. Transporting bicycles is free.

Visitor Information

Services operate through the local chamber of commerce or general store on individual islands (see "Essentials," throughout the chapter, for the island in question). You can also check out **www.gulfislandstourism.com** or **www.gulfislands.net** for general information. Not all islands have public campgrounds, and moorage facilities for pleasure craft vary in size and amenities considerably.

Salt Spring Island

The largest of the Gulf Islands, Salt Spring is—to the outside world—a bucolic getaway filled with artists, sheep pastures, and cozy B&Bs. While this image is mostly true, Salt Spring is also a busy cultural crossroads: Movie stars, retirees, high-tech telecommuters, and hippie farmers all rub shoulders here. The hilly terrain and deep forests afford equal privacy for all lifestyles, and that's the way the residents like it.

With a year-round population of 10,000 residents, Salt Spring is served by three ferries, making it by far the easiest of the Gulf Islands to visit. Not coincidentally, Salt Spring also has the most facilities for visitors. The center of island life is **Ganges,** a little village with gas stations, grocery stores, and banks, all overlooking a busy pleasure-boat harbor. You can easily spend from an hour to most of a day poking around the art galleries, boutiques, and coffee shops here.

In fact, the island is famed across Canada as an artists' colony and many people visit expressly to see the studios of local artists and craftspeople. Stop by the visitor center for the **Studio Tour Map,** which pinpoints nearly 50 island artists—glass blowers, painters, ceramists, weavers, carvers, and sculptors, many of whom are available to visit.

ESSENTIALS

GETTING THERE BC Ferries sails to **Fulford Harbour,** in the southern part of Salt Spring, or **Long Harbour,** toward the north. Seaplanes land in **Ganges Harbour,** in the center of the island. See "Getting There," above, for information about fares and schedules.

VISITOR INFORMATION Head to the **Salt Spring Island Chamber of Commerce** (121 Lower Ganges Rd.; ✆ **866/216-2936** or 250/537-5252; www.saltspringtourism.com), in the village of Ganges. Open daily, year-round, from 11am to 3pm (10am–4pm in July and Aug). Another good online resource is **www.saltspringtourism.com.**

GETTING AROUND The introduction of public transit is one of the more significant changes on Salt Spring in recent years. Buses loop around the island with Ganges as the major destination on schedules that are conveniently tied in with arrivals and departures of ferries at Fulford Harbour, Vesuvius, and Long Harbour. **Silver Shadow Taxi** (✆ **250/537-3030**) services the island. If you want to rent a car, **Salt Spring Marina Rentals** (✆ **800/334-6629** or 250/537-3122) in downtown Ganges can set you up with a mid-range vehicle for about C$60 a day. This company also rents scooters for C$50 per hour or C$70 for 24 hours. **Salt Spring Adventure Co.,** at Salt Spring Marina, 7-126 Upper Ganges Rd. (✆ **877/537-2764** or 250/537-2764; www.saltspringadventures.com), rents both bikes (C$25 per day) and kayaks (C$60–C$90 per day), and will deliver them to anywhere on Salt Spring Island for a nominal charge. Although there are no boat rentals available anywhere on the island, **Salt Spring Marina** at Harbour's End (124 Upper Ganges Rd.; ✆ **800/334-6629** or 250/537-5810) does offer fishing charters. Costs start at C$450 for 4 hours for two people.

EXPLORING SALT SPRING ISLAND

The bustling seaside village of **Ganges ★★★** belies the notion that the Gulf Islands are sleepy hideaways. Historic buildings and bright new commercial structures harbor banks and shopping malls, liquor stores, cafes, bakeries, and a busy marina. A favorite stop is **Sabine's** (115 Fulford-Ganges Rd.; ✆ **250/538-0025**), one of the best fine used bookstores in the Pacific Northwest. Two floors are filled to the rafters with contemporary used and antiquarian books in all categories, and is home of the works of Nick Bantock, creator of *Griffin & Sabine* (Raincoast Books), among others, and who is often on hand to chat and sign books.

Salt Spring's Saturday **farmers' market,** held in Centennial Park in the heart of Ganges, is another summer must-see. This weekly gathering is a glorious melee of islanders and visitors, dogs and children, craftspeople, food vendors, jugglers, and musicians. Everything for sale must be handmade or homegrown, so it's as much a feast for the eyes as for the stomach. If you're looking to snatch up some of the freshly baked goods, arrive before 10am, as they're often sold out within an hour or so of opening. The crowds stay until late afternoon, when fresh-produce vendors, start to drift away. Go to **www.saltspringmarket.com** for more information.

As good as it is, the farmers' market pales in comparison to the **Salt Spring Island Fall Fair,** an annual weekend event held toward the end of September at the Farmers' Institute Fairgrounds (351 Rainbow Rd.). Filled with all the sights, sounds, tastes, and smells of a good old-fashioned country fair, it showcases award-winning livestock and home-baked pies, alongside rides and classic games like balloon darts. A shuttle runs from Ganges to the fairgrounds; call ✆ **250/537-2484** for fair information.

RUCKLE PROVINCIAL PARK ★★

This 433-hectare (1,070-acre) park starts out along 8km (5 miles) of shoreline around **Beaver Point** and sweeps up to an expanse of open and grassy meadow. Once owned by the Ruckle family, Irish immigrants in the late 1800s, part of the park is still operated as a sheep farm by the Ruckle family. Several of the original buildings, including a barn and an old residence, still stand. Ruckle Park is by far the easiest hiking ground on Salt Spring Island, offering more than 15km (9.3 miles) of trails, the favorite being a shoreline trail than runs 4,400m (14,436 ft.) from the heritage farm area right through to Yeo Point. You're also likely to see scuba divers in the waters off Ruckle Park, where castle-like underwater caves and a profusion of marine life create intriguing dives.

The park has 75 walk-in campsites with fire pits (firewood is provided in the summer), 8 RV sites without hook-ups, plus some group sites, a picnic area, a large kitchen shelter, drinking water, several pit toilets, and a security patrol for the entire camping area. The park attracts eco-adventurers and families alike, though for young children, you would be better off heading for **Cusheon Lake.** Ruckle Park has no designated swimming and playground areas, and no interpretive programs. From mid-March to October, a camping fee of C$16 per day applies, and you must reserve your campsite in advance. Camping is free from November to mid-March, on a first-come, first-served basis. No firewood is supplied November through mid-March. Call (✆ **877/559-2115** or 250/539-2115) for local reservations and information, or log on to www.discovercamping.ca.

OUTDOOR ADVENTURES

Although sea kayaking has always been popular, now it proliferates professionally. **Island Escapades** (163 Fulford Ganges Rd.; ✆ **250/537-2553;** www.islandescapades.com) offer harbor tours (from C$50 adults) to full day paddles, including lunch, for C$150 adults. At the north end of Salt Spring, **Andale! Kayaking** (1484 North Beach Rd.; ✆ **250/537-0700**) is another reliable outfitter.

If letting the topsails catch the wind is your preference, **L'Orenda Sailing** (Moby's Dock; ✆ **250/538-0084;** www.lorenda.ca) offers daily afternoon sails aboard a 12m (39-ft.) Classic North Sea double-ended yawl. Sailors can help hoist the sails or do nothing but enjoy the passing scenery. Sails cost C$69 adults; children 12 years and under are half price. One of the more unique land tours is with the

Sidecar Touring Company (✆ **250/538-7981**), which really feels like a throwback to the 1940s. One passenger rides the sidecar, the other takes the pillion seat behind the driver. Tours are C$65.

WHERE TO STAY

Blackberry Glen ★ An idyllic setting sets the tone for this stylish inn. The orchard gardens are gorgeous, and the rooms are finessed with tasteful color schemes, luxurious linens, and hardwood floors. All have queen beds, except the Long Harbour Suite, which has its own terrace balcony, cathedral ceilings, and a sitting area in front of a wood-stove fireplace. The Fulford Suite has a private bathroom across the hall. Refreshments and cookies are always available in the tiny library, and there's a main floor lounge crammed with books and DVDs. For breakfast, you may have orange-liqueur French toast or stinging nettle quiche and lemon balm tea. At press time, two cabins were under renovation: One floats on a tranquil pond, decorated with colorful art and vintage nautical pieces; the other cabin has a more lodge-style ambiance with gorgeous fir floors and elegant furnishings.

156 Quebec Dr., Salt Spring Island, BC V8K 2P4. ✆ **877/890-0764** or 250/537-0764. www.blackberryglen.com. 6 units. May–Sept C$99–C$169 double; Oct–Apr C$89–C$149 double. Rates include breakfast. MC, V. Children 12 & under not accepted. **Amenities:** 2 lounges; hot tub. *In room:* Hair dryer, no phone, Wi-Fi.

Hastings House ★★★ A member of the exclusive Small Luxury Hotels of the World, this sophisticated inn overlooks Ganges Harbour and lies an olive pit's throw from the village itself. First a Hudson's Bay Company trading post, then a farm, and then the homestead of Warren Hastings and his bride, Barbara Wedgwood, the British pottery heiress, the property and magnificent orchard gardens were transformed into a replica of a 16th-century Sussex estate. Since then, the Tudor-style manor house, farmhouse, barn, and trading post have been turned into cottages and suites, each charged with character and filled with original art and antiques, and all the modern luxuries of a first-class hotel (including bathrooms large enough for deep soaking tubs). A two-room spa, with steam shower, offers quality treatments. A somewhat incongruous sculpture garden gives purpose to a wilder part of the property. When it comes to dining here (see "Where to Dine," below), reserve 6 months in advance for summer visits and check out the "Catch your own Dungeness crab" add-on package. After you trap your crab, you have the option of either learning to clean and prepare the crab yourself, or have the chef create a crab specialty for you to enjoy.

160 Upper Ganges Rd., Ganges, Salt Spring Island, BC V8K 2S8. ✆ **800/661-9255** or 250/537-2362. Fax 250/537-5333. www.hastingshouse.com. 18 units. July–Sept C$495–C$895 double; early-Apr to June & Oct C$395–C$715 double. Closed Nov to early-Apr. Rates include afternoon tea & breakfast. Additional adult C$75. AE, DC, MC, V. Children 16 & under not accepted. **Amenities:** Restaurant; lounge w/honor bar; spa. *In room:* CD player, fridge, Wi-Fi.

WHERE TO DINE

Hastings House ★★ PACIFIC NORTHWEST Impeccable cuisine, attentive service, and a gracious setting have made Hastings House one of the most sought-after destination restaurants—and inns—in the Pacific Northwest (see "Where to Stay," above). In addition to a la carte selections, there's a superb, multi-course menu that changes daily; many of the ingredients come from the estate itself. Dinner can be an elegant, evening-long affair with an excellent wine list. The choice of entrees nearly always features Salt Spring lamb, the house specialty (try it grilled with rosemary spaetzle and a grainy mustard jus). Wild spring salmon, perhaps with a sweet soya emulsion, or a pan-seared duck breast with port wine jus and filet of Alberta beef, with duck liver and apricot mousse, are other possibilities. In warm weather, the best tables are on the veranda overlooking the gardens and harbor.

160 Upper Ganges Rd. ✆ **250/537-2362.** Reservations required. Main courses C$12–C$48; 3- to 4-course prix fixe dinner C$65–C$80. AE, DC, MC, V. Mid-Mar to mid-Nov daily 6–10pm. Closed mid-Nov to mid-Mar.

House Piccolo ★ CONTINENTAL This small blue-and-white heritage farmhouse-turned-restaurant is wonderfully intimate. Two-person tables are scattered through two connecting country-style dining rooms accented with copper kettles set high on shelves. Everything on the European-style menu is enticing, particularly the fresh bread, broiled prawn and sea-scallop brochettes, and wiener schnitzel. Save room for homemade ice cream or the chocolate terrine, both of which are Piccolo institutions. House Piccolo is a member of Chaine des Rôtisseurs, an international gastronomic society dedicated to the promotion of fine dining around the world.

108 Hereford Ave. ✆ **250/537-1844.** www.housepiccolo.com. Reservations recommended July–Sept. Main courses C$25–C$36. DC, MC, V. May–Sept daily 5–10pm; Oct–Apr Wed–Sun 5–8pm.

Galiano Island

Galiano Island is a magnet for outdoor enthusiasts. It's a long, skinny island that stretches more than 26km (16 miles) from top to bottom, and is no more than 2km (1¼ miles) across. Two harbors and several parks provide abundant opportunity to hike, camp, fish, boat, and bird-watch—activities that have, in fact, been hard won. Logging was once Galiano's biggest industry, and when clear-cutting almost destroyed the wilderness, the community rallied, purchasing key tracts of land that have now returned to wilderness. Remnants of lumber operations are still evident in parts, including a shoreline strewn with salt-laden, sun-bleached logs.

Most of the 1,100 or so permanent residents live on the southern part of the island, close to **Sturdies Bay,** which, for all intents and purposes, is the island's downtown. So, it's here that you'll find most of the accommodations and a handful of restaurants and stores, as well as in the surrounding areas of **Georgeson Bay, Montague Harbour,** and **Spotlight Cove.** North Galiano is much wilder, and although there are pockets of housing, the country is dense with cedar and fir trees, maple and alder stands.

VISITOR INFORMATION Contact **Galiano Island Chamber of Commerce** (2590 Sturdies Bay Rd.; ✆ **866/539-2233;** www.galianoisland.com). It's open in July and August daily from 9am to 5pm and September to June on occasional weekends from 9am to 5pm.

EXPLORING GALIANO ISLAND

In and around **Sturdies Bay,** you'll find picturesque B&Bs, a few galleries, and a handful of shops. Nearby, **Bellhouse Provincial Park** is one of the prettiest settings on the island, with a rocky, moss-covered peninsula, sculpted sandstone, and magnificent groves of copper-red arbutus trees. Situated at the entrance to **Active Pass,** here's where to linger for an hour or two over a picnic, watching the myriad kinds of wildlife. Tides run up to 5 knots here, and the shoreline drops sharply into deep water, making it an excellent point to spin-cast for salmon.

Galiano Bluffs Park, another favorite area, is also at the entrance to Active Pass but sits 120m (394 ft.) above it. The views from the bluffs deserve rave reviews. Watch BC Ferries' largest ships rumble past and grab your binoculars to see eagles riding the updrafts, as well as seals, sea lions, and other marine life. Seasonal wildflowers are an equal delight. **Montague Harbour Marina** (✆ **250/539-5733**) is a fun place to visit, if only to yacht-watch or catch a light meal in the marina restaurant. While there, check out **Galiano Island Kayaking** (✆ **250/539-2442;** www.seakayak.ca). The 3-hour rentals are C$55 a person; full-day paddles are C$85 a person. You can also rent canoes. **Gulf Island Safaris** (✆ **888/656-9878**) runs wildlife and whale-watching tours that get you up close with marine life aboard rubber Zodiac boats, with pre-arranged pickups from Galiano.

MONTAGUE HARBOUR PROVINCIAL MARINE PARK ★★

One of the Gulf Islands' most popular provincial parks, Montague Harbour is where to watch giant yachts arriving and chattering kingfishers diving for salmon. Swim and beach comb to your heart's content along gorgeous shell and gravel beaches, enjoy a picnic on the bluff, and search through shell middens dating back 3,000 years. The protected waters are perfect for beginner rowers, and hiking trails include an easy 3km (1.9-mile) forest and beach walk that loops around Gray Peninsula, originally inhabited by First Nations peoples. Along the northwest edge of the peninsula are spectacular rippled rock ledges, as well as white shell beaches, and along the southern shore are two caves that can be reached by foot at low tide, or by boat.

If you want to stay awhile, the park has two year-round campgrounds: one with 15 walk-in sites for boaters and cyclists, another with 25 drive-in sites for motorists. ***Note:*** There are no RV hookups. There's a boat ramp, 35 mooring buoys, and a store. Free interpretive talks are offered during July and August. Check the **Nature House** for schedules. Buoys are C$12 per vessel; campsites are C$21 a day. Call **Discover Camping** at ✆ **800/689-9025** or 250/391-2300 for information and reservations, or go online to www.discovercamping.ca.

WHERE TO STAY

Driftwood Village Resort ★ ☺ Set in a delightful garden filled with fruit trees, the Driftwood Village Resort epitomizes Galiano's easy-going attitude, making for relaxed, stress-free family vacations. Each of the studio, one-, and two-bedroom cottages is charming, cozy, and decorated with original artwork. While various bed-linen combinations give each cabin a different feel, all have oceanfront views, private bathrooms, well-equipped kitchens, and private decks with barbecues. All but one of the cottages have wood-burning fireplaces. There's a Jacuzzi in the center of the garden from which to stargaze or watch deer meandering by. A footpath leads down to a sandy beach on Matthews Point, one of Galiano's many bird-watching spots. The "Ocean" cottages, which come with skylights and a private Jacuzzi, are especially nice.

205 Bluff Rd. E., Galiano Island, BC V0N 1P0. ✆ **866/502-5457** or 250/539-5457. www.driftwoodcottages.com. 10 units. Mid-June to mid-Sept C$129–C$160 cottage; mid-Sept to mid-June C$85–C$135 cottage. Additional adult C$10–C$20. Children 12 & under stay free in parent's cottage. MC, V. Pets accepted (C$10). **Amenities:** Jacuzzi; Wi-Fi. *In room:* TV, DVD player (in some), kitchen, no phone.

Galiano Inn & Spa ★★★ A cosmopolitan boutique destination spa resort, every room is its own tranquil, eco-conscious retreat overlooking Active Pass. Each room is invitingly uncluttered with open-beam ceilings and decor that includes chocolate-brown cork floors and a ledge-rock wood-burning fireplace that conceals a plasma TV/DVD player. At a push of a button, a hidden table emerges from the cherry-wood wall for intimate, in-suite dining. A push of another button reveals a massage table for in-room spa services. All beds have silk stuffed duvets (versus allergenic down duvets). En-suite bathrooms feature heated floors, air-jetted Jacuzzis or soaker tubs, separate showers—and 24-karat gold fixtures. New 1-bedroom villas have virtually doubled the inn's capacity. The Atrevida! restaurant is an island favorite (see "Where to Dine," below), and the Madrona del Mar Spa, with its Zen garden, showcases exclusive hemp-inspired spa treatments, which give a whole new dimension to the infamous BC bud. In winter, they include several extra-value items to their rates, such as certificates to the spa. ***Tip:*** The inn is a 5-minute walk from the ferry terminal, so if you're staying here, leave your car behind and explore the island using one of the resort's Smart Car runabouts.

134 Madrona Dr., Galiano Island, BC V0N 1P0. ✆ **877/530-3939** or 250/539-3388. www.galianoinn.com. 18 units. July to mid-Sept C$249–C$299 suite, C$425 villa; mid-May to June & mid-Sept to Oct C$199–C$249 suite, C$299 villa; Nov to mid-May C$179–C$199 suite, C$199 villa. Rates include breakfast. Additional adult C$25. MC, V. **Amenities:** Restaurant; lounge; hot tub; room service; spa. *In room:* TV/DVD player, hair dryer, Wi-Fi.

WHERE TO DINE

Atrevida! ★ PACIFIC NORTHWEST Galiano Island's only oceanfront restaurant is a treat. Watch the ferries ply through Active Pass as you enjoy rock crab croquette with cilantro chipotle tamarind; grilled beef tenderloin with green peppercorns, crème fraîche, and lobster sweet-pea risotto; or sandalwood-smoked salmon with brown butter. The vegetarian Moroccan *tajine* is rich and aromatic, served in the traditional pottery *tajine* with eggplant, zucchini, red peppers, butternut squash, couscous, garbanzo beans, carrot, grape tomatoes, almonds, and spices of every description. It's a very exotic, flavorful experience. The wine list focuses on special orders from British Columbia, some of which you can purchase from the wine store. If you've a ferry wait, park your car in the lineup and head over to the outdoor patio to chill out over a cold drink.

In the Galiano Inn, 134 Madrona Dr. ✆ **250/539-3388.** Reservations required. Main courses C$18–C$29. MC, V. Daily 5:30–9:30pm.

La Berengerie ★ FRENCH Shrouded by evergreen clematis, this tiny log cabin is a jewel in the forest. Floral linen tablecloths, soft classical music, and watercolor paintings by local artists set a romantic tone. The food rarely disappoints. Described as French-Algerian, the cuisine uses herbs to bring Middle Eastern flavor to classics such as duck *a l'orange, coq au vin,* and red snapper with gingered tomato sauce. La Berengerie also does an excellent bouillabaisse. The seafood gratiné is delicious—creamy and light, with a host of delicate flavors. A four-course menu features a choice of appetizers, entrees, and desserts. The homemade breads and comfort desserts are yummy. In July and August, the vegetarian sundeck opens up, as does a garden patio. The drawback is that it closes in winter. ***Tip:*** There are three quaint bedrooms upstairs, often available for rent.

2806 Montague Harbour Rd. ✆ **250/539-5392.** www.galianoisland.com/laberengerie/. Reservations recommended on weekends. Main courses C$15–C$22; 4-course prix-fixe dinner C$31. MC, V. July & Aug daily 5–9pm; Apr–June & Sept–Oct Fri–Sun (call for hours). Closed Nov–Mar.

Mayne Island

Mayne has always been a transfer point between islands. This began in the 1860s, when prospectors rested up in Miners Bay before crossing the Georgia Strait on their way to the gold mines in the Fraser Valley and the Cariboo. Back then, this rowdy social and drinking hub was known as "Little Hell," but as gold fever faded, so did Mayne's importance. Today, stopovers are much tamer. The 900 permanent residents like it this way, as it's enabled the island to retain much of its charm and heritage.

Because most of Mayne Island is privately owned, there are few public trails, so walkers and cyclists take to the network of hilly roads, traveling past 19th-century buildings, farms, beaches, and home studios. Cyclists could complete Mayne's 25km (16-mile) circuit in a day. Some of the more "natural" walks are along the pathways of yet-to-be-developed areas, where locals have created impromptu trails through the forest. Hendersen Hills is one example. There are numerous sheltered bays, including **Village Bay, Miners Bay,** and **Horton Bay,** all with docking facilities and accommodations that run the gamut from bare bones to luxurious.

GETTING THERE **BC Ferries** sails to **Village Bay,** on the northwest side of the island. Pleasure boaters dock at **Horton Bay,** at the southwest corner of the island. Floatplanes arrive at the docks at **Miners Bay.**

VISITOR INFORMATION **Mayne Island Community Chamber of Commerce** (✆ **250/539-5034**) doesn't have a bricks-and-mortar headquarters but does maintain a resource site at www.mayneislandchamber.ca. Useful maps and event information are usually posted on bulletin boards in the windows of the gas station (which doubles as a video-movie rental place) and the grocery store. This is where you can also purchase a copy of *The Mayneliner* (C$3.50), a monthly publication of gossip, happenings, and island issues.

HIKING The roads on Mayne are usually quiet enough that they can also serve as paths for hikers. Those looking for more solitude should consider **Mount Parke Regional Park,** off Fernhill Road in the center of the island. The park's best views reward those who take the 1-hour hike to Halliday Viewpoint.

EXPLORING MAYNE ISLAND

Miners Bay is the hub of Mayne, housing a surprisingly well-stocked supermarket, a small library, and a bakery-cafe. On summer Saturdays, a small farmers' market is held outside the **Agricultural Hall,** which on other days doubles as a theater, bingo hall, and exhibition center. The **Mayne Island Museum** is in a former one-room jail dating from 1896 and displays all manner of local artifacts from the early 1900s. It usually opens on July and August weekends, as well as holiday weekends, from 10am to 3pm. Admission is by donation; C$2 is suggested. Kayak and canoe rentals are available at **Mayne Island Kayaking** (✆ **250/539-0439**) which launches from Bennett Bay and Oyster Bay. Rates range from C$48 adults for a 2-hour rental to C$78 adults for a 24-hour rental of a fiberglass kayak, with an option to extend the rental. Guided tours include a 2½-hour Discovery tour (C$49), and a 5-hour paddle to Saturna's winery for a tasting (C$110). The company also offers bike rentals at C$18 for a half-day or C$25 for a full-day.

The road from Miners Bay to **Georgina Point** and the **Active Pass Lighthouse** is the most picturesque on Mayne Island. En route, you'll pass **St. Mary Magdalene Anglican Church,** built in 1898, on a hill amid a grove of red arbutus trees. The steeple of the church overlooking Active Pass has been a landmark for sailors for more than a century. Established in 1885, the lighthouse marks the entrance to Active Pass and, now automated, is open daily from 9am to 3pm, with free admission. You'll likely see seals, seabirds, and the occasional whale.

Although many islanders have "back routes" to the top of **Mount Parke Park** (www.crd.bc.ca/parks/mountparke), officially, there's only one public hiking trail up, and it's a fairly strenuous 30- to 40-minute uphill hike. (Cyclists must leave their bikes at the trail-head rack.) At 255m (837 ft.), the end of the trail is the highest point on Mayne, and if you can forgive the obligatory antennae towers, you'll be rewarded with wonderful views and maybe an air show of soaring eagles and turkey vultures.

WHERE TO STAY & DINE

Oceanwood Country Inn ★ This waterfront English country inn is as posh as it gets on Mayne. New owners have enhanced the old charm with a contemporary feel. The living room features a crackling fireplace, full bookshelves, a DVD library, board games, and a nice selection of music. Each guest room is as comfortable as ever. Most are romantic, with deep-soaker bathtubs and private balconies. Many have fireplaces. The Geranium is particularly large and also has a private outdoor soaking tub—on a rooftop deck, no less. Continental breakfast includes hot-from-the-oven croissants, homemade granola, and exotic fruit juices.

Now that Oceanwood has a patio license, it's become the "in" place for sharing ocean-view sunsets and a glass of wine—BC vintages, as well as labels from Italy, Chile, France, and California. Add a variety of tapas plates and quesadillas, and it's the only elegant inside/outside locale on the island for stylish afternoon munchies. Come dinner, a new a la carte menu is presented every day. It's casual, but for dinner and Sunday brunch, you might want to doff your muddy Reeboks for something a little smarter—or at least wear clean jeans.

630 Dinner Bay Rd., Mayne Island, BC V0N 2J0. ✆ **250/539-5074.** Fax 250/539-3002. www.oceanwood.com. 12 units. Mid-June to mid-Sept C$125–C$250 suite; mid-Sept to mid-June C$110–C$225 suite. 2-night minimum. Single nights C$40 extra. MC, V. Children 12 & under not accepted. **Amenities:** Restaurant; lounge; complimentary bikes; hot tub; sauna. *In room:* TV/DVD player, fridge, hair dryer, iPod dock, no phone, Wi-Fi.

The Pender Islands

Known for their secluded coves, beautiful beaches, and islets, the Penders are a tranquil escape, and a boater's nirvana. With a population of barely 2,000, they remain small enough that, as one resident says, "The sight of another human being still conjures up a smile!"

The Penders are actually two islands, linked by a short wooden bridge that spans a canal between **Bedwell and Browning harbors.** With several parks, picnic areas, and overnight camping facilities, the Penders are threaded with meandering, illogical roads that are a delight to tour by car or bicycle. The Penders have more public beach access points for their size than any other Gulf Island—37 in all, with plenty of picturesque cottages, orchards, and a dozen or so artisans' home galleries to enjoy en route.

GETTING THERE

BC Ferries sails to **Otter Bay,** on the northwest side of North Pender Island. Pleasure boats can dock at **Bedwell Harbour,** on the southern cove where North and South Pender meet.

VISITOR INFORMATION

There is no formal visitor information center on Pender Island, although you can pick up brochures at the "mall," **The Driftwood Centre** (4605 Bedwell Harbour Rd.; ✆ **250/629-6555**). Or contact the **Pender Island Chamber of Commerce** (✆ **866/468-7924;** www.penderislandchamber.com).

GETTING AROUND

Pender Island Cab Company (✆ **250/629-2222;** www.penderislandcab.com) provides service to various points around the islands. Bike and scooter rentals are available in season at **Otter Bay Marina** (✆ **250/629-3579**) at a daily rate of C$25 and C$85, respectively. Hourly rentals are C$8 for bikes and C$25 for scooters.

EXPLORING THE PENDERS

The larger of the two islands, **North Pender** is more populated and more developed than its southerly neighbor. There's no real town center in the traditional sense on North Pender, so the modern **Driftwood Centre** (4605 Bedwell Harbour Rd., near Razor Point Rd.), in the center of the island, is the nucleus of island life. Here's where to stock up on groceries and gift items, and indulge in your sweet tooth at the must-visit **Pender Island Bakery** (✆ **250/629-6453;** www.penderislandbakery.com). The **Saturday Market** (May–Oct 9:30am–12:30pm) is a fine place for mixing with the locals, sampling island-grown produce, and browsing through artisan stalls. Continue on along Razor Point Road toward Browning Harbour, and you'll find **Morning Bay Vineyard** (6621 Harbour Hill Dr.; ✆ **250/629-8352;** www.morningbay.ca). Overlooking Plumber Sound and with a main building designed to look like a barn, it features 20 terraces that climb up the south side of Mount Menzies. In 2007, the vineyard delivered its first estate wines. Its Gerwürztraminer-Riesling (the first vintage) has since won a silver medal in the 2008 All-Canadian Wine Championships, and its Reserve Merlot was awarded a bronze medal at the prestigious New York–based Finger Lakes competition. Tastings are Wednesday through Saturday, 10am to 5pm.

Away from the Driftwood, most activity happens around **Otter Bay,** where the ferries arrive; **Port Browning;** and **Hope Bay.** At **Port Washington,** northwest of Otter Bay, you'll find orchards and charming old cottages reminiscent of a turn-of-the-20th-century coastal village; the village has a pretty dockside, a couple of galleries, and a water's-edge bistro cafe. Check out **Pender Island Kayak Adventures** at the Otter Bay Marina (✆ **250/629-6939;** www.kayakpenderisland.com) for kayak rentals, and guided kayaking tours and lessons in and around island coves and to neighboring Mayne and Saturna islands. Two-hour guided tours are C$45 adults, C$30 children 11 and under; 3-hour guided tours are C$60 adults; and all-day paddles are C$105 adults. **Port Browning Marina** (4605 Oak Rd.; ✆ **250/629-3493**), on the northern cove where North and South Pender meet, is an inviting "watering hole" with First Nations decor, including a totem pole. North Pender parks include **Medicine Beach,** one of the last wetlands in the Gulf Islands, and home to many native plants once used for food and medicine. The beach is within walking distance of **Prior Centennial Provincial Park,** a forest of cedar, maple, fir, and alder trees. Located 6km (3¾ miles) from the ferry terminal, Prior Centennial can also be reached off Canal Road.

South Pender has always attracted independent, sometimes eccentric, fun-loving spirits who don't mind the isolation. Although the only services to be found are at the **Poets Cove Marina** (9801 Spalding Rd.; ✆ **250/629-3212**), there are lots of beaches, parks, and trails to enjoy. Hikers should head for **Mount Norman Regional Park** (www.britishcolumbia.com/parks). At 244m (801 ft.), Mount Norman is the highest point on the Penders.

From Mount Norman Regional Park, you can access **Beaumont Marine Provincial Park,** without a doubt the prettiest marine park in the Gulf Islands, its picturesque coastal wilderness seemingly tamed by gentle waters, moss-covered rocks, and grassy verges. It's now a part of the **Gulf Islands National Park Reserve** (✆ **250/629-6139;** www.pc.gc.ca/eng/pn-np/bc/gulf/index.aspx) and is a moderate, 40-minute hike from Mount Norman.

Unlike the limited facilities of most of these parks, nearby Prior Centennial (also a part of the Reserve) includes 17 vehicle/tent sites, pit toilets, water, fire pits, and picnic tables and is operated by Parks Canada (✆ **877/737-3738** for reservations; www.pccamping.ca). Sites average C$36 per day, depending on the site size required, plus a nonrefundable reservation fee of C$11. Another favorite recreation area, **Brookes Point,** is one of the last undeveloped headlands in the Gulf Islands. The coastal bluff is ecologically important, as it hosts rare types of native grass and more than 100 bird species, some of which are endangered. Large pods of **killer whales** sometimes swim right under the point in the nearby kelp beds, as do mink, seal, otter, and Dall's porpoises. If you have good shoes, the walk along the shoreline from here to Gowlland Point is captivating.

WHERE TO STAY

Poets Cove Resort & Spa ★★ ☺ As one of the most upscale, year-round destinations in the Gulf Islands, this resort offers so much to do that you never have to leave its confines. Accommodations range from 22 modern lodge rooms (they all face west to catch glorious sunsets) to deluxe two- and three-bedroom cottages (best for romantic getaways), and spacious and family-oriented villas complete with kitchens, dining rooms, living rooms with fireplaces, balconies, and BBQs. Most have private hot tubs. Children's programs and a 110-slip marina make Poets Cove popular with families and boaters. The bright, airy **Aurora Restaurant** (see "Where to Dine," below) features French-influenced fine dining, and Syrens Lounge & Bistro offers casual dining inside or on the enormous deck. The menu includes kid-friendly burgers and pint portions of other selections for smaller appetites. If you're staying in a cottage or villa, you can order items from the "raw menu" to barbecue yourself. The Susurrus Spa is a destination unto itself, with six large treatment rooms, a steam cave, and oceanfront Jacuzzi.

Tip: The "Poets Cruises" is an excellent 3-hour island hop and eco-adventure (C$109) with different itineraries that include stopovers at historic Hope Bay on North Pender, the vineyard on Saturna Island, and places to spot wildlife in the area.

9801 Spalding Rd., South Pender Island, BC V0N 2M3. ✆ **888/512-7638** or 250/629-2100. Fax 250/629-2105. www.poetscove.com. 22 rooms, 15 cottages, 9 villas. C$189–C$299 double; C$359–C$699 cottage; C$239–C$529 villa. Children 17 & under stay free in parent's room. AE, MC, V. Pets accepted (C$50 per stay). **Amenities:** Restaurant; pub; large heated outdoor pool; spa; 2 outdoor tennis courts. *In-room:* TV/DVD player, fridge, hair dryer, Wi-Fi.

WHERE TO DINE

Aurora ★ PACIFIC NORTHWEST By far the most sophisticated dining room you'll find anywhere on the Penders, Aurora serves food to match the great marine views. There's a French influence to the menu items, which lean to local produce. Standouts include the Salt Spring goat-cheese tart and herb salad, seared Qualicum scallops (the catch of the day is always a good choice), and Pender Island lamb. For dessert, sample local creations on the cheese plate. The restaurant is romantic, whether you sit by the huge stone fireplace that dominates an entire wall or beside the floor-to-ceiling windows. If you're an oenophile, you'll probably prefer a table near the wall of wine bottles—the wine list is extensive.

In Poets Cove Resort & Spa, 9801 Spalding Rd. ✆ **250/629-2100.** Reservations recommended. Main courses C$24–C$35. AE, MC, V. Daily 5:30–10pm.

Saturna Island

Time seems to have bypassed Saturna Island, making remote tranquility the island's star attraction. Home to approximately 350 permanent residents, Saturna is still fairly primitive. There are no banks, no pharmacies, or drug stores; the library's located in the church basement, and the general store doubles as a tiny coffee shop. In fact, Jose Maria Narvaez would probably still recognize the forests and shorelines of the island named after his ship, Santa Saturnina, even though his last visit was in 1791. The Gulf Islands National Park Reserve protects some 44% of Saturna's 49 sq. km (19 sq. miles), earning the island an elevated status for hiking, boating, and communing with nature. Of all the Gulf Islands, Saturna is the most ecologically vigilant.

Laced with trails through mixed forest and marshland, hikers rarely tire of this island's topography. Most head for **Winter Cove Marine Park,** a sanctuary to eagles, shorebirds, kingfishers, seals, and otters; or up to the summit of Mount Warburton. Kayakers will prefer **Thomson Park** or **Cabbage Island Marine Park,** near **Tumbo Island,** and **Veruna Bay** and **Russell Reef** are the hot choices for family swimming. What commerce there is happens around the community center at **Lyall Harbour,** where you'll find a grocery store, pub, gas station, kayak rentals, and a gallery, as well as a couple of B&Bs. ***Note:*** There are no public campgrounds.

GETTING THERE

BC Ferries sails to **Lyall Harbour.** Most trips involve a transfer at Mayne Island. Boaters dock at **Winter Cove Marine Park,** north of Lyall Harbour. Seaplanes can dock at Lyall Harbour.

VISITOR INFORMATION

Head to the **Saturna Island General Store** (101 Narvaez Bay Rd.; ✆ **250/539-2936;** www.saturnatourism.com). The **Saturna Point Lighthouse Pub** (✆ **250/539-5725**) at the Ferry Dock is home to the island's only ATM.

GETTING AROUND

The island has no pickup or touring service, although your B&B may step in to fill this need on an as-required basis. Bring your own bike (there are no rentals) or come to kayak. **Saturna Sea Kayaking** (✆ **250/539-5553**) is located in the village and can fit you out with single and double fiberglass kayaks from C$30 to C$65 for 2 hours, C$40 to C$70 for 4 hours. Multiple-day rates are available.

EXPLORING SATURNA ISLAND

East Point Regional Park ★★, on the island's southeastern tip, is a naturalist's delight. It starts with the ocean views from the sculptured sandstone headlands and just gets better. Take the very short trail down to the **East Point Lighthouse,** built in 1888, and you'll be standing at the easternmost edge of the Gulf Islands, looking over to **Patos Island Lighthouse,** on the U.S. side of the border. Together, the lighthouses guide large vessels through the channel's surging waters. Some of the area is on private land; be careful not to trespass off the trails. A longer trail (300m/984 ft.) leaves the parking lot and heads north to a viewpoint of Tumbo Channel and the Strait of Georgia.

If you've time, make the 4.5km (2¾-mile) drive or hike up to the 497m (1,631-ft.) summit of **Warburton Pike.** If you can disregard the unbecoming sprawl of TV towers, the sweeping vistas from the top are nothing short of fantastic. The way up is via a winding gravel road that's narrow and sometimes slippery in wet weather, but the beautiful Douglas fir forest more than makes up for the occasional rough patch of road.

WHERE TO STAY & DINE

Saturna Lodge Set amid the rustic, rural charms of the island, a stone's throw from the Saturna Island Vineyards, this casual country inn is an unexpected delight. Guest rooms are named after wine grapes and are comfortably appointed with duvet-covered queen-size beds (twin beds in the Ambrosia Suite) and private en-suite bathrooms. This and the Napa Suite share a bathroom and can be joined for family accommodation. All have views of Plumber Sound (though some more than others), and the Riesling Suite has a private deck. TV-hungry urbanites can cozy up in front of the fireplace in the downstairs lounge, or pick a DVD/VHS title from the lodge's small library. In shoulder season, the lodge discounts its rate by C$20 per night.

130 Payne Rd. (P.O. Box 54), Saturna Island, BC V0N 2Y0. ✆ **866/539-2254** or 250/539-2254. Fax 250/539-3091. www.saturna.ca. 6 units. June to early Sept C$119–C$169 double; Apr, May, Sept & Oct C$99–C$135 double; Nov–Mar C$79–C$119 double. Rates include full breakfast. Additional adult C$35. Discounts for longer stays. MC, V. **Amenities:** Restaurant; lounge; complimentary bikes; Jacuzzi; Wi-Fi. *In room:* TV/DVD player (on request), no phone.

VANCOUVER ISLAND'S WEST COAST ★★★

The scenic drive through the center of Vancouver Island is only a taste of what's to come once you reach the wild coast of Western Canada. Here, the Pacific Ocean rollers crash against the shore, beaches stretch for miles, and the mist clings to the rainforest like cobwebs. Most of what you'll see is part of **Pacific Rim National Park.** In winter, you'll witness some of the best storms in the world—as dramatic and angry as a Turner landscape. In summer, families play alongside surfers, kayakers, and others enjoying this Valhalla for outdoor activities. **Tofino** has long been the commercial center of the region and as such, has many services to offer visitors, including a sushi restaurant and decent, albeit small, shops and galleries. Tofino is the gateway to **Clayoquot Sound,** North America's largest remaining expanse of low-elevation old-growth temperate rainforest and a UNESCO World Biosphere Reserve. It's a "living laboratory," where you'll find isolated resorts and cabins clinging to the edge of the wilderness and bears scavenging the shoreline for tasty delicacies, flipping rocks like flapjacks. Unfortunately, Tofino becomes so busy in summer that its popularity is eroding its charm.

For many, the town of **Ucluelet,** 42km (26 miles) away, is a quieter choice. It's a little rougher around the edges, but you can link up with the Wild Pacific Trail and find B&Bs that are truly away from the madding crowd—although judging from new developments such as Black Rock Resort, it's only a matter of time until eco-adventurers and urban escapees start to influence the wilderness here, too. Wherever you decide to stay, to get from A to B, you really do need a set of wheels, or strong legs, to explore the area fully. If driving, be careful. Black bear and deer are common, and at times, the roads can be windy and unexpectedly foggy.

Essentials

VISITOR INFORMATION The **Tofino–Long Beach Chamber of Commerce** is located at 1426 Pacific Rim Hwy. (✆ **250/725-3414;** www.tourismtofino.com); open hours are March through September daily 11am to 5pm. Another good resource is www.gotofino.com. **The Pacific Rim Visitor Centre** (✆ **250/726-4600**), at the junction of Highway 4 and Pacific Rim Highway, is a good stop for an overall orientation to the area, plus a chance to use the washroom after the cross-island drive.

GETTING THERE BY BUS **Greyhound Canada** (✆ **800/661-8747;** www.greyhound.ca) operates regular daily service between Victoria and Tofino-Ucluelet, departing at 8:30am and arriving in Tofino about 2:30pm. The bus stops in Nanaimo and will drop off/pick up at Port Alberni. Fares from Port Alberni to Tofino are C$28 nonrefundable, C$32 refundable adults. **The Tofino Bus Company** (✆ **866/986-3466;** www.tofinobus.com) also runs a daily service from Vancouver and Victoria to Tofino-Ucluelet. From Port Alberni to Tofino-Ucluelet, single adult fare is C$26 nonrefundable, C$24 refundable. **Island Link Bus** (✆ **250/954-8257;** www.islandlinkbus.com) runs a passenger express service between BC Ferries' terminals, and Vancouver, Victoria, and Comox airports to Tofino and Ucluelet.

BY CAR Tofino and Long Beach all lay near the end of Highway 4 on the west coast of Vancouver Island. From Nanaimo, take the Island Highway (Hwy. 19) north for 52km (32 miles). Just before the town of Parksville is a turnoff for Highway 4, which leads first to the midisland town of Port Alberni (38km/24 miles) and then to Tofino (135km/84 miles west of Port Alberni). The road is paved the whole way but gets windy and rough after Sproat Lake.

BY FERRY A 4½-hour ride aboard the **Alberni Marine Transportation** (✆ **250/723-8313;** www.ladyrosemarine.com) passenger ferry MV *Lady Rose* takes you from Port Alberni through Alberni Inlet to Ucluelet, 41km (26 miles) south of Tofino. It makes brief stops along the way to deliver mail and packages to solitary cabin dwellers along the coast and to let off or pick up kayakers bound for the Broken Islands Group. The *Lady Rose* departs three times a week to each destination from Alberni Harbour Quay's Angle Street. The fare to Ucluelet is C$37 one-way and C$74 round-trip. The service operates in summer only; however, the same company offers year-round mail delivery trips to/from Port Alberni and Bamfield—check the website for details.

BY PLANE **Orca Airways** (✆ **888/359-6722;** www.flyorcaair.com) flies year-round between Vancouver and Tofino; one-way fares are about C$199 adults, with discounts offered on advanced bookings. The airline also offers a Victoria–Tofino schedule during the summer months at C$225 each way. **Tofino Air** (✆ **866/486-3247** or 250/725-4454; www.tofinoair.ca) provides charters and scenic tours. For both carriers, discounts for seniors and children are 5% to 10% off listed price.

Exploring Tofino & Long Beach

Pacific Rim National Park has three units, though only one, Long Beach ★★, is easily accessed by the average traveler. Long Beach is a stretch of coastal wilderness at the outer edge of a peninsula about halfway up Vancouver Island's western shore. The beach is more than 16km (10 miles) long, broken here and there by rocky headlands and islands and bordered by tremendous groves of cedar and Sitka spruce. The beach is popular with countless species of birds and marine life, and, lately, with wet-suited surfers as well. Hiking trails wind through coastal rainforests and mossy bogs. Per day entry to the park is C$7.80 for adults, C$6.80 seniors, C$3.90 youths, and C$19.60 families.

Two former fishing villages serve as entry points to Long Beach. The town of **Ucluelet** (pronounced You-*clue*-let, meaning "safe harbor" in the local Nuu-chah-nulth dialect) sits on the southern end of the Long Beach peninsula, on the edge of Barkely

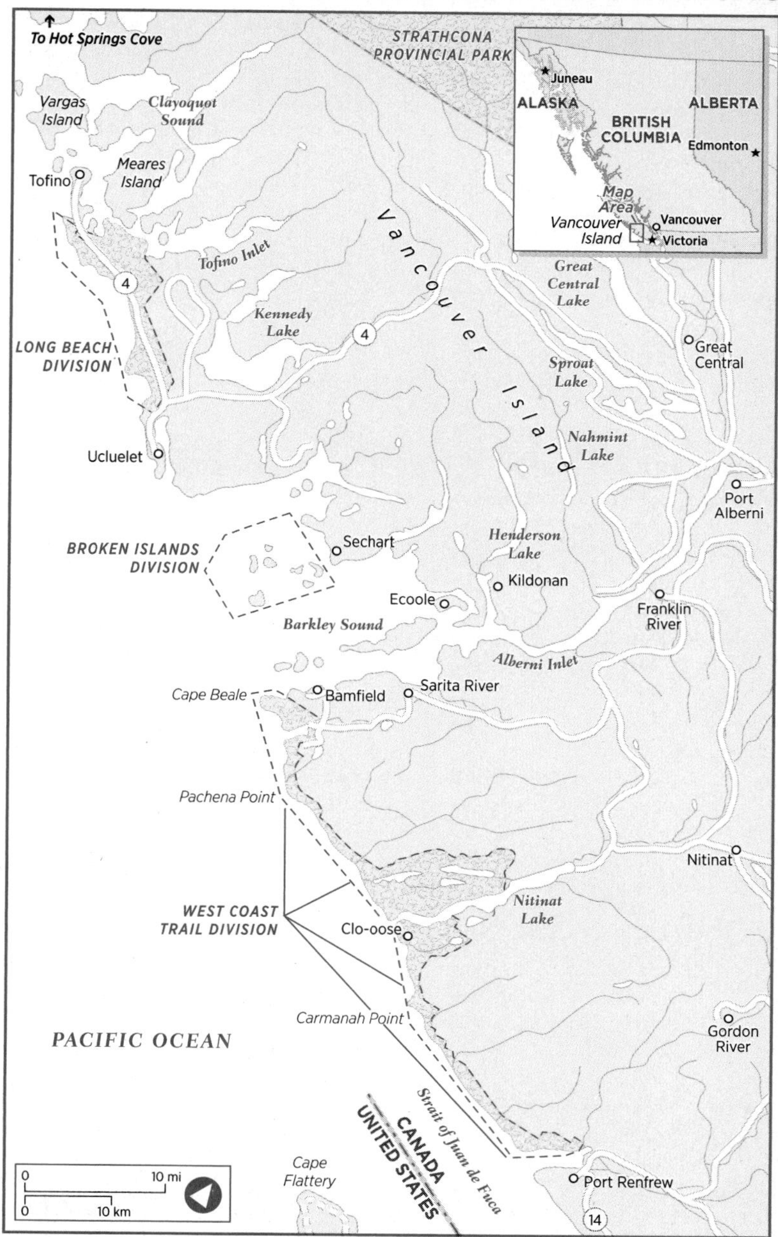
To Hot Springs Cove
STRATHCONA PROVINCIAL PARK
Vargas Island
Clayoquot Sound
Meares Island
Tofino
Tofino Inlet
Vancouver Island
Kennedy Lake
4
LONG BEACH DIVISION
Ucluelet
Great Central Lake
Great Central
Sproat Lake
Nahmint Lake
Port Alberni
BROKEN ISLANDS DIVISION
Sechart
Henderson Lake
Kildonan
Ecoole
Barkley Sound
Franklin River
Alberni Inlet
Cape Beale
Bamfield
Sarita River
Pachena Point
Nitinat
WEST COAST TRAIL DIVISION
Nitinat Lake
Clo-oose
Carmanah Point
Gordon River
PACIFIC OCEAN
Strait of Juan de Fuca
CANADA
UNITED STATES
Cape Flattery
Port Renfrew
14
0
10 mi
0
10 km
Juneau
ALASKA
ALBERTA
BRITISH COLUMBIA
Edmonton
Map Area
Vancouver Island
Vancouver
Victoria

Sound. At the far-northern tip of the peninsula, **Tofino** (pop. 1,600) borders on beautiful Clayoquot Sound and is the center of the west coast eco-tourism business. It's a schizophrenic kind of town: Half is composed of eco-tourism outfitters, nature lovers, activists, and serious granolas; the other half is composed of loggers and fishers.

The reason for Tofino's popularity is not hard to fathom. Tofino offers incredible marine vistas at the end of a thin finger of land, battered by the Pacific to the west and lapped by Tofino Sound on the east. The town is notched with tiny bays and inlets, with a multitude of islands, many of them very mountainous, just offshore. Further east, the jagged, snow-capped peaks of Strathcona Park fill the horizon.

Tofino is becoming more crowded and subject to a particular brand of gentrification. On the beaches south of town, luxury inns serve the rarified demands of upscale travelers attracted to the area's scenery. There are more fine-dining restaurants and boutiques here than can possibly be justified by the town's size. Dining is as big a draw as sea kayaking for many Tofino visitors.

With all the bustle, it can be difficult at times to find solitude in what's actually still an amazingly beautiful and wild place. Accordingly, more people decide to avoid the crowds and visit Tofino in winter, to watch dramatic storms roll in from the Pacific.

Outdoor Pursuits

BIRDING ★ With the rapidly aging baby-boomer generation, less strenuous pursuits like bird-watching have garnered an enthusiastic following. **Just Birding** (**✆ 250/725-2520;** www.justbirding.com) provides guided birding tours for novice and expert birders (sometimes called "twitchers"). Tours are year-round and range from early-bird, half-day excursions to shorebird walks, full-day paddles with eagles, and mountain birding. Rates vary depending on the tour, but they start at C$100. The annual Shorebird Festival, in late April, is a big draw.

BIKING Biking along the flat stretch of paved road that connects Tofino, the Pacific Rim National Park Reserve, and Ucluelet, is an easy and scenic 42km (26-mile) ride. Rent bikes in Tofino at **Eco Everything**, 150 4th St., (**✆ 250/725-2193**). In Ucluelet, from **Ukee Bikes**, 1559 Imperial Lane, (**✆ 250/726-2453**). If you're a runner, check out the annual marathon at www.edgetoedgemarathon.com.

FISHING Tofino and Ucluelet are at the heart of the region's commercial fishing industry, and you'll find a number of sport-fishing charters in both marinas. The main hooks are salmon, steelhead, rainbow trout, Dolly Varden char, halibut, snapper, and cod. **Jay's Clayoquot Ventures** (561 Campbell St.; **✆ 888/534-7422** or 250/725-2700; www.tofinofishing.com) is an experienced and reputable company that organizes fishing charters throughout Clayoquot Sound—both deep-sea and freshwater excursions. Saltwater fly-fishing trips start at C$115 per hour for a 5-hour minimum and include equipment and flies. **Lance's Sportfishing Adventures** (120 4th St.; **✆ 888/725-6125** or 250/725-2569; www.fishtofino.com) combines fishing trips aboard 7.3m (24-ft.) offshore vessels with a visit to Hot Springs—the advantage being you'll enjoy the springs before the crowds. Rates are C$110 per hour for a 6-hour minimum and include all gear. This outfitter also packages overnight deals with **Weigh West Marine Resort** (www.weighwest.com). In Ucluelet, **Roanne Sea Adventures** (**✆ 250/726-4494;** www.roanne.ca) or **Long Beach Charters** (**✆ 877/726-2878;** www.longbeachcharters.com) are respected outfitters with competitive rates that average C$600 per 7-hour trip.

HIKING **Tla-ook Cultural Adventures** (✆ **877/942-2663** or 250/725-2656; www.tlaook.com) offer guided hikes and walks for a variety of fitness levels, including boat trips to nearby islands. Led by First Nations guides, trips include cultural teachings, history, storytelling, identification of rainforest "medicines," and tide pool exploration. Rates are C$50 per hour. A full program of guided beach and rainforest walks, land-based whale-watching tours, and storm-watching hikes are available through **Oceans Edge** (855 Barkley Crescent, Ucluelet; ✆ **250/726-7099;** www.oceansedge.bc.ca). All excursions are 3 to 6 hours over moderate terrain, and prices vary according to activity; budget around the C$225 mark for a half-day tour. Book well in advance or just hope for cancellation when you arrive. Other star hikes include the 3.5km (2.2-mile) **Gold Mine Trail** near Florencia Bay, so called for its gold-mining heritage; the partially boardwalked **South Beach Trail** (about 1.5km/.9 mile); and the even shorter **Schooner Beach Trail,** both of which take you through rainforest before opening up onto sandy beaches.

KAYAKING Kayaking through Clayoquot Sound is one of the most intimate ways to experience its history, serenity, and natural beauty. The trick is to find an outfitter who can enrich the experience beyond just a paddle. The owners of **Rainforest Kayak Adventures** (✆ **877/422-WILD** [877/422-9453]; www.rainforestkayak.com) helped set the benchmark for sea-kayak instruction in BC more than 20 years

HIKE OF A lifetime: THE WEST COAST TRAIL

The rugged West Coast Trail has gained a reputation as one of the world's greatest extreme hiking adventures. Each year, about 9,000 people tackle the entire challenging 75km (47-mile) route, and thousands more hike the very accessible 11km (6¾-mile) **ocean-front stretch** at the northern trail head near Bamfield. Imperative for the full hike are a topographic map and tidal table, stamina for rock climbing as well as hiking, and advanced wilderness-survival and minimum-impact camping knowledge. Go with at least two companions, pack weatherproof gear, and bring 15m (50 ft.) of climbing rope per person. Only 52 people per day are allowed to enter the main trail (26 from Port Renfrew, 26 from Bamfield), and registration with the park office is mandatory. Most people make the hike in 5 to 7 days.

The West Coast Trail land is temperate coastal rainforest dominated by old-growth spruce, hemlock, and cedar. The topography ranges from sandy beaches to rocky headlands and wide sandstone ledges. Caves, arches, tidal pools, and waterfalls add variety to the shoreline. If you hike the trail from May 1 through June 14 or September 16 to September 30, which the park service considers shoulder season, you no longer need reservations. Simply show up at one of the trail **information centers** at Gordon River in the south or Pachena Bay in the north, attend the orientation session, and set off. You will need reservations if you intend to hike the trail in high season, from June 15 through September 15. Call **Super Natural BC** (✆ **800/435-5622** or 250/387-1642) after April 1 to schedule your entry reservation for the coming high season. In summer, you can also contact the **parks service** (✆ **250/728-3234** or 250/647-5434; www.pc.gc.ca) for information. Make your reservations as early as possible. There's a C$25 booking fee and C$128 trail-use fee. If you want to try your luck, there are 10 daily first-come, first-served wait-list openings at each trail head information center. The park service says you'll probably wait 1 to 3 days for an opening.

ago and have been guiding the area for almost as long. These are the folks to see if you're looking to become a guide or instructor yourself (C$685 to C$1,550 and up). The **Tofino Sea-Kayaking Company** (320 Main St.; ✆ **800/863-4664** or 250/725-4222; www.tofino-kayaking.com) also offers guided tours, ranging from a 2½-hour paddle at C$60 to all-day excursions at C$135, as well as daily rentals (C$40 single and C$74 double). **Remote Passages** (✆ **800/666-9833;** www.remotepassages.com) leads guided kayaking to Meares Island (2½ hours at C$64) and to Clayoquot (4 hours at C$79). If you're based in Ucluelet, **Majestic Ocean Kayaking** (1167 Helen Rd., Ucluelet; ✆ **800/889-7644** or 250/726-2868; www.oceankayaking.com) might be more convenient. They have a range of ecotourism adventures to Barkley Sound, Pacific Rim National Park, and Deer Group Islands. Prices start at C$60 for a 3-hour paddle around Ucluelet Harbour to a full-day trip to Broken Group Islands (including cruiser transport there) at C$235 adults. All-inclusive, multi-day wilderness camping and overnight trips to Vargas Island and others around Clayoquot Sound start at C$250 per day adults. For a blended paddle of environment and authentic First Nations culture, travel with **Tla-ook Cultural Adventures** (✆ **877/942-2663** or 250/725-2656; www.tlaook.com), where Nuu-chah-nulth First Nations guides take you aboard stylized dugout canoes, sharing their deep-rooted cultural history of the area and weaving in stories of aboriginal folklore (C$55 for 2½ hours; C$74 for 4 hours).

SURFING The heavy, constant rollers of the Pacific Ocean against wide expanses of beach have made this one of the world's hot spots for surfing. Whether beginner or experienced, you'll find outfitters to help you catch the wave, year-round. **Live to Surf** (1180 Pacific Rim Hwy.; ✆ **250/725-4463;** www.livetosurf.com) is Tofino's original surf shop and offers rentals of boards and wetsuits, as well as daily surf lessons through its Westside Surf School (✆ **250/725-2404**). Two-hour lessons include all the gear (wetsuit, booties, gloves, and board) and cost C$100 adults, with longer lessons offered for experienced and ultra-fit surfers. **Pacific Surf School** (440 Campbell St.; ✆ **888/777-9961** or 250/725-2155; www.pacificsurfschool.com) holds 3-hour lessons (C$79) and provides private tutoring (C$135); and **Surf Sister** (625 Campbell St.; ✆ **877/724-SURF** [7873] or 250/725-4456; www.surfsister.com) is, as the name suggests, geared to women, with its mother-daughter camps and yoga surf retreats (C$75 includes a surfboard and C$65 if you have your own board). **Inner Rhythm Surf Camp** (✆ **877/393-SURF** [877/393-7873]; www.innerrhythm.ca) and **Relic Surf** (✆ **250/726-4421;** www.relicsurfshop.com) are based in Ucluelet, and each offers 2-hour winter sessions at C$69 adults, 3-hour summer sessions at C$79.

WHALE-WATCHING Operating out of Tofino and Ucluelet, **Jamie's Whaling Station** (606 Campbell St., Tofino, ✆ **800/667-9913** or 250/725-3919; 168 Fraser Lane, Ucluelet, ✆ **877/726-7444** or 250/726-7444; www.jamies.com) is a pioneer of the adventure business. It's been around since 1982 and has evolved a full roster of whale-watching, bear-watching, and other wildlife tours. Venture out in 12-passenger Zodiacs—C$79 adults, C$65 children 4-12 years—or in the comfort of a 65-foot vessel—C$99 adults, C$65 children 4-12 years—complete with snack bar, inside heated seating, and washrooms. A C$2 surcharge is added, contributing to local wildlife research and rescue programs, and the local bird hospital. ***Note:*** Jamie's also has a 35-foot cabin cruiser for the 1¼-hour boat ride up to Hot Springs Cove, where you can soak up the waters for a couple of hours before the return trip, either by boat or by seaplane. The boat has space for sea kayaks. **Ocean Outfitters** (368 Main St., Tofino; ✆ **877/906-2326** or 250/725-2866; www.oceanoutfitters.bc.ca) is another popular option, also featuring Zodiac and family-travel vessels. In Ucluelet, **Archipelago Cruises** (Whiskey Landing Wharf; ✆ **250/726-8289**) operates a 16m (53-ft.) Canoe Cove motor yacht; come rain or shine, cruising on the yacht includes sights, as well as a glass of champagne.

RAINY-DAY ACTIVITIES: SHOPPING, STORM-WATCHING & MORE

When you'd rather be indoors, snuggle up with a book at the **Wildside Booksellers and Espresso Bar,** 320 Main St. (✆ **250/745-4222**), or get a massage or salt glow at the **Ancient Cedars Spa** at the Wickaninnish Inn (✆ **250/725-3100**).

Or, check out the galleries. The **Eagle Aerie Gallery,** 350 Campbell St. (✆ **250/725-3235**), constructed in the style of a First Nations longhouse, features the innovative work of Tsimshian artist Roy Henry Vickers. The **House of Himwitsa,** 300 Main St. (✆ **250/725-2017;** www.himwitsa.com), is also First Nations owned/operated. The quality and craftsmanship of the shop's artwork, masks, baskets, totems, gold and silver jewelry, and apparel are excellent. The **Reflecting Spirit Gallery,** 441 Campbell St. (✆ **250/725-4229**), offers medicine wheels, rocks, and crystals, as well as a great selection of Native art, carvings, wood crafts, and pottery.

Watching the winter storms from big windows has become very popular in Tofino. For a slight twist on this, try the outdoor storm-watching tours offered by the **Long Beach Nature Tour Co.** ★ (✆ **250/726-7099;** www.oceansedge.bc.ca). Owner Bill McIntyre, former chief naturalist of Pacific Rim National Park, can explain how storms work and the best locations to get close to them without getting swept away.

Where to Stay

The 94 campsites on the bluff at **Green Point** are maintained by Pacific Rim National Park (✆ **250/726-7721**). The grounds are full every day in July and August, and the average wait for a site is 1 to 2 days. Leave your name at the ranger station when you arrive to be placed on the list. You're rewarded for your patience with a magnificent ocean view, pit toilets, fire pits, pumped well water, and free firewood (no showers or hookups). Sites are C$18 to C$24. The campground is closed October to March.

The **Bella Pacifica Resort & Campground,** 3.5km (2 miles) south of Tofino on the Pacific Rim Highway (P.O. Box 413), Tofino, BC V0R 2Z0 (✆ **250/725-3400;** www.bellapacifica.com), is privately owned and has 165 campsites from which you can walk to Mackenzie Beach or take the resort's private nature trails to Templar Beach. Flush toilets, hot showers, water, laundry, ice, fire pits, firewood, and full and partial hookups are available. Rates are C$24 to C$48 per two-person campsite. Reserve at least a month in advance for a summer weekend; open mid-February to mid-November.

Clayoquot Wilderness Resort ★★★ "Glamping" (glamorous camping) was invented here, beneath canvas accommodations that are geared to tender-footed eco-adventurers and seekers of a one-of-a-kind experience. Reached either by floatplane or 25-minute boat ride out of Tofino, the resort's splendid isolation means at night, the darkness is blacker than ebony, the stars brighter than diamonds, and the silence deliciously deafening. Nestled on wooden platforms in the trees, the Rockefeller-style safari sites are all opulently furnished with antiques, handmade furniture, Persian rugs, four-poster beds topped with down duvets, and freestanding propane and wood stoves. The cuisine is spectacular, as is the wine list, from pancakes made with freshly picked blueberries to alder-smoked grilled salmon over wild greens, or four-peppercorn-crusted tenderloin medallions in the evening. Stays are sold only as all-inclusive, multi-night packages. Trails around the resort invite mountain biking and horseback riding. Other activities include a trip to Hot Springs Cove as well as kayaking, fishing, and wildlife-viewing excursions. Prices include a 3% sustainability fee, which also covers an environmental legacy program for habitat restoration and wildlife studies. Everything about this resort is as green as you will find, from innovative compostable plastics made from corn and potato to its own sustainable run-by-the-river hydropower generator. This is the place to visit if you're looking for cocktail-party bragging rights.

Bedwell River, Clayoquot Sound (P.O. Box 728), Tofino, BC V0R 2Z0. ✆ **888/333-5405** or 250/725-2688. Fax 250/725-2689. www.wildretreat.com. 21 outpost tents. Mid-May to Sept C$4,750–C$11,000 3-, 4- & 7-night stays per person. Rates include 3 meals/day, plus transport to & from Tofino. AE, MC, V. Parking in Tofino. **Amenities:** Restaurant; lounge; bike rental; hot tubs; spa; kayak rentals; free canoes; Wi-Fi. *In room:* Hair dryer, no phone.

Inn at Tough City 🎁 Take a close look, and you'll see this inn for what it is—a recycled treasure, and one of the quirkiest small inns in downtown Tofino. Constructed with over 45,000 recycled bricks, refurbished hardwood floors, and original stained-glass windows from as far away as Scotland, the Inn at Tough City is a find. You've got to love the vintage collection of advertising signs and old tins. All guest rooms have their own color scheme, accented with stained glass and antique furniture. They also have decks or balconies with water views, though room nos. 3 and 6 have only peek-a-boo ones. The upstairs guest rooms have fireplaces. All have custom-made bed linens in soft, environment-friendly, unbleached cotton. The inn doesn't provide breakfast but does have the only authentic sushi restaurant in town (see "Where to Dine," later in this chapter).

350 Main St. (P.O. Box 8), Tofino, BC V0R 2Z0. ✆ **250/725-2021.** Fax 250/725-2088. www.toughcity.com. 8 units. July–Sept C$179–C$229 double; Oct, Nov & Mar–June C$109–C$179 double. Closed Dec–Feb. AE, MC, V. **Amenities:** Restaurant; lounge. *In room:* TV, hair dryer.

Long Beach Lodge Resort ★★ This upscale resort lies on the beach at Cox Bay, between Pacific Rim National Park and Clayoquot Sound. Set among towering trees and taking full advantage of the rugged coastline and sandy beach, the cedar-shingled lodge rivals the Wickaninnish Inn (reviewed below) for views and service that here rates two staff for every three guests. The welcoming Great Room—with its dramatic First Nations art, oversize granite fireplace, and deep armchairs—is an ideal spot to relax overlooking the bay and sample the chef's daily, fresh, and organic creations for lunch, dinner, or as shared plates of hors d'oeuvres. Accommodations include 41 beachfront lodge rooms with oversize beds, fireplaces, Jacuzzis or extra-deep-soaker bathtubs, and private balconies, as well as 20 two-bedroom cottages nestled in the rainforest. Surfers opt for the ground floor, beachfront rooms that literally put the rollers on their doorstep. Rain gear is provided to guests who want to venture forth into the storms. Rates include a buffet breakfast.

1441 Pacific Rim Hwy., Tofino, BC V0R 2Z0. ✆ **877/844-7873** or 250/725-2442. www.longbeachlodgeresort.com. 61 units. Mid-Oct to mid-Mar C$159–C$249 double, C$269 cottage, C$469 suite; mid-Mar to May C$189–C$289 double, C$319 cottage, C$469 suite; June to mid-Oct C$289–C$389 double,

C$489 cottage, C$579 suite; year-round C$629 penthouse. Rates include continental breakfast buffet. Additional adult C$30. Children 6–15 C$15 extra. AE, MC, V. Pets accepted (C$50). **Amenities:** Restaurant; lounge; oceanfront health club. *In room:* Hair dryer.

A Snug Harbour Inn ★ Set on a 26m (85-ft.) cliff overlooking the pounding Pacific, A Snug Harbour Inn is a romantic oasis that takes the credit for at least 85 wedding engagements. Each guest room is decorated a little differently: One has an Atlantic nautical theme, a three-level Lighthouse Suite boasts the best views, and the Sawadee tops the list for snuggly comfort. One suite was built for wheelchair accessibility, including a walk-in shower; and another is pet friendly. All have fireplaces, down duvets over queen- or king-size beds, double-jet bathtubs, and private decks boasting vast ocean views. For a nominal extra charge, you can order up items such as roses, champagne, and other gifts to add to your stay. There's a powerful telescope in the Great Room, through which you can watch sea lions on the rocks below, or at night, with no light pollution, enjoy some unparalleled stargazing. Outside, there's a trail of 75 steps down to the pebbly beach, appropriately called "Stairway from the Stars." It's worth the descent, but it's a bit of a hike back up—take it in the morning to whet your appetite for a terrific breakfast.

460 Marine Dr. (P.O. Box 367), Ucluelet, BC V0R 3A0. ✆ **888/936-5222** or 250/726-2686. Fax 250/726-2685. www.awesomeview.com. 6 units. June–Sept C$270–C$355 double; Oct & Mar–May C$215–C$280 double; Nov–Feb C$190–C$225 double. MC, V. Pets accepted. **Amenities:** Lounge; Jacuzzi. *In room:* TV/DVD player, hair dryer, Wi-Fi.

Wickaninnish Inn ★★★ Perched on a rocky promontory overlooking Chesterman Beach, between old-growth forest and the Pacific Ocean, this Relais & Châteaux inn continues to set and refresh the standard by which other fine hoteliers seem to judge themselves. It describes itself as rustically elegant, which translates into handmade driftwood furniture; local artwork in every room, alongside fireplaces, big-screen TVs, richly textured linens and furnishings, and en suite bathrooms with double soakers; and all with breathtaking views of the ocean. The corner suites have an additional wall of windows that seems to beckon the outside in. Adjacent to the original lodge is the **Wickaninnish on the Beach,** with even more luxurious two-level guest suites and a health club.

In summer, the sprawling sands of Chesterman Beach are littered with sandcastles, tidal pools, and sun worshippers. In winter, it's quite a different story. As thundering waves, howling winds, and sheets of rain lash up against the inn's cedar siding, storm-watching becomes an art. Every guest room provides grandstand views through triple-glazed, floor-to-ceiling windows. The result is a surreal feeling of being enveloped by a storm in virtual silence, especially when snuggled up in front of the fire. Rain gear is provided for those brave souls who want to take on the elements first-hand. The **Ancient Cedars Spa** will mellow your mood, especially since each treatment begins with an aromatic footbath; the private massage hut on the rocks rocks. Cuisine is another one of the inn's draws. Reservations at the **Pointe Restaurant** (see "Where to Dine," below) are sought after, so be sure to make them when you book your room.

Osprey Lane at Chesterman Beach (P.O. Box 250), Tofino, BC V0R 2Z0. ✆ **800/333-4604** or 250/725-3300. Fax 250/725-3110. www.wickinn.com. 75 units. June–Sept C$420–C$580 double, C$540–C$620 suite; Oct–May C$340–C$440 double, C$460–C$975 suite. Rates may vary over holiday periods. Storm-watching, spa & other packages available. AE, MC, V. **Amenities:** Restaurant; bar; coffee lounge; health club; spa. *In room:* TV/DVD player, hair dryer, minibar, iPod dock, Wi-Fi.

Where to Dine

IN TOFINO

If you're just looking for a cup of java and a snack, it's hard to beat the **Caffé Vincenté,** 441 Campbell St. (✆ **250/725-2599**), a touch of urban hip near the entrance to town. The cafe also does an excellent breakfast and lunch and serves afternoon dessert. **The Wildside** (1180 Pacific Rim Hwy; ✆ **250/725-9453**), tucked in a small cluster of buildings just off the highway on the way to Tofino where surfers tend to congregate. Don't be put off by the shack-like appearance: The pulled-pork sandwich is yummy, and the fresh-from-the-ocean fish is served tempura-style. The complex is also home to **The Tofitian,** a computer cafe with free Wi-Fi and the area's finest espresso (Lavazza).

Pointe Restaurant ★★★ WEST COAST If the 240-degree view of the Pacific Ocean pounding at your feet doesn't inspire, then the food and award-winning wine list certainly will. The menu is an imaginative showcase of fresh coastal food and seafood that's caught within a stone's throw of the inn. Chanterelles, boletus, angel wings, and pine mushrooms are brought in from neighboring forests. Gooseneck barnacles come off the rocks on the beach, and Indian Candy, made from salmon marinated and smoked for 6 days, comes from Tofino. Everything is exquisitely presented—an endive and berry salad with lavender, buttermilk, and wildflower honey is perfectly combined with tempura oysters, and the prosciutto-wrapped pork loin is especially tasty. A chef's four-course tasting menu showcases the best of the season for C$150 with wine pairings, C$80 without. And if the tempest outside is brewing over your meal, take note. The restaurant has surround-sound to make it feel as if you're eating in the eye of a storm. Be sure to book a table well in advance, or at least when you book your room, or you might be disappointed.

At Wickaninnish Inn, 500 Osprey Lane at Chesterman Beach. ✆ **800/333-4604** or 250/725-3100. www.wickinn.com. Reservations required. Main courses C$34–C$49. AE, MC, V. Daily 8am–9:30pm.

Shelter ★ PACIFIC NORTHWEST Polished wood dominates the decor of this cozy spot, which also features a large stone fireplace. Although there's meat on the menu, fish is the specialty here, which is done to perfection, whether seared albacore tuna, steamed mussels with caramelized onion and roasted garlic, or the yellow Thai seafood curry served with sticky rice steamed black in a banana leaf. Don't leave without at least trying the bouillabaisse (tasters are by request). It's the signature dish crammed with local fish, from sable and Chinook salmon to prawns, clams, and mussels that have simmered away in a fire-roasted tomato sauce. Fish aside, the Angus rib-eye with Panko onion rings is pretty darn good, as is the best vegetarian dish on the menu: a char-grilled vegetable ratatouille. Most wines are award-winning whites from BC vineyards; nearly all are available by the glass.

601 Campbell St. ✆ **250/725-3353.** www.shelterrestaurant.com. Reservations recommended. Main courses lunch C$11–C$18, dinner C$13–C$32. MC, V. Daily 11am–10pm.

Sushi Bar at Tough City ★ SUSHI A hard-won reputation for authenticity has grown a small bar to the entire main floor of this popular B&B, and in warmer weather, customers spill onto the outdoor patio. The menu has all the traditional favorites: sushi rolls, tempura rolls, *nigiri,* and sashimi, as well as other Japanese dishes such as teriyaki salmon, chicken, and beef. If you're not a fan of sushi but love crab, the Dungeness crab dinner (C$34) is one of the best, in part because it's so simply prepared—steamed and served cold with melted garlic butter and a fresh Caesar salad. In July and August, the bar opens for lunch, as well as dinner.

350 Main St. © **250/725-2021.** www.toughcity.com. Main courses C$10–C$24. AE, MC, V. Year-round daily 5:30–9pm; July–Aug daily 11:30am–9pm.

IN UCLUELET

Ukee Dogs ★★ CANADIAN Operating out of a converted gas station and garage, there's a delicious informality about this cafe where tables are within spitting distance of the open kitchen. Everything's made from scratch, and chef-owner Stephanie Deering chats to you over her hot stove about your order. You want onions? How about some cilantro? She gave up a long and lucrative career in fine dining to set up shop away from the rat race, so you can be assured her no-frills dishes will please. The hearty bean chili and cheddar is so good that many of the fishermen have it for breakfast in addition to the various breakfast scramblers on offer. The vegetable curry pie is simmered in a creamy Madras sauce; and the hot dogs? Well, they're what made Ukee's a household name in these parts, so they're a have-to-have. Everything on the menu is under C$7, and each meat item has a vegetarian counterpart.

1576 Imperial Lane. © **250/726-2103.** Main courses C$2–C$7. Cash only. Fall–spring Mon–Fri 8:30am–3:30pm; summer Mon–Sat 8:30am–3:30pm. Closed Sun.

VANCOUVER ISLAND'S EAST COAST

Vancouver Island's east coast is lined with long sandy beaches, world-class golf courses, and fishing resorts. Parksville and neighboring Qualicum Beach are longtime favorites for family vacations. With miles of beach for the kids and six local golf courses for the parents, these twinned towns are the perfect base for a relaxing vacation. Comox and Courtenay, 61km (38 miles) north, are another set of intergrown beach towns with access to great sea kayaking and tours to fossil digs. Campbell River (pop. 29,000), 46km (29 miles) farther north, is by far the most famous salmon-fishing center in British Columbia, with many long-established fishing resorts that have hosted everyone from the shah of Iran to John Wayne to Goldie Hawn.

Essentials

VISITOR INFORMATION For information on Qualicum Beach, contact the **Qualicum Beach Visitor Information Centre,** 2711 W. Island Hwy., Qualicum Beach, BC V9K 2C4 (© **250/752-9532;** www.qualicum.bc.ca). For information on Parksville and to get a free visitor's guide, contact the **Parksville Visitor Info Centre,** 1275 East Island Hwy., P.O. Box 99, Parksville, BC V9P 2G3 (© **250/248-3613;** www.chamber.parksville.bc.ca). For more information on the Comox/Courtenay area, contact the **Comox Valley Visitor Info Centre,** 2040 Cliffe Ave., Courtenay, BC V9N 2L3 (© **888/357-4471** or 250/334-3234; www.discovercomoxvalley.com). The **Campbell River Visitor Info Centre** is at 1235 Shopper's Row, Campbell River, BC V9W 2C7 (© **250/287-4636;** www.campbellriverchamber.ca), or you can write for information to Box 400, Campbell River, BC V9W 5B6.

GETTING THERE BY PLANE The **Campbell River and District Regional Airport,** located south of Campbell River off Jubilee Parkway, has regularly scheduled flights on commuter planes to and from Vancouver and Seattle.

KD Air (✆ **800/665-4244,** 604/688-9957, or 250/752-5884; www.kdair.com) offers several daily flights from Vancouver to the Qualicum Beach Airport for C$250 round-trip, with discounts for seniors and children. **Orca Airways** (✆ **888/359-6722** or 604/270-6722; www.flyorcaair.com) also provides service between these two points.

BY TRAIN VIA Rail's **Malahat** (✆ **888/842-7245;** www.viarail.com) stops in Parksville and Qualicum Beach on its daily trip from Victoria to Courtenay.

BY BUS **Greyhound** (✆ **800/661-8747**) operates one bus daily with service from Victoria all the way to Port Hardy. There are three buses daily between Nanaimo, Parksville, Qualicum Bay, Courtenay, and Campbell River. One-way fare from Nanaimo to Campbell River is C$39. **Island Link Bus** (✆ **250/954-8257;** www.islandlinkbus.com) also runs a passenger express service between BC Ferries' terminals and Vancouver, Victoria, and Comox airports to Parksville and Qualicum. One-way fares are slightly less than Greyhound, but schedules may not be as convenient.

BY CAR From Nanaimo, the Island Highway (Hwy. 19) links Parksville, Courtenay, and Campbell River with points north. Campbell River is 52km (32 miles) north of Courtenay and 266km (165 miles) north of Victoria.

Exploring the East Coast

Parksville (pop. 9,576) and **Qualicum Beach** (pop. 6,874) are near the most popular beaches on Vancouver Island: Spending a week on the beach here is a family tradition for many BC families. Parksville claims to have the warmest ocean-water beaches in all Canada. **Rathtrevor Beach Provincial Park** is a popular place for swimming and sunbathing.

Facing each other across the Courtenay River Estuary, the twin towns **Comox** (pop. 11,847) and **Courtenay** (pop. 18,420) provide a bit of urban polish to a region rich in beaches, outdoor recreation, and dramatic land- and seascapes. The highlight of the **Courtenay District Museum & Paleontology Centre,** 207 Fourth St. (✆ **250/334-0686;** www.courtenaymuseum.ca), is a 12m (39-ft.) cast skeleton of an elasmosaur, a crocodile-like Cretaceous marine reptile. With four departures daily in July and August, the museum leads 3-hour **fossil tours** of its paleontology lab and to a local fossil dig; C$25 adults, C$20 seniors and students, C$15 children, or C$75 per family. Call ahead for reservations; tours also run on Saturdays April through June. Admission to the museum alone is by donation. Summer hours are Monday to Saturday 10am to 5pm and Sunday noon to 4pm. Winter hours are Tuesday to Saturday 10am to 5pm.

The Museum at Campbell River ★, 470 Island Hwy. (✆ **250/287-3103;** www.crmuseum.ca), is worth seeking out. This large and captivating museum is devoted to carvings and artifacts from the local First Nations tribes; especially fine is the display of contemporary carved wooden masks. Also compelling is the sound-and-light presentation *The Treasures of Siwidi,* which uses masks to retell an ancient Native Indian myth. Another gallery houses a replica of a pioneer-era cabin and a collection of photos and tools from the early days of Vancouver Island logging. The 30-seat theater offers a couple of short films; one, *War of the Land Canoes,* is a 1914 documentary shot in local Native villages. The gift shop is one of the best places in Campbell River to buy authentic Native art and jewelry. The museum is open daily mid-May through September 10am to 5pm, and October through mid-May Tuesday to Sunday noon to 5pm. Admission is C$6 adults, C$4 students, C$15 family, free for children under 6.

Sports & Outdoor Activities

DIVING The decommissioned **HMCS *Columbia*** was sunk in 1996 near the sea-life-rich waters of Seymour Narrows off the Quadra Island's west coast. For information on diving to this artificial reef and on other diving sites (with enticing names like Row and Be Damned, Whisky Point, Copper Cliffs, and Steep Island) in the Campbell River area, contact **Beaver Aquatics** (© **250/287-7652;** www.connected.bc.ca/~baquatics).

FISHING Between Quadra Island and Campbell River, the broad Strait of Georgia squeezes down to a narrow mile-wide passage called Discovery Channel. All the salmon that entered the Strait of Juan de Fuca near Victoria to spawn in northerly rivers funnel down into this tight constriction, a churning waterway with 4m (13-ft.) tides.

However, fishing isn't what it once was in Campbell River, when tyee and coho salmon regularly tipped the scales at 34kg (75 lb.). Some salmon runs are now catch-and-release only, while others are open for limited catches; many fishing trips are now billed as much as wildlife adventures as hunting-and-gathering expeditions.

If you'd like to get out onto the waters and fish, be sure to call ahead and talk to an outfitter or the tourist center to find out what fish are running during your visit and if the seasons have been opened. Because of plummeting numbers of salmon and of recent treaties with the United States, the next few years will see even more greatly restricted fishing seasons in the waters off Vancouver Island. Don't be disappointed if there's no salmon fishing when you visit or if the salmon you hook is catch-and-release only. For one thing, there are other fish in the sea: Not all types of salmon are as threatened as the coho and tyee, and fishing is also good for halibut and other bottom fish. And if you really just want to get out on the water and have an adventure, consider a wildlife-viewing boat tour, offered by many fishing outfitters.

There are dozens of fishing guides in the Campbell River area, with a range of services that extend from basic to pure extravagance. Expect to pay around C$100 per hour for 4 to 5 hours of fishing with a no-frills outfitter. A flashier trip on a luxury cruiser can cost more than C$120 per hour. The most famous guides are associated with the Painter's Lodge and its sister property, April Point Lodge on Quadra Island. A few smaller fishing-guide operations include Coastal Wilderness Adventures © **866/640-1173** or 250/287-3427, www.coastwild.com) with both salt water and freshwater fly-fishing trips; **CR Fishing Village,** 260 Island Hwy. (© **250/287-3630;** www.fishingvillage.bc.ca); and **Coastal Island Fishing Adventures,** 663 Glenalan Rd. (© **888/225-9776** or 250/923-5831; www.coastalislandfishing.com), with operations in Campbell River and at Gold River, on Vancouver Island's west coast.

You can also check out the info center's directory to fishing guides by following the links at www.campbellriverchamber.ca. Most hotels in Campbell River also offer fishing/lodging packages; ask when you reserve.

GOLF Greens fees at the following courses are C$50 to C$85 for 18 holes.

There are six courses in the Parksville–Qualicum Beach area, and more than a dozen within an hour's drive. Here are two favorites: The **Eagle Crest Golf Club,** 2035 Island Hwy. (© **250/752-6311**), is a 18-hole, par-71 course with an emphasis on shot making and accuracy; and the public **Morningstar Golf Club,** 525 Lowry's Rd. (© **250/248-8161**), is an 18-hole, 7,018-yard course with a par-72 rating.

One of the finest courses on Vancouver Island is the **Crown Isle Resort & Golf Community,** 339 Clubhouse Dr., Courtenay (© **888/338-8439** or 250/703-5050; www.crownisle.com). This lavish 18-hole links-style championship golf course has already hosted the Canadian Tour and Canadian Junior Men's Tournament. Because it was carved out of a dense forest, you may see wildlife grazing on the fairway and roughs at the **Storey Creek Golf Club,** Campbell River (✆ **250/923-3673**). Gentle creeks and ponds also wind through this course.

KAYAKING With the Courtenay Estuary and Hornby, Tree, and Denman islands an easy paddle away, sea kayaking is very popular in this area. In fact, you might consider it **Kayak Utopia,** which is the new business name used by **Comox Valley Kayaks,** 2020 Cliffe Ave., Courtenay and **Campbell River Kayaks,** 1620 Petersen Rd., Campbell River, (✆ **888/545-5595** or 250/334-2628; www.comoxvalleykayaks.com). Both locations offer rentals, lessons, and tours. A 2-hour introductory lesson is C$40. A day trip to Tree Island goes for C$72. Rentals start at C$15 for 2 hours.

SKIING **Mount Washington Alpine Resort** ★ (✆ **888/231-1499** or 250/338-1386; 250/338-1515 for snow report; www.mtwashington.bc.ca) is a 5-hour drive from Victoria and open year-round (for hiking or skiing, depending on the season). The summit reaches 1,588m (5,210 ft.), and the mountain averages 860cm (339 in.) of snow per year. A 505m (1,657-ft.) vertical drop and 60 groomed runs are served by eight lifts and a beginners' tow. Fifty-five kilometers (34 miles) of Nordic track-set and skating trails connect to Strathcona Provincial Park. The **Raven Lodge** has restaurants, equipment rentals, and locker rooms. Lift rates are C$64 for adults, C$52 for seniors and students, and C$33 for kids 7 to 12. Take the Strathcona Parkway 37km (23 miles) to Mount Washington, or use turnoff 130 from Inland Highway 19.

Where to Stay & Dine

IN PARKSVILLE & QUALICUM BEACH

Tigh-Na-Mara Seaside Resort & Spa ★★ ☺ Romantic family getaways might sound like an oxymoron, but not at Tigh-Na-Mara, Gaelic for "the house by the sea." Established in the 1940s on an 11-hectare (27-acre) forested waterfront beach near Rathtrevor Beach Provincial Park, this time-honored resort just keeps getting better. Romantics gravitate here for the Grotto Spa; it's the largest spa in British Columbia and offers a mineral pool and exceptional spa services. Tigh-Na-Mara's range of accommodations means that guests can stay in intimate one- or two-bedroom log cottages in a forest setting, luxuriate in spa bungalows, or splurge on the ocean-view condominiums (many with Jacuzzis). All guest accommodations have fireplaces, and some have kitchen facilities. The three- and four-room cottages can sleep up to eight. Families rave about Tigh-Na-Mara's supervised child-friendly programs as much as for its stunning location. The resort includes a newly-renovated lounge and a welcoming cedar-paneled **Cedar Restaurant** (with summer BBQs). For its spa clients, the **Treetops Tapas & Grill** is a huge draw.

1155 Resort Dr., Parksville, BC V9P 2E5. ✆ **800/663-7373** or 250/248-2072. Fax 250/248-4140. www.tigh-na-mara.com. 192 units. July & Aug C$179–C$299 double, suite & bungalow; C$199–C$359 cottage. May, June & Sept C$159–C$259 double, suite & bungalow; C$189–C$309 cottage. Oct–Apr C$129–C$209 double, suite & bungalow; C$169–C$289 cottage. 3- to 7-night minimum stay July & Aug. Seasonal & spa packages available. AE, MC, V. Pets accepted Sept–May (C$30). **Amenities:** 3 restaurants; lounge; babysitting; mountain bike rentals; fitness center; Jacuzzi; heated indoor pool; sauna. *In room:* TV, fridge, kitchen, Wi-Fi.

IN COURTENAY

Kingfisher Oceanside Resort & Spa ★★ Located 7km (4¼ miles) south of Courtenay, this adult-oriented destination resort is a winner. Bright and colorful rooms tend to be extra-large, and many come with balconies or patios overlooking the ocean. The even roomier beachfront suites come with kitchenettes and heated bathroom floors; you'll pay more, of course, but you can save dollars by cooking your own meals. Most people come for the impressive spa, which includes a heated outdoor pool with a shoulder-massaging waterfall, a cave steam-room and sauna, and spa services that range from thalassotherapy wraps, Reiki, and reflexology to facials and drop-in yoga classes. A complimentary shuttle runs between the resort and downtown, to the Comox Valley Airport, and to Mount Washington Alpine Resort (see "Mount Washington Alpine Resort," above). The Kingfisher Oceanside Restaurant is one of the better places to dine in the area (see "Where to Dine," below).

4330 Island Hwy. S., Courtenay, BCV9N 9R9. ✆ **800/663-7929** or 250/338-1323. Fax 250/338-0058. www.kingfisherspa.com. 64 units. C$170 double; C$220–C$350 suite; C$455 deluxe suite. Additional adult C$25. Low-season discounts available; spa, ski & golf packages available. AE, DC, DISC, MC, V. **Amenities:** Restaurant; lounge; health club; room service; spa; unlit outdoor tennis court; canoe & kayak rentals. *In room:* TV/DVD player, hair dryer, Wi-Fi.

IN CAMPBELL RIVER

Painter's Lodge Holiday & Fishing Resort ★★ An international favorite of avid fishermen and celebrities, Painter's Lodge has welcomed the likes of Bob Hope, Julie Andrews, Goldie Hawn, and the Prince of Luxembourg. Its location overlooking Discovery Passage is awesome, and its rustic grandeur has a West Coast ambience, with comfortable lounges, large decks, and roomy accommodations decorated in natural wood and outdoorsy colors. Wrapped in windows, the lodge's restaurant, **Legends,** boasts a view of the Passage from every table (see "Where to Dine," below). One of the neatest dining experiences is to take the speedboat trip (10 min. in each direction) over to **April Point Resort & Spa on Quadra Island** for a pre-dinner martini at their sushi bar before returning to Legends for the catch of the day. The trip is included in hotel rates.

1625 MacDonald Rd. (P.O. Box 460, Dept. 2), Campbell River, BC V9W 4S5. ✆ **800/663-7090** or 250/286-1102. Fax 250/286-0158. www.painterslodge.com. 94 units. Early Apr–mid Oct C$139–C$159 double; C$219 cabin. Additional adult C$20. AE, DC, MC, V. Closed mid-Oct to early Apr. **Amenities:** Restaurant; pub; lounge; babysitting; children's center; health club; 2 Jacuzzis; heated outdoor pool; 2 outdoor tennis courts. *In room:* TV, hair dryer, Wi-Fi.

WHISTLER ★

The premier ski resort in North America, according to *Ski, Snow Country,* and *Condé Nast Traveler* magazines, the **Whistler/Blackcomb** complex boasts more vertical feet, more lifts, and more ski terrain than any other ski resort in North America. And it isn't all just downhill skiing: There's also backcountry, cross-country, snowboarding, snowmobiling, heli-skiing, and sleigh riding. In summer, there's mountain biking, rafting, hiking, golfing, and horseback riding. The area got the ultimate seal of approval from the International Olympic Committee when Whistler landed the opportunity to stage many of the alpine events for the 2010 Winter Games. So come test yourself on the same slopes that Olympic champions have skied on. And then there's **Whistler Village,** a resort town with a year-round population of 10,000—plus 115 hotels and lodgings and myriad restaurants—arranged around a central village street in a compact enough fashion you can park your car and remain a pedestrian for the duration of your stay.

THE INSIDE passage & NORTHERN BC

Most of this chapter's towns and sights are geographically in British Columbia's midsection. By the time you reach **Prince Rupert** in northern BC, however, you'll feel the palpable sense of being in the north: The days are long in summer and short in winter, and the spruce forestlands have a primordial character. First Nations peoples make up a greater percentage of the population here than in more southerly areas, and Native communities and heritage sites are common.

One of the most dramatic ways to reach northern British Columbia is by ferry. The BC Ferries **Inside Passage** route operates between Port Hardy, on Vancouver Island, and Prince Rupert, on the mainland; this 15-hour, 491km (305-mile) ferry run passes through mystical land- and seascapes, combining the best scenic elements of Norway's rocky fjords, New Zealand's majestic South Island, Chile's Patagonian range, and Nova Scotia's wild coastline, with excellent wildlife-viewing opportunities. Prince Rupert is a feisty little seaport on the northwestern edge of Canada, a perfect spot to explore deep-sea fishing, learn about ancient Native culture or perfect your sea kayaking skills. Inland from Prince Rupert, the Yellowhead Highway (Hwy. 16) follows the mighty Skeena and Bulkley rivers past First Nations villages and isolated ranches, finally reaching Prince George, the largest city in northern British Columbia. Prince George is also a transportation gateway.

THE INSIDE PASSAGE ★★ Fifteen hours may seem like a long time to be on a ferry. But you'll never get bored as the MV ***Northern Adventure*** noses its way through an incredibly scenic series of channels and calm inlets, flanked by green forested islands. Whales, porpoises, salmon, bald eagles, and sea lions line the route past the mostly uninhabited coastline. This BC Ferries run between Port Hardy and Prince Rupert follows the same route as expensive Alaska-bound cruise ships, but at a fraction of the cost. And in midsummer, with the north's long days, the trip is made almost entirely in daylight.

The ferry north from Port Hardy initially crosses a couple hours' worth of open sea—where waters can be rough—before ducking behind Calvert Island. Except for a brief patch of open sea in the Milbanke Sound north of Bella Bella, the rest of the trip follows a narrow,

Essentials

VISITOR INFORMATION The **Whistler Visitor Info Centre,** easy to find on the Village Bus Loop at 4230 Gateway Dr., Whistler, BC V0N 1B4 (✆ **877/991-9988** or 604/935-3357; www.whistler.com), is open daily 9am to 5pm. **Tourism Whistler** is at the Whistler Conference Centre at 4010 Whistler Way, Whistler, BC V0N 1B0, open daily 9am to 5pm (✆ **800/944-7853;** www.tourismwhistler.com). Both offices can assist you with event tickets, reservations for recreation, and last-minute accommodations bookings.

GETTING THERE BY CAR Whistler is about a 2-hour drive from Vancouver along Hwy. 99, also called the **Sea-to-Sky Highway ★**. The drive is spectacular, winding along the edge of Howe Sound before climbing up through the mountains.

Parking at the mountain is free for day skiers; there are large parking lots along Fitzsimmons Creek between Whistler Village and Upper Village. However, most hotels will charge a fee for overnight parking.

protected channel between the mainland and a series of islands.

The actual Inside Passage begins north of Bella Bella, as the ferry moves behind mountainous Princess Royal and Pitt islands. The passage between these islands and the mainland is very narrow—often less than a mile wide. The scenery is extraordinarily dramatic: Black cliffs drop thousands of feet directly into the channel, notched with hanging glacial valleys and fringed with forests. Powerful waterfalls shoot from dizzying heights into the sea. Eagles float along thermal drafts, and porpoises cavort in the ferry's wake. Even in poor conditions (the weather is very unpredictable here), this is an amazing trip.

WHERE TO STAY IN PORT HARDY The night before the 15-hour Inside Passage ferry runs, Port Hardy is booked up and reservations are needed at most restaurants. If you are taking the ferry north in summer, you'll definitely need reservations the evening before the 7:30am departure; try the **Glen Lyon Inn,** 6435 Hardy Bay Rd. (✆ **877/949-2395** or 250/949-2395, www.glenlyoninn.com), an attractive hotel and restaurant development right above the marina with doubles from C$110.

WHERE TO STAY & DINE IN PRINCE RUPERT One and a half kilometers (1 mile) from the ferry terminal, the **Park Avenue Campground,** 1750 Park Ave. (✆ **250/624-5861;** mailing address: Box 612, Prince Rupert, BC V8J 4J5), has 97 full-hookup and tenting sites. Facilities include a laundry, hot showers, flush toilets, a playground, mail drop, and pay phones. Make reservations in advance during summer because this campground is the best in the area. Rates are C$20 for tenters to C$32 for RVs.

Hotel options include **Coast Prince Rupert Hotel,** 118 Sixth St. (✆ **800/663-1144** or 250/624-6711; www.coasthotels.com), with well-maintained rooms right downtown for C$130 double; and the **Crest Hotel ★**, 222 First Ave. W. (✆ **800/663-8150** or 250/624-6771; www.cresthotel.bc.ca), which offers the best views in town, good dining, and beautifully furnished rooms for C$129–C$169 double. Best dining bets include the **Breakers Pub ★**, 117 George Hills Way, on the Cow Bay Wharf (✆ **250/624-5990**), a popular pub with a harbor view and well-prepared international food; and **Cow Bay Café ★**, 205 Cow Bay Rd. (✆ **250/627-1212**), a homey place with lots of vegetarian options.

BY BUS **Whistler Express,** 8695 Barnard St., Vancouver (✆ **604/266-5386** in Vancouver, or 604/905-0041 in Whistler; www.perimeterbus.com), operates door-to-door bus service from Vancouver International Airport to over 25 lodgings in Whistler. With advance reservations, some buses will pick up passengers at downtown Vancouver hotels. Buses depart seven times daily in the summer and 12 times in winter. The trip typically takes 3 hours, though weather and construction on the Sea-to-Sky Highway may delay the bus; one-way fares are C$49 to C$59 for adults and C$25 to C$35 for children. Kids under 5 ride free. Reservations are required year-round. **Greyhound,** Pacific Central Station, 1150 Station St., Vancouver (✆ **604/662-8051** in Vancouver, or 604/482-8747 in Whistler; www.greyhound.ca), operates service from the Vancouver Bus Depot to the Whistler bus depot at 2029 London Lane. The trip takes about 2½ hours; one-way fares are C$21 for adults and C$16 for children ages 5 to 12. **Pacific Coach Lines** (✆ **800/661-1725** or 604/662-7575; www.pacificcoach.com) operates one-way and return bus service from Vancouver International Airport and Vancouver hotels to Whistler area hotels for C$37 each way. **Snowbus**

(✆ **604/685-7669;** www.snowbus.ca) offers service to/from Whistler and Vancouver area suburbs (Richmond, Burnaby, North Vancouver) and other neighborhood locations in addition to downtown Vancouver and the airport. On Friday and weekend morning departures, riders have the option of hot breakfasts; free movies are offered during the journey. Also available from the website is a C$20 SnowCard (free to BC residents), which offers discounts on Snowbus transportation and lift ticket packages, as well as discounts at Vancouver and Whistler area restaurants, recreational clothing stores, and ski and board shops. One-way fare between Vancouver and Whistler is C$23. Snowbus operates daily, but only during ski season.

BY TRAIN The **Whistler Sea to Sky Climb,** a new route from Rocky Mountaineer Vacations (✆ **877/460-3200** or 604/606-7245; www.whistlermountaineer.com), offers service between Vancouver and Whistler along the highly scenic Sea-to-Sky corridor. There's one train in each direction daily, departing 8:30am from North Vancouver Station, arriving at Whistler Station at 11:30am. The train returns in the afternoon, departing Whistler Station at 2:30pm and arriving at North Vancouver Station at 6pm. Currently, the train operates mid-May to late September only. The least expensive fair is C$129 adults, C$90 children 2 to 11 one-way; or C$219 adults, C$153 children round-trip.

GETTING AROUND Be sure to pick up a map when you get to Whistler and study it—the curving streets are made for pedestrians but defy easy negotiation by drivers, particularly in the winter darkness. **Whistler Village** is at the base of the ski runs at Whistler Peak. **Upper Village,** at the base of Blackcomb ski runs, is just across Fiztsimmons Creek from Whistler Village. As development continues, the distinction between these two "villages" is disappearing, though Whistler Village is the center for most independent restaurants, shopping, and the youthful nightlife scene. Upper Village, centered on the Four Seasons and Fairmont Chateau Whistler hotels, is quieter and more upscale. However, both villages are compact, and signed trails and paths link together shops, lodgings, and restaurants in the central resort area. The walk between the two village resort areas takes about 10 minutes.

Many smaller inns, B&Bs, restaurants, and services are located outside the nucleus of Whistler Village and Upper Village. **Creekside** is a large development east (downhill) from Whistler Village (there are lifts onto Whistler Mountain from Creekside—in fact, this was the original lift base for the resort), while the shores of **Alta Lake** are ringed with residential areas and golf courses.

BY BUS The year-round Whistler and Valley Express (WAVE) **public bus system** (✆ **604/932-4020**) offers 14 routes in the Whistler area. Buses have both bike and ski racks. Most routes cross paths at the Gondola Transit Exchange off Blackcomb Way, near the base of the Whistler Mountain lifts. One-way fares are C$2 for adults and C$1.50 for seniors and students. For a route map, go to www.busonline.ca.

BY TAXI The village's taxis operate round-the-clock. Taxi tours, golf-course transfers, and airport transport are also offered by **Airport Limousine Service** (✆ **604/273-1331**), **Whistler Taxi** (✆ **604/938-3333**), and **Sea to Sky Taxi** (✆ **604/932-3333**).

BY CAR Rental cars are available from **Avis** in the Cascade Lodge, 4315 Northlands Blvd. (✆ **800/TRY-AVIS** [879-2847] or 604/932-1236).

SPECIAL EVENTS Downhill ski competitions are held December to May, including the **TELUS Winter Classic** (Jan), and the **TELUS World Ski & Snowboard Festival** (Apr). In August, mountain bikers compete in **Crankworx.**

The **Whistler Summit Concert Series** (✆ **604/932-3434**) is held during August weekends. The mountains provide a stunning backdrop for the on-mountain concerts.

The second weekend in September ushers in the **Whistler Jazz & Blues Festival** (✆ **604/932-2394**), featuring live performances in the village squares and the surrounding clubs. **Cornucopia** (✆ **604/932-3434**) is Whistler's premier wine-and-food festival. Held in November, the opening gala showcases top wineries from the Pacific region plus lots of food events and tastings from local chefs.

Skiing & Snowboarding

CROSS-COUNTRY SKIING The 32km (20 miles) of easy-to-very-difficult marked trails at Lost Lake start at the Lorimer Road bridge over Fitzsimmons Creek, just west of Upper Village. Passes are C$18 per day. The Lost Lake trails link to the Nicklaus North Golf Course, with cross-country ski trails leading through the undulating golf course grounds along the shores of Green Lake. The **Valley Trail System** in the village becomes a well-marked cross-country ski trail during winter.

A 1-hour cross-country lesson runs about C$39 and is available from **Cross Country Connection** (✆ **604/905-0071;** www.crosscountryconnection.bc.ca), also at the trail head. They also offer Nordic ski rentals, though customers having lessons have dibs on rentals. The website also has a downloadable map of the trail system.

New in 2010 was **Whistler Olympic Park** and **Callaghan Country** (✆ **877/764-2455** or 604-964-2455; www.whistlerolympicpark.com), developed for the cross-country, biathlon, Nordic combined, and ski jumping events for the Vancouver 2010 Olympic and Paralympic Winter Games. Located 10km (6¼ miles) southwest of Whistler, these two areas combine to offer 70km (43 miles) of cross-country ski trails and 10km (6¼ miles) for snowshoeing. A cross-country day pass is C$20 adults; lessons and tours are also available.

DOWNHILL SKIING The **Whistler/Blackcomb Mountains,** 4545 Blackcomb Way, Whistler, BC V0N 1B4 (✆ **866/218-9690** or 604/932-3434, snow report 604/687-1032; www.whistlerblackcomb.com), are jointly operated by Intrawest, so your pass gives access to both ski areas. You can book nearly all accommodations and activities in Whistler from their website.

From its base in Whistler Village, **Whistler Mountain** has 1,530m (5,020 ft.) of vertical and over 100 marked runs that are serviced by a total of 20 lifts. From its base in Upper Village, **Blackcomb Mountain** has 1,610m (5,282 ft.) of vertical and over 100 marked runs that are served by a total of 17 lifts. Both mountains also have bowls and glade skiing, with Blackcomb offering glacier skiing well into August. Together, the two mountains comprise the largest ski resort in North America, offering over 3,378 skiable hectares (8,100 acres)—1,214 hectares (3,000 acres) more than the largest U.S. resort.

During winter, lift tickets for 2 days of skiing on both mountains range from C$125 to C$178 for adults, C$106 to C$152 for seniors, and C$65 to C$92 for children 7 to 12. Lifts are open 8:30am to 3:30pm (to 4:30pm mid-Mar to season closing, depending on weather and conditions). Whistler/Blackcomb offers ski lessons and guides for all levels and interests. Phone **Guest Relations** at ✆ **604/932-3434** for details. Ski, snowboard, and boot rentals are available from the resort, and can be booked online. In addition, dozens of independent shops provide equipment rentals. **Affinity Sports** (www.affinityrentals.com) has seven locations in the Whistler area, with online reservations available. **Summit Ski** (✆ **604/938-6225** or

604/932-6225; www.summitsport.com) has three locations in Whistler and rents high-performance and regular skis, snowboards, cross-country skis, and snowshoes.

HELI-SKIING & BOARDING Forget lift lines and crowds. Ride a helicopter to the crest of a Coast Range peak and experience the ultimate in powder skiing. If you're a confident intermediate-to-advanced skier in good shape, consider joining a heli-ski trip. **Whistler Heli-Skiing** (✆ **888/HELISKI** [435-4754] or 604/932-4105; www.whistlerheliskiing.com) offers a three-run day, with 1,400 to 2,300m (4,593–7,546 ft.) of vertical helicopter lift, which costs C$795 per person. **Coast Range Heli-Skiing** (✆ **800/701-8744** or 604/894-1144; www.coastrangeheliskiing.com) offers a four-run day, with 1,800 to 4,000m (5,906–13,123 ft.) of vertical helicopter lift, which costs C$880 per person. Both trips include a guide and lunch.

SNOWCAT SKIING & BOARDING Lifts and choppers aren't the only way up a mountain. **Powder Mountain Catskiing** (✆ **877/PWDRFIX** [793-7347] or 604/932-0169; www.powdermountaincatskiing.com) uses snowcats to climb up into a private skiing area south of Whistler where skiers and boarders will find 1,740 skiable hectares (4,300 acres) on two mountains. The price, C$499 per person, pays for a full day of skiing, usually six to ten runs down 2,100 to 3,000 vertical meters (6,890–9,942 ft.) of untracked powder, plus transport to/from Whistler, breakfast, lunch, and guides.

Other Winter Pursuits

DOG SLEDDING Explore the old-growth forests of the Soo Valley Wildlife Preserve while mushing a team of eager Huskies. Soo Valley Quest offers a choice of dog-sledding trips, and if the weather and terrain permit, you may even get to drive the dogs yourself. A 2½-hour Woof Pack tour costs C$280 for two people sharing a sled; book through the central booking agency ✆ **888/403-4727;** www.whistlerblackcomb.com.

ICE CLIMBING Climb a frozen waterfall with **Coast Mountain Guides** (✆ **604/932-7711;** www.coastmountainguides.com). Guides provide all equipment; beginners welcome. Climbs start at C$347 per person.

SLEIGH RIDING For an old-fashioned horse-drawn sleigh ride, contact **Blackcomb Horsedrawn Sleigh Rides,** 103–4338 Main St., Whistler, BC V0N 1B4 (✆ **604/932-7631;** www.blackcombsleighrides.com). Giant Percheron horses lead the way, and comfortable sleighs with padded seats and cozy blankets keep you warm. A number of tours are available, starting with basic half-hour rides for C$55 for adults, and C$35 for children 3 to 12. Longer rides and dinner sleigh-ride combos are also available.

SNOWMOBILING The year-round ATV/snowmobile tours offered by **Canadian Snowmobile Adventures Ltd.,** Carleton Lodge (✆ **604/938-1616;** www.canadiansnowmobile.com), are a unique way to take to the Whistler Mountain trails. Exploring the Fitzsimmons Creek watershed, a 2-hour tour costs C$125 for a driver and C$99 for a passenger. If you're up for more adventure, consider a nighttime snowmobile tour to a remote mountain cabin, where a fondue dinner awaits, for C$225 driver, C$189 passenger.

SNOWSHOEING Snowshoeing makes a great family outing; kids really enjoy the experience of walking on snow. Most ski rental outfits also offer snowshoe rentals, so you won't have to look far to find a pair. If you want to just rent the snowshoes and find your own way around, rentals are typically C$15 per day. **Outdoor Adventures@Whistler,** P.O. Box 1054, Whistler, BC V0N 1B0 (✆ **604/932-0647;** www.adventureswhistler.com), has guided tours for novices at C$79 for 1½ hours.

Warm-Weather Pursuits

BIKING Whistler is world famous for its mountain biking. While many gonzo riders come from around the world to test themselves on the many technical trails, others come to enjoy the gentler pleasures of simply biking through the forest.

Some of the best mountain-bike trails in the village are in Whistler and Blackcomb mountains' **Bike Park** (✆ **866/218-9690** or 604/904-8134; www.whistlerbike.com), which offers more than 200km (124 miles) of lift-serviced trails and mountain pathways with more than 1,490m (4,888 ft.) of vertical drop. The park has three access lifts and two jump areas; the trail system is labeled from green circle to blue square to black diamond. High season per-day lift tickets and park admission are C$51 adults, C$45 seniors and youths 13 to 18, and C$28 children 7 to 12. There's also the **Air Dome,** a 780-sq.-m (8,396-sq.-ft.) covered indoor mountain bike training facility with a huge foam pit, ramps, and a quarter pipe and half pipe. A 3-hour pass is C$16. If you're not ready for daredevil riding on the mountain, the 30km (19-mile) paved **Valley Trail** is a pedestrian/bicycle route linking parks, neighborhoods, and playgrounds around Whistler Village. For other biking trails, check out the comprehensive Whistler biking website at www.whistlermountainbike.com.

In summer, nearly every ski shop switches gears and offers bike rentals. You'll have absolutely no problem finding a bike to rent in Whistler Village. If you want to call ahead and reserve a bike, try **Whistler Bike Co.,** 4205 Village Square (✆ **604/938-9511;** www.bikeco.ca). Prices range from C$33 per half-day for a commuting-style bike to C$45 to C$85 per half-day for a high-end mountain bike.

CANOEING & KAYAKING The 2-hour River of Golden Dreams Kayak & Canoe Tour offered by **Whistler Outdoor Experience,** P.O. Box 151, Whistler, BC V0N 1B0 (✆ **604/932-3389;** www.whistleroutdoor.com), is a great way to get acquainted with an exhilarating stretch of slow-moving glacial water that runs between Green Lake and Alta Lake behind the village of Whistler. Packages range from C$54 per person unguided to C$84 per person with a guide. **Outdoor Adventures Whistler** (✆ **604/932-0647;** www.adventureswhistler.com) leads canoe trips down the Lillooet River. A guided, 3-hour sunset cruise in six-person canoes is C$99 for adults, C$49 kids ages 4 to 12.

GOLF Robert Trent Jones, Jr.'s, **Fairmont Chateau Whistler Golf Club,** at the base of Blackcomb Mountain (✆ **604/938-2092,** or pro shop 604/938-2095), is an 18-hole, par-72 course. The 6,067m (6,635-yd.), par-72 signature course was selected in 1993 as Canada's best new golf course by *Golf Digest* magazine. Greens fees are C$79 to C$195 in high season. A multiple-award-winning golf course, **Nicklaus North at Whistler** (✆ **604/938-9898**) is a 5-minute drive north of the village on the shores of Green Lake. The 6,317m (6,908-yd.), par-71 course's mountain views are spectacular. Greens fees are C$75 to C$175. The 6,105m (6,676-yd.) **Whistler Golf Club** (✆ **800/376-1777** or 604/932-4544), designed by Arnold Palmer, features nine lakes, two creeks, and magnificent vistas. In addition to the 18-hole, par-72 course, the club offers a driving range, putting green, sand bunker, and pitching area. Greens fees are C$79 to C$159.

HIKING There are numerous easy hiking trails in and around Whistler. (Just remember—never hike alone, and bring plenty of water with you.) You can take ski lifts up to Whistler and Blackcomb mountains' trails during summer, but you have a number of other choices as well. The **Lost Lake Trail** starts at the northern end of the Day Skier Parking Lot at Blackcomb. The 30km (19 miles) of marked trails that wind around creeks, beaver dams, blueberry patches, and lush cedar groves are ideal for biking, cross-country skiing, or just strolling and picnicking.

The **Valley Trail System** is a well-marked paved trail connecting parts of Whistler. The trail starts on the west side of Hwy. 99 adjacent to the Whistler Golf Course and winds through quiet residential areas, as well as golf courses and parks. Garibaldi Provincial Park's **Singing Pass Trail** is a 4-hour hike of moderate difficulty. The fun way to experience this trail is to take the Whistler Mountain gondola to the top and walk down the well-marked path that ends in the village.

The Whistler Village Gondola (Whistler Base) and Wizard Express-Solar Coaster Express (Blackcomb Base) are open in summer and provide access to the Peak to Peak Gondola as well as miles of alpine hiking trails, including the Peak Interpretive Walk; guided hikes are available.

Nairn Falls Provincial Park is about 33km (21 miles) north of Whistler on Hwy. 99. It features a 1.5km-long (1-mile) trail leading you to a stupendous view of the icy-cold Green River as it plunges 60m (197 ft.) over a rocky cliff into a narrow gorge on its way downstream. On Hwy. 99 north of Mount Currie, **Joffre Lakes Provincial Park** is an intermediate-level hike leading past several brilliant-blue glacial lakes up to the very foot of a glacier. The **Ancient Cedars** area of Cougar Mountain is an awe-inspiring grove of towering cedars and Douglas firs. Some of the trees are over 1,000 years old and measure 2.5m (8 ft.) in diameter.

HORSEBACK RIDING **Adventure Ranch** near Pemberton (✆ **604/894-5200;** www.adventureranch.net) leads 2-hour horseback tours for C$69 from its Lillooet River–side ranch, 30 minutes from Whistler.

JET BOATING **Whistler River Adventures** (✆ **604/932-3532;** www.whistler river.com) takes guests up the Lillooet River from near Pemberton. The tour surges past large rapids, spectacular glacier peaks, and traditional Native fishing camps. Deer, bear, osprey, and spawning salmon are frequently seen. This 3-hour-long trip is C$109; kids 5 to 15 get a C$10 discount.

RAFTING **Whistler River Adventures** (see "Jet Boating," above) offers five different day trips on local rivers, ranging from a placid all-generation paddle to a roaring white-water adventure. Four-hour paddle trips on the Cheakamus River are gentle enough for families (C$89 adults, C$69 kids ages 10–16, and C$54 kids ages 5–9), while the 8-hour round-trip Elaho-Squamish River white-water trip is for those seeking an adrenaline high (C$159 adults, C$149 kids 10–16). All trips include equipment and ground transport. The 8-hour trip includes a salmon barbecue lunch.

ZIP-LINING One of Whistler's most popular year-round thrills is the steel zip-line rides offered by **Ziptrek Ecotours** (✆ **866/935-0001** or 604/935-0001; www.zip trek.com). Zip-lining involves gliding along a suspended steel cable using a pulley and climbing harness at speeds up to 89kmph (55 mph). Guided tours include the Bear Tour that links five zip-lines that range in height and length from 24 to 610m (79–2,001 ft.), spanning 11 hectares (27 acres) in the valley between Whistler and Blackcomb Mountains, an area of untouched coastal temperate rainforest. The adrenaline-pumping Eagle tour extends 1,828 meters (5,997 ft.) and drops 20 stories to end in Whistler Village itself. Tickets are C$99 (Bear Tour) and $119 (Eagle Tour) adults, C$79 and C$99, respectively, for seniors and youths 6 to 14. For those not up to zip-lining, Ziptrek also offers **TreeTrek,** a network of suspended boardwalks, aerial stairways, and bridges at heights of over 182m (597 ft.) in the tree canopy. Tickets are C$39 adults and C$29 seniors and youth 14 and under.

Exploring the Town

SEEING THE SIGHTS The **Squamish Lil'wat Cultural Centre** (**© 866/441-7522** or 604/898-1822; www.slcc.ca) is an architecturally stunning showcase of soaring glass and stone, designed to celebrate the joint history and living cultures of the Squamish and Lil'wat Nations. The facility includes both indoor and outdoor space, anchored by the monumental Great Hall with traditional artifacts and 66m (217-ft.) glass plank walls revealing spectacular mountain and forest views. The center also features a gallery of Squamish and Lil'wat sacred cultural treasures and icons, plus a shop for First Nations art. Outdoors is a Squamish longhouse, which was the traditional dwelling of the Squamish people, and a replica Lil'wat "ístken" or "Pit House," which was the traditional dwelling of the Lil'wat people. The center is open daily 9:30am to 5pm, and admission is C$18 adult, C$14 seniors and students, C$11 youths 13 to 18, and C$8 kids 6 to 12.

To learn more about Whistler's heritage, flora, and fauna, visit the **Whistler Museum & Archives Society,** 4329 Main St., off Northlands Boulevard (**© 604/932-2019;** www.whistlermuseum.com). June to Labour Day, the museum is open daily 10am to 4pm; call ahead for winter opening hours. Admission is C$5 for adults, C$4 seniors and students, and C$3 youths 7 to 18.

The **Path Gallery,** 4338 Main St. (**© 604/932-7570**), is devoted to Northwest Coast Native art, including totem poles, carved masks, and prints. **Gallery Row** in the Hilton Whistler Resort consists of three galleries: the **Whistler Village Art Gallery** (**© 604/938-3001**), the **Black Tusk Gallery** (**© 604/905-5540**), and the **Adele Campbell Gallery** (**© 604/938-0887**). Their collections include fine art, sculpture, and glass.

SHOPPING **Whistler Village,** and the area surrounding the **Blackcomb Mountain lift,** brim with clothing, jewelry, craft, specialty, gift, and equipment shops open daily 10am to 6pm. You'll have absolutely no problem finding interesting places to shop in Whistler—both quality and prices are high.

SPAS Spas are definitely a growth industry in Whistler. Nearly all the large hotels now feature spas, and a number of independent spas line the streets of Whistler Village. The **Vida Wellness Spa** at Chateau Whistler Resort (**© 604/938-2086**) is considered one of the best in Whistler. Open daily 8am to 9pm, it offers massage therapy, aromatherapy, skin care, body wraps, and steam baths. Another noteworthy hotel spa is the Westin Resort's **Avello Spa,** 400–4090 Whistler Way (**© 877/935-7111** or 604/935-3444; www.whistlerspa.com), which offers a host of spa services as well as holistic and hydrotherapy treatments. **The Spa at Four Seasons Resort** (**© 604/966-2620**) has 15 treatment rooms, a Vichy shower, yoga and fitness classes, and a vast assortment of luxurious treatments from mineral scrubs to wildflower baths. **Solarice Wellness Centre and Spa,** with locations at 4308 Main St. (**© 866/368-0888** or 604/966-0888), and 4230 Gateway Dr. (**© 888/935-1222** or 604/935-2222; www.solarice.com), is a highly atmospheric day spa with exotic-themed treatment rooms and a wide selection of beauty and relaxation treatments.

The therapists at **Whistler Physiotherapy** (© **604/932-4001** or 604/938-9001; www.whistlerphysio.com) have a lot of experience with the typical ski, board, and hiking injuries. There are three locations: 339–4370 Lorimer Rd., at Marketplace; 202–2011 Innsbruck Dr., next to Boston Pizza in Creekside; and 4433 Sundial Place in Whistler Village.

Where to Stay

For a first-time visitor, figuring out lodging at Whistler can be rather intimidating. One of the easiest ways to book rooms, buy ski passes, and plan activities is to visit the official Whistler Blackcomb Resort website at **www.whistlerblackcomb.com.** Most hotels and condo developments are represented at this one-stop shopping and information site.

Lodgings in Whistler are very high quality, and the price of rooms is equally high. The hotels listed below offer superlative rooms with lots of extras. However, the smaller inns offer great value and excellent accommodations, often with services and options that can, for many travelers, make them a more attractive option than the larger hotels. At these smaller, owner-operated inns, rates typically include features that are sometimes available for an extra fee at hotels. These inns are located outside of the central villages and usually offer a quieter lodging experience than the hotels in Whistler Village.

In addition to the hotels and inns below, Whistler is absolutely loaded with condo developments. To reserve one of these units—which can range from studios, to one- to five-bedroom fully furnished condos, to town houses and chalets, with prices from around C$175 to C$1,500 a night—many travelers find the easiest thing to do is simply decide on a price point and call one of the central booking agencies, such as **Whistler Superior Properties** (© **877/535-8282** or 604/932-3510; www.whistler superior.com) or **WhistlerCanada.net** (© **888/905-0434** or 604/905-0434; www.whistlercanada.net); **Whistler Accommodations** (© **866/905-4607** or 604/905-4607; www.whistleraccommodation.com) focuses on condos and hotels in the Upper Village.

Reservations for peak winter periods should be made by September at the latest.

IN THE VILLAGE & UPPER VILLAGE

Fairmont Chateau Whistler ★★★ Perennially rated the top ski resort hotel in North America by reader surveys in such magazines as *Condé Nast Traveler,* the Fairmont re-creates the look of a feudal castle at the foot of Blackcomb Mountain, but with every modern comfort added. Massive wooden beams support an airy peaked roof in the lobby, while in the hillside Mallard Bar, double-sided stone fireplaces cast a cozy glow on the couches and leather armchairs. Rooms and suites are very comfortable and beautifully furnished, and feature duvets, bathrobes, and soaker tubs (some offer stunning views of the slopes). Fairmont Gold service guests can have breakfast or relax après-ski in a private lounge with the feel of a Victorian library. All guests can use the heated outdoor pool and Jacuzzis, which look out over the base of the ski hill. The hotel's **Vida Wellness Spa ★** is among the best in town. The Fairmont pays attention to the needs of skiers, with a recreation concierge, ski storage next to the slopes, and ski valets to help make pre- and après-ski as expeditious and pleasant as possible.

4599 Chateau Blvd., Whistler, BC V0N 1B4. © **800/606-8244** or 604/938-8000. Fax 604/938-2058. www.fairmont.com/whistler. 550 units. Winter C$399–C$669 double, C$499–C$1,809 suite; summer C$119–C$379 double, C$275–C$1,409 suite. AE, MC, V. Underground valet parking C$25. Pets are welcome. **Amenities:** 4 restaurants; bar; babysitting; children's programs; concierge; concierge-level rooms; health club; 18-hole golf course; Jacuzzi; heated indoor/outdoor pool; room service; outstanding spa facility; 2 tennis courts; secure ski and bike storage; rooms for those w/limited mobility. *In room:* A/C, TV w/movie channels, hair dryer, minibar, Wi-Fi.

Four Seasons Resort Whistler ★★★ The Four Seasons Resort Whistler is a très chic, très elegant monument to refinement. Easily the most refined and elegant of Whistler's hotels, the Four Seasons is monumental in scale—the expansive stone, glass, and timber lobby is like a modern-day hunting lodge—while maintaining the atmosphere of a very intimate and sophisticated boutique hotel—a rare achievement. The Four Season's urbane good taste extends to the large guest rooms, decorated in wood and cool earth tones and beautifully furnished with rich fabrics and leather furniture. All rooms have a balcony, fireplace, and very large, amenity-filled bathrooms with soaker tubs. The standard room is a very spacious 46 sq. m (495 sq. ft.), and superior and deluxe level rooms are truly large. A separate wing of the hotel contains private residences—139 to 344-sq.-m (1,496–3,703-sq.-ft.) apartments with two to four bedrooms. With 15 treatment rooms, the exquisite **Spa at the Four Seasons Resort ★** is Whistler's largest, and a heated outdoor pool and three whirlpool baths fill half the hotel courtyard.

4591 Blackcomb Way, Whistler, BC V0N 1B4. ✆ **888/935-2460** or 604/935-3400. Fax 604/935-3455. www.fourseasons.com/whistler. 273 units. Mid-June to mid-Sept and Nov 27–Dec 19 C$305–C$670 double; mid-Sept to late Nov and mid-Apr to mid-June C$265–C$435 double; Dec 20–Jan 1 C$1,025–C$1,775 double; Jan 2 to mid-April C$405–C$920 double. AE, DC, DISC, MC, V. Underground valet parking C$28, self-park C$23. **Amenities:** Restaurant; lounge; concierge; health club; Jacuzzis; heated outdoor pool; room service; superlative spa; ski and bike storage; rooms for those w/limited mobility. *In room:* A/C, TV/DVD, CD player, hair dryer, minibar, Wi-Fi.

Pan Pacific Whistler Mountainside ★★ The Pan Pacific's slightly older and more family-oriented Mountainside all-suite property has a lot going for it, with top-notch furnishings, kitchenettes, and loads of amenities. Comfortable as the rooms are, however, the true advantage to the Pan Pacific Mountainside is its location at the foot of the Whistler Mountain gondola. Not only can you ski right to your hotel, but thanks to a large heated outdoor pool and Jacuzzi deck, you can sit at the end of the day sipping a glass of wine, gazing up at the snowy slopes, and marvel at the ameliorative effects of warm water on aching muscles. With sofa beds and fold-down Murphy beds, the studio suites are fine for couples, while the one- and two-bedroom suites allow more space for larger groups or families with kids.

4320 Sundial Crescent, Whistler, BC V0N 1B4. ✆ **888/905-9995** or 604/905-2999. Fax 604/905-2995. www.panpacific.com. 121 units. Jan 1 to late Apr C$199–C$849 studio, C$299–C$1,049 1-bedroom, C$599–C$1,499 2-bedroom; late Apr to late Nov C$129–C$329 studio, C$169–C$429 1-bedroom, C$229–C$529 2-bedroom; late Nov–Dec 31 C$199–C$849 studio, C$299–C$1,049 1-bedroom, C$399–C$1,499 2-bedroom. AE, DC, MC, V. Underground valet parking C$20. **Amenities:** Restaurant; pub; concierge; fitness center w/whirlpool and steam room; Jacuzzi; heated outdoor pool; room service; ski, bike, and golf bag storage; rooms for those w/limited mobility. *In room:* A/C, TV w/pay movie channels, fridge, hair dryer, Wi-Fi, stove w/oven, microwave, dishwasher, pay Nintendo.

The Pan Pacific Whistler Village Centre ★★★ The Pan Pacific chain has two handsome properties in Whistler, both just steps off Blackcomb Way in Whistler Village. The all-suite Pan Pacific Whistler Village Centre is an imposing structure with curious gables and a dormered roofline, underscoring the fact that this is anything but an anonymous corporate hotel. All in all, suites in the Village Centre are more like apartments than hotel rooms; it's also more couples-oriented than its family-friendly sister property. All one-, two-, and three-bedroom suites have a balcony, fireplace, flatscreen TV, full kitchen with granite counters, soaker tub, bathrobes, handsome furniture, and floor-to-ceiling windows to let in the amazing mountain vistas. The penthouse suites are truly magnificent, with cathedral ceilings, massive stone fireplaces, multiple balconies, and loads of room—the Blackcomb Suite has 156 sq. m (1,679 sq. ft.)! The Village Centre has a fitness center with sauna, massage therapy and spa treatment rooms, a lap pool, and two hot tubs. Rates include a full breakfast buffet and afternoon/evening hors d'oeuvres in the Pacific Lounge, a guest-only facility with an outdoor patio.

4299 Blackcomb Way, Whistler, BC V0N 1B4. ✆ **888/966-5575** or 604/966-5500. Fax 604/966-5501. www.panpacific.com. 83 units. Jan 1 to late Apr C$249–C$999 1-bedroom, C$499–C$1,399 2-bedroom, C$1,299–C$2,799 3-bedroom penthouse; late Apr to late Nov C$179–C$429 1-bedroom, C$249–C$529 2-bedroom, C$699–C$999 3-bedroom penthouse; late Nov–Dec 31 C$249–C$999 1-bedroom, C$349–C$1,399 2-bedroom, C$799–C$2,799 3-bedroom penthouse. AE, DC, DISC, MC, V. Underground valet parking C$20. **Amenities:** Restaurant; pub; concierge; fitness center; Jacuzzi; heated outdoor pool; room service; sauna; ski, bike, and golf bag storage; rooms for those w/limited mobility. *In room:* A/C, TV w/pay movie channels and Web TV, fridge, hair dryer, stovetop, microwave convection oven, dishwasher, Wi-Fi, pay Nintendo.

The Westin Resort and Spa Whistler ★★★ Talk about location: The all-suite Westin Resort snapped up the best piece of property in town and squeezed itself onto the mountainside at the bottom of the Whistler gondola. It's central to all the restaurants and nightspots in Whistler Village, yet slightly apart from the crowds. The two-towered hotel is built in the style of an enormous mountain chalet with cedar timbers and lots of local granite and basalt finishings. All 419 suites received an update in 2007 and offer full kitchens, soaker tubs, slate-lined showers, and an elegant and restful decor; there are even "workout" suites with an array of fitness equipment. The beds, Westin's signature Heavenly Beds, are indeed divine. If you're here to ski, expect little luxuries including a ski valet service and (no more cold toes!) a boot-warming service. That is certainly one of the reasons why the Westin has already grabbed several top awards; the hotel's **Avello Spa ★** is extremely well-appointed for après-ski pampering and the indoor/outdoor pool, hot tubs, steam baths, and sauna will warm up ski-weary limbs.

4090 Whistler Way, Whistler, BC V0N 1B4. ✆ **888/634-5577** or 604/905-5000. Fax 604/905-5589. www.westinwhistler.com. 419 units. Mid-Apr to late Nov C$179–C$489 junior suite, C$269–C$599 1-bedroom suite, C$429–C$1,049 2-bedroom suite; late Nov to mid-Apr C$209–C$589 junior suite, C$319–C$689 1-bedroom suite, C$539–C$1,519 2-bedroom suite. Children 17 and under stay free in parent's room. AE, DC, DISC, MC, V. Parking C$32. **Amenities:** Restaurant; bar; babysitting; bike rental; children's program; concierge; health club; indoor and outdoor Jacuzzi; indoor and outdoor pool; room service; sauna; spa. *In room:* A/C, TV w/pay movies, hair dryer, fully appointed kitchen, Wi-Fi.

OUTSIDE THE VILLAGE

Alpine Chalet Whistler ★★ This cozy alpine-style lodge sits in a quiet location near Alta Lake and the Whistler Golf Club. The entire inn is designed to provide luxurious lodgings, privacy, and a welcoming sense of camaraderie in the comfortable, fireplace-dominated guest lounge. There are three room types: alpine rooms, comfortable lodge rooms that will suit the needs of most skiers and travelers; chalets, which are larger and feature fireplaces and other extras; and the master suite, the largest and most opulent room, with a fireplace, cathedral ceiling, Jacuzzi, and large private balcony. All rooms have balconies or terraces, fine linens, bathrobes, and other upscale amenities you'd expect at a classy hotel. Evening meals are available by reservation.

3012 Alpine Crescent, Whistler, BC V0N 1B3. ✆ **800/736-9967** or 604/935-3003. Fax 604/935-3008. www.whistlerinn.com. 8 units. Early Jan to Apr C$189–C$269; mid-Dec to early Jan C$259–C$399; May to mid-Dec C$149–C$229. Rates include full breakfast. MC, V. Free parking. **Amenities:** Guest lounge; 8-person hot tub; steam room; heated ski lockers. *In room:* A/C, TV/DVD, hair dryer, Wi-Fi, heated floor.

Cedar Springs Bed & Breakfast Lodge ★ ☺ The no-children policy at many Whistler inns can be a real challenge for families, but the Cedar Springs provides an excellent solution. Guests at this large and charming lodge a mile north of Whistler Village have a choice of king-, queen-, or twin-size beds in comfortably modern yet understated surroundings. Two family suites, with two queen-size and two twin beds, are just the ticket for families. What's more, the lodge is just next door to a park, biking paths, and a sports center with swimming pool. Cedar Springs also offers excellent accommodations for couples and solo travelers. The large honeymoon suite boasts a fireplace and balcony. Most rooms feature handmade pine furniture; all have bathrooms with heated tile floors. The guest sitting room has a TV, VCR, fireplace, and video library. A sauna and hot tub on the sun deck overlooking the gardens add to the pampering after a day of play. A gourmet breakfast is served by the fireplace in the dining room, and guests are welcome to enjoy afternoon tea. Lodge owners Jackie and Jeorn offer lots of extras such as complimentary shuttle service to ski lifts, heated ski gear storage, bike rentals, and free Wi-Fi.

8106 Cedar Springs Rd., Whistler, BC V0N 1B8. ✆ **800/727-7547** or 604/938-8007. Fax 604/938-8023. www.whistlerinns.com/cedarsprings. 8 units. High winter season C$175–C$285 double; spring, summer, fall C$95–C$169 double. Rates include full breakfast and afternoon tea. MC, V. Free parking; 2-minute walk to public transport. Take Hwy. 99 north toward Pemberton 4km (2½ miles) past Whistler Village. Turn left onto Alpine Way, go a block to Rainbow Dr., and turn left; go a block to Camino St. and turn left. The lodge is a block down at the corner of Camino and Cedar Springs Rd. **Amenities:** Jacuzzi; sauna; guest lounge w/TV/VCR/DVD; secure ski and heated gear storage. *In room:* Hair dryer, no phone, Wi-Fi.

Durlacher Hof Pension Inn ★★ 🎁 This lovely inn boasts both an authentic Austrian feel and a sociable atmosphere. Both are the result of the exceptional care and service shown by owners Peter and Erika Durlacher. Guests are greeted by name at the entryway, provided with slippers, and then given a tour of the three-story chalet-style property. The rooms vary in size from comfortable to quite spacious and come with goose-down duvets and fine linens, private bathrooms (some with jetted tubs) with deluxe toiletries, and incredible mountain views from private balconies. Better still is the downstairs lounge, with a welcoming fireplace and complimentary après-ski appetizers baked by Erika; likewise, breakfasts are substantial and lovingly prepared. Peter and Erica are fonts of knowledge about local restaurants and recreation; they will happily arrange tours and outings.

7055 Nesters Rd., Whistler, BC V0N 1B7. ✆ **877/932-1924** or 604/932-1924. Fax 604/938-1980. www.durlacherhof.com. 8 units. Mid-Dec to Mar 31 C$139–C$499 double; mid-June to Sept 30 C$109–C$299 double. Discounted rates for spring and fall. Extra person C$35. Rates include full breakfast and afternoon tea. MC, V. Free parking. Take Hwy. 99 about 1km (⅔ mile) north of Whistler Village to Nester's Rd. Turn left and the inn is immediately on the right. **Amenities:** Jacuzzi; sauna; 1 room for those w/limited mobility. *In room:* TV, hair dryer, no phone, Wi-Fi.

Hostelling International Whistler 🏷 One of the few inexpensive spots in Whistler, the hostel also happens to have one of the nicest locations: on the south edge of Alta Lake, with a dining room, deck, and lawn looking over the lake to Whistler Mountain. Inside, the hostel is extremely pleasant; there's a lounge with a wood-burning stove, a common kitchen, a piano, Ping-Pong tables, and a sauna, as well as a drying room for ski gear and storage for bikes, boards, and skis. In the summer, guests have use of a barbecue, canoe, and rowboat. As with all hostels, most rooms and facilities are shared. Beds at the hostel book up very early. Book by September at the latest for the winter ski season.

5678 Alta Lake Rd., Whistler, BC V0N 1B5. © **604/932-5492.** Fax 604/932-4687. www.hihostels.ca. 25 beds in 1- to 6-bed dorms. C$30–C$33 IYHA members; C$33–C$36 nonmembers. Family and group memberships available. MC, V. Free parking. **Amenities:** Bike rental; sauna; canoe and kayak rental; fireplace; Wi-Fi.

Inn at Clifftop Lane ★★ This large home, built as a B&B, sits above the Whistler Village on a quiet side street just south of Whistler Creekside, and offers large and beautifully furnished rooms. The inn strikes that perfect balance between the hominess of a B&B and the formality of a small boutique hotel. Each of the guest rooms is spacious, with an easy chair and living area, plus a bathroom with a jetted tub and bathrobes. The home is filled with books and decorated with antiques and folk art collected during the owners' travels, lending a cheerful élan to the breakfast rooms and guest lounge. Outdoors, steps lead through the forest to a hot tub and a private deck. This is a great choice for travelers seeking understated comfort and elegance with friendly, professional service.

2828 Clifftop Lane, Whistler, BC V0N 1B2. © **888/281-2929** or 604/938-1229. Fax 604/938-9880. www.innatclifftop.com. 5 units. Summer from C$119–C$139 double; winter from C$145–C$259. Ski packages available. Rates include full breakfast. AE, MC, V. Free parking. **Amenities:** Lounge; hot tub; library. *In room:* TV, hair dryer, Wi-Fi, robes, jetted tub.

Where to Dine

Whistler overflows with dining choices: Whistler Village alone has over 90 restaurants. You'll have no trouble finding high-quality, reasonably priced food. **Ingrid's Village Café,** just off the Village Square at 4305 Skiers Approach (© **604/932-7000**), is a locals' favorite for simple, homelike food, for both quality and price. A large bowl of Ingrid's clam chowder costs just C$5, while a veggie burger comes in at C$6.50. It's open daily 8am to 6pm.

The **Citta Bistro,** in the Whistler Village Square (© **604/932-4177**), has a great patio and serves thin-crust pizzas such as the Californian Herb, topped with spiced chicken breast, sun-dried tomatoes, fresh pesto, and mozzarella, as well as gourmet burgers such as the Citta Extraordinaire, topped with bacon, cheddar, and garlic mushrooms. Main courses are C$7 to C$14; it's open daily 11am to 1am. The **Whistler Brewhouse,** 4355 Blackcomb Way (© **604/905-2739**), is a great spot for a microbrew ale, a plate of wood-fired pizza or rotisserie chicken (C$15–C$23), and a seat on the patio; open daily 11:30am to midnight, until 1am on weekends. **Sachi Sushi,** 4359 Main St. (© **604/935-5649**), is the best of Whistler's many sushi restaurants—the udon noodles and hot pots are excellent as well. Sushi rolls cost from C$8 to C$17; open Monday to Thursday 11am to 10pm, Friday and Saturday 11am to 11pm, and Sunday 11:30am to 9pm.

Araxi Restaurant & Bar ★★★ CONTEMPORARY CANADIAN Frequently awarded for its wine list, as well as voted best restaurant in Whistler, this is one of the resort's top places to dine. Outside, the heated patio seats 80 people, while inside, the artwork, antiques, and terra-cotta tiles provide a subtle Mediterranean ambience that serves as a theater for the presentation of extraordinary food. Diners have a choice of a la carte items or a four-course tasting menu, which changes monthly, for C$68. The kitchen makes the most of local ingredients such as house-smoked trout, Pemberton cheese and lamb, and Howe Sound oysters. Chef James Walt has a deft hand, producing dishes that are inventive yet tradition-based and full of flavor: Boudin blanc sausage is fashioned from squab and foie gras, and presented with Jerusalem artichoke puree; delicate lamb meat rilletts come with a single, perfect pumpkin ravioli. Don't hesitate to ask for a suggestion when contemplating the nearly encyclopedic wine list—the wine staff here is exceedingly friendly and knowledgeable.

4222 Village Sq. ✆ **604/932-4540.** www.araxi.com. Main courses C$29–C$45. AE, MC, V. Mid-May to Oct daily 11am–3pm and 5–11pm. Mid-Oct to Mid-May 5–11pm.

Bearfoot Bistro ★★★ PACIFIC NORTHWEST One of the very best in Whistler, Barefoot Bistro has created an enormous following for its regional, seasonal cuisine. The emphasis is on innovation, new flavors, and unusual preparations—in short, this is a cutting-edge restaurant for serious gastronomes. In the dining room, choose either three or five courses from the admirably broad menu, with selections such as lobster with Meyer lemon fava-bean risotto, popcorn-crusted lingcod with littleneck clam corn chowder, or braised pork belly with Dungeness crab grapefruit salad. There's nothing ordinary about the food, or the wine list, which has earned awards from *Wine Spectator* magazine. A number of specialty tasting menus are also available. Appetizers and more casual meals are available in the fireside room and the cozy Champagne Bar.

4121 Village Green. ✆ **604/932-3433.** www.bearfootbistro.com. Reservations required on weekends. 3-course menu C$39–C$98 (low–high season); 5-course menu C$98–C$148. AE, MC, V. Daily 5–10pm.

Mountain Club ★ CONTEMPORARY CANADIAN The dining room is chic, with feints toward woodsy decor, but the food at Mountain Club is at once casual and serious. Most of the menu is served small-plates style, and even the main courses are available in half portions, so this is a good destination if you want a light meal or wish to sample a number of dishes. For a hearty side dish, the truffled vegetables are a real pleasure; the Asian-style prawn dumplings are served in a delicate lemon-grass broth; beef tenderloin is served with tangy blue cheese bread pudding. A lot of care goes into the food, but the ambiance is anything but fussy, as the restaurant's ironic design provides a youthful, high-spirited vibe.

#40 4314 Main St. ✆ **604/932-6009.** www.themountainclub.ca. Main dishes C$15–C$28. MC, V. Mon–Sat 5pm–1am; Sun 5pm–midnight.

Rimrock Cafe and Oyster Bar ★★ SEAFOOD Upstairs in a long, narrow room with a high ceiling and a massive stone fireplace at one end, Rimrock is very much like a Viking mead hall of old. It's not the atmosphere, however, that causes people to hop in a cab and make the C$5 journey out from Whistler Village. What draws folks in is the food. The first order of business should be a plate of oysters. Chef Rolf Gunther serves them up half a dozen ways, from raw with champagne to cooked "in hell" (broiled with fresh chiles). For my money, though, the signature Rimrock oyster is still the best: broiled with béchamel sauce and smoked salmon. Other appetizers are lightly seared ahi tuna or Quebec foie gras with apple raspberry salad. Main dishes are focused on seafood and game. Look for lobster and scallops with toasted almond butter and crispy leeks or grilled Arctic caribou with porcini cream and orange cranberry relish. The accompanying wine list has a number of fine vintages from BC, California, New Zealand, and Australia.

2117 Whistler Rd. ✆ **877/932-5589** or 604/932-5565. www.rimrockwhistler.com. Main courses C$24–C$40. AE, MC, V. Daily 11:30am–11:30pm.

Whistler After Dark

For a town of just 10,000, Whistler has a more-than-respectable nightlife scene. You'll find concert listings in the ***Pique,*** a free local paper available at cafes and food stores. **Tommy Africa's,** 4216 Gateway Dr. (✆ **604/932-6090**), and the dark and cavernous **Maxx Fish,** in Whistler Village Square below the Amsterdam Cafe (✆ **604/932-1904**), cater to the 18- to 22-year-old crowd; you'll find lots of beat and not much light. The crowd at **Garfinkel's,** at the entrance to Village North (✆ **604/932-2323**), is similar, though the cutoff age can reach as high as 26 or 27. **Buffalo Bills,** across from the Whistler Gondola (✆ **604/932-6613**), and the **Longhorn,** 4284 Mountain Sq. (✆ **604/932-5999**), cater to the 30-something crowd. Bills has a pool table, a video ski machine, and a smallish dance floor. The Longhorn usually has live music or entertainment on the weekends, when it's jammed with partiers.

THE OKANAGAN VALLEY ★★

Just south of the High Country on Hwy. 97, the arid Okanagan Valley, with its long chain of crystal-blue lakes, is the ideal destination for freshwater-sports enthusiasts, golfers, skiers, and wine lovers. Ranches and small towns have flourished here for more than a century; the region's fruit orchards and vineyards will make you feel as if you've been transported to the Spanish countryside. Summer visitors get the pick of the crop—at insider prices—from the many fruit stands that line Hwy. 97. Be sure to stop for a pint of cherries, homemade jams, and other goodies.

An Okanagan-region chardonnay won gold medals in 1994 at international competitions held in London and Paris. In 2000, several other Okanagan vintages picked up quite a number of medals at international competitions. And more than 100 other wineries produce vintages that are following right on their heels. Despite these coveted honors, the valley has only recently begun to receive international publicity. Most visitors are Canadian, and the valley isn't yet a major tour-bus destination. Get here before they do.

Many retirees have chosen the Okanagan Valley as their home for its relatively mild winters and dry, desert-like summers. It's also a favorite destination for younger visitors, drawn by boating, water-skiing, sportfishing, and windsurfing on 128km-long (80-mile) Okanagan Lake. The town of Kelowna in the central valley is the hub of the province's winemaking industry and the area's largest city.

Essentials

VISITOR INFORMATION Contact the **Thompson Okanagan Tourism Association,** 2280 Leckie Rd., Kelowna (✆ **250/860-5999;** www.totabc.com), which is open daily from 8am to 4:30pm. For information about the Okanagan wineries, contact **Penticton & Wine Country Chamber of Commerce,** 553 Railway St., Penticton (✆ **800/663-5052** or 250/493-4055; www.tourismpenticton.com). The friendly staff at its Wine Country Visitor Centre can help you with itineraries, restaurants, activities, and lodging. The center also has an excellent wine shop, filled with the best of BC wines and regional cheeses.

GETTING THERE BY PLANE **Air Canada Jazz** (✆ **888/247-2262;** www.aircanada.ca) and **WestJet** (✆ **888/937-8538;** www.westjet.com) offer frequent daily commuter flights from Calgary and Vancouver to Penticton and Kelowna. **Horizon Air** (✆ **800/252-7522;** www.alaskaair.com), a division of Alaska Air, provides service to and from Seattle and Kelowna.

BY CAR The 387km (240-mile) drive from Vancouver via the Trans-Canada Highway (Hwy. 1) and Hwy. 3 rambles through rich delta farmlands and the forested mountains of Manning Provincial Park and the Similkameen River region before descending into the Okanagan Valley's antelope-brush and sagebrush desert. For a more direct route to Kelowna, take the Trans-Canada Highway to the Coquihalla Toll Highway, which eliminates more than an hour's driving time. The 203km (126-mile) route runs from Hope through Merritt over the Coquihalla Pass into Kamloops.

BY BUS **Greyhound Canada** (✆ **800/661-8747;** www.greyhound.ca) runs daily buses from Vancouver to Penticton and Kelowna, with service continuing on to Banff and Calgary. The one-way fare to Penticton is C$67.

SPECIAL EVENTS Be the first to taste the valley's best chardonnay, pinot noir, merlot, and ice wines at the **Okanagan Wine Festival** (✆ **250/861-6654;** www.owfs.com), during the first and second weeks in October at wineries and restaurants throughout the Okanagan Valley.

Tasting the Fruits of the Vineyards

British Columbia has a long history of producing wines, ranging from fantastic to truly bad. In 1859, missionary Father Pandosy planted apple trees and vineyards and produced sacramental wines for the valley's mission. Other monastery wineries cropped up, but none worried about the quality of their bottlings. After all, the Canadian government had a reputation for subsidizing domestic industries, such as book publishing and cleric wineries, to promote entrepreneurial growth.

In the 1980s, the government threatened to pull its support of the industry unless it could produce an internationally competitive product. The vintners listened. Rootstock was imported from France and Germany, and European-trained master vintners were hired to oversee the development of the vines and the winemaking process. The climate and soil conditions turned out to be some of the best in the world for winemaking, and today, British Columbia wines are winning international gold medals. Competitively priced, in the range of C$10 to C$50, they represent some great bargains in well-balanced chardonnays, pinot blancs, and Gewürztraminers; full-bodied merlots, pinot noirs, and cabernets; and dessert ice wines that surpass the best muscat d'or.

Most Okanagan wineries are found between the U.S. border and Kelowna along Highway 97, 130km (81 miles) of stunning lake and mountain scenery. Just across the U.S. border from Washington State, **Osoyoss** is a small agricultural town on Osoyoos Lake that's making a rapid transition to wine-country-resort destination. Just to the north, the unfussy town of **Oliver** was once mostly known for apricots and peaches, but now it's generally considered the top terrior for growing grapes in the Okanagan Valley.

Many Canadian retirees have chosen **Penticton** as their home because it has relatively mild winters and dry, desert-like summers. It's also a favorite destination for younger visitors, drawn by boating, water-skiing, sportfishing, and windsurfing on 128km-long (80-mile) Lake Okanagan. On the east shores of the lake, just past Penticton, is the Naramata Bench, another highly favored location for vineyards.

The town of **Kelowna** in the central valley is the hub of the BC winemaking industry and the valley's largest city, with a population of 105,000.

The valley's more than 100 vineyards and wineries conduct free tours and wine tastings throughout the year. Here are a few favorite stops; each of the following wineries is open daily for tastings from spring through late fall. Call ahead for winter hours.

Just north of Osoyoos, **Burrowing Owl Winery ★**, halfway between Osoyoos and Oliver at 100 Burrowing Owl Pl. (✆ **877/498-0620** or 250/498-6202; www.bovwine.ca), makes exceptional wines; its award-winning merlot is one of BC's top wines. Their **Sonora Room** dining room is an equally excellent vineyard restaurant (closed in winter), and the 10-bedroom **Guest House at Burrowing Owl** (p. 758) is a top boutique lodging.

The town of **Okanagan Falls** is 20km (12 miles) south of Penticton along Highway 97. Adjacent to a wilderness area and bird sanctuary overlooking Vaseaux Lake, **Blue Mountain Vineyards & Cellars,** Allendale Road (✆ **250/497-8244;** www.bluemountainwinery.com), offers tours by appointment and operates a wine shop and tasting room. Blasted Church Vineyards ★, 378 Parsons Rd. (✆ **250/497-1125;** www.blastedchurch.com), has impossible-to-miss wine labels, and delicious and affordable wines. One of my favorites.

Near Oliver, **Tinhorn Creek Vineyards,** Road 7 (✆ **888/846-4676;** www.tinhorn.com), is one of the top Okanagan wineries. Specialties include Gewürztraminer, pinot gris, chardonnay, pinot noir, cabernet franc, merlot, and ice wine. Also near Oliver, the **Hester Creek Estate Winery,** Road 8 (✆ **250/498-4435;** www.hestercreek.com), has a wine boutique open daily 10am to 5pm, and tours of the winemaking area are available by appointment; especially nice here is the grapevine-shaded patio that invites picnickers.

Penticton is at the lower shores of Okanagan Lake, and rising immediately to the east is the Naramata Bench, home to some of the best Okanagan wineries. **La Frenz Winery,** 740 Naramata Rd. (✆ **250/492-6690;** www.lafrenzwinery.com), makes excellent small-lots bottlings of semillion, viognier, and merlot. **Poplar Grove Winery ★**, 1060 Poplar Gove Rd. (✆ **250/493-9463;** www.poplargrove.ca), produces a top-notch claret-style wine; try the cabernet franc if it's available—it's a wonderful wine that sells out every year.

Traveling north from Penticton on Highway 97 (the west side of the lake), you'll find other notable wineries. **Sumac Ridge Estate Winery,** 17403 Hwy. 97 (✆ **250/494-0451;** www.sumacridge.com), operates a wine shop and tasting room, plus the winery features a fine dining room, the **Cellar Door Bistro.**

Across Okanagan Lake from Kelown is **Westbank,** home to a number of well-established wineries. **Mission Hill Wines,** 1730 Mission Hill Rd. (✆ **250/768-7611;** www.missionhillwinery.com), was established in 1981 and has one of the most opulent wineries in BC. The cabernet sauvignon and syrah is excellent. The **Hainle Vineyards Estate Winery,** 5355 Trepanier Bench Rd. (✆ **250/767-2525;** www.hainle.com), was the first Okanagan winery to produce ice wine. The winery's **Amphora Bistro** is open daily for lunch and dinner. **Quails' Gate Estate ★**, 3303 Boucherie Rd., Kelowna (✆ **250/769-4451;** www.quailsgate.com), has a beautiful new tasting room overlooking vineyards and the lake. If ice wines (made with grapes that have been allowed to stay on the vine through several frosts, dehydrating them and intensifying the sugars) are your favorite dessert potable, you'll want to taste the vintages here. An excellent restaurant, **Old Vines Patio and Restaurant,** is open year-round for lunch and dinner.

In and around **Kelowna** are some of the biggest names in British Columbia's winemaking industry. **Calona Vineyards,** 1125 Richter St., Kelowna (✆ **250/762-3332;** www.calonavineyards.ca), conducts tours and tastings through western Canada's oldest (since 1932) and largest winery. South of Kelowna on the east side of the lake is **Cedar Creek Estate Winery,** 5445 Lakeshore Rd. (✆ **250/764-8866;**

www.cedarcreek.bc.ca), which produces notable pinot noir, chardonnay, and meritage blends. The Terrace Restaurant is open for lunch daily.

Sports & Outdoor Activities

BIKING The best Okanagan Valley off-road bike trail is the Kettle Valley Rail Trail. The tracks and ties have been removed, making way for some incredibly scenic biking. The most picturesque and challenging section of the route is from Naramata, north of Penticton along the east side of Okanagan Lake. The rails-to-trails route climbs up steep switchbacks to Chute Lake and then across 17 trestles (recently rebuilt after burning in a forest fire) as it traverses Myra Canyon. The entire mountain bike route from Naramata to Westbridge in the Kettle River Valley is 175km (109 miles) and can take from 3 to 5 days. For more information on cycling the route, contact the visitor center above, or contact the **Bike Barn,** 300 W. Westminster (✆ **250/492-4140**), which has bike rentals and lots of friendly advice. Also check the website at www.spiritof2010trail.ca.

BOATING & WATERSPORTS The Okanagan Valley's numerous local marinas offer full-service boat rentals. The **Marina on Okanagan Lake,** 291 Front St., Penticton (✆ **250/492-2628**), rents ski boats, Tigersharks (similar to jet skis or Sea-Doos), fishing boats, and tackle. In Kelowna, the marinas at the Grand Okanagan Resort and the Hotel Eldorado offer boat and watercraft rentals.

GOLF The Okanagan's warm climate is good for more than just growing grapes and apricots. The valley also boasts 50 golf courses; for complete information, contact www.totabc.com/trellis/golf. Here are two of the best. Les Furber's **Gallagher's Canyon Golf and Country Club,** 4320 McCulloch Rd., Kelowna (✆ **250/861-4240**), has an 18-hole course that features a hole overlooking the precipice of a gaping canyon and another that's perched on the brink of a ravine. It also has a 9-hole course, a midlength course, and a new double-ended learning center. Resting high on a wooded ridge between two lakes, Les Furber's **Predator Ridge,** 360 Commonage Rd., Vernon (✆ **250/542-3436**), has hosted the BC Open Championship in recent years. The par-5 4th hole can be played only over a huge midfairway lake; it's a challenge even for seasoned pros. The greens fees throughout the Okanagan Valley range from C$65 to C$175 and are a good value not only because of the beautiful locations but also for the quality of service you'll find at each club.

SKIING Cross-country and powder skiing are the Okanagan Valley's main winter attractions. Intermediate and expert downhill skiers frequent the **Apex Resort,** Green Mountain Road, Penticton (✆ **800/387-2739,** 250/492-2880, 250/292-8111, or 250/492-2929, ext. 2000, for snow report; www.apexresort.com), with 56 runs and 52km (32 miles) of cross-country ski trails. Day passes are C$60 adults, C$49 seniors and ages 13 to 18, and C$37 kids 12 and under. Facilities include an ice rink, snow golf, sleigh rides, casino nights, and racing competitions.

Where to Stay

The **BC Provincial Parks Service/Okanagan District** (✆ **250/494-6500;** www.discovercamping.ca) maintains a number of provincial campgrounds in this area. They're open April to October, and fees are C$10 to C$30 per night. There are 41 campsites at **Haynes Point Provincial Park** in Osoyoos, which has flush toilets, a boat launch, and visitor programs. This campground is popular with naturalists interested in hiking the "pocket desert." **Vaseaux Lake Provincial Park,** near Okanagan

Falls, offers 12 campsites and great wildlife-viewing opportunities; deer, antelope, and even a number of California bighorn sheep live in the surrounding hills. And **Okanagan Lake Provincial Park** has 168 campsites nestled amid 10,000 imported trees. Facilities include free hot showers, flush toilets, a sani-station, and a boat launch.

IN & AROUND OSOYOOS

Guest House at Burrowing Owl ★★ The top-echelon Burrowing Owl Winery offers 10 spectacular guest rooms in the midst of a vineyard. This newly constructed boutique inn has large and airy rooms, filled with light, fine art, native stone, and gracious good taste. Most rooms have king-size beds (two have two doubles), and all have balconies overlooking the grape vines and the nearby desert hills. Relax by the 25m (82-ft.) outdoor pool and patio, and definitely have dinner at the **Sonora Room ★**, the winery's excellent New Canadian restaurant.

100 Black Sage Rd. (R.R. 1, Comp 20, Site 52), Oliver, BC V0N 1T0. ✆ **877/498-0620** or 250/498-0620. www.bovwine.ca. 11 units. July 1 to mid-Oct C$325. 2-night minimum stay in high season. Lower off-season rates. AE, MC, V. Free parking. **Amenities:** Restaurant; guest lounge; hot tub; outdoor pool; wine shop and tasting bar. *In room:* A/C, flatscreen TV, fridge, Wi-Fi, fireplace.

IN PENTICTON

Naramata Heritage Inn & Spa ★★ Built in 1908, the Naramata Inn served as a hotel, private residence, and girls' school before undergoing extensive and loving renovation as a classic wine-country inn. This inn is a half-hour northwest of Penticton on the quiet side of Lake Okanagan in the tiny community of Naramata. It offers very charming rooms (note that some are authentically small), restored to glow with period finery, but modern luxury—the linens are top-notch and the bathroom's heated tile floors are a nice touch on a cool morning. In addition to en suite bathrooms with showers, rooms also have a claw-foot tub in the bedroom for soaking and relaxing. The inn also offers a spa for upscale pampering, plus the best dining in the area. There are few places in the otherwise utilitarian Okanagan as unique as this.

3625 First St., Naramata, BC V0H 1N0 (19km/12 miles north of Penticton on the east side of Okanagan Lake). ✆ 866/617-1188 or 250/496-6808. www.naramatainn.com. 12 units. High season C$182–C$510 double. Rates include continental breakfast. Lower off-season rates. AE, MC, V. Amenities: Restaurant (see "Where to Dine," below); wine bar; limited room service; spa; Wi-Fi. In room: A/C, hair dryer.

Penticton Lakeside Resort Convention Centre & Casino Set on the water's edge, the Penticton Lakeside Resort has its own stretch of sandy Lake Okanagan beachfront, where guests can sunbathe or stroll along the adjacent pier. The deluxe suites feature Jacuzzis, and the lakeside rooms are highly recommended for their view. All rooms and suites are smartly furnished with quality furniture; all rooms have balconies (some suites have two-person Jacuzzi tubs). The menus at the Hooded Merganser Restaurant and the Barking Parrot Bar & Patio feature locally grown ingredients. Other facilities include an extensive pool and health club facility, and a casino.

21 W. Lakeshore Dr., Penticton, BC V2A 7M5. ✆ **800/663-9400** or 250/493-8221. Fax 250/493-0607. www.rpbhotels.com. 204 units. C$226–C$273 double. Lower off-season rates. AE, DC, DISC, MC, V. Free parking. When you arrive in town, follow the signs to Main St. Lakeshore Dr. is at the north end of Main St. Pets accepted with C$20 fee. **Amenities:** Restaurant; lounge; babysitting; children's center; concierge; health club; Jacuzzi; indoor pool; room service; sauna; tennis courts; watersports equipment rental; volleyball court. *In room:* A/C, TV/VCR w/pay movies, hair dryer, Wi-Fi.

IN KELOWNA

Delta Grand Okanagan Lakefront Resort & Conference Centre ★★★ ☺ This elegant lakeshore resort sits on 10 hectares (25 acres) of beach and parkland, but it's an easy walk to downtown restaurants and the arts district. The recently updated rooms are spacious and regally outfitted with opulent furniture and upholstery, with knockout views from every window. Suites offer Jacuzzi tubs and separate showers, and deluxe condos offer full kitchens—good for families. Grand Club rooms occupy the top two floors of the resort, and offer secured access and a private lounge (with complimentary breakfast). Two-bedroom units come with full kitchen, fireplace, three TVs, and washer and dryer. Even more fabulous are the Royal Private Villas, sumptuous guest units in their own building that are essentially luxury apartments, with access to a private infinity pool. This is an ideal location for visitors who want to feel pampered in sophisticated surroundings while maintaining easy access to the waterfront. The restaurant and lounge overlook the resort's private marina, where guests can moor their small boats. Motorized swans and boats sized for kids offer fun for children in a protected waterway. The state-of-the-art fitness room and spa offers a variety of wellness and aesthetic treatments.

1310 Water St., Kelowna, BC V1Y 9P3. © **800/465-4651** or 250/763-4500. Fax 250/763-4565. www.deltahotels.com. 390 units. High season C$239–C$384 double; C$359–C$1,639 suites, condos, or luxury villas. Extra person C$15. Off-season discounts available. AE, DC, MC, V. **Amenities:** 3 restaurants; pub; lounge; concierge; health club w/spa; indoor and outdoor pool; room service; watersports equipment rentals; casino. *In room:* A/C, TV, hair dryer, minibar (on request), Wi-Fi.

Hotel Eldorado ★★ This is one of the most charming places to stay in Kelowna if you like historic inns. With a history dating back to 1926, the waterfront Eldorado has been fully restored and is now decorated with a unique mix of antiques; a wing with 30 new guest rooms and six luxury suites was added in 2005. All rooms are individually decorated, and there's a wide mix of floor plans and layouts, some with CD players and fridges. The third-floor guest rooms with views of the lake are the largest and quietest. Some rooms also feature lakeside balconies. On the premises are a boardwalk cafe, lounge, spa, and dining room. The staff can arrange boat moorage, boat rentals, and water-skiing lessons.

500 Cook Rd. (at Lakeshore Rd.), Kelowna, BC V1W 3G9. © **866/608-7500** or 250/763-7500. Fax 250/861-4779. www.eldoradokelowna.com. 55 units. C$179–C$449 double. Lower off-season rates available. AE, DC, MC, V. From downtown, follow Pandosy Rd. south 1.5km (1 mile). Turn right on Cook Rd. **Amenities:** Fine-dining restaurant; bar; boardwalk cafe; fitness center; Jacuzzi; indoor pool; spa services; steam room; marina. *In room:* A/C, TV, hair dryer, Wi-Fi.

Where to Dine

A number of vineyards in the Okanagan Valley now have restaurants; in fact, in good weather, these winery dining rooms are extremely charming places to eat, as most dining is alfresco (there are no bad views in the valley) and there's an explosion of local boutique and organic market produce available to young chefs. Of the wineries noted above, Sumac Ridge's **Cellar Door Bistro** (© **250/494-0451**) is open daily year-round for lunch and dinner; Quails' Gate's **Old Vines Patio and Restaurant** (© **800/420-9463** or 250/769-4451) is open year-round for lunch and dinner; Hainle's **Amphora Bistro** (© **250/767-2525**) is open Tuesday through Friday for lunch, and nightly for dinner; and Burrowing Owl's very impressive **Sonora Room** (© **877/498-0620** or 250/498-0620) is open daily for lunch, and Wednesday through Sunday for dinner (closed in winter).

IN & AROUND PENTICTON

Naramata Inn ★ PACIFIC NORTHWEST Built in 1908, the Naramata Inn is resplendent in early-20th-century character. The Cobblestone Wine Bar serves some of the most sophisticated food in the Okanagan Valley, and with a very impressive wine list. Using only the freshest ingredients—many from its own garden—the Cobblestone offers a selection of tasting menus that focus on regional ingredients; wine pairings are available for each of the menus. Expect such refined dishes as seared deep sea scallop and kurobuta pork belly confit with parsnip ravioli, and double smoked bacon-wrapped quail breast with matsutake mushrooms. At lunch, expect soup, salads, and delicious hearth breads.

3625 First St., Naramata (19km/12 miles north of Penticton on the east side of Okanagan Lake). ✆ **250/496-5001.** www.naramatainn.com. Reservations required. 5-course menu C$70. MC, V. Apr–Oct daily 11:30am–10pm. Call for winter hours.

IN KELOWNA

Bouchons Bistro ★ FRENCH This Gallic transplant offers classic French bistro fare just a few blocks from the Okanagan lakefront. The dining room, with ocher walls, stained-glass panels, and handwritten menus, actually feels Parisian. The menu doesn't stray far from classic French cuisine, though dishes are prepared with the freshest and best of local products—the level of cooking at Bouchons will make you appreciate French cuisine once again. Cassoulet is a house specialty, and you can't go wrong with duck confit glazed with honey and spices. A recent game-meat-focused menu offered wonderful wild fowl consommé with foie gras wontons. There's also a five-course table d'hôte for C$39. The wine list is half French, half Okanagan vintages. In summer, there's alfresco dining in the garden-like patio.

1180 Sunset Dr. ✆ **250/763-6595.** www.bouchonsbistro.com. Reservations suggested. Main courses C$20–C$36. MC, V. Daily 5:30–10pm.

RauDZ Regional Table ★★ CONTEMPORARY CANADIAN This is the hottest of dining spots in Kelowna, and the second solo venture (after multi-starred Fresco, in this same space) of chef/owner Rod Butters, who has worked at some of western Canada's top restaurants. The cooking focuses on fresh, relatively unfussy regional cuisine sourced from local farmers, ranchers, fishers, and food artisans. Start with a salmon "BLT" with crispy pancetta and fig-anise toasts and move on to duck meatloaf served with garlic-oil-roasted beets and turnips, or oat-crusted arctic char, with maple butter and potato, spinach, and bacon sauté. Service is top-notch; the wine list celebrates the vintages of the Okanagan Valley.

1560 Water St. ✆ **250/868-8805.** www.raudz.com. Reservations recommended. Main courses C$14–C$30. Daily 5–10pm.

THE YUKON, NORTHWEST TERRITORIES & NUNAVUT

17

by Kirsten Murphy

The Far North of Canada is one of North America's last great wilderness areas. The Yukon, the Northwest Territories, Nunavut, and northern British Columbia are home to the Inuit, Inuvialuit, and northern First Nations peoples like the Dene, as well as vast herds of wildlife and thousands of square miles of tundra and stunted subarctic forest. For centuries, names such as the Klondike, Hudson's Bay, and the Northwest Passage have conjured up powerful images of rugged determination in an untamed and harsh wilderness. For an area so little visited and so distant, the North has long played an integral role in the history and imagination of the Western world.

Yet the North has been changing rapidly, creating a whole pattern of paradoxes. The Arctic is a hotbed of mineral, oil, gas, and diamond exploration. Jobs and schools have brought aboriginal people from their hunting camps to town, where they live in modern, centrally heated homes. A minority of people still support their families with ancestral hunting and artisan skills, but most Northerners are engaged in the wage economy and pursue wild game and marine mammals—an activity that remains an integral part of their culture—on weekends and days off.

Inuit, Inuvialuit, Dene, and Métis—the latter being offspring of European and aboriginal couples—make up the majority of the North's population. All of Canada's indigenous peoples were originally nomadic, traveling enormous distances in pursuit of migrating animals. And though the Inuit no longer live in igloos, these snow houses are still built as temporary shelters. Survival is the key word for Aboriginal Canadians. They learned to survive in conditions that seem unimaginably harsh to more southerly peoples, relying on skills and technologies that become more wondrous the better you know them. Early European explorers quickly learned that, in order to stay alive, they had to adopt those skills and technologies as best they could. Those who refused to listen to the traditional knowledge of the elders rarely survived in the great Canadian North.

Norse merchants and explorers traveling from Greenland may have been the first non-aboriginal visitors to the Canadian North, as long as 800 years ago, but the first non-aboriginal known to have penetrated the region was Martin Frobisher. His written account of meeting the Inuit, over 400 years old, is the earliest on record. At about the same time, European whalers, hunting whales for their oil, were occasionally forced ashore by storms or shipwrecks, and depended on the Inuit and Inuvialuit knowledge of the land and sea, and their hospitality, for survival. This legendary hospitality, extended to any stranger who came to them, remains an outstanding characteristic of the Inuit. Western Europeans began to move into the Canadian Arctic in greater number during the "fur rush" of the late 18th century. In the wake of the fur hunters and traders came Roman Catholic and Anglican missionaries, who built churches and opened schools.

For most of its recorded history, the Far North was governed from afar, first by Great Britain, then by the Hudson's Bay Company, and from 1867, by the new Canadian government in Ottawa. At that time, the Northwest Territories included all of the Yukon, Saskatchewan, Alberta, and huge parts of other provinces. Then, in 1896, gold was discovered on Bonanza Creek in the Midwestern Yukon region of Klondike. Tens of thousands of people flocked to the Yukon in a matter of months, giving birth to **Dawson City** in northern Yukon**, Whitehorse** (later the capital) in south-central Yukon, and a dozen other tent communities, many of which eventually went bust along with the gold veins. The Yukon Gold Rush was the greatest in history; prospectors washed more than C$500,000 in gold out of the gravel banks along the Klondike before industrial mining moved in to reap in the millions. With its new wealth and population, the Yukon split off from the rest of the Northwest Territories in 1898.

The Northwest Territories didn't receive its own elected government until 1967, when the center of government was moved from Ottawa to the new territorial capital of **Yellowknife** and a representative assembly was elected. In 1999, the eastern section of the Northwest Territories, almost 2 million sq. km (about 772,000 sq. miles), became a separate and autonomous territory known as **Nunavut** (meaning "our land" in the Inuit language of Inuktitut), with its capital of **Iqaluit** (formerly Frobisher Bay) on Baffin Island. The rest of the pre-Nunavut Northwest Territories—1.2 million sq. km (463,322 sq. miles) of land that contains the drainage of the Mackenzie River, a sizeable portion of Arctic coast, the Great Slave and Great Bear lakes, and a few Arctic island territories—has retained the Northwest Territories name.

EXPLORING THE NORTH

The Arctic isn't like any other place. That observation may seem elementary, but even a well-prepared first-timer will experience many things here to startle—and perhaps offend—the senses.

No matter where you start from, the Arctic is a long way away. By far the easiest way to get there is by plane. Whitehorse, Yellowknife, and Iqaluit all have airports with daily service from major Canadian cities. Each of these capital cities is a center for a network of smaller airlines with regularly scheduled flights to yet smaller communities; here you'll also find charter services to take you to breathtaking glaciers, mountain ranges, old whaling camps, and majestic fjords.

The Yukon, the Northwest Territories & Nunavut

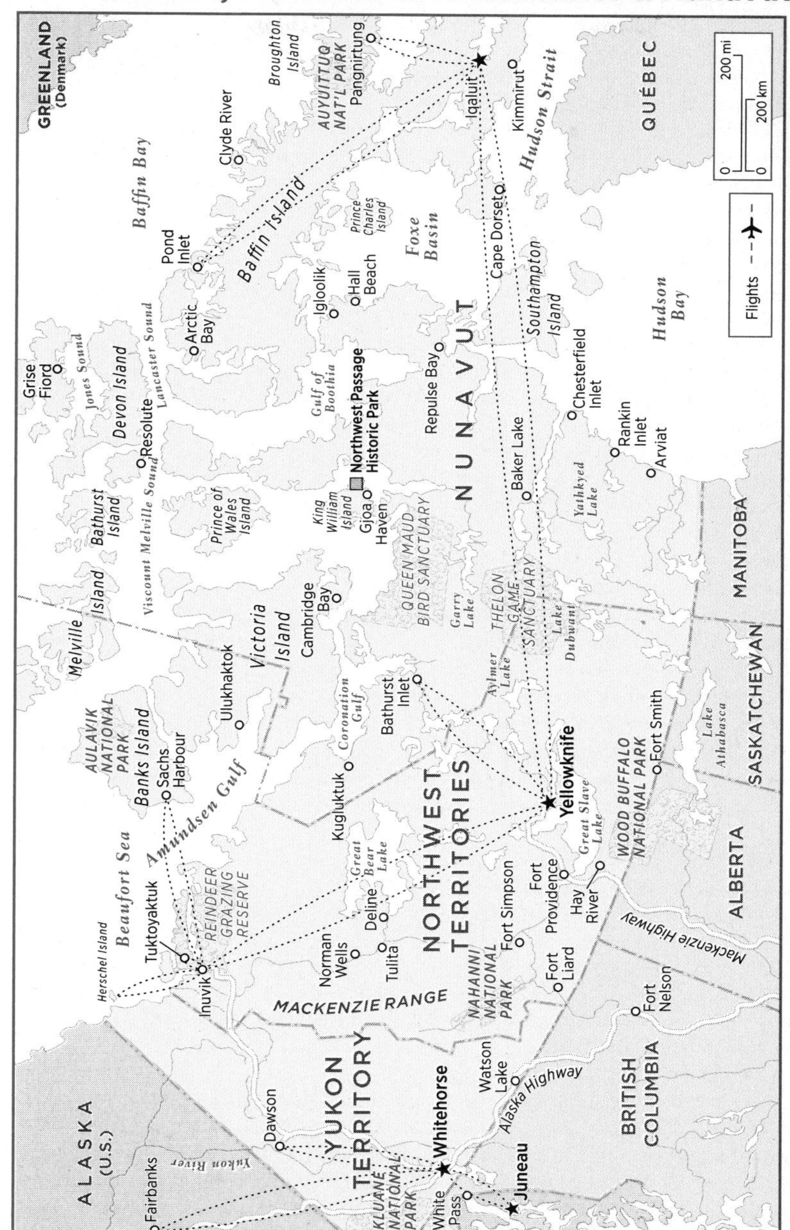

Tucked inland just east of Alaska, the Yukon is home to one of the most notable fortune hunts of all times: the Klondike Gold Rush. From 1898 to 1920, Dawson City was the destination of tens of thousands of prospectors—and other types of gold diggers—who were lured north by the dream of easy wealth. Today, Dawson City and territorial capital Whitehorse are still very lively and filled with history, though many of today's travelers are drawn as much to recreation on the Yukon's rivers, lakes, and mountains as to the trail of bonanza gold.

Until 1999, the Northwest Territories encompassed the entire northern tier of Canada (except the Yukon). Then Nunavut, comprising the eastern mainland and many of the arctic islands, split away (or was "created" if you live in Nunavut) to form a separate territory and a de facto homeland for the Inuit peoples. Centered on Baffin Island and the capital Iqaluit, Nunavut is an extremely far-flung territory made of up remote communities, expanses of tundra, and craggy, glacier-crowned islands.

The remaining Northwest Territories is sometimes referred to as the Western Arctic, although that term belongs to communities north of the Arctic Circle. Government, and gold and silver mining, were once the prime economic drivers. That distinction now goes to diamond mining. The capital of Yellowknife is a modern city, born of a gold rush and sustained by high-paying government and mining-industry jobs. Vast glacier-dug lakes provide lakefront for rustic to ritzy fishing lodges.

Visitor Information

For information, contact **Tourism Yukon** (P.O. Box 2703, Whitehorse; ✆ **800/661-0494;** www.travelyukon.com). Be sure to ask for a copy of the official vacation guide, *Yukon: Canada's True North.*

For the Northwest Territories, contact **Northwest Territories Tourism** (P.O. Box 610, Yellowknife; ✆ **800/661-0788,** 867/873-7200, or 867/873-5007; www.spectacularnwt.com). They no longer provide free maps of the territory, but they will send you *The Explorers' Guide,* with full listings of accommodations, services, and outfitters, which is updated every year.

Information on Nunavut is at **www.nunavuttourism.com**, where you can download a copy of the *Nunavut Travel Planner.* You can also call ✆ **866/686-2888** or e-mail info@nunavuttourism.com to make inquiries or request the travel planner.

Climate & Seasons

During summer, the farther north you travel, the more daylight you get. Yellowknife and Whitehorse bask under 20 hours of sunshine a day, followed by 4 hours of milky twilight bright enough to read a newspaper by. In Inuvik, Northwest Territories, the summer sun shines around the clock for 6 weeks, starting in June. Even further north, in Sachs Harbour and Uluhaktok, there is 24-hour daylight for close to 3 months. In midwinter, however, these communities experience 24-hour darkness for the same length of time.

The North is divided into two climatic zones: **subarctic** and **arctic,** but the division doesn't follow the Arctic Circle. And while there are permanent ice caps in the far-northern islands, summer in the rest of the land gets considerably hotter than you might think. The average high temperatures in July and August for many subarctic regions can be in the 70s and 80s (20s Celsius), and the mercury has been known to climb into the 90s (30s Celsius). However, even in summer, you should bring a warm sweater or ski jacket—and don't forget a pair of really sturdy shoes or boots.

In winter, weather conditions are truly arctic. Winter is ideal for northern-lights viewing, dog sledding, ice fishing, snowmobiling, and driving ice roads. The mercury may dip as low as –60°F (–51°C) for short periods. You'll need heavily insulated clothing and footwear to travel during this time of year. Spring is an increasingly popular time to visit, with clear sunny skies, highs around 20°F (–7°C), and spring festivals that incorporate traditions such as skinning and wood chopping in just about all of the 33 communities.

Driving the North

Setting out to drive the back roads of the Far North has a strange fascination for many people, most of whom own RVs. The most famous route through the North is the **Alaska Highway,** which was built during World War II to link the continental United States with Alaska via northern British Columbia and the Yukon. Today, the route is mostly paved and isn't the adventure it once was. Off-road enthusiasts may prefer the **Mackenzie Highway,** linking **Edmonton** to **Yellowknife.** But even this road is entirely paved nowadays, which leaves the **Dempster Highway** ★ (✆ **867/456-7623** for highway information; www.511yukon.ca), between **Dawson City** and **Inuvik,** as one of the few real back roads left.

Much of the North is served by good roads, though driving up here demands different preparations than you might be used to. It's a good idea to travel with a full 20L (5¼-gal.) gas can, even though along most routes gas stations appear frequently. However, there's no guarantee these stations will be open in the evenings, on Sunday, or at the precise moment you need to fill up. By all means, fill up every time you see a gas station in remote areas.

In summer, dust can be a serious nuisance, particularly on gravel roads. When it becomes a problem, close all windows and turn on your heater fan. This builds up air pressure inside your vehicle and helps to keep the dust out. Keep cameras in plastic bags for protection.

It's a good idea to attach a bug or gravel screen, and plastic headlight guards, to your vehicle. And it's absolutely essential that your windshield wipers are operative and your washer reservoir full. In the Yukon, the law requires that all automobiles drive with their headlights on; it's a good idea while traveling on any gravel road.

April and May are the spring slush months, when mud and water may render some road sections hazardous. The winter months, December through March, require a lot of special driving preparations but can provide a breathtaking experience.

Shopping for Northern Arts & Crafts

The handiwork of the Dene, Inuvialuit, and Inuit people is absolutely unique. There is moose-hair tufting, birch-bark baskets, quillwork, and beadwork, as well as soapstone carving and prints representing mythical and oral traditions. Some of it has utility value—you won't get finer, more painstakingly stitched cold-weather clothing anywhere in the world.

Most arts-and-crafts articles are handled through community cooperatives, thus avoiding the cut of the middleman. Official documentation will guarantee that a carving or a painting is genuine Aboriginal Canadian art. Don't hesitate to ask retailers where a particular piece comes from, what it's made of, and who made it. They'll be glad to tell you and frequently will point out where the artist lives and works. In the eastern Arctic, particularly, artists will often approach tourists in the streets, or in bars and restaurants, seeking to sell their goods. While these articles may lack the official paperwork, the price is often right; use your judgment when deciding to buy.

Before investing in aboriginal art, make sure you know what the **import restrictions** are in your home country. In many countries, it's illegal to bring in articles containing parts of marine mammals (this includes walrus or narwhal ivory, as well as whale bones or polar-bear fur). Sealskin products are commonly prohibited. Consult a Customs office to find out what restrictions are in place.

Food, Drink & Accommodations

Northerners traditionally lived off the land by hunting and fishing (many still do, to some degree), and Arctic specialties have now worked their way onto many fine-dining menus. **Char, buffalo,** and **musk ox** may be available on some menus and offer a different taste and texture for meat eaters. **Caribou** is delicious but hard to find because of hunting restrictions and federal food-inspection regulations. If you're lucky enough to find it on a menu, good caribou, sometimes dressed in sauces made from local berries (wild blueberries or Saskatoon berries) tastes like mild venison and is usually cheaper than beef or lamb in the North. Musk ox is rather stronger tasting, with a chewy texture, and is often served with wild mushrooms. **Arctic char** is a mild pink-fleshed fish, rather like salmon but coarser grained and less oily. You won't find the mainstays of the Inuit diet—seal and whale meat—on most restaurant menus, but in outlying communities, you won't have to look hard to find someone able to feed you some ***maktaaq*** (whale blubber and skin) or ***igunaq*** (aged, fermented meat, of walrus or seal). **Bannock,** a type of baking-powder biscuit, and so-called **Eskimo doughnuts,** a cousin of Indian fry bread, are popular snacks to feed tourists. You'll have to decide how appetizing you find the delicacy known as **Eskimo ice cream *(akutuq)*,** a mousse-like concoction made of whipped animal fats (caribou fat and seal oil, for instance) and berries. It is definitely an acquired taste.

Vegetarians aren't going to find much variety in the North. The traditional Arctic diet doesn't include much in the way of fruits or vegetables, and green stuff that's been air-freighted to the smaller communities can be rather sad-looking by the time it reaches the table. However, fresh produce in the capital cities is as good as produce from the south. Bring your own dietary supplements if you have a restricted diet.

No matter what you eat in the North, it's going to be expensive. In towns like Yellowknife or Inuvik, a normal dinner entree at a decent hotel restaurant will cost at least C$25; at outlying communities where hotels offer full board, a sandwich with fries will also often run C$25. Chances are excellent that, for the money, your food will be very pedestrian in quality. In most towns, the grocery-store chain The Northern shelters a few fast-food outlets, usually the only other dining option.

Alcohol flows freely in the Yukon and four communities in the Northwest Territories: Yellowknife, Inuvik, Fort Smith, and Hay River. The rest of the territory and all of Nunavut have liquor restrictions. In some locales, RCMP officers will check the baggage of incoming travelers at the airport and confiscate alcohol. In other communities, alcohol is legal but regulated to such a degree the casual visitor will find it impossible to get hold of a drink. In other communities, alcohol is available in hotel bars or restaurants, but not in stores (or even through room service). Alcohol is a major social problem in the North, so by all means, respect the local laws regulating alcohol consumption. Details can be found at www.fin.gov.nt.ca/liquor/restrictions.

Warning: Get Thee to an Outfitter

Outdoor enthusiasts who want to get out onto the land, the water, or the glacier will need to have the assistance of a licensed outfitter or a local licensed tour provider. There are no roads to speak of here, so you'll need help simply to get wherever you're going. This usually involves a boat or an airplane trip. Sports-equipment rental is all but unheard of, and it's very foolish to head out into the wilds (which start at the edge of the village) without the advice and guidance of someone who knows the terrain, weather, and other general conditions. For all these reasons—and for the introduction you'll get into the community—you should hire a licensed outfitter. You'll end up saving money, time, and frustration.

Accommodations are the most expensive day-to-day outlay in the North. Almost every community, no matter how small, will have a hotel, but prices are very high. You can save some money with B&Bs or home stays, which also have the advantage of introducing you to the locals.

The Great Outdoors

SEASONAL TRAVEL Hiking and naturalist trips are popular in late July, August, and early September, when there is maximum daylight and the warmest weather. The ice is off the ocean and lakes, allowing access by boat to otherwise-remote areas. Naturalist-led hikes out onto the tundra make great day trips.

While it may seem natural to plan a trip to the Arctic in summer, the Far North is a year-round destination. Late-winter dog-sledding trips out into the frozen wilderness are popular with adventurous souls. North of Inuvik, in May and June, dog-sled or snow-machine trips visit the edge of the ice floe, where wildlife viewing is superb. And in the dead of winter, there is the 24-hour darkness and the northern lights that lure people north.

MOSQUITOES, DEERFLIES & OTHER CRITTERS During summer especially, two of the most commonly heard sounds in the North are the rhythmic buzzing of winged biting insects and the cursing of their human victims. **Insect repellent** is a necessity, as is having a place you can get away from the mosquitoes for a while. Some hikers wear expedition hats or head nets to ward off the worst attacks. These work well. Mosquitoes can go through light fabric, which is why it's better to wear sturdy clothes, even on the hottest days. Wasps, hornets, and other stinging insects are common. If you're allergic, be ready with your serum.

CANOEING & DOG SLEDDING If you want to see the land as early explorers and Dene did, try exploring the North via these two traditional methods. The following outfitters usually offer recreation in more than one part of the North or different recreational pursuits, depending on the season.

CANOEING The early French-Canadian trappers, or ***voyageurs,*** explored the North—particularly the Yukon—by canoe, and outfitters now offer multiday expeditions down the region's wide powerful rivers. A good place to go for some advice on guided tours on Yukon and Northwest Territories rivers is **Paddle Canada**

(✆ **888/252-6292** or 613/269-2910; www.paddlingcanada.com). **Kanoe People** (✆ **867/668-4899;** www.kanoepeople.com) offers both custom and guided canoe trips on Yukon rivers and lakes. River trips pass historic mining ghost towns and First Nation villages. A guided trip on the Yukon goes for 8 days and costs C$1,596, and one on the Telsin lasts 10 days at C$1,649. Bring your own sleeping bag, pad, and small personal gear (including fishing tackle) of choice; everything else—including camping equipment, food, and transportation from Whitehorse—is included.

DOG SLEDDING An even more indigenous mode of transport in the North is travel by dog sled. While few people run dogs as their sole means of getting around any longer, the sport of dog sledding is hugely popular, and dog-sledding trips to otherwise-snowbound backcountry destinations make a great early-spring adventure. In the Northwest Territories, world champion musher Grant Beck of Yellowknife owns and operates **Beck's Kennels and Aurora Watching** (124 Curry Drive, Yellowknife; ✆ **867/873-5603;** www.beckskennels.com). Take a spin around Grace Lake by dog team for C$60. Or spend a couple of hours ice fishing on Great Slave Lake for C$90. Some packages range from C$170 to C$320 and include aurora watching on the tundra. In Inuvik, **Arctic Adventures** (25 Carn St.; ✆ **800/685-9417;** www.arcticchalet.com) offers tour packages that include accommodations, meals, and guided trips. They will also customize trips. Rates range from C$125 to C$500.

In the Yukon, **Uncommon Journeys** (✆ **867/668-2255;** www.uncommonyukon.com) offers 7- and 10-day guided backcountry dog-sledding trips out into the northern wilderness. Seven-day trips start at C$3,290. The company was listed as one of Canada's "top 25 coolest adventures" in the popular Canadian outdoors magazine *Explore*.

WILDLIFE It's easy to confuse **caribou** with European reindeer, as the two look very much alike and, in fact, are generally classified as the same species. But while reindeer are mostly domesticated animals, caribou are wild and still travel in huge migrating herds that stretch to the horizon, sometimes numbering 100,000 or more. Caribou form the major food and clothing supply for many Inuit, Inuvialuit, and Dene, whose lives cycle around the movements of the herds.

The mighty **musk ox** is indigenous to the Arctic. About 12,000 of them live on the northern islands. Immense and prehistoric-looking, the bulls weigh up to 590kg (1,301 lb.). They appear even larger because they carry a mountain of shaggy hair. Underneath the coarse outer coat, musk oxen have a silky-soft layer of under-wool, called ***qiviut*** in Inuit. One pound of qiviut can be spun into a 40-strand thread 40km (25 miles) long! As light as it is soft, a sweater made from the stuff will keep its wearer warm in subzero weather. And it doesn't shrink when wet. *Qiviut* is extremely expensive. Once spun, it can sell for as much as C$90 for 28g (1 oz.).

The monarch of the Arctic, the **polar bear** roams the coast and the shores of Hudson Bay and the High Arctic; you'll have to travel quite a way over mighty tough country to see one in its habitat. Weighing up to 658kg (1,450 lb.), they're the largest land predators in North America. **Grizzly bears** are found in the boreal forests and river basins. Both animals are very dangerous; if you encounter them, give them a wide berth. The North is full of other animals much easier to observe than the bears. In the wooded regions, you'll come across **wolves** and **wolverines** (harmless to humans, despite the legends about them), **mink, lynx, otter, ptarmigan,** and

beaver. The sleek and beautiful white or brown **arctic foxes** live in ice regions, as well as beneath the tree line and near settlements.

Mid-July to late August, **seals, walruses, narwhals,** and **bowhead** and **beluga whales** are in their breeding grounds off the coast of Baffin Island and in Hudson Bay. And in the endless skies above there are **eagles, hawks, owls, razor-billed auks,** and **ivory gulls.**

THE ALASKA HIGHWAY: ONTO THE LAST FRONTIER ★

Constructed as a military freight road during World War II to link Alaska to the Lower 48, the Alaska Highway—also known as the Alcan Highway, and Highway 97 in British Columbia—has become something of a pilgrimage route. The vast majority of people who make the trip are recent retirees, who take their newly purchased RVs and head up north; it's a rite of passage.

Strictly speaking, the Alaska Highway starts at the Mile 1 marker in **Dawson Creek,** on the eastern edge of British Columbia, and travels north and west for 2,242km (1,393 miles) to **Delta Junction,** in Alaska, passing through the Yukon along the way. The **Richardson Highway** (Alaska Rte. 4) covers the additional 158km (98 miles) from Delta Junction to **Fairbanks.** As recently as 25 years ago, much of the talk of the Alaska Highway had to do with conditions of the road itself, the freak rain and snowstorms, and the far-flung gas pumps. However, for the road's 50th anniversary in 1992, the final stretches of the road were paved.

While the days of tire-eating gravel roads and extra gas cans are largely past, there are several things to consider before setting out. First, this is a very *long* road. Popular wisdom states that if you drive straight out, it takes 3 days between Dawson Creek and Fairbanks. But much of the road is very winding, slow-moving RV traffic is heavy, and considerable portions are under reconstruction every summer. If you try to keep yourself to a 3-day schedule, you'll have a miserable time.

What to Expect

Summer is the only opportunity to repair the road, so construction crews really go to it; depend on lengthy delays and some very rugged detours. Visitor centers along the way get faxes of daily construction schedules and conditions, so stop for updates or follow the links to "Road Conditions" from the website **www.themilepost.com.** You can also call ✆ **867/456-7623** for 24-hour highway information.

While availability of gasoline isn't the problem that it once was, there are a couple of things to remember. Gas prices can be substantially higher than in, say, Edmonton or Calgary. Although there's gas at most of the communities that appear on the road map, most close up early in the evening. You'll find 24-hour gas stations and plenty of motel rooms in the towns of Dawson City, Fort St. John, Fort Nelson, Watson Lake, and Whitehorse.

Try to be patient when driving the Alaska Highway. In high season, the entire route, from Edmonton to Fairbanks, is one long caravan of RVs. Many people have their car in tow, a boat on the roof, and several bicycles chained to the spare tire. Thus encumbered, they lumber up the highway; loath (or unable) to pass one another. These convoys of RVs stretch on forever, the slowest of the party setting the pace for all.

Driving the Alaska Highway

This overview of the Alaska Highway is not meant to serve as a detailed guide for drivers. For that, you should purchase the annual *Alaska Milepost* (www.themilepost.com), which offers exhaustive, mile-by-mile coverage of the trip (and of other road trips into the Arctic of Alaska and Canada).

The route begins (or ends) at Dawson Creek, in British Columbia. Depending on where you start from, Dawson Creek is a long 590km (367-mile) drive from Edmonton or a comparatively short 406km (252 miles) from Prince George on Highway 97. Dawson Creek is a natural place to break up the journey, with ample tourist facilities. If you want to call ahead to ensure a room, try the **Ramada Limited Dawson Creek** (1748 Alaska Ave.; ✆ **800/663-2749** or 250/782-8595).

From Dawson Creek, the Alaska Highway soon crosses the Peace River and passes through **Fort St. John,** in the heart of British Columbia's far-north ranch country. The highway continues north, parallel to the Rockies. First the ranches thin, and then the forests thin. Moose are often seen from the road.

From Fort St. John to **Fort Nelson,** you'll find gas stations and cafes every 65 to 80km (40–50 miles), though lodging options are pretty dubious. Fort Nelson is thick with motels and gas stations; because it's hours from any other major service center, this is a good place to spend the night. Try the **Woodlands Inns and Suites** (3995 50th Ave.; ✆ **866/966-3466** or 250/774-6669; www.woodlandsinn.ca). At Fort Nelson, the Alaska Highway turns west and heads into the Rockies; from here, too, graveled **Liard Highway** (BC Hwy. 77; Northern Territories Hwy. 7) continues north to Fort Liard and Fort Simpson, the gateway to **Nahanni National Park,** a very worthy 284km (176-mile) side trip on an unpaved road.

A breathtaking, unspoiled wilderness of 4,766 sq. km (1,840 sq. miles) in the southwest corner of the Northwest Territory, Nahanni National Park is accessible only by foot, motorboat, canoe, or charter aircraft. Within the park, the South Nahanni River claws its path through the rugged Mackenzie Mountains, at one point, charging over incredible Virginia Falls, at 105m (344 ft.), twice as high as Niagara Falls and carrying more water. Below the falls, the river surges through one of the continent's deepest gorges, with canyon walls up to 1,333m (4,373 ft.) high. For most travelers, a flight-seeing day trip to the falls is adventure enough, though white-water raft trips from the base of the falls through the canyon (requiring 6 days or more) may be tempting to enthusiasts. **South Nahanni Airways** (✆ **867/695-2007;** southnahanniairways@canada.ca); **Simpson Air** (✆ **867/695-2505** or www.simpsonair.ca); and **Wolverine Air** (✆ **888/695-2263;** www.wolverineair.com), in Fort Simpson, offer charter drop-offs to various park destinations or sightseeing day trips to the falls; a 3-hour flying-only tour costs C$1,095 for up to five people, while a 5½-hour flying tour with a stopover at the falls costs C$1,295 for up to three people. For a full listing of licensed rafting outfitters and for details about the park, contact **Nahanni National Park** (✆ **867/695-3151;** http://www.pc.gc.ca/pn-np/nt/nahanni/index.aspx).

From Fort Nelson, the Alaska Highway through the Rockies is mostly narrow and winding; you can depend on finding a construction crew working along this stretch. The Rockies are relatively modest mountains in this area, not as rugged or scenic as they are farther south in Jasper National Park. Once over the Continental Divide, the Alaska Highway follows tributaries of the Liard River through **Stone Mountain** and **Muncho Lake** provincial parks. Rustic lodges are scattered along the road. The lovely log **Northern Rockies Lodge ★**, at Muncho Lake (✆ **800/663-5269** or 250/776-3481; www.northern-rockies-lodge.com), offers lodge rooms and log cabins for C$105 to C$125 and campsites for C$35.

At the town of **Liard River,** stop and stretch your legs or go for a soak at **Liard Hot Springs.** The provincial parks department maintains two nice soaking pools in the deep forest; the boardwalk out into the mineral-water marsh is pleasant, even if you don't have time for a dip.

As you get closer to **Watson Lake** in the Yukon, you'll notice that mom-and-pop gas stations along the road will advertise that they have cheaper gas than at Watson Lake. Believe them, and fill up: Watson Lake is an unappealing town whose extortionately priced gas is probably its only memorable feature. **The Belvedere Motor Hotel** (609 Frank Trail; ✆ **867/536-7714**) is the best spot to spend the night, with a restaurant and coffee shop on-site and rooms starting at C$89.

The long road between Watson Lake and **Whitehorse** travels through rolling hills and forest to Teslin and Atlin lakes, where the landscape becomes more mountainous and the gray clouds of the Gulf of Alaska's weather systems hang menacingly on the horizon. Whitehorse is the largest town along the route of the Alaska Highway, and unless you're in a great hurry, plan to spend at least a day here. See the Whitehorse section (below) for lodging suggestions.

Hope for good weather as you leave Whitehorse; the trip past **Kluane National Park** is one the most beautiful parts of the entire route. Tucked into the southwestern corner of the Yukon, a 2-hour drive from Whitehorse, these 22,015 sq. km (8,500 sq. miles) of glaciers, marshes, mountains, and sand dunes are unsettled and virtually untouched—and designated as a **UNESCO World Heritage Site.** Bordering on Alaska in the west, Kluane contains **Mount Logan** and **Mount St. Elias,** respectively the second- and third-highest peaks in North America.

Because Kluane is largely undeveloped and is preserved as a wilderness, casual exploration of Kluane is limited to a few day-hiking trails and aerial sightseeing trips on small aircraft and helicopters. The vast expanse of ice and rock in the wilderness heart of Kluane is well beyond the striking range of the average outdoor enthusiast. The area's white-water rafting is world-class but likewise not for the uninitiated (for information on white-water expeditions in Kluane, see "Sports & Outdoor Activities," in the section on Whitehorse, below).

Purists may object, but the only way the average person is going to have a chance to see the backcountry of Kluane Park is by airplane or helicopter. Located at the **Haines Junction** airport, **Trans North Helicopters** (✆ **867/668-2177;** www.tntaheli.com) offers a 1-hour flight into Kluane Park and over Lowell Glacier and Lowell Lake. The fare is C$319 per person, based on a minimum group of four (for a minimum total cost of C$1,276).

The park's one easy day hike is at lovely **Kathleen Lake,** where there's an interpreted hike which is several hundred meters of boardwalk or a longer 10 km trail along the lake's south bank. Rangers at the **visitor center** (Haines Junction; ✆ **867/634-7250**) can offer advice on other hikes; they also show an award-winning audiovisual presentation on the park. For more information on recreation in Kluane, see the website at **www.pc.gc.ca/pn-np/yt/kluane/index.aspx.**

After Kluane, the Alaska Highway edges by Kluane Lake before passing Beaver Creek and crossing over into Alaska. From the border crossing to Fairbanks, it's another 481km (299 miles).

WHITEHORSE: CAPITAL OF THE YUKON ★

Born of the Klondike Gold Rush, Whitehorse was the head of riverboat navigation on the Yukon River for the thousands of prospectors who came north seeking fortunes. Just south of the city (upriver), the Yukon River's treacherous Miles and White Horse Rapids (so called for white-capped waves that resembled horses' manes) blocked riverboat transport. When the White Pass and Yukon Route railway arrived in Whitehorse from Skagway in 1902, the city's role as the transportation hub of the Yukon was cemented. Whitehorse boomed again during the 1940s, when thousands of U.S. Army personnel arrived to complete the Alaska Highway, and by 1953, Whitehorse became the capital of the Yukon after Dawson City fizzled out along with its gold.

With a population of about 26,000, Whitehorse is home to almost three-quarters of the Yukon's population. It's no longer a frontier settlement, and food, lodging, and hospitality are all of a high standard.

Essentials

GETTING THERE **Whitehorse Airport** (✆ **867/667-8440**), just off the Alaska Highway on a rise above the city, is served by **Air Canada Jazz** (✆ **888/247-2262;** www.flyjazz.ca) from Vancouver. **Air North** (✆ **800/661-0407** in Canada or 800/764-0407 in the U.S.; www.flyairnorth.com) flies into Whitehorse from Juneau and Fairbanks, Alaska, plus Edmonton, Calgary, and Vancouver. **Condor Air** (✆ **800/524-6975;** www7.condor.com), in summer, offers weekly nonstop flights between Whitehorse and Frankfurt, Germany (the Yukon is a very popular destination for German outdoor adventurers). Cab fare to downtown Whitehorse from the airport is around C$15. Whitehorse is 458km (285 miles) southeast of Beaver Creek (the Alaskan border).

VISITOR INFORMATION Your first stop should be the **Yukon Visitor Information Centre** (2nd and Hanson sts.; ✆ **867/667-3084**). The third week in May to the third week in September, the center is open daily 8am to 8pm; winter hours are Monday to Friday 9am to 4:30pm. A bounty of information can be found at **www.visitwhitehorse.com, www.yukoninfo.com,** and **www.travelyukon.com.**

GETTING AROUND Public transit is handled by **Whitehorse Transit** (✆ **867/668-7433**); fare is C$2.50. Car rental is available from **Budget** (✆ **800/858-5377** or 867/667-6200), **Hertz** (✆ **800/654-3131**), and **National** (✆ **867/456-2277** in Canada or 800/764-2277 in the U.S.). If you need a taxi, try **Yukon Taxi** (✆ **867/667-6677**).

SPECIAL EVENTS February is a happening month in Whitehorse. One of the top dog-sled races in North America, the **Yukon Quest** (www.yukonquest.com), runs 1,610km (1,000 miles) between Whitehorse and Fairbanks, Alaska. The town is filled with hundreds of yapping dogs and avid mushers, eager to vie for the C$150,000 top prize. Making even more noise is the **Frostbite Music Festival** (www.frostbitefest.ca), which attracts musicians and entertainers from across Canada. Immediately afterward is the **Yukon Sourdough Rendezvous** (www.yukonrendezvous.com), a midwinter festival commemorating the days of the Gold Rush with various old-fashioned competitions, like dog pulls, fiddling and costume contests, and a "mad trapper" competition.

In early summer, Whitehorse hosts the **Yukon International Storytelling Festival** (www.storytelling.yk.net), the third-largest event of its kind in the world. The festival highlights ancient stories of First Nations and Native circumpolar peoples, but features traditional stories from all over the world. Many stories are performed theatrically, with song, music, and dance.

Exploring Whitehorse

Whitehorse has a large collection of historic Gold Rush buildings and landmarks scattered throughout the city, though without context, they may just seem like old buildings. The **Yukon Historical and Museums Association** (Donnenworth House, 3126 3rd Ave., next to Le Page Park and behind the T. C. Richard's Building; ✆ **867/667-4704;** http://heritageyukon.ca) offers Whitehorse Heritage Buildings walking tours June to August. Monday through Saturday, the hour-long tours are at 11am, 1, and 3pm by donation. They pass many of the Gold Rush–era structures and historic sites, such the unusual log cabin skyscrapers, and are a good introduction to the town.

Be sure to stop by city hall, on 2nd Avenue, between Steele and Wood streets, for a free 3-day parking permit.

MacBride Museum ★ Covering half a city block, this log-cabin museum is crammed with relics from the Gold Rush era and has a large display of Yukon wildlife and minerals, all lovingly arranged by a nonprofit society. Within the museum compound, you'll find Sam McGee's Cabin (read Robert Service's poem on the cremation of same) and the old Whitehorse Telegraph Office. The MacBride has four galleries, open-air exhibits, and a gift shop.

1124 1st Ave. (at Wood St.). ✆ **867/667-2709.** www.macbridemuseum.com. C$8 adults, C$7 seniors, C$4.50 children 6–16, free for children 5 & under. Mid-May to Aug daily 10am–5pm; Sept daily noon-5pm; winter Thurs–Sat noon–5pm.

Old Log Church Museum The first resident priest of Whitehorse arrived in 1900, and the town immediately proceeded to build a log church and rectory to house him and his services. They're now some of the oldest buildings in the city. The Old Log Church was once the Anglican cathedral for the diocese—the only wooden cathedral in the world—and today, it is a museum of the Yukon's early missionaries, whalers, and explorers, and their contact with indigenous First Nations people. The collection of Inuvialuit artifacts from Herschel Island (off the Yukon's Arctic Ocean shore) is especially interesting. (On the next block over are two "log skyscrapers"—old two- and three-story log cabins used as apartments and offices.)

Elliott St. (at 3rd Ave.). ✆ **867/668-2555.** C$8 adults, C$7 seniors & students, C$4.50 children 17 & under. Mid-May to mid-Sept daily 9:30am–5:30pm; Mid-Sept to mid-May 10am–4pm or by appointment. Closed Dec 24 to Jan 2.

SS *Klondike* Take a tour of the largest of the 250 riverboats that chugged up and down the Yukon River between 1929 and 1955, primarily as a cargo transport. Actually, the one on view was built in 1936 to replace the first *Klondike,* which ran aground. The *Klondike* is now permanently dry-docked beside the river and is a designated National Historic Site. The boat has been restored to its late-1930s glory.

Anchored at the Robert Campbell Bridge. ✆ **867/667-4511** in summer or 867/667-3910 in the off-season. C$6.05 adults, C$1.90 children. Tours on the hour. May 15 to June 11 daily 9am–6pm; June 12 to Aug 21 daily 9am–7:30pm; Aug 22 to Sept 15 daily 10am–4pm. Closed mid-Sept to mid-May.

Takhini Hot Springs A swimming pool fed by natural hot springs and surrounded by rolling hills and hiking trails, the developed Takhini Hot Springs might be just what you need after days on the Alaska Highway. After swimming, you can refresh yourself at the restaurant. Depending on the season, wall climbing, zip lining, camping, horseback riding, hiking, cross-country skiing, and wagon or sleigh rides are also available.

10 Hotsprings Rd. (off of the N. Klondike Hwy., 27km/17 miles north of Whitehorse). ✆ **867/633-2706.** www.takhinihotsprings.yk.ca. Pool C$11 adults, C$9 seniors, C$8 youth 8-18, C$7 children 4-7, free children under 3. Late May to mid-June daily noon–10pm; mid-June to mid-Sept daily 8am–10pm.

Whitehorse Fishway Narrowly bounded by high basalt walls and once one of the roughest sections of the Yukon River, Miles Canyon is now the site of a hydroelectric dam and the world's longest wooden fish ladder. The native Chinook salmon that migrate past Whitehorse use the fishway to bypass the dam, on their way to completing one of the longest fish migrations in the world. Mid-July to mid-August, you can view these magnificent fish through windows looking in on the ladder. Interpretive displays and an upper viewing deck show you the entire process by which the dam has ceased to be an obstruction to the salmon migration.

At the end of Nisutlin Dr., Riverdale. Free admission. Fish ladder open late June to early Sept daily 8:30am–8:30pm.

Yukon Arts Centre This is the hub of visual and performance arts in Whitehorse and the Yukon. The gallery hosts 10 to 17 rotating exhibits yearly, featuring both regional and international artists, photographers, and themes. It also offers workshops, lectures, and children's programs. You can see world-class, local and touring theatrical, musical, and dance performances year-round in the center's 424-seat theater.

Yukon Place (at Yukon College, off Range Rd. N.). ✆ **867/667-8575.** www.yukonartscentre.com. Free admission (donation required). Tues–Fri noon–6pm; Sat & Sun noon–5pm. Call or visit website for performance calendar.

Yukon Beringia Interpretive Centre ★ ☺ During the last Ice Age, a land bridge joined Asia to Alaska and the Yukon, forming a subcontinent known as Beringia. Bordered on all sides by glaciers, Beringia was once home to woolly mammoths and other fascinating Pleistocene-era animals, as well as to cave-dwelling humans. This museum presents the archaeological and paleontological past of Beringia, with life-size exhibits of ice-age animals, multimedia displays, films, and dioramas on its prehistoric people, animals, plants, and ecosystems. Try your hand at hurling an atlatl, which is a sling and spear weapon that early hunters used in these parts 10,000 years ago.

Adjacent to the Yukon Transportation Museum, on Electra Crescent (Mile 917 on the Alaska Hwy.). ✆ **867/667-8855.** www.beringia.com. C$6 adults, C$5 seniors, C$4 students, free for children 5 & under; combo ticket w/Yukon Transportation Museum C$9 adults, C$25 families. Mid-May to Labour Day daily 9am–6pm; winter Sun and Mon 1–5pm.

Yukon Transportation Museum ★ ☺ This fascinating museum presents the development of travel, from dog sled to railway to bush plane, through to the building of the Alaska Highway. You'll come away with a new appreciation of how adventurous and arduous it once was to travel to the Yukon. The exhibits and vintage photos on travel by dog sled are especially interesting. There's also a replica of the historic aircraft *Queen of the Yukon,* the sister aircraft of *The Spirit of St. Louis.* A film details the building of the White Pass Railroad from Skagway to Whitehorse, and a model recreation of that railway features a replica of downtown Whitehorse in the 1920s and 1930s. Step outside the museum, and you'll see its DC-3 weathervane, the world's largest, at the entrance of the Whitehorse airport.

30 Electra Crescent (Mile 917 on the Alaska Hwy., adjacent to Whitehorse Airport & the Beringia Centre [see above]). ✆ **867/668-4792.** www.yukontransportationmuseum.ca. C$6 adults, C$5 seniors, C$4.50 students 12-17, C$3 children 6–12, free for children 5 & under; combo ticket w/Yukon Beringia Interpretive Centre C$9 adults, C$25 families. Mid-May to Labour Day daily 10am–6pm.

Tours & Excursions

NORTHERN TALES (P.O. Box 31178, Whitehorse; ✆ **867/667-6054;** www.northerntales.ca) offers year-round outdoor adventures. Aurora-watching packages in the winter start at C$125 and run as high as C$800, depending on number of nights. There is also snowmobiling and dog sledding. Between October and March, you can combine two natural phenomena in one great trip with northern-lights viewing in the Yukon and storm watching on the west coast of Vancouver Island for C$1,980.

WILDLIFE TOURS North of Whitehorse 26km (16 miles), the **Yukon Wildlife Preserve** (Mile 5, Takhini Hot Springs Rd., 1.5km/1 mile east of the Takhini Hot Springs; ✆ **867/456-7400;** www.yukonwildlife.ca) manages populations of many different indigenous animal species for breeding and conservation purposes, and is open for public viewing. The preserve covers hundreds of acres of forests, marshes, and meadows, and features such animals as bison, moose, musk ox, elk, mountain goats, and rare peregrine falcons. Local wildlife also frequents the preserve. From mid-June to August, the preserve offers five guided 90-minute driving tours; cost is C$22 adults, C$20 seniors, C$10 children 6–17, free for children 5 & under; C$50 families.

RIVER CRUISES The **MV *Schwatka*** (✆ **867/668-4716** for reservations) is a river craft that cruises the Yukon River through the famous Miles Canyon. This stretch—once the most hazardous section of water in the territory—is now dammed and tamed, though it still offers fascinating wilderness scenery. The cruise takes 2 hours, accompanied by narration telling the story of the old "wild river" times. Adults pay C$30; children 11 and under pay half price. Trips are offered late May through September 15. The boat leaves 5km (3 miles) south of Whitehorse; follow the signs for Miles Canyon.

SHOPPING The **Yukon Gallery** (2054 2nd Ave; ✆ **867/667-2391;** www.yukongallery.ca) is Whitehorse's best commercial visual-arts gallery, featuring a large show space devoted to Yukon and regional artists. There's an extensive display of paintings and prints, as well as some ceramics and Northern crafts, like moose-hair tufting. **Mac's Fireweed Books** (203 Main St.; ✆ **800/661-0508,** 867/668-6104, or 800/661-0508; www.yukonbooks.com) is the best bookstore in town, specializing in Yukon-related books and "Arcticana," as well as a vast selection of magazines.

Sports & Outdoor Activities

CANOEING The rivers of the Yukon were once navigated only by aboriginal canoeists, and the Yukon's swift-flowing wide rivers still make for great canoe trips. In addition to its multiday expeditions (see "The Great Outdoors," earlier in this chapter), **Kanoe People** (✆ **867/668-4899;** www.kanoepeople.com) offers a variety of planned, self-guided day trips on the Yukon River for C$60 to C$95 per person. It also rents canoes, sea kayaks, and other equipment by the day or week. For day rentals costing C$40 for either canoes or kayaks, as well as a selection of easy day canoe trips, contact **Up North Adventures** (✆ **867/667-7035;** www.upnorth.yk.ca), on the Yukon River across from the MacBride Museum (86 Wickstrom Rd.). You can also rent a canoe for a day and shoot the once-harrowing 40km (25-mile) Miles Canyon—C$75 pays for two shuttles and the canoe rental. Other day trips on the Yukon and multiday trips on the Teslin and Pelly rivers are also offered. In winter, Up North offers ice fishing, snowshoeing, and snowmobile tours, including multiday trips that trace a circuit of backcountry cabins and wall tents.

HIKING If you're looking for a short loop hike from downtown, the **Millennium Trail** (www.city.whitehorse.yk.ca) is an excellent choice. Begin on either side of the Robert Campbell Bridge (the extension of 2nd Ave., south of Whitehorse) and follow the paved accessible foot path to a new footbridge directly below the Whitehorse Dam. The entire loop is 5km (3.1 miles). A longer loop is the Yukon River Loop Trail, which continues from the Millennium Trail on either side, passing the dam and the fish ladder, and following Schwatka Lake to Miles Canyon. Here, the Yukon River cuts a narrow passage through the underlying basalt. Though not very deep, the canyon greatly constricts the river, forming rapids that were once the object of dread to the greenhorn 98ers in their homemade boats. A footbridge crosses the river above Miles Canyon, making a 15km (9.3-mile) loop.

During July and August, the **Yukon Conservation Society** (302 Hawkins St.; ✆ **867/667-5678;** www.yukonconservation.org) offers free, guided nature walks in the Whitehorse area. Contact them weekdays between 10am and 2pm for details. Hikes are given Monday to Friday, and on most days, several destinations are offered, including the **Whitehorse Rapids Dam** and **Miles Canyon.** Most walks are only a couple of hours long. You must get yourself to the departure point for any hike, and be sure to bring comfortable shoes and insect repellent.

HORSEBACK RIDING At Fish Lake, just 20 minutes from Whitehorse, **Sky High Wilderness Ranches** (✆ **867/667-4321;** www.skyhighwilderness.com) offers a variety of guided horseback rides starting at C$35 an hour. The 3-hour Midnight Sun ride is a top choice, costing C$95. Sky High Wilderness Ranches also offers hostel lodging and cabins ranging from C$50 to C$150 per person, per day, plus fishing in aptly named Fish Lake. The operation is 24km (15 miles) northwest of Whitehorse on the Fish Lake Road.

RAFTING Whitehorse-based white-water outfitter **Tatshenshini Expediting** (1602 Alder St.; ✆ **867/633-2742;** www.tatshenshiniyukon.com) offers a fantastically exciting day trip down Kluane National Park's Tatshenshini River for C$125. The rate includes lunch and paddling gear, but does not include transportation to/from Whitehorse. Participants must be 14 years of age or older. Longer trips from this outfitter include an 11-day trip down the Tatshenshini from Dalton Post and down the Alsek River to the Pacific for C$3,600. Four- and six-day trips down the Alsek are also available. Call ahead because trip offerings vary from year to year and fill up fast.

Where to Stay

There are a great number of campgrounds in and around Whitehorse; they represent the best alternative for travelers watching their money.

Tenters will like the **Robert Service Campground** (South Access Rd.; © **867/668-6678** or 867/668-3721; www.robertservicecampground.com), close to downtown and free of RVs. There are 68 unserviced tent sites, plus fire pits, washrooms, showers, and a picnic area. The rate is C$18 per tent. Just north of Whitehorse, on the Dawson City road, are a number of lakeside territorial parks with campgrounds. At Lake Laberge Park, you can camp "on the marge of Lake Lebarge" with the creatively spelled verses of Robert Service filling your thoughts. There's also camping at Takhini Hot Springs (see "Exploring Whitehorse," above).

Whitehorse has more than 40 hotels, motels, B&Bs, and chalets in and around the downtown area, including a couple opposite the airport. This is far more than you'd expect in a place its size, and the standards are mostly high. If you're on a budget, check out the **Beez Kneez Bakpakers Hostel** (408 Hoge St.; © **867/456-BEEE** [867/456-2333]; www.bzkneez.com), near the south entrance to Whitehorse, with a large deck, full kitchen, and lots of friendly travelers to befriend; C$30 per person for co-ed bunk accommodations, C$65 double, C$55-C$65 double cabin.

Airport Chalet The Airport Chalet is located directly across from the Whitehorse Airport on the Alaska Highway, only 3.2km (2 miles) from the city center. It's a full-service hotel, offering a licensed family restaurant, cocktail lounge, and a choice of hotel-, motel-, family-, or kitchenette-style rooms. Rooms are basic but spacious with two double beds. All the hotel rooms have extended cable and free local calling.

91634 Alaska Hwy., Whitehorse, YT, Y1A 3E4. © **866/668-2166** or 867/668-2166. Fax 867/668-2173. www.airportchalet.com. 29 units. C$89–C$129. AE, MC, V. **Amenities:** Restaurant; cocktail lounge. *In room:* TV, fridge (in some), kitchenette (in some).

Best Western Gold Rush Inn Modern, but with a Wild West motif, the Gold Rush Inn is one of the largest and most central lodgings in Whitehorse, within easy walking distance of attractions and shopping. All of the guest rooms are recently remodeled; a few come with cots and cribs for kids. Some rooms have Jacuzzis, and all have microwaves.

411 Main St., Whitehorse, YT Y1A 2B6. © **800/661-0539** in the Yukon or northern BC, 800/764-7604 in Alaska, or 867/668-4500. Fax 867/668-7432. www.goldrushinn.com. 99 units. C$165–$225 double. Children 11 & under stay free in parent's room. Weekend specials in the off-season. Senior discounts. AE, DC, DISC, MC, V. Free parking. Pets accepted in certain rooms. **Amenities:** Restaurant; tavern. *In room:* A/C (in some), TV, fridge, hair dryer, Wi-Fi (free).

Casa Loma Located conveniently along the Alaska Highway, Casa Loma is just a 5-minute drive to the airport and downtown Whitehorse. The rooms are basic, but clean and comfortable. Some units have kitchenettes.

1802 Centennial St. (Mile 921 on the Alaska Hwy.), Whitehorse, YT, Y1A 3Z4. © **867/633-2266.** Fax 867/668-4853. www.yukoninfo.com/casaloma. 24 units. C$84–C$99 double. Children 11 & under stay free in parent's room. Winter weekly & monthly rates. AE, MC, V. Free parking & plug-ins. Pets accepted (C$5 per day, per pet). **Amenities:** Restaurant; lounge. *In room:* TV, Wi-Fi.

Edgewater Hotel ★★ This small, vintage boutique hotel was operated by the same family for three generations but was recently sold to new owners. It's in a location central to historic Whitehorse; overlooking the Yukon River across from the handsome (now defunct) rail station. A favorite of traveling businesspeople and government officials, the Edgewater has more polish than the other downtown hotels that focus on summer coach tours. Guest rooms are comfortably furnished: Standard rooms have one bed but no air-conditioning (rarely an issue at this latitude), while

Deluxe rooms have two beds, double sinks, and A/C. The two suites are essentially one-bedroom apartments with full kitchens and two beds in the bedroom. All rooms have high-speed Internet, a flat-screen TV, a fridge, and a large work table. The Edgewater's two in-house restaurants, the **Cellar Steakhouse & Wine Bar** (✆ **867/667-2572**) and the **Edge Bar and Grill**, are among Whitehorse's finest.

101 Main St., Whitehorse, YT Y1A 2A7. ✆ **877/484-3334** or 867/667-2572. Fax 867/668-3014. www.edgewaterhotel.yk.ca. 30 units. C$169–C$189 double; C$289 suite. Discounts for seniors & AAA/CAA members. AE, DC, MC, V. Free parking. **Amenities:** 2 restaurants. *In room:* A/C (in some), TV, hair dryer, Internet.

High Country Inn ★ One of the newest hotels in Whitehorse, the High Country Inn is attached to a small convention center just south of downtown. After staying in historic Gold Rush–era rooms across the North, the High Country Inn's very comfortable, corporate hotel rooms may be enticing. There's variation in room size; if you want extra space, ask for a room on the third or fourth floor, which have executive, Jacuzzi, and kitchenette suites. In summer, the deck at the Yukon Mining Company, the hotel's restaurant, is one of the city's most popular outdoor dining and drinking venues.

4051 4th Ave., Whitehorse, YT 1A 1W2. ✆ **800/554-4471** or 867/667-4471. Fax 867/667-6457. www.highcountryinn.yk.ca. 81 units. C$135–C$235 double. Reduced rates in off-season. AE, MC, V. Free parking. Pets accepted on the 2nd floor. **Amenities:** Restaurant; lounge; complimentary airport shuttle. *In room:* TV, fridge, hair dryer, Wi-Fi (free).

Inn on the Lake For a treat, consider this gorgeous cedar lodge, just a 35-minute drive (55km/34 miles) from Whitehorse. It was recognized by *Martha Stewart Living* and *National Geographic Traveler* as one of the top 150 places to stay in 2009. There are no phones or televisions in the rooms. The location is ideal for day trips to Whitehorse, Atlin, British Columbia, and Skagway, Alaska. The resort has several room and cottage options. The dining room serves breakfast (C$13), lunch (C$17), and dinner (C$34). In the summer, guests have access to mountain bikes, canoes, kayaks, and peddle boats. There is year-round access to a fitness center, a hot tub, and a sauna. Complimentary golf passes for Meadow Lakes Golf Resort are included for stays of 3 days or longer. In the winter, guests can drive a dog sled, ice fish, and snowmobile. The restaurant features locally grown organic vegetables, meats, and Arctic char, complemented with a selection of Yukon beers and Canadian wines.

P.O. Box 10420, Whitehorse, YT, Y1A 7A1. ✆ **867/660-5253.** Fax 867/660-5259. www.innonthelake.com. 15 units. C$179–C$290 double. Special 3-day packages w/airport pickup, aurora viewing, golf pass & meals C$950. AE, MC, V. **Amenities:** Restaurant; Wi-Fi. *In room:* Kitchen (in cabins), no phone.

Midnight Sun Bed & Breakfast This B&B is within walking distance of downtown and offers four large guest rooms, all with private bathrooms, phones, high-speed Internet, and TVs. Continental or full breakfast is included. There's a guest lounge, plus a do-it-yourself barbecue area. Absolutely everything is shipshape and comfortable, and the welcome is hearty—you'll feel right at home.

6118 6th Ave., Whitehorse, YT Y1A 1N8. ✆ **866/284-4448** or 867/667-2255. Fax 867/668-4376. www.midnightsunbb.com. 4 units. C$120–C$150 double. Rates include breakfast. Reduced rates available in off-season & senior discount available. AE, MC, V. Free parking. *In room:* TV, Internet.

Mountain Ridge Motel and RV Park Just a 7-minute drive to Whitehorse and close to the airport, this motel has great mountain views and offers rooms, cabins, and full-service RV sites. It's basic, but clean and quiet.

Mile 91297 on the Alaska Hwy., Whitehorse, YT, Y1A 7A3. ✆ **888/667-4202** or 867/667-4202. www.mtnridge.ca/accommodation. C$99–C$126 double; C$69–C$89 cabin; C$35 RV site. AE, DC, DISC, MC, V. Pets accepted. *In room:* TV, Wi-Fi.

River View Hotel Don't let looks deceive. One of the oldest establishments in the Yukon, completely rebuilt in 1970, the River View breathes territorial tradition. The nondescript exterior belies comfortable, large, and fully modern guest rooms that represent a good deal in an otherwise expensive town. The lobby is crowded with Old Yukon memorabilia, from hand-cranked phones to moose antlers, and the Talisman Café has one of the best ethnic and vegetarian menus in town. You can't beat the location either: It's on the Yukon River, across from the MacBride Museum, and only 1 block from Main Street.

102 Wood St., Whitehorse, YT Y1A 2E3. ✆ **867/667-7801.** Fax 867/668-6075. www.riverviewhotel.ca. 53 units. Fall & winter C$79–C$139 double; spring & summer C$109–C$149 double. Additional adult C$10. DC, DISC, MC, V. Heated underground parking C$6. Pets accepted C$10 per night. **Amenities:** Restaurant; room service. *In room:* TV, hair dryer, Wi-Fi (free).

Stop In Family Hotel This full-service hotel is within walking distance of shopping, restaurants, and tourist attractions. It offers clean, simple, and affordable accommodations. The real draw is its East Indian restaurant, a popular eatery among locals and tourists.

314 Ray St., Whitehorse, Y1A-5R3. ✆ **867/668-5558.** Fax 867/668-5568. 44 units. C$89–C$149 double. AE, MC, V. **Amenities:** Restaurant. *In room:* TV, hair dryer.

202 Motor Inn This place offers quality accommodation at affordable rates, but not much variety—all the rooms are the same, although some rooms have two queen beds instead of one. On the plus side, it's centrally located, within walking distance of the MacBride Museum, downtown shopping, and the waterfront trolley.

206 Jarvis St., Whitehorse, Y1A 2H1. ✆ **800/365-0405** or 867/668-4567. Fax 867/667-6154. www.202motorinn.com. C$119 double. Additional adult C$10. Off-season rates available. AE, MC, V. Free parking. **Amenities:** Restaurant; lounge. *In room:* A/C, TV, Internet.

Westmark Whitehorse Hotel ★ Centrally located in downtown Whitehorse, this regional chain has one of the busiest lobbies in town—the Gray Line/Holland America/Westours tour-booking office is located here. In addition, the hotel hosts one of Whitehorse's popular musical revues, the *Frantic Follies.* This is ground zero for bus-tour travelers, though there's plenty of reason to call for reservations if you're just traveling through. The guest rooms are spacious and well maintained, and many accommodate travelers with disabilities.

201 Wood St., Whitehorse, YT Y1A 2E4 ✆ **800/544-0970** or 867/393-9700. Fax 867/668-2789. www.westmarkhotels.com. 180 units. From C$149 double. Children 11 & under stay free in parent's room. Off-season rates available. AE, DC, MC, V. Free parking. **Amenities:** Restaurant; lounge. *In room:* TV, hair dryer, Wi-Fi (C$6/day).

Yukon Inn Rooms here are attractively appointed with natural or blush oak finish, and guests are greeted by West Coast Aboriginal art work at the front desk. Beds are either extra long double or king size (some have twin beds and double- or queen-size sofa beds). Each room has a writing desk for those who like to work a little or write a letter or two.

4220 4th Ave., Whitehorse, YT, Y1A 1K1. ✆ **800/661-0454** or 867/667-2527. Fax 867/668-7643. www.yukoninn.com. 95 units. C$119 double. Children 15 & under stay free in parent's room. AE, MC, V. Free parking. **Amenities:** Restaurant; lounge. *In room:* TV, fridge, hair dryer, Wi-Fi (free).

Where to Dine

Food is generally more expensive in Whitehorse than in the provinces, and this goes for wine, as well. Be happy you didn't come during the Gold Rush, when a meal of beans, stewed apples, bread, and coffee could cost $5—the equivalent of as much as C$125 today!

Whitehorse is going through a coffeehouse craze, which is great for travelers wanting lattes, pastries, and inexpensive lunches. **Backerei** (100 Main St.; © **867/633-6299**) has an alternative feel, with home-baked breads, and soups and salads for lunch. For straight-up Yukon java, go to **Midnight Sun Coffee Roastery** (4168-C 4th Ave.; © **867/633-4563**), a bohemian hangout specializing in fresh-roasted coffees—made in an antique roaster on the premises—as well as freshly baked muffins, croissants, cookies, pastries, and breakfast and lunch sandwiches.

Whitehorse is lucky to have an excellent local brewery, the **Yukon Brewing Company,** which makes "beer worth freezing for." It's available on draft at most bars and restaurants. Unfortunately, there's no brewpub, but if you enjoy the ales, consider a tour of the brewery at 102 Copper Rd. (© **867/668-4183**).

EXPENSIVE

Cellar Steakhouse & Wine Bar ★ CANADIAN This plush lower-level dining room at the Edgewater Hotel has a big local reputation. Steaks, prime rib, and other hearty dishes are the specialty, though fresh local fish plays a big role on the menu, too. In addition, there is a selection of tapas and appetizers (C$12–C$16)—oysters casino, seared ahi tuna, chicken wraps, and so on—to accompany a glass of wine or make a light meal. The dining room is refined and elegant, with a casual sophistication largely lacking at other Whitehorse restaurants that play at fine dining. The wine list is the city's finest. Upstairs, the Edge Bar & Grill offers more casual dining for three meals a day.

101 Main St. (in the Edgewater Hotel). © **867/667-2572.** www.edgewaterhotel.yk.ca. Reservations recommended. Main courses C$28–C$47. AE, DC, MC, V. Mon–Fri 11:30am–1:30pm; daily 5–10pm.

G and P STEAK/PIZZA A refined, family owned restaurant specializing in rich and delicious steaks, ribs, seafood, pizza, and Mediterranean dishes. The ceiling is sprinkled with tiny glowing lights, creating the illusion of dining under the stars.

91888 Alaska Hwy. (in the Kopper King Complex). © **867/668-4708.** www.gandpsteakhouse.com. Reservations recommended. Main courses C$24–C$52; pizza C$16–C$30. MC, V, AE. Tues–Sun 4–10pm.

MODERATE

Antoinette's ★ CARIBBEAN/FRENCH/THAI Your taste buds will tingle with delight at the savory soups, salads, and quiches flying out of this newly opened kitchen—it's so popular that people sometimes share tables at lunch just to make sure they can dine here. Centrally located on Steele Street, favorite choices include curry chicken or ginger black bean beef with jasmine coconut rice. The dinner takes more chances, with choices like Trinidadian prepared halibut and free range ostrich.

312 Steele St. © **867/668-3505.** Lunch main courses C$8–C$15; dinner main courses C$21–C$29. MC, V. Tues–Sat 11am–2pm & 5–9pm.

Klondike Rib & Salmon BBQ ★ BARBECUE/STEAK/SEAFOOD One of the most popular places to eat in Whitehorse, but open only from May to September, this fast-paced restaurant looks a bit worn from the outside—no wonder, as it's in one of the city's oldest remaining buildings (a bakery from 1900)—but there's nothing old-fashioned about the quality or execution of the food served. Both ribs and chicken are smoked in house and are outstanding, and even standards like beef tenderloin get updated with apricot-mustard glaze and fresh pineapple salsa. Fresh wild local salmon is also excellent, as is Arctic char and halibut. It wouldn't be Northern food without game, and diners should consider wild stroganoff, with bison, caribou, and other wild meats in mushroom and brandy sauce. Even the burgers go Northern—would you like fries with your caribou or musk-ox burgers? The dining room is delightfully atmospheric, but the real action is on the two small outdoor heated decks that flank the dining room.

Corner of 2nd Ave. & Steele St. ✆ **867/667-7554.** Reservations recommended. Main courses C$24–C$35. MC, V. Daily 11am–2pm & 4–9pm. Closed mid-Sept to mid-May.

Lil's Place DINER If Elvis was alive, he'd be sipping on a milkshake and chomping on a hamburger at this authentic 1950s diner. The decor includes a black-and-white checkered floor, servers in poodle skirts, and a juke box. Come hungry on the weekends for their all-you-can-eat breakfast buffet.

209 Main St. ✆ **867/668-3545.** www.lilsplace.ca. Main courses C$8–C$21. AE, MC, V. Daily 7am–9pm.

Sam N' Andy's ★ MEXICAN This place serves up delicious tacos, burritos, Tex Mex, homemade burgers, and vegetarian dishes. It offers inside seating and an outdoor patio (voted "Favourite Yukon Patio" in 2008).

506 Main St. ✆ **867/668-6994.** Main courses C$14–C$19. AE, MC, V. Mon–Sat 11am–9pm.

Sanchez Cantina ★ MEXICAN Savor the spicy flavors of Mexico at this cool Whitehorse restaurant. In the summer, guests have a choice of the cozy dining room inside or the sunny deck. The food here is authentic—from homemade salsa and guacamole to Mexican ceviche, enchiladas, mole poblano, and adobo.

211 Hanson St. ✆ **867/668-5858.** Main courses C$14–C$19. AE, MC, V. Mon–Sat 11am–9pm.

Wolf Den ★ EUROPEAN This comfortable, friendly restaurant serves up traditional Swiss bubbling cheese and meat fondues, raclette and Tartar's Hat. It's a 15-minute drive south of Whitehorse but certainly worth the trip, especially in the summer, when T-bone steaks are sizzling on the barbeque.

Mile 904 on the Alaska Hwy. ✆ **867/393-3968.** www.wolfsden.ca. Main courses C$5.50–C$39. MC, V. Daily 8am–10pm. Closed early Oct to mid-Nov.

Whitehorse after Dark

The top-of-the-bill attraction in Whitehorse is the ***Frantic Follies*** ★ (✆ **867/668-2042;** www.franticfollies.com), a singing, dancing, clowning, and declaiming Gold Rush revue that has become famous throughout the North. The show is an entertaining mélange of skits; music-hall drollery; whooping, high-kicking, garter-flashing cancan dancers; sentimental ballads; and deadpan corn, interspersed with rolling recitations of Robert Service's poetry. Shows take place nightly May through September at the **Westmark Whitehorse Hotel** (✆ **800/544-0970**). Tickets are C$24 adults, C$10 children 12 and under.

Whitehorse has quite the local music scene. The bar at the **Capital Hotel** (103 Main St.; ✆) **867/667-2565**) has live music nightly, while **Lizards Lounge,** at the Town and Mountain Hotel (401 Main St.; ✆ **867/668-7644**), also has live bands frequently. Also, check out what's happening at the **Boiler Room,** at the Yukon Inn, (4220 4th Ave.; ✆ **867/667-2527**), which has live music and DJs.

THE CHILKOOT TRAIL & WHITE PASS

South of Whitehorse, massive ranges of glacier-chewed peaks rise up to ring the Gulf of Alaska; stormy waters reach far inland as fjords and enormous glaciers spill into the sea (the famed Glacier Bay is here). This spectacularly scenic region is also the site of the **Chilkoot Trail,** which in 1898 saw 100,000 Gold Rush stampeders struggle up its steep slopes. Another high mountain pass was transcribed in 1900 by the White Pass and Yukon Railroad on its way to the goldfields; excursion trains now run on these rails, considered a marvel of engineering.

To see these sites, most people embark on long-distance hiking trails, rail excursions, or cruise boats. Happily, two highways edge through this spectacular landscape; if you use the **Alaska Marine Highway ferries** (✆ **800/642-0066;** www.dot.state.ak.us/amhs), this trip can be made as a loop from either Whitehorse or Haines Junction. Because the ferries keep an irregular schedule, you'll need to call or check the website to find out what the sailing times are on the day you plan to make the trip.

The Chilkoot Trail

In 1896, word of the great gold strikes on the Klondike reached the outside world, and nearly 100,000 people set out for the Yukon to seek their fortunes. There was no organized transportation into the Yukon, so the stampeders resorted to the most expedient methods. The **Chilkoot Trail,** long an Indian trail through one of the few glacier-free passes in the Gulf of Alaska, became the primary overland route to the Yukon River, Whitehorse, and the gold fields near Dawson City.

The ascent of the Chilkoot became the stuff of legend, and pictures of men and women clambering up the steep snowfields to Chilkoot Summit are one of the enduring images of the stampeder spirit. The Northwest Mounted Police demanded that anyone entering the Yukon carry a ton of provisions (literally); there were no supplies in the newly born gold camps on the Klondike, and malnutrition and lack of proper shelter were major problems. People were forced to make up to 30 trips up the trail in order to transport all their goods into Canada. Once past the RCMP station at Chilkoot Summit, the stampeders then had to build some sort of boat or barge to ferry their belongings across Bennett Lake and down the Yukon River.

Today, the Chilkoot Trail is a national historic park jointly administered by the Canadian and U.S. parks departments. The original trail is open year-round to hikers who wish to experience the route of the stampeders. The route also passes through marvelous glacier-carved valleys, coastal rainforest, boreal forest, and alpine tundra.

However, the Chilkoot Trail is as challenging today as it was 100 years ago. Though the trail is only a total of 53km (33 miles) in length, the vertical elevation gain is nearly 1,128m (3,700 ft.), and much of the path is very rocky. Weather, even in high summer, can be extremely changeable, making this always-formidable trail sometimes a dangerous one.

Most people make the trip from **Dyea,** 15km (9¼ miles) north of Skagway in Alaska over the Chilkoot Summit (the U.S.-Canadian border) to **Bennett** in northwest

British Columbia, in 4 days. Many shuttles and taxis run from Skagway to the trail head at Dyea. The third day of the hike is the hardest, with a steep ascent to the pass and a 12km (7.5-mile) distance between campsites. At Bennett, there's no road or boat access; from the end of the trail, you'll need to make another 6km (3.7-mile) hike out along the rail tracks to Highway 2 near Fraser, British Columbia (the least expensive option), or you can ride the **White Pass and Yukon Railway** (✆ **800/343-7373;** www.whitepassrailroad.com) from Bennett out to Fraser for C$50 or down to Skagway for C$90. There's an C$18 surcharge for tickets purchased in Bennett, so plan ahead. Remember to take a passport with you on this hike—you're crossing an international border.

The Chilkoot Trail isn't a casual hike; you'll need to plan and provision for your trip carefully. And it isn't a wilderness hike because between 75 and 100 people start the trail daily. Remember that the trail is preserved as an historic park; leave artifacts of the Gold Rush days—the trail is strewn with boots, stoves, and other effluvia of the stampeders—as you found them.

Permits are also required to make the hike. The U.S. and Canadian parks authorities cooperate to administer these permits, and they can be obtained on either side of the border. Only 50 hikers are allowed per day from each side of the pass, and 42 of the permits may be reserved for $12 each—the other eight are held for last-minute hikers. The permits cost $53 adults, $26 children 6 to 17; the fees are the same in U.S. and Canadian dollars.

For details on the Chilkoot Trail, contact the **Klondike Gold Rush National Historic Park** (✆ **907/983-2921;** www.nps.gov/klgo/index.htm) or the **Canadian Parks Service** (✆ **800/661-0486;** www.nationalparks.org/discover-parks).

White Pass & the Yukon Route

In 1898, engineers began the task of excavating a railway line up to **White Pass.** Considered a marvel of engineering, the track edged around sheer cliffs on long trestles and tunneled through banks of granite. The train effectively ended traffic on the Chilkoot Trail, just to the north.

The White Pass and Yukon Route railroad now operates between Skagway, Alaska, and Bennett, British Columbia. Several trips are available on the historic line. Trains travel twice daily from Skagway to the summit of White Pass; the 3-hour return journey costs US$98 for adults. As this trip does not cross the U.S./Canadian border, U.S. citizens do not require a passport for passage. Late May through early September from Sunday to Friday, trains make a 6-hour one-way trip from Skagway to Lake Bennett, the end of the Chilkoot Trail, costing US$165 adults for diesel-powered engines; it's US$125 for a 4-hour round-trip journey (offered Sat and Sun) on a steam-powered engine from Skagway to Fraser Meadows. As these trips cross an international border, passports are required. Connections between Fraser and Whitehorse via motor coach are available daily. Prices for children 3 to 12 on all rides are half the adult fare, and infants ride free.

The White Pass and Yukon excursion trains operate mid-May to the last weekend of September. Advance reservations are required; for details, contact the **White Pass and Yukon Route** (✆ **800/343-7373;** www.whitepassrailroad.com).

DAWSON CITY: AN AUTHENTIC GOLD-RUSH TOWN ★★

Dawson City is as much of a paradox as it is a community today. Once the biggest Canadian city west of Winnipeg, with a population of 30,000, it withered to practically a ghost town after the stampeders stopped stampeding. In 1953, the seat of territorial government was shifted to Whitehorse, which might've spelled the end of Dawson—but didn't. For now, every summer, the influx of tourists more than matches the stream of gold rushers in its heyday. The reason for this is the remarkable preservation and restoration work done by Parks Canada. Dawson today is the nearest thing to an authentic Gold Rush town the world has to offer.

However, Dawson City is more than just a Gold Rush theme park; it's a real town with 1,800 year-round residents (though population triples in summer with seasonal workers), many still working as miners (and many as sourdough wannabes). The citizens still like to party, stay up late, and tell tall tales to strangers, much as they did a century ago.

Essentials

GETTING THERE From Whitehorse, you can catch an **Air North** plane for C$300 (✆ **800/764-0407** in the U.S. or 800/661-0407 in Canada) for the 1-hour hop. You can also fly round-trip from Fairbanks, Alaska. Call the Visitor Information Centre (see below).

The scenic 537km (334-mile) drive on the North Klondike Highway from Whitehorse to Dawson City takes 6 to 8 hours. If you're driving from the upper part of Alaska, from Chicken, take the chip-sealed **Taylor Highway** across the border, where it becomes the paved **Top of the World Highway,** completing the trip to Dawson.

VISITOR INFORMATION The **Visitor Information Centre** (Front and King sts.; ✆ **867/993-5566**) provides details on all historic sights and attractions; the national park service also maintains an information desk here. It's open mid-May to mid-September daily 8am to 8pm. Walking tours of Dawson City, led by highly knowledgeable guides, depart from the center daily in summer, costing C$6. Visit **www.dawsoncity.ca** for current information.

SPECIAL EVENTS **Discovery Days** in mid-August commemorates the finding of the Klondike gold a century ago with dancing, music, parades, and canoe races. In mid-July, the city hosts the **Dawson City Music Festival** (www.dcmf.com), featuring rock, folk, jazz, blues, world-beat, and traditional music from across Canada and beyond. Dawson also hosts a variety of winter events. In late February and early March, the **Trek over the Top** (www.trekoverthetop.com) features snowmobile races from Tok, Alaska, to Dawson City, and vice versa, via the Top of the World Highway. In mid-March, the **Percy De Wolfe Memorial Race and Mail Run,** a 336km (209-mile) dog-sled race from Dawson City to Eagle, Alaska, commemorates the route of historic Dawson mail carrier Percy De Wolfe.

Exploring Dawson City & Environs

All of Dawson City and much of the surrounding area is preserved as a National Historic Site, and it's easy to spend a day wandering the boardwalks, looking at the old buildings, shopping the boutiques, and exploring vintage watering holes. About half of the buildings in the town are historic; the rest are artful contemporary reconstructions. **Dawson Historical National Historic Site Complex** (✆ **867/993-7200** or 867/993-7237; www.pc.gc.ca/lhn-nhs/yt/dawson/natcul.aspx) preserves 8 blocks, and sites in and around Dawson City. The Parks Service fees are usually C$6 for each guided tour. A variety of tours are available, and combination tickets are available; tours are available June through mid-September. For current Parks Canada program information and tickets, head over to the Visitor Information Centre at Front and King streets.

Between the town and the mighty Yukon River is a dike channeling the once-devastating floodwaters. A path follows the dike and makes for a nice stroll. The **SS *Keno,*** a Yukon riverboat, is berthed along the dike (near Front and Queen sts.). Built in Whitehorse in 1922, it was one of the last riverboats to travel on the Yukon—there were once more than 200 of them.

Dänojà Zho Cultural Centre The name of this new First Nations center translates as "Long Time Ago House." Built to celebrate and share the traditional lifestyle and history of the Tr'ondëk Hwëch'in people (more commonly referred to as the Hän), the center offers archeological artifacts, costumes, tools, photos, and presentations that tell the story of the Native inhabitants of the Klondike area. Especially interesting is the Hammerstone Gallery, which relates the events of the last century from a First Nation perspective. Ticket price includes a guided tour; the gift shop carries handmade clothing, books, music, and gifts.

On Front St. (across from the Visitor Information Centre). ✆ **867/993-6768.** www.trondek.com. C$5 adults, C$2.50 children 12–18, free for children 11 & under. June–Sept daily 10am–6pm.

Dawson City Museum ★ In the grand old Territorial Administration building, this excellent museum should be your first stop on a tour of Dawson City. Well-curated displays explain the geology and paleontology of the area (this region was on the main migratory path between Asia and North America during the last Ice Age), as well as the history of the Native Hän peoples. The focus, of course, is the Gold Rush, and the museum explains various mining techniques; one of the galleries is dedicated to demonstrating the day-to-day life of early-1900s Dawson City. Various tours and programs are offered on the hour, including the excellent Oscar-nominated short documentary from 1957, *City of Gold.* Costumed docents are on hand to answer questions and recount episodes of history. On the grounds are early rail steam engines that served in the mines.

5th Ave. (at Minto Park). ✆ **867/993-5291.** http://users.yknet.yk.ca/dcpages/Museum.html. C$9.45 adults, C$7.35 students & seniors, free for children 5 & under; C$16 families. Mid-May to Mid-Sept daily 10am–6pm.

Robert Service Cabin Poet Robert Service lived in this two-room log cabin from 1909 to 1912. Backed up against the steep cliffs edging Dawson City, Service's modest cabin today plays host to a string of pilgrims who come to hear an actor twice daily recite some of the most famous verses in the authentic milieu. Oddly enough, the bard of the Gold Rush neither took part in nor even saw the actual stampede. Born in England, he didn't arrive in Dawson until 1907—as a bank teller—when the rush was well and truly over. He got most of his plots by listening to old prospectors in the saloons, but the atmosphere he soaked in at the same time was genuine enough—and his imagination did the rest.

8th Ave. ✆ **867/993-7200.** C$6. June to mid-Sept daily 9am–5pm; recitals daily 10am & 3pm.

Jack London's Cabin and Interpretive Centre American adventure writer Jack London lived in the Yukon less than a year—he left in June 1898 after a bout with scurvy—but his writings immortalized the North, particularly the animal stories like *The Call of the Wild, White Fang,* and *The Son of Wolf.* The cabin contains more than 60 photos, documents, newspaper articles, and other London memorabilia.

8th Ave. © **867/993-5575.** C$5 adults. Mid-May to mid-Sept daily 11am–3pm; recitations daily at 12:30pm.

Bonanza Creek The original Yukon gold strike and some of the richest pay dirt in the world were found on **Bonanza Creek,** an otherwise-insignificant tributary flowing north into the Klondike River. A century's worth of mining has left the stream bed piled into an orderly chaos of gravel heaps, the result of massive dredges. The National Park Service has preserved and interpreted a number of old prospecting sites; however, most of the land along Bonanza Creek is owned privately, so don't trespass, and by no means should you casually pan gold.

The **Discovery Claim,** about 16km (10 miles) up Bonanza Creek Road, is the spot, now marked by a National Historic Sites cairn, where George Carmack, Skookum Jim, and Tagish Charlie found the gold that unleashed the Klondike stampede in 1896. They staked out the first four claims (the fourth partner, Bob Henderson, wasn't present). Within a week, Bonanza and Eldorado creeks had been staked out from end to end, but none of the later claims matched the wealth of the first. Just over 12km (7½ miles) up Bonanza Creek, Parks Canada has preserved **Dredge no. 4** (© **867/993-7200**), the largest wooden-hulled gold dredges ever used in North America; it's open June through early to mid-September daily 9am to 5pm, with tours (C$6) offered hourly to 4pm. Dredges—which augured up the permafrost, washed out the fine gravel, and sifted out the residual gold—were used after placer miners had panned out the easily accessible gold along the creek. Dredge no. 4 began operation in 1913 and could dig and sift 13,800 cubic m (487,342 cubic ft.) in 24 hours, thus doing the work of an army of prospectors. You can do some free panning yourself at Claim 6, 15km (9¼ miles) up Bonanza Road. Bring your own pan (BYOP)!

Bonanza Creek Rd., about 2km (1¼ miles) south of Dawson City.

The Klondike Gold Rush

The Klondike Gold Rush began with a wild war whoop from the throats of three men—two First Nations Canadians and one white—that broke the silence of Bonanza Creek on the morning of August 17, 1896: "Gold!" they screamed, "Gold, gold, gold!" That cry rang through the Yukon, crossed to Alaska, and rippled down into the United States. Soon, the whole world echoed with it, and people as far away as China and Australia began selling their household goods and homes to scrape together the fare to a place few of them had ever heard of before.

Some 100,000 men and women from every corner of the globe set out on the Klondike stampede, descending on a territory populated by a few hundred souls. Tens of thousands came by the Chilkoot Pass from Alaska—the shortest route, but also the toughest. Canadian law required each stampeder to carry a ton—literally 909kg (2,004 lb.) of provisions up over the 914m (2,999-ft.) summit. Sometimes, it took 30 or more trips up a 45-degree slope to get all the baggage over, and the entire trail—with only one pack—takes about 3½ days to hike. Many collapsed on the way, but the rest slogged on—on to the Klondike and the untold riches to be found there.

For some, the riches were real enough. The Klondike fields proved to be the richest ever found anywhere. Klondike stampeders were netting $300 to $400 in a single pan (and gold was then valued at around C$15 for 28g/1 oz.)! What's more, unlike some gold that lies embedded in veins of hard rock, the Klondike gold came in dust or nugget forms buried in creek beds. This placer gold, as it's called, didn't have to be milled—it was already in an almost-pure state!

The trouble was that most of the clerks who dropped their pens and butchers who shed their aprons to join the rush came too late. By the time they had completed the backbreaking trip, all the profitable claims along the Klondike creeks had been staked out and were defended by grim men with guns in their fists.

Almost overnight, Dawson boomed into a roaring, bustling, gambling, whoring metropolis of 30,000 people, thousands of them living in tents. And here gathered those who made fortunes from the rush without ever handling a pan: the supply merchants, saloonkeepers, dance-hall girls, and cardsharps. There were also some oddly peripheral characters: a bank teller named Robert Service who listened to the tall tales of prospectors and set them to verse (he never panned gold himself). And a stocky 21-year-old former sailor from San Francisco who adopted a big mongrel dog in Dawson, then went home and wrote a book about his canine companion that sold half a million copies. The book was *The Call of the Wild;* the sailor, Jack London.

By 1903, more than C$500 million in gold had been shipped south from the Klondike, and the rush petered out. A handful of millionaires bought mansions in Seattle, tens of thousands went home with empty pockets, and thousands more lay dead in unmarked graves along the Yukon River. Within a decade, Dawson became a dreaming backwater haunted by 30,000 ghosts.

Tours & Excursions

From June to mid-September, the National Park Service offers C$6 **daily walking tours ★** of Dawson City; check for hours and sign up for the tours at the **Visitor Information Centre,** at Front and King streets (© **867/993-5566**). Up to eight different tours are offered in high season.

The ***Yukon Queen II*** is a "fast cat" catamaran that can carry 104 passengers over the 173km (107-mile) stretch of river from Dawson City to Eagle, Alaska. Tickets include meals; mid-May to mid-September, the 1-day round-trip journeys run daily. Adults pay C$90 each way. (Travelers can also fly back.) Book the boat trip and return flights through **Gray Line Yukon/Yukon Queen River Cruises** (© **867/993-5599**) on Front Street (First Ave.) near the Visitor Information Centre; tickets go quickly, so reserve well in advance in high season; at all times, you'll need to reserve 1 day in advance for U.S. immigrations preapproval. If paying in cash, only U.S. dollars are accepted, even in Dawson City. If you want to stay overnight in Eagle, you'll have to make arrangements separately.

If you just want to get out on the Yukon River without the trip to Alaska, **Fishwheel Charters** (© **867-993-6237**) offers a fascinating 2-hour river journey into the traditional Hän culture that existed here long before the Klondike Gold Rush. The tour operator, himself a member of the Hän First Nation, provides background on traditional lifestyles and takes visitors past the Hän village of Moosehead, historic Fort Reliance, and a traditional fish camp. On the way back, the tour stops at Dog Island for tea and bannock. During high season, three trips daily are offered; cost is

C$32 adults, C$10 children 10 and under. Inquire at the Visitor Information Centre for the location of ticket office.

Where to Stay

The **Dawson City River Hostel** (✆ **867/993-6823** summer only; www.yukonhostels.com) is just across from the Dawson Ferry. Beds are available in a variety of shared and private rooms in riverfront cabins. There's no electricity (though there is the midnight sun for a nightlight), and wood fire heats the sauna and the prospector's bath house. The rate for Hostelling International members is C$18, C$22 for non-members; private rooms cost C$46. The **Gold Rush Campground** (✆ **867/993-5247;** www.goldrushcampground.com), at the corner of 4th Avenue and York Street, is right in Dawson and operated by very friendly folks; rates range from C$20 to C$40

Each of the following, except the Dawson City Bunkhouse and the Westmark Inn, are open year-round.

Aurora Inn ★ If the Gold Rush theme prevalent in much of Dawson isn't your thing, then try the bright, airy rooms at the Aurora Inn, a cosmopolitan country inn in the Swiss tradition. The large guest rooms are furnished with locally made pine furniture and come in a variety of configurations, including top-of-the-line king suites with Jacuzzi tubs. Everything is notably well maintained and shipshape—you'll need to remove your shoes before going to your room. All rooms have private bathrooms and TVs, and there's also a common area with a large-screen TV and VCR. The dining room here is one of Dawson's best.

5th Ave. & Harper St., Dawson City, YK Y0B 1G0. ✆ **867/993-6860.** Fax 867/993-5689. www.aurorainn.ca. 20 units. Summer C$149–C$209 double; winter C$129–C$169 double. Additional adult C$30. Children 11 & under stay free in parent's room. MC, V. Free parking. **Amenities:** Restaurant; free airport shuttle. *In room:* TV, Wi-Fi.

Bombay Peggy's Inn & Pub ★ Surprise your friends and family—and maybe yourself—by spending a few nights in a brothel. The structure that houses Bombay Peggy's was built in 1900 and served multiple purposes before becoming one of Dawson City's most notorious houses of ill repute. In its current incarnation, Bombay Peggy's takes the name of one of the brothel's leading madams and celebrates the building's long association with the hospitality industry. Rebuilt and modernized, Bombay Peggy's is now a small inn with large and stylish guest rooms, plus a pub and martini lounge on the main floor. The rooms are decorated with antiques, Oriental carpets, and tongue-in-cheek Victorian boudoir élan (you might choose to spend the night in the Lipstick Room, for instance); all rooms but the three "Snugs" have private bathrooms.

2nd Ave. & Princess St., Dawson City, YK Y0B 1G0. ✆ **867/993-6969.** Fax 867/993-6199. www.bombaypeggys.com. 9 units. C$99–C$199 double. Lower rates in off-season. AE, MC, V. **Amenities:** Pub. *In room:* A/C, Wi-Fi.

Dawson City B&B This nicely decorated, large home fronted by two stories of decks is on the outskirts of Dawson City, beside Gateway Park and overlooking the Klondike and Yukon rivers, with excellent views. The grounds are very attractively gardened. Rooms are ample size, very clean, and simply but attractively furnished. Breakfasts are bounteous. Smoking is not permitted inside the house.

451 Craig St., Dawson City, YT Y0B 1G0. ✆ **867/993-5649.** Fax 867/993-5648. www.dawsonbb.com. 4 units (3 w/bathroom). C$165 double. Senior & AAA/CAA discounts available. DC, MC, V. Free parking. Children 11 & under not accepted. **Amenities:** Free bicycles; free fishing rods. *In room:* TV.

Dawson City Bunkhouse One of the good lodging values in town, this handsome hotel looks Old West but is just a decade old. Guest rooms are small, but bright and clean; the beds come with Hudson's Bay Company blankets. The cheapest rooms don't have private bathrooms, but toilets and showers are down the landing. Only the queen (sleeps three) and king (sleeps four) suites have private bathrooms. There's no heat in the rooms, so check Dawson temperatures before making a reservation—though it's rarely a problem under the summer's midnight sun.

Front & Princess sts., Dawson City, YT Y0B 1G0. ✆ **867/993-6164.** Fax 867/993-6051. info@dawsoncitybunkhouse.com. 32 units (20 w/bathroom). C$-75–C$109 double. Senior discounts available. MC, V. Free parking. Closed mid-Sept to mid-May.

Downtown Hotel One of Dawson City's originals, the Downtown has been completely rebuilt, refurbished, and updated with all modern facilities, yet it preserves a real Western-style atmosphere. The Jack London Grill and Sourdough Saloon (with its Sourtoe Cocktail) look right out of the Gold Rush era; they're definitely worth a visit.

2nd Ave. & Queen St., Dawson City, YT Y0B 1G0. ✆ **867/993-5346.** Fax 867/993-5076. www.downtownhotel.ca. 59 units. C$118–C$163 double. Children 5 & under stay free in parent's room. Senior discounts available. AE, DC, DISC, MC, V. Transportation available for travelers w/disabilities. **Amenities:** Restaurant; lounge; Internet access (in saloon); Jacuzzi. *In room:* TV w/pay movies.

Eldorado Hotel ★ Another vintage hotel made over and modernized, the Eldorado offers clean and nicely appointed guest rooms in its original building or in an adjacent modern motel unit. Some rooms feature kitchenettes. The Eldorado also manages a true antique, the Yukon Hotel on Front Street. Built in 1897, the old two-story Eldorado hotel is completely modern inside, and all rooms have kitchens. The Eldorado represents a good lodging value for the independent travelers—and if you wish, you can still pay for your room in gold dust.

902 3rd Ave. & Princess St., Dawson City, YT Y0B 1G0. ✆ **800/764-3536** or 867/993-5451. Fax 867/993-5256. www.eldoradohotel.ca. 46 units. C$138–C$269 double. Children 11 & under stay free in parent's room. Senior discounts available. AE, DC, DISC, MC, V. **Amenities:** Restaurant; lounge; courtesy airport pickup; executive-level suites. *In room:* TV, kitchenette (in some), Wi-Fi (free).

Klondike Kate's Cabins Near the well-loved restaurant with the same name (see below), these recently built modern log cabins are clean and full of character, all with private bathrooms and cable TV. Some cabins have fridges and microwaves, and some can sleep up to four. In summer, the cabins are cheerful with pots of flowers and chairs on porches; nonsmoking cabins are available.

1102 3rd Ave., Dawson City, YT Y0B 1G0. ✆ **867/993-6527.** Fax 867/993-6044. www.klondikekates.ca. 15 units. C$140–C$160 double. MC, V. Free parking. Closed Oct–May. Pets accepted (C$20). **Amenities:** Restaurant; airport pickup. *In rooms:* TV, Internet.

Westmark Inn Dawson City ★★ The Westmark is Dawson City's largest and most comfortable hotel, with an entire street of newly constructed guest rooms added to their existing units in 2005. However, the hotel is only open from May to

September. The Westmark is owned by the Holland America cruise line, so the hotel serves a lot of bus tour passengers, but if Dawson's antique hotels don't appeal, then call ahead and reserve brand-new rooms at this top-notch accommodation. Most rooms have two queen beds, though kings and triples are also available. Belinda's, the dining room, extends out onto a very large heated and covered deck, which overlooks a charming courtyard garden. A second-story lounge has a patio with views over Dawson.

5th Ave. & Harper St., Dawson City, YT Y0B 1G0. ✆ **800/544-0970** or 867/993-5542 (summer only). www.westmarkhotels.com. 179 units. C$140–C$189 double. AE, MC, V. Free parking. Closed mid-Sept to mid-May. **Amenities:** Restaurant; lounge. *In room:* TV.

Where to Dine

Food is generally good in Dawson City and, considering the isolation and transport costs, not too expensive. The Downtown and Eldorado hotels both have good dining rooms and are open for three meals a day. Many restaurants close in winter or keep shorter hours. The **River West Bistro** (Front and Queen sts.; ✆ **867/993-6339**) is the hub of the town, with excellent baked goods and espresso drinks in the morning, and burgers and sandwiches available the rest of the day. It's open 7am to 8pm Monday through Friday, and 8am to 8pm on Saturday and Sunday.

Aurora Inn ★ CONTINENTAL/GERMAN The sunny, cheerful dining room at the Aurora Inn serves expertly prepared German- and Swiss-style food—the only cooking that approaches Euro-style cuisine in Dawson. The menu ranges from schnitzels to lamb chops and cheese fondue for two. Local salmon is pan-fried and served with homemade tartar sauce. All breads and desserts are homemade.

5th Ave. & Harper St. ✆ **867/993-6860.** Main courses C$20–C$32. MC, V. Daily 4–9pm.

Bonanza Dining Room CANADIAN This dining room is a bustling hive in the summer when locals come to swap stories and share gossip. It is a great place to start the day with a hearty breakfast or end a day with a buffalo burger or salmon steak. The steaks are charbroiled to perfection, and there's also a solid wine list.

902 Third Ave., (part of the Eldorado Hotel) ✆ **867/993-5451.** Main courses C$14–C$40. MC, V. Sun–Thurs 6am–10pm; Fri & Sat 6am–11pm.

Jack London Grill CANADIAN This full-service restaurant, with seating for 75 people, is known for its salmon dinners. It's part of the Downtown Hotel and takes its name from the famous American writer who penned *Call of the Wild* after visiting the Klondike during the 1890s Gold Rush. In the summer, the patio offers BBQ salmon, steak, and hamburgers with assorted salads, as well as beverages, including wine and beer.

2nd Ave. & Queen St. ✆ **867/993-5346.** Main courses C$14–C$40. MC, V. Sun–Thurs 6am–10pm; Fri & Sat 6am–11pm.

Klondike Kate's Restaurant ★ CANADIAN This friendly and informal cafe is in one of Dawson's oldest buildings, with a covered and heated deck off the side. The menu offers well-prepared standard Yukon fare—steak, salmon, ribs—plus more inventive specials that take advantage of seasonal and regional ingredients, including fresh morel mushroom soup, and a tomato–and–goat cheese salad with port and beet-juice vinaigrette. Reservations are a good idea because this is a very popular place—and with good reason.

3rd Ave. & King St. Reservations recommended. ✆ **867/993-6527.** Main courses C$15–C$38. MC, V. Apr–Sept daily 6:30am–11pm.

Dawson City after Dark

"After dark" is oxymoronic in summertime Dawson—the midnight sun brings out the partier in the residents, and you'll find plenty of late-night action. We overheard in one bar, "In summer, Dawson doesn't sleep. We have all winter for that." Dawson City is still full of honky-tonks and saloons, and most have some form of nightly live music. On warm summer evenings, all the doors are thrown open, and you can sample the music by strolling through town on the boardwalks; the music is far better than you'd expect for a town with fewer than 2,000 people. Some favorites: Both the lounge bar and the pub at the **Midnight Sun** (✆ **867/993-5495**), at 3rd Avenue and Queen Street, have live bands nightly. The tavern at the **Westminster Hotel,** between Queen and Princess streets on 3rd Avenue, often features traditional Yukon fiddlers, as well as other local and touring musical acts. The pub at **Bombay Peggy's** (2nd Ave. and Princess St.; ✆ **867/993-6969**) has occasional live music and a very lively and youthful cocktail crowd—don't be surprised when this spot gets raucous.

Diamond Tooth Gertie's (4th and Queen sts.; ✆ **867/993-5575**) is Dawson City's one remaining gambling hall, and it has an authentic Gold Rush decor, from the shirt-sleeved honky-tonk pianist to the wooden floorboards. The games include blackjack, roulette, and poker, as well as slot machines; the minimum stakes are low, and the ambience is friendly, rather than tense. The three nightly floor shows combine cancan dancing, throaty siren songs, and ragtime piano. May through September, Gertie's is open daily 2pm to 2am, and admission is C$6. An interesting side note: Gambling revenues from Gertie's support historic preservation in the Klondike.

It's said that "strange things are done under the midnight sun," but there's nothing much odder than the **Sourtoe Cocktail** at the Sourdough Saloon in the Downtown Hotel (2nd Ave. and Queen St.). You can join 65,000 members of the Sourtoe Cocktail Club by tossing down a drink into which the bartender places a preserved human toe. Yes, a real human toe. Apparently, in the 1970s, a habitué of the saloon, Dick Stevenson, discovered a severed human toe preserved in alcohol while cleaning out an old cabin (the story of this original severed toe involves a tale of frostbite and amputation during the 1920s). Remembering the poem *Ballad of the Ice-Worm Cocktail* by Robert Service, Stevenson came up with the idea for a very unique specialty cocktail. The toe makes the ultimate garnish for the cocktail of your choice; pick your liquor, and the bartender will slip in the digit. The toe, which is about as disturbing looking as you are currently imagining, must touch the drinker's lips during the consumption of the alcohol before he or she can claim to be a true Sourtoer. A Sourtoe Cocktail costs C$5, and after you finish the drink, you'll receive a certificate plus the right to disgust listeners for the rest of your life. For more on the Sourtoe Cocktail, see the website at **www.sourtoecocktailclub.com.**

THE TOP OF THE WORLD HIGHWAY & THE DEMPSTER HIGHWAY

The scenic **Top of the World Highway** links Dawson City to Tetlin Junction in Alaska. After the free Yukon River ferry crossing at Dawson City (depending on weather conditions, open mid-May to mid-Oct), this 282km (175-mile) paved or chip-sealed road rapidly climbs above the tree line, where it follows meandering ridge tops—hence the name. The views are wondrous: Bare green mountains undulate for hundreds of miles into the distance; looking down, you can see clouds floating in deep valley clefts.

After 106km (66 miles), the road crosses the U.S.-Canadian border; the border crossing is open mid-May through the first weekend in October, 8am to 8pm Pacific Standard Time (note that the time in Alaska is an hour earlier). There are no restrooms, services, or currency exchange at the border.

The free ferry at Dawson City can get very backed up in high season; delays up to 3 hours are possible. Peak traffic in mid-summer is from 7 to 11am and 4 to 7pm. Commercial and local traffic has priority and doesn't have to wait in line. The Top of the World Highway isn't maintained during winter; it's generally free of snow April through mid-October.

Forty kilometers (25 miles) east of Dawson City, the famed **Dempster Highway** ★ heads north 735km (457 miles) to **Inuvik,** Northwest Territories, on the Mackenzie River near the Arctic Ocean. The most northerly public road in Canada, the Dempster is another of those highways that exudes a strange appeal to RV travelers; locals in Inuvik refer to these tourists as "end of the roaders." It's a beautiful drive, especially early in the fall, when frost brings out the color in tiny tundra plants and migrating wildlife is more easily seen. The Dempster passes through a wide variety of landscapes, from tundra plains to rugged volcanic mountains; in fact, between Highway 2 and Inuvik, the Dempster crosses the Continental Divide three times. **North Fork Pass** in the Ogilvie Mountains, with the knife-edged gray peaks of Tombstone Mountain incising the horizon to the west, is especially stirring. The Dempster crosses the Arctic Circle—one of only two roads in Canada to do so—at Mile 252.

The Dempster is a gravel road open year-round. It's in good shape in most sections, though very dusty; allow 12 hours to make the drive between Inuvik and Dawson City. There are services at three points only: Eagle Plains, Fort McPherson, and Tsiigehtchic (formerly known Arctic Red River). Don't depend on gas or food outside of standard daytime business hours. At the Peel and Mackenzie rivers are free ferry crossings in summer; in winter, vehicles simply cross on the ice. For 4 weeks, during the spring thaw and the fall freeze-up, through traffic on the Dempster ceases. For details on ferries and road conditions, call ✆ **877/456-7623** in the Yukon or 800/661-0752 in the Yukon or Northwest Territories.

INUVIK

Inuvik, 771km (479 miles) from Dawson City, is the town at the end of the long Dempster Highway—the most northerly road in Canada—and the most-visited center in the Western Arctic. Because of its year-round road access from the Yukon and frequent flights from Yellowknife, Inuvik is becoming a tourist destination in itself and is the departure point for tours out to more far-flung destinations. Inuvik is on the Mackenzie River, one of the largest rivers in the world. Here, about 129km (80 miles) from its debouchment into the Arctic Ocean, the Mackenzie flows into its vast delta. At 13,000 sq. km (5,019 sq. miles), the Mackenzie Delta is the largest delta in Canada and the third largest in the world, after the Lena Delta in Russia and the Mississippi Delta in the United States. It's a mind-boggling maze of channels and interconnecting lakes. Even the most seasoned boaters find it challenging to navigate through the delta, and that's with a map! Inuvik is also right at the northern edge of the taiga, near the beginning of the tundra, making this region a transition zone for a number of the larger Northern animals, such as musk ox, caribou, bears, and wolves.

The town is home to a population of 3,500, composed mostly of **Inuvialuit,** the Inuit people of the western Arctic, and **Gwich'in,** a Dene tribe from south of the Mackenzie River Delta. In the last 10 to 20 years, Inuvik has become a surprisingly multicultural community. "Non-aboriginals" make up a growing part of the population, and the term includes Inuvik's long-time residents of European descent, as well as the newer members from the Middle East and North Africa, the Philippines, and even the Dominican Republic.

Essentials

The Inuvik airport is 14km (8¾ miles) from town. The two cab companies are **Delta Cabs** (**✆ 867/777-5100**) and **United Taxi** (**✆ 867/777-5050**). Fares are regulated by the town government and are based on the number of people in the cab, starting at C$25 for one person, C$14 each for two people, and C$10 per person for three. There is no public bus service.

If you've flown in, you will want to rent a vehicle, even if just for 1 day. There are no car rental kiosks at the airport, but you can prearrange a vehicle drop-off for a fee. Otherwise, it will cost you C$25 to cab it to one of two car rental locations. The closest one is **National Car Rentals** (170 Airport Rd.; **✆ 877-881-5398** or 867/777-2346; www.nationalcar.ca), which is about 10km (6¼ miles) from the airport and operates out of Norcan Leasing. The other is **Arctic Chalet Car Rentals** (25 Carn St., part of Arctic Chalet cabins; **✆ 800/685-9417** or 867/777-3535; www.arcticchalet.com), which rents 4×4 trucks and SUVs. Rates range from C$75 to C$150 per day.

For more information about Inuvik and the surrounding area, go to the town's website at **www.inuvik.ca,** which includes a link to the **Midnight Sun Recreation Complex** (**✆ 867/777-8600**). The complex is a modern multi-use recreation center with an indoor swimming pool, hockey arena, curling rink, and fitness center.

CBC North (www.cbc.ca/north) or **News/North and the Inuvik** (www.nnsl.com) provides the best online news, weather, and road reports. Bulletin boards at the Post Office on the corner of Mackenzie Road and Veteran's Way, and the Rexall Drug Store (125 Mackenzie Rd.), are also great sources for what's happening in town.

Exploring Inuvik

Your first stop should be the **Western Arctic Visitor Centre** (**✆ 867/777-4727;** www.spectacularnwt.com), located at the entrance to town. Plan to spend at least an hour looking at stuffed caribou, musk ox, arctic foxes, and diagrams of the area. The staff is exceptionally friendly and will happily explain recreation and

HISTORIC streets

Want a quick lesson in Inuvik history and culture? Try walking down the street. Kingmingya ("cranberry") Road and Kugmallit ("local tribe") Road are Inuvialuit names, while Bonnetplume Road refers to a prominent local Gwich'in family. Berger Street was named after the judge appointed to the Mackenzie pipeline inquiry in the 1970s. Early European explorers also get their due: Dolphin, Reliance, and Union streets are named after three ships connected to British explorer John Franklin.

sightseeing options. It's open from June 15 to early September from 9am to 7pm. While you are there, pick up an Arctic Crossing certificate and get a Dempster Highway passport stamped.

The most famous landmark in Inuvik is the **Igloo Church** (180 Mackenzie Rd.; ✆ **867/777-2236**), formally known as Our Lady of Victory Catholic Church, a large round structure with a glistening dome resembling an igloo. The iconic church is one of the few buildings on the ground (most buildings are built on pilings because of the permafrost). Tours of the church are available through the Western Arctic Visitor's Centre. The acoustics in the church are amazing, and catching a visiting concert is a real treat. Inuvik also has the world's most northerly **mosque**. The 144-sq.-m (1,554-sq.-ft.) mosque made the 4,000km (2,485 mile) trip from Winnipeg in September 2010. Prior to that, the Muslim community celebrated Ramadan in the town's curling hall.

Another landmark is **Ingamo Hall Friendship Centre** (20 Mackenzie Rd.; ✆ **867/777-2166**); the former Hudson's Bay warehouse is the largest log building north of the Arctic Circle. It was renovated in 1979 using 1,000 logs that were rafted 1,300km (808 miles) down the Mackenzie River from Fort Simpson to Inuvik. The hall is one of the oldest buildings in Inuvik and is used for dances, talent shows, meetings, and bingo.

An ideal way to learn more about the Beaufort Delta region is by paging through the **Dick Hill Northern Collection** at the **Inuvik Centennial Library** (100 Mackenzie Rd.; ✆ **867/777-8620**). The collection has thousands of photos, maps, and memorabilia of the area from 1958 to 2008. The library also has free high-speed Internet access.

The **Inuvik Greenhouse,** on the corner of Loucheux Road and Breynat Street (✆ **867/777-3267**), is home to towering sunflowers and rows of organically grown vegetables in the summer. The greenhouse is a converted hockey arena that was scheduled for demolition until a group of community-minded green thumbs stepped up in 1999. It is the northernmost greenhouse in North America; it's open May to early September.

Several art and gift shops offer carvings and crafts from the Beaufort Delta region; the best is the third floor of the **Inuvialuit Regional Corporation** (289 Mackenzie Rd.; ✆ **867/777-2737;** www.irc.inuvialuit.com). It's normally open Monday to Friday 9am to 5pm, but it's a good idea to call ahead. The "craft closet," as some call it, is continually getting new soapstone carvings, beaver-fur mitts, beaded slippers, seal-skin vests, prints, paintings, and traditional Inuvialuit parkas. One hundred percent of the sales are paid to the artists.

Originals (171 Mackenzie Rd.; ✆ **867/777-2433**) has a fine selection of carvings, prints, key chains, and souvenirs. The store is also stocked with Northern diamonds to make your heart skip and your wallet thinner. **Northern Images** (15 Mackenzie Rd.; ✆ **867/777-2786**) primarily features high-end prints, carvings, and clothing from the Eastern Arctic.

Where to Stay

Inuvik has several good hotels, all located on the town's one main street, Mackenzie Road. However, beware: They all book up in the last week of June during the annual Inuvik Petroleum Show. To check conference dates, go to **www.inuvik.ca.**

Arctic Chalet ★ Here, you can find a truly rustic Northern experience, with some modern conveniences. Choose from one of six stand-alone, duplex, or triplex cabins just a stone's throw from a quiet lake. Each cabin and room has satellite TV and a telephone. Most cabins have private baths and kitchenettes with dishes and cookware, but rooms in the main lodge do not (the main log house has two upstairs rooms that have a shared common area, kitchenette, and bath). In the winter, you can enjoy watching the northern lights, try dog sledding, and take ice-road tours. Airport shuttle service is provided for C$25, as well as shuttle service into town, which is about 5km (3 miles) from the property. Car rentals are also available on-site (see p. 793).

25 Carn St., Inuvik, NT X0E 0T0. ✆ **800/685-9417** or 867/777-3535. Fax 867/777-4522. www.arcticchalet.com. 11 units. C$110 double w/shared bathroom; C$130 double w/private bathroom; C$130–C$150 cabin. AE, MC, V. *In room:* TV, Internet.

The Capital Suites This hotel offers a little bit more than a traditional hotel room. Even the most basic suites have a separate living and sleeping area, as well as a full kitchen. The rooms are clean and modern, and part of a hotel chain that boasts of their signature Aurora beds, which feature 200-thread-count cotton-polyester-blend linen sheets. The pillows and duvet are hypoallergenic and antibacterial.

198 Mackenzie Rd., Inuvik, NT X0E 0T0. ✆ **800/669-9444** or 867/678-6300. Fax 867/678-6309. www.capitalsuites.ca. 82 units. C$184–C$255 double. AE, MC, V. *In room:* A/C, TV, hair dryer, Wi-Fi.

Mackenzie Hotel This hotel is the most centrally located of the local hotels and within walking distance of the Mackenzie River and a number of recreational lakes. Standard rooms feature one or two queen-sized beds, a coffee station with microwave, a refrigerator, cable TV, and on-demand movies. The executive suites include a king-sized bed, separate living room area, and Jacuzzi tub. This is the only hotel in town with an on-site restaurant and lounge.

185 Mackenzie Rd., Inuvik, NT X0E 0T0. ✆ **867/777-2861.** Fax 867/777-3317. www.mackenziehotel.com. 96 units. C$189–C$240 double. AE, MC, V. **Amenities:** Restaurant; lounge; exercise room. *In room:* A/C, TV, hair dryer, Wi-Fi.

Nova Inn ★ The Nova Inn has 42 clean, well-appointed rooms and suites, designed with relaxation and comfort in mind. Queen Rooms are spacious and elegantly laid out with a gas fireplace and writing desk. Junior Suites are ideal for people who need a little more room for longer stays. They have a queen-sized pull-out sofa, range-top stove, microwave, and refrigerator. Executive Suites are the "home away from home" option, offering a private and separate bedroom, in addition to a living area. Executive suites have a fully equipped kitchenette, including a range-top stove, microwave, and refrigerator. Historic black-and-white photos of the early fur traders and dog teams from the region line the hallways and rooms. The hotel is on the outskirts of town, and in the winter, the 10-minute walk to the restaurants and shops in –22°F (–30°C) or –40°F (–40°C) feels a lot longer. Corporate and federal rates are available.

288 Mackenzie Rd., Inuvik, NT X0E 0T0. ✆ **866/374-6682** or 867/777-6682. Fax 867/777-4522. www.novainninuvik.ca. 42 units. C$184–C$255 double. AE, MC, V. *In room:* A/C, TV, fridge, hair dryer, Internet.

Campers have two territorial campgrounds to choose from. **Jak Park** is 5km (3 miles) south of Inuvik on Airport Road leading into town (✆ **867/777-7353**). It has 36 sites, toilets, showers, firewood, and an impressive view of the Mackenzie Delta from an observation tower—as well as excellent cranberry-picking in September. **Happy Valley Park** (✆ **867/777-7353**) is right in town and located on a bluff overlooking the Mackenzie Delta. The site is walking distance to shopping and attractions. It offers 27 sites with a laundromat, hot showers, and RV hook-ups from May to early September. Territorial Park camping fees: Tent pads are C$15 per day, non-powered RV sites are $23 per day, and powered RV sites are C$28 per day. Reservations are recommended, which you can make at www.nwtparks.ca, or order a free Road and Campground guide by calling ✆ **800/661-0788.**

Where to Dine

Café Gallery This cafe serves up the best lattes in town. The staff is friendly and chances are that after only a couple of days, they will know your name and your order when you walk in the door. The bright, upbeat cafe is decorated with local art and offers fresh sandwiches, pizza by the slice, salad, muffins, and delicious cheesecakes with seasonal wild berries. Entire pre-cooked pizzas are available for C$36, they just need to be reheated.

84 Mackenzie Rd. ✆ **867/777-4985.** Main courses C$3–C$36. MC, V. Mon–Sat 8am–6pm. Closed Sun.

Café 222 As is the case in many Northern communities, the local branch of the Royal Canadian Legion offers the best bang for your luncheon buck. Café 222 (named after the Legion's branch number) serves daily hot lunches for under C$12. The hall fills up for "beef on a bun" for C$6 on Friday night. A Legion membership is not required, as there is usually a member there who will happily sign you in. There's also free Internet access. This is more of a licensed community hall than a restaurant, so the hours of operation are limited.

118 Veteran's Way. ✆ **867/777-2300.** Main courses C$5–C$11. MC, V. Mon–Fri 11am–1pm; Fri-Sat 5–9pm. Closed Sun.

The Roost ★ The Roost serves up fast food such as hamburgers, fried chicken, subs, and lasagna, but is best known for pizzas and Chinese food. Eat in or delivery available until 3am on the weekends.

106 Mackenzie Rd. ✆ **867/777-2727.** Main courses C$7–C$17; pizzas C$26–C$40. MC, V. Mon–Fri 11 am–midnight; Sat & Sun 11 am–3am.

Tonimoes This is a 100-seat dining room at the **Mackenzie Hotel,** and the only actual sit-down, licensed restaurant in town. The stone doorway and dark woodwork create a warm, cozy atmosphere. The restaurant features prime rib dinners on Friday night and Sunday brunches. Just across the hall, lunch and dinner are served in **Shivers** lounge. The lounge is popular with the after-work crowd and tourists. It is easy to relax and unwind in the wing-back chairs.

185 Mackenzie Rd. © **867/777-2861.** www.mackenziehotel.com. Main courses C$15–C$40. AE, MC, V. Tonimoes daily 7am–10pm; Shivers Mon–Sat 11am–midnight.

At the airport, **Cloud Nine** (© **867/777-3541**) is a small cafeteria-like restaurant with soups, sandwiches, and huge burgers with crinkle fries (C$8–$18). And a trip to Inuvik is not complete without a visit and a spin on the dance floor at the **Mad Trapper Pub** (124 Mackenzie Rd.; © **867/777-5853**), usually the last stop of the evening, where you can enjoy live music and a game of pool.

Inuvik has three supermarkets. **Northmart** (160 Mackenzie Rd.; © **867/777-2582**), **Arctic Foods** (182 Mackenzie Rd.; © **867/777-2880**) and **Stantons** (49 Navy Rd.; © **867/777-4381**). The **"Fruit Man"** (Bill Rutherford) sets up a fruit-and-vegetable stand in a truck across from Northmart throughout the year. It is a treat when he's in town, but his work takes him on the road for several weeks at a time.

Inuvik's one **Liquor Store** is at 27 Distributor St. (© **867/777-4974**). The store is well-stocked with a modest supply of beer, wine, and spirits.

Outdoor Recreation, Events & Festivals

Boot Lake Park is a 5-minute walk from downtown. It is a day-use park popular for hiking, kayaking, sightseeing, canoeing, and picnicking in the summer. During the winter, after the snow has fallen, the trail and lake become snowshoe and cross-country ski destinations. The park has two gentle recreational walking trails. One is the 10km (6.2-mile) **Boot Lake Trail,** made up of boardwalk and dirt trail. Footbridges protect the sensitive ecosystem, which is home to wild flowers, waterfowl, and arctic spruce trees. The other hike is **Jimmy Adams Peace Trail,** which is Inuvik's contribution to the Trans-Canada Trail. The 12 km (7.4 mile) Jimmy Adams Trail follows the shores of Boot Lake and leads to viewpoints, footbridges, and lookouts of the wetlands, the town of Inuvik, and the east channel of the Mackenzie River. Like many areas in the NWT, the northern lights can be enjoyed from Boot Lake during the winter months.

If you visit Boot Lake in the summer, you may want to visit **Inuvik Rentals** (8 Reliance St.; © **867/678-0013;** www.inuvikrentals.com) for the appropriate gear: They rent bikes for C$15 a day, canoes for C$25 a day, and small motorized boats for C$99 to C$119 a day. Weekly rates are also available. (They accept Visa and MasterCard.)

Golfing north of the Arctic Circle is growing in popularity. **The End of the Road Golf Course** is at the junction of Airport Road and Franklin Avenue (© **867/678-0083**). They advertise having a 9-hole course, but as of 2010, only 3 holes and a driving range were in place. It's open June to August daily 3 to 9pm. The signs advising golfers to watch out for bears is a reminder of how far North you are.

At the **End of the Road Music Festival,** you can grab a lawn chair and listen to music while bathed in the midnight sun. The highly anticipated 3-day festival is organized by the town of Inuvik (© **867/777-8600;** www.inuvik.ca) and is held on the second or third week of August at Jim Koe Park in the heart of Inuvik. There are also shows at the Midnight Sun Recreation Complex just a couple of blocks away.

The festival showcases music ranging from fiddlers to punk rockers. Check www.inuvik.ca for dates.

The **Great Northern Arts Festival** (✆ **867/777-8638;** www.gnaf.org) offers visitors the rare opportunity to watch and take part in drum dancing, carving, and aboriginal craft making. For 10 days in mid-July, the festival features up to 60 visual artists and 40 performing artists from all three territories and as far as Greenland and Alaska. The festival celebrates the artistic traditions of the Inuit, Inuvialuit, Gwich'in, Dene, and Métis. ***Beware:*** This is prime mosquito season, so pack lots of repellent and a bug jacket.

The **Muskrat Jamboree** (muskratjamoree@hotmail.com) takes place the last weekend in March and marks the long-awaited return of spring. The volunteer-run carnival unites people after the long, dark days of winter. The weekend kicks off with a free community feast at the **Midnight Sun Recreation Complex** (95 Gwich'in Rd.; ✆ **867/777-8640**), followed by a weekend of tea-boiling contests (participants race to build a fire and bring a campfire kettle of water to a rumbling boil), muskrat skinning, harpoon throwing, and dog-team races. Dress warmly: Spring by Western Arctic standards still means –22°F (–30°C).

Outfitters

Up North Tours (✆ **867/678-0510;** www.upnorthtours.ca) operates out of the Nova Inn (288 Mackenzie Rd.). One of the most popular tours is the Tuktoyaktuk Delta Cruise. You travel by boat up the East Channel of the Mackenzie River along the Arctic Coast, stopping in Tuktoyaktuk. After a guided tour of the community, you fly back to Inuvik for a very different perspective of the Mackenzie Delta. The 6-hour tour is C$499, with discounts for online bookings. There are also tours of Herschel Island and Dempster Highway, and fishing trips.

Arctic Adventure Tours (which operates out of Arctic Chalet cabins) is also known as **White Huskey Tours** (✆ **867/777-3535;** www.whitehuskies.com). They also offer tours to Tuktoyaktuk, Herschel Island, and the Dempster Highway in the summer. In the winter, experience the thrill of dog sledding by day or by moonlight, or both. Other winter tours include reindeer viewing, driving the Mackenzie ice road, and aurora watching. Owners and operators Judi and Olav Falsnes will also customize tours. See the website for pricing of individual tours.

Exploring Outside Inuvik

Inuvik may be the end of the road, but tour operators continue out from here to truly remote destinations. Two of the best companies are **Up North Tours** (see above) and **Arctic Adventure Tours** (✆ **867/777-3535;** www.whitehuskies.com), both of which offer tours by air and boat. Be warned, however, that schedules may not be what you're used to: Because minimum numbers are necessary for all tours, sometimes trips may be delayed a couple of hours, or even a couple of days, until the minimum number of passengers is reached. Make sure you inquire about refund policies because each company is different.

TUKTOYAKTUK On the shores of the Arctic Ocean's Beaufort Sea, the little Inuvialuktun town known as "Tuk" is a 1-hour flight from Inuvik over the Beaufort Delta and Arctic coastline. The two tour operators in Inuvik—Up North Tours and Arctic Adventure Tours—offer half-day tours of Tuk (including the flight) starting at C$400. The ideal trip is a full-day tour that involves a 1-hour flight to Tuk and a

A TRIP FOR every SEASON

Kyle Kisoun-Taylor, owner of Up North Tours, is part of a family that has hunted caribou and boated in the Beaufort Delta region for generations. His advice? Winter is ideal for northern-lights viewing, dog sledding, and driving the Mackenzie Ice Highway to Tuktoyaktuk. June and July are when the midnight sun, fishing, boating, flights to Herschel Island, Tuktoyaktuk, wild flowers—and yes mosquitoes—are at their peak. But if your mission is to see wildlife, the best time to come is August and September, when caribou, wolves, and bears migrate across the Dempster Highway.

6-hour (weather depending) return trip by boat. The tours focus on the curious "pingos" (volcano-like formations made of buckled ice that occur only here and in one location in Siberia) and the Inuvialuit culture. Stops are made at fish shacks and the workshops of stone carvers and other artisans, and you'll get the chance to stick your toe in the Arctic Ocean. A highlight of any Tuk tour is the 13m (43-ft.) descent by ladder into an underground community freezer—where whale, caribou, and other wild meat is kept frozen.

The community also has two replicas of sod houses, one of which was built for Queen Elizabeth II's royal visit in 1970. Sod houses were dome-shaped traditional Inuvialuit summer homes framed with driftwood and whale bone. Most people visit Tuk only for a day. But if you decide to stay overnight, there are a number of locally owned and operated bed and breakfasts. For more information, click on "Accommodations" at http://tuk.ca/welcome. Unfortunately, the town's one hotel, quaintly named the "Tuk Inn," is closed.

MACKENZIE DELTA TRIPS When the Mackenzie River meets the Arctic Ocean, it forms an enormous basin filled with a multitude of lakes, river channels, and marshlands that are summer nesting grounds for waterfowl, shorebirds, muskrats, and aquatic insects. It is the second largest delta in North America (after the Mississippi Delta). Year after year, the Mackenzie brings sediments toward the ocean, where it creates islands and extends the delta into the Beaufort Sea. Although the delta extends across the tree line, most of it is covered with spruce trees that give way to willow bushes. Four-hour wildlife-viewing trips on the mazelike delta begin at C$185.

HERSCHEL ISLAND This former whaling camp, 240km (149 miles) northwest of Inuvik, sits just off the northern shores of the Yukon in the Beaufort Sea. The island is a 90-minute flight in a single engine plane, or a 1- to 2-day boat trip, depending on weather. July is breathtaking, when the island is carpeted with purple saxifrage and icebergs float by. A thousand years ago, the Thule and Inuvialuit used the island as a base for whale hunting, trapping, fishing, and social gatherings. Then, in the late 1800s, Herschel Island became a camp for American and Hudson's Bay Company whalers, and then became a community of 2,000 people. The Inuvialuktun word for Herschel Island is Qikiqtaruk, which simply means "island." Today, it's a territorial park, preserving both the historic whaling camp and abundant tundra plants and wildlife (including musk ox, arctic fox, caribou, grizzly bear, and many shorebirds).

ORIGINS OF tuktoyaktuk

Many Tuktoyaktuk residents are descendents of the Kitigaaryumiut people who gathered seasonally along Kittigazuit Bay to hunt beluga whales. In 1850, the population was estimated to be 2,500. That number plummeted to less than 300 in 1905 after American whaling ships introduced diphtheria, measles, and flu epidemics that killed off most of the nomadic community. The area is now a designated National Historic Site, located 30km (19 miles) west of Tuk and consisting of graves and ruins of traditional Inuvialuit houses, as well as a Hudson's Bay Company log house.

Flight tours with Up North Tours and Arctic Adventure Tours to Herschel island generally begin in July, when the Arctic ice floes move away from the island sufficiently to allow floatplanes to land in **Pauline Cove,** near the old whaling settlement. Trips continue as late as mid-September, but the park guides usually pack up by Labour Day. A day trip to the island starts at C$800 and includes a brief tour of the whaling station, as well as a chance to explore the tundra landscape and Arctic shoreline. On the flight to the island, there's a good chance of seeing musk ox, nesting arctic swans, caribou, and grizzly bears in the Mackenzie River Delta.

AKLAVIK There are no scheduled tours to this picturesque Gwich'in community, 116km (72 miles) west of Inuvik. Aklavik is accessible by ice road from December to late April and by plane the rest of the year. Its history of resilience and survival makes it an interesting place to visit. In the 1950s, the federal government attempted to relocate the town's 1,500 residents to Inuvik because of dangerous spring flooding. However, many families with traditional camps and trap lines steadfastly refused, giving rise to Aklavik's famous motto, "Never say die." A popular attraction is the grave of Albert Johnson, the Mad Trapper of Rat River. Johnson is the mysterious loner who fatally shot an RCMP officer in 1932. His life and death was the focus of the 2009 Discovery Channel documentary "The Hunt for the Mad Trapper." Another attraction is the town's spring carnival, the **Mad Trapper Jamboree,** named after Albert Johnson. Two airlines offer daily scheduled flights from Inuvik for about C$280 round trip: **North-Wright Air** (✆ **867/777-2220;** www.north-wrightairways.com) and **Aklak Air** (✆ **866/707-4977** or 867/777-3555; www.aklakair.ca). There are no campgrounds; **Aklavik Inn** (✆ **867/978-2414**) is the only hotel in town. It has two single rooms. Lunches and dinners are optional. You can prepare your own, or the owners will provide meals at an additional cost. The rate is C$250 and includes breakfast. The Inn does not have a website, but details can be found on the territory's tourism website (www.spectacularnwt.com) under "Where to Stay."

FORT MCPHERSON The town (180km/112 miles from Inuvik) is known as Tetlit Zheh in Gwich'in, which means "house above the river." It's worth a stop for several reasons. The **Nitainlaii Visitor's Centre** (✆ **867/777-3652**, travel_westernarctoc@gov.nt.ca) showcases Gwich'in traditions and tools, including a birch-bark water pail, caribou-legging sled, and moose-hide boat. Some summers, Gwich'in elders are hired to provide guided tours and explain the traditional uses of local plants and animals. It is open 9 am to 9 pm daily from June 1 to Sept 15. The **Fort McPherson Tent and Canvas Company** (Lots 17–19; ✆ **867/952-2179**) is one of the greatest aboriginal business success stories in the Northwest Territories. The modest but busy warehouse produces hundreds of canvas tents and toboggan covers each year that are sold across Canada and Europe. The gift shop features jackets, hats, and canvas bags. Another attraction is the **Midway Lake Festival** (✆ **867/952-2017**) in the last week of July, which brings together fiddlers and musicians from across the North. For more information about the community, visit www.fortmcpherson.ca.

TSIIGEHTCHIC Formerly known as Arctic Red River, the town name means "at the mouth of the iron river" in Gwich'in. With just 130 residents, and 120km (75 miles) from Inuvik, it is one of the smallest communities in the Northwest Territories. It's an easy drive from Inuvik, or by ferry in the summer. The town is built on a hill overlooking the confluence of the Arctic Red and Mackenzie rivers, which is where the community's 144-year-old Catholic Church sits. The area has a long history as a summer fish camp for the Gwichya Gwich'in ("people of the flat lands") and was the site of many gatherings and trade with Slavey and Inuvialuit families. For more information, contact the Charter Community of Tsiigehtchic (✆ **867/953-3201;** www.gwichin.ca).

ULUHAKTOK Unlike Tsiigehtchic, the only way to reach Uluhaktok is to fly. Formerly known as Holman, this tiny town on Victoria Island is known for its **Craft and Printmaking Co-Op** (✆ **867/396-3531**) and the most northerly 9-hole golf course in North America. The **Uluhaktok Golf Course** (✆ **867/396-8000**) hosts the Billy Joss Open Celebrity Golf Tournament in mid-July. Participants tee off in the midnight sun while keeping a close eye out for nearby musk ox. Because the golf course is tundra, golfers carry specially woven mats for teeing off. Another worthwhile event is the **Kingalik Jamboree,** which takes place during Father's Day weekend in June. Come prepared to square dance, saw logs, and throw a harpoon. Because of its remoteness, it is an expensive place to visit, but it is certainly a unique Arctic adventure. Flights on Aklak Air cost approximately C$2,000 round-trip from Inuvik. The town's one hotel, the **Arctic Char Inn** (✆ **867/396-3501;** www.arcticcharinn.com; C$219 per person) has a restaurant and Wi-Fi. Each of the nine rooms has two twin beds (no queen-size beds). **Kuptana's Lodging** (✆ **867/396-3561**) is a bed and breakfast with two separate rooms that have double beds and a shared bathroom for C$170.

SACHS HARBOUR This is another expensive place to reach, but well worth the cost if you want to see, hear, and experience life in the Arctic. Sachs Harbour is on Banks Island and is known as the musk ox capital of the world; the Inuvialuit name for the island is Ikaahuk, meaning "a place where they cross." Archeological evidence suggests the Thule people migrated from Asia to Banks Island 3,400 years ago. Anyone with an interest in archeology or Arctic history will be blown away by the stamina and determination required to hunt and survive in this relentlessly cold climate. Information about guided tours and hunts is available through the Hamlet of Sachs Harbour (✆ **867/690-4351;** www.maca.gov.nt.ca under "Local and Regional Governments"). The **Aulavik National Park** is part of the island, 200km (124 miles) north of Sachs Harbour. For flights to Sachs Harbour, call Akalak Air (✆ **866/707-4977** or 867-777-3555; www.aklakair.ca) they generally cost about C$1,449 round-trip from Inuvik. The one place to stay in Sachs Harbour's is **Kuptana's Polar Grizzly Lodge** (✆ **867/690-4151**). The lodge has five rooms that each have 2 or

3 twin beds. C$245 per person buys you one night in one of those twin beds, with free but limited Internet access and a shared kitchen and bathroom.

YELLOWKNIFE: CAPITAL OF THE NORTHWEST TERRITORIES ★

Yellowknife's appeal is its simple but stark beauty. When arriving by plane, the city suddenly pops out of bedrock in the tundra. It is a small, modern sub-arctic capital city on Great Slave Lake and the largest of the Territories' 33 communities. The city first boomed when bush pilots and gold-hungry prospectors arrived in the early 1930s; very little of those pioneering days remains, but a spirit of adventure and love of the outdoors lives on. Of today's 20,000 residents, many are government workers and artists who live within the city limits and the outlying communities of Dettah and N'dlio. The Dene of the region are proud descendants of the Chipewyan and Tlicho people who first inhabited the area and are known as the Yellowknives Dene. They call Yellowknife Sombe'Ke—or "where the money is"—and their language and culture remain strong. Traditional Dene languages can be heard when the legislative assembly sits, or in grocery stores and on the radio.

Miramar Con and Giant Yellowknife gold mines defined the community for 40 years, but today, Yellowknife styles itself as Canada's diamond capital. Gold played out just as geologists traced a trail of micro-diamonds to kimberlite pipes out on the tundra. As the seat of government, the city is at the center of a transportation network that connects communities across the Arctic.

The bordellos, gambling dens, log-cabin banks, and never-closing bars of the gold-boom days are merely memories now. But the original **Old Town** is here, a crazy tangle of wooden shacks hugging the lakeshore rocks, surrounded by small commercial airlines that supply mining camps and transport hunters and fishermen to wilderness lodges—on floats in summer, on skis in winter.

Yellowknife is a vibrant, youthful place, made expensive by isolation and high salaries paid to transient young professionals and local entrepreneurs who pay big-city prices for homes. A significant portion of Yellowknife consists of people in their late 20s and 30s. Yellowknife attracts young people just out of college looking for high-paying public-sector jobs, wilderness recreation, and the adventure of living in the Arctic. After a few years, however, many of them head back south to warmer climes. Yellowknife is also the center for a number of outlying Dene communities, which roots the city in a more long-standing traditional culture.

People are very friendly and outgoing, and seem genuinely glad to see you. The party scene here is just about what you'd expect in a town surrounded by Dene villages and filled with geologists and young bureaucrats. There's a more dynamic nightlife here than the size of the population could possibly justify. It's a city of contrasts. One night, you can listen to classical music, while the next night, you are sipping hot chocolate in wolf-skin mitts under the northern lights.

Essentials

GETTING THERE Most people fly to Yellowknife. **Air Canada** (✆ **888/247-2262;** www.aircanada.com) and **West Jet** (✆ **800/538-5696;** www.westjet.com) keep prices competitive. Many locals prefer to support the Northern-owned airlines: **Canadian North** (✆ **800/661-1505;** www.canadiannorth.com) and **First Air**

(© **800/267-1247;** www.firstair.ca), which still provide hot meals and complimentary newspapers on certain routes. However, when it comes time to leave, Air Canada has the only regular early morning departures, which will affect connecting flights upon departure. Canadian North has morning flights on Monday only.

The alternative to flying is an 18-hour drive 1,524km (947 miles) from Edmonton. Take Highway 16 to Grimshaw, where the **Mackenzie Highway** leads to the Northwest Territories border, 475km (295 miles) north, and on to Yellowknife via Fort Providence. There is very little to see in the last 450km (280 miles). In the summer, a ferry runs across the Mackenzie River, and in winter, an ice road provides access across the river. However, both the road and the ferry close for several weeks between seasons. Best to check with the territory's transportation road and ferry report for conditions ((©) **800/661-0750**). The entire road is now paved, and the trip from Edmonton is a comfortable 2-day trip. If you are driving in the winter, the majority of your driving will be in the dark. Many car rental companies in Alberta and other provinces specifically prohibit travel to the Northwest Territories with their vehicles. If you are considering driving North with a rental vehicle, make sure you read the rental policy in advance. There is a good chance you will see herds of wood buffalo between Ft. Providence and Yellowknife.

VISITOR INFORMATION For information about the territory, in general, or Yellowknife, in particular, contact one of the following: **NWT Tourism** (P.O. Box 610, Yellowknife; © **800/661-0788** or 867/873-7200; www.spectacularnwt.com) or the **Northern Frontier Regional Visitors Centre** (No. 4, 4807 49th St., Yellowknife; © **877/881-4262** or 867/873-4262; www.northernfrontier.com).

A useful phone number for motorists is the **ferry information line** at © **800/661-0750** (NT only), which lets you know the status of the various car ferries along the Dempster and Mackenzie highways. At breakup and freeze-up time, there's usually a month's time when the ferries can't operate and the ice isn't yet thick enough to drive on.

CITY LAYOUT The city's expanding urban center, **New Town**—a busy hub of modern hotels, shopping centers, office blocks, and government buildings—spreads above the town's historic birthplace, called **Old Town.** Together, the two towns count about 20,000 inhabitants, by far the largest community in the Territories. The real attractions are in Old Town, a section of the city on Great Slave Lake that includes the famous Ragged Ass Road, rustic but livable shacks, and art galleries featuring traditional aboriginal art and furs. Old Town features large modern homes that tower beside the few remaining trappers' cabins. Because much of the city limits are part of the Yellowknives Dene ongoing land claim, residential development has been limited. Houses are surprisingly expensive, and $300,000 trailer homes are not uncommon.

Most of New Town lies between rock-lined Frame Lake and Yellowknife Bay on Great Slave Lake. The main street in this part of town is **Franklin Avenue,** also called **50th Avenue,** where a half-dozen high-rises anchor a small downtown core. Oddly, early town planners decided to start the young town's numbering system at the junction of 50th Avenue and 50th Street; even though the downtown area is only 10 blocks square, the street addresses give the illusion of a much larger city.

The junction of 48th Street and Franklin (50th) Avenue is pretty much the center of town. A block south are the post office and a number of enclosed shopping arcades (very practical up here, where winter temperatures would otherwise discourage shopping). Turn north and travel half a mile to Old Town and **Latham Island,** which stick out into Yellowknife Bay. This is still a bustling center for boats, floatplanes, B&Bs, and food and drink.

South of Frame Lake is the modern residential area, and just west is the airport. If you follow 48th Street out of town without turning onto the Mackenzie Highway, the street turns into the **Ingraham Trail,** a bush road heading out toward a series of lakes with fishing and boating access, hiking trails, and a couple of campgrounds. This is the main recreational playground for Yellowknifers, who love to canoe or kayak from lake to lake or all the way back to town.

GETTING AROUND **Yellowknife Airport** is 5km (3 miles) northeast of the town. Monday through Saturday, **Yellowknife City Transit** (contact Cardinal Coach Lines at ✆ **867/873-4693** or city hall at ✆ **867/920-5653**) loops through Yellowknife once an hour—sometimes with a bus available every half-hour—with stops at the airport and throughout downtown. The fares are C$2.50 adults, C$1.50 children 6 to 17, and free for children 5 and under; tickets are available at City Hall and at various local shops.

For car rentals, **Budget** (✆ **800/527-0700** in the U.S., 800/472-3325 in Canada, or 867/920-9209) and **Hertz** (✆ **800/527-0700** or 867/766-3838) have offices at the airport. **National** (✆ **888/878-5557** or 867/920-2970) has an office in town but will drop off and pick up the vehicle at the airport. **Rent-A-Relic** (356 Old Airport Rd.; ✆ **867/873-3400**) offers older models at substantial savings—and they'll pick you up and drop you off at the airport. **Yellowknife Motors** (49th Ave and 48th St.; ✆ **867/766-5000**) also has vehicles for lease and rent. At all these operations, the number of cars available during summer is rather limited and the demand very high. Try to book ahead as far as possible.

Taxis are pretty cheap in Yellowknife; call **City Cabs** (✆ **867/873-4444**) or **Diamond Cabs** (✆ **867/873-6666**) for a lift. A ride to the airport costs about C$15.

SPECIAL EVENTS The **Caribou Carnival** (✆ **867/873-9698;** www.caribou carnival.ca), in late March, is a burst of spring fever that morphs into a month-long celebration of all things Northern: aurora viewing, film festivals, and rock concerts at the **Snow King's** (www.snowking.ca) ice castle on Yellowknife Bay, igloo-building contests, and Inuit wrestling. The highlight is the **Canadian Championship Dog Derby** (www.spectacularnwt.com/wheretoexplore/yellowknife/dogteams), a 3-day, 240km (149-mile) dog-sled race. Summer begins with the chance to tee off at midnight at the **Canadian North Midnight Classic Sun Golf Tournament** (✆ **867 /873-4326;** www.yellowknifegolf.com) on June 21, summer solstice. This is no ordinary 18-hole golf course. It is a large, lakeside sand pit that requires each golfer to carry a square piece of artificial turf for teeing off. Ten days later, if you're lucky enough to find a ticket to the **Beer Barge** on Canada Day (July 1), grab it. Tickets are hard to come by. The highlight is the beer garden and people dressed up in period costumes from the gold prospecting days. Beer Barges were a big deal in the 1950s and '60s, before roads into the territory were built. The **Festival of the Midnight Sun** is an arts festival in mid-July. There are a one-act play competition, various arts workshops (including lessons in Native beading and carving), and fine art on display all over town. The must-see event of the summer, also in mid-July, is **Folk on the Rocks Music Festival** (✆ **867/920-7806;** www.folkontherocks.com), which features a mix of Northern (Arctic) and Southern Canadian folk, rock, blues, and other genres, plus Native musical performances. Past headliners include Jim Cuddy, Sam

Roberts, and Buffy Saint Marie. The Canadian Snowbirds flight team flies into town for the **Yellowknife International Air Show** every 2 years on the last weekend in July. The air show is organized by the City of Yellowknife (✆ **867/920-5600;** www.yellowknife.ca). During the alternating summers, the **Midnight Sun Float Plane Fly In** (✆ **867/873-4036;** www.floatplaneflyin.com) is held. The city is abuzz, with float planes arriving from across North America. And when you're not marveling at a C46 water bomber or Cessna Caravan, you can enjoy any number of outdoor concerts. The fly-in coincides with Folk on the Rocks.

Exploring Yellowknife

Stop by the **Northern Frontier Regional Visitor Centre** (✆ **877/881-4262** or 867/873-4262; www.northernfrontier.com), on 49th Street (just north of 49th Ave.) on the west edge of town, to see a number of exhibits explaining the major points of local history, ecology, and Native culture. You'll want to put the kids on the "bush flight" elevator, which simulates a flight over Great Slave Lake while slowly rising to the second floor. The center also has a video library and information on walking trails, parks, and outdoor activities. Also, pick up a free parking pass, enabling you to escape the parking meters. It's open May through August daily 8:30am to 6pm, and the rest of the year Monday through Friday 8:30am to 5:30pm and weekends noon to 4pm. In many ways, Yellowknife is a city of one: one movie theatre (**Capital Theatre;** 4920 52nd St.; ✆ **867/873-2302**), one book store (**Yellowknife Book Cellar;** 4923 49th St.; ✆ **800/944-6029** or 867/920-2220), one swimming pool (**Ruth Inch Memorial Pool;** 4807 52nd St.; ✆ **867/920-5682**), and one must-see museum (**Prince of Wales Northern Heritage Centre;** 4750 48th St.; ✆ **867/873-7551;** www.pwnhc.ca). The museum highlights the history, artifacts, and Aboriginal languages of the Northwest Territories. Permanent collections include a northern Aviation Gallery; an exhibit about Yamoga, the legendary Dene traveler and lawmaker; and a narrated documentary about a handmade moose-hide boat. You'll also learn about local hunters and early prospectors. Admission is free. June to August, it's open daily 10:30am to 5:30pm; September to May, it's open Tuesday to Friday 10:30am to 5pm and on weekends noon to 5pm. For information about new collections, visit http://pwnhc.learnnet.nt.ca. The museum's **Heritage Cafe** (✆ **867/873-7570**) serves lunch Monday to Friday from 11:30am to 2pm and features homemade soups, sandwiches, and desserts. It's so popular with locals, reservations are recommended, especially on Fridays. While at the museum, drop by the **NWT Legislature** (✆ **800/661-0784** or 867-669-2230; www.assembly.gov.nt.ca) for a guided tour. The building is shaped like an igloo and looks like a giant glowing flying saucer at night. Free guided tours are held Monday to Friday at 10:30am. Additional tours are offered in the summer. Reservations are recommended for large groups.

Yellowknife honors its bush pilots in a number of ways. **Bristol Monument** is the actual airplane of legendary pilot Max Ward, founder of the now-defunct Wardair, which served international destinations in the 1980s after starting as a humble local air charter business. The aircraft was retired in 1968 after touching down at the North Pole. Rising above Old Town, the **Bush Pilot's Monument** is a stone pillar paying tribute to the little band of airmen who opened up the Far North. The surrounding cluster of shacks and cottages is the original Yellowknife, built on the shores of a narrow peninsula jutting into Great Slave Lake. Sprinkled along the inlets are half a dozen bush-pilot operations, minuscule airlines flying charter planes, as well as scheduled routes to outlying areas. The little floatplanes shunt around like taxis, and you can watch a landing or takeoff every hour of the day. Off the tip of the Old Town peninsula lies **Latham Island,** which you can reach by a causeway. The island includes N'dilo, a small aboriginal community with a few luxury homes and a number of B&Bs.

Tours & Excursions

Yellowknife Outdoor Adventures (3603 Franklin Ave.; ✆ **867/444-8320;** www.yellowknifeoutdooradventures.com) offers fishing trips ranging from C$125 to C$350, bird watching from C$100 to C$180, ice road tours for C$185, city tours for C$220, aurora watching by dog sled for C$155, and bison-viewing tours for C$195. Rates are per person but depend on a minimum of three people. The company will also customize an overnight trip to Hay River aboard a **Buffalo Air** DC-3 airplane for C$1,000 (which includes the flight and hotel). **Buffalo Airways** (✆ **867/873-6112;** www.buffaloairways.com) is the airline profiled in the History Channel's smash hit *NWT Ice Pilots*.

DogPaddle Adventures (✆ **867/444-2242;** www.dogpaddleadventures.com) offers, by season, canoe fishing trips or winter excursions involving dog-sled rides, snowmobiling, ice-fishing, and snow-shoeing, plus a primer on dog handling for mushers. Rates range from C$50 for an hour's dog-sled ride to C$250 per person for a day of ice-fishing and dog-sledding at a remote day camp.

Shopping

Yellowknife is a principal retail outlet for Northern artwork and craft items, as well as for the specialized clothing the climate demands. Some of it is so handsome that sheer vanity will make you wear it in more southerly temperatures.

Down to Earth Gallery (5007 Bryson Dr.; ✆ **867/920-0711;** www.downtoearthgallery.blogspot.com) in Old Town is a cooperatively owned and operated gallery with more than 60 aboriginal and contemporary artists from the Yukon, NWT, and Nunavut. The gallery has an impressive and affordable selection of pottery, paintings, photography, jewelry, beadwork, and glasswork. And speaking of glasswork, make sure you check out the **Yellowknife Glass Recyclers Co-Op** (3510-A McDonald Dr.; ✆ **867/669-7654**) just down the street. The shop carries drinking glasses, vases, bowls, and candleholders of various-colored recycled glass. For just C$40, you can sandblast your own personalized glass. Inquire about workshops.

Also in Old Town is **Just Furs** (3602 Franklin Ave.; ✆ **867/873-6748**). This store is for people who see fur as a renewable resource that was and is an integral part of the Dene and Inuit culture. You'll find gorgeous sheared beaver hats, scarves, and gloves. **Northern Images** (4801 Franklin Ave.; ✆ **867/873-5944**) features authentic Native Canadian (Inuit and Dene) articles: apparel and carvings, graphic prints, silver jewelry, ornamental moose-hair tuftings, and porcupine-quill work. Proceeds from sales go directly to Native artisans.

Gallery of the Midnight Sun (5005 Bryson Dr.; ✆ **867/873-8064)** has a great selection of Northern sculptures (mainly Inuit stone carvings), and also sells a variety of apparel, paintings, and Arctic crafts. To browse an excellent selection of paintings and other artworks by Northern artists of all cultural backgrounds, visit **Birchwood Gallery** (26–4910 50th Ave.; ✆ **867/873-4050;** www.birchwoodgallery.com).

Arrowmakers Art Gallery (4825 49th Ave., in the lobby of the Explorer Hotel; ✆ **867/920-7002**) specializes in Northern Aboriginal art. It has original fish-skin prints, moose-hair tufting, birch-bark baskets, and an extensive collection of paintings by Chipewyan artist John Rombough.

Sports & Outdoor Activities

The town is ringed by hiking trails: some gentle, some pretty rugged. Most convenient for a short hike or a jog is the 9km (5.6-mile) trail around **Frame Lake,** accessible from the Northern Heritage Centre, the Prince of Wales Heritage Centre, and other points. Don't forget insect repellent and watch for black bears that wander close to the city and parks.

The other major focus of recreation in the Yellowknife area is the **Ingraham Trail,** a paved and then gravel road starting just northwest of town and winding east over 73km (45 miles) to Tibbett Lake. En route lay a string of lakes, mostly linked by the Cameron River, making this prime canoe and kayak country. Ingraham Trail also crosses by several territorial parks, two waterfalls, the Giant Mine, and waterfowl habitat, plus lots of picnic sites, camping spots, boat rentals, and fishing spots.

One of the largest lakes along the trail is **Prelude Lake,** 32km (20 miles) east of town; it's a wonderful setting for scenic boating. For boat rentals, you might check out **Overlander Sports** (✆ **867/873-2474;** www.overlandersports.com). For other rental providers, contact the visitor center (✆ **877/881-4262** or 867/873-4262; www.northernfrontier.com).

CANOEING & KAYAKING When you fly into Yellowknife, you'll notice that about half the land surface is composed of lakes, so it's no wonder that canoeing and kayaking are really popular here. **Narwal Adventure Training and Tours** (101–5103 51st Ave.; ✆ **867/873-6443;** www.ssimicro.com/~narwal), offers canoe and kayak rentals and instruction, and can provide guided tours of Great Slave and Prelude lakes. A daylong rental from Narwal is around C$45. The Northern Frontier Regional Visitor Centre offers maps of seven canoe paths through the maze of lakes, islands, and streams along the Ingraham Trail; with a few short portages, it's possible to float just about all the way from Prelude Lake to Yellowknife, about a 5-day journey.

FISHING TRIPS Traditionally, fishing has been the main reason to visit the Yellowknife and the Great Slave Lake area. Lake trout, arctic grayling, northern pike, and whitefish grow to storied size in these Northern lakes; the pristine water conditions and general lack of anglers mean fishing isn't just good, it's great. Both **Bluefish Services** (✆ **867/873-4818**) and **Barbara Ann Charters** (✆ **867/873-9913**) offer fishing trips on Great Slave Lake directly from town, but most serious anglers fly in floatplanes to fishing lodges, either on Great Slave or on more remote lakes, for a wilderness fishing trip.

One of the best of the lodge outfitters on Great Slave Lake is the **Frontier Fishing Lodge** (✆ **780/465-6843;** www.frontierfishinglodge.com), 185km (115 miles) southeast of Yellowknife and accessible only by floatplane or boat. With comfortable lodge rooms or freestanding log cabins, a 3-day all-inclusive guided fishing trip costs around C$1,795. Nearly two dozen fishing-lodge outfitters operate in the Yellowknife area; contact the visitor center for a complete listing.

HIKING The most popular hike along the **Ingraham Trail** is to **Cameron River Falls.** The well-signed trail head is 48km (30 miles) east of Yellowknife. Although not a long hike—allow 1½ hours for the round-trip—the trail to the falls is hilly. An easier trail is the 3 km (1.8 miles) **Prelude Lake Nature Trail,** winding along Prelude Lake through wildlife habitat. The 90-minute hike begins and ends at the lakeside campground. Closer to Yellowknife, the 4 km (2.4 miles) **Prospectors Trail** at Fred Henne Park is an interpreted trail through gold-bearing rock outcroppings; signs tell the story of Yellowknife's rich geology.

Where to Stay

The campground most convenient to Yellowknife is **Fred Henne Park** (✆ **867/920-2472** for information on all territorial parks), just east of the airport on Long Lake. The campground is a popular summer recreation area for local residents and a destination for tourists. The Park has 104 campsites, with 54 electrical sites and 50 non-powered sites. Both RVs and tents are welcome; there are showers, kitchen shelters, potable water, camp stoves, and electrical outlets, but no RV hookups. At **Prelude Lake Territorial Park,** 29km (18 miles) east of Yellowknife, there are 28 rustic campsites, with no facilities beyond running water and firewood. **Reid Lake Territorial Park,** 61km (38 miles) east of Yellowknife, is near the opposite end of the Ingraham Trail, and is the starting point for popular canoe trips on the Cameron River. Reid Lake also has 28 campsites with running water and firewood. All three territorial park campsites are open mid-May to mid-September and charge the same fees: C$15 for a tent pad, C$23 for unpowered sites, or C$28 for powered sites, except Fred Henne, where powered sites are C$32. All these territorial parks accept online reservations at www.campingnwt.ca.

EXPENSIVE

Chateau Nova ★ Archival photos of Yellowknife's days of yore grace the walls of one of the town's newest hotels, which has Papa Jim's Restaurant, known for its hand-rolled pizzas, steak, chicken, and ribs. The restaurant offers excellent amenities in a pleasant location right downtown. Guest rooms are large and comfortable, and have such amenities as bathrobes. Suites include a kitchenette, and a queen sleeper sofa in addition to a queen bed.

4401 50th Ave., Yellowknife, NT X1A 2N2. ✆ **877/839-1236** or 867/873-9700. Fax 867/873-9702. www.chateaunova.com. 80 units. C$149–$159 double, suites C$180-C$200. Additional adult C$10. Children 11 & under stay free in parent's room (maximum of 2 children). AE, DC, DISC, MC, V. **Amenities:** Restaurant; lounge; courtesy airport shuttle; executive-level rooms; exercise room; limited room service; sauna. *In room:* A/C, TV/VCR, hair dryer, Internet.

Explorer Hotel ★★ The Explorer is a commanding snow-white structure overlooking both the city and a profusion of rock-lined lakes. It has long been Yellowknife's premier hotel—Queen Elizabeth herself has stayed here—and after a complete top-to-bottom renovation in 2005, the Explorer sparkles with renewed style and comfort. Guest rooms are spacious, many with kitchenettes. If you've arrived with business to do, you'll like the large desks, voicemail, and other business services. Two wheelchair-accessible rooms are also available. The Trader's Grill and Trapline Lounge are among the Territories' finest restaurants.

4825 49th Ave., Yellowknife, NT X1A 2R3. ✆ **800/661-0892** in Canada or 867/873-3531. Fax 867/873-2789. www.explorerhotel.ca. 178 units. C$198–C$210 double; from C$220 suite. AE, DC, MC, V. Free parking w/winter plug-ins for car head-bolt heaters. **Amenities:** 2 restaurants; free airport shuttle; executive-level rooms; exercise room; limited room service. *In room:* TV, hair dryer, Wi-Fi.

Yellowknife Inn ★ This inn is right in the center of Yellowknife and has recently been completely refurbished and updated. The new lobby is joined to a large shopping-and-dining complex, the Centre Square Mall, making this the place to stay in winter. Guest rooms are a fair size, some with minibars, and offer amenities that have won an International Hospitality award. The walls are decorated with Inuit art. Guests receive a pass to local fitness facilities. The hotel will also store extra luggage or equipment if you're off to a secondary destination for a while.

5010 49th St., Yellowknife, NT X1A 2N4. ✆ **800/661-0580** or 867/873-2601. Fax 867/873-2602. www.yellowknifeinn.com. 120 units. C$160–C$175 double, C$168–C$194 executive suites. Rates include breakfast. AE, DC, MC, V. Free parking. **Amenities:** Restaurant; lounge; fitness center nearby. *In room:* TV, minibar (in some), Wi-Fi.

MODERATE

Arnica Inn An attractive two-story red structure, the Arnica Inn has undergone a complete renovation. Within walking distance to both downtown and Old Town, the Arnica is also just around the corner from Great Slave Lake. Many units have pleasantly spacious kitchenettes stocked with electric ranges and all the necessary utensils. All rooms have two double beds, flat-screen TVs, and private full bathrooms. There are smoking and nonsmoking rooms available. Room rate includes continental breakfast.

4115 Franklin Ave., Yellowknife, NT X1A 2N4. ✆ **867/873-8511.** Fax 867/873-5547. www.arnicainn.com. 42 units. C$149–C$159 double. Rates include continental breakfast. Additional adult C$15. Senior & corporate rates available. MC, V. Free parking w/plug-ins. *In room:* TV, Wi-Fi (free).

Where to Dine

EXPENSIVE

Bullock's Bistro NORTHERN This bustling little restaurant offers the most expensive and undoubtedly the best fish and chips north of 60. It doesn't have a lengthy menu, but it's doing something right: The dining room is usually filled to capacity for lunch and dinner. The secret is that Bullock's serves fish taken from Great Slave Lake—trout, cod, pike, pickerel, and whitefish—in simple but delicious preparations. Go for the fish and chips, stay for the various fish chowders. The fish is always fresh, and the ambience vibrant but informal. Visitors are encouraged to leave their mark by signing the walls or ceiling. The restaurant usually shuts down for the month of October.

3534 Weaver Rd. ✆ **867/873-FISH** (867/873-3474). Reservations recommended. Main courses C$18–C$44. MC, V. Tues–Sat 11am–10pm; Sun & Mon 5–10pm.

Le Frolic Bistro & Bar ★ BISTRO/PUB FARE This has the look and feel of a French eatery. It's one of the most established restaurants and upscale eateries in Yellowknife, and the menu has such classics as foie gras, musk-ox tenderloin, various wines, and crème brûlée. Bustling and convivial, this popular watering hole is a great spot to have an informal meal or to enjoy a drink and appetizer—there's a menu of dishes meant for sharing, in addition to burgers and French bistro favorites. The atmosphere is friendly, with stained glass and dark paneling lending a pleasant air of formality.

5019 49th St. ✆ **867/669-9852.** www.lefrolic.com. Main courses C$14–$42. AE, DISC, MC, V. Mon–Sat 11am–1am.

Fuego ★ INTERNATIONAL/NORTHERN This funky restaurant in downtown Yellowknife serves the best steaks and rack of lamb in town. It is below ground, with a dark but comfortable decor. The service is friendly, and the live music is excellent.

4915 50th St. (downstairs). ✆ **867/873-3750.** Reservations recommended. Main courses C$23–C$42. AE, MC, V. Mon–Fri 11:30am–2pm; Sat & Sun 5–10pm.

Thorton's Wine and Tapas Room ★ INTERNATIONAL Here, you'll find an extensive wine list and a selection of tapas and main courses sure to make your mouth water. It's easy to lose yourself in conversation while enjoying a fireside chat and nibbling on tempura-dipped sushi rolls or lightly seasoned char cakes. Traditionally, it closes from May to September while the owners sniff out new wines.

52 Ave. & 51 St. (next to King Pin bowling alley). ✆ **867/669-9463.** Reservations recommended. Tapas C$8–C$33; main courses C$23–C$42. AE, MC, V. Tues–Sat 5–10 pm; Sun brunch 11am–2pm. Closed May–Sept.

Trader's Grill and Trapline Lounge ★ INTERNATIONAL/NORTHERN These two interlinked restaurants in the Explorer Hotel offer some of the best Northern cooking in the Northwest Territories. The menu lists a number of game dishes peculiar to the region, such as caribou, char, and musk ox (depending on availability), but prepared with French sauces and finesse. Other dishes—steaks, pasta, and seafood—have a more international provenance.

4825 49th Ave. (in the Explorer Hotel). ✆ **867/873-3531,** ext. 7121. Reservations recommended. Main courses C$18–C$40. AE, DC, MC, V. Trader's Grill Mon–Sat 7am–2pm & 5–10pm, Sun 8am–10pm; Trapline Lounge Mon–Sat 11am–11:30pm.

Twist ★ ECLECTIC Upstairs from Fuego, Twist is known for an ever-evolving tapas menu and award-winning Caesar cocktail. However, it also has its own fully functional kitchen and a delicious Saturday brunch. Wednesday night is "pierogie night," and the lounge fills up early.

4915 49th Ave. (upstairs). ✆ **867/873-3573.** Main courses C$15–C$34. AE, DC, MC, V. Mon–Thurs 11am–midnight; Fri & Sat 11am–2am.

Wildcat Cafe ★ NORTHERN This slanting log cabin built in 1937 is a designated heritage site. It's great place to try Northern fare, such as bison, musk ox, and arctic char. Because it seats only about 40 people, you may be asked to share your table if it's busy; the outdoor deck has additional seating for 20 to 25 people and is a great place to watch float planes take off and land. Unfortunately, the restaurant is open only from May to early September.

3904 Wiley Rd. ✆ **867/873-4004.** Main courses C$15–C$42. MC, V. Daily 10am–10pm.

MODERATE

Diamantes Restaurant ★ ITALIAN/INTERNATIONAL The specialty here is pasta and Italian dishes. It also has the most consistently available menus of northern meat, such as buffalo, musk ox, char, and pickerel. The decor includes large black-and-white photos of Northern mining. It is a 5-minute cab ride from downtown.

483 Range Lake Rd. ✆ **867/920-2971.** Reservations recommended. Main course C$24–C$37. MC, V. Mon–Fri 11am–2pm & 4–11pm.

Gold Range Bistro ★ DINER This is a popular breakfast and lunch stop with the locals that specializes in hamburgers, clubhouse sandwiches, and Chinese food. Don't miss the comical signage above the front door that reads, "You want more pork, order a pork chop."

5051 50th St. ✆ **867/873-4567.** Main courses C$10–C$18. MC, V. Mon–Fri 5:30–10:30pm; Sat & Sun 7:30–9pm.

Main Street Donair MIDDLE EASTERN Smack in the middle of town, this is the only place in Yellowknife serving authentic Middle Eastern *donairs* and *shawarmas.* It has big windows looking onto Franklin Avenue and is a great place to people watch. Eat in or take out.

4905 Franklin Ave. ✆ **867/766-3910.** Main courses C$8–C$14. AE, MC, V. Mon–Fri 10am–6pm; Sat 11am–5pm. Closed Sun.

Sushi North ★ JAPANESE This place offers rolls, *nigiri,* and combination meal sets. The restaurant overlooks downtown Yellowknife. Service is polite and speedy. It's great for a fast sit-down meal or take-out.

#200, 4910 50 Ave. ✆ **867/669-0001.** Fax 867/669-0012. Main courses C$7–C$20. No credit cards. Mon–Sat 11:30am–7pm. Closed Sun.

A Taste of Saigon ★ VIETNAMESE This popular lunch spot is known for its spicy satay, lemon-pepper chicken, and noodle dishes. It is always packed midday, so lunch reservations are strongly recommended; or arrive after 1pm, when the office workers have cleared out.

4913 50 St. ✆ **867/873-9777.** Reservations recommended. Main courses C$10–C$25. MC, V. Mon–Sat 11am–9pm. Closed Sun.

There are also a number of Chinese restaurants, including the **Jade Garden** (5309 Franklin Ave.; ✆ **867/873-3339**) and **Mark's Family Restaurant** (5102 Franklin Ave.; ✆ **867/920-7878**). **The Red Apple** (4701 50th Ave.; ✆ **867/766-3388**) has great lunch and dinner buffets.

INEXPENSIVE

The **Heritage Café** at the **Northern Heritage Centre,** on Frame Lake (✆ **867/873-7551**), has a good selection of inexpensive lunch items; this is a fine place to go for soups, salads, sandwiches, and pasta dishes, whether or not you plan on visiting the museum. It's open Tuesday through Friday 11am to 4pm and Sunday noon to 4pm.

Brand-name fast food is present in Yellowknife, and for people on a tight budget, this is probably the way to avoid the otherwise rather high cost of dining. All the downtown shopping arcades have inexpensive food outlets, as well.

Yellowknife After Dark

By and large, people in Yellowknife aren't scared of a drink, and nightlife revolves around bars and pubs. Increasingly, there's a live music scene in Yellowknife.

The Black Knight (4910 49 St.; ✆ **867/920-4041**) has an English-pub feel to it and is one of the few places in Yellowknife serving Guinness beer on tap. It also has the largest selection of scotches in town (somewhere around 120). The pub is open 11am until 2am every day except Sunday. The **Top Knight,** a nightclub upstairs from the pub, offers dancing and informal dining.

Surly Bob's (4910 50th Ave.; ✆ **867/873-5626**) is a sports bar full of loud and proud sports fans during the playoff seasons. On a good night, Bob has been known to crack a smile. The bar has a full kitchen, and Friday and Saturday nights are Lobster Night for C$35.

The 20-something crowd can be found dancing to Lady Gaga and Kanye West, and drinking at the **Raven** (5030 50th St.; ✆ **867/669-9755**).

The city's infamous bar the **Gold Range** (5010 50th St.; ✆ **867/873-4441**), also known as the "Strange Range," has live music and local characters. Many locals make the Gold Range the last stop during a night out; you can't say you've seen Yellowknife if you haven't seen the Strange Range. ***Take note:*** The bar is on a street more derelict than dangerous.

If you are looking for a place to dance the night away, check out **Sam's Monkey Tree** (483 Range Lake Rd.; ✆ **867/920-4914**), but be prepared to stand in line after 10:30pm in the summer. It's a popular spot with university students home for the summer.

NATIONAL PARKS

The Northwest Territories has five national parks, three of which are north of the Arctic Circle, and two that border on Alberta.

Aulavik (✆ **867/690-3904;** www.pc.gc.ca) on Banks Island is the territory's most northerly national park. Aulavik means "place where people travel" in Inuvialuktun. It is the burial site for the 155-year-old HMS *Investigator,* a British exploration sailing ship that sank in 1854 after being trapped in year-round ice for two winters. The wreck was discovered in the summer of 2010. The only way to get to the park is to charter a plane from Inuvik. This will cost in excess of C$20,000 (including canoes), but it is possible to split the cost with other groups. Parks Canada maintains a list of groups willing to split flight costs. For more information, contact **Parks Canada** in Inuvik (✆ **867/777-8800**). Aulavik is home to musk ox, bears, arctic wolves, lemmings, Peary caribou, and migratory sea birds. There are no hiking trials and no visitor centers in the park. However, **Parks Canada** staff in Inuvik or Sachs Harbour (✆ **867/690-3904**) can help plan hiking routes. The prime hiking season is late June to mid-August, when there is 24-hour daylight. It is a great time for canoeists and kayakers to paddle the Thomsen River, a Class 1 waterway and one of the most northerly navigable rivers in the world. Guided paddling trips are available through **Whitney and Smith Legendary Expeditions** (✆ **800/713-6660** or 403/678-3052; info@legendary.ca).

Tuktut Nogait (✆ **867/777-8800;** www.pc.gc.ca) is 40km (25 miles) east of Paulatuk. The name means "young caribou" in Inuvialuktun. Three main rivers have carved deep, dark canyons throughout the park where peregrine falcons and golden eagles nest. The **Paulatuk Hunters and Trappers Committee** (✆ **867/580-3004**) or the **Paulatuk Community Corporation** (✆ **867/580-3601**) have organized boat tours into the park. The Parks office is in Paulatuk (✆ **867/580-3233**). The relatively flat terrain, number of campsites, spectacular scenery, and wildlife viewing make it a worthwhile destination. The best time to arrive is between late June and early August, when the ground is carpeted with wildflowers and fauna. The Hornaday River is a world-class white-water–kayaking destination, suitable for experienced paddlers. Tuktut Nogait is home to musk ox, grizzly bears, wolves, red foxes, and ground squirrels. The one airline with scheduled service to Paulatuk is **Aklak Air** (✆ **866/707-4977** or 867/777-3555; www.aklakair.ca). Airfare from Inuvik to Paulatuk is about C$1,200.

Ivvavik (✆ **867/777-8800;** www.pc.gc.ca) belongs to the Yukon but is administered by Parks Canada staff in Inuvik. The 100,000-sq.-km (38,610-sq.-mile) park means "a place for giving birth" because it overlaps on the calving grounds of the Porcupine caribou herd. It is the first national park that was created because of a land claim settlement—the Inuvialuit Final Agreement, signed in 1984. The Firth River has rapids ranging from Class 2 to Class 4. Only experienced rafters and guiders should attempt the river without a guide. There is good fishing and hiking, although like Aulavik, there are no designated trails in Ivvavik. The **Parks Canada** staff in Inuvik can help plan hiking routes. Three companies offer guided trips on the Firth River. **Rivers, Oceans and Mountains,** in Vancouver, BC (✆ **888/639-1114;** www.iroamtheworld.com); **Explorers League World and Wilderness Rafting Expeditions,** in Nelson, BC (✆ **778/785-0469;** www.explorersleague.ca); and **Nahanni River Adventures,** in Whitehorse (✆ **867/668-3180;** www.nahanni.com).

In the southern part of the territory, the **Nahanni National Park Reserve** (✆ **867/695-3151;** www.pc.gc.ca) is Canada's Grand Canyon, where the river passes through four sets of miles-long towering canyons. It's unique geography made it the first place on Earth to receive a UNESCO World Heritage Site designation, and a canoe or rafting trip down the river is considered one of Canada's iconic adventures. The park's boundary expanded from just less than 5,000 sq. km (1,931 sq. miles) to 30,000 sq. km (11,583 sq. miles), approximately the size of Belgium, in 2009. There are hiking and hot springs, but the real draw is paddling the South Nahanni River, which, with a guide, is possible for just about anyone. You may also see grizzly bears, woodland caribou, and Dall sheep while you do it. The most established tour companies are **Nahanni River Adventures** (✆ **867/668-3180;** www.nahanni.com), **Black Feather** (✆ **888/849-7666;** www.blackfeather.com), and **Nahanni Wilderness Adventures** (✆ **867/678-3374;** www.nahanniwild.com).

Wood Buffalo (✆ **867/872-7960)** is the largest national park in Canada. From short strolls on secluded forested trails to rugged canoe trips on meandering rivers of the boreal plains, there is a little something for outdoor enthusiasts of all ages and abilities. Photographers will be made snap-happy by the estimated 6,000 bison roaming within the park's 44,807 sq. km (17,300 sq. miles). The park is geographically split between the Northwest Territories and northern Alberta. Several hundred whooping cranes nest in the park each summer. One of Wood Buffalo's most interesting geological features is the Salt Plains, which proved an ideal habitat for bison and pelicans. For most of the year, the only way in is through Fort Smith or Chipewyan by plane or boat. However, there is a short window in the winter when you can drive from Fort McMurray, Alberta to Fort Chipewyan.

INTO THE wild

Only experienced wilderness travelers with advanced wilderness first aid should visit the national parks north of the Arctic Circle. Registration and deregistration is mandatory, both upon entering the park and leaving it. Search and Rescue will come looking for visitors if they fail to deregister or are more that 48 hours late.

Northern Nation Parks fees are C$147 per person for the year or C$25 per person per day, except Wood Buffalo Park, where the annual fee is C$69 and the daily rate is C$9.80. Because of the remoteness, satellite phones are highly recommended for Aulavik, Tuktut Nogait, or Ivvavik parks. **New North Networks** (74 Firth St., Inuvik; ✆ **867/777-2111;** www.newnorth.ca) rents satellite phones and devices similar to Emergency Locator Devices (ELTs). For more information about Parks Canada, go to www.pc.gc.ca.

NUNAVUT: THE INUIT HOMELAND

By Jillian Dickens

Nunavut is a vast region—more than one-fifth of Canada's land mass and 40% of its coastline. It is also one of the world's most remote and uninhabited areas, but one that holds many rewards for the traveler willing to get off the beaten path. Arctic landscapes can be breathtaking, traditional Inuit villages retain age-old hunting and fishing ways, and the artwork of the North is famous worldwide. In almost every community, artists engage in weaving; print making; or stone, ivory, and bone carving. Locally produced artwork is available from community co-ops, galleries, or from the artists themselves.

Compared to most Indigenous languages, the Inuit language of Inuktitut is holding up strong. With more than 90% of Nunavummiut (residents of Nunavut) fluent Inuktitut speakers, it is the language of the street in most communities. The Nunavut government has made Inuktitut preservation a priority and plans to make it the working language of the region by 2020.

But while Nunavut Inuit are preserving ancient traditions, they are balancing this with a modern lifestyle, complete with cars, cable television, and Internet—some communities even have cellphone capability.

What to Expect

Traveling the wilds of Nunavut is a great adventure, but frankly, it isn't for everyone. It is still a young territory (established in 1999), which is apparent in the lack of infrastructure and development. The Arctic is a very expensive place to travel. Airfare is very high—for example, flights between Ottawa and Iqaluit are usually more than C$1,500, and it will cost even more again to fly from Iqaluit to Pond Inlet in the high Arctic. While almost every little community has a serviceable hotel/restaurant, room prices are shockingly high; a hostel-style rustic room with shared facilities and full board costs as much as a decent room in Paris. Food costs are equally high (remember that food must be air-freighted in), and the quality is poor.

To reach anywhere in Nunavut, you'll need to fly on floatplanes, tiny commuter planes, and aircraft that years ago passed out of use in the rest of the world. Of course, all aircraft in the Arctic are regularly inspected and regulated for safety, but if you have phobias about flying, you may find the combination of rattling aircraft and changeable flying conditions unpleasant.

Nunavut is the homeland of the Inuit. Travelers are made welcome in nearly all Inuit villages, but it must be stressed that these communities aren't set up as holiday camps for southern visitors. Many people aren't English speakers; except for the local hotel, there may not be public areas open for visitors. You're definitely a guest here; while people are friendly and will greet you, you'll probably feel like an outsider.

The key to traveling here is flexibility. The elements—wind, rain, snow, and ice—alter travel plans more often than not. Mechanical breakdowns on flights occur regularly, and maintenance takes much, much longer than in the south. But most important to remember is Nunavummiut operate on "northern time," so pre-planning is difficult. Best to have a-take-things-as-they-come attitude and leave southern sensibilities (and watches) at home.

Baffin Island: Adventure & Inuit Art

One of the most remote and uninhabited areas in North America, rugged and beautiful **Baffin Island** is an excellent destination for the traveler willing to spend some time and money for an adventure vacation; it's also a great place if your mission is to find high-quality Inuit arts and crafts.

It's easy to spend a day or two exploring the galleries and museums of **Iqaluit,** the capital, but if you've come this far, you definitely should continue on to yet more remote and traditional communities. Iqaluit is the population and governmental center of Baffin, but far more scenic and culturally significant destinations are just a short plane ride away.

For information about travelling throughout Nunavut and for a copy of the latest travel planner, contact **Nunavut Tourism** (© **866/686-2888** or 867/979-6551; www.nunavuttourism.com). Any serious traveler should get hold of *The Nunavut Handbook,* an excellent government-sponsored guide loaded with information on Nunavut's land, wildlife, history, people, and culture, and practical tips for travelers. The handbook is available from local bookstores and from www.nunavuthandbook.com.

GETTING THERE Iqaluit, 2,266km (1,408 miles) from Yellowknife, is the major transport hub on Baffin and is linked to the rest of Canada by flights from Montréal, Ottawa, and Yellowknife on Inuit-owned **First Air** (© **800/267-1247** or 613/254-6200; www.firstair.ca) or **Canadian North** (© **800/661-1505;** www.canadiannorth.com); there are also flights from Ottawa or Montréal to Iqaluit on **Air Canada** (© **888/247-2262;** www.aircanada.com).

Because there are no roads linking communities here, travel between small villages is also by plane (some locals and very adventurous visitors will travel by boat or snowmobile between communities, but this takes time, skill, and preparation). First Air is the major local carrier, centering out of Iqaluit; a bevy of smaller providers, like **Calm Air** (© **800/839-2256;** www.calmair.com) and Inuit-owned **Air Inuit** (© **800/361/2965**; www.airinuit.com), fill in the gaps.

Iqaluit: Gateway to Baffin Island

On the southern end of the island, Iqaluit (pronounced Ee-ka-loo-eet), meaning "place of many fish" in Inuktitut, is the capital of Nunavut and, like most Inuit settlements, is quite young; it grew up alongside a U.S. Air Force airstrip built here in 1942. The rambling community overlooking Frobisher Bay now boasts a rapidly growing population of more than 7,000 and is a hodgepodge of weather-proofed government and civic buildings.

GETTING AROUND There is no public transit, but about 80 licensed taxis serve the population. A flat rate of C$6 will take you anywhere in town, but you may have to share the ride with others. There are street names, but no one uses them; all addresses go by building number (with little logic behind the numbering), and cabbies have the buildings memorized. **Pai Pa** (© **867/979-2585**) and **Caribou Cabs** (© **867/979-4444**) are the two main companies.

SPECIAL EVENTS April is when Iqaluit comes out to play. The weather is warming up (about 14°F/–10°C, on average), and it's the perfect time of year to get out on the land for cross-country skiing, snowmobiling, and dog-sledding. **Toonik Tyme,** Nunavut's biggest festival celebrating the return of spring, takes place in April, although the exact dates often change. Check www.tooniktyme.com to confirm dates. Events range from traditional (bannock making, seal skinning, and dog-sledding contests) to modern (an uphill snowmobile climb and the popular Fear Factor, where people eat all sorts of nasty things for a chance at the grand prize).

In early summer, from Nunavut Day (June 21) to Canada Day (July 1), Iqaluit hosts the **Alianait Arts Festival** (www.alianait.ca), an arts mash-up with performers from around the North, and select international artists performing music, storytelling, film, and circus acts.

EXPLORING IQALUIT

Begin at the **Unikkaarvik Visitor/Information Centre** (© **866/NUNAVUT** [866/686-2888] or 867/979-4636), overlooking the bay, with a friendly staff to answer questions or suggest guiding companies to take you around, and a series of displays on Inuit culture, natural history, and local art. Watch one of the hundreds of Nunavut videos, read from the various books on the North, and pick up some souvenirs. There's even an igloo to explore. June to Labour Day, the center is open daily 10am to 5pm; the rest of the year, it's open Monday through Friday the same hours.

Next door is the **Nunatta Sunakkutaangit Museum** (© **867/979-5537**), housed in an old Hudson's Bay Company building. The collection of Arctic arts and crafts on display and for sale here is excellent, and this is a good place to observe the stylized beauty of Inuit carvings. It also hosts traveling exhibits, the most popular being the world-famous annual Cape Dorset Print Collection, and displays local and regional Inuit artifacts—tools, skin clothing, or a sealskin kayak. It's open Tuesday through Sunday 1 to 5pm.

The **Legislative Assembly** (Building 926, near Four Corners; © **867/975-5000;** www.assembly.nu.ca) has an impressive display of Inuit tapestries and carvings, and the pièce de résistance—an intricately carved Narwhal tusk, embedded with gems, and crowned with a Western Nunavut diamond at its tip. Tours (by appointment) of the "Leg" are worthwhile and free. The public can sit in on legislative sessions, conducted mainly in Inuktitut with English translations. Contact the assembly for session schedules.

Apex (5km/3 miles southwest of town via the road to Apex), the quaint satellite community in the valley southeast of Iqaluit, resembles the small hamlets that make up the rest of Nunavut. On the beach are two former Hudson's Bay buildings, one converted to a private home, and the other used as an artist's studio. This is a picturesque place to walk along the shore.

Sylvia Grinnell Territorial Park (✆ **867/975-7700;** www.nunavutparks.com), a 30-minute walk from Iqaluit or C$6 cab ride (1km/½ mile northeast of town, along the road past Discovery Lodge Hotel), is an ideal spot for a light hike on the rolling tundra and pathways, or alongside the meandering Sylvia Grinnell River. There's a lovely look-out spot at the base of the park, where you might want to have a picnic and watch for caribou and Arctic fox. The river's abundant char population gave Iqaluit its name, and in summer, it's crowded with eager fishers casting along the river's edge. You need a license to fish here, and the easiest way to get one is at **Arctic Ventures** (Building 192, 5-minute walk east of Four Corners; ✆ **867/979-5992**). Canadian residents pay C$20 for the season or C$15 for 3 days, and non-residents pay C$40 for the season and C$30 for 3 days.

Qaummaarviit Territorial Park (✆ **867/975-7700;** www.nunavutparks.com), the tiny rock island to the west of Iqaluit, is an archeological goldmine. About 12km (7½ miles) from town by boat (or dogsled in winter), it's the best place near the capital to see ancient remains of the Thule people, ancestors of Inuit. Arctic conditions are ideal for preservation, and the remains of 11 sod houses bring you back to what life was like before European contact. It's a boat ride away, so hire a guide to take you there and interpret the site. **Inuksuk Adventures** provides tours here, including transportation, guides, and a snack, but not every day. You must book in advance (✆ **867/979-2113;** www.inuksukadventures.ca).

WHERE TO STAY

Nunattaq Suites (4141 Lake View Rd.; ✆ **867/979-2221;** www.nunattaqsuites.com) offers comfortable, clean, and cozy bed-and-breakfast style accommodations with spectacular views. Rooms come with a queen-size bed, private bathroom, and wireless Internet. A family kitchen and living room are available for use. It's a nice alternative to the hotels in town, but it's a 15-minute walk from downtown. Rooms start from C$175 for a double.

Frobisher Inn (✆ **867/979-2222;** www.frobisherinn.com), atop Iqaluit's Astro Hill—or the "Frobe," as it's known by regulars—is in a massive complex that houses a cinema, a small shopping arcade, and the municipal pool, and is easy to see from just about anywhere in town. Guest rooms on the bay side are quite panoramic. There's a very lively bar, the **Storehouse** (✆ **867/979-1105**), as well as a decent restaurant, the **Gallery** (✆ **867/979-2222** ext. 608), with a mix of French and Northern choices. Double rooms begin at C$250.

The **Nova Inn** (923 Federal Rd.; ✆ **866/497-6933** or 867/979-6684; www.novainniqaluit.ca) is Iqaluit's newest hotel, with one pub, the Kickin' Caribou Lounge; a pretty good restaurant, the Waters' Edge (both at ✆ 867/979-4726); and a small fitness center. All rooms are equipped with kitchenettes, including a refrigerator, microwave, toaster, and dishes, and competitive pricing, starting at C$195 for a double.

The Faroese innkeeper converted an old nursing station in Apex to the gorgeous **Rannva's B&B** (✆ **867/979-3184;** me@rannva.com), designed with Scandinavian simplicity and style. The rate is C$145 for a double, with a hearty, delicious breakfast and strong coffee included. You will need to depend on taxis to get to and from town.

WHERE TO EAT

Dining choices are limited, even in the capital. You'll find prices are sometimes double that of more southern locales, and the quality is often low. But there are a few spots that beat out the rest.

The Grind 'n Brew (Building 116B; ✆ **867/979-0606**), essentially a shack across the street from the Bay, is a local favorite. Don't let the clutter and kitsch throw you off: This is the best place in town to get a pizza, and the early morning "Eye Opener" breakfast sandwiches are delicious, especially before a day out on the land. Sit down at one of the tables for a coffee, and you'll learn all the local gossip.

Water's Edge (✆ **867/979-4726**), in the Nova Inn, is Iqaluit's newest and arguably most up-scale dining establishment, and has menu items on par with anything you'd find in the south. You can order salads, crab cakes, and even filet mignon and live lobster, and they sometimes have local cuisine (called "Country Food") like caribou, musk-ox, and Arctic char on offer.

Two local classics sure to cure junk food cravings are the **Snack** (Building 163; ✆ **867/979-6767**) and the Chinese food at the **Captain's Table Dining Room** at the **Navigator Inn** (Building 1036; ✆ **867/979-8833**). You'll see Snack delivery jeeps riding all through town 24 hours a day, so getting delivery is a popular option, or you can slide into one of the red patent-leather booths at the restaurant and treat yourself to Québécois favorites like *poutine* (C$9.25) or submarine sandwiches (C$21 for the steak sub). The "Nav's" buffet (C$21 Mon–Fri noon–1pm, C$31 Fri 5–8:30pm) has all you'd imagine—chow mein, sweet-and-sour pork, deep-fried chicken balls, spicy calamari, and won ton soup. It's a good value, but get there at noon to beat the office crowd.

SHOPPING

There are more artists per capita in Nunavut than anywhere in the world, and Iqaluit is the primary center for Baffin Island art. During most months, except mid-winter, you will see artists carving caribou antler and soapstone outside their homes. You may be approached in bars and restaurants, and on the street, to buy art, crafts, and clothing (seal-skin mitts are common). The quality is usually high, and the price much cheaper than elsewhere in Canada. Artists will typically give you two prices for their wares, what they feel it's worth and what they will accept if you can't afford it. You can haggle a bit, but probably shouldn't too hard—you are already getting a good deal. Local galleries carry works from communities around the island; ask at the visitor center for a *Discover Nunavut Arts and Culture* pamphlet and contact the **Nunavut Arts and Crafts Association** (✆ **867/979-7808;** www.nacaarts.com) for a list of all retail outlets selling Inuit art around Nunavut.

Arctic Ventures (Building 192; ✆ **867/979-5992**) is mainly a grocery store, but the top level has an impressive selection of Arctic literature. There's also some fun Nunavut-inspired t-shirts—think wolves, polar bears, and snowmobiles.

SPORTS & OUTDOOR ACTIVITIES

Spring (Apr–June) is the peak time for outdoor sports in Nunavut. The bay is still frozen and snow still covers the ground, but the days are warmish (about 14°F/–10°C) and the sun doesn't set until late. You know it's spring when the high-pitched sounds of ski-doos touring the streets ramp up and every third person has raccoon eyes from their snow goggles.

DOG-SLEDDING The traditional mode of transport has been largely replaced by snowmobiles, ATVs, and cars. But some die-hards are keeping the sport alive, and in Iqaluit, there are still a handful of dog teams. The wide-open spaces of the tundra and the flat, pristine ice surface on the Bay make for ideal sledding conditions—there are no trees to get in the way. Polar adventurer Matty McNair, owner of **Northwinds** (✆ **867/979-0551;** www.northwinds-arctic.com), operates guided Tea on the Sea day trips on Frobisher Bay for C$175 per person (minimum two people). For a more intense, dedicated experience, Northwinds offers The Baffin Challenge, a 16-day trek through traditional Inuit routes near Iqaluit (C$7,500) or the Northern Lights package (a six-day version) for C$4,000. Your guide and equipment—supplies, tents, and, of course, dogs—are included, but the work (harnessing dogs, hiking up hills, and leading the pack) is a shared duty.

KITE-SKIING In the past few years, this adventurous sport, which has people being towed along the ice and snow strapped to a kite, has really taken hold, and in the spring, you can often see heaps of enthusiasts playing on the Bay. Guided trips and lessons, however, are harder to come by. Northwinds runs 12-day training courses and mini-expeditions (C$3,500).

During summer months, popular sports are boating, hiking, and fishing. Guided hiking and fishing trips are hard to find and not entirely required. Grab a picnic and head to the rolling hills near Apex or to Silvia Grinnell Park. Boating is a different story. **Inuksuk Adventures** (✆ **867/979-2113;** www.inuksukadventures.ca) does various boat trips throughout Frobisher Bay, but not every day. Call to book.

Other Baffin Island Destinations

If you've come as far as Iqaluit, don't stop now. Smaller communities on Baffin Island are far more scenic and compelling than Iqaluit, and with excellent recreational opportunities. Each of the following Inuit communities is served by scheduled air service and will have a small hotel, store, and guide services. For current information on these communities, consult the Nunavut tourism website at www.nunavuttourism.com.

PANGNIRTUNG & AUYUITTUQ NATIONAL PARK

Called "Pang" by locals, Pangnirtung is at the heart of one of the most scenic areas in Nunavut. Located on a deep, mountain-flanked fjord, Pang is the jumping-off point for the 19,089-sq.-km (7,370-sq.-mile) Auyuittuq National Park.

Pang itself is a lovely little village of 1,200 people, with a postcard view up the narrow fjord to the glaciered peaks of Auyuittuq. The local population is friendly and outgoing, which isn't always the case in some other Inuit villages. The **Angmarlik Interpretive Centre** (✆ **867/473-8737**) is definitely worth a stop, with well-presented displays on local Inuit history and culture.

Just across the street is the **Uqqurmiut Centre for Arts and Crafts** (✆ **867/473-8669;** www.uqqurmiut.com), where Pang artisans create stunning hand-woven tapestries sold around the world. The center is a huge economic driver in a region with few active industries. You can meet the artists at work on the large looms and view their wares in what may be the best gift shop in Nunavut, with its selection of tapestries, woven belts, and the ubiquitous Pang hats. There are also carvings and prints for sale, made in the adjoining print shop.

Most people go to Pang to reach Auyuittuq National Park, 31km (19 miles) farther up Pangnirtung Fjord. This is Nunavut's most popular national park, with 400 people visiting a year! Auyuittuq (pronounced Ow-you-ee-tuk) means "the land that never melts" and refers to the 5,698-sq.-km (2,200-sq.-mile) Penny Ice Cap, which covers the high plateaus of the park, and the glaciers that edge down into the lower valleys and cling to the towering granite peaks. The landscapes are extremely dramatic: Cliffs rise from the milky-green sea, terminating in hornlike glacier-draped peaks 2,333m (7,654 ft.) high; in fact, the world's longest uninterrupted cliff face on Thor Peak (over 1km/½ mile of sheer rock) is in the park. Auyuittuq is largely the province of long-distance hikers and rock climbers; if you're looking for an adventurous walking holiday in magnificent scenery, this might be it. The best times to visit are March until early April for skiers or day trips by snow machine to the Arctic Circle, and July to mid-August, when the days are long and afternoons bring short-sleeve weather. You must register and complete an orientation before entering the park, and you need to hire an outfitter to get you to the entrance. For details, contact the Auyuittuq National Park Office (✆ **867/473-2500;** www.parkscanada.gc.ca/auyuittuq).

HIKING THE PARK The Arctic Circle is about 14km (8¾ miles) from the entrance to the park, so a hike there and back makes a nice day trip. But beyond this point is where the landscape gets really interesting. You can even hike through the entire 97km (60-mile) Ashuyuk Pass, clear to the neighboring village of Qikiqtarjuaq, which will take you just under 2 weeks. Parks Canada recommends hikers completing the entire pass begin in Qikiqtarjuaq and hike south towards Pang. No matter which hike you choose, guides are advised. You need a boat or snow machine in spring to take you to the park entrance—about a 40-minute ride from Pang and almost 3 hours from Qikiqtarjuaq—and the park terrain can be challenging, at times (from the Pang side, even at the start of the hike, waist-deep river water flowing from the glaciers above is a likely possibility).

The most experienced guide in Pang, Joavee Alivaktuk of **Alivaktuk Outfitting** (✆ **867/473-8721**) provides transport to and from the park (C$110 per person each way; C$220, including tax, round trip). **Black Feather** (✆ **888/849-7668;** www.blackfeather.com) outfits and guides small groups for multiday hikes through the park (14 day hikes are C$3,395, plus tax and C$150 park fee).

POND INLET

In many ways, the best reason to make the trip to Pond Inlet on Baffin's northern shore is simply to see the landscape. On a clear day, the 4-hour flight from Iqaluit up to Pond is simply astounding: hundreds of miles of knife-edged mountains, massive ice caps (remnants of the ice fields that once covered all North America), glacier-choked valleys, and deep fjords flooded by the sea. It's an epic landscape—in all the country, perhaps only the Canadian Rockies can match the eastern coast of Baffin Island for sheer scenic drama.

Pond Inlet sits on **Eclipse Sound,** near the top of Baffin Island, in the heart of this rugged beauty. Opposite the town is **Bylot Island,** a wildlife refuge and part of **Sirmilik (North Baffin) National Park** (✆ **867/899-8092;** www.parkscanada.gc.ca/sirmilik). Its craggy peaks rear 2,167m (7,110 ft.) straight up from the sea; from its central ice caps, two massive glaciers pour down into the sound directly across from town. Before entering Sirmilik, you must register and do an orientation session.

Considering the amazing scenery in the area, Pond Inlet is relatively untouristy, though it has seen an increase in summer visitors in the last few years with the rise of cruise traffic. The peak tourist season is May and June, when local outfitters offer trips out to the edge of the ice floes, the point where the ice of the protected bays meets the open water of the Arctic Ocean. In spring, this is where you find much of the Arctic's wildlife: seals, walruses, bird life, polar bears, narwhals, and other species converge here to feed, often on one another. A wildlife-viewing trip out to the floe edge (by snowmobile or dogsled) requires at least 3 days, with 5-day trips advised for maximum viewing opportunities. Other recreation opportunities, like kayaking and biking, open up in August, when the ice clears out of Eclipse Sound. Bird-watching boat trips to Bylot Island are offered (the rare ivory gull nests here), as well as narwhal-watching trips in the fjords. It's best to allow several days in Pond Inlet if you're coming for summer trips; the weather is very changeable this far north.

Polar Sea Adventures (✆ **867/899-8870;** www.polarsea.com) is probably the most prominent operator in Pond, delivering safe, very well-planned and high-quality multiday trips in spring and summer. Among the scheduled offerings are dog-sledding, skiing, camping on the floe edge, hiking, and sea kayaking trips. The company also customizes trips, so if you want to bicycle across the sea ice, this is the place to call.

Enookie Inuarak of **Inuarak Outfitting** (✆ **867/899-8551;** inuarak@gmail.com) offers floe-edge tours, dog-team tours, and fishing expeditions near Pond.

KIMMIRUT & KATANNILIK TERRITORIAL PARK

The center for Baffin Island's famed stone-carving industry, **Kimmirut** is located along a rocky harbor, directly south of Iqaluit on the southern shore of Baffin Island. While many people make the trip to this dynamic, picturesque community to visit the workshops of world-renowned carvers, there are other reasons to make the trip. **Katannilik Territorial Park** is a preserve of Arctic wildlife and lush tundra vegetation and offers access to Soper River. The Soper, a Canadian Heritage River, is famed for its many waterfalls in side valleys and for its long-distance float and canoe trips.

Many people visit Katannilik Territorial Park for a less-demanding version of rugged Auyuittuq National Park farther north. Wildlife viewing is good, and hiking trails wind through the park. Canoeing or kayaking the Soper River is a popular 3-day trip that's full of adventure but still suitable for a family. For more information on the park, contact the Katannilik Park manager (✆ **867/939-2084;** www.nunavutparks.com).

Getting to the starting point of your Soper journey is tricky, and you would do well with a guide throughout the 3-day adventure. **Northwinds** (✆ **867/979-0551;** www.northwinds-arctic.com) is there to help with customized tours.

CAPE DORSET

The rolling tundra surrounding Cape Dorset is similar to that of Iqaluit or Kimmirut; what makes Dorset stand out is the artists who live there. This is the home of the **West Baffin Eskimo Co-Operative** (✆ **867/897-8827;** wbec@interhop.net), where fine soapstone carvings, stone-cut printing, etchings, and most famously, the

Cape Dorset Print Collection, are created, marketed, and sold. Mid–20th-century artist James Houston put Dorset art on the map in the 1950s, when he recognized its brilliance and helped establish what came to be a world-famous, thriving collection. The prints are characterized by abstract, brightly colored portrayals of Inuit culture, Northern wildlife and scenery, and the more seemingly mundane aspects of Northern life, like shopping at the Northern store or lining up at the ATM. Art buffs flock to the village for tours of the co-op, to view artists at work, and to shop.

Other Nunavut Destinations

BATHURST INLET

One of the most notable arctic lodges, Bathurst Inlet Lodge (✆ **867/873-2595;** www.visitnunavut.com/bathurstinletlodge.html) was founded in 1969 for naturalists and those interested in the Arctic's natural history and ecology. The lodge is at the mouth of the Burnside River on an arm of the Arctic Ocean in a rugged landscape of tundra and rocky cliffs. The lodge is housed in the historic buildings of a former Oblate mission and the old Hudson's Bay Company trading post.

The lodge is open for a brief mid-summer season only. Rates will depend on the activities available during your visit, but are typically C$4,995 a week, which includes charter air transportation to/from Yellowknife, all meals, and programs. The lodge can make arrangements to suit your individual interests, including fishing, hiking, flight seeing, wildlife photography, and river floating.

QUTTINIRPAAQ (ELLESMERE ISLAND) NATIONAL PARK RESERVE

A good part of the intrigue of Ellesmere Island is its absolute remoteness. A preserve of rugged glacier-choked mountains, ice fields, mountain lakes and fjords, and Arctic wildlife, **Ellesmere Island National Park** is the most northerly point in North America. During the short summer, experienced hikers and mountaineers make their way to this wilderness area to explore some of the most isolated and inaccessible land in the world.

History is well-preserved this far north. Archeological sites dating back to Independence I culture (Paleo-Eskimo peoples from 2400–1000 BCE) all the way to the Dorset culture (500 BCE–CE 1500) are scattered throughout the park, as are endless ancient fossils. Fort Conger, the site of Nares, Greely, and Peary explorations in the late 1800s and early 1900s, still stands as it was when left by Peary.

Getting to Ellesmere is neither easy nor cheap. From Resolute Bay (served by regularly scheduled flights on First Air), park visitors must charter a private airplane for the 3-hour, 960km (597-mile) flight farther north. Facilities are limited to shelters at Tanquary Fiord Operations Station and outhouses at Lake Hazen and Ward Hunt Island stations, so you must be prepared for extremes of weather and physical endurance. The most common activity is hiking from Lake Hazen at the center of the park to Tanquary Fjord in the southwest corner. This 129km (80-mile) trek crosses rugged tundra moorland, as well as several glaciers, and demands fords of major rivers. Needless to say, Ellesmere Island Park isn't for the uninitiated.

Kenn Borek Air (✆ **867/252-3845;** www.borekair.com) charters Twin Otters from Resolute to the park. The craft will carry 907kg (2,000 lb.)—equal to 8 to 10 people with gear—and costs about C$50,000. A more feasible option is sharing the charter with other visitors, which you can coordinate through Kenn Borek, but make sure to do so well in advance.

For more information and an up-to-date listing of outfitters who run trips into the park, contact Quttinirpaaq National Park (✆ **867/975-4673;** www.parkscanada.gc.ca/quttinirpaaq).

Northwest Passage

The hotly contested waterway snaking between the high Arctic archipelago connecting the Atlantic and Pacific oceans is fast becoming a tourist destination. Although the landscape is bleak (think flat, brown expanses) and wildlife sightings rather unimpressive compared to elsewhere in Nunavut, the passage still holds its own, if only for sheer historic and symbolic significance. Between the 15th and 20th centuries, European explorers tried in vain to find a short route to the riches of Asia, each failing miserably. Sir John Franklin's plight may have been the worst, with his sailors eating their leather boots as a last resort. Finally, in 1906, Norwegian explorer Roald Amundsen, using skills garnered from the Inuit, completed the first Northwest Passage crossing. There are a great number of historical sites dotting the passage, namely the graves of four Franklin sailors on Beechey Island.

The little community of **Gjoa Haven,** approximately midway along the Passage, was named after Amundsen's ship, the *Gjoa.* One resident even boasts being Amundsen's grandson. Gjoa Haven is also home to the **Northwest Passage Territorial Trail** (✆ **867/975-7700;** www.nunavutparks.com), a collection of six sites significant to the Passage's history, including a museum with a replica of the *Gjoa,* shelters used by Amundsen during his quest, and grave sites believed to be where more members of Franklin's crew were buried.

In recent years, the Passage has become popular for its current affairs, as well. Recent easing of ice-pack conditions has made the passageway more accessible to marine traffic, and many nations are staking its claim. One of the only ways to visit the Passage is by ship, and cruise ship visits have increased rapidly.

CRUISING ACROSS THE top OF THE WORLD

Given the challenge of traveling to Nunavut—expensive flights, limited accommodations and restaurants, and few packaged touring options—another worthwhile option is taking an expedition cruise to Nunavut. It's a more affordable way to see vast landscapes of the territory, wildlife colonies, and villages, all in one pop. The cruises are typically on small ships with other like-minded travelers and include daily landings to hike around and explore. Itineraries vary, but most start in Western Greenland and traverse across Northern Baffin Island, through the Passage, ending in Cambridge Bay or Kugluktuk. Prices start at about C$7,500 for a 12-night journey throughout Nunavut's coastal areas. **Adventure Canada** (✆ **800/363-7566;** www.adventurecanada.com) is a family-owned business with 20 years experience offering small-ship expedition cruising in the Arctic. **Cruise North Expeditions** (✆ **866/263-3220;** www.cruisenorthexpeditions.com) is an Inuit-owned and -operated company that also offers expedition-style cruises through Nunavut and the Arctic.

APPENDIX: CANADA IN DEPTH

by Andrew Hempstead

18

Canada's sheer amount of elbow space can make you dizzy. At 6.1 million sq. km (2.4 million sq. miles), 322,000 sq. km (124,325 sq. miles) more than the United States, this colossal expanse contains only 33 million people—fewer than the state of California alone. Most of the population is clustered in a relatively narrow southern belt that boasts all the nation's large cities and nearly all its industries. The silent Yukon, Northwest Territories, and Nunavut—where 100,000 people dot 2.4 million sq. km (926,645 sq. miles)—remain a frontier, stretching to the Arctic shores and embracing thousands of lakes no one has ever charted, counted, or named.

It's impossible to easily categorize this land or its people—just when you think you know Canada, you discover another place, another temperament, a hidden side.

HISTORY 101

The Founding of New France

The Vikings landed in Canada more than 1,000 years ago, but the French were the first Europeans to get a toehold in the country. In 1608, Samuel de Champlain established a settlement on the cliffs overlooking the St. Lawrence River—today's Québec City. This was exactly a year after the Virginia Company founded Jamestown. Hundreds of miles of unexplored wilderness lay between the embryo colonies, but they were inexorably set on a collision course.

The early stages of the struggle for the new continent were explorations—and the French outdid the English. Their fur traders, navigators, soldiers, and missionaries opened up not only Canada but also most of the United States. Relying on canoes for transport, these *voyageurs* discovered, mapped, and settled at least 35 of the 50 United States. Gradually, they staked out an immense colonial empire that, in patches and minus recognized borders, stretched from Hudson Bay in the Arctic to the Gulf of Mexico. Christened New France, it was run on an ancient seigniorial system, whereby settlers were granted land by the Crown in return for military service.

The military obligation was essential, for the colony knew hardly a moment of peace during its existence. New France blocked the path of western expansion by England's seaboard colonies with a string of forts that lined the Ohio-Mississippi Valley. The Anglo-Americans were determined to break through, and so the frontier clashes crackled and flared, with the native tribes participating ferociously. These miniature wars were nightmares of savagery, waged with knives and tomahawks as much as with muskets and cannons, characterized by raids and counter-raids, burning villages, and massacred women and children.

The French retaliated in kind. They converted the Abenaki tribe to Christianity and encouraged them to raid deep into New England territory, where, in 1704, they totally destroyed the town of Deerfield, Massachusetts. The Americans answered with a punitive blitz expedition by the famous green-clad Roger's Rangers, who wiped out the main Abenaki village and slaughtered half its population.

By far the most dreaded of the tribes was the Iroquois, who played the same role in the Canadian east as the Sioux (another French label) played in the American West. Astute politicians, the Iroquois played the English against the French and vice versa, lending their scalping knives first to one side, then to the other. It took more than a century before they finally succumbed to the whites' smallpox, firewater, and gunpowder—in that order.

The Fall of Québec

There were only about 65,000 French settlers in the colony, but they more than held their own against the million Anglo-Americans, first and foremost because they were natural forest fighters—one French trapper could stalemate six redcoats in the woods. Mainly, however, it was because they made friends with the local tribes whenever possible. The majority of tribes sided with the French and made the English pay a terrible price for their blindness.

Even before French and English interests in the New World came to the point of armed struggle in the Seven Years' War, the British had largely taken control of Acadia (as the area of coastal Nova Scotia and New Brunswick was then known), though its lush forests and farmlands were dotted with French settlements. The governors knew there would be war, so, suspicious of Acadia's French-speaking inhabitants, they decided on a bold and ruthless plan: All Acadians who wouldn't openly pledge allegiance to the British sovereign would be deported. The order came in 1755, and French-speaking families throughout the province were forcibly moved from their homes, many resettling in the French territory of Louisiana, where their Cajun language and culture are still alive today. To replace the Acadians, shiploads of Scottish and Irish settlers arrived from the British Isles, and the province soon acquired the name Nova Scotia—New Scotland.

When the final round of fighting began in 1754, it opened with a series of shattering English debacles. The French had a brilliant commander, the Marquis de Montcalm, exactly the kind of unorthodox tactician needed for the fluid semi-guerrilla warfare of the American wilderness. Britain's proud General Braddock rode into a French-Indian ambush that killed him and scattered his army. Montcalm led an expedition against Fort Oswego that wiped out the stronghold and turned Lake Ontario into a French waterway. The following summer he repeated the feat with Fort William Henry, at the head of Lake George, which fell amid ghastly scenes of massacre, later immortalized by James Fenimore Cooper in *The Last of the Mohicans*

(Signet Classics). Middle New York now lay wide open to raids, and England's hold on America seemed to be slipping.

Then, like a cornered boxer bouncing from the ropes, the British came back with a devastating right-left-right that not only saved their colonies but also won them the entire continent. The first punches were against Fort Duquesne, in Pennsylvania, and against the Fortress of Louisbourg, on Cape Breton, both of which they took after bloody sieges. Then, where least expected, came the ultimate haymaker, aimed straight at the enemy's solar plexus—Québec.

In June 1759, a British fleet nosed its way from the Atlantic down the St. Lawrence River. In charge of the troops on board was the youngest general in the army, 32-year-old James Wolfe, whose military record was remarkable and whose behavior was so eccentric he had the reputation of being "mad as a March hare." The struggle for Québec dragged on until September, when Wolfe, near desperation, played his final card. He couldn't storm those gallantly defended fortress walls, though the British guns had shelled the town to rubble. Wolfe therefore loaded 5,000 men into boats and rowed upriver to a cove behind the city. Then they silently climbed the towering cliff face in the darkness, and when morning came Wolfe had his army squarely astride Montcalm's supply lines. Now the French had to come out of their stronghold and fight in the open.

The British formed their famous "thin red line" across the bush-studded Plains of Abraham, just west of the city. Montcalm advanced on them with five regiments, all in step, and in the next quarter of an hour, the fate of Canada was decided. The redcoats stood like statues as the French drew closer—100 yards, 60 yards, 40 yards. Then a command rang out, and (in such perfect unison it sounded like a single thunderclap) the English muskets crashed. The redcoats advanced four measured paces, halted, fired, advanced another four paces with robot precision—halted, fired again. Then it was all over.

The plain was covered with the fallen French. Montcalm lay mortally wounded, and the rest of his troops fled helter-skelter. Among the British casualties was Wolfe himself. With two bullets through his body, he lived just long enough to hear that he'd

DATELINE

1608 Samuel de Champlain founds the settlement of Kebec—today's Québec City.

1642 The French colony of Ville-Marie established, later renamed Montréal.

1759 The British defeat the French at the Plains of Abraham. Québec City falls.

1763 All "New France" (Canada) ceded to the British.

1775 American Revolutionary forces capture Montréal but are repulsed at Québec City.

1813 Americans blow up Fort York (Toronto) in the War of 1812.

1841 The Act of Union creates the United Provinces of Canada.

1855 Ottawa becomes Canada's capital.

1869 The Hudson's Bay Company sells Rupert's Land to Canada. It becomes the Province of Alberta.

won. Montcalm died a few hours after him. Today, overlooking the boardwalk of Québec, you'll find a unique memorial to these men—a statue commemorating both the victor and vanquished of the same battle.

A Confederation of Provinces

Canada has always been a loosely linked country, a confederation of provinces, not a union of states. Canadians are quick to tell you theirs is a "cultural mosaic" of people, not a "melting pot." These factors account in great part for two of Canada's most striking characteristics: its cultural vitality and its habits of mistrust and contention.

THE U.S. INVASION

The capture of Québec determined the war and left Britain ruler of all North America down to the Mexican border. Yet, oddly enough, this victory generated Britain's worst defeat. For if the French had held Canada, the British government would certainly have been more careful in its treatment of the American colonists. As it was, the British felt cocksure and decided to make the colonists themselves pay for the outrageous costs of the French and Indian Wars. The taxes slapped on all imports—especially tea—infuriated the colonists to the point of open rebellion against the Crown. The rest of this story—the America Revolution of 1775 to 1783—is, as they say, history.

But if the British misjudged the temper of the colonists, the Americans were equally wrong about the mood of the Canadians. General George Washington felt sure the French in the north would join the American Revolution, or at least not resist an invasion of American soldiers. He was terribly mistaken on both counts. The French had little love for either of the English-speaking antagonists. But they were staunch Royalists and devout Catholics, with no sympathy for the "godless" republicans from the south. Only a handful changed sides, and most French Canadians fought grimly shoulder to shoulder with their erstwhile enemies.

Thirty-eight years later, in the War of 1812, another U.S. army marched up the banks of the Richelieu River where it flows from Lake Champlain to the St. Lawrence.

1873 The Northwest Mounted Police (the Mounties) are created.

1875 The west coast community of Gastown is incorporated as the city of Vancouver. The Northwest Mounted Police build the log fort that will develop into the city of Calgary.

1885 Under Louis Riel, the Métis rebel in western Saskatchewan.

1887 The transcontinental railroad reaches Vancouver, connecting Canada from ocean to ocean.

1896 The Klondike Gold Rush brings 100,000 people swarming into the Yukon.

1914 Canada enters World War I alongside Britain. Some 60,000 Canadians die in combat.

1920 The Northwest Territories separate from the Yukon.

1930 The Great Depression and mass unemployment hit Canada.

1939 Canada enters World War II with Britain.

continues

And once again, the French Canadians stuck by the British and flung back the invaders. The war ended in a draw, but with surprisingly happy results. Britain and the young United States agreed to demilitarize the Great Lakes and to extend their mutual border along the 49th parallel to the Rockies.

LOYALISTS & IMMIGRANTS

One of the side effects of the American Revolution was an influx of English-speaking newcomers for Canada. About 50,000 Americans who had remained faithful to George III, the United Empire Loyalists, migrated to Canada because they were given rough treatment in the States. They settled mostly in Nova Scotia and began to populate the almost-empty shores of what's now New Brunswick.

After the Napoleonic Wars, a regular tide of immigrants came from England, which was going through the early and cruelest stages of the Industrial Revolution. They were fleeing from the hideously bleak factory towns, from workhouses, starvation wages, and impoverished Scottish farms. Even the unknown perils of the New World seemed preferable to these blessings of the Dickens era. By 1850, more than half a million immigrants had arrived, pushing Canada's population above 2 million. The population centers began to shift westward, away from the old seaboard colonies in the east, opening up the territories eventually called Ontario, Manitoba, and Saskatchewan.

With increased population came the demand for confederation, largely because the various colony borders hampered trade. Britain complied rather promptly. In 1867, Parliament passed an act creating a federal union out of the colonies of Upper and Lower Canada, Nova Scotia, and New Brunswick. British Columbia hesitated over whether to remain separate, join the United States, or merge with Canada, but finally voted itself in. Remote Newfoundland hesitated longest of all, a distinct colony until 1949, when it became Canada's 10th province.

THE METIS REBELLION

Geographically, Canada stretched from the Atlantic to the Pacific, but in reality, most of the immense region in between lay beyond the rule of Ottawa, the nation's capital. The endless prairies and forest lands of the west and northwest were inhabited by

1947 Huge oil deposits are discovered at Leduc, southwest of Edmonton. The Alberta oil boom begins.

1959 The opening of the St. Lawrence Seaway turns Toronto into a major seaport.

1967 Montréal hosts the World Expo.

1968 The Parti Québécois is founded by René Lévesque. The separatist movement begins.

1970 Cabinet Minister Pierre Laporte is kidnapped and murdered. The War Measures Act is imposed on Québec.

1976 Montréal becomes the site of the Olympic Games.

1988 Calgary hosts the Winter Olympics.

1989 The Canada-U.S. Free Trade Agreement eliminates all tariffs on goods of national origin moving between the two countries.

1995 Québec votes narrowly to remain in Canada.

1999 Nunavut severs itself from the rump Northwest Territories to become a self-governed territory and Inuit homeland.

about 40,000 people, more than half of them nomadic tribes pushed there by the waves of white settlers. They lived by hunting, fishing, and trapping, depending largely on buffalo for food, clothing, and shelter. As the once-enormous herds began to dwindle, life grew increasingly hard for the nomads. Adding to their troubles were whiskey traders peddling poisonous rotgut for furs and packs of outlaws who took what they wanted at gunpoint.

Ordinary law officers were nearly useless. In 1873, the federal government created a quite extraordinary force: the Northwest Mounted Police, now called the Royal Canadian Mounted Police (and now rarely mounted). The scarlet-coated Mounties earned a legendary reputation for toughness, fairness, and the ability to hunt down wrongdoers. And unlike their American counterparts, they usually brought in prisoners alive.

But even the Mounties couldn't handle the desperate uprising that shook western Saskatchewan in 1885. As the railroad relentlessly pushed across the prairies and the buffalo vanished, the people known as the Métis felt they had to fight for their existence. The Métis, offspring of French trappers and Native women, were superb hunters and trackers. The westward expansion had driven them from Manitoba to the banks of the Saskatchewan River, where some 6,000 of them now made their last stand against iron rails and wooden farmhouses. They had a charismatic leader in Louis Riel, a man educated enough to teach school and mad enough to think God wanted him to found a new religion.

With Riel's rebels rose their natural allies, the Plains tribes, under chiefs Poundmaker and Big Bear. Together, they were a formidable force. The Métis attacked the Mounted Police at Duck Lake, cut the telegraph wires, and proclaimed an independent republic. Their allies stormed the town of Battleford, then captured and burned Fort Pitt. The alarmed administration in Ottawa sent an army marching westward under General Middleton, equipped with artillery and Gatling machine guns. The Métis checked them briefly at Fish Creek but had to fall back on their main village of Batoche. There the last battle of the west took place—long lines of redcoats charging with fixed bayonets, the Métis fighting from house to house, from rifle pits and crude trenches, so short of ammunition they had to shoot lead buttons instead of bullets.

2003 Tourism starts to rebound following major drop due to SARS outbreak in Toronto and discovery of mad cow disease in some Alberta cattle.

2005 Canada's Civil Marriage Act, legalizing same-sex marriage, receives royal assent. Michaëlle Jean, born in Haiti, becomes the 27th governor general of Canada, the first black person to hold that position.

2007 The Canadian dollar reaches, then exceeds, the value of U.S. dollar for the first time since 1957.

2010 Vancouver/Whistler host the Winter Olympics.

Batoche fell (you can still see the bullet marks on the houses there), and the rebellion was completely crushed shortly afterward. Louis Riel was tried for treason and murder. Though any court today probably would've found him insane, the Canadian authorities hanged him.

RAILROADS, WHEAT & WAR

The reason the army crushed Riel's rebellion so quickly was also the reason for its outbreak: the Canadian Pacific Railway. The railroad was more than a marvel of engineering—it formed a steel band holding the country together, enabling Canada to live up to its motto, *A Mari Usque ad Mare* ("From Sea to Sea").

Though the free-roaming prairie people hated the iron horse, railroads were vital to Canada's survival as a nation. They had to be pushed through, against all opposition, because the isolated provinces threatened to drift into the orbit of the United States. Without the western provinces, the Dominion would cease to exist. As one journalist of the time put it: "The whistle of a locomotive is the true cradle song and anthem of our country." As Canada's transportation system developed, the central provinces emerged as one of the world's biggest breadbaskets. In just a decade, wheat production zoomed from 56 million bushels to more than 200 million, putting Canada on a par with the United States and Russia as a granary.

And despite the bitterness engendered by Riel's execution, in the following year, Canada elected its first prime minister of French heritage. Sir Wilfrid Laurier had one foot in each ethnic camp and proved to be a superlative leader—according to some, the best his country ever produced. His term of office (1896–1911) was a period in which Canada flexed its muscles like a young giant and looked forward to unlimited growth and a century of peaceful prosperity—just like an equally optimistic American neighbor to the south.

With the onset of World War I, the Dominion went to war allied with Britain and likewise tried to fight it on a volunteer basis. It didn't work. The tall, healthy Canadians, together with the Australians, formed the shock troops of the British Empire and earned that honor with torrents of blood. The entire western front in France was littered with Canadian bones. The flow of volunteers became a trickle, and in 1917, the Dominion was forced to introduce conscription. The measure ran into violent opposition from the French-speaking minority, who saw conscription as a device to thin out their numbers.

The draft law went through, but it strained the nation's unity almost to the breaking point. The results were ghastly. More than 60,000 Canadians fell in battle, a terrible bloodletting for a country of 250,000. (In World War II, by contrast, Canada lost 40,000 from a population of 11.5 million.)

TOWARD WORLD POWER

Between the World Wars, the fortunes of Canada more or less reflected those of the United States, except that Canada was never foolish enough to join the "noble experiment" of Prohibition. Some of its citizens, in fact, waxed rich on the lucrative bootlegging trade across the border.

But the Great Depression, coupled with disastrous droughts in the western provinces, hit all the harder in Canada. There was no equivalent of Roosevelt's New Deal in the Dominion. The country staggered along from one financial crisis to the next until the outbreak of World War II totally transformed the situation. The war provided the boost Canada needed to join the ranks of the major industrial nations. And the surge of postwar immigration provided the numbers required to work the new industries. From 1941 to 1974, Canada doubled in population and increased its gross national product nearly tenfold.

With the discovery of huge uranium deposits in Ontario and Saskatchewan, Canada was in the position to add nuclear energy to its power resources. And the opening of the St. Lawrence Seaway turned Toronto—more than 1,600km (994 miles) from the nearest ocean—into a major seaport. All these achievements propelled Canada into its present position: a powerhouse of manufacturing and trade, with a standard of living to exceed that of the United States. But, simultaneously, old ghosts were raising their heads again.

Trouble in Québec

As an ethnic enclave, the French Canadians had more than won their battle for survival. From their original 65,000 settlers, they had grown to more than 6 million, without receiving reinforcements from overseas. They had preserved and increased their presence by means of large families, rigid cultural cohesion, and the unifying influence of their Catholic faith. But they had fallen far behind the English-speaking majority economically and politically. Few held top positions in industry or finance, and they enjoyed relatively little say in national matters.

What rankled them most was that Canada never recognized French as a second national language; the French were expected to be bilingual if they wanted good careers, but the English-speakers got along nicely with just their own tongue. On a general cultural basis, as well, the country overwhelmingly reflected Anglo-Saxon attitudes, rather than an Anglo-French mixture.

By the early 1960s, this discontent led to a dramatic radicalization of Québécois politics. A new separatist movement arose that regarded Québec not as simply 1 of 10 provinces, but as *l'état du Québec,* a distinct state that might, if it chose, break away from the country. The most extreme faction, the Front de Liberation du Québec (FLQ), was frankly revolutionary and terrorist. It backed its demands with bombs, arson, and murder, culminating in the kidnap-killing of Cabinet Minister Pierre Laporte in October 1970.

The Ottawa government, under Prime Minister Pierre Trudeau, imposed the War Measures Act and moved 10,000 troops into the province. The police used their exceptional powers under the act to break up civil disorders, arrest hundreds of suspects, and catch the murderers of Laporte. In the 1973 provincial elections, the separatists were badly defeated, winning only 6 seats from a total of 110.

The crisis eventually calmed down. In some ways, its effects were beneficial. The federal government redoubled its efforts to remove the worst grievances of the French Canadians. Federal funds flowed to French schools outside Québec (nearly half the schoolchildren of New Brunswick, for example, are French-speaking). French Canadians were appointed to senior positions. Most important, all provinces were asked to make French an official language, which entailed making signs, government forms, transportation schedules, and other printed matter bilingual. Civil servants had to bone up on French to pass their exams, and the business world began to stipulate bilingualism for men and women aiming at executive positions. All these measures were already afoot before the turmoil began, but there's no doubt that bloodshed helped to accelerate them.

Union or Separation?

Ever since the violent crisis, Canadian politicians of all hues have been trying to patch up some sort of compromise that would enable their country to remain united. They appeared close to success when they formulated the so-called Meech Lake Accord in the 1980s. Québec's premier set up a commission to study ways to change the province's constitutional relationship with Ottawa's federal government. This aroused the ire of other provinces, which failed to see why Québec should be granted a "special" position in Canada. During this time, the separatist Parti Québécois rallied its forces and staged a political comeback. The Meech Lake agreement became too unwieldy to pass muster, and an alliance of French Canadians, Native Canadian groups, western Canadian libertarians—and the province of New Brunswick—drove a stake through the heart of the accord. So the proposals, memorandums, and referendums go on and on; each one vetoed by the other camp and none coming closer to a solution.

The rift between Québec's French and English speakers—and between Québec and the other provinces—is still wide, though an improving Québec economy has generally muted resentments in the past few years. To make the situation even more complex, the only population segment in Québec that's growing is that of non-English- and non-French-speaking immigrants. Winning over the immigrant vote is suddenly big political business in Québec.

In October 1995, Québec again faced a referendum asking whether the French-speaking province should separate from the rest of Canada, and suddenly Canada

CANADA'S cultural MOSAIC

Canada has sought "unity through diversity" as a national ideal, and its people are even more diverse than its scenery. In the eastern province of Québec live 6 million French Canadians, whose motto, *Je me souviens* ("I remember"), has kept them "more French than France" through 2 centuries of Anglo domination. They've transformed Canada into a bilingual country where everything official—including parking tickets and airline passes—comes in two tongues.

The English-speaking majority of the populace is a mosaic rather than a block. Two massive waves of immigration—one before 1914, the other between 1945 and 1972—poured 6.5 million assorted Europeans and Americans into the country, providing muscles and skills, as well as a kaleidoscope of cultures. The 1990s saw another wave of immigration—largely from Asia, and particularly from Hong Kong—that has transformed the economics and politics of British Columbia. Thus, Nova Scotia is as Scottish as haggis and kilts, Vancouver has the largest Chinese population outside Asia, the plains of Manitoba are sprinkled with the onion-shaped domes of Ukrainian churches, and Ontario offers Italian street markets and a theater festival featuring the works of Shakespeare at, yes, Stratford.

You can attend a Native Canadian tribal assembly, a Chinese New Year dragon parade, an Inuit spring celebration, a German Bierfest, a Highland gathering, or a Slavic folk dance. There are group settlements on the prairies where the working parlance is Danish, Czech, or Hungarian, and entire villages speak Icelandic.

teetered on the brink of splitting apart. The vote went in favor of the pro-unity camp by a razor-thin margin, but the issue was hardly resolved: In all likelihood, it lives to be reborn as another referendum. Meanwhile, as public officials debate separatism, Québec's younger generation is voting with its feet. Many of its brightest and best are heading west, particularly to more prosperous BC and Alberta. However, these western provinces—no lovers of Ottawa—themselves dream of loosening the federal laws binding them to eastern Canada.

By now, most Canadians are heartily tired of the Québec debate, though nobody seems to have a clear idea how to end it. Some say secession is the only way out; others favor the Swiss formula of biculturalism and bilingualism. For Québec, the breakaway advocated by Francophone hotheads could spell economic disaster. Most of Canada's industrial and financial power is in the English-speaking provinces. An independent Québec would be a poor country. But all Canada would be poorer by losing the special flavor and rich cultural heritage imparted by the presence of La Belle Province.

ONWARD INTO THE 21ST CENTURY: THE CREATION OF NUNAVUT & MORE

Elements of the Canadian economy are still adapting to the landmark North American Free Trade Agreement concluded with the United States in 1989. While free trade hasn't done much to revive the smokestack industries that once were the engines of eastern Canada, the agreement, combined with a weak Canadian dollar in the 1990s, was actually good for much of Canada's huge agricultural heartland. However, the globalization of trade is transforming the Canadian economy in ways that produce confusion and hostility in some citizens. Many Canadians are deeply ambivalent about being so closely linked to their powerful southern neighbor, and the trade agreement (and U.S. culture, in general) often gets the blame for everything that's going wrong with Canada. Yet 85% of Canada's trade is with its southern neighbor—so it's a relationship that will need to be worked out in some form or other.

Public interest in protecting the environment runs high, as reflected in public policy. Recycling is commonplace, and communities across the country have made great strides in balancing economic interests with environmental goals. On Vancouver Island, for example, environmentalists and timber companies agreed in 1995 on forestry standards that satisfy both parties. When salmon fishing boats blockaded an Alaska ferry in Prince Rupert in 1997, the issue for the Canadians was perceived overfishing by Americans. Salmon have been reduced to an endangered species in much of the Pacific Northwest, and the Canadians consequently don't think much of U.S. fisheries' policies.

In 1999, the vast Northwest Territories was divided in two. The eastern half, which takes in Baffin Island, the land around Hudson's Bay, and most of the Arctic islands, is now called Nunavut and essentially functions as an Inuit homeland. The rump Northwest Territories officially retains the territory's old name, though many refer to the region as the Western Arctic.

The success of the Nunavut negotiations has emboldened other Native groups to settle their own land claims with the Canadian government. While many of the claims in northern Canada can be settled by transferring government land and money to Native groups, those in southern Canada are more complex. Some tribes assert a prior claim to land currently owned by non-Natives; in other areas, Native groups refuse to abide by environmental laws that seek to protect endangered runs of salmon. The situation in a number of communities has moved beyond protests and threats to armed encounters and road barricades. The path seems set for more and increasingly hostile confrontations between official Canada and its Native peoples.

The first decade of the 21st century was generally positive for Canada, which distanced itself from the dictates of Washington and charted its own path on international issues. Much to the chagrin of its southern neighbor, Canada did not join the U.S.-led "Coalition of the Willing" in its war against Iraq, although it has had a significant role in Afghanistan peacekeeping efforts. Canada's support for Israel and generally unpopular stance on climate change are two of the factors that many experts blame for the country's failure to win a seat on the United Nations Security Council in 2010, further marking a newfound Canadian policy of independence. Indeed, as the U.S. follows an increasingly unilateralist international program and as Canada embraces progressive policies in issues such as the legalization of marijuana and sanctioning of same-sex unions, Canada at times finds itself at odds with its powerful neighbor.

Reflecting the strength of the Canadian economy, in 2007 the Canadian dollar pulled ahead of the U.S. dollar in value for the first time since 1957, and has remained at or near parity since. Although Canada posted its first fiscal deficit in over a decade in 2009, conservative lending practices meant that Canada mostly avoided the banking crisis experienced by many other countries during the most recent global economic crisis. Since the financial crisis hit, the Canadian economy has rebounded better than most other Western nations and most of the jobs lost since late 2008 have been recovered.

Index

A

B

D

E

F

G

L

M

N

O

P

T

W

Y